# Critical Essays on Jonathan Edwards

# Critical Essays on Jonathan Edwards

## William J. Scheick

G. K. Hall & Co.   •   Boston, Massachusetts

Library of Congress Cataloging in Publication Data
Main entry under title:
Critical essays on Jonathan Edwards.
   (Critical essays on American literature)
   Includes bibliographical references and index.
   1. Edwards, Jonathan, 1703–1758—Addresses, essays, lectures. I.
Scheick, William J. II. Series.
BX7260.E3C67      285′.8′0924      79-17053
ISBN 0-8161-8304-X

*This publication is printed on permanent/durable acid-free paper*
MANUFACTURED IN THE UNITED STATES OF AMERICA

For Nathan Andrew

# CRITICAL ESSAYS ON AMERICAN LITERATURE

This series seeks to publish the most important reprinted criticism on writers and topics in American literature along with, in various volumes, original essays, interviews, bibliographies, letters, manuscript sections, and other materials brought to public attention for the first time. William J. Scheick's volume on Jonathan Edwards is the most substantial collection of criticism yet assembled on this important writer. Scheick's introduction represents a definitive assessment of the place of Jonathan Edwards in American letters and a survey of the critical record on this writer. In addition, the volume presents a significant original essay, Wayne Lesser's "Jonathan Edwards: Textuality and the Language of Man." We are confident that this collection will make a permanent and valuable contribution to American literary scholarship.

JAMES NAGEL, GENERAL EDITOR

*Northeastern University*

# CONTENTS

# INTRODUCTION

An attempt to collect significant critical essays on Edwards' life and work inevitably conveys a degree of presumption. The task requires a keen sensitivity to two and a half centuries of commentary as well as an informed awareness of at least the five disciplines—theology, philosophy, history, American studies, and literary criticism—which have principally generated that commentary. Not only do critical remarks range from general appreciations to highly specialized discussions, but they reflect a wide variety of idiosyncratic reaction, or of internecine conflict, over such issues as whether Edwards' thought was empirical or idealistic, whether it was progressive or conservative, whether it influenced American culture negatively or positively, or not at all. So the choices made by an editor, who may wish his selection to evince a certain catholicity within the single criterion of excellence in the scholarship on Edwards, implicitly reveal a confidence in knowing enough to participate intimately in the complex issues involved as well as in comprehending these intricacies sufficiently to make proper decisions. Herein lies a double-edged presumption, sharpened by the editor's tacit assumption of his audience's good will. With this dilemma in mind, I cautiously offer the selections printed in this volume as *representative* of notable commentary on Edwards, notable because they define very well some feature of Edwards' thought or art, they proved to be seminal or are likely to open new vistas, or they invite, however idiosyncratic the solicitation may be, further attention to some neglected particulars of Edwards' life and work.

Evidence of my editorial presumption appears as well in the arrangement of the selections in this book. It would have been easiest merely to reprint the essays in chronological order. In an attempt to be more instructive, however, I devised categories emphasizing the specific area in which the contribution was made or, at least, suggesting more clearly lines of development within a given topic. Of course no section can in fact be satisfactorily separated from any other: Edwards' life is related to his thought; his theological concepts merge with his philosophical and historical notions, and all three intrinsically involve the influences on Edwards and his influence on others; and the artistry of Edwards' work depends on the context provided by his life, thought, and sources. The categories presented here, consequently, are designed as an aid, their boundaries quite imaginary but theoretically useful in a *survey* of scholarship on Edwards.

## I

Of all the concerns of Edwards studies, the area of biography is *editorially* the simplest to manage. This is the result, I suspect, of the difficulties scholars have encountered in making new contributions to the subject. Reports on Edwards' life appear very early, indeed occur even in his own work not only explicitly in such autobiographical revelations as the *Personal Narrative* or *A Faithful Narrative of the Surprising Work of God* but also implicitly in his most public and personally guarded works. After his death in 1758, the first full and noteworthy account was written by Samuel Hopkins in *The Life and Character of the Late Reverend Mr. Jonathan Edwards* (1765).[1] During the next sixty-four years lesser versions of Hopkins' portrait appeared, until the publication of Sereno E. Dwight's long biography, printed as the first volume of *The Works of President Edwards* (1829–1830). The importance of Dwight's edition in reviving interest in Edwards during the early nineteenth century has never been investigated, any more than has the effect of earlier editions by Edward Williams and Edward Parsons (1806–1811; reprinted at least twice in the first half of the century) and by Samuel Austin (1808–1809; reprinted frequently during the century). Yet a glance, for instance, at the *Christian Examiner* and the *Christian Review* from 1833 to 1848 reveals an extensive renewed concern with Edwards' thought; even an abbreviated but entertaining version of Edwards' life was printed in the *Christian Examiner*.[2] Near the close of the century Alexander V.G. Allen's noteworthy *Jonathan Edwards* (1889) appeared, but it focuses more on intellectual rather than on biographical matters. Forty years later Henry B. Parker's misinformed *Jonathan Edwards: The Fiery Puritan* (1930) was published, followed by Arthur Cushman McGiffert's *Jonathan Edwards* (1932), which presents a benign but modest portrait of the theologian as a religious psychologist. The next major synthesis of biographical study was Ola E. Winslow's *Jonathan Edwards, 1703–1758* (1940), still a basic resource for scholars.

Since the appearance of Winslow's work, little has been added to the ascertainable facts of Edwards' life. The task of unveiling more details has apparently proven quite difficult, even though large areas of Edwards' career remain mysterious or, at least, undisclosed. Many of Edwards' actions, their timing and their effect, as well as his journeys to different towns and his relationships with specific individuals, all warrant further investigation. Recently, in a review-essay on Edwards scholarship, Everett Emerson remarked how little is known of Edwards' Northampton years,[3] which unfortunately are not illuminated by Edwin Sponseller's thirty-two page *Northampton and Jonathan Edwards* (1966). We do indeed need to know more about the Northampton community, as the background for Edwards' performance as pastor; in fact we need to know much more in general about Edwards' milieu. Doubtless the occasional publication of "excavated" manuscripts will help fill in Edwards' biography piece by tiny piece, as do the recent appearance of Edwards' letter of invitation to George Whitefield[4] and of a letter by Timothy Cutler.[5]

The essays I have chosen for this category focus on the Reverend Robert Breck affair and on Edwards' dismissal from Northampton. In the passage reprinted from *The Evangelical and Literary Magazine* (1822) Edwards appropriately is permitted to have the opening word in a letter (complementing those printed in Clarence H. Faust and Thomas H. Johnson's *Jonathan Edwards: Representative Selections*, 1935, 1962) exploring job opportunities after the Northampton fiasco. Ezra Hoyt Byington's forgotten study (1890) of Robert Breck is, I admit, a somewhat eccentric inclusion, for it mentions Edwards only in passing. But when its discussion and the documents presented in *The Evangelical and Literary Magazine* are combined with Charles Edwin Jones's recent account (1978) of Edwards' role in the Breck affair, and of Breck's subsequent role in Edwards' dismissal, the resultant wealth of detail yields new depths of insight into the interface of these two episodes.

Seen collectively, the three selections implicitly dramatize the slowness of advances in factual studies of Edwards' life and indicate as well how even a single, seemingly minor event like the Breck affair can be most illuminating when placed in context.

Some Edwards critics have ventured into the realm of interpretative biography. Undoubtedly the most important and influential book in this mode is Perry Miller's *Jonathan Edwards* (1949). During the last three decades, every serious student of Edwards' thought has referred to this work as a point of departure. It gave Edwards' scholarship renewed respectability, and the renaissance of current interest in Edwards draws its energy from it. Its deserved stature notwithstanding, Miller's study exhibits an overstated, sometimes hyperbolic claim for Edwards' modernity. But this very distortion wrested academic interest in Edwards out of its lethargy, and whatever its limitations today, the book still generates comment and remains in many respects seminal. Because the effect of Miller's chapters is cumulative and because Miller is, in my opinion, better represented elsewhere in this collection, I do not reprint an excerpt from his book on Edwards. Nevertheless its presence is felt here when time and again other authors refer to it in the reprinted selections.

Edward H. Davidson's *Jonathan Edwards: The Narrative of a Puritan Mind* (1966, 1968) is a interpretative biography in the Millerian mode. The passage reprinted from it focuses on the curious and little-understood description of Sarah Pierrepont that Edwards wrote when he was about twenty years old (he later married her). Emphasizing images of light and the centrality of the eye in the work, Davidson speculates about how its meditative style reflects a tension between the doctrine of divine sovereignty and Edwards' sense of wonder. Davidson's study, it might be noted parenthetically, could have been included in the category of literary criticism.

Interpretative biographies more concerned with the psychological than with the intellectual side of Edwards' mind date from Joseph H. Crooker's view of the theologian as a monomaniac.[6] They range from studies of the disruptive power of emotion in Edwards,[7] to Freudian readings,[8] to an Eriksonian analysis. The last, as exemplified by Richard L. Bushman's long essay (1969), is reprinted here because it is the best of its kind, presenting a provocative yet reasonable speculative reading of Edwards' life.

## II

When one turns to Edwards' thought, the fiction of my categories—especially of the subcategories of theology, philosophy, and history—becomes most difficult to maintain. The topic of Edwardsean ideas is enormous, and no introduction to a collection of essays can do justice to it.

Comment by Edwards' contemporaries responding to his theology appeared frequently enough. Much of it was reactionary, most notably Charles Chauncy's *The Late Religious Commotion in New-England Considered* (1743), Thomas Clap's *A Letter from the Reverend Mr. Clap* (1745), and sundry articles printed in the Old Light publication *The Boston Evening-Post* during 1743 and 1744. The passages reprinted in this volume from works by Solomon Williams and Ebenezer Frothingham represent the typical level on which the debate was conducted as well as indicate the degree to which Edwards provoked both the Old Lights and the New Lights. As an Old Light, Williams worried about what seemed to be his cousin's advocacy of excessive religious enthusiasm, and he wished to preserve what he saw as a more rational, orthodox approach to determining church membership, including a defense of the Half-Way Covenant. Associated with the Separate Church of Wethersfield, New Light Frothingham considered Edwards' views to be too cautious and he emphasized religious enthusiasm as a manifestation of the saint's personal communion with God. Seeking, as usual, to locate some middle ground between these proximal Arminian and Antinomian positions, Edwards tried to bridge the gap between the notions of a visible and an invisible sainthood, a very old problem dating back to at least St. Augustine. But by their nature moderates find themselves in the middle of a fray; and as the passages by Frothingham and Williams indicate, Edwards' theological views were caught in the crossfire emanating from opposing sides.

The debates continued after Edwards' death. His ideas were attacked in such works as James Dana's *An Examination of the Late Rev. President Edwards' Enquiry on Freedom of the Will* (1770), which was followed by a second volume in 1773. They were defended, albeit sometimes in modified form, in such books as Stephen West's *An Essay on Moral Agency* (1772, 1794) and Samuel Hopkins' *An Inquiry into the Nature of True Holiness* (1773). Hopkins and the New Divinity transmitted Edwards' theological ideas, though not always in pure form, well into the nineteenth century.

In the early nineteenth century American attention to Edwardsean theology was primarily sustained by religious journals. In *The Christian Spectator* an early Edwards' resolution served as a point of departure, his understanding of religious revivals was probed, and his view of original sin was considered.[9] The 5 July 1822 issue of *The Evangelical and Literary Magazine* has already been remarked, though we ought to add the interesting detail that this journal was published in Richmond, Virginia. During the next decade *The Christian Examiner* printed an imaginary reply by Edwards to Professor Stuart's notion of original sin and, in the same year in which an Emerson work was reviewed in the journal, provided favorable discussions of Edwards' ideas on conversion and religious affections.[10] And the *Literary and Theology Review* presented Enoch Pond's analysis of Edwards' concept of the will.[11]

During the 1840s, *The Christian Examiner* printed W.H. Channing's "Jonathan Edwards and the Revivalists" as well as a biography of the theologian; and *The Christian Review* provided a discussion of Edwards' approach to religious affections and a long defense of his view of the will.[12] Articles on Edwards appeared in *Bibliotheca Sacra*, *New Englander*, *North American Review* and *Princeton Theological Review*, among others, from the 1850s through the turn of the century. These facts are worth noting because they are little recognized, because they demonstrate that no break occurred in the transference of Edwards' thought (however modified), and because they belong to an area of Edwards scholarship in dire need of careful investigation. Edwards' theology was transmitted to our time without interruption.

In the late nineteenth and early twentieth centuries the journals continued to keep Edwardsean ideas current. Leslie Stephen's essay (1876), in part reprinted in this volume, first appeared in *Fraser's Magazine* and in *Littell's Living Age*.[13] As the excerpt shows, Stephen provides lucid, if not always favorable, commentary on the interface of Edwards' metaphysical theory and his theology, especially on the relation between pantheism and virtue. Also representative of the high quality of some late nineteenth-century studies of Edwards is Allen's book (1889), referred to earlier and excerpted elsewhere in this collection.

Of works treating, in some fashion, Edwards' theology shortly after the turn of the century, William James' *The Varieties of Religious Experience* (1902) comes to mind, but Edwards plays only a contributory role in the book. Published shortly thereafter, I. Woodbridge Riley's *American Philosophy: The Early Schools* (1907) and *American Thought from Puritanism to Pragmatism* (1915) are better identified with the philosophical category. During the 1920s and 1930s studies of Edwards' theology often reflect a warp characteristic of the cultural and political concerns of many critics during that time, as exemplified by Vernon Louis Parrington's *The Colonial Mind, 1620-1800* (1927; later incorporated in *Main Currents in American Thought*, 1930). The distortion is interesting but not very useful to the student of Edwards. Two major exceptions in this period are Joseph Haroutunian's *Piety Versus Moralism: The Passing of the New England Theology* (1932) and Faust and Johnson's edition of Edwards' writings (1935). Stimulated by these and by Miller's book (1949), studies of Edwards' theology improved during the next three decades, highlighted by Conrad Cherry's *Jonathan Edwards: A Reappraisal* (1966). Emphasizing the Calvinist side of Edwards' views, Cherry treats a wide variety of theological concerns with enviable clarity. In the chapter on nature and grace, reprinted here, Cherry discusses in detail Edwards' sense of a gap between nature and grace (a thesis worth debating) and of the nature of conversion.

Interest in Edwards' theology includes, for some, an attempt to place it in the history of American religion. After Haroutunian's work, such studies as

Conrad Wright's *The Beginnings of Unitarianism in America* (1955), Edwin Scott Gaustad's *The Great Awakening in New England* (1957), C.C. Goen's *Revivalism and Separatism in New England, 1740–1800* (1962), Alan Heimert's *Religion and the American Mind: From the Great Awakening to the Revolution* (1966), William A. Clebsch's *American Religious Thought: A History* (1973), and Robert L. Berner's disappointing "Grace and Works in America: The Role of Jonathan Edwards,"[14] represent a wide range of approach to this subject. The best of these works notwithstanding, current studies of Edwards on the whole tend away from general estimates. They incline to be highly specialized, often engaged in defining in detail one or another specific theological point. Gerhard T. Alexis' "Jonathan Edwards and the Theocratic Ideal" and David Weddle's "Jonathan Edwards on Men and Trees, and the Problem of Solidarity" are indicative.[15] A list of such articles would indeed be very long, but would testify to the liveliness of current discussions of Edwards' religious ideas.

Edwards' philosophical views are not, properly speaking, separable from his theological beliefs, though scholarly debate over the former has been more extreme and acquired depth only after the late nineteenth century. Interest in Edwards' philosophy, as somewhat distinct from his theology, developed after the appearance of several essays on Edwards' idealism in the 1870-1890s, through the publication of Allen's book on Edwards (1889) and Riley's study of American philosophy (1907). Allen penetrates into several corners of Edwards' thought with admirable perception, with the consequence that his reaction to what is disclosed is not altogether favorable. His account of Edwards' metaphysical arguments is rich in detail, and in the passage on freedom of the will, reprinted here, Allen exhibits his wide breadth of philosophical knowledge when suggesting fascinating similarities between Edwards' thought and that of Hobbes, Hume, Mill, and the Scotch philosophical necessitarians. Allen's comments on *Freedom of the Will* may not completely satisfy today, in that they seem insensitive to certain features of Edwards' thought in the book, but they remain richly allusive and suggestive. Riley's chapter on Edwards, reprinted here in part, demonstrates an even more remarkable range, providing a clear-headed discussion of the similarities and differences between Edwards' thought and Berkeley's, of Edwards' alleged pantheism, and particularly of the connection between Edwards' idealism and his mysticism. Questions concerning influences on Edwards are also raised, making Riley's chapter equally suitable for the intellectual lineage category elsewhere in this book.

At the turn of the century discussions of Edwards' philosophy stressed his idealism, a trend evident as well in much of the commentary written on Edwards during the first half of the twentieth century. Reaction eventually set in, a counterforce sensitive to what appeared to be the empirical thrust of Edwards' thinking. This argument was epitomized in Perry Miller's writings on Edwards. "Edwards, Locke, and the Rhetoric of Sensation" (1950), reprinted with an abbreviated title in *Errand into the Wilderness* (1956), provides a synopsis of Miller's view of the issue, as it is argued at length in his intellectual biography of the theologian. The argument of the essay, reprinted here, is clear and vigorous; although it may require some qualification, it offers a cogent approach to one side of Edwards' thought, which is why it appears here rather than under the equally suitable category of intellectual lineage. The essay, it might also be remarked, evinces a power of persuasion characteristic of Miller's technique, a contributing factor to the tremendous influence nearly all of his studies of Puritan culture exert on interested members of the academic community.

In one form or another the debate continues. More recent scholars have advanced modified versions of Miller's interpretation of Lockean influence on Edwards, most notably Edward H. Davidson and Claude A. Smith.[16] Others still wrestle with the evidence for idealism in Edwards' thought: for instance, Wallace E. Anderson's "Immaterialism in Jonathan Edwards' Early Philosophical Notes," George Rupp's "The Idealism of Jonathan Edwards," and (notably) Michael J. Colacurcio's "The Example of Edwards: Idealist Imagination and the Metaphysics of Sovereignty."[17] In "The Sixth Sense of Jonathan Edwards"[18] David Lyttle reasonably places Edwards between both extremes, advancing the view that for the theologian the encounter with grace is similar to sensory experience but qualitatively distant from it as it engages a supernatural aesthetic sensitivity in the saint.

Studies of Edwards' philosophical ideas have gone in other directions. In the area of aesthetics the landmark work is Roland André Delattre's *Beauty and Sensibility in the Thought of Jonathan Edwards* (1968). Because the argument of Delattre's book is complex and necessarily self-referential, it is not easy to follow nor does it readily yield an excerpt. The selection by Delattre reprinted in this collection originally appeared in *Soundings* (1968), is drawn from the analysis presented in the book, and typifies the new level (beyond Cherry, for instance) to which discussions of Edwards' aesthetics has been elevated. In fact the question of Edwards' aesthetics touches every feature of his thought, which is why Delattre systematizes what informs but is not always explicitly treated in Edwards' works. Delattre's book is especially important, I think, to studies of Edwards' writings from a literary point of view, though at the moment it has not exerted a noticeable influence in this area. A more recent, less ambitious and generally disappointing related work is Clyde A. Holbrook's *The Ethics of Jonathan Edwards: Morality and Aesthetics* (1973).

Other philosophical concerns have emerged. Some inquiry has been made into whether Edwards was philosophically progressive or conservative. Arguments for a forward-looking Edwards have been advanced, for example, by Perry Miller and by Douglas J. Elwood (*The Philosophical Theology of Jonathan Edwards*, 1960); arguments for a reactionary Edwards have been made by, among others, Robert C. Whittemore and David C. Pierce.[19] In his pamphlet on Edwards (1971) Edward M. Griffin provides an overview of this controversy, and several other features of it are implicit in Thomas Werge's "Jonathan Edwards and the Puritan Mind in America: Direction in Textual and Interpretive Criticism."[20] Some scholars have searched for philosophical influences on Edwards beyond that of Berkeley and Locke. This interest is exemplified by studies of similarities between Edwards' ideas and those of the Cambridge Platonists, studies ranging from Clarence Gohdes' "Aspects of Idealism in Early New England" to Emily S. Watts' recent "The Neoplatonic Basis of Jonathan Edwards' 'True Virtue.' "[21] Attention has also been given to the philosophical implications of Edwards' faculty psychology in such articles as Harvey G. Townsend's "The Will and the Understanding in the Philosophy of Jonathan Edwards," Norman S. Fiering's "Will and Intellect in the New England Mind," and J. Rodney Fulcher's "Puritans and Passions: The Faculty Psychology in American Puritanism."[22] A wide variety of interest has been expressed concerning the relation between Edwards' thought and the intellectual milieu of the eighteenth century, some measure of which can be taken from Faust and Johnson's *Jonathan Edwards: Representative Selections* (1935, 1962) and Alfred Owen Aldridge's *Jonathan Edwards* (1964).

Although an attempt has been made to show that the theologian's ontology derived from his cosmology and harmonized with his theology, all of which depends on the trinitarian model,[23] similar efforts to systematize Edwards' thought will, it would appear, not comprise a major trend in future studies. The wide range of controversy over Edwards' philosophical views suggests that they are the product of various influences and that they are less systematic than we might wish. Doubtless, disagreements over Edwards' philosophical concepts will continue, even if the controversy is likely to be characterized by dwindling vigor.

In-depth studies of Edwards' thought about history have appeared even more recently than serious investigations of his philosophy. Like the latter, however, the gamut of commentary on Edwardsean history ranges from Perry Miller's reading of it as forward-looking (*Jonathan Edwards*, 1949) to Peter Gay's dismissal of it as the curious production of "the last medieval American— at least among the intellectuals."[24] The first significant study of the eschatological and millennial implications of Edwardsean history was made by C.C. Goen (1959). Goen's observations may now require modification here and there, but they were seminal to subsequent studies, register a sensitivity to influences on Edwards, and still remain suggestive—good reasons for reprinting the work in this volume.

In his long introduction to the fifth volume of the Yale edition of Edwards' works (*Apocalyptic Writings*, 1977), Stephen J. Stein admirably advances Goen's discussion. Stein's findings had been suggested in previously published essays, one of which bears the unassuming title "A Notebook on the Apocalypse by Jonathan Edwards" (1972). This essay, reprinted here, revises Goen's article and replies to Alan Heimert's *Religion and the American Mind*, particularly concerning the view that Edwards and the Great Awakening had a formative effect on new eschatological notions in eighteenth-century America. Stein's essay also necessarily challenges the Miller and the Heimert portraits of Edwards as innovatively progressive. Heimert does not appear in this collection, an omission which might raise an eyebrow. Heimert's reading of Edwards was anticipated by Miller and Goen, who are represented in this volume, and is questioned by Stein and Joseph Conforti, who also appear in this collection. On the whole Heimert's book is undeniably informed and valuable, but its depiction of Edwards as an archetypal evangelical providing "pre-Revolutionary America with a radical, even democratic, social and political ideology" remains, for me at least, very problematic.

Edwards' historical views have been approached from various angles. A German professor of American studies, for instance, recently tried to connect Edwardsean history with the tradition of Puritan historical narration. A meandering, long book, Karl Dieterich Pfisterer's *The Prism of Scripture: Studies on History and Historicity in the Work of Jonathan Edwards* (1975) fails to close with its subject in a satisfying or significant manner, though it does give some insight into Edwards' *A Faithful Narrative*. My essay on *History of the Work of Redemption* (1975), reprinted here, examines two interrelated motifs in the work in terms of Edwards' correlation of the conversion process to historical progress. Still another approach is reflected in Mason I. Lowance's studies of Edwards' use of typological history as a manifestation of the divine truth revealed in Scripture and in nature.[25] His most recent essay (1977) on the subject is reprinted in this collection. Several features of Edwards' millennial notions are discussed in the context of the views of his contemporaries in James West Davidson's *The Logic of Millennial Thought: Eighteenth-Century New England* (1977).

Within the category of Edwards' thought it would be reasonable to include a section for miscellaneous topics. I decided against this subcategory because these topical discussions, however interesting and potentially valuable, have not yet managed a depth of perception evident in considerations of Edwardsean theology, philosophy, and history.

On the question of scientific influences, Clarence H. Faust has attacked the belief that Edwards was a remarkable scientific observer, whereas Theodore Hornberger has argued for the strong effect of science on Edwards' mind. The debate continues.[26] Following Hornberger and Miller (1949), Henry J. Laskowsky has suggested that the sophisticated sense of causality informing *Freedom of the Will* is indebted to Newtonic influence, and Ron Loewinsohn speaks similarly about Edwards' writings in general.[27] However, David Scofield Wilson undercuts claims for the remarkableness of Edwards' early essay on arachnids, and in a general essay Jean-Pierre Martin discounts the significance of scientific influences on the theologian.[28] The questions raised by these studies require more attention. Another topical approach appears in Sang Hyun Lee's "Jonathan Edwards' Theory of the Imagination," which interprets Edwards' understanding of habit as the mind's real and active power to order and relate events.[29] My "Family, Conversion, and the Self in Jonathan Edwards' *A Faithful Narrative of the Surprising Work of God*"[30] assesses the concept of family as an index to Edwards' thought. Another topic is emphasized in Christopher R. Reaske's "The Devil and Jonathan Edwards,"[31] which indicates that Edwards' interest in demons derived from the Bible, John Flavel, and Milton and that this concern underwent a transformation from a mild preoccupation with devils, to an heated engagement with the subject during the Great Awakening, to a subdued awareness of it during his later life. In "Social Criticism and the Heavenly City of Jonathan Edwards"[32] Robert B. Westbrook finds an Edwardsean social vision implicit in three primary theological concepts. James Carse has written an entertaining, if somewhat misleading book on the subject of *Jonathan Edwards and the Visibility of God* (1967).

A most interesting topic is treated in Gail Thain Parker's "Jonathan Edwards and Melancholy,"[33] which provides a good overview of the Puritan attitudes toward melancholy possibly underlying Edwards' handling of the subject. Another concern, one rather limited in value to the scholar, includes Edwards' relevance today, as exemplified by Benjamin Wisner Bacon's "The Theological Significance of Jonathan Edwards" and Clyde A. Holbrook's "Edwards and the Ethical Question."[34]

This sample by no means exhausts the scope of topical interest in Edwards. Subsequent critical activity should deepen the level of insight into several of these areas of inquiry. Approaching Edwards in terms of specific subjects is one direction in which future studies must go if we are to understand and assess his thought better than we do at present.

# III

Perhaps of all the fields of interest in Edwards scholarship, the ones in greatest need of further exploration include the influences upon him and his influence upon others. Neither subject is easy to pursue.

Just how, if at all, a work has influenced an author, even when one can verify it had been read by him, remains problematic. Yet the question of background and context can become crucial, as is evidenced whenever untested critical claims are made for Edwards' originality. Research for instance, suggests that Perry Miller's reading of Edwards' view of the sensation of grace as an innovative adaptation of Lockean psychology becomes less conclusive in the light of similar notions and language in the work of, say, Thomas Hooker, Anne Bradstreet, and Solomon Stoddard, not to mention even such earlier precedents as the Cambridge Platonists, John Calvin, and the Bible. One side of this large question, Edwards' intellectual correspondence to the thinkers of his day, is explored in John Opie's anthology, *Jonathan Edwards and the Enlightenment* (1969), which emphasized the theologian's acute awareness of eighteenth-century intellectual achievements. From a different angle of vision, Edwards' thought has been contrasted to that of Samuel Johnson.[35]

A major benefit to emerge from the Yale edition of Edwards' works has been the editors' effort to acknowledge influences on Edwards. In the first volume (1957) Paul Ramsey points to Locke's effect on *Freedom of the Will* and differentiates between Edwardsean concepts and those of Thomas Chubb, Daniel Whitby, and Isaac Watts. John E. Smith, in the second volume (1959), comments briefly on sixteen authors contributing to the background of *Re-*

*ligious Affections*, including Thomas Shepard and Solomon Stoddard; as Fulcher's essay (cited earlier) and Robert Lee Stuart's " 'Mr. Stoddard's Way': Church and Sacrament in Northampton" imply,[36] we need to know considerably more about the effect of both Shepard and Stoddard on all aspects of Edwards' thinking. Several sources, including John Taylor, Francis Hutcheson, and John Locke, affecting *Original Sin* are discussed by Clyde A. Holbrook in the third volume of the Yale edition (1970). Whereas influences are generally ignored in C.C. Goen's introduction to the fourth volume (1972), they emerge prominently in Stephen J. Stein's commentary in *The Apocalyptic Writings* (1977).

The Yale edition, in short, provides some valuable leads for future students of Edwardsean thought, as indeed does Thomas H. Johnson's infrequently cited but valuable study of Edwards' reading and William S. Morris's neglected essay on the possible influence of Burgersdychian thought on Edwards.[37] Demonstrating the degree of mastery requisite to a serious comparative study, Morris's essay would have made a good addition to the lineage category, or that of theology, did not its size make its reprint fee prohibitive. From such studies it is evident that much needs to be done. Certainly one of the most significant topics requiring development includes Stoddard's influence on his grandson, not an easy subject to research because Stoddard's published works reveal the fewest clues, most of which are either lost or presumably buried in manuscript material.

An excerpt from Alexander Allen's book provides the first entry in the category of influences on Edwards because it sheds light into a very obscure corner of the theologian's mind. Tracing similarities between the thought of Edwards and of Scotchman Andrew Ramsay, Allen suggests the need for more research, especially concerning the late works, on several points, including Edwards' trinitarian beliefs.

David Scofield Wilson's "The Flying Spider," mentioned in passing earlier, has received very little recognition in scholarship on Edwards. Yet, it is, simply, a very admirable study of works precedent to and quite likely influential upon Edwards' youthful essay on spiders. Revisionist in effect, the essay comes at Edwards from a distinctive but instructive angle, which alone should endear it to Edwards scholars.

Which brings to mind an important matter: disclosure of Edwards' sources, even exposing his derivativeness, will not endanger his significance. Such revelations only illuminate his mind, permitting us to detect and to appreciate, with more accuracy and deeper sensitivity, just what his contribution is. A concentrated focus on Edwards' work, with at best only a brief consideration of its background and context, can be myopic. Whatever we learn about the influences on it, Edwards' mind will continue to strike us as brilliant. What we may lose in the alleged originality of one or another feature of his thought, we shall gain elsewhere in his work; and our admiration will be more firmly founded and greater as a result.

The matter of Edwards' influences on others has proven equally troublesome. Various speculations have emerged, most insufficiently substantiated.[38] There is a need for a careful consideration of Edwards' influence on Scotch clergy, a subject briefly addressed in James Orr's "Jonathan Edwards: His Influence in Scotland."[39] It is mentioned, in a perverse way, in Oliver Wendell Holmes' essay on Edwards, reprinted in part here from *Pages from an Old Volume of Life* (1883). Including Holmes in this collection may be another editorial eccentricity, but in spite of its substantial shortcomings the essay makes an intriguing comparison of Pascal and Edwards and, inadvertently, stimulates interest in what even his late nineteenth-century detractors perceived as his genuine influence on Scotch clergy and as the influence of that clergy on him (cf.Allen, above, on Kames and Ramsey).

Edwards' authority in America is the subject of Joseph A. Conforti's recent essay on Samuel Hopkins, reprinted here. Taking exception to Heimert's view of Edwards' effect on the New Divinity, Conforti indicates how the New Divinity extended and modified Edwards' thought, especially in the matter of social activism. Cogently Conforti contributes to an argument descending from Charles Hodge's attack on Edwards as an old-fashioned Calvinist at odds with the New Divinity and from Noah Porter's defense of Edwards as the founder of that school.[40] Edwards' thought, however modified, was transmitted to later times principally through the New Divinity, as Joseph Haroutunian (1932) and more recently Ann Douglas (*The Feminization of American Culture*, 1977) have reminded us, and it is very important to observe this fact when speaking of his influence in the nineteenth century. Edwards' presence can be detected in several nineteenth-century works, but this influence is more often indirect (through, for instance, the New Divinity) than direct. It is a genuine influence nonetheless, though it might best be referred to as the effect of Edwardsean tradition.

The role of Edwardsean tradition in nineteenth-century writings is a subject of increasing interest. Certainly the best known inquiry of this kind is Perry Miller's "From Edwards to Emerson,"[41] a favorite with teachers of American literature. By the time he reprinted the essay in *Errand into the Wilderness* (1956) Miller confessed his discomfort with it, particularly with what seemed to some to be its implicit argument for direct intellectual descent from Edwards to Emerson. Miller had in mind "certain basic continuities" in American culture, though even some of the specific connections he makes can be questioned in terms of more recent inquiries into Edwards' alleged pantheism. Others, several of whom might have benefited by distinguishing between Edwards and Edwardsean tradition, have tried similar exercises. Representative attempts to discern cultural continuities between Edwards and nineteenth-century authors include, with varying degrees of success, Mason I. Lowance's "From Edwards to Emerson to Thoreau: A Revaluation," Charles T. Samuels' "Usher's Fall: Poe's Rise," John N. Serio's "From Edwards to Poe," Robert E. Morsberger's "'The Minister's Black Veil': Shrouded in a Blackness, Ten Times Black," Walter R. Patrick's "Melville's 'Bartleby' and the Doctrine of Necessity," Daniel Stempel and Bruce M. Stillians' mention of Edwards' difference from

Schopenhauer in the use of the words *will* and *prefer* in "Bartleby the Scrivener,"[42] Albert J. Gelpi's *Emily Dickinson, The Mind of the Poet* (1965), and Lawrence Buell's "Calvinism Romanticized: Harriet Beecher Stowe, Samuel Hopkins, and *The Minister's Wooing*" (1978). Buell's good essay, which looks forward to a fuller treatment of the subject, appears in this collection.

The influence of Edwards or, more properly, of Edwardsean tradition on modern authors is an infrequent subject for critics. George S. Lensing's disappointing "Robert Lowell and Jonathan Edwards: Poetry in the Hands of an Angry God" reminds us of a well-known instance.[43] And William Hoffa has inconclusively joined Edwards and Norman Mailer through a subjectivist tradition.[44]

The items included in the lineage category of this book are representative, and it should be recalled that essays entered elsewhere in the volume might well have appeared at this point: Cherry's emphasis on the theological context of Edwards' understanding of conversion, Allen's suggestion of similarities between Edwards and other thinkers on the will, Riley's disclosure of the roots of Edwards' idealism, Miller's account of Edwards' use of Lockean psychology, Goen's reading of the background behind and the alleged progressive nature of Edwards' eschatology, Stein's remarks on the deviation of Edwards' apocalyptic notions, and Wilson H. Kimnach's (to be discussed shortly) questioning of influences on Edwards' sermonic manner. Although infrequently given its due as a topic in its own right, the subject of Edwards' sources and influence remains of major consequence and deserves much more concentrated attention.

## IV

Of the five disciplines exhibiting a sustained interest in Edwards, literary criticism is the most recent to develop. Certainly Faust and Johnson's introductory comments on Edwards as a man of letters, in their anthology (1935, 1962) remarked earlier, set a precedent, even discussing Edwardsean style. And Miller's intellectual biography (1949) offered several remarks in passing on the stylistic implications of Locke's influence on Edwards. However, Edwin H. Cady's "The Artistry of Jonathan Edwards" (1949) actually demonstrated Edwards' writing to be a *bona fide* area for literary investigation. (Incidentally, 1949 also was the year in which Kenneth B. Murdock published *Literature and Theology in Colonial New England*.) Cady's essay, reprinted here, considers the images in "Sinners in the Hands of an Angry God" as they relate to the social and religious context of the sermon.

The article was seminal, and subsequent studies expanding Cady's concern with imagery to include tone, word choice, and sentence structure, clearly reveal their debt. Representative of these later efforts, and evincing an extremely varied degree of success, are Paul R. Baumgartner's "Jonathan Edwards: The Theory behind His Use of Figurative Language," James C. Cowan's "Jonathan Edwards' Sermon Style: 'The Future Punishment of the Wicked Unavoidable and Intolerable,' " Willis J. Buckingham's "Stylistic Artistry in the

Sermons of Jonathan Edwards" and Annette Kolodny's "Imagery in the Sermons of Jonathan Edwards."[45] Various artistic features of Edwards' work, particularly as they relate to his theology, are considered in my *The Writings of Jonathan Edwards: Theme, Motif, and Style* (1975).

Edwards' *Personal Narrative* has been especially attractive to critics concerned with literary structure. In "The Art and Instruction of Jonathan Edwards' *Personal Narrative*" (1965)[46] Daniel Shea made a new contribution to our understanding of the work's literary merits. Shea's essay, reprinted here, emphasizes how narrative structure and manner embody Edwards' intention to affect his readers by integrating content and presentation. In "Jonathan Edwards' *Personal Narrative*: Dynamic Stasis"[47] Norman S. Grabo perceives the structure of the work to exhibit a paradoxical relation between its four repeated cycles and its emphasis on pure stasis. For David L. Minter, in *The Interpreted Design as a Structural Principle in American Prose* (1969), the *Personal Narrative* reveals Edwards' attempt to apply the conventional form of Puritan spiritual autobiography to a formless experience, resulting in an adaptation of that form combining traditional indications of divine design and the aesthetic dimension of authorial design. In *The Design of the Present: Essays on Time and Form in American Literature* (1969) John F. Lynen argues that the *Personal Narrative*, among other examples of Edwards' writings, correlates divine truth and the present moment; though the experience recounted falls short of the truth, it serves as a potential summary of reality—a dualism Edwards resolved somewhat by making point-of-view an answer. The *Personal Narrative* and *The Nature of True Virtue* provide the focus for John Griffith's "Jonathan Edwards as a Literary Artist,"[48] a reading of the former work as a literary act of worship in which a spare form becomes a literary equivalent for spiritual awareness.

Structure in Edwards' sermons is the subject of Wilson H. Kimnach's "The Brazen Trumpet: Jonathan Edwards' Conception of the Sermon" (1975). This essay, reprinted here, opens a new dimension in literary studies of Edwards' writings because it combines a concern with Stoddardean influence and manuscript evidence to suggest how Edwards modified the traditional sermon form. It is only a step toward a very large subject, but an important one nonetheless. Less suggestive is Robert Lee Stuart's "Jonathan Edwards at Enfield: 'And of the Cheerfulness and Pleasantness . . . ,' " which argues that certain passages, however few, appear in "Sinners in the Hands of an Angry God" in a manner indicative of how "the entire structure of Edwards' preaching is planned to allow release of tension by the offering of hope."[49]

Wayne Lesser's "Jonathan Edwards: Texuality and the Language of Man," published here for the first time, applies a deconstructionist method and combines critical interest in the language and the structure of the *Personal Narrative*. Making good use of previous scholarship on Edwards, it emphasizes the strategy of language in the work, stressing a narrative duality embodied in Edwards' verbal performance undertaken to measure the limits of language. Specifically Edwards' language conveys the gap between speaking self and desired transcendent self, between that self's fallen inaccessible past and possibly redeemed present, which at every moment of self-awareness is displaced into pastness—a dilemma making self-reflection and language, as its vehicle, indicative of humanity's fallen condition. Lesser applies special critical terminology, which may not be to everyone's liking but which should be accorded its due for the purpose of probing the language of the *Personal Narrative* in an informing way quite distinct from previous literary criticism on the work.

## V

Kimnach's essay concludes with an invitation to others to delve into the extensive Edwards manuscripts, and in his "Jonathan Edwards' Sermon Mill,"[50] which documents changes Edwards made to adapt sermons for differing audiences, he again demonstrates the value of the manuscripts. The importance of manuscript material is evident as well in Stein's essay, discussed earlier. As Thomas Shafer has observed, of more than two hundred and fifty sermons composed by Edwards during the first decade of his career, only nine have been published.[51] As long as this material, written in virtually illegible hand, remains in manuscript—which is to say generally unavailable—the advancement of scholarship on Edwards faces a major obstacle. A related problem, not to be completely resolved by the Yale edition, is the unreliability of many of the editions of Edwards' work upon which scholars must rely, versions often silently modified by eighteenth-century editors.

A second major problem confronting Edwards scholarship is less technical. As I observed at the opening of this introduction, Edwards has attracted interest from scholars in at least five disciplines. A person studying Edwards in terms of one discipline needs, then, to familiarize himself with the concerns, language, and methods of others approaching the theologian from other disciplines. This is not always easy to do, and instances of misunderstanding can already be documented. Edwards was not merely a theologian, a philosopher, a historian, or an artist, nor are the influences on him or his on others (either directly or through Edwardsean tradition) monolithic. Future studies of Edwards must, then, combine these varied interests if they are to be true to the community of Edwards scholarship as a whole and if they are to be true to the complexity of Edwards' mind, which after all spawned the very diversity that the scholar must now take into account.

Even as our collective portrait of the man and his mind gets clearer, Edwards will, I suspect, continue to elude us. He has always been more than the sum of the critical particulars derived from his life and work, and so is he likely to remain. Herein lies his essential mystery and, as well, the enigmatic source of the commentary which has been lavished upon him during the last two and a half centuries.

## Notes

1. Reprinted most recently in *Jonathan Edwards: A Profile*, ed. David Levin (New York: Hill and Wang, 1969).

2. S.O., "Jonathan Edwards," *Christian Examiner*, 44 (1848), 367–86.

3. "Jonathan Edwards," *Fifteen American Authors before 1900*, ed. Robert A. Rees and Earl L. Harbert (Madison: University of Wisconsin Press, 1971), pp. 169–84.

4. Henry Albelove, "Jonathan Edwards' Letter of Invitation to George Whitefield," *WMQ*, 29 (1972), 487–89.

5. Douglas C. Stenerson, "An Anglican Critique of the Early Phase of the Great Awakening in New England: A Letter by Timothy Cutler," *WMQ*, 30 (1973), 475–82.

6. "Jonathan Edwards: A Psychological Study," *New England Magazine*, N.S. 2 (1890), 159–72.

7. Frederick J.E. Woodbridge, "Jonathan Edwards," *PhR*, 13 (1904), 393–408.

8. E.g., Edwin E. Slosson, "Jonathan Edwards as a Freudian," *Science*, 52 (24 December 1920), 609.

9. *The Christian Spectator*, 7 (1825), 14–17; N.S. 1 (1827), 295–308, 625–29.

10. *The Christian Examiner*, 14 (1833), 235–40; 18 (1835), 52–54, 72–78, 256–57.

11. *Literary and Theology Review*, 1 (1834), 523–34.

12. *The Christian Examiner*, 43 (1847), 374–94; 44 (1848), 367–86; *The Christian Review*, 6 (1841), 192–206; 8 (1843), 367–402.

13. *Fraser's Magazine*, N.S. 8 (1873), 529–51; *Littell's Living Age*, 120 (1874), 219–36.

14. *SoQ*, 15 (1977), 125–34.

15. Alexis, *CH*, 35 (1966), 328–43; Weddle, *HTR*, 67 (1974), 155–75.

16. Davidson, "From Locke to Edwards," *JHI*, 24 (1963), 355–72; Smith, "Jonathan Edwards and 'the Way of Ideas,' " *HTR*, 59 (1966), 153–74.

17. Anderson, *JHI*, 25 (1964), 181–200; Rupp, *HTR*, 62 (1969), 209–26, Colacurcio, in *Puritan Influences in American Literature*, ed. Emory Elliott (Urbana: University of Illinois Press, 1979).

18. *Church Quarterly Review*, 167 (1966), 50–59.

19. Whittemore, "Jonathan Edwards and the Theology of the Sixth Way," *CH*, 35 (1966), 60–75; Pierce, "Jonathan Edwards and the 'New Sense' of Glory," *NEQ*, 41 (1968), 82–95.

20. Griffin, *Jonathan Edwards* (Minneapolis: University of Minnesota Press, 1971); Werge, *Reformed Review*, 23 (1970), 153–56, 173–83.

21. Gohdes, *PhR*, 39 (1930), 537–55; Watts, *EAL*, 10 (1975), 179–89.

22. Townsend, *CH*, 16 (1947), 210–20; Fiering, *WMQ*, 29 (1972), 515–58; Fulcher, *Journal of the History of Behavior Sciences*, 9 (1973), 123–39.

23. Leonard R. Reforgiato, "The Unified Thought of Jonathan Edwards," *Thought*, 47 (1972), 599–610.

24. *A Loss of Mastery: Puritan Historians in Colonial America* (Berkeley: University of California Press, 1966; New York: Vintage, 1968), p. 116. For a reaction see John F. Wilson, "Jonathan Edwards as Historian," *CH*, 46 (1977), 5–18.

25. "The Images or Shadows of Divine Things: The Typology of Jonathan Edwards," *EAL*, 5 (1970), 141–81; rptd. in *Typology and Early American Literature*, ed. Sacvan Bercovitch (Amherst: University of Massachussetts Press, 1972), pp. 209–49; "Typology and Millennial Eschatology of Early New England," *Literary Uses of Typology from the Late Middle Ages to the Present*, ed. Earl Miner (Princeton: Princeton University Press, 1977), pp. 228–73.

26. Faust, "Jonathan Edwards as a Scientist," *AL*, 1 (1930), 393–404; Hornberger, "The Effect of the New Science upon the Thought of Jonathan Edwards," *AL*, 9 (1937), 196–207.

27. Laskowsky, "Jonathan Edwards: A Puritan Philosopher of Science," *ConnR*, 4 (1970), 33–41; Loewinsohn, "Jonathan Edwards' Optics: Images and Metaphors of Light in Some of His Major Works," *EAL*, 8, (1973), 21–32.

28. Wilson, "The Flying Spider," *JHI*, 32 (1971), 447–58; Martin, "Edwards' Epistemology and the New Science," *EAL*, 7 (1973), 247–55.

29. *MichA*, 5 (1972), 233–41.

30. *TSL*, 19 (1974), 79–89.

31. *JHI*, 33 (1972), 123–38.

32. *Soundings*, 59 (1976), 396–412.

33. *NEQ*, 41 (1968), 193–212.

34. Bacon, *Proceedings at the Dedication of the Memorial Gateway to Jonathan Edwards at the Old Burying Ground, at South Windsor* (25 June 1929); Holbrook, *HTR*, 60 (1967), 163–75.

35. Joseph J. Ellis, "The Puritan Mind in Transition: The Philosophy of Samuel Johnson," *WMQ*, 28 (1971), 26–45.

36. Stuart, *AQ*, 24 (1972), 243–53.

37. Johnson, "Jonathan Edwards' Background of Reading," *PCSM*, 28 (1931), 193–222; Morris, "The Genius of Jonathan Edwards," in *Reinterpretations in American Church History*, ed. Jerold C. Brauer (Chicago: University of Chicago Press, 1968), pp. 29–65.

38. An example of a weak attempt is William H. Parker's "Jonathan Edwards: Founder of the Counter-Tradition of Transcendentalist Thought in America," *GaR*, 27 (1973), 543–49.

39. *Congregationist and Christian World*, 88 (3 October 1903), 467–69.

40. Hodge, "Jonathan Edwards and the Successive Forms of the New Divinity," *Biblical Repertory and Princeton Review*, 30 (1858), 585–620; Porter, "The Princeton Review on Dr. Taylor and the Edwardsean Theology," *New Englander*, 18 (1860), 726–73.

41. *NEQ*, 13 (1940), 589–617.

42. Lowance, *ATQ*, 18 (1973), 3–12; Samuels, *GaR*, 18 (1964), 208–16; Serio, *ConnR*, 1 (1972), 88–92; Morsberger, *NEQ*, 46 (1973), 454–63; Patrick, *AL*, 41 (1969), 39–54; Stempel and Stillians, "*Bartleby the Scivener*: A Parable of Pessimism," *NCF*, 27 (1972), 268–82;

43. *SCR*, 6 (1974), 7–17.

44. William Hoffa, "Norman Mailer: *Advertisements for Myself* or a Portrait of the Artist as a Disgruntled Counter-Puncher," in *The Fifties: Fiction, Poetry, Drama*, ed. Warren French (Deland, Florida: Everett/Edwards, 1970), pp. 73–82.

45. Baumgartner, *PMLA*, 78 (1963), 321–25; Cowan, *SCB*, 29 (1969), 119–22; Buckingham, *PLL*, 6 (1970), 136–51; Kolodny, *EAL*, 7 (1972), 172–82.

46. Reprinted in Shea's *Spiritual Autobiography in Early America* (Princeton: Princeton University Press, 1968), pp. 187–208.

47. *LWU*, 2 (1969), 141–48.

48. *Criticism*, 15 (1973), 156–73.

49. *AL*, 48 (1976), 46–59.

50. *EAL*, 10 (1975), 167–78.

51. "Manuscript Problems in the Yale Edition of Jonathan Edwards," *EAL*, 3 (1968), 159–71.

# I  BIOGRAPHY

# Biography: Factual

## Original Letter
## From President Edwards

Anonymous[*]

To the Publisher of the Ev. and Lit. Mag.

SIR,

All who have read the Life of President Edwards, have a lively and painful recollection of his dismission from Northampton. The following papers, in his own hand writing, will throw some light on the subject, and will, at the same time, let many understand better than they do, the mode of doing business in the New-England churches. It is by no means insinuated that the spirit manifested in this case is a *fair sample* of the New-England spirit—by no means; but the case affords an example of the manner in which the pastoral relation between a minister and his people is dissolved.

This case affords an opportunity of instituting a comparison between the Constitutions of Presbyterian and Congregational Churches. But I leave it to others to pursue this subject, and make suitable reflections for themselves. I think indeed that the advantage is on the side of Presbyterianism. But while I am decided in this opinion, I hesitate not to say that many brethren mistake the true state of the case. In this country all submission to ecclesiastical authority is *purely voluntary* on the part both of people and ministers. And if any choose to throw off allegiance, there is no power to restrain them. They may sin by doing so; but that is between themselves and their God. The church can do nothing but declare their sin, and refuse to commune with them. I have dropped these hints purely for the sake of setting others to thinking on the true state of the case, and preventing them from indulging in a fancied security. The real strength of Presbyterianism consists in the power which it has to keep out error, and not in its power to crush it when it has come in and spread widely. This shows the necessity of vigilance and care. No matter to what society any people belong, whether Episcopal, Presbyterian, Congregational, Baptist or Methodist, if they choose to break or change their ecclesiastical connexions, they can do so and none can prevent them—that is, the Church has none but moral or declarative power. In this respect, it is, in this country, precisely in the state of the primitive Church; with this most important advantage on behalf of the latter, that it was not divided into various separate and independent denominations, as

[*]Reprinted from *The Evangelical and Literary Magazine*, 5 (5 July 1822), 365–69.

is the case with us, but was considered as ONE; so that all parts respected the discipline, of any particular church judicatory, and thus rendered discipline efficient. *There ought to be such unity now.* This indeed cannot exist among those who regard the Church as a separate society, and those who hold that there is no difference between the church and the world. But these last are comparatively few; and can, in cases of this sort, by no means be taken into the account.

But this is a digression. The antagonists of President Edwards were the *liberal men* of 1750. Their spirit is the same with that of the *liberales* of the present day. The following documents afford a fine specimen of the fierce, intriguing, uncompromising temper of that sort of liberality which obtrudes itself on the world's notice, trumpets its own praises, and anathematizes all that will not walk according to its course.

I have no doubt but that many of your readers will thank me for enabling you to publish the following letter with its appendages.

Respectfully, &c.        H.

*Northampton June 25, 1750.*

DEAR SIR,

I here send you an account of the doings of the council that sat here last week.

The council consisted of 19 members, which came to pass through one of the churches that I chose, refusing to send a delegate; viz. the church of Cold-Spring, which there is reason to think was through the practices of some of the Northampton people, privately with the people of Cold-Spring. So that I had one less of those that I chose in the council than the people, and the event was accordingly. The vote for my separation from the people was passed by the majority of one voice. When the question was put, the ministers were equally divided upon it, 5 on the one side and 5 on the other; but of the messengers (among whom I had the least interest) 5 were on the one side and 4 on the other, so that thus the vote was carried. Of the five ministers, and four delegates that dissented, four ministers and three messengers entered their protestation against the result. Mr. Reynolds being a very timorous, cautious man, he and his delegate, though they dissented, yet did not join in the protest.—I have here enclosed a copy of the result of the council, and also of the protestation against it.—There were about 23 of the church that voted for my continuing their minister. Some staid away from the meeting, because they would not appear to act either way, but most of the rest voted for my being dismissed with great alacrity.—Sir, I desire to hear from you at all opportunities; we are now thrown upon the ocean of the wide world, and have nothing to depend upon but God who is all sufficient; I desire your prayers for us in our present circumstances.

I am, sir, your peculiarly obliged loving brother,

JONATHAN EDWARDS.

*The Rev. Mr. Bellamy.*

# THE RESULT OF THE COUNCIL.

At a Council of Nine Churches, viz:—
The Church of Enfield, Rev. Mr. Peter Reynolds, *Pastor*;
                    Mr. Edwards Collings, *Delegate.*
        Sheffield,    Jonathan Hubbard, *Pastor*; Mr.
                    David Kellog, *Delegate.*
        Sutton,       David Hall, *Pastor*; Mr. Jonathan
                    Hale, *Delegate.*
        Reading,      William Hobby, *Pastor*; Mr. Sam'l
                    Bancroft, *Delegate.*
First Church in Springfield, Robert Breck, *Pastor*; Mr. Thos.
                    Stebbins, *Delegate.*
First Church in Sunderland, Joseph Ashley, *Pastor*; Mr. Sam'l
                    Montague, *Delegate.*
        Hatfield,     Timothy Woodbridge, *Pastor*;
                    O. Partridge, Esq. *Delegate.*
First Church in Hadley, Chester Williams, *Pastor*; Mr.
                    Enos Nash, *Delegate.*
        Pelham,       Robert Abercrombie, *Pastor*; Mr.
                    Matthew Graw, *Delegate.*
Convened at the call of the first Church in Northampton, together with the Elder of the Church in Cold-Spring, added by the consent of both the Pastor and Church in Northampton; in order to advise to a remedy from the calamities arising from the unsettled, broken state of the first Church in Northampton, by reason of a controversy subsisting about the qualifications for full Communion in the Church.

The Rev. Mr. Hubbard was chosen *Moderator*, and the Rev. Mr. Williams, *Scribe.*

The Council, after seeking the divine presence and direction, had the matter in controversy laid before them: and finding the sentiments of the Pastor and Church, concerning the qualifications necessary for full Communion, to be diametrically opposite to each other; the Pastor insisting upon it as necessary to the admission of Members to full Communion, that they should make a profession of sanctifying Grace; whereas the brethren are of opinion that the Lord's Supper is a converting ordinance; and consequently, that persons, if they have a competency of knowledge, and are of a blameless life, may be admitted to the Lord's Table, although they make no such profession; and also finding that, by reason of this diversity of sentiments, the doors of the Chruch have been shut for some years, so that there has been no admission; and not being able to find out any method, wherein the pastor and brethren can unite, consistent with their own sentiments, in admitting members to full communion. The council did then, according to the desire of the church, expressed in their letters missive, proceed to consider of the expediency of dissolving the relation between pastor and people, and after hearing the church upon it, and mature deliberation of the case, the questions were put to the members of the council severally;

1. Whether it be the opinion of this council, that the Rev. Mr. Edwards persisting in his principles, and the church in theirs in opposition to his, and insisting on a separation, it is necessary that the relation between pastor and people be dissolved? Resolved in the affirmative.

2. Whether it be expedient that this relation be immediately dissolved? Passed in the affirmative.

However we take notice, that notwithstanding the unhappy dispute which has arisen and so long subsisted between the pastor and church of Northampton, upon the point before mentioned, that we had no other objection against him, but what relates to his sentiments upon the point aforesaid, laid before us; and although we have heard of some stories spread abroad, reflecting upon Mr. Edwards's sincerity, with regard to the change of his sentiments about the qualifications for full communion; yet we have received full satisfaction that they are false and groundless. And although we don't all of us agree with Mr. Edwards in our sentiments upon the point, yet have abundant reason to believe that he took much pains to get light in that matter, and that he is uprightly following the dictates of his own conscience; and with great pleasure reflect upon the christian spirit and temper he has discovered in the unhappy controversy subsisting among them; and think ourselves bound to testify our full charity towards him, and recommend him to any church or people agreeing with him in sentiments, as a person eminently qualified for the work of the gospel ministry. And we would recommend it to the Rev. Mr. Edwards and the first Church in Northampton, to take proper notice of the heavy frown of divine Providence in suffering them to be reduced to such a state, as to render a separation necessary, after they have lived so long and amicably together, and been mutual blessings and comforts to each other. And now recommending the Rev. Mr. Edwards and the Church in Northampton to the Grace of God,

We subscribe,                                                    JONA. HUBBARD, Moderator,
                                                                     in the name of the Council.

Northampton, June 22d, 1750.

## PROTESTATION AGAINST THE COUNCIL'S RESULT, BY SOME OF THE MEMBERS.

We cannot agree to a dismission of the Rev. Mr. Edwards, at least for the present, for the following reasons; previous to which we observe, that though we presume not to infringe the rights of other consciences, yet we beg leave to enjoy our own, and being sought to offer advice and counsel at Northampton, are constrained to say to this church.

1. That we disapprove of the separation of the Rev. Mr. Edwards from his people, because that in the nature of the thing there is no just cause therefor, his sentiments being, as we apprehend, perfectly harmonious with the mind of the Lord Jesus Christ, and strictly conformable to the practice of the apostles, and that of the reformed churches in general.

2. Upon supposition that Mr. Edwards were in the wrong in the present controversy, yet there is, as we apprehend, no proportion between the importance of the controversy, and that of his dismission.

3. It appears that there have been no proper essays, in the way of fair reasoning, with or before the parties, to convince either of them of the truth or falseness of their principles, which love to the truth itself, and their souls requires.

4. Because the Church, or at least its committee, while they offer to us reasons for separating them from their pastor, yet will not suffer us so to enter into the grounds of those reasons, as to offer to them that light which the word of God affords; which we esteem an imposition on our consciences, and does but tend to keep them in the dark.

These, brethren, are some of the reasons, for which we can by no means approve a separation, at least at present, but if such separation should eventually come on, we bear a free and cheerful testimony in favour of our dearly beloved brother, and your once dearly beloved Pastor; though now esteemed your enemy, because (as we apprehend) he has told you the truth. He needs not indeed any recommendation of ours, which is more properly commendation of ourselves than of him, nor need we say much to others, for that his praise is in most of our churches through the land. Yet we are constrained to say to the world, that God has furnished him with those ministerial gifts and graces, by which he has hitherto shone as a burning and shining light, and though his people in general cease to rejoice in his light, yet we hope and trust others may rejoice in it for a long season. So wishing that the dear people of God in this place may take the point in controversy into a meek, calm, serious and prayerful consideration; and that so truth with holiness may greatly prevail in this place, we subscribe,

Yours in the bond of the Gospel.

> DAVID HALL,
> WILLIAM HOBBY,
> EDWARD BILLING,
> ROBERT ABERCROMBIE,
> JONATHAN HALE,
> MATTHEW GRAY,
> SAMUEL BANCROFT.

Northampton, June 22, 1750.

# The Case of Rev. Robert Breck

Ezra Hoyt Byington[°]

One of the best ways to gain a vivid and correct impression of the manners and opinions of our forefathers, and of the institutions under which they lived, is to explore the history of some single event, important enough to have connections with a large number of people, in various stations of life, and of various opinions. Such an event was the controversy which arose in Springfield, Massachusetts, in 1734, and continued for two years, in respect to the settlement of Robert Breck as pastor of the church in that town; an event which had a certain importance, in its time, for the people of Springfield, but which interests us mainly on account of the light it casts upon the way of life of the people a century and a half ago.

The town of Springfield was then one hundred years old. There were about a thousand people living within the present limits of that city.[1] Mr. Breck was the fourth pastor of the church. The average length of the pastorate had been thirty years. The number of members of the church was sixty-seven. The valley of the Connecticut was already full of thriving towns and villages. We read in the pamphlets of that time of Longmeadow and Westfield and Hadley, Northampton, Hatfield, and Deerfield among other places in the vicinity. The Hampshire Association of Ministers was a vigorous organization, made up of thirteen pastors, among whom were Jonathan Edwards, of Northampton, Isaac Chauncy, of Hadley, William Williams, of Hatfield, Stephen Williams, of Longmeadow, Samuel Hopkins, of West Springfield, and Ebenezer Devotion, of Suffield. This association, though organized for the mutual improvement of its members, like similar bodies in our own time, was accused of seeking to control the action of the churches in the selection of their pastors. It was alleged that some of these pastors were Presbyterians, and that they took it for granted that an association had powers like those of a presbytery. Their theological views were, for the most part, those of the earlier Puritans, which are moderately stated in the Westminster Confession of Faith. It was before the time of the "Improvements in theology" set forth by President Edwards. But even then, as we shall see, there was a difference in theological opinion among the pastors, and a still greater difference in their views of Christian liberty. For the most part they were devoted to their religious work. The years 1734 and 1735 were the years of the Great Awakening at Northampton, and Mr. Edwards was too

[°]Reprinted from *The Andover Review*, 13 (May 1890), 517–33.

fully absorbed in his work at home to enter very fully into the affairs of the church in Springfield.

The ministers and churches of Massachusetts were profoundly affected by the connection of the church with the state. The laws of the *Colony* of Massachusetts Bay had limited even the right of suffrage to members of the church. The charter of the *Province* of Massachusetts, which was granted by William and Mary in 1691, extended the suffrage to all male freeholders who possessed an estate worth two pounds a year. This provision of the charter opened the way for giving to those who were not communicants a voice in the selection of their ministers, and in the direction of the pecuniary interests of the parish. All this tended to liberalize the spirit of legislation. The General Court of the Province never enacted a law for the punishment of heresy[2] by fine and banishment, such as that under which William Pyncheon was summoned to appear before the General Court in 1650 to answer for his book entitled "The Meritorious Price of our Redemption."

Still, the legislation of the provincial period of our history was designed to bring the church under the fostering care and protection of the state. The basis of this legislation was a law passed in 1692, at the second session of the General Court, under the provincial charter, for the settlement and support of ministers.[3] It requires the inhabitants of each town to be constantly provided with "an able, learned, and orthodox minister, or ministers, of good conversation, to dispense the word of God to them." The minister was to be chosen by the church, "according to the directions given in the Word of God." The inhabitants of the town or precinct "who usually attend on the public worship of God," were to be called together to accept or reject the candidate whom the church had chosen. If they accepted him he became the legal minister of the town or precinct. If they rejected him, the church might still refer the matter to a council of neighboring churches, and if the council approved the choice of the church, the minister, accepting the call,[4] and duly installed, became the legal pastor, and was entitled to his salary. The amount both of the "settlement" and of the "maintenance" of the minister was fixed by a contract before his introduction to his office, and the people were required to pay toward his settlement and maintenance, "each man his several proportion thereof." The Court of General Sessions of the county was required to see that the contract was fulfilled. If any town or precinct should neglect to provide itself with a suitable minister, the Court of Quarter Sessions was required to "make order upon them speedily to provide themselves with a minister." If this order was disregarded, it was the duty of the court to procure and settle a minister, and order the charge of such minister's settlement and maintenance to be levied on the inhabitants of such town. At a later time, it was made the duty of the General Court itself, on receiving notice from the court of any county that a town or precinct was destitute of a minister, to provide and send to every such town or precinct an able, learned, and orthodox minister, of good conversation, and to provide for his support by adding to the taxes of such town or precinct so much as they should judge sufficient for this end.

These laws assumed a definite method of procedure on the part of churches and congregations, such as is marked out in the Cambridge Platform. This Platform had a quasi-legal authority, having been commended to the churches by the General Court, and it was constantly appealed to as the standard in the discussions of those days.

Thus the churches of the olden time were accustomed to depend on the authority of the state for raising the money to support public worship. In the course of time they learned to follow legal forms and precedents, and to transact much of their most important business in a legal spirit and environment. There would sometimes be a doubt whether a council called to settle a minister had been legally called, and whether its proceedings were regular and valid; whether a minister had been "duly settled according to law;" whether a minister was "orthodox, able, learned, and of good conversation," within the meaning of the law; and whether he *continued* to possess all these excellent qualities. On the decision of these questions would depend his right to his *salary*, and also the right of the town, or parish, to assess a tax for his support. Sometimes the question would be raised whether a *town* which was supporting a minister had such a minister that it was not liable to be presented by the grand jury, and prosecuted as a destitute town. These discussions and litigations were among the most characteristic things relating to the life and manners of our fathers.

Robert Breck, of Springfield, was the son of Robert Breck, of Marlboro', of whom the "Boston News-Letter" said: "He was an able minister, a man of great learning in the original languages of the Bible, and in philosophy, and also a man of great courage and prudence." His grandfather was Captain John Breck, "a very ingenious and worthy man." His great-grandfather was Edward Breck, a man of wealth and influence in England, who came to this country in 1636, and settled in Dorchester.

Robert Breck was born in Marlboro', Massachusetts, July 25, 1713, and entered Harvard College at the age of thirteen. His rank as a scholar is indicated by the fact that the President and Fellows awarded to him the honorary prize of thirty pounds as a "sober, diligent, and promising student, and candidate for the ministry." He was graduated with honor in 1730. It has been stated that he studied theology with his father, but as the father died the year after his son was graduated, it is probable that he continued his studies without an instructor. He began to preach while he was very young, according to the custom of those times. He was hardly more than twenty when we find him preaching in Scotland, a parish in Windham County, Connecticut, and at various other places in that colony. The young and untrained preacher was very free and bold in his utterances, and very early subjected himself to the charge of heresy, a charge which some of the pastors of the vicinity were disposed to press to his injury.

Some time in May, 1734, the First Church in Springfield invited him to preach as a candidate for settlement. He came, and preached to the acceptance of the people, so that after about three months the church and parish gave him a call, and proposed terms of settlement. He had then just passed his twenty-first birthday.

Soon after he came to Springfield there were reports passing from one to another that he was not sound in the faith. The people listened to his sermons, but failed to detect anything that savored of heresy. So far as the pamphlets[5] which were published at the time, on both sides, give us information, it was not claimed that there was anything unsound in his religious teachings after he came to Springfield. The reports all came from Connecticut. A letter was received from a minister in that colony, which stated that "Mr. Breck was not a suitable person to be employed in the ministry," and named Rev. Thomas Clap, of Windham, afterward President of Yale College, and two others, as persons who were responsible for the charges. This letter was put into the hands of Mr. Breck, who went at once to Windham to confer with Mr. Clap in respect to the accusations. Mr. Clap was not satisfied with the result of the conference, and so wrote a long letter to the Hampshire Association of Ministers, in which he set forth the four charges against the young candidate for the pastorate.

1. That he had denied that the passage in 1 John v.7, concerning the "three that bear record in heaven," and also the passage in John VIII., concerning the woman taken in adultery, were of divine inspiration.

2. That he had also denied the necessity of Christ's satisfaction to divine justice for sin, and had said that God might, consistent with his justice, forgive sin without any satisfaction.

3. That he had preached that the heathen, who lived up to the light of nature, would be saved. Christ would be in some way revealed to them; or they would be saved in some other way.

4. That there was a general report that he had stolen books from the college library, while a student, and that he had been expelled from college for this offense; and further, that when Mr. Clap had informed him of these reports, he had denied them, a denial which was now known to be false.

In addition to all this it was stated in other letters that Mr. Breck had said publicly, that "if the decrees of God were absolute, he saw no encouragement for men to try to do their duty, for let them do what they would, they could not alter their condition; and that we were not under obligation any further than we had power."

The charges were the basis of the opposition to the settlement of Mr. Breck. In reply to the charges, he claimed that it was unjust to use against him expressions which he might have used in his earliest sermons, at a time when his views were quite immature; that these expressions did not express his settled opinions; that some of them had never been used in his sermons, but only in oral discussion with pastors with whom he was discoursing, for the sake of clearing his own mind; and also, that some of these statements were not inconsistent with the Confession of Faith. He asked to be judged, not by these early sermons, but by the sermons he had preached in his present pulpit, and he repeatedly invited those who questioned his orthodoxy to satisfy themselves by an examination as to his views in theology.

In respect to the charge of taking books from the library, he admitted that there had been a technical offense, which gave some color to the charge, but claimed that the offense, such as it was, was the fault of a boy of thirteen, and that it was so trivial that the faculty did not make it a matter of formal discipline, and that his subsequent deportment has been so exemplary that they had selected him as the student most worthy to receive the honorary prize. Mr. Breck also stated that he had never denied that there had been some foundation for the story, but had only denied it in the exaggerated form in which it had been reported. These are the leading points in the case as it is presented in the pamphlets and in the manuscripts which have been preserved.

Mr. Breck was informed that these reports had excited a degree of prejudice against him among the ministers of the vicinity, and that if he were to accept the call they might refuse to ordain him. He was also informed that they had exerted more or less influence with some members of his congregation. He therefore decided to refer the matter again to the people. He knew that he had the confidence of a large majority of his congregation, and that some of the pastors of the vicinity were satisfied as to his integrity and his orthodoxy, so that there would be no serious difficulty in securing ordination. "If one council will not do it," he said, "another will." With these views, he stated, in his reply to the call, that while he was disposed, on some accounts, to accept their invitation, he did not think the provision for his temporal support was sufficient, and that he could not accept the call unless they should see the way clear to increase it. The people were not quite agreed in the matter, and did not think it expedient to increase the salary. So that Mr. Breck finally declined the call and returned to his friends in Boston.

But the people were not satisfied. The records of the parish show that the majority believed that his settlement had been prevented by the intermeddling of "some persons of note who had sent writings to some of the ministers of this vicinity." The parish, therefore, appointed a committee, November 8th, to find out how much ground there was for the charges against Mr. Breck, and also to learn more definitely the views of the ministers. In response to their inquiries six of the pastors, among whom we find the name of Jonathan Edwards, signed a paper, which reads as follows:—

"Upon consideration of the case of Mr. Robert Breck, represented to us in some letters from Windham and Norwich, we think it advisable that the people of Springfield do no further make their application to him."

The committee reported, and the people considered the advice. Six weeks later the freeholders and other inhabitants assembled according to law, voted "that application be made to the worthy Mr. Robert Breck to preach the word of God to us in this place, in order to a settlement." This vote was passed by a decisive majority, and a committee was chosen to proceed to Cambridge, make investigations, ask advice, and act according to their best judgment. The result was that Mr. Breck returned to Springfield, and began to preach again. This open disregard of the advice of the ministers of the vicinity seems to have been unusual, and it had the effect to lead them to enter more directly into the case. A majority of them seem to have thought that it would be an infringement of their rights to settle a minister within the county in opposition to their advice. The next stage in the business was the effort of the association to investigate the charges against Mr. Breck. They entered into correspondence with various parties in Connecticut; and also induced Mr. Breck to write to Mr. Clap, and endeavor to make his peace with him. They invited Mr. Breck to attend the meeting of the association in April, 1735, and make such statement as he thought proper with reference to the charges. He seems to have accepted their proposals in good faith. He wrote a letter to Mr. Clap in which he made such acknowledgments and concessions as he thought proper, but he failed to satisfy that gentleman. He also read to the association a paper which was quite satisfactory to some of the pastors, but not to the majority. Six out of thirteen ministers now took his part, and remained his friends to the end. He next asked the association to satisfy themselves as to his theological views by an oral examination. The majority declined to do this, on the ground that charges were already pending against him. At this stage of the business a committee from the First Parish appeared before the association to inquire "what impediment, if any, there was to the settlement of Mr. Breck; and if such impediment existed, how it could be removed."

This was designed to open the way for a formal examination of the charges of Mr. Clap and others from Connecticut. Mr. Breck and his friends were prepared to welcome such an investigation, but they asked to be permitted to name one or two of the persons who were to pass upon the case. The association appointed seven of their own members to hear the whole case and to give their judgment. It was pointed out to them that several of these gentlemen had already prejudged the case, and expressed their opinion publicly. Mr. Breck offered to go on with the investigation if one of the committee would retire, or if, that gentleman remaining, he might call in two unprejudiced persons from outside the county. These propositions were declined by the majority, and so the proposed investigation failed.

At this stage of the business the First Church in Springfield, on the 17th of April, renewed their call to Mr. Breck, and one week later the parish voted to concur. It appeared that a decided majority of the church and congregation were very earnest to secure the permanent settlement of the young preacher as their pastor. It remained to be seen whether the minority of the people, aided by the majority of the association, would be able to prevent it. Mr. Breck, made wiser by the experiences of the year, acted with a degree of prudence and foresight which he had not before shown. He first sent a communication to the people, in which he said that, in the peculiar circumstances of this case, he should seek advice from his friends before he gave an answer to their call. He went soon after to Boston, and requested the pastors of that city, who were well known throughout the Province, to examine him as to his views in theology. This they did, and as a result gave him a certificate[6] that they had found him sound in the faith. They say: "These may certify that on the 8th day of May, 1735, we discoursed with Robert Breck, M. A., to our good satisfaction, concerning his orthodoxy in the great doctrines of Christianity, as believed and professed in the churches of Christ in New England, agreeable to the Westminster

Confession of Faith; and so recommend him to the grace of God, and are his brethren in Christ."

With this indorsement he returned to Springfield, and on the 28th of July accepted the call. The next step was to select a council for his ordination. The excitement in Springfield ran very high. Four members of the church presented a protest, which was entered upon the records. Twenty-seven members of the parish sent to Mr. Breck a remonstrance against his course in accepting the call before submitting himself to the judgment of the ministers of the association as to his orthodoxy and as to his character. Mr. Breck replied that the Council would be the proper tribunal to pass upon all these questions.

In the end the church voted, by a decided majority, to call a council for his installation. They selected four churches within the county, designating them by the names of their pastors, and left it with the pastor-elect, with a committee of the church, to select an equal number of churches outside the county. The council, as finally agreed upon, consisted[7] of the church in Hatfield, Rev. William Williams, pastor; Hadley, Rev. Isaac Chauncy, pastor; Suffield, Rev. Ebenezer Devotion, pastor; Sunderland, Rev. William Rand, pastor; Brattle Street Church, Boston, Rev. William Cooper, pastor; Second Church, Boston, Rev. Samuel Mather, pastor; the New Brick Church, Boston, Rev. William Welstead, pastor; and the church in Sudbury, Rev. William Cooke, pastor. The council was to meet October 7th.

Those who opposed the settlement of Mr. Breck denied the legality of the council for two reasons: First, because the votes of the church designated the pastors, instead of the churches to which they ministered; and because these votes left it with the pastor-elect and a committee of the church to select a part of the churches; and, secondly, because the church had no right to call churches from outside Hampshire County. It was replied, on the part of the church, that what was done by its committee, chosen for the purpose, was done by itself,— that the letter missive, which went in the name of the church, was addressed to all the churches, by name, and that they had elected delegates to the council, showing that they understood the invitation. It was also claimed that they had a right to go outside the county for members of the council, as there was nothing in the Cambridge platform to forbid it; and that in this case it was necessary in order to secure an impartial council.

It is not easy to understand, at this distance of time, the intense interest which this case excited, not only at Springfield, but in other parts of New England. The members of the council from Boston went to Springfield a week in advance of the meeting of the council, in order to consult with the ministers of the vicinity, and learn from them directly the grounds of their opposition. How abundant the leisure of those pastors of the olden time! It is a hundred miles from Boston to Springfield, and the stagecoaches, or ministerial chaises, of those days would be more than one day on the journey. Yet they went from town to town in the Connecticut valley, and tried to induce the pastors to submit their complaints against Mr. Breck to the council. When the time for the meeting of the council came, the ministers of the county were present in

Springfield to watch the proceedings, and to use their influence to prevent the ordination. The President of Yale College was also there, as the champion of orthodoxy, to direct the measures of the opposition. Rev. Thomas Clap and a number of other pastors from Connecticut were there, with documents to be presented to the council. It was confidently asserted by the opponents of Mr. Breck that whatever the council might do, "there would be no ordination."

In order to secure the fulfillment of this prediction, the dissatisfied members of the parish had induced three justices of the Court of Sessions to come from Northampton to Springfield, with the purpose of using the authority of the court, if necessary, to prevent the council from completing the service for which it had been convened. It was afterwards proved before the General Court that it was at first intended to arrest all the members of the council who had come from outside the county, and lock them up in jail, on the ground that their attempt to sit as members of a council in Hampshire County was an unlawful act,—an usurpation of power,—to the great injury of the minority. Warrants were actually made out for their arrest, but as one of the justices was doubtful as to their right to issue them, this plan was abandoned. The second plan was to arrest Mr. Breck, and hold him in custody until the council should adjourn.

We may well suppose that when the day for the meeting of the council came business was suspended in Springfield, and that the people were eagerly watching the proceedings. The council met in the morning, not in the church, but in the house of Madam Brewer, the widow of the last pastor. Seven of the eight churches invited were represented by pastors and delegates. The church in Hatfield, of which the venerable William Williams was pastor, declined to respond, on the ground that the council was irregular and illegal. The council organized by choosing Rev. William Cooper, of Boston, Moderator. Their first act was to invite the church—as well the minority as the majority—to lay all the facts in the case before them. Two papers were presented. The first was a remonstrance against the right of "the body calling itself a council" to ordain Mr. Breck, signed by William Pyncheon, Jr., Esq., and others of the minority of the parish. The second was a protest against the right of the council to act in the case, signed by six pastors of the county. The council, after considering these papers, and the reasons which were set forth in support of them, voted: "That the elders and other delegates here assembled are an ecclesiastical council, properly called by the First Church in Springfield to join in the regular carrying on of the ordination of Mr. Breck, and are ready to hear, judge, and act in the case."

The council next called upon those who objected to Mr. Breck to present the evidence in support of the charges which they made against him. This they declined to do, on the ground that they could not recognize the body then in session as a regular and legal council. The Moderator next asked Rev. Mr. Clap and Rev. Mr. Kirkland, the authors of the charges, to let the council know whatever they knew against the candidate, which might disqualify him for the ministry. Mr. Clap proceeded to read a number of documents, most of them sworn to before a magistrate, with reference to the preaching of Mr. Breck while he was in Connecticut. These papers cover the whole case, and constitute the evidence on which the minority based their opposition. They are printed in full in the pamphlet published by the Hampshire ministers. Just as Mr. Clap finished reading the papers, and before Mr. Breck had commenced his reply, an officer entered the room with a warrant for the arrest of "Robert Breck, gentleman," and for bringing him forthwith before the court then in session in the town-house, "To answer for such things as should be objected to him." Mr. Breck was taken by the officer from the council, and carried to the town-house. Proclamation was made that any persons who knew about the principles or the character of Mr. Breck should come forward and give testimony. Mr. Clap and Mr. Kirkland came forward and presented the evidence which they had just read to the council, with some additional statements. Mr. Breck was also examined by the justices as to his theological opinions. The evidence tended to show that he was not sound in the faith, and also that he had charged various persons with misrepresentation and falsehood. The old charge of taking books from the college library was also referred to in the testimony as a matter of common report. The proceedings seem to have been of the nature of an inquiry into the character of the candidate and his fitness to be a settled minister under the laws of the Province.

These proceedings of the secular power had the effect, of course, of suspending the session of the ecclesiastical court. Before adjourning, however, they sent a vigorous protest to the court, in which they say that they "consider it a duty not only to the church in Springfield, but to the churches which they represent, and to all the churches of Christ throughout the Province, to inform the court that when they sent their officer to apprehend Mr. Breck they were regularly and legally convened in council, at the desire of the church in Springfield, for the regular carrying on of the ordination of said Mr. Breck, according to the order of the gospel in the churches of New England, and were actually hearing the charges against him when the court saw fit to wrest the case out of their hands." Having sent their protest, the council waited for the result. Mr. Breck was held in custody until night, and the justices gave orders to their officer to hold him till the next day. But certain members of the council gave their word that he should appear when called for, and he was permitted to go to his lodgings.

The council reassembled early in the morning, and continued the hearing of the case. Mr. Clap and Mr. Kirkland made oral statements as to the additional testimony they had given in court. The justices soon sent for Mr. Breck, and held him until late in the afternoon, when they made out a warrant which directed the sheriff to take him to Windsor, in the Colony of Connecticut, and deliver him into the custody of the County Court, "there to answer for those things which might be objected against him." He was taken to Windsor, and delivered to the officers of the court. He was permitted to give bonds for his appearance at a subsequent time to answer to a charge concerning the doctrines which he had preached while within that colony.

These proceedings increased very much the excitement among the people at Springfield. The church appointed a committee to attend him, "in token of respect as their pastor-elect, and the people gave evident marks of their affection for him as he went through the town." The next day they assembled in the meeting-house to pray for his safe return. The record says: "It was a large and weeping assembly." A day or two later Mr. Breck returned to Springfield, and the council resumed its sessions. They considered more fully the charges and the testimony for and against him, and listened to his reply. The decisive paper in the case was a Confession of Faith which he drew up for the satisfaction of the council, as a statement of his mature opinions concerning the leading truths of the gospel.[8] It is a serious and definite statement, following substantially the Westminster Confession, and, by implication, renouncing most of the errors which he had been accused of preaching in Connecticut. After reciting the statement of his belief, he said: "This is the scheme of Christian doctrine which I have learned from the Holy Scriptures, and which I shall think myself obliged to teach others in the best manner I am able, while at the same time I put them that profess to believe in mind that they be careful to maintain good works. It is my prayer that my knowledge of these things may be enlarged, my faith of them confirmed, and that I may be enabled always to keep the mystery of the faith in a pure conscience." This confession was satisfactory to the whole council. It was read to a great crowd of people who assembled in the street in front of the house in which the council was holding its sessions; and was subsequently read by the candidate to the congregation at his ordination. The council, after a full consideration of the case, came to a Result, in which they said, that they found that Mr. Breck had been regularly called by a very great majority of the church and precinct of Springfield; and also that he was sound in the faith, and of good conversation; so that they advise the people "to continue their regards for him." "Nevertheless," they say, "having met with an unusual interposition and hindrance in carrying on the work upon which we were called, we do not think it advisable to proceed further herein at this time, but that this council be adjourned" to meet in Boston, October 21st. The Moderator remained in Springfield over the Sabbath, and read this result to the congregation.

The object of the adjournment was not only to allow time for the excitement to subside, but also to test the legality of the interference of the secular authorities with the work of the council. Two weeks later the church appointed a committee to bring the matter before the General Court. This committee presented a memorial to the General Court on the 25th of November, in which they stated the fact of the call of Mr. Breck by a very great majority of the church and precinct, and the convening of a council for his ordination, and say that "on the day appointed for that solemnity John Stoddard, Ebenezer Pomeroy, and Timothy Dwight, Esqrs., his Majesty's justices of the peace for the County of Hampshire, had caused him to be arrested and taken from the aforesaid ecclesiastical council, and brought before them, and that they examined him touching divers points of doctrine; and, further, that by a warrant from the said justices, he was sent to Windsor, in the Colony of Connecticut, where he was bound over by the County Court to answer to a charge touching his doctrines." They ask the General Court to decide whether these proceedings have been according to law, and if not, to grant such redress as the case admits.

The journals of the General Court show that the case was very fully considered by that body. It was first assigned to the 5th of December, at which time the papers were read. It was voted to inquire into the matter of complaint, and to appoint a committee to report what action ought to be taken. Notice was sent to the justices at Northampton, and to other parties interested. The General Court heard not only the committee from Springfield, but Mr. Breck, and the Moderator of the council, and various other persons. The matter was before the Court December 5th and 6th, 9th, 24th, 26th, and 27th. The decision was, first, that the council was duly called, and was properly and legally a council, according to the usages of the churches; and, secondly, that the justices had no right to "interrupt the church and ecclesiastical council, while they were, in the exercise of their just rights, investigating the case."

Strengthened by this decision, the council, which had been continued by successive adjournments, reassembled at Springfield on the 27th of January, 1736, and "finding that the people did abide firm in their choice of Mr. Breck, and their desire to have him as their pastor," they proceeded to ordain him as pastor of the church. The sermon was preached by Mr. Cooper, the Moderator, from Matthew XIII. 3. In this sermon, which was printed, Mr. Cooper bears this testimony in respect to the young pastor: "I think myself bound to testify, on this occasion, that in all this time I never heard one hard word drop from you respecting any person of any order. I have seen your tears, admired your silence, and hope God has heard your prayers. May the fruit of all be to humble you, to prove you, and to make you a greater blessing to this church and people."

Those who were opposed to Mr. Breck made one more effort to prevent him from continuing as the minister of the church. They signed a complaint to the Court of Sessions for the county, which set forth that the church in Springfield was destitute of a minister duly settled according to law; that one Robert Breck had taken upon himself the office of pastor, under pretense that he had been ordained; that the said Breck is not qualified, according to the laws of this Province, to be a gospel minister, inasmuch as he is not orthodox in his belief, and not of good conversation; that, according to law, there can be no money raised for the settlement and support of any person in the ministry but such as are orthodox and of good conversation. They therefore ask the court to make such order in the premises "that some suitable person may be settled in the pastoral office in said church, it being contrary to the law of this Province, and the peace of the king, that a person of such principles and conversation should take upon himself the office of a minister, or that the said church should be destitute of a settled minister." The Court took this petition into consideration on the 2d of March, and summoned the church and parish to appear and answer the complaint. The parish appointed a committee of five, of which William

Pyncheon, Jr., Esq., was chairman, to represent them before the court, and instructed them to "carry the case as far as necessary, from court to court, in order to a *final* determination of the matter." As there is no further reference to the case in the records of the parish, it is probable that it never came before the court for trial.

These proceedings were followed by a number of pamphlets, which are the authentic sources of information concerning these matters. The first was published in Boston, 1736, a few months after the ordination had taken place. It is entitled "A Narrative of the Proceedings of those Ministers of the County of Hampshire that have disapproved the Settlement of Mr. Robert Breck." It is a vigorous pamphlet of about one hundred pages. This was followed the same year by "An Answer to the Hampshire Narrative." This also contains one hundred pages. It is said to have been written by Rev. William Cooper, of Boston. The next year appeared another thick pamphlet, with the title, "A Letter to the Author of the Answer to the Narrative."

While these proceedings in court and this war of pamphlets were going on, the young pastor set himself to conciliate the opposition among his people. He gave himself to the duties of his office with exemplary fidelity. It is said of him, that if he wished any favor he would ask it from some one of his people who had been unfriendly. Such an expression of his confidence won their good will. He chose his wife wisely also. He married, a few weeks after his ordination, Eunice Brewer, the daughter of his predecessor, who had been universally loved and revered. He invited Rev. Stephen Williams, of Longmeadow, who had been one of the most decided of his opponents, to perform the marriage ceremony, and this act of courtesy is said to have modified his opposition. In a few years he was accepted by his brethren in the ministry, as well as by his people, as a minister "able, learned, orthodox, and of good conversation."

Mr. Breck was the pastor of the church in Springfield forty-eight years. The church grew with the town, and its minister became a man of great influence in the Connecticut valley. It is more than a hundred years since his death, but the traditions concerning him at Springfield are still fresh, and he is held in great esteem and veneration. His funeral sermon was preached by Dr. Lathrop, of West Springfield, who had been a student in divinity under him. In this sermon he said: "His intellectual powers were naturally superior, and were brightened by his education, and enlarged by an extensive acquaintance with men and books. He accustomed himself to a close manner of reasoning and thinking, and filled up his time with diligent application. History was his amusement, divinity his study; he excelled in both, especially the latter. He was an accomplished gentleman, and an exemplary Christian. His attendance on the duties of his profession was constant, his preparations for the sanctuary were mature, his public prayers were deliberate and solemn, his sermons were full of thought,—dressed in the most proper language, and communicated in the easiest manner. His religious sentiments were formed on a careful examination of the Scriptures, without servile attachment to sects or systems. His turn of thinking was liberal yet Scriptural, exalted yet humble."

Such was the man as he seemed to his contemporaries at the close of a pastorate of half a century.

## Notes

1. Judge Morris's *Historical Address*, 1875.

2. *Andover Review*, 9 (1886), 248.

3. These laws may be found in the *Province Laws*, I. 62, 102, 506, 216, 597 and II. 58; III. 288.

4. The first law gave the choice to the people of the town. This was amended at the next session so as to give the church the right to lead in the choice.

5. *Narrative of the Proceedings of those Ministers of Hampshire County that have disapproved the Settlement of Mr. Robert Breck* (Boston, 1736); *Answer to the Above* (Boston, 1736); *Letter to the Author of the Answer* (Boston, 1737).

6. This was signed by Benjamin Coleman, Joseph Sewall, John Webb, William Cooper, Thomas Foxcroft, Samuel Checkley, Joshua Gee, and Mather Byles. One of them said afterwards: "I can assure you that his examination was not a slighty one, if the ability and fidelity of the eight ministers that were concerned in it can be relied on."

7. Mr. Williams was the oldest minister in the county, being 70; Isaac Chauncy (H. C., 1693) was grandson of President Chauncy; Ebenezer Devotion, H. C., 1707; William Rand, H. C., 1724; William Cooper, born 1694, H. C., 1712, junior pastor with Dr. Coleman,—"there was not a more decided Calvinist than he, yet he was a staunch advocate of religious liberty,"—was elected President H. C. 1737; Samuel Mather, son of Cotton Mather, H. C., 1723; D.D.,—"was charged with looseness of doctrine;" William Welstead, H. C., 1716, "an excellent Christian gentleman, and an exemplary minister;" William Cooke, H. C., 1716.

8. In this confession, which is too long to insert entire, he declares his belief in one God, who is also triune; in the Holy Scriptures, which are of divine authority, and which have been preserved by God's providence "pure and uncorrupt;" in the decrees of God, by which, whatsoever comes to pass in time has been foreordained from all eternity,— "yet so as not to take away the will of His creatures, or make Himself the Author of sin;" in the providential government of the world; in the first covenant with Adam; in his fall from his first estate, which involved the race "in his guilt and corruption;" in the covenant of redemption, and the vicarious sacrifice of the God-Man, "which satisfied divine justice for the sins of the elect, and reconciles them to God;" in the work of the Holy Spirit, "who makes effectual application of the benefits of Christ's redemption to the souls of men;" in the inability of fallen man to that which is spiritually good, and the necessity of effectual calling by the Almighty Spirit; in the imputation of the righteousness of Christ for their justification; in the work of sanctification; in the final perseverance of the saints; the eternal separation of the righteous from the wicked; the righteous for life eternal, and the wicked for everlasting punishment.

# The Impolitic Mr. Edwards:
# The Personal Dimension of the
# Robert Breck Affair

Charles Edwin Jones*

In 1729 Jonathan Edwards was installed as his grandfather Solomon Stoddard's successor. Inheritance of Stoddard's prestigious Northampton pulpit, however, in no way implied inheritance of his grandfather's preeminence among western Massachusetts clergy. Long before the end of Stoddard's fifty-eight-year pastorate, his son-in-law, William Williams of Hatfield, had come to share leadership of the Hampshire Association of Ministers. And upon the death of "Pope" Stoddard, Williams stepped into the senior minister's shoes. Far from challenging his uncle, Jonathan Edwards not only acquiesced in his ascendancy, but actively supported Williams' leadership. The actions of the old guard under Williams contributed to the factionalism which characterized the Connecticut Valley churches in the decade of the Great Awakening, and prepared the way for Jonathan Edwards' dismissal from Northampton in 1750. Edwards' participation in the Robert Breck affair during his first decade in Northampton, set in motion forces which later would victimize him.[1]

The solidarity between Edwards and his uncle was achieved during the first year of Edwards' Northampton pastorate. John Williams, pastor at Deerfield, died in 1729, and during the search for a successor, William Williams' son Elisha, rector of Yale College, the associated ministers of New Haven County, Connecticut, and Edwards all backed Edwards' brother-in-law, Benjamin Pierpont, for the position. William Williams, who had at first also favored Pierpont, suddenly turned on him. Ignoring Edwards with whom Pierpont was then living, the "Hatfield Mr. Williams" insisted the candidate "was not of Prudent, Grave & Sober Conversation," but "vain, apish & jovial, particularly among females." At least one young lady was said to be "afraid" of him. In face of the elder Williams' opposition, the Deerfield congregation rescinded its invitation.[2] Mr. Williams' nephew at Northampton never again opposed him.

In 1733, four years after Jonathan Edwards succeeded his grandfather, Daniel Brewer, pastor of the First Church in Springfield, died. Robert Breck, a graduate of Harvard, was invited to try out as a candidate and on July 30, 1734, the church called him as pastor. Although the congregation approved, a minister could not settle permanently without ordination. Hardly had Breck begun

*Reprinted, with permission, from *The New England Quarterly*, 51 (March 1978), 64–79.

preaching at Springfield, however, when rumors about his past reached Hampshire County. This gossip served not only as the prelude to Robert Breck's initiation at Springfield, but also marked the beginning of the collapse of Stoddardism in the church politics of western Massachusetts.

Early in 1734, despite significant opposition, the Scotland, Connecticut church had called Breck as pastor and had offered him a generous 250-pound annual salary to settle. Opponents of Breck in the congregation charged the candidate had boasted that, given the opportunity, "he would preach People out of those false and stingy Notions" they had been taught.[3]

Catching wind of the dispute and having questions of his own to put to Breck, Thomas Clap, pastor of the First Church in Windham, decided to visit Scotland to investigate. Upon his arrival, the two men retired to Breck's quarters where an all-night inquisition ensued. Clap questioned not only the validity of the candidate's theological position, but also the propriety of his past conduct. Setting aside the young man's explanation that an extended absence from Cambridge while he was a student there had been occasioned by smallpox, the older man suggested that Breck had been expelled for stealing and had been readmitted only after his father interceded on his behalf with college authorities. Clap's charges so infuriated Breck that finally he exploded, "I suppose you wou'd have it here, as it is in Scotland; there the young Ministers cannot think freely for themselves; but must think as the old Ministers do, or else they will not ordain them."[4]

Apparently Robert Breck's assessment of Thomas Clap's motives was correct. After Clap convinced the Scotland church that the candidate was unsuitable, the church withdrew its offer,[5] and Breck left town, riding toward the Connecticut River and Springfield.

Word of the Connecticut fiasco followed fast after Breck. Eleazer Williams, one of Clap's ministerial neighbors, wrote his brother, Stephen Williams, pastor in the third parish of Springfield, "I am very much afraid" Breck is "not a suitable Person to be employ'd in the Ministry."[6] Stephen Williams circulated his brother's letter among Hampshire Association ministers,[7] who in turn appointed Samuel Hopkins and Ebenezer Devotion to question Breck.

When confronted, the youth denied he had been expelled from Harvard, claiming he had taken the unorthodox positions cited by Clap and Williams merely for argument's sake. The ministers' representatives demanded a letter signed by a minister of unassailable integrity certifying Breck's orthodoxy.[8] Otherwise they would not ordain him.

On October 8, the Hampshire Association of Ministers met and prepared to deal with the Springfield problem. In the organizing session which in keeping with congregationalist practice preceded the meeting, the group for the first time passed over William Williams,[9] an opponent of Breck, and elected Isaac Chauncy,[10] a believer in the candidate's innocence, as moderator. They then elected Jonathan Edwards, who sided with Williams, as scribe. During the business session, the group voted to add proof of orthodoxy to previously adopted requirements for ordination.[11] Since negotiations between Breck and the church had stalemated over salary, the meeting adjourned without further action.[12]

Still favoring Breck and believing his statement that Clap had lied, the church voted on November 8 to send a committee[13] of community leaders to negotiate with the Association ministers. The ministers advised against further efforts to settle Breck, and sent the church a letter signed by William Williams, Jonathan Edwards, Stephen Williams and three other ministers to this effect.[14] Nevertheless, on January 1, 1735, the church voted to ask Breck to preach again with a view to settling.

Since the candidate now said he would stand behind previous statements, Stephen Williams advised him to seek a character reference from Thomas Clap. As a result Breck wrote his Connecticut adversary explaining that while his theology was now as always unimpeachable, he had not in fact told the whole truth in regard to his college troubles. In response Clap wrote the neighboring clergy they were in a better position to judge the candidate's character than he was.[15]

When the Hampshire Association met at West Springfield on April 8, William Williams resumed his role as moderator, and proceeded to a formal examination of the candidate. Breck continued to hedge about his past, however, and the ministers decided he would have to face Thomas Clap before a committee of the Association.[16] Then, as if to substantiate the youth's charge that local ministerial leaders were biased, the Association chose a six-member committee of whom only Isaac Chauncy and Ebenezer Devotion could be said to favor Breck. Later, "to Remove the Difficulty" of a "Committee consisting of an Even number,"[17] Jonathan Edwards was added. By appointment of a one-sided committee, the Hampshire ministers showed their subservience to William Williams, who like his father-in-law before him, was determined to control pastoral appointments in western Massachusetts.[18]

Like Solomon Stoddard, William Williams skillfully used family connections, professional courtesies, and the friendship of leading merchants—the so-called "River Gods"—to political advantage.[19] During a forty-three-year apprenticeship under Stoddard, Williams had gathered a coterie of strong allies. At Stoddard's death in 1729, he commanded the allegiance of scores of followers by means of kinship, marriage, and professional obligation. Within the fourteen-member Hampshire Association of Ministers, he was the father-in-law of Jonathan Ashley and the uncle of Jonathan Edwards, Stephen Williams, and Samuel Hopkins' wife. He had been a participant in the ordinations of Stephen Williams, Samuel Hopkins, Nehemiah Bull, Jonathan Edwards, and Jonathan Ashley. All would stand with the Hatfield pastor in resisting outside intervention in the Connecticut Valley churches.[20]

On April 17 the Springfield church again extended a call to Robert Breck. The terms were not attractive. Realizing that he must be ordained now or never, Breck accepted and left for Boston where he hoped to persuade leading ministers to support him.[21]

In Boston Breck gained the endorsement he sought. Because of the strong local opposition, the eastern clergy advised that some ministers from outside Hampshire County be placed on the ordination council. Breck agreed. On July 28 he observed that while "many obstacles" remained yet to be surmounted, the "uneasiness" of "some of the neighboring ministers" might be overcome by association with Boston ministers who approved his candidacy.[22]

In making arrangements for the examination and ordination, the Springfield church followed Breck's instructions. Ignoring congregational tradition, it sent the letters of invitation to the ordination council to ministers, not churches. Ordinarily only neighboring churches would be chosen to participate. The Springfield congregation, however, selected four ministers from the Hampshire Association and four from the outside whom "Mr. Breck shall chuse to ordain him."[23] Of the eight thus chosen, only William Williams could be said to represent the traditional view. From Boston Benjamin Colman wrote Stephen Williams:"I beseech you Sir . . . be tender of him. A young Mans Reputation & Usefulness is of the highest price."[24]

Western feelings, however, were not to be easily assuaged. The delegates from eastern Massachusetts had scarcely settled in their rooms at Madame Brewer's (Robert Breck was already boarding with the widow of the deceased pastor) when local clergy registered a formal protest against outside clergy being called in. They also contacted county officials, alleging the ordination would constitute a violation of the peace. (The justices of Hampshire County: Seth Pomeroy, Timothy Dwight, and Jonathan Edwards' uncle, John Stoddard, were all members of Edwards' Northampton congregation.)[25]

On the morning of October 7 the council met to examine Robert Breck. As soon as organization was completed, a group representing the minority in the Springfield congregation appeared against Breck. The candidate, they charged, had all but called the doctrine of predestination absurd, and had failed to keep his promise to postpone seeking ordination until he answered the charges against him. They claimed the council assembled was illegal and, as constituted, was prejudiced in favor of Breck. Next, a committee from the parish (not church members) testified that it would refuse to submit to the council's judgment.[26]

When on the second day the council set aside time to hear Thomas Clap, Elisha Williams, then head of the New Haven school, was present. (The younger Williams, Jonathan Edwards' cousin, had been Edwards' teacher at Wethersfield when for a few years Yale students resided wherever the teachers lived.) Rector Williams' presence witnessed obliquely to the intercollegiate as well as the intersectional rivalry represented in the Springfield case, but had little effect on the proceedings. Even before Thomas Clap was allowed to speak, the council voted that, provided no "Proofs & Evidences" against the candidate were forthcoming, it would ordain him.[27] Meeting in closed session, the ministers had scarcely finished hearing Clap when the sheriff interrupted the meeting, and, to the surprise of the Hampshire delegation, arrested Breck. (Williams backers had prearranged the arrest, but had instructed the justices to have the Boston ministers, not Breck, arrested.)[28] The arrest threw the meeting into consternation and the puzzled councillors followed the sheriff's party to the Town House.[29]

The justices of the peace were themselves in a quandary. Originally they had planned to have the sheriff arrest the outside ministers for illegal intrusion. When the sheriff, fearful of the political consequences, arrested Breck instead, he placed the other justices and the local clergy in an embarrassing position. To gain time, the justices announced that the ordination council would reconvene in the afternoon to allow "any in the Assembly to testifie" concerning "the Principles &c of Mr. Breck." At dark the justices ordered their officers to take custody of Breck, but some of the council members assured them "he should be forthcoming when call'd for," and he was allowed to go home for the night.

The next morning, while Breck's opponents met inside the Town House to seek a civil charge against him, "a young Gentleman" mounted a horse in front of the building and read "Mr. Breck's confession of faith" to the assembled crowd. The orator, Edwards later claimed, used the pious reading "to blacken" the reputations of Breck's "good and worthy" opponents. Even the horse sensed the "vile Errors" being promulgated and "stood astonished" at what was going on. "If he had had the Tongue of Balaam's Ass," Edwards quipped, "he would have reproved the madness of the Prophet."[30]

In the meantime the justices decided that while still in Connecticut, Robert Breck had violated the Massachusetts statute against atheism and blasphemy. So that afternoon, while the candidate's backers conducted a tearful prayer meeting for his safety, the Hampshire County sheriff set off with Breck for Connecticut. There, officials accepted Breck's bond to appear before the Windham County court in December and released him. As a result, four days after the ordination council began, Breck was back in Springfield. The council reconvened and swiftly endorsed the candidate's character and doctrine. This much accomplished, it recessed to meet October 21 in Boston.

The departure of the eastern clergy signaled the beginning of a battle of words and litigation which would prove an embarrassment to Connecticut Valley ministers and politicians for several decades to come. Newspapers in Boston and at least one in New York reported the affair. In an action fit only for "Knaves and Ruffians," a Boston paper published a letter of Thomas Clap which Hampshire partisans insisted had been pilfered from the mails. On November 22 the Springfield congregation petitioned the Massachusetts General Court to uphold its rights as a congregational church against intrusion by magistrates. And in December the House of Representatives ruled that the county authorities, being limited by law to investigation, had no right to intervene in the council's deliberations.[31] Thus vindicated, the church proceeded to prepare for the ordination, and on January 26, 1736, Robert Breck was "Publickly and Quietly" installed as pastor of the First Church in Springfield.[32]

Breck soon found, however, that even his most ardent supporters had reservations about his faithfulness. In the ordination sermon, William Cooper of Boston formulated his own partially suppressed doubt when he declared to Breck:

> Of your adherence to the doctrines of the gospel, as they are . . . received in the Churches of New-England, you have given the fullest satisfaction: And we dare not allow a suspicion, that you don't believe in your Heart, what you have confess'd with your Mouth.[33]

If in victory even his staunchest friends questioned the young man's integrity, what reaction would his enemies have in defeat?

For the next two years Boston printers kept busy printing charges and countercharges of the warring factions. First the Hampshire ministers issued a documented account: *A Narrative of the Proceedings of those Ministers . . . That Disapproved of the Late Measures Taken in Order to the Settlement of Mr. Robert Breck, in the Pastoral Office in the First Church in Springfield, With A Defence of Their Conduct in That Affair* (1736). Breck's supporters struck back in *An Examination of and Some Answer to a Pamphlet, Intitled, A Narrative and Defence of the Proceedings . . . With a Vindication of those Ministers and Churches that Approv'd of and Acted in the Settlement of Said Mr. Breck* (1736). Jonathan Edwards had been away from home during the uproar in Springfield. Censure of the local authorities by the General Court and defeat of the western clergy in their attempt to block Breck's ordination, had deep personal implications for Edwards. His uncles, John Stoddard and William Williams, had led Hampshire attempts to thwart Breck. More than family pride was at stake. Stoddard, unquestioned political leader of Hampshire County and Edwards' mainstay in the Northampton congregation, and Williams, "Pope" Solomon Stoddard's successor, held the keys to Jonathan Edwards' future. At the insistence of his uncle Williams, in 1737 Edwards wrote a ferocious apologetic in the Hampshire defense. Published nearly two years after the fact, *A Letter to the Author of the Pamphlet Called an Answer to the Hampshire Narrative* did little more than sort out previous arguments. Its actual effect was to underscore the powerlessness of the Hampshire Association of Ministers and the lack of grace with which William Williams accepted defeat. In writing, Jonathan Edwards identified himself conspicuously with the old guard, and became the champion of an already lost cause.[34]

A year before the pamphlet warfare subsided, Robert Breck and some of his supporters tried rapprochement. On April 28, 1736, Breck married Eunice Brewer, daughter of his predecessor. He asked Stephen Williams, one of his Hampshire opponents, to officiate. Williams consented, later explaining that although he had objected to Breck's ordination, he saw no reason to oppose his marriage.[35] Soon after the ordination, Benjamin Colman, pastor of the Brattle Street Church in Boston, set out to heal the east-west division. Early in 1736 Colman, who later claimed Breck had "dealt Fallaciously and Injuriously" with him to gain his support, wrote William Williams suggesting that the annual ministerial convocation at the Harvard commencement turn from wrangling over church offices to seeking more effective ways to spread the gospel. On March 16 the Hampshire Association went on record in favor of the proposal and declared its willingness to adopt methods "proper" to the attainment of the goal. Seeing no incongruity between spreading the gospel and scrambling for ecclesiastical power, the Association then requested William Williams to collect Hampshire opinion on the appropriate "power of Ecclesiastical Councils," and chose Jonathan Edwards to assist in assembling the data.[36]

Neither improved relations with Boston nor strengthened legal defenses could reinstate the old order. The Springfield fiasco laid bare the frailty of ministerial solidarity, an Achilles heel visible to any congregation seeking endorsement for unconventional arrangements.

In forming an ordination council for John Ballantine in 1740, the church at Westfield invited Robert Breck and some Boston area ministers to participate. The candidate's home church, the Brattle Street Church in Boston, declined representation, and William Cooper, one of its ministers, advised that, in light of the Springfield dispute, the Westfield congregation limit Ballantine's examiners to ministers who had opposed Breck. At first Breck himself declined to serve, but pressed by his congregation, he reversed his decision. When Breck appeared at Westfield, however, Jonathan Edwards, Stephen Williams, Jonathan Ashley, and other Williams-allied ministers withdrew, leaving only Breck and two other ministers to ordain Ballantine.[37]

In the years following Springfield, the Williams-dominated group became involved in two other parish squabbles. In 1739 a minority within the Northfield congregation alleged that their pastor, Benjamin Doolittle, was tainted with Arminianism and requested the Hampshire Association to call an ecclesiastical council. Unwilling in the circumstances to proceed against one of its own number, the Association advised the aggrieved brethren to pursue a conciliatory course. For his part, Doolittle succeeded so well in dealing with the situation that he remained as pastor at Northfield until his death.[38]

At South Hadley, the dissatisfied element proved more difficult to manage. Before a council which met May 3, 1737, members complained that Grindall Rawson was an unlearned sluggard who neglected "Study," plagiarized sermons, and "Squandered" time "in unnecessary Journeys & other Recreations." They averred also that Rawson had lied in claiming he was free of debt when he settled. The pastor, they said, had "so Alliannated" their affections as to negate any future benefit from his ministry. As at Northfield, the council (William Williams again serving as moderator, and Jonathan Edwards as scribe) recommended forbearance. Three years later, however, the church called another council which delivered the desired verdict. Despite this action and the discontinuance of his salary, when Rawson continued to preach, the church again asked the Hampshire Association for advice. At the Association meeting on April 7, 1741 (the last one William Williams attended), the motion prevailed that the church call another council. To be composed of member churches "only," it should include representatives of all Hampshire County congregations except Elbonos and Springfield. The council met against the church's will in September. With Edwards acting again as scribe, the council reviewed the charges and concurred with the previous verdict. Hastily the church called another pastor. In preparation for his arrival, the precinct appropriated ten pounds to have Rawson forcibly dragged from the pulpit.[39]

In the dozen years following the Breck crisis, Jonathan Edwards witnessed a transformation in the leadership of the Hampshire churches. His Uncle John Stoddard, stalwart of the old guard in western Massachusetts politics and the "strong rod" of Edwards' support in the Northampton congregation, died in 1748.[40] Death and the addition of pastors of newly organized churches also radically altered the Hampshire Association. Nehemiah Bull of Westfield died in 1740; Ebenezer Devotion of Suffield and William Williams of Hatfield in 1741; Isaac Chauncy of Hadley in 1745; and Benjamin Doolittle of Northfield in 1748. Speaking at the funeral of William Williams in 1741, Edwards pointed to the change in leadership. "What a great alteration is made in a little time, in the churches in this part of the land!" Williams' strength, his nephew declared, had been the ministers' "strength." They had been able always "to resort" to him "in difficult cases for instruction and direction." Following in the steps of Solomon Stoddard, he had been "the head and ornament" of the Hampshire Association.[41]

On October 13, 1741, six weeks after William Williams died, Robert Breck was admitted to membership in the Hampshire Association of Ministers.[42] Forces were even then at work which would result in Jonathan Edwards' dismissal from Northampton in 1750. The Robert Breck affair was but one of them. Breck's admission to the Association was undeniable proof, nevertheless, that the power of the Stoddard-Williams faction had been broken. Opportunity for retribution still lay in the future.

Nearly nine years later, Robert Breck served on the ecclesiastical council which dismissed Jonathan Edwards from Northampton. Senior majority member, he signed the tracts which defended the council's action.[43] Since the council vote was 10-9, Breck's opinion was decisive. Commenting on the congregation's 200-20 vote for dismissal,[44] Breck said he had expected people to vote reluctantly against their pastor. To his amazement, when the vote was called for, "their Arms flew as if they went with Springs."[45]

## Notes

1. Following Perry Miller, most recent writers have implied that Jonathan Edwards inherited his grandfather's power in ecclesiastical affairs along with his pulpit. See Alan Heimert, *Religion and the American Mind from the Great Awakening to the Revolution* (Cambridge, Mass., 1966), pp. 124, 131, 154 and *passim*; Robert J. Taylor, *Western Massachusetts and the Revolution* (Providence, 1954), pp. 45–51; and Edwin Scott Gaustad, *The Great Awakening in New England* (New York, 1957), pp. 105–106.

2. George Sheldon, *A History of Deerfield, Massachusetts* (Deerfield, Mass., 1895), I, 467–469. Pierpont "seems never to have recovered from the blow dealt him by Mr. Williams. He went to the West Indies, where he died within four or five years" (p. 469).

3. *A Narrative of the Proceedings of those Ministers of the County of Hampshire, &c. That*

*have Disapproved of the Late Measures Taken in Order to the Settlement of Mr. Robert Breck* (Boston, 1736), pp. 4, 5, 10.

4. *A Narrative of the Proceedings*, 6, 56.

5. Biography of Thomas Clap in *Sibley's Harvard Graduates* (Boston, 1945), VII, 27-50. Clap's connection with Breck, 30–31; also see Louis Leonard Tucker, *Puritan Protagonist: President Thomas Clap of Yale College* (Chapel Hill, 1962), pp. 47–58.

6. *Narrative of the Proceedings*, 2–3.

7. Association members present were: William Williams of Hatfield, Ebenezer Devotion of Suffield, Samuel Hopkins of West Springfield, Peter Reynolds of Enfield, Nehemiah Bull of West-field, Jonathan Ashley of Deerfield and, of course, Stephen Williams of Longmeadow. Devotion was married to Robert Breck's aunt. His son, Ebenezer (Yale, 1732), was ordained first pastor at Scotland, Oct. 22, 1735. Thomas Clap preached the ordination sermon.

8. Hearing the tales which were following him, Breck wrote Clap and accused him of falsehood and misrepresentation. Hardly had Clap received the letter, however, when Breck arrived in Windham asking for a letter of recommendation to the Hampshire Association. Naturally, Clap refused to write one. Breck's letter to Clap is printed in Mason A. Green, *Springfield* (Springfield, Mass., 1888), pp. 230–231.

9. During the period covered by Hampshire Association records (1731–1741), William Williams was chosen moderator at every Association meeting he attended except this one. The Association records are in the Forbes Library, Northampton, Massachusetts.

10. Isaac Chauncy (1670–1745), grandson of President Chauncy of Harvard, served as pastor at Hadley from 1696 until his death. Popular with his parishioners, Chauncy never had the struggle over his salary which many of the ministers of the time had. His son, Israel (Harvard, 1724), served as Stoddard's assistant at Northampton in 1725–1726. Later, however, Israel lost his mind and stayed in an outbuilding near his father's house. During fits of insanity he would cry "Fire!" One night in 1736 the building where Israel stayed actually caught on fire. Thinking that the fire was imaginary as usual, his father ignored his cries and Israel burned to death. Isaac Chauncy never recovered from the shock. See biographies of Isaac Chauncy in *Sibley's Harvard Graduates*, IV, 160–162; and of Israel Chauncy in *Sibley's Harvard Graduates*, VII, 325–326.

11. Two years before, the Association had adopted rules to be followed in examining prospective ministers:

"1. They ought to have so much knowledge in the learned Languages as to be able to search and enquire into the Hebrew and Greek original of the Scriptures.

"2. They ought to consent to the Confession of faith agreed upon by the [Westminster] Assembly of Divines, or show an orthodox one of their own.

"3. They ought to be well skilled in Divinity.

"4. They ought to be members in full Communion with some particular Church.

"5. They ought to be persons of Regular Conversation.

"6. They ought to Declare that they Design to Devote themselves to the work of the Ministry, both publick and private.

"7. It is further expected that they Common-place upon any Scripture that is assigned to them." Hampshire Association of Ministers, "Records," Oct. 13, 1732.

12. Hampshire Association of Ministers, "Records," Oct. 8, 1734.

13. The committee was composed of Jonathan Chapin, Luke Hitchcock, and Thomas Stebbins. The families of all three had been leaders in Springfield for several generations. See "Biographical and Genealogical" section in Henry W. Burt, *The First Century of the History of Springfield* (Springfield, Mass., 1899), p. 11.

14. Signers of the letter sent on Nov. 20 were: William Williams, Isaac Chauncy, Jonathan Edwards, Stephen Williams, Samuel Hopkins, and Peter Reynolds. Since the letter was addressed from Hadley, it is assumed that Isaac Chauncy, often scribe for the Association, wrote it. It is also

possible that Jonathan Edwards, scribe for the previous meeting, wrote the letter. The text of the letter is in *Narrative of the Proceedings*, pp. 13–14.

15. *Narrative of the Proceedings*, pp. 17–18.

16. Hampshire Association of Ministers, "Records," April 8, 1735.

17. Edwards was added to eliminate the parliamentary inconvenience of an even-numbered committee, not to break a tie between pro-Breck and anti-Breck members. The Association's apologist, probably Edwards, claimed that three Association ministers: Isaac Chauncy, Ebenezer Devotion, and William Rand, thought Breck was innocent of Clap's charges. Rand, however, was not a member of the Association committee. See *Narrative of the Proceedings*, p. 28.

18. In the Hampshire Association as a whole the anti-Breck group included William Williams of Hatfield, Stephen Williams of Longmeadow, Samuel Hopkins of West Springfield, Peter Reynolds of Enfield, Nehemiah Bull of Westfield, Jonathan Ashley of Deerfield, and Jonathan Edwards of Northampton. See *Narrative of the Proceedings*, 40. Neutral or pro-Breck members included: Isaac Chauncy of Hadley, Ebenezer Devotion of Suffield, William Rand of Sunderland, Benjamin Doolittle of Northfield, Grindall Rawson of South Hadley, and Samuel Allis of Somers. Clifford Shipton, a recent commentator, thought the division in the Association was seven to six. See his biography of Breck in *Sibley's Harvard Graduates*, VIII, 666. No commentator, however, rules out the possibility of apathy on the part of some who have been classified as favoring Breck.

19. See Robert J. Taylor, *Western Massachusetts in the Revolution*, pp. 11–12, 48.

20. Perhaps William Williams had preached the ordination sermons for several others. Since the Association records did not always include what ministers participated in ordination ceremonies, this gauge to Williams' prestige can only be approximate. Usually he was a principal participant. In 1724 the Sunderland church bypassed William Williams and chose Isaac Chauncy to preach at the ordination of William Rand. After his rise to power in Stoddard's declining years, this is the only instance found where Williams was not chosen.

21. Robert Breck, *An Examination of, and Some Answer to a Pamphlet, Intitled, A Narrative and Defence of the Proceedings of the Ministers of Hampshire, who Disapproved of Mr. Breck's Settlement at Springield. With a Vindication of those Ministers and Churches that Approv'd of and Acted in the Settlement of said Mr. Breck* (Boston, 1736), p. 87. Boston ministers signing Breck's certificate of orthodoxy included: Benjamin Colman, Joseph Sewell, John Webb, William Cooper, Thomas Foxcroft, Samuel Checkley, Joshua Gee, and Mather Byles.

22. Letter quoted in Henry Morris, *History of the First Church in Springfield* (Springfield, Mass., 1875), pp. 56–57.

23. *Narrative of the Proceedings*, 33; see also *A Letter to the Author of the Pamphlet Called An Answer to the Hampshire Narrative* (Boston, 1737), 38; and Josiah Gilbert Holland, *History of Western Massachusetts* (Springfield, Mass., 1855), I, 200.

24. An excerpt from Colman's letter is in the biography of Breck in *Sibley's Harvard Graduates*, VIII, 668.

25. John Stoddard, a leading figure in western Massachusetts politics, was the strongest supporter Edwards ever had. See Benjamin W. Dwight, *The History of the Descendants of John Dwight, of Dedham, Mass.* (New York, 1874), I, 113–117.

26. *Narrative of the Proceedings*, pp. 34, 37, 41–46.

27. The ordination council's statement is quoted in the biography of Breck in *Sibley's Harvard Graduates*, VIII, 669.

28. The petition which stated that Breck, not the church, had set up the council, is quoted in Green, *Springfield*, p. 248.

29. *An Examination of, and Some Answer to a Pamphlet, Intitled, A Narrative and Defence of the Proceedings*, pp. 88–89.

30. *Narrative of the Proceedings*, pp. 65–66. Breck's confession of faith is in *An Examination of, and Some Answer to a Pamphlet, Intitled, A Narrative and Defence of the Proceedings*, pp. 88–89.

31. Massachusetts Bay, House of Representatives, *Journal, 1735–1736*, XIII, 115, 145–146, 151–152, 184, 185, 187.

32. See biography of Breck in *Sibley's Harvard Graduates*, VIII, 673.

33. William Cooper, *The Work of Ministers* (Boston, 1736), pp. 20–21.

34. Sereno Dwight, *Life of President Edwards* (Jonathan Edwards, *Works*, edited by Sereno Dwight, I) (New York, 1830), pp. 125–126.

35. Stephen Williams, who died in 1782, requested that Robert Breck preach his funeral sermon.

36. Hampshire Association of Ministers, "Records," March 16, 1736.

37. See biography of John Ballantine in *Sibley's Harvard Graduates*, IX, 468–472.

38. Franklin Bowditch Dexter, *Biographical Sketches of the Graduates of Yale College* (New York, 1885), I, 151–154. Hampshire Association of Ministers, "Records," May 2, 1739 and April 8, 1740.

39. See biography of Grindall Rawson in *Sibley's Harvard Graduates*, VIII, 476–480.

40. Jonathan Edwards, "God's Awful Judgment in the Breaking and Withering of the Strong Rods of a Community," in his *Works*, edited by Sereno Dwight, VI, 217–231. Sermon preached at John Stoddard's funeral.

41. Jonathan Edwards, "The Sorrows of the Bereaved Spread before Jesus," in his *Works*, edited by Sereno Dwight, VIII, 482.

42. Hampshire Association of Ministers, "Records," Oct. 13, 1741.

43. Robert Breck and others, *An Account of the Conduct of the Council which Dismissed the Rev. Mr. Edwards from the Pastoral Care of the First Church of Northampton; with Reflections on the Protestation Accompanying the Printed Result, of that Council, and the Letter Published Relating to that Affair, In a Letter to a Friend* (Boston, 1750); and Robert Breck and others, *A Letter to the Reverend Mr. Hobby, in Answer to his Vindication of the Protest, against the Result of an Ecclesiastical Council, met at Northampton, &c.* (Boston, 1751).

44. Edwards said there were 229 male members in 1750.

45. Letter of Samuel Hopkins to Ezra Stiles, June 23, 1750, in Ezra Stiles, *Extracts from the Itineraries and other Miscellanies* (New Haven, 1916), pp. 501–503.

# Biography:
# Interpretative

## Sovereign God
## and Reasoning Man

Edward H. Davidson[*]

During his undergraduate years Edwards began to keep a record of his daily life contained under a set of double entries. One he called "Resolutions"; these were advices to himself, statements of his condition on this or that day, and exhortations that he strive to do better than he had been doing. Some of these notations were in the manner of any young man—Benjamin Franklin perhaps—advising himself on ways of becoming successful: "Never to lose one moment of time, but to improve it in the most profitable way I possibly can"; or, "To maintain the strictest temperance, in eating and drinking."[1] The tone is so well-known in the lives of successful men that these entries seem hardly more than codicils in the documents of the American dream. Most of them are, however, of quite a different character, for they were jottings made in keeping with and at the same time as a "Diary" Edwards began in December, 1722, and maintained intermittently for two years. They range over a wide variety of meditation, insight, speculation, wonder, joy, and despair; they form one of the most interesting and valid records we have of Edwards's mind in one of its crucial periods.

Over and over again Edwards stressed the absolute importance of a man's belief in God's sovereignty. It was a doctrine he made into a keystone of his own theology, and it was one that, when he became a minister, he drilled into his hearers as the primary necessity for their salvation. Yet much as he later came to "love" that doctrine, the youthful Edwards felt a strong repugnance to it: "From my childhood up," he wrote later in his *Personal Narrative*, "my mind had been full of objections against the doctrine of God's sovereignty, in choosing whom he would to eternal life, and rejecting whom he pleased; leaving them eternally to perish, and be everlastingly tormented in hell. It used to appear like a horrible doctrine to me."[2] Here was the great stumbling block in the way of his personal faith; no amount of reasoning could overcome it. Indeed, reason was but another obstacle in the solving of this great issue. Faith, and faith alone, was the way out of the difficulty; but a man might wait a lifetime to gain enough faith, and his end might find him still resisting and unrepentant.

[*]Reprinted, with permission, from *Jonathan Edwards: The Narrative of a Puritan Mind* (Boston: Houghton-Mifflin, 1966), pp. 20–28.

At the time of his greatest resistance to this doctrine, the youthful Edwards was twice afflicted with illness; once it was a pleurisy sometime before he entered Yale College; the second occasion was in 1725. In both instances Edwards feared, as his Resolutions and Diary suggest, not that he would die: death seems not to have darkened his mind as he lay helpless; rather, he feared that he might not find in the illness and affliction that humility of mind and soul which was the first requisite for overcoming his resistance. Arrogance of heart, willful self-righteousness, the young man's passionate need for self-realization and self-fulfillment—these were the darkenings of the way which Edwards knew he must travel before he could finally recognize the truth that God is Almighty and that man is even less than the blade of grass or the speck of dust. God's sovereignty was a gospel truth; it was also the first test of a man's seeking salvation; and it was, most importantly, the primary condition for self-knowledge. To be abased and to rise, to be humbled until one cried in anguish and then to be lifted up by that very power one had feared and even loathed, was the central act in Christian experience. Whatever one's destiny in life, one did not shape one's course; everything one did, from the first infant's cry to the last gasp of mortal life, was foreordained by a deity who, if He should vary His intention by so much as a single atom's motion, would deny His godhead. Thus God's sovereignty is not only what one is as a human being, but it also measures what one is not in the eyes of God. It echoes Luther's cry when he fell in a faint in the choir loft, *"Ich bin's nit! Ich bin's nit!"* or *"Non sum! Non sum!"*, either of which can be translated "It's not I" or "I am *not*."[3]

The nearly violent opposition to the idea of God's sovereignty was very like Satan's and the unregenerate man's hatred of God. It was the presence of that dross and waste in life, that unbidden fear of losing one's spiritual energy and of "falling away," which haunted Edwards in his youth and demanded of him the most arduous exertions. When he could not meet that exacting requirement, he weakened and became ill. Yet the illness had a palliative and recovering force; for in the descent of the flesh to the submission of sickness, that dark and obsessive resistance to the true light was softened. In the second of the two major illnesses (that of 1725 which laid him low "for about a quarter of a year") "God was pleased," he afterward recalled, "to visit me again, with the sweet influences of his Spirit. My mind was greatly engaged there in divine pleasant contemplations, and longings of soul. I observed that those who watched with me, would often be looking out wishfully for the morning . . . ; and when the light of day came in at the windows, it refreshed my soul from one morning to another. It seemed to me some image of the light of God's glory." The recovery and the acceptance of God's sovereignty came about because of what William James called "letting go"; Edwards did not think; he simply felt, and the presence of God's being became apparent. Thus, after his recovery from the illness, he wrote: "The doctrines of God's absolute sovereignty, and free grace, . . . and man's absolute dependence on the operations of God's Holy Spirit, have very often appeared to me as sweet and glorious doctrines. These doctrines have been much my delight."[4]

The awesome doctrine of God's sovereignty—a subject on which . . . Edwards wrote his first published work—was counterbalanced for Edwards in these early years by several modes of thought. One was his understanding of mental perception by means of his assumptions of and revisions in Locke's theory of the mind. Another, perhaps equally important was what Edwards knew from British thinkers who had already considered the question of God's incoming spiritual light. Among these were the group known as the Cambridge Platonists—Ralph Cudworth chiefly, but also Henry More and Benjamin Whichcote. Indeed, Edwards inherited the intellectual foreground of seventeenth-century English Puritans; as one commentator has correctly stated, there is "little distinction . . . between the writers of New England and the particular English theologians and teachers of the . . . seventeenth century under whom New Englanders studied, whom they read and digested before their migration and continued to read for over a century thereafter." Nothing supports this statement better than Edwards's "Catalogue of Books" with its many references to seventeenth-century British religious writers. In this list the name of Richard Baxter, the English theologian, appears seven times, one less than the references to Newton and one more than to Locke's name; the thought of Baxter can be taken as part of the intellectual and spiritual ancestry of Edwards's ideas.[5]

Yet Edwards's reading in the English theologians was not wholly for the confirmation of ideas he already had; apparently he was attracted to these books because they spoke to him in a language he was himself using. God's sovereignty and His majesty in the world were not merely dogmas: they were modes of feeling; they were activities of the senses. Even though the language of Baxter and others may come from Scripture and from the great tradition of Christian apologetics stemming from Augustine, the words have a haunting resonance and a design which make them felt and seen. The references to light and to color are regular and pervasive. For Baxter "the Spirit giveth light"; for John Owen, "Light requires neither proofe nor Testimony for its Evidence. Let the Sun arise in the firmament, and there is no need of Witnesses to prove and confirm unto a seeing man that it is day." Light does not seize and envelop a man, as it did in Augustine's vision of God's power; rather, light explains the continuing effects which God's world has on the intransigent or the enlightened man; it may shine into the heart and transform a man's life. Thus for Baxter and the Cambridge Platonists light is a link in thought between the act of intuition by which grace is received and the continuing effects on the senses with which a man lives. Human reason arrives at a knowledge of God and, at its best, reaches salvation when it is moved from without and when it comes to open its lifelong dialogue with the world of facts and ideas.

This sensuous and, by turns, mystical activity is nowhere better disclosed in Edwards's youthful writings than in that extraordinary paragraph which has afterward been known as "Sarah Pierrepont."

Edwards wrote it when he was twenty. The girl was only thirteen. To the modern reader, to express love for a presumably gracious and lovely young woman by recounting that girl's extraordinary sensitivity to divine impulses seems strange indeed. The single paragraph of approximately one hundred words tells us almost nothing about the person who was Sarah Pierrepont; it does tell us a great deal about Jonathan Edwards in this crucial time of his life when he was seeking some sense of his place and being in the world.

The curious opening of the confession—"They say there is a young lady in [New Haven] who is beloved of [the] Great Being . . ."—suggests that the writer is himself at a distance and unempowered to approach or write about such a saintly being. The distance is metaphysical only; for the movement of the confession is away from the brusqueness, the sternness, the masculinity of the world and ever toward the sweetness, sensitivity, and delicacy of the woman's appreciation: "this Great Being, in some way or other invisible, comes to her and fills her mind with exceeding sweet delight. . . . She expects after a while," the meditation goes on, "to be raised up . . . out of the world and caught up into heaven. . . . There she is to dwell with him, and to be ravished with his love and delight forever."[6] The tone is that of the rapture of the flesh and the mystical wonder which come to the soul, both well known in the writings of Christian saints; the commonplaces of ecstasy are all through the brief and tantalizing paragraph.

The crux of the confession is its opposition to the formal statements Edwards was writing on the doctrine of God's sovereignty. Sarah Pierrepont is a refuge from the harshness, the terror, and the abject feeling of inconsequence which came to Edwards every time he pondered that awesome question of God's infinite majesty. The "objections" and resistances to the sovereignty of God broke down not only because Edwards made his peace with the domineering image of the father which loomed so long for him but because the wondrous joy and delicacy of the feminine counterpart to God the Father came in the form and the presence of an extraordinary girl who, as Edwards wrote of her, "is of a wonderful sweetness, calmness and universal benevolence of mind; especially after this Great God has manifested himself to her mind. She will sometimes go about from place to place, singing sweetly; and seems to be always full of joy and pleasure. . . ."[7]

The figure of the woman, whether saintly or earthly, has been for ages man's refuge from the brute realities of himself and his world. The Roman Church had long made this feminine gentleness a dogma, for the Mother sat at the right hand of God as an intercessor for fallible men on this earth. Edwards may be discovering what human longing had once resolved in a doctrine; but, as in so many things, Edwards had to discover the meaning for himself. That he discovered it in the person of the young woman with whom he would enjoy the privileges of the nuptial bed might suggest a lurking tendency to masquerade fleshly desires behind the vesture and rhetoric of spirituality, even mystical rapture. Yet as men have long known, flesh and spirit are in mystical experience and in mystical writing so close as to be indistinguishable. The ravishment which Sarah enjoyed with God was not very far from the physical union she would have with her young husband; and the young Edwards's ecstatic vision of his beloved in the passionate fulfillment with God was little different from his own erotic-mystical dream. Men do not deceive themselves and find their frustrated yearnings in sublimated guises of the union of the soul with God; they find resolutions for their deepest despairs in evocations which, for a time, appease their doubts and relieve their fallen hopes. From the sovereign father and God to the winsome, alluring, spiritualized girl, Edwards moved from the darkness into the light. It was, perhaps, not quite the light of this world, but it was light nevertheless and it shone all the more brightly for its being lodged in a person of such appeal and wonder.

The light which shines throughout "Sarah Pierrepont" is not only the light of God's benign grace; it is also a rhetorical brightness, a language of wonder and joy and love which would become, in the after years of Edwards's ministry, one of the key manners of his preaching style. The device is the vision of sinful man ringed with the brilliant light of God's restoring grace; man can do nothing for himself; the light does all. But, on the instant or for the hour of its shining, miracles are wrought, and anguished man knows, however fitfully and briefly, that he is saved of God. Edwards developed a meditative style which begins with "Sarah Pierrepont" and remained with him throughout his life.

One sign of this style is Edwards's poetic eye-mindedness; it is a Romantic poet's insistence that the object is the word, and the word is the instant conveyor of the object to the inward sight of the mind. The paragraph is keyed to a language of seeing: light shines, the darkness flees; the girl goes about, she sees and is full of sweet delight; the paths and the groves are ringed with joy, and the unseen becomes a presence as real as if it were there to be touched. The verbs are all in the present tense, a now of seeing and speculation, as if everything from the past to the future could be lived instantly; the radiance of the girl's presence is like the line between visibility and invisibility and between what "seems" and "is." If the modern reader misses the stages in comprehension, the tension between the slowly opening wonder and the dazzling fulfillment, Sarah Pierrepont was for Edwards the soul's immediate presence in divine things. God fills His universe, and His presence is there to be known. Man, feeble and obtuse, resists the moment, but this divinely inspired girl sees everything.

"Sarah Pierrepont" is indeed very close to Edwards's meditations on spiders and his conjectures on "The Mind." They have the same subject: the mind's and the soul's apprehension of divine things. In "Sarah Pierrepont" Edwards had, as it were, someone else to undergo the experience for him and then stand on the other side waiting for him to follow. In his more formal and logical excursions on this question Edwards had to present the experience as he was living it. Yet in both instances the emphasis is on the mind's seeing—on a visionary present of such intensity that things are not merely felt and known; they are seen as mediatorial relevances between what lies like dross in the mind and what exists forever in the phenomenal universe of God. The meditation is swift, hardly more than an instant, but in its coming it suddenly invests the world with splendor and light, and in its going it leaves the mind just that much more alive than it was. The visionary dream of "Sarah Pierrepont" was Edwards's poem to the most elevated and intoxicating physical response to the world; that he should have put his dream of wonder in the person of a young girl might suggest his unwilling awareness bordering on shame that he was seldom, if ever, in his own life and being, capable of such ecstasy.

The doctrine of God's sovereignty was the counterstatement to wonder; it was that dark, unbidden side of a young man's life when the despair became a real illness and the doubt was like the coming of the night. Indeed, the doctrine of God's sovereignty might well represent the mind against the flesh; it could also spell, as Edwards's later life disclosed, a waning of his power of visionary insight: the world became less and less ringed with light, and the remarkable young man's responses to the physical world faded. Despite several occasions when he may have felt the coming and then the presence of the Light, Edwards never again had quite the visionary ecstasy of "Sarah Pierrepont." The girl became the woman; the young man became an older man; and, with the waning of a profound awareness of this world in all its magic and divine grace, Edwards slowly lost what he had so much enjoyed in his youth. The dogmatist and, more especially, the intellectual disputant triumphed over the poet, not because an angry God shut the valves of the youth's attention but because Edwards suffered that inevitable wastage of sensual delight. As it left him, he did what many another first-class mind has done: he tended, as we shall see, more and more to intellectualize perception and to fashion, not vivid lineaments of this world in its light, but well-lighted principles and fully seen ideas.

Edwards was learning, both by living it and writing about it, the meditative way. It is a "way," and each man must learn it for himself. In Edwards's time it had been so long practiced in England and America that a sensitive young person hardly needed to look beyond the shelves of books in his home or in his school library to find texts for comparison and instruction. Indeed, the manner of meditation had become a mode of poetry which the English poets of the sixteenth and seventeenth centuries had exhibited with such imagination that a poet like the Puritan Edward Taylor had found it wholly effective to his thought. Each Sunday when the Lord's Supper was to be celebrated, he penned his Preparatory Meditation in verse on the same text he had used in his sermon: a formal, logical disquisition from the pulpit was one way of presenting an idea; but a quiet, inner colloquy with oneself was another, and perhaps the second was more necessary to the soul's vitality than the first.

What Edwards learned in his young manhood was not only the meditative manner—the apposite phrasing of a thought, however that thought might bear overtones of Scripture, and the location of that thought in the recesses of one's private being—but a meditative style. The style is not easily apparent in Edwards's Diary and Resolutions, for they are couched in a language which bears all the colors of copybooks and good advice. Yet the beginnings and the development of that style are there nonetheless.

Edwards learned that experience, which necessarily comes from the outside (Locke had proved that truth), turns inward: it moves from fact to idea, from substance to concept; it conforms to a logic which God has implanted in

His universe since the beginning of time. Yet the inward turning of experience is the translation of facts and human acts into words. The use of the right word, the turn of the phrase, the winding of the thought through a sentence could be the tentative or ultimate resolution of that activity God has implanted in His universe and the intelligence He expects men to develop. A word, a sentence, a paragraph or a page could be that ever-widening possibility for the mind to live within itself or to go outward and do the work which it should perform. Edwards thus began in his youth to develop a style which would open the world and yet which would somehow relate that world to one's own will. To the extent that words can organize, however variously and even for a time falsely, a realm of meaning, then words are man's way to control fate.

Thus Edwards's style had a limpidity and grace, even from the beginning, which are missing from other Puritan meditative writings. The Lockean effect was already apparent: words are not simply "real" reflections of real things; they are relevances which the mind establishes between itself and what lies all around it. As relevances they may relate only as God has prescribed—for God, in the beginning, made the Word just as He made atoms; nevertheless, the possibility for variety and for fresh incentives is endless. Words became, therefore, modes of discovery—a discovery of objects in relation to the world and of ideas which only those words, in just their right order, could convey. In 1725 Edwards noted: "There are a great many exercises, that for the present, seem not to help, but rather impede, Religious meditation and affections, the fruit of which is reaped afterwards, and is of far greater worth than what is lost; for thereby the mind is only for the present diverted; but what is attained is, upon occasion, of use for the whole life-time." It was not the impediment or the diversion which mattered; it was the "affection" or the soul's learning which could be "reaped afterwards" that made the difference, and the only means of so catching thought in its passage was to give it its true and memorable word. Even Edwards's private, cautionary advices to himself are couched in this ambience of meditative possibility: "A virtue which I need in a higher degree," he noted, "to give a beauty and lustre to my behaviour, is gentleness. If I had more of an air of gentleness, I should be much mended."[8] Edwards's style was a way of turning experience in upon one's self and of refining that sensible comprehension into the language of introspection. Words became the ever-widening and ever more personal possibility that one could, and indeed must, build a world from within.

## Notes

1. Sereno E. Dwight, *The Life of President Edwards* (New York: S. Converse, 1830), pp. 68, 69.

2. *The Works of President Edwards*, Samuel Austin (Worcester, Mass., 1808), I, 33. (This edition is hereinafter cited as *Works*.)

3. *Dokumente zu Luthers Entwicklung*, ed. Otto Scheel (Tübingen, 1929), II, 116; see Erik H. Erikson, *Young Man Luther: A Study in Psychoanalysis and History* (New York, 1958,) p. 23.

4. *Works*, I, 41.

5. Thomas H. Johnson, "Jonathan Edwards' Background of Reading," *Publications of the Colonial Society of Massachusetts*, 28 (1931), 193-222.

6. Dwight, p. 114.

7. *Ibid.*, pp. 114–15.

8. *Ibid.*, pp. 106, 105.

# Jonathan Edwards as Great Man: Identity, Conversion, and Leadership in the Great Awakening

Richard L. Bushman°

Erikson's *Young Man Luther* has raised again the question of the great man's part in history.[1] The early nineteenth-century fascination with heroes who bent the course of events through sheer determination and personal force later faded as new conceptual tools enabled historians to calculate more precisely the impact of social forces. The times, it was then believed, thrust forward the great men, and rather than shaping events to their wills, heroes were as much determined by their environments as the mass. Erikson's biography of Luther does not restore the hero to his former eminence nor discount the weight of social conditions, but it does assert that the relationship of a man and his times is an exchange that goes both ways. A single individual can bring to his age powers that enable him to mobilize forces latent in the mass of men. Not just any power, however imposing, will do. The great man's capacities must be congruent with the needs of his age; when he speaks the age must respond. But his presence does make a difference. The force of one man's will, as Erikson shows in the case of Luther, can shape history.

Through Luther, Erikson examines the nature of the great man's power and shows that his compelling qualities may grow out of his anxieties as much as his strengths. His virtue lies in his unrelenting determination to settle psychological controversies which others experience but face less decisively. While most men conceal their anxieties and compromise rather than reconcile internal conflicts, an unusual integrity in the great man compels him to harmonize the warring elements. From his anguished quest for peace comes a new personal identity and with it a magnificent release of energy and determination. The combination of a compelling new identity and individual magnetism galvanizes others, and the great man, often without calculation, finds himself at the head of a movement.

All this is extrapolation from the one biography Erikson has published, but the notions are so intriguing and *Young Man Luther* so rewarding that similar works on other men seem in order. Only when applied to a number of figures can the merit of Erikson's implicit hypotheses be measured. While of lesser

°Reprinted, with permission, from *Soundings*, 52 (Spring, 1969), 15–46.

magnitude than Luther and Protestantism, Jonathan Edwards and the Great Awakening of 1740 in New England were similarly related. The revivals of 1735 which foreshadowed the greater outburst in 1740 began in Edwards's parish, and for many years he was called to preach wherever ministers wished their congregations to join the movement. No one compelled sinners to face their doom more relentlessly, and no one told better the sweet raptures of grace or explained more precisely where to place one's trust. He was by common consent the most powerful spokesman for the reborn men of his generation.

To understand the sources of this influence, Erikson's model of leadership calls for a reconstruction of the leader's identity and of the emotional needs of his age, for the great man has access to the hearts of other men at the point where the spiritual needs of leader and people converge. In Erikson's scheme, identity is the shape that an individual gives to his life to satisfy himself and his society. It is constituted both by his personal likes, dislikes, habits, attitudes, fears, hopes, and capacities, and by the way he manages all these internal resources within the limitations of his social environment. As Erikson puts it, identity in the maturing person is "the accrued experience of the ego's ability to integrate all identifications with the vicissitudes of the libido, with the aptitudes developed out of endowment, and with the opportunities offered in social roles."[2] To work with this model in Edwards's case we must delineate the emerging patterns of his thought and feeling and the roles he assumed in his father's parsonage as he grew up. We must also look for strains among these components, for it was the resolution of tensions in conversion which both shaped his personal identity and prepared him for leadership in the Great Awakening.

Erikson draws heavily on psychoanalysis for his insights into Luther, and among psychological systems psychoanalysis is unusually helpful in enlarging the historian's understanding of human character. But more important than the system employed is the ability to enter into the consciousness of another person and to respond to his feelings. Psychoanalysis is particularly useful in the interpretation of early childhood, where an adult imagination is most likely to fail; but so little information on that period remains in most cases, and virtually none for Edwards, that the beginnings perforce must be neglected. Psychoanalytic insights can also help to discover patterns in the materials on later life, and in the analysis that follows I have relied more than once on Erikson's reformulation of Freud to interpret the data.[3] But sensitivity of the sort exhibited by novelists or the best literary critics is the skill most evident in Erikson's work and the one required of historians who would follow him. Effective application of his model of leadership depends mostly upon the exercise of historical imagination in translating the raw facts of a biography into a coherent and believable human experience.

I

Jonathan Edwards was born in 1703 in East Windsor, Connecticut, in the household of the Reverend Timothy Edwards.[4] East Windsor had separated from Windsor in 1694, and in the first year of its independence the parish settled Timothy Edwards as its minister. Fresh from Harvard, he soon married and moved into the house which his father, a prosperous Hartford merchant, built for him in the center of the village. Jonathan was his fifth child and first son, the only son, as it turned out, among eleven children.

The most evident import of Jonathan's genealogy is that he would be expected to attain to eminence. Differing circumstances on the ancestral lines of both mother and father pointed in the same direction: Jonathan would have to be powerful and successful, especially intellectually, to fulfill his family's hopes. Jonathan's mother, Esther, was the daughter of Solomon Stoddard and Esther Warham Mather Stoddard, a very imposing pair of parents. Solomon Stoddard was the dominant ecclesiastical figure in the Connecticut Valley and a powerful man throughout New England. His voice could disturb the Mathers in their Boston stronghold and was regarded respectfully everywhere. Most noted for successfully challenging the "New England Way" of admitting only visible saints to communion, Stoddard believed that true saints could not be discovered and that upright and orthodox people should be accepted into the Church in the hope that communion would help convert them, a view that many churches in the Connecticut Valley adopted. Solomon was also renowned for the fervency of his preaching and for the recurrent revivals in his Northampton congregation, a tradition Jonathan was to inherit and culminate.

When Solomon accepted the pulpit at Northampton, he met and soon married his predecessor's widow. The daughter of a famed Connecticut minister, and a powerful person in her own right, Esther Stoddard was widely known for her vigorous mind, strength of will, and considerable learning, traits which, along with her name, she gave to Jonathan's mother.

Esther Edwards was remembered by her friends as "tall, dignified and commanding in her appearance," yet "affable and gentle in her manners." Solomon sent her to Boston for her education, and she became especially well acquainted with the Scriptures and with theological writers. After Timothy's death she would ask in the neighborhood ladies to listen to her comments on theology. Some of the listeners thought Esther Edwards surpassed her husband in "Native vigor of understanding."[5]

Knowing this much, it seems safe to say that Esther wanted Jonathan to embody the qualities notable in her father, her mother, herself, and the man she chose to marry. To please his mother fully Jonathan would have to be a man of unusual force and intellect. Values so thoroughly inbred and virtually unchallenged through at least two generations could exert an intense pressure, all the greater because Jonathan was the only son among eleven children. The hopes which only a man child could fulfill necessarily focused on a boy who arrived after four daughters, and the hopes grew more intense as six daughters followed.

A rivalry with the other Stoddard daughters may have heightened Esther's ambition for her son. A hint of this competition infuses all the family relationships. Perhaps the goal was to produce a worthy successor to Solomon; if so, Esther triumphed, for Jonathan was chosen to take the Northampton pulpit.

But he paid dearly for his success. His cousins harried him whenever he was in trouble. During the dismissal proceedings at Northampton, one cousin, Joseph Hawley, was the leading spokesman for the opposition. Another, Solomon Williams, wrote the refutation of Edwards's plea for a church of visible saints, pointedly rebuking him for attacking his honored grandfather. Still another cousin, Israel Williams, a powerful figure in civil and commercial affairs in Northampton, had a long record of opposing Edwards' ministry on various counts. As early as the college years, Elisha Mix, a roommate and a cousin on Esther's side, fell out with Jonathan and wanted to move. Jonathan's father complained to Elisha's mother of his bad conduct and reproved her for speaking ill of Jonathan before strangers.[6] This collective animus may measure the determination of the Stoddard daughters to have their sons achieve the stature of Solomon and the disappointment of Esther's sisters at seeing one who was not their own excel.

Timothy's predilections reinforced Esther's high expectations for Jonathan. Timothy was the first in his family to attend college in three generations. His great-grandfather, Richard Edwards, was an ordained minister, a university graduate, and the teacher in the Cooper's Company school in London. He died young, and his widow married a cooper. With him and William, her only son by Richard, she migrated to Connecticut. William would have gone to college had his own father lived, but in America he took up his stepfather's trade. Whatever educational values may have been transmitted across the generations were twice focused on only sons, for William's wife bore him a single son who was named Richard in memory of a father and perhaps of a way of life not wholly forgotten. Timothy remembered of this Richard that, beside the Bible, "Other Good books were in the Season thereof Much Read in his house," providing some evidence of values surviving.[7]

William could not afford college for his son, but in the cooper's shop Richard prospered. He also built up a mercantile business that eventually outgrew one warehouse and required another. Meanwhile he rose through town offices into colonial politics, holding positions as selectman, as deputy to the General Court, and in his later years as Queen's Attorney. When it came time to choose a career for his eldest son, Richard sent Timothy to Harvard to study for the ministry, and perhaps to recover the honor and refinement of the first Richard's station. Timothy's aspirations for Jonathan were at least tinged with the frustrated desires of two generations finally promised fulfillment in a brilliant scion.

After settling in East Windsor, Timothy became well known for his great skill in preparing boys for Harvard and Yale. He simply assumed that Jonathan would be a scholar too and assimilate his father's learning in Latin, Greek, and Hebrew. All of the Edwards children studied the classical languages under Timothy, and even the girls went on for more schooling. The desks lining the parlor were constant reminders of family expectations. Jonathan quite naturally began Latin at age six when his precocity was fast becoming evident. In the family of Esther and Timothy, the early discovery of Jonathan's great abilities only heightened the parents' hopes and intensified the pressure for achievement.

More remains than the meager information about Esther and Jonathan to tell us about the probable effects of Timothy's character on his son. Timothy was a compulsively exact and exacting man. He schooled his students so well because he tolerated no errors in their recitations, just as he allowed none to himself. He memorized every word of his sermons and delivered them letter-perfect. Measuring corn for barter or in lieu of money payment on his salary, he "made the negro sweep it up very clean" and then measured the sweepings.[8] He delighted in classifying thoughts, arranging them in numbered lists. His tribute to his father "ends with a list of seventeen mercies attending the manner of his death, separates his dying words into thirty-five items, works out six ways in which he glorified God at his death, and proceeds to supply numbered particulars under each."[9]

Timothy displayed all the classic compulsive traits, order, thrift, and obstinacy. When inflation depreciated the value of his salary, he prepared lengthy comparisons of purchasing power at the time he was settled and afterwards to prove he was being cheated. He was never one to yield in disputes with his congregation, either. In the 1730's a young man in town married a local girl without her parents' permission. Timothy wished to censor the boy, but the congregation refused to concur. Considering the case a matter of conscience, Timothy denied communion to the entire town for over three years while the controversy dragged on.

Jonathan's mind, though far more sweeping, poetic, and profound than his father's, bore the marks of its training under Timothy. Jonathan too refused to give an inch when challenged. In the dismissal controversy at Northampton he would not compromise with his parishioners, nor would he yield a point in the debate with Solomon Williams on admission to communion. In all intellectual disputes Edwards stubbornly beat down his opponents, demolishing even the slightest contradictions. He had to prove himself right in every detail. Even in non-combative writings, his arguments were exhaustive. What often appears as repetition was part of a massive effort to block every conceivable loophole. The careful definitions, the close reasoning, the piling up of proofs and illustrations were the natural ways of his thorough and fastidious mind. The truth had to be expressed immaculately and in perfect order, leaving no gaps for error to invade.

His father's parsimony shaped not only Jonathan's attitude toward money—he too argued with his parish over salary—but toward ideas. Ideas were poetry and power for Edwards; with them he negotiated his peace with the universe. But they were also things to be possessed. His delight in discovering Locke was greater "than the most greedy miser finds, when gathering up handsful of silver and gold, from some newly discovered treasure."[10] He pinned papers to his coat while riding as reminders of his thoughts so that none would be lost. All of his ideas, along with many he read, were written down and carefully preserved in notebooks that came to contain many thousands of pages.

The productions of mind were hoarded and treasured as valued possessions in a vast miser's store of thoughts.

Timothy's exactions were moral as well as intellectual. He required perfect obedience as well as perfect accuracy. The detailed instructions contained in letters to his family were presumably no less thorough when he was at home. Jonathan's behavior for the most part appears to have satisfied his parents. In one letter, when Jonathan was eight, Timothy said, "I hope thou wilt take Special care of Jonathan that he dont Learn to be rude and naught etc., of which thee and I have Lately Discoursed."[11] But the tenor of the comment was that naughtiness was exceptional. Not until late adolescence did the strains which Timothy's high standards imposed come out. Jonathan gratefully acknowledged that his parents' "counsel and education" had been his "making," but confessed that "in the time of it, it seemed to do me so little good."[12] The entire diary testified of the "good" of that sort of upbringing. Timothy's education implanted a conscience as meticulous and demanding as his standards of scholarship. The comment "it seemed to do me so little good" speaks of long struggles in which part of the self was hopelessly resistant to the pressures of conscience. By the time of the diary, Jonathan had conquered all obvious forms of sin and was struggling with the fine points, like wanting to stop to eat when mealtime came and an occasional listlessness in his studies. But his conscience kept asking for perfection, and he obediently renewed the daily examinations of his soul. He thought once that he must live as if he were to be the only true Christian on the earth in his generation. Timothy's education placed that much of a burden on his boy. Throughout his life, Jonathan continued to abhor himself as a "miserable wretch," "base and vile," and unworthy of God.[13]

There is some evidence that a peculiar combination of fear and love enforced Timothy's exactions. He displayed an extraordinary anxiety for his children's physical safety. An excerpt from a letter to Esther illustrates the point.

> I hope God will help thee to be very careful that no harm happen to the little Children by Scalding wort, whey, water, or by Standing too nigh to Tim when he is cutting wood; and prithee take what care thou canst about Mary's neck, which was too much neglected when I was at home. . . . And Let Esther and Betty Take their powders as Soon as the Dog Days are Over, and if they dont help Esther, talk further with the Doctor about her for I wouldnt have her be neglected. . . . If any of the children should at any time Go over the River to meeting I would have them be exceeding carefull, how they Sit or Stand in the boat Least they should fall into the River."[14]

That passage may be read as the loving concern of an oversolicitous father, but, as Ola Winslow commented, "instead of quieting childish fears he raised them, as though parental guidance consisted in advance notice of potential disaster."[15] If the attitude was typical, Timothy's anxieties would have reinforced in the Edwards children the ordinary apprehensions of violent destruction. Perhaps on an unconscious level they sensed that under Timothy's apparent strength was a lively sense of the precariousness of existence. At the very least they imbibed a sense of their vulnerability. Small wonder that thunder terrified Jonathan and raised apprehensions of divine wrath.

Timothy's own vulnerability made resistance still more hazardous. Fears for his own destruction arose with anxieties about the children. The myth of his boyhood, based perhaps on fact, perhaps on his own febrile imagination, had him narrowly escaping calamities ranging from drownings and freezings to swallowing peach stones. His letters home from the military expedition which he accompanied as chaplain admonish Esther not to be "discouraged or over anxious concerning me," and follow with such quavering reassurances as, "I have still strong hopes of seeing thee and our dear children once again." His life, like the letters, was suffused with the conditional, "if I Live to come home." Or, again: "Tell the children, that I would have them, if they desire to see their father again, to pray daily for me in secret."[16] The conventional sentiment may have had deeper significance in the Edwards household where the children were made to feel some of the responsibility for preserving his rather frail being, making resistance fraught with danger.

Timothy's fragility and perfectionism were slight defects, and the burdens he imposed on his children surprisingly light, considering the emotional hardships of his own childhood. Richard Edwards was one of the few men in seventeenth-century New England to seek and obtain a divorce. After three appeals and a special investigation, his complaints finally moved the magistracy. Timothy's mother, Elizabeth Tuttle, confessed pregnancy by another man three months after her marriage and was unfaithful periodically throughout the twenty-four years of her life with Richard. He never forgave her infidelity and besides bore other perversities "too grievous to forgitt and too mutch here to Relate."[17] Elizabeth's trouble was not mere weakness but a violent malice, bordering on or perhaps symptomatic of insanity. Her brother Benjamin killed their sister with an axe. Another sister killed her own son. Elizabeth threatened Richard with physical violence. Timothy grew up in the presence of distrust and hatred, dependent almost wholly on his father for steady affection and exposed to visible and explosive hostility in his mother. The insistence on rigid control and the precautions Timothy urged on the patient Esther out of fear for his own and his children's safety were modest demands from such a man.

The fear of destruction was always wrapped and muffled in love. Timothy Edwards was indeed an oversolicitous parent, moved by genuine affection and concern. Another letter asks Esther to "remember my love to each of the children, to Esther, Elizabeth, Anne, Mary, Jonathan, Eunice and Abigail," in his usual thorough way naming each individually in order of birth, and then adding, "the Lord have mercy on and eternally save them all, with our dear little Jerusha," the most recent. The next sentence tells much about the warmth of his household: "The Lord bind up their souls with thine and mine in the bundle of life."[18]

Any contemplated disobedience faced this love as well as the implicit danger of destruction. Overt rebellion struck at the loving and loved parent. Jonathan's doctrine that sin was all the more heinous for offending a God who loved the sinner with infinite compassion expressed the anguish felt by rebels in the Edwards household. Unjustifiable resistance wholly deserved its punishment, even if it were complete destruction. All of the Edwards children remained loyal to their parents and their parents' values. The resentments arising from discipline were necessarily turned inward or diverted to other objects.

A chance event in the family history may have accentuated the apprehensions which Timothy aroused. When Jonathan was seven he passed through a rare naughty spell, resisting for a moment his father's strict control. Immediately afterwards Timothy left with the military expedition for Canada and soon wrote home his quavering hopes for a safe return and the admonitions to pray for his safety. Jonathan's wish to overthrow his father's government seemed to enjoy remarkable success. Suddenly his father was gone and Jonathan was the only male in the house, a situation perfectly designed to revive the furtive romance with the mother characteristic of boyhood a few years earlier. With his conscious mind, Jonathan knew well enough where his father was and that he intended to return, but the direct fulfillment of secret wishes heightened fantasies with immense appeal to the unconscious. When word came back that Timothy had fallen ill and nearly died, the rational faculty would have to struggle desperately to convince itself that those deep wishes had not come precariously close to fulfillment. The brief release of passionate hopes compelled the internal restraining forces to grow all the stronger. All this was stored away in the expanding armory of Jonathan's exceedingly aggressive conscience.

Recreating what we can, then, from the meager facts of Jonathan's childhood, a few themes begin to emerge:

1) Both father and mother had unusually high hopes for Jonathan's intellectual prowess and for the possibility of his becoming eminent.

2) Timothy exacted extraordinarily precise moral and intellectual behavior from his son.

3) Timothy's feelings for his children were an ambivalent mixture of high demands, intense love, and fear of destruction, both theirs and his own.

## II

Three essays written by Jonathan, probably between his eleventh and thirteenth years, open a window on his character as it took shape amid the high expectations of the Edwards household. One was an unfinished set of observations on the rainbow, foreshadowing the later notes on natural science. The second was the famous essay on spiders, and the third a facetious rebuttal to the notion of a material soul. The hand of Timothy encouraging and guiding Jonathan's development is seen behind the spider essay, "Of Insects." Like many other New England ministers, Timothy cultivated English correspondents, offering them, in return for their interest, notes on natural phenomena in the New World. More ambitious for his son than himself, Timothy urged Jonathan to write up his observations and send them to England where conceivably they might impress "the Learned world."[19]

"Of Insects" demonstrates how precocious Jonathan was both intellectually and socially. In the letter accompanying the essay, he self-consciously presented himself in a stylized guise suitable for his tender age and also in accord with the conventional proprieties of authorship.

> Forgive me, sir, that I Do not Conceal my name, and Communicate this to you by a mediator. If you think the Observations Childish, and besides the Rules of Decorum,—with Greatness and Goodness overlook it in a Child and Conceal Sir, Although these things appear very Certain to me, yet Sir, I submit it all to your better Judgment and Deeper insight. . . .[20]

Particularly the sentence, "Forgive me, sir, that I Do Not Conceal my name, and Communicate this to you by a mediator," was an affectation entirely appropriate for his century, but one that had to be learned. Somehow from the books or the guests in the East Windsor parsonage Jonathan had picked up the mannerism and made it his own.

Obviously as Jonathan wrote this essay he did not think of himself as a young future pastor, as might be expected from his upbringing and later life. He accepted that role too; a contemporaneous letter to his sister triumphantly recounted the conversions during a revival time in East Windsor.[21] But in the essay on spiders he appeared as a natural philosopher, and the essay on the soul was weighted heavily with the gestures of an eighteenth-century man of letters.

> I am informed that you have advanced an Notion that the soul is materiall and attends the body till the resurection as I am a profest Lover of novelty you must immagin I am very much entertained by this discovery (which however [old] in some parts of the world is new to us) but suffer my Curiosity a Littel further I would know the manner of the kingdom before I swear alegance.[22]

The casual, satirical tone, so redolent of fashionable prose postures, stands in marked contrast to the earnest, straightforward style of Edwards' maturity and comes as something of a relief in an anthology of his writing. The two pages on "The Soul" suggest that he toyed with more sprightly life-styles and was for a moment light-hearted before settling down to the life and death issues.

The parenthetical comment, "which however [old] in some parts of the world is new to us," indicates that imitating English manners was more than an amusing posture. Jonathan was a provincial, painfully aware that there were brilliant centers of culture and learning where ideas had grown old before the provinces even heard them. He wanted access to those centers and recognition from them. The roles of man of letters or natural philosopher were acceptable in the capitals of the English community, and, with Timothy's help, Jonathan cultivated the parts. If Timothy's expertise was limited to ancient languages, he knew of larger fields for the mind and aspired to see his son enter them.

Jonathan's strategy is reminiscent of Benjamin Franklin's, to name but one of Edwards' contemporaries with a similar youthful outlook. Franklin too was industriously perfecting his style, using Addison and Steele as his masters, with the intent of winning the attention of great ones. Success in the *New England Courant* fostered high hopes which led first to Philadelphia and then to London, where he introduced himself to polite society with a philosophical essay and a natural curiosity, a piece of asbestos. Defeated for the most part in this first assault, Franklin returned to Philadelphia and built a solid provincial base before trying again and succeeding magnificently as a natural philosopher. His scientific experiments won the recognition of the learned world and helped to establish him as the most cosmopolitan of provincials. In social terms, scientific speculation and experimentation can be interpreted as providing entry to the intellectual life beyond the provinces. Far from being unique, Edwards and Franklin simply took more seriously activities in which many educated Americans dabbled. Science and letters were avenues which talented young men could follow into the great world.

In Edwards's case, the social opportunity must also be related to his personal situation. Ascent into the great world was the fulfillment of his parents' high expectations, or, more accurately, a natural sequel to the rewards his intelligence had won at home. As his parents' ambitions for him became his own ambitions for himself, success in meeting their expectations encouraged him to aspire to success in broader spheres.

The spheres he hoped to conquer grew ever larger after he entered Yale at age thirteen and learned about the marvels of Locke and Newton. Sometime during his college years he began the notes on mind and on natural science which reveal how seriously Edwards took the work of these two intellects. The natural science notes show Edwards exploring every physical phenomenon he observed and in his usual thorough and rational way explaining the facts of physics, biology, and astronomy. "The Mind" contained observations on psychology and metaphysics after the manner of Locke's *An Essay Concerning Human Understanding*. In it Jonathan laid the groundwork of his philosophical idealism.

Both sets of notes were meant to be more than a record of observations. Edwards planned two massive treatises for publication. At the head of the notes on "The Mind" is a formal title: "The Natural History of the Mental World, or of the Internal World: being a Particular Enquiry into the Nature of the Human Mind." The relationship of this work to the notes on natural science was to be explained in the introduction: "Concerning the two worlds—the External and the Internal: the External, the subject of Natural Philosophy; the Internal, our own Minds."[23] With his two volumes Edwards planned to encompass the whole of existence, the internal and external worlds. He aimed to enlarge upon and perhaps advance beyond Locke and Newton, grounding all in theological metaphysics. Edwards was well aware that his undertaking was presumptuous and cautioned himself "not to insert any disputable thing, or that will be likely to be disputed by learned men; for I may depend upon it, they will receive nothing, but what is undeniable, from me."[24] And yet confidence in his own powers and mastery of every intellectual task Connecticut had presented encouraged him to go ahead with his *Summa*. This young provincial aimed high.

The picture of Edwards thus far is relatively conflict-free. Past performance promised future fulfillment of his parents' hopes. His natural gifts and temperament suited perfectly the life they foresaw for him. Even the legacy of compulsive thoroughness and logic were put to the service of his identity as scholar and philosopher. In the family, at Yale, and hopefully in the greater

English community, society confirmed his belief that the works of his mind were worthy and important and would assure him a place of high respect.

But the promise was not fulfilled exactly as forecast. The two treatises were never published. Although Edwards steadily added to his scientific and philosophical notes, they remained notes. He never publicly assumed the role of natural philosopher, and he dropped the fashionable style of a man of letters in favor of a more somber voice as preacher. His career as pastor and divine absorbed his entire life. The early work was put aside except when it served religion.

The main turning came during the conversion years, but the earliest writings reflect the tensions conversion had to resolve. More was at stake, of course, than boyish dreams of fame. The essay on spiders particularly points to the pitfalls which the high-strung Edwards conscience created even for a boy as obedient as Jonathan and which compelled him to change his life. "Of Insects" is most useful to a biographer if it is read as an unconscious allegory of human existence. Such an interpretation is not far-fetched considering that later Edwards consciously made a spider the emblem of man's plight. Aside from purely scientific curiosity, something held Edwards' attention on spiders hour after hour. During his observations he continually drew parallels with people, and at the end he discussed the ways of God with small creatures in the universal moral order.

The quality which first intrigued him was the "truly very Pretty and Pleasing" ability of spiders to swim through the air from tree to tree and float high in the sky toward the sun. By careful experimentation, he discovered that spiders emitted a fine web which the air bore upwards and which, when it grew long enough, carried away the spider. He hypothesized that it spun the web from "a certain liquor with which that Great bottle tail of theirs is filled," and which dried and rarefied when exposed. He saw the spiders on these webs "mount away into the air" and thought it afforded them "a Great Deal of their sort of Pleasure." Their delight disclosed "the exuberant Goodness of the Creator" who provided for the necessities and also "the Pleasure and Recreation of all sorts of Creatures."[25]

The pleasures of ascent, however, were short-lived, for as the spiders mounted toward the sun in the fair summer weather, they were caught in the prevailing westerly winds and carried to the sea with a great stream of other insects to be "buried in the Ocean, and Leave Nothing behind them but their Eggs." "The End of Nature in Giving Spiders this way Of flying Which though we have found in the Corollary to be their Pleasure and Recreation, yet we think a Greater end is at last their Destruction."[26] The "Greater end" of the pleasing rise was eventual destruction.

The spider's nature made him worthy of this fate. At first appearance "no one is more wonderful than the Spider especially with Respect to their sagacity and admirable way of working." Its maneuvers were "truly very Pretty." But the inner nature of the spider warranted a violent burial at sea, for in essence it was "the Corrupting Nauseousness of our Air." Were spiders in any number to die inland in winter, the spring sun would revive "those nauseous vapours of which they are made up."[27] To prevent them from smelling up the country they were taught to rise and then destroyed.

Edwards here dwelt somewhat pathetically on two themes which sound again more stridently through the "Diary": a pleasurable ascent ends in destruction, and nauseousness lies beneath the pretty appearances. In the "Diary" Jonathan firmly renounced the pleasures of rising as he saw that pride led to destruction. His schemes to achieve eminence in the world had to be abandoned in favor of a life devoted wholly to religion. A loathing of his own vileness also came to obsess him. Later he spoke of sensuality as pollution. "How sensual you have been!" he told one audience. "Are there not some here that have debased themselves below the dignity of human nature by wallowing in sensual filthiness, as swine in the mire, or as filthy vermin feeding with delight on rotten carrion?"[28] "Of Insects" suggests that Jonathan's conscience was already disturbing his complacency in prideful achievement and that the underside of the compulsive perfectionism Timothy implanted was a fear of concealed filth.

Another portentous theme appeared in the early writings. Comparing spiders to humans, Edwards said, "the soul in the brain immediately Percieves when any of those little nervous strings that Proceed from it are in the Least Jarrd by External things." In the essay on the material soul, he asked facetiously if the soul is "a number of Long fine strings reaching from the head to the foot." The image of strings suggests how delicately responsive was his nervous system and how easily jarred. When the spiders were jarred in the course of the experiments, they spun a web and drifted off. The material soul was less mobile, and the main point of the essay concerned the discomforts it suffered "when the Coffin Gives way" and "the earth will fall in and Crush it." Or more excruciating, when other souls were buried in the same grave, they "Quarril for the highest place." "I would know whether I must Quit my dear head if a Superior Soul Comes in the way." When twenty or thirty souls occupied the spot, "the undergoing so much hard Ship and being deprived of the body at Last will make them ill temper'd."[29]

The satirical portrayal of a discontented, nervous soul, growing ill-tempered as it struggled for a place in the narrow confines of the grave, suggests some of the contrasting pleasures of Edwards' famous booth in the woods. The large family of girls, the guests, the students, and the watchful, demanding eyes of Timothy left little room in the house for peaceful worship. With his boyhood friends, Jonathan built a "booth in a swamp, in a very retired spot, for a place of prayer. And besides, I had particular secret places of my own in the woods, where I used to retire myself."[30] Personal relations all too easily jarred "the little nervous strings" proceeding from his brain, and Edwards struggled hard for mastery of his responses. His diary discloses that he suffered particularly from a "disposition to chide and fret." His own overweening conscience inclined him to snap at others' weaknesses and "to manifest my own dislike and scorn."[31] He eventually decided he could permit himself no evil speaking, not even that which he once thought to be righteous reproof. The dangers of slander or undue vehemence were all too apparent. Even public worship tried him, until by concerted effort he learned to overcome his impatience.[32] Throughout his life he often walked in the fields or rode in the woods, where alone under the sky he more easily composed his soul and made peace with God.

In sum, these early writings confirm to some extent and elaborate the previous speculations on the emotional import of Edwards' early life:

1) For a time anyway, Jonathan aspired to fulfill family expectations through his philosophic writings.

2) The pleasure and excitement of rising was counter-balanced by a fear of destruction because of unworthiness or inward filthiness.

3) The tendency to chide and fret made close personal relations uncomfortable.

## III

Edwards' conversion, which drew on all of these themes, occurred over a period of years in his early manhood. Near the end of his college, a case of pleurisy brought him "nigh to the grave" and shook him "over the pit of hell." After that he grew steadily more uneasy about religion, going through "great and violent inward struggles" until he finally broke off "all ways of known outward sin." The "inward struggles and conflicts, and selfreflections" continued, and he made "seeking my salvation the main business of my life" but still did not consider himself converted.[33] Meanwhile he was studying theology in New Haven and preparing to take a temporary pulpit in New York City.

Sometime in his eighteenth or nineteenth year began a series of experiences which he later believed to be gracious. Two slightly differing accounts survive. Edwards wrote the *Personal Narrative* nearly twenty years later, after the first revivals in Northampton. What remains of the "Diary" begins in December of 1722 when he was in New York City and when he had reason to believe grace had already touched him. It records his struggles with sin and his further experiences with grace.

In the "Diary" Edwards charted his cycles of spiritual decay and recovery, the movement from spiritual dullness to the exhilarating moments of rededication. On Saturday, January 12, 1723, in the morning, he enjoyed one of the seasons of grace, and the comment he wrote directly afterwards indicates the nature of the experience. The paramount issue was renunciation of self and complete surrender to God.

> I have this day, solemnly renewed my baptismal covenant and self-dedication, which I renewed, when I was taken into the communion of the church. I have been before God, and have given myself, all that I am, and have, to God; so that I am not, in any respect, my own. I can challenge no right in this understanding, this will, these affections, which are in me. Neither have I any right to this body, or any of its members—no right to this tongue, these hands, these feet; no right to these senses, these eyes, these ears, this smell, or this taste. I have given myself clear away, and have not retained any thing, as my own. I gave them to God, in my baptism, and I have been this morning to him, and told him, that I gave myself *wholly* to him. I have given every power to him; so that for the future, I'll challenge no right in myself, in no respect whatever.[34]

Edwards felt compelled to offer more than perfect obedience to God. He searched his soul to be sure nothing was left for himself; everything was given to God, his body and all its senses, all his powers, all enjoyments, the credit for all his efforts, the right to complain or rest, the right to seek anything for himself. He could not permit himself to be "in any way proud." At issue in conversion was the willingness to obliterate selfishness and give up all to God. During the controversy over admission to communion in Northampton, he summarized in a public profession what was expected of saints and put this surrender and the accompanying obedience at the heart. The profession read in the whole:

> I hope, I truly find in my heart a willingness to comply with all the commandments of God, which require me to give up myself wholly to Him, and to serve Him with my body and my spirit; and do accordingly now promise to walk in a way of obedience to all the commandments of God, as long as I live.[35]

The *Personal Narrative* shifted the stress somewhat to emphasize Edwards' reconciliation with the doctrine of "God's sovereignty, in choosing whom he would to eternal life, and rejecting whom he pleased, leaving them eternally to perish, and be everlasting tormented in Hell." Edwards did not consciously experience the intense fear of divine wrath which usually preceded conversion. He thought his "great and violent inward struggles" were not properly called terror, but as these comments reveal, the fear of punishment was there, probably buried too deep to be felt. The doctrine of election "used to appear like a horrible doctrine," and filled his mind with objections from his childhood up.[36]

For no discernible reason, Edwards suddenly became convinced of God's justice in election. Objections ceased and he rested easy in assurance of divine justice. In connection with this alteration, he tells of his first experience with "that sort of inward, sweet delight in God and divine things" that he later called grace. It came as he read the passage in Scripture saying, "Now unto the King eternal, immortal, and invisible, the only wise God, be honor and glory for ever and ever, Amen." As he read these words, there diffused through his soul "a sense of the glory of the Divine Being; a new sense, quite different from any thing I ever experienced before."[37] As far as Edwards could tell that was the moment of his conversion, and reconciliation with divine power was the critical issue. After that, the thunder that had once terrified aroused sweet contemplations of God's glory.

The two accounts of the experience with grace are easily reconciled, for they have in common a submission to God. The "Diary" stresses the surrender of self and renunciation of pride. The *Personal Narrative* emphasizes the discovery of beauty in God's sovereign right to punish. Both forms of submission can be seen as aspects of a single experience, especially if one remembers how some common vicissitudes of childhood could prepare the way for this very combination. While engaged in passionate rivalry with his father for the love of his mother, a boy imagines himself rising in pride and power to displace his father, thereby evoking paternal wrath. Peace negotiations require both the renunciation of pride and acceptance of the father's superior power, a double surrender morally symmetrical with the two issues in Edwards' conversion.[38]

Edwards' pride could easily have awakened these old memories and their attached apprehensions because his ambition was tied so closely to intellectual achievement, which was also his father's source of pride and a form of accomplishment his mother prized. In seeking to excel as a scholar he inevitably outdid his father and won the favor of his mother. The audacity of the act, though wholly symbolic and unconscious, released the fears which Timothy's compulsive demands and the implicit threats of destruction had formed in Jonathan's conscience. The "torments of hell" included the terror the Edwards children felt toward the imminent possibility of hurting and being hurt by their loving, profoundly fragile, and threatening father. In yielding all to God, Jonathan disclaimed the old rivalry, again symbolically and unconsciously, and placated his archaic fears. The danger of rising to destruction was averted.

Edwards wanted God to sanctify every level of his being, down to the deepest, and the glory of conversion was the comprehensive transformation it wrought. Its power lay in the affinity between theological notions and intimate personal tensions. In conversion Jonathan reconciled himself to God and universal being but the religious symbols also formed bonds with long forgotten memories and with buried conflicts too explosive for consciousness to touch. Conversion resolved tensions along the full range of experience. Until that moment God was the sovereign who judged and punished, shaking men over the pit until they obeyed. The relationship was one of king to subject. As the new "sense of the glory of the Divine Being" came over Edwards upon reading the first epistle to Timothy, he felt a happy yearning to enjoy God, to "be rapt up to him in heaven" and to be "swallowed up in him forever." He prayed "In a manner quite different" from before and "with a new sort of affection." The beauty and loveliness of Christ instead of the fierce power of God impressed his mind. All of Canticles occupied him and especially the verse, "I am the Rose of Sharon, and the Lily of the valleys." These symbols and the whole perception of the divine was softer, warmer, more sensuous.[39] The new relationship was one of lovers. At times the tone was frankly sexual. Some passages in the *Personal Narrative* overflow with a lover's passion.

> The inward ardor of my soul, seemed to be hindered and pent up, and could not freely flame out as it would. I used often to think, how in heaven this principle should freely and fully vent and express itself. Heaven appeared exceedingly delightful, as a world of love; and that all happiness consisted in living in pure, humble, heavenly, divine love.[40]

Or in a different mode: "My heart panted after this, to lie low before God, as in the dust; that I might be nothing, and that God might be ALL, that I might become as a little child."[41] One of the rewards of conversion was that feelings otherwise tightly suppressed flowed freely toward God.

The venting of emotion was possible because vileness was changed to sweetness. The nauseousness of the spider was banished. Whereas sensuality had been and under that name was still described as filth and defilement, the new "delights" were of a "pure, soul-animating and refreshing nature." The happiness of heaven where the inward ardor could "freely flame out" consisted "in pure, humble, heavenly, divine love." The "ravishingly lovely" beauty of holiness was "far purer than any thing here upon earth"; everything else was "mire and defilement" in comparison.[42] In grace emotions were sweet and calm and flowed freely without polluting. Sensuality was purely joyous.

One final issue came to resolution during conversion. Edwards overcame, partially at least, his uneasiness among people. His disposition to chide and fret had disturbed his personal relations, and he had found peace most easily in solitude. In conversion he still envisioned himself "alone in the mountains, or some solitary wilderness, far from all mankind, sweetly conversing with Christ, and wrapt and swallowed up in God." But loving and even ardent relations with other Christians were possible. Another of his poetic visions pictured the soul of a true Christian as "a little white flower" standing "peacefully and lovingly, in the midst of other flowers round about." In New York he drew very close to the two saintly people with whom he lived and delighted in long intimate discussions about heaven and holiness.[43]

Edwards' social discomforts did not disappear, for his "heart was knit in affection" only "to those, in whom were appearances of true piety." Indeed he "could bear the thoughts of no other companions, but such as were holy, and the disciples of the blessed Jesus." He disliked visiting among his parishioners where small talk of the world was a necessity. Instead he invited them to his study where he could keep the discussion on religion. The woman he married, Sarah Pierrepont, had been widely reputed for her piety, and even before he met her Edwards wrote a tribute to her "wonderful sweetness" and "singular purity."[44] He could enjoy the intimacies of marriage and friendship only with those whom grace had sanctified, but at least conversion afforded that measure of untroubled intercourse.

IV

The happy visitations of grace continued during his stay in New York and into the following summer spent at his father's house. By the fall of 1723 he had agreed to settle in Bolton, a new town not far from East Windsor, but before his installation, a tutorship opened at Yale, and Edwards persuaded Bolton to release him. From June of 1724, after a winter of private study, until September of 1726, he was the senior tutor and acting Rector, with responsibility to discipline the students as well as to instruct them. After one week on the job, "despondencies, fears, perplexities, multitudes of cares, and distractions of mind" weighed him down and convinced him "of the troublesomeness and vexation of the world." For the three years of his tutorship he was in a "low, sunk estate and condition, miserably senseless" about "spiritual things."[45] The only respite came in the fall of 1725 when he fell ill at North Haven on his way home and his mother came to nurse him.

For many reasons Edwards welcomed the offer which came in 1725 to assist aging Grandfather Stoddard in Northampton. The new position took him away from Yale, and it made him heir-apparent to Solomon Stoddard's immense power. Nothing could have thrilled his mother more. The summer following his ordination, Edwards married Sarah Pierrepont, whose piety he had admired from afar and whose life in the Northampton parsonage bore out the promise of her early godliness and aristocratic upbringing. She was deeply devoted to her husband—one of her deepest sorrows was to displease "Mr. Edwards"—and her saintliness fully matched his own.[46] A daughter, the first of eleven children, was born in 1728.

Solomon Stoddard died in 1729 and Edwards became chief pastor. He seems never to have regretted the subordination of his youthful ambitions to be a natural philosopher. A ministerial career was perfectly suited to the religious identity formed in conversion. In the pulpit the lonely quest for salvation entered onto a broad stage. His office permitted him to talk freely of God's wrath, of human defilement, and of the exquisite joys of grace. Speaking objectively as pastor, Edwards exposed his soul publicly as he could never do privately. The secret yearnings and dread so long stored in the recesses of his heart became the bread and wine of an open communion with the world. Even the disposition to chide and rebuke was dignified to a duty. When he admonished, he spoke for God, expressing the righteous wrath of a Holy Father, commanding rather than being commanded, pure instead of vile, terrifying rather than being terrified. And the whole was sanctified and purged of pride because done for God and not for self.

The congregation responded to his quiet, intense preaching. From time to time under Stoddard, revivals had brought unusually large numbers into the Church. Five years after Edwards became pastor, the town experienced a livelier concern with religion than any known before. Two sudden deaths contributed to "the solemnizing of the spirits" of the young, and a controversy over Arminianism set many to asking the true way of salvation. Before long "among old and young, and from highest to the Lowest; all seemed to be siezed with a deep concern about their Eternal salvation."[47] The concern spread from town to town until churches all up and down the Connecticut Valley were reporting revivals. The suicide of Edwards' Uncle Hawley in a fit of melancholy over his state slowed the work, but five years later in 1740, when Whitefield visited New England, Northampton and other towns were ripe. The concern spread more widely than ever, engaging thousands of souls this time, and Edwards was in great demand as a preacher and counselor.

Edwards identified these conversions as being of the same species as his own. People felt the same "utter helplessness, and Insufficiency for themselves, and their Exceeding wickedness and Guiltiness in the sight of God," each one considering himself worse than all others just as he had. They were eventually brought to "a Lively sense of the Excellency of Jesus Christ" and "to have their Hearts filled with Love to God and Christ, and a disposition to Lie in the dust before him." In the procss of conversion people were also "brought off from their Inordinate Engagedness after the world," though obviously in different ways from Edwards' renunciation of achievement as a philosopher. The same love for others and concern for their souls, the same heightened sense of personal wickedness, the same variations in intensity of devotion all linked the common experience to Edwards' conversion.[48]

His personal influence, of course, does not begin to explain the prevalence of the revivals. All over New England people underwent rebirth in the period of a few years. They followed Edwards, or others like him, because they were ready, not because he personally overpowered them. Something common to all, some prevailing strain on their institutions, some pressure in the culture prepared people for the new life he urged upon them. They listened because the truth of his experience was also the truth of theirs.

I have treated the consciousness of this period at length elsewhere, but even in outline the parallels with Edwards can be seen.[49] In Edwards' psyche the most serious conflict leading to conversion was the tension between prideful ambition and the fear of suffering God's wrath for indulging in pride. Conditions in New England in the early eighteenth century put large segments of the population in a similar predicament. The paramount fact of the common life after 1700 was rapid expansion—in population, in the number of new settlements, in commercial opportunities and involvements, and in the economic horizons of the ordinary man. In Connecticut, for example, population grew nearly five times as fast in the thirty years after 1700 as in the thirty years before; the number of new towns settled doubled; the number of debt cases per capita—a measure of increasing prosperity and commercial growth—increased five times.

The most important and obvious effect on most lives was to broaden economic opportunities. The new towns offered a host of tantalizing possibilities for incipient merchants. The growing markets outside New England, in Newfoundland and Halifax, in the West Indies, and in Europe, along with the expanding needs of the prospering fishing fleet provided growing outlets for farmers, and the rapid growth of population made speculation in new land very enticing. These developments permitted young men to dream dreams utterly unfeasible earlier. New England had visited a few men with prosperity from the beginning, but very few ordinary men could hope for more than a decent living. William Edwards, for example, had carried on his trade without making great advances. Richard had fared better, building on his father's business, but in the seventeenth century he was exceptionally fortunate. Not everyone could elevate himself in the eighteenth century either, but new opportunities increased the incidence of success. Examples multiplied of small storekeepers who became wealthy merchants and of thrifty farmers who doubled their estates through speculation. By later standards the stakes were small, but the prospects dazzled the first generation of the new century.

Expansion stimulated the desire to rise in the world and yet implicitly threatened destruction, the very ambivalence prominent in Edwards' life. Commercial and agricultural expansion depended heavily on risk-laden spec-

ulations: natural disasters, debt foreclosures, and unforeseen calamities of various kinds could wipe out farmers and traders. The psychic hazards were as
great as the economic ones. Puritan preachers urged men to follow their callings
industriously and to rise through their enterprise. But they condemned men for
setting their hearts on wealth and making it their god. The increasing luxury of
the eighteenth century and its "Cursed Hunger of Riches" evoked the most
bitter indictments. A man never knew exactly where he stood. At one moment
he rested in the assurance of his virtuous diligence and of the prosperity heaven
had bestowed. At the next a warning from the pulpit started fears that the lust
for gold had hopelessly corrupted his soul. Men found themselves in a dilemma
comparable to the plight of Robert Keayne, a Boston merchant of the seventeenth century. Keayne prospered in Boston and maintained a respectable
reputation until he was accused of unfair dealing and reprimanded in the
courts. The confrontation with his guilt put him in fear for his salvation. In
hopes of recovering his peace of mind, Keayne wrote an interminable testament justifying his conduct.[50] In the seventeenth century distress like his hung
over the few who prospered; in the eighteenth century economic expansion
exposed the entire population to these unsettling apprehensions.

Conflicts with authority magnified the guilt and fears of the ambitious.
Aspiring men fought with established authority at every level of government, in
the town, in the church, and in the colonial government. With innumerable
variations, involving large and small enterprises, the pattern repeated itself:
ambitious men in pursuit of wealth broke through conventional restrictions and
clashed with authorities bent on preserving order. The conflicts were psychi-
cally debilitating because the magistracy and ministry were thought to rule by
virtue of divine investiture. Authority had a counterpart in individual consciences, and when men resisted they fought against themselves. Opposition,
however well justified, partook of sinful rebellion.

Another theme in Edwards' life, his prickly relations with associates, appears in the social record also. New Englanders were notoriously litigous, quick
to criticize, to sue, or to ask the church to censure. Economic expansion increased the occasions for misunderstandings and ill feeling. The competition
for land and trade and for every conceivable economic advantage made enemies of former friends. Every debt case, for example, represented a dispute. A
creditor always preferred to settle privately to avoid court costs. Only when
prolonged appeals failed did he sue. The storekeeper or wealthy farmer grew
exasperated at the delays in payment; the debtor for his part felt the terms
unjust, the request for payment over-hasty, or the creditor unsympathetic. The
fivefold increase in debt cases per capita in Connecticut between 1700 and 1730
represented at least as large an increase in personal quarrels arising for economic reasons.

The whole society suffered from a painful confusion of identity. People
were taught to work at their earthly callings and to seek wealth; but one's
business had to remain subservient to religion and to function within the bounds
of seventeenth-century institutions. The opportunities constantly prompted

people to overstep both boundaries, thereby evoking the wrath of the powerful men who ruled society. Even relations with neighbors deteriorated as expansion multiplied the occasions for hard feelings. At some indeterminate point social values and institutions stopped supporting the man who placed his confidence in worldly success and instead obstructed and condemned his actions. The pleasurable rise which prosperity afforded carried one at last to destruction.

A widespread uneasiness put people "upon Enquiring, with concern and Engagedness of mind, what was the way of salvation, and what were the Terms of our acceptance with God."[51] The revival preachers confronted their audience with the darkest possible view of their sins and hopeless future. They had fought against God, were filled with pride and vileness, and were worthy of unending torment in the pit of hell. This frank exposure of their dark inward side gave people the courage to bring their sins and insecurity to the surface. The man in the pulpit assuring them that he understood their guilt and the presence of others publicly manifesting their anguish provided communal support for the agonizing confrontation.

The preachers required total humiliation and submission before promising peace. The only hope for reconciliation with God was to confess to utter helplessness and to depend wholly on his grace. For those who heard, moral rectitude and a measure of prosperity suddenly furnished neither peace in this world nor a promise of God's favor in the world to come. Men stood naked under the heavens, helplessly exposed to divine wrath. Edwards noticed people passing from despair to passivity as they recognized the impossibility of earning salvation and gave themselves up to be damned or saved at God's pleasure. Then almost surprisingly hope revived. The good news of the Gospel was heard as if for the first time. The gift of grace seemed sufficient to redeem, and the convert rejoiced in new confidence, founded now on God's loving mercy. They were brought to a "Lively sense of the Excellency of Jesus Christ" and "of the Truth of the Gospel." The sense of sin continued and increased, but now contrition was combined with love and joy.[52] Men felt that they were saved.

With a new identity founded in God's gracious love, converted men renounced their former sources of confidence. The world's wealth no longer appeared so enticing. Edwards noted that in Northampton "People are brought off from Inordinate Engagedness after the World, and have been Ready to Run into the other Extreme of Too much neglecting their worldly Business and to mind nothing but Religion." People seemed to "dread their former Extravagances" and wanted to strip themselves of worldly luxury.[53] After the frenetic itinerant James Davenport urged a New London audience to discard their wigs, fine clothing, and worldly books, the people piled their possessions in a public place and burned them.

Conversion also relieved tensions with neighbors and with authority. The infusion of God's love sweetened all personal relations. "Persons are soon brought to have done with their old Quarrels: Contention and Intermeddling with other mens matters seems to be dead amongst us," Edwards wrote. He cited a number of parishes where old contentions vanished and the congregation was "universally united in hearty affection to their minister." In 1735 his own people "Generally seem to be united in dear Love, and affection one to another," and he "never saw the Christian spirit in Love to Enemies so Exemplified, in all my life." Indeed Northampton "never was so full of love, nor so full of distress as it has Lately been."[54] He composed a covenant to which his congregation subscribed in 1742, pledging themselves not to "overreach or defraud" their neighbors, or "wilfully or negligently" to default on their honest debts. They promised not to "feed a spirit of bitterness, ill will, or secret grudge," and in the management of public affairs not to let private interest and worldly gain lead them into "unchristian inveighings, reproachings, bitter reflectings, judging and ridiculing," but do everything with "christian humility, gentleness, quietness and love."[55]

The results of the revival deeply gratified Edwards. A barely suppressed elation runs throughout *A Faithful Narrative of the Surprising Work of God*, the essay in which he described the love of God and men which came over Northampton in 1735. The Spirit of God appeared to be creating an entire society of saintly men, submissive to God and exquisitely sensitive to religion, a society which confirmed and supported the identity Edwards had assumed in his own conversion. The resonance between Edwards and his people did not continue as perfect harmony. Eventually he demanded more saintliness than they could muster, and his congregation voted 200 to 23 to dismiss him. But for more than a decade, while his words shaped the innermost lives of the reborn, his heart and theirs were as one.

V

Edwards' influence arose from the emotional congruities of his life and his people's; both felt a tension between the yearning to rise in the world and the fear of being destroyed for their pride. In a time of newly opened possibilities for success, heightened aspirations ineluctably entangled men in conflicts with established institutions and values. Widespread contention filled people with guilt, just as the stresses in Edwards' life brought him to an obsession with his unworthiness. The conflict might have been resolved by rationalizing self-interest or by justifying the right to resist authority, and many Americans followed that very course. Edwards, however, admitted his utter sinfulness, submitted all to God, and was rewarded with love, joy, and peace. The conversion of thousands during the Awakening signified the general applicability of Edwards' personal solution to the common problem and the implicit acceptance of his leadership.

The sources of pride and guilt doubtlessly varied. Edwards' intellectual ambitions and the peculiar combination of enveloping love, moral precision, and fear in his father were unique. Strictly personal circumstances could have generated pride and guilt in other lives as well. But the susceptibility to revival preaching in a large proportion of the population, more than chance can account for, is a puzzling fact. Apart from Providence, which can never be ruled out, general social conditions offer the most plausible explanation. The widening economic opportunities of the early eighteenth century, pressing men against rulers, against established institutions like town and church, and against the moral restrictions on covetousness, seem to be the most likely sources of the prevailing distress. Circumstances converged to generate tensions whose psychological structure happened to coincide with that which life in the Edwards' household formed in Jonathan.

Insofar as this analysis is convincing, it confirms Erikson's conception of leadership as the application of the leader's personal identity resolution to the needs of his age. Anyone approaching the problem of leadership, of course, must proceed with humility. Because the influence of one person on another works along subterranean psychological channels, the difficulties in arriving at uncontestable conclusions are immense. The explanation for the power of Joseph McCarthy in the fifties remains conjectural, even when responses from actual participants are still available. But if we are not to abandon all efforts in despair, Erikson's model merits attention. Without claiming scientific certainty for its conclusions, it provides a frame within which to draw together the remaining evidence and to reconstruct lives as imaginatively and as completely as possible.

One virtue of Erikson's work is the incorporation of the personal emotional struggles of which our lives are composed into a coherent system of historical analysis. Attempts to make history "human," to "breathe life" into it, so often lead only to anecdotes or colorful quotations. Erikson's vigorous and well-articulated treatment of human feeling in the framework of his model of leadership makes the moral vicissitudes of life a central component of fundamental historical processes. He helps the historian to describe the bearing of emotions and will as coherently as the impact of the impersonal economic and social forces which once threatened to eliminate personality from historical writing altogether. This entrenchment in an analytical structure is the best assurance possible that personality will be given its due.

It should be apparent that Erikson's model does not apply to every kind of leadership. Most authorities operate within conventions which assure a measure of obedience apart from any personal qualities, and for the most part social forms contain people's anxieties without any extraordinary direction from a gifted man. But at those critical junctures where old values fail and a new order is coming, the way is open for a leader of greater charisma. Then the man of unusual courage and integrity, who successfully contends with the sufferings, self-doubts, and hopes of his time, may, more than we have imagined, exert an influence on the course of events.

Notes

1. Erik H. Erikson, *Young Man Luther: A Study in Psychoanalysis and History*, Austen Riggs Monograph No. 4 (New York, 1958).

2. Erik H. Erikson, *Childhood and Society*, 2nd ed. (New York, 1968), p. 261. Erikson also

discusses identity in "Identity and the Life Cycle: Selected Papers by Erik H. Erikson," *Psychological Issues*, I (1959), and in Richard I. Evans, *Dialogue with Erik Erikson* (New York, 1967).

3. I give an example of how psychoanalysis can illuminate incidents from adult life in "On the Uses of Psychology: Conflict and Conciliation in Benjamin Franklin," *History and Theory*, 5 (1966), 225–240.

4. Three biographies of Edwards' life are useful for different purposes. Ola Elizabeth Winslow, *Jonathan Edwards, 1703–1758: A Biography* (New York, 1940), places Edwards in his social setting. Perry Miller, *Jonathan Edwards* (New York, 1949), is a brilliant interpretation of Edwards' thought with suggestive comments on the social structure in the Connecticut Valley. S.E. Dwight, *The Life of President Edwards* (New York, 1830), reprints much of the source material.

5. Dwight, *Edwards*, pp. 16, 18.

6. Jonathan Edwards to Timothy Edwards, Nov. 1, 1720; fragment of a letter from Timothy Edwards to Mrs. Mix. Both are in the Andover collection now on deposit at the Edwin J. Beinecke Library at Yale. I am grateful to Andover-Newton Theological Seminary for permission to refer to this letter and also to Miss Marjorie Wynne of the Beinecke Library for giving me access to it.

7. Quoted in Winslow, *Edwards*, p. 16.

8. Quoted in Winslow, *Edwards*, p. 21.

9. Quoted in Winslow, *Edwards*, p. 22.

10. Quoted in Miller, *Edwards*, p. 52.

11. Winslow, *Edwards*, p. 41.

12. From the "Diary," in Dwight, *Edwards*, p. 86.

13. Ibid., pp. 81–83.

14. Winslow, *Edwards*, pp. 41, 42.

15. Ibid., p. 43.

16. Dwight, *Edwards*, p. 14; Winslow, *Edwards*, p. 41.

17. Quoted in Winslow, *Edwards*, p. 18.

18. Dwight, *Edwards*, p. 14.

19. Winslow, *Edwards*, p. 36.

20. Ibid.

21. Dwight, *Edwards*, p. 21.

22. *Jonathan Edwards: Representative Selections, with Introduction, Bibliography, and Notes*, ed. Clarence H. Faust and Thomas H. Johnson, rev. ed. (New York, 1962), p. 11.

23. The intended title page is reprinted in Dwight, *Edwards*, p. 664.

24. From the "Notes on Natural Science," reprinted in Dwight, *Edwards*, p. 702.

25. *Representative Selections*, pp. 3, 6, 7.

26. Ibid., pp. 10, 8.

27. Ibid., pp. 3, 10.

28. *The Works of President Edwards, in Four Volumes* (New York, n.d.), IV, 234.

29. *Representative Selections*, pp. 5, 11, 12.

30. Ibid., p. 57.

31. Dwight, *Edwards*, pp. 84–85.

32. Ibid., pp. 85, 88, 89, 90, 94.

33. *Representative Selections*, pp. 57, 58.

34. Dwight, *Edwards*, pp. 78–79.

35. *Works*, I, 202.

36. *Representative Selections*, p. 58.

37. Ibid., p. 59.

38. A more elaborate explication of Edwards' conversion and the psychoanalytic elements involved may be found in Richard L. Bushman, "Jonathan Edwards and Puritan Consciousness," *Journal for the Scientific Study of Religion*, 5 (1966), 383-396.

39. *Representative Selections*, pp. 59, 60.

40. Ibid., p. 63.

41. Ibid., pp. 63–64.

42. Ibid., pp. 62, 63.

43. Ibid., pp. 60, 63, 64, 65.

44. Ibid., pp. 64, 65.

45. Dwight, *Edwards*, pp. 106, 103.

46. Ibid., pp. 171–172.

47. *Representative Selections*, pp. 74, 75.

48. Ibid., pp. 77, 78.

49. Richard L. Bushman, *From Puritan to Yankee: Character and the Social Order in Connecticut, 1690-1765* (Cambridge, 1967).

50. Bernard Bailyn, "The Apologia of Robert Keayne," WMQ,7 (1950), 568-587.

51. *Representative Selections*, p. 74.

52. Ibid., pp. 77, 78.

53. Ibid., pp. 76, 77.

54. Ibid., pp. 76–78.

55. Dwight, *Edwards*, pp. 165–167.

# II   THOUGHT

# Thought:
# Theological

## [On Edwards' *An Account of the Life of the Late Reverend Mr. David Brainerd*]

Ebenezer Frothingham°

I shall make some Observations from what Mr. *Edwards* has wrote in pag. 294, and no doubt his Aim was at the Separates; and when I read it, my very Soul trembled, and was in Pain for poor deluded formal Hypocrites, and the dear Saints of God, that are in woful Captivity, by Men's Inventions; for in that Page, there is no proper Distinction made between Truth and Error; and the natural Tendency of such Writing, is to Prejudice the poor ignorant Persons against the Power of God, and all the powerful Appearances of the Goings of our God and King in his Sanctuary, *Psa. 63. 2. To see thy Power and thy Glory, so as I have seen thee in the Sanctuary.* And also to seal down poor formal deluded Hypocrites in Hundreds, for Damnation: May God in Mercy prevent it. Again. What is there writ, is exceedingly likely to perplex and intangle the Saints of God, and wound some who may be longing and thirsting to see God's Power and Glory again; and also to harden others who have got a Prejudice against the Power of God, and thereby to keep them still under that cruel Spirit, *&c.* Now had Mr. *Edwards* applyed what he has writ upon the Top of the next Page, to himself, and others that oppose the Separates, he would no doubt have hit the right Nail in the Head (as we used to say). He has writ thus: 'Or 'tis like the Conduct of some unskilful rash Person, who finding himself deceived by some of the Wares he had bought at that Shop, should at once conclude that all he there saw, was of no Value, and pursuant to such a Conclusion, when afterwards he has true Gold and Diamonds offered him, enough to inrich him, and enable him to live like a Prince all his Days, he should throw it all into the Sea, *&c.*' Now if this is not the very Case to a Tittle, of those that oppose the Separates, I think I am greatly mistaken indeed: For observe; because there has sometimes been among the Separates, a false Power and Zeal, Hay, Wood, and Stubble (which God is in Mercy, a consuming and purging out of our Hearts and Practices); therefore Mr. *Edwards* and others, are rashly refusing the true Gold,

°Reprinted from *The Articles of Faith and Practice with the Covenant, That Is Confessed by the Separate Churches of Christ in General in This Land* (Newport, R.I., 1750), pp. 423–27, 432. (Evans, 6504)

or Religion, which is from the Divine Influènce of the Spirit of all Grace, which if they would heartily receive, would enable them to live more like the Priests of the most high God (1 *Pet.* 2 chap. 9) and remove away that Barrenness,[1] and hard Temper of Mind, which we abundantly fear they are chiefly under. But not to inlarge: I readily grant, that there is such a Thing as Satan's bringing Scripture to Persons Minds, upon which, they may be transported, and filled with Joy, and they may have sudden Impulses also, and Satan may transform himself into an Angel of Light, and delude Persons; but then I would observe, that the Scripture that Satan brings, does not come with any renewing, instructing, or sanctifying Influence upon the Heart, neither is a Person, by such sudden Impulses upon the Mind, brought to see the Divinity and Connection of the Scriptures: But when the Spirit of God brings or applies Scriptures to a Person, these Things are wrought more or less upon the Heart; so also the Joy that is raised from vain Imaginations, or Sparks of a Person's own kindling, such Joy has no Substance in it, nor does it yield any solid Comfort; and when such Joys go off a Person, there is no more Tenderness nor Watchfulness wrought in the Person's Mind, of sinning against an holy God; nor have they a Thirst increased in their Minds after Holiness and Likeness to God, which the true Believer has when his Joys go off. Again. The sudden Impulses upon the Mind, that come from a false Spirit, serve to lead a Person away from God, and not to cleave to the Scriptures, but to puff them up with Pride, and lead them out of the Pathway of Duty; but the sudden, immediate Influences of the Spirit of God, always more or less, leads the Heart towards God, and seizes the Mind with Reverence, and the Fear of God, and inclines the Person to search, that he might know the Mind and Will of God in the Path-way of Duty; and there is a tender Care begotten in the Mind, lest he should go contrary to the Will of God: These sudden Influences that are from God's Spirit, never lead a Person contrary to the Scriptures. . . .

But Mr. *Edwards* and others, have mustered up a Number of Errors, and made a Scarecrow of them, by not making proper Distinctions; so that tender Lambs of Christ's Flock are scared from the Gospel Fold, and are almost worried out of all the powerful Influences and Operations of the Spirit of God; and in his Application of these Errors, saith, 'It is the Separates Religion.' So also in his trying to cut off our Religion, he cuts a-cross the Spirit of God in its divine Teaching, and sealing Influences, and, as it were, takes away the Key of Knowledge, and shuts up the Way to Heaven, and will neither enter in himself (for the present) nor suffer them that have a Mind to enter, to go in; and therefore makes sad the Hearts of the Righteous, and strengthens the Hands of the Wicked; And will the Lord in Mercy look upon him, and forgive him this great Sin.

The Reader may remember, if he has read Mr. *Brainerd's* Life, that Mr. *Edwards* improves Mr. *Brainerd's* Experiences and Religion, in order to shew that the Separates Experiences, is Delusions, and their Practice, Erroneous; and he has not writ one Word, as I remember, but what the learned Ministers in the Land, and their Congregations hold with, and experience the same Religion that Mr. *Brainerd* had, and the Separates are the only Persons that are deluded, and out of the Way, in the Land: Therefore this brings me to make a brief Inquiry, who it is that holds to and professes that Religion, and them Influences, or Experiences, and Practice, that Mr. *Brainerd* had from time to time: And here first; Did not Mr. *Brainerd* from time to time, experience and express a great Sense of his own Nothingness, and great Vileness, and his intire Dependance upon God, for Help to assist him in the Discharge of all Duties that lay before him? Now is this the Experiences of the learned Ministers, and their Churches in general in the Land; or is it not rather the daily Experience of the Saints in the Separates?[2]

So I conclude; earnestly praying, That God would give Mr. *Edwards* to see wherein he has opposed and stood against God's Work of late in the Land; and that he might have a Pardon sealed to his Soul; and that God would once more make his Face as Flint and his Brow as Brass, against the Enemies of God and his Church, and that he might be made as a Flame of Fire, in dispensing the everlasting Gospel. *Amen.*

Notes

1. The text reads *Barrennels*, a printing error resulting from the resemblance between the letter *l* and the long *s*.

2. The errata page reads, Separation.

# [On Edwards' *An Humble Inquiry into the Rules of the Word of God*]

Solomon Williams*

I agree with my dear Brother *Edwards*, that if Men should set their own Wit and Wisdom in Opposition to God's revealed Will, there's no End of Objections which may be raised against any of God's Institutions, and if we lift up our Tool to mend God's Altar, we shall pollute it.—And I am of Opinion that Inconveniencies both real and imaginary may attend the Scheme which he has undertaken to maintain: And that they are not only equal to the manifest Conveniences and happy Tendencies of it, or to the Inconveniencies and bad Consequences of the other, but vastly greater, and that it is a Scheme contrary to God's Dispensation to his Church in all Ages, and inconsistent with it self.

The outward Duties of Morality and Worship, when to Appearance they are sincerely performed, are by the Church in their publick Judgment to be charitably thought to be the Product of the great inward Duties of the Love of God, and Acceptance of Christ. The latter ought not only to be pretended to, but exhibited by the former; and God never appointed any other Way of their being made visible to the World: And he who is the Searcher of Hearts has only a Right and Ability to determine of them otherwise. But in this State of Things, he neither has given us a Rule, nor will allow us to judge otherwise in order to Persons being taken into his Family, and to the outward Priviledges of his House.—The Notion of Men's being able and fit to determine positively the Condition of other Men, or the certainty of their gracious Estate; has a direct Tendency to decieve the Souls of Men; to harden some in Hypocrisy, and lift up others with Pride and Self-Conceit. The Effect of such a Way and Practise in Admission of Persons into the visible Church seems naturally this, and these Effects speak out themselves: That since the outward Duties of Morality and Worship may proceed from other Causes than the Love of God, and Faith in Christ, therefore some Persons look upon these as not giving any Evidence at all of those Graces: But judge of some Accounts which they hear of Persons relating their Experiences, or some inward Feelings; (which can only be said to evidence their Grace if they be not decieved themselves, nor aim to decieve others) and

*Reprinted from *The True State of the Question Concerning the Qualifications Necessary to Lawful Communion in the Christian Sacraments* (Boston, 1751), pp. 140–43. (Evans, 6798)

which without those Duties of Morality and Worship, or separate from them, can't be so good Evidences of Grace as these are without them. And so they determine that if Men live never so strictly conformable to the Laws of the Gospel, and never so diligently seek their own Salvation to outward Appearance, they give no more publick Evidence that they are not Enemies of God, and Haters of Jesus Christ, than the very worst of the Heathen. Nor do they stick any more to speak of them, and act openly towards them in such a Manner; thereby violating in the most open & scandalous Manner the Law of Christ, wherein he solemnly forbids them to judge one another: Which yet they continually do in open Defiance of his Law, the Rules of his visible Kingdom, and his own Example as King of the visible Church. And the greatest Part of those who are in Covenant with God, and to whom Christ has commanded Baptism the Seal of the Covenant to be administered, whom he hath bound by the most solemn Engagements to attend all his Ordinances, and wait at his Foot for all the Blessings of the Covenant of Grace; are forbidden to do it by their Brethren, tho' they own them at the same Time to be in Covenant with God; because they think them not good enough to recieve the Food which Christ has provided for them.

Mr. *Edwards* proposes one of two Evil Consequences inevitably following the Method of Proceeding which he opposes.—"Either there must be no publick Notice given of the Conversion of a Sinner, or else this Notice must be given in a Way of Conversation by the Parties themselves."

And how are these Evils remedied upon his Scheme? Supposing it be necessary that some publick Notice be given of the Conversion of every Person in a Town, what Way can it be done? According to him the best visible Exercise of the Worship of God, and most sincere Practise of moral Virtues to outward Appearance; the greatest visible Appearance of the Love of God, and Concern to please him that is compatible to the State of an unconverted Man, is not so much as the least Evidence of any Pretence to Godliness.

What other Way is there left but a Declaration of inward Experiences? For as to Persons saying they are converted, this I believe will by few be thought to be so good an Evidence as the former. Now what Way has the Church to judge of these Experiences? Are they to take the Minister's Word for them; and so admit the Person? If this is the Way, it may indeed give him as great Advantage in some Respects as the Romish Priests have, or make him something like *Nebuchadnezzer, Dan.* 5. 19. But it will leave the Church as much in the Dark as they were before; and if they offer unto God Thanksgiving upon his Information, it must surely be done upon an implicit Faith; if the Church are to judge for themselves, there can be no Way but by hearing the Man relate his Experiences. "And this must be done by Persons declaring their Experiences from Time to Time, and Place to Place," or else the Church must all meet together to hear them, and this amounts to the same Thing. So that I can't see how one of these Evil Consequences is avoided by Mr. *Edwards*'s Scheme. "He supposes the Matter ought to be under some Regulation, and the Direction of skilful Guides &c."—Shall these skilful Guides direct every Man, Woman and Child, what Experiences to relate, and what to omit, what are fit to be published, and what not? If so, I believe the Church will soon judge, or if they don't others will, that this is as artificial a Sort of Conversion, as the making a common Draught, and Formula, for the Experiences of all that are to be taken into the Church. Whether this is like to promote the Honour of God, or be a Scandal & Reproach to his Name, seems not very difficult to determine.—One would think the late dreadful Consequences of such Sort of Doings in this Land had been enough to convince every judicious Christian of the Sinfulness of it. Neither upon Mr. *Edwards*'s Scheme can I conceive the making two distinct Kinds of visible Churches, or visible Bodies of professing Saints any more unavoidable than on the other. Indeed the very Doctrine itself makes two such Bodies within one another, and openly distinguish'd one from another. One Company consisting of such as openly declare that they judge themselves gracious Christians: And the other of those whom these own to be in Covenant with God, who have been sealed with the Seal of his Covenant, and Christ has taken into his Family, but only they have no Right to so much as the outward Priviledges of it belonging to the visible Kingdom of Christ, and yet at the same Time visibly and openly belonging to the Kingdom of the Devil; declaring that they desire above all Things in the World to partake and enjoy the Blessings of the Kingdom of Christ, having sworn that they will make it their chief Business to obtain them, and use every Method which Christ has appointed therefor; moral or visibly Religious in their Conversation, and yet treated as open and avowed Enemies of Jesus Christ, and his Kingdom, making no Pretence to Godliness; and this by the declared & publick Judgment of the Church, in the same visible Covenant with them. I appeal also to the common Sense of Mankind, whether this be not the Case where that Method of Proceeding Mr. *Edwards* contends for, is established; and with Mr. *Edwards*, leave it to the judicious Reader to make his own Remarks, whether there be a just Foundation in Scripture or Reason for such a State of Things; and whether this is the comely Order of the Gospel which Christ hath instituted.

How much my good Brother *Edwards* has had to prejudice his Mind on one Side or other of this Question, I know not: Altho' I cannot but wonder, "he has thought himself constrained to act as he has done in this Controversy, from the clear Evidences of the Word of God," and to make such a Use and Application of Scripture as he has done, when he has so little to say from Scripture or [Reaso]n, for the maintaining the Cause he has espoused.

# Jonathan Edwards

Leslie Stephen°

Edwards often shows himself a worthy successor of the great men who led the moral revolt of the Reformation. Amongst some very questionable metaphysics and much outworn—sometimes repulsive—superstition, he grasps the central truths on which all really noble morality must be based. The mode in which they presented themselves to his mind may be easily traced. Calvinism, logically developed, leads to Pantheism. The absolute sovereignty of God, the doctrine to which Edwards constantly returns, must be extended over all nature as well as over the fate of the individual human soul. The peculiarity of Edwards' mind was, that the doctrine had thus expanded along particular lines of thought, without equally affecting others. He is a kind of Spinoza-Mather; he combines, that is, the logical keenness of the great metaphysician with the puerile superstitions of the New England divine; he sees God in all nature, and yet believes in the degrading supernaturalism of the Salem witches. The object of his faith, in short, is the "infinite Jehovah" (vi. 170), the God to whose all pervading power none can set a limit, and who is yet the tutelary deity of a petty clan; and there is something almost bewildering in the facility with which he passes from one conception to the other without the smallest consciousness of any discontinuity. Of his coincidence in the popular theories, and especially in the doctrine of damnation, I have already given instances. His utterances derived from a loftier source are given with equal emphasis. At the age of fifteen or sixteen he had said, "God and real existence are the same; God is, and there is none else."[1] The same doctrine is the foundation of the theories expounded in his treatises on Virtue and on the End of God in Creation. In the last of these, for example, he uses the argument (depending upon a conception familiar to the metaphysicians of the previous age), that benevolence, consisting in regard to "Being in general," must be due to any being in proportion to the degree of existence (ii. 401). Now "all other being is as nothing in comparison of the Divine Being." God is "the foundation and fountain of all being and all perfection, from whom all is perfectly derived, and on whom all is most absolutely and perfectly dependent; whose being and beauty is, as it were, the sum and comprehension of all existence and excellence, much more than the sun is the fountain and summary comprehension of all the light and brightness of the

°Reprinted, in part, from *Hours in a Library* (Second Series) (London: Smith, Elder, & Co., 1876), pp. 85–90.

day" (ii. 405). As he says in the companion treatise, "the eternal and infinite Being is, in effect, being in general, and comprehends universal existence" (vi. 59). The only end worthy of God must, therefore, be His own glory. This is not to attribute selfishness to God, for "in God, the love of Himself and the love of the public are not to be distinguished as in man, because God's being, as it were, comprehends all" (vi. 53). In communicating His fulness to His creatures, He is of necessity the ultimate end; but it is a fallacy to make God and the creature in this affair of the emanation of the Divine fulness "the opposite parts of a disjunction" (vi. 55). The creature's love of God and complacence in the Divine perfections are the same thing as the manifestation of the Divine glory. "They are all but the emanations of God's glory, or the excellent brightness and fulness of the Divinity diffused, overflowing, and, as it were, enlarged; or, in one word, existing *ad extra*" (vi. 117). In more familiar dialect, our love to God is but God's goodness making itself objective. The only knowledge which deserves the name is the knowledge of God, and virtue is but the knowledge of God under a different name.

Without dwelling upon the relations of this doctrine to modern forms of Pantheism, I must consider this last proposition, which is of vital importance in Edwards' system, and of which the theological and the metaphysical element is curiously blended. God is to the universe—to use Edwards' own metaphor—what the sun is to our planet; and the metaphor would have been more adequate if he had been acquainted with modern science. The sun's action is the primary cause of all the infinitely complex play of forces which manifest themselves in the fall of a raindrop or in the operations of a human brain. But as some bodies may seem to resist the action of the sun's rays, so may some created beings set themselves in opposition to the Divine Will. To a thorough-going Pantheist, indeed, such an opposition must appear to be impossible if we look deep enough, and sin, in this sense, be merely an illusion, caused by our incapacity of taking in the whole design of the Almighty. Edwards, however, though dimly aware of the difficulty, is not so consistent in his Pantheism as to be much troubled with it. He admits that, by some mysterious process, corruption has intruded itself into the Divine universe. The all-pervading harmony is marred by a discord due, in his phraseology, to the fall of man. Over the ultimate cause of this discord lies a veil which can never be withdrawn to mortal intelligence. Assuming its existence, however, virtue consists, if one may so speak, in that quality which fits a man to be a conducting medium, and vice in that which makes him a non-conducting medium to the solar forces. This proposition is confounded in Edwards' mind, as in that of most metaphysicians, with the very different proposition that virtue consists in recognising the Divine origin of those forces. It is characteristic, in fact, of his metaphysical school, to identify the logical with the causal connection, and to assume that the definition of a thing necessarily constitutes its essence. "Virtue," says Edwards, "is the union of heart to being in general, or to God, the Being of beings" (ii. 421), and thus consists in the intellectual apprehension of Deity, and in the emotion founded upon and necessarily involving the apprehension. The doctrine that whatever is done so as to promote the glory of God is virtuous, is with him identified with the doctrine that whatever is done consciously, in order to promote the glory of God, is virtuous. The major premise of the syllogism which proves an action to be virtuous must be actually present to the mind of the agent. This, in utilitarian phraseology, is to confound between the criterion and the motive. If it is, as Edwards says, the test of a virtuous action that it should tend to "the highest good of being in general," it does not follow that an action is only virtuous when done with a conscious reference to that end. But Edwards overlooks or denies the distinction, and assumes, for example, as an evident corollary, that a love of children or friends is only virtuous in so far as it is founded on a desire for the general good, which, in his sense, is a desire for the glory of God (ii. 428). He judges actions, that is, not by their tendency, but by their nature; and their nature is equivalent to their logic.

His metaphysical theory coincides precisely with his theological view, and is generally expressed in theological language. The love of "Being in general" is the love of God. The intellectual intuition is the reflection of the inward light, and the recognition of a mathematical truth is but a different phase of the process which elsewhere produces conversion. Intuition is a kind of revelation, and revelation is a special intuition.

## Note

1. See an interesting article in the "American Cyclopaedia." which has, however, this odd peculiarity, that it never mentions Hell in discussing the theories of Edwards.

# Conversion: Nature and Grace

Jonathan Edwards' depiction of faith supposes at every point that faith is a gift of God; it is a possibility only as God gives it through Word and Spirit. In fact, the keystone of Edwards' Calvinist theology is the unremitting insistence that God is sovereign in man's salvation. Man is absolutely dependent upon the sovereign will of God for everything belonging to his salvation, "from the foundation to the top stone."[1] Edwards was, indeed, a revivalist who called men to conversion; but he was of what William McLoughlin has called "the old revival tradition." Edwards could not have dreamed of saying with Charles Grandison Finney, the father of modern American revivalism, that conversion to saving faith "is not a miracle, or dependent on a miracle in any sense" but "is a purely philosophical result of the right use of the constituted means."[2] Edwards spoke of the "surprising work of God" when he referred to the conversions elicited by his preaching in Northampton—they were miracles of grace, not results "worked up" by revivalist methods.[3]

In accordance with his Calvinist view of the sovereignty of God in conversion to faith, Edwards appeals to a doctrine of predestination. His doctrine is supralapsarian with respect to election and sublapsarian with respect to reprobation: God decreed from eternity to save certain men, apart from any consideration of the state of their lives; but he decreed the rejection of others only on the basis of their sin.[4] In certain periods of the history of Calvinism the theory of predestination assumed primarily speculative, nonexistential value. It was used as the fundamental doctrine on which to erect an elaborate scheme for the explanation of the mind of God and the soteriological status of every man in the universe.[5] This was at some remove from the use predestinarians like Augustine, Luther, and Calvin had made of the doctrine. As Dillenberger and Welch have said, for Luther "predestination is a confession about the trustworthy character of God . . ."; and "Calvin moved from faith to an elaboration of predestination as a way of showing that God is wholly the author of our faith and that every notion of work or merit must be rejected."[6] For Edwards also predestination is an existential affirmation that what a man is in faith, he is by the sovereign will of a trustworthy God. It is a way of affirming that faith is not a product of human nature, that it is not achieved through man's obedience to the

[*]Excerpted from *The Theology of Jonathan Edwards: A Reappraisal* by Conrad Cherry. Copyright © 1966 by Conrad Cherry. Reprinted by permission of Doubleday & Company, Inc.

law. Saving faith is predestined: it is by grace alone; a free, undeserved gift of God.

Regenerative conversion by grace, therefore, in which man is turned to a life of faith, is "immediate." We have seen how Edwards applies the term "immediate" to the work of God's Spirit to stress that He is unmediated by the natural power of His means. To emphasize much the same thing, "immediate" can take on the meaning of "instantaneous." As in the creation scene in Genesis, in the new birth "something is brought out of nothing in an instant. God speaks and it is done."[7] Regeneration by Word and Spirit is instantaneous in that it is a leap from an old way of being into a new way of being which is irreducible to the potentialities of the old way. There is a moment "when" the transition is made from old to new creaturehood. "God speaks and it is done." Conversion as an instantaneous transition does not mean, however, what it so often came to mean for revivalists: that the whole of regeneration is collapsed into one irrecoverable moment of time; or that the Christian should search out a moment of religious conversion-experience for his own assurance. Though instantaneous conversion is of the essence of regeneration, it does not exhaust the meaning of the new birth. There is in regeneration the progressive sanctification in which God continues throughout life to cleanse the elect of sin and assist them in the "race of life." In one sense, says Edwards, "grace is growing: from its first infusion, till it is perfected in glory, the kingdom of Christ is building up in the soul."[8] Although Edwards does select out of his surroundings certain instances of conversion as examples of the surprising work of God and does not deny that one may be able to state when his new birth occurred,[9] still the time of a person's reception of grace is not always obvious to him since the manner of the Spirit's operation is often "unsearchable and untraceable." And above all, one is to avoid a confidence in his religious experience since it breeds religious pride and a confidence in oneself rather than in God.[10] Within these circumscriptions Edwards affirms that regeneration is done at once and not gradually: it begins from the gift of grace and not from any gradual improvement of human nature prior to grace. When the elect are effectually called into faith by Word and Spirit, "there is something immediately put into their hearts, at that call, that is new, that there was nothing of there before, which makes them so immediately act in a manner altogether new, and so alien from what they were before."[11] In one respect the new birth is as gradual as the growth of the fetus in the womb; yet like the beginning of the fetus its actual beginning is all at once. "In the new birth there is certainly a very great change made in the soul" just as in the natural birth "when the rational soul is first infused, the foetus immediately upon it becomes a living creature and a man, that before had no life."[12]

Edwards' conception of instantaneous conversion, then, is grounded in the conviction that an immense chasm exists between nature and grace, a chasm that can be bridged only from the side of grace. Human nature's gradual improvement of itself can never produce the movements into saving faith. Like Augustine and Luther, Edwards rejects any Pelagian (for Edwards, "Arminian") scheme that allows men to take chief credit for their salvation by at-

tributing the dawn of faith to natural human powers.[13] The new life in faith is
given from beyond the capacities of human nature, no matter how those capacities are gradually improved.

A. B. Crabtree, in his interpretation of Edwards' theological anthropology,
has claimed that Edwards "steps over the threshold of Catholic anthropology,
and approaches the very center" of it when, in his doctrine of the Fall, he argues
that man's natural abilities are retained but his spiritual principles lost through
Adam. Edwards even contends, Crabtree continues, "that human nature is
complete as human nature without the supernatural principles"; yet "instead of
traversing from this point the road of semipelagianism as Catholic theology had
so often done, he identifies human nature with radical and unmitigated evil and
reaches a position scarcely to be distinguished from that of Flacius."[14] This
claim is certainly correct to the extent that Edwards does employ the scholastic
distinction between natural and supernatural principles in his description of the
results of the Fall. But the distinction results in neither Pelagianism nor a
devaluation of human nature as such. Edwards' explanation of the consequences of the Fall is:

> The case with man was plainly this: when God made man at first he implanted in him
> two kinds of principles. There was the *inferior* kind, which may be called NATURAL,
> being the principles of mere human nature; such as self-love, with those natural
> appetites and passions, which belong to the *nature of man*, in which his love to his
> own liberty, honour, and pleasure, were exercised. . . . Besides these, there were
> *superior* principles, that were spiritual, holy, and divine, summarily comprehended
> in divine love; wherein consisted the spiritual image of God, and man's righteousness
> and true holiness. . . . Which though withdrawn, and man's nature forsaken of these
> principles, human nature would be human nature still. . . . When man sinned and
> broke God's covenant, and fell under his curse, these spiritual principles left his
> heart. . . .[15]

On the one hand, the corruption of the *imago dei* through the withdrawal of the
spiritual principles means that man and his natural powers avail nothing before
God for salvation; on the other, however, it means that man still remains man
after the Fall—*on one level at least*—on the level of natural human concerns.
Edwards does not attempt, through the notion of the retained natural principles, to preserve the Semi-Pelagian "natural inclination to virtue" after the
Fall.[16] Edwards' language is unambiguous: man is "naturally blind in the things
of religion";[17] "all that a natural man doth is sin."[18] "The inside of the body of
man is full of filthiness, contains his bowels that are full of dung, which represents the corruption and filthiness that the heart of man is naturally full of."[19]
Because of this filth and corruption, fallen man is hardly "inclined naturally to
virtue"; on the contrary, he is inclined away from love of God and his glory, i.e.,
away from true virtue.[20]

The corruption of the *imago*, however, does not spell the destruction of the
goodness of human nature. It will become clear in the next chapter that the
"natural principle of self-love" retained by sinful man is not, in and of itself, an
evil. Above all, the human faculties are not destroyed in their natural operations
by the removal of the supernatural principles. Natural man is still capable, for

example, of the reasoning power which sets him apart from inferior animals.[21] To be sure, the supernatural operations of the faculties are lost. When fallen man sets himself to worship God through the employment of his natural faculties, he worships not the true God but idols. Natural man is so constituted that his faculties are hindered *about the things of religion*.[22] Edwards has in mind much the same notion championed by Luther and Calvin: fallen, unenlightened reason is of use and value in the Kingdom of Earth or in the realm of man's political, domestic, and natural affairs; but in the Kingdom of Heaven, or *coram deo*, it is of itself a servant of sin and avails nothing for righteousness.[23] Every man's loss of supernatural principles through Adam's fall does not signify that men thereby become something less than men by becoming absolute instances of evil. Rather, the evil arises when man turns to "things religious"; then the natural human principles are not kept in their proper place.

> These inferior principles are like *fire* in a house; which we say is a good servant, but a bad master; very useful while kept in its place, but if left to take possession of the whole house, soon brings all to destruction. Man's love to his own honour, separate interests, and private pleasure, which before was *wholly subordinate* unto love to God and regard to his authority and glory, now disposes and impels him to pursue those objects, without regard to God's honour, or law. . . .[24]

The result is idolatry. On the basis of his natural principles, man sets up his "separate interests" and "private pleasure" in the room of the Creator; in this the "apostasy of man does summarily consist."[25]

Edwards' view of the fallenness of man and of the sovereignty of God's grace in saving faith is the basis for his approach to a question made momentous by the Reformed stress on the "immediacy" of the Spirit. What is the role of the "means of grace," of the vehicles of grace in history? The subject of the means of grace became all the more problematic as some groups growing out of the Puritan tradition queried: If God's Spirit is not efficacious by power inhering in the means, why not dispense with those means altogether? We discussed in the preceding chapter how Scripture and preaching may be understood as means of grace. There are for Edwards other means of grace as well: the Christian Sabbath, prayer, the instruction of Christian parents, and the Church in its worship and practice.[26] Baptism and the Lord's Supper are means of grace only in a very restricted sense: they are instituted as seals of faith for professors of faith (in the case of infant baptism, for children of professors) rather than, like preaching, as converting ordinances for those outside faith as well.[27] At this point Edwards set himself against the position of his grandfather Stoddard, involving himself in a controversy that resulted in his dismissal from the Northampton pulpit in 1750—a controversy that will occupy us in our concluding part. "Seeking," or the attendance on the means of grace to the end of finally receiving faith, is itself also a means of grace. Seeking salvation is a means when it brings man to an awareness of his own helplessness and to a despair in his own strength. Finding is not guaranteed by the seeking; God converts in his own good time. Intense seeking after faith—say through prayer—does not guarantee faith; nevertheless seeking can be a valid means of grace.

It is therefore quite a wrong notion that some entertain, that the more they do, the more they shall depend upon it. Whereas the reverse is true: the more they do, or the more thorough they are in seeking, the less will they be likely to rest in their doings, and the sooner will they see the vanity of all that they do. . . . You must undertake the business of seeking salvation upon these terms, and with no other expectations than this, that if ever God bestows mercy it will be in his own time; and not only so, but also that when you have done all, God will not hold himself obliged to show you mercy at last.[28]

Douglas J. Elwood has suggested that Edwards joined that line of Puritan theologians who inclined away from outward means of grace by emphasizing the internals of grace in the immediate operation of the Holy Spirit.[29] But Edwards makes it quite clear that the internal, immediate operation of the Holy Spirit replaces neither the outward means of grace nor the human seeking through the means. He joins a host of other Puritans in holding that God operates within man immediately but always in conjunction with the external means of grace. External means, particularly church forms and ceremonies, prevent grace from "disordering" the personal and social aspects of human life: regeneration by the Holy Spirit is ordered by being given in conjunction with the ordinances and means of grace established historically in the Church.[30] And the human seeking of salvation within the means of grace provides the framework within which God chooses to work by his Holy Spirit when converting man.[31] Nevertheless—and this is Edwards' principal point on this subject—*God has sovereign disposal over the means and the striving attached to them*. It is the power of God alone which decides the efficacy of the means. In fact, "God may sometimes make use of very unlikely means, and bestow salvation on men, who are under very great disadvantages; but he does not bestow grace wholly without any means."[32] At all times "it is of God that we have these means of grace, and it is God that makes them effectual. . . .It is of God that we have ordinances, and their efficacy depends on the immediate influence of the Spirit of God."[33] Hence means are not unnecessary, but it is the height of pride and "vain self-flattery" for a man to believe that seeking salvation in the means will itself give him the salvation:

Some hope by their strivings to obtain salvation of *themselves*. They have a secret imagination, that they shall by degrees, work in themselves sorrow and repentance of sin, and love towards God and Jesus Christ. Their striving is not so much an earnest seeking to God, as a striving to do themselves that which is the work of God.[34]

There is in Edwards' thought, therefore, no devaluation of the outward means of grace or of attendance on them but, rather, a typically Calvinist confession that only by the power of the grace of God do they become means of evoking faith and repentance.

Puritan theology had frequently articulated the relation between nature and grace, and between striving for faith and the actual receipt of faith, in terms of a doctrine of "preparation for salvation." This doctrine became the focus of some important controversies within the Puritan fold, and it caused Jonathan Edwards no little concern in his attempt to formulate his theory of conversion. The doctrine of preparation was part of what E. S. Morgan has called a Puritan "morphology of conversion," a formal structure in which each stage in the conversion of a sinner could be located and distinguished from the next stage; "so that a man could check his eternal condition by a set of temporal and recognizable signs."[35] The morphology was made up of a stage of preparation, divided into various steps, which preceded the stage of saving faith. For Richard Sibbes and Thomas Shepard, the steps in preparation were conviction of sin, compunction for sin and humiliation or self-abasement before God.[36] For William Perkins they were man's living under the outward means of grace, man's consideration of the law in relation to his own practice, his recognition of his particular sins and his fear of punishment in view of that recognition.[37] Whatever individual steps were enumerated, Puritan theologians were usually agreed that God first prepares man for the reception of faith through the law. As William Ames said, "that man be prepared to receive the promises, the application of the Law doth ordinarily goe before to the discovery of sin, and inexcusableness and humiliation of the sinner. . . ."[38]

In a diary entry of August 12, 1723, Edwards indicates that his acquaintance with the Puritan morphology of conversion was anything but passing or insignificant for his life and thought:

> The chief thing, that now makes me in any measure to question my good estate, is my not having experienced conversion in those particular steps, wherein the people of New England, and anciently the Dissenters of Old England, used to experience it. Wherefore, now resolved, never to leave searching, till I have satisfyingly found out the very bottom and foundation, the real reason, why they used to be converted in those steps.[39]

Edwards did witness the steps, to a degree, in his own religious experience and in the "surprising conversions" which occurred in his parish in the 1730s. Prior to his receiving the "new sense" of faith, Edwards suffered legal convictions and "violent inward struggles" over his sinful state;[40] and in his account of conversions in Northampton, he refers to "distressing apprehensions of the anger of God," terrors and fears which grew out of conviction of sin and which preceded the sense of God's grace and mercy.[41] Theologically also Edwards must have discovered, at least partially, the "bottom and foundation" of the steps in conversion, for he definitely incorporated three steps of preparation in his scheme of salvation. God's usual manner of bringing man to faith is to convict him of his sin, give him displeasure against that sin, and make him humble through an awareness of his unworthiness of salvation.[42] In short, Edwards contended, in agreement with his forefathers, that man is prepared by the law for the reception of grace and that usually this preparation involves legal conviction, compunction, and humiliation.

Yet the matter could not rest there for Edwards. The "bottom and foundation" of the problem lies not simply in *whether* there is a legal preparation for faith but more pertinently in the *manner* and *nature* of the preparation. Two consequences could, and sometimes did, follow from the Puritan notion of preparation, consequences which must have continued to plague Edwards as he sought to apply the steps to his "own estate": (1) so structuring conversion that the scheme of salvation becomes frozen into a *fixed* and *necessary order* of steps; and (2) confusing law with gospel by forcing the beginnings of saving faith back into legal preparation itself. Both became results in some of the seventeenth-century American Puritans' elaborate defense of the preparation scheme over against the antinomianism of Anne Hutchinson and her associates, who inclined away from any legal preparation and toward an unprepared gift of grace in conversion.[43] Edwards sought to avoid both consequences while embracing a doctrine of legal preparation for salvation.

Admitting that man is normally convicted and humbled by the divine law written into nature and Scripture before he receives grace, Edwards refuses to grant that this process can be so universalized that it must of necessity apply to every man, or to different men in the same way. In the first place, the work of the Holy Spirit cannot be so schematized that its *modus operandi* is fixed to a definite, rigid, and clearly discernible pattern:

> . . . nothing proves it to be necessary, that all those things which are implied or presupposed in an act of faith in Christ must be plainly and distinctly wrought in the soul, in so many successive and separate works of the Spirit that shall be, each one, plain and manifest, in all who are truly converted. . . . What we have principally to do with, in our inquiries into our own state, or directions we give to others, is the nature of the effect that God has brought to pass in the soul. As to the steps which the Spirit of God took to bring that effect to pass, we may leave them to him.[44]

The great terrors of conscience, which normally arise out of being struck by God's demands prior to the gift of converting grace, *may* come *after* conversion.[45] Though it may be properly argued that one will never really receive Christ in faith until he is humbled to the extent of depending no longer on his own righteousness, "yet this won't prove that pride must first be mortified and humility infused in a distinct work before conversion."[46] Furthermore, against the attempt to stretch *all* legal preparation over a long period of trial and struggle, Edwards points out that in many accounts of conversion in the Scriptures the whole of conversion is wrought "in a few hours" without any lengthy period of conviction and humiliation,[47] and that some genuine conversions in Northampton had not been preceded by lengthy preparations.[48] Edwards' argument on this point is a considered rejection of the view of Solomon Stoddard, who, in his concern to embrace in the visible church not only professing believers but also those long struggling in preparation, had insisted that "ordinarily we find that much time is consumed in the work of preparation."[49] Therefore, while recognizing that preparation for salvation *usually* involves certain steps, Edwards will neither fix the work of the Spirit to an inflexible series of stages nor confine human experience to a universal pattern of conversion.

Those Puritan theologians who were prone to see the beginnings of faith in legal preparation usually claimed that there was a chasm separating preparation and justifying faith; but the chasm was bridged—perhaps unintentionally—from the side of preparation in the attempt to stress the necessity of the law in conversion. Thomas Shepard, for example, remarked that a gulf separated the last step of preparation (humiliation) from faith, but the gap was filled when he said, "Faith . . . is to be expected, not only as begotten in us, but as it is in the begetting of it in the conviction and humiliation of every sinner."[50] Edwards holds with the English Puritan John Owen that although the sinner convicted by the law may be capable of justifying faith, he does not yet have that faith through the conviction.[51] Edwards will turn neither to the antinomian extreme of eliminating legal preparation as the normal antecedent of faith, nor to the legalistic extreme which posits the beginning of faith in legal conviction. The work of the law on natural man in preparing him for faith through conviction, compunction, and humiliation still leaves him as natural man. He is not yet a recipient of "special grace"; he receives only "common grace" or the common operation of the Spirit. The Spirit simply assists the natural human principles "against the prejudicing, blinding tendency of sin" so that one is aware of his sin, guilt, and impending eternal misery.[52] The faculties do not have in legal preparation that new spiritual basis which founds the act of faith; they are assisted to do what they do naturally or from themselves.

> That conviction of guilt which a natural man may have from the Spirit of God is only by the Spirit's assisting natural conscience the better and more fully to do its office. Therein common grace differs from special. Common grace is only the assistance of natural principles; special is the infusing and exciting supernatural principles; or, if these words are too abstruse, common grace only assists the faculties of the soul to do that more fully which they do by nature. . . . But special grace causes the faculties to do that that they do not by nature. . . .[53]

The *source* or *origin* of conviction, humiliation, and faith is therefore of determinative significance for Edwards.[54] With regard to the New England revivals this meant that the terrors of conscience, experienced at the hands of the revivalist who proclaimed the threats of the law and God's judgment, were not marks of conversion to faith. When one is prepared for faith by the law or by the Spirit's "common" operation through the law, this preparation is not yet what is prepared for, viz., the faith given through the saving work of the Spirit.

Put another way, one is not truly or *savingly* convicted and humbled in legal preparation. One's heart is not "wean'd" by the law from sin and self-righteousness.

> No sound divine will assert that sin is mortified in order of time before grace is infused. The truth is that the case is the same with regard to the objects of his lusts and a man's own righteousness. There is a legal work commonly preparing the way for a man's being weaned from each. A legal conviction to beat and force him from his own righteousness and a legal repentance to beat him off from the objects of his lust. But the heart is not truly wean'd from either till grace is infused.[55]

It follows that there is need for not only a legal but also an "evangelical" conviction, humiliation, and repentance. In the latter only is the soul really weaned from sin. Only in conjunction with faith does the law complete its work. Conviction of and compunction for sin, to the extent not only of recognizing one's sin but of sensing it in all of its depth as an affront to God, is a companion of the sensing of the gospel-comforts in faith. Similarly, evangelical humiliation and joyful faith "keep company together." "So that at the same time that God lifts up the soul with comfort, and joy, and inward sweetness, he casts it down with abasement."[56] Repentance can be taken in two ways for Edwards: to connote a sense of and sorrow for our sinfulness; and to refer to the actual turning to the mercy of God for the remission of sin. When the latter, and for Edwards the more proper, sense is intended, "faith is in it."[57] Evangelical repentance is, in fact, part of the whole movement of faith. One must still distinguish between faith and repentance since their immediate objects are different: repentance has reference primarily to the evil to be delivered from (sin), while faith has reference to both "evil to be delivered from and good to be obtained" (salvation).[58] "It is true, repentance, in its more general, abstracted nature, is only a sorrow for sin and foresaking of it, which is a duty of natural religion"; but evangelical repentance is a movement of faith; that is, "a dependence of soul on the Mediator for deliverance from sin, is of the essence of it."[59] Edwards' distinction between the legal and the evangelical relation to sin is not an attempt to undercut the need for the terrorizing and convicting work of the law: much of Edwards' preaching indicates the belief that legal preparation is God's usual way of dealing with sinful man. But law finds its end and fulfillment only in gospel; conviction, humiliation, repentance, and faith become "like strings in concert: if one is struck, others sound with it,"[60] when experienced through faith in the good news of the Christ.

Edwards' position on "preparation" provides the context in which he is to be appraised regarding the role for which he has so often been remembered: a proclaimer of the terrors of the law and the wrath of God. Leonard Trinterud points out that the object of eighteenth-century preaching of the terrors of the law, which was indigenous to Puritan theology, was "not to frighten men into heaven, but that they might be 'slain by the Law' " or "be compelled to abandon, in the face of the law's requirements, any pretense of not needing salvation through grace."[61] Edwards was fully in sympathy with such preparatory preaching, and there is no denying that in many of his sermons God's wrath and the sinner's jeopardy and condemnation before the law are depicted in vivid images. It is really inaccurate to subsume all these homilies under the category "hell-fire sermons." Even the famous Enfield sermon, "Sinners in the Hands of an Angry God," does not have hell-fire as its predominating image. As E. H. Cady has discerned in his study "The Artistry of Jonathan Edwards," "by almost any count, fire-imagery amounts to little more than a quarter of the total figures" in the Enfield sermon. "Hell is in [the] picture, but only at the periphery. The focus is on the predicament of the sinner, how dreadfully he dangles *just before* he plunges to eternal agony, and while he has time to repent and be saved." Edwards employs the metaphors of the spider dangling over a fire by a thin thread and of man's walking on slippery places where a quick fall is always a live possibility, when speaking of the sinner's predicament—rather than dwelling on "color words" or "objective heat words."[62] But Edwards did intend to represent in this and other imprecatory sermons man's condemnation by the unfulfilled demands of God's law, and the wrath of God that burned toward the sinner. He intended to represent, in H. Richard Niebuhr's words, "the precariousness of life's poise . . . the utter insecurity of men and of mankind which are at every moment . . . ready to plunge into the abyss of disintegration. . . ."[63] By being so brought to an awareness of the life of sin, natural man may be legally prepared for the reception of grace and mercy. The wonder and joy of God's grace in Christ are more readily sensed when sinners are "brought to reflect upon the sins of their lives, and to see the wickedness of their hearts."[64]

Edwards sometimes preached sermons which tended to dwell on God's wrath without much reference to God's mercy, sermons explicitly preparatory and legal rather than evangelical.[65] On the basis of such sermons one might argue with some justification that, in these sermons themselves at least, the fulfillment of law in gospel, the *telos* of legal preparation in faith, is not always apparent. But Edwards conceived the task of the preacher to be not simply the awakening of terrors in the conscience of the sinner through such exposition of the law. In his own words, ministers "are set in the church of God . . . to be the instruments of leading souls to the God of all consolation . . . they are sent as Christ was, and as coworkers with him, to preach good tidings to the meek, to bind up the broken hearted. . . ."[66] And running through many of those sermons which on the surface are concerned exclusively with God's wrath, is a proclamation of the merciful God whose wrath yet burns toward sin. There is in "Sinners in the Hands of an Angry God," the sermon so often taken as representative of Edwards' pathological preoccupation with a God of wrath, a stream of hope and mercy running through the exposition of the wrath of God. *If* God should withdraw his hand, the sinner would fall into destruction. *If* God should let sinful man go, he would swiftly "descend and plunge into the bottomless gulf."[67] This is a "big *if*": it points to the angry God who is yet merciful even in his wrath. As W. L. Anderson has said, "God's hand is the sole power that prevents the fall into perdition. It is indeed the hand of 'an angry God,' yet its grasp is so controlled by mercy that the sinner 'has not dropped into hell.' "[68] Certainly, the sinner is not to ignore his precariousness by assuring himself that God is merciful—at any moment God could let him drop. God's mercy does not cancel His wrath. But the God whose ire is thoroughly provoked by sin is the same God who grants "pardon for the greatest sinner."[69] Edwards never loses sight of this promise. And for him the end of being awakened by the law to the wrath of God is not that awakening itself but the reception of grace in the gospel.[70] The fulfillment of legal preparation lies in evangelical conviction, humiliation, and repentance; only in this fulfillment is the soul really "wean'd" from sin.

Edwards does not confine the use of the law to its preparatory work in conversion. The law is not only the "schoolmaster" which leads men to Christ by flailing them into a conviction of their helplessness and need for a Saviour; it is also "a rule of life," a "directory" according to which the people of God are to walk.[71] Edwards has in mind what were for John Calvin the "first" and "third" functions of the law: the function of condemning man of his unrighteousness;

and that of teaching believers God's will and arousing them to obedience.[72] But Edwards will not identify faith with a living under the law according to either of the law's functions. The terrors of conscience which spring from the first function are only *preparation* for saving faith; and, though the man of faith has in the law a guide for his life as a Christian, the good moral life lived according to the law is not itself justifying faith and is not productive of the salvation received in faith. Man is not saved by any goodness or righteousness arising from his obedience to the law, "let it be an obedience to the ceremonial law, or a gospel obedience, or what it will. . . ."[73]

## Notes

1. Sermon: "God's Sovereignty in the Salvation of Men," *Works*, ed. Sereno E. Dwight (New York: Converse, 1829), VIII, 119. Henceforth WD.

2. Quoted in William G. McLoughlin, Jr., *Modern Revivalism: Charles Grandison Finney to Billy Graham* (New York: Ronald Press, 1959), p. 11.

3. *Ibid.*

4. "Miscellaneous Remarks on Important Doctrines," WD, VII, 434.

5. See the elaborate scheme of Calvin's successor in Geneva, Theodore Beza, which is entitled "The Sum of all Christianity, or the Description and Distribution of the Causes of the Salvation of the Elect and of the Destruction of the Reprobate, Collected from the Sacred Writings." Heinrich Heppe, *Reformed Dogmatics* (London: Allen & Unurn, 1950), pp. 147–48.

6. John Dillenberger and Claude Welch, *Protestant Christianity, Interpreted Through Its Development* (New York: Charles Scribner's Sons, 1954), p. 34.

7. "Treatise on Grace," pp. 25–26.

8. "A History of the Work of Redemption," WD, III, 186.

9. See "Narrative of Surprising Conversions," *Works* (New York: Leavitt & Trow, 1843–1844) III, 260 ff. Henceforth WW.

10. *Affections*, WY, II, 162, 170–71, 329.

11. "Observations Concerning Efficacious Grace," WW, II, 591.

12. Misc. no. 241, Yale MSS.

13. "Observations Concerning Efficacious Grace," WW. II, 590. Cf. Augustine, "On Grace and Free Will," *Basic Writings of Saint Augustine*, ed. W. J. Oates (New York: Random House, 1948), I, 738, 753–54; and Luther, *On the Bondage of the Will*, trans. J. I. Packer and O. R. Johnston (Westwood, N.J.: Fleming H. Revell Co., 1957), p. 253.

14. A. B. Crabtree, *Jonathan Edwards' View of Man, A Study in Eighteenth Century Calvinism* (Wallington, England: Religious Education Press, 1948), pp. 25–26.

15. "The Great Doctrine of Original Sin Defended," WD, II, 534–37.

16. Aquinas, *Nature and Grace*, pp. 126, 128.

17. Sermon: "Man's Natural Blindness in the Things of Religion," WD, VII, 3–30.

18. Misc. no. 676, Townsend, p. 244.

19. *Images or Shadows of Divine Things*, ed. Perry Miller (New Haven: Yale University Press, 1948), p. 91.

20. "Original Sin," WD, II, 537.

21. "Man's Natural Blindness in the Things of Religion," WD, VII, 4.

22. "Man's Natural Blindness in the Things of Religion," WD, VII, 5.

23. See B. A. Gerrish, *Grace and Reason, A Study in the Theology of Luther* (Oxford, England: Clarendon Press, 1962), pp. 72–73; and Wendel, *Calvin*, pp. 192 ff.

24. "Original Sin," WD, II, 537.

25. Sermon: "Men Naturally God's Enemies," WW, IV, 42.

26. "A History of the Work of Redemption," WD, III, 333; "An Humble Attempt to Promote Explicit Agreement and Visible Union of God's People in Extraordinary Prayer," WD, III, 450; "God's Sovereignty in the Salvation of Men," WD, VIII, 115, Cf. Thomas A. Schafer, "Jonathan Edwards' Conception of the Church," CH 24 (1955), 62.

27. Edwards recognized that the Lord's Supper might indeed *tend* toward conversion, but this was, he felt, no argument that it was instituted for that *purpose* in Scripture. "Qualifications for Communion," WD, IV, 412–13, 423 ff.

28. Sermon: "Pressing into the Kingdom of God," WD, V, 464, 467. J. H. Gerstner believes, on the basis of statements in some of Edwards' sermons which speak of a "possible" and even a "probable" finding in the seeking, that for Edwards "any serious seeking would probably issue in salvation." John H. Gerstner, *Steps to Salvation, The Evangelistic Message of Jonathan Edwards* (Philadelphia: Westminster Press, 1960), pp. 101–2. But for Edwards the possibility or probability of finding does not inhere in the seriousness of the seeking but in the free grace of God. This is especially apparent in Edwards' understanding of "preparation for salvation," considered below.

29. Elwood, *The Philosophical Theology of Jonathan Edwards* (New York: Columbia University Press: 1960), p. 147. For this interpretation of English Puritanism see Geoffrey Nuttall, *The Holy Spirit in Puritan Faith and Experience*, (Oxford: Blackwell, 1947), pp. 91–92.

30. "Some Thoughts on the Revival," WD, IV, 216–17. Cf. the agreement of the main-line English Puritans on this point in Perry Miller, *Errand into the Wilderness* (Cambridge: Harvard University Press, 1956), pp. 67–68.

31. Sermon: "The Manner in which the Salvation of the Soul is to be Sought," WW, IV, 370–71.

32. "God's Sovereignty in the Salvation of Men," WD, VIII, 112.

33. "God Glorified in Man's Dependence," WW, IV, 171.

34. Sermon: "The Vain Self-Flatteries of the Sinner," WD, VI, 419.

35. Edmund S. Morgan, *Visible Saints, The History of a Puritan Idea* (New York: New York University Press, 1963), p. 66.

36. Richard Sibbes, *Works*, I, 47; Thomas Shepard, *Works*, I, 116–84.

37. William Perkins, *Works*, II, 13.

38. William Ames, *Marrow of Sacred Divinity* (London, 1643), p. 111.

39. Dwight, *Life of President Edwards*, WD, I, 93.

40. *Ibid.*, pp. 58–60.

41. "Narrative of Surprising Conversions," WW, III, 240 ff. Cf. C. C. Goen, *Revivalism and Separatism in New England, 1740–1800* (New Haven: Yale University Press, 1962), p. 13.

42. See Misc. nos. r, 116b, 255, 337, 354, 1019, Yale MSS; see also the sermon: "Hope and Comfort Usually Follow Genuine Humiliation and Repentance," WD, VIII, 72, 95.

43. See Perry Miller, " 'Preparation for Salvation' in Seventeenth-Century New England," JHI, 4 (1943), 268 ff.

44. *Affections*, WY, II, 161–62.

45. "Narrative of Surprising Conversions," WW, III, 244.

46. Misc. no. 470, Yale MSS.

47. Misc. no. 317, Yale MSS.

48. "Narrative of Surprising Conversions," WD, IV, 35–36.

49. Solomon Stoddard, *The Nature of Saving Conversion* (Boston, 1770), p. 2.

50. Shepard, *Works*, I, 237. It is by no means to be suggested that the Puritans before Edwards were unanimous on this subject. During the seventeenth-century controversy over antinomianism in Massachusetts, Thomas Hooker, who was in agreement with Shepard, found an opponent in John Cotton, who refused to grant that faith can be initiated by preparation in "natural" man. And Giles

Firmin attacked Shepard "for demanding too much of natural man before grace." Miller, *Errand into the Wilderness*, p. 87, n. 154.

51. Owen, *Works*, V, 74–75.

52. Misc. no. 732, Townsend, pp. 112–13.

53. Misc. no. 626, Townsend, p. 111.

54. William James's contention that finally Edwards' distinction between converted and unconverted man must fall to the ground is an inevitable ramification of James's position that "the worth of a thing" cannot "be decided by its origin." James believes that in Edwards' *Religious Affections* "one could hardly read a clearer argument than this book unwittingly offers in favor of the thesis that no chasm exists between the orders of human excellence, but that here as elsewhere, nature shows continuous differences, and generation and regeneration are matters of degree." But Edwards, unlike James, presupposes that the value of a thing *is* decided by its origin, a presupposition made quite explicit in the *Affections* and one of the pillars on which the entire treatise rests. In terms of Edwards' "first sign" of gracious affections, the gracious is distinguished from the natural human affection by its *divine* or *supernatural origin*, which precludes Edwards' arguing, even "unwittingly," that the difference between natural generation and saving regeneration is simply a "matter of degree." In short, Edwards is irredeemably "supernaturalist," if we take this now hackneyed and ambiguous term to mean that whatever human nature is and does from itself is qualitatively different from what it is and does from beyond itself or from the Spirit of God. And the difference is owing to the difference between natural and supernatural origins.

See William James, *The Varieties of Religious Experience* (New York: Collier Books, 1961), pp. 194–96.

55. Misc. no. 1019, Yale MSS.

56. "Hope and Comfort Usually Follow Genuine Humiliation and Repentance," WD, VIII, 96.

57. Misc. no. 669, Yale MSS.

58. *Ibid.*

59. "Justification by Faith Alone," WW, IV, 119.

60. Misc. no. 393, Yale MSS.

61. Leonard J. Trinterud, *The Forming of an American Tradition* (Philadelphia: Westminster Press, 1949), p. 183.

62. Edwin H. Cady, "The Artistry of Jonathan Edwards," *NEQ*, 22 (1949), 69. Cf. "Sinners in the Hands of an Angry God," WW, IV, 313–21.

63. H. Richard Niebuhr, *The Kingdom of God in America* (Chicago: Willett, Clark, & Co., 1937), p. 137.

64. Sermon: "God Makes Men Sensible of Their Misery Before He Reveals His Mercy and Love," WD, VIII, 62.

65. See sermons: "Wicked Men Useful in Their Destruction Only," WW, IV, 300–12; "The Portion of the Wicked," WD, VIII, 195–226.

66. "The True Excellency of a Gospel Minister," WD, VIII, 443.

67. "Sinners in the Hands of an Angry God," WW, IV, 317.

68. Wilbert L. Anderson, "The Preaching Power of Jonathan Edwards," *Congregationalist and the Christian World*, 88 (October 3, 1903), 464.

69. Sermon: "Great Guilt no Obstacle to the Pardon of the Returning Sinner," WW, IV, 422.

70. "Sinners in the Hands of an Angry God," WW, IV, 316.

71. "A History of the Work of Redemption," WD, III, 211.

72. Calvin, *Institutes*, II, vii, 6, 12.

73. "Justification by Faith Alone," WW, IV, 85.

# Thought: Philosophical

## The Freedom of the Will

Alexander V. G. Allen[°]

Edwards was now at leisure to take up some larger work than any which he had hitherto attempted. At this time, also, he seems to have reverted to the speculations which had interested him when he was a boy in college writing his notes upon the Mind. But the gulf of more than a quarter of a century lay between him and that early dream, so suddenly and strangely relinquished, of interpreting the universe in accordance with the absolute reason. Meantime his thoughts had been running so long in the grooves of a religious controversy which was still unfinished, that he could not escape the fascinations which it offered,—the temptation to make some final and permanent effort for the maintenance of the Calvinistic theology. So far as he reverted to his early speculations, it seems to have been mainly for the purpose of laying a deeper basis for the argument against Arminianism.

Hitherto he had assaulted the foe chiefly on religious grounds. But it had long been apparent to him that the hinge of the whole controversy was the speculative issue regarding the freedom of the will. Out of the Arminian doctrine that the will was free, in the sense of possessing a self-determining power, grew, as he thought, the arrogant disposition to despise the Calvinistic notions of God's sovereignty and moral government, the contempt for "the doctrines of grace," the dislike to experimental religion, the cultivation of a morality which read out the divine existence from the sphere of human interests. Everything vital was at stake in the doctrine of the human will. So strongly was he convinced of this that in his most impressive manner he declared himself ready to admit, that if the Arminians could demonstrate the self-determining power of the will, they had an impregnable fortress against every Christian doctrine which he held most dear. To the task, then, of demolishing this stronghold he devoted himself with the momentum of thought, and energy, and indignation which had been gathering for many years. So intense was the spirit with which he labored that in four months he finished the composition of the work on which, more than on any other of his writings, his world-wide reputation has rested,—a work which produced so deep an impression that it still continues to be spoken of as "the one large contribution which America has made to the deeper philosophic thought of the world."

[°]Reprinted from *Jonathan Edwards* (Boston: Houghton-Mifflin, 1889), pp. 281–99.

The treatise on the Will was published in 1754, and may be regarded as one of the literary sensations of the last century. It was more than that,—it was, to a large part of the religious world, a veritable shock, staggering alike to the reason and the moral sense. The age was accustomed to similar views from infidels and free-thinkers such as Hobbes, and Collins, and Hume were reputed to be. There were others, too, calling themselves Christians, such as Hartley, and Tucker, and Priestley, who denied the freedom of the will, but without awakening the indignation which was caused by Edwards' assertion of the same principle. For here was one who rose up in the name of religion and morality, whose high character was acknowledged by all, whose genius was indisputable, whose reasoning seemed invincible, and who seemed to be clasping hands with materialists and atheists in behalf of the doctrine that the will was not free to choose between good and evil. Edwards' teaching, also, was associated in the public mind with his other beliefs,—the divine sovèreignty, decrees of election and reprobation, an everlasting hell which was yawning for the reception of a majority of the human race. It now added an element of inexpressible horror to the situation if it was also true that the will was not free to choose between good and evil.

Edwards' work on the Will was but the culmination of the reaction which he had signalled when he preached his Boston sermon on Dependence in 1731. His work was received by his fellow-religionists with exultant testimonies to its power and value. There was among the Calvinists a general conviction that he had annihilated Arminianism. From being ashamed of their cause, they now felt themselves forever absolved from the disgraceful necessity of bowing in the house of Rimmon, which had led so many of their number, a Doddridge or a Watts, to admit the self-determining power of the will. In the enthusiastic words of Jonathan Edwards the Younger: "Now, therefore, the Calvinists find themselves placed upon firm and high ground. They fear not the attacks of their opponents. They face them on the ground of reason as well as of Scripture. Rather have they carried the war into Italy and to the very gates of Rome."[1] Long after its first appearance the same testimony continued to be borne. "There is no European divine," said Dr. Chalmers, "to whom I make such frequent appeals; no book of human composition which I more strenuously recommend than his Treatise on the Will, read by me forty-seven years ago, with a conviction that has never since faltered, and which has helped me more than any other uninspired book to find my way through all that might otherwise have proved baffling, and transcendental, and mysterious in the peculiarities of Calvinism."[2] In a passage frequently quoted, Sir James Mackintosh speaks of Edwards' power of subtle argument as "perhaps unmatched, certainly unsurpassed, among men."[3] Dugald Stewart regarded him as not inferior to disputants bred in the best universities of Europe. It is said that in conversation he once remarked that the argument of the Freedom of the Will had not been and could not be answered. The late Isaac Taylor, who edited an English edition of the work, esteemed it "a classic in metaphysics," though regretting the mixture of the metaphysical with the Scriptural argument. He also thought that Edwards had achieved his immediate object of demolishing the Arminian notion of contingency, and that his influence had been much greater than those who had yielded to it had always confessed. Among other things which Edwards had taught the world was "to be less flippant."[4] A writer in the Christian Spectator for 1823 expressed the prevalent opinion when he remarked that it was curious to observe how few attempts had been made formally to answer any of those larger works in which Edwards put forth his strength. "Nibbling enough about the points of his arguments there has certainly been, but for the most part it has been extremely chary; and we suspect that the few who have taken hold in earnest have in the end found pretty good reason to repent of their temerity." The general impression that Edwards' argument was invincible drove those who resisted his conclusion to making an appeal to the consciousness in opposition to the intellect, as the only available alternative; or, in the words of Dr. Johnson to Boswell, "We know that we are free and there 's an end on 't." Even so late as 1864, a distinguished American writer, Mr. Hazard, introduced his Review of Edwards on the Will by remarking that the soundness of his premises and the cogency of his logic were so generally admitted that "almost by common consent his positions are deemed impregnable, and the hope of subverting them by direct attack abandoned."

In view of these tributes of admiration, and many others which could be adduced, it is unnecessary to remark that high place must be assigned in literature to Edwards on the Will. Like Butler's Analogy, it belongs among the few great books in English theology. It may claim the great and peculiar honor of having first opened up to the world a new subject of interest,—the neglected and almost unknown sphere of the human will in its vast extent and mystery. It attempted to fill an empty niche in the corridors of human thought. From an historical point of view, no one can question its significance. Whether its importance is now more than historical, it is fairly open to doubt. The book is a difficult one to read, and this difficulty has been generally supposed to lie in the nature of the subject rather than in the author's method of exposition. But the close scrutiny to which it has been subjected has revealed a confusion in Edwards' mind as one source of the difficulty which the student encounters.[5] The work starts out with a definition of the will as "that by which the mind chooses anything,"—a definition which might be allowed to stand, though far from being an adequate one. But even to this definition Edwards does not adhere. Hardly is he launched in his argument when he is found resting upon another ground,—that the will is that by which the mind desires or inclines to anything; and this ambiguity of the word "choice" runs throughout the treatise. In his Notes on the Mind he had identified inclination with will: to this principle he had clung throughout his career as a practical theologian; it now turns up again in this speculative treatise, and becomes the basis of his opinion regarding the nature of freedom and of human responsibility. If a man possesses an inclination, however derived, and has the natural power to gratify it, he is free. If his inclination be evil, he is a proper subject of condemnation, or of approval if his inclination be right. But the ability to reverse the inclination, or to choose between the good and the evil, is no prerogative of the will.

The most striking feature of Edwards' position is its close agreement with the attitude of the physical or materialistic school of philosophy in his own and in a later age. There is no difference between his doctrine and that of the ancient Stoics, or of the famous philosopher Hobbes, who shocked the religious world of his day by his unspiritual method of dealing with religious things.[6] There is no perceptible difference between Edwards and David Hume on the vital question of the nature of causation. A cause is defined to be, not only that which has a positive tendency to produce a thing, but it includes also all antecedents with which consequent events are connected, whether they have any positive influence in producing them or not. He assumes that uniform causes are followed by uniform results. In this respect he is also at one with the late John Stuart Mill, affirming the common principle that the life of humanity, like that of outward nature, is involved in the meshes of necessity. The invariableness of the order of nature, man as the creature of outward circumstance, the iron chain of necessity which controls human character and conduct,—these things, as Mr. Mill has taught them, are paralleled by Edwards' view of a world in which every event in nature or in human experience is decreed by an Infinite Will, and in the nature of the case cannot be otherwise than it is.

Edwards' argument against the freedom of the human will, in the sense of a power to choose between good and evil, gains its force from the assumption of the thing to be proved. There is no movement in his thought beyond this assumption that every event must have some external cause. But the question at issue is, whether the will be not itself a creative cause, endowed with the power of initiating acts, of choosing between motives, nay, even of creating a motive to itself. The illusion under which Edwards labors is in looking at man as part of nature, instead of as a personal being, who, rising above nature, has in himself the power of new beginnings. It is unnecessary to follow him in the phases of his argument as with matchless subtilty he reiterates the principle that every event must have a cause. It only requires to start with another definition of the will, as, like the divine will, "a creative first cause,"—wherein also lies the image of God in the creature,—and Edwards' objections not only fail to overcome this counter principle, but even tend to its confirmation.

But it is, after all, the religious argument, and not the metaphysical, upon which Edwards' chief reliance depends in refuting the doctrine of the self-determining power of the will. If the will were free to choose between good and evil, then there would be uncertainty as to the result of its choice, and God's foreknowledge of the volitions of moral agents would be impossible. If the Divine Mind could not foreknow with infallible certainty the acts of the creature, how could events be decreed with the infallible certainty of their accomplishment? The divine action must in consequence be subject to constant revision, the divine immutability give way to infinitely numerous changes of intention. But this seemed to Edwards as contradictory to Scripture as it was to reason and to the moral sense. The Bible, as he read it, abounded in the prediction of events attributed to God. To admit the possibility of the uncertainty of human actions seemed also to involve a tacit atheism. Such an admission limited the divine omniscience, and endangered the omnipotence of God. The divine

Being would then be conceived as standing at the mercy of man, waiting for the human will to determine its course. For such a deity, too feeble to govern the world which He had made, a Calvinist like Edwards could have no respect. The God of the Arminians was to him no God at all.

The issue which is here raised is a serious one, confronting every earnest thinker. While we are concerned in this discussion, not so much with the replies that have been or may be made to Edwards' position, yet it may be said in passing that we are not necessarily shut up to the alternatives of sacrificing human freedom, or limiting the divine omniscience. It is not difficult to conceive that the Infinite Mind may be competent to take into account every use that man may make of his freedom, and to govern the world accordingly. Even if it were required to conceive the divine omniscience as self-limited in order to the free development of the creature, this does not make impossible the divine moral government. It then would become a feature of the world-process as God has ordered it, that the free will of man shall be the means through which the divine purpose is to be accomplished. To govern the world, and yet allow full scope to human freedom, is a task more difficult, and therefore worthier of God. It is a grave objection to Edwards' conception of the universe that, when God has once decreed the course of human affairs down to its smallest detail, there remains no further opportunity for the creative divine activity. The same result would be obtained if for God were substituted the action of force or of unchanging law.[7]

It had formed an essential part of Edwards' plan in the treatment of his subject, to show that the Arminian idea of the freedom of will—as implying a self-determining power, or power to choose between good and evil—was not only untrue in itself, but was not necessary to moral agency. He had done this, apparently to his entire satisfaction, in the third part of his book, where he elaborates his thought at some length. But the scholarly recluse may become so accustomed to his own line of reflection as to be out of touch with the popular mind, which draws inferences from premises of its own, the ground of which lies too deep to be disturbed by speculative discussion. The popular inference from Edwards' argument was, that he had denied the freedom of the will, and in so doing had shaken the truth of moral accountability. In Scotland, where his work had been long expected and was eagerly received, this inference was also drawn by the celebrated Lord Kames, who was entangled in speculations of his own on the same subject, and who hailed Edwards as a kindred spirit coming to his relief. Lord Kames had deduced the natural conclusion that, "if motives are not under our power or direction, we can at bottom have no liberty." He also reasoned that the human consciousness, which attests a sense of liberty, must be therefore a delusion, implanted in the soul in order to give men a sense of responsibility for their acts. An anonymous pamphlet was also issued in Scotland in which it was maintained that, if Edwards' teaching were true, it was better that it should not be known, as it would endanger the feeling of human accountability. Edwards seems to have been surprised and indignant when he learned through his friend and correspondent, Dr. Erskine, how his views were interpreted by those with whom he had no sympathy. In order to put his meaning beyond the power of misinterpretation, he wrote an open letter, which has ever since been appended to his treatise on the Will, in which he defined his attitude against those who understood him to hold that the will was not free.

How, then, did he discriminate his position from philosophical necessitarians, as they are called, who agreed with him in holding that the will has no power to choose between good and evil? It is a curious and remarkable case of how a subtle and powerful mind may fall into captivity to the bondage of words. Edwards now declared that he held to the freedom of the will, because freedom consisted, not in one's power of choosing between alternatives, but in his power to pursue his inclination without restraint. Because a man's actions were necessitated, or certain to take place just as they did, it did not follow that he acted under compulsion. Indeed, he was quite willing to give up all such words as "necessity" or "inability" when applied to the will. What he contended for was only the certainty that men's actions would take the shape they did, and that without any feeling, on their part, of compulsion or restraint. So long as there was no sense of compulsion, a man was free, no matter how he came by his inclination, or how infallibly certain that his action should be what it was.

It is rather to the credit of the necessitarians, with whose principles Edwards agreed while he disliked their alliance, that they refused to escape the consequences of their theory by what seems a hollow evasion or mere jugglery with words. Calvin also had held consistently to the same conviction that the will did not possess the power to choose between good and evil. He had even denounced with something of scorn in his tone the manner of those who, while accepting this view, still maintained that a man was free "because he acts voluntarily and not by compulsion." "This is perfectly true," he adds, "but why should so small a matter have been dignified with so proud a title? An admirable freedom!—that man is not forced to be the servant of sin, while he is, however, a voluntary slave; his will being bound by the fetters of sin. I abominate mere verbal disputes, by which the church is harassed to no purpose; but I think we ought religiously to eschew terms which imply some absurdity, especially in subjects where error is of pernicious consequence. How few there are who, when they hear free will attributed to man, do not immediately imagine that he is the master of his mind and will, and can incline himself either to good or evil!"[8] But this small matter, as Calvin rightly deemed it, Edwards chose to dignify, in the emergency of his conflict, with the proud title of freedom. There is even a tone of passion in its advocacy. He contends that he differs from necessitarians like Lord Kames by holding to freedom in the highest sense. "No Arminian, Pelagian, or Epicurean," he exclaimed, "can rise higher in his conception of freedom than the notion of it which I have explained. . . . And I scruple not to say, it is beyond all their wits to invent a higher notion or form a higher imagination of liberty; let them talk of sovereignty of the will, self-determining power, self-motion, self-direction, arbitrary decision, liberty *ad utrumois*, power of choosing differently in given cases, etc., as long as they will." But Calvin was right when he foresaw the consequences of dignifying so small a matter with so proud a title. From a fear of being understood to deny the freedom of the will, coupled as it was in the popular mind with the sense of responsibility, the preachers who followed Edwards magnified his meagre conception of freedom, and felt justified in using the Arminian nomenclature. In this way Edwards' idea of freedom became a bridge of transition to a modern Calvinism in which liberty is conceded in the fuller sense as a power to choose between good and evil.

But we reach the momentous outcome of Edwards' argument when he applies this same idea of freedom to the sovereign will of God. To the conclusion that this was the only freedom predicable of God, he was driven by the necessities of his thought. He was laboring to show that man is free, although possessing no power to choose between good and evil,—free even though his action be necessary or certain; and if free, then responsible for his action, and deserving of praise or blame. To establish this point he drew an illustration from the person of Christ, with whom there was a necessity to the right and an impossibility to sin, and yet He was morally responsible, and his conduct a proper subject of moral approval. From this very inadequate conception of the personality of Christ, he passed on to the consideration of the being of God. God also is free only to do what is right,—free only in the sense that He has the power to carry out the divine inclination. The divine freedom is therefore but another name for a divine and eternal necessity. Behind the divine will there lies an immutable divine wisdom, to which the will of God must in the nature of the case conform. But here one is forced to ask what becomes of the doctrine of the divine sovereignty, which played so large a part in Edwards' earlier writings, which, as he had presented it, implied in the divine will a power to the contrary. How often had he asserted, that God was under no obligation to save man after the fall; that when, in the exercise of His sovereign will, He had determined to do so, it was still a matter of His arbitrary will whom He would save and whom He would reject! "He chooseth whom He will, and whom He will, He hardeneth." The two doctrines are plainly incompatible. Sovereignty, as he had preached it, contradicts necessity. The divine sovereignty was the last relic of freedom, when it had been denied elsewhere. But it now appears as having no justification at the bar of reason. Even in Edwards' consciousness from the first, it had been a mysterious conviction, the genesis of which he could not explain. It is plain that a change is now taking place in his mind as to the nature of God, which is fundamental and revolutionary in its character. The Augustinian idea of God as arbitrary, unconditioned will, is growing weak in the presence of another conception,—the definition of God as the one substance of whose thought the world of created things is the necessary manifestation. But throughout the universe there is no place for the freedom of the will.

At this point, which is the culmination of Edwards' argument, there opened before him diverging lines of thought, and which of them he should take depended on whether his interest was stronger in following out the line of speculation about the nature of God and its relation to man, or in tracing the origin and history of that evil inclination in humanity which is known as Original Sin. The discussion of the latter topic was required in order to supplement the treatise on the Will. For it is a noticeable feature of this treatise that no effort is made to account for that inclination to evil in every man, which man does not originate within himself, which he is not free to reverse or overcome. Elsewhere Edwards had boldly declared that the will is determined by God. But we do not meet this statement in any such emphatic form in his work on The Will. He preferred to abide by the negative demonstration that the acts of the will are rendered certain by some other cause than the mere power of willing. What that remoter cause may be is not specially considered. He does not go beyond the statement that the will is determined by that motive which, as it stands in the mind, is the strongest, or that the will always is as the greatest apparent good is. In the vast and obscure region of human motives there is disclosed an ample sphere where God may work unfelt or unperceived, where He may so influence or direct the agencies which control the will that a man shall do the divine bidding while still acting in accordance with his own inclination. To the natural objection that such a view makes God the author of sin, he offers a brief reply, at the same time remarking that he has not space to consider at length the question of the first entrance of sin into the world. The subject of original sin was then clearly before his mind. But the idea of God had a deeper charm than the nature of man, and its exposition more imperatively demanded his attention. Before writing his work on Original Sin, he stopped to consider the nature of True Virtue and the Last End of God in the Creation.

## Notes

1. Edwards the Younger, *Works* (Boston, 1854), I, 484.

2. Thomas Chalmers, *Works*, vol. i. p. 318.

3. *Progress of Ethical Philosophy* (Philadelphia, 1834), p. 108.

4. Introductory Essay to his edition of *Freedom of the Will*, p. xxv.

5. Among other American critics of Edwards' argument besides the late Mr. Hazard, are Bledsoe, *Examination of Edwards on the Will*; Whedon, *The Freedom of the Will as a Basis of Moral Responsibility*; Tappan, *Review of Edwards' Inquiry*, etc. In Mr. Martineau's recent work, *A Study of Religion*, there is an admirable criticism of Edwards' attitude. Cf. vol. ii. chap. 2.

6. Edwards declared that he had not read Hobbes. Hume he seems to have read after his own work was published. One would like to know whether he had read Collins' *Philosophic Inquiry Concerning Human Liberty*, in which views identical with his own are advocated. It has been remarked that Collins' little work would have made an admirable introduction to Edwards' treatise. Edwards makes no allusion to him, though his book must have been widely known. Cf. Professor Fisher's valuable remarks in *Discussions in History and Theology* (New York: Scribners, 1880), pp. 234, 235.

7. Edwards' biblical argument is a defective one. But it involves questions of Biblical criticism,—the relation between the revelation and its record,—and cannot here be criticised. According to Edwards, Scripture reads like one continuous chapter of fulfilled prophecy. His interpretation of history is in harmony with his view of life, as ordered by divine decrees.

8. *Institutes of Christian Religion*, book ii. ch. ii. p. 7.

# Jonathan Edwards

I. Woodbridge Riley°

Jonathan Edwards (1703–1758), the most subtle of New England idealists, was the quintessence of Puritan culture. Of mingled English and Welsh blood, the Saxon and Celtic strains appeared in his dual nature, with its conflicting logical and imaginative powers. Outwardly Edwards was an advocate of cold ratiocination, of the strict metaphysical way of reasoning; inwardly, a philosopher of the feelings, a fervent exponent of the dialectic of the heart; traditionally he has been known as the preacher of the cold austerities of Puritanism; in reality he was an advocate of the interior or hidden life which results in an intimate union between the individual and the absolute. To judge from his private journal, which presents a series of exquisite miniatures, this saint of New England may be fitly described in the words upon his memorial window: *Dei cultor mystice amantissimus*.

As in the case of the *Confessions* of Saint Augustine, to whom the Puritan divine has been often compared, these early experiences were significant in setting the tone and colour of his subsequent intellectual life.[1] In this life three phases have been recognised, for Edwards has been entitled a mystic because of his wonderful sense of the immediateness of the Divine Presence and agency; an idealist, because of his agreement with Plato's conception of God as the idea of the good; a pantheist, because of his approximation to Spinoza's doctrine of the one substance, of which the universe is the manifestation. All these comparisons have been made, but not all have been correlated. In presenting these as the progressive stages in the philosopher's thinking, it is reasonable to hold that the first is the most fundamental, inasmuch as it goes far to explain both that precocious postulate that 'the material universe exists nowhere but in the mind,' and the final conclusion that 'existence is constantly proceeding from God.' And so, broadly considered, Edwards' philosophical career may be distributed into three phases of belief: first, the idealism of his youth and early manhood, when a student at Yale College; second, the determinism of his middle period, when the professional exigencies of his ministry kept him within the rigid bounds of Calvinism; third, the tentative pantheism of his maturity, when a recrudescence of certain primary convictions led to such a view of God's last end in creation as to constitute an almost monistic doctrine of immanence.

° Reprinted, with permission, from *American Philosophy: The Early Schools* (New York: Dodd, Mead, & Co., 1907), pp. 126–27, 129–30, 142–59, 169–80, 184–87.

How may these varying phases of belief be harmonized? Between Edwards the philosopher and Edwards the theologian there may be granted a certain intellectual duality, yet in Edwards the ecstatic there is little variableness, since there is a common element which, like a subterranean stream, flows steadily beneath the entire field of his speculations. This common element is Edwards' mysticism, for his idealism appears to be based upon a mystic form of phenomenalism, his determinism upon a mystic doctrine of passivity, his pantheism upon a mystic absorption of the individual into the absolute. . . .

The problem of Edwards' idealism is the most difficult in the history of American philosophy. Was it his own, or borrowed, or both? Was it the product of precocious genius, or an adaptation of the Berkeleian system, or a blending of the idealistic hints and suggestions then in the air? In the absence of a definitive edition of Edwards' works, no final answer can be given to these questions. Nevertheless one may present the materials already published, review the history of the case, and suggest a principle which may throw a little new light on this vexed controversy. For a full understanding of the completed Edwardean scheme there are four sets of records to be examined: first, the early theoretical presentation of his idealism; then his account of his youthful ecstasies and mystic raptures; next, his maturer treatises, such as the *Inquiry on the Freedom of the Will;* finally, his posthumous publications, such as that on *God's Chief End in the Creation.* . . .

While it may be allowed that this series of metaphysical definitions and discussions as emanating from an undergraduate are truly marvellous, yet it is now pretty well agreed that they were written before Edwards left college. Indeed, it has been argued from the forcing process of Edwards' youth, the stimulating atmosphere of theological speculation in which he was brought up, that there is no improbability that at seventeen he reached his idealistic conceptions, just as Berkeley himself began his *Commonplace Book,* containing the material for his *Theory of Vision* and his *Principles,* shortly after taking his first degree, at the age of nineteen.[2] But leaving aside all comparison in the somewhat futile problem of precocity, the contention that Edwards' idealism was as early as it has been traditionally claimed, receives further vindication by referring to the fourth series of notes which have been assigned to the last two years of college life and the two following of graduate residence. It is the *Miscellanies* which possess that familiar air of retrospection, that way of pointing back to previous views, indicative of the fact that the youthful author's mind was already set in an idealistic direction. As taken from the originals, which are not in Edwards' collected works, two of these earlier observations may here be cited:

> Spiritual happiness, as we have shown and demonstrated—contrary to the opinion of [most who believe] that nothing is substance but matter—that no matter is substance but only God, who is a Spirit, and that other spirits are more substantial than matter; so also it is true that no happiness is solid and substantial but spiritual happiness, although it may seem that sensual pleasures are more real, and spiritual only imaginary; just as it seems as if sensible matter were only real and spiritual

substance only imaginary. . . . We know there was Being from eternity; and this being must be intelligent, for how doth the mind refuse to believe that there should be being from all eternity, without its being conscious to itself that it was; that there should be from all eternity, and yet nothing known, all that while, that anything is. This is really a contradiction; and we may see it to be so, though we know not how to express it. For in what respect has anything had a being, when there is nothing conscious of its being; for in what respect has anything a being that [of which] angels nor men, nor created intelligences know nothing, but only as God knows it to be? Not at all more than there are sounds where none hears it, or colour where none sees it. Thus, for instance, supposing a room in which none is; none sees the things in the room; no created intelligence. The things in the room have no being any otherways than only as God is conscious [of them]; for there is no colour there, neither is there any sound, nor any shape, &c.[3]

With these citations which reaffirm the thought and even the argumentative illustration of the earliest essay on *Being*, the idealistic thinking of Edwards is brought through the year 1722, and thereby into the first probable point of historical connection with the kindred immaterialism of Berkeley, for it was in the following year that Edwards' former tutor, Samuel Johnson, of Yale College, was reported to have first heard of Berkeleism when he went to England for episcopal ordination.[4] While the evidence that the American idealist drew on the Irish idealist prior to this date is highly problematical, one must needs review the arguments on both sides before proceeding to what may possibly furnish a new clue to the problem of Edwards' originality, namely, those mystic expressions which go far to explain the generation and growth of the later immaterialistic doctrines. As to the sources whence the young undergraduate derived his idealistic notions, it has been variously said[5] that in recent years there has grown up what may be regarded as a history of opinion on this difficult point. On the one hand, it is maintained that Edwards had no acquaintance with the writings of Berkeley, and that it is not necessary to suppose such an acquaintance in order to explain this reproduction, almost complete, of a philosophy which is identified with Berkeley's name. The former was the view of Dr. Sereno Edwards Dwight,[6] the latter the view of President Noah Porter of Yale College, who argued that, being surrounded as it were by similar logical and spiritual impulses, Jonathan Edwards drew the same conclusions as Berkeley had done from the same data in Locke's *Essays*.[7]

On the other hand, those who hold that Edwards may have read Berkeley's works can bring no direct evidence to substantiate their opinion. Professor A. Campbell Fraser, the biographer and editor of Berkeley, was the first to advance the opinion that Edwards, the most subtle reasoner that America has produced, adopted and professed Berkeley's great philosophical conception,[8] but is now less disposed to this conjecture than formerly.[9] So, too, Professor Fisher was once of the opinion that it was from Berkeley that the youthful American philosopher imbibed his views, but further investigations have proved it to be in the highest degree probable that this inference is a mistaken one. It was owing to the powerful stimulus imparted to the young Yale student by the writings of Locke that he was prompted to move on in a path of his own, while the 'new philosophy,' to which Edwards afterwards refers with approval, appears to have been the publications of Sir Isaac Newton.[10] So, too, Professor George Lyon in treating of Edwards as a representative of the English idealism of the eighteenth century has declared that the dependence on Berkeley is unmistakable, and has even undertaken to point this out in some detail. He quotes, for example, the following: 'The ideas we have by the sense of feeling are as much mere ideas as those we have by the sense of seeing,' remarking that this is precisely the position whereby Berkeley in his *Principles* did away with what was equivocal in his *Theory of Vision*. He refers to Edwards' arguments for the merely mental existence of all the objects of vision, because, namely, 'all these things . . . do exist in a looking-glass,' as almost a phrase of Berkeley's, and, at any rate, one of his favourite proofs. He also considers the argument to be similar to Berkeley's in which Edwards maintains the unlikeness between our ideas of space and those which a man born blind would have.[11]

But in view of the later negative evidence, the dissimilarities between the principles of Berkeley and of Edwards, it has been asserted that these parallelisms of language and argument cited by Lyon appear trivial. How could any idealist fail to observe that ideas of touch are as much ideas as those of sight? And, what more natural illustration of the ideality of objects of vision than their reflection in a looking-glass? Or, what more likely an observation than the difference between a blind man's idea of space and ours? This last, moreover, he could have got, and probably did get, from Locke.[12]

Thus far all the evidence for this alleged influence of Berkeley is entirely internal. There is no external evidence that is worth considering. The suggestion that Edwards may have become acquainted with Berkeley's philosophy through Samuel Johnson, who was tutor at Yale between 1716 and 1719, fails when it is put to the test. Johnson was *persona non grata* to Edwards, for he remained at New Haven while Edwards withdrew, with other disaffected students, to Wethersfield. Nor is there any evidence that Johnson was at this time acquainted with Berkeley's writings. Johnson's own manuscript, entitled 'A Catalogue of Books read by me from year to year since I left Yale Colledge,' contains no mention of anything of Berkeley's before 1727–28. In that year and the year following the *Principles* are entered, and in 1729–30 the *Dialogues* and the *Theory of Vision*.[13] Finally certain recently discovered manuscripts confirm one's opinion of the lateness of the date in Johnson's mastery of Berkeley's works, for on September 10, 1729, he writes to the Dean 'a letter . . . upon reading his books of the *Principles of Human Knowledge* and *Dialogues*.'[14]

If it now seems highly improbable that Edwards could have become acquainted with the Irish metaphysician through his casual tutor Johnson, there nevertheless remains the possibility that he could have known Berkeley's works at first hand, for from four to seven years elapsed between the publication of Berkeley's early philosophy and the earliest date claimed for these writings of Edwards.[15] But here the suggestion of Johnson's biographer, Beardsley, that the 'new philosophy,' against which the students were warned, when Johnson graduated in 1714, was Berkeley's, has been demolished;[16] and the opinion of President Porter that there is no evidence that any of Berkeley's works were known at Yale College when Edwards was a student is hardly tenable,[17] for the fact that a book is not catalogued is no proof that it was not in a library. So, too, with the argument from silence in Edwards' own works. He paid an ample tribute to Locke, but nowhere does he mention Berkeley, to whom lay the greater indebtedness. Although in his relations to other writers Edwards may have been candid in some respects, he was not in all. In corroboration of the opinion that he was not the man to conceal a real obligation has been cited his remark at the end of his notes in *Natural Science*: 'This has been thought of before.' But as a sort of psychological explanation as to the silence on the name of Berkeley, it has been said that, frank as these early writings of Edwards may seem, they contain intimations of a reserved and even secretive temperament. He has recourse now and then to shorthand, in which he buried in oblivion his most intimate thoughts or feelings. He charges himself not to allow it to appear as if he were familiar with books or conversant with the learned world. He seems to feel that he has a secret teaching which will create opposition when revealed and clash with the prejudices and fashions of the age.[18] In all this quandary one is not helped out by the articles and meagre references to Edwards' unpublished writings. What has been called the most interesting manuscript of the Yale collection, a memorandum book labelled simply 'Catalogue,' has as the opening leaf a record of 'legenda,' but what was the complete list of philosophical works mentioned in this reading list the editor has not divulged.[19]

Under these various difficulties and limitations as to the external evidence, one is forced to fall back upon the internal, the similarities or discrepancies between the immaterialistic doctrines of Edwards and of Berkeley. Here, too, the evidence is mainly negative as to any direct dependence of the younger upon the older idealist. In a general way it has been argued that the student who had read Berkeley must surely have felt himself under a real obligation. But there is nothing whatever of this in Edwards. On the contrary, there is evident consciousness of independence. He is preparing to write a book in which these views of his will be given to the world. He is aware of their novelty. He is careful, therefore, to guard himself against misapprehension, especially in the matter of the seeming denial of the existence of bodies outside the mind. 'It is from hence I expect the greatest opposition,' he writes.[20] Interpreting this as an expression of a sense of personal ownership in his ideas, it is further argued that if Edwards had derived his idealism from Berkeley, we should expect a much more direct reflection of Berkeley's thought and language. How, for instance, could he have written as he did on the subject of universals, if he had been acquainted with Berkeley's vigorous polemic against the doctrine of abstract ideas? No ideas are more characteristic and oft-repeated in the early works of Berkeley than the following: The impossibility of perceiving distance by sight, the arbitrariness of God in connecting ideas of sight and ideas of touch, the influence of suggestion in perception, the objects of sight a divine visual language. Is it conceivable or to be regarded as a mere accident that a young student, reproducing ideas derived from the reading of Berkeley, should have given no hint of being affected by such all-pervading and altogether fascinating conception?

... But we can go further. Not only is there no proof that Edwards derived his idealism from Berkeley, but it is clearly evident that his idealism has, to say the least, a different accent and character from that of the author of the *Principles of Human Knowledge* and the *Dialogues of Hylas and Philonous*. Berkeley's early doctrine is, as everyone knows, that the *esse* of material things consists in their *percipi*. Now it is no doubt true that in urging this doctrine his main object was to establish the reality of the divine being and action, and the substantiality and causality of spirit. That spirit is alone substantial and causal is indeed the real Berkeleian idealism. But the relation of things sensible to spirits, and especially to the mind of God, is hardly considered by Berkeley in his early writings; he contents himself with the thought that God imprints the ideas of material things on our senses in a fixed order. To the objection that material things when not actually perceived by us must be non-existent he can only reply that 'there may be some other spirit that perceives them, though we do not.' The *esse* of things is thus their *percipi*. Later in life Berkeley went beyond this, and taught that the *esse* of things is not their *percipi*, but their *concipi*; that the world in its deepest truth is a divine order eternally existing in the mind of God. But it is this doctrine which, along with the phenomenalism which he shares with Berkeley, is the characteristic doctrine of Jonathan Edwards. It is implied in his conception of the real, as distinguished from the nominal, essence, in his conception of truth as the agreement of our ideas with the ideas of God, and it is definitely expressed in various passages, best perhaps in the formulation of his idealism already quoted: 'That which truly is the substance of all bodies is the infinitely exact, and precise, and stable Idea, in God's mind, together with His stable Will, that the same shall gradually be communicated to us, and to other minds, according to certain fixed and established Methods and Laws.' The phenomenalism in Edwards is relatively subordinate. But similar ideas are not at all prominent in Berkeley before the *Siris*, which was not published till 1744.[21]

Further divergences between Edwards and Berkeley which have been pointed out do not especially concern the early idealism, for the doctrine that space is divine, which Berkeley denounces as absurd, is traceable to Newton, and the doctrine of necessitated volition, wherein Edwards differed from both Berkeley and Johnson, is to be referred to the later determinism of the *Inquiry Into the Freedom of the Will*. But if the hypothesis of Berkeleian influence be surrendered, although it is not certain that Berkeley had absolutely nothing to do with Edwards' early idealism,[22] that surrender weakens but does not necessarily preclude the hypothesis of a borrowing from other sources. Here four philosophers have been suggested. These are, in their historical order: Descartes, with his problematical idealism in the early part of the *Meditations*;[23] Malebranche, with his supposition that God is the only agent and does everything upon occasion of certain events in the mundane sphere;[24] Norris, whose

*Theory of the Ideal or Intelligible World*, published in 1701, reproduced ideas of Malebranche; and Arthur Collier, whose *Clavis Universalis* of 1713 propounded a theory of absolute idealism.[25] Between these thinkers and Edwards there are affinities, yet as actual connections they have been declared highly problematic and quite gratuitous,[26] and for such reasons as these. Against Descartes the students of Yale had been warned as early as 1714 as one of those bringing in a corrupting new philosophy;[27] in behalf of Malebranche there is no proof positive, for Edwards makes no reference to him;[28] and the same is true of Norris, except for Edwards' chance use of the phrase, 'the ideal world';[29] while as for Collier's pamphlet, which, like Edwards' early note on 'Existence,' compares the sensible world to a looking-glass,[30] at this time that rare work was unknown even in England and Scotland.[31]

Although these arguments from silence may be deemed inconclusive, since the tendency among writers to assume that the New England scholars cannot have been acquainted very largely with the literature of their times is unfounded,[32] nevertheless, in the absence of definite references, recourse must be had to those authors whom it is known that Edwards read as an undergraduate. These were Cudworth, with his diffused Platonism; Newton, with his doctrine of colours; Locke, with his doctrine of ideas. As to the last of the given authorities, it is well argued that, when one considers the nature of the mind of Edwards, there is no difficulty in believing that although isolated in a new world he advanced upon Locke in a way similar to that of Berkeley, and propounded elements of idealism that have entered into the most recent thought. That there is no difficulty in drawing idealism from the writings of Locke has been pointed out by Sir William Hamilton, and Reid thought it strange that Locke, who wrote so much about ideas, should not see those consequences that Berkeley thought so obvious.[33] However, this is arguing from mere probability. Therefore, in default of a careful re-editing of the unpublished manuscripts and since it is impossible to determine all that was in the air of the Connecticut Valley in Edwards' youth, it has been similarly declared that we need, in order to account for his idealism, to recognise only these forces: The early fascination for him of Newton's discoveries respecting light and colours; the philosophy of Locke, especially the stress laid upon sensation as explaining the origin of ideas; his own extraordinary deductive power, so early exhibited and henceforth at once his strength and his weakness, and his wonderful sense of the Divine Presence and agency.[34]

Assuming these three factors as making up the character of Edwards as idealist, one may say that his learning appears to have been less than his logical powers and his intuitive greater than either. Such an evaluation has at least the merit of correlating the various opinions of the man and his works. First, there is the native opinion that since he knew Plato but partially, Aristotle hardly at all, could not read French and was ignorant of the Schoolmen and the Catholic theologians since Augustine,[35] and since the search for his indebtedness to others has been vain, his early notes are all the greater warrant for ranking him among the great, original minds.[36] Again, there is the foreign opinion of Dugald Stewart that in logical acuteness and subtlety Edwards does not yield to any disputant bred in the universities of Europe;[37] this is borne out by Edwards' early confession that one reason why, at first, before he knew other logic, he used to be mightily pleased with the Old Logic, was because it was very pleasant to see his thoughts, that before lay in his mind jumbled without any distinction, ranged into order and distributed into classes and subdivision, so that he could tell where they all belonged and run them up to their general heads.[38] Finally there is the opinion of Sir James Mackintosh, that Edwards' power of subtle argument was joined, as in some of the ancient mystics, with a character which raised his piety to fervour. This sentiment is repeated in the most recent study of Edwards, which contends that is was not in the realm of the discursive but of the intuitive understanding that he has his pre-eminence; for his mind in early years seems to have been dominated by the sense of the sublime and beautiful, proportion and symmetry.[39]

Whether or not this element of the mystical and transcendental thought was at variance with his own logic, that element has received considerable recognition. Most pertinent is the opinion that in the critical analysis of the mental outfit of Edwards it would be a gross mistake to overlook the spiritual insight and capacity of feeling, which is one part of the truth in the remark of Mackintosh concerning him, that he was a rationalist and mystic. . . . Let any discerning student take up the treatise on the *Will* and observe the sharp, unrelenting logic in which the author hunts down his opponents, and then let him take up the same author's sermon on the *Nature and Reality of Spiritual Light*, or passages in his book on the *Affections*, or some of the extracts from his *Diary*. It is like passing from the pages of Scotus or Aquinas to Thomas à Kempis or Saint Augustine or Saint Francis of Assisi.[40] This is a suggestion of the psychological side of Edwards' mysticism; what was its correlated philosophical significance has also been recognised. For example, in the early note on 'Excellence,' it is argued that God being Infinite Being, all other being must necessarily be considered as nothing, that 'in metaphysical strictness and propriety, He is and there is no other.' In the latest of the treatises the whole system of created beings is spoken of 'as the light dust of the balance (which is taken no notice of by him that weighs), and as less than vanity. . . .' In harmony with these views, Edwards' type of piety is thoroughly the mystic type, the enjoyment of God in complete self-surrender to His Spirit and the communication of God himself to spirits directly by an immediate illumination. Now, this conception of God is what underlies Edwards' conception of the ideality of the material universe. It is not that the phenomenalism brings with it the idealism: it is the deeper idealism of the thought of God which brings in the phenomenalism.[41] Further recognition of the significance of Edwards' mysticism is given in the suggestion that Edwards may have drawn his conclusion that all existence is mental, the existence of all things ideal, by combining his idea of God as universal existence with the principle derived from Locke that all ideas begin from external sensation; and that with Edwards' premises the transition seems an easy one from the popular belief in the externality of the objects of our sense to a disbelief in the existence of matter.[42]

That Edwards' mysticism was behind his idealism has received abundant recognition, yet what were the more precise relations between the two elements needs fuller elaboration. In a general way, the belief in God as universal existence has been attributed to an high aesthetic interest as the most prominent characteristic. Thus, in the very first of the notes on the *Mind,* essaying to define Excellency, or that which is beautiful and lovely as a thing he is concerned with more than anything else whatsoever, the youthful enthusiast concludes: 'As nothing else has a proper being but spirits, and as bodies are but shadows of being, therefore the consent of bodies one to another, and the harmony that is among them, is but the shadow of excellency. The Highest Excellency, therefore, must be consent of spirits one to another.'[43] In this initial definition there is, indeed, much of the aesthetic; at the same time there is more of the mystical, for the personal insight or direct intuition of the truth is based upon a feeling of union between the self and the absolute. Here Edwards' universal definition of excellency, as the consent of being to being, falls in with his definition of inspiration as an absolute sense of certainty, a knowledge in a sense intuitive, wherein such bright ideas are raised, and such a clear view of a perfect agreement with the excellencies of the Divine Nature, that it is known to be a communication from him; all the Deity appears in the thing, and in everything pertaining to it.[44]

How subtle, pervading and profound was this transcendental element in the development of Edwards' thought may be gathered only in a final review of his system; meanwhile, how fundamental it was, is to be seen in the very earliest of his idealistic fragments, that essay on *Being* which concluded that spirits only are properly substances. In a complete retrospection it is seen that all of Edwards' reflections are marked by aesthetic, intuitive, transcendental characteristics. Upon what were these characteristics based? Leaving aside the external sources as problematical, recourse may be had to the internal, those precocious mystic experiences which have been broadly likened to those of Thomas à Kempis and Francis of Assisi. In their highest manifestations these are ecstasies, transports of feelings, in which thought and will are merged;[45] in their origin and development they pass through a prescribed course or succession. Here the true mystic figures his path as a ladder reaching from earth to heaven; this *scala perfectionis* is usually divided into three stages: the first, the purgative, brought about by contrition and amendment, is valuable in teaching self-discipline and the meaning of order and limitation; the second stage, the illuminative, being the concentration of all the faculties upon God, assumes that to the individual there are vouchsafed intuitive visions of truth, and that feeling is a direct source of knowledge; the last stage, the contemplative, or intuitive, is one wherein man beholds God face to face and is joined to him. The means by which this vision is manifested to consciousness is in ecstasy, which begins where thought ceases to our consciousness; it differs from hallucination because there is no organic disturbance and because it claims to be, not a partial disintegration, but a temporary enhancement of the mental faculties.[46]

Whether or not the Saint of New England was familiar with this mystic progression as presented in the ancient manuals,[47] the record of his interior life, written for his own private benefit, some twenty years after the earliest of the events narrated, falls most naturally into the three given stages, purgative, illuminative and intuitive. As to the first, he tells how he had a variety of concerns and exercises about his soul from his childhood, and two remarkable seasons of awakening before he was brought to that new sense of things which he had since had. But after great and violent inward struggles and the gaining of a spirit to part with all things in the world, there came the first instance of that sort of inward sweet delight in God and divine things.[48] This was the illuminative stage, intimately conjoined and blended with the intuitive. Along with this new sense,—a kind of vision or fixed ideas and imaginations of being alone in the mountains or some solitary wilderness far from all mankind,— there came a thought of being wrapt up to God in heaven, being, as it were, swallowed up in Him forever.[49] This is the extremity of mysticism. What was its entire significance had best be given in Edwards' very words:

> After this my sense of divine things gradually increased, and became more and more lively, and had more of that inward sweetness. The appearance of every thing was altered; there seemed to be, as it were, a calm, sweet cast, or appearance of divine glory, in almost every thing. God's excellency, his wisdom, his purity and love, seemed to appear in every thing; in the sun, moon, and stars; in the clouds, and the blue sky; in the grass, flowers, trees; in the water, and all nature; which used greatly to fix my mind. I often used to sit and view the moon for continuance; and in the day, spent much time in viewing the clouds and sky, to behold the sweet glory of God in these things: in the mean time, singing forth, with a low voice, my contemplations of the Creator and Redeemer. And scarce any thing, among all the works of nature, was so sweet to me as thunder and lightning; formerly, nothing had been so terrible to me. Before, I used to be uncommonly terrified with thunder and to be struck with terror when I saw a thunder-storm rising; but now, on the contrary, it rejoiced me. I felt God, so to speak, at the first appearance of a thunder-storm; and used to take the opportunity, at such times, to fix myself in order to view the clouds, and see the lightnings play, and hear the majestic and awful voice of God's thunder, which oftentimes was exceedingly entertaining, leading me to sweet contemplations of my great and glorious God. While thus engaged, it always seemed natural to me to sing, or chant forth my meditations; or, to speak my thoughts in soliloquies with a singing voice. Holiness, as I then wrote down some of my contemplations on it, appeared to me to be of a sweet, pleasant, charming, serence, calm nature; which brought an inexpressible purity, brightness, peacefulness, and ravishment to the soul. In other words, that it made the soul like a field or garden of God, with all manner of pleasant flowers; all pleasant, delightful, and undisturbed; enjoying a sweet calm, and the gently vivifying beams of the sun. The soul of a true Christian, as I then wrote my meditations, appeared like such a little white flower as we see in the spring of the year; low, and humble on the ground, opening its bosom, to receive the pleasant beams of the sun's glory; rejoicing, as it were, in a calm rapture; diffusing around a sweet fragrancy; standing peacefully and lovingly, in the midst of other flowers round about; all in like manner opening their bosoms, to drink in the light of the sun.

There was no part of creature-holiness, that I had so great a sense of its loveliness, as humility, brokenness of heart, and poverty of spirit; and there was nothing that I so earnestly longed for. My heart panted after this,—to lie low before God, as in the dust; that I might be nothing, and that God might be ALL.[50]

In the concluding passage of this exquisite ecstasy, with its implication of union with the deity, of absorption into the inmost essence of the divine, there appear what have been called the unmistakable marks of the mystic in every age. But in Edwards' full narrative there are also to be found the marks of mysticism from the more modern point of view, and it is by combining the old and the new that there may be gathered some hints as to the idealistic bases of Edwards' philosophy. The psychological marks of mysticism have been recently given as four in number: Ineffability,—the subject of it immediately says that it defies expression, that no adequate report of its contents can be given in words. In this peculiarity mental states are more like states of feeling than like states of intellect. The noetic quality,—although so similar to states of feeling, mystical states seem to those who experience them to be states of knowledge; they are states of insight, illuminations, revelations, full of significance and importance, all inarticulate though they remain. Transiency,—mystical states cannot be sustained for long, their quality can be but imperfectly reproduced in memory, yet this is susceptible of continuous development in what is felt as inner richness and importance. Passivity,—the oncoming of mystical states can be facilitated by preliminary voluntary operations, yet when the characteristic sort of consciousness has once set in, the mystic feels as if his own will were in abeyance.[51]

To apply these criteria to the record of Edwards' inner life is to gain a further insight into those mental processes leading to his idealism. The mark of transiency may be neglected. The brief duration, the constant intermittance, is an accident not an essential of the mystic state. Edwards complained that his earlier affections were lively and easily moved, and that it was only after he had spent most of his time, year after year, in meditation and soliloquy that his sense of divine things seemed gradually to increase. Leaving aside, then, the mark of transiency, one comes to the more important mark of passivity. Here Edwards says in his early notes on the *Mind*: Our perceptions or ideas that we passively receive through our bodies are communicated to us immediately by God. There never can be any idea, thought or action of the mind unless the mind first received some ideas from sensation, or some other way equivalent, wherein the mind is wholly passive in receiving them.[52] Although these particular notes were probably written under the influence of the *Human Understanding*, yet the virtual contradiction of the Lockean sensationalism was not so easy a transition unless the young thinker had some other and deeper basis upon which to rest. This basis appears to have been the mystic experience indirectly referred to in the alternative offered in the foregoing passage; for besides the reception of ideas 'from sensation' there was 'some other way equivalent, wherein the mind is wholly passive in receiving them.'

It is in this emphasis on the passive attitude in the reception of ideas that one fundamental source of Edwards' idealism is to be found. Being essentially subjective, the quietistic state readily lends itself to a sense of the unreality of the external world. In Edwards' language this takes the form of a belief that corporeal things could exist no otherwise than mentally, and that other bodies have no existence of their own; in modern psychological terms the recognition of the unreal sense of things may be laid to a temporary absence of conaesthesia, a transient loss of the sense of the compact reality of the bodily organism. Furthermore, this indirect phenomenalism, this extreme subjectivism, being carried to its logical extreme, might well lead to the conclusion embodied in Edwards' first fragment, the corollary of the essay on *Being*, which protested against the view that material things are the most substantial, and affirmed that spirits only are properly substances.

If these conjectures be true, if Edwards' mystic ecstasies furnished a personal ground for the earliest of his idealistic fragments, the question of originality receives a new light, for that question is shifted from external to internal sources, from a later period of general learning to an earlier period of individual experience. The reading of other authors may have given a form of expression, but a vivid, intense, personal impression furnished in largest measure the substance of Edwards' idealism. Here the convincement of the sovereignty of God had as its philosophical equivalent the belief in the universality of the divine existence, and the ravishment of the spirit, the corresponding assurance of the superiority of the ideal over the material world. Now, if these inferences be true, the probability of the use of external authorities assumes less importance. It may be granted, indeed, that some of the notes on the *Mind* were written so much later than is traditionally allowed, that Edwards was already enabled to learn of Malebranche, with his vision of all things in God, of Norris, with his kindred doctrine of the ideal world, and even of Berkeley, with his divine language of signs. These writers may have furnished Edwards with the outward form of his philosophy, they do not entirely account for the inner substance. In fine, whatever the dress in which his thoughts were clothed, the body of philosophy was the author's own. . . .

That Edwards' thinking is thus far of one texture, that his mysticism and his idealism are most intimately interwoven, is clear from this familiar recurrence, this repeated reminder of the problem of being. Yet, although in his doctrine of the transcendence of divine archetypes, the philosopher has drawn legitimate conclusions from his early idealism, this has not yet issued in a correlated pantheism. Up to this point his interests have lain rather in an illuminative theory of knowledge than in an intuitive theory of being. To explain the impartation of the spiritual sense he has used such significant terms as the communication of the divine, that fulness of all things, that infinite fountain of good, but he has not yet essayed to make an identification of his divinity with the totality of existence. In his posthumous *Dissertation Concerning the End for Which God Created the World*, it would appear that he would fain make that identification, but in the next treatise published in his lifetime there is apparent a certain conscious fear of an issue so fatal to his orthodoxy. In the most famous of his public writings, the *Inquiry on the Will*, there is evident that diversity of thought, that vacillation between two poles of speculation—Augustinianism and pantheism—which renders Edwards liable to the charge of metaphysical duality, a fatal diremption in an otherwise coherent system. This is the duality between Edwards the theologian and Edwards the philosopher. In the one case there is a tendency toward a consistent monism, a doctrine of the absolute based on the mystic longing for the ultimate unity of all existence; in the other, there is a tendency toward an uncritical dualism, a doctrine of immanence being sacrificed to the conventional Calvinistic transcendence. The former doctrine, based on his more personal and more ultimate experiences, may have been one which Edwards preferred for himself; but the latter, being called for by the exigencies of his theological position, he was obliged to teach to others. Nevertheless, beneath this well-worked mine there lay hidden a most precious vein of speculative metal. The chief value of this careful and strict inquiry was long considered to be in its demolition of the Arminian notion of contingency; its chief interest now consists in its disclosure of the personal idealism of its author. Here, it has been asserted that the two elements of this work, its determinism and its idealism, are discrepant and irreconcilable, because they are juxtaposed, not united.[53] But a more genetic view of Edwards' system, as not to be fully understood, except in connection with his inward experiences, makes this position untenable. Traces of Edwards' previous thought have been recognised in the very beginning of the essay, for the initial definition of cause is but the expansion of the former definition in the notes on *Mind*. The latter had briefly said: Cause is that after or upon the existence of which, or the existence of it, after such a manner, the existence of another thing follows. And the former continues:

> Therefore I sometimes use the word *Cause*, in this inquiry, to signify any *antecedent*, either natural or moral, positive or negative, on which an Event, either a thing, or the manner and circumstance of a thing, so depends, that it is the ground and reason, either in whole, or in part, why it is, rather than not; or why it is as it is, rather than otherwise; or, in other words, any antecedent with which a consequent Event is so connected, that it truly belongs to the reason why the proposition which affirms that Event is true; whether it has any positive influence, or not. And agreeably to this, I sometimes use the word effect for the consequence of another thing, which is perhaps rather an occasion than a Cause, most properly speaking.[54]

What is the significance of these kindred definitions some three decades apart? The most recent investigation of the *Inquiry* has brought the pertinent conclusion that upon the idea of cause as thus defined the whole treatise rests, for an event in the realm of mind without a cause is as inconceivable to Edwards as such an one in the realm of matter. This is a great positive argument of the discussion, though rather an assumed axiom than the subject of prolonged elaboration. And thus it comes to pass that into the very foundation of the whole argument there is inserted an ambiguity which, doubtless, deceived Edwards himself, and has given rise to two distinct interpretations of the work. Motives are 'causes' determining the will. Is the motive an occasion upon which the efficient will acts, or itself an efficient cause operating upon the will? Edwards' definition gives no answer to this question, for he has wrapped up in one term both efficient and occasional causes. It is doubtless true that his idealism had much to do with this. If God were the only agent; if, according to the occasionalism of Malebranche, God does everything upon occasion of certain events in the mundane sphere, then there is no essential difference between the occasional and what seems to us to be the efficient cause. But, however the ambiguity was introduced into his thinking, there it was, at the very foundation of the edifice he was about to rear, and destined to make its whole structure insecure to the highest pinnacle.[55]

That the necessarian's earlier metaphysics blended with the later theology is further illustrated by the congruity between his theory of causality and his theory of perception. Here it has been well argued that in Edwards' idealistic opinion as to all external things, perception by created beings is owing to the stable will of God, who not only produces ideas, but, as to things perceived, causes them to be the objects of perception. The question naturally arises whether motives, the antecedents of voluntary action, and their relative strength, are not likewise understood by him as the effect of the stable, constant exercise of the divine will? It must be borne in mind that his usual answer to the objection that if there were no power of alternative choice we should not be responsible for wrong moral choices, is that the wrong of a choice lies not in its cause, but in its nature.[56]

Although the idealistic elements in Edwards' best known treatise may be thus correlated, such a correlation does not explain the occasion, the animus or the extent of that work. Written hurriedly in some four months, while engaged in his missionary labours among the Indians at Stockbridge, the writer acknowledges his purpose to be the bringing of the late objections and outcries against Calvinistic divinity to the test of the strictest reasoning. Here, against the objection that such reasoning is metaphysical and abstruse, he proceeds:

> The question is not, whether what is said be metaphysics, physics, logic, or mathematics, *Latin, French, English,* or *Mohawk?* But whether the reasoning be good, and the arguments truly conclusive? The foregoing arguments are no more metaphysical, than those which we use against the papists, to disprove their doctrine of transubstantiation; alleging it is inconsistent with the notion of corporeal identity, that it should be in ten thousand places at the same time. It is by metaphysical arguments only we are able to prove, that the rational soul is not corporeal, that lead or sand cannot think; that thoughts are not square or round, or do not weigh a pound. The arguments by which we prove the being of God, if handled closely and distinctly, so as to show their clear and demonstrative evidence, must be metaphysically treated. It is by metaphysics only that we can demonstrate, that God is not limited to a place, or is not mutable; that he is not ignorant, or forgetful; that it is impossible for him to lie, or be unjust; and that there is one God only, and not hundreds or thousands. And, indeed, we have no strict demonstration of anything, excepting mathematical truths, but by metaphysics. We can have no proof, that is properly demonstrative, of any one proposition, relating to the being and nature of God, His creation of the world, the dependence of all things on Him, the nature of bodies or spirits, the nature of our own souls, or any of the great truths of morality and natural

religion, but what is metaphysical. I am willing my arguments should be brought to the test of the strictest and justest reason, and that a clear, distinct, and determinate meaning of the terms I use should be insisted on; but let not the whole be rejected, as if all were confuted, by fixing on it the epithet, *metaphysical*.[57]

That in this relish for metaphysics the scholastic theologian was in his element is clear from this defence of his philosophic method; but that he had more than a dialectical interest in his subject is proven by the relentless rigidity with which he pursued the opponents of Calvinism. Owing to the prevailing deism the danger Edwards feared was that men would think that God had left the world to take care of itself.[58] Moreover, as the Arminian idea of freedom of the will seemed an assertion of man at the expense of God, and a self-determining human will a limit placed by the finite upon the infinite, Edwards' object was to bring liberty within limitations, to establish ultimately the absoluteness of the deity. However, before this ultimate purpose can be affected, the ground must be cleared of the old issues. Here the specific question was the Arminian notion of liberty, which is the will's power of determining itself in its own acts, the being wholly active in it without passiveness and without being subject to necessity.[59] Expressed in more modern phrase, the question at issue might be framed as to whether the will be not itself a creative first cause, endowed with the power of initiating acts, of choosing between motives *de novo*.

To this question Edwards' answer was in general that philosophical necessity belongs to the very nature of the will, there having been no loss of liberty, no forfeiture of a prerogative once possessed. Now, as always, man's will is guided by the last dictate of his understanding, and those last dictates depend upon a Providential disposing and determining of men's moral actions.[60] Here the will is defined as that power or principle of the mind by which it is capable of choosing, and the last dictate, as that motive which, as it stands in the view of the mind, is the strongest; that is, the will always is as the greatest apparent good is, the good being that which is agreeable, pleasing and suits the mind. Furthermore, in every volition there is a preference or a prevailing inclination of the soul, whereby at that instant it is out of a state of perfect indifference. These inclinations depend upon moral necessity or causes such as habits and dispositions of the heart, whence moral inability consists in a want of inclination or the strength of a contrary inclination, being opposed to natural inability or some impeding defect or obstacle that is extrinsic to the will.[61]

Given these definitions, one may meet the Arminian notions concerning the will's self-determination, indifference, and contingence. As to the first possibility, it is to be argued that the will is not a self-determining power in and of itself, because we must consider how the person came to have such a volition, whether it was caused by some external motive or habitual bias. Then, too, if the dictate of the understanding be the same as the determination of the will, this is to make the determination of choice prior to the dictate of the understanding. But how can the mind first act and by its act determine what motives shall be the ground for its volition and choice?[62] Arguing against those who say that spirits, which are spirits of an active nature, have the spring of action within themselves, and can determine themselves, the strict necessarian is forced to identify a logical statement with the steps in a chronological process, and, at the same time, artificially to separate volition and determination, as if they were separately process and product. This was a weak argument against those advocates of the sovereignty of the will, who said that the determination of volition must be itself an act of the mind; for an act of the will being a mode of the mind's functioning, if it be free in this functioning, it is free in the act.

But secondly, continues Edwards, to suppose the will to act at all, in a state of perfect indifference, not inclining one way more than another, is to assert that the mind chooses without choosing, whereas the mind must be influenced in its choice by something that has a preponderating influence. Here there is no great difficulty in showing not only that it must needs be so, but also how it is so; for example, being asked to touch some square on a chessboard, my mind is not given up to vulgar accident, but makes the choice from foreign considerations, such as the previous determination to touch that which happens to be most in my eye.[63] In this criticism Edwards appears safe in asserting that the mind can [n]ever be in a perfect state of equilibrium, for, as he says, even the involuntary changes in the succession of our ideas, though the cause may not be observed, have as much of a cause as the continual, infinitely various, successive changes of the unevennesses on the surface of the water. Thirdly, against the belief that an event is not dependent on a cause but, as it were, loose from its influence, it may be argued that the will is not contingent as opposed to all necessity, for the volition must come to pass from some adequate cause, or otherwise the mind would be given up to a wild contingence, as the smoke that is driven by the wind.[64]

With arguments like these does Edwards fill his polemical treatise against such writers as Whitby and Collins, who hold loosely defined notions of free will as including the choosing of choices, choice from a previous indifference or choice apart from all influence of motives. Now, in all this minute and painstaking argumentation, it is evident that recourse has been had to the author's earlier studies, for between Edwards and Locke, as has been pointed out, there is substantial similarity: in both the idea of liberty is the same; of determination by motive; of the different weight of different motives; of the causal relation between motive and action; the argument from causation is in Locke, though obscured by his sensational philosophy; the general conception of the inconceivability of the Arminian position is Locke's; and even the argument of the *reductio ad absurdum*.[65]

And yet for all these similarities and agreements, Edwards' most laboured work cannot be pronounced entirely unoriginal. The weapons of his dialectic may have been borrowed, but the ardour with which he wielded them sprang from a personal conviction. The sharp and relentless determinism of this treatise is one thing, its inward and impelling spirit another. Outwardly the author seems but a man in an iron mask; within there were impulses and feelings more congruous with the beaming eye and sensitive mouth of his portrait. Between Edwards the logician and Edwards the mystic there is here an apparent, but not a real, duality. The view of moral necessity as determining voluntary action appeared hard and mechanical, yet it had a vital connection with that profound belief of the immanence of the deity which was Edwards' earliest achievement. The steps in this conviction are somewhat involved; they may nevertheless be explicated. In giving a double definition of the will, as both that by which the mind chooses anything, and also that by which it desires or inclines to anything, Edwards superimposes the emotional upon the voluntary. This has been generally considered the ordinary eighteenth-century confusion between the sensibility and the will, but for that confusion there was more than a conventional reason. It is indeed a fatal logical error to confound the feelings, the action of which is necessary, with the will, the action of which is free; but that error lay at the bottom of Edwards' peculiar personal experiences. As in his doctrine of mystical insight through sensible knowledge, he had blended the functions of sensibility and intellect, so in his use of the word inclination, as both a preferring and a choosing, he introduces an ambiguous middle term which partakes of the nature of both the involuntary and the voluntary. But to Edwards that ambiguity was no undesirable thing; the identification of inclination with the will, of the passive with the active, was a reminiscence of the receptive attitude of him who sought spiritual co-operation with the deity. That this twofold theory of the will, like a twofold theory of knowledge, seemed no incongruity, is borne out by two previous statements of the author. And he had already said that in sense-impressions the mind is abundantly active, so he had defined an inclination as nothing but God's influencing the soul according to a certain law of nature.[66] In fine, Edwards' ambiguities, the duplications both in his theory of causation and in his theory of knowledge, are to be explained from his idealistic mysticism, for both are founded in a conviction that with complete self-surrender there come not only pure impulses, but attendant reflection.

While in such a double occasionalism Edwards' indebtedness to his mystic experiences has been neglected, his resemblance to other idealists has nevertheless been pointed out. In subordinating his system to the divine will, he has been likened to Berkeley and Johnson; in combining the Platonism of the notes on *Mind* with the moral theory of the treatise on the *Will*, to Malebranche.[67] With these resemblances acknowledged, there still remains the further question of the ultimate issues of this treatise, since it has been suggested that the idealism of Edwards, his view of the immanence of God, and his doctrine of moral necessity as connected with voluntary action would seem to involve pantheism.[68] Edwards, like Geulincx, might seem to teach that men's actions are but modes of the divine mind, but as for teaching a doctrine of blind necessity, the author is at pains to defend his treatise. As he answered the objection to being a Hobbite, by saying that it happens that he never read Hobbes, so he answers the charge of being one of the Stoics, by saying that if they held any such doctrine of Fate, as is inconsistent with the world being in all things subject to the disposal of an intelligent, wise agent, that presides—not as the *soul* of the world, but—as the Sovereign *Lord* of the Universe, governing all things by proper will, choice, and design, in the exercise of the most perfect liberty conceivable, without subjection to any constraint, or being properly under the power or influence of anything before, above, or without himself; I wholly renounce any such doctrine.[69]

In spite of the author's denial of the charge of Stoicism, the tendency of the treatise on the *Will* toward pantheism has been declared probable, because in both earlier and later writings he uses language which identifies God with the world. In his early Notes on the *Mind* he writes: 'God and real existence are the same; God is and there is none else. . . . It is impossible that God should be otherwise than excellent, for He is infinite, universal and all-comprehending excellence.' In his treatise on *Virtue* he writes, that God 'is, in effect, being in general, and comprehends universal existence.' In his late posthumous treatise on the *End of God in Creation* he says of God, that His 'being and beauty is, as it were, the sum and comprehension of all existence and excellence,' much more than the sun is 'the comprehension of all light and brightness of the sky.'[70] Similar views, which would identify God with the totality of the world, have been pointed out as follows: In his initial note on Excellency in *Mind*, as in his sermon on *Divine and Supernatural Light*, Edwards has been said to have manifested his deep aesthetic contemplation, whereby nature, man and God are synthesised, or, more exactly, man and nature are one in God.[71] In like manner, concerning a very early *Observation* that 'the mere exertion of a new thought is a certain proof of a God, and that the substance which brings that thought forth is God,'[72] it has been asserted that such an occasionalistic view might easily pass on to an idealistic pantheism.

In view of these numerous citations, it can hardly be allowed that the grand heroic conception of God comprehending and fulfilling the existence of the infinite variety of the concrete was too sublime a conception for Edwards to have continued to hold.[73] It is true that in the treatise on the *Will* he momentarily forsakes the argument for the existence of God based on the category of substance for the more commonplace argument based on the category of causation; but it is not true that he loses the more poetic and more pantheistic notion of God's all-comprising substance. Indeed, Edwards' most boldly speculative work, *God's Last End in Creation*, has been more adequately described as one whose whole trend is toward a comprehensive idealism which makes God all in all.[74] Here, as Edwards' chief expositor affirms, there appeared, with something of the beauty which had fascinated the vision of his youth, that other element of his thought which, though subordinated, was never annihilated, that conception of God which Plato, Spinoza or Hegel might have held,—the idea of the good, the one substance, the absolute thought unfolding itself or embodying itself in a visible and glorious order. Furthermore, the very title of the work is declared to suggest the profound speculations of Gnostic theosophies, to recall the mystic thinkers of the Middle Ages, for throughout this treatise the Neo-Platonic word 'emanation' is the one about which the thought revolves, and the old phrases, such as the overflow of the divine fulness, diffusion of the divine essence, emanation from God compared with the light and heat which go forth from the sun,—these constitute the verbal signs of Edwards' thought. It is possible that he might have avoided them had he known their earlier associa-tion. But they represent truly the tendency of his mind; they stand for princi-ples which had been lying for years beneath his practical theology.[75]

Further corroboration of the opinion that this same treatise represents an intellectual growth towards a pantheistic form of belief is to be found in the assertion that it was not an unpremeditated work, but largely a construction from his earlier writings, exhibiting a real simplification of his thought and suggestive indications of almost conscious attempts at unification. This intellec-tual growth, it is further explained, would remain altogether enigmatic were it not for the early notes on the *Mind*. Here the trend of Edwards' thinking is not so much disclosed in such Berkeleian expressions as that the 'material universe exists nowhere but in the mind,' as in such pantheistic expressions as these: 'Seeing God has so plainly revealed himself to us, and other minds are made in his image, and are emanations from him; we may judge what is the excellence of other minds by which is his, which we have shown is Love. His Infinite Beauty is his Infinite Mental Love of himself. Now God is the Prime and Original Being, the First and Last, and the Pattern of all, and has the sum of all perfections. We may, therefore, doubtless conclude, that all that is the perfec-tion of spirits may be resolved into that which is God's perfection, which is Love'[76]. . . .

In these passages the New England saint has reached a system more mysti-cal than rational, more in the nature of the ineffable knowledge than in har-mony with what reason dictates in the affair. This he appears to realise in a subsequent question-begging defence, and in a final confession of the inade-quacy of his previous answer: If any are not satisfied with the preceding answer, he continues, let them consider whether they can devise any other scheme of God's last end in creating the world but what will be equally obnoxious. . . . I confess there is a degree of indistinctness and obscurity in the close considera-tion of such subjects, and a great imperfection in the expressions we use con-cerning them, arising unavoidably from the infinite sublimity of the subject and the incomprehensibleness of those things that are divine.[77]

With its final note of ineffability, which marks the transition from the rationalistic to the theological portion of his dissertation, Edwards has reached the height of his philosophical speculation, inasmuch as the other posthumous treatises offer no real solution of the dualistic problem involved, but only a specious promise of an advance in speculation. It has been said that if the Calvinistic theology should be eliminated from the dissertation on the *Nature of True Virtue*, there would remain a conception almost identical with that of Spinoza,[78] but such an elimination was not made.

Disinterested love of God on the part of man, love to being in general on the part of God, are presented as the respective ideals; but it can scarcely be held, as the younger Edwards held, that this is a successful union of two here-tofore supposedly mutually exclusive explanations of the universe, as created either for happiness of finite beings, or as a manifestation of the glory of God.[79] These two contrasted views, the one Arminian, the other Calvinistic, were not harmonised by Edwards, unless a certain passage expounding a sort of aesthetic mysticism be considered the key to the dissertation.[80] After having shown how that love, wherein true virtue consists, respects both the Divine Being and created beings, it is added: That consent, agreement, or union of being to being, which has been spoken of, namely, the union or propensity of *minds* to mental or spiritual existence, may be called the highest and primary beauty; being the proper and peculiar beauty of spiritual and moral beings, which are the highest and first part of the universal system, for whose sake all the rest has existence. . . . The reason, or at least one reason, why God has made this kind of mutual agreement of things beautiful and grateful to those intelligent beings that perceive it, probably is, that there is in it some image of the true, spiritual, original beauty, which has been spoken of, or the union of spiritual beings in a mutual propensity and affection of the heart.[81]

These reasonings constitute an attempt to solve the dualistic problem of God's relation to the ideal and actual worlds, of the infinite to finite minds, yet they are no advance on previous thought. Indeed, they are little but a combination of the author's former conclusions, and may be referred, first, to the incipient Platonism of his essay on *Being*, whereby he puts in the divine mind infinite archetypes, on which the creation is fashioned; next, to the initial topic in his Notes on *Mind*, wherein excellency is defined as the loving consent of spirits one to another; and finally, to his mystical epistemology, a sensible knowledge, or knowledge of the heart, expounded in the *Religious Affections*. Dealing then, as he does, with the immanence of God in nature, Edwards should logically reach the issue of a speculative mysticism which makes the relation of the individual to the absolute less an ethical harmony of two mutually exclusive wills than a fusion of personalities, a union in which there is no longer a consciousness of a distinct life, but a real substitution of divine for human nature.[82] Nevertheless, to make such a transfusion or identification, even the mystic hesitated. His ecstatic desires tended towards the unitive state, his Calvinistic beliefs resulted in a dualism. How his theology thus overshadowed his philosophy has been pointed out in a certain contradiction in the treatise on *Virtue*. If Edwards had said plainly what his theology implies, that the creature has no existence outside of God, his attitude would have been clear and consistent. But he seems also to grant an infinitesimal portion of an independent existence to humanity. He halts between these two opinions, neither of which is quite acceptable to him.[83]

So, too, a certain vacillation on the allied question, whether the creation was an eternal necessity in the nature of the divine being, receives no corrective in the other treatises. A recently recovered manuscript on the *Trinity* deals with the problem of God and his relation to the mundane sphere, but here the author reasons more as a thelogian than a philosopher. In the opening section there is indeed an implication of a cosmic principle immanent in the world, but the unity of that principle is sacrificed to a conventional duality, for that immanence is rendered possible only by supposing that:

God Perpetually and Eternally has a most Perfect Idea of himself, as it were, an exact Image and Representation of himself ever before him and in actual view, & from hence arises a most pure and Perfect act or energy in the Godhead, which is the divine Love, Complacence and Joy. . . . However, if God beholds himself so as thence to have delight & Joy in himself he must become his own Object. There must be a duplicity. There is God and the Idea of God, if it be Proper to call a conception of that that is purely spiritual an Idea.[84]

By adopting a traditional doctrine of the logos as a mediating principle between Creator and creation, Edwards has sacrificed the philosophical unification of his system to theological teaching. Moreover, he finally confesses that he does not pretend to explain his subject so as to render it no longer a mystery, for he thinks it to be the highest and deepest of all divine mysteries still.[85] With this note of ineffability, denoting a certain metaphysical impotence, one may leave the writings of Jonathan Edwards. His unpublished manuscripts may afford some corrective to the grave deficiencies of his philosophical system, but, until they are given to the public, one is forced to the abrupt conclusion that, while the Saint of New England was a precocious idealist and a profound mystic, he was not a consistent philosopher.

## Notes

1. V. G. Allen, *Jonathan Edwards* (Boston, 1889), p. 12.

2. H. N. Gardiner, *Jonathan Edwards: A Retrospect* (New York, 1901), p. 144.

3. E. C. Smyth, *Jonathan Edwards' Idealism, American Journal of Theology*, 1 (1897), p. 953, quoting MS. copy of 'Miscellanies,' f. p. 1173, and pp. p. 1.

4. Noah Porter, *Discourse at Yale College on the 200th Birthday of Bishop Berkeley* (New York, 1885), p. 71.

5. This summary is taken chiefly from the views of Allen, Curtis, Fisher, Gardiner and Smyth.

6. Cf. his *Life of Edwards* (New York: Converse, 1829), p. 40.

7. *Discourse at Yale College on the 200th Birthday of Bishop Berkeley*, 1885, p. 71.

8. *Life of Berkeley*, p. 182; Berkeley's *Principles*, 1871, p. xviii.

9. Fraser's 1901 edition of Berkeley's *Works*, III, 398. Compare also a letter to the writer, 9th July, 1906, in which Professor Fraser says: 'Edwards too (at least in his youth) embraced Berkeley, although I do not think he has named him.'

10. G. P. Fisher, *An Unpublished Essay of Edwards on the Trinity* (New York, 1903), p. 18.

11. Gardiner, p. 138.

12. Gardiner, p. 147.

13. Gardiner, p. 141.

14. See preceding chapter.

15. Gardiner, p. 140.

16. E. C. Smyth, *PAAS*, 10 (1900), 251.

17. Porter, p. 71.

18. Allen, p. 19 note.

19. F. B. Dexter, *The Manuscripts of Jonathan Edwards*, p. 15, reprint from the *PMHS*, 15 (1902).

20. Gardiner, pp. 145–146.

21. Gardiner, pp. 147–149.

22. So H. N. Gardiner in a letter to the writer, 14th May, 1906.

23. Gardiner, p. 151.

24. Frank Hugh Foster, *Genetic History of New England Theology* (Chicago, 1907), p. 64.

25. J. H. MacCracken, *Jonathan Edwards' Idealismus* (Halle, 1899), p. 32.

26. M. M. Curtis, *Kantean Elements in Edwards* (Berlin, 1906), p. 40.

27. Smyth, *Early Writings*, p. 234.

28. Lyon, *Idéalisme*, p. 433.

29. *Mind*, § 40.

30. *Mind*, § 27.

31. Curtis, p. 40.

32. Foster, p. 48 note.

33. Curtis, p. 40. Cf. below book V, Chapter VI.

34. Smyth, *Early Writings*, pp. 235–236.

35. F. B. Sanborn, *Journal of Speculative Philosophy* 17 (1883).

36. F. J. E. Woodbridge, *PhR*, 13 (1904), 407.

37. Cf. W. H. Squires, *The Edwardean* 1 (1903), 32–50, for the panegyrics of Maurice, Blakey, Morrell, A. Campbell Fraser, Leslie Stephen, Fichte, etc.

38. *Mind*, § 17.

39. Curtis, p. 35.

40. Fisher, *Edwards on the Trinity*, pp. 14, 21.

41. Gardiner, pp. 158–159.

42. Allen, pp. 12–13.

43. *Mind*, § 1.

44. *Ibid*, § 20.

45. G. P. Fisher, *History of Christian Doctrine* (New York, 1896), p. 12.

46. W. R. Inge, *Christian Mysticism* (London, 1899), Chapter I.

47. In his *Diary*, December 18th, 1722, Edwards says that he does not remember that he experienced regeneration exactly in those steps, in which divines say it is generally wrought, but in his *Affections* he refers to the ancient anchorites and hermits.

48. Edwards, *Diary*, pp. LIV, LV.

49. *Diary*, LV.

50. *Diary*, p. LV.

51. William James, *Varieties of Religious Experiences* (Boston, 1902), pp. 380–381.

52. Allen, pp. 12–13.

53. F. J. E. Woodbridge, p. 399.

54. *Will*, p. 15.

55. Foster, pp. 64–65.

56. Fisher, *Trinity*, p. 39.

57. *Will*, p. 85.

58. For an exposition of Edwards' anti-deistic opuscle, 'The Insufficiency of Reason as a Substitute for Revelation,' cf. Curtis, p. 49 ff.

59. *Will*, p. 40.

60. *Ibid*, pp. 17, 40, 68, 78.

61. *Ibid*, pp. 5–11.

62. *Will*, pp. 14, 26, 27.

63. *Ibid*, pp. 12, 20, 21, 22, 41.

64. Will, p. 41.

65. Foster, p. 76.

66. *Miscellanies*, No. 301 (MS.).

67. Lyon, pp. 435–437.

68. Fisher, *Trinity*, p. 40.

69. *Will*, p. 69.

70. Fisher, *Trinity*, p. 40.

71. Curtis, p. 36.

72. Smyth thinks that this *Observation* was composed not far from the year 1727 (p. 957).

73. J. H. MacCracken, *The Sources of Jonathan Edwards' Idealism, PhR*, 11 (1902), 32.

74. Gardiner, pp. 156–157.

75. Allen, pp. 21, 327–331.

76. Woodbridge, pp. 399–407.

77. *Creation*, pp. 102, 106.

78. Woodbridge, p. 402.

79. Jonathan Edwards, Jr., in Williston Walker, *Ten New England Leaders* (New York, 1901), p. 254.

80. A. T. Ormond (*PhR*, 13 [1904], 181) considers the key to Edwards' philosophy to be found in his treatise on *Decrees and Election*, § 58, in a passage similar to the above.

81. *Virtue*, pp. 125, 127, 128.

82. Cf. Inge, *Christian Mysticism*, pp. 28, 29.

83. Allen, p. 319 note.

84. *Trinity*, pp. 77, 80.

85. *Ibid*, p. 117.

# Edwards, Locke, and
# the Rhetoric of Sensation

Perry Miller°

## I

"Tell me, Hylas," demands the interlocutor in Bishop Berkeley's *Three Dialogues,* the Socratic Philonous who is the transparent disguise for Berkeley himself, "hath every one a liberty to change the current proper signification attached to a common name in any language?" Can he call fire water, or trees men? The hapless Hylas, who perfectly embodies the received, enlightened, respectable opinion of 1713, is bound to answer in only one way, bound to fall into Philonous' trap, for Hylas is, inevitably, a reader of John Locke. Of course not, he replies, such conduct would not be rational, because "common custom is the standard of propriety in language."[1]

Neither Berkeley nor his alter ego had any intention—indeed they were not capable—of refuting Locke. Men of the early eighteenth century were not so much the beneficiaries of Locke as they were his prisoners. Try as he might, Berkeley could not transcend the *Essay Concerning Human Understanding;* he could only alter a few emphases and enlarge the method. So, being resolved to deny the existence of "an absolute external world," not only did he have to commence with the sensational psychology, not only did he have to borrow Locke's method even while extending the critique to primary as well as secondary qualities, but he had, still more unavoidably, to accept Locke's third book, the treatise on the nature of language, and then try to bend it to his own devices. He had to prove upon sound Lockean principles that even Locke, by persisting in his belief in material substance, was, despite his own Book III, entangled in "the embarras and delusion of Words."[2]

For two or three generations after 1690 practically all the theorizing upon language attempted by English or colonial American writers, and much of that on the Continent, was a reworking or reinterpretation of Locke. Vast differences slowly began to emerge, but the starting points remained, into what we call the romantic era, those of Book III; perhaps these are even yet the tacit

° Reprinted by permission of the publisher from *Errand into the Wilderness* by Perry Miller (Cambridge: The Belknap Press of Harvard University Press). Copyright (c) 1956 by the President and Fellows of Harvard College.

assumptions of schools that are hostile to the Lockean temper. Locke's own motive for devoting a section to language (he says that he had not intended such a discussion, but that as he proceeded he found "so near a connexion" of words, which interpose themselves between the understanding and truth, with knowledge that he could not escape the challenge)[3] was simple: he blamed theological disputatiousness, the word-spinning of "schoolmen," for the commotions of Europe. If words could be reduced to what in fact they are, mere sounds, which "in their first original, and their appropriated use" do not stand for clear or distinct ideas, then the "disputing natural and moral philosophers of these latter ages" could be silenced and the soft voice of reason at last be heard.[4] "The multiplication and obstinacy of disputes, which have so laid waste the intellectual world, is owing to nothing more than to this ill-use of words."[5] More than any other influence, except perhaps sheer exhaustion, Locke's treatise brought about that cessation from acrimonious theological pamphleteering with which English Protestantism greeted the new century. But John Locke, who died in 1704, did not live long enough to see that, whereas his downright and common-sensical doctrine delivered men from the wrangling of theologians, it raised up as many problems as it solved and condemned mankind to a new, and almost as bad-tempered, warfare of rhetoricians.

After a century of it, human endurance weakened, and the reëxamination of Locke became a revulsion, identifying him and all his commentators with an era declared to have been dead to the things it knew not and wed to "musty laws lined out with wretched rule." Only in our own day, when one may safely suggest that the romantic denunciation was possibly excessive, can it be perceived that the Lockean analysis actually posed the very terms in which the romantic counterrevolution was phrased, and that, with all its fatal limitations, his was a heroic effort to come to grips with the problem of language. To the extent that our own conception of speech has become less transcendental, that the Coleridgean and Emersonian belief in the word becoming one with the thing no longer seems plausible, we find ourselves, to some extent, facing once more the issues posed by the third book of the *Essay Concerning Human Understanding*.

Locke's treatise exerted so profound an influence on the eighteenth century not only because of his felicity in phrasing the doctrine, but because the doctrine itself was the culmination and synthesis of a development that had been gathering way for a century. It was, one might say, the final recognition and acceptance of the consequences for philology of the scientific revolution. The essence of Locke's theory is that language, like government, is artificial; it rests upon contract, and neither vocabulary nor syntax have any inherent or organic rationale. By themselves, words are only noises, having no transcendental or preternatural correspondence with articulate sounds and certain ideas," and a specific word serves as the sensible mark of a particular idea only "by a perfect voluntary imposition."[6] Meaning is arbitrary, the result of social convention. And therefore—to Locke's adherents this was the liberating discovery—words are *separable* from things. They are related to reality according to nothing more than their conscious designation by society, and no utterance can convey meaning to anyone who does not accept, who is too boorish or too eccentric to accept, the manners of society.

Behind this formulation lay the long effort of the partisans of nature to achieve, against the futilities of the Scholastics and the pretensions of sectaries, what they fondly expected would be the serenity of a universal and sane truth, a truth that would have the further advantage of utility in mechanics and accounting. By making words their target, they executed a flank attack on theologians. "Words," said Bacon, setting the theme his followers were assiduously to enlarge, "as a Tartar's bow, do shoot back upon the understandings of the wisest, and mightily entangle and pervert the judgment." Verbiage is the enemy, which makes it impossible for men "to follow and as it were to hound nature in her wanderings."[7] By the middle of the seventeenth century, the chorus was swelling: the "guardians and tutors" of mankind, said Cowley, have withheld him from nature's endless treasure by distracting him with painted scenes, but Bacon at last has turned his mind from words, "which are but Pictures of the Thought," to things, "the Mind's right object"; he who now would make "an exact Piece" must disregard the images of fancy, and

> before his sight must place
> The Natural and Living Face;
> The real Object must command
> Each Judgment of his Eye, and Motion of his Hand.[8]

The manifesto of the Royal Society, Bishop Sprat's *History* of 1667, was studied with condemnations of "notional wandrings," "imaginary ideas of conceptions," demonstrations "onely fitted for talk," and proudly asserted that the aim of the society was "to separate the knowledge of Nature, from the colours of Rhetorick, the devices of Fancy, or the delightful deceit of Fables."[9] In Locke, therefore, Sprat's ideal of style, freed from the domination of colors, devices, and deceits, maintaining "an inviolable correspondence between the hand and the brain," received at last a psychological and physiological justification. Locke proved by the nature of things that when men "set their thoughts more on words than things," they are employing terms learned "before the ideas are known for which they stand," and therefore could not possibly know what was being talked about.[10] Fortified by his authority, the doctrines of the separableness of words from objects and of the artificial origin of language became the dominant stereotypes of the eighteenth century. Gathering up the platitudes of the new criticism, Alexander Pope declared in 1711,

> Words are like leaves; and where they most abound,
> Much fruit of sense beneath is rarely found.[11]

Typical spokesmen, like Adam Smith in 1759, declared that the names of objects are merely "assigned,"[12] and Hugh Blair in 1783 epitomized the whole theory in a sentence: "Words, as we now employ them, taken in general, may be considered as symbols, not as imitations; as arbitrary, or instituted, not natural signs of ideas."[13]

Hence Berkeley, who may be said to inaugurate a minority report in the "age of reason," executed a strategic maneuver when, far from calling in question the fundamental premises of Locke, as a Cambridge Platonist might or as Leibniz did, he accepted entirely the analysis of language and then proceeded to argue that from it followed consequences utterly opposite to the comfortable assurances of Locke and the popularizers of Newton. Granted that language is a social convention, as arbitrary as one wished, had not Locke, by the rigor of his own logic, been forced to assert that the correspondence was arranged not between the word and a material object, but between the word and an idea in a man's head? Locke's "new way of reasoning by ideas" had to see words as simply impacts on the senses that were artificially linked with other impacts derived from objects; what men experienced as gold they called "gold," but properly speaking, the word applied to the experience, not to the material. Locke could not see why anyone should be disturbed over this consideration. As he worked out his psychology, he found that the basic components of thought were "simple ideas," which did come directly into the mind from concrete objects; hence the elements of speech, the vocabulary of basic English, so to speak, would be attached to those mental entities "only to be got by those impressions objects themselves make on our minds, by the proper inlets appointed to each sort."[14] Since all men possess the same inlets, they would get the same impressions; gold would be experienced as gold, and the word "gold," though in itself simply a vibration of the ether, would stand securely for one, and only for one, thing. This was an adequate basis for coherent society—or for "the comfort and advantage of society,"[15] which was all Locke wanted. The social compact and the rights of property rested firmly on the assurance, given by psychology, that a man can make articulate signs "stand as marks for the ideas within his mind."[16]

There was one slight danger to guard against. Even Cowley, naïvely assuming that the real object could directly command the judgment, had still confessed, although in parentheses, that we do "perversely" draw our thoughts sometimes from words. Sociable creature though he was, Locke was obliged to perceive that the process of attaching words to ideas might be reversible. A name is normally affixed to the idea derived from experience, but in the temporal order of experience the name may come first and so excite the idea, or some idea, before the object has even been met. By custom and education, Locke agreed, words are indeed assumed to stand for the things; the connection between "certain sounds and the ideas they stand for" becomes, by constant use, so intimate "that the names heard, almost as readily excite certain ideas as if the objects themselves, which are apt to produce them, did actually affect the senses." Obviously, children learn many words before they know the things, and adult discourse, consisting largely of general terms, actually requires that speakers do not perpetually have in mind, or put into words, all the component ideas, let alone the myriad sensations, that enter into an "abstract idea."[17] If they did, they would be bores!

Locke had no intention of augmenting boredom. In fact, by the mechanics of his psychology, an elision of detail was eminently to be expected: "ideas become general, by separating from them the circumstances of time and place, and any other ideas that may determine them to this or that particular existence."[18] The principle of separation, which accounts for the origin of language in general, also operates within language; thus a generalized name—honor, truth, regeneration, grace, matter—becomes affixed to this or that abstract idea. So far, so good; but did not Locke run the danger, at the end of his subtlety, of introducing by the back door the very "imaginary ideas of conceptions" he and the scientists had expelled by the front? Was he admitting, after all, that there are some words, the very words over which the wars had been fought, from which men might legitimately, instead of perversely, draw their thoughts?

Locke's answer was emphatically no. He protected his argument against this objection by his ingenious distinction between simple ideas and all the forms of complex ideas: mixed modes, relations, and substances. Simple ideas are the hard pellets of sensation, the irreducible atoms of impression, out of which complex ideas are built; simple ideas—this is the heart of Locke's conception—can be given a name only by those who have first had the sensation. No word alone can impart a simple idea, and therefore such ideas "are not capable of any definition"; "all the words in the world, made use of to explain or define any of their names, will never be able to produce in us the idea it stands for." He who has never tasted "pine apple" cannot get, from any number of words, "the true idea of the relish of that celebrated and delicious fruit."[19] This was Locke's major contribution to the Enlightenment, his weapon against enthusiasm, incantation, and priestcraft, his guarantee against perversity. The primary alphabet of thought simply cannot be taken from words; words can only be attached subsequently, by public agreement, to indubitable shocks of sense. This was the way to achieve what Sprat had defined as the goal of the Royal Society, the correspondence of hand and brain, the way—once and for all—to emancipate the solid knowledge of nature from the frivolous and discordant colors of rhetoric.

Thereafter the sailing was clear. Complex ideas are mechanical compositions of the simples, made not from new or unitary sensations but by "putting together those which the mind had before." They are wholly, completely "voluntary," "put together in the mind, independent from any original patterns in nature." Complex ideas do not need to correspond to real conjunctions of simple ideas in nature; they are "always suited to the end for which abstract ideas are made"—which is to say, for counters in civilized conversation—and as long as everybody is agreed, they will serve.[20] They are economical, because they collect an abundance of particulars into "short sounds," and they can never (except to enthusiasts!) become the instigators of perverse thoughts, because they are always definable. That is, they can always be resolved back into their components. Since they "depend on such collections of ideas as men have made, and not on the real nature of things,"[21] there is no need to fight about them: if a dispute threatens, all we need do is to take apart the complex idea in question, see what differences appear in our respective inventories of impressions, and so come to an accommodation. "A definition is best made by enumerating those simple ideas that are combined in the signification of the term defined."[22]

That the terms of theology and ethics, the words over which Christendom had been rent, were "mixed modes," Locke was well aware; he thought he might do "some service to truth, peace, and learning, if, by any enlargement on this subject, I can make men reflect on their own use of language," because this would be to make them aware that both they and their opponents might have good words in their mouths "with very uncertain, little, or no signification."[23] They might even, he insinuated, begin to suspect that because the revealed will of God happens to be clothed in words, doubt and confusion unavoidably attend that sort of conveyance; whereas in nature, in the realm of the simple ideas, "the precepts of Natural Religion are plain, and very intelligible to all mankind, and seldom come to be controverted."[24] If the concept of predestination, for instance, is in fact nothing but a bundle of particulars, then unloosening the thongs and spreading out the collection of elements may make for pleasant discourse over the port—"for easier and readier improvement and communication of their knowledge"[25]—but surely not for the splitting of skulls.

Berkeley improved upon this logic by insisting that Locke did not go far enough. The premise being that language is separable from reality, a word would therefore have meaning only so long as it could be attached, either immediately or by stopping to think, to an idea framed in the mind of speaker and listener; consequently, the name of a complex idea would be viable only so long as both agreed that if they took the time to investigate it they would turn up the same array of simple ideas. Thereupon Berkeley pounced upon Locke's admission that in social intercourse, men do get along without the investigation, that for indefinite periods the word serves from man to man without anybody's really entertaining the idea. If the idea can be dispensed with temporarily, need it ever be required? If it is unnecessary, does it exist? "It is one thing for to keep a name constantly to the same *definition*, and another to make it stand everywhere for the same *idea*: the one is necessary, the other useless and impracticable."[26] In other words, it is entirely logical, on the basis of the sensational psychology, to argue that the names of complex ideas, being only human constructions for social ends, for converse over the port, do not stand for any ideas at all and never have stood for any; that they are merely words and nothing but words. If a bundle has to be resolved back into its particulars in order to be defined, the particulars are the definition, and bundles are simply "fictions and contrivances of the mind."[27]

For certain words—Berkeley concentrated on "matter"—there obviously are no corresponding ideas; the whole business is a social makeshift, and Locke, for all his precaution, had failed to hound nature in her wanderings. Those indeed advise well, Berkeley continued, who tell us to attend our ideas and not the absurd opinions which grow out of words, but they have not heeded their own counsel "so long as they thought the only immediate use of words was to signify ideas, and that the immediate signification of every general name was a determinate abstract idea."[28] Locke and the Lockeans had, in short, fallen into the error of contending, in the face of their own logic, that whereas no word can engender a simple idea, a word standing for an intricate conception, if susceptible of definition, can communicate a nexus of ideas. The result was that they still tried to use such a word as "matter" as though it could summon up an idea, when to the simplest introspection it was evident that no such idea ever had existed or could exist. But Locke, we remember, had classified the concept of matter, along with all mixed modes and substances, under the head of complex ideas, which included also the propositions of Christian theology, such as resurrection, regeneration, and reprobation. Was Berkeley alone or peculiar in sensing a terrible deficiency in the very center of the rational optimism? Did he, in fact, realize how enormous the deficiency was? Was it the century's desire for stability and its want of logical acumen that induced so many businessmen and divines to accept Locke with a sigh of relief, in the confidence that life could now become genial, enthusiasm unfashionable, and Christianity reasonable, that language could at last be so brought under control that it would no longer "insinuate wrong ideas, move the passions, and thereby mislead the judgment"?[29]

Suppose there were a mind as acute as Berkeley's, no less prepared to seize upon the weakness of the sensational rhetoric and yet equally convinced that the terms of the analysis were correct; and suppose that this mind, not so much concerned with the purely metaphysical issue of materialism and appreciating that there never had been an age "wherein strength and penetration of reason, extent of learning, exactness of distinction, correctness of style, and clearness of expression, did so abound," was also convinced that never was there an age "wherein there has been so little sense of the evil of sin"? If this mind, fully possessed of the doctrine of the sensational rhetoric, were also persuaded that "our people do not so much need to have their heads stored, as to have their hearts touched; and they stand in the greatest need of that sort of preaching, that has the greatest tendency to do this,"[30] would he be content with refinements on the Lockean metaphysics, or would he see in the Lockean theory of language a help to that of which the people had greatest need? What would he therefore do with it? What could he do?

## II

There is no evidence that Jonathan Edwards ever read Berkeley. He did read Locke, probably in 1717 when he was fourteen years of age—read him with more pleasure, he recollected, "than the most greedy miser finds, when gathering up handfuls of silver and gold, from some newly discovered treasure."[31] In 1727 he went up the river to become colleague pastor with his magnificent grandfather at Northampton, and two years later to assume the sole spiritual dictatorship of the most turbulent town in New England. He went there to preach, to touch the people's hearts and not to store their heads, but his own head was full of Newton and Locke; while Newton had impressed upon him the inviolable connection of cause and effect, Lock had taught him that in general the words used by parsons "signified nothing that really existed in nature."[32] The frontiersmen, farmers, aspiring merchants, and land speculators who made up pioneer Northampton existed in nature, and to them Edwards was to preach the New England theology, as complicated a collection of mixed modes as could be imagined. Meanwhile, he had read in Locke that the mixed modes which constitute the propositions of theology are "for the most part such whose component parts nowhere exist together." Hence his mission was defined for him: "It is the mind alone that collects them, and gives them the union of one idea: and it is only by words enumerating the several simple ideas which the mind has united, that we can make known to others what their names stand for."[33]

As a student and tutor at New Haven, Edwards had already jotted down his *Notes on the Mind,* which to historians have seemed so to echo Berkeley that they have supposed an influence; in fact the similarity stems from Edwards' having also, and precociously, grasped the implication of the Lockean postulate. For Berkeley it led inescapably to a stylistic injunction: "Whatever ideas I consider, I shall endeavour to take them bare and naked into my view";[34] for the young Edwards, acceptance of the sensational psychology was a commitment, for a lifetime of effort, "to extricate all questions from the least confusion of ambiguity of words, so that the ideas shall be left naked."[35]

Within a few years at Northampton he was preaching naked ideas in this fashion:

> How dismal will it be, when you are under these racking torments, to know assuredly that you never, never shall be delivered from them; to have no hope: when you shall wish that you might but be turned into nothing, but shall have no hope of it; when you shall wish that you might be turned into a toad or a serpent, but shall have no hope of it; when you would rejoice, if you might but have any relief, after you shall have endured these torments millions of ages, but shall have no hope of it; when after you shall have worn out the age of the sun, moon, and stars, in your dolorous groans and lamentations, without any rest day or night, or one minute's ease, yet you shall have no hope of ever being delivered; when after you shall have worn out a thousand more such ages, yet you shall have no hope, but shall know that you are not one whit nearer to the end of your torments; but that still there are the same groans, the same shrieks, the same doleful cries, incessantly to be made by you, and that the smoke of your torment shall still ascend up forever and ever; and that your souls, which have been agitated with the wrath of God all this while, yet will still exist to bear more wrath; your bodies, which shall have been burning and roasting all this while in these glowing flames, yet shall not have been consumed, but will remain to roast through an eternity yet, which will not have been at all shortened by what shall have been past.[36]

By such rhetoric he whipped up a revival in 1734, and a still greater one in 1740, which, with the help of Whitefield, spread over all New England, became a frenzy and a social upheaval, and then burned itself out in a sullen resentment against its begetter and resulted in Edwards' expulsion from Northampton. Students have worried over how Edwards ever got from his early devotion to Locke, with the denunciation of "magisterial, positive, and imperious" ways of "imposing our own sense and interpretation"[37] on the Bible, to his later and indubitably imperious utterance. They have assumed that he could not have read Locke carefully; actually, he read Locke so profoundly that the progress from Book III of the *Essay* to the apocalyptic terrors of his revival sermons seemed to him not only logical but irresistible.

Edwards became a revolutionary artist in the midst of the eighteenth century because he took with painful seriousness Locke's theory that words are separable from all reality, natural or spiritual, and in themselves are only noises. "Sounds and letters are external things, that are the objects of the external senses of seeing and hearing"; therefore, he told his people, "ideas of certain marks upon paper, such as any of the twenty-four letters, in whatever order, or any sounds of the voice, are as much external ideas, as of any other shapes or sounds whatsoever."[38] Hence, "words are of no use any otherwise than as they convey our own ideas to others."[39] Out of the Lockean psychology, for instance, he could readily explain the failure of the educational methods employed by his enemies in Stockbridge upon the Indian children, who were being taught, Edwards reported, to read words merely as sensations and not as signs of ideas, "without any kind of knowledge of the meaning of what they read." They were being permanently disabled from ever getting knowledge by their "habit of making such and such sounds, on the sight of such and such letters, with a perfect inattentiveness to meaning." The proper method, "a rational way of teaching" either in the schoolroom or in the pulpit, would be to attach every word to an idea, so that eventually the words would provoke the concept: "Being long habituated to make sounds without connecting any ideas with them, they so continue until they come to be capable of well understanding the words, and would perhaps have the ideas, properly signified by the words, naturally excited in their minds on hearing the words, were it not for an habitual hearing and speaking them without any ideas." Edwards was an unbreakable, and unbendable, man; he would never admit that the methods he used to instigate the Awakening were wrong, even after they failed him; in the midst of his bitter exile, he unrepentantly insisted, "The child should be taught to understand *things*, as well as *words*."[40]

In his notebooks Edwards came back again and again to the troubling theme which was the crux, as he saw it, not only of his own problem but, in view of what the people most needed, of that of the age. The one incontrovertible and yet disastrous fact, "duly considering human nature," was simply that a great part of our discourse about things can be conducted without "the actual ideas" of the things in our mind, that "the mind makes use of signs instead of the ideas themselves."[41] This ability was obviously a consequence of the sensational psychology; it was immensely useful in practical affairs because it saved time; it enabled a man to run his eye down a page and take in a staggering array of abstract terms—"God, man, angel, people, misery, happiness, salvation, destruction, consideration, perplexity, sanctification"—without having to stop and frame a conception for every word. "If we must have the actual ideas of everything that comes in our way in the course of our thoughts, this would render our thoughts so slow as to render our power of thinking in great measure useless."[42] But granted these conveniences, nevertheless a terrible prospect followed: thinking can get along without being employed about things or ideas; it can operate entirely with those artificial signs which the mind habitually substitutes for reality. Profitable though the device may be for warfare, business, and speculation, what is it but the supreme manifestation of original sin? It is the negation of life, the acceptance of substitutes, of husks without the corn. Actually to know something, actually to live, is to deal with ideas themselves, for which words must remain forever the inadequate, because arbitrary, symbols:

> To have an actual idea of a thought, is to have that thought we have an idea of then in our minds. To have an actual idea of any pleasure or delight, there must be excited a degree of that delight. So to have an actual idea of any trouble or kind of pain, there must be excited a degree of that pain or trouble. And to have an idea of any affection of the mind, there must be, then present, a degree of that affection.[43]

In one of the several astonishing passages of his notebooks, Edwards worked out in a significant image the immense distinction between knowledge of the word and knowledge of the actuality for which the word is a substitute:

> When we have the idea of another's love to a thing, if it be the love of a man to a woman [whom] we are unconcerned about, in such cases we have not generally any further idea at all of his love, we only have an idea of his actions that are the effects of love, as we have found by experience, and of those external things which belong to love and which appear in case of love; or if we have any idea of it, it is either by forming our ideas so of persons and things as we suppose they appear to them that we have a faint vanishing notion of their affections, or—if the thing be a thing that we so hate that this can't be—we have our love to something else faintly and least excited: and so in the mind, as it were, referred to this place, we think this is like that.[44]

To know the love of a woman only from the *signs* displayed by another man in love, and to deduce from this that what he feels must resemble some lesser feeling of one's own, bears the same relation to one's actually loving a woman that the word bears to the idea.

When we come to the words of theology, the problem of getting from the term to the idea becomes difficult in the extreme. Instead of striving with ourselves to excite in ourselves the constituent ideas of the complex conception, "and so having actually such an abstract idea as Mr. Locke speaks of," we content ourselves with "only an idea of something in our mind, either a name, or some external sensible idea, that we use as a sign to represent that idea."[45] But in the face of this dilemma, it never occured to Edwards, as it had to Berkeley, to solve his problem by denying the reality of the abstract idea—which is presumptive proof that Edwards was unaffected by Berkeley. He remained, on this point, faithful to Locke: the way to comprehend an abstract idea was, for him, not to deny it, but to define it. "If we are at a loss concerning a connection or consequence, or have a new inference to draw, or would see the force of some new argument, then commonly we are put to the trouble of exciting the actual idea, and making it as lively and clear as we can; and in this consists very much of that which we call attention of the mind in thinking."[46] But to excite the actual idea of certain realities, of the love of woman or the fear of God, for example, does indeed put us to "trouble." And it was precisely here that Edwards went beyond Locke, far beyond him! He reached into a wholly other segment of psychology, the realm of the passions, and linked the word not only with the idea but also with that from which Locke had striven to separate it, with the emotions.

Edwards' great discovery, his dramatic refashioning of the theory of sensational rhetoric, was his assertion that an idea in the mind is not only a form of perception but is also a determination of love and hate. To apprehend things only by their signs or by words is not to apprehend them at all; but to apprehend them by their ideas is to comprehend them not only intellectually but passionately. For Edwards, in short, an idea became not merely a concept but an emotion. Thus he could achieve, to the bewilderment of his opponents, his radical definition of grace as "a new simple idea," and thereby elevate the central Christian experience entirely above the ambiguities of the mixed modes. He went so far as to distinguish the emotional from the intellectual apprehension by calling it the truly "sensible" method, and to whisper to himself in the seclusion of his study, "Perhaps this distribution of the kinds of our knowledge into Speculative and Sensible, if duly weighed, will be found the most important of all."[47] For Edwards it was the most important achievement of his life and the key to his doctrine and practice.

Again he presents a strange parallel to Berkeley, though now with an important difference. As soon as Berkeley had proved, out of Locke's own principles, that words can function in communication without there being any idea involved or, as with abstractions, even existing, he was ready to suggest that words, simply as physiological stimuli, could operate not by actually communicating anything but by "the raising of some passion, the exciting to or deterring from an action, the putting the mind in some particular disposition." He entreated his readers to answer honestly if they had not, upon hearing certain discourses, experienced passions of fear or love or admiration "without any ideas coming between." Yet even with his logical destruction of abstract ideas to support him, Berkeley knew that when he claimed for language the right of working as a mere provoker of emotion, without the intermediacy of concepts, he was challenging the reigning complacency of the age: it is "commonly supposed," he noted, that "the communicating of ideas marked by words is . . . the chief and only end of language."[48] The Lockeans were positive on this point: consigning emotion to the pathology of enthusiasm, Locke explicitly limited the function of language to making known one man's thoughts or ideas to another, to doing it easily, and to conveying the knowledge of things.[49] Once more Locke was resolutely consolidating the gains of the recent scientific offensive; Sprat, for example, had lamented that tropes and figures, which originally had been intended to "bring Knowledge back again to our very senses, from when it was at first deriv'd," were in this degenerate age being used, in defiance of reason, to correspond "with its Slaves, the Passions!"[50] Locke's triumph, by restricting the validity of words to their matching ideas, seemed to preclude their ever being used again by civilized men as the goads of passion; and yet by 1710 Berkeley was soberly maintaining that, since there are words which symbolize abstract ideas, when in reality no such ideas can be conceived, at least such words must be used in the ordinary affairs of life only to "excite in us proper sentiments or dispositions to act in such a manner as is necessary for our well-being, how false soever they may be if taken in a strict and speculative sense."[51]

Edwards, as we have seen, remained a true Lockean, in that he persisted in taking abstract ideas for realities; had he in other respects remained as literal a disciple of Locke he would have frowned, as did his opponents in Boston, Lockeans like Chauncy and Mayhew, upon any use of words to arouse affections. On the other hand, had he followed the line of Berkeley and denied the existence of complex abstractions, he might have given way entirely to employing words for their emotional excitement without bothering about ideas, and so have gone along with the enthusiasts who turned the Awakening into an orgy. His greatness is that he did neither. Instead, he redefined "idea." He so conceived it that it became a principle of organization and of perception not only for the intellectual man but for the passionate man, for the loving and desiring man, for the whole man. He conceded readily that a word can act as an emotional stimulus, not because like Berkeley he separated emotion from the mind, but because, having consolidated the mind with the passions, he was ready to maintain that an emotional response is also an intellectual, or that an intellectual, in the highest sense, is also emotional. A passionate grasping of meaning from a thing or a word is as much an idea—a more clear and distinct idea—as a theoretical grasping. He argued that the purport of a symbol can be appreciated not only by the human head but more accurately by the human heart. An "ideal apprehension" is not only a proposition, it is a "sense"— "whereby things are pleasing or displeasing, including all agreeableness and disagreeableness, all beauty and deformity, all pleasure and pain, and all those sensations, exercises and passions of the mind that arise from either of those."[52]

In other words, Edwards did not deny what Berkeley maintained, that the noise of a word can produce a visceral response which has nothing to do with any intelligibility. He was too rigorous a sensationalist not to see that such a phenomenon was altogether likely, and had he been doubtful, the extremists of the Awakening gave him empirical verification. What Edwards saw was that a purely physiological—or, as we might say, "aesthetic"—reaction to a word is of no use to anybody; what he denied was that the appeal to the emotions must always be made at the cost of the idea; what he insisted upon was that by the word (used in the place of a thing) an idea can be engendered in the mind, and that when the word is apprehended emotionally as well as intellectually, then the idea can be more readily and more accurately conceived. When the word sets in train a sequence of passions, out of it—not invariably, but frequently—

there emerges, like Venus from the foam, a "sensible" concept. This was possible, he argued, because an idea is a unit of experience, and experience is as much love and dread as it is logic. To go from the word to a mechanical response, in preaching or in literary criticism, is a direct, natural, scientifically explicable process; but to get from the sensational impact of a word, through the emotion, to the saving, comprehending idea, there must be an indirect, a supernatural, a mysterious leap. And yet, wonder of wonders, it happens! It happens because, while the saving and comprehending idea is not an effect of which the word is the cause, still, in the marvelous order of divine providence, the preliminary application of the word is, for the producing of that idea, absolutely indispensable.

Hence is seemed obvious to Jonathan Edwards that the sounding of the word, out of which the new simple idea would or might be born, had to be of a word that stood for reality; and reality, to any objective consideration, is grim as well as beautiful. "I am not afraid to tell sinners, that are most sensible of their misery, that there case is indeed as miserable as they think it to be, and a thousand times more so; for this is the truth."[53] Edwards was the heir of a tradition which often found its happiest formulations in the terms of formal logic, and he sometimes expounded the rationale of his apocalyptic preaching by drawing upon old distinctions: the nature of a cause, he pleaded, is not always to be deduced from the nature of an effect, not that of an effect from the cause, "when the cause in only *causa sine qua non*, or an occasional cause: yea, that in such a case, oftentimes the nature of the effect is quite contrary to the nature of the cause."[54] But Edwards could not have explained by the logic of federal Puritanism and by the scholastic psychology of the "faculties" how his naked preaching of terror could become an "occasional cause"; federal Puritanism would have suspected, as Edwards' opponents in fact did during the 1740's, that the effect was merely the efficient work of the word and so was entirely "natural." Edwards decisively departed from the old Puritanism by his appropriation of the new psychology of sensation. By defining grace in this novel frame of reference as a new simple idea, and by keeping in the center of this thinking the principle that an undefinable simple idea can be learned only from experience, he committed himself as a preacher to a rhetoric in which words were obliged to stand in the place of engendering objects, in spite of the fact that there is never any inherent reason why any particular word should stand for any specific object. He was prepared to stake his life upon the assurance that words which were disciplined into becoming "naked" embodiments of ideas could thence become, at least for those capable of receiving the concept, the source or the occasion of an ideational discovery. But if his rhetoric was to achieve such an effect, it had to be not only naked, but so passionately presented that the passions of listeners would heed it. "I should think myself in the way of duty, to raise the affections of my hearers as high as I possibly can, provided that they are affected with nothing but truth, and with affections that are not disagreeable to the nature of what they are affected with."[55] Because the terror of damnation is a truth, and fear is an affection agreeable to it, Edwards preached terror and fear.

To step for a moment outside history, let us look a century ahead of Edwards to Kierkegaard's observation that the teacher can give the learner not truth but only the condition necessary for understanding truth. By conceiving of the word as the occasional rather than the efficient cause, Edwards was maintaining, in the idiom of colonial New England, essentially Kierkegaard's position; in their different phrases both claimed that there is a fundamental limitation upon all literature, namely, that after the artist has provided the verbal environment, at this point another power must intervene if the beholder is to collect out of it the true conception.

> But one who gives the learner not only the Truth, but also the condition for understanding it, is more than teacher. All instruction depends upon the presence, in the last analysis, of the requisite condition; if this is lacking, no teacher can do anything. For otherwise he would find it necessary not only to transform the learner, but to recreate him before beginning to teach him. But this is something no human being can do; if it is done, it must be done by God himself.[56]

In Edwards' version, the statement runs that a person can indeed respond to words in terms of his knowledge of natural good or evil, but for him to react to the spiritual import of rhetoric—since spiritual good or evil will never consist in any consonancy whatsoever with human nature—"it must be wholly and entirely a work of the Spirit of God, not merely as assisting and coworking with natural principles, but as infusing something above nature."[57]

Yet this did not mean for Edwards—any more than for Kierkegaard—that the rhetorician simply builds up a wall of words around the listener, and then reclines, to let the Spirit of God work or not work. Had Edwards evaded the issue by taking so easy a way out, he too could be accused, as have most of the followers of Locke, for having surrendered to a "passive"notion of intelligence and to a naïve environmentalism. Edwards' point was that the sensory impression, and especially the sensible word, comes to the human spirit bearing significances of love or terror, and the leap to a saving understanding proceeds out of the natural. Though a sense of spiritual excellency is required for salvation, it is not the only kind of ideal apprehension that is concerned in conviction: "It also partly depends on a sensible knowledge of what is natural in religion." The mind, being convinced of the truth, "thence naturally and immediately infers from this fitness" what is originally beyond the contrivance of man.[58] So the word must be pressed, and rhetoric must strive for impression; it is a strength, not a weakness, of language that no matter how sensational it becomes, it has to depend upon something happening to the recipient outside and above its own mechanical impact. If this fact imposes a limitation upon the efficacy of art, it bestows at the same time an infallible criterion for its success: "There is a great difference between these two things, viz., lively imaginations arising from strong affections, and strong affections arising from lively imaginations." If

Edwards' artistry was an accidental effect or a consequence of real passion, it would be genuine; but if it produced in the listener or reader an emotion that contained no more than what the rhetoric imparted, "then is the affection, however elevated, worthless and vain."[59] I think Edwards meant the affection of both speaker and listener, for he never spared himself. To this paradoxical and yet logical conclusion, this desperate and yet exhilarating insight, the sensational concept of language led to the reasoning of America's greatest sensationalist.

## Notes

1. *Dialogues*, ed. Mary Whiton Colkins (New York, 1929), 281–82.

2. Berkeley, *Dialogues*, 123.

3. *An Essay Concerning Human Understanding*, book III, chap. 9, par. 21.

4. *Essay*, book III, chap. 10, par. 2.

5. *Essay*, book III, chap 10, par. 22.

6. *Essay*, book III, chap. 2, pars. 1, 8.

7. Bacon, *Works*, ed. Spedding, Ellis, and Heath (Boston, 1857), VII, 412.

8. Preface to Thomas Sprat, *The History of the Royal Society* (London, 1667).

9. *The History of the Royal Society*, 62.

10. *Essay*, book III, chap. 2, par. 7.

11. *An Essay on Criticism*, vv. 309–10.

12. Adam Smith, "Considerations on the First Formation of Languages," reprinted in *Essays Philosophical and Literary* (London, n.d.).

13. Hugh Blair, *Lectures on Rhetoric and Belles Lettres* (Dublin, 1783), I, 115.

14. *Essay*, book III, chap 4, par. 11.

15. *Essay*, book III, chap 2, par. 1.

16. *Essay*, book III, chap. 1, par. 2.

17. *Essay*, book III, chap. 2, par. 6; chap. 3, par. 7.

18. *Essay*, book III, chap. 3, par. 16.

19. *Essay*, book III, chap. 3, pars. 4, 11.

20. *Essay*, book III, chap. 5, pars. 4, 7.

21. *Essay*, book III, chap. 6, par. 1.

22. *Essay*, book III, chap 3, par. 10.

23. *Essay*, book III, chap. 5, par. 16.

24. *Essay*, book III, chap. 4, par. 23.

25. *Essay*, book III, chap. 3, par. 20.

26. Berkeley, *A Treatise Concerning the Principles of Human Knowledge* (London, 1710), intro., par. 18.

27. *Treatise*, intro., par. 13.

28. *Treatise*, intro., par. 23.

29. *Essay*, book III, chap. 10, par. 23.

30. Jonathan Edwards, *Works* (New York, 1844), III, 336.

31. Sereno F. Dwight, *The Life of President Edwards* (New York, 1830), 30.

32. *Essay*, Book III, chap. 10, par. 16.

33. *Essay*, Book III, chap. 11, par. 18.

34. *Treatise*, intro., par. 21.

35. Dwight, *Life*, 702.

36. *Works*. IV, 278.

37. *Essays*, book III, chap. 9, par. 23.

38. *Works*, III, 80.

39. *Works*, I, 532.

40. Dwight, *Life*, 475–76.

41. Perry Miller, "Jonathan Edwards on the Sense of the Heart," *H T R*, 41 (1948), 129.

42. Miller, 133.

43. Miller, 131.

44. "Miscellanies, No. 288," Jonathan Edwards Manuscripts, Yale University Library (quoted by permission).

45. Miller, 131.

46. Miller, 134.

47. Miller, 138.

48. *Treatise*, intro., par. 20.

49. *Essay*, book III, chap. 10, par. 23.

50. Sprat, *History, 112*.

51. *Treatise*, part I, par. 52.

52. Miller, 136.

53. *Works*, III, 338.

54. *Works*, III, 290.

55. *Works*, III, 335.

56. Robert Bretall, *A Kierkegaard Anthology* (Princeton: Princeton University Press, 1946), 158.

57. Miller, 141.

58. Miller, 143, 145.

59. *Works, III, 124*.

# Beauty and Theology:
# A Reappraisal
# of Jonathan Edwards

Roland André Delattre[°]

BEAUTY IS ONE OF THE THINGS Jonathan Edwards was most concerned to understand. Identifying beauty radically with excellence, Edwards finds that "it is what we are more concerned with than any thing else whatsoever: yea, we are concerned with nothing else."[1] If we wish to understand and appreciate Edwards we must dare to take seriously his frequent suggestion that beauty is the central clue to the nature of reality. We must pursue the possibility that the aesthetic aspect of his thought and vision, which finds its definitive formulation in his concepts of beauty and sensibility, provides a larger purchase upon the essential and distinctive features of his thought than is provided by any of the alternatives explored by Edwards scholars—such as the interpretation of Edwards as idealist, empiricist, sensationalist, Platonist, scholastic, Calvinist, mystic, or some combination of these.

The significance of beauty for Edwards is difficult to overstate. It is, for him the first principle of being, the inner, structural principle of Being-itself by virtue of which all things that are have their being, and according to which the universal system of being is articulated. Beauty is not the only kind of order or perfection Edwards finds in reality, but it does provide the primary model of order in terms of which he seeks to understand all forms of order and disorder, concord and discord, in the whole system of being under God. Beauty is in fact fundamental to Edwards' understanding of divine being: it is, he says, that "wherein the truest idea of divinity does consist";[2] it is first among the perfections of God; it provides the foundation for his doctrine of the Trinity; and it defines his understanding of the nature of divine transcendence and immanence, and of the relation between transcendence and immanence in God with respect to his creation, governance, and redemption of the world.

Furthermore, beauty is fundamental to Edwards' understanding of human being and perfection. Virtue and holiness are forms of beauty, as are the varieties of justice and the fruits of conscience. He finds in beauty the central clue to the nature and meaning of conversion, the new life in Christ, and the holiness and joy given in the indwelling of the Holy Spirit. Beauty provides the

[°] Reprinted, with permission, from *Soundings*, 51 (Spring, 1968), 60–79.

model in terms of which Edwards understands the nature of community—social, civil, and religious. In sum, beauty is for Edwards the key to the structure and the dynamics of the moral and religious life, and more particularly to the manner of the divine governance and its relation to human freedom and responsibility. For it is his view that God governs the moral world not by brute force but by the attractive power, that is, the beauty of the apparent good.

How all this is so can only be partially demonstrated in this essay. But it is worth stating the case in these comprehensive terms because my argument runs so sharply against the grain of what was until recently—and in many quarters apparently remains—the received wisdom of our culture regarding the essential character of Edwards' thought. According to that view, Edwards saw God as a terrifying and arbitrary sovereign whose providential and predestinarian governance of the world is so unbendingly deterministic in its power as to deny to his creatures the least fragment of freedom and to leave them no sure hope but to throw themselves upon the divine mercy in an ecstasy of conversion. If even the first generation of Edwardseans could regard themselves as being faithful to their master when they made the acid test of religious sincerity a willingness to be damned for the glory of God—a notion which Edwards himself explicitly rejected as absurd[3]—it is no wonder that it has taken two hundred years for us to cut through our preconceptions about what a man like Edwards *must* have believed in order to recover a more accurate picture of what he *did* believe and think.

Edwards scholars, of course, have long sought to dispel this popular impression of Edwards, one which has made it easy for philosophers, moralists, and theologians to ignore him. Nineteen years ago, in his ground-breaking intellectual biography of Jonathan Edwards, Perry Miller wrote that Edwards' conception of beauty is "the crown of his thought."[4] Since that time one of the major achievements of Edwards scholarship has been the growing recognition of the enormous significance of the twin aesthetic concepts of beauty and sensibility in his thought.[5] More attention has been given, however, to the sensibility than to the beauty, to the sense of beauty in Edwards' thought than to the beauty itself and Edwards' conception of it. This is unfortunate, particularly since his concept of beauty is primarily objective, structural, and relational rather than subjective, emotional, and relativist.

My main purpose in this essay is to correct this imbalance by, first, elucidating Edwards' conception of beauty and then, second, exhibiting the operation of this concept of beauty in his thought by following some of the ways in which it informs his understanding of God's perfections and the manner in which God governs the moral world. In conclusion I shall offer some brief suggestions regarding the historical and contemporary significance of this interpretation of Edwards. I take as my text and platform his declarations that "God is God, and distinguished from all other beings, and exalted above 'em, chiefly by his divine beauty," and that this divine beauty is that "wherein the truest idea of divinity does consist," and furthermore that "he that sees not the beauty of holiness . . . in effect is ignorant of the whole spiritual world."[6]

## I

Edwards distinguishes between two major forms of beauty. The form that comes most readily to mind, the beauty of harmony and proportion, he calls *secondary or natural beauty,* for he finds in it but an image of another and higher form of beauty, a *primary or spiritual beauty,* which he defines as being's cordial consent to being in general.

It is relatively easy to understand Edwards' definition of secondary beauty as harmony or proportion. But his definition of primary beauty as being's cordial consent to being in general presents greater difficulty. And yet "consent" is the key to his understanding of beauty, the common denominator among all the varieties of beauty which he distinguishes.

> There are two sorts of agreement or consent of one thing to another. (1) There is a *cordial* agreement; that consists in concord and union of mind and heart. . . . (2) There is a *natural* union or agreement; which, though some image of the other, is entirely a distinct thing; the will, disposition, or affections of the heart having no concern in it, but consisting only in uniformity and consent of nature, form, quality, etc.[7]

There are, accordingly, two principal kinds of beauty, each a variety of the single rule of beauty as "agreement or consent" as opposed to "discord and dissent." Primary beauty consists in one kind of consent: the cordial or heartfelt consent of being to being. It is essential to primary beauty that the will, disposition, or affection of the heart be involved in the consent. Secondary beauty consists in an inferior and very different sort of consent, although it is one which may be an image or shadow of primary beauty: namely, "a mutual consent and agreement of different things, in form, manner, quantity, and visible end or design; called by various names of regularity, order, uniformity, symmetry, proportion, harmony," and "uniformity in the midst of variety."[8]

The object of consent is as essential to the definition of beauty as is the character of the consenting being. In the case of primary or spiritual beauty, that object must be either other minds or other things. If the consent be "of mind towards minds, it is love, and when of minds towards other things, it is choice."[9] Love and choice, then, are forms of consent and beauty.

Primary beauty is peculiar to moral agents and relations, while secondary beauty is found in all kinds of beings and relations. Secondary beauty alone provides no guarantee of true virtue, holiness, or conformity to God; these are all measured by the primary beauty of a disposition to consent cordially to the universal system of being. Edwards thought Francis Hutcheson had mistaken shadow for substance, and accordingly rejected his moral theory because Hutcheson accepted as his primary model and norm the very proportion or harmony which Edwards found to be a distinctly secondary kind of beauty.[10]

Edwards also distinguishes between particular and general beauty. Particular beauty may be affirmed of whatever "appears beautiful when considered only with regard to . . . a limited and private sphere," while general beauty includes only that which "appears beautiful when viewed most perfectly, comprehensively and universally with regard to its tendencies and connections."[11]

The essential thing to note is the "limited and private sphere" sufficient to the former, in contrast with the wider "tendencies and connections" essential to the definition of the latter. Any particular beauty, when viewed as a part of some more comprehensive system of being may be found to dissent from that larger system, in which case it must be pronounced false or confined or partial beauty; otherwise it qualifies as true or universal beauty.

Two further principles essential to Edwards' definition of beauty must be introduced now in order to anticipate possible misconceptions about his thought—misconceptions flowing from apprehensions about the presumed subjectivism sometimes regarded as necessarily attendant upon the "intrusion" of aesthetic notions into ethics and theology, or else misconceptions flowing from the wide diversity of ways in which men have thought about beauty.

The first of these two principles is that beauty is objective for Edwards. This does not mean that beauty is in the thing, if the thing be finite, for only God has beauty in himself.[12] Nor is beauty therefore only in the eye of the beholder. For, although Edwards does trace to the eye of the beholder much that passes for beauty and much that is limited or partial beauty, he does not accept this as the only alternative to regarding beauty as an immediate property of the object. Beauty is objective for Edwards because it is constituted by objective relations of consent and dissent among beings, relations into which the subject or beholder may enter and participate, but relations the beauty of which is defined by conformity to God (consent to being in general) rather than by degree of subjective pleasure. Beauty is, in other words, a *structural* concept, the nearest synonym for which is excellence rather than pleasantness. Edwards avoids subjectivism and aestheticism in his deployment of the concept of beauty by his objectivist definition of beauty and by his systematic insistence that, while virtue and holiness and spiritual beauty necessarily involve consent to beauty (complacence), their foundation and essential definition consists rather in consent to being (benevolence).

The objectivist character of Edwards' thought is manifest in his view that deformity rather than ugliness is the opposite of beauty. Although the notions of form and deformity involve the presence of a subject, deformity refers to the object and to *objective relations,* while ugliness refers to the subject and to *subjective responses.* If the measure of beauty is found primarily in the response of the subject, then the opposite of beauty will be designated as ugliness, as in the subjectivist theory of beauty developed by Edwards' contemporary, Edmund Burke.[13] But if the measure of beauty is found to be objectively determined by the relation of being to being, then the opposite of beauty will be designated as deformity, as in Edwards' objectivist theory of beauty. Beauty is defined as the consent of being to being; dissent from being constitutes deformity.

A second definitive principle for Edwards' conception of beauty is that the model of beauty is the beautifying rather than the beautified. This distinction corresponds to the one between primary and secondary beauty. Edwards' conception of primary beauty is more fully exemplified by the creative and dynamic idea of the beautifying, while his conception of secondary beauty corresponds more closely to the more static and passive idea of the beautified. He would have agreed with Shaftesbury that "the beautifying, not the beautified, is the really beautiful,"[14] for beauty functions in Edwards' thought more as a formative principle of being than as a principle of well-formed being; it is more fully exhibited bestowing beauty than in receiving it. Beauty is more properly and fully exhibited in creative spiritual relations of consent than in created material relations of proportion. The beauty of the well-formed is created more than it is creative, while the real model of beauty for Edwards is the creative.y beautifying—that which has the power to consent to being, to beautify, to bestow beauty. Accordingly, God is most beautiful, for he is the effulgent fountain of all being and beauty, the beautifying one, the bestower of all beauty.

The above distinction and order or priority corresponds closely to Henry Nelson Wieman's distinction between creative and created good,[15] and even more closely to Alfred North Whitehead's distinction between the major and minor forms of beauty. Particularly if Edwards' definition of primary beauty appears arbitrary, it may be helpful to note its remarkable similarity to Whitehead's definition of beauty as "the mutual adaptation of the several factors in an occasion of experience."[16] The correspondence between Edwards' definition in terms of consent to being and Whitehead's definition in terms of mutual adaptation is especially interesting since Whitehead too finds in beauty the primary model of order for his metaphysics and his theology. "All order," he finds, "is . . . aesthetic order, and the moral order is merely certain aspects of aesthetic order. The actual world is the outcome of the aesthetic order, and the aesthetic order is derived from the immanence of God."[17] Whitehead's minor form of beauty, defined as "the absence of mutual inhibition,"[18] is a mode of "mutual adaptation" which corresponds closely with Edwards' view of harmony and proportion as a secondary form of beauty; and his major form of beauty as "the inherent capacity for the promotion of Beauty"[19] corresponds closely to Edwards' conception of beauty as the structural, creative principle of being in his system. The differences between Edwards' aesthetic philosophy of being and Whitehead's aesthetic philosophy of process do not stand in the way of Edwards sharing Whitehead's conviction that "beauty, moral and aesthetic, is the aim of existence."[20]

To summarize this much: Edwards' conception of beauty is primarily objective, structural, relational, and creative or formative, rather than primarily subjective, emotional, relativist, and created or well-formed. Primary beauty consists in the cordial consent of being to being; secondary beauty consists in harmony and proportion.

I turn now to the manner in which this conception of beauty informs the Edwardsean view of God. With his objectivist, structural concept of beauty Edwards is able to insist upon the objectivity of God while also affirming that God cannot be adequately known without being enjoyed. For beauty is objective with respect to the self, and yet it is available only in and through the enjoyment of it. Beauty is not discernible to the indifferent eye. Though indifferent men may know many things about beauty, they do not and cannot know beauty itself. For beauty is the very model of that which cannot be known without being enjoyed.

## II

The following proposition should be placed at the center of our thinking if we would understand Edwards' conception of God, namely, that "God is God, and distinguihed from all other beings, and exalted above 'em, chiefly by his divine beauty."[21] For Edwards does not confine his claim to the relatively simple idea that along with and along side of several other things, God is also beautiful. Many poets, saints, and theologians have said as much. Edwards says much more. When, in his preaching and writing, he invokes the divine beauty with which he is so much affected, it is not so much in order to sing God's praises as it is to speak as truly as he can about the nature of God and his relation to the world. For Edwards, the divine beauty is not simply one alongside the other attributes or perfections of God. He goes further and says that from among all God's perfections it is by his beauty that he is primarily distinguished as God.

Certainly one of the distinguishing marks—if it is not indeed the distinctive feature—of Edwards' theology, when looked at in relation to the whole history of Christian thought, is this radical elevation of beauty to preeminence among the divine perfections. Certainly the beauty of God and of divine things has long been a recurrent theme of religious piety all around the world, including Christendom. But the concept of beauty has rarely found an important— not to speak of a secure—place in Christian theology, especially within the main line of Christian orthodoxy, and even more especially within Protestant Reformed or Calvinist orthodoxy.

Despite its appearance in a marginal way in the thought of such theologians as Thomas Aquinas, and its more important appearance in the tradition of Christian Platonism from Augustine through Pseudo-Dionysius to the Cambridge Platonists and their British heirs—to carry the story no further than Edwards' own day—the concept of beauty, when it has not been completely ignored, has had at most a very insecure position among theological concepts in Christian thought. Any serious development of the concept of beauty as a divine perfection has, in fact, been looked upon as a mark of heterodoxy, if not indeed of heresy. Anders Nygren, the contemporary Lutheran theologian, expresses himself on the matter rather more forcefully than is customary, but his judgment is not untypical of orthodoxy's suspicion regarding beauty as a divine perfection. In his influential study, *Agape and Eros*, in which he sets these two conceptions of love radically over against each other, Nygren says: "Eros is of a markedly aesthetic character. It is the beauty of the divine that attracts the eye of the soul and sets its love in motion." It is therefore permissible to speak of beauty in the context of Eros. "To speak of the 'beauty' of God in the context of Agape, however, sounds very like blasphemy."[22] We may, with one exception, agree with Karl Barth's judgment regarding the theological appropriation of the concept of beauty, that "Reformation and Protestant orthodoxy, so far as I can see, completely ignored it."[23] Obviously Barth did not see across the Atlantic and back into eighteenth-century New England, for it appears that he is not acquainted with Jonathan Edwards.

Not until Karl Barth has any theologian of Reformed orthodoxy besides Edwards made significant theological use of the concept of beauty. It is a mark of Edwards' theological boldness and imagination that European Protestantism should have had to wait two hundred years longer than New England for the subject to be even seriously broached by a major orthodox theologian. That it should take one as daring as Barth to do so is not surprising. As Barth himself observes,

> owing to its connection with the ideas of pleasure, desire and enjoyment (quite apart from its historical connection with Greek thought), the concept of the beautiful seems to be a particularly secular one, not at all adapted for introduction into the language of theology, and indeed extremely dangerous.[24]

Despite these and other considerations, Barth characteristically refuses to be put off, though he does not give the concept of beauty anything approaching the rich theological development it receives from Edwards. Dangers there surely are, but, says he, "the aestheticism which threatens here is no worse than the other 'isms' or any 'ism'. They are all dangerous."[25]

In his development of beauty as a divine perfection Edwards, unlike Barth, did not feel himself to be involved with an especially dangerous concept. As a latter-day Puritan he was nurtured in a tradition rich in resources for just such a development by virtue of Puritanism's unprecedented stress on immediate experience and its aesthetic and even sensual vocabulary for expressing that experience, not to speak of Puritanism's sympathetic relationship to Cambridge Platonism. Also, it must be remembered that Puritan simplicity of worship and life was a function of its opposition to idolatry, pride, and self-indulgence, and is not to be attributed to any supposed opposition to beauty. On the contrary, the Puritan's sense of life as a pilgrimage of spiritual training and discipline for a more lovely world to be opened up to the saints was tempered by a sometimes mystical sense of the beauty of things natural as well as divine. In matters aesthetic, the Puritan canons of beauty and taste compare favorably with those of many movements and periods which are frequently regarded (or regard themselves) as aesthetically more cultivated—a judgment which would probably find wider acceptance if we did not tend to accept as definitive of Puritanism what became of it by the early or mid-nineteenth century, rather than what it was at its zenith.

### III

Jonathan Edwards employs two different but closely related formulations of the divine perfections. In each formulation beauty emerges as preeminent among the perfections of God. For our purposes it will be enough to follow just one of them, in which he distinguishes between two kinds of perfections or attributes in God: "his moral attributes, which are summed up in his holiness,

and his natural attributes of strength, knowledge, etc. that constitue the greatness of God."[26] Just as men distinguish between natural and moral good—

> So divines make a distinction between the natural and moral perfection of God: by
> the *moral perfections* of God, they mean those attributes which God exercises as a
> moral agent, or whereby the heart and will of God are good, right, and infinitely
> becoming, and lovely; such as his righteousness, truth, faithfulness, and goodness; or,
> in other words, his holiness.

> By God's *natural attributes* or perfections [Edwards continues], they mean those
> attributes wherein, according to our way of conceiving God, consists, not the holiness
> or moral goodness of God, but his greatness; such as his power, his knowledge
> whereby he knows all things, and his being eternal, from everlasting to everlasting,
> his omnipresence, and his awful and terrible majesty.[27]

All the divine perfections, as Edwards conceives them, are to be referred to one
or the other of these two comprehensive classes—all, that is, except the beauty
of God,° which is related to these two classes of perfections in that God's natural
attributes manifest his secondary or natural beauty, while God's moral perfections constitute his primary or spiritual beauty. We must distinguish, then, not
only between the natural and the moral perfections of God, but also between
these and the beauty of God. There is a difference which I now want to examine
between the moral perfections of God and the beauty of those moral perfections. And this difference pertains to the substantial being of God, rather than to
any change in view on the part of the perceiver—though the latter difference or
change is so important that the former can easily be missed.

　　To apprehend the beauty of the holiness or moral perfection of God is not,
in Edwards' view, simply a subjective matter of being affected and pleased with
God, or of being inclined to him as holy and beautiful. It is rather to apprehend
something about God himself, to be instructed about the being of God in such a
fashion as not only to open up and unfold to view a whole new dimension of the
divine being, but also to open up to view a whole new world. To come to an
apprehension or sense of the beauty of God is not simply to change one's
attitude towards God, even though a transformation of inclination and self-
disposition towards God is an essential part of such an apprehension. It is also,
and more importantly, to apprehend something about God himself. After enumerating a variety of other things that are brought into view through an apprehension of the divine beauty, Edwards is carried to heights of eloquence in
the following passage:

> He that sees *the beauty of holiness*, or true moral good, sees *the greatest and most
> important thing in the world*, which is the fulness of all things, without which all the
> world is empty, no better than nothing, yea, worse than nothing. Unless this is seen,
> nothing is seen, that is worth the seeing: for there is no other true excellency or
> beauty. Unless this be understood, nothing is understood, that is worthy of the exer-

---

° The divine glory is another exception, but does not need separate treatment because glory and
beauty are virtually identical in Edwards' conception of God. The evidence for this is examined in
my forthcoming book on Edwards.

cise of the noble faculty of understanding. *This is the beauty of the Godhead, and the divinity of Divinity* (if I may so speak), the good of the infinite Fountain of Good; without which God himself (if that were possible to be) would be an infinite evil: without which, we ourselves had better never have been; and without which there had better have been no being. He therefore in effect knows nothing, that knows not this: his knowledge is but the shadow of knowledge.[28]

"He that sees not the beauty of holiness . . . in effect is ignorant of the whole spiritual world," for from this sense of spiritual beauty arises "all true experimental knowledge of religion."[29]

Now, it is important to note that this thing which is "the greatest and most important thing in the world, . . . the beauty of the Godhead, and the divinity of Divinity" is not simply the holiness or the moral perfection of God, but is rather the *beauty* of that holiness and of the moral perfections summed up in his holiness. If it be felt that this is a distinction without a difference, let the following evidence be carefully considered. The failure to perceive this distinction goes a long way towards explaining the failure of earlier interpreters of Edwards to understand his conception of the priority of beauty among the perfections of God. What I want to show now is that beauty is, for Edwards, not simply a quality attached to the natural and (especially) to the moral perfections of God, but that beauty is itself a substantive perfection of God, and that it is the highest and central, the first and most distinguishing perfection of God, the knowledge and enjoyment of which constitutes the most intimate knowledge of God.

If, as Edward says, "the beauty of the divine nature does primarily consist in God's holiness," which is the sum of his moral perfections, then it is to these that men must attend if they would apprehend the divine beauty. But there is a difference between the moral perfections of God and his beauty, for his moral perfections may be apprehended and known, as we shall see in a moment, and still the beauty of God not be seen. To see and have a sense of the one is not necessarily to see and have a sense of the other. To see and have a sense of God's *natural* perfections (such as his greatness, power, and knowledge), certainly, is not yet to see God's true beauty; this is at best to apprehend only God's natural beauty, that secondary beauty which is defined by proportion rather than consent. Nor does an apprehension of God's true beauty necessarily follow from seeing or having a sense of his *moral* perfections or attributes (such as his justice, righteousness, goodness, and holiness), as can be seen from passages such as the following ones, the meaning of which for the point now under consideration is clear, though their own immediate concern is rather with the significance of the sense than with the status of the beauty:

If persons have a great sense of the natural perfections of God, and are greatly affected with them, or have any other sight or sense of God, than that which consists in, or implies a sense of the beauty of his moral perfections, it is no certain sign of grace: as particularly, men's having a great sense of the awful greatness, and terrible majesty of God; for this is only God's natural perfection, and what men may see, and yet be entirely blind to the beauty of his moral perfections.

In the end, Edwards continues—

Wicked men and devils will see, and have a great sense of *everything* that appertains to the glory of God, but only [i.e., except for] *the beauty of his moral perfections*. They will see his infinite greatness and majesty, his infinite power, and will be fully convinced of his omniscience, and his eternity and immutability; and *they will see and know everything appertaining to his moral attributes themselves, but only* [i.e., except for] *the beauty and amiableness of them;* they will see and know that he is perfectly just and righteous and true; and that he is a holy God, . . . and they will see the wonderful manifestations of his infinite goodness and free grace to the saints; and there is nothing will be hid from their eyes, but only [i.e., except for] the beauty of these moral attributes, and that beauty of the other attributes, which arises from it. And so natural men in this world are capable of having a very affecting sense of everything else that appertains to God, but this only [i.e., except only his beauty][30]

It is clear from this that there is something very special about beauty as divine attribute or perfection. There is nothing very remarkable about the view that God's natural perfections may be apprehended without having a sense of the divine beauty, though Edwards finds there is in these natural perfections a derivative and secondary beauty. But that God's infinite goodness and grace and his other moral attributes, even his holiness, may be known while yet the divine beauty remains hidden to view—this is what is remarkable in Edwards' scheme! If even the holiness of God may (according to this passage) be apprehended while one is still blind to the divine beauty; and if, as is the case in Edwards' scheme, beauty is actually a perfection of God—something "without which God himself . . . would be an infinite evil"[31]—and not simply a name for a form of human response to God; then surely the divine beauty must be seen as having a peculiar or unique place among the divine perfections.

There are, then, in Edwards' view, three stages or moments in our knowledge of God, each of which corresponds to and designates at once something about the divine being and something about the manner of our relation to him: the knowledge of God's natural perfections, the knowledge of his moral perfections, and finally the knowledge of his beauty. Power may, for the present purpose, be taken as representative of the natural perfections of God. And goodness may, in the same manner, be taken as representative of the moral perfections of God—goodness rather than holiness, since holiness, though it is the sum of the moral perfections of God, also has a wider than moral significance. Beauty, goodness, and power may be taken as representative of the three kinds of divine perfections into which all of them may be resolved, according to this formulation. And their rank among the divine perfections is first beauty, then goodness, then power, in descending order.

Edwards sees this focus upon God's beauty and his moral perfections as standing in sharp contrast with a major prevailing tendency of his day to stress instead what he regards as merely natural perfections in God. "'Tis beyond doubt," he writes in the course of his maturest analysis of the Great Awakening, "that too much weight has been laid, by many persons of late, on discoveries of God's greatness, *awful* majesty, and natural perfections . . . without any real view of the holy, *lovely* majesty of God."[32]

Though some of Edwards' impact upon his own age, and—even more so— much of his reputation in ages since his own, rested upon his capacity to make the terrors of hell and separation from God real and apparent to his hearers, it was the divine beauty and the real good in God rather than the horrors following upon sin which he sought most passionately to make apparent to those in his spiritual care. It was the beauty of God and of all things in God, rather than the fires of hell, that most moved his mind to dialectics and his tongue to eloquence. In fact it was one of the central and recurring themes of his whole work as a moralist, preacher and theologian, that he who is moved in what he does by fear rather than by love, by a fear, e.g., of God's awful power rather than by a sense of God's even more awesome beauty, is precisely to that extent already alienated from God and, but for the grace of God, separated from his holiness and redeeming presence.

If the divine being is rightly to be discerned, Edwards felt, more must be made of God's goodness than of his greatness, more made of his "holy, lovely majesty" and moral perfection than of his "awful majesty and natural perfection." To this end it is not enough to look beyond the natural to the moral perfections of God. A further requirement is that the *beauty* of those moral perfections must be seen, for "if the moral beauty of God be hid," not only will "the enmity of the heart. . . remain in its full strength" whatever else be known of God's greatness and goodness, but also, that "wherein the truest idea of divinity does consist" and by which God is most distinguished from all other beings will remain unknown.[33] That is, Edwards' conception of the divine beauty provides the most critical measure, not only of our existential response to God, but also of our philosophical and theological conception of God. This would not be so if Edwards' definition of beauty were subjective, emotional, and relativist rather than objective, structural, and relational, for in that case the attribution or predication of beauty to God would be only an expression of our existential response to the divine reality, and would involve no cognitive claim about the divine being itself. But Edwards sees beauty as the central clue not simply to the appropriate human response to God, as in a right inclination of the will, true religious affections, and true virtue. He wants to insist over and beyond this that beauty is the central clue to the divine object of that response, as definitive a clue to the inner nature of the divine being as is available to men.

## IV

Beauty is preeminent among the perfections of God. Because Edwards always seeks to understand all things in relation to God, his whole theological-philosophical-ethical program rests upon his vision of the beauty of the divine being. It is, for example, Edwards' view that God's governance and redemption are exercised not by arbitrary and brute force, but by the attractive and creative power of God's own beauty. "'Tis by a sight of the beauty and amiableness of God's holiness," Edwards finds, "that the heart is transformed into the same image and strongly engaged to imitate God."[34] It is by this divine beauty, perceived as a *"bonum formosum,* a beautiful good in itself . . . that the true saints have their hearts affected, and love captivated by the free grace of God in the first place."[35] Nothing less than a manifestation and communication of the divine beauty itself has the creative, transforming power sufficient to the reconciliation of the sinner with God.

Edwards mobilizes the doctrine of the Trinity and his conception of the beauty of God to interpret the manner in which this decisive act of redemption is accomplished. His formulation can be summarily expressed in terms of the same "is as" volitional equation—"the will always is as the greatest apparent good is"[36]—by which the moral world is governed generally. Edwards finds that beauty is essential to the determination of both sides of this equation—that is, both the moral condition of the will and the attractive power of the apparent good which the will "is as." The decisive act of redemption is accomplished by God's communicating his own beauty immediately to both sides of the equation. With respect to one side of the equation (the moral condition of the will), true virtue and holy affections rest upon the indwelling of the Holy Spirit "which *is* the divine excellency and beauty itself";[37] such virtue and affections are forms of primary beauty. With respect to the other side of the equation (the attractive power of the good), it is in the beauty of Jesus Christ that God presents himself objectively as the creature's real good made manifest as the apparent good. "It is this sight of the divine beauty of Christ," says Edwards, "that bows the will and draws the hearts of men," and it is in a "sight or sense" of this beauty that consists "the saving grace of God's Spirit."[38] The divine beauty which, for Edwards, is the Holy Spirit appears in Jesus Christ.

We cannot here pursue any further the theological and ethical reformulation which follows from placing the concept of beauty at the center of Edwards' program and vision. But the spirit of that program may be summed up in the form of an Edwardsean response to the first question of the Westminster catechism. What is the first end of man? It is to glorify God (that is, celebrate his being) and enjoy him forever (that is, delight in his beauty).

There are at least two broad areas of contemporary thought to which the interpretation of Jonathan Edwards developed in this essay should prove peculiarly relevant.

(1) There is a growing recognition among Americans engaged in the work of theology and of theological ethics as well as "American studies" that there is a substantial American theological tradition, that it has done considerably more than reflect the European theological scene, and that it deserves and will reward careful study.[39] The greatness of some of the principal contributors to this tradition—from the first-generation Puritan divines, through Edwards, Chan-

ning, Emerson, Bushnell, William James, and Royce, to Wieman and the Niebuhr brothers, not to speak of literary figures such as Melville, Whitman, and Faulkner—is in large part defined precisely by their theological appropriation of what may be called "the American experience." The interpretation of Edwards is probably the single most important factor in assessing this tradition.

By placing his structural, relational, objective concept of beauty at the center of his thought we shall be able to appreciate hitherto neglected contributions Edwards makes to this American theological tradition of discourse. In particular, this opens up for reevaluation the relation of Edwards' thought and vision to that of others in this tradition in whose thought the aesthetic dimensions of experience and of reality have played a significant part—the early Puritans, Channing, Emerson and other transcendentalists, Bushnell, Wieman, Whitehead, and H. R. Niebuhr.° Also calling for fresh investigation are those (often the same ones as above) for whom a relational theory of being and good is a significant feature of their thought—most porminently Bushnell, Royce, James, Wieman, and H. R. Niebuhr. Such studies are of more than historical interest because this is a tradition of discourse defined rather by common concerns and problems than by a common position.

(2) It is my view that by attending to the critical importance of beauty in Edwards' vision of reality we are not only able to discern more accurately what he thought; we are also able to appreciate more fully precisely those dimensions of his intellectual achievement which hold the greatest promise of relevance to theological and moral reflection in our own time. I have in mind particularly the relevance of these aspects of Edwards' thought to some of the problems H. Richard Niebuhr was working on when he died—the relation between being and value or good, the "responsible self" as a model for understanding moral agency, and problems involved in an adequate "resymbolization" of Christian faith,[40] possibilities for which are opened up by Edwards' deployment of beauty as a central category of being and of interpretation. Professor Albert Hofstadter, for whom "beauty is the revelation of the truth of (spiritual) being,"[41] is, in terms of rather different (Hegelian, phenomenological) resources, at work on these same issues in ways which might well benefit by being drawn into intellectual companionship with Niebuhr and Edwards.

I have in mind also Hannah Arendt,[42] who deploys the concept of beauty most creatively and suggestively in relation to the human cultural world in much the same way that Edwards does in relation to the universal system of being. These thinkers and a growing company of others are addressing themselves to issues on which Jonathan Edwards' thought gives promise of shedding important light when approached in terms of its aesthetic dimensions, particularly where the issues involve the development of models for the structure and dynamics of the moral life.

---

° There are of course others, not American, with whom Edwards can profitably be drawn into constructive conversation by virtue of the approach to his thought taken in this essay—Spinoza, Kant, Kierkegaard, and Schleiermacher, among them.

# Notes

1. "Notes on the Mind," No. 1 in *The Philosophy of Jonathan Edwards From His Private Notebooks*, ed. Harvey G. Townsend (Eugene, Oregon, 1955), p. 21 (hereinafter cited as *Mind*).

2. Jonathan Edwards, *Religous Affections*, ed. John E. Smith (New Haven, 1959), p. 298 (hereinafter cited as *RA*).

3. "Miscellanies," No. 530. The Yale University Collection of Edwards Manuscripts.

4. Perry Miller, *Jonathan Edwards* (New York, 1959), p. 241.

5. See especially Douglas J. Elwood, *The Philosophical Theology of Jonathan Edwards* (New York, 1960); John E. Smith's Introduction to the Yale Edition of the *Religious Affections*; and Alan Heimert, *Religion and the American Mind: From the Great Awakening to the Revolution* (Cambridge, 1966).

6. *RA*, pp. 298, 275.

7. Jonathan Edwards, *The Nature of True Virtue* (Ann Arbor, 1960), p. 31, italics added (Hereinafter cited as *TV*).

8. *Ibid.*, p. 28.

9. *Mind*, No. 45.

10. Francis Hutcheson, *An Inquiry Into the Original of Our Ideas of Beauty and Virtue* (London, 1725).

11. *TV*, pp. 2–3.

12. " 'Tis peculiar to God that He has beauty within Himself.' " *Mind*, No. 45.

13. Edmund Burke, *A Philosophical Enquiry Into the Origin of Ideas of the Sublime and Beautiful*, ed. J. T. Boulton (London, 1958).

14. Anthony Ashley Cooper, Third Earl of Shaftesbury, *The Moralist, A Philosophical Rhapsody* (Treatise Five of *Characteristics* [London, 1732]), p. 404. Edwards would have disagreed, however, with Shaftesbury's reasons for coming to such a pregnant conclusion.

15. Henry Nelson Wieman, *The Source of Human Good* (Chicago, 1946).

16. Alfred North Whitehead, *Adventures of Ideas* (New York, 1933), p. 324.

17. Whitehead, *Religion in the Making* (Cleveland, 1960), p. 101.

18. Whitehead, *Adventures of Ideas*, p. 324.

19. *Ibid.*, p. 329.

20. *Whitehead, Essays in Science and Philosophy (New York, 1948), p. 8.*

21. *RA*, p. 298.

22. Anders Nygren, *Agape and Eros* (London, 1953), pp. 223–224.

23. Karl Barth, *Church Dogmatics* (Edinburgh, 1957), II/I, 651. Barth goes on to observe that "even Schleiermacher, in whom we might have expected something of this kind," that is, some positive development and deployment of the concept of beauty, "did not achieve anything very striking in this direction."

24. *Ibid.*

25. *Ibid.*, p. 652.

26. *RA, p. 256.*

27. *RA*, p. 255, italics added.

28. *RA*, p. 274, italics added.

29. *RA*, p. 275.

30. *RA*, pp. 263, 264, italics added.

31. *RA*, p. 274.

32. *RA*, p. 265, italics added.

33. *RA*, pp. 264, 298.

34. "Miscellanies," No. 1127. The Yale University Collection of Edwards Manuscripts.

35. *RA*, pp. 262–273.

36. Jonathan Edwards, *Freedom of the Will*, ed. Paul Ramsey (New Haven, 1957), p. 142.

37. Jonathan Edwards, *An Unpublished Essay of Edwards on the Trinity*, ed. G. P. Fisher (New York, 1903), pp. 118–119, italics added.

38. Jonathan Edwards, "True Grace," *Works* (New York, 1843), IV, 469–470.

39. See the fine introductory essay and collection of readings in Sydney E. Ahlstrom, ed., *Theology in America: The Major Protestant Voices from Puritanism to Neo-Orthodoxy* (Indianapolis, 1967). See also Daniel D. Williams, "Tradition and Experience in American Theology," in James W. Smith and A. Leland Jamison, eds., *The Shaping of American Religion* (Princeton, 1961), pp. 443–495; Joseph Haroutunian, "Theology and American Experience," *Criterion*, 3 (1964), 3–12; James Sellers, *Theological Ethics* (New York, 1966); and Herbert Richardson, *Toward an American Theology* (New York, 1967).

40. Among the works of H. R. Niebuhr, see especially *The Meaning of Revelation* (New York, 1941); *Radical Monotheism and Western Culture* (New York, 1960), particularly the essay on "The Center of Value," reprinted as a Supplementary Essay, pp. 100–113; and *The Responsible Self* (New York, 1963). Edwards became an increasingly important resource and intellectual companion to Niebuhr in his later years.

41. Albert Hofstadter, "Validity Versus Value: An Essay in Philosophical Aesthetics," *The Journal of Philosophy*, 59 (1962). 615. Professor Hofstadter's views are more fully developed in *Truth and Art* (New York, 1965).

42. Hannah Arendt, *The Human Condition* (Chicago, 1958); and *Between Past and Future* (New York, 1961).

# Thought: Historical

## Jonathan Edwards: A New Departure in Eschatology

C. C. Goen°

The current revival of interest in both Jonathan Edwards and eschatology points up the fact that there has been no deliberate effort to bring these two subjects together. The only previous attempt to treat Edwards' doctrine of the last things is that by Frank Hugh Foster, in a series of articles on "The Eschatology of the New England Divines."[1] Unfortunately, the title promises more than the discussions afford; because Foster's interest is confined almost entirely to the problem of Universalism, his section on Edwards treats only of the doctrine of eternal punishment and serves to perpetuate the common notion that the great Puritan was little more than a preacher of damnation. This overlooks the fact (as do many other studies) that Edwards had a fully developed and closely reasoned eschatology, every part of which was buttressed with ponderous proofs from Scripture and logic. He based his argument for a future life on the rational nature of man and the moral government of God, and drew on the biblical imagery for detailed descriptions of the destiny of both the redeemed and the damned. His farewell sermon to the Northampton congregation reveals that he was not simply a cold-blooded logician but a warm-hearted pastor-evangelist tenderly concerned for the souls committed to his care. If he made hell "real enough to be found in the atlas,"[2] he did so with a profound conviction of God's justice in the eternal doom of the unrepentant, as well as with the earnestness of one persuaded of the certainty of eternal felicity for the redeemed.[3] And if he subsumed his eschatological doctrines under the rubrics of a pre-scientific world view, he still saw clearly that the redemption which proceeded from the heart of a just and merciful God was being realized progressively in the drama of history and would be consummated on the grand scale of eternity.

But there is another side to his eschatological thought which has not been adequately explicated. Edwards' doctrine of the last things, so far as it describes the final End beyond history, is but a full and realistic elucidation of concepts generally accepted in the othodox Calvinistic tradition. When he undertakes to construct the historical events preceding the final consummation, however, he

° Reprinted, with permission, from *Church History*, 28 (March, 1959), 25–40.

introduces a radical innovation which had decisive consequences for the future. This centers around his millennial speculations, which are anything but "old-fasioned chiliasm."[4] It is the purpose of the present study to subject these speculations to a fresh analysis in order to determine their content, novelty and source, and to suggest something of their influence on subsequent American thought. It will point to the probability that Edwards' proposal of an imminent millennium within ordinary history was a definitive factor in the religious background of the idea of progress.

## A HISTORICAL MILLENNIUM

In the *History of Redemption*, which, had he lived to complete it, was to have been Jonathan Edwards' *magnum opus*, he relates the story of salvation from the beginning to his own day, and then turns to the biblical prophecies to fill out the remainder of historical time. To read him correctly at this point, one must understand his method of prophetic interpretation, especially as it applies to the Revelation. He adopted the so-called "Historical" mode of interpretation which had been generally in vogue since the Reformation.[5] This approach regards the Revelation (along with Daniel) as predicting the apostasy of the Roman Catholic Church; the papacy is identified with the beast, commonly called Antichrist, and the latter half of Revelation is thought to describe his downfall.[6] Inasmuch as this view was the standard Protestant belief in Edwards' day, it is only natural that he should outline the periods of the Christian era thus:

1. From Christ's resurrection to the destruction of Jerusalem
2. From the destruction of Jerusalem to Constantine
3. From Constantine to the rise of Antichrist (the papacy)
4. From the rise of Antichrist to the Reformation
5. From the Reformation to the present time
6. From the present time to the fall of Antichrist

But there is a significant departure from traditional interpretation in that these periods are subsumed under the *suffering* state of the church, while the seventh (and last) period comprises the *prosperous* state of the church—and this without the personal return of Christ or the end of history as such. That is to say, Edwards foresaw a golden age for the church on earth, within history, and achieved through the ordinary processes of propagating the gospel in the power of the Holy Spirit. This is commonly designated postmillennialism, and its novelty in eighteenth-century New England will be shown shortly. For the present, attention is called to Edwards' view of events surrounding the supposed fall of Antichrist, the subsequent prosperity of the church, and the final conflict with evil just before the end. These are adjuncts of the historical millennium.

According to Edwards, the golden age is ushered in by the fall of Antichrist. This adversary, in the common view, is the papacy, through which the devil has smuggled back into Christendom the paganism that had been purged from the empire by Constantine. Thus, says Edwards, by these means the head of the beast which was wounded unto death in Constantine, has his deadly wound healed in Antichrist, Rev. xiii. 3. And the dragon that formerly reigned in the Heathen Roman empire, being cast out thence, after the beast with seven heads and ten horns rises up out of the sea, gives him his power, and seat, and great authority; and all the world wonders after the beast.[7]

Having arisen gradually to a position of power and perversity, Antichrist is due to reign 1260 years, during which time the true church is suppressed and "in a state of great obscurity, like the woman in the wilderness."[8] The overthrow of Antichrist is predicted in Rev. 16:1 ff., where the vials represent the unleashing of God's wrath against the beast. Edwards felt that things were already far along on this timetable.

By the consent of most divines, there are but few things, if any at all, that are foretold to be accomplished before the beginning of that glorious work of God [the millennium]. Some think the slaying of the witnesses, Rev. xi. 7, 8, is not yet accomplished. So divines differ with respect to the pouring out of the seven vials, of which we have an account, Rev. xvi, how many are already poured out, or how many remain to be poured out; though a late expositor [Moses Lowman] . . . seems to make it very plain and evident, that all are already poured out but two, viz. the sixth on the river Euphrates, and the seventh into the air. But I . . . only would say, that it seems to be something immediately preparing the way for the destruction of the spiritual Babylon.[9]

Just as the rise of Antichrist was gradual, so will be his fall. This makes the determination of the dates of the rise and fall difficult, but they are certain to be 1260 years apart. There shall be a great outpouring of the Spirit of God to empower the instruments of His will; and in spite of strenuous resistance by Antichrist, his kingdom of darkness will fall before the advance of the light. "And doubtless one nation shall be enlightened and converted after another, one false religion and false way of worship exploded after another."[10] In the conflict, true Christians will experience many difficulties, but

the kingdom of Antichrist shall be utterly overthrown. His kingdom and dominion has been much brought down already by the [fifth] vial poured out on his throne in the Reformation; but then it shall be utterly destroyed. Then shall be proclaimed, "Babylon is fallen, is fallen." When the seventh angel sounds, the time, times, and a half, shall be out, "and the time shall be no longer." Then shall be accomplished concerning Antichrist the things which are written in the 18th chapter of Revelation, of the spiritual Babylon, that great city Rome, or the idolatrous Roman government, that has for so many ages been the great enemy of the Christian church, first under Heathenism, then under Popery. That proud city, which lifted herself up to heaven, and above God himself, in her pride and haughtiness; that cruel, bloody city, shall come down to the ground. . . . She shall be thrown down with violence, like a great millstone cast into the sea, and shall be found no more at all, and shall become a habitation of devils, and the hold of every foul spirit, and a cage of every unclean and hateful bird. Now shall she be stripped of all her glory, and riches, and ornaments, and shall be cast out as an abominable branch, and shall be trodden-down as the mire of the streets. All her policy and craft, in which she so abounded, shall not save her. And God shall make his people, who have been so persecuted by her, to come and put their foot on the neck of Antichrist, and he shall be their foot-stool. All the strength and wisdom of this great whore shall fail her, and there shall be none to help her. The

> kings of the earth, who before gave their power and strength to the beast, shall now
> hate the whore, and shall make her desolate and naked, and shall eat her flesh, and
> burn her with fire, Rev. xvii. 16.[11]

It hardly need be said that the language here, though suggested by the biblical passage itself, is strongly reminiscent of "Sinners in the Hands of an Angry God."

A remarkable concomitant of the new influx of the Spirit of power into the true church is the mass conversion of the Jews. Though they have obstinately rejected Christ for centuries, yet the veil shall be removed from their eyes and their infidelity dispelled. "Nothing is more certainly foretold than this national conversion of the Jews is in the 11th chapter of Romans."[12] This will be truly life from the dead, and is in fact what is meant by "the first resurrection," Rev. 20:4. Moreover, heathen nations will be enlightened with the glorious gospel and respond in wonderful fashion. "There will be a wonderful spirit of pity towards them, and zeal for their instruction and conversion put into multitudes, and many shall go forth and carry the gospel unto them, and then shall the joyful sound be heard among them, and the Sun of righteousness shall then arise with glorious light shining on those many vast regions of the earth that have been covered with Heathenish darkness for many thousand years . . . under the cruel tyranny of the devil, who has all this while blinded and befooled them, and domineered over them, and made a prey of them from generation to generation."[13]

After Satan's visible kingdom is universally overthrown through the destruction of the apostate church, the conquest of Jewish infidelity, and the dispelling of heathen darkness, the church enters into the millennial reign of righteousness. Divine and human learning will spread over all the world: "the most barbarous nations shall become as bright and polite as England," ignorant and heathen lands shall bask in the brightest light of gospel truth, men shall live as brothers in a world of love, "and they shall all join the facets of their minds in exploring the glories of the Creator, their hearts in loving and adoring Him, their hands in serving Him, and their voices in making the welkin ring with His praise!"[14] It shall be a glorious time, "wherein the whole habitable world shall be blessed with honourable tokens of God's presence, not only as the Land of Canaan, but as the Temple; yea, as the holy of holies and the ark that had God's glory upon it."[15]

> 'Tis probable that the world shall be more like Heaven in the millennium in this
> respect: that contemplation and spiritual employments, and those things that more
> directly concern the mind and religion, will be more the saint's ordinary business
> than now. There will be so many contrivances and inventions to facilitate and expe-
> dite their necessary secular business that they shall have more time for more noble
> exercise, and that they will have better contrivances for assisting one another through
> the whole earth by more expedite, easy, and safe communication between distant
> regions than now. . . . And so the country about the poles need no longer be hid to us,
> but the whole earth may be as one community, one body in Christ.[16]

In this time will be fulfilled those prophecies of the Old Testament which speak of glory in the "latter days." It will be a time of great learning, of great holiness, of the universal regnancy of religion, of widespread peace and love, of excellent order and beauty in the church, of the greatest temporal prosperity, and of great rejoicing everywhere. Then at the close of this halcyon era, presumably of one thousand years duration, the smoldering embers of wickedness burst forth into flame once more; Satan comes forth to lead a widespread apostasy in fierce opposition to the church of God. The rebellion is short-lived, however, for Christ returns in person to subdue his enemies, raise the dead, and dispense judgment in the final consummation of the historical order.[17]

## THE IMMINENCY OF THE MILLENNIUM

Edwards considered that the most likely time for the end of the reign of Antichrist was 1260 years after either A.D. 606 (the recognition of the universal authority of the bishop of Rome), or A.D. 756 (the acceding of temporal power to the pope). In spite of the fact that either date would place the event far beyond his own lifetime, the revival stirrings on both sides of the Atlantic fired his imagination with the thought that the millennium might be in the immediate offing. He began to entertain the idea that God might have purposed to realize the biblical prophecies in America as a land destined to accomplish the renovation of the world. The year following the series of sermons that comprise the *History of Redemption*, which Perry Miller (perhaps too sanguinely) says "brought the people to the very threshold of the millennium,"[18] Edwards published his *Thoughts on the Revival of Religion in New England* (1740). Here he openly espouses the imminency of the golden age and attempts to show that many things make it probable that this work will begin in America. "This new world is probably now discovered, that the new and most glorious state of God's church on earth might commence there; that God might in it begin a new world in a spiritual respect, when he creates the *new heavens* and *new earth*."[19] Many contrasts between the scenes of the church's formation and those of its reformation suggest themselves to his mind. The old world had brought forth the historical Christ, but it had slain him too; the new world had received him and would offer him to all as the hope of the world.

The passing of the Great Awakening dimmed these hopes somewhat. But there still remained the possibility that the sweeping revivals were but forerunners of a greater movement—just as the wind and fire and earthquake had heralded at Horeb the coming of the Lord. This made Edwards most receptive to the proposal of the Scottish divines that true Christians everywhere unite in prayer for an outpouring of the Spirit that would bring in the great day of the Lord. Prayer would not necessarily hasten the day—that was settled in the inscrutable counsels of God—but it could prepare Christian hearts for its approach, and might even be part of the means God ordained for the fulfilling of his decree. "It is proper to pray for the general outpouring of the divine Spirit in the world, because there are many signs that such an event is near,—so very near that before the appointed seven years of prayer are ended, the day determined by divine decree may be ushered in."[20]

Edwards' correspondence with religious leaders in Scotland reveals his deep longing to see the millennial harbinger. Writing in 1743 to the Rev. William M'Culloch, he recounts the recent showers of blessing on New England, along with the ill winds which were threatening to drive them away.

> But yet I cannot think otherwise, than that what has now been doing, is the forerunner of something vastly greater, more pure, and more extensive. . . . I live upon the brink of the grave, in great infirmity of body, and nothing is more uncertain, than whether I shall live to see it: but I believe God will revive his work again before long, and that it will not wholly cease till it has subdued the whole earth.[21]

The present spiritual drouth, he opined, is likely sent to humble us ere God return with greater mercies. But—and here again he departs for conventional beliefs—*the worst of our troubles is already past*. In reply, M'Culloch cites the common expectation that before the overthrow of Antichrist and the dawning of the millennial day, the church will face extremely severe trials resulting in its almost total extinction and requiring direct divine intervention to save it. This was considered to be the import of the slaying of the two witnesses by the beast, Rev. 11. Edwards' answer of 1744 rejects this view by pointing out that the same passage goes on to predict the rising up of the witnesses after their attempted suppression. It is more than likely that this has already happened: "I humbly conceive that we can justly infer no more from this prophecy than this, viz, that the one thousand two hundred and sixty days is the proper time (as it were) of the Church's trouble and bondage, or being clothed in sackcloth, because it is the appointed time of the reign of antichrist; but this don't hinder but that God, out of great compassion to his Church, should, in some respect, *shorten the days*, and grant that his Church should, in some measure, anticipate the appointed great deliverance that should be at the end of these days, *as he has in fact done* in the Reformation; whereby his Church has had a great degree of restoration granted her, from the darkness, power and dominion of antichrist, before their proper time of restoration, which is at the end of one thousand two hundred and sixty days; and so the Church through the compassion of her Father and Redeemer, anticipates her deliverance from her sorrows; and has, in some respects, an end put to her testifying in sackcloth, as many parts of the Church are henceforward brought out from under the dominion of the antichristian powers, into a state of liberty; though in other respects, the Church may be said still to continue in her sackcloth, and in the wilderness, (as Chap. xii. 14,) till the end of the days."[22] In view of these thoughts, he concludes,

> 'Tis pity that we should expect such a terrible devastation of the Church, before her last and most glorious deliverance, if there be no such thing to be expected. It may be a temptation to some of the people of God, the less earnestly to wish and pray for the near approach of the Church's glorious day, and the less to rejoice in the signs of its approach.[23]

This, then, was the practical aspect of the problem. The commonly received opinion that the millennial age could be ushered in only by the most formidable and grievous trials the church had ever known was an error that seriously discouraged all efforts to advance the kingdom of Christ on earth. It was to answer this objection that Edwards composed in 1747 *A Humble Attempt to Promote Explicit Agreement and Visible Union of God's People in Extraordinary Prayer, for the Revival of Religion and the Advancement of Christ's Kingdom on Earth, Pursuant to Scripture Promises and Prophecies Concerning the Last Time*. The occasion was the "Memorial from Several Ministers in Scotland,to Their Brethren in Different Places, on Continuing a Concert for Prayer." (1744) To this proposal Edwards heartily acceded, for "it is evident from the Scripture, that there is yet remaining a great advancement of the interest of religion and the kingdom of Christ in this world, by an abundant outpouring of the Spirit of God, far greater and more extensive than ever yet has been."[24] After expatiating on the various motives for the proposed union in prayer, and on some of the more puerile objections, Edwards undertook to show that most Protestant interpreters before him had misread prophecy. "Another objection, that is very likely to arise in the minds of many against such extraordinary prayer as is proposed for the speedy coming of Christ's kingdom, is that we have no reason to expect it, until there first come a time of most extreme calamity to the church of God, and prevalence of her Antichristian enemies against her; even that which is represented, Rev. xi., by the slaying of the witnesses; but have reason to determine the contrary."[25] This objection, if allowed, would drastically inhibit earnest prayer. "For they that proceed on this hypothesis in their prayers, must, at the same time that they pray for this glorious day, naturally conclude within themselves, that they shall never live to see on the earth any dawning of it, but only to see the dismal time that shall precede it, in which the far greater part of God's people, that shall live until then, shall die under the extreme cruelties of their persecutors."[26] And the more God answers their prayers, the more must they expect to see themselves involved in catastrophe. It was a formidable objection.

Edwards answered it by expanding the position he had taken a few years earlier in his correspondence with M'Culloch. The events of Rev. 11:7–11 are regarded as already fulfilled. The time when the two witnesses lie dead is the time when the true gospel is suppressed by the Antichristian church; the Reformation marks their return to life and the beginning of the downfall of Antichrist. As in *History of Redemption*, the emptying of the vials of God's wrath on the throne of the beast is thought to be far along, and his fall, though gradual, will be swift and sure. "As the power of Antichrist, and the corruption of the apostate church, rose not at once, but by several notable steps and degrees; so it will in like manner fall: and that divers steps and seasons of destruction to the spiritual Babylon, and revival and advancement of the true church, are prophesied of under one."[27] The final stage of papal decline, in fact, may be at hand. "There are, as I apprehend, good reasons to hope, that that work of God's Spirit will begin in a little time, which, in the progress of it, will overthrow the kingdom of Antichrist, and in its issue destroy Satan's visible kingdom on earth."[28] The sixth vial, which Edwards viewed as predicting the drying up of the streams of revenue by which the rapacious papacy had glutted itself for centuries, is probably already in progress. Here he follows Moses Lowman, who had identified the fifth vial with the Reformation.

It also appears satisfyingly, by his late exposition, that, take one vial with another, it has not been two hundred years from the beginning of one vial to the beginning of another, but about one hundred and eighty years. But it is now about two hundred and twenty years since the fifth vial began to be poured; and it is a long time since the main effects of it have been finished. And therefore if the sixth vial has not already begun to be poured out, it may well be speedily expected.[29]

Edwards proceeded to draw evidences from recent history to indicate the shrinking income and influence of the papacy: witness especially the political and military reverses of France, one of Rome's mainstays.

Lest, however, he become intoxicated with the prospect of standing on the threshold of the millennium, he reminds himself at the last that no man makes a timetable for Jehovah. Would it not still be a wonderful thing if in one half-century Protestantism could be purified and Spirit-filled, in another half-century the power of popish abominations broken, in a third half-century the Mohammedans subdued and the Jews converted? "And then in the next whole century [which would extend to the year 2000], the whole heathen world should be enlightened and converted to the Christian faith, throughout all parts of Africa, Asia, America and Terra Australis, and be thoroughly settled in the Christian faith and order, without any remainders of their old delusions and superstitions, and this attended with an utter extirpation of the remnant of the church of Rome, and all the relics of Mahometanism, heresy, schism and enthusiasm [!], and a suppression of all remains of open vice and immorality, and every sort of visible enemy to true religion, through the whole earth, and bring to an end all the unhappy commotions, tumults, and calamities occasioned by such great changes, and all things so adjusted and settled through the world, that the world thenceforward should enjoy a holy rest or sabbatism?"[30]

This points up the fact that Edwards allowed no discontinuities in history; the victory was to be won gradually, whether the battle be long or short. "But whatever our hopes may be in this respect, we must be content to be ignorant of the times and seasons, which the Father hath put in his own power; and must be willing that God should answer prayer, and fulfill his own glorious promises, in his own time."[31] He was content to wait on the Lord, believing in the *certain* coming of the kingdom and hoping for its *soon* coming.

## THE NOVELTY OF THIS IDEA

It is worth repeating that Edwards was an able exponent of traditional orthodoxy regarding the future state. This should negate the usual allegation that postmillennialism is always allied with liberal thought. But because his millennial ideas constitute a major innovation, it may be well to explore more his relation to his own tradition and inquire into the source of the new departure.

To begin with, since Edwards is recognized generally as a Calvinist in theology, one might ask how his eschatology comports with that of the Reformer. There is no noteworthy difference between the two as far as their beliefs concerning the eternal order are concerned; but their views diverge markedly with respect to the millennium. Calvin decisively rejected all chiliastic notions as impoverishing, if not destroying, the Christian hope.[32] He followed Augustine in making the "first resurrection" refer to individual regeneration; and the "thousand years" are simply a period of church history (the present and last) during which Christ reigns in the hearts of individual believers and over the church, his body. The very word "millennium" is foreign to his thought except as a symbolic term to be used guardedly and always in a spiritualized sense. He certainly would not endorse Edwards' sanguine speculations regarding the golden age of the church as a still future period of history. Calvin thought the people of God were destined to wander as pilgrims on the earth until the end of time.

> The church lives under the sign of the cross, so that it dies daily, and is resurrected again and again only by the wondrous grace of God until the day of its ultimate and perfect resurrection. "God is the Saviour of His church until the end, but the manner in which He saves it must not be judged according to our natural feeling; for until the time of its final victory the church will ever resemble a dead corpse."[33]

Edwards was likewise at odds with the Westminster Confession, on which the orthodoxy of his day ultimately rested. It simply is not true to say with Foster that his eschatology represents no new departure from this historic symbol. The Westminster Confession mentions the return of Christ at the end of the age for judgment, asserts the eternal destinies of the righteous and the wicked in unequivocal terms, identifies the pope as the man of sin and the son of perdition, and so forth. But it is completely silent on the subject of the millennium, and taken as a whole, is actually amillennial in import—as are all the historic creeds of Christendom before it.[34]

The pastor at Northampton, of course, lived in the milieu of the Saybrook Platform, which brought the Westminster standards to Connecticut via the Cambridge Platform and the Savoy Declaration.[35] Although these recensions hesitated to take too many liberties with the parent creed, the Savoy Declaration (1658) added a significant paragraph to the article on the church: "As the Lord is in care and love towards his Church, and hath in his infinite wise providence exercised it with great variety in all ages, for the good of them that love him, and his own glory; so, according to his promise, we expect that in the latter days, Antichrist being destroyed, the Jews called and the adversaries of the kingdom of his dear Son broken, the churches of Christ being enlarged and edified through a free and plentiful communication of light and grace, shall enjoy in this world a more quiet, peaceful, and glorious condition than they have enjoyed."[36] This is the first creedal statement by any confessional group to embody definite millennial presuppositions. Its repetition at Cambridge and Saybrook brought it within the purview of Jonathan Edwards, who was first to give full explication to its more radical suggestions.[37]

Edwards was not unconscious that in assigning the darkest days of the Christian church to the past and transposing the return of Christ to the close of the millennium he was going counter to Protestant opinion for two centuries. Moreover, those who eagerly read and disseminated his works were not slow to recognize the discrepancy. The preface to the American edition of *Humble Attempt* states: "As to the author's ingenious observation on the *prophecies*, we entirely leave them to the reader's judgment; with only observing, though it is the apprehension of many learned men, that there is to be a very *general slaughter of the witnesses of* CHRIST, when about finishing their testimony to the pure worship and truths of the gospels, about three or four years before the *seventh angel* sounds his trumpet for the ruin of antichrist. . . ." Dwight is at pains to show that the new departure rested on a careful fresh exegesis of the prophetic Scriptures.

> In the course of this Treatise, Mr. Edwards was led, in answering objections, to examine an Interpretation of Prophecy, until then most generally if not universally received: viz. *That the kingdom of Christ could not come, until there had previously been a time of most extreme calamity to the Church of God, and prevalence of her Antichristian enemies against her, as represented in* Rev. xi. *by the Slaying of the Witnesses.* Some years before this, Mr. Edwards had examined the Apocalypse with great care, in connexion with the Prophecy of Daniel; in order to satisfy himself whether the *Slaying of the Witnesses* was to be regarded as past, or future. This he did with his pen in his hand; and a brief abstract of his views on this point, is found in the answers to the 4th and 5th objections in the Humble Attempt. The views of prophecy, here presented by Mr. Edwards, were, I believe, at the time wholly new to the Christian world, and were at first regarded by many as doubtful, if not erroneous; but have since produced the general conviction, that the downfall of Popery and the ultimate extension of the kingdom of Christ, are far less distant than has been supposed—a conviction remarkably supported by the whole series of Providential dispensations. And there can be no doubt that this conviction has been a prime cause, of the present concentrated movement of the whole Church of God, to hasten forward the Reign of the Messiah.[38]

Other biographers of Edwards join Dwight in regarding this innovation as a distinct contribution to Christian thought, in that it removed fears of the near approach of the end and encouraged Christian effort in the extension of the kingdom. Could one expect less from the theologian of the Great Awakening?

## SOURCE OF THE NEW IDEAS

Although contrary to then current opinion on two major counts, Edwards' prophetic interpretation was not entirely unprecedented. Opinions vary, however, regarding the source of his innovations. Perry Miller suggests that he took his cue from the apocalyptic speculations of the physicists. Isaac Newton, whom Edwards read avidly, had advanced a mechanistic hypothesis for the cataclysmic destruction of the world, and had even tried to calculate the time of the end from the prophecies in Daniel and the Revelation. In this theory he was followed by William Whiston, who envisioned a social and political millennium on the earth after a "celestial flamethrower" had withered all wickedness. Thomas Burnet had preceded both of these with a mechanical theory of world destruction by natural causes. In reading these eminent men, Edwards sensed that their lack of ethical insight had led them to abandon the concept of judgment. According to Miller, he was a "latecomer to the apocalyptic tradition, approaching it at the moment when the scientists were bent upon appropriating it into the area of causation."[39] He therefore sought to modify the apocalyptic physicists by

> accepting the whole suspect [?] doctrine of the millennium, which Whiston had fastened upon the conception by making it the reward of destruction. But Edwards puts it historically on this side of the apocalypse, allowing the thousand years of earthly virtue to be produced through natural causes; only thereafter does he call in the Judgment. He gives humanity all that Whiston and the mechanists demanded: he gives them their millennium, and lets it be shown that even with so long a conditioning in righteousness, mankind will still fall back into depravity, from which there can be no escape except the cry at midnight. . . . By then the saints will know—as indeed they know even now—that they must ascend into Heaven, leaving this world, with all its beauty to the flames, "there being no further use for it."[40]

The exact method of the final conflagration is not a necessary object of speculation.

This is an intriguing theory, but it does scant justice to some of the more obvious evidence. One should not overlook the explanation which lies closer to the surface, namely, Edwards' familiarity with the biblical commentaries of Daniel Whitby, Charles Daubuz, and Moses Lowman. These men are landmarks in the development of an entirely new pattern of eschatological thought which arose in the Middle Ages, a pattern which can be suggested here only in barest outline. After popular expectations of the world's end in the eleventh century (based on an erroneous reading of Augustine) had failed of realization, hopes for the personal return of Christ shaded over into a longing for purification of the corrupt ecclesiastical system. Joachim of Flora, who articulated the new expectancy, shifted the emphasis from the Apocalypse to the promise of the coming Comforter, and predicted a final glorious age of the Spirit before the end. Orthodox Catholics continued to hope for the eventual world-wide domination of the Roman Church as envisioned by Aquinas. Reformation revolutionaries attempted to force a speedy inauguration of the kingdom by taking matters into their own hands. *All of these developments implied definitely postmillennial assumptions.* Although the Reformers sought to recover the realistic eschatology of the early Christian era by reasserting the apocalyptic elements, anticipations of a palmy period of earthly bliss to precede the return of Christ continued to find sporadic expression. Lutheran Pietism, for example, betrays postmillennial predilections; and the subtle chiliasm of the Savoy Declaration has already been noticed.

The man who is generally regarded as the originator of post-millennialism in its modern form is Daniel Whitby (1638–1725). An English latitudinarian, he published in 1703 a mammoth two-volume work, *Paraphrase and Commentary on the New Testament,* to which was appended (in lieu of a commentary on the Revelation) "A Treatise of the Millennium: Shewing That It Is Not a Reign of Persons Raised from the Dead, but of the Church Flourishing

Gloriously for a Thousand Years after the Conversion of the Jews, and the Flowing-in of All Nations to Them Thus Converted to the Christian Faith." The popularity of this work may be judged by the fact that it reached its seventh printing the year after Jonathan Edwards died. Its purport is clearly indicated in the cumbersome title. Whitby regards the "first resurrection" as the wholesale conversion of the Jews, under whose leadership the church flourishes throughout the earth with the consequent obedience of the Gentiles to the gospel. This is the reign of the saints on earth, a reign of Christ only in the spiritual sense. It lasts for a thousand years, closing with a brief insurrection of wickedness which is subdued by Christ as he returns to put an end to time and history.

Whitby was followed in this general scheme by two of his contemporaries, Charles Daubuz and Moses Lowman. Edwards read and quoted all three (Whitby was his arch-enemy in the Arminian controversy), but it was the commentary of Lowman on Revelation, published in 1737, which appealed to him most.[41] Copious references to Lowman as "a learned expositor" appear in both *History of Redemption* and *Humble Attempt*. Edwards recognized that Lowman differed from most other commentators, and indeed, he did not hesitate to differ with Lowman where he felt it necessary. But at the crucial point concerning the church's golden age within history, he is in complete agreement. The whole tenor of Edwards' eschatology so comports with the Whitby-Lowman exegesis that one must regard this, more than any Puritan attempt to ethicize the apocalyptic physicists, as the immediate source of his millennial speculations.

## INFLUENCE ON LATER THOUGHT

Although Jonathan Edwards is not regarded as the founder of a "school" of theology in the formal sense, most of his ideas were reproduced—albeit in modified form—by one or another of the New England theologians. For the most part, such men as Joseph Bellamy, Jonathan Edwards, Jr., Timothy Dwight, and Samuel Hopkins were content to follow their master in eschatology. They relied on the same commentators and in general articulated the same scheme. One or two observations may suffice to point out the new directions of eschatological thought as influenced by the elder Edwards.

The rising tide of Universalist sentiment forced the followers of Edwards to a new defense of the doctrine of eternal punishment. Here they found it necessary to abandon his arbitrary rationalization about an infinite sin as the violation of an infinite obligation to the infinite Being and therefore deserving an infinite, i.e., an eternal punishment. Rather, they shifted the argument to more biblical grounds and sought to establish by exegesis that God has declared that eternal punishment is just, and thus the matter was settled. But even while refusing to surrender the basic doctrine, they found a way to relax the rigor of a stern eschatological dualism; and it was the new idea of a historical millennium which gave them the opportunity. Whereas Edwards had maintained that relatively few would be saved, his successors argued that probably the greater part of the human race would find mercy because of wholesale conversions during the millennium. Bellamy even undertook to show arithmetically how this could be; assuming the population to be the same throughout the six thousand years of world history [sic!] as at the beginning of the millennium, and to double every fifty years during the thousand-year reign, the ratio of the saved to the lost in the final total would be more than seventeen thousand to one![42] Hopkins acquiesced in this notion, though perhaps with less mathematical precision. Both seemed to take comfort in relegating to eternal misery only a few incorrigibles and thus they softened the severity of God's wrath while continuing to uphold the theory of justice. It is one of the ironies of history that Edwards himself, by his doctrine of the millennium, supplied this escape mechanism. Perhaps he gave away his argument unintentionally—or was he ever the *philosophe?*

At all events, he gained the distinction of being America's first major postmillennial thinker. As such, he may be said to have furnished a religious philosophy for responding to the challenge of "manifest destiny." The importance of the religious background of the idea of progress can never be disparaged; and though direct evidence may be lacking, it is difficult to believe that Edwards' historicizing of the millennium did not furnish a strong impetus to utopianism in America. His novel interpretation took hold readily. Hopkins' 142-page "Treatise on the Millennium" appended to his two-volume work, *The System of Doctrines,* is unapologetically Edwardsean; and others besides theologians were ready to espouse the new theory, too. Though Edwards knew it not, his historical millennium was of a piece with the liberalizing thought which came to full flower in the following century. The encouragement it gave to the efficacy of human effort made it a natural ally to the new doctrine of human ability which already had begun to make inroads on the older Calvinism. Bellamy called the saints to action, "because there is so much to be done, and the glorious Day is coming on!"[43] In another context, this was exactly suited to the American nationalistic temper: the new world was to be the scene of dawning glory and no hand could stay its coming. Whatever the tragedy of the ultimate secularization of the millennial hope, it becomes an integral part of the optimistic activism which was destined to crown with success the "errand into the wilderness." This is Jonathan Edwards' contribution to the radical utopianism which is part of the American tradition.

## Notes

1. *Bibliotheca Sacra*, 43 (1886), 1–32, 287–302, 711–728, and continued in subsequent volumes.

2. Ola Elizabeth Winslow, *Jonathan Edwards* (New York: The Macmillan Co., 1941), p. 193.

3. Cf. *Charity and Its Fruits* (London, 1851). The last chapter alone is sufficient to contradict Miss Winslow's judgment that Edwards' treatment of heaven was two-dimensional and prosaic.

4. Perry Miller, *Jonathan Edwards* (New York: William Sloan Associates, 1949), p. 310.

5. Other modes of interpreting Revelation are the Preterist, which regards nearly all of its prophecies as already fulfilled, the Futurist, which place fulfillment largely at the end of the age, and the Historical Background, which seeks to understand its message in terms of the situation in which it was written and received.

6. These ideas have their source in the chiliastic sects of the Middle Ages, notably the Franciscan Spirituals, who espoused Joachimite doctrine in the thirteenth century. They are common notions of Wycliffe, Huss, the Taborites, some of the Anabaptists, and the Reformers generally.

7. Jonathan Edwards, *Works* (New York: Robert Carter and Bros., 1881), I, 457. This is a reprint of the Worcester edition, which has been considered more or less standard, although it has some variations in arrangement.

8. *Ibid.*, p. 456. Interpreters of the "Historical" School assign to the reign of Antichrist 1260 years by the application of the year-day principle to Rev. 12:6, 14; 13:5; etc.

9. *Ibid.*, p. 480.

10. *Ibid.*, p. 482.

11. *Ibid.*, p. 486.

12. *Ibid.*, p. 487.

13. *Ibid.*, pp. 487 ff.

14. Harvey G. Townsend (ed.), *The Philosophy of Jonathan Edwards from His Private Notebooks* (Eugene: University of Oregon Press, 1955), p. 207.

15. Alexander B. Grosart (ed.), *Selections from the Unpublished Writings of Jonathan Edwards* (private printing, 1865), p. 128.

16. Townsend, *op. cit.*, pp. 207 f.

17. Edwards believed that the personal, visible return of Christ at the end of the age is prefigured by several other crises in history: the destruction of Jerusalem, the victory of Constatine, the time of the Reformation.

18. Miller, *op. cit.*, p. 318.

19. Edwards, *Works*, III, 314.

20. Alexander V. G. Allen, *Jonathan Edwards* (Boston: Houghton, Mifflin and Co., 1890), p. 236.

21. S. E. Dwight, *The Life of President Edwards* (New York: G. and C. and H. Carvill, 1830), p. 197. This sentiment appears often.

22. *Ibid.*, p. 217. Italics mine.

23. *Ibid.*, p. 218.

24. Edwards, *Works*, III, 439.

25. *Ibid.*, p. 471.

26. *Ibid.*, p. 472.

27. *Ibid.*, p. 491.

28. *Ibid.*, p. 494.

29. *Ibid.*, p. 500.

30. *Ibid.*, p. 493.

31. *Ibid.*, p. 507. Perry Miller accuses Edwards of believing, for a time at least, that the millennium had actually begun in Northampton. (*Op. cit.*, p. 318.) Edwards answers this himself: "It has been slanderously reported and printed concerning me, that I have often said, that the Millennium was already begun, and that it began at Northampton. A doctor of divinity in New England, has ventured to publish this report to the world, for a single person, who is concealed and kept behind the curtain: but the report is very diverse from what I have ever said. Indeed I have often said, as I say now, that I looked upon the late wonderful revivals of Religion as forerunners of

those glorious times so often prophesied of in the Scripture, and that this was the first dawning of that light, and beginning of that work, which, in the progress and issue of it, would at last bring on the Church's latter day glory; but there are many that know that I have from time to time added, that there would probably be many sore conflicts and terrible convulsions, and many changes, revivings and intermissions, and returns of dark clouds, and threatening appearances, before this work shall have subdued the world, and Christ's kingdom shall be every where established and settled in peace, which will be the lengthening of the Millennium or day of the Church's peace, rejoicing and triumph on earth, so often spoken of." (Dwight, *op. cit.*, p. 213.)

32. *Institutes of the Christian Religion* iii. 25. 5. It should be stated that Calvin knew millennial faith only as exhibited in the carnal chiliasm of the revolutionary Anabaptists, and he pictured them (probably erroneously) as believing in nothing beyond the earthly kingdon which they were bent on setting up by force.

33. Heinrich Quistorp, *Calvin's Doctrine of the Last Things,* trans. Harold Knight (Richmond: John Knox Press, 1955), p. 177.

34. Cf. J. A. Brown, "The Second Advent and the Creeds of Christendom," *Bibliotheca Sacra* 24 (1867), 629–51.

35. After Cutler's defection to episcopacy in 1722 (just before Edwards entered Yale), orthodoxy in Connecticut was strictly defined as complete acceptance of the Saybrook Platform. In this rigorous doctrinal environment, "by both precept and example, he was predisposed to subscribe to the Saybrook Platform . . . before he was asked." (Winslow, *op. cit.*, p. 85.)

36. Philip Schaff, *Creeds of Christendom* (New York: Harper and Bros., 1877), III, 723. The article on the return of Christ precedes this in the confession; whether a temporal precedence is intended or not is impossible to say.

37. This is not to say that either Edwards' predecessors or contemporaries eschewed chiliasm. Early colonial writings are replete with references to prophecy; legislators and educators, historians and theologians wrote on prophecy with the general framework of the "Historical" School. But virtually every one holds to the premillennial return of Christ, and most of them place it far in the future. Postmillennialism as an explicit tenet was unknown. "The founders of New England were not social radicals—they preached the millennium as far off, so that for the present we must be visible saints and submit to church discipline." (Miller, *op. cit.*, p. 320.)

38. Dwight, *op. cit.*, p. 246. See also pp. 211, 219.

39. Perry Miller, "The End of the World," *Errand into the Wilderness* (Cambridge: Belknap Press of Harvard University Press, 1956), p. 239.

40. *Ibid.*, p. 235.

41. In Jonathan Edwards' list of books "to be enquired after" is "the best exposition of the Apocalypse." My guess is that he found Lowman's work nearest to this desideratum. Cf. Thomas H. Johnson, "Jonathan Edwards' Background of Reading," PCSM, 27 (1931), 193–222.

42. Joseph Bellamy, "The Millennium," *Sermons* (Boston: Edes and Gill, 1758), pp. 62 ff.

43. *Ibid.*, p. 69.

# A Notebook on the Apocalypse
# by Jonathan Edwards

Stephen J. Stein°

In 1723 at the age of nineteen, Jonathan Edwards drew together his reflections on the book of Revelation and penned the following private conjecture concerning the millennium: "And what further confirms that the sabbath of the world will begin near about the beginning of the seventh thousand years of the world, is because we are sure, it cannot be far from it. For we are coming near it already; so that the beginning of this glorious time, cannot be very far on this side."[1]

Nearly twenty years later during the heat of the Great Awakening, he published a glowing report suggesting that the "glorious day" may have dawned with the outbreak of the revivals. Edwards calculated the general evangelical successes of the day, particularly those in New England, to be "the beginning or forerunner of something vastly great."[2] In subsequent generations such speculations were sometimes a shibboleth for Edwards's disciples, other times a source of embarrassment. His detractors in every age make them the object of ridicule and derision. Neither detractors nor disciples, however—nor scholars, for that matter—have invested heavily in a close examination of his commitment to biblical prophecy.[3]

The contemporary convergence of several movements in American scholarship promises to alter the situation by providing a new assessment of Edwards's apocalypticism within the larger context of colonial thought and life. One converging force is the strong continuing interest in Puritan studies, a movement which now has entered a second and more sophisticated phase.[4] Another contributory trend is signaled by the growing importance accorded the interpretation of the Bible in literary circles concerned with early America.[5] Thirdly, the forthcoming bicentennial celebration of the birth of the nation will aid indirectly in the reassessment by means of the examination of eighteenth-century life which is being carried out, including the religious dimensions of colonial existence.[6] Finally and perhaps most importantly, the Yale edition of *The Works of Jonathan Edwards* will contribute substantially by providing public access to Edwards's unpublished writings, an essential prerequisite for any serious reappraisal.

°Reprinted, with permission, from *The William and Mary Quarterly*, 29 (October 1972), 623–34.

Even without such materials being available, the process of reassessment has begun. Alan Heimert, for one, has theorized concerning the larger significance of Edwards's apocalypticism. Flying in the face of a body of established literature, he assigns primary responsibility for the formation of Revolutionary ideals in eighteenth-century America to the evangelical party born and nurtured in the Great Awakening. Heimert underscores the role played by the apocalypticism of Edwards and other evangelicals: "Whether the millennial theory of post-Awakening Calvinism was intellectually respectable may be questioned, but what cannot be gainsaid is that the expectancy expressed in that theory controlled the mind of the period."[7] Despite several frontal attacks upon his thesis, Heimert's revisionary proposal has succeeded in delineating a major point of debate for the coming decade.[8] To date, however, the scholarly exchanges have not drawn upon the full wealth of potential resources. Little or no reference, for example, has been made to the private reflections of Edwards upon apocalyptic themes and texts. Furthermore, a principal repository of his writings on the subject, the unpublished "Notes on the Apocalypse," has not even been introduced. The balance of this essay is a description of Edwards's private notebook on the Revelation, its appearance and history, composition and dating, and its potential significance for colonial studies.

In its present form, the "Apocalypse" is the product of thirty-five years of study and reflection. The manuscript is a quarto measuring approximately six and one-half by eight inches; it consists of 208 numbered pages which are stitched together into six quires of unequal size. Fifteen of the pages remain blank. In addition, a gathering of eight unnumbered, unattached pages has been inserted at the end of the notebook. The volume was assembled over a period of many years as the different kinds of paper, the contrasting inks, the assorted threads and twines, and the varied styles of stitching attest. The notebook is in remarkably good repair with only a few edges on the first pages seriously frayed, the result of a missing front cover. A few wormholes aside, the "Apocalypse" remains substantially intact.

The table of contents for the manuscript is as follows:

The contents of the "Apocalypse" are a highly diverse lot, held together less by actual integration in the notebook and more by the integrity of Edwards's interests and intentions.

The manuscript displays numerous changes in Edwards's handwriting, further documenting the gradual compilation of the notebook. Modifications in the size and formation of the written characters chart the various periods of his lifetime. The earliest entries are written in a very small but well-formed script of a circular nature. As the years passed, Edwards adopted a more angular style. The letters became larger and were not formed as carefully: less precision and more haste are apparent on his part. The changes in writing style produced a substantial decline in the average number of words on a page, from more than 1,150 words per page in the opening section of the notebook to less than 450 words near the end of the manuscript. Despite these wide variations, at no point is the usefulness of the "Apocalypse" impaired by illegibility; in fact, the changes in the hand are important clues for dating the various parts of the notebook.[9]

Legibility aside, prior to the decade of the 1960s the "Apocalypse" was virtually an unknown notebook. The history of the manuscript is the tale of a document hidden from public view which narrowly avoided several potential mishaps. Initially the "Apocalypse," together with the majority of Edwards's manuscripts, passed through the hands of faithful admirers such as Samuel Hopkins, his closest disciple; Jonathan Edwards, Jr., his son and theological heir; and Sereno E. Dwight, grandson and editor of his works. The only identifiable reference to the "Apocalypse" in their writings come from the hand of Dwight, who wrote as follows in his biography of Edwards:

> Some years before this, Mr. Edwards had examined the Apocalypse with great care, in connexion with the Prophecy of Daniel; in order to satisfy himself whether the *slaying of the witnesses* was to be regarded as past, or future. This he did with his pen in his hand; and a brief abstract of his views on this point, is found in the answers to the 4th and 5th objections in the Humble Attempt.[10]

Note No. 90 in the "Apocalypse" is a detailed examination of the slaying of the two witnesses (Rev. 11).[11] The *Humble Attempt*, published in 1748, was Edwards's plea for a concert in prayer among evangelicals throughout the world.[12] This reference notwithstanding, the point is that in the early years of its existence the "Apocalypse" attracted little attention.

During the balance of the nineteenth century, the "Apocalypse" with the other manuscripts passed through increasingly perilous times, bouncing between factious family members and would-be editors. To good fortune and the concern of some of the family must be credited its continued existence. Once in the decade before the Civil War, an editor of *The Congregational Review* happened to see the notebook on the Revelation. "We wish," he wrote, "that the work on the Apocalypse might be transcribed and given to the world, and that speedily."[13] Such, however, was not its destiny. The "Apocalypse" escaped the pirating hands of Alexander B. Grosart, who wanted to produce a Scottish edition of Edwards's works,[14] only to fall into the clutches of Edwards Amasa Park of Andover Seminary, scion of the family and would-be biographer. Park's projected biography of Edwards kept the manuscripts away from the public for more than a quarter of a century, a period of careless guardianship in which survival was something of a miracle in itself. Park's death sealed the fate of his biography which never advanced much beyond the drawing board.[15] His death also led directly to the deposition of the main body of Edwardsiana in the libraries of Yale University in August 1900, thanks to the continuing interest of a group within the surviving family.[16] More than sixty years of quiet followed before the "Apocalypse" and the other papers took their place in the Beinecke Rare Book and Manuscript Library at Yale, their present location.

That the "Apocalypse" remained hidden from public view is understandable, considering this history. That it escaped the net of researchers in the field is more surprising. Alan Heimert, who makes the eschatological ideas of Edwards so primary in his argument, shows no awareness of the notebook. His oversight is puzzling on two counts. In the first place, Ola E. Winslow's prizewinning biography published in 1940 lists "Notes on Revelation" in the catalogue of Edwards's manuscripts.[17] Secondly, Heimert was the student and professed protégé of Perry Miller, the first general editor of the Yale edition of *The Works of Jonathan Edwards*, who had direct knowledge of the existence of the "Apocalypse." Miller's own intellectual biography of Edwards, however, also did not mention the notebook.[18] Even C. C. Goen's essay on Edwards's eschatology, the only scholarly article directly related to the topic, does not acknowledge the existence of the manuscript, although he wrote the essay while a graduate student at Yale University.[19] Therefore Thomas Schafer's work with the manuscripts of Edwards was the first scholarly examination of the "Apocalypse." His investigations are being followed, in turn, by preparation of a critical edition of the text by this essayist as part of the Yale edition of the *Works*.

Edwards wrote the opening section of the manuscript in 1723, the year in which he returned to New England after serving a short stint as a supply minister in New York. Later he reminisced in his spiritual autobiography about those days:

> If I heard the least hint of any thing that happened, in any part of the world, that appeared, in some respect or other, to have a favorable aspect on the interests of Christ's kingdom, my soul eagerly catched at it; and it would much animate and refresh me. I used to be eager to read public news letters, mainly for that end; to see if I could not find some news favorable to the interest of religion in the world.[20]

The "Apocalypse" establishes that Edwards persisted in this particular habit until his death. The last entry in the notebook is a citation taken from the *Connecticut Gazette* of December 10, 1757, published slightly more than three months before he died at Princeton. The excerpt tells of new plans by the king of Spain to tax the Spanish clergy, a move Edwards regarded as contributing to the weakening and eventual overthrow of the antichristian papal forces.[21]

Edwards began the notebook intending to compile a private commentary on the Apocalypse. The first twelve pages of the manuscript are a chapter-by-chapter discussion of the book of Revelation, most of which was written in a relatively short time. In this opening synopsis he penned the youthful conjecture concerning the millennium quoted in the initial paragraph of this essay. His early reflections in the "Apocalypse" dovetail directly with even earlier comments on similar topics located among the first entries of his "Theological Miscellanies."[22] The first section of the "Apocalypse," as a systematic treatment of a book in the Bible, is unmatched by any other piece of exegetical writing in Edwards's corpus. Here is detailed the fullest picture of the young exegete at work.

The chapter-by-chapter synopsis is followed in the manuscript by a series of successively numbered random notes on various passages in the book of Revelation. The random procedure is typical of Edwards's notebooks. Entries vary in length, from only a few lines to nearly thirteen pages. They also vary in nature, with excerpts quoted verbatim from his reading alongside highly speculative original passages based on his own reflections. The series of ninety-three entries spans more than three decades of his life, some late notes and addenda being written in the mid-1750s. The numbered series is, therefore, a primary measure of Edwards's changing thoughts on the Revelation. Sometimes these notes served as preparatory sketches for parts of essays published subsequently. The seventy-eighth entry, for example, a discussion of the pouring of the sixth vial upon the great River Euphrates (Rev. 16:12), appeared in a later redaction in the *Humble Attempt*.[23]

In another major section of the notebook entitled "Extracts from Mr. Lowman," Edwards copied extended passages from a commentary on the Revelation by Moses Lowman (1680–1752), a dissenting English divine who was the author of several works related to antiquity.[24] During the mid-1740s Edwards filled forty pages with excerpts from Lowman relating to the historical interpretation of the apocalyptic visions of the seals, the trumpets, and the vials in the Revelation (Rev. 6:1–17, 8:1–5; 8:6–9, 12; II:15–19; 15:1–16:21). He added another version in which he evaluated the nature and adequacy of Lowman's exegesis, rendering substantive criticism of his historical, theological, and hermeneutical perspectives. His reading of Lowman had a dual effect upon him, confirming his own convictions regarding the nature and importance of apocalyptic but also causing him to alter some details in his eschatological timetable.

The pace of entries in the "Apocalypse" was irregular in the years between 1723 and 1747. Edwards wrote the early pages of the notebook in a relatively short period of time, but subsequent portions were completed more sporadically. Time gaps, for example, are evident when he assumed the responsibilities as tutor at Yale in the middle of 1724 and when he shouldered the full burden of parish activities in Northampton at the beginning of 1729 following the death of his grandfather and associate, Solomon Stoddard.[25] The entries made intermittently during the next years show Edwards returning at times to focus anew upon aspects of apocalyptic. After October 1747 his steady use of the notebook can be tracked through the dates of newspaper and magazine excerpts.

The most unusual portions of the "Apocalypse," setting it apart from Edwards's other manuscripts, are the sections resembling a scrapbook used for recording data from contemporary affairs. These parts of the notebook contradict the common stereotype of Edwards the scholar, buried in theological tomes from morning to night, oblivious to all activity in the world around him. From the pages of the "Apocalypse" emerges Edwards the student of contemporary affairs. Beginning in October 1747, he regularly transcribed excerpts from newspapers and magazines, gradually filling a section entitled "An Account of Events Probably Fulfilling the Sixth Vial on the River Euphrates." According to his interpretation of the Revelation, the stage was being set for an overthrow of the forces of evil and antichristianism. The final blow will fall with the pouring of the seventh vial (Rev. 16:17). The sixth vial, however, "is the last thing that shall be done against her, before the very stroke is given by which she shall be destroyed."[26] This vial of God's wrath weakens and undermines the temporal power and authority of the papacy and Roman Catholic nations. In this fashion Edwards fitted the international imperial struggles of the day into a providential view of history through which God worked out his preconceived economy. Edwards used the "Apocalypse" to keep score in the cosmic struggle being waged on the earthly stage with human dramatis personae. Naval successes by Protestant powers—the English, the Dutch, and the colonists in America— were evidence of weakening the antichristian forces. For this reason he entered into his notebook a list of French men-of-war with their armaments and crews captured by the English.

|                    | Guns | Men     |
| ------------------ | ---- | ------- |
| Le Grand Monarque  | 74   | 620     |
| Le Terrible        | 74   | 620     |
| Le Neptune         | 70   | 620     |
| Le Trident         | 64   | 500     |
| Tonond             | 80   | 750     |
| Le Severn          | 50   | 480     |
| Intrepid           | 74   | 620[27] |

"Drying up the River Euphrates" was equivalent to choking off "the outward carnal supplies and incomes of the false antichristian church."[28] The list of events fulfilling the sixth vial is the negative side of a divine ledger maintained by Edwards.

After March 1748 Edwards began to compile a second, smaller list on the positive side of the ledger, showing the advances of Christ's kingdom. Under the heading "Events of an Hopeful Aspect on the State of Religion," he tallied favorable occurrences which came to his attention through newspapers, correspondence, or personal activity. To him these positive signs signaled the spread of a gospel kingdom and the consequent approach of the end time. He attached special importance to accounts of missionary successes among the Indians, the Turks, Russians, or Jews; each of these groups at one time or another had assumed special apocalyptic significance in the Protestant exegetical tradition.[29]

For example, he copied an account of a conversion from the *Boston Gazette* of May 3, 1748:

> London, February 3. Last Wednesday afternoon, a Jew, eminent for his great knowledge of the Hebrew and Chaldee languages, was after a proper confession of his faith, publicly baptized at the meetinghouse in Paul's Alley, Barbican.[30]

In the "Apocalypse" is reflected the image of Edwards watching providence in action, keeping track of the score as the millenium gradually approached. But he was not content to watch on the sidelines. In the *Humble Attempt* he called for concerted prayer and lively preaching, two positive steps which will hasten the coming of the glorious day.[31]

The dating of individual entries in the "Apocalypse" occasionally assumes special importance, as in the case of the earliest parts of the manuscript; but the most significant chronological observation about the notebook is more general.[32] The "Apocalypse" stretches across thirty-five years of Edwards's life, nearly his entire period of maturity. This long span of time makes possible an assessment of change and development, thereby enhancing the value of the notebook as a tool in the evaluation of the apocalypticism of Edwards. The notebook functioned in various ways during different periods of Edwards's life: as a discursive commentary on the Revelation, as a copybook for transcribing authors whom he found insightful on topics related to apocalyptic, as a scrapbook for collecting accounts from his reading in contemporary affairs, and for listing evidences of progress in God's kingdom, and as a sketchbook for developing thoughts on eschatological matters. The passage of years saw the stress shift from one function to another.

The significance of the "Apocalypse" in the reassessment of the apocalypticism of Edwards hinges directly on the use he ultimately intended for the materials in the notebook. A major clue to his plans for the manuscript is contained in the letter which he sent to the trustees of the College of New Jersey at Princeton before he accepted the presidency of that institution. Edwards forecasted a prospective work relating directly to the "Apocalypse":

> But beside these, I have had on my mind and heart, (which I long ago began, not with any view to publication,) a great work, which I call a *History of the Work of Redemption*, a body of divinity in an entire new method, being thrown into the form of a history; considering the affair of Christian Theology, as the whole of it, in each part, stands in reference to the great work of redemption by Jesus Christ; which I suppose to be, of all others, the grand design of God, and the *summum* and *ultimum* of all the divine operations and decrees; particularly considering all parts of the grand scheme, in their historical order.[33]

He proposed to examine the principal events in the development of the church as revealed in history and prophecy, from the beginning of time into the future, "till at last, we come to the general resurrection, last judgment, and consummation of all things; when it shall be said, *It is done.*"[34] The intent of the proposal is clear, but he did not spell out fully the precise substance of the work. The "Apocalypse" supplements his sketch of the projected "History of Redemption" by providing the fullest picture available of his eschatological views.[35] Therefore, in the first case, the notebook is significant for the reassessment because it reveals something of the probable substance of his proposed magnum opus.

Secondly, the manuscript is important by virtue of its documentation of the high priority which Edwards himself attached to apocalyptic reflections. The "Apocalypse" provides a striking measure of his lifelong preoccupation with the book of Revelation, the only book of the Bible for which he deemed it necessary to construct a separate notebook. He normally recorded scriptural reflections and commentary in one of two general exegetical series, the "Notes on Scripture" or the "Miscellaneous Observations on Scripture," also known as the "Blank Bible."[36] But his consuming interest in biblical prophecy and a fixation with the last book of the Bible were responsible for the early inauguration of the special notebook devoted to ruminations on the Revelation. Biblical prophecy remained a formative influence upon him. His continuous preoccupation with it suggests a way to integrate more closely Edwards's theological studies with his daily activities as a minister and preacher during the period of the Great Awakening.

Thirdly, the "Apocalypse" provides a corrective to one major premise of Alan Heimert's thesis, namely, the idea that the Great Awakening was the formative influence in the development of new eschatological ideas in eighteenth-century America.[37] The notebook establishes that in the case of Edwards, whom Heimert regards as the archetype of all evangelicals, new ideas had been brewing long before the awakening of the 1740s. Edwards's early reflections on the Revelation contributed substantially to the formation of his eschatological ideas. The revivals confirmed and strengthened him in his opinions. The "Apocalypse" therefore underscores the exegetical base of his eschatological views.

On the other hand, and in the fourth place, the notebook corroborates an important part of Heimert's hypothesis, his conclusion about the generality of interest in eschatological affairs during the eighteenth century. The "Apocalypse" pointedly documents the fact that many like-minded evangelicals were watching history, waiting on the doorstep of the eschaton. An international community of evangelicals spanned the Atlantic, forming a tight web by means of the exchange of correspondence and publications and by cooperation and mutual prayer.[38] Edwards was not alone in his concern with events favorable to religion.

Finally, the "Apocalypse" is significant because it offers a needed balance to the abundance of adulatory writing about Edwards. The reputation of America's greatest Calvinist will not be enhanced by the eventual publication of the notebook, for it contains little creative theological reflection equivalent to that which brought him fame and theological renown, such as *Freedom of the Will* and *The Nature of True Virtue*.[39] This manuscript discloses Edwards's participation in an unattractive aspect of the Protestant exegetical tradition, namely, its religiously sanctioned prejudice and anti-Catholicism. Edwards stands in a long line of bigoted polemicists who drew upon the Revelation for inspiration. He drank deeply from the tradition and added his own imaginative contributions as well as a new sense of urgency. Such apocalyptic speculation, while it has little to commend itself to the modern reader, does have the advantage of bringing a new dimension of realism to the assessment of Edwards.

The tides of scholarship have washed hard against the image of Edwards, each generation wearing away certain features and highlighting others. The piety, the precocity, the idealistic philosophy, and the Enlightenment psychology attributed to Edwards now have simply become part of the larger view. The lesson is clear: filiopietism, uncritical adulation, and scorn are equally inappropriate responses. The "Apocalypse" has a part to play in the ongoing revision of Edwardsian scholarship and in the larger study of early America.

## Notes

1. Jonathan Edwards, "Notes on the Apocalypse," 13, Edwards Papers, Beinecke Rare Book and Manuscript Library, Yale University, New Haven. Hereafter cited as "Apocalypse." Quotations from the manuscript are edited in accordance with the style sheet of the Yale edition of *The Works of Jonathan Edwards*.

2. *The Works of President Edwards* . . . (New York, 1881), III, 316. Hereafter cited as Worcester rev. ed.

3. One noteworthy exception to the scholarly pattern is C. C. Goen, ,"Jonathan Edwards: A New Departure in Eschatology," *CH*, 28 (1959), 25–40.

4. See Michael McGiffert, "American Puritan Studies in the 1960's" *WMQ*, 3d Ser., 27 (1970), 36–67.

5. For example, *EAL*, 5 (1970–1971), is devoted to the topic of biblical typology in colonial America and includes a massive bibliography compiled by Sacvan Bercovitch, a "Selective Checklist of Typology," continued as a supplement to 6 (1971–1972).

6. A model for such study is Edmund S. Morgan, "The Puritan Ethic and the American Revolution," *WMQ*, 3d Ser., 24 (1967), 3–43. See also Richard Hofstadter, *America at 1750: A Social Portrait* (New York, 1971).

7. Alan Heimert, *Religion and the American Mind: From the Great Awakening to the Revolution* (Cambridge, Mass., 1966), 66.

8. For negative critiques of Heimert, see Edmund S. Morgan, *WMQ*, 3d Ser., 24 (1967), 454–459; and Sidney E. Mead, "Through and beyond the Lines," *Journal of Religion*, 48 (1968), 274–288. A more sympathetic appraisal is William G. McLoughlin, "The American Revolution as a Religious Revival: 'The Millennium in One Country,' " *NEQ*, 40 (1967), 99–110. Heimert's impact is graphically documented in Cedric B. Cowing, *The Great Awakening and the American Revolution: Colonial Thought in the 18th Century* (Chicago, 1971), esp. Chap. 6.

9. Full credit must be given here to the prodigious accomplishment of Professor Thomas A. Schafer of McCormick Theological Seminary, editor of the forthcoming "Theological Miscellanies" in the Yale edition of *The Works of Jonathan Edwards* (New Haven, 1957–    ). His comprehensive

dating of the early manuscripts is foundational for all serious contemporary scholarship on Edwards, including this piece. He has kindly allowed me to read portions of unpublished materials and to use edited texts. Although he has been my principal tutor in the technical study of the manuscripts, giving generously of his time and knowledge, he is obviously not responsible for any specific statements in this essay.

10. Sereno E. Dwight, ed., *The Works of President Edwards: with a Memoir of His Life*, I (New York, 1830), 246.

11. Edwards, "Apocalypse," 74–81.

12. The 4th and 5th objections in the Humble Attempt are in *Works*, Worcester rev. ed., III, 471–504.

13. G. F. Magoun, "The Manuscripts of President Edwards," *The Independent*, 212 (1852), 208. The article was reprinted in *Littell's Living Age*, 36 (1853), 180–181.

14. The lone product of Grosart's effort was the *Selections from the Unpublished Writings of Jonathan Edwards* . . . (Edinburgh, 1865). In the 1890s he returned some manuscripts to the family. He suggested, however, that the failure to complete the project was "*the* disappointment of my life." See "The Handwriting of Famous Divines: Jonathan Edwards, M.A.," *The Sunday at Home*, 31 (1897), 459.

15. On Park, see D. L. Furber, ed., *Professor Park and His Pupils: A Biographical Sketch* (Boston, 1899); and Frank Hugh Foster, *The Life of Edwards Amasa Park* (New York, 1936).

16. There is a large body of correspondence among the Edwards Papers in the Beinecke Library at Yale University relating to the decision of the family.

17. Ola Elizabeth Winslow, *Jonathan Edwards, 1703–1758: A Biography* (New York, 1940), 374.

18. Perry Miller, *Jonathan Edwards* (New York, 1949).

19. Goen, 29–45.

20. Edwards, "Personal Narrative," in *Works*, Worcester rev. ed., I, 19.

21. Edwards, "Apocalypse," 167.

22. Before he began the "Apocalypse," Edwards wrote the following related miscellanies: No. k, EXPOSITION; No. hh, ANTICHRIST; No. uu, APOCALYPSE; No. 22, FOUR BEASTS; No. xx, VIALS; No. yy, WOMAN IN THE WILDERNESS; and No. 26, MILLENNIUM. The "Theological Miscellanies" are located among the Edwards Papers in the Beinecke Library.

23. See Edwards, "Apocalypse," 55–63, for the text of No. 78. The "Tractate on Revelation 16:12," comprised of the eight unattached pages inserted at the end of the notebook, is a reworking of the same materials. The parallel discussion in the *Humble Attempt* is in *Works*, Worcester rev. ed., III, 494–504.

24. Moses Lowman, *A Paraphrase and Notes on the Revelation of St. John* (London, 1737; 2d ed., 1745). On Lowman, see *Dictionary of American Biography*, s.v. "Lowman, Moses."

25. Edwards wrote the following entry in his "Diary" during 1724: "*Saturday night, June 6.* This has been a remarkable week with me, with respect to despondencies, fears, perplexities, multitudes of cares and distraction of thought; being the week I came hither (to New Haven) in order to entrance upon the office of tutor of the college. I have now abundant reason to be convinced of the troublesomeness and perpetual vexation of the world." *Works*, Worcester rev. ed., I, 13.

26. Edwards, "Apocalypse," 55.

27. *Ibid.*, 136.

28. *Ibid.*, 58.

29. For an overview of the development of diversity within the tradition of Christian eschatology, see the slanted but valuable four volumes of LeRoy Edwin Froom, *The Prophetic Faith of Our Fathers: The Historical Development of Prophetic Interpretation* (Washington, D.C., 1946–1954). Aspects of Edwards's more immediate background in the Protestant tradition are detailed in

the essays included in Peter Toon, ed., *Puritans, the Millennium, and the Future of Israel: Puritan Eschatology 1600–1660* (Cambridge, 1970). For reflections on the use of apocalyptic in colonial America, see Jesper Rosenmeier, "The Teacher and the Witness: John Cotton and Roger Williams," *WMQ*, 3d Ser., 25 (1968), 408–431.

30. Edwards, "Apocalypse," 186.

31. See esp. Part II, "Motives to a Compliance with what is proposed in the Memorial," in *Works*, Worcester rev. ed., III, 439–464.

32. Thomas Schafer's closely reasoned literary history of Edwards's early years has overturned many long-standing chronological assumptions held since the publication of Sereno F. Dwight's biography of 1829. Schafer places the beginning of the "Apocalypse" in late spring or early summer 1723. My studies suggest that Edwards probably wrote the opening entries some time after May 1, when he returned to Windsor from New York. Several early notes are heavily dependent upon Matthew Poole, *Annotations upon the Holy Bible* (London, 1683), a copy of which his father Timothy Edwards is known to have owned. For some hint of the impact of the new chronology, see Thomas A. Schafer, "The Role of Jonathan Edwards in American Religious History," *Encounter*, 30 (1969), 212–222.

33. Dwight, ed., *Works*, I, 569.

34. *Ibid.*, 570.

35. The common assumption that the sermons preached by Edwards in 1739 and published posthumously, John Erskine, ed., *A History of the Work of Redemption. Containing The Outlines of a Body of Divinity. In a Method entirely new* (Edinburgh, 1774), are the projected work is misleading. A sizable amount of manuscript evidence relating to the proposal remains from Edwards's later years.

36. Both manuscripts are among the Edwards Papers, Beinecke Library. Entires in the "Notes on Scripture" are arranged chronologically, as Edwards wrote them from 1723 until the end of his life. The contents of the "Blank Bible" are ordered canonically; Edwards did not possess the interleaved Bible until 1730. He wrote notes relating to the Revelation in both of these series. For an inaccurate edition of the "Notes on Scripture," see Dwight, ed., *Works*, IX. A small number of notes from the "Blank Bible" were published in Grosart, ed., *Selections from the Unpublished Writings*. Eschatological motifs pervade many of Edwards's sermons and some of his other private writings in addition to the manuscripts and published works cited here and elsewhere in this essay.

37. Heimert writes, "The watershed in American history marked by the 1740's can be understood best in terms of the degree to which, *after the Great Awakening* [italics mine], the American populace was filled with the notion of an impending millennium." *Religion and the American Mind*, 59.

38. Unfortunately, there is no adequate account of the relationships among evangelicals in different nations during the 18th century.

39. See Jonathan Edwards, *Freedom of the Will*, ed. Paul Ramsey, in *The Works of Jonathan Edwards*, I (New Haven, 1957); and Edwards, *The Nature of True Virtue*, ed. William K. Frankena (Ann Arbor, Mich., 1960).

# The Grand Design: Jonathan
# Edwards' *History of the Work*
# *of Redemption*

William J. Scheick[*]

In 1739 Jonathan Edwards gave a series of discourses on the continuity of divine providence as disclosed by history. Although he never published these sermons during his life, Edwards saw in them the nucleus of a major treatise. In fact, partly owing to his wish to rework this study, he was many years later initially disinclined to accept the position of president of the College of New Jersey. In a letter to the trustees of the college he wrote: "I have had on my mind and heart, (which I long ago began, not with any view to publication,) a great work, which I call a *History of the Work of Redemption*, a body of divinity in an entire new method, being thrown into the form of a history."[1] The unfinished project, only slightly revised by Edwards, was published posthumously in 1774 in Scotland under the title its author had designed for it.

The *History* has proved troublesome to many of Edwards' critics. The major difficulty has been to discover what Edwards could have meant by his claim to "an entire new method." One critic, in despair, proclaims the study to be "a thoroughly traditional book."[2] Others try to exonerate Edwards, noting that he had not had a chance to perfect the work or that he had set himself a task beyond realization.[3] Nagged by the same problem, another scholar sidesteps the issue: "If the *History* reads like the most conventional Puritan typology, it glows with the clear insight Edwards had into the meaning of history to the individual man."[4] Other responses range from the relatively mild conclusions that the book expresses further Edwards' belief in the visibility of God[5] and that it "can be considered the first venture in 'thesis history' in the New World, about the best that can be said for it,"[6] to the startling assertions of Perry Miller. Miller speaks of the document as "a pioneer work in American historiography," concluding that it presents the revolutionary insight "that what man sees as the truth of history is what he wills to prevail."[7] Although this appraisal is unpalatable to most current students of Edwards' work, it has proved seminal to the more refined observations of C. C. Goen and Alan Heimert. In a convincing essay Goen reads the book as a prediction of "a golden age for the church on earth, within history, and achieved through the ordinary processes of propagat-

[*]Reprinted, with permission, from *Eighteenth-Century Studies* 8 (Spring, 1975), 300–14.

ing the gospel in the power of the Holy Spirit."⁸ Similarly, for Heimert, insofar as the *History* suggests a "vision of mankind moving in nearly linear progress toward felicity," it represents "a scenario for American social and political history in the last half of the eighteenth century."⁹

In spite of these perceptive remarks, however, the reader still must wonder what Edwards intended as his new method. Goen acknowledges sources for Edwards' postmillennial reading of history and Heimert cautiously intimates that Edwards' prediction was largely unconscious. I would like to suggest, without repudiating the contributions of these preceding discussions, that Edwards thought of his study as innovative because in it he treats history as an allegory of the conversion experience. History, in his view, merely manifests in large the experiences of the individual soul undergoing the regenerative process. Like nature, history evinces a symbolic representation of the spiritual progress of the saint. It was the vision of merging the motions of nature, of history, and of the saint's private self into one theological tract, "shewing the admirable contexture and harmony of the whole,"¹⁰ that Edwards considered the original facet of his proposed treatise.

## I

The *History* describes three periods of time. The first era, spanning four thousand years, extends from the fall of Adam to the Incarnation. It includes five principal subdivisions: Adam and Eve after the fall; Noah after the flood; patriarchs Abraham, Isaac, and Jacob and their special calling by God; Moses in the wilderness; and David's reign over the Jews. The second epoch is comprised of the incarnation and the resurrection of Christ. The final period encompasses, in phases balancing those of the first period, all history subsequent to the resurrection: the destruction of Jerusalem, the rise of Constantine, the dominance of the Roman Catholic Church, the emergence of the Reformation, and the ultimate conquest of the Antichrist. Edwards' overall purpose in this account is to reveal the continuity of history, to indicate how every historical event contributes to one "grand design."¹¹

In theological terms this design emerges from the covenant made between the Father and the Son to redeem certain men from their fallen condition. Edwards endorses the traditional Puritan understanding of this contract as an "eternal covenant of redemption which was between the Father and the Son before the foundation of the world. Every decree of God is in some way or other reducible to that covenant" (II, 378). This work of redemption, Edwards explains, is only virtually, not actually, completed by Christ's resurrection. Salvation occurs within the total fullness of time or history: "the whole dispensation, as it includes the preparation and the purchase, and the application and success of Christ's redemption, is here called the work of redemption" (II, 13).

The preparation and application of Christ's work involve another contract, the covenant of grace. Only those chosen by God, for reasons He alone knows, share in this relation. The saints in no way merit their election; they remain utterly dependent upon God's arbitrary will. If they are chosen, however, they eventually receive special grace and are slated for eternal life in heaven. The covenant of grace supersedes the covenant of works which was in effect before the fall. The older covenant permitted Adam some power of his own in that he could maintain his Edenic existence as long as he voluntarily obeyed God's laws. When he disobeyed, Adam lost this ability for himself and the rest of mankind, with the consequence that since the fall all men are completely helpless spiritually. The covenant of works was abrogated, replaced by the new covenant. Both are part of the grand design Edwards perceives in history. History is the actualization of Christ's covenant of redemption.

The underlying pattern of history is so concrete for Edwards that he turns to architecture (suggested no doubt by I Cor. iii. 10–17) for many of the images he associates with it:

> Like an house or temple that is building; first, the workmen are sent forth, then the materials are gathered, then the ground fitted, then the foundation is laid, then the superstructure is erected, one part after another, till at length the top stone is laid, and all is finished. Now the work of redemption in that large sense that has been explained, may be compared to such a building, that is carrying on from the fall of man to the end of the world. God went about it immediately after the fall of man . . . and so will proceed to the end of the world; and then will come when the top stone shall be brought forth, and all will appear complete and consummate. (II, 18)

Satan, in instigating "the ruins of the fall," endeavors "to frustrate [God's] design . . . , to destroy his workmanship" (II, 19, 20). But Satan's efforts are doomed, for God's "glorious building" is solidly founded on "the first stone" of Christ's covenant of redemption (II, 31). Christ is "the chief corner stone" of "this great building of redemption"; and, Edwards explains, "if we are Christians, we belong to that building of God" (II, 96, 172). In order to read history properly, therefore, we must first discover its architectural blueprint. Once we perceive this underlying design, then we shall realize how, in the structural scheme of providence, all historical events are "united, just as the several parts of one building: There are many stones, many pieces of timber, but all are so joined, and fitly framed together, that they make but one building: They have all but one foundation, and are united at last in one top stone"(II, 382).

References to streams and oceans also frequently occur in the *History*. Though conventional Puritan images, they are put to good use by Edwards. At one point in the work he reviews what he has previously written: "We began at the head of the stream of divine providence, and have followed and traced it through its various windings and turnings, till we are come to the end . . . where it issues. As it began in God, so it ends in God. God is the infinite ocean into which it empties itself" (II, 380). In another passage Edwards develops the image still further:

> God's providence may not unfitly be compared to a large and long river, having innumerable branches, beginning in different regions, and at a great distance one from another, and all conspiring to one common issue. After their very diverse and [apparent] contrary courses . . . they all gather more and more together, the nearer they come to their common end, and all at length discharge themselves at one mouth into the same ocean. The different streams of this river are apt to appear like mere

> jumble and confusion to us, because of the limitedness of our sight, whereby we
> cannot see from one branch to another, and cannot see the whole at once. . . . A man
> who sees but one or two streams at a time, cannot tell what their course tends to. Their
> course seems very crooked, and different streams seem to run for a while different
> and contrary ways: And if we view things at a distance there seem to be innumerable
> obstacles and impediments in the way to hinder their ever uniting and coming to the
> ocean, as rocks and mountains and the like; but if we trace them, they all unite at last,
> and all come to the same issue, disgorging themselves in one into the same great
> ocean. (II, 382–83)

It is, then, in terms of the grand design that historical events must be interpreted, otherwise they "will all look like confusion, like a number of jumbled
events coming to pass without any order or method, like the tossing of the waves
of the sea" (II, 381). These traditional images, the special significance of which
we will discuss shortly, prove structurally useful to Edwards, as do the architectural analogies, because they too convey an impression of the radical order,
unity, and pattern at the core of history. So closely joined are they in Edwards'
mind, in fact, that he readily mixes metaphors, as in the following passage
concerning the end of time: "now the whole work of redemption is finished . . . .
Now the top stone of the building is laid. In the progress of the discourse on this
subject, we have followed the church of God in all the great changes, all her
tossings to and fro that she has been subject to, in all the storms and tempests
through the many ages of the world, till at length we have seen an end to all
these storms. We seen her enter the harbor, and landed in the highest
heavens, in complete and eternal glory" (II, 372–73). God's edifice, like Noah's
ark, is brought safely home over the perilous waves of the world.

The function of these images as organizational motifs is not unique in
Puritan writings. Their subtle dimension in the *History* surfaces when we
realize that usually they are associated with the soul. In other words, Edwards
presents the construction of God's building of redemption in terms exactly
identical to those he and countless other divines before him used to describe the
effects of grace in the soul. Traditionally the soul is spoken of as the temple of
the Holy Spirit and frequently it is depicted as a pilgrim tossed about on the seas
of experience. One of Ann Bradstreet's meditations, for instance, reads: "That
house which is not often swept makes the cleanly inhabitant soon loath it, and
that heart which is not continually purifying itself is no fit temple for the spirit
of God to dwell in." Elsewhere, discerning an "emblem true" in how "brooks in
thy clear waves do meet," she laments: "O could I lead my rivulets to rest."[12]
Edward Taylor, a Puritan poet who occasionally describes the soul in terms of
architectural imagery, likewise writes of how it is tossed amid the "Worlds wild
waves" despite Christ's "sea of Electing Grace, and Love."[13] Such imagery
abounds in New England Puritan writings. By using these motifs in the *History*
Edwards intended, in short, to portray, through identical imagery, a correspondence between Christ's covenant of redemption with regard to history (including the church, which exists in and fulfills time) and His Covenant of grace with
regard to the individual elect soul. He explicitly declares his intention when he
remarks: "I would observe, that the increase of gospel light, and the carrying on
the work of redemption, as it respects the elect church in general, from the first

erecting of the church to the end of the world, is very much after the same manner as the carrying on of the same work and the same light in a particular soul, for the time of its conversion, till it is perfected and crowned in glory" (II, 40). History, particularly as reflected in the progress of the church, possesses a collective self—for Edwards it was most evident in New England Puritan tradition—akin to the inner self of the saint.[14] They are mutually aligned.

A clue to his approach to history may come from the writings of such divines as Thomas Hooker. Although Edwards' regard for the writings of earlier Puritan thinkers is well known, arguments for Hooker's specific influence on him cannot be made. Nevertheless a glance at Hooker's typological method is instructive and may illuminate a tradition in which Edwards was working. Hooker's typology is not limited to Scripture or nature. Time and again he reads biblical events not only as historical facts but also as allegories of the spiritual experiences of the soul. A type, strictly speaking, is something that is historically true which symbolizes at the same time other historical truths, whereas allegory points to spiritual truths beyond the temporal world.[15] For Hooker, the image of Israel is less significant as a type for New England (as apparently it predominantly is for many of his Puritan contemporaries) than as an allegorical representation of the experiences of the soul:

> There must be Contrition and Humiliation before the Lord comes to take possession; the House must be aired and fitted before it comes to be inhabited, swept by brokenness and emptiness of Spirit, before the Lord will come to set up his abode in it. This was typified in the passage of the Children of Israel towards the promised Land; they must come into, and go through a vast and a roaring Wilderness, where they must be bruised with many pressures, humbled under many overbearing difficulties, they were to meet withal before they could possess that good Land which abounded with all prosperity, flowed with Milk and Honey. The truth of this Type, the Prophet Hosea explains, and expresseth at large in the Lords dealing with his People in regard of their Spiritual Condition.[16]

Edwards expands this technique to include secular as well as biblical history, though the uniformity and intensity of his application are quite different from that of Hooker's analogy. For Edwards all of history comprises a coherent allegory of the soul's experience of grace.

## II

As Edwards made clear in *A Divine and Supernatural Light* the reception of special grace by the soul is an immediate experience, not necessarily preceded by the enlightenment of reason and the conviction of conscience (the effects of common grace). He agreed, however, that normally preparatory stages will be involved:

> This with me is established, that grace and the exercise of grace is given entirely by the Spirit of God by His free and most arbitrary motions; but that His ordinary method, notwithstanding, is to give grace to those that are much concerned about it, and earnestly and for a considerable time seek it or continue to do things in order to do it. That is, 'tis the Spirit's ordinary method first to make them concerned about it so as to convince them that 'tis best to seek it, so far as to make them seek it much, and

then to bestow it . . . . So that there is doubtless in God's ordinary way a preparatory
conviction of sin . . . . For God makes use of things, viz., good nature, a good understanding, a rational brain.[17]

Nevertheless such a sequence is not requisite. Sometimes, Edwards explained,
"God, if he pleases, can convince men without such endeavours of their own . . .
as must be the case in many sudden conversions."[18] In fact, too great a reliance
on these preparatory stages may lead to the sort of error Edwards perceived in
Arminian notions. This precaution explains why Edwards became particularly
disturbed by the attitude of many members of his Northampton congregation,
as a letter he sent to the Reverend Thomas Gillespie indicates: "Particularly it
was too much their method to lay almost all the stress of their hopes on the
particular steps and method of their first work, i.e. the first work of the Spirit of
God on their hearts in their convictions and conversion."[19] Edwards sought to
undercut this notion in *Distinguishing Marks of a Work of the Spirit of God,
Some Thoughts Concerning the Present Revival of Religion in New-England,*
and *Treatise Concerning Religious Affections.* Even in his edition of the
memoirs of David Brainerd he asserted: "I do not suppose, a sensible distinct-
ness of steps of the Spirit's operation and method of successive convictions and
illuminations, is a necessary requisite to persons being received in full charity,
as true saints; provided the nature of the things which they profess be right, and
their practice correspondent."[20] Although God may employ preparatory stages,
the actual reception of divine light is not dependent on them: "He imparts this
knowledge immediately, not making use of any intermediate natural causes, as
he does in other knowledge."[21] The truly converted, he reported in *A Faithful
Narrative of the Surprising Work of God,* "have intuitively beheld, and immediately felt, most illustrious works and powerful evidence of divinity in
them."[22]

Although he never wished to dismiss the concept of stages with regard to
the conversion experience (there was too much Puritan tradition, which he
respected, behind the idea),[23] Edwards found it necessary to shift the locus of
this sequence. He had become increasingly certain that any dependence on *a
priori* preparatory steps led to self-deluding pride. From what he had witnessed, in himself as well as in others, he concluded that preparatory stages may
exist but for the most part such phases remain imperceptible. On the other
hand, *a posteriori* stages of spiritual development, albeit never perfectly clear,
always made themselves evident in one form or another. In fact, frequently
those very steps generally thought to be preparatory were actually the effects of
grace. Although immediate, the influx of grace does not blind or ravish the soul.
It tends to be a gentle sensation giving rise to progressive stages of *a posteriori*
development. As Edwards explained in *A Faithful Narrative,* the chosen "have
a little taste of the sweetness of divine grace, and the love of a Saviour, when
terror and distress of conscience begins to be turned into an humble, meek sense
of their own unworthiness before God; and there is felt inwardly, perhaps, some
disposition to praise God; and after a little while the light comes in more clearly
and powerfully."[24] He similarly wrote elsewhere: "The gradual progress we

make from childhood to manhood is a type of the gradual progress of the saints in grace."[25]

That "the manner of God's work on the soul is (sometimes especially) very mysterious"[26] formed a fundamental tenet of Edwards' understanding of conversion. The Holy Spirit is so "exceeding various in the manner of his operating, that in many cases it is impossible to trace him, or find out his way"; "sometimes the change made in a saint, at first work, is like a confused chaos; so that the saints know not what to make of it. The manner of the Spirit's proceeding in them that are born of the Spirit, is very often exceeding mysterious and unsearchable."[27] This point of view accounts for Edwards' avoidance of a neat linear sequence of events and his use of a seemingly amorphous, even fragmentary narrative method in the "Personal Narrative." While in the temporal world, the saint must constantly grope for insight into his spiritual condition. Indeed, although assurance is attainable in some extraordinary instances, the elect must generally eschew presumptuous certainty and simultaneously maintain a constant hope in salvation. "The saints cannot always take comfort, and do not always taste the sweetness that there is in store for them," Edwards explained, "by reason of the darkness and clouds that sometimes interpose."[28] The elect, consequently, catch only glimpses into the state of their soul, and such insight always derives from hindsight. This means, among other things, that conversion must be evaluated *a posteriori* or according to its effects.

The unfolding of history, as Edwards perceives it, presents an allegory of this drama of conversion. Historical progress is also "accomplished in various steps" and "by degrees" (II, 231, 235). The ultimate pattern or scheme of history likewise tends to remain obscure to man, so murky that (as a long quotation from Edwards cited earlier makes clear) he may subjectively see it as manifesting apparent "contrary courses." Yet in fact, as Edwards notes elsewhere, "God is continually causing revolutions. Providence makes a continual progress, and continually is bringing forth things new in the state of the world, and very different from what ever were before. He removes one that He may establish another. And perfection will not be obtained till the last revolution, when God's design will be fully reached."[29] In another place Edwards speaks of the turmoil of historical events as God's new creation, a gradual re-creation, which image equally applies to the renovation of the soul through special grace:

> As after nature has long been shut up in a cold dead state, in time of winter, when the sun returns in the spring, there is, together with the increase of the light and heat of the sun, very dirty and tempestuous weather, before all is settled calm and serene, and all nature rejoices in its bloom and beauty. It is in the new creation as it was in the old: the Spirit of God first moved upon the face of the waters, which was an occasion of great uproar and tumult, and things were gradually brought to a settled state.[30]

Bereft of any knowledge of this "design, it would all appear to him confusion" (II, 19), Edwards indicates in the *History*; for "the work in a particular soul has its ups and downs; sometimes the light shines brighter, and sometimes it is a dark time; sometimes grace seems to prevail, at other times it seems to languish for a great while together. . . . But in general, grace is growing: From its first infusion, till it is perfected in glory, the kingdom of Christ is building up in the soul" (II, 40). Like the saintly self, the collective self of history must be appraised retrospectively with regard to its fruits. Thus, for instance, at the very beginning of *Some Thoughts* Edwards vehemently argues that religious revivals are to be judged *a posteriori* rather than *a priori*.

The equation of the progress of time and the experience of the gracious soul illustrates Edwards' proneness to read history allegorically. For him history may be real, but ultimately its meaning (like that of nature) derives from its correspondence to and revelation of the spiritual growth of the gracious soul. The saint's soul, like history, possesses meaning or identity because Christ informs its center or foundation. As the phrase "building up in the soul" implies, Edwards ultimately grounds the architechtonics of the history of redemption within the terrain of the regenerate self. Thus, in explaining why God constructs Christ's building of redemption so gradually, he actually probes the mystery of the conversion experience:

> In this way the glory of God's wisdom . . . is more visible to the observation of creatures. If it had been done at once, in an instant, or in a very short time, there would not have been such opportunities for creatures to perceive and observe the particular steps of divine wisdom, as when the work is gradually accomplished, and one effect of his wisdom is held forth to observation after another. It is wisely determined of God, to accomplish his great design by a wonderful and long series of events, that the glory of his perfections may be seen, appearing, as it were, by parts, and in particular successive manifestations. For if all that glory which appears in all these events had been manifested at once, it would have been too much for us . . . ; it would have dazzled our eyes, and overpowered our sight. (II, 240)

Whatever apparent meanderings the saint's life or his emotions may take, the fact remains that the rivulets of his inner being steadily flow, along with everything else in nature and history, toward God: "gracious affections are more a natural motion, like the stream of a river; which though it has many turns hither and thither, and may meet obstacles, and run more freely and swiftly in some places than others; yet in general, with a steady and constant course, tends the same way, till it gets to the ocean."[31]

A principle of ascendancy informs the steady progress evinced by nature, history (including the church), and the gracious self. As the saint's soul becomes aligned with the divine will, as his heart is "more and more conformed to God," it is steadily attuned to the underlying principle of creation: "the eternally increasing union of the saints with God, by something that is ascending constantly towards that infinite height, moving upwards with a given velocity, and that is to continue thus to move to all eternity."[32]

## III

Because he discerns this correspondence, it is not surprising that Edwards refers to history in terms of his favorite image for depicting the saint. In *God Glorified in the Work of Redemption by the Greatness of Man's Dependence upon Him in the Whole of It*, for example, he portrays the elect as "beautiful and blessed by a communication of God's holiness and joy, as the moon and planets are bright by the sun's light. The saint hath spiritual joy and pleasure by a kind of effusion of God on the soul."[33] As he notes in *A Divine and Supernatural Light*, special grace "assimilates the nature [of the soul] to the divine nature, and changes the soul into an image of glory that is beheld."[34] Again, in a thanksgiving sermon delivered on 7 November 1734, he remarks: "the saints see the glory of God but by a reflected light, as we in the night see the light of the sun reflected from the moon."[35] The image appears throughout Edwards' writings in reference to the gracious condition of the soul and is, perhaps, most completely presented in *Religious Affections:*

> Grace in the soul is as much from Christ, as the light in a glass, held out in the sunbeams, is from the sun. But this represents the manner of the communication of grace to the soul, but in part; because the glass remains as it was, the nature of it not being at all changed, it is as much without any lightsomeness in its nature as ever. But the soul of a saint receives light from the Sun of Righteousness, in such a manner, that its nature is changed, and it becomes properly a luminous thing: not only does the sun shine in the saints, but they also become little suns, partaking of the nature of the fountain of their light.[36]

Likewise in history, as an allegory of the blessed soul, "the light that the church enjoyed from the fall of man, till Christ came, was like the light which we enjoy in the night; not the light of the sun directly, but as reflected from the moon and stars; which light did foreshow Christ, the Sun of righteousness" (II, 32). In his notes on the Bible Edwards speaks of Christ as "the Sun from whom the Church borrows her light. The gospel light granted to the Old Testament church in its different successive ages, was very much like the light of the moon in the several parts of the revolution it performs, which ends in its conjunction with the sun."[37] Even full conjunction, however, proves inadequate in terms of the total overview, as he suggests in the *History*: "The proper time of the success or effect of Christ's purchase of redemption is after the purchase has been made, as the proper time for the world to enjoy the light of the sun is the day time, after the sun is risen, though we may have some small matter of it reflected from the moon and planets before" (II, 229).

Thus, just as the elect soul does not become totally illuminated until it reaches heaven, so too history is not suddenly and maximally made lucid by Christ's incarnation. History, like the elect soul, must advance by degrees, for "the success of Christ's redemption while he himself was on earth, was very small in comparison of what it was after the conclusion of his humiliation" (II, 229). Christ's incarnation, in short, is an act affecting history directly in a way similar to the immediate communication of special grace to the soul; but with regard to both the inner self of the saint and the collective self of history, the actualization of this influence is progressive. As the soul grows in grace and as history approaches eternity, both by means of *a posteriori* phases, the more luminous they become.

This was Edwards' new method, and indeed there is, to my knowledge, nothing else quite like it in New England Puritan literature. Had he lived to develop this early collection of sermons, had he had an opportunity especially to perfect many of the images which clearly convey much of his argument, he no doubt would have produced the major treatise he envisioned. By discerning in all of history an allegory of the spiritual progress of the saint's self, he sounded a prophetic note. The Old Testament prophets, he believed, "were the stars that reflected the light of the sun" (II, 95). Ministers, "set by Christ to be lights or luminaries in the spiritual world," represent modern-day prophets: "they are set to be that to men's souls, that the lights of heaven are to their bodies."[38] As he expressed the image elsewhere, "the moon well represents the glory of the prophets and apostles and other ministers of Christ that have been improved as such lights of his church and instruments of promoting and establishing his kingdom and glory, and so have been luminous to enlighten the world by reflecting the light of the sun that is of Christ, and conveying his beams to them."[39]

Edwards too, as an ambassador of Christ, sought to shed light on the darkness he thought overshadowed New England and the world in 1739: "It is now a very dark time with respect to the interests of religion . . . wherein there is but a little faith, and a great prevailing of infidelity on the earth" (II, 330). He was certain that "God in his providence now seems to be acting over again the same part which he did a little time before Christ came" (II, 313). As a latter-day prophet Edwards announced the second coming of Christ. He prophesied that the progress of history and the regeneration of the soul are "swiftly, yet gradually" coming to an end (II, 330). He readily confessed that "whether the times shall be any darker still, or how much darker, before the beginning of this glorious work of God, we cannot tell" (II, 330). Yet his message was clear: just as the final stage of history will include "times of great peace and love" (II, 350), so too will the soul of the saint at last achieve an "inward quietness," something "of the tranquility of heaven, the peace of the celestial paradise, that has the glory of God to lighten it."[40]

Edwards' prophetic duty was to help communicate Christ's redemption, both in the souls of his parishioners and thereby in the church and in history. "This is a work which will be accomplished," he told his audience, "by the preaching of the gospel, and the use of the ordinary means of grace, and so shall be gradually brought to pass" (II, 330–31). Hence Edwards' prophetic *persona* in the *History of the Work of Redemption* is most appropriate. By this means he personally merged, as it were, his private self and the collective self of history into a single voice. As a spiritual father of New England he derived his authority not only from Scripture but also from the twin luminaries of an inspired inner self and history, the latter an allegory of the former. As a prophetic agent of divine will he joined the two together. In a very real sense Edwards had come to think of himself as a luminary, like the prophets of old, shedding light on God's grand architectural design.

Notes

1. Sereno E. Dwight, *The Life of President Edwards* (New York, 1830), p. 569. This is the first volume of *The Works of President Edwards* edited by Dwight. The other nine volumes are hereafter cited as *Works* (Dwight). Whenever possible, quotations will be drawn from *The Works*

*of President Edwards*, ed. Samuel Austin (Worcester, Mass., 1808), hereafter cited as *Works* (Austin). Italics have been deleted from the passages I cite.

2. Peter Gay, *A Loss of Mastery: Puritan Historians in Colonial America* (New York, 1968), p. 94.

3. See, for instance, Ola Elizabeth Winslow, *Jonathan Edwards, 1703–1758: A Biography* (New York, 1940), pp. 309–310.

4. Edward H. Davidson, *Jonathan Edwards: The Narrative of a Puritan Mind* (Cambridge, Mass., 1968), p. 61.

5. James Carse, *Jonathan Edwards and the Visibility of God* (New York, 1967).

6. Alfred Owen Aldridge, *Jonathan Edwards* (New York, 1964), p. 162.

7. *Jonathan Edwards* (New York, 1949), pp. 311–12.

8. "Jonathan Edwards: A New Departure in Eschatology," *Church History*, 28 (March 1959), 26.

9. *Religion and the American Mind: From the Great Awakening to the Revolution* (Cambridge, Mass., 1966), pp. 66, 99.

10. As expressed in the letter to the trustees of the College of New Jersey (Dwight, p. 570).

11. *Works* (Austin), II, 377. Subsequent page references to the *History* will be noted parenthetically in the text.

12. *The Works of Ann Bradstreet*, ed. Jeannine Hensley (Cambridge, Mass., 1967), pp. 275, 211.

13. *The Poems of Edward Taylor*, ed. Donald E. Stanford (New Haven, Conn., 1960), p. 284; *Edward Taylor's Christographia*, ed. Norman S. Grabo (New Haven, Conn., 1962), p. 305. For a discussion of this image in Taylor's work, see my *The Will and the Word: The Poetry of Edward Taylor* (Athens, Georgia, 1974), pp. 150–68.

14. Of related interest is the recent observation that in writing history the Puritans "expanded the spiritual autobiography to include not only the individual but the tribal society," with the result that the motifs of spiritual biography pervade their histories (Cecelia Tichi, "Spiritual Biography and the 'Lords Remembrancers,' " *WMQ*, 28 [1971], 64–85). Other facets of the Puritan idea of a collective self are presented in my "Anonymity and Art in *The Life and Death of That Reverend Man of God, Mr. Richard Mather*," *AL*, 42 (1971), 457–67 and "Standing in the Gap: Urian Oakes's Elegy on Thomas Shepard," *EAL*, 9 (1975), 301–306.

15. Differences in New England typological methods have not yet received sufficient critical attention. An important contribution toward an understanding of these differences is Sacvan Bercovitch's distinction between historical and allegorical modes in "Typology in Puritan New England: The Williams-Cotton Controversy Reassessed," *AQ*, 19 (1967), 166–91. Mason I. Lowance, Jr., discusses these two modes with regard to Edwards' references to nature in "Images or Shadows of Divine Things: The Typology of Jonathan Edwards," *EAL*, 5 (1970), 141–81. This essay and several others of interest on the subject appear in *Typology and Early American Literature*, ed. Sacvan Bercovitch (Amherst, Mass., 1972).

16. *The Application of Redemption* (London, 1656), p. 5.

17. *The Philosophy of Jonathan Edwards from His Private Notebooks*, ed. Harvey G. Townsend (Eugene, Oregon, 1955), pp. 109–10.

18. Untitled sermon on Hosea v. 15, *Works* (Dwight), VIII, 59.

19. *The Great Awakening*, ed. C. C. Goen (New Haven, Conn., 1972), p. 564.

20. Sereno E. Dwight, ed., *Memoirs of the Rev. David Brainerd: Missionary to the Indians on the Border of New-York, New-Jersey, and Pennsylvania: Chiefly Taken from His Own Diary. By Rev. Jonathan Edwards, of Northampton* (New Haven, Conn., 1822), p. 442.

21. *A Divine and Supernatural Light*, in *Works* (Austin), VIII, 292.

22. *The Great Awakening*, p. 179.

23. In *The Heart Prepared: Grace and Conversion in Puritan Spiritual Life* (New Haven, Conn., 1966) Norman Pettit writes: "With the downfall of the Hutchinsonians the preparationists

felt compelled not only to defend their doctrine but to advance it as dogma. In time it became an established prerequisite for full church membership as well as an integral part of New England theology. But as the century wore on, it never ceased to be a source of controversy," for the notion that conversion may happen by degrees and the "extreme emphasis on covenant ideals were fundamentally opposed to the basic tenets of Reformed theology" (pp. 20, 217–18). Pettit briefly notes that Edwards asserted a Reformed position on grace and discarded the concept of conversion through efficacious stages (pp. 208–12). For a discussion of how Thomas Hooker and Thomas Shepard departed from Calvin by defining (in the binary forms of Ramist logic) the process of conversion as a recognizable sequence of events, see David L. Parker, "Petrus Ramus and the Puritans: The 'Logic' of Preparationist Conversion Doctrine," *EAL*, 8 (1973), 140–162.

24. See my "Family, Conversion, and the Self in Jonathan Edwards' *A Faithful Narrative of the Surprising Work of God*," *TSL*, 19 (1974), 79–89.

25. *Images or Shadows of Divine Things*, ed. Perry Miller (New Haven, Conn., 1948), p. 53.

26. *A Faithful Narrative*, in *The Great Awakening*, p. 177.

27. *Religious Affections*, ed. John E. Smith (New Haven, Conn., 1959), pp. 161–62.

28. Untitled sermon on Romans ii.10, *Works* (Dwight), VIII, 232. Two essays bearing on this matter with regard to the "Personal Narrative" are Daniel B. Shea, "Jonathan Edwards' *Personal Narrative*," *Spiritual Autobiography in Early America* (Princeton, N.J., 1968), pp. 187–208; and Norman S. Grabo, "Jonathan Edwards' *Personal Narrative*: Dynamic Stasis," *LWU*, 2 (1969), 141–48.

29. *The Philosophy of Jonathan Edwards*, p. 135.

30. *Some Thoughts*, in *The Great Awakening*, p. 318.

31. *Religious Affections*, p. 374.

32. "Dissertation Concerning the End for Which God Created the World," *Works* (Austin), VI, 41, 123.

33. Ibid., VII, 478.

34. Ibid., VIII, 312.

35. *Works* (Dwight), VIII, 308.

36. *Religious Affections*, p. 342.

37. *Works* (Dwight), IX, 559.

38. *The True Excellency of a Minister of the Gospel*, in *Works* (Austin), VIII, 368.

39. *Images or Shadows of Divine Things*, p. 60.

40. "The Peace Which Christ Gives His True Followers," *Works* (Austin), VIII, 242.

# [Typology, Millennial Eschatology, and Jonathan Edwards]

Mason I. Lowance, Jr.°

If the typical efficacy of the Sabbath as a figure of the millennium was extended into modern times, and if the moral authority of the Old Testament types was employed as an example for the magistrates of New England, the renewed prophetic power endowed typology by Jonathan Edwards gave it an even greater scope. Moreover, Edwards' declaration that the millennium would occur on earth before the Second Coming and Judgment nurtured utopian enthusiasm during the Great Awakening and foreshadowed a society of God's saints out of which the millennium would emerge. This progressive and evolutionary view of prophetic fulfillment was fully developed in Edwards' theology, making him the most prominent exponent of millennial utopianism in America before the Revolution. His writings on the millennium and his many attempts to construct a synthetic typological doctrine were centered on a transformation of the typological figures themselves to give meaning to the events of contemporary history. For Edwards the types were instituted to be organic and vital; they became richer images than the static metaphors of the jeremiad tradition, exceeding the extension of typical efficacy into modern cycles of history because they were not just reflections of God's grand design but harmonious prophecies of the world's redemption.

Edwards extended typology beyond the boundaries of the two Testaments by minimizing the distinction between the figure and the thing figured.[1] However, he always retained an eschatological sense of a future fulfillment of the promises made through *natural and scriptural revelation*. Although orthodox typology applied to this historical scheme established between the Old and New Testament dispensations, for Edwards it also embraced correspondences between external representations and the spiritual ideas they shadow forth. Typology was for Edwards "a denial of the possibility that the universe is devoid of meaning ... it served the classic purpose of giving coherence and unity to history. Just as the events and personages of the Old Testament fore-

°Reprinted, with permission, from Part VI of "Typology and Millenial Eschatology of Early New England," in *Literary Uses of Typology from the Late Middle Ages to the Present*, ed. Earl Miner (Princeton: Princeton University Press, 1977), pp.262–73.

shadowed the Redeemer, so too did all that transpired in Edwards' own day strike him as being prophetic of the coming Kingdom."[2] Edwards perceived a progressive "harmony between the methods of God's Providences in the natural and religious worlds, in that as when day succeeds the night, and the one comes on, and the other gradually ceases, those lesser lights that served to give light in the absence of the sun gradually vanish as the sun approaches. . . ."[3] Edwards was not allegorizing the types into static metaphors or emblems; rather, he was revitalizing them by using typology as a renewed prophetic language for God's promises revealed in nature.

Unfortunately, some of his most illuminating passages on the subject of typology remain in manuscript. In Miscellany 119, for example, he observed:

> The things of the ceremonial law are not only things whereby God designedly shadowed forth spiritual things; but with an eye to such a representation were all the transactions of the life of Christ ordered. And very much of the wisdom of God in the creation appears, in his so ordering things natural, that they livelily represent things divine and spiritual, [such as] sun, fountain, vine; as also, much of the wisdom of God is in his Providence, in that the state of mankind is so ordered, that there are innumerable things in human affairs that are lively pictures of the things of the gospel, such as shield, tower, and marriage, family.[4]

Edwards' ultimate aim throughout his unpublished writing on typology was "to show how there is a medium between those that cry down all types, and those that are for turning all into nothing but allegory and not having it to be true to history. . . ."[5] His reasoning about the distinctions between typology and allegory was always clear, and he restored to typology its original historical and prophetic meaning while applying earlier dispensations to contemporary and future ones. He gave a cautious warning in his "Notebook on the Types," that "persons ought to be exceeding careful in interpreting of types, that they don't give way to a wild fancy; not to fix an interpretation unless warranted by some hint in the New Testament of its being the true interpretation or a lively figure and representation contained or warranted by an analogy to other types that we interpret on sure ground."[6] However, he regarded typology to be a "certain sort of language, as it were, in which God is wont to speak to us."[7]

Consistently with his published declarations about the natural universe being typical and prophetic of God's future redemption of the world, he concluded the "Types" notebook by observing:

> To say that we must not say that such things are types of those and these things unless the Scripture has expressly taught us that they are so, is as unreasonable as to say that we are not to interpret any prophecies of Scripture or apply them to those and these events, except we find them interpreted to our hand, and must interpret no more of the prophecies of David, etc. For by the Scripture it is plain that innumerable other things are types that are not interpreted in Scripture (all the ordinances of the law are all shadows of good things to come), in like manner as it is plain by Scripture that those and these passages that are not actually interpreted are yet predictions of future events.[8]

Several clear declarations of typological doctrine illuminate Edwards' theory of God's revelation in cycles of historical dispensation. His writings frequently offer conclusions about the coming millennium, and they also abound in typological proofs of its imminent fulfillment that show how the biblical figures were revitalized to strengthen the case for the coming kingdom.

Two published documents are central to Edwards' millennial prophecies: the *History of the Work of Redemption*, a series of sermons first preached in 1739 but not published until after his death, and *An Humble Attempt to Promote Explicit Agreement and Visible Union Among God's People*, which gave the Awakening a prophetic role in calling for civil as well as religious union. Edwards declared: "*Union* is one of the most *amiable* things that pertains to human society; yea, it is one of the most beautiful and happy things on earth, which indeed makes earth most like heaven"; and thus he suggested not only the image of God's perfection that would be reflected in a perfect civil union, but also prophesied the harmonious earthly kingdom that is to be an image of heavenly beauty.

This kind of millennial emphasis was exceedingly strong throughout Edwards' writing. For example, in *Some Thoughts Concerning the Present Revival of Religion in New England* (1742), we find:

> It is not unlikely that this work of God's spirit . . . is the dawning or at least a prelude of that glorious work of God, so often foretold in Scripture . . . and there are many things which make it probable that this work will begin in America . . . . And if we may suppose that this glorious work of God shall begin in any part of America, I think if we consider the circumstances of the settlement of New England, it must needs appear the most likely of all the American colonies.[9]

In the same year that he had preached the History of Redemption sermons, 1739, he stated in his *Personal Narrative* that the relation he perceived between the present and the future could be determined by analyzing prophetic images in Scripture:

> My heart has been much on the advancement of Christ's Kingdom in the world. The histories of the past advancement of Christ's Kingdom have been sweet to me. When I have read the histories of past ages, the pleasantest thing in all my reading has been, to read of the kingdom of Christ being promoted. And when I have expected, in my reading to come to any such thing, I have rejoiced in the prospect, all the way as I read. And my mind has been much entertained and delighted with the Scripture promises and prophecies, which related to the future glorious advancement of Christ's Kingdom upon earth.[10]

It should not be surprising, then, that Jonathan Edwards' central spiritual and intellectual endeavor became the discovering of those harmonious correspondences prophesied in Scripture and, in his resurrection of typological patterns, that he should apply the types and antitypes to the natural world. The close relationship he understood to exist between Scripture, history, and nature is clearly seen in the well-known letter he wrote to the Trustees of the College of New Jersey (later Princeton University) when they offered him its presidency:

> I have had it on my mind and heart (which I long ago began, not with any view to publication), a great work, which I call a *History of the Work of Redemption*—a body of divinity in an entire new method, being thrown into the form of a history . . . wherein every divine doctrine will appear to the greatest advantage, in the brightest

> light, in the most striking manner, shewing the admirable contextual harmony of the whole . . . . I have also for my profit and entertainment, done much towards another great work, which I call the *Harmony of the Old and New Testaments*, in three parts. The first, considering the Prophecies of the Messiah, his redemption and kingdom . . . showing the universal, precise, and admirable correspondence between predictions and events. The second part, considering the Types of the Old Testament shewing the evidence of their being intended as representations of the great things of the gospel of Christ; and the agreement of type and antitype. The third and great part, considering the Harmony of the Old and New Testament, as to Doctrine and precept.[11]

Edwards' assumption of the Princeton presidency prevented his completing this ambitious work.[12] But at his death, a few months later, he did leave us the redemption sermons and some manuscript fragments of the "Harmonies" in addition to the manuscripts called "Prophecies of the Messiah" and "Fulfillment of the Prophecies of the Messiah," all of which corroborate with detail those exegetical principles advanced in the *Types of the Messiah* and the posthumously published *History of the Work of Redemption*. The vision of the last days provided by the *History* is yet more important, since it may be explicated by those assertions in the typology and prophecy manuscripts. Although his son, Jonathan Edwards, Jr., and his friend, John Erskine, had a substantial hand in reshaping some of the sermons to complete the book, finally published in 1774, the views are those of Edwards and may be checked by opinions he offered elsewhere on the same subject.

Following the example of the "late expositor" Moses Lowman, whose *Paraphrase and Notes on the Revelation of St. John* had been to Edwards' eschatology what John Locke's *Essay Concerning Human Understanding* had been to his epistemology, Edwards asserted that the fifth vial (of the seven prophesied in Revelation which would destroy Satan's kingdom) had already been unleashed.[13] This interpretation, incorporated into the redemption sermons, placed the work of redemption very far along in its progressive course. The prophecy was proved by a scheme of typological adumbration and antitypical fulfillment. In the events of the last days, Edwards saw an extension of the prophetic fulfillment that has been progressive and continuous from the Creation. In the figure of David, for example, he perceived a foreshadowing of Christ and His Kingdom:

> David, as he was the ancestor of Christ, so he was the greatest personal type of Christ of all under the Old Testament. The types of Christ were of three sorts: instituted, providential, and personal. The ordinance of sacrificing was the greatest of the *instituted* types; the redemption out of Egypt was the greatest of the *providential*; and David the greatest of the *personal* ones. Hence Christ is often called David in the prophecies of Scripture.[14]

Another typological correspondence Edwards developed fully is that of the Holy City. The traditional conception of Jerusalem as a prefiguration of the Heavenly City is repeated in the *History*, but it is not merely a literal reincarnation, as some earlier millennial typologists had suggested. Rather, it is both a *literal and a spiritual* city, a "type" of God's spiritual kingdom, which was to be established after the defeat of Satan at the end of human time. That the Jerusalem of the Old Testament was prophetic of this spiritual state in Edwards' vision is made quite clear:

> This city of Jerusalem is therefore called the *holy city*; and it was the greatest type of the Church of Christ in all the Old Testament. It was redeemed by David, the Captain of the Hosts of Israel, out of the hands of the Jebusites, to be God's city, the holy place of his rest forever, where he would dwell. So Christ, the Captain of his people's salvation, redeems his church out of the hands of devils, to be his holy and beloved city. And therefore how often does the Scripture, when speaking of Christ's redemption of his church, call it by the names of Zion and Jerusalem? This was the city that God had appointed to be the place of the first gathering and erection of the Christian church after Christ's resurrection, of that remarkable effusion of the spirit of God on the apostles and primitive Christians, and the place whence the gospel was to sound forth into all the world; the place of the first Christian church, that was to be, as it were, the mother of all other churches through the world.[15]

Edwards' perception of the church as a progressive historical movement leading to the gathering of the saints in Christ was supported by his reading of the biblical types. Just as Jerusalem signified typologically the Holy City and the center of Christ's spiritual kingdom on earth in the continuum of human time, so it would also signify the coming of the church kingdom that will be established for eternity at the end of human time.

Throughout the *History of the Work of Redemption*, these typological associations abound. Edwards envisions the setting up of Christ's kingdom as a succession of great events, each revealed in the prophecies of Scripture and each having a spiritual significance for his own time. The *History*, moreover, contains a vivid description of the arrival of millennial peace and the coming of the kingdom. This conclusive interpretation of the prophecies and the types is dramatically conceived and beautifully preached; the conviction with which Edwards approached his own last days is resonant throughout the climactic scenes depicting the arrival of God's glory. The gathered church of God's elect saints is brought forward to enjoy forever the beauty of redeemed creation in a period of perfect peace. "Then shall the whole church be perfectly and forever delivered from this present evil world," Edwards says, and the sense of religious community that has characterized the Puritan vision of God's holy city from primitive times to the present echoes throughout his vision of the end:

> . . . now they shall all be gathered together, never to be separated any more. And not only shall all the members of the church now be gathered together, but all shall be gathered unto their Head, into his immediate glorious presence, never to be separated from him any more.[16]

Similarly, in Miscellany 262, Edwards developed a millennialism that clearly suggests the fusion of civil and religious forces in the fulfillment of God's glory:

> Millennium: Tis probable that the world shall be more like Heaven in the millennium in this respect: that contemplation and spiritual enjoyments, and those things that

more directly concern the mind and religion, will be more the saint's ordinary business than now. There will be so many contrivances and inventions to facilitate and expedite their necessary secular business that they shall have more time for more noble exercise, and that they will have better contrivances for assisting one another through the whole earth by more expedite, easy, and safe communication between distant regions than now. The invention of the mariner's compass is a thing discovered by God to the world to that end. And how exceedingly has that one thing enlarged and facilitated communication. And who can doubt that yet God will make it more perfect, so that there need not be such a tedious voyage in order to hear from the other hemisphere? And so the country about the poles need no longer be hid to us, but the whole earth may be as one community, one body in Christ.[17]

Thus the millennial vision and progressive eschatology were joined in a comprehensive image of a future paradise in which human relations, scientific invention, and earthly achievement would be developed under the guidance of divine Providence. The vision was progressive and utopian. The proof of its revealed promise was governed, however, by the truths Edwards received from Scripture and nature, and from the typological associations he perceived between the two.

For Edwards, the prophetic language of the Bible, this "language of Canaan," which John Cotton knew the saints would all speak at the final resurrection, was instituted at the beginning of time in the building of the natural world in God's image, so that all Creation resonates with prophetic images of God's ultimate glory and his redemption of the saints. Similarly, the incarnation was more than the arrival of the Word as flesh; the antitype is eternal, not temporal, so that Christ's fulfillment of the prophetic figures, like the figures themselves, operates throughout human time, from *alpha* to *omega*. In a little-known passage from the *Miscellanies* that confirms this view, Edwards says:

479. WORK OF REDEMPTION: TYPES. Things even before the fall were types of things pertaining to the gospel redemption. The old creation, I believe, was a type of the new. God's causing light to shine out of darkness, is a type of his causing such spiritual light and glory by Jesus Christ to succeed, and to arise out of, the dreadful darkness of sin and misery. His bringing the world into such beautiful form from out of a chaos without form and void, typifies his bringing the spiritual world to such divine excellency and beauty after the confusion, deformity, and ruin of sin.[18]

If the millennial writers of the first and second generations had restricted their arguments to specific scriptural promises or to the allegorical metaphors derived from them, and if those millennial seers during the eighteenth century had also viewed the historical process as a fulfillment of specific passages in the Bible, seeking "signs of the times" that would corroborate their predictions, Edwards also found scriptural authority for his vision of the millennium, but he transformed the typological system by extending it to embrace the natural and historical universe. And the "typology" of nature set forth in Edwards' numerous writings on the subject becomes more than an academic extension of the biblical figures into modern time. It is an original epistemology by which Edwards and his successors learned to read the vast and complex Book of Nature, in which they found prophetic figures of the imminent millennium and the kingdom of Christ. Like John Cotton, they envisioned a time when all the saints would understand and speak this prophetic language of Canaan, by which God's revealed will had been dispensed to regenerate perceivers through a glass, darkly. And they looked forward with joy to that time when the veil would be lifted, and all the prophecies and types would be fulfilled in a time of peace and harmony. It is the vitality of this millennial vision, recalling the conviction with which the first New England Puritans had interpreted their Bibles, that gives Edwards' typological argument an organic life that would later inspire Emerson's reading of nature and Whitman's millennial vision of America's promise.

## Notes

1. A treatment of Edwards' epistemology and reading of the book of nature lies beyond the scope of this essay. But for some discussion, see Roland Delattre, *Beauty and Sensibility in the Thought of Jonathan Edwards: an Essay in Aesthetics and Theological Ethics* (New Haven and London, 1968); and my own essay, "The *Images* or *Shadows of Divine Things* in the Thought of Jonathan Edwards," in Bercovitch. *Typology and Early American Literature* (Amherst, 1972), pp. 209–249.

2. Alan Heimert, *Religion and the American Mind* (Cambridge, Mass., 1966), p. 68.

3. Jonathan Edwards, "Miscellany Number 638," as quoted by Perry Miller, *Images or Shadows of Divine Things* (New Haven, 1948), pp. 52–53n.

4. I am indebted to professor Thomas Shafer of the McCormick Theological Seminary, Chicago, for allowing me to use his personal transcriptions of these miscellaneous entries, which will appear in his edition of Edwards' miscellaneous notebooks for the Yale edition of the *Works of Jonathan Edwards*.

5. This observation Edwards made in his manuscript "Notebook on the Types," a small gathering of observations about typology that contains some of his most succinct statements of theory. It is largely unknown, but is being edited for the Yale edition by Professor Wallace Anderson of the Ohio State University, and should be published soon as part of the volume on prophetic miscellanies. The manuscript of "Types" is part of the Andover Collection, never before published.

6. "Types" typescript, p. 4.

7. *Ibid.*, p. 8.

8. *Ibid.*, p. 10.

9. Jonathan Edwards, "Paradise in America," ed. Michael McGiffert, *Puritanism and the American Experience* (Reading, Mass., 1969), pp. 160–163.

10. Jonathan Edwards, *Personal Narrative*, in *Selections from Jonathan Edwards*, ed. Clarence H. Faust and Thomas H. Johnson (New York, 1962), p. 68.

11. Jonathan Edwards, *The Works of Jonathan Edwards* (Worcester, Mass., 1820), I, pp. 569–570. See also C. C. Goen, "Jonathan Edwards: A New Departure in Eschatology," *CH*, 27 (1959), 32.

12. Of Edwards' work on the *Harmony*, Jesper Rosenmeier remarks: "Had Edwards lived to complete the Harmony, he would have made the most exhaustive compendium of Biblical metaphors yet undertaken in America. His purpose, however, went far beyond working out the precise meanings and correspondences between Old Testament prefigurations and their New Testament fulfillments. Rather, Edwards was interested in the harmony and beauty of the relationships, for he was convinced that it would continue to grow in the future, and that whoever understood the present divine communications might gain a view of the harmony that would be manifest in the New Jerusalem. So dynamic did Edwards consider the process of redemption to be that he perceived not only the Bible but Nature as a prophetic part of the gyre of salvation" (unpublished manuscript, p. 17).

13. I am indebted to Mr. Christopher Jedrey for a close comparison of Lowman's *Paraphrase* and Edwards' *Redemption*, which he prepared as a course paper in 1972. Although Lowman's study is not concerned with typological figuralism, it is very concerned with the interpretation of symbols and figures that appear in the Book of Revelation as they apply to literal events of the future. See Moses Lowman, *A Paraphrase and Notes of the Revelation of St. John*, 2nd ed. (London, 1745).

14. Jonathan Edwards, *A History of the Work of Redemption*, in *Works*, ed. Sereno Dwight (Hartford, 1820). Vol III, p. 227.

15. *Ibid.*, III, p. 233.

16. *Ibid.*, III, p. 417.

17. Jonathan Edwards, Miscellany 262, as quoted by Douglas Ellwood; *The Philosophical Writings of Jonathan Edwards* (New York, 1961), p. 74.

18. Jonathan Edwards' miscellaneous notebooks. Again, I am grateful to Thomas Shafer for the use of these entries that treat typology.

# III  LINEAGE

# Lineage: Influences on Edwards

## The Philosophical Theologian

Alexander V. G. Allen[*]

Toward the close of his life, and within perhaps four or five years of his death, Edwards became acquainted with one of the most remarkable theological works of the last century,—The Philosophical Principles of Natural and Revealed Religion, unfolded in Geometrical Order by the Chevalier Ramsay, author of the Travels of Cyrus. Glasgow, 1747.[1] From a notice which Edwards saw of the work in the Monthly Review, he became aware of its significance and was desirous to purchase it. The book may have been in his possession by 1754. Its author must have been a man closely resembling Edwards in the type of his mind,—a speculative thinker aiming at a system of absolute Christian thought. But if the Chevalier Ramsay had been familiar with Edwards' books he could not have more directly opposed Edwards' methods and conclusions. His Philosophical Principles combats the theories of Berkeley and Malebranche, as tending directly toward Pantheism, which he regarded as an immoral fatalism as well as a practical atheism. Predestination, also, and the denial of freedom of the will, he condemned, tracing them to the principle which, as he sought to show, led back ultimately to Spinoza's doctrine of the one substance, with its two attributes of thought and extension.

Edwards does not seem to have been influenced at all by these denunciations of his favorite doctrine. But while these two minds were at the antipodes of speculation on these profound issues, they had also much in common, and at one point their thought tended to coalesce in a common conviction. Both had been going through a similar theological experience, in that they had recoiled from the deism of the eighteenth century, which relegated God to some remote spot outside of His creation. The Scotchman, however, had first fallen into deism, accepting its postulate of Diety as singleness of essence, and reducing religion to a reverence for and the practice of virtue. All religions, as he then thought, contained these simple ideas, but were also full of false theories and evil superstitions, with a complicated ritual which obscured the essential truth. Ramsay did not long remain in this position. Under the influence of Poiret, he encountered the fascination of French mysticism, which led him in 1710 to seek an interview with Fénelon. The story of his conversion to Roman Catholicism is told in his Life of Fénelon,[2] by whom he was convinced that there was no

[*]Reprinted from *Jonathan Edwards* (Boston: Houghton-Mifflin, 1889), pp. 346–57.

middle ground between deism and the Catholic faith. After his conversion, as he pursued his great inquiry regarding the nature of God, he discerned that the pantheism in which thoughtful minds were taking refuge from an impossible deism was also but a makeshift, and like deism resulted in a loss of the consciousness of the living God. It was at this point that he met Edwards, who had also arrived by a process of his own at conclusions which are closely related to Spinoza's doctrine of the one substance.

The issue which Ramsay had confronted, and which Edwards must also have seen, even if at a distance, was no passing mood in human thought. It involves the same essential condition in which the early fathers of the Christian church had found themselves when they felt the necessity of reconciling the truth in Stoic pantheism with Jewish monotheism. If the idea of God as infinite personality was lost in Stoicism, which conceived of Diety as universally diffused, permeating the universe as all-pervading breath, equally difficult was it to find satisfaction in the deistic conception of the Jew. A Diety idle or dormant, silently reposing in Himself until he comes forth for the creation, must be a being without relationships, and therefore without consciousness. It was here that Platonism came to the rescue of embarrassed thinkers, with its idea of a Logos which bridged the gulf between pantheism and deism. Or, as transmuted by Christian thought, the true Logos was the Christ, the Son eternally generated from the Father, God's second self, in whom He saw Himself reflected, between whom and Himself there existed from eternity the activity of divine communication and love. The doctrine of eternal distinctions within the divine essence satisfied the necessity of early Christian thought, as it sought some adequate conception of God.

The following sentence from Ramsay's book had first arrested the attention of Edwards:— "The Infinite Spirit, by a necessary, immanent, eternal activity, produces in Himself His consubstantial image, equal to Himself in all His perfections, self-origination only excepted; and from both proceed a distinct, self-conscious, intelligent, active principle of love, coequal to the Father and the Son, called the Holy Ghost. This is the true definition of God in His eternal solitude, or according to His absolute essence distinct from created nature." This passage Edwards had copied from a notice in the Monthly Review, before he was yet in possession of Ramsay's work. When he had secured the book, he copied out other passages which bear upon this leading thought. Among them are the following sentences:—

> "Such inactive powers as lie dormant during a whole eternity in God, are absolutely incompatible with the perfection of the divine nature, which must be infinitely, eternally, and essentially active . . . . Since God cannot be eternally active from without, He must be eternally active from within. . . . An absolutely infinite mind supposes an absolutely infinite object or idea known . . . . Hence this generation of the Logos or of God's consubstantial idea is sufficient to complete the perfection of the divine understanding . . . . Thus it is certain that, antecedent to all communicative goodness to anything external, God is good in Himself . . . . He does not, therefore, want to create innumerable myriads of finite objects to assert His essential beneficence and equity; since he produces within Himself from all eternity an in-

finite object that exhausts, so to speak, all His capacity of loving, beatifying and doing justice. The Deists Socinians, and Unitarians, who deny the doctrine of the Trinity, cannot explain how God is essentially good and just, antecedently to, and independently of, the creation of finite things; for God cannot be eminently good and just where there is no object of His beneficence and equity . . . . To complete the idea of perfect felicity there must be an object loving as well as an object loved . . . . There is a far greater felicity in loving and in being loved than in loving simply. It is the mutual harmony and correspondence of two distinct beings or persons that makes the completion of love and felicity. Hence God could not have been infinitely and eternally loved if there had not been from all eternity some being distinct from Himself and equal to Himself that loves Him infinitely. The eternal, infinite, and immutable LOVE which proceeds from the idea God has of Himself is not a simple attribute, mode, or perfection of the divine mind; but a living, active, consubstantial, intelligent being or agent . . . . We may represent the divine essence under these three notions,—as an infinitely active mind that conceives; or as an infinite idea that is the object of this conception; or as an infinite love that proceeds from this idea . . . . There are three; there can be but three; and all that we can conceive of the Infinite mind may be reduced to these three: infinite LIFE, LIGHT, and LOVE . . . . These three distinctions in the Diety are neither three independent minds, . . . nor three attributes of the same substance, . . . but three coeternal, consubstantial, coördinate persons, coequal in all things, self-origination only excepted . . . . All those who are ignorant of the doctrine of the Trinity, of the generation of the Logos, of the procession of the Eternal Spirit, and of the everlasting commerce among the sacred three, look upon God's still eternity as a state of inaction or indolence."

Exactly how much Edwards may have meant by copying into his notebook passages like these from Ramsay, it is not easy to determine. At least he was interested in the thought they contained; to a certain extent it must have been new to him. How far its influence may be traced in his later writings remains to be considered. The Observations on the Scriptural Economy of the Trinity shows that a profound change was passing over the mind of its author in regard to the nature of the divine existence. Although, as has been remarked, this work created a sense of disappointment when it appeared, yet the disappointment is only an evidence how thought has moved since Edwards' day. Had it been published in his lifetime it might have involved him in another controversy, and that with his own household of faith. A passage like the following shows him to be aware that he is making an innovation on views which were widely prevalent: "It appears to be unreasonable to suppose, as some do, that the Sonship of the second person of the Trinity consists only in the relation He bears to the Father in His mediatorial character."[3] Edwards was contending for the Trinity as grounded in the nature of things, or in the necessity of God's being. Although he could not have been acquainted with the process of historical theology, yet the working of his mind was leading him into the same path through the mazes of thought, which Origen and Athanasius had also followed. The way in which he was travelling was by no means a familiar one in the Calvinistic churches, and by many it was regarded with distrust or mislike. The method of Calvin had been for the most part prevalent, which waived aside the doctrine of the eternal generation of the Son as unnecessary or unprofitable, or even as "an absurd fiction."[4] Such a method as Calvin's might answer the practical needs of the church, so long as thought lay dormant, or tradition and Scripture possessed an unquestioned authority. In the eighteenth century, when the appeal was carried to the reason, the divnity of Christ was endangered by the silence of those who refused to follow the voice of reason as it pointed toward Christ as the eternal Son, without whose coequal and coeternal presence with the Father even the thought of God was becoming impossible. To maintain the divinity of Christ, as was then the custom, solely on the ground that it was essential to His making an adequate atonement for sin, was to involve the rejection of His divinity if such a theory of atonement should become obnoxious. If the Spirit of God, as popularly conceived, was but the divine energy applying the benefits of Christ's atonement, there would be no necessity for His existence as a coequal factor or distinction in the divine essence, when some different and higher view of human nature should have arisen in place of the doctrine of original sin. Such was the process by which, in the mind of the last century, the doctrine of the Trinity was undermined. Not to ground the distinctions in the divine essence by some immanent, eternal necessity was to make easy the denial of what has been called the ontological Trinity, and then the rejection of the economical Trinity was not difficult or far away.

This little treatise of Edwards, then, is far from being unimportant or comonplace. It adds to our estimate of his work as a theologian. He was stemming the theological tide instead of yielding to it. He was asserting a doctrine of the Trinity which implied its eternal necessity in the nature of God, even had there been no fall, no need of an atonement for human redemption. Had his thought been fully developed, it must have led him to the recognition of Christ as sustaining an organic relation to the world of outward nature. As Christ is the creative wisdom of God in whom God saw Himself reflected, so the beauty and the glory of Christ is visible in the world of created things. The following exquisite passage deserves no apology for being reproduced at length. It does not belong to the Observations, but has been recently recovered from Edwards' manuscripts:—

> "We have shown that the Son of God created the world for this very end, to communicate Himself in an image of His own excellency. He communicates Himself properly only to spirits, and they only are capable of being proper images of His excellency, for they only are properly *beings*, as we have shown. Yet He communicates a sort of a shadow or glimpse of His excellencies to bodies which, as we have shown, are but the shadows of beings and not real beings. He who, by His immediate influence, gives being every moment, and by His spirit actuates the world, because He inclines to communicate Himself and His excellencies, doth doubtless communicate His excellency to bodies, as far as there is any consent or analogy. And the beauty of face and sweet airs in men are not always the effect of the corresponding excellencies of mind; yet the beauties of nature are really emanations or shadows of the excellency of the Son of God.
>
> "So that, when we are delighted with flowery meadows and gentle breezes of wind, we may consider that we see only the emanations of the sweet benevolence of Jesus Christ. When we behold the fragrant rose and lily, we see His love and purity. So the green trees and fields, and singing of birds, are the emanations of His infinite

joy and benignity. The easiness and naturalness of trees and vines are shadows of His beauty and loveliness. The crystal rivers and murmuring streams are the footsteps of His favor, grace, and beauty. When we behold the light and brightness of the sun, the golden edges of an evening cloud, or the beauteous bow, we behold the adumbrations of His glory and goodness; and in the blue sky, of his mildness and gentleness. There are also many things wherein we may behold His awful majesty: in the sun in his strength, in comets, in thunder, in the hovering thunder-clouds, in ragged rocks and the brows of mountains. That beauteous light with which the world is filled in a clear day is a lively shadow of His spotless holiness, and happiness and delight in communicating Himself. And doubtless this is a reason that Christ is compared so often to those things, and called by their names, as the Sun of Righteousness, the morning-star, the rose of Sharon, and lily of the valley, the apple-tree among trees of the wood, a bundle of myrrh, a roe, or a young hart. By this we may discover the beauty of many of those metaphors and similes which to an *unphilosophical person do seem so uncouth*.

"In like manner, when we behold the beauty of man's body in its perfection, we still see like emanations of Christ's divine perfections, although they do not always flow from the mental excellencies of the person that has them. But we see the most proper image of the beauty of Christ when we see beauty in the human soul."[5]

This beautiful passage, which illustrates the poetic temperament of Edwards, has also its theological significance. He was reproducing the Christ of the early church, who is organically related to nature and to man,—the manifestation of the wisdom of God. But he was resuming also, though he may not have known it, the discussion of the Trinity at the point where it was dropped in ancient controversies, developing the doctrine after a manner of his own which deserves the closest attention.

## Notes

1. Andrew Michael Ramsay, commonly called the Chevalier Ramsay, was born in Ayr, Scotland, 1686. After studying at Edinburgh and St. Andrews he went abroad, residing mainly in France, where he died 1743. Among other positions which he held was that of tutor to the children of the Pretender, called James III.; and it has been thought that the doctorate conferred on him by Oxford was partly owing to his Jacobite relations. His *Philosophical Principles* is hardly orthodox from the Roman Catholic stand-point, as it urges a final restoration of all souls to God. A copy of it is in the library of Harvard College, which is rich in the theological literature of the last century.

2. *Life of François de Salignac de la Mothe Fénelon* (London, 1723), pp. 180–247.

3. *Observations*, etc., p. 56. The opinion which Edwards was controverting was advanced by Dr. Thomas Ridgeley in 1731. In 1792 Dr. Samuel Hopkins speaks of it "as gaining ground and spreading of late." Cf. Prof. E. C. Smyth, Appendix to *Observations*, etc., p. 91, for a list of references bearing on this point. But Edwards was also controverting his own earlier view. Cf. the passages where he alludes to the Trinity, *ante*, p. 99.

4. "I do not undertake," says Calvin, "to satisfy those who delight in speculative views . . . . Studying the edification of the church, I have thought it better not to touch on various topics which could have yielded little profit, while they must have needlessly burdened and fatigued the reader. For instance, what avails it to discuss, as Lombard does at length, Whether or not the Father always generates? This idea of continual generation becomes an absurd fiction from the moment it is seen that from eternity there were three persons in one God."—Calvin, *Institutes*, book i. ch. 13.

5. *Observations*, etc., Appendix, pp. 94–97. When this passage was written there is no means of

determining without further appeal to the manuscripts. I should like to think that it belonged to Edwards' later years, and was nearly contemporaneous with his writings on the Trinity. But it may have belonged to his youth, and have been written not long after the *Notes on the Mind*. For similar expressions of thought regarding the relation of Christ to the creation, the reader may be referred to Dorner, *Person of Christ*, Eng. trans., vols. i. and ii. Cf., also, Twesten, *Vorlesungen*, vol. ii. pp. 199, ff., for an admirable statement of how the second person in the Trinity is organically related to the external world.

# The Flying Spider

By David Scofield Wilson[*]

... I saw him suddainly in the mid-work to desist, and turning his taile into the wind to dart out a thred . . ., by and by the Spider lept into the air, and the thread mounted her up swiftly . . . . I found the Air filled with young and old sailing on their threads, and undoubtedly seizing Gnats and other Insects in their passage; there being often as manifest signes of slaughter, as leggs, wings of Flyes &c. on these threads, as in their webbs below. (Martin Lister, 1669)[1]

Jonathan Edwards' youthful essay on the "Ballooning" or "Flying" spider has been much praised by Edwards scholars, for it is minutely accurate in concrete particulars while sweepingly speculative in the corollaries, tightly reasoned but felicitously expressed, and it conveys the emotional as well as intellectual engagement of the boy as he studies the spider and speculates about its meaning.[2] In addition, modern appreciation of the piece derives in part from the praise of Edwards' scientific accuracy and originality of observation voiced by Henry C. McCook and other qualified arachnologists.[3] However, an unfortunate effect of their testimony has been to create the impression that Edwards' piece is original in both senses of that term, not only genuinely the product of Edwards' youthful, firsthand observation, but also the first such description of ballooning spiders in Western literature.[4] While refraining from the extravagant praise of Edwards' scientific precocity that marked most of the nineteenth-century comments upon the piece, Clarence H. Faust and Thomas H. Johnson nevertheless report in their notes to their American Writers Series *Jonathan Edwards* that, "Professor H. C. McCook believed himself to be the first who had made certain of the observations, until he discovered that Edwards had anticipated him by one hundred and sixty years."[5] The reader is left to infer, reasonably, that Edwards was indeed a pioneering observer of nature in this instance. It is not true. Instead, Jonathan Edwards' "Flying Spider" is one specimen only, albeit a felicitous and precocious one, of a well-established genre of whose existence Edwards was probably aware, for his essay was composed in response to a request from England for just such "observations" as he penned and his essay shows marked similarities to earlier examples of the genre.

A note which explicitly recognizes the existence and similarities of several English antecedent productions must be added to the scholarship surrounding the "Flying Spider" so that future students will not be allowed to infer an

[*]Reprinted, with permission, from *Journal of the History of Ideas*, 32 (July, 1971), 447–58.

unwarranted uniqueness in the Edwards piece they study. But beyond that, some thought must be given to the categorical assumptions and implicit definitions that have operated in the past to allow Edwards' youthful piece to be treated as a unique rather than typical item—i.e., as a cultural curiosity instead of as a specimen of a functioning genre. How has it happened, one must ask, that such a gem of youthful composition by one of America's most powerful and significant eighteenth-century thinkers has been allowed to stand out of context for over two hundred and fifty years? What attitudes toward nature, natural philosophy, national boundaries, and literature have clouded full perception of the place of Edwards' piece in the fabric of eighteenth-century culture and may continue to operate in the future to becloud our understanding of the cultural significance of similarly fine but less famous documents of natural philosophy? The questions are sweeping and the answers complex, but it seems clear that a central error has been the failure to read natural-philosophy documents with the same sophistication and care that is devoted to belles lettres.

The scholarly world would be justly indignant with one who presumed to evaluate Freneau's pastoral creations without reference to their English and continental precedents and scornful of another who judged Franklin's satire without reference to Swift, Addison, and Steele. The whole meaning and significance of a piece can never be fully appreciated or justly assessed without reference to its genre, for the elements of tone, form, diction, imagery, and logic that make up the piece do not exist in a vacuum of time or culture but proceed from established traditions or from the intent of an author who accepts or rejects those traditions. Like belles lettres, natural history essays are cultural products; natural facts may or may not be timeless, acultural, and universal, but the observation, perception, and expression of those facts are cultural. As such the essays must be submitted to the critical procedures developed by humanists to protect against temporary fashions in taste and the tendency to couch such taste in the language of universal, natural truth. Consequently, in addition to documenting the existence of precedents to Edwards' piece, this article seeks (1) to demonstrate some of the generic elements that link it to others on similar topics, (2) to speculate on the significance of the genre, its cultural role, and the meaning of its persistence into the twentieth century, and (3) to attempt to suggest relevant, additional ways in which natural-philosophy documents may be explored by students of culture and the natural environment.

1. *The Specimen.* Jonathan Edwards' essay appears in two forms; the first, an essay which he titled "Of Insects" and wrote in 1715 at the age of eleven, and the second, a letter to an English correspondent of his father's, generally titled "The Flying Spider."[6] "Of Insects" is fuller and longer and is the more interesting to study; its tone is less formal, the *persona* more involved and ingenuous, and the "corollaries" more bold and synthetic; whereas "The Flying Spider" is Edwards' condensation of the original essay and has been self-consciously adjusted to epistolary form ("May it please your Honour," "Now, Sir . . .," "And this, Sir . . .," "But yet, Sir . . .") and "improved" by elevating the diction (e.g. substituting "vault of Heavens" for "Sky") and by eliding much of the corollary

material.[7] Comparison of the essay and the letter reveals that Edwards was a conscious literary craftsman, shifting, condensing, reforming, deleting and adding material, and adjusting the tone; comparison reveals, in other words, the interposition of a critical mind between the original essay and the eventual letter. Edwards, himself, probably was the major critic, but his father or another adult may well have made suggestions for improvement. At any rate, his letter demonstrates an eager desire to express himself in the generalized diction and ponderous tone that he or his adviser thought appropriate to correspondence on important topics. His eagerness to appear mature and knowledgeable may account for the digressive allusions to optics, gravity, and bouyancy to explain and clarify the mystery of the spider's behavior (AR. 14–15). In this latter action he parallels the practice of contributors to the *Philosophical Transactions* of the Royal Society of London who frequently attempted to explain, rather than simply report, phenomena.

The first five hundred words of the essay and of the letter reveal about Edwards' practice what is typical of virtuosi's amateur literary attempts, namely, their informal, unpolished, innocent prose is frequently superior to that which is "improved."[8] In the essay, Edwards moves quickly from "all Insects" to spiders, from the several types of spiders to those that "keep" in grass, and from that class to the species that "march[es] in the air from tree to tree" and leaves webs that all can observe on a "Dewey morning towards the latter end of august or at the beginning of september." He expands briefly on gossamer and then specifically exemplifies the phenomena in a brief narrative that includes personal as well as descriptive material:

> ... I have severall times seen in a very Calm and serene Day at that time of year, standing behind some Opake body that shall Just hide the Disk of the sun and keep of[f] his Dazling rays from my eye and looking close by the side of it, multitudes of little shining webbs and Glistening Strings of a Great Length and at such a height as that one would think they were tack'd to the Sky by one end were it not that they were moving and floating, and there Very Often appears at the end of these Webs a Spider floating and sailing in the air with them ... (AR, 6).

The syntax may be loose but the imagery is both accurate and evocative, and the report, while focussing on the object of the spider, still comfortably includes the *persona's* stance and response. The reader can both feel the wonder stirred in the *persona* by the phenomenon and scrutinize the objective facts as well. Furthermore, the *persona's* presence within the description functions in the rhetoric of the genre to validate the descriptive statements for those readers who had become conditioned to skepticism by exotic and fanciful travelers' tales. While such pathetic and ethical content was increasingly to be cleansed from scientific prose during the following two-and-a-half centuries, it formed an integral part of the best natural-philosophy prose of the seventeenth and eighteenth centuries and is one of the qualities of such reportage that justifies its treatment as literature.

In the letter, Edwards announces his subject in a general way, omitting the earlier version's mention of the several types of other spiders. He reduces by half the number of words required to arrive at his specific object of interest, but in so doing he makes the language more abstract, thereby dininishing its effect for description. He follows with nearly two hundred words of general comments upon gossamer (when it is made and how best to view it) before narrating his own experience with it. One sentence of this "philosophical" fill sufficiently exemplifies the more complex syntax, strained diction, and generalized imagery of the letter:

> Nor Can One Go Out in A Dew'y Morning at the Latter End of August And the beginning of September but he Shall see multitudes of webbs made visible by the Dew that hangs on them, Reaching from one tree branch & shrub to Another which webbs Are Commonly thought to be made in the Night, because they appear only in the morning wheras [sic] none of them Are made in the night, for these Spiders never Come Out in the night when it is Dark and the Dew falling, but these webbs may be seen well enough in the Day time by An observing Eye by their Reflection of the Sunbeams (AR, 13).

This is not the quality of prose that has excited readers of Edwards' "Of Insects." However, the narration that follows is still the charmingly personal report of his observation of gossamer in the sky. It is nearly identical to that of the essay in content, but the syntax and expression have been revised:

> Standing at Some Distance behind the End of an house or some other Opake body so as Just to hide the Disk of the sun and keep off his Dazling Rays, and looking along Close by the side of it, I have seen vast multitudes of little shining webbs, and Glistening strings *brightly Reflecting the Sunbeams and some of them*, of a Great length and at such a height that One would think they were tacked to the *vault of the heavens* and would be burnt like tow in the Sun And make a very beautiful, pleasing, as well as surprizing Appearance (AR, 13–14; italics mine).

Besides adding "brightly Reflecting the Sunbeams and some of them" and elevating "sky" to "vault of the heavens" Edwards has tightened the syntax and revised the rhythms of the sentence. The "I have seen" has been brought forward into juxtaposition with its complement "multitudes of little shining webbs" at the middle of the long sentence. The opening adjectival phrases introduce the vision, and the concluding phrases drop gradually back into generalization at the end. Regrettably, this revision destroys the dramatic effect and emotional truth of his earlier version, which opened with *I*, yet kept the reader suspended during the qualifying phrases so that he felt released by the appearance of the complement "multitudes . . ." and further stimulated by the climactic appearance of the spider. In the revised version, the rhythm is interrupted and the spider does not appear till the next paragraph.

The purpose of this comparison of the opening portions of the two documents is to demonstrate economically two propositions: (1) that the essay and the letter are different in tone, imagery, diction, and details of order; and (2) that a richer understanding of the documents' meaning occurs when they are studied together and compared. Both propositions sound obvious, and they ought to have been, but the fact is that Edwards' two documents on the flying spider have generally been used interchangeably, and one or the other reprinted simply as a proof of Edwards' precocity. There is no operative principle evident, for example, in the anthologies which reprint Edwards' observations; some print the essay, others the letter.

Apparently, as Martin Lister earlier said of the spider itself, Edwards' observations too are a "strange puzel to the wiser World." Many anthologies do not print either of them, presumably because the editors think them fragments of his "corpus" irrelevant to the larger themes the editors seek to exemplify by their selections from Edwards in particular, or think eighteenth-century American natural philosophy irrelevant in general except where it neatly illustrates social, theological, or philosophical themes.[9] Such documents of natural philosophy as are reprinted today are scattered about through anthologies and illustrated histories as were the actual stuffed birds, fossils, and rock samples in the "cabinets" of eighteenth-century virtuosi. They await the synthesizing genius of a Linneaeus or Darwin to put them into a coherent order. Before a new synthesis of these scattered fragments can come about, individual specimens such as Edwards' must be analyzed, first by critics as fully engaged by the piece and as interested in its history and development as are critics who devote their attention to chronicling the development of an Edward Taylor poem; and second, by critics familiar with the literature of natural philosophy.

2. *The Genre.* To read the accounts of flying spiders which antedate Edwards' is to discover that they are often as accurate as his, frequently as precisely and effectively expressed, and no more free from culturally conditioned errors of interpretation than are his.[10] In fact, comparison of Edwards' piece to others on the same topic written by respected adult virtuosi allows one to perceive the irrelevance of complaints such as Faust's that Edwards' corollaries are "theological" and hence inappropriate to natural philosophy, as if theologically tinged speculation has no more place in eighteenth-century natural philosophy than in twentieth-century science.[11]

As early as Robert Hooke's *Micrographia* (1665) virtuosi had published their fascination with the delights and beauties of the minute natural world. By 1701, thirteen years before Edwards' pieces, the genre had already become so sophisticated with microscopical observation that Anthony van Leeuwenhoek published a twenty-two page "Letter . . . concerning Spiders . . ." in the *Philosophical Transactions*. But the most remarkable observations upon the flying spider particularly, and those most enlightening for Edwards scholars, are those published between 1669 and 1671 by Martin Lister in the *Philosophical Transactions*.

Interest in spiders that "dart" their webs into the air preparatory to sailing or as bridges across empty space is first manifest in the Society's publications by a letter (1668) from Richard Stafford in Bermuda, who reports that some Bermuda spiders "spin their Webbs betwixt Trees standing seven or 8 fathom asunder; and they do their Work by spirting [sic] their Webb into the Air, where the Wind carries it from Tree to Tree" (*PT*, III, 795). Then in the 1669 volume of the *Philosophical Transactions* (*PT*, IV, 1014–15), John Ray communicates to the Society a description by Martin Lister, later F.R.S. and according to the

*DNB* "one of the earliest students" of spiders. It is a piece that deserves extended quotation for it is not well known to students of American literature but will be recognized by scholars familiar with Edwards' work as remarkably similar in tone, descriptive precision, and content:

> The *long Threads* in the Air in Summer, and especially towards *September*, have been a strange puzel to the wiser World. It would divert you, though you know them as well as I, if I here reckoned up the ridiculous opinions concerning them; but I omit them, and proceed to tell you the certain and immediate Authors of them, and how they make them. ° ° ° ° °
> I had exactly mark'd all the ways of Weaving, used by any sorts of them, and in those admirable works I had ever noted that they still let down the Thread, they made use of; and drew it after them. Happily at length in neerly attending on one, that wrought a nett, I saw him suddainly in the mid-work to desist, and turning his taile into the wind to dart out a thred with the violence and streame, we see water spout out of a spring: This thread taken up by the wind, was in a moment emitted some fathoms long, still issuing out of the belly of the animal; by and by the Spider lept into the air, and the thread mounted her up swiftly. After this first discovery, I made the like Observation in almost all sorts of Spiders, I had before distinguished; and I found the Air filled with young and old sailing on their threads, and undoubtedly seizing Gnats and other Insects in their passage; there being often as manifest signes of slaughter, as leggs, wings of Flyes &c. on these threads, as in their webbs below . . . . I observed them to get to the top of a stalk or bough, or some such like thing, where they exercise this darting of threads into the air, and if they had not a mind to saile, they either swiftly drew it up again, winding it up with their fore-feet over there head into a lock, or break it off short, and let the air carry it away . . . . ° ° ° ° °
> In Winter and at Christmas I have observed them busy a darting, but few of them saile then . . .; it is more than probable, that the great ropes [of webbing] of Autumne are made only by the [older spiders], and upon long passages and Summer weather, when great numbers of prey may invite them to stay longer up.

Both Edwards and Lister communicate the delight and wonder with which they perceive the heretofore puzzling pheonomena: Edwards through adjectives like "Pretty" and "Pleasing," through figures ("one would think they were tack'd to the Sky"), and by establishing a *persona* to discover the secret; Lister, with words like "puzel" and "admirable," with the extravagant figure which compares the spider's darting of web to the "violence . . . we see water spout out of a spring," and through establishment of a stationary *persona* to whom the "suddain" darting of a thread and swift "mounting up" of the spider come as a scientific revelation and emotional climax.

Edwards has been much admired, by McCook and others, for his meticulous description (accompanied by sketches here omitted) of the way in which he investigated the spider's method of darting out threads and sailing away. He says in the essay:

> I Repeated the traill Over and Over again till I was fully satisfied of his way of working which I Dont only Conjecture to be on this wise viz they . . . let themselves hang Down a little way by their webb and then put out a web at their tails which being so Exceeding rare when it first comes from the spider as to be lighter than the air so as of itself it will ascend in it (which I know by Experience) the moving air takes it by the End and by the spiders Permission Pulls it out of his tail to any length and If

the further End of it happens to catch by a tree or any thing, why there's a web for him to Go over upon and the Spider immediately perceives it and feels when it touches, much after the same manner as the soul in the brain immediately Percieves [sic] when any of those little nervous strings that Proceed from it are in the Least Jarrd by External things; and this very way I have seen Spiders Go from one thing to another I believe fifty time[s] at least since I first Discovered it . . . (AR, 7).

This piece is remarkable, but an equally remarkable description of the same phenomenon had appeared half a decade earlier when the *Philosophical Transactions* printed "*A Discourse upon the Usefulness of the Silk of Spiders. By Monsieur Bon, President of the Court of Accounts, Aydes and Finances, and President of the Royal Society of Sciences at* Monpellier":

> They hang themselves perpendicular by a Thread, and turning their Head towards the Wind, they shoot several others from their *Anus*, like so many Darts: And if by chance the Wind, which spreads them abroad, fastens them to any solid Body, (which they perceive by the resistance they find in drawing them in from time to time with their Feet) they can make use of this kind of Bridge to pass to the place where their Threads are fixt. But if these Threads meet with nothing to fix on, the Spiders continue to let them out further, until their great length and the force with which the Wind drives them, surpassing the weight of their Bodies, they find themselves to be strongly drawn; and then breaking the first Thread, which they hung by, they let themselves loose to be driven by the Wind, and flutter on their Backs in the Air with their Legs stretch'd out. [12]

The startling congruity of these two descriptions provokes the inference that young Edwards knew and incorporated Bon's earlier description into his own. The similar imagery and nearly identical order of the descriptive elements support the inference; and yet, dissimilarities of diction, phrasing, and interpretation make caution necessary, at least until more conclusive proof is found. Furthermore, it may be argued that French and American aeronautic spiders exhibit sufficiently identical behavior to make plausible the assertion that coincidence only, and not imitation, is demonstrated by the evidence.

Though direct influence on Edwards is unproven, it is nevertheless clear that the pieces by Lister, Bon, and Edwards are similar enough to justify talk of a genre whose diction, imagery, and expression echo each other, and that Edwards' essay and letter must be viewed as specimens of that genre if any conclusions about his precocity, originality, observation, expression, and speculations are to be attempted. A further indication that these several pieces on the spider were indeed generically related is that the pieces composed by Bon and Edwards in the early eighteenth century self-consciously address themselves to queries published by Lister in 1671. Lister had asked, for example, "Whether the thread formed in the Body of the Animal . . . be drawn off of a liquid mass, as in spinning of Glass or melted Wax, which seems to have been *Democritus's* sense, in saying, it was excrement corrupted or fluid at certain times?" (*PT*, VI, 2173.) Edwards remarks:

> . . . in all Probability the Web while it is in the Spider is a certain liquour with which that Great bottle tail of theirs is filld, which immediately upon its being Exposed to the air turns to a Dry Substance and very much raifies, and extends itself (AR, 9).

Lister had asked "What difference 'twixt the thred of Spiders, and that of the Silk-worm or Caterpillars?" (*PT*, VI, 2173.) Bon, as the title of his essay indicates, answered at length in 1710, and van Leeuwenhoek, while never specifically referring to silk, describes the spider's threads and spinning apparatus in great detail. And Lister had asked "the reason why Spiders sail not in the air until Autumn . . .?" (*PT*, VI, 2174.) Edwards addressed himself to the problem and joined in his answer all that he knew of New England's prevailing winds, autumnal aridity, and spider behavior to his belief that a Divine purpose operated to maintain a balance of nature by lofting the spiders, after their eggs were laid, and blowing them on seaward breezes to their interment in the ocean (*AR*, 10–13): The point here is not Edwards' teleological inference, but the fact that his explanation is a direct attempt to answer a question first voiced by Lister.

One further example of the similarities between these several specimens of the genre must be considered. None of the virtuosi thought inferences of minute volition in the Spider or Divine Design in their behavior inappropriate or irrelevant to natural-philosophy speculation. Lister speaks of the spiders' "delight in sailing" and their ability to "*steer* their Course, and perhaps *mount* and *descend* at pleasure" (*PT*, XIV, 593–4). Anthony van Leeuwenhoek climaxes his extended description of the spider's spinning by asserting that "we may hereby discover the Wisdom of God in the Perfection of his Creatures, tho we little regard such a Thread as this, because it escapes our naked sight" (*PT*, XXII, 874). Apparently then, Edwards' presumption of Divine purpose in his spider's sailing is neither a product of his Calvinism nor a flaw in his science. On the contrary, the more one reads descriptions of minute, animate nature, the more he comes to recognize that these virtuosi of the late seventeenth and early eighteenth centuries investigated natural microcosms in the same spirit as their poetic fathers who scrutinized minute nature for the vehicles to their metaphysical metaphors. That is to say, they described spiders, partly to understand spiders, but also to understand God and God's principles of life in the world. This intention of the authors who contributed to the genre must be understood if we are to avoid the shallow condemnation of portions of their work as "unscientific" or "primitive" natural history.

Proof that such theological inferences are no necessary hindrance to accurate and responsible scientific work is provided by Henry C. McCook's speculation that the spider's habit of gathering in its threads and descending suggests "an act of volition on the part" of the spider and by his assertion that the similarity between the spider's sophisticated ballooning skill and man's similar achievements "strikes into a profounder depth than curious wonderment, and touches the problem of a Supreme Mind over Nature."[13] Such assertions may indeed be inappropriate in twentieth-century science, but they were integral elements of the genre for more than two hundred years. Apparently the flying or ballooning spider has served western man as a reminder of the marvellous extremes in the great chain of being and of the equally instructive brotherhood of man and spider within that chain. Thus the spider may serve present-day scholars as a provocative link between the seventeenth-century metaphysical, eighteenth-century rational, and nineteenth-century transcendental students of nature and "nature's people."

3. *Culture and Natural Philosophy*. Spiders may well be "a matter of taste," as W. S. Bristowe declares at the beginning of his superb *A Book of Spiders*, but the more "spider literature" one reads, including Bristowe's own literate, entertaining, thoroughly informed, and exquisitely illustrated volume, the more the indifference and distaste of the reading public in general and of all but a few naturalists seems another "strange puzel."[14] The lore of spiders is rich in superstitious, theological, allegorical, and satirical associations which bolster the repulsion many members of western culture feel regarding the spider. And yet, the works of Topsell, Edwards, Lister, Hulse, Bon, McCook, and others demonstrate (1) that spiders have often functioned to focus the delight and intellect of exceptional men, and (2) that the flying spider particularly has served as a symbol of aspiration, minute volition, and cosmic design. It was surely a vestige of such metaphysical inclination that led Whitman to identify with the darting spider in "The Noiseless Patient Spider,"[15] Similarly, an attenuated metaphysical sentiment appears to lie behind the description of twentieth-century ballooning spiders in Manhattan by the modern naturalist, author, and insect photographer, Edwin Way Teale:

> . . . against the high-piled background of the buildings, . . . a gossamer shower [was] descending from the sky. Baby spiders . . . had ridden like dandelion seeds across the [Hudson] and above the skyscrapers . . . . The tiny aeronauts were descending slowly, the rays of the sun glinting on the threads as they turned in midair. Journey's end for these spiders was amid the inhospitable concrete and asphalt of Times Square.[16]

Such spider descriptions, which attempt to fuse scientific and cultural modes of perception, speculation, and expression may function culturally in much the same way that metaphysical poetry did; perhaps such descriptions occupy a niche in the nonpoet's cosmos congruent to that filled for the literati by the poem.

Study of Edwards' piece and its Royal Society antecedents has obvious applicability to Edwards scholarship. However, it may serve a broader scholarly mission as well, for the tunnel vision, whether nationalistic or disciplinary, that allowed generations to virtually ignore the generic precedents for Edwards' work shows that categorical traditions have operated to obscure an important area of colonial prose. "The Flying Spider" case indicates the likelihood that identical habits of thought and expectation have probably operated in other cases and allowed similar documents of comparable cultural interest and importance to remain undiscovered and unappreciated simply because they resisted easy integration into accepted categories of belles lettres, science, or intellectual history. Even the small fame of Edwards' spiders is certainly a function of the author's later importance in other areas of cultural expression, not a response to the material primarily. Naturally enough, then, the even more delightful and mature productions of less well-known colonial virtuosi like Paul Dudley will continue to be overlooked unless scholars prepared and inclined to study cross-disciplinary documents discover them.

The time is ripe for rediscovering the riches of natural philosophy that lie gathering dust in the cabinets of antiquarians and ripe for the invention of fresh ways of revealing their relevance. Within the academic community the growing respectability of interdisciplinary research and publication raises the hope that scholars of broad, cross-disciplinary competence and inclination will search out such cultural documents as Edwards' and those from the *Philosophical Transactions* and make of them test cases that display the origins and developments of cultural patterns whose beginnings reside in colonial times but whose effects are felt still. The celebrated schism between science and literary culture, for example, has been well documented, but these materials exemplify ways in which the chasm was deliberately and satisfactorily bridged during the battle of the ancients and moderns; i.e., they present for our inspection models of successful integration of the objective and subjective modes of perception and expression. The present momentum of inter-disciplinary ecological scrutiny of man and his environment further suggests that the ecologists with the breadth of vision to seek not only the biological and physical parameters of the ecosystem but, also, the cultural variables and constants of our imagined ecosystem, could discover in the literature of natural philosophy evidence of the ways in which culture and the natural world external to man have interacted in the past.

Interdisciplinary studies of American culture and the American environment exemplify what bold synthesis can do to reveal the texture, tone, and organization of a system through careful investigation of a small portion of it. Students of culture have found worlds of meaning in such facts and symbols as Andrew Jackson's life, Lindbergh's flight, and the nineteenth-century dime novel, and the attitudes toward herbs of Jefferson's circle. Students of biological ecosystems have extracted revelations about the ecosystem from study of spider mites and DDT, the lake as microcosm, and the social behavior of starlings. Other students might now begin to fuse analyses of socio-cultural phenomena and processes with analyses of physical and biological phenomena and processes by similarly investigating some of the seemingly insignificant and minor documents of natural history in order to perceive the interrelations of cultural, historical, and natural ingredients in the total ecosystem. The rattlesnake, for example, evoked from even the most sober and rational colonial virtuosi a mixture of horror and delight that led them to adopt figurative language and elements of literary form in an attempt to express their sense of the beast's full meaning. With imagination, that rattlesnake, or the medicinal herbs of the new world, its birds of passage, its marsupials or its beavers could be shown to be the "real toads" that invaded the "imaginary gardens" of the American mind to fill the niches carved out by other species, natural or supernatural, and to modify by their residence the organization and texture of the world as man perceived it.

Notes

1. Martin Lister "Concerning the odd Turn of some Shell-snails, and the darting of Spiders, made by an Ingenious Cantabrigian and by way of Letter communicated to Mr. I. Wray [i.e., John

Ray], who transmitted them to the Publisher for the R.S.," *Philosophical Transactions* of the Royal Society of London, 4 (1669), 1014–15; The Cantabrigian is identified as Lister by Ray in *Phil. Trans.*, 5 (1670), 2103–05. Pagination is often misleading in these early volumes of the Society and there are two series of pages which include 2103; I refer to the second.

2. Carl Van Doren, *Benjamin Franklin and Jonathan Edwards: Selections From Their Writings* (New York, 1920), xi; Clarence H. Faust and Thomas H. Johnson, *Jonathan Edwards: Representative Selections* (New York, 1962), p. 417; Perry Miller, *Jonathan Edwards* (New York, 1949), pp. 37, 146; Alfred Owen Aldridge, *Jonathan Edwards* (New York, 1966), pp. 3–5; and Edward H. Davidson, *Jonathan Edwards: The Narrative of a Puritan Mind* (Boston, 1966), pp. 3–4.

3. Henry C. McCook, "Jonathan Edwards as a Naturalist," *Presbyterian and Reformed Review*, 1 (1890), 393–402, and *American Spiders and their Spinning-Work* (Philadelphia, 1889–93), I, 68–69, 280–82; Benjamin Julian Kaston, *Spiders of Connecticut* (Hartford, 1948), p. 31.

4. Sereno E. Dwight, in his *The Works of President Edwards: With a Memoir of His Life* (New York, 1830), p. 28, appears to have originated the error, but see also Benjamin Silliman, "Juvenile Observations of President Edwards on Spiders," *The American Journal of Science and Arts*, 21 (1832), 109–11, in which he claims Edwards could have been "another Newton." Other nineteenth-century comments on Edwards and the flying spider are in Moses Coit Tyler, *A History of American Literature*, 1607–1765 (New York, [1878], 1962), pp. 415–16; I. N. Tarbox, "Jonathan Edwards as a Man; and the Ministers of the Last Century," *New England and Yale Review*, 43 (1884), 630; and Egbert C. Smyth, "The Flying Spider—Observations By Jonathan Edwards When A Boy," *The Andover Review*, 13 (1890), 1–19, and "Some Early Writings of Jonathan Edwards," *American Antiquarian Society*, n.s. 10 (1895), 213.

5. Faust and Johnson, p. 417; the impression conveyed by this note must be corrected so that this instance of Edwards' interests in natural philosophy will be properly interpreted. Nevertheless, in "Manuscript Problems in the Yale Edition of Jonathan Edwards," *EAL* 3 (1969), 159-68, Thomas A. Shafer makes it clear that the scholarly energy devoted to the Yale Edition is almost exclusively invested in textual matters. While he grants that "part of the work of an editor is to supply an introduction in which are treated such matters as date, purpose, meaning, and influence of the writing under discussion," (p. 168) his statement that "explanatory notes are to be kept to a minimum" (p. 167) suggests that full attention cannot economically be granted to the research required to produce new explanatory notes. Generally the priority thus given to validating the text is appropriate, for responsible interpretation cannot proceed otherwise, but in the case of Edwards' essay on the spider the text has long been sufficiently established to allow priority to be given to the writing of new notes which comment upon the meaning and significance of the piece and identify for the reader its generic status and cultural niche.

6. Faust and Johnson provide a brief history and bibliography of the piece, p. 417, and reprint "Of Insects," pp. 3–10; also Aldridge, p. 3. "The Flying Spider" can be found in Van Doren, *op. cit.*, pp. 203–08; also Carl Bode, Leon Howard, and Louis B. Wright, *American Literature: The 17th and 18th Centuries* (New York, 1966), pp. 261–67.

7. Smyth. "The Flying Spider . . ." pp. 6, 14, 16: since Smyth printed both the essay and letter in *The Andover Review*, 13 (1890). 1–19, subsequent references (designated *AR*) in my text are to this version.

8. Cf. John Bartram's letters in William Darlington, *Memorials of John Bartram and Humphry Marshall* (Philadelphia, 1849), pp. 194–95, 382–88.

9. Among anthologies which print neither are: Roy Harvey Pearce, *Colonial American Writing* (New York, 1950); Norman Foerster, *American Poetry and Prose* (Boston, 1957); Milton R. Stern and Seymour L. Gross, *American Literature Survey* (New York, 1962); Russel B. Nye and Norman S. Grabo, *American Thought and Writing* (Boston, 1965); George F. Horner and Robert A. Bain, *Colonial and Federalist American Writing* (New York, 1966); Sculley Bradley, Richmond C. Beatty, and E. Hudson Long, *The American Tradition in Literature* (New York, 1967); and Harrison T. Meserole, Walter Sutton, and Brom Weber, *American Literature: Tradition and Innovation* (Lexington, Mass., 1969).

10. Of a Letter . . . by Richard Stafford . . . Strange Spiders-Webbs," *Phil. Trans.* of the Royal

Society of London, 3 (1688), 795; "Some Observations Concerning . . . the darting of Spiders, made by an Ingenious Cantabrigian and by way of Letter communicated to Mr. I. Wray, who transmitted them to the Publisher for the R.S.," *Phil. Trans.*, 4 (1669), 1014–16; "A Confirmation . . . about the manner of Spiders projecting their Threds . . .," *Phil. Trans.*, 5 (1670), 2103–05; "A Letter . . . together with a Set of Curious Inquiries about Spiders . . . By Mr. Martyn Lister," *Phil. Trans.*, 6 (1671), 2170–74; "A Letter . . . containing the Projection of the Threds of Spiders . . . by Dr. M. Lister," *Phil. Trans.*, 14 (1684), 592–94; "A Letter from Mr. Anthony van Leeuwenhoek, F.R.S. concerning Spiders . . .," *Phil. Trans.*, 22 (1701), 867–81; "A Discourse upon the Usefulness of the Silk of Spiders, by Monsieur Bon . . .," *Phil. Trans.*, 27 (1710), 9–10. References in my text are designated *PT*.

11. Clarence H. Faust, "Jonathan Edwards as a Scientist," *AL*, I (1930), 395; also Henry B. Parkes, *Jonathan Edwards, The Fiery Puritan* (New York, 1930), p. 37.

12. *Phil. Trans.*, 27 (1710) 9–10; *The Dictionnaire de Biographie Française (Paris, 1954), VI, 898, contains a brief biography of* François-Xavier Bon (1678–1761).

13. McCook, *American Spiders*, 261, 256.

14. In addition to *A Book of Spiders* (New York, 1947) and McCook's *American Spiders*, see Bristowe, *The Comity of Spiders* (2 vols.; London, 1939, 1941); John Henry Comstock, *The Spider Book* (New York, 1912); and for a French example of the genre, J. Henri Fabre (1823–1915), *The Insect World of J. Henri Fabre*, trans. Alexander Teixeira de Mattos, ed. Edwin Way Teale (New York, 1966), 294–95. Eleazar Albin, *A Natural History of Spiders, and other curious Insects*, with fifty copper plates (London, 1736), is an excellent early illustrated work. An especially literate and sensitive modern treatment of aeronauts occurs in John Crompton's Lamburn, *The Spider* (London, 1950), pp. 136–44; Crompton cites numerous descriptions of spiders in English literature, including Gilbert White's entry for Sept. 21, 1741, in *The Natural History of Selborne*.

15. John Burroughs, the American naturalist, admirer of Gilbert White, and friend of Walt Whitman for several years before Whitman wrote the poem, was also interested in spider behavior: *Writings of John Burroughs* (Boston, 1913), II, 117; V, 129; VII, 189; IX, 237; and XI, 209.

16. Edwin Way Teale, *The Lost Woods, Adventures of a Naturalist* (New York, 1945), pp. 169–70.

# Lineage:
# Edwardsean Influences

## Jonathan Edwards

Oliver Wendell Holmes[*]

As the centennial anniversaries of noteworthy events and signal births come round, frequent and importunate as tax-bills, fearful with superlatives as schoolgirls' letters, wearisome with iteration as a succession of drum-solos, noisy with trumpet-blowing through the land as the jubilee of Israel, we are, perhaps, in danger of getting tired of reminiscences. A foreigner might well think the patron saint of America was Saint Anniversary. As our aboriginal predecessors dug up the bones of their ancestors when they removed from one place to another, and carried them with the living on their journey, so we consider it a religious duty, at stated intervals in the journey of time, to exhume the memories of dead personages and events, and look at them in the light of the staring and inquisitive present, before consigning them again to the sepulchre.

A recent centennial celebration seems to make this a fitting time for any of us, who may feel a call or an inclination, to examine the life and religious teachings of a man of whom Mr. Bancroft has said, referring to his relations to his theological successors, that "his influence is discernible on every leading mind. Belamy and Hopkins were his pupils; Dwight was his expositor; Smalley, Emmons, and many others were his followers; through Hopkins his influence reached Kirkland, and assisted in moulding the character of Channing."

Of all the scholars and philosophers that America had produced before the beginning of the present century, two only had established a considerable and permanent reputation in the world of European thought,—Benjamin Franklin and Jonathan Edwards. No two individuals could well differ more in temperament, character, beliefs, and mode of life than did these two men, representing respectively intellect, practical and abstract. Edwards would have called Franklin an infidel, and turned him over to the uncovenanted mercies, if, indeed, such were admitted in his programme of the Divine administration. Franklin would have called Edwards a fanatic, and tried the effect of "Poor Richard's" common-sense on the major premises of his remorseless syllogisms.

We are proud of the great Boston-born philosopher, who snatched the thunderbolt from heaven with one hand, and the sceptre from tyranny with the other. So, also, we are proud of the great New England divine, of whom it might be said quite as truly, "Eripuit coelo fulmen." Did not Dugald Stewart and Sir

[*]Reprinted from *Pages from an Old Volume of Life* (1883), in *The Complete Works* (Boston: Houghton-Mifflin, 1889), 8: 361–66, 384–87, 394.

James Mackintosh recognize his extraordinary ability? Did not Robert Hall, in one of those "fits of easy transmission," in which loose and often extravagant expressions escape from excitable minds, call him "the greatest of the sons of men"? Such praise was very rare in those days, and it is no wonder that we have made the most of these and similar fine phrases. We always liked the English official mark on our provincial silver, and there was not a great deal of it.

In studying the characteristics of Edwards in his life and writings, we find so much to remind us of Pascal that, if we believed in the doctrine of metempsychosis, we could almost feel assured that the Catholic had come back to earth in the Calvinist. Both were of a delicate and nervous constitution, habitual invalids. Their features, it is true, have not so much in common. The portrait prefixed to Dwight's edition of Edwards's works shows us a high forehead, a calm, steady eye, a small, rather prim mouth, with something about it of the unmated and no longer youthful female. The medallion of Pascal shows a head not large in the dome, but ample in the region of the brow, strongly marked features, a commanding Roman nose, a square jaw, a questioning mouth, an asserting chin,—a look altogether not unlike that of the late Reverend James Walker, except for its air of invalidism. Each was remarkable for the precocious development of his observing and reflecting powers. Their spiritual as well as their mental conditions were parallel in many respects. Both had a strong tendency to asceticism. Pascal wore a belt studded with sharp points turned inward, which he pressed against his body when he felt the aggressive movements of temptation. He was jealous of any pleasure derived from the delicacy of his food, which he regarded solely as the means of supporting life. Edwards did not wear the belt of thorns in a material shape, but he pricked himself with perpetual self-accusations, and showed precisely the same jealousy about the gratification of the palate. He was spared, we may say in parenthesis, the living to see the republication in Boston of his fellow-countryman, Count Rumford's, essay "Of the Pleasure of Eating, and of the Means that may be employed for increasing it." Pascal and Edwards were alike sensitive, pure in heart and in life, profoundly penetrated with the awful meaning of human existence; both filled with a sense of their own littleness and sinfulness; both trembling in the presence of God and dwelling much upon his wrath and its future manifestations; both singularly powerful as controversialists, and alive all over to the *gaudia certaminis,*—one fighting the Jesuits and the other the Arminians. They were alike in their retiring and melancholy kind of life. Pascal was a true poet who did not care to wear the singing robes. As much has been claimed for Edwards on the strength of a passage here and there which shows sentiment and imagination. But his was in his youthful days, and the "little white flower" of his diary fades out in his polemic treatises, as the "star of Bethlehem" no longer blossoms when the harsh blades of grass crowd around it. Pascal's prose is light and elastic everywhere with *esprit;* much of that of Edwards, thickened as it is with texts from Scripture, reminds us of the unleavened bread of the Israelite: holy it may be, but heavy it certainly is. The exquisite wit which so delights us in Pascal could not be claimed for Edwards;

yet he could be satirical in a way to make the gravest person smile,—as in the description of the wonderful animal the traveller tells of as inhabiting Terra del Fuego, with which he laughs his opponents to scorn in his treatise on the "Freedom of the Will." Both had the same fondness for writing in the form of aphorisms,—natural to strong thinkers, who act like the bankers whose habit it is to sign checks, but not to count out money,—and both not rarely selected the same or similar subjects for their brief utterances.

Even in some external conditions Pascal and Edwards suggest comparison. Both were greatly influenced by devout, spiritually-minded women. Pascal, who died unmarried, had his two sisters,—Gilberte and Jacqueline,—the first of whom, afterwards Madame Périer, wrote the Memoir of her brother, so simply, so sweetly, that one can hardly read it without thinking he hears it in her own tender woman's voice,—as if she were audibly shaping the syllables which are flowing through his mute consciousness. Edwards's wife, Sarah Pierrepont, was the lady of whom he wrote the remarkable account (cited by Mr. Bancroft in his article on Edwards, as it stands in the first edition of Appleton's "Cyclopaedia") before he had made her acquaintance,—she being then only thirteen years old. She was spiritual to exaltation and ecstasy. To his sister Jerusha, seven years younger than himself, he was tenderly attached. She, too, was of a devoutly religious character.

There were certain differences in the midst of these parallelisms. Auvergne, with its vine-clad slopes, was not the same as Connecticut, with its orchards of elbowed apple-trees. Windsor, a pleasant name, not wanting in stately associations, sounds less romantic than Clermont. We think of Blaise and Jacqueline, wandering in the shadow of *Puy de Dome*, and kneeling in the ancient cathedral in that venerable town where the first trumpet of the first crusade was blown; and again we see Jonathan and Jerusha straying across lots of Poquannock, or sitting in the cold church, side by side on the smileless Sabbath. Whether or not Edwards had ever read Pascal is not shown by any reference in his writings, but there are some rather curious instances of similar or identical expressions. Thus the words of his sermon, in which he speaks of sinners as "in the hands of an angry God," are identical in meaning with Pascal's "dans les mains d'un Dieu irrité." His expression applied to man, "a poor little worm," sounds like a translation of Pascal's "chétif vermisseau." A paragraph of his detached observations entitled "Body Infinite," reminds one of the second paragraph of the twenty-fourth chapter of Pascal's "Pensées." These resemblances are worth noting in a comparison of the two writers. Dealing with similar subjects, it is not strange to find them using similar expressions. But it seems far from unlikely that Edwards had fallen in with a copy of Pascal, and borrowed, perhaps unconsciously, something of his way of thinking . . . .

A chief ground of complaint against Edwards is his use of language with reference to the future of mankind which shocks the sensibilities of a later generation. There is no need of going into all the plans and machinery of his "Inferno," as displayed in his sermons. We can endure much in the mediaeval verse of Dante which we cannot listen to in the comparatively raw and recent prose of Edwards. Mr. John Morley speaks in one of his Essays of "the horrors of what is perhaps the most frightful idea that has ever corroded human character,—the idea of eternal punishment." Edwards has done his best to burn these horrors into the souls of men. A new organic and a new inorganic chemistry are brought into the laboratory where "the bulk of mankind" have been conveyed for vivisection or vivicombustion. The body is to possess the most exquisite sensibilities, is to be pervaded in every fibre and particle by the fire, and the fire is to be such that our lime-kilns and iron-furnaces would be refrigerators in comparison with the mildest of the torture-chambers. Here the great majority of mankind are to pass the days and nights, if such terms are applicable to it, of a sleepless eternity. And all this apparatus of torture in full operation for "four thousand years," none of its victims warned of it or knowing anything about it until the "good news" came which brought life and immortality to light,—an immortality of misery to "the bulk of mankind!"

But Edwards can be partially excused for doing violence to human feelings. It is better, perhaps, to confess that he was an imitator and a generous borrower than to allow him the credit of originality at the expense of his better human attributes. Very good men are sometimes very forgetful. The Rev. Thomas Scott was a very good man, no doubt, in many respects, but that excellent old friend of the writer, the late learned and amiable Dr. Jenks, says in an Editor's Notice, to be found in the fifth volume of "The Comprehensive Commentary": "Nothing but such a diligent comparison as this work necessarily required, of the labors of Henry and Scott, could have shown how greatly the latter was indebted to the former, especially in the Old Testament; and the lack of acknowledgment can be accounted for, and reconciled with principle, only by the consideration, that, possibly, if it had been made in every case where it was due, the work would have been less acceptable to persons of the 'establishment' whom the writer was desirous to influence favorably." Was ever an indictment drawn in language more tenderly modulated?

The Rev. Mr. Gillespie of Scotland, writing to Edwards, asks him, "Are the works of the great Mr. Boston known in your country, namely, the 'Fourfold State of Man?' " etc. To which Edwards replies: "As to Mr. Boston's 'View of the Covenant of Grace,' I have had some opportunity to examine it, and I confess I do not understand the scheme of thought presented in that book. I have read his 'Fourfold State of Man,' and liked it exceedingly well. I think in that he shows himself to be a truly great divine."

The Rev. Thomas Boston of Ettrick, Scotland,—an Ettrick shepherd very different from "Jamie the Poeter," as James Hogg was called by his rustic neighbors,—may be remembered as one of the authors largely cited by Mr. Buckle in his arraignment of the barbarous theology of Scotland. He died in 1732, but the edition before the present writer, though without date, is evidently a comparatively recent one, and bears the impress, "Philadelphia: Presbyterian Board of Publication."

Something of the mild surprise which honest old Dr. Jenks experienced when he found the property of Matthew Henry on the person of Thomas Scott may be felt by scrupulous individuals at recognizing a large part of the awful language, with the use of which Edwards is often reproached, as the property of Thomas Boston. There is no mistaking the identity of many of these expressions and images. Some, besides the Scriptural ones, may have been borrowed by both writers from a common source, but there is a considerable number which confess their parentage in the most unequivocal way. The argument for infinite punishment is the same; the fiery furnace the same; the hair suspending a living soul over it the same; reptiles and other odious images belong to both alike; infinite duration is described in similar language; the natural affections no longer exist: the mother will not pity the daughter in these flames, says Boston; parents, says Edwards, will sing hallelujahs as they see their children driven into the flames where they are to lie "roasting" (Edwards) and "roaring" (Boston) forever. This last word, it may be remarked, has an ill sound on the lips of a theologian; it looks as if he were getting out of the reach of human sympathies. It sounds very harshly when Cotton Mather says of a poor creature who was accidentally burned to death,—being, it seems, a little in liquor at the time, poor soul!—that she "went roaring out of one fire into another."

The true source of Edwards's Dante-like descriptions of his "Inferno" is but too obvious. Whatever claim to the character of a poet is founded on the lurid brilliancy of these passages may as well be reconsidered in the red light of Thomas Boston's rhetorical *autos-da-fé*. But wherever such pictures are found, at first or second hand, they are sure causes of unbelief, and liable to produce hatred not only of those who teach them, but of their whole system of doctrines. "Who are these cruel old clerical Torquemadas," ask the ungodly, "who are rolling the tortures of ourselves, our wives and children, under their tongues like a sweet morsel?" The denunciations of the pulpit came so near the execrations of the street in their language, and sometimes, it almost seemed, in their spirit, that many a "natural man" must have left his pew with the feeling in his heart embodied in a verse which the writer of this article found many years ago in a psalm-book in a Glasgow meeting-house where he was attending service, and has remembered ever since:

> "As cursing he like clothes put on,
>     Into his bowels so
> Like water, and into his bones
>     Like oil down let it go.". . .

The truth is, Edwards belonged in Scotland, to which he owed so much, and not to New England. And the best thing that could have happened, if it had happened early enough, both for him and for his people, was what did happen after a few years of residence at Stockbridge, where he went after leaving Northampton,—namely, his transfer to the presidency of the college at Princeton, New Jersey, where the Scotch theological thistle has always flourished, native or imported,—a stately flower at present, with fewer prickles and livelier bloom than in the days of Thomas Boston, the Ettrick shepherd of old. Here he died before assuming the duties of his office; died in faith and hope,—hope for himself, at any rate, perhaps, as we shall see, with less despairing views for the future of his fellow-creatures than his printed works have shown us.

# Samuel Hopkins and the New Divinity: Theology, Ethics, and Social Reform in Eighteenth-Century New England

Joseph A. Conforti°

The intellectual stress of the Great Awakening of the eighteenth century was simultaneously divisive and creative. It split New England theologians into contending camps, one of which grew from the teachings of Jonathan Edwards and represented the first indigenously American school of Calvinism. Proponents of the New Divinity, as the doctrines of this Edwardsian party came to be called, attempted to build a complete, consistent system of evangelical Calvinism around such critical issues of the Awakening as the nature of and need for spiritual rebirth, the authenticity of mass conversions, the role of means (prayer, Bible reading, and church attendance) in regeneration, and the coming of the millennium.

In the years after the Awakening, and particularly during his Stockbridge exile (1751–1757), Edwards assumed the task of refining and systematizing the revival's theological implications. His untimely death at the height of his creative power in 1758 left his ambitious project uncompleted. But in the years since the revival Edwards had attracted clerical followers who aided him in his efforts and continued his work.

Edwards's closest friend and disciple was Samuel Hopkins. Born in Waterbury, Connecticut, in 1721, Hopkins graduated from Yale in 1741, studied for the ministry in Edwards's Northampton parsonage, and was ordained at Housatonic (renamed Great Barrington in 1761), Massachusetts, in 1743.[1] Eight years later, when Edwards settled in Stockbridge, Hopkins renewed their friendship and frequently made the thirty-minute horseback ride from Housatonic to the Indian mission. Upon Edwards's death, all of his unpublished papers were placed under Hopkins's care. From 1770 to 1803 Hopkins served the First Congregational Church of Newport, Rhode Island, where his theological concerns became focused on social reform.

°Reprinted, with permission, from *The William and Mary Quarterly*, 34 (October, 1977), 572–89.

In the late 1750s Hopkins and other ministers began to publish tracts and tomes which were designed to complete Edwards's theological work. In so doing, these New Divinity clerics, or "Consistent Calvinists" as they were also called, so radically extended and modified their teacher's ideas that many New Lights, such as the Baptist leader Isaac Backus, claimed for themselves the name of Edwardsians and rejected the New Divinity as a bastardizing of Edwards's thought.[2]

The New Divinity's alterations of Edwardsianism have allowed historians to heap praise on Edwards while belittling the school he helped to found. In this standard view, Edwards marks the apex and the New Divinity the nadir of colonial New England's intellectual history.[3] For some historians, the Consistent Calvinists lacked Edwards's piety; they could rationally grasp his doctrines but could not plumb the depths of the religious experience upon which he based his theology. For others, the New Divinity men lacked not only Edwards's piety but his acumen as well. Their commitment to consistency betrayed intellectual debility. Absorbed in exploring minute and subtle details, they retreated into a rarefied intellectual world and lost contact with social reality. They promoted a "paper war" of religious polemics, created abstract metaphysical systems, and thereby alienated the laity. They discoursed with one another, oblivious to the expanding and changing society around them. In the end, the subtle differences of their discourses and systems became obscure to the participants themselves, and few New Englanders grieved over the passing of the New England theology.[4]

In reality, however, Consistent Calvinism was far from simply a body of abstract metaphysical arguments which contemporaries might justly dismiss as intellectually absurd and socially irrelevant. When one focuses on the problem of true virtue and especially on Hopkins's original interpretation of the doctrine of disinterested benevolence, the social context and meaning of the New Divinity come into view. The debate over the nature of true virtue derived from efforts to define authentic spiritual sentiments in light of what many saw as the false piety and emotional excesses of the Awakening. The controversy also had a social dimension; it was in part a response to what the New Divinity men viewed as a crisis in social thought in mid-eighteenth-century New England. Hopkins, for example, was disquieted by the conflict between traditional social values and the behavior of New Englanders in a time of critical change. Like other evangelicals, he inherited a social ethic that stressed corporate obligation, personal restraint, and communal harmony and simplicity. But the economic and demographic expansion of New England during his lifetime promoted acquisitive, egocentric patterns of behavior at odds with those norms.[5]

The doctrinal "paper war" revolving around the problem of true virtue arose from attempts to close the gap between values and experience by formulating new theological legitimations for behavior.[6] With his doctrine of disinterested benevolence, Hopkins endeavored to discredit liberal. Old Light, and even New Light compromises of inherited social thought. In the process he gave evangelical Calvinism an activist social thrust—a development which some historians, most notably Alan Heimert,[7] would lead us to believe flowed directly from Edwardsianism and not by way of the New Divinity movement. While in fundamental respects Hopkins was a follower of Edwards, he nevertheless found serious flaws in his mentor's theology. Specifically, Hopkins concluded that Edwards's interpretation of true virtue was deficient on several counts. Not only did it tend toward abstraction, but it mixed ethics with aesthetics, made unnecessary concessions to rational moral philosophers, and did not provide an adequate spur to social action.

Edwards's *Dissertation concerning the Nature of True Virtue* was written in 1755 but did not appear in print until 1765. It provoked responses from Old Light Calvinists who had been carrying on a theological controversy with the New Divinity men for several years. In 1770, for example, William Hart of Saybrook, Connecticut, published his *Remarks on President Edwards's Dissertation concerning the Nature of True Virtue*. Hart intended his work to be a final moderate Calvinist assault on the theology of the Great Awakening. He wanted to demonstrate how the New Divinity as a whole, and particularly Edwards's concept of true virtue, were "wrong, imaginary and fatally destructive of the foundation of morality and true religion."[8] Hart was especially disturbed that Edwards had replaced the biblical God with the abstract metaphysical concept of "Being in general." Furthermore, Hart argued, a penchant for metaphysics and aesthetics had led Edwards to deny that social morality was true virtue and to "involve practical religion . . . in a cloud." Most of Edwards's dissertation was vitiated, Hart suggested, because he had confused aesthetics with ethics.[9]

Such criticism helped clarify for Hopkins the deficiencies in Edwards's ethical theory and convinced him that his own work should be an improvement on, not simply a defense of, Edwards. Hopkins focused on Edwards's interpretation of Being in general as one of the central areas in need of improvement. "True virtue," Edwards began his dissertation, "most essentially consists in benevolence to *Being in general*," and he went on to explain that "I shall not be likely to be understood, that no one act of the mind or exercise of love is of the nature of true virtue, but what has Being in general or the great system of universal existence, for its direct and immediate object." While Edwards seemed to equate Being in general with God, he described an ultimate reality different from traditional notions of the Deity. God was not only "the *head* of the system [of universal being] and the chief part of it,"[10] but the source of all being. Hopkins found this conception of Being in general both amorphous and abstract. He attempted to correct Edwards—and thus silence Edwards's critics—by redefining Being in general as "God and our neighbors," that is, God and mankind.

Hopkins was also dissatisfied with Edwards's handling of the subjective nature of true virtue. Love of Being in general, Edwards argued, originated in a "relish," "propensity," or "inclination" of the will or heart. In short, true virtue was essentially a matter of motivation. While natural principles governed the will of an unconverted person, through regeneration an authentic Christian had a benevolent affection implanted in his heart which motivated him to love Being in general.[11]

At this point, critics such as Hart charged that Edwards transformed his analysis into a discussion not of ethics but of aesthetics. To ask what is the nature of true virtue, Edwards wrote, "is the same as to inquire, what that is which renders any habit, disposition, or exercise of the heart truly *beautiful*."[12] The major alteration produced by regeneration, and thus the distinguishing feature of true virtue, Edwards concluded, consisted in a "comprehensive view"[13] of spiritual reality, which the saint relished and loved for its beauty. Edwards's overly aesthetic interpretation of true virtue was another element of his theology which Hopkins undertook to improve.

Both Hopkins and the critics of *True Virtue* saw that Edwards's emphasis on the beatific nature of regeneration militated against worldly action. Edwards left an ambiguous legacy for Christian ethics.[14] In the 1740s he had attempted to counteract a new wave of revival-inspired antinomianism by insisting upon the importnce of evangelical activity as a fruit of conversion. But a decade later, New England's religious life had changed dramatically, and the emphasis of Edwards's theology changed with it. A sharp decline in conversions put an end to the antinomian menace. Anti-revival rationalism now posed the major threat to evangelical Calvinism. Indeed, it seemed to Edwards that the spiritual delights of regeneration had been largely forgotten. In this sense, the dominant theme of *True Virtue*—that regeneration culminates in relishing the beauty of Being in general—was intended as an antidote to rationalist thought.

Edwards's approach, however, placed theological obstacles in the way of evangelical activism.[15] In Hopkins's view, the quietistic emphasis of *True Virtue* made Edwards vulnerable to the charge that he had involved practical religion in a cloud. Edwards's detailed descriptions of the subjective nature of regeneration, when combined with the mystical quality of his concept of Being in general, encouraged passive contemplation and rapt otherworldiness. Through his doctrine of disinterested benevolence Hopkins endeavored to remove the ambiguity in Edwards's theology on the issue of ethics. The cause of religious reform profited from this shift.

When Edwards did discuss social morality in *True Virtue*, he made clear that he was talking about an inferior, secondary order of virtue and beauty. Hopkins found Edwards's analysis of secondary virtue the most deficient part of his ethical theory. In his judgment, it was objectionable in general because it borrowed too much from the views of contemporary moral philosophers whose thought was essentially rationalistic and in particular because it embraced a concept of self-love that was ethically as well as spiritually dangerous.

Religious rationalists in Europe and America—as advocates of what was called natural theology—held that man had the natural ability to understand scripture, judge right from wrong, and attain salvation. Edwards's concept of secondary virtue incorporated the views of such exponents of natural theology as the earl of Shaftesbury and the Scottish philosopher Francis Hutcheson.[16] Responding to the moral cynicism of Thomas Hobbes, Shaftesbury and

Hutcheson rested their sanguine hopes for mankind on belief in an innate "moral sense" capable of regulating the behavior of individuals without the need for supernatural grace.[17] Many eighteenth-century moral philosophers reacted to Hobbesian pessimism by basing the regulation of social behavior on another natural faculty in man—self-love. Not always carefully distinguishing this principle from selfishness, they described it as an inclination to seek one's own happiness and avoid misery. Moses Hemmenway, an Old Light critic of Edwards and the New Divinity who adopted the view of most rational, common-sense philosophers, and of most moderate and liberal Calvinists, defined self-love in reply to Hopkins in 1772 as "that affection or propensity of heart to ourselves, which causes us to incline to our own happiness." Rationalists maintained that self-love did not conflict with the public good. It was a form of enlightened self-interest in which individual happiness was part of the public good. Selfishness, Hemmenway argued, was a much narrower affection; it was "a regard to ourselves and our own good, exclusive of all regard to others or their good."[18] In short, self-love, like man's reason and moral sense, was a natural principle implanted in human nature by God; upon it, both true virtue and social order were established.

Edwards countered by arguing that natural principles played an important role on the level of secondary virtue. Not true virtue but an inferior form of virtue resulted from the operation of reason, conscience, moral sense, and even self-love. To Hopkins's disappointment, Edwards agreed with many rationalists that "self- love is a principle that is exceeding useful and necessary in the world of mankind." Self-love may promote social harmony, Edwards asserted, because unregenerate men "are most affected towards, and do most highly approve, those virtues which agree with their interest most, according to their various conditions in life."[19] What Edwards was saying in his attempt to assimilate the natural theology of the rationalists into his ethical theory was that God had provided for the organization of society on the basis of a kind of virtue and beauty inferior to true virtue and its beauty. While the realization of a thoroughly virtuous social order depended upon mass revivalism, the realization of a basically harmonious society did not have to wait for a new Awakening, because natural principles such as reason, moral sense, and self-love were at work in the world. Even though the human race suffered from natural depravity, Edwards reminded the readers of *True Virtue* that "the present state of mankind is so ordered and constituted by the wisdom and goodness of its supreme Ruler, that these natural principles for the most part tend to the good of the world of mankind."[20]

To Edwards, secondary virtue established negative moral goodness as the normative ethical condition of natural man. "By negative moral goodness," Edwards wrote, "I mean the absence of true moral evil." Although secondary virtue "be not of the nature of real positive virtue or true moral goodness, yet it has a negative moral goodness, because in the present state of things it is evidence of the absence of that higher degree of wickedness which causes great insensibility or stupidity of conscience."[21]Furthermore, in practice, secondary and true virtue often resembled one another. Trying objectively to differentiate one moral state from the other was comparable, Edwards suggested, to attempting to distinguish between invisible and visible saints. At bottom the difference was not external but resided in the motive or inclination of the heart or will.[22] Thus, he concluded, rationalists were labeling as true virtue what in reality was only secondary virtue.

Hopkins discovered a number of defects in Edwards's concept of secondary virtue. He feared that while Edwards had denied the rationalists' contention that natural man was not capable of true virtue, he had nevertheless conferred theological legitimacy on natural principles. Hopkins was especially alarmed by Edwards's acceptance of self-love. It appeared to him that Edwards's position played into the hands of the rationalists who, by distinguishing self-love from selfishness, were developing a social ethic that was facilitating the transition from communal to individualistic social ethics. The concept of self-love as differentiated from selfishness served as the underpinning of the rationalist clergy's social thought in the second half of the eighteenth century. Their "realistic" social perspective held that the best possible society and the greatest good to the greatest number would result from the operation of self-love, that is, from the individualistic pursuit of happiness.[23] Hopkins's identification of all virtue with disinterested benevolence was an attempt to shore up traditional social thought and block the advance of self-love theories. His radical call for self-denial, in conjunction with his efforts to amend what he saw as the abstract and aesthetic qualities of Edwards's interpretation of true virtue, broadened the theological base for social reform within the New Divinity movement.

In 1773 Hopkins entered the theological paper war over the nature of true virtue with the publication of *An Inquiry into the Nature of True Holiness*. Where Edwards located true virtue in exalted consciousness, Hopkins placed it in elevated social behavior. Consequently, evangelical activism superseded mystical quietism. In one respect, then, Hopkinsianism did indeed liberalize Calvinism—or, as one critic of the New Divinity prefers to put it, moralize Edwardsianism—and looked forward to modern humanized religion.[24] But the weight of theological tradition prevented an easy slide into Enlightenment humanism. The social ideals which Hopkins's *Inquiry* endorsed, for example, were reactionary; that is, the work marshaled old and new theological arguments to reaffirm the legitimacy of New England's communal values against lay desertion and clerical compromise.

Edwards described Being in general as a comprehensive ontological reality, and true virtue as an aesthetic perception of this universal being. Hopkins, on his part, stressed that Being in general was the tangible reality of God and our neighbors. As a result, Hopkins saw true virtue as more an ethical than an aesthetic ideal. Universal benevolence or "love to God and our neighbour, including ourselves . . . or friendly affection to all intelligent beings"[25] constituted Hopkins's definition of true virtue.

On the question of God's moral nature and its relation to true virtue,

Hopkins arminianized Edwards's thought. For Edwards, God's glory did not depend upon His benevolence toward His creatures. Although God desired man's happiness, His "goodness and love to created beings is derived from, and subordinate to his love of himself." While self-centered existence was morally reprehensible in man, Edwards argued, it was appropriate in the Deity. God did not exercise disinterested benevolence toward earthly beings; rather, He loved Himself as the "chief part" and source of all being. Though he acted benevolently toward mankind, He was not morally obliged to promote their happiness.[26]

For Hopkins, on the other hand, God's moral nature circumscribed His sovereignty. God was not a self-centered deity but a benevolent governor whose glory depended upon the happiness of mankind.[27] Disinterested benevolence was His primary moral attribute: "the holiness and perfection of God and his people, consists, so much at least, in disinterested benevolence, that there is no moral perfection without it, in God or the creature."[28] Hopkins joined liberal Arminian Calvinists in linking divine perfection to human happiness. Benevolence was such an important part of God's moral nature that He had always to act in accordance with the moral interests of His creatures.[29]

Edwards would not have recognized his concept of Being in general or the God of his Calvinism in Hopkins's *Inquiry*. On these two points Hopkins had greatly altered Edwards's thought. But Hopkins's most important refashioning of Edwards's definition of true virtue—and his major contribution to an evangelical theology of social reform—dealt with the opposition of disinterested benevolence to self-love. Here he not only parted ways with Edwards but dismissed out of hand the views of the rational moral philosophers. Hopkins refused to give even the slightest theological sanction to the self-interested behavior which he saw undermining New England society, particularly that of Newport.

Hopkins contended that no middle ground such as secondary virtue and beauty existed between true virtue and selfishness. Every human being's heart was filled with either totally self-interested or totally disinterested affections, and a gulf existed between these moral states which only the Holy Spirit could close. Hopkins confidently rejected Edwards's claim that the secondary virtue which natural principles produced was morally and socially valuable even though it fell short of true virtue. He maintained that secondary virtue and the "negative moral goodness" it established in the world were irreconcilably opposed and in no way analogous to the disinterested benevolence of true virtue: "There is, however, a great difference, and opposition in these two kinds of affections; . . . This selfish affection, though extended to the whole community with which the selfish man is connected, is at bottom nothing but love to himself. This is the foundation and center of his love. He in reality loves nothing but himself, and regards others wholly for his own sake."[30] Hopkins created a complete disjunction between true and secondary virtue, because every affection that fell short of disinterested benevolence was rooted in selfishness. He argued, for example, that self-love, far from restraining wickedness, "is the source of all the profaneness and impiety in the world; and of all pride and ambition among men; which is nothing but selfishness acted out in this particular way."[31]

Hopkins's strictures on self-love led ultimately to the most famous tenet of his theological system: a regenerate person must be willing to be damned for the glory of God. "He therefore cannot know that he loves God and shall be saved," Hopkins argued in A *Dialogue between a Calvinist and a Semi-Calvinist*, written in the late 1780s and published posthumously in 1805, "until he knows he has that disposition which implies a willingness to be damned, if it be not most for the glory of God that he should be saved."[32] In other words, one could not avoid damnation except by being willing to be damned. Lay and clerical opponents of the New Divinity (and some modern historians as well) tore this doctrine out of context and used it to portray Consistent Calvinism as an absurd system. Hopkins's position becomes intelligible, however, when it is related to the eighteenth-century debate on the nature of true virtue and to the crisis of social thought in New England.

After rejecting Edwards's contention that natural principles, including self-love, resembled true virtue and brought secondary virtue into the world, Hopkins reassessed the larger role of self-love in his mentor's theology. Few New Englanders other than Hopkins had access to the unpublished writings of Edwards that supplemented *True Virtue*. In these manuscripts Hopkins found Edwards arguing that self-love not only produced secondary virtue but operated on the level of true virtue. "That a man should love his own happiness," Edwards noted in *Charity and Its Fruits*, written in 1738 (but not published until 1851), "is as necessary to his nature as the faculty of the will is; and it is impossible that such a love should be destroyed in any other way than by destroying his being."[33] Self-love, like the will, was a faculty common to all members of the human race. The converted as well as the unconverted were moved by it to desire their own happiness. The essential difference was that the regenerate, having gained a new disposition of the heart, identified their interest and happiness with love of Being in general. On the basis of this view of self-love, which was grounded in Lockean sensationalism, Edwards found it inconceivable that a person could be willing to be damned. In "Miscellany 530" Edwards stated the matter clearly: "Love to God, if it be superior to any other principle, will make a man forever unwilling, utterly and finally, to be deprived of that part of his happiness which he has in God's being blessed and glorified, and the more he loves Him, the more unwilling he will be. So that this supposition, that a man can be willing to be perfectly and utterly miserable out of love to God, is inconsistent with itself."[34] Regeneration disposed the faculty of self-love to relish, delight, and seek happiness in eternal harmony with God. While not going as far as theological utilitarians, Edwards did argue that "wicked men do not love themselves enough"[35] or else they would seek their own eternal happiness by avoiding sin.

Hopkins countered by arguing that a Christ-like disposition to self-denial, rather than an inclination flowing from self-love to identify ultimate happiness with Being in general, was the hallmark of true virtue. He rejected all ethical theories that approved self-centered inducements to salvation: "to give up our temporal interest, worldly interest, for the sake of eternal happiness, wholly under the influence of self-love, is as real an instance of selfishness, as parting with all we have now, to possess a large estate next year."[36] Love of God and neighbor, and not the saving of one's soul, became the core of Hopkinsianism. The true Christian must lose himself in a cause higher than his own salvation— namely, the temporal and eternal well-being of others.[37] Thus the most peculiar tenet of Hopkinsianism, and the one most offensive to the rational mind, reinforced the social activism which his redefinition of Being in general and his criticism of secondary virtue encouraged.

Taken together, Hopkins's innovations represented an important shift away from the equivocal theological legacy of Edwards on the issue of worldly action toward an emphatic endorsement of social reform.[38] Where Edwards saw true virtue as essentially a matter of right affections, Hopkins viewed it as right actions. God's moral law, Hopkins concluded, "leads us to consider holiness as consisting in universal disinterested good will considered in all its genuine exercises and fruits, and acted out in all its branches toward God, and our neighbor."[39]

In reinterpreting true virtue as radical disinterested benevolence, Hopkins was not simply responding to Edwards's positions. He was also attempting to furnish a corrective to the increasingly fashionable theological notion of self-love. As in Edwards's theology, self-love in the eighteenth century was at times viewed as a mediating moral state between selfishness and true virtue, and at others as part of true holiness itself. In either case it appeared to the New Divinity men to be a doctrine that promoted and legitimized avaricious, egoistic patterns of behavior. Their apprehensions had considerable justification, for the concept of self-love proved to be an intellectual way station on the road to a full-fledged theory of self-interest. By removing much of the moral obloquy attached to egocentric behavior, it eased the passage from traditional communal ideals to a new ideology of individualism and self-interest. As the rational clergy saw it, the idea of self-love brought about greater coherence between social theory and social reality. At the same time, they argued, it denied the legitimacy of naked self-interest (selfishness) and would create a more stable social order since, in theory at least, self-love would promote the public good. To the structural forces in eighteenth-century New England that encouraged individualistic, self-centered behavior—economic and demographic expansion, and land hunger—the rationalists now added a theoretical argument that may have allowed many people to allay feelings of guilt for having violated social tradition and to rationalize self-interest.[40]

To be sure, all of this was not self-evident in the middle of the eighteenth century. Rather, as Richard L. Bushman has pointed out, "the 1750s and 1760s were a period of experimentation in social theory because everyday experience confronted people with the problem" of contriving "a new rationale for the social order . . ."[41] But the New Divinity man perceived present and potential dangers in such experimentation. Liberal and Old Light Calvinists drew their self-love social theories directly from rational moral philosophers like Shaftesbury and Hutcheson. Many New Lights, on the other hand, gave self-love a role in human behavior based upon the views of Edwards in *True Virtue*.[42] It remained for the New Divinity men to protest what they saw as theological concessions to selfish social behavior.

To this task Hopkins brought a strong sense of moral urgency. In growing numbers ministers chose "to represent the hopes and fears, joys and sorrows, and all the exercises of the Christian as wholly selfish," he protested, "and treat of all the doctrines and duties of christianity in this light! How common to find arminians, neonominists, professed calvinists, antinomians, or whatever other name they may bear, and however they may differ in other things, all agreeing in this!"[43] The New Divinity men held that self-love ethical theories, whether Edwardsian or Hutchesonian, were contributing to the failure of communal ideals. As Hopkins reasoned, "if no person can renounce his eternal interest, in opposition to a selfish regard to it, there is no such thing in nature as self-denial, or public, disinterested affection."[44] Furthermore, if the new social morality was anchored in egocentricity, then the truly benevolent man was required to battle that false morality in all its social manifestations. Hopkins's theology thus obliged him to oppose the emergent values of commercial Newport; in particular, it inspired his assault on slavery and the slave trade.

Hopkins's repudiation of the new morality derived from his rural upbringing and twenty-five-year pastorate in the backcountry. It was intensified by his experience of the worldly society and mercantile economy of Newport, with its involvement in the slave trade and the production of rum which was used to secure human cargo on the coast of Africa. To the rustic theologian, committed to a simple, even ascetic socio-religious tradition, Newport appeared a symbol of what America was in danger of becoming. Moreover, the behavior of Newport slave merchants underlined the importance of distinguishing secondary virtue from true virtue. In terms of conventional social morality the respectable slave traders, most of whom were practicing Christians, seemed to be virtuous men. Measured against the yardstick of disinterested benevolence, however, their virtue fell far short of love to Being in general. Finally, Hopkins linked his attack on Newport's slave traders and the social order they represented with the Revolutionary struggle against Great Britain.

In the early 1770s Hopkins preached to his congregation on the iniquity of the slave trade, and he published his first important antislavery tract, *A Dialogue Concerning the Slavery of the Africans*, in 1776. The work was dedicated to the Continental Congress, from which he sought reassurance that a 1774 resolution prohibiting the slave trade issued "not merely from political reasons; but from a conviction of the unrighteousness and cruelty of that trade and a regard to justice and benevolence." He urged the delegates not to divorce politics from morality but rather to promote the moral regeneration of America and guarantee the success of the Revolution by "bring[ing] about a total abolition of slavery, in such a manner as shall greatly promote the happiness of those oppressed strangers, and [the] best interest of the public."[45]

With the mode of life of Newport's wealthy merchant class undoubtedly in mind, Hopkins challenged the American people not only to abolish slavery but also to launch a "thorough reformation" of all "public sins."[46] For several years he had seen the promise of radical social regeneration held out by resistance to Great Britain. "The struggle is like to prove fatal to tea drinking in America which will save much needless expense," he had written to the Reverend John Erskine in Scotland in 1774, adding that "there is a hopeful prospect of its putting an end to many other extravagances, unless accommodation should take place soon."[47] In his *Dialogue* Hopkins urged Americans to reform all their selfish, profligate ways. By concentrating on the evil of slavery he did "not mean to exclude other public, crying sins found among us, such as impiety and profaneness—formality and indifference in the service and cause of Christ and his religion—and various ways of open opposition to it—intemperance and prodigality; and other instances of unrighteousness." Slavery and all the sins of America were "the fruits of a most criminal, contracted selfishness."[48]

Through the 1780s and 1790s Hopkins remained committed to the abolition of slavery and the slave trade, and continued to see these evils in the larger context of a social order rooted in self-interest and extravagance rather than true virtue.[49] The Revolutionary dedication to simplicity and the public good had been abandoned, Hopkins wrote in an antislavery essay in 1787, and Americans were spending their money "for foreign luxuries or unnecessaries, and those things which might have been manufactured among ourselves."[50] The continuing oppression of the blacks became for Hopkins the main sign that the Revolution had failed to reform thoroughly the indulgent self-centered behavior of the American people and to reconstruct the social order on the basis of love to Being in general. Hopkins singled out Newport, where the slave trade had been resumed, as "the most guilty . . . of any [community] on the continent, as it has been in great measure built by the blood of the poor Africans, and the only way [for it] to escape the effects of Divine displeasure is to be sensible of the sin, repent and reform."[51] Although Hopkins persevered to the end of his life in supporting the antislavery cause, when the federal constitutional convention prevented congressional interference with the slave trade until 1808, he became pessimistic about America's immediate future and transferred to the millennium his hope for a society held together by self-sacrificing love of God and our neighbors.

The idea of disinterested benevolence, as one critic of Hopkins has recently reminded us, was not exclusively of New England origin. Francis Hutcheson, George Whitefield, John Wesley, and the Quakers, for example, all developed notions of benevolence in the eighteenth century that inspired the crusading reformers of the next century.[52] No theories of disinterested benevolence, however, not even that of Edwards, approached the self-denying idealism of Hopkins's views. For this reason, many of New England's future religious reformers, particularly the next generation of young, pietistic, Congregational clerics, would come to see the doctrine of disinterested benevolence as a unique contribution of the New Divinity movement.[53]

Far from losing contact with social reality by spinning a metaphysical cocoon around itself, the New Divinity movement, as this analysis of the debate over the problem of true virtue has tried to suggest, was in constant dialogue with the clerical spokesmen for, and the lay representatives of, an emerging secular social order. New Divinity theology struck a responsive chord among certain segments of New England society. The movement increasingly captured the allegiance of aspirants to the Congregational ministry, especially in the years leading up to and following the founding of the predominantly Hopkinsian Andover Seminary in 1808.[54] Moreover, on the lay level, the New Divinity appealed to and was welcomed by congregations throughout rural New England. Thus, surveying the backcountry from his pastorate in Salem in 1813, liberal Calvinist William Bentley reluctantly concluded that Hopkins's "System of Divinity is the basis of the popular theology of New England."[55]

From the vantage point of rural New England, and in light of the region's crisis in social thought, it is interesting to speculate on the intellectual consequences of the New Divinity's triumph. For many pious young men, religious reform provided an outlet for the tension between Christ and culture to which the New Divinity was addressed and which it encouraged. But for most inhabitants of rural New England who supported the New Divinity, the conflict between normative values and new patterns of behavior was not so easily resolved. For these people the Second Great Awakening, like the First, may have been a vent for the moral uneasiness that characterized a continuing crisis of religious legitimation. If this is so, then the New Divinity did not betray its origins in experimental religion by over-intellectualizing the piety of the First Awakening but preserved, for the backcountry at least, the revival's creative tension between social tradition and social practice.

## Notes

1. On Hopkins see Edwards A. Park, *Memoir of the Life and Character of Samuel Hopkins, D.D.* (Boston, 1854), and Joseph A. Conforti, "Samuel Hopkins and the New Divinity Movement: A Study in the Transformation of Puritan Theology and the New England Social Order" (Ph.D. diss., Brown University, 1975), upon which this essay is based.

2. See William G. McLoughlin, *Isaac Backus and the American Pietistic Tradition* (Boston, 1967), 184–185.

3. The classical statement of this view is Joseph Haroutunian, *Piety versus Moralism: The Passing of the New England Theology* (New York, 1932).

4. In addition to Haroutunian, *Piety versus Moralism*, expressions of the views summarized above may be found in Sidney Earl Mead, *Nathaniel William Taylor, 1786–1858: A Connecticut Liberal* (Chicago, 1942), *passim*, esp. p. 96; Herbert Wallace Schneider, *The Puritan Mind* (Ann Arbor, Mich., 1958 [orig. publ. New York, 1930]), pp. 222–223; Douglas J. Elwood, *The Philosophical Theology of Jonathan Edwards* (New York, 1960), p. 154; Edmund S. Morgan, *The Gentle Puritan: A Life of Ezra Stiles, 1727–1795* (New Haven, Conn., 1962), pp. 313–315; Morgan, "The American Revolution Considered as an Intellectual Movement," and Donald Meyer, "The Dissolution of Calvinism," in Arthur M. Schlesinger, Jr., and Morton White, eds., *Paths of American Thought* (Boston, 1963), pp. 18–22, 77–80; Cedric Cowing, *The Great Awakening and the American Revolution: Colonial Thought in the Eighteenth Century* (Chicago, 1971), pp. 197–198; and Stephen E. Berk, *Calvinism versus Democracy: Timothy Dwight and the Origins of American Evangelical Orthodoxy* (Hamden, Conn., 1974), chap. 6. Two exceptions to the views found in these works are Edwin Scott Gaustad, *The Great Awakening in New England* (New York, 1957), pp. 126–140, and Richard D. Birdsall, "Ezra Stiles versus the New Divinity Men," *AQ*, 18 (1965), 248–

258. For a theological compendium that falls somewhere between the competing interpretations of the New Divinity movement see Frank Hugh Foster, *A Genetic History of New England Theology* (Chicago, 1907).

5. Jack P. Greene, "Search for Identity: An Interpretation of the Meaning of Selected Patterns of Social Response in Eighteenth-Century America," *Journal of Social History*, 3 (1970), 190–224, esp. 191–205. For other interpretations of this cleavage see Richard L. Bushman, *From Puritan to Yankee: Character and the Social Order in Connecticut, 1690–1765* (Cambridge, Mass., 1967), chaps. 12–16; Edward M. Cook, Jr., "Social Behavior and Changing Values in Dedham, Massachusetts, 1700 to 1775," WMQ, 3d Ser., 28 (1970), 546–580; and Kenneth A. Lockridge, "Social Change and the Meaning of the American Revolution," *Jour. Soc. Hist.*, 4 (1973), esp. 423–424. On the traditional New England social values see Michael Zuckerman, *Peaceable Kingdoms: New England Towns in the Eighteenth Century* (New York, 1970), and Stephen Foster, *Their Solitary Way: The Puritan Social Ethic in the First Century of Settlement in New England* (New Haven, Conn., 1971).

6. On the problem of legitimation in the sociology of religion see Peter L. Berger, *The Sacred Canopy: Elements of a Sociological Theory of Religion* (New York, 1967), chaps. 2, 7.

7. Alan Heimert, *Religion and the American Mind: From the Great Awakening to the Revolution* (Cambridge, Mass., 1966).

8. William Hart, *Remarks on President Edwards's Dissertation concerning the Nature of True Virtue . . .* (New Haven, Conn., 1771), p. 41.

9. *Ibid.*, pp. 9, 21, 45–46.

10. Jonathan Edwards, *Works*, ed. E. Hickman (New York, 1843), II, 262, hereafter cited as Edwards, *Works*. The concept of Being in general may be traced back to Edwards's early theological efforts. See, for example, his essay "Of Being" in Harvey G. Townsend, ed., *The Philosophy of Jonathan Edwards from His Private Notebooks* (Eugene, Ore., 1955), pp. 1–20. The best modern interpretation of the concept is in Elwood, *Philosophical Theology of Edwards*, esp. pp. 22–23.

11. *True Virtue*, in Edwards, *Works*, II, 261–266.

12. *Ibid.*, 261. Roland André Delattre, *Beauty and Sensibility in the Thought of Jonathan Edwards* (New Haven, Conn., 1968), offers an excellent analysis of the role of aesthetics in Edwards's theology. See also Clyde A. Holbrook, *The Ethics of Jonathan Edwards: Aesthetics and Morality* (Ann Arbor, Mich., 1973), esp. pp. 104–105.

13. *True Virtue*, in Edwards, *Works*, II, 262.

14. This conflict in Edwards's thought between quietism and activism is best revealed in the *Religious Affections*. Holy action is the last of the 12 distinguishing signs of conversion that Edwards discusses. Many of the other signs (4 and 10, for example) are existential states and aesthetic perceptions. Edwards, *Works*, III. esp. 108, 171.

15. Heimert in *Religion and the American Mind* exaggerates the role of evangelical activism in Edwards's theology and in the process creates an overdrawn portrait of the social and political implications of Edwards's thought. As Delattre notes, Heimert's chapter on "The Beauty and Good Tendency of Union" shows an understanding of the place of aesthetics in Edwards's theology, "but he overstates his case for the location of that divine beauty in human community" (*Beauty and Sensibility*, pp. 10–11).

16. Edwards's *True Virtue* was intended in part to refute Hutcheson's *An Inquiry into the original of our ideas of Beauty and virtue* (London, 1725). In his reply Edwards incorporated aspects of Hutcheson's ethical theory. See A. Owen Aldridge, "Edwards and Hutcheson," HTR, 44 (1951), 35–53, and Clarence H. Faust and Thomas H. Johnson, eds., *Jonathan Edwards: Representative Selections . . .* (New York, 1935), pp. lxxv–xciii.

17. Conrad Wright, *The Beginnings of Unitarianism in America* (Boston, 1955), chap. 6. On the "common-sense" philosophy see Gladys Bryson, *Man and Society: The Scottish Inquiry of the Eighteenth Century* (Princeton, N.J., 1945), pp. 1–28; Douglas Sloan, *The Scottish Enlightenment and the American College Ideal* (New York, 1971), esp. chaps. 3, 4; Henry F. May, *The Enlighten-*

*ment in America* (New York, 1976), pp. 341–358; and Sydney E. Ahlstrom, "The Scottish Philosophy and American Theology," *CH*, 24 (1955), 257–272.

18. Moses Hemmenway, *A Vindication of the Power, Obligation and Encouragement of the Unregenerate to attend the Means of Grace. Against the Exceptions of the Rev. Mr. Samuel Hopkins* . . . (Boston, 1772), p. 63. On self-love theorists in the 18th century see Jacob Viner, *The Role of Providence in the Social Order: An Essay in Intellectual History* (Philadelphia, 1972), pp. 62–85, and Wright, *Beginnings of Unitarianism*, pp. 142–145.

19. *True Virtue*, in Edwards, *Works*, II. 283–299.

20. *Ibid.*, p. 299.

21. *Ibid.*

22. *Ibid.*, p. 297.

23. Bushman, *Puritan to Yankee*, pp. 278–279. On clerical and lay use of the concept of self-love in economic and social theory at mid-century see J. E. Crowley, *This Sheba, Self: The Conceptualization of Economic Life in Eighteenth-Century America*, The John Hopkins University Studies in Historical and Political Science (Baltimore, 1974), pp. 72–73, 91–92; also see Henry W. Sams, "Self-Love and the Doctrine of Work," *JHI*, 4 (1943), 320–332.

24. Haroutunian, *Piety versus Moralism, passim*, esp. pp. 83–84.

25. Samuel Hopkins, *An Inquiry into the Nature of True Holiness* . . . (Newport, R.I., 1773), 11, hereafter cited as *True Holiness*. Hopkins's phrase "including ourselves" was not an acceptance of self-love. According to him, a man should have a "regard" to himself only as part of Being in general, "so that all his own particular interest is subordinate to that of the whole" (*ibid.*, 24).

26. *True Virtue*, in Edwards, *Works*, II, 268–270.

27. *True Holiness*, 53. At times Edwards moved closer to Hopkins's position. See, for example, "Miscellany 3" in Townsend, ed., *Philosophy of Edwards*, p. 193.

28. *True Holiness*, p. 45.

29. For the liberal Calvinists' interpretation of the benevolence of the Deity see Wright, *Beginnings of Unitarianism*, chap. 7.

30. *True Holiness*, p. 23.

31. *Ibid.*, p. 29.

32. The *Dialogue* was printed in Stephen West, ed., *Sketches of the Life of the Late Rev. Samuel Hopkins, D.D.* . . . (Hartford, Conn., 1805); quotation on p. 150.

33. Jonathan Edwards, *Charity and Its Fruits; or, Christian Love as Manifested in the Heart and Life* (New York, 1851), p. 229.

34. Townsend, ed., *Philosophy of Edwards*, p. 204; Holbrook, *Ethics of Edwards*, esp. pp. 56–63.

35. Edwards, *Charity and Its Fruits*, p. 236.

36. *True Holiness*, p. 70.

37. On this and several other suggestive implications of Hopkins's interpretation of disinterested benevolence see Oliver Wendell Elsbree, "Samuel Hopkins and His Doctrine of Benevolence," *NEQ*, 8 (1935), 534–550.

38. Heimert detects such a trend toward activism in the thought of Edwards's followers: "Within Calvinist doctrine itself, the 1750s witnessed something of a redefinition of Christian virtue, making 'zeal' a more distinguishing affection . . . than love. The changing emphasis reflected the shift in focus from the heart to the will implicit in the *Religious Affections*" (*Religion and the American Mind*, p. 311). Such a shift occurred somewhat later than Heimert believes, largely, as I have tried to show, as a result of Hopkinsianism.

39. *True Holiness*, p. 41.

40. This was particularly true in commercial areas, where, by the 1760s, the crisis in social thought was adjusted and a modified corporate ethic (self-love) was in conflict with naked self-

interest (see Crowley, *This Sheba, Self*, pp. 96–97). But as Kenneth A. Lockridge has recently argued, the rural world that spawned the New Divinity clung to an idealized corporate perspective that made even relatively minor social changes seem like "catastrophic alterations of an idyllic and holy past" ("Social Change and the Meaning of American Revolution," *Jour. Soc. Hist.*, 6 [1973], 423–424); see also Zuckerman, *Peaceable Kingdoms, passim*. In both commercial and rural New England, the republican ideology of the Revolution, with its emphasis on public virtue and simplicity, heightened the conflict between social theory and social practice, and fired the hopes of evangelicals like Hopkins.

41. Bushman, *Puritan to Yankee*, p. 272.

42. On the use of the concept of self-love by both Old Lights and New Lights see, for example, Samuel Cooper, *A Sermon Preached in Boston, New England, before the Society for Encouraging Industry and Employing the Poor* (Boston, 1753), pp. 2–3, and Thomas Clap, *An Essay on the Nature and Foundation of Moral Virtue and Obligation . . .* (New Haven, Conn., 1765), pp. 13–17.

43. *True Holiness*, p. 78.

44. *Ibid.*, p. 70. For an interesting debate on self-love between Hopkins and a prominent secular leader see the correspondence with Roger Sherman in Andrew P. Peabody, ed., "Hopkinsianism." *PAAS*, 5 (1889), 437–461.

45. Hopkins, *A Dialogue Concerning the Slavery of the Africans; Shewing it to be the Duty and Interest of the American Colonies to emancipate all their African Slaves . . .* (Norwich, Conn., 1776), p. iii. Two recent essays briefly analyze Hopkins's antislavery thought and actions. See David S. Lovejoy, "Samuel Hopkins: Religion, Slavery, and the Revolution," *NEQ*, 40 (1967), 227–243, and David E. Swift, "Samuel Hopkins: Calvinist Social Concern in Eighteenth-Century New England," *Journal of Presbyterian History*, 47 (1969), 31–54. Also see Bernard Bailyn, *The Ideological Origins of the American Revolution* (Cambridge, Mass., 1967), pp. 232–241, and David Brion David, *The Problem of Slavery in the Age of Revolution, 1770–1823* (Ithaca, N.Y., 1975), pp. 293–299.

46. Hopkins, *Dialogue Concerning Slavery*, p. 53.

47. Hopkins to John Erskine, Dec. 27, 1774, Gratz MSS, Historical Society of Pennsylvania, Philadelphia. For similar hopes and their implications for the Revolution see Edmund S. Morgan, "The Puritan Ethic and the American Revolution," *WMQ*, 3d Ser., 24 (1967), 3–43, and Lockridge, "Social Change and the Meaning of the American Revolution," *Jour. Soc. Hist.*, 6 (1973), p. 424.

48. Hopkins, *Dialogue Concerning Slavery*, p. 52.

49. For a full discussion of Hopkins's antislavery position in relation to the Revolution and the central themes of this essay see Conforti, "Samuel Hopkins and the New Divinity Movement," chap. 8. One important antislavery consequence of his theology was the institution of ecclesiastical sanctions against the holding and trading of slaves in his own church. Under his prodding the church voted in 1784 "that the slave trade and the slavery of the Africans, as it has taken place among us, is a gross violation of the righteousness and benevolence which are so much inculcated in the gospel; and therefore we will not tolerate it in this church" (Jan. 30 and Mar. 4, 1784, First Congregational Church Records, Newport Historical Society, R.I.).

50. This essay, signed "Crito," appeared in two installments in the *Providence Gazette: and Country Journal* (R.I.), Oct. 6, 13, 1787. It was reprinted under the title "The Slave Trade and Slavery" in *Timely Articles on Slavery by the Rev. Samuel Hopkins* (Boston, 1854), a collection of Hopkins's antislavery writings. The quotation is on p. 619.

51. Hopkins to Moses Brown, Apr. 29, 1784, Moses Brown Papers, Rhode Island Historical Society, Providence; "The Slave Trade and Slavery," in *Timely Articles on Slavery*, p. 615.

52. Lois W. Banner, "Religious Benevolence as Social Control: A Critique of an Interpretation," *Journal of American History*, 60 (1973), 25–41.

53. For a recent assessment of the influence of Hopkins and the New Divinity on 19th-century reform see Davis, *Problem of Slavery in the Age of Revolution*, p. 296. Two 19th-century reformers left glowing testimonies to the influence of Hopkins; see William Ellery Channing to E. A. Park,

Feb. 14, 1840, Yale MSS, Sterling Memorial Library, New Haven, Conn., and John Greenleaf Whittier, *Works*, VI, (New York, 1888), pp. 130–140.

54. By 1792, for instance, Ezra Stiles reported that more than one-third of the Congregational clergy in Connecticut identified themselves as New Divinity men. In the same year, Stiles noted, the Consistent Calvinists claimed to have the allegiance of all new Congregational ministerial candidates in the state. Franklin Bowditch Dexter, ed., *The Literary Diary of Ezra Stiles, D.D., LL.D.,* III (New York, 1901), pp. 463–464. For other evidence documenting the growth of the New Divinity see *ibid.*, pp. 247, 363; *The Diary of William Bentley, D.D.: Pastor of the East Church, Salem, Massachusetts* (Salem, 1905–1914), I, p. 161, III, p. 364; West, ed., *Sketches of the Life of Hopkins*, pp. 102–103; Park, *Memoir of Hopkins*, pp. 236–237; Leonard Bacon *et al., Contributions to the Ecclesiastical History of Connecticut* (New Haven, 1861), p. 240; and Charles Keller, *The Second Great Awakening in Connecticut* (New Haven, 1942), pp. 36–37, 50–52. On Hopkins's influence over the Andover seminarians see Wolfgang E. Lowe, First American Foreign Missionaries: The Students, 1810–1829: An Inquiry into their Theological Motives" (Ph.D. diss., Brown University, 1962).

55. *Diary of Bentley*, IV, p. 302; see also Foster, *Genetic History of New England Theology*, p. 1.

# Calvinism Romanticized: Harriet Beecher Stowe, Samuel Hopkins, and *The Minister's Wooing*

Lawrence Buell[*]

The importance of the Puritan imagination in shaping New England's literary Renaissance of the mid-nineteenth century has been widely and justly proclaimed. In the process, however, much more attention has been paid to the liberal Unitarian-Transcendentalist impact upon literary aesthetics than to the impact of the conservative Calvinist theological mainstream, the influence of which (as measured by denominational statistics) was much stronger in the region as a whole throughout the antebellum period. Significantly, the literary figure whose "Puritan" roots have most often been examined is Nathaniel Hawthorne, who in real life attended Unitarian churches—when he attended at all—and had no visible sympathy for contemporary Calvinist sects. Students of American Romanticism have in general been uninterested in tracing the legacy of Edwardseanism, which used to be known as *the* "New England theology," except insofar as it may have led from Edwards to Channing to Emerson—a tenuous genealogy at best.[1] As a result, most American literary scholars, even specialists in New England Romanticism, have only a sketchy understanding of the period's overall religious climate.

The situation is in a sense justified by the fact that the liberal, Arminian mentality which led to the Unitarian and Transcendentalist movements was far more hospitable to art than was orthodoxy. One recalls Timothy Dwight's dictum: "Between the Bible and novels, there is a gulf fixed."[2] Theological liberalism, by contrast, tended to erase the distinction between sacred and profane forms of expression, devaluing the importance of doctrinal content and attaching a significance at least in principle to art as a means of inspiration. Small wonder, then, that among the region's major literary figures who matured before the Civil War, only Emily Dickinson and Harriet Beecher Stowe were reared under Calvinist influences. Orthodox littérateurs were numerous but largely strait-jacketed by conventional pietistic formulas. To create the imaginative free play of an Emerson or a Hawthorne, a generation or more of

[*]Reprinted, with permission, from *ESQ: A Journal of the American Renaissance*, 24 (3rd Quarter 1978), 119–32.

secularism or urbanity normally seems required. Religious orthodoxy of any sort seldom inspired great art during the nineteenth century until the artist had begun to view his subject ambivalently.

Whether for these or other reasons, few literary historians have cared to investigate the theological opinions of Edwards' major successors—Joseph Bellamy, Samuel Hopkins, the younger Edwards, Timothy Dwight (whose poetry is enough of a chore for most readers), Nathaniel Emmons, and N. W. Taylor. Horace Bushnell, revived by Charles Feidelson in the 1950's as an "interesting" parallel "exhibit" to Emerson, is a partial exception,[3] but the aesthetic implications of his thought have been much less explored than those of, say, William Ellery Channing. Evidently it is assumed that Edwards' Calvinist progeny made little or no distinctive contribution to the style or vision of subsequent writers of quality. Yet the truth is that the gradual secularization of Edwardseanism is, in its own way, just as important to the history of American literature as the earlier, better-understood process of secularization in the liberal ranks. This claim has been impressively documented, at least in a negative sense, by Ann Douglas' *The Feminization of American Culture*, which shows that writers of orthodox and liberal background alike contributed importantly to the groundswell of sentimental literature in nineteenth-century New England, as doctrinal structures began to erode.[4] On a more limited scale, it has been shown that the style of Second Awakening Calvinism had a distinct impact upon the inner lives of both Stowe and Dickinson.[5] But the full importance of the New England theology as muse, model, and censor for the workings of the New England imagination remains to be described; and until it is, the dynamics of American Romanticism cannot be fully understood.

The present essay attempts to further this rehabilitation process by surveying the creative uses of orthodoxy in the one serious novel of the period which deals most directly with the Edwardsean tradition, Harriet Beecher Stowe's *The Minister's Wooing*. Though it has always had its admirers, Stowe's third novel has been unjustly overshadowed by the fame of *Uncle Tom's Cabin* and by the tendency of American criticism to limit itself to commentaries *ad nauseam* on the same handful of texts.[6]

The titular hero of Stowe's historical romance is Samuel Hopkins (1721–1803), Edwards' most controversial disciple. Taking considerable liberties with the facts, Stowe presents Hopkins as a middle-aged bachelor, boarding in the house of his pious Newport parishoner, the widow Katy Scudder, who is intent on marrying him to her saintly daughter Mary. Mary really loves her attractive but as yet unconverted cousin James Marvyn, but when James is believed to be lost at sea Mary reluctantly submits to her mother's matchmaking. On the eve of the wedding, James of course returns. Mary self-denyingly rejects him in order to keep her word to Hopkins, but when the minister learns of her true feelings, he generously releases her and performs the wedding in which he was to have been the bridegroom. In a semi-related subplot, Stowe has Jonathan Edwards' grandson, Aaron Burr, the symbolic opposite of Hopkins, attempt to seduce both Mary and *her* counterpart, a young Frenchwoman suggestively named Virginie, who is somewhat more vulnerable for having as an innocent girl made the kind of mismarriage with a kindly father-figure which threatens Mary herself. Immaculate Mary easily resists Burr and helps her friend to do the same.

Criticism of *The Minister's Wooing* has centered around the heroine and primary center of consciousness, Mary Scudder, viewing her either as Stowe's idealized self-image or as a cultural symbol and literary type.[7] From this perspective, the role of Hopkins seems rather circumscribed: his gawkiness is contrasted with her beauty, his theological legalism with her spontaneous piety. This and the fact that the triangulated love affair was almost total fabrication[8] suggest that Stowe's interest in Hopkins himself was limited at best. Sentimental characterization and melodramatic plot do indeed usurp the book to such an extent that it is easy to understand why Hopkins' mid-nineteenth-century counterparts felt that he had been reduced to caricature. Yet in another sense the book is built around him, and he must be regarded as its central figure. What distinguishes *The Minister's Wooing* is not its hackneyed plot but Stowe's recreation of post-Revolutionary New England and in particular its rapidly secularizing yet still evangelical milieu, in which Hopkins is the local pontiff. A close examination of Stowe's Hopkins in relation to the original, indeed, illuminates not only what is of lasting interest about the novel but also its flaws.

As Charles Foster notes, Stowe was "almost certainly" drawn to Hopkins as a fictional subject because of his role as an early anti-slavery crusader.[9] This is the context of her first published sketch of him, in a review article on "New England Ministers" written shortly before she began *The Minister's Wooing*;[10] and this is the aspect of his career described most exhaustively in her chief source for the facts of his life, the *Memoir of the Life and Character of Samuel Hopkins*, by Edwards A. Park, who edited what is still the standard edition of Hopkins' works.[11] Park, the Stowes' neighbor and "closest friend" on the Andover faculty, lent her his memoir, which she ransacked for anecdotes.[12] The story of Newport Gardner, whose master decided to free him at the very moment he was praying for his liberty; the story of Hopkins persuading his friend Joseph Bellamy to free his slave on the spot; the allusion to a wealthy family who left Hopkins' church "in disgust" when he preached against slavery—these are a few examples of passages which Stowe lifted or transposed in the manner familiar to those acquainted with her *Key to Uncle Tom's Cabin*.[13] Even the idea of writing a fiction about Hopkins would have been reinforced by a passage in Park summarizing an 1843 short story about the supposed sale of the slave Hopkins owned during his pastorate at Great Barrington (1743–69), as well as "the mental depression of the good man in consequence of his bargain, and the subsequent history of the negro who was sold. The scene of the narrative is laid at Newport" (*Memoir*, p. 114).

In addition to reading Park, Stowe familiarized herself with Hopkins' anti-slavery writings. The minister's discussion, in Chapter 10, with his obdurate slave-holding parishioner Simeon Brown, parallels the arguments in Hopkins' *Dialogue Concerning the Slavery of the Africans* (*Works*, II, pp. 556–557, pp.

563–565; *MW*, pp. 119–120). His sermon in Chapter 15 consists entirely of excerpts taken from Hopkins' newspaper denunciation of "The Slave Trade and Slavery" (*Works*, II, pp. 614–615; *MW*, pp. 177–178), his most incendiary essay. In the novel, this is Hopkins' finest moment as a public figure. When he asserts his convictions without heeding in the slightest the hostility of the town and the temporizing advice of his friends, he seems commanding, noble, almost God-like in his fidelity to absolute truth, whatever the practical consequences. Altogether, Stowe was faithful to a fault to Park's characterization of Hopkins as "the first of the American divines" to campaign effectively against slavery, "unless we include . . . a few estimable Quakers" (*Memoir*, p. 161). Her image of Hopkins as lonely giant led her, for example, to distort the conservatism of his Newport colleague Ezra Stiles, whom she transforms from a supporter of Hopkins' humanitarianism into an apologist for slavery.[14]

Hopkins' anti-slavery efforts are finally, however, a secondary theme in *The Minister's Wooing*, unless one reads his act of releasing Mary from her bond as a blow for emancipation parallel to his sermon—an analogy Stowe leaves wholly implicit. The full extent of Stowe's interest in Hopkins is much more complex, involving her personal history as well as her public convictions. The figure of Hopkins can be associated with her father Lyman Beecher, as a representative of Edwardsean Calvinism, and secondarily with her husband Calvin Stowe, who like her father amply illustrated the trait of eccentric individualism which she attributed to New England ministers in general.[15] Although Stowe began writing sketches of turn-of-the-nineteenth-century New England figures in the early 1830's, shortly after her family's removal to Cincinnati, her serious investigations of family and regional history started with her role in the preparation of Lyman Beecher's *Autobiography*. Beecher was trained at Yale by another disciple of Edwards, Timothy Dwight. Though not precisely a Hopkinsian, in his early ministry Beecher was " 'a friend to Hopkinsianism' " who " 'took great pains' " to see that his people were " 'converted in Hopkins' way.' " Beecher later insisted, however, that he " 'never carried [Hopkins'] views to an extreme.' "[16] He did not, for instance, insist so heavily upon the doctrine that God has ordained sin and damnation for the ultimate good of the universe. From the viewpoint of family history, then, Hopkins would have seemed a somewhat reactionary force, a stern great-uncle who helped place restraints on the more generous-minded Beecher's views. The prime instance of this in *The Autobiography*, and one of the chief sources of *The Minister's Wooing*, is the drowning of the upright but apparently unconverted fiancé of Harriet's older sister Catherine. Beecher was exceedingly tender and patient in his attempts to deal with Catherine's resentment against the creed that would consign her lover to damnation, but, like Stowe's Hopkins in the case of James Marvyn's grieving mother, Beecher could ultimately do no more than counsel unconditional submission to God's will.[17] Catherine eventually became a shrewd and vocal critic of Calvinism. Stowe underwent a similar crisis when her son Henry drowned in 1858, an event which merged with her memory of her sister's loss to form the basis of the pseudo-tragedy of James Marvyn in the

novel. Somewhat like Catherine, Stowe improvised her own *ad hoc* modification of Calvinism to assuage her doubts about Henry's salvation. Foster aptly
describes this improvisation as a "homemade doctrine of special privilege,"
whereby Henry's salvation was guaranteed by his mother's prior loyalty to
God.[18]

In *The Minister's Wooing* itself, the pattern of the daughter with spiritual
insight upstaging the ministerial father figure is of course crucial. It is Mary
who protects Virginie against Burr, Mary who converts the unregenerate hero,
for whom Hopkins' sermons are empty words. When Hopkins questions Mary
about her "evidences" of regeneration, she replies with a letter that in effect
rejects the basic criterion by which he would distinguish true assurance from
false—that is, the idea that the unconditional submission to God which marks
the truly regenerate person includes "a willingness to be left to eternal sin" if
God deems it necessary for the greater glory of the universe (*MW*, p. 214). As
Foster discovered, Mary's response comes straight from a 1799 letter to Lyman
Beecher written by his then-fiancée, Roxana Foote, Harriet's mother,
posthumously canonized by her husband and children.[19] In both contexts the
minister figures as logician, the maiden as intuitive thinker; the minister is
assailed by periodic self-doubt, the maiden remains serene; and the minister
considers himself unworthy of her. In short, the maiden-as-evangelist device
was for Stowe not only a stock gimmick of sentimental fiction that she herself
had used with popular success in the characterization of Eva in *Uncle Tom's
Cabin*; it was also a fact of family history. On the basis both of such correspondences and of Stowe's habit of composing in erratic bursts of emotional energy,
Foster understandably reads the book as the "semi-lyrical expression [of] her
own inner crisis," interpreting the figure of Mary as an idealized compound of
mother, sister, and self, half embracing and half resisting Calvinism as person-
ified by Hopkins.[20]

Yet *The Minister's Wooing* is finally not spiritual autobiography but historical fiction. Even its fantasy elements are responses to history as well as
expressions of the author's psychic needs. For example, in her fictionalization of
Hopkins' life, Stowe predictably exaggerates the pattern of the female lay
evangelist by making the minister seem hopelessly dependent upon the women
around him for his daily needs. Stowe would have been encouraged in this
portrayal by certain features of the historical record itself. The historical
Hopkins expressed, to begin with, great admiration for a series of exemplary
pious women, beginning with Sarah Pierrepont Edwards and her daughter
Esther Burr, Aaron Burr's grandmother and mother, whom the narrator sees as
prototypes for Mary Scudder (*MW*, pp. 159, 193–194, 265–266). Park even
credits Mrs. Edwards with suggesting "the germ of one branch of Hopkinsianism"—ironically the same idea of unconditional submission which Mary
Scudder rejects.[21] Hopkins later edited the spiritual autobiographies of two of
his women parishioners, Sarah Osborn and Susanna Anthony, leaders of a
female "Praying Circle" which was extremely influential in Hopkins' Newport
church and probably decisive in persuading a divided parish to accept him as

pastor. In the early years of Hopkins' Newport ministry, the regular monthly meetings of the "church" (that is, the members in full communion) were held at Mrs. Osborn's house.[22] Park emphasizes that "long before Mr. Hopkins went to Newport, Madam Osborn had been esteemed as the spiritual advisor of the church," that "she was consulted . . . as if she had been a minister" (*Memoir*, p. 99). Stowe could easily have translated such details into an image of female dominance over Hopkins. Finally, Hopkins' eulogies of the piety of Osborn and other female saints whom he admired contrast markedly with his own habitual self-deprecation, his evaluation of himself as a "low and shameful christian," and his assessment of his ministry as a failure. Mary Scudder's sublime assurance of grace might have derived not only from Lyman Beecher's report of Roxana's unique serenity, but also from Hopkins' description of Mrs. Osborn's "almost unparalleled assurance" or from Jonathan Edwards' avowal that his wife had "the greatest, fullest, longest continued, and most constant Assurance of the favour of God, and of a title to future glory, that he ever saw any appearance of, in any person."[23]

Stowe's imposition of feminine spiritual leadership upon Hopkins' life cannot, then, be understood solely in terms of her personal history and the conventions of sentimental literature. Her broader artistic purpose was, as Alice Crozier puts it, "to recreate the life of New England" in the last quarter of the eighteenth century "as a complete historical experience . . . important in and of itself."[24] This holistic vision is in many respects a highly personal one, but Stowe is most truly presented if it is approached as fictionalized history rather than as veiled confession. For much of the book, the narrative line clearly interests Stowe less in itself than as an occasion for limning representative characters, scenes, activities, and views. She specializes in short tours-de-force-like essays on the New England kitchen; thumbnail biographies of secondary characters who are also social types (the Widow Scudder, the New England farmer Zebedee Marvyn, the busybody dressmaker Miss Prissy); and genre sketches of ministerial teas and quilting bees—all of these interspersed with reflections on the rigor, simplicity, charm, and privations of "pre-railroad times." Such unity as this rather miscellaneous ensemble possesses is furnished mainly by Stowe's use of the figure of Hopkins both as individual and as cultural representative.

The extent of Stowe's understanding of Hopkinsianism has not been rightly appreciated by her critics, possibly because Hopkins himself is so often dismissed unread as the bogeyman of late Puritan theology. Not only had Stowe studied his anti-slavery writings, she also knew his *Treatise on the Millennium*, from which she has Hopkins quote several times; and she had at least a limited acquaintance with his *Inquiry into the Nature of True Holiness* and his magnum opus, the *System of Doctrines*, the first (1793) *summa theologia* by an Edwardsean divine.[25] It is not accidental that the novel is set on the eve of the joint publication of the *System* and the *Treatise*.

The vital center of Hopkins' system, and of the novel itself, is his idea of holiness. Hopkins believed that true holiness consists in a special kind of love. His characteristic term for it is "disinterested benevolence," which he defines as "friendly affection to all intelligent beings" or—more abstractly—as "affection" for "the greatest good of the whole." Christ's voluntary sacrifice as the willing victim of God's wrath is the model of disinterested benevolence. The truly regenerate person is one who would submit unconditionally to the conviction of God's benevolent purposes even if he knew this meant his own damnation. He would continue, that is, to "be a friend of God, and to be pleased with his moral perfection" even though he saw no sign that he himself was saved. To love God because you think he loves you is, for Hopkins, mere self-love: "He who does not know how to deny himself with respect to his eternal interest, is really a stranger to self-denial."[26]

This doctrine, which Hopkins derived from Edwards' *The Nature of True Virtue* and which Stowe inherited as a living reality from her father, seemed to her both noble and appalling. On the negative side, it made an almost impossible demand on human nature, as Stowe points out through the famous image of Hopkins placing a rungless ladder from earth to heaven and commanding sinners to climb it (*MW*, p. 66). On the other hand, she also found something sublime in Hopkins' idea of disinterestedness. "No real artist or philosopher ever lived," insists the narrator, "who has not at some hours risen to the height of utter self-abnegation for the glory of the invisible" (*MW*, p. 18). The structure of the novel is set up in such a way as to deny "unconditional submission" as theological dogma but to affirm it as ethical imperative. On the theological level, even Saint Mary Scudder balks at it; and the characters of James Marvyn and his grieving mother are portrayed so sympathetically that the reader hardly accepts the possiblity of James' death, much less his (or her) damnation. On the other hand, the characters are distinguished according to their capacities for total self-surrender. The noble characters all deny themselves in order to reach a final transfiguration. James yields himself up to God in the shipwreck, after which he is spiritually reborn (*MW*, p. 376); Mary renounces her love for James in order to keep her word to the Doctor, and thereby passes the ultimate test of her purity; Hopkins shows that he can resist emotional as well as economic self-interest when he returns Mary to James. With Mary's help, Virginie gives up Burr. The villains, Simeon Brown and Aaron Burr, enact parodies of disinterested benevolence—Brown, with his lip-service assent to the doctrine which ceases as soon as Hopkins urges him to act contrary to self-interest, Burr, with his ironical acceptance of Virginie's renunciation of him: " 'I bow to it in submission' " (*MW*, p. 345).

Stowe develops the benevolence theme in a series of polarities. Hopkins, the spiritual heir and literary executor of Edwards, is played off against the unworthy blood relative, Burr. "Both had a perfect *logic* of life, and guided themselves with an inflexible rigidity by it. . . . Burr rejected all sacrifice; Hopkins considered sacrifice as the foundation of all existence" (*MW*, p. 349). The unhistorical encounter between them in the novel would have been suggested not just by their common tie to Edwards but by a naive and touching letter Hopkins, at the very end of his life, wrote to Burr, urging the then-vice-president to remember the ways of his ancestors and attend to matters of religion.[27] James, the worthy infidel-lover, experiences the conversion which the hardened Burr cannot. Virginie, as her name implies, is a Catholic version of the Puritan Virgin Mary, misguided but ultimately correctible in her affections. Both are saint-like in their willingness to sacrifice their own salvation for the sake of their lovers, but Mary's sanctified devotion is distinguished sharply from Virginie's amorousness. And of course Hopkins and Mary are contrasted as representing "male" and "female" types of piety: the rational/speculative versus the intuitional/experiential (*MW*, p. 19).

At least superficially, the latter puts the former to rout. Not only is Mary the more visibly successful minister, she is also a kind of Beatrice to Hopkins' Dante. Stowe suggests that she inspires the millennial visions which are about to appear in his theological writings (*MW*, pp. 17, 92). His theological masterwork is a sublimation of sexual feeling which can never find a direct outlet (*MW*, pp. 69–70, 400). Here and elsewhere, the novel shows that, Puritanism notwithstanding, human and divine love are hopelessly intermixed. James cannot be converted without Mary as intermediary; her love for him, conversely, is really "the love of something divine and unearthly, which, by a sort of illusion, connects itself with a personality" (*MW*, p. 95).

This humanitarianism, however, was in a sense not a rejection of Hopkins but an adaptation of a principle for which he himself stood. To be sure, Hopkins regarded love "which is limited to particular objects" as falling short of true holiness (*Works*, III, 16). But he considered "the holiness of creatures" as "not different in nature and kind from the holiness" of God (*Works*, III, 11). The idea that others may be brought to a sense of true holiness at least in part through appreciation of the lives of exemplary Christians is an entirely traditional Puritan idea,[28] which is illustrated in Hopkins' publication of the lives of his two parishioners. His notion of holiness, moreover, actually represents a humanization of Edwardsean doctrine. As Joseph Haroutunian points out, Hopkins probably felt he was simply following in the footsteps of Edwards' *The Nature of True Virtue* (for Hopkins, holiness equaled Edwards' "virtue"), but in the process of re-stating Edwards' definition of virtue as "benevolence to Being in general," Hopkins in effect "equated 'Being in general' with 'God and our fellow creatures,' and thus made it stand for the *sum* of all being" rather than a truly transcendent spiritual entity. Hopkins' idea of holiness, Haroutunian continues, amounts to much the same thing as " 'friendly affection,' and benevolence is very much like the love of a friend, a kindly regard for the good of others."[29] Hopkins' resolution of all sin into self-love is in keeping with this. Haroutunian sees this shift as a deplorable shrinking of the scope of the Edwardsean vision, but from Stowe's perspective the slight but significant humanization of the concept of benevolence would have been most welcome.

Certain other aspects of Hopkins' theology reveal a similar humanitarian emphasis when viewed in historical perspective. One was his modification of the doctrine of original sin. Hopkins taught that although Adam's posterity are inevitably sinful, sin really begins only with sinful acts when the child becomes "capable of any thing of a moral nature" (*Works*, I, 225). Although Hopkins' main reason for taking this position was probably to counter the anti-Calvinist argument that men cannot morally be held responsible for their sins in the Calvinist scheme of things, his position also lent support to liberals within Calvinism, like Lyman Beecher, who denied the necessity of infant damnation and, eventually, original sin itself. Of more immediate interest to Stowe in *The Minister's Wooing* was the millennial motif in Hopkins' thought. Though much of Hopkins' writing on this subject consists of a combination of biblical exegesis and jeremiad, he also shows a strong utopian tendency. Hopkins sees the millennial society as evolving from the present-day church: "every true member of the church belongs to the new creation, and is part of it; and this new creation of the new heaven and new earth goes on and makes advances as the church is enlarged and rises to a state of greater prosperity, and proceeds towards perfection" (*Works*, II, 265), which Hopkins sees as coming near the end of the twentieth century. One of the most charming portions of Hopkins' works—and there are such, though few—is his description of the ideal society of the future: its agricultural and industrial improvements, domestic life, literary activity, and so forth. Here is one passage which Stowe used almost verbatim (*MW*, pp. 100–101).

> It will not be necessary for each one to labor more than two or three hours in a day, and not more than will conduce to the health and vigor of the body; and the rest of their time they will be disposed to spend in reading and conversation, and in all those exercises which are necessary and proper in order to improve their minds and make progress in knowledge, especially in the knowledge of divinity. . . . (*Works*, II, 287)

Stowe balances her disapproval of the Gothic side of Hopkins' theology and her awareness of his failure as a pulpit orator by stressing, perhaps overstressing, his enthusiasm for the subject of the millennium. Sometimes she does this for comic purposes, as an example of his pedantic tunnel vision, but at least in principle Stowe regards this side of Hopkins sympathetically—and perceptively—as "the solace and refuge of his soul, when oppressed with the discouragements" which beset his daily labors (*MW*, p. 100).

Hopkins' millennialism is also of great importance to Stowe in illustrating what she rightly felt was one of the most distinctive features of the traditional New England character. "New England," the narrator notes, "presents probably the only example of a successful commonwealth founded on a theory, as a distinct experiment in the problem of society." Hence it was natural for its "great thinkers" to dwell "so much on the final solution of that problem in this world" (*MW*, p. 100). Likewise, the spiritual leaders of this holy commonwealth "sought to make religion as definite and as real to men as their daily affairs."[30] The historical Hopkins fascinated Stowe as an example par excellence of a New Englander who sought to live his life on a millennial scale. "His minutest deeds were the true results of his sublimest principles" (*MW*, p. 134). All of the biographical sources available to Stowe stress this quality in Hopkins, making him out to be an example of his own doctrine of disinterested benevolence. Even in the days when he was convinced he himself was unregenerate, Hopkins worked to bring others to Christ; he never flinched from preaching unpopular doctrines, and in fact went out of his way to do so for the sake of emphasis; he donated income from his publication for Afro-American relief when he could not make ends meet; unlike Ezra Stiles he stayed loyal to his Newport congregation when it was decimated by the Revolutionary War, and he generously passed up the opportunity to consolidate it with another congregation under his leadership. He adhered to a daily regimen of Spartan simplicity, which included fourteen hours or more of study per day. Above all, he labored with great earnestness in the Lord's vineyard for sixty years despite the fact that both the churches over which he presided dwindled away under his leadership. In short, a purer example of selfless, unworldly dedication could scarcely be found. His very failures seemed to establish his sainthood.

Most important for Stowe's purposes was the fact that Hopkins was *both* a model of the unworldly utopian thinker—the relentless codifier of divinity into an abstract system—*and* a man of action. "He did not, like some in our day, confine himself to analyzing virtue in the abstract, but took upon himself the duty of practicing it in the concrete."[31] Stowe's critics have generally assumed that she sought to oppose these two sides of Hopkins and present the impression of an essentially good man caught pathetically in his own sophisms, a man whose heart was better than his head. Admittedly the text lends some support to this reading. Characters like James Marvyn and Miss Prissy, for example, cannot accept or understand Hopkins' theology but come to admire him for his good deeds. Yet the narrator says explicitly in connection with both Burr and Hopkins that one must "take their lives as the practical workings of their respective ethical creeds" (*MW*, p. 349). Hopkins' decision to preach against slavery is seen as having been made possible by the very limitations of his mind: "With him logic was everything, and to perceive a truth and not act in logical sequence from it a thing so incredible, that he had not yet enlarged his capacity to take it in as a possibility" (*MW*, p. 112). Similarly, his renunciation of Mary is the proof of the unconditional submission to the "disinterested love" he has been preaching (*MW*, p. 411), made possible by life-long habits of mental self-discipline.

This view of Hopkins closely follows the interpretation in Park's *Memoir*, which is much concerned to demonstrate to a skeptical audience that "the men who originated the Hopkinsian peculiarities were men of warm hearts as well as cool heads" (*Memoir*, p. 89). Far from viewing Hopkins' philanthropy as an incidental virtue redeeming an inhumane theology, Park insists that "his philanthropy was his theology drawn out into practice, and that his theological speculations were prompted and followed by philanthropic aims. We cannot understand him as a theologian, without examining his life of beneficence; and we cannot appreciate his activities in doing good, without studying his peculiarities as a divine" (*Memoir*, pp. 169–170). Despite Hopkins' defenses of chilling theses like the benefits of sin and damnation in the divine economy, at bottom his "benevolence and sense of justice and equity moulded his theological belief" (*Memoir*, p. 172). Indeed his attempts to justify sin arose from his sense of justice—his need to understand the ways of God as not simply mysterious but morally justifiable. Altogether Park and Stowe are essentially alike in devoting limited space to the repellent aspects of Hopkins' harshness and rigidity in order to stress the generous-minded aspects of his central doctrine that men must, as Park rather euphemistically puts it, be "willing to lose themselves in the divine glory" (*Memoir*, p. 172).

It was not simply the pietistic basis of Hopkins' uncompromising integrity that would have attracted Stowe to him as a subject for a fiction about traditional New England manners. His resoluteness also exemplified a more general characteristic of the traditional New Englander: his simplicity. Stowe repeatedly contrasts the wholesome austerity of late eighteenth-century society with the more comfortable but oversophisticated present. Newport under the theocracy versus the latter-day Newport as a fashionable watering place; Mary Scudder's wardrobe versus the frivolous garb of present times—these are two of many examples, typically handled in a seriocomic tone which makes the old ways seem quaint but purer than our own. The element of naïveté is a potential source of tragedy, as when Mrs. Marvyn falls into despair because she cannot see beyond the logic of Hopkins' system, but for the most part it is treated with gentle humor and nostalgia.

Perhaps more than any other aspect of the book, this myth of simplicity accounts for the strengths and limitations of *The Minister's Wooing*. On the positive side, it enables Stowe to portray the world of the novel as an organic whole, whose minute particulars are charged with ritual significance, and to illuminate those particulars with a sense of reverence and detachment which at best is exceedingly sensitive. On the negative side, the myth short-circuits the creative process in some crucial areas. The characters are artificially flattened, a technique which succeeds with the Dickensian secondary figures who illustrate social traits (Miss Prissy, Simeon Brown) but not with the main actors, in whom we expect greater psychological complexity. More important, the narrator remains too self-conscious of the gap between her world and theirs; she can reconstruct the latter in great measure, but she does not really enter it. Perhaps for this reason, perhaps because Stowe is conscious of writing for an audience that knows little and cares less about Samuel Hopkins, her tone is disconcertingly inconsistent. The minister is sometimes an object of filiopietistic reverence, sometimes a buffoon.

One is reminded of Stowe's essay on old "New England Ministers," which moralistically admonishes us that "a want of reverence threatens now to become the besetting sin of America," and then proceeds to spend much of its time retailing droll anecdotes about the colonial clergy.[32] In our first glimpse of Hopkins, for example, he seems a picture of Laputan absent-mindedness. The heroine must repeatedly call and nudge him in order to make him understand that it is time for him to take tea (*MW*, pp. 45–46). The narrator habitually refers to him patronizingly as "the good Doctor," "the simple-minded Doctor," the "honest old granite boulder" (*MW*, pp. 93, 189, 111), even as she is about to relate some action which we are supposed to accept as truly noble.

Indeed the Scudder residence, where most of the action takes place, is in many respects Stowe's equivalent of the House of the Seven Gables. We savor the quaint gloom for awhile, but we are happy to escape it in the end. The two romances end with much the same sort of sentimental compromise. In the present case, James (like Hawthorne's Holgrave) must submit to his bride's conventionalism before he can have her, and he replaces Simeon Brown as the leading financial benefactor of Hopkins' church; but it is clear that James and Mary, as representatives of the younger generation, are ushering in an era of natural piety as opposed to Hopkins' scholasticism. The effect, as in Hawthorne, is to impose an unworthily facile closure on a complex situation and reinforce the suspicion that the author was never fully serious in the first place.

Stowe's storybook ending, however, is quite in keeping with her myth of simplicity. Her New England Arcadia is finally a world of Romantic tragi-comedy, in which, after a suitable amount of tribulation, even the apparent incompatibilities of Calvinism and sentimentalism can be reconciled. Iron-ically, Stowe's researches on Hopkins could have lent support to such an ap-proach. His systematic approach to divinity, particularly his attempts to spell out the details of the millennium, and his biographers' presentation of him as a simple-hearted soul who fully reconciled theory and practice, would have rein-forced Stowe's inclination to make a fable out of his life, to present him as a stylized figure on a non-mimetic level while at the same time professing that she had written a realistic novel. In order to do this, Stowe had only to quote Hopkins' writing. For instance, she has him open a breakfast "conversation" with a passage from his *Treatise on the Millennium* which Stowe presents as oral dialogue (*MW*, p. 99). This in a way is unfair practice. The data are accurate, but the context is distorted; the effect is to exaggerate the sense of Hopkins as pedantic and archaic. In doing so, however, Stowe was merely imitating the flavor of the ecclesiastical biographies with which she was famil-iar, including *The Autobiography of Lyman Beecher*. Such works were them-selves nostalgia pieces, calculated to appeal simultaneously to the reader's historical sense, his filiopietism, and his relish for out-of-the-way excerpts and anecdotes. Whether they primarily seek to portray the subject as a model Christian or as a striking and colorful character (and usually they do both), they inevitably have an archaeological aura to them which puts the subject at a certain distance and makes him seem somewhat two-dimensional.

Altogether, the figure of Samuel Hopkins, not only as thinker and actual person but also as an artifact transmitted to Stowe from sources like Park's *Memoir*, was well suited to serve her as representative of what she found most significant in traditional New England. By following lines of interpretation others had laid down, Stowe could legitimately view Hopkinsianism as foster-ing elements in that tradition which ought to be vital to her own generation—for example, activism, self-sacrifice, and millennial aspiration—while at the same time she could smile at or satirize obsolete or harmful aspects of the New England theology by appealing to the already current stereotype of Hopkins as the harshest and crankiest follower of Edwards. In particular, Hopkins seemed perfectly to illustrate the simplicity which again could legitimately serve at once as the occasion for laughter, as an escape fantasy, and as a theme for homilies on the desirability of a spartan moral life.

What then does *The Minister's Wooing* finally say about the aesthetic uses of Edwardsean theology? To begin with, Stowe's handling of the latter obviously links the novel to Puritan literature in general ways also characteristic of American Romantic literature as a whole. For instance, its uneasy combination of the motifs of jeremiad and progress is typical of co-temporary historical romances of the Puritan era, all of which take their cue ultimately from the ambivalent view of the past versus the present displayed by Scott (the romancers' sourcebook and a favorite of Stowe's) and from the Puritans' interpretation of New England as uniquely favored but errant.[33] Again, Stowe's use of culturally representative characters, with two complementary models of piety at the center (Mary and Hopkins), draws on the Puritan tradition of *exemplum fidei* which Sacvan Bercovitch rightly sees as informing the New England Romantics' definition of the self.[34] His paradigmatic case, significantly, is the life of John Winthrop in Cotton Mather's *Magnalia Christi Americana*, a work much read by Stowe's characters and a lineal ancestor of ecclesiastical biographies like Stowe's sources, Park, Patten, and Sprague.

But the literary implications of Stowe's particular branch of New England thought, the late Edwardsean sensibility, may perhaps be spelled out more distinctly. I shall venture to suggest several characteristic traits. First, this sensibility implies a literary universe in which supernatural religion is basically accepted as a given, so that belief in a personal God, miracles, hell, and the interposition of divine grace are accepted as emotional realities if not as positive articles of faith. Secondly, this in turn implies a dramatic situation in which a religion of doctrinal rigor, defined as the communal standard, is played off against a religion of love in such a way that the claims of both are deeply felt and the first is compromised but not discredited by the other. Third, we may expect such works to set up on some level an equation between self-fulfillment and self-denial rather than self-assertion or self-reliance in the Emersonian sense. These three motifs, clearly operative in *The Minister's Wooing*, all relate to key concerns of the New England theology as it was painstakingly but insistently modified in the direction of the religion of the heart. The first relates to the problem of assurance; the second, to the tension between piety and doctrine, between the potentially antinomian value of holiness and the need to view God systematically; the third, to the concept of disinterested benevolence.

Besides Stowe, the major American Romantic in whom these motifs figure most importantly is Emily Dickinson. The elusive possibility of a direct relation with a personal, sovereign God; the sharp juxtaposition of the probing intellect and utter sentimentalism; and the almost voluptuous celebration of self-denial in the role of New England nun—these are significant features of Dickinson's poetic landscape which have their counterparts in Stowe. In Hawthorne and Melville one finds them to a less marked extent; in Emerson, Thoreau, and Whitman, hardly at all. All five of these writers, for example, tend more quickly to equate doctrine with rigidity or hypocrisy and to reduce the supernatural dimension of religious experience to naturalistic terms. Only in late Whitman (after his Wordsworthian lapse into semi-orthodoxy) does the concept of a personal God become a felt reality; only in Thoreau's "Higher Laws" does the idea of self-denial take on an erotic appeal.

All this is not to say that the Calvinist and liberal elements in American Romanticism can be neatly separated. The purpose of making such distinctions should not be to simplify but to complicate our understanding of the period. Consider the relation between *The Minister's Wooing* and *The Scarlet Letter*, another historical romance with a love plot involving an orthodox minister and a female parishioner who presents an alternative model of sainthood that seems more attractive than his. It would be silly to insist that Hawthorne's work is "Unitarian" rather than "Edwardsean," for the world of *The Scarlet Letter* corresponds much more closely to the Calvinist view of man's fallen nature than does the world of *The Minister's Wooing*. Yet we also see marked differences along the lines which have been discussed. Hester Prynne's self-abasement is not accompanied by the mood of exaltation that one often finds in Dickinson's poems of renunciation and which always accompanies Stowe's treatment of self-sacrifice. For Hester, repression is chiefly a mixture of strategic retreat and penitential gesture. The character of Dimmesdale is much closer to the refined, man-of-sensibility preacher stereotype popular among Unitarians of the day than to the genuine Puritan article, which Hopkins more faithfully approximates.[35] Finally, doctrine as such is of little interest to Hawthorne. There is nothing in Hawthorne like Stowe's chapter on "Views of Divine Government" (*MW*, pp. 242–255), which interprets the significance of James Marvyn's supposed death from the standpoint of Edwardsean theology. Although it seems clear, as Michael Colacurcio has convincingly shown,[36] that the Hester-Dimmesdale affair is in some sense a stylized meditation on the Antinomian controversy (Hester recalls Anne Hutchinson, Dimmesdale recalls John Cotton), Hawthorne's emphasis is much more upon the psychological consequences than upon the theological implications themselves.

Such differences in portrayal certainly relate in some way to the differences in basic intellectual stance between the two authors. A thorough study of both, and of similar parallels and contrasts (Stowe and Dickinson, Stowe/Dickinson vs. Melville, and so forth) would go far toward clarifying our understanding of American Romanticism. In particular, it might help us to put in proper perspective the increasingly influential arguments of those who, with excess of pardonable zeal, would interpret American Romanticism (indeed all of American literature) as an emanation from or reaction to Emerson. This approach does not begin to explain Stowe, or Dickinson, or the Melville of *Clarel*, or for that matter the post-Calvinist milieu of late-century regionalists like Mary Wilkins Freeman. As their relationship to the full extent of nineteenth-century religious thought becomes better appreciated, the whole map of American literary history is likely to become less parochial.

## Notes

1. All recent efforts of this kind derive ultimately from Perry Miller's essay, "From Edwards to Emerson," *NEQ*, 13 (1940), 589–617. Some of the weaknesses of his thesis, which Miller himself saw more clearly than many of his successors, are sensitively pointed up by Conrad Wright's essay on "The Rediscovery of Channing" in *The Liberal Christians* (Boston: Beacon, 1970), pp. 22–40. The best extant histories of theological developments inspired by Edwards are Frank Hugh

Foster, *A Genetic History of the New England Theology* (Chicago: Univ. of Chicago Press, 1907); Joseph Haroutunian, *Piety versus Moralism: The Passing of the New England Theology* (1932, rpt. 1970; New York: Harper); and Sydney Ahlstrom, "Theology in America," in *The Shaping of American Religion*, ed. James Ward Smith and A. Leland Jamison (Princeton: Princeton Univ. Press, 1961), I, 232–321.

2. *Travels in New England and New York*, ed. Barbara Solomon (Cambridge: Harvard Univ. Press, 1969), I, 374. I have described the contrast in receptivity to art between liberal and orthodox Congregationalists from 1790–1830 in *Literary Transcendentalism* (Ithaca and London: Cornell Univ. Press, 1973), pp. 21–28, 106–112; and in "The Unitarian Movement and the Art of Preaching in 19th Century America," *AQ*, 24 (1972), 166–190.

3. *Symbolism and American Literature* (Chicago: Univ. of Chicago Press, 1953), p. 151.

4. *The Feminization of American Culture* (New York: Knopf, 1977), chs. 1–4, appendices, and *passim.*

5. On Stowe, see especially Charles Foster, *The Rungless Ladder: Harriet Beecher Stowe and New England Puritanism* (Durham, N.C.: Duke Univ. Press, 1954). On Dickinson, see, for instance, George F. Whicher, *This Was a Poet* (1938; rpt. Ann Arbor: Univ. of Michigan Press, 1957), pp. 58–76; and Richard B. Sewall, *The Life of Emily Dickinson* (New York: Farrar, Straus, 1974), I, 17–27, 235–243, and *passim.*

6. Nineteenth-century tributes include James Russell Lowell, quoted in Charles Edward Stowe, *Life of Harriet Beecher Stowe* (Boston: Houghton, 1889), pp. 327–336; J. Henry Jones, "Mrs. Stowe and Her Critics," *University Quarterly*, 2 (1860), 1–33; 3 (1861), 93–115; and Florine Thayer McCray, *The Life Work of the Author of Uncle Tom's Cabin* (New York: Funk and Wagnalls, 1889), pp. 249–287. In our century there have been only a few important readings of the book: Charles Foster, "The Genesis of Harriet Beecher Stowe's *The Minister's Wooing*," *NEQ*, 21 (1948), 493–517, considerably revised as ch. 4 of *The Rungless Ladder*; Paul John Eakin, *The New England Girl* (Athens: Univ. of Georgia Press, 1976), pp. 27–48; and Alice Crozier, *The Novels of Harriet Beecher Stowe* (New York: Oxford Univ. Press, 1964), ch. 4 *passim*—a discussion of Stowe's New England fiction as a whole. Foster's essays are particularly excellent. Estimates of the book have varied widely. Alexander Cowie called it "the best-known of Mrs. Stowe's works" apart from *Uncle Tom's Cabin* in *The Rise of the American Novel* (New York: American Book Co., 1948), p. 455, but a decade later Lillian Beatty termed it an "almost forgotten book," in "The Natural Man vs. the Puritan," *Personalist*, 40 (1959), p. 22. The latter assessment is more accurate. Recent praise of the book is somewhat apologetic and defensive, the present essay not excepted. Stowe leans heavily upon the stock devices of sentimental fiction; see Herbert Brown, *The Sentimental Novel in America* (Durham, N.C.: Duke Univ. Press, 1940), pp. 195, 197, 281, 290, 321.

7. Foster takes the former, Eakin the latter approach. Feminist criticism, which is rediscovering so much of the neglected fiction of the period, seems likely to reinforce them. See, for example, Douglas, pp. 64–65.

8. Its only factual basis was an anecdote of Hopkins' short-lived engagement as a *young* man to a woman who jilted him when her former lover unexpectedly returned. Stowe probably found the story on p. 55 of Edwards A. Park's *Memoir* of Hopkins (see note 11).

9. Foster, "Genesis," p. 510.

10. *Atlantic Monthly*, 1 (1857), 490. The work reviewed, the first two volumes of William B. Sprague's monumental *Annals of the American Pulpit*, a compedium of short informal memoirs of eminent ministers, probably influenced the tone of her thinking about the novel.

11. *The Works of Samuel Hopkins*, 3 vols. (Boston: Book and Tract Society, 1852). Park's *Memoir* comprises pp. 1–266 of vol. I but was also published separately, with the same pagination. These sources are cited below as *Works* and *Memoir* respectively. Stowe also had access to other lives of Hopkins. In addition to the brief sketches in Sprague's *Annals*, I, 428–435, Stowe would have read *Sketches of the Life of the Late Rev. Samuel Hopkins, D.D.*, ed. Stephen West (Hartford: Hudson and Goodwin, 1805), a spiritual autobiography; William Patten, *Reminiscences of the Late Rev. Samuel Hopkins* (Providence: Isaac Cady, 1843); and perhaps also John Ferguson, *Memoir of*

the *Life and Character of Rev. Samuel Hopkins* (Boston: Leonard Kimball, 1830). Ferguson, however, contains nothing used in *The Minister's Wooing* that Stowe could not have found in other sources; and she used only one passage which Park or the *Sketches* does not include—an anecdote of Sarah Edwards' extraordinary religious sensitivity: see Patten, pp. 23–24, and Stowe, *Minister's Wooing*, (Boston: Houghton, 1896), pp. 265–266. All citations are from this edition, which will be abbreviated *MW;* quotations, however, have been checked against the first edition (New York: Derby and Jackson, 1859), and, in the one instance of discrepancy, the wording of the first edition has been adopted.

12. Forrest Wilson, *Crusader in Crinoline: The Life of Harriet Beecher Stowe* (Philadelphia: Lippincott, 1941), p. 299; McCray, p. 281. McCray, pp. 281–282, prints a letter from Park describing how he lent Stowe the *Memoir* and was later somewhat disconcerted by the liberties she took with the historical record. Park reports that she wrote him 'a very beautiful letter,' now lost, defending what she had done on grounds of poetic inspiration.

13. *Memoir*, pp. 154–156, 118, 116; *MW*, pp. 393, 126–129, 120–121.

14. Stowe would also have inherited an anti-Stiles bias from her father, Lyman Beecher, whose *Autobiography* (New York: Harper, 1865), which she helped prepare, describes Yale's transition from Stiles' presidency to that of Beecher's mentor Timothy Dwight in terms very unfavorable to Stiles—a typical Edwardsean disparagement of middle-of-the-roaders like Stiles (*Autobiography*, I, 38–49).

15. Stowe, "New England Ministers," pp. 487–489. The following discussion of the autobiographical basis of *MW* is indebted at a number of points to Foster's two essays.

16. *Autobiography*, I, 160, 121, 168.

17. *Autobiography*, 478–516; *MW*, p. 241.

18. *Rungless Ladder*, p. 102. Charles Stowe, *Life of Harriet Beecher Stowe*, pp. 320–322, 339–340, prints the relevant mss.

19. "Genesis," pp. 502–504; *Rungless Ladder*, pp. 114–116; *Autobiography of Lyman Beecher*, I, 83–86.

20. "Genesis," p. 513.

21. *Memoir*, p. 22; see also pp. 19–21, 254–257; and Hopkins, ed., *The Life and Character of the Late Reverend, Learned and Pious Mr. Jonathan Edwards* (Northampton: Andrew Wright, 1804), pp. 93–95, 98–104, as well as Sereno Dwight, *Life of President Edwards*, in *The Works of President Edwards*, ed. Dwight (New York: S. Converse, 1824). I, 113–115, 171–190. Stowe certainly knew Hopkins' work (from which she quotes, *MW*, pp. 193–194); If she did not know Dwight's directly, she would have known of it from Park's liberal excerpts. The related concepts of unconditional submission and disinterested benevolence are discussed below.

22. Ezra Stiles, *Literary Diary*, ed. Franklin B. Dexter (New York: Scribner, 1901), I, 44; Hopkins, ed., *Memoirs of the Life of Mrs. Sarah Osborn* (Catskill, N.Y.: N. Elliot, 1814), p. 83. During the late eighteenth and early nineteenth centuries, the number of women members in New England's Congregational churches tended far to exceed the number of men; see Edmund Morgan, *The Gentle Puritan: A Life of Ezra Stiles* (Chapel Hill: Univ. of North Carolina Press, 1962), p. 188; and especially Douglas, *Feminization*, pp. 97–99.

23. *Sketches of the Life of Samuel Hopkins*, p. 86; *Autobiography of Lyman Beecher*, I, 88; *Memoirs of . . . Sarah Osborn*, p. 332; Dwight, *Life of President Edwards*, p. 188.

24. *Novels*, p. 99. Crozier comments thoughtfully on the novel's documentary aspect.

25. Here are some significant instances in which Stowe makes verbatim use of the works just mentioned: *MW*, p. 245 (*cf. Works*, II, 245); *MW*, pp. 99–100 (*cf. Works*, II, 286–287); *MW*, pp. 191–192 (*cf. Works*, II, 289–290, 312–313).

26. Quotations from *Works*, II, 16; I, 386, 389; III, 59–60. See in general *Works*, I, 378–421; III, 3–66.

27. *Memoir*, pp. 257–258. Like Hopkins, Burr was also bound up with Beecher family legend. Burr's sister was the first wife of Judge Tapping Reeve, Lyman Beecher's " 'chief counselor and

friend' " (*Autobiography*, I, 223) in Harriet's girlhood town of Litchfield, Connecticut. As the narrator says, Burr lived "in the private annals of many an American family" (*MW*, p. 154).

28. The nature and importance of the Puritan concept of the *exemplum fidei* is brilliantly discussed in Sacvan Bercovitch, *The Puritan Origins of the American Self* (New Haven and London: Yale Univ. Press, 1975), pp. 1–34 and *passim*.

29. Haroutunian, *Piety to Moralism*, pp. 82, 84.

30. "New England Ministers," p. 491.

31. "New England Ministers," p. 490.

32. "New England Ministers," p. 486.

33. The best study of the New England romancers is Michael Bell, *Hawthorne and the Historical Romance of New England* (Princeton: Princeton Univ. Press, 1971).

34. Bercovitch, pp. 148–186.

35. For a sense of the relation between Dimmesdale and Unitarian ministerial stereotyping, see Daniel Howe, *The Unitarian Conscience* (Cambridge: Harvard Univ. Press, 1970), pp. 151–204; and Lewis Simpson, *The Man of Letters in New England and the South* (Baton Rouge: Louisiana State Univ. Press, 1973), pp. 3–31.

36. "Footsteps of Ann Hutchinson: The Context of *The Scarlet Letter*," *ELH*, 39 (1972), 459–494.

# IV LITERARY CRITICISM

# Literary Criticism: Language

## The Artistry of Jonathan Edwards

Edwin H. Cady*

From what is now increasingly apparent of Jonathan Edwards, it surprises that so quiet, academic, and sweet-natured a man could have preached sermons which broke his contemporaries down into storms of distress. Perhaps the most intriguing of these is "Sinners in the Hands of an Angry God." It is known even to those who have never read Edwards. It has been the focus of much of the disapproval showered on him as "the salamander of divines," and it raises fascinating problems even for the objective or sympathetic reader. Biographers agree that Edwards recoiled from the Billy Sunday type of sweaty-shirt oratory and dramatic shouting of his colleagues in the Great Awakening. He was always the Puritan academic, the Brahmin, reading his sermons quietly from a digni-fied, motionless stance in the pulpit. Why, then, was "Sinners in the Hands of an Angry God" so successful in its mission of reducing previously blasé Enfield, Connecticut, to shuddering terror? Why has it become the classic of hell-fire-and-brimstone preaching which so long shut out our view of the tender-minded and philosophic Edwards? It is perhaps too easy to lay the blame for the latter fact on readers who would not read aright. At any rate, we are left with the fundamental question: what made the sermon so very effective? Where lie the springs of its success?

The answer, I think, is that it is in the widest sense a work of literary art. It uses all the weapons, conscious and subconscious, verbal, emotional, and sen-suous, of the author at his best. This is a statement which a generation or more ago might well have been hooted at. Now, thanks to the distinguished work of many scholars in restoring for us the man and his times, it may be entertained. But it must be demonstrated.

In the light of Edwards' reputation as polemicist one looks first to the intellectual structure of the sermon. Perhaps it is another example of his devas-tatingly tight, crushing logic. But a glance at the rational structure of the sermon shows it to be comparatively insignificant. In traditional form, Edwards gives his text (much more suggestive than doctrinal), four implications of the text, and ten "observations" upon his reading of it, before he passes on to its "application" to his audience. In the most simple fashion available to the Pu-

*Reprinted, with permission, from *New England Quarterly*, 22 (March, 1949), 61–72.

ritan homiletic tradition, the argument clusters about Edwards' "proposition":
" 'There is nothing that keeps wicked men at any one moment out of hell, but
the mere pleasure of God.' " From this the argument runs: God can and should
let them fall; He has already passed sentence on them; their natures are wicked,
their claims on God and their powers of self-preservation worse than nothing;
indeed, although God's rightful anger burns against their wickedness, nothing
but His inscrutably capricious hand supports them. Let every sinner strive for
grace while yet there is time.

As reasoning this was elementary for Edwards. But it was the word he had
come to Enfield to speak with the hope that "the use of this awful subject may
be for awakening unconverted persons in this congregation." He knew he
addressed a conspicuously "unawakened" audience. Enfield had resisted the
revivalism which was sweeping the Connecticut Valley like a forest fire. Edwards had come to kindle them, too, and his experience as a preacher as well as
his religious and homiletic theories told him that it was no use to argue. His aim
was to stir the heart, to stimulate the soul, to turn the whole man to a devoted
search for the springs of grace within him. There were generations of Puritan
preaching behind both speaker and crowd; he shared a wide context of understood reference with his hearers. When they were converted it would be time to
feed them the meat of doctrine. Now the aim was the most powerful use of all
the weapons of appeal at his command. He did not lose dignity, academic poise,
or logic. But he did blend thought, imagery, allusion, and personal reference in
a way which can only be called organic, artistic, and poetic. And he did kindle
Enfield.

Although thought, form, and imagery in the sermon are one, the great
emotional power of the discourse comes primarily from the rich and versatile
imagery. For "image" in this connection I mean a literary device by which the
writer likens an inward state, that subjective fusion of sense, emotion, and
recognition which we call experience, to something outward which can be used
to convey approximately the same experience into the subjective inwardness of
the reader. There are about twenty-five important "images" in "Sinners in the
Hands of an Angry God." Not all of them are good: that is, artistically effective.
Some are failures because they were mere clichés, others because they are not
realized by the author, still others because they are somehow fumbled. But
much the greater portion of them do work successfully, and their success carries
Edwards' excruciatingly vivid vision alive into the minds of his hearers.

Perhaps the meaning of this can be clarified by turning first to some of
Edwards' images which fail. Immersed in the highly figurative tradition both of
the Bible and of seventeenth-century preaching, Edwards often thought naturally and unconsciously in metaphor—as his audience must also have done. And
sometimes even so careful a stylist as he slipped into the use of outworn convention. In the second sentence of the sermon, for example, he observes that in
despite of God's grace the Israelites of old by sin had "brought forth bitter and
poisonous fruit." The second of his "observations" remembers "the sword of

divine justice," and in the fifth he recalls that sinners are even in life the possessions of Satan:

> The devils watch them; they are ever by them at their right hand; they stand waiting for them, like greedy hungry lions that see their prey. . . .The old serpent is gaping for them; hell opens its mouth wide to receive them. . . .

There is nothing stupid about such images, but they were not calculated to awaken Enfield. Enfield must have heard them from the same pulpit many times before; and they must have slipped through the minds of Edwards' hearers like waterworn pebbles, not arousing sensation or stimulating reaction. To the modern reader they seem casual and dim, as indeed they most probably were to the temporarily nodding preacher.

Almost equally footless are the images which Edwards began to develop into means of true communication and then fumbled. Warning, for example, that there is "no security to wicked men," he noted that: "The arrows of death fly unseen at noon-day; the sharpest sight cannot discern them." Like the devil as a roaring lion, the arrows of death by disease were too-familiar Biblical allusions. Edwards moved slightly toward realizing them for his listeners' imaginations but dropped the effort short of success. A failure more interesting because it is more ambitious is the metaphor which appears early in the "Application."

> There are black clouds in God's wrath now hanging directly over your heads, full of the dreadful storm, and big with thunder. . . .The sovereign pleasure of God, for the present, stays his rough wind; otherwise it would come with fury, and your destruction would come like a whirlwind, and you would be like the chaff of the summer threshing floor.

This one simply shows a failure of Edwards' imagination to carry through to artistic success a genuinely poetic impulse. In its context, as we shall see, the image is perfectly placed. It begins well, taking the storm-clouds black and pregnant with thunder as symbols of the ineffable wrath of God. But it weakens as it ceases to elaborate itself into objective terms of awe and terror. The real impulse fades out in the abstractions of "rough wind" and "whirlwind," and the scriptural clichés of chaff and threshing floor supply blank counters to fill in an imaginative void. Edwards could hardly have moved his audience with such imagery.

Inescapably, Edwards was addicted to the use of Biblical quotation and allusion with suggestive, figurative intent. Occasionally he was successful, especially with the text of his sermon. But for the most part he fails when he depends upon them rather than upon the careful, artistic elaboration of the symbols of his own imagination. An excellent case in point is section 2 of the "Application." Built around Scriptural references, it is emotionally frayed and flat in spite of Edwards' uncommon effort to heighten its effect with exclamation marks. Even the elaborate apocalyptic imagery at the end, of God trampling out the vintage of the blood of sinners, seems remote and unconvincing.

This example, like the first paragraph of section 4 of the "Application," goes to show how unimpressive Edwards' message can be when the images fail to come, when his abstractions are not fleshed with the symbols of his passionate vision.

For Edwards' imagery is predominantly successful, and from its success springs the long-famed power of the sermon. By skilful timing and neat fitting into the context, he could pack even conventional images with meaning, as in the telescoped figures of his "observation" number 1.

> Sometimes an earthly prince meets with a great deal of difficulty to subdue a rebel. . . .But it is not so with God. . . .Though hand join in hand, and vast multitudes of God's enemies combine and associate themselves, they are easily broken in pieces. They are as great heaps of light chaff before the whirlwind, or large quantities of dry stubble before devouring flames. We find it easy to tread on and crush a worm that we see crawling on the earth; so it is easy for us to cut or singe a slender thread that any thing hangs by: thus easy is it for God... to cast his enemies down to hell.

Yoked with the frustrated metaphor of the storm treated above, are two others, equally conventional to begin with, which grow and elaborate from within to fresh and muscular conclusions:

> The wrath of God is like great waters that are dammed for the present; they increase more and more, and rise higher and higher, till an outlet is given; and the longer the stream is stopped, the more rapid and mighty is its course, when once it is let loose . . . the waters are constantly rising, and waxing more and more mighty; and there is nothing but the mere pleasure of God, that holds the waters back, that . . . press hard to go forward. If God should only withdraw his hand from the flood-gate, it would immediately fly open, and the fiery floods of the fierceness and wrath of God, would rush forth with inconceivable fury . . . .

Here was an old image redesigned to startle Enfield out of its smugness. Every New Englander was intimate with his community's use of water power at the mill if nowhere else. The dramatic peril of floods as well as the daily power of the falling waters were familiar and exciting. And Edwards took the stuff of his hearers' own minds, raised it to the plane of his own intensity, and made his vision live in those minds. Picture, idea, and emotion existed together in the minds of speaker and listeners; the work of artistic communication had been done.

Much the same thing can be said of the accompanying image of God's wrath as an arrow bent on the creaking bow. It is a traditional picture to which is brought a sudden access of fresh terror by its notation of the vast tension of divine anger which may find shocking release when the arrow is "made drunk with your blood."

By the same token, the images which, being fresh, came most natively from Edwards' imagination and tallied most familiarly with the lives of his hearers, remain the most successful. They are individually the most memorable. Yet they are also the most organically fused with the message and the structural intent of the sermon as a whole. Like many of the images of the major poets, these of Edwards are surprisingly homely and immediate. At the very beginning, illustrating the text, "Their foot shall slide in due time," is a sort of generic picture of him that "walks in slippery places": a condition then as now realizable every New England winter. The walker is "every moment liable to fall, he cannot foresee one moment whether he shall stand or fall the next; and when he does fall, he falls at once without warning . . . without being thrown by the hand of another." He "needs nothing but his own weight to throw him down." Then, as the thought has developed, Edwards applies it to sinners generally. "God will not hold them up in these slippery places any longer, but will let them go; and then, at that very instant, they shall fall into destruction; as he that stands on such slippery declining ground, on the edge of a pit, he cannot stand alone, when he is let go he immediately falls and is lost." The fact that this has been expanded and elaborated step by step in conjunction with the four logical stages of the "implications" Edwards finds in his text makes it the more effective. And what member of the audience could fail to participate imaginatively, as he had often done physically, in the act of slipping to a fall? What hearer so dull that the sense of the slippery nature of worldly security did not begin to creep up the back of his mind?

Equally fresh is the "observation" 7 which sees "Unconverted men walk over the pit of hell on a rotten covering, and there are innumerable places in this covering so weak that they will not bear their weight, and these places are not seen." And, of course, there is the climactic figure of the entire sermon, the image known to almost all literate persons, even those who have not read Edwards. To a people who lived long months by the hearth, whose leisure moments would often have been taken up in playing with the fire, it must have been horrifying to participate imaginatively (on both ends of the web) in the metaphysical *and* physical experience denoted in Edwards' saying

> The God that holds you over the pit of hell, much as one holds a spider, or some loathsome insect over the fire, abhors you, and is dreadfully provoked: . . . you are ten thousand times more abominable in his eyes, than the most hateful venomous serpent is in ours. . . .
>
> O sinner! Consider the fearful danger you are in: it is a great furnace of wrath. . . . You hang by a slender thread, with the flames of divine wrath flashing about it, and ready every moment to singe it, and burn it asunder; and you have no interest in any Mediator, and nothing to lay hold of to save yourself, nothing to keep off the flames of wrath, nothing of your own, nothing that you ever have done, nothing that you can do, to induce God to spare you one moment.

If one had to guess the place where Edwards was forced to request silence from "a breathing of distress, and weeping" as Eleazar Wheelock remembered, it would be here, one supposes, beyond question. Certainly he temporarily changed direction to a more conventionally logical exposition before coming back again to the *ad hominem* attack. Much of the power of the figure is no doubt derived from its climactic position, its elaboration, and its composite admixture of other elements. But surely that all-too-empathic, homely picture of the disgusted Power, the flames, and the imminently shrivelling insect is the most potent factor.

A look at the kinds of imagery used in the sermon is revealing also. It is not surprising to find political and juridical imagery reflecting the covenant traditions of New England theology and politics. The theme of righteous king against rebellious subject is significantly used four times, including once as a sub-strand of the spider metaphor and again as the key to the whole of section 1 of the "Application." The rather distantly Swiftian theme of disgust comes forward from "We find it easy to tread on and crush a worm" of "observation" 1, and "the world would spew you out" of the third paragraph of the "Application," to its climax in the spider metaphor. There is one sea image beside the "great waters dammed" figure, and a couple of swords of divine justice, including one fairly vivid "the glittering sword is whet, and held over them."

But the most telling images fall into three main groups: the fires of hell; the tension-pressure symbols of God's wrath; and suspension-heaviness symbols of the predicament of the sinner. Contrary to the accepted traditions about "Sinners in the Hands of an Angry God," pictures of hell-fire appear to be neither its most vivid nor its most numerous images. By almost any count, fire-imagery amounts to little more than a quarter of the total of figures. Further, Edwards made surprisingly little effort to actualize fire for his audience. He used no color words and no objective heat words. Occasionally the flames "flash" or "glow," but there is no attempt to make the reader see their infinite billows and feel their deathless, terrible pain comparable to that made in the sermon called "The Future Punishment of the Wicked Unavoidable and Intolerable."

Actually, "Sinners in the Hands of an Angry God" is not directly concerned to create Hell imaginatively. Hell is in its picture, but only at the periphery. The focus is on the predicament of the sinner, how dreadfully he dangles *just before* he plunges to eternal agony, and while he has time to repent and be saved. The most striking and distinctive images in the work fall into two groups: (1) those which display the fearful wrath of God, and (2) those which portray dramatically (they seldom paint) the sinner shakily hanging. The tension-pressure images of wrath (those of the threatening sword, the storm, the flood, the bow, the wine-press, the grape-treading Deity) we have already examined. While they are pervasive and do much to suggest the emotional tension raised by the sermon, it is noteworthy that they are all fairly conventional, even when effectively used.

The freshest imagery, and the most essential to the peculiar success of the sermon, communicates Edwards' sense of the eerie suspension of the sinner upon almost nothing and intensifies it by adding a nightmarish feeling of his fatal weight. Dominantly these are kinesthetic, almost visceral, in their effects, rather than visual. Thus they appeal to the most fundamental human sense, one which is all too seldom commanded by writing. We have already seen the squeamish feelings of treacherous footing and dangerous weight given by the thought of him "that walks in slippery places" and of the unconverted who "walk over the pit of hell on a rotten covering." Edwards also sees "that natural men are held in the hand of God, over the pit of hell." In the third pragraph of the "Application" he points out with unusual kinesthetic effect:

> Your wickedness makes you as it were heavy as lead, and to tend downwards with great weight and pressure towards hell; and if God should let you go, you would immediately sink and swiftly descend and plunge into the bottomless gulf, and your healthy constitution, and your own care and prudence, and best contrivance, and all your righteousness, would have no more influence to uphold you and keep you out of hell, than a spider's web would have to stop a fallen rock.

From those points it is only a normal imaginative extrapolation to the magnificent, fearful drama of God and his loathsome, dangling spider.

Deriving necessarily and directly from the fusion of message and image is Edwards' "Application" to his hearers. From the announcement that the "use of this awful subject may be for awakening unconverted persons in this congregation," the point of attack in the sermon is personal. The second person pronoun predominates. Into the middle of the climactic metaphor come the expressions of wonder that "you did not go to hell the last night," this morning, as you came blasphemously to God's house, or, indeed, "why you do not this very moment drop into hell." Then, however directed, Edwards works through four points of exposition before he returns to "this congregation." Now he appeals to its small-town curiosity: "If we knew that there was one person and but one, in the whole congregation [going to hell] . . . what an awful sight would it be to see such a person!" He appeals separately to the old, the young, the children. He even appeals to Enfield's local pride by pointing out that the day of Christ has come to the perennially rival town of Suffield. And at last he comes down gradually, passion spent, to a quiet and rather literary ending.

Doubtless the very sobriety of Edwards' voice and manner gave all the force of effective understatement to his agonizing dream. No dramatics in the pulpit could have been adequate to his symbols. And doubtless also his working within the conventions of the old manner and the traditional sermon method gave him an access to the religiously innured but not rebellious minds of the Enfield parishioners which might have been closed to an obvious innovator. But all these factors aside, the secret of the effectiveness, then and since, of "Sinners in the Hands of an Angry God" resides first in the organic oneness of theme, image, and "application." More directly, the emotional force of the sermon springs from the imagery itself, especially from the freshly imaginative, native figures which burned into the minds of his audience Edwards' vision of the horrible predicament of the sinner without grace.

Although this is not the occasion to defend Edwards from popular misconceptions, it should be apparent that he was not motivated by sadism, a rebellious libido, or any other psychiatric perversion. He was a mystic profoundly convinced of the reality of his subjective experience of God (and psychiatry has most unfortunately as yet neglected to tell us whence come creative and integrative personality forces). He was also a tender-minded pastor of the souls God and society had entrusted to him, and a responsible intellectual leader. As all these, he was faced with the problem of moving an audience left calloused, by generations of ordinary preaching, against the traditional appeals of Edwards' (and their) faith. It was his duty and his opportunity to throw all his imaginative and literary resources into the creation of a metaphysical *tour de force* which would provide profound conceptual and emotional experience for his audience so armored in ennui. His problem of expression was precisely that of a metaphysical poet: to find a means to drive out into effective form his overpowering sense of an inward reality. His problem of communication was even more exacting: to find "objective correlatives" which would carry his own experience into the minds of an audience bored with many repetitions of traditional Biblical and Puritanic conventions but otherwise unliterary. That he solved both problems brilliantly is attested both by contemporary evidence and by the eminence, savory or not, of the work ever since. By all the ordinary tests, "Sinners in the Hands of an Angry God" is a genuine work of literary art and testifies to Jonathan Edwards' right to the name of artist.

# Literary Criticism: Structure

## The Art and Instruction of Jonathan Edwards' *Personal Narrative*

Daniel B. Shea°

Although the first editor of Jonathan Edwards' *Personal Narrative* described this spiritual autobiography as written for "private Advantage," he also seems to have felt that Edwards had given him implicit permission to make the document serve a public purpose. The sometimes baffling resemblance between authentic and fraudulent spirituality was, said Samuel Hopkins, "a point about which, above many other[s], the protestant world is in the dark, and needs instruction, as Mr. Edwards was more and more convinced, the longer he lived; and which he was wont frequently to observe in conversation."[1] As Hopkins was aware, Edwards' essential act throughout a large body of his published work had been to set nature apart from supernature in the domain of religious experience. The act was no less central to the *Personal Narrative* than it was to other works in which Edwards promoted experimental religion and instructed readers on its glories and pitfalls.

In the controversy between himself and opposers of the Great Awakening, Edwards had put to good use his accounts of the gracious experience of Abigail Hutchinson, Phebe Bartlett, and his own wife, Sarah. But a narrative told in the first person, as Sarah's had been originally,[2] was immensely more valuable to his cause than even the best job of evangelistic reporting. Let the reporter be a "true saint," said Edwards, still he can only judge "outward manifestations and appearances," a method "at best uncertain, and liable to deceit."[3] No such objection could have been made against his *Account* of the life of David Brainerd, in which Edwards allowed the Indian missionary's diary to speak for itself. A reader's view of "what passed in [Brainerd's] *own heart*" would thus be cleared of such obstacles as an impercipient narrator; yet the reader would be in the hands of a perfectly reliable guide. As a student, Brainerd may have been rash in remarking that one of his Yale tutors had "no more grace than this chair," but Edwards could only praise the discretion he revealed when considering "the various exercises of *his own mind*": "He most accurately distinguished between real, solid piety, and enthusiasm; between those affections that are rational and scriptural—having their foundation in light and judg-

°Reprinted, with permission, from *American Literature*, 37 (March, 1965), 17–32.

ment—and those that are founded in whimsical conceits, strong impressions on the imagination, and vehement emotions of the animal spirits."[4] In the *Personal Narrative* Edwards had performed exactly those functions for which in 1749 he was praising Brainerd. Both men gave their readers, as Edwards said of Brainerd, an "opportunity to see a confirmation of the truth, efficacy, and amiableness of the religion taught, in the practice of the same persons who have most clearly and forcibly taught it."[5]

Because Edwards could not have introduced his own autobiography in such glowing terms, Samuel Hopkins admiringly supplied the deficit in 1765. But set next to the cautious distinction-making of the narrative itself, his words were superfluous. Since the manuscript of the *Personal Narrative* is lost, we shall never know just how much care Edwards took in composing it. In fact, the text printed by Hopkins gives the appearance of hurried writing.[6] But if Edwards spent only a day with his spiritual autobiography, he had spent twenty years or more arriving at the criteria by which he judged his experience. It is possible, of course, that we read precision back into the *Personal Narrative* after watching Edwards at work in, say, the *Treatise Concerning Religious Affections*, but the distinction between autobiography and formal argument, especially for an eighteenth-century New England divine, should not be exaggerated. Edwards' narrative is not identical with his spiritual experience but represents a mature articulation of that experience, its form and language determined in varying degrees by the author's reading of sacred and secular writers, interviews with awakened sinners, and his concerns at the time of composition. The Edwards of the *Personal Narrative* bears more resemblance to the author of the *Religious Affections* than to the young student at Yale who entered the perplexing data of daily spiritual upheavals in his diary.[7]

Edwards set down his spiritual autobiography with more than "private advantage" in mind, then, and he seems in fact to have been governed by the purposes that informed most of his work during the period of the Great Awakening. By narrative example he will teach what is false and what is true in religious experience, giving another form to the argument he carried on elsewhere; and he hopes to affect his readers by both the content and the presentation of his exemplary experience.

I

Something of what Edwards was trying to accomplish in the *Personal Narrative* emerges from a comparison with the *Diary*, which he kept regularly from the last year of his studies at Yale until his settlement in Northampton. The two are profitably read together, but not as if they formed a continuous and coherent piece of writing. A sense of their separate identities is necessary, not only because the *Diary* instructed Edwards alone, while the *Personal Narrative* extends and formalizes its instruction, but also because Edwards was bound to tell his story differently after twenty additonal years of introspection and a good deal of pastoral experience. In 1723, for instance, he was greatly troubled by "not having experienced conversion in those particular steps, wherein the people of New England, and anciently the Dissenters of Old England, used to experience it."[8] Subsequent events, however, revealed a great variety in the Spirit's operations, so that in 1741 Edwards allowed that a given work might be from the Spirit even though it represented a "deviation from what has hitherto been usual, let it be never so great."[9] He may even have reached by this time the more radical conclusion announced in the *Religious Affections,* that although Satan can only counterfeit the Spirit's saving operations, he has power to imitate exactly the order in which they are supposed to appear (pp. 158–159). In any case, the *Personal Narrative* reveals no more brooding on Edwards' part over the absence of "particular steps."

The *Diary* exhibits, in general, considerably more doubt, sometimes approaching despair, than could be inferred from an isolated reading of the *Personal Narrative.* Periods of spiritual crisis were marked by such tortured complaints as: "This week I found myself so far gone, that it seemed to me I should never recover more"; and "Crosses of the nature of that, which I met with this week, thrust me quite below all comforts in religion."[10] There are, in addition, all the entries in which, as a kind of running theme, Edwards agonizes over dead, dull, and listless frames of mind. The *Personal Narrative* reflects little of the intensity or number of these entries. Edwards mentions only that at New Haven he "sunk in Religion" as a result of being diverted by affairs; and in a subsequent paragraph he rounds off a similar recollection with the comment that these "various Exercises . . . would be tedious to relate" (pp. 32–33).

The difference between the two versions is striking, yet understandable, if we assume that as Edwards grew in his assurance of grace, these drier seasons lost, in recollection, their original impact. But since Edwards seems to have consulted his diary as he wrote ("And my Refuge and Support was in Contemplations on the heavenly State; as I find in my Diary of *May* 1, 1723"), it is more likely that deletions and new emphases were intentional—the choice, for example, to minimize emotions arising from dullness and insensibility in a narrative intended to be affecting. The lingering memory of his uncle Hawley's suicide in 1735 would certainly have enforced Edwards' decision: "He had been for a Considerable Time Greatly Concern'd about the Condition of his soul; till, by the ordering of a sovereign Providence he was suffered to fall into deep melancholly, a distemper that the Family are very Prone to; he was much overpowered by it; the devil took the advantage & drove him into despairing thoughts."[11]

Whatever the proximate reason, Edwards felt strongly enough about the dangers of melancholy to edit out any hint of it in the record of his conversion experience, just as in the preface to Brainerd's memoirs he forewarned readers that melancholy was the sole imperfection in an otherwise exemplary man, and just as in his *Thoughts* on the revival of 1740–1742 he excepted melancholy as the "one case, wherein the truth ought to be withheld from sinners in distress of conscience."[12] It was sufficient for readers to know that a Slough of Despond existed, the foul and miry byproduct, as John Bunyan explained, of conviction of sin. Nothing was to be gained, and much would be risked, by bringing on stage the youth who once found himself "overwhelmed with melancholy."[13]

Seen from another point of view, the youth of the *Diary* might by the very miserableness of his seeking illustrate an important lesson. The characteristic of the *Diary* which the author of the *Personal Narrative* apparently found most repugnant was its tendency toward spiritual self-reliance. For even as he reminded himself that effort was ineffectual without grace, the young diarist had also been busy drawing up his "resolutions," seventy of them eventually. In the *Personal Narrative*, Edwards reached back twenty years to untangle these cross-purposes, simplifying his experience somewhat as he fitted it for instruction. Spiritual industry could not be despised; its products were real and of value: "I was brought wholly to break off all former wicked Ways, and all Ways of known outward Sin." What had to be emphasized was that the sum of resolutions and bonds and religious duties was not salvation. Edwards spoke beyond the limits of his own case when he concluded, "But yet it seems to me, I sought after a miserable manner: Which has made me some times since to question, whether ever it issued in that which was saving; being ready to doubt, whether such miserable seeking was ever succeeded."[14]

## II

While the pattern that emerges from Edwards' reshaping of some of the materials of his diary helps suggest the more formal, public nature of the autobiography, the later document represents in most ways a fresh beginning on the analysis of his spiritual experience. The first sentence of the *Personal Narrative* reveals Edwards' anxiety to get at major issues, prefacing the entire narrative with a declaration that nearly sums it up: "I Had a variety of Concerns and Exercises about my Soul from my Childhood; but had two more remarkable Seasons of Awakening, before I met with that Change, by which I was brought to those new Dispositions, and that new Sense of Things, that I have since had." A Northampton reader ought not to have missed the distinctions being made, or the ascending order of importance in the three clauses. Certainly he would have known that in the 1735 awakening more than three hundred persons appeared to have been "savingly brought home to Christ," but that in the minister's *Faithful Narrative* of the work he had dismissed some as "wolves in sheep's clothing," while discovering in those for whom he was more hopeful "a new sense of things, new apprehensions and views of God, of the divine attributes." For the reader of shorter memory, who might have withdrawn from a battle he thought won at an early age, Edwards was ready at the end of the paragraph to deny that a boy who prayed five times a day in secret, who abounded in "religious Duties," and whose affections were "lively and easily moved" had anything of grace in him. He had already explained in "A Divine and Supernatural Light" (1734) that emotions raised by the story of Christ's sufferings or by a description of heaven might be no different in kind from those elicited by a tragedy or a romance.[15] And it was unnecessary to introduce psychology here, since the course of the narrative itself revealed the nature of these early affections. In time, Edwards says, they "wore off," and he "returned like a Dog to his Vomit." It was characteristic of Edwards not to hesitate in applying a text (Proverbs 26:11) to himself, but he may already have conceived an extended application for this simile. In 1746, after his last awakening had ebbed, he used the same expression in charging that persons "who seemed to be mightily raised and swallowed with joy and zeal, for a while, seem to have returned like the dog to his vomit."[16]

When Edwards testifies that a sickness so grave it seemed God "shook me over the Pit of Hell" had only a passing effect on resolution, the implication is undoubtedly both personal and general. The emotion aroused by this image could have no other name but terror, but at almost the same time that he preached "Sinners in the Hands of an Angry God" (1741), Edwards was disclosing that terror had been irrelevant in his own experience. Whatever moved him in his New Haven years, "it never seemed to be proper to express my Concern that I had, by the name of Terror" (p. 24). Thus an important distinction was laid down. The experience of terror gave no cause for self-congratulation, since there were persons, like the younger Edwards, "that have frightful apprehensions of hell . . . who at the same time seem to have very little proper enlightenings of conscience, really convincing them of their sinfulness of heart and life."[17]

Edwards' technique through the initial paragraphs of the *Personal Narrative* is to separate the "I" of the narrative from his present self and to characterize the younger "I" as a less reliable judge of spiritual experience than the mature narrator. Thus, Edwards the boy takes much "self-righteous" pleasure in his performance of religious duties, or Edwards the young man seeks salvation as the "main Business" of his life, unaware that his manner of seeking is "miserable." Soon the reader must adjust his attitude even more carefully, for the mature Edwards will begin to describe genuinely gracious experience, while the "I" remains largely ignorant of what has happened. Edwards compiles sufficient evidence for a reader to draw his own conclusions from the passage, but subordinates himself to the mind of a youth who was not yet ready to draw conclusions when he says, "But it never came into my Thought, that there was any thing spiritual, or of a saving Nature in this" (p. 25).

One reason for so oblique an approach may be traced, not to the autobiographer's ignorance of his subject, but to the pastor's close acquaintance with the hypocrite, a brash, colloquial figure who appears often in the *Religious Affections*, drawn no doubt from models near at hand. That part of Edwards' purpose which was public and exemplary dictated that he give a wide margin to the "bold, familiar and appropriating language" of those who condemned themselves by announcing, " 'I know I shall go to heaven, as well as if I were there; I know that God is now manifesting himself to my soul, and is now smiling upon me' " (pp. 170–171). At the same time, Edwards remains faithful to personal experience, accurately reflecting the uncertainty and inconclusiveness he could see in his diary; and by preserving intact the uncertain young man, he provided a character with whom readers similarly perplexed could identify.

The evidence that counters and overwhelms the disclaimers attached to these paragraphs emerges from the history Edwards gives of his assent to the doctrine of God's sovereignty. Even after childhood, his mind, which was "full of Objections," and his heart, which found the doctrine "horrible," had struggled against accepting the notion that God in his sovereign pleasure should choose to save some and leave the rest to be "everlastingly tormented in Hell." Suddenly and inexplicably the objections had evaporated, but at the time Edwards found it impossible to describe "how, or by what Means." Only the effects were clear: "I saw further, and my Reason apprehended the Justice and Reasonableness of it" (p. 25). Because the next and most significant stage of his conviction deserved separate treatment, Edwards is content for the moment to imply its essential difference: the doctrine that was now reasonable would latter appear "exceedingly pleasant, bright and sweet." In short, common grace had assisted natural principles by removing prejudices and illuminating the truth of the doctrine; saving grace had infused a new spiritual foundation that underlay a wholly different mode of perception through the "new sense" or "sense of the heart" that characterized genuinely spiritual experience.[18]

## III

How far Edwards exceeded his Puritan predecessors in the art of uniting instruction with spiritual autobiography, the one reasoned and objective, the other felt and subjective, appears most impressively when he begins to document the experience of the "new man." As he relives the first instance of an "inward, sweet Delight in GOD and divine Things," his prose rises gradually to a high pitch of joyous emotion, sustained by characteristic repetitions and parallelisms and by an aspiring and exultant vocabulary. The paragraph takes its shape so naturally that one nearly overlooks the emergence of relationships that received their fullest elaboration in the *Religious Affections*. Edwards' first ejaculation, "how excellent a Being that was," is a response to the first objective ground of gracious affections, "the transcendently excellent and amiable nature of divine things." When he continues, "and how happy I should be, if I might enjoy that GOD and be wrapt up to GOD in Heaven, and be as it were swallowed up in Him," Edwards proceeds according to the order of true saints, whose apprehension of the excellency of divine things "is the foundation of the joy that they have afterwards, in the consideration of their being theirs." The affections of hypocrites, on the other hand, are aroused in a contrary order; they find themselves "made so much of by God" that "he seems in a sort, lovely to them."[19]

To make clear the order of his own affections became crucial for Edwards as he went on to report his visions, "or fix'd Ideas and Imaginations." He ran the risk, after all, of becoming a chief exhibit in the case against enthusiasm should his narrative have fallen into the wrong hands. Nevertheless, when judging experiences similar to his own he was satisfied that lively imaginations could arise from truly gracious affections; and in adding, "through the infirmity of human nature,"[20] he claimed less for his "visions" than some who read him later. Class distinctions and hierarchies in spiritual experience held little interest for Edwards, because all distinctions resolved finally into the ultimate one between the old and the new man. It was less difficult, however, to point out what was not spiritual experience, even in personal narrative, than it was to render the perceptions of the "new sense" with an instrument so imperfect as human language and so indiscriminate in itself as to be the common property of both spiritual and natural men. Moreover, narrative prose was only Edwards' second choice to convey what he felt. Insofar as the medium approached anything like satisfactory expression it was by compromise with another that seemed more natural: "to sing or chant forth my Meditations; to speak my Thoughts in Soliloquies, and speak with a singing Voice." In admitting that the "inward ardor" of his soul "could not freely flame out as it would," Edwards reconciled himself to one kind of defeat, but the attempt, if skillfully managed, might prove affecting to others.

The impossible aim Edwards set for himself in the *Personal Narrative* was to articulate his totally new delight in "things of religion" for readers who could have "no more Notion or idea" of it than he had as a boy, no more "than one born blind has of pleasant and beautiful Colours." He might have taken solace in the consideration that since all expression was in this case equally imperfect, any expression would do. The prose of the *Personal Narrative* deserves respect to the degree that Edwards refused to avail himself of this consolation or to accept language that by this time flowed easily from his pen. Edwards' continual use of the word "sweet," for instance, points up some of the difficulty of judging his art and rhetorical effectiveness in the narrative. If the word seems at one moment to derive from a sensationalist vocabulary, we may regard its use as part of his unique project to make Lockean psychology serve the interests of experimental religion. Simply through repetition the word tends to gather to itself all the sensible difference Edwards was trying to express when he said that the easily moved affections of his youth "did not arise from any Sight of the divine Excellency of the Things of GOD; or any Taste of the Soul-satisfying and Life-giving Good, there is in them." But Edwards' reading of Locke only added new significance to scriptural passages long familiar to him. In the *Religious Affections* he refers the reader to Psalm 119 for a striking representation of "the beauty and sweetness of holiness as the grand object of a spiritual taste" (p. 260), and goes on to paraphrase verse 103 ("How sweet are thy words unto my taste! Yea, sweeter than honey to my mouth"). In this light Edwards appears only to be indulging in the kind of reverent plagiarism common to many spiritual autobiographies, among them that of Sarah Edwards.[21]

Occasionally, too, Edwards declines the full potential of personal narrative by taking over, with little change, passages from his 1737 account of Northampton conversions, making them his own by the mechanical act of altering the pronoun. He could not have avoided reporting that in his own experience, as in that of the converts, "the Appearance of every thing was altered"; but he expands the point by again simply listing natural phenomena over which the "new sense" played, without vitalizing and re-viewing them through personal expression: "God's Excellency, his Wisdom, his Purity and Love, seemed to appear in every Thing; in the Sun, Moon and Stars; in the Grass, Flowers, Trees; in the Water, and all Nature; which used greatly to fix my Mind."[22] However, when Edwards dramatizes a new kind of perception and so involves divine attributes with natural phenomena that abstraction is made vivid and concrete, he begins to communicate something of what it was to confront nature as, in the strictest sense, a new beholder:

> "I used to be a Person uncommonly terrified with Thunder: and it used to strike me with Terror, when I saw a Thunder-storm rising. But now, on the contrary, it rejoyced me. I felt GOD at the first Appearance of a Thunder-storm. And used to take the Opportunity, at such Times, to fix myself to view the Clouds, and see the Lightnings play, and hear the majestick & awful Voice of God's Thunder: which often times was exceeding entertaining, leading me to sweet Contemplations of my great and glorious GOD." (p. 27)

Taken together, these successive views of nature in its placid and then terrible beauty would adumbrate the symmetry of the divine attributes. Edwards noted as much in another manuscript not published in his lifetime,[23] but the narrative of his conversion imposed special conditions on viewing "shadows of divine things." When he scrutinized his own spiritual "estate," it was absolutely necessary that he be able to acknowledge a view of God's loveliness and majesty in conjunction, for even "wicked men and devils" were sensible of His "mighty power and awful majesty." Against the background of the recent awakening Edwards was moved to observe in the *Religious Affections* that "too much weight has been laid, by many persons of late, on discoveries of God's greatness, awful majesty, and natural perfection . . . without any real view of the holy, lovely majesty of God" (p. 265). To express the ideal vision in the *Personal Narrative*, Edwards chose the language of theological paradox over that of sensationalism, although we do hear symmetry and can observe the proportion Edwards maintains through a dexterous manipulation of his terms. The passage also reveals an infiltration into prose of the "singing voice," whose rhythms were still alive in the memory, inseparable from the experience that originally provoked them:

> "And as I was walking there, and looked up on the Sky and Clouds; there came into my Mind, a sweet Sense of the glorious Majesty and Grace of GOD, that I know not how to express. I seemed to see them both in a sweet Conjunction: Majesty and Meekness join'd together: it was a sweet and gentle, and holy Majesty; and also a majestic Meekness; an awful Sweetness; a high, and great, and holy Gentleness."
> (p. 26)

Through heightened paradox the unawakened reader might be brought to see dimly and to seek the same sense of God's natural and moral perfections balanced and intermingled with each other. Edwards strove to make the path more clear and more inviting as well when he singled out for relatively extensive treatment that which constituted "in a peculiar manner the beauty of the divine nature." At its center the *Personal Narrative* focuses on the experiential realization that holiness is the divine attribute which primarily elicits the love of the true saint. God's underived holiness could not, of course, be encompassed by words; it could only be loved. But the holiness of creatures, deriving from the divine object of their love, yielded to definition in the *Religious Affections* as "the moral image of God in them, which is their beauty" (p. 258).

In the *Personal Narrative*, Edwards had already embodied the relationship between the holiness of God and the holiness of man in two successive and integrally related "moral images." The first describes the soul as "a Field or Garden of GOD," its multitude of flowers representative of individual moral excellencies. Since holiness comprehends all these excellencies, as its beauty sums up their individual loveliness, Edwards closes in immediately on a single, consummate flower: ". . . such a little white Flower, as we see in the Spring of the Year; low and humble on the Ground, opening its Bosom, to receive the pleasant Beams of the Sun's Glory; rejoycing as it were, in a calm Rapture; diffusing around a sweet Fragrancy; standing peacefully and lovingly, in the midst of other Flowers round about; all in like Manner opening their Bosoms, to drink in the Light of the Sun" (pp. 29–30). Each felt quality that Edwards noted in his perception of holiness—"Purity, Brightness, Peacefulness & Ravishment to the Soul"—finds its correspondent physical detail in the image. The life of the flower, as it drinks in light and sustenance from the sun and returns its own fragrance, is the life of grace, continuous in God and the regenerate man; and the second image is finally enlarged to the scope of the first to include a fellowship of saints. Edwards' tendency toward pathetic fallacy, the flower's "rejoycing as it were, in a calm rapture," only reminds the reader that this is personal narrative and not an exercise in typology.

## IV

Not every sight to which the "new sense" gave access evoked an ectasy of joy. Acuteness of spiritual perception could also compel disgust and nausea when eyes seeing for the first time began to search the depths of one's depravity. So hideous a view as Edwards reported would have taxed any vocabulary, but his own had so far been richest and most novel when he expressed the affection of love. For this other task he might have been forced to depend entirely upon the communal vocabulary of the Calvinists vis-à-vis man's corruption had his sensitivity to language not intervened. Edwards' awareness of the problems involved in verbal self-chastisement compares with that of his fictional fellow minister, Arthur Dimmesdale, who found that he could excoriate himself as the "vilest of sinners," not only with impunity, but with the ironic dividend of being revered the more for his sanctity. Regardless of their denotative content, formulary expressions, given wide currency, were quickly emptied of meaning—as Edwards well knew from his experience with hypocrites, men fluent in "very bad expressions which they use about themselves . . . and we must believe that they are thus humble, and see themselves so vile, upon the credit of their say so."[24]

When Edwards is most likely to suggest to modern readers an inverse pride in his corruption rather than the "evangelical humility" (the sixth sign of gracious affections) he hoped he had, we discover that a question of language is at the root of the difficulty. It is not the rank of "chief of sinners" that he covets, nor is Edwards vying with his fellow townsmen for a place in the last ring of hell when he rejects their expression, "as bad as the Devil himself," because it seemed "exceeding faint and feeble, to represent my Wickedness." The full text of this passage, as printed by Hopkins, makes clear that Edwards is in fact rejecting language he thought inadequately proportioned to its object: "I thought I should wonder, that they should content themselves with such Expressions as these, if I had any Reason to imagine, that their Sin bore any Proportion to mine. It seemed to me, I should wonder at my self, if I should express *my* Wickedness in such feeble Terms as they did." (p. 37)

The rationale that lies behind Edwards' greater dissatisfaction with attempts to convey a sense of his wickedness than with parallel attempts to express his delight in divine things is given fully in the *Religious Affections*. There Edwards explained that to the saint the deformity of the least sin must outweigh the greatest beauty in his holiness, because sin against an infinite God is infinitely corrupt, while holiness cannot be infinite in a creature (p. 326). No expression, then, could take the measure of infinite corruption, and before accepting a simile that only traded on the reputation of Satan, Edwards preferred to draw on the resources of his own rhetoric. He begins by bringing together two images that suggest physical immensity, and then associates them with the key word "infinite," which is extracted at last from its concrete associations and made to reproduce itself rhythmically:

> "My Wickedness, as I am in my self, has long appear'd to me perfectly ineffable, and infinitely swallowing up all Thought and Imagination; like an infinite Deluge, or infinite Mountains over my Head. I know not how to express better, what my Sins appear to me to be, than by heaping Infinite upon Infinite, and multiplying Infinite by Infinite. I go about very often, for this many Years, with these Expressions in my Mind, and in my Mouth, 'Infinite upon Infinite. Infinite upon Infinite!' " (p. 37)

Even if he had improved on pallid representations of wickedness, Edwards only pushed the question one step further. Did the improvement arise from a greater conviction of sin or from a natural ability in prose expression? Just how rigorously Edwards dealt with himself in answering such questions appears in a subsequent reflection that immediately dissipated any complacency in mere verbal skill: "And yet, I ben't in the least inclined to think, that I have a greater Conviction of Sin than ordinary. It seems to me, my Conviction of Sin is exceeding small, and faint." Typically enough, Edwards' ruthlessness here is a double-edged sword that also cuts away from himself. As a public document, the *Personal Narrative* might only provide hypocrites with a new model for their deceptions, a thesaurus of expressions (such as "infinite upon infinite") that proclaimed conviction or other classic signs of grace. Edwards could not prevent a prostitution of his narrative, but he knew that the hypocrite found it difficult to claim anything in small amounts, and he would explain in the *Religious Affections* how mimicry eventually confounded itself: "But no man that is truly under great convictions, thinks his conviction great in proportion to his sin. For if he does, 'tis a certain sign that he inwardly thinks his sins small. And if that be the case, that is a certain evidence that his conviction is small. And this, by the way, is the main reason, that persons when under a work of humiliation, are not sensible of it, in the time of it."[25]

Simultaneously, then, Edwards convinces the reader that his self-scrutiny has been unremittingly honest, while he offers instruction that is meticulous in its distinctions, and affecting in its language. The *Personal Narrative* is relatively brief, set against Mather's "Paterna" or Shepard's "My Birth & Life"; but it is not incomplete. Like all autobiographers, secular or spiritual, Edwards fashioned a coherent narrative by using his total experience selectively; we judge it incomplete only by our curiosity about the interior life of his last harrowing years. He could scarcely have added a word to the felt distillation of all he ever thought on all that finally mattered.

## Notes

1. *The Life and Character of the Late Reverend Mr. Jonathan Edwards* (Boston, 1765), p. iii.

2. *The Works of President Edwards: With a Memoir of his Life*, ed. Sereno E. Dwight (New York, 1829–1830), I, 171–186; hereafter cited as *Works*. Sarah's original relation was drawn up, according to Dwight, at the request of her husband. Edwards then retold her experiences as part of his attempt to vindicate experimental religion in *Some Thoughts Concerning the Present Revival of Religion* (*Works*, IV, 110–118).

3. *A Treatise Concerning Religious Affections*, ed. John E. Smith (New Haven, 1959), p. 181.

4. From Edwards' "Preface" to the *Account* of Brainerd's life, "chiefly taken from his own diary and other Private Writings," *Works*, X, 29.

5. *Works*, X, 27.

6. Although anthologies of American literature continue to reproduce the *Personal Narrative* from the Austin (Worcester, 1808) or Dwight editions, the text printed by Hopkins in his 1765 *Life* of Edwards is clearly preferable. As was their habit, the nineteenth-century editors "improved" Edwards' style and also omitted several important passages. All my references are to the Hopkins text, but it is beyond the scope of this study to call attention to all the omissions and revisions of later editions. The indications in the Hopkins text of relatively hasty composition are: (1) the number of sentences lacking a pronominal subject ("On one Saturday Night, in particular, had a particular Discovery . . ."), more than appear in later editions; (2) redundancy of a sort that invites improvement and that Edwards himself might have revised had he taken a second look ("my Concern that I had," or the phrase just quoted). If Edwards intended to make the manuscript more fit for posthumous publication, he apparently never found time to do so.

7. It is very doubtful that the *Personal Narrative* was written after the *Religious Affections* appeared in 1746, but it might conceivably have been written as Edwards prepared a series of sermons given in 1742–1743, on which the *Religious Affections* is based. The only absolute certainty, of course, is that he did not conclude the narrative before January 1739, the date he mentions in its final paragraph.

8. *Works*, I, 93.

9. *Works*, I, 93.

10. *Works*, III, 561.

11. *Jonathan Edwards: Representative Selections*, ed. Clarence Faust and Thomas Johnson (Rev. ed.; New York, 1962), p. 83.

12. *Works*, IV, 163.

13. Entry for Jan. 17, 1723, *Works*, I, 81.

14. Hopkins, *Life of Edwards*, p. 24. By deleting "was" from the final phrase of this sentence, editors after Hopkins also silenced the passive voice that reminded readers, however awkwardly, whence grace originates.

15. *Works*, VI, 175–176.

16. *Religious Affections*, p. 119.

17. *Religious Affections*, p. 156.

18. The full context for these distinctions may be found in the "Miscellanies" published in *The Philosophy of Jonathan Edwards From His Private Notebooks*, ed. Harvey G. Townsend (Eugene, 1955), pp. 249–251. See especially numbers 397, 408, 628.

19. *Religious Affections*, pp. 240–250.

20. *Religious Affections*, 291.

21. The word "sweet" is used frequently in Sarah's first person narrative.

22. The comparable passage in the *Faithful Narrative* reads: "The light and comfort which some of them enjoy . . . cause all things about them to appear as it were beautiful, sweet, and pleasant, All things abroad, the sun, moon, and stars; the clouds and sky, the heavens and earth, appear as it were with a cast of divine glory and sweetness upon them." *Works*, IV, 50.

23. "As thunder and thunder clouds, as they are vulgarly called, have a shadow of the majesty of God, so the blue skie, the green fields, and trees, and pleasant flowers have a shadow of the mild attributes of God, viz., grace and love of God, as well as the beauteous rainbow." *Images and Shadows of Divine Things*, ed. Perry Miller (New Haven, 1948), p. 49.

24. *Religious Affections*, pp. 316–317.

25. *Religious Affections*, p. 334. The relationship between Edwards' personal experience and his public pronouncements on experience often presents interesting problems. In the passage quoted above, Edwards almost seems to be settling for himself the question of why he could record no more conviction of sin than we find described in the *Personal Narrative*. But another cross-reference, a sentence from the narrative, printed only by Hopkins, contains the essential logical distinction he employed to discuss conviction in the *Religious Affections* (pp. 323–336): "That my Sins appear to me so great, don't seem to me to be, because I have so much more, Conviction of Sin than other Christians, but because I am so much worse, and have so much more Wickedness to be convinced of" (p. 37).

# The Brazen Trumpet: Jonathan Edwards's Conception of the Sermon

Wilson H. Kimnach°

The author of *Sinners in the Hands of an Angry God* has been credited with a high degree of conscious literary artistry in recent years; however, the genre in which Jonathan Edwards most excelled, the sermon, is still handled very gingerly, if not actually ignored, by being undifferentiated from the essay. It is as if it were a sub-genre, the rules and conventions of which mean little and perhaps never meant much anyway. This reluctance to take Edwards's literary form seriously, like the relative tardiness in appreciating his conscious artistry, may have its origins as readily in the professions of Edwards himself as in a modern bias. He wrote extensively on ministers and their duties, yet he wrote little on the sermon, and more than once he actually professed indifference to any literary art in his own writings.[1] As a result of these factors, it seems timely to attempt an assessment of Edwards's conception of the literary form in which he most commonly worked, even though much of his attitude must be inferred from practice. Specifically, I shall consider what the Edwardsean sermon is, where Edwards got his notion of it, and what he did with the form.

A particular form of the sermon was obviously clear in the mind of the young Jonathan Edwards as he wrote his first sermons, in 1721 and 1722, perhaps for candidating appearances.[2] Its conventional structure may not have been so limited as the sonnet, but it was hardly closer to the liberal spaciousness of the essay. This form, used by Edwards throughout his life, has a tripartite structure, comprising a Text, a Doctrine, and an Application. It must have those basic divisions in order to be a fully developed Edwardsean sermon. Although Edwards eventually exploited the limited flexibility of the form in a great many ways, it is possible to abstract a paradigm.

The Text—sometimes called the Opening or Explication, though never labeled by Edwards—provides the formal foundation of the sermon. It consists of a passage from the Bible, sometimes as much as three or four verses, though not infrequently as little as a phrase. Edwards almost always supplies a commentary—defining words, clarifying the context, supplying historical back-

°Reprinted, with permission, from *Jonathan Edwards: His Life and Influence*, ed. Charles Angoff (Rutherford: Fairleigh Dickinson University Press, 1975), pp. 29–44.

ground, and so forth—which anticipates, and culminates in, the statement of the sermon's doctrine. The Text is always in a sense the most "academic" portion of the sermon, yet it has been observed that some of Edwards's most beautiful passages of narration and description occur there, particularly when he is attempting to give a lively portrait of a biblical event.[3]

The statement of doctrine—carefully labeled "Doc." by Edwards—is the evident thematic implication of the examined Scripture text; indeed, Perry Miller has characterized Edwards's doctrinal statements as "the baldest, most obvious,"[4] though a little game of guessing the sermon's text from reading its statement of doctrine will soon convince one that Edwards was an ingenious and imaginative textuary. In culminating the explication of the Text, the concise statement of doctrine formulates the thesis of the entire sermon and introduces its formal heart, the Doctrine. Usually constituting a little less than half the body of the sermon, the Doctrine is immediately divided into two, three, or more major propositions, the first one or two of which present an exposition of the doctrinal idea, while the remainder offer the Reasons of the Doctrine. All of these major propositions are subdivided further into numbered subheads, often on three levels of subdivision. As a structure of thought, the Doctrine develops, as often as not, from negation to affirmation, and from assertion to confirmation through appeals to common sense, experience, and the authority of Scripture. Although the term *reason* and the reputation of the Puritans for "iron logic" have fostered the notion that something approximating modern academic logic exists in the arguments of these sermons, the burden of proof is actually carried by authority—that of the ministerial "voice" and that of the Word of God. The "logic" is primarily a matter of the methodical formal structure of the sermon and the associational logic of modern advertising. Much of the power of the proof to persuade is, moreover, directly attributable to certain rhetorical and even poetic devices: particularization, repetition, vivid images and metaphors, and pungent phrasing.

All in all, the primary function of the Doctrine division of the sermon is clarification and amplification of the thesis, the statement of doctrine.

The third division of the sermon, the Application or Improvement (always boldly labeled by Edwards), generally accounts for over half the total sermon. Its relationship with the Doctrine division is a little different from that between the Doctrine and the Text. Whereas the Doctrine appears to fulfill and extend the Text, the Application is, in a sense, parallel to the Doctrine, rendering abstract principles as concrete experiences, indicating the point of the Gospel's impingement upon life, and focusing the metaphysical doctrine upon a social, or even personal situation. The Application does not extend the theological scope of the Doctrine, but ultimately reduces the doctrinal burden of the sermon to a few specific injunctions. Within, the Application is formally structured much as the Doctrine, the primary divisions being three or four Uses (Instruction, Examination, Exhortation), each of which is divided into numbered subheads. Frequently, the Application concludes with a brief series of Directions.

Text, Doctrine, and Application, if well contrived, fit one another like rings in a pool of water. Of course, the sermon was most frequently likened to a silver trumpet by Puritan typologists, and Cotton Mather's manual for ministerial students, *Manuductio ad Ministerium*, contains the running title, "The Angels preparing to Sound the Trumpets."[5] It is an appropriate image, for the tripartite sermon is a dynamic instrument: intellectual and emotional "vibrations" receive their fundamental character in the small mouthpiece, the Text; they acquire timbre as they pass through the Doctrine, and realize their full effect only in the bell of the Application. Literally, the center of attention in the sermon moves from *statement* in the Text to *concept* in the Doctrine, and finally to *experience* in the Application. The trumpet of the Connecticut River Valley, from Thomas Hooker to Jonathan Edwards, was an instrument of peculiar power, although it seems to have been made of brass rather than silver.

As the son of the Reverend Timothy Edwards, Jonathan witnessed innumerable sermons during his formative years, and later as a colleague and "journeyman preacher" under his renowned grandfather, the Reverend Solomon Stoddard of Northampton, he rapidly developed and perfected his sermon style. This background certainly contributed more to the character of Edwards's sermons than any rhetoric or homiletics texts that he may have studied at Yale College. Indeed, there are many indications that Timothy Edwards and Solomon Stoddard were the determinative factors in Jonathan Edwards's ultimate conception of the sermon.

> Let us labour in a very particular, convincing and awakening manner to dispense the Word of God; so to speak as tends most to reach and pierce the Hearts and Consciences, and humble the Souls of them that hear us.

The words are Timothy Edwards's, though they might have been Stoddard's. They occur in the one sermon he published, *All the Living Must Surely Die*,[6] and they remind us that, although Timothy never attained widespread fame, he was a powerful evangelical preacher. Indeed, Benjamin Trumbull, in his *History of Connecticut*, attests that "no minister in the colony had been favoured with greater success than he [in promoting awakenings during the years before the Great Awakening] . . ."[7] Whether or not he was so outstanding, he certainly did use the basic sermon form later adopted by his son.

The five or six extant sermons by Timothy Edwards reveal him to have been a rather pedestrian, if intelligent and learned, preacher.[8] The form of his sermons might be described as classical Puritan, corresponding in principle and structure to the Ramistic diagrams in John Wilkins's seventeenth-century homiletics text, *Ecclesiastes* (a middle-of-the-road Puritan text, if such there be).[9] His sermons have the three basic divisions of Text, Doctrine, and Application, each structured internally through a succession of brief, numbered heads. In comparison with Jonathan's sermon structure, however, Timothy's is extremely bifurcated. For instance, in a sermon of moderate length,[10] Timothy employs no fewer than twenty-three numbered heads in the Doctrine and forty-four in the Application; moreover, many of these heads (averaging less than one hundred words each) contain numbered subheads within them. One does not move far without a "2dly" or "3rdly." The argument is abstract and unencumbered by imagery or metaphor; it is heavily laden with Scripture citations throughout; the language is so "plain" as to be almost unnoticeable, and the tone is forthright and serious. The most obvious source of vitality is the frequent explicit references to men and events in the town. On the whole, it is a Puritan's purist form, embodying the classic Perkinsian virtues, and what it lacks in imagination and beauty in the superstructure, it makes up in the solidity of its foundation.

Jonathan Edwards's first sermon,[11] written after he left home but before he came under the influence of Stoddard, shows that he immediately reduced the number of heads and subheads to permit greater development within heads; likewise, he reduced the frequency of Scripture citation. Perhaps these moves reflect the influence of his training in rhetoric at Yale, but the form is obviously that which was branded deep in his mind by his father's example, whatever refinements may have been acquired at college.

When Edwards joined his grandfather as colleague in 1727, he had written over thirty sermons, though his style was not yet fully developed. In these early sermons, the preoccupation with formal structure and the transitions it required is manifested in a certain woodenness in the diction. There are some effective passages and even some fine sermons, but professional consistency and polish are not yet evident. During the next two years, however, Edwards was to develop with great rapidity under Stoddard, so that he was possessed of much of his ultimate mastery by the time of the old master's death in 1729.

Solomon Stoddard was probably the most impressive man Edwards met in his youth—perhaps in his life. Stoddard was one of the great preachers of the latter days of the Theocracy, and it was largely because of him that the atmosphere of theocracy lingered a little longer in the Connecticut Valley than in the East. "Pope Stoddard," as he was only half-irreverently called, evidently preached in a manner in some respects reminiscent of Thomas Hooker. The form of his sermons is the same as that used by Timothy Edwards, the only notable difference being a reduced number of heads and subheads: Stoddard also apparently needed more space for development than Timothy Edwards. Still, in comparison with the sermons of Jonathan Edwards, those of Stoddard are heavily structured and formally conservative.

Within the formal structure, however, Stoddard found ample range for the exercise of his oratorical and literary powers. He infused the "plain style" with a strong tincture of his own personality and, being gifted with a capacity for pungent, epigrammatic expression, he created, without relying extensively on the graces of imagery and metaphor, a colloquial idiom that is still vital. Not infrequently, the tone of his sermons is that of a Teutonic professor before a group of humble students, holding the spirit of inquiry in the iron vise of pedagogical drill:

> Q. On what Terms doth God offer Deliverance from this Captivity [in the hands of Satan]?

A.1. Not upon the Condition of their laying down the Price of their Deliverance . . .

2. Nor upon Condition of their Recompencing God for it afterwards . . .

3. But on Condition of accepting it as a free Gift through Christ.

In *The Benefit of the Gospel to those that are Wounded in Spirit*, as in many other sermons, Stoddard asks all the "right" questions and supplies all the answers.[12] The very momentum of successive answers carries the minds of the congregants from stage to stage of the argument. It is not logic, but a rhetorical structure that has some of the inevitability of logic. Very often, moreover, the conclusion of an inquiry is vigorously propounded in an epigrammatic climax, corresponding in effect to the conclusion of a syllogistic demonstration:

> If they were thoroughly scared, they would be more earnest in their Endeavours; Senselessness begets Slightliness.[13]

Or in another passage:

> The Pretence that they make for their Dullness, is that they are afraid there is no Hope for them . . . but the true Reason is not that they want Hope, but they want Fears.[14]

Such expressions are not soon forgotten; like his grandson and successor in the Northampton pulpit, Stoddard reveals his notion of religion to have been sensational.

Stoddard could also use imagery and metaphor with real artistry when the occasion arose:

> their hearts be as hard as a stone, as hard as a piece of the nether milstone, and they will be ready to laugh at the shaking of the Spear.[15]

Finally, he could employ repetition effectively, often achieving striking results through incremental repetition involving an important word, but one not necessarily "poetic":

> They may have a large understanding of the Gospel, yet not be set at Liberty by it. Men may be affected with it, yet not be set at Liberty by it. Men may be stirred up to reform their Lives, yet not be set at Liberty. There be but a few comparatively that are set at Liberty by it.[16]

In technique—and indeed in theme—Stoddard's sermons are strikingly close to those later preached by Edwards. His grandson never used the Question-Answer device as much as he, preferring the continuous line of argument, but certainly all of the above passages are more than a little reminiscent of Jonathan Edwards.

In addition to being an excellent example of the Puritan preacher himself, Stoddard was something of a critic and even a theorist in the art of prophesying. For instance, in 1724 he published a sermon, *The Defects of Preachers Reproved*, which elucidates the paradoxical doctrine, "There may be a great deal of good Preaching in a Country, and yet a great want of good Preaching." In this sermon Stoddard equates good preaching with revival preaching, insists upon the minister's preaching from personal experience rather than from a mere theoretical understanding, and fervently advocates the "hellfire" strategy. Thus, he argues:

> When men don't Preach much about the danger of Damnation, there is want of good Preaching.[17]

More than that:

> Men need to be terrified and have the arrows of the Almighty in them that they may be Converted.[18]

He urges preachers to deal "roundly" with their congregations, and "rebuke sharply" those who need reproof. Finally, he defends his conception of the sermon from the accusations of a new faction arising in the East:

> It may be argued, that it is harder to remember Rhetorical Sermons, than meer Rational Discourses; but it may be Answered, that it is far more Profitable to Preach in the Demonstration of the Spirit, than with the enticing Words of man's wisdom.[19]

"Rational Christianity" and the essay-sermon may have been riding the tides into Boston harbor at the beginning of the eighteenth century, but they would not inundate the Connecticut Valley if Solomon Stoddard could help it. In his hands, the traditional Puritan sermon retained the outward form of Ramistic logic, but it had become a meticulously prepared instrument of psychological manipulation; consequently, he was not about to trade it for what he saw as a psychologically superficial and intellectually simplistic, though stylish, mode of discourse. For Solomon Stoddard, rhetoric was power.

There can be little doubt that Stoddard made a great impression on his grandson through his advice and example, shaping Edwards's conception of the sermon at a crucial point in his literary development. Without really deviating from the sermon form that Timothy Edwards employed, Stoddard discovered hidden rhetorical resources in the "plain style" by insisting upon the evaluation of rhetoric in psychological terms that were more comprehensive and subtle than either the old logic or the new Reason. Although widely divergent in talents and personalities, Timothy Edwards and Solomon Stoddard fortuitously complemented one another in their sequential impact upon Edwards. Most important of all, perhaps, is their insistence upon the sermon as a heart-piercing implement (represented by the image of the arrow or spear), a simple, efficient, yet terrible device.

To these combined influences, Jonathan Edwards of course contributed his own peculiar qualities. Among them he had one in particular which I shall call *pursuit*. A quality of the spirit as much as the intellect, "pursuit" is not a matter of brilliance, originality, or inspiration, though it obviously involves a considerable degree of highly disciplined imagination. Essentially, it is the tendency to explore an idea or experience, in all of its ramifications, through a process of extrapolation much more sustained than is usually appealing—or even bearable—to mere men.

Having apparently accepted what was virtually a family literary tradition, the "awakening sermon," Edwards characteristically explored, extended, and pursued the ultimate implications of the form. Some fourteen years after his Northampton ordination, he preached and published what was for him the apotheosis of the revival sermon, *Sinners in the Hands of an Angry God*. This shattering blast of the Gospel trumpet before the walled citadel of the natural heart marks the climax of Edwards's efforts in the genre of the sermon. Although he was to write a number of fine sermons after 1741, study of the extant sermon manuscripts in the Yale Beinecke Library reveals that the years between that date and Edwards's expulsion from the Northampton pastorate in 1750 were a denouement so far as the art of the sermon is concerned.

Three manuscript notebooks, now in the Yale collection, contain all of Edwards's extant working notes for sermons that were made during and after the years of the Great Awakening. The notes constitute a kind of literary diary, revealing Edwards's thoughts on the sermon and the preacher's duties, week in and week out. The sermon notes include entries for sermons that were never written, and there are entries for sermons that have been lost. Studying these entries enables one to assess the overall role of preaching in Edwards's pastorate, his attitude toward the sermon itself, and his handling of certain of the technical problems involved in sermon composition.

One of the first points the notebooks make clear is that, even during the Awakening years, the hortatory sermons were supplemented by a large number of instructional, corrective, and ceremonial sermons. Everything from the nature of biblical tropes to the fundamentals of the faith is carefully propounded and explained; the daily lives of the congregants are examined, and even such pecadilloes as the swiping of Farmer Smith's apples occasion entire sermons. Of course, the sacrament services, fast days, funerals, and Indian skirmishes get their homiletical due. The sermon is invariably occasional, it seems, always a kind of response to a particular situation, although, like many an occasional poem, it may have literary value that transcends its origin. The picture of Edwards implicit in the notebooks is not at variance with a rather surprising image that occurs in an entry in another notebook, his interleaved Bible:

> The business and labours of a minister of the Gospel is on many accounts fitly compared to that of the ox that labours in a man's husbandry, and particularly to . . . [the] treading out the corn, his chief work being to explain and apply the word of God to his Hearers and, as it were, bringing out that spiritual food from the veil or husk it is wrapped up in on the Plant whereon it grew, that it might be fitted for our use.[20]

Neither the conception of the minister's primary duty nor the agricultural analogy is unusual or original. Still, not many persons, contemporary or subsequent, would think of attaching the image of an ox to Jonathan Edwards, even when they would attach a less amiable one. As usual, however, he is peculiarly apt in his choice of images: the sermon notebooks chronicle twenty years of patient, plodding service in a narrow round as Edwards again and again attempted to make the sermon both an instrument of instruction and an efficient talisman of the divine light.

Long before the climax of his preaching career, however, there are signs that he was impatient with the inevitable limitations of the sermon form. On the one hand, he relentlessly pursued the perfection of the awakening sermon and diligently preached the required pastoral sermons; on the other hand, starting in 1730, he began to experiment in the form. For the most part, these experiments can be described as efforts to enlarge the metaphysical scope of the sermon by simply expanding the form, accordion-fashion. Edwards began to write sermons of greater length than he could preach even within the two-stage sabbath service. The result is a single sermon that had to be divided into three or more preaching units. As the years passed, the tendency to pack more and more thought into his sermons resulted in longer and longer sermons, literary forms that have no correlation with the unit of the pulpit oration. In the middle and late 1730s he began to divide the long sermons into sermon series—that is, three or more sermons with the same general text but separate (though related) doctrinal statements. Among the more notable of these series are *Charity and its Fruits* (16 sermons), written in 1738, and *A History of the Work of Redemption* (30 sermons), written in 1739.[21] The latter series, although written in the little sermon booklets, was written as a continuous work, and the preaching unit divisions were made within the completed text. Obviously, what Edwards did—intentionally or despite himself—was to press the instructional sermon or lecture into the treatise by simply developing more and more elaborate, sustained arguments. As a matter of fact, one of his most famous treatises, *A Treatise Concerning Religious Affections* (1746), was apparently first preached as a sermon series in 1742 and 1743.[22]

The significance of these developments is apparent: in the course of his first decade as a preacher, Edwards gradually differentiated the hortatory element from the philosophical element. More and more, the hortatory sermon became an instrument of manipulation, appealing to the senses with its imagery and the emotions with its incantatory rhythms. At the climax of his preaching career, Edwards observed that

> the main benefit that is obtained by preaching, is by impression made upon the mind in the time of it, and not by any effect that arises afterwards by a remembrance of what was delivered.[23]

This view obviously stresses the sensational value of sermonic literature.

On the other hand, during these same years the inclination to pursue issues of theological controversy and develop his own philosophical theology caused Edwards to present some of his best ideas in sermonic treatises that violate the fundamental requirements of relative simplicity, brevity, and unity of effect implied by his own analysis of the sermon just cited. Significantly, he devoted less attention to the composition of sermons in the middle and late forties and gave minimal effort after his remove to Stockbridge in 1751. At the same time, he began the ambitious series of treatises that continued to the end of his life.

Somewhere along the line, Jonathan Edwards fell into the peculiarly modern trap of overspecialization. That is, he ultimately sacrificed the traditional Puritan sermon form—a wonderfully adaptable, though neither remarkably dramatic nor capacious genre—in his efforts to fulfill the role assigned him by his father and grandfather, on the one hand, and his need to exercise his philosophic creativity on the other. His streamlined hortatory sermon, exemplified by the printed version of *Sinners in the Hands of an Angry God,* is virtually monotonic, fusing the Doctrine and Application in such a way that the full blast of emotional appeal begins immediately after the Text and does not cease until the end of the sermon.[24] This is the ultimate weapon in colonial homiletics, and it established the literary technology of American revivalism.

The more philosophical writings simply drifted away from the sermon form as if Edwards felt that his profoundest thoughts were unsuitable to it. He was correct, in a sense, for his profoundest thoughts were the *long* thoughts of one trained primarily in the Ramistic technique of exposition through dichotomization and particularization. However, Edwards never found a form to replace that of the sermonic system of proliferating heads and subheads. In his last years, he seems to have grappled fruitlessly with the problem of a form adequate for his projected *magnum opus.*[25]

With the end of the Great Awakening, Jonathan Edwards turned away from the art of the sermon, his creative impulse in homiletics having been either fulfilled or stifled in the upheaval. Today, surveying his 1200 manuscript sermons in the Yale Beinecke Library, I am inclined to think that the period of Edwards's greatest achievement in the sermon was relatively early, perhaps beginning as far back as 1725 and ending in the early 1740s. Only a few of these sermons have been printed; thus, a full revelation of the richness and beauty of Edwards's earlier sermons—where doctrine and passion are often harmoniously realized within a traditional form—is yet to come.

## Notes

1. For Edwards's most vehement rejection of "style," see the Preface to *Discourses on Various Important Subjects* (Boston: Kneeland and Green, 1738), p. v.

2. For the dating of sermon manuscripts written before 1733, I am wholly indebted to Prof. Thomas A. Schafer of McCormick Theological Seminary.

3. Ola Elizabeth Winlsow, *Jonathan Edwards, 1703–1758: A Biography* (New York: Macmillan, 1940), p. 140.

4. *Jonathan Edwards* (1949; rpt. New York: World, 1963), p. 48.

5. *Manuductio ad Ministerium* (Boston: Printed for Thomas Hancock, 1726). This is one preaching manual that Edwards certainly read.

6. *All the Living Must Surely Die: Election Sermon* (New London: T. Green, 1732), p. 25.

7. *History of Connecticut* (New Haven, Conn.: Maltby, Goldsmith, and Wadsworth, 1818), 2:140.

8. Four sermons were printed from manuscripts by John A. Stoughton in *"Windsor Farmes": A Glimpse of an Old Parish* (Hartford: Clark & Smith, 1883), pp. 121–45.

9. *Ecclesiastes, or, A Discourse concerning the Gift of Preaching as it fals under the rules of Art,* 2nd ed. (London: Printed by M. F. for Samuel Gellibrand, 1647), pp. 5–7.

10. A sermon on Isa. 26:9, printed in Stoughton, pp. 121–32.

11. A manuscript sermon in the Yale Beinecke Library on Isa. 3:10, probably composed in 1721.

12. *The Benefit of the Gospel to those that are wounded in Spirit* (Boston: Printed by Thomas Fleet, 1713), pp. 116–17.

13. *Ibid.,* p. 180.

14. *Ibid.*, p. 181.

15. *The Defects of Preachers Reproved* (New-London, Conn.: Printed and Sold by T. Green, 1724), p. 13.

16. Stoddard, *Benefit*, pp. 175–76.

17. Stoddard, *Defects*, p. 13.

18. *Ibid.*, p. 14.

19. *Ibid.*, pp. 24–25.

20. "Miscellaneous Observations on the Holy Scriptures" (manuscript notations), p. 814.

21. Tryon Edwards edited and published *Charity and Its Fruits; or, Christian Love as Manifested in the Heart and Life* (New York: Robert Carter & Bros., 1852), as John Erskine had earlier edited and published *A History of the Work of Redemption* (Edinburgh: Printed for W. Gray, *et al.*, 1774).

22. This is asserted by Sereno E. Dwight in his *Life of President Edwards* (New York: S. Converse, 1829), p. 223.

23. *Thoughts on the Revival of Religion in New England* (1742, rpt. in vol. 3 of *The Works of President Edwards* (New York: Leavitt & Allen, 1843), p. 342.

24. At least two versions of this sermon have been printed. That in the *Works* (1843), 4:313–21, is abridged. A good text is available in *The American Tradition in Literature*, 3rd ed., ed. S. Bradley, R. C. Beatty, and E. H. Long (New York: Norton, 1967), 1:109–24.

25. Edwards early projected "A Rational Account of Christianity," apparently a metaphysical treatise in form. In later years, however, he became more preoccupied with a "History of the Work of Redemption," suggesting a narrative form. Edwards did not live to write this work.

# Jonathan Edwards: Textuality and the Language of Man

Wayne Lesser[*]

Friedrich Nietzsche was obsessed with the inseparable relationship between his life history and the history of his books. In *Ecce Homo,* he concludes that his life, rather than being represented by his books, now actually performs his books.[1] While it might seem odd to open a discussion of Jonathan Edwards with a reference to Nietzsche, I do so to make two basic observations which, although implicit in all significant Edwards scholarship, are rarely made explicit. First, any assessment of Edwards' spiritual belief and practice must recognize that his life—on psychological, social, and religious levels—was as much a life verbalized as spiritualized. And second, the Jonathan Edwards we know is not just the man who wrote tracts, sermons, narratives, and a diary; he is a man whose life, we infer, was the performance—written, oral, psychological, social, and spiritual—of those works.

The obviousness of these assumptions, however, is somewhat belied by a problem of interpretation that issues from them. Our understanding of Edwards, as it is grounded in his philosophic argumentation and sermonizing, his spiritual and psycho-social inquiries, his overt and veiled references to other thinkers, and his commitment to matters theologic and aesthetic, is in large measure predetermined by the principles of textual analysis we attach to these assumptions. More directly, we know Jonathan Edwards through his texts, and the modes of reading and analysis we bring to these texts have a profound influence upon what we find in them. As readers, we must do more with his texts than extract a historically and ideologically plausible system of belief from them, do more than read them in cultural context, and do more than trace their formal and rhetorical attributes. Perhaps more so for Edwards than for any other Puritan thinker, we must try to grasp the significance of the act of writing and the nature of the human word (as opposed to the scriptural word) *for him.* I say "for him" because the notions of textuality and language which have informed our appreciation of Edwards have been more ours than his. We have not, in fact, regarded these matters with the same commitment to "contextualism" that we have regarded matters of history, culture, theology, and biogra-

[*] This essay was written specifically for this volume and appears here for the first time with the permission of its author.

phy. In the following pages, then, I want to suggest a change in our perception of the relationship between theological principle and the verbal dimension of religious practice—a change which will allow us to understand more fully the connection between the "spiritual" and the "aesthetic" dimensions of Edwards' verbal activity. But before elaborating upon this thesis, I wish to look briefly at those canons of inquiry and method upon which some of the most synthetic and sophisticated textual analyses have been based.

## I

It would be unfair to say that the views of textuality and language which have operated in our evaluations of Edwards are incorrect because they are based upon arbitrary judgments or misreadings. The weakness in our present understanding of these matters is a blindness in our perception of Edwards as an acting human self, a limitation of our vision which, paradoxically, issues from that very commitment to theological, historical, and biographical breadth animating the finest scholarship. In one sense, the root of the problem is Edwards himself. The complexity of his ideas and the various specific issues and occasions addressed in individual texts have made attempts at a synthetic appraisal quite difficult. In order to read the individual text, we must view it in its relation to a larger system of thought; and to determine such a system, we must hypothesize a particular canon of belief and test it through an *a posteriori* analysis of the textual evidence. While this Aristotelian approach has indeed allowed us to acquire a synthetic understanding of Edwards as a thinker, it has also encouraged us to assume that verbal *praxis* is a localized and congruent expression of the Logos of Edwards' religious *theoria*. And this assumption has blinded us to the drama of the writing self played out in Edwards' texts. In the attempt to find an enabling perspective for Edwards' complex thought, we have derived our views of textuality and language more from the necessities of our models than from the texts themselves.

For Perry Miller, the point of intelligibility for reading Edwards is a particular view of his place in intellectual history; for Conrad Cherry it is the concept of faith; and for Roland Delattre it is the concept of beauty.[2] In Miller's work, which precedes the attention to aesthetic matters in Edwards by Davidson and Cady,[3] the intellectual-historical matrix rests upon a group of ideas whose problematic is created more by the ideological conflict among them than by any difficulty of their written presentation. Thus, Miller makes virtually no attempt to define a relationship between the ideas Edwards received and the particular difficulties of their verbal expression. In Cherry's case, the concept of faith is used to explain the "internal dynamics of the faith act" in a manner which clarifies the ontological, epistemological, and psychological relations among man, Christ, and God. Here, the act of faith is a mode of being-belief which involves the total man and informs all his worldly endeavors. Cherry employs his model to define the elusive notion of sanctification (a divine light or holy gift) as the animating principle of faith: a principle which grounds the ontology of man's faith in the Holy Spirit and connects him to God, and yet also defines a difference between the human and divine essences. This difference is bridged, but not effaced, by the totality of sanctified human behavior and scripture. Cherry's model explains man's difference from and connection to God, and it also locates the operation of the human "faculties" and the significance of love and good works in a scheme of conversion where man cannot earn his salvation. The problem, however, is that this model is uncritically extended to include the undefined "faculties" of language-making and writing. Such an extension yields the reasonable, but unearned conclusion that man can find "acceptable words" which would appeal to the whole man in a manner analogous to the word of scripture: "Like the words of scripture, the words of the preacher may cease to be simply means of grace and become truly the word of God when joined with God's Spirit."[4]

I find a similar problem in Delattre's position, even though it more explicitly attends to matters of aesthetics. For Delattre, beauty is the controlling philosophic principle of Edwards' thought because it captures the ontological priority of Being-God while allowing for the visible realization of grace in the human fields of aesthetic perception and moral reflection simultaneously. Man's achievement of an aesthetic and moral order constitutes a version of human holiness, the essence of which consents to and participates in the beautiful essence of divine Being. Here, the act of writing is an emblematic expression of a larger aesthetic sense which constitutes the potentiality of man's spiritual being—the representational power as well as the structural and affective proportion achieved in writing enable man to participate in an aspect of divine excellence.[5]

I take Cherry and Delattre admiringly to task because it is the very inclusiveness and appropriateness of their models that make the extension of such explanatory structures into the area of textuality appear so sensible. Each model issues from a particular conception of the texture of man's being and is employed to characterize the dynamic relationship between that essence and the concepts of sanctification, regeneration, and justification. In the enterprise of interpretation, each scholar takes his particular view of that dynamic relationship and utilizes it as both a principle of textual analysis *and* as the constitutive attribute of the texts themselves. From one standpoint such a methodology is indeed suitable. To regard the essence of man in a particular way, to posit that essence as the subject or a text of corpus, and then to see the constitutive attributes of the subject as the informing principle of the text's structure, characterize an exegetical strategy which comports comfortably with Edwards' intellectual orientation. Interested in conversion as a change in man's very mode of being, Edwards tries to understand this change as a fundamental alteration in an entity's principles of motion and rest (its nature). Thus, it would seem that the congruence of human nature and the structure of verbal expression assumed by the models in question is valid. In terms of the models we have just seen, this principle of being-verbal structure would be either faith or beauty, and it would be fully realized in the experience of conversion and more modestly realized in a formally coherent and rhetorically effective written exercise. While Cherry and Delattre would disagree with one another about the origin of this informing principle and the relation of man's converted self to God's Being, they both see the written act as a representation of man's being, changed or changing. I want to suggest that, for Edwards, man's written enterprise does not, in fact *cannot* describe or represent the sanctified morphology of being. The writing self, unlike the self engaged in the act of reading scripture, is constituted by language, is weighed down in a mode of existence named and nameable by discourse, and cannot bring a consciousness of the self as saved to a presence. The language of man is an expression of fallen man, and the act of writing, rather than representing the teleology of conversion (change in one's mode of being), discloses the fluctuation of the human entity away from and toward its own *human* mode of being—the essence of the human dilemma.

The distinction I am asserting between the living man whose being is tied to language and a saintly man whose essence is beyond language (and, therefore, beyond the scope of man in his worldly existence) complements the most traditional views of Edwards' religious thought, can be supported textually and historically, and even exists as a sort of veiled possibility in Cherry and Delattre when they foray briefly into the issue of verbal potentiality. Cherry, for instance, focuses on the inspirational possibilities of preaching and mentions Edwards' desire to "raise the affection of my hearers as high as possibly I can, provided they are affected with nothing but the truth." Explaining that this rhetorical heightening can be more than mere theatrics, Cherry also makes the point that it will produce an impact beyond rhetoric if supplemented by a "plus" which is the work of God's Spirit. By asserting that "the words of Scripture and of preaching become the Word of God when they are 'idealized' by God's spirit," and by placing the final judgment that such a Spirit is present in the listener's belief that he has "vitally" perceived "new ideas," Cherry actually equates the prior authority of scripture with the problematic validity of human performance in a social context—a context which, as Edwards often remarked, encouraged the sinful self-assertion of both speaker and listener.[6] More important, Cherry assumes that words can, under certain circumstances, become man's saving objects. He is correct, but he works from the incorrect supposition that such an effect is realized when charged words make the Spirit present to the listener, when language represents the Spirit. What actually occurs, I believe, is that the human word, unlike scripture, makes the writer-listener aware of the *absence* of the Spirit, of the absence of an ineffable holiness, the presence of which then becomes the object of intense desire. This object, however, is attainable only in a human-Spirit intimacy of the heart that transcends language and, I might add, one man's judgment of another man's spirituality.

Although, I suspect, Delattre would find this notion as inappropriate as Cherry would, he nonetheless flirts with the idea in a footnote. Admitting that "the relationship among beauty, holiness, excellence, goodness, and value and among their corresponding concepts is one of family resemblance" which defies

schematization, he tries to argue that such a relationship does not create semantic chaos or a representational-figural indeterminacy which problematizes language as a spiritual instrument. In one sense he is absolutely correct. In matters
of religious doctrine such words have an ontological referent which hypostas-
izes their meanings. But he, too, in spite of insisting that the status of words is
ontological rather than linguistic, is forced to admit that "the precarious relationship between language and reality continued to concern him [Edwards] to
the end," and that "the answer to the question of wherein excellence consists
was . . . linguistic only on the way to being ontological."[7] Delattre's reluctance
to grant words a linguistic priority is logical when one considers the importance
of human aesthetic endeavor to his model of beauty and sensibility. But it is
necessary only if we again insist that language must represent things spiritual in
order to help in the spiritual sensitization of man—an assumption we need not
accept and which Edwards had historic as well as theologic reasons for
questioning.

Trying to elucidate the engagement of valid affections in his treatise on
*Religious Affections*, Edwards writes: "It must be confessed, that language is
here somewhat imperfect, and the meaning of words in a considerable measure
loose and unfixed, and not precisely limited by custom, which governs the use of
language."[8] The distinction Edwards makes between the semantic and social
fields of language is a microcosm of a complex oppositional relationship that
permeates the treatise. For Edwards, the genuine movement of affections involves one's discovery of a new essence (or nature) in two related, but opposing
fields simultaneously: the human field of rational thought and action and the
spiritual field where feelings of the self as subject are transvalued into a selfless
love for and joy in God. This is not, as some have thought, a simple dichotomy of
the subjective and objective dimensions of sanctification. Instead, to borrow a
phrase from Baudelaire, it is the exercise of "a self insatiable for non-selfhood,"
an oscillating endeavor both to realize the physical existence of a self changed
by faith while desiring the effacement of that self as a human consciousness
infected with an ineradicable degree of mortal sinfulness.

John Smith, in his introduction to the *Religious Affections*, makes the point
that "the more clearly divine excellence is grasped, the more obvious does the
distance between God and man appear."[9] For Edwards, the issue of religious
consciousness and exercise pivots on the concepts of difference and sublation.
Man's sense of spirituality (manifested in opposite feelings of security-love-joy
and personal worthlessness) is based upon his perception of a change in his own
nature—a change made acute by an ever-increasing sense of the difference
between the unconverted self, the sanctified (but still flawed) self, and the self
subsumed into non-existence by the perfection of God. The acting human self,
since it cannot achieve perfect holiness while alive, enhances its apprehension
of the divine by means of sublation: it perpetuates dialectical oppositions which
refer to the difference between the mortal and the divine so as to heighten the
desire for a synthesis (identity) which it recognizes and sustains as unachievable. The language of man—which strives to define those spiritual things it

cannot name, which strives to detach itself from ordinary speech and usage, but which also relies upon such custom for its communicative power (to the self or another audience)—embodies such oppositions and sublations and, therefore, refers indirectly to the existential dynamics of Puritan theology. Those Puritan works which strike us as having a particularly selective or "aesthetic" sensitivity to language are works which are self-conscious of language in this way. And for Edwards, perhaps the greatest eighteenth-century American religious thinker, the written text is a palimpsest whose original markings were (are) the essences of man in their difference from the essence of God. In the most self-conscious writings of Edwards, the text is an expression of human-divine difference which refers allegorically—in the differential play of language—to a holiness un-nameable, unverifiable, and unattainable in discourse.

On the simplest level, we might say for Edwards that human perception works by the contrasting of essences and that his texts capture the self's encounter with its own modes of being and its aspirations for a divine Being through a rhetoric of difference and sublation. While the language of man discloses competing desires for individuality (a consciousness of the self as a religious-social entity) and selflessness, the Word of scripture has no such split intentionality and, therefore, inspires man by emphasizing yet another field of difference between the human and the divine. Although this theory of language and writing can be found in the linguistics of Saussure and has been adapted by Derrida and others for a radical upending of the Western metaphysical tradition,[10] there is strong reason to believe that Edwards anticipated certain features of these views and found a way to employ them within the most conservative Puritan theologic tradition.

The heart of Edwards' theology—his conception of the Trinity, his sense of the limitations of natural human powers for the achievement of grace, his definition of the relationship between the divine grace and the human act of faith—is remarkably close to that of Augustine.[11] Recent views of Augustine, expecially studies of the *Confessions,* have demonstrated the way in which he tested the problematic relations among memory, the present self, and the wish for spirituality within the context of a linguistic performance which recognizes the limitations of man *in* language.[12] While it is certainly plausible that Edwards, so sympathetic to Augustine, would have seen the Saint's contemplative activity in these terms, it is even more reasonable to assume that Edwards perceived the complementariness of those views to his own meditative temperament.

Conrad Cherry makes the observation that "rather than being possessed of sinless perfection, the man of faith lives in the tension between grace and the sin remaining in his heart. . . . Old man and new man 'subsist together in the same person'—this forms the dialectic characteristic of true saints; in whom 'grace dwells with so much corruption'."[13] In the sense that language and its use in the act of writing (diary, sermon, tract, personal narrative) were religious activities as persistently significant to the Puritan as "good works," it is reasonable to assume that self-conscious writing played out this very "tension." In fact, one might well take up Norman Grabo's concern for "the emotional matrix or affective structure from which ideas arise"[14] and argue that this matrix is indeed a "tension" which, on the verbal level, is realized in the differential structure of the linguistic performance. When we think about Edwards' obsession with the morphology of conversion,[15] the problematic correspondence between words and truth which must have informed all attempts to deal with this issue verbally,[16] and his distrust of established patterns of religious exercise (the habitual practice of which would de-sensitize rather than intensify self-confrontation), it appears quite logical that Edwards would employ writing as a means of testing the self—of testing the depth and range of his perception of human and divine difference and, in the process, intensifying the commitment to holiness.

The testing of the faithful self, the problematizing of religious exercise, the perception of difference, and the value of sublation can nowhere be seen more vividly than in Edwards' *Personal Narrative*. This text actually investigates the relations among man's modes of being, his desire for non-being, and the languages of man and scripture. The *Personal Narrative* is the most sophisticated example of the dynamics of self-reflection in early American literature; for it shows how one man, constituted by language and caught in a verbal reality, can, to borrow an idea from Louis Renza's comments on Augustine, interpret his own existence as a self-experienceable sign of God's creation.[17]

## II

Although it is embarrassingly fashionable these days to say that all texts are about their own origins in a writing consciousness constituted by language, such a generalization about the *Personal Narrative* would be more than suitable. The *Personal Narrative* is addressed to the most persistent question of Puritan self-reflection and religious exercise: how can a man, in reviewing his life, document a change in his mode of being (the essence of conversion) when, as a writing and thinking self, he is still constituted by language? To put this another way: how can a man express the fact that he writes, thinks, and lives with the sense of himself as a decadent (aspiring toward a secret expression of the self in writing as well as in his other sins) and a beginning (discovering a holy essence constituted previous to and outside language) simultaneously? I say the *Personal Narrative* addresses itself to this question because its autobiographical format, its non-linear presentation of event and spiritual growth, its problematizing of its own figurative language, its use of scriptural reference, and its curiously truncated ending are the integral parts of a single enterprise: Edwards' attempt "to write of his own existence as if it were not radically grounded in his own existence."[18]

The complexity of this enterprise and its manifestation in the structure of the *Personal Narrative* can perhaps be most clearly explained in the context of a more traditional interpretation. Daniel B. Shea, in what is probably the authoritative analysis of the text, argues that it has a dual intention.[19] It is, first, a fresh analysis of Edwards' spiritual experience based, in large part, on a mature reconsideration of the material in his diary. Secondly, it is an instructive work which aspires toward two pedagogic ends: to inspire those readers with no notion of the delight in "things of religion" by a compelling account of his own discovery; and to depict an exemplary engagement of true religious affections, over years of introspection, in a manner which vivifies the corruptions as well as the commitments of human spiritual aspiration. Shea's argument, and it is a strong one, rests upon his perception of Edwards' sensitivity to the possibilities of language—its objective potential for purposes of instruction, its subjective dimensions for conveying the felt perceptions of a "new man," its supplemental relation to scripture, and its dangerous capacity for misrepresentation, inadequate description, and rhetorical deception. Shea asserts that the multiple intention of the *Personal Narrative* is realized through a sequence of ideational concerns, each of which is tied to a particular notion of language potential and to stylistic procedure. The problem with his analysis is that the connection between matters of style, self-expression, and religious instruction is far more problematic than Shea would have us believe.

In his discussion of the *Personal Narrative*, William Scheick seems to sense the problems in Shea's reading.[20] First, Scheick places more emphasis upon Edwards' warning about language: "language communicates only reflections of these spiritual influences upon the soul. . . . [It] cannot finally cope with God's sovereign and mysterious providence, even though it is divinely ordained to provide clues to the spiritual condition of one's will." Furthermore, he makes an observation about the opening sentence of the text which reveals the incompleteness of Shea's view of the narrative voice, a view from which all the notions of thematics and language derive: "This sentence implies that the phases [of the "I" over time] are more merged than unique, more like the indistinguishable waves of the sealike 'process of time' in which the narrator finds himself." Although Scheick finally concludes, along with Shea, that the narrative voice is a unified expression of Edwards in the present, he seizes upon this conflation of time to imply that the *Personal Narrative* allegorizes the eschatology of Church history in its history of individual conversion. I, too, regard the issue of time as pivotal, but would also argue that it is central to the dynamics of autobiographical disclosure, that it problematizes the narrative "I" in a manner which allows Edwards to test the relationship of being to language within the context of spiritual belief.[21] The *Personal Narrative* is indeed a sort of allegory, for its sublation of time present and past refers allegorically to a spirituality which lies outside of both time and language.

The opening sentence of the *Personal Narrative* reads as follows:

> I had a variety of concerns and exercises about my soul from my childhood; but had two more remarkable seasons of awakening, before I met with that change, by which I was brought to those new dispositions, and that new sense of things, that I have since had.[22]

The convoluted structure of the phrases and the present perfect construction of the final clause—which might have been more simply expressed as "that I have now"—reveal Edwards' perception of the duality inherent in memory acts and give us a clue to the reason he chose autobiographical disclosure as a means for testing the relations among self, language, and faith. He does not say that he is writing from a sense of himself "now" because the sanctified Jonathan Edwards who is writing this essay is involved in a verbal activity which necessarily and intentionally occludes his continuity with the "I" conveyed in the narrative performance. The problem for Edwards, and for all writers involved in such autobiographical acts, is that he cannot accurately verbalize the past; all he can express is the relation between his present discursive intention and a "gestalt of pastness," a framed sense of that past which is no more than a signification of it made by the present self. Although the source of the essay is his diary, Edwards, the early diarist, is "Other" to his present self—and it is this very "Otherness" that he plays upon for the purposes of religious exercise.[23]

By writing of his own past under such epistemological conditions, Edwards can demonstrate that his past, as it really was, is not recoverable—thus, he can enlarge the distance between an unregenerated past self and a possibly regenerated present self. Since the memory act also reveals more about the writer's present signification of the past than of the past itself, the autobiographical activity refers indirectly to a positive change in Edwards' patterns of perceiving and thinking—a change which suggests a transformation of his very nature. Perhaps most important, the act of writing gives Edwards the chance to go beyond writing, through writing, to capture a felt difference between a consciousness constituted outside of language by God (transcendent and unnameable) and a recounting "I" of the narrative who exists only within the limits of language. This idea is central to the dynamics of autobiographical disclosure and it operates as the central structural principle of the *Personal Narrative*. Each time the pronoun "I" is used, it denominates a new and different narrative consciousness which is "Other" to Edwards himself. The moment Edwards (who wishes to disclose himself as a sanctified interiority constituted by God's grace outside language) uses the word "I," he is displacing something unnameable with something nameable. As soon as the self (man as a transcendental sign created by God) is named "I," that self is converted into a mere lexical "I," or verbal fiction constituted by language. Thus, as soon as the recounting "I" of the text relates what happened to him, he is no longer the one recounted.[24] The centrality of this principle to Edwards' self-reflection is obvious: man's very need for self-reflection is evidence of his sinfulness, and every verbal act of self-reflection is necessarily a religious transgression. The recollective activity, by its very nature, posits an independent self (a lexical "I") as its subject, and sets up the religious felicity of the self as the object of its desire. In the true act of faith, however, God's holiness is the subject and man's love for His perfection constitutes desire. The *Personal Narrative* is not an attempt at unifying past and present selves; it is an attempt to confess the sins of a consciousness determined by language and to separate the present self from earlier modes of word-bound being.

The *Narrative* is more a discovery of conversion than a history of it. Edwards' verbal performance is as much an attempt to create the interpenetration of self-reflection and spiritual exercise as it is an effort merely to document or assert the interdependence of the personal and the religious in the true believer. In short, the *Personal Narrative* is Edwards' attempt to use the introspective endeavor as a mode of self-realization consistent with the self-effacing philosophic emphasis of his theology. The *Narrative* is, first, his attempt to express spiritual commitment by de-centering himself as the subject of the inquiry and by displacing his wish for his own good estate as the object of desire. Second, it is an attempt to intensify his apprehension of the spiritual by differentiating, on philosophic levels, human potential from holy perfection and excellence. Finally, it is an attempt to find a language through which he can express himself as a writing consciousness in the act of spiritual growth. Any state of being named in discourse asserts the speaker's self as it exists in language and, consequently, apart from God. For this reason, Edwards seeks a language which will capture the self becoming less a self and more a part of God, a language which does not purport to define what is, but to suggest what is coming into being.

In his *Narrative*, Edwards accomplishes these tasks by developing two points of personal-spiritual intelligibility at once. First, the text is characterized by a repetitive pattern of failure which allows him to confess, on the most subtle level, the sin of regarding himself as the origin of consciousness and the center of reality. But at the same time, the structure of the text is also teleologic, enabling Edwards to dissociate himself from this sinfulness by relocating his verbal performance—the referent of which was the self and its aggrandizement—in a new verbal field where his words are more truly those of holy worship. Both of these patterns—the repetitive and the teleologic—are created by the progression of "I"s in the text. But in order to understand how these "I"s constitute such movements, we must realize that each use of the pronoun denominates more than the Jonathan Edwards of a certain age and place. The "I" is not so much an autobiographical fact as a lexical sign which signifies a flawed relationship between Edwards' consciousness of self and his consciousness of God. Thus, the *Personal Narrative* is actually the story of three main "I"s. The first refuses to recognize his limitations in a word-bound reality. In his efforts at purification, he repeatedly exposes himself as an unself-conscious creation of language whose gestures at spiritual transformation are self-deceiving and must end in failure. The second accepts his inability to voice his spiritual commitment without secretly expressing himself and, thereby, aggravating his distance from God. With this knowledge, he is able to fulfill his urge for religious expression by referring indirectly to a transformation of being he knows he cannot name—a transformation he allegorizes through the manipulation of figurative language. The third "I," Edwards the writing consciousness, is unnamed and forever must remain so. He exists as a potentiality beyond, but related to the characters of his text. He is known to himself only in terms of his absence from his own text, both from his past and the "I" of the narrative. In other words, Edwards the writer is a consciousness effaced by the religious preparation of his narrative, a non-being who is absent from his worldly self, who is an "emptiness" waiting to be filled (fulfilled) by the grace (presence) of God.

Although the repetitive and teleologic movements within the *Narrative* intertwine helix-like throughout the text, it would be fair to say that the repetition of failure is the dominant organizational principle of the first half until it is displaced by a more persistent teleology in the second. Basically, the first thirteen paragraphs constitute one conceptual area of the text through which Edwards investigates the relationship between sin and self expression. Although there are many reversals in this section, there are two principal repetitions which ultimately force the speaker's recognition of his spiritual limitations as a consciousness within language. In the first of these, he discovers that increasing intellectual maturity and self-consciousness do not necessarily purify the quality of religious commitment, that his actions as a young adult were in fact repetitions of an earlier childish self-righteousness. In the second, his attempt to personalize religious "delight"—produced by acceptance of God's sovereignty and the authority of Scripture—through his own romantic use of language is exposed as a mode of self-induced excitement akin to the self-centered activities of the earlier "I"'s.

In the first four paragraphs, Edwards recollects a boyhood enthusiasm for religious devotion and a period of spiritual rejuvenation at the conclusion of his college years. There are three "I"'s in this segment, and each fails in his religious commitment: 1) a boyhood "I" who possesses a self-righteous delight "when engaged in religious duties" but whose diminished enthusiasm is compared to a dog's return to its vomit; 2) a repentant "I" whose uneasy thoughts about his soul are stimulated during a near fatal bout with pleurisy, but whose repentance wanes after his recovery; and 3) a seeking "I" whose "violent inward struggles" lead him to make a formal vow to seek salvation by breaking off "all former wicked ways, and all ways of known outward sin." In a sense, the chronological movement from the "delighter" to the "repenter" to the "seeker" suggests a certain maturation in Edwards' sense of his religious commitment. Indeed, he says of the seeker: "But yet I was brought to seek salvation, in a manner that I never was before." Nevertheless, from the vantage point of the present he is uncertain whether his vow ever issued from the infusion of grace, and he admits that his calculated quest for salvation was a miserable one. The failure of this seeker problematizes for Edwards the whole notion of a growing spirituality based upon the increasing self-consciousness which attends intellectual maturity. The chartered vow made by the seeker is a formal confession of his earlier sinfulness, but it does not newly constitute or prove a change in his fundamental mode of being. The very formality of the contract exposes it as a worldly ritual which, in spite of its origin in soulful anguish, has no real spiritual legitimacy. Thus, the delighting boy's return dog-like to his sinful ways is repeated in the young adult's reliance upon a human contract; the child's delight in building secret places in the woods simply becomes an adult's certainty in the words written by his own hand; and the simile of a dog returning to its vomit is merely repeated in a vocabulary suitable for the business-like approach of the seeker—"miserable."

The second repetition—including an account of his comprehension of God's sovereignty, an expression of his "delight" and its sources, and a description of his intense desire for "soul-satisfying and life giving good"—is a response to the problem of self-assertion and language posed in the first section. In this portion of the text, Edwards replaces the discredited idea of a congruence between intellectual growth and spiritual commitment with another view. Instead, he works from the assumption that a return to spontaneous and effusive religious feeling will efface that secret selfishness which undermined his earlier enterprise. He traces a transformation in his appreciation of the doctrine of God's sovereignty, a transformation which begins with his early belief that the doctrine is God's abuse of His power. Gradually, he comes to see it as a just doctrine, and finally he delights in it as a manifestation of God's nature and presence. The movement here—from judgment to assent to delight—is a reversal of the debilitating rationalism which informed his earlier activities, and it is a far more intense and legitimate engagement with matters of the spirit than his previous ones. Indeed, Edwards takes pains to emphasize the difference between this experience and those of his childhood and college years: "The delights which I now felt in things of religion, were of an exceeding different kind, from those forementioned, that I had when I was a boy. . . . They were of a more inward, pure, soul-animating and refreshing nature." In spite of this assertion (and the poetic eloquence depicting his delight in God's handiwork in the preceding paragraphs), this "I" ("almost constantly in ejaculatory prayer") is caught in the same pattern of failure as his predecessors. He is the most important "I" in the text, for he is the one who truly discovers a holy essence different from his worldly self, and yet who also commits the sin of trying to attach himself to this godliness through the power of his own language.

Through engagement with scripture, he discovers both a new delight in God (I Tim. i. 17) and a source for the enhancement of that delight ("I am the Rose of Sharon, the lily of the valleys"). As a consequence of this enhancement, he has a vision of God as "majesty and meekness join'd together," a vision which suggests a paradoxical opposition whose result is a perfect union. Although this vision may have been the most important one of his life, Edwards responds to it inappropriately, in a manner "which afterwards proved a great damage to me." Basically, he tries to transform himself into something akin to this paradoxical holy essence by polarizing his life into moments of "ejaculatory" ecstasy and agonized longing. His efforts, as well as the words he uses to express them, portray a man with "too great a dependence upon my own strength." His "longing," "pursuing," and "pressing" are earnest on the surface but solipsistic underneath: "My experience had not then taught me, as it has done since, my extreme feebleness and impotence, every manner of way; and the innumerable and bottomless depths of secret corruption and deceit, that there was in my heart." The failure of this "I"—who "sought an increase of grace and holiness. . .with vastly more earnestness, than ever I sought grace, before I had it"—initiates the pivotal moment in the text. For it is here that a self who knows that he is saved, and who knows what it means to love Christ, actually calls his own mode of being, as a consciousness capable of expressing that love, into question:

The Heaven I desired was a heaven of holiness: to be with God, and to spend my eternity in divine love, and holy communion with Christ. My mind was very much taken up with contemplations on heaven, and the enjoyments of those there; and living there in perfect holiness, humility and love. *And it used at that time to appear a great part of the happiness of heaven, that there the saints could express their love to Christ. It appeared to me a great clog and hindrance and burden, that what I felt within, I could not express to God, and give vent to, as I desired*. . . . I used often to think, how in heaven, this *sweet principle* should freely and fully vent and express itself. Heaven appeared to me exceeding delightful as a world of love. It appeared to me, that all happiness consisted in living in pure, humble, heavenly, divine love (p. 30; emphasis mine).

In this key paragraph, Edwards defines the problem of devotion as a problem of language; he apprehends the difference between the kingdoms of earth and heaven in terms of the difference between a human condition limited by language and a holy reality beyond language and, therefore, beyond the frustrations of spiritual isolation and aphasia. Furthermore, with the words "sweet principle" he discovers a rhetorical solution to his dilemma and initiates the assertive teleology of the latter portion of the text. Specifically, he discovers the possibility for a language of devotion which does not secretly assert the self and, of consequence, will allow for an effacement of the lexical "I."

The phrase "sweet principle" refers to that expression of love to Christ possible in heaven but impossible on earth. But it is more complicated than this. The expression of love to Christ not only characterizes existence in heaven, it also constitutes heaven as a place where there is no gap between self and God that requires words. Heaven is a state of being where perfect expression is *no* expression, where there is no separation of entities to be bridged by language. Since such a state of being is unattainable on earth, the goal of worship is an understanding of such impossibility, not a self-deluding attempt to convert it into a possibility. In other words, devotion is not an attempt to represent divine love or earn it; rather, devotion is an attempt to differentiate divine love from man's expression of love and to work against the human tendency toward self-love. The extraordinary importance of the phrase "sweet principle" is that Edwards uses it as the basis of an allegory—an allegory through which he can refer indirectly to a oneness which cannot be named and earned, to a love the desire for which will displace concerns of his own selfhood. To make this rather cryptic observation clearer: with the phrase "sweet principle," Edwards begins to manipulate language for the purpose of referring, on the linguistic level, to a state of being where opposites unite in perfect harmony and where differences are simultaneously maintained and reconciled. Through such maneuvering, Edwards finds a way to worship and to yearn for an essence ("majesty and meekness") without secretly claiming to be already *of* it.

When he uses the phrase "sweet principle" to name the concept of divine love, Edwards is transvaluing the previous meaning of the word "sweet," a word used many times in the preceding text. Earlier, "sweet" was used as an adjective the referent of which was the tasting human self; namely, the word was used to make God known to the speaker by drawing a comparison between the worldly pleasure of taste and the pleasure of faith. Now, however, the most immediate referent of the word is divine love—a love the constitutive characteristic of which is its perfection beyond the words (or appetites) of man. Whereas "sweet" was once used to reduce holiness to human terms, it is now used to emphasize a holiness outside the bounds of human reference; whereas "sweet" once asserted the role of man's *presence* (as a taster) in God's existence, it now asserts the *absence* of human essence from things divine. By transvaluing the word in this manner, Edwards is able to do three things through its adjectival use. First, he can use the word to signify ineffability and impossibility—thereby referring to the inimical attributes of God and pointing toward his own sense of absence, his yearning for a oneness, the presence of which does away with the need for the word "sweet." Second, he can use the word both to remind himself of and distance himself from the sins of the past—sins reducible to his earlier use of the word "sweet" and the implications of that use. Third, through the use of a word laden with references to past decadence and present longing, he can know his own essence in a manner which refers by allegorical indirection to God's essence. In other words, he recognizes himself—through the word "sweet"—as a sublation of decadent self-expression and faithful self-effacement, and he knows that this sublation will forever produce feelings of absence and unfulfilled need. Such knowledge heightens his apprehension of God, for it refers to Him as a sublation of "majesty and meekness," the nature of which produces "all happiness," not perpetual desire. In this way, he can make God known to himself by a negative self-reference (an allegory of human-divine difference) far different from his self-indulgent comparison of holy sweetness and the delights of the human tongue.

The teleological portion of the text grows out of this language play in that such manipulation frees Edwards to use an "I" who both is and is not the subject of discussion—to write of his own existence as if it were not radically grounded in his own existence. I say this conceptual area of the text is teleological because it is a portrayal of spiritual growth allegorized in the tale of an escape from language. There is a progression of three "I"s in this tale—a passive "I", a seeking "I", and a choosing "I"—and each asserts the nature of his belief in his own peculiar manner. Each "I" has a different essence—or controlling principle of selfhood—and each contemplates this essence as a way to apprehend God and focus attention upon Him. Thus, each "I" offers a brief manifesto of his belief in a language suitable to his particular sense of the difference between holy and human essences. In the course of their narration, however, both the passive and seeking "I"s lose clear hold of their enterprise. Each forgets that he is merely using linguistic maneuver to comprehend a reality beyond expression; both lose sight of themselves and their language as fictional constructs because their commitment to the enterprise of holy worship is so intense. The last, or choosing "I" earns a pyrrhic solution to this dilemma, a solution which explains the language of the *Narrative*'s final two paragraphs and Edwards' puzzling observation "that in some respects I was a far better Christian, for two or three years after my first conversion, than I am now."

The passive "I" uses the concept of sweetness to denominate a humility and passivity which will overcome previous self-assertions. He sets out to apprehend God in terms of holiness, the primary attribute of which is its divine beauty, and the essence of which is the "sweet calm" of the believer. He draws an analogy between the blossoming of a little white flower and a childhood helplessness, a comparison he locates within the figural context of a sweet fragrance animated, or brought into being by the beams of God's glory. In this way, he is able to talk about knowing God through his own passive-essence as a child-flower blooming with "sweet fragrancy" only upon the offering of God's light. The problem for this "I" is created by his inability to sublimate the previous connotation of "sweet." His very use of the word reminds him of his absence from the "sweet calm" of a heavenly existence where words are not the foundation of communication. Thus, the glory of his figurative identity as a passive being is immediately upended by a despair at his entrapment in a word-bound reality, by the onset of feelings of a "brokenness of heart and poverty of spirit." Unwilling to accept the paradox of glory and despair, he replaces the figurative representation of himself as a child-flower with a view of himself as a servant of God—a redefinition he seals with a written oath on January 12. This tactic fails, for it encourages him to lose sight of the figurative origin and nature of his contemplation. Specifically, he begins contemplating this absence from God in the objective terms of his separation from friends, and his wordliness precipitates, "greatly to the wounding of my soul," an even greater diversion from religious commitment. Ultimately, his commitment is re-kindled by the words of scripture. The "sweet and powerful words" give him a sense of God which his soul (not his writing hand) "with sweetness made its own language." But more of this later.

The seeking "I," who is not satisfied with a "sweet complacence" procured only through the words of scripture, employs yet another verbal strategy for dealing with the paradox of glory-despair—now re-conceptualized in terms of passivity and thirst. He transvalues the concept of sweetness to denominate a kind of heavenly introspection where "sweet communications" with oneself *in* God express one's love for Him. With this manipulation, he can refer to the "infinite foundation of divine glory and sweetness" in the indirect terms of a contemplation on the equally "ineffable" and "infinite" magnitude of his own sinfulness. In this way, the greater his self-abasement, the greater his apprehension of God's perfection; the more revolting the view of himself, the sweeter the nature of life in God's kingdom. But he too forgets that this is all verbal maneuvering. Thus, he participates in the onerous activity of comparing himself to others, a comparison which, following the figurative logic of his exercise, actually asserts his superiority to those without such "infinite" apprehensions. His plaintive lament—"I am greatly afflicted with a proud and self-righteous spirit; much more sensibly, than I used to be formerly"—is quite justified.

The final "I" of the text recognizes the failure of his predecessors. He understands that the attempt to represent one's love for God in human language is unachievable without a secret assertion of the self. He also knows that the expression of one's love by figurative indirection is equally untenable; for man will be inevitably victimized by that very language he believes he is using for spiritual purposes. The "serpent rising and putting forth it's head, continually, everywhere, all around me" is the language of man—it lures man into displays of "a proud and self-righteous spirit" just as the serpent of the Garden tricked Adam and Eve. The final "I," recalling the return to scripture by the passive "I" and the employment of the serpent metaphor with its scriptural referent by the seeking "I," abandons the risky attempt to sustain his belief through his own linguistic powers. In doing so, he leaves behind him a "delight and pleasure" possible only when he believed in his own expressive abilities. He also, perhaps, leaves behind him a capacity for passionate spiritual encounters; for the knowledge he now holds would reveal the hidden flaw at the base of all such verbally centered wonderments. Although he suspects that his earlier religious fervor made him a "better Christian" (in the sense that his religious commitment was more overtly manifested in his worldly conduct), he knows that he is more pious now: "I have had a more full and constant sense of the absolute sovereignty of God, and a delight in that sovereignty; and have had more of a sense of the glory of Christ, as a mediator, as revealed in the gospel."

The final "I," unlike his predecessors, understands the complex relationship between the "will" and language. To be inclined towards God (with all the loving and self-effacing ramifications of such inclination), is also to be inclined towards His Word. But the linguistic dimension of volition is not just manifested in one's enjoyment of scripture, it is exercised through one's recognition of the difference between human communicative endeavor and the disclosive potentiality of the Word. Man knows his world and himself through a language which names the elements of his universe on the basis of their instrumentality. For this reason, the man who insists upon grasping at his spiritual essence through his language only reveals the extent to which he is still an instrument of his own world: a consciousness which knows itself and God only in terms of their functionality. The proof of man's will to God is his full receptivity to the enabling Word, for it is only this language which will heighten perception and disclose his essence simultaneously. In other words, scripture is more than a means of conversion; it discloses a principle of being beyond human language that man must accept as his own essence. When the choosing "I" says that "this is my chosen light, my chosen doctrine," and "this is my chosen prophet," he is expressing the free inclination of his will toward a new mode of being and a new language. His utterance of the recollected scripture is intended to express *and* constitute his essence as a true believer; it is intended as a constative *and* performative expression of religious commitment simultaneously.[25]

I say that the choosing "I" *intends* a verbal utterance of this variety because it is an effort incompletely realized. It is impossible to make a verbal statement which says what one means, performs what one promises, and characterizes completely what one is. What separates the choosing "I" from all the other "I"s in the text is his very perception of the relationship between holy oneness and the nature of language. All his predecessors try to apprehend the spiritual by increasing the connotations of words, by freeing words from their traditional contexts for the purposes of semantic and figurative play. The choosing "I," however, sees his enterprise as one of limiting the field of connotation. He seeks a language, like that of the Word, in which words have only one referent—God. Thus, his recollection of scripture in the next to last paragraph of the *Narrative* is followed by an attempt to refer to holy oneness by linguistic restraint. First, he elaborates upon the nature of his choice with verbs, not adjectives: "to follow Christ, and to be taught and enlighten'd and instructed by Him; to learn of Him, and live to Him." Second, he tames the semantic chaos engendered by the word "sweet" by linking it with the inclusive concept of blessedness: "Another Saturday night, January, 1738-9, had such a sense, how sweet and blessed a thing it was, to walk in the way of duty." Finally, he verbalizes the conflated concepts of blessedness and happiness with a formulaic paraphrase of religious belief: "I had at the same time, a very affecting sense, how meet and suitable it was that God should govern the world, and order all things according to his own pleasure; and I rejoiced in it, that God reigned, and that his will was done" (p. 39).

The choosing "I" is the most pious figure of the text. He finds a way to use legitimately the trusted formulas of religious expression without falling into enthusiastic excess on the one hand, or the complacency of rote memorization on the other. Nevertheless, he too is caught by the necessity of language, and this entrapment is suggested by the fact that the final words, although formulaic, are his own. Edwards, the writing consciousness, is separated from even this final "I." By distancing himself from an "I" who has gone as far as possible toward coping with the dilemma of his human essence in language, Edwards actually places himself beyond language and beyond man's world. In emptying himself of language, Edwards confesses his sins, negates his worldly self, and opens himself for a completely new existence.

## Notes

1. See Michael Ryan's essay on Nietzsche, "The Act," *Glyph*, 2 (1977), 65-87.

2. Perry Miller, *Jonathan Edwards* (New York: Meridan Books, 1959); Conrad Cherry, *The Theology of Jonathan Edwards: A Reappraisal* (New York: Anchor Books, 1966); Roland Delattre, *Beauty and Sensibility in the Thought of Jonathan Edwards* (New Haven: Yale University Press, 1968).

3. Edward Davidson, *Jonathan Edwards* (Cambridge: Harvard University Press, 1968); Edwin Cady, "The Artistry of Jonathan Edwards," *NEQ*, 22 (1949), 61-72.

4. Cherry, p. 52.

5. Delattre, especially Chapter 3 on beauty and being.

6. Cherry, especially Chapter 3 on the Word and spirit.

7. Delattre, pp. 32-33n.

8. Jonathan Edwards, *Religious Affections*, ed. John Smith (New Haven: Yale University Press, 1959), p. 97.

9. Edwards, p. 39.

10. I am referring here to the deconstructive readings by such recent philosophic critics as Jacques Derrida, Paul deMan, and Roland Barthes.

11. See Cherry, especially his discussions of illumination and infusion, the nature of grace, and trust and humility.

12. See Eugene Vance, "Augustine's *Confessions* and the Grammar of Selfhood," *Genre,* 6 (1973), 1-28; Louis Renza, "The Veto of the Imagination: A Theory of Autobiography," *New Literary History* 9 (1977), 1-26.

13. Cherry, p. 78.

14. Norman Grabo, "The Veiled Vision: The Role of Aesthetics in Early American Intellectual History," in *The American Puritan Imagination,* ed. Sacvan Bercovitch (London: Cambridge University Press, 1974), p. 24.

15. See William Scheick, *The Writings of Jonathan Edwards: Theme, Motif, and Style* (College Station: Texas A&M University Press, 1975).

16. See Bercovitch, "The American Puritan Imagination: An Introduction," in his *The American Puritan Imagination,* p. 3.

17. See Louis Renza, "The Veto of the Imagination," especially his comments upon Augustine, p. 3.

18. I take this phrase also from Renza's discussion of Augustine, "The Veto of the Imagination," p. 9.

19. Daniel B. Shea, Jr., "The Art and Instruction of Jonathan Edwards' *Personal Narrative,*" in Bercovitch, *The American Puritan Imagination,* pp. 159-72.

20. Scheick, pp. 59-66.

21. The issue of time is addressed by John Lynen in *Design of Present: Essays on Time and Form in American Literature* (New Haven: Yale Univ. Press, 1969). While Lynen is also concerned with the problem of autobiographical disclosure in relation to the self over time, he does not treat this as a grammatological problem. Rather, he offers an account of the way in which Edwards (and Benjamin Franklin, too) posits himself in the provisional role of a transcendental consciousness through the use of narrative point of view. Because he views the text in terms of more traditional notions of narration, he is able to make a strong argument that Edwards, through the act of writing, achieves a unity of consciousness. This, of course, is exactly the opposite conclusion one arrives at if one sees the text in terms of a linguistic problematic. In a sense, Lynen's position is very close to David Minter's: *The Interpreted Design as a Structural Principle in American Prose* (New Haven: Yale Univ. Press, 1969). Minter, starting from similar assumptions about the nature of narrative, asserts that the text enacts a dialectic between Edwards' impotent design and God's universal design. These two designs play out a sort of "divine comedy" through which man's plans are undone at the very time he is being led by God to paradise. In spite of the undeniable strength of Minter's reading, I would again assert that the design of the text is all Edwards' and that the oppositions man encounters, while he exists in language, cannot be resolved into a synthesis. The text, rather than unifying Edwards' consciousness or bringing his own design under the aegis of God's design, depicts an inescapable dynamics of separation.

22. My source for the *Personal Narrative* is Samuel Hopkins' *Life and Character of Jonathan Edwards,* reprinted in *Jonathan Edwards, A Profile,* ed. David Levin (New York: Hill and Wang, 1969), pp. 24-39. All parenthetical numbers in the text refer to this edition.

23. See Renza for an excellent generic discussion of this principle, especially as it pertains to Augustine, Rousseau, and St. Theresa, pp. 1-26.

24. Renza, pp. 1-26.

25. The clearest example of a performative utterance is the statement "I do" uttered by the participants in a wedding ceremony. The words both answer the question put to the participants and seal, or perform the marriage act. For a discussion of this principle, see J.L. Austin, *Philosophical Papers,* ed. J.O. Urmson and G.J. Warnock (Oxford: Oxford University Press, 1970), pp. 233-52.

# INDEX

*The Politics of*
*Literary Reputation*

# The Politics of Literary Reputation

*The Making and Claiming of 'St. George' Orwell*

*John Rodden*

New York    Oxford
*Oxford University Press*
1989

Oxford University Press

Oxford   New York   Toronto
Delhi   Bombay   Calcutta   Madras   Karachi
Petaling Jaya   Singapore   Hong Kong   Tokyo
Nairobi   Dar es Salaam   Cape Town
Melbourne   Auckland

and associated companies in
Berlin   Ibadan

Library of Congress Cataloging-in-Publication Data
Rodden, John.
The politics of literary reputation : the making and claiming
of 'St. George' Orwell / John Rodden.
p.    cm.
Bibliography: p.    Includes index.
ISBN 0-19-503954-8
1. Orwell, George, 1903–1950—Criticism and interpretation—History.
2. Canon (Literature) I. Title.
PR6029.R8Z776 1989                          88-22721
828'.91209—dc19                             CIP

Parts of Chapters Two to Five have previously appeared, in slightly different form, in *Philosophy and Literature, Biography, Papers in Comparative Studies, College English, Commonweal, The German Quarterly, Queen's Quarterly, Canadian Journal of History, Four Quarters,* and *College Literature.*

Permission to reprint from the following is gratefully acknowledged:

*frontis:* Jim Borgman, © 1983 *Cincinnati Enquirer;* p. 14: *Punch,* 21/28 Dec. 1983; p. 31, *top:* Herblock, Universal Press Syndicate, 17 Oct. 1986; *bottom:* Paul Conrad, Los Angeles Times Syndicate, 20 April 1981; p. 38, *top:* John Trever, *Albuquerque Times,* 1983; *bottom:* Associated Press, 22 Dec. 1983; p. 172, *top: The Spectator,* 7 Jan. 1984; *bottom:* Mike Mosher, in David Smith and Mike Mosher, eds., *Orwell for Beginners* (London: W.W. Norton, 1984); p. 186, *top:* Tom Wilson, © 1982 Universal Press Syndicate; *bottom:* Tom Wilson, © 1984 Universal Press Syndicate; p. 234: Einstein Moomjy, New York; p. 235: Charles Schulz, © 1983 United Feature Syndicate, Inc.; p. 236; Boise Cascade Corporation, Boise, Idaho; p. 237, *top:* Gary Larson, Universal Press Syndicate; *bottom:* Sandra Boynton; p. 245: *Time* magazine, 28 Nov. 1983, copyright Time, Inc.; p. 256, *top:* Etta Hulme, *Fort Worth Star-Telegram,* 29 Jan. 1984; *bottom:* Noel Watson, *The Financial Post,* 7 Jan. 1984; p. 257: Docutel/Olivetti Corporation, Dallas, Texas; p. 276, *top:* David Low, *Manchester Evening Guardian,* 17 Dec. 1954; *bottom: Daily Mail,* 14 Dec. 1954; p. 277: BBC Archive; p. 299: *Der Spiegel,* 3 Jan. 1983; p. 323: David Astor/Orwell Archive, University of London.

9 8 7 6 5 4 3 2 1

Printed in the United States of America
on acid-free paper

*In memory of*
*Catherine McGinley*

# Contents

# Preface

I

Literary reputations are made, not born. But to the outsider or latecomer, the canon of great names often looms like a canopy of fixed and shining stars, so that socially constructed reality appears a law of nature. Or like inherited titles, reputations seem not so much "established" as "acquired," a matter of birthright vaguely ascribed to some dateless anointing. Literary histories have traditionally nourished these illusions by treating the rise and fall of reputations as a matter of "taste," a subject best left to the curious sociologist and the omniscient "verdict of posterity," outside the bounds of literary scholarship proper. One of the most difficult problems for literary and cultural historians is to cast light on the making of reputation as a social process while not ignoring that intrinsic, sometimes indefinable, aesthetic attributes of works contribute to authors' reputations. For we should neither reduce reputation merely to an interaction among institutional forces nor presume cynically that all established judgments are largely groundless, the products of ruling class "mystifications" which demand "unmasking" and "demythologizing." The problem is further complicated by the common supposition, repeatedly contradicted by experience, that literary reputation and value rest almost exclusively upon literary productions: the works of the writer, not the image of the man.

The subject of George Orwell's reputation raises all these issues with the man and writer's characteristic directness. Within little more than four years in the late 1940s, Orwell rose from a position of relatively modest standing

as a London journalist and minor English novelist to a writer of international stature during the last months of his life and a symbolic figure from virtually the moment of his death. If he had never written his last two books, quite probably he would be largely unknown today, even within the literary academy, his brilliant essays and trenchant journalism notwithstanding. But in the aftermath of what the press came to call "the countdown to 1984" and "The Year of Orwell," Orwell's name is once again, as it was in the mid-1950s, recognizable to millions. Unlike so many acclaimed modern writers, his critical reputation has suffered no periods of sharp decline since his death; and although his popular standing is again in descent from its high-water mark of the early 1980s, he has remained a permanent fixture in the media's pantheon of literary figures.

Still, it is questionable, almost painfully so for some admirers, whether Orwell's literary achievement—except perhaps in the essay form, where his compelling ethos so strongly appeals—can bear the weight of esteem and significance which successive generations have bestowed upon him. Indeed the virtues cited as characteristic of the writer's style have all been claimed as the man's personal qualities: clarity, simplicity, honesty, plainness, vigor, passion. Even some of the most prominent champions of Orwell's work have maintained, often with regret, that he was much more important for how he lived than for what he wrote. Whether true or not, as a critic remarked of Camus shortly after his death, many readers *want* Orwell to be a great writer, not just a very good one. The disarming candor, the fervent commitment, the innate decency, and always the living voice conspire so pardonably to rationalize such a critical judgment, even to demand it.

Orwell himself frequently bemoaned book reviewers' inflated, cultish praise of other writers, once caustically reminding a star-struck critic to "remember the difference between hagiography and criticism."[1] The advice is worth recalling when we come to 'St. George' Orwell, lionized as the "quintessentially English" patriot, the fearless slayer of the Red dragon, the socialist paragon, the pure stylist, the model of intellectual integrity—and vilified with a sling of his own adjective "Orwellian" back upon him. Certainly Orwell's ubiquity during the early 1980s in classrooms and academic journals, in the press, and on airwaves was incontestable; but no extended discussion has dealt with the making of his extraordinary public reputation and its attempted "claiming" by numerous political and commercial interests, with how Orwell has come to represent so much in a personal way to intellectuals both of the Left and Right, and with how his rhetoric and vision have so deeply penetrated our consciousness that they have been assimilated, often without attribution, into the Western political lexicon and imagination.

The following chapters are the story of that process. "Making" and "claiming" are broad and colloquial terms for the process, yet their scope and informality at least respect the theoretical complexities and heated polemics involved. Reputations come into being in different ways at different times under different conditions. They are radically contingent—partly make-believe and always makeshift and made over—being variously cre-

ated, fashioned, built, manufactured, suppressed, and distorted—in a constant interaction of images and information in and through social relations. Ordinary usage, which characterizes reputations as "monuments," disguises this sociohistorical process as an inherited product, thereby veiling the fact that reputations emerge over time and leading us to project a single aspect for the diverse whole.

The situation is all the more complicated in Orwell's case, for the remarkable fact about his posthumous history is that he has been cast not in one but in several vivid, distinct images since his death. And not only have changing historical conditions spotlighted various of these images, but the tendency has persisted to read all the images backwards from the Cold War, the widely quoted obituaries, *Nineteen Eighty-Four,* and *Animal Farm,* thus obscuring or confusing Orwell's earlier work and life. Some of these images are mere caricatures, bearing little direct relation to George Orwell, as man or writer. Most people familiar with his life and work know, for instance, that he was no "difficult saint" or "doomsday prophet."[2] But the matter begins, not ends there. All the important issues still remain; and even such a knowing dismissal of these characterizations may be ill-founded or premature. The original contexts of such characterizations, how they became established as images of the author, what such images indicate about author-reader relationships, and how they bear on the uses and abuses to which a writer's name and work are put: however laborious, investigation of the dense, intricate web of relations which constitutes these processes is our historical and sociological task. It is to identify both the immediately and less obviously recognizable faces in the Orwell family album and to trace their lines of descent and divergence. As such, it lies beyond both the erection and razing of literary monuments.

Thus my project is cultural criticism directed at recovery and clarification. For as a negotiated process of selection and exclusion, history is indeed not only a repository of events but a giant dustbin, and contemporary interests have a way, even without writers like Winston Smith at work, of "rectifying" reputations in line with present-day preoccupations. Part of the task with Orwell is therefore to retrieve the scraps of his early reputation from the memory holes of history.

II

This book aims chiefly to describe the making and claiming of a reputation, rather than to argue a specific case for its upward or downward revaluation. Inasmuch as I am implicated in the very processes I am describing, of course, these chapters do reflect and will inevitably contribute to Orwell's changing value and repute. So while my goal is certainly not to refurbish Orwell with a new image or set of images, let alone to coopt him for one political camp or another, I am fully aware that the act of tracing and appraising his historical images will influence their development and figure in the emergence of new images of him. To chronicle the "making" of a reputation inescapably influ-

ences its "remaking." Moreover, the incremental, near-invisible historical process and the tissue of interacting influences which bear on it are hardly intelligible without some arrangement into stages and lines of development. And this arrangement is invariably related to one's own critical location and consciousness. One of this project's contentions is that the historical-institutional locations of certain of Orwell's observers have decisively influenced the course of his reputation. Likewise, my own politico-historical and cultural-professional location—as a left-of-center white male of working-class origins, a post- Vatican II Catholic liberal, an academic in English and Communication Studies, and an American who came to Orwell's work in the 1970s—has obviously borne on my reconstruction of his reputation, as the succeeding chapters make clear.

In the widest and most explicit senses of the word, then, the case of Orwell raises the "politics" of literary reputation. For no reputation germinates in a value-free environment; all reputations flourish or perish in light of relations and access to power and influence. Reputations are invariably "political," enmeshed in ideological beliefs and emergent from within concrete forms of social and institutional life. Even beyond such conditioning structures, however, so political is Orwell's reputation that its history is inextricably bound up in postwar cultural politics and his politicized legacy is a minor political issue in its own right.

### III

Much discussion about Orwell has involved the transformation of Eric Blair into "George Orwell." Our concern is chiefly with the metamorphosis of "Orwell" into 'St. George'—and the so-called grave-robbing which has attended it. Although this study treats selected aspects of Orwell's reputation from several perspectives through the year 1988, much of my attention is focused upon two periods: the postwar decade and the months before and during 1984. These two periods are particularly important as the key years of the emergence and expansion, and then re-emergence and re-expansion, of Orwell's reputation. The former period spans the term of his critical ascension and sudden growth in popular reputation, a decade stretching roughly from the mid-1940s to the mid-1950s. In 1945–46 the U.K. and U.S. editions of *Animal Farm* appeared. The years 1953–56 saw the production of three film/TV adaptations of *Nineteen Eighty-Four* and an animated cartoon of *Animal Farm*. By the late 1950s almost all of Orwell's early out-of-print books (some of them never published in America) had come back into print, four essay collections had appeared, and his books had been translated into more than thirty languages. In the single year 1949–50, during which occurred the publication of *Nineteen Eighty-Four* and Orwell's death, his reputation penetrated beyond intellectual circles into the wider public domain and his predominant public images of "prophet" and "saint" began to take firm shape. By 1956 one old friend could observe that "as his reputation soared after the publication of *Nine-

*teen Eighty-Four*," an "almost" "unknown" writer seemed suddenly transformed into "the Orwell legend."³

The countdown to 1984 similarly witnessed Orwell's popular reputation re-emerge far beyond even its dimensions in the mid-1950s. Press articles, television and radio programs, plays and movies, academic conferences and commercial spinoffs devoted or pegged to *Nineteen Eighty-Four* testified that Orwell and his work were subjects of global interest. "1984" was Orwell's year all right: he was even drafted as a favorite-son candidate for the White House by "The Orwell for President Committee."⁴ One headline in a small U.S. daily newspaper fairly summed up Orwell's Anglo-American status for at least a few weeks in early 1984: "Orwell Becomes A Household Word."⁵

## IV

Although these chapters are first a study of one writer's history of repute, the protean shape and broad scope of Orwell's reputation makes him an especially worthwhile case for insight into the general processes involved in making literary reputations. For Orwell poses unusual, and valuable, difficulties by virtue of the complex, highly personal response to him by readers; and he offers unusual, if complicated, opportunities by his politicized reception and the diversity of his audiences. The rare and auspicious fact is that Orwell has been both an extraordinarily popular serious writer and a critically acclaimed one. A study of his reputation thus promises to illumine not only the cultural significance of the most widely read serious writer and the most celebrated English political writer of our century. It also lends itself to careful speculation about the social processes governing the personal response to and the public impact of the writer in the modern age. Perhaps through Orwell we can begin to understand, in Malcolm Muggeridge's phrase about his friend, "how the legend of a human being is created"⁶—how history makes figures and how biography and society interrelate.

*The Politics of*
*Literary Reputation*

*Not what the Saint is but what he*
*represents in the eyes of the non-sanctified*
*gives him his world-historical importance.*
            *Nietzsche*
            Human, All Too Human


*. . . no decent person cares tuppence for the*
*opinion of posterity.*
            *Orwell, "As I Please"*

# Introduction

## Appraising Famous Men:
## Mediating Biography and Society

I

Literary reputations get made, but how? How does a writer become, in Lionel Trilling's famous characterization of Orwell, "a figure in our lives"?[1]

Much has been written about Orwell as a man and as a writer, and much also about the general relation of the contemporary writer to his culture. Most commentaries on Orwell, however, are biographical discussions or literary criticism not directed to his cultural significance; and most discussions of "the writer in society" are not so much the outgrowth of specialized individual studies as an attempted substitute for them. The need is to see how the complex relations between writers and cultures work themselves out in an individual life and legacy. The nature and development of Orwell's public reputation are first his own special case, for Orwell's career constitutes one man's response to a particular historical situation. Yet because of his polarized reputation among intellectuals and extensive media exposure, Orwell also furnishes perhaps the best opportunity among modern authors for exploring how patterns of interpersonal and institutional relations transform a writer into a literary figure.

What do we mean when we call a writer a "literary figure"? How in fact does a "literary" reputation differ from other sorts of reputation? How does a writer achieve not just a standing in literary circles but a public reputation? How does response to a writer's work and personality interact with cultural and political history to shape his reputation? What bearing do the social-institutional affiliations of audiences have upon the forma-

3

tion of literary reputation? And how in turn do their responses to a writer re-form them as readers and reshape history itself? The arrival and enactment of Orwell's fated year made such questions about him not only timely but collectively self-revealing. One index to a culture is the figures it exalts.

Literary critics and sociologists have scarcely touched upon these questions. No study has directly addressed the processes by which writers' images and identities are formed and literary reputations are gained, lost, consolidated, revised, and deformed—important issues located in what Orwell called, during the early years of the Cold War in postwar Britain, "that painful and . . . almost insoluble problem, the relation of literature to society."[2] Although Marxist literary criticism, literary sociology, and German reception aesthetics have all explored this relation from various vantage points,[3] literary critics have frequently regarded the institutional processes of "reputation-formation" and "canon-formation" as extraneous to artistic production and critical acclaim. Indeed literary criticism and literary sociology have traditionally behaved like estranged bedfellows. Invariably segregated as "intrinsic" and "extrinsic" approaches to literature, each has kept its back to the other. Empirical sociology and Marxist theory have too often tended to dissolve the experience of art into statistics or social structures, and to defer to criticism for literary interpretation; criticism has tended to regard interpretation as its private turf and to acquiesce to sociology on "external" matters of literary production and reception.

"[R]eal criticism," pronounced Northrop Frye in his *Anatomy of Criticism* (1957), had nothing to do with "all the literary chit-chat which makes the reputations of poets boom and crash in an imaginary stock-exchange." Criticism was as yet still "a primitive science," said Frye, whose "materials, the masterpieces of literature," could only yield their natural fruits and ground a "systematic" field of study ("criticism") if reputation and the history of taste ("where there are no facts, and where all truths have been split . . . into half-truths") were "snip[ped] off and throw[n] . . . away."[4] How the nascent science's "materials," its "masterpieces," gained their status, whether there might not be "half-truths" in the history of reputations of relevance to critics, and how one could even speak about the comparative maturities of disciplines without some understanding of their institutional histories: these questions did not detain Frye.

"A book never *is* a masterpiece," wrote the elder Goncourt. "It *becomes* one."[5] It is a widely believed, though still little-examined, generalization that "producers," "distributors," and "consumers" in the "literary industry"— publishers, censors, agents, book clubs, libraries, reviewers, academic critics, the mass media—partly determine a book and writer's success with the public.[6] Not only the quality or "genius" of a writer's work earns him and it a literary reputation, but also an institutional network of production, distribution, and reception which circulates and values his achievement. What needs systematic study is how books and authors emerge through this web of relations and through institutional history, what roles specific audiences play in

the formation of popular images, and how critical and popular influences interact to transform critical acclaim into public reputation.

This study addresses some elementary patterns of interaction in this intricate process as it concentrates upon literary reception. The aim is to make sense of the reputation of a single controversial and significant literary figure, and in turn to shed some light on the reputation process generally. Reputations are perceived and disseminated in and through images, as Chapter Two will argue, and since the project reconstructs not the story of a man's life but the vicissitudes of his reputation, it pursues not the fates of historical individuals but of historical images. It is a tour of a portrait gallery. Our focus widens and narrows—we step up and step back—as we scrutinize each picture, and move on from one to the next.

Rather than a straightforward chronology of Orwell's history of repute, therefore, I have approached his reputation by the more painstaking route of the dominant historical images in which various readers and groups have cast him, insofar as the available record of his historical reception has permitted. Critics and the media have indeed treated Orwell via a number of sharply defined images as "essences" characterizing him and his work. Based on these repeated characterizations, I have reconstructed the commentary (or "imagery") on Orwell into four metaphors as public "faces," limiting the number as the reception evidence suggested and for heuristic purposes and reasons of economy. Each of these faces must be examined, insofar as possible, against Orwell's own view of what he was doing, or trying to do. Like all of us, Orwell presented in his personal life and in his work different yet not incommensurable views of himself to different people at different times. Yet criticism, unlike hagiography, must not avoid the most insistent questions: To what degree is a writer responsible for the uses to which his name and work have been put? And which portraits of him are "forgeries"?

Friends have waylaid me repeatedly with these questions, and in the course of these pages I have tried to respond to the pertinent issues, but the questions themselves are too baldly put. Orwell is arguably partly "responsible" for or complicitous in some of the abuses of his work, but the life and writings of every writer condition the course of his reputation. No political writer can avoid ideological distortion, let alone posthumous confiscation of his name, for no one can prevent observers from seizing on perceived affinities between his work and that of groups whom he opposed, from linking his position on one issue with a range of other allegedly related issues, or from ignoring or disregarding his stated intentions and/or the original context in which he wrote. Likewise, metaphors or images or "portraits" are neither "true" nor "false"; only the factual claims made via them possess or lack validity. Portraits are good or poor likenesses; no image of Orwell in this study captures all of him. We should speak of "partial" portraits, rather than "authentic" ones and "forgeries": the man was the original, not some prose description. This is not to say that we cannot reject illegitimate claims to a legacy. Or that we cannot distinguish between "por-

traits" and "caricatures." Every portrait selects and emphasizes, but caricatures are at wide variance with the available biographical and critical evidence, clearly less inclusive, coherent, fair-minded, and convincing. Finally,
however, though these distinctions are important for conceptual clarification, the most that one can do in drawing them in the particular case is to
make one's own interpretations clear, to stay close to the author's writings,
to weigh the (often conflicting) testimony about his life, to appreciate the
context in which he wrote and was received—and thereby expose the
grosser attempts to claim his mantle, for whatever camp. Many of the unfortunate misconceptions about Orwell have arisen because his declared political positions altered somewhat during World War II and after, and because
his acquaintances have differed in their reports of his political sympathies.

Orwell is one of the few literary men who stands with modern thinkers of
the stature of Hegel, Marx, Nietzsche, Freud, Bergson, and Sorel as writers
whose work has undergone distortion by disciples and colleagues. Notably,
he is the only imaginative writer—and the only English-language writer—in
this group. Since most of Orwell's work was fiction and journalism, he has
been in certain respects even more susceptible to misinterpretation and misuse than these other figures. His last two works are variously taken for direct
political statements or prophecies or satires, his fictional characters are read
as autobiographical mouthpieces, his nonfiction is invoked where expedient
to buttress both practices, and his "failure" to provide any comprehensive
*summa* of his politics is exploited as a rationale for "extending" his ideas in
various partisan directions. Whereas these other thinkers are read only by an
intellectual minority, with their work often perceived as not easily accessible,
argument about Orwell's writings has frequently entered the conversation of
the wider public, as the letter columns of Anglo-American newspapers from
the mid-1950s and early 1980s attest. In a September 1983 Harris Poll an
astounding 27 percent of Americans claimed (perhaps doubtfully) to have
read *Nineteen Eighty-Four*—well before the novel began to sell more than
50,000 copies per day in early 1984 and became a subject of New Year
television specials and advertising promotions.[7]

One recalls the comment of a Whitehall official in a wartime dossier on
Orwell: "As to use, we already know by personal acquaintance, making use of
him is difficult."[8] Political and commercial interests have found it less difficult
since the publication of *Nineteen Eighty-Four* and Orwell's death. Indeed the
"Orwell phenomenon" and the contested legacy of 'St. George' are so intertwined with the complexities of postwar Anglo-American ideological and
cultural politics that an intellectuals' holy war has periodically flared as to
which groups possess the right to claim his rich bequest. Numerous American and European academic conferences on Orwell during 1984 featured old
friends, biographers, and academic "experts," many of whom were deferred
to as vicars of Orwell and treated as his voices from beyond the grave—which
of course only served to increase the cacophony and the number of competing claims. On a much larger scale, the bitter volleying of Orwell's name and
catchwords between the West and the Communist bloc constitutes an extra-

ordinary instance of what political scientists have recently come to call "word politics."[9]

Thus the politics of Orwell's reputation represents far more than a battle for the ghost of 'St. George' himself. An extended study of his heritage offers several revealing perspectives on the main political and cultural developments of the postwar West. *George Orwell: An Afterlife* would in many ways be an even more complicated and rewarding book than Bernard Crick's *George Orwell: A Life*. The present study consists of a variety of sharply focused scenes from that afterlife, rendering a world-historical, primarily posthumous Orwell.

## II

A study in the historiography of reputation, or what we might call "reputation-history," proposes to act as a bridge connecting cultural history, literary biography, and literary and historical sociology. It is an effort to relocate literary history within intellectual and social history. I am less concerned here with what the literary critics usually examine, those subtleties of the writer's art so often lost on the non-specialist and the non-reader, and more concerned with what critics pay little heed to but wider audiences mainly experience, the public images of writers transmitted through their work and through re-presentations of their work and personalities by critics and the mass media. In many respects the project is similar to Orwell's own "semi-sociological literary criticism,"[10] and it is the sort of undertaking which I believe that Orwell himself would have endorsed and which his essay "Charles Dickens" exemplified in its attention to Dickens' social origins and politicized reception. Orwell often wondered how and why reputations changed, and he answered in "Inside the Whale," as I have done in this study, that first and foremost "one has to take account of the *external* conditions that make certain writers popular at certain times." Indeed his essays bear out the judgment of John Atkins, Orwell's friend and *Tribune* colleague, that he was "not really a literary critic" at all but a "literary sociologist": "All his best criticism was sociological."[11]

Insofar as an historiography of literary reputation seeks to bridge biography and society, it poses what Sartre saw as "the problem of mediations," or phrased more challengingly, what C. Wright Mills called "the task and promise" of "the sociological imagination": "to understand the intersections of biography and history within society," "to shift from one perspective to another [and] thereby to know the social and historical meaning of the individual in society and in the period in which he has his quality and his being."[12]

The critical point with Orwell, as with so many other historical figures, however, is that his "period" is at least as much his posthumous history as it was his living one. Orwell continues to exert influence because what he said to his age still somehow speaks to our own, and because the force of his example and the symbolic power of his work upon his contemporaries

somehow grip us too. Thus the posthumous history needs close examination not only for itself but to better understand how general history gets concretely realized in personal histories and how living and posthumous reputations interrelate. Bernard Crick drew back from subtitling his biography of Orwell a "Life and Times" on the sound theoretical principle that "such a formula, unless a man has a great effect on events, is mainly padding." Nor could Crick comfortably write a "Life and Works," he said, because he saw his task not as "literary criticism" but as a chronicle of Orwell the man and writer. Crick settled finally, and simply, for "A Life."[13]

Yet the fact is that since his death at mid-century, Orwell has indeed had a major impact on events, attributable not just to the books he wrote but to the sort of life he led, or which people think he led. Today only the books remain. But for all the capacity of the writer's clear voice to evoke a sense of the man within the work, the books alone cannot fully account for his cultural influence or inspirational power. To understand Orwell's impact one must instead look back and forth between the life and books and times. How the life and works were influenced by the times, and in turn have influenced the times—both Orwell's and ours—is the dynamic, reciprocal process which repeatedly requires examination in his case. It is the process of a man making and remaking himself and thereby remaking his world and ours; of a writer's reception by, impact upon, and re-formation of and through his culture.

These processes return us by a different route to intrinsic and extrinsic considerations, and to the problem of mediations. With every person, and Orwell was no exception, there is an "inside" and "outside" view: how he saw himself and how the world has seen him. This distinction between inside and outside views, and the practice of shuttling between them, is fundamental to social psychology and the sociology of symbolic interaction, resonant with Mills's description of the personal "troubles" of milieu and the public "issues" of social structure. "Troubles" have to do with the individual's self, arising with him "as a biographical entity"—within his character and within the range of his immediate relations with others. "Issues" have to do with institutions and their interpenetration, transcending the individual's local environments and pertaining to a society's organization and history. Mediating this rich field of relations between the self and social structure is the social group, that pivotal region in which the formation of self-images and public images is endlessly renegotiated and transformed. Mills himself believed strongly that "the problems of history-making" necessitated an understanding of group relations, of both the institutional dimensions of personal troubles and the human meaning of public issues.[14] Orwell the literary sociologist certainly would have agreed. In choosing to study a writer's history of reputation, we have the advantage (not without its interpretive difficulties) of having his self-estimations at different times preserved in his own words, rather than needing to judge him exclusively by the reports or memories of others. As we examine the Orwell portraiture, we will pay particularly close attention in certain sections to Orwell's self-images and to the reference group as a unit of

study, seeing how the group relations and social-institutional affiliations of Orwell and his audiences have conditioned their images of him.

Literary transfiguration is, then, a process with a large institutional component. Occasionally the process bears some marks of a consciously coordinated effort among several of the industry's spheres to "manufacture a reputation"—i.e., among interested parties in publishing, book reviewing, academic criticism, literary and critical movements, and the mass media. But such orchestrations are probably far less frequent than the conspiracy-minded would have us believe.[15] All of these agents of influence have interacted (though in my judgment not colluded) to build Orwell's critical reputation into a wide public one. The estimates and characterizations of early book reviewers and literary critics have substantially determined the distinctive shape of his reputation; the mass media's assimilation of his works has been mainly responsible for its size. Because of their historical importance and general availability, materials connected with these three agents of influence (reviewers, critics, mass media) receive special attention in this study. I have found autobiographies, biographies, and memoirs invaluable for interpreting the larger social-institutional contexts of observers' responses to Orwell. Indeed my reconstruction of the formation of Orwell's reputation could not have proceeded without these materials. Newspaper columns, general circulation periodical articles, letters to the editor, and transcripts of radio and television broadcasts have enabled a few forays into Orwell's reputation at the widest spheres of public response. Such "marginal" reception materials puncture the fiction of the homogeneity of the reading "public," that easily held academic illusion of a single, intellectual audience.[16] They also give empirical support to the common-sense view—whose implications have gone largely unaddressed in reception aesthetics and literary sociology—that intellectual audiences are themselves multiple and in any case are by no means the exclusive receivers of "public" writers like Orwell.

### III

In his essay on Henry Miller, Orwell remarks on "one of those revealing passages in which a writer tells you a great deal about himself while talking about somebody else."[17] Just as some of Orwell's critical statements on Dickens, Swift, Tolstoy, and Kipling tell us more about him than about them, observers' comments on Orwell not infrequently amount less to literary criticism than to self- and group-analysis. Such "revealing passages" written by Orwell are obviously of special interest; but so too are such passages in the commentary of Orwell's observers. For when many observers tell us, however knowingly or unawares, as much about themselves as about their ostensible subject, it suggests a great deal about how readers identify with authors as intellectual models and rivals.

The sense of passionate identification expressed toward Orwell by some observers and the variety of inspirational images in which they have cast him sometimes make him appear almost like Joseph Campbell's "hero with

a thousand faces." "Kidnaping Our Hero" is in fact a subtitle of one of Irving Howe's discussions of Orwell's controversial postwar legacy. Indeed the typically unscholarly question of heroes and hero worship hovers at the border of any study of the making of a literary figure. "The need for heroism is not easy to admit," wrote Ernest Becker in *The Denial of Death.* "To be conscious of what one is doing to earn his feeling of heroism is the main self-analytic problem of life." Each of the historical faces which I have reconstructed from the Orwell commentary is a characteristic image of the Hero—as Rebel, Common Man, Prophet, and Saint. Despite the diverse judgments of observers on Orwell, there is seldom far removed from their remarks about him the search for, appeal of, or anxiety toward the heroic— manifested with their preoccupation with Orwell the man, or with the man in the writings.[18]

Such a focus upon a writer as a heroic character in his society was frequent, though often wholly uncritical, in nineteenth-century biography, and it is central to the philosophizing of Carlyle, Emerson, Nietzsche, and others on "great men." Contemporary biographers, on the other hand, influenced by the psychohistorian's practice of locating extraordinary adult achievement in childhood conflicts and by the social historian's emphasis on ordinary lives and on socioeconomic forces as historical determinants, often shrink great men and women. The crucial task in writing biography and history is to address the institutional conditions which bear on the making of reputations while retaining the generosity of spirit to recognize the he- roic in its many guises. For Becker, societies are not merely systems of symbolic interaction and role-typing but "cultural hero systems." They are theatres for the heroic which give people feelings of specialness and useful- ness by carving out "roles for performance of various degrees of heroism." People play their roles on different stage levels, from the "high" heroism of an Orwell to the "low" heroism of a Wigan coal miner.[19]

Perhaps the frequent characterizations of Orwell as an intellectual "con- science" and "voice" by so many of his admirers constitute a baring of one dimension of our modern culture's hero system: the making and recogni- tion of the intellectual hero. Sometimes the acknowledgments by other writers of Orwell's "presence" in their lives are startlingly open and unre- strained. Characterizations of Orwell by Anglo-American intellectuals of the Left and Right—to Lionel Trilling the figure of "the man who tells the truth," to Irving Howe an "intellectual hero," to T.R. Fyvel a "literary hero," to Angus Wilson "one of my great heroes," to John Atkins a "social saint," to Stephen Spender "an example of 'the lived truth', " to George Woodcock a "conscience," to Alfred Kazin "a hero whom I shall always love," to Joseph Epstein and Malcolm Muggeridge a "hero of our time," to Richard Rees a "spiritual hero," to John Wain a "moral hero"—indicate that for many intellectuals, regardless of their politics or even generation, Orwell has stood as nothing less than an heroic model and ethical guide.[20] Such a relationship between a writer and his culture demands explanation of what various group and cultural needs have so powerfully and frequently drawn

observers to him. It is not enough to say that a person is an heroic figure because other people have named him as such: the task is to see both *why* they so named him and what specific *elements* in his life and work apparently fulfilled their needs and aspirations. Of course, like all figures, "George Orwell" has been a mutable, pulsating "figure in our lives"—or in some people's lives. He is nothing like the unchanging wax figure now installed at Madame Tussaud's in London, but rather a fluid, if more or less continuous, presence in recent Anglo-American cultural life and a periodically prominent habitation and name in our culture.

## IV

The value of the insights derived from studying Orwell's reputation will possess general relevance insofar as Orwell's widely recognized importance as a modern literary figure suggests questions much larger than his own case. "[G]et to really know something about yourself—and thru yourself the world," Henry Miller told Orwell in 1938. "Everyone is micro- and macrocosm both, don't forget that. . . ."[21] Miller's posture of political detachment aside, the substance of this advice is worth our consideration in approaching a figure of Orwell's dimensions and significance. For it is paradoxically true that the general is sometimes best approached by way of the particular. A writer can be peculiarly representative of his age or craft by the very fact of his distinctiveness; Orwell's single history remarkably touches, often in the capacity of the writer as participant-witness, practically all the pressing issues facing his generation—and ours: poverty, imperialism, war, revolution, socialism, mass culture, totalitarianism. "His history," declared the narrator of one Orwell TV special in 1984, "is the history of the twentieth century." Indeed, from the standpoint of the 1980s, Orwell appears very much like a Sartrean "singular universal," an individual through whom the "universal" spirit of an age finds expression and from whose "singular" experiences the character of the age is forged. Or as one critic dubbed him in 1984: "The Political Secretary of the Zeitgeist."[22]

In confronting the problem of mediations—in framing the task of getting to know something about a self and a reputation, and through it something about a society and an age—one could boil down the questions on Orwell already posed in this introduction to four key ones worthy of extended exploration:

- What sort of "reputation-history" does Orwell possess?
- How should a writer with this particular history of reputation be approached?
- Why has this writer, George Orwell, been the occasion for such wide-ranging symbolic transformation?
- In what images have observers cast him?

Part One furnishes a preliminary answer to these questions and a critical perspective useful for investigating them further. Chapter One offers

the long view to the first question, including a capsule history of Orwell's reputation. Chapter Two addresses questions two through four, examining reputation as a literary issue, offering a framework for discussing it, and introducing the Orwell gallery. Part Two tours each room portrait by portrait, slowly encircling each face and inspecting each from shifting angles of vision. We will be assaying the efficacy and limitations of the critical concepts broached in Chapter Two as we probe the features and blemishes of the Orwell physiognomy.

Thus we are exploring the reputation process in a single instance, looking for ways of conceptualizing some of its general implications and identifying its distinctive features, and seeking to return to the instance with some helpful theoretical instruments. The first tasks are to clarify the dimensions of and the issues bearing on Orwell's reputation, and thereby provide a background from which larger questions about the making of reputation will emerge. Our consequent starting point is a brief and concrete discussion of Orwell's history of reputation and ambiguous legacy.

*Part One*

# Anatomy of Reputation

*... later on* [he may] *attain a brilliant reputation. And if
it should come only after he is no more, well!...
He may console himself by thinking of the saints, who are
canonized only after they are dead.*
                    Schopenhauer,
                        *"On Reputation,"* The Art of Literature


*No doubt alcohol, tobacco and so forth are things
that a saint must avoid, but sainthood is also a thing that
human beings must avoid.*
                        Orwell, *"Reflections on Gandhi"*

Swaddling 'St. George' ushers in the New Year: the countdown to 1984
was finally over.

# ONE

# *Orwell into the Nineties*

## 1. Reputation, Legacy, Historiography

I

"Saints should be judged guilty until they are proved innocent," Orwell said of Gandhi,[1] and probably no one would have been more surprised (and disquieted) than Orwell himself at critics' posthumous discovery and spontaneous proclamation of his heroic sanctity. He was eulogized majestically by V.S. Pritchett as a "saint" and "the conscience of his generation";[2] his beatification as a writer followed in upward revaluations of his work a few months later by leading British and American intellectuals;[3] and his canonization in school curricula and in the popular press during the 1950s was conducted by acclamation rather than audit. Periodic impieties from the far Left about a "reactionary petit-bourgeois" Orwell and from psychoanalytic critics about a "sadomasochistic" Orwell merely reinforced the image established among many liberal and conservative intellectuals of a lonely, embattled hero persecuted for having spoken the truth.[4] Even occasional revelations about Orwell's shortcomings in private life have only served to reaffirm for his admirers his genuine and fallible humanity.[5] Many reviewers have depicted him simply as a man among saints. Certainly more than one Orwell-watcher has assumed 'St. George' innocent until proven guilty—and skipped trial proceedings altogether.* Such uncritical hagiography, as will soon be-

---

*As one worshipful reviewer of *Such, Such Were the Joys* put it in 1953: "In this case at least I do not even have to read the book, I like it in advance. One should not prejudge—with the exception of George Orwell!"[6]

15

come apparent, is only one manifestation of a recurring contrast between images of the man and images of his work.

Still, it would be no exaggeration to say that Orwell merits his own fond benediction to Kipling as "the most popular English writer of our time."[7] *Animal Farm* and *Nineteen Eighty-Four* have sold almost 40 million copies in sixty-odd languages, more than any other pair of books by a serious *or popular* postwar author. One sign and secret of Orwell's appeal for new generations of readers may lie in the widespread, pleasurable association of his name with our earliest reading experiences, and in the feeling that he speaks directly to every stage of our reading lives. Schoolchildren find *Animal Farm* a beguiling fantasy, and then learn to delight in the neatness of its allegory. Many of the fable's mature readers vividly recall having burst through it in a single sitting as youngsters, and sometimes also remember seeing the animated cartoon version, with its happy ending. High school students read *Nineteen Eighty-Four*, often identifying with rebellious Winston and Julia, and afterwards spotting adult Newspeak and doublethink everywhere. College students in introductory composition classes are reminded by their instructors that "Good prose is like a windowpane" and "What is above all needed is to let the meaning choose the word," and then given assignments to model their themes on "Shooting an Elephant," "Politics and the English Language," or other of Orwell's frequently anthologized autobiographical and expository essays. More advanced students of history, politics, and literature not only read these works but also the social documentaries, the literary criticism, and the fiction in order to understand better the nature of poverty, imperialism, war, and totalitarianism; the intellectual and cultural climate of the British 1930s and '40s; and the interrelations among politics, art, and language. And sometimes just for the pure pleasure of the bracing prose.

Probably no other modern English-language writer's work has been so woven into the texture of the popular imagination. Teenagers have tuned out and floated off on the waves of rock star David Bowie's apocalyptic hits, "Nineteen Eighty-Four" and "Big Brother." Concerned citizens, alarmed about reports of massive CIA-FBI-KGB computer files and worldwide undercover spying operations, have warned that the spectre of Oceania is not just far-fetched science fiction.[8] The words *vaporized, thoughtcrime*, and *Hate Week* suddenly come to life for many of us when televised nightmares like *Holocaust* enter our living rooms. Indeed, as he once said of Kipling's rhetorical impact upon the pre- World War I era, Orwell today may also stand as "the only English writer of our time who has added phrases to the language."[9] Bureaucrats traffic in Newspeak, politicians orate in doublespeak, government agents eavesdrop like Thought Police—even "Some are more equal than others" has become a knowing put-down for hypocrisy and a discrimination story headline, making the phrase sometimes sound more native than the Jefferson original. Perhaps not a few youngsters have even wondered, when watching commercials for the nationwide Big Brothers organization for fatherless boys, what "Big Brother Is Watching You" really meant.

So thoroughly have the catchwords and mood of Orwell's dystopia permeated our collective consciousness that "1984" immediately evokes—or did until the long-awaited arrival of the year—numerous fearful associations. The date is part of Western folklore. Many people don't know it is a book title; still more have no idea of the name of the book's author. No matter: the numeral became, as it were, a man-made Friday the 13th. The title of a 1983 Smithsonian Institute panel made the point: "1984 as a Universal Metaphor."[10] Even people who have never read the book will admit to having paused momentarily in vague anxiety at the mere mention of that numerical swastika of the totalitarian age. Now that we have lived through the year (and recorded it countless times on our letters, checks, and computer terminals), the figure haunts us no longer; instead it may seem to most of us no more than four ordinary numbers, a historical relic, or a hackneyed joke. And yet even our new nonchalance or jadedness toward "1984" testifies in a way to the numeral's wide currency: surely it is the only number that has ever become a cliché.

In addition to the general impact of Orwell's last two books, there are the documentaries and essays, with their appeal of Orwell's accessible, gripping prose style and his apparent rootedness in the culture of ordinary people's lives. Even Orwell's casual journalism often gives the impression of freshness, although some of it is now almost a half-century old. Orwell subtitled his first American essay collection "Studies in Popular Culture,"[11] and his anthropological pieces on boys' weekly newspapers, detective stories, and penny postcards in some ways mark him as the grandfather of the field. One is hard-pressed to think of another English writer who has managed to survive and bridge the ever growing chasm between high and mass culture, his work being not only assigned in the universities but widely read by the general public.

Others have paved the trails Orwell blazed. The present-day orientation of academic fields studying issues in communication, sociology, and journalism is partly connected with the history of Orwell's example and influence. Much of his fiction and journalism carefully explores the subtle interconnections between linguistic and political manipulation, and has spawned English followers like Henry Fairlie and Kenneth Hudson. One critic has maintained that even Orwell's realistic fiction and documentaries constitute a searching investigation of the failures of language to promote interpersonal intimacy and social harmony.[12] Best-selling anti-jargon vigilantes like Edwin Newman (*Strictly Speaking, A Civil Tongue*) and William Safire (*New Language of Politics, What's the Good Word?*) are directly descended from (though far less serious than) Orwell. Studies in political rhetoric on the government jargon used during the Vietnam War and Watergate Affair have unearthed a mountain of euphemism and doublespeak that makes them seem like research projects documenting our regress toward Newspeak. Sociology textbooks have excerpted chapters of Orwell's novels and documentaries, and Dwight Macdonald called Orwell's documentary writing "the best sociological reporting I know."[13] Orwell's practices of "living

his research," presenting sociological types like the "tramp-monster" and miner, and offering detailed subjective descriptions of his situations and subjects bear clear affinities with the best-written early fieldwork of the Chicago School of interpretive sociology.[14] More recognizably, Orwell's energetic prose, his unusual openness about how he may be influencing his own reporting, and his characteristic preference for describing society "from below" by way of lower-class and deviant life mark him as a forerunner of the New Journalism of Tom Wolfe and Jack Newfield.[15] It is doubtful that any other recent English literary man has served as the subject or springboard for academic studies in such wide-ranging fields as political thought, journalism and media studies, rhetoric and semantics, futurology, popular culture, and even religious studies.[16]

## II

Not all of these legacies, however, have been as widely acknowledged as they might, nor are those which *are* claimed necessarily the ones which Orwell actually left. Orwell's predicament four decades after his death is not unlike what he called Kipling's "peculiar position of having been a byword for fifty years." "Before one can speak about Kipling," wrote Orwell in a prophetically self-reflexive moment, "one has to clear away a legend that has been created by . . . sets of people who have not read his works." Moreover, as he said of Stendhal, the great majority of those who *have* read his books know him for only two famous ones, a circumstance that has added half-truth to ignorance and turned Orwell legend into chimera.[17]

All writers are selectively read and esteemed, of course, according to a plethora of sociohistorical variables. But the point with Orwell is that the popularity of *Animal Farm* and *Nineteen Eighty-Four* has both made his name familiar across a broad spectrum of the international reading public and has helped generate widely variable popular and critical attitudes toward him. "Orwell" and his coinages are recognizable on a worldwide scale. But most people know nothing about Orwell's life: the man has been eclipsed by the power and notoriety of his masterworks. Among intellectual readers, similar discrepancies prevail. Intellectuals of the Left (Bernard Crick, Irving Howe) and Right (Norman Podhoretz) have judged him the best political writer of the century. Yet some radicals (John Casey) and more literary-minded intellectuals (T.A. Birrell) have regarded him as a ("mere") journalist.[18]

The variations in Orwell's reputation in the educational community are perhaps most striking. Orwell's canonization in English curricula was immediate, but it has also been eclectic. *Animal Farm* is a high school staple. (A former college chairman of the Advanced Placement Program could write in the 1970s, with noticeable chagrin, that Orwell's beast fable was the only book previously read by every student of the eighty-five in his freshman literature class.[19]) Orwell's essays are likewise standard requirements in introductory university composition classes. Yet these writings are rarely encountered in more advanced courses. Nor, apart from the

special attention to Orwell's *oeuvre* in 1984, are any of his other works usually taught in the academy. Nor are there any Orwell journals or literary societies.[20] (Admittedly, one can hardly imagine anything he would have more disliked.) And yet, except possibly for Lawrence, it is likely that Orwell has exerted deeper influence on young Anglo-American writers than any other English writer of the last half-century. Several postwar British writers more widely taught in university literature courses, such as the so-called Angry Young Men and Movement writers (Kingsley Amis, John Wain, John Osborne, Robert Conquest), acknowledge their indebtedness for style and subject matter to Orwell's early fiction and essays. But he made a first appearance in *The Norton Anthology of English Literature* only after some of them (fourth edition, 1980).

Statements from those inside and outside the academy on Orwell's standing as a "canonized" author highlight these oddities in reputation. One coordinator of an American academic conference on Orwell's work in 1984 told me that, of more than a dozen academic symposia she had organized in the previous three years, no figure or issue had attracted so many international participants as the Orwell symposium. Such testimony stands in apparent opposition to the verdict of several U.S. English professors in a 1983 interview. They agreed that Orwell was a "journalist" and "didactic writer" who "failed to live up to top literary standards," with *Nineteen Eighty-Four* in particular "lacking in literary sophistication."[21] Readily conceding Orwell's exclusion from the modern British novel's "great tradition," even so ardent an Orwell admirer as Richard Rovere reflected these same assumptions and the prevailing consensus on Orwell's fiction ("of the second rank") in his introduction to *The Orwell Reader* (1956).[22] Others have dismissed Orwell's fiction as being not even third-rate, with his documentaries qualifying him as a lesser Mayhew.[23] I have heard *Animal Farm* and *Nineteen Eighty-Four* patronized as "high school reading." (Even though *Nineteen Eighty-Four* has been one of the books most frequently banned from U.S. secondary schools.[24]) And since a fable and a dystopia do not fit easily into standard fiction categories, the result is that Orwell the fiction writer is reduced to a "Thirties writer"—his work falling, most inconveniently for reading lists in college literature courses, between the end of the modernist movement and the return to more traditional, realistic fiction in the 1950s.

Some readers, having encountered *Animal Farm* or *Nineteen Eighty-Four* and an Orwell essay or two as teenagers, vaguely think of "Orwell" and his "old-fashioned plain style" as adolescent fare. Others faintly remember him and his work as something from the dim past. (As one journalist wrote, mockingly, of this feeling in early 1983: "Oh yeah, there's that book I read in high school. It's that 'Big Brother thing'—George . . . what's his name . . . wrote it."[25]) To many Britons and most Americans he is a sort of icon. Even after (or because of) the publicizing of *Nineteen Eighty-Four* during the title year, they know relatively little about the real life of George Orwell, the ephemera of the year and the hype behind the popular biographical treatments ("Do *you* know who George Orwell is?" asked a *People* magazine

cover) having effectively obscured the few substantive press discussions and radio-TV documentaries on Orwell.[26] But, given the newspaper headlines, many people know the sinister meaning of "Orwellian" and feel a twinge of discomfort at the mention of the adjective's reference, assuming *l'adjectif c'est l'homme*. Readers of *Animal Farm* and *Nineteen Eighty-Four* who are slightly acquainted with the myth of Orwell's "saintly" life often perceive the breach between the man's character and the writer's vision as near-absolute. As we will soon see in detail, their Orwell is a schizoid figure, the "honest, decent man who wrote the abject, ruthless books."

All this raises the issue of Orwell's relation to mass culture and his place in the English literary canon. These subjects can, however, wait; thus far we have merely indicated the boundaries and terrain of a writer's reputation. Topography now equips us for geology. The incongruities in Orwell's reputation from one region to the next should refocus our attention on two partially submerged issues: the heterogeneity of Orwell's audiences and the problematic relation between the man and the works. The implications for canon-formation and of the discrepancies in Orwell's reputation among different spheres of reception are discussed in Chapter Two, an instance of what I term "the problem of reputation." Here we need note only that differences from one sphere of reception to another are characteristic of all authors' reputations; my present aim is to mark, not to decry or contest, the peculiar "tri-furcation" in Orwell's reputation among popular, intellectual, and academic spheres of reception, including many notable variations in all three. Orwell's reputation turns out to be of special interest precisely because its sharp discontinuities illustrate so graphically the heterogeneous receptions of all writers.

The multiformity in Orwell's reputation has arisen at least partly because his readership, unlike most, spans the continuing, probably widening, split among "highbrow," "middlebrow," and "lowbrow" audiences. Various of Orwell's works are read primarily in the critical community, still living in the shadow of the modernist revolution and its formalist assumptions; *Animal Farm, Nineteen Eighty-Four,* and (to a lesser extent) the documentaries and essays are read by the literary-minded public, usually favoring non-experimental, more accessible writings; and Orwell's coinages, often along with information about his last two books and his life, have reached the general public either in the press or through the broadcast media.

The impression of a "schism" between "the man" and "the works"— usually portrayed as corresponding to the supposed rift between "Eric Blair" and "George Orwell"—has further contributed to his highly ramified reputation. Information about "Orwell" often fails to travel far beyond intellectual circles; as a result, the public is left to judge Orwell primarily by *Nineteen Eighty-Four* and infer the man from it. This is not to say, however, that there is anything like a consensus among intellectuals and academics as to the relation of the man to the works. Just the reverse. The sense of a disjunction between the man and his writings is reflected in the long-standing argument among critics as to which of the two is the more signifi-

cant accomplishment. Literary and biographical critics have been at pains
for years to show that Orwell was more important for what he wrote than
for how he lived. "The achievement is more important than the man,"
biographer Bernard Crick has insisted. The compulsion to argue the point
testifies in itself, however, to the power of Orwell's personal example. Old
Orwell acquaintances have usually argued exactly the reverse of Crick, supporting their views with some "revealing" personal anecdote or conversation "with Eric," implying that only they are really qualified to decide the
man-versus-writer issue. "The greatest thing about Orwell was Orwell,"
concluded poet-friend Paul Potts. "He was ultimately better than anything
he wrote. . . . In this man's presence there have been kings who would have
looked parvenus." Adding still further to the confusion is testimony from
other Orwell friends like Jacintha Buddicom that *Animal Farm* and the
nonfiction "exactly" capture the man, indeed that, in George Woodcock's
judgment, Orwell's "crystalline prose" exemplifies that "the style is the
man."[27]

The mass media have redoubled and recast the confusion by trumpeting
all these judgments and simultaneously taking the Orwell of *Nineteen Eighty-
Four* for the whole literary personality, thus transmitting to the public a
grotesque twin profile: the 'St. George' caricature of the nonfiction and
acquaintances' testimonies crouches in the shadow of The Prophet of *Nineteen Eighty-Four*. In the 1950s and early '60s, magazine reviewers paid tribute in the literary pages to Orwell as Lionel Trilling's "virtuous man" even
as reporters writing for the political pages bandied "1984" in Cold War
arguments and casually linked "Big Brother" to Orwell's character. These
opposing practices further contributed to the sense of a "split" between
Orwell's life and work. Meanwhile, just as friends of Orwell like Woodcock
sometimes implied that the man and works were a seamless, transparent
unity, hostile Left critics like Isaac Deutscher and James Walsh asserted the
same identity to merge the man and *Nineteen Eighty-Four* into a bogeyman
figure. Woodcock's pure, clean stylist was Walsh's "hysterical, shrieking"
slogan-monger and anti-socialist duckspeaker.[28] ("The style is the unperson"?) 'St. George' as Defender of the King's English was thus coming to be
viewed by admirers as a paladin of good prose and by enemies as a pillar of
Establishment reaction.

## III

With the exception of the Marxist Left, however, the coveted (and presumed) patronage of the patron saint was to know no bounds. "George died
on Lenin's birthday, and is being buried by the Astors," wrote Malcolm
Muggeridge in his diary in January 1950, "which seems to me to cover the
full range of his life." Or perhaps better, his afterlife. Prominent Labour
Party supporters and democratic socialists, liberals and neoliberals, conservatives and neoconservatives, anarchists, the "younger" generation of writers, composition teachers, journalists, literary intellectuals and leading

opinion-makers, Catholics and Protestants, Humanists and Personalists all soon beat a path to Orwell's grave, exalting him not only as a literary model but also as a human one. "The most heterogeneous following a writer can ever have accumulated," Woodcock called Orwell's "faithful." Many newcomers to the flock elaborated tortuous, and heretofore overlooked, parallels between Orwell and themselves. Even *The Bookseller* took to reminding readers on one occasion that Orwell too was "a bookseller."[29]

The historical emergence of the "claiming" of Orwell is worth pursuing here, for its study illumines the problem of intellectual grave-robbing and the hidden concatenations between Orwell's afterlife and his life. Equally important, it takes us a step further toward understanding the first critical issue which we have discussed, the heterogeneity of Orwell's reception, and opens out onto the second issue, the "paradoxical" relation of the man to the works, suggesting an avenue for approaching its tensions.

What Orwell wrote of Dickens soon applied to himself: "the very people he attacked have swallowed him so completely that he has become a national institution himself."[30] Each new publication by or about Orwell in the early 1950s further enlarged his reputation and also further complicated it by serving as the occasion for political and commercial interest groups to claim him as a partisan. To *Time,* flagship publication of the conservative Luce press, Orwell demonstrated in his 1950 and 1953 essay collections that he was "The Honest Witness," "one of the few genuinely important writers of these times," the fearless patriot who "car[ried] out a guerrilla campaign against the woolheaded fellow travelers who were poisoning English life." The *New Republic,* organ of the American liberal intelligentsia, treated the 1950 republication of *Burmese Days* and *Coming Up for Air* as occasions for "Homage to George Orwell," for "less vain, less subjective a writer never lived." But *Newsweek* and the popular press were not to be outdone: *Homage to Catalonia,* appearing in its first American edition in 1952, was "a great, even saintly, sort of recollection. . . . Orwell in no place in his account of his war experiences in Spain betrays the least malice. Of such, perhaps, is the Kingdom of Heaven." The battle for the mantle of 'St. George' Orwell had begun.[31]

The making of Orwell into a patron saint of the Left and Right, however, was not a matter of ideological factions simply claiming a champion. It was the outcome of a complicated conjunction of the Cold War, two powerful satires, and an ailing writer's (perhaps understandable) carelessness with regard to the possibilities for ideological and commercial exploitation of his work. Orwell's conflicting posthumous images before the public in the early '50s were matters of timing as much as critics' or the media's design.|Contributing mightily to the anomalies was Orwell's meteoric climb to fame during his last years, arising from the sudden successes of *Animal Farm* and *Nineteen Eighty-Four,* which were his darkest works and were written in large part as broadsides against Russian state socialism and therefore highly susceptible by their negative thrust to misinterpretation. Orwell's untimely death from tuberculosis in January 1950, just seven months after the publication of

*Nineteen Eighty-Four,* made the book seem to many people (even some friends)[32] the parting testament of a dying man in despair, and it further confused Orwell's legacy. These varied developments made it easier for anti-socialist and conservative critics, especially those unfamiliar with the London literary scene, to misconstrue Orwell, willfully or not, as an ally. His determination to complete *Nineteen Eighty-Four,* and then retype it himself when no secretary could be found to do the job, was also interpreted by many observers as evidence of his "death wish." Isaac Rosenfeld could "not conceive of a greater despair" than Orwell's, and he speculated in 1950 about Orwell's "suicide," his masochistic drive as "a dying man" to finish the masterpiece in which he had "cast his own sickness [as] the world's."[33] Jeffrey Meyers later expressed the prevalent view that *Nineteen Eighty-Four* was the killing blow in Orwell's "mad and suicidal sojourn" to his "bleak" Hebrides isle.[34] Orwell had finished *Nineteen Eighty-Four,* went some verdicts, and *Nineteen Eighty-Four* had finished him. (The view has persisted. "Consumed by His Book, George Orwell Died for It," ran one press headline in 1984.[35])

These widely circulated speculations generated a romantic myth about Orwell as a man who literally lived and died for his work, just as his dystopia was becoming embroiled in Cold War argument. Furthermore, Orwell's request in his will that no biography of him be written was respected by his acquaintances and energetically enforced by his widow Sonia. Yet Orwell's work had also given the impression that there was hardly need for a biography; much of his writing seemed straightforwardly autobiographical to most readers. So acquaintances reminisced about Orwell and wrote about his work, constructing along the way what amounted to a haphazard composite biography. They used his work to talk about his life, often casually treating his essays and fiction as if they were unreconstructed reports about the poverty and Burmese police work of his younger days, i.e., as if his fictional heroes Gordon Comstock and John Flory *were* George Orwell.[36] And they similarly used his life to talk about his work, but of course relying upon exaggerated stories of his boyhood poverty and down-and-out days. Usually these stories were quoted not from actual conversations with Orwell, who was extraordinarily reticent even with close friends about his personal life, but based upon ostensibly autobiographical passages in his books or on hearsay.[37] Literary critics and reviewers who had not known Orwell followed these leads and operated similarly.[38] New editions of Orwell's work, new collections of his essays, and new books of literary/ biographical criticism on him kept his name continually in book review pages during the 1950s. But his early work frequently received belated and flattering attention at least partly on account of the growing reputations of his last two books. The complex and partial truths making for Orwell's posthumous fame often overwhelmed responses to Orwell's prewar work, obscuring or distorting his early career and reputation.

Even before Orwell's death, the political claims and counter-claims were being lodged to both the man and the work. Almost immediately the notoriety of *Animal Farm* turned "Orwell" into an issue in international cultural

politics. Published in Britain in the same month (August 1945) as the dropping of the atom bombs, *Animal Farm* exploded on the cultural front. Orwell's little fable seemed to signal the end of one era of East-West relations and the beginning of another: the Cold War. One historian has judged that *Animal Farm,* along with Arthur Koestler's *Darkness at Noon,* "probably did more to make Western public opinion *feel* the unique Stalinist combination of equalitarian myth and new privileges than any historical or sociological explanation." *Animal Farm*'s plot and characterizations closely corresponded to the Russian Revolution, its aftermath, and its principals; understandably, it was taken—as Orwell intended—as first and foremost an assault on the Soviet Union. Anglo-American Communist reviewers denounced Orwell's "pig's eye view." Equally predictably, anti-Stalinist radicals in London and New York greeted *Animal Farm* enthusiastically.[39]

Quite disturbing to Orwell, however, was his fable's celebrated reception in conservative circles. Some conservative reviewers read it as a criticism of the Soviet Union from the Right; noting that it was set in England (with the lyrics of the animal hymn "Beasts of England" modeled on the *Internationale*), they welcomed it as not only anti-Stalinist but anti-socialist, as not only pro-libertarian but pro-American. Or they coupled Orwell with his friend Koestler as a disillusioned former Communist Party member. Orwell reportedly told Stephen Spender that he "had not written a book against Stalin in order to provide propaganda for capitalists." Nevertheless, he fell victim to a process whose dangers he often discussed in conversation: how difficult it is, in an ideologically polarized climate, to take up any position without being presumed to hold (or being deliberately tagged with) the current string of "party line" views conventionally associated with the position. It was not well understood outside the literary Left in London and New York that Orwell was an internal critic of the Left and yet not a bitter ex-socialist.[40]

Part of Orwell's problem was that he was now addressing a much wider audience, politically and culturally, than earlier in his career. His clear style implied a clear message. No reader needed to make a special effort to read Orwell's prose. But the plain style can mask a submerged complexity, and this was the case with the relation of Orwell's political fable to the emergent Cold War. For an allegory like *Animal Farm* which seemed so straightforward—the best example of Orwell as "The Crystal Spirit," in Woodcock's estimation—made one assume that one *did* understand the man and the book, and need not acquaint oneself with its historical-political context. The point here is not that Orwell was disingenuous or his persona false, as some radical Left critics have argued. It is simply that the man, his work, and political events so converged as to make Orwell both famous and widely misunderstood at the same time.

*Nineteen Eighty-Four* suffered similar ideological misreadings. Indeed the book became known almost immediately not by its original and proper title, but simply as "1984," a distillation which ironically outdid even the bareness of Newspeak by dispensing with words altogether. This abridgement both

reflected and facilitated the encapsulation, oversimplification, and distortion of his work in the following decade. Whatever Orwell's anger at the use of *Animal Farm* as "propaganda for capitalists," however, he appears to have taken no special steps to avoid the same consequences with *Nineteen Eighty-Four*. In 1947, responding to his literary agent's news that a "reactionary" Dutch paper was serializing *Animal Farm*, Orwell answered, "I don't know if we can help that. Obviously a book of that type is liable to be made use of by Conservatives, Catholics, etc."[41] This casual (though perhaps also cynically pragmatic) attitude toward the abuse of his work suggests that Orwell may indeed have inadvertently contributed to the misreadings of *Animal Farm* and *Nineteen Eighty-Four* which arose even during his life. Clearly, Orwell as polemicist was willing to sacrifice precision of aim for rhetorical power, as his incautious name for the Party, "Ingsoc" (= English socialism) suggests.*
Not surprisingly, as with *Animal Farm, Nineteen Eighty-Four* was warmly welcomed on the Right as not only anti-Communist but also anti-socialist.[43] Even Orwell's publisher, Fredric Warburg, interpreted *Nineteen Eighty-Four* in his in-house report as "a deliberate and sadistic attack on socialism and socialist parties generally." Warburg attributed Orwell's vitriol entirely to his ill health and feared that *Nineteen Eighty-Four* was "worth a cool million votes to the Conservative party."[44]

However erroneous Warburg's judgments, his reading merits notice: if Orwell's publisher could so grossly misinterpret his intentions, how likely was it that others would not? Although many intellectuals on the anti-Stalinist Left (Pritchett, Trilling, Philip Rahv) immediately saw what Orwell was up to and shared his political stance, confusions like Warburg's—far more serious and widespread than with *Animal Farm* because the Cold War was now nearing its peak (June 1949) and because the slogans of *Nineteen Eighty-Four* were so inviting as press headlines—soon developed. What has gone unnoticed is the extent to which Warburg's actions contributed to their development. Orwell issued a press release, through Warburg, and later a *dementi*, often quoted by scholars though not widely heeded at the time, that *Nineteen Eighty-Four* was "NOT intended as an attack on Socialism or on the British Labour Party, of which I am a supporter. . . . "[45] No statement, seemingly, could have been clearer. But Warburg apparently continued to advertise *Nineteen Eighty-Four* with promotions from conserva-

---

*The lack of caution, however, is partly why *Nineteen Eighty-Four* penetrated so deeply into the Western imagination. The book facilitated the immediate and only half-conscious transferal and superimposition of the West's wartime horror of Nazi Germany onto Stalinist Russia. Orwell's dystopia could be taken as the nightmare of Nazism and Bolshevism rolled into one: "Red Fascism." The "enigma" of Russia and of Stalin's postwar actions were then comprehensible as the aggressive acts of a Hitler. By fusing some tendencies common to Nazism *and* Bolshevism into a model of "totalitarianism," *Nineteen Eighty-Four* thus inadvertently lent coherence and force to the simplistic Nazi-Stalinist analogy, whereby Russia in the 1950s was a carbon copy of Germany in the 1930s, with "Yalta" and "Greece" feared as a replay of "Munich" and "appeasement." Needless to say, Orwell's swipes at Britain and the U.S.—e.g., the fact that "Airstrip One" was England, that its currency was "dollars," and its national anthem was "Oceania, 'tis of thee"—were largely ignored in the Western media.[42]

tive papers like Lord Beaverbrook's *Evening Standard,* which had named *Nineteen Eighty-Four* its Book of the Month that June. The literary editor of the *Evening Standard* wrote that *Nineteen Eighty-Four* "shows how 'the abolition' of private property means the concentration of property in fewer hands than before," and he sarcastically prescribed it as "required reading" for Labour Party M.P.s. The *Evening Standard* subheadline that *Nineteen Eighty-Four* was "the most important book published since the war" also appeared on the dust jacket of the Uniform Edition of *Nineteen Eighty-Four* printed in late 1949.[46]

Whether all or some or none of this was done with Orwell's knowledge is impossible to say. The Irish writer Frank O'Connor, however, has expressed doubt whether Orwell's *dementi* was "altogether candid." A self-described "non-political man," O'Connor claims that Warburg also sent out—at least to the conservative paper for which O'Connor reviewed *Nineteen Eighty-Four,* if not others, though it is unclear whether this promotion too continued after Orwell's *dementi*—"a cover letter in which Secker & Warburg implied that *1984* was an anti-Labour polemic" and which estimated "the number of votes it was believed [the book] would cost the Labour Party in the next General Election."[47] In addition, before the misinterpretations of *Nineteen Eighty-Four* began to appear (though admittedly, after the confusions with *Animal Farm,* his decision shows, at minimum, poor judgment) Orwell did arrange with the conservative *Reader's Digest* to print a 25-page condensation of *Nineteen Eighty-Four,* and with Henry Luce's *Life* to run an illustrated summary in its July 4 issue.[48] These organs, and some American and Canadian newspapers, told the public that Orwell's book was a vision of a future police state "under socialism."[49] As the subheadline of *Life*'s story put it, *Nineteen Eighty-Four* portrayed "The Cruel Fate of Man In A Regimented Left-Wing Police State Which Controls His Mind and Soul." Soon thereafter pro-McCarthyite organs like *The Freeman* began suggesting that Adlai Stevenson's advisers were "sicklied over" with the vision of a nation "wet-nursed by a Big Brother that may, in 1984, turn out to be Big Brother: Orwell style."[50]

The elevation of the man by various intellectual groups followed apace with Orwell's death. Only the Marxist Left dissented from the chorus of acclaim. After the lavish praise bestowed on Orwell in obituaries and reviews by his London acquaintances (Pritchett, Spender, Koestler, Herbert Read, Bertrand Russell), Orwell stood before readers on both sides of the Atlantic as an heroic figure, or in the phrase of *Tribune* editor John Atkins, "a social saint."[51]

The encomia soon spread outward—and took flight. Anglo-American liberals honored Orwell wistfully as a fellow thinker whose calling as a writer had not compromised his "manhood" and as a man of action who had fought in the Spanish Civil War against fascism, lived among the poor and the working classes, and never hesitated to tell his fellow leftists—many of them now guilt-ridden over the Soviet "betrayal of the Left"—when and where they were wrong. "If there were a competition for saints in which

liberals could bid," Philip Rieff mused in 1954, "Orwell would be their man; he satisfies at once the liberal nostalgia for action and their resignation to despair."[52] If so, he also satisfied the conservative hunger for order and their aversion to change. More interested in *Nineteen Eighty-Four* as an anti-Communist statement and less so in the man's character, conservatives nevertheless held up Orwell as an "honest" radical, who became "disillusioned" with socialism, and some conservatives implied or argued that he was tending toward Conservatism or religious belief during his last years. Conservative intellectuals (Christopher Hollis, Russell Kirk) argued that Orwell's outlook "coincided" with many conservative principles; the Luce press and anti-Communist periodicals like *The Freeman* went much further, explicitly appropriating Orwell as a bulwark against the threat of socialism and communism alike. The John Birch Society offered *Nineteen Eighty-Four* for sale; its Washington branch adopted "1984" as the last four digits of its telephone number.[53] Thus, whereas to liberals Orwell appeared an exemplary role model, to many conservatives and right-wing anti-Communists he stood as a defender of democracy and an implacable, clear-sighted foe of socialist experiments. Before the Left and Right, he was 'St. George,' Heroic Truth-teller and Fearless Patriot.

And to the literate public too these tableaux of Orwell became recognizable, though largely overshadowed by the darkness of his final vision in *Nineteen Eighty-Four*. Cast against the luminous white of Orwell's "exemplary life," the blackness of his nightmare vision in *Nineteen Eighty-Four* projected a kind of silhouette. The press was chiefly (if not intentionally) responsible for distributing the image of the "fatalistic" Orwell (though some of Orwell's closest acquaintances had subscribed to it too) by employing the coinages of Oceania as shorthand for the perceived Red menace. TV and film adaptations of *Animal Farm* and *Nineteen Eighty-Four* in the mid-'50s made Orwell's slogans familiar to millions of nonreaders. Soon after the unprecedented controversy over the BBC's 1954 adaptation of Orwell's dystopia, in which outraged viewers claimed that the program upset them physically and warped youngsters' minds with its pessimism, "1984" became in Britain what Isaac Deutscher called "The Black Millennium," lodged in the imagination as the horrific Year of Judgment, when our technology and our leaders and our very spouses and children betray us.*[54] As associations multiplied and quickened between the world of Orwell's novel and the world of the 1950s—the budding American "computer state," the Soviet occupation of Eastern Europe, the McCarthy "witchhunts," Khrushchev's revelations of Stalin's crimes, the Soviet invasion of Hungary, the erection of the Berlin Wall—clock-watchers began to wonder whether their anxious present could really become Orwell's terrifying future. As they did so, Orwell himself started to take on the image not just of the secular saint but of the gloomy clairvoyant, Prophet of the Future Imperfect.

*See Chapter Five, Section 16, "Media Prophet": Orwell on the Telescreen (pp. 273–87).

This twin profile of the haloed Saint and the dark Prophet gradually became the public image by which Orwell was chiefly known. The two faces gained prominence not only because of the charged characterizations— "saint," "virtuous man," "prophet," "fatalist"—which the critics and the media applied to Orwell, but also because these images correlated with the developing rift between the life and works, i.e., between the man and the author of *Nineteen Eighty-Four*. Likewise the two faces corresponded to the central division in Orwell's reception between intellectual and popular audiences. For intellectuals of the Left and Right, Orwell was a moral hero. For the public at-large, he was either "the author of *Nineteen Eighty-Four*" or, more likely, a vague and shadowy figure.

Thus, by the mid-'50s, the nomenclature which a few major commentators had applied to Orwell shortly after his death had set the main outlines of his reputation. It remained for other critics, and especially the mass media, to fill out, modify, retouch, and popularize these sketches. The images of Orwell and the disputes and confusions about his legacy which emerged in the early 1950s have followed along these lines into the 1980s. The only real change has been the increased number of claimants and the heightened determination of would-be political beneficiaries to gain exclusive possession of the Orwell halo.

The tug-of-war between the Right and Left climaxed during late 1983 and early 1984. Norman Podhoretz, neoconservative editor of *Commentary*, argued that "If Orwell Were Alive Today," he "would be taking his stand with the neoconservatives and against the Left" on everything from the nuclear freeze to the (alleged) failure of democratic socialism. The conservative *National Review* offered similar "Homage to Orwell," claiming that Orwell in the 1980s would be denouncing left-wing "liberation movements and the whores' allegiance" of "the forces of darkness. . . . The [right-wing] forces of light have Orwell on their side and draw strength from it." On the liberal-Left, Irving Howe insisted that Orwell's "conservative sentiments" in *Nineteen Eighty-Four* "not only aren't in conflict with his socialist opinions, they can be seen as sustaining them." To the radical-liberal *Village Voice*, Orwell's travels to and from Wigan Pier were the "Chronicles of a Decent Man."[55]

The press meanwhile invoked Orwell to denounce Newspeak of the East and West, from the mysterious deaths of dissidents in Soviet mental hospitals ("negative patient care outcomes") to the Reagan administration's MX "Peacekeeper" missile and "revenue enhancements." ("Nothing is certain but negative patient care outcome and revenue enhancements.") Almost every major issue or topic of joint interest to the East and West between the late 1970s and 1984—the Soviet occupation of Afghanistan, the Iranian hostage crisis, the politicized 1980 and 1984 Olympics, the imposition of martial law in Poland and the Philippines, the Soviet shooting of Korean air liner 007, the U.S. military involvement in Lebanon and El Salvador and Nicaragua,[56] the re-election of Reagan—became an occasion in the American or another national press to rail at doublethink and the "Orwellian"

spectre of Big Brother. "Happy 1984," proclaimed a *New York Times* editorial which criticized Ronald Reagan's "Orwellian arguments" for the U.S. "invasion" (or "rescue mission") of Grenada in 1983.[57] Proponents and opponents of the nuclear freeze, abortion, the ERA, and the Reagan administration's proposed "squeal rule" (intended to inform parents whether their teenagers received contraceptives from federal clinics) all adopted Orwell's name and catchwords to adorn their arguments. Freezing our arms stockpile in the face of the steady buildup by totalitarian Russia, murdering innocent human life, eliminating gender distinctions, and letting government secretly usurp parents' duties in their children's sexual education meant capitulating to the "Big Brother" without and creating the conditions for Oceania within. Right? Or did practicing "continuous warfare" while millions starved, invading a woman's body, relegating half the population to second-class status, and violating the confidence and rights of young people signify the apotheosis of blackwhite, the loss of ownlife, the existence of female proles, and the coming of "1984"? It depended on whom you listened to.[58]

On the question of Orwell's excellence as a political writer, however, most political intellectuals and most journalists managed to agree—and it is, as Podhoretz has admitted, partly Orwell's "enormous reputation" that has made him "well worth stealing" by intellectuals intent upon adding authority to their positions.* In Howe's estimation, Orwell is "the best English essayist since Hazlitt, perhaps since Dr. Johnson." Crick has ranked Orwell with Hobbes and Swift as one of the greatest "political writers" in English. Podhoretz himself has placed Orwell almost this high, and the neoconservative Committee of the Free World has published under the imprint "Orwell Press."[59]

IV

Not only *Nineteen Eighty-Four* but also Orwell himself, therefore, have been pressed into the service of rival factions and diametrically opposed causes. "Emasculation through Canonisation," Leopold Labedz, the neoconservative editor of *Survey* magazine, has called the process of Orwell's appropriation. Labedz bemoans that Orwell, once a "democrat and libertarian," was "reassessed" and "expropriated" in the late 1960s and '70s by the very sort

---

*Podhoretz's remark about Orwell's "enormous reputation" among intellectuals calls attention to the chief irony in Orwell's "high culture" reception, the gap between his "academic" and "intellectual" reputation. Orwell's absence from the literary "high canon" testifies to the academy's relative *disesteem* for his achievement—as a "political" writer and realistic novelist; and the battles for his mantle among non-academic intellectuals testify equally to their *presumption* of his stature. Quite possibly, the professors have undervalued Orwell and the political intellectuals have overvalued him; but both groups have tended more to *assume* his reputation than to re-evaluate it. Such a "freezing" of reputation within particular domains of reception is, as we will see in Part Two, a typical development. For a discussion of Orwell's reputation in the literary academy, see Chapter Six, Section 22, Canonization and the Curriculum: Orwell in the Classroom (pp. 382–98).

of radical "progressive" intellectuals whom he (and Labedz) despised. Pretending that Orwell was a latter-day pacifist and that there had never been any differences between them, socialists have castrated Orwell, once an uncompromising anti-pacifist and anti-Communist, and have hoisted him to their fashionable Left pedestals, argues Labedz. Neoconservative Irving Kristol has taken a similar line, commenting that Orwell would be "slowly spinning in his grave" if he knew into whose hands he had fallen.[60]

If, that is, the grave-robbers of the Left *and* Right hadn't run off with him already. For conservatives and neoconservatives have also "emasculated" Orwell, downplaying his pamphleteering for an "English socialist revolution" during World War II and his expression of support for the Labour Party even after the publication of *Nineteen Eighty-Four,* among their other omissions or distortions. Nor is what Labedz calls the "Orwellization" of Orwell—a neologism which would itself leave Orwell spinning in his grave—limited to ideological groups, to the media fanfare attending the "countdown" to 1984, or even to the last two decades. Moreover, "emasculation" suggests a process much too explicit and calculated for characterizing much of the subtle incorporation of "Orwell" and his coinages into the rhetoric of many political and commercial interest groups. Except within contentious intellectual circles, the refurbishing and sanctifying of Orwell have not entailed the kind of castration-by-the-pen—through detailed rewriting of his positions—that Labedz charges. For the most part, Orwell's coopting has simply proceeded by ritual invocation. His canonization has not so much left him an ideological eunuch as a prefab cultural commodity.

"Assimilation Through Canonization" might therefore better describe Orwell's posthumous fate, at least at the wider levels of reception (letters to the editor, lobbying by political interest groups, commercial promotions), where no deliberate "Orwellizing" has occurred. Particularly in the 1980s and in non-intellectual groups, "Orwell" is merely mouthed, like a Party chant in *Nineteen Eighty-Four.* He has become part of the repertoire of the duckspeaker, similar to the political quacking of the names "Edmund Burke," "Thomas Jefferson," "Abraham Lincoln." (Or, more recently, the bleating of "Franklin Roosevelt," "John F. Kennedy," and "Scoop Jackson" by Republicans as well as Democrats in the 1984 and 1988 presidential campaigns.) It is true, of course, that the *precondition* for this sort of reflex supplication is a filing down of a figure's edges. To accommodate him to (nearly) all groups and interests, the figure must transcend ideology—and transcend history too, so that he comes to represent a timeless virtue (Truth, Freedom, Democracy, Unity) rather than a party or partisan cause. He must be, as Orwell would put it, "lifted clean out of the stream of history" and remade into an all-purpose Comrade Ogilvy, the valiant Party hero whom Winston "creates" at the Ministry of Truth.

The most remarkable thing with the use of "Orwell" is not just that all this has happened—and happened so fast and happened not to a political leader but to a literary man—but that the process has served the ends of *both* acclaim *and* detraction. The edges of "Orwell" have been "filed down" in *two*

Orwell is victimized as a quacker of Reaganite duckspeak and classic Newspeak.

During the 1984 countdown, George Orwell, the dissident atheistic socialist, became— voila!—Moral Majority preacher Jerry Orwell.

directions, both in regard to the man's life and to the complexity of *Nineteen Eighty-Four*. People have used "Orwell" (and especially "Orwellian") to praise and to bury, making it a kind of oddly reversible figure of epideictic rhetoric. In intellectual circles, "Orwell" is typically a kind of blessing, a rhetorical flourish, an appeal to the sainted. But in the popular press, "Orwell" and, even more so, "Orwellian" are sometimes confused with "Big Brother."

Consider the following examples of the latter use of "Orwell," all from press reports or broadcasts in the 1980s:

"Orwell Takes Over as Philippine Society Crumbles." A 1981 headline describing the corruptions of the Marcos regime.

"Who Needs Orwell When We Have Schweiker?" From a 1982 column in which Richard Schweiker, Secretary of Health and Human Services in the Reagan Administration, was attacked as a Big Brother figure for pushing the Administration's so-called "squeal rule" proposal, which would have mandated government-supported clinics to report distribution of contraceptives to teens.

"Orwell in Warsaw." A 1982 headline pertaining to Government repression in Poland.

"George Orwell would be proud of our *1984*-ish ways. I am horrified." From a 1982 column criticizing new state restrictions on the insanity plea.

"Orwell in the Classroom." A 1982 letter warning against the perils of mandatory school prayer.

"An Antidote to Orwell." A 1983 editorial from the chief of the New York Tourist Bureau on tourism's role in promoting international understanding. "A world in which tourism thrives is not the world of 1984."

"We might agree to let Reagan be Reagan, but it is frightening to think about letting Reagan be Orwell." From Senator Edward M. Kennedy's speech to the National Press Club in February 1983, in which Kennedy voiced disapproval of the Reagan Administration's plans to affix dissenting labels to three Canadian films critical of U.S. nuclear policy.

"This is Moscow TV Eyewash News, with George Orwellski." From a 1983 *Albequerque Journal* cartoon attacking TASS's explanation for the Kremlin's shooting of the Korean 007 airliner, killing 269 people. Here Orwell, the BBC broadcaster, is cast as a broadcaster at the Ministry of Truth—a Winston Smith of the airwaves.

"The George Orwell Memorial Administration." Headline caption in a 1986 editorial cartoon, ridiculing Ronald Reagan's statement that the inconclusive arms summit in Iceland with General Secretary Gorbachev was a "success." Below the headline are purported examples of Reagan Newspeak: "A Summit is Not A Summit," "Disinformation is Truth," "Falling Flat On The Face Is Standing Tall," "Failure Is Success."[61]

Such usages demonstrate that "Orwell" has become classic blackwhite, possessed of two mutually contradictory meanings. Not only does it signify a virtuous white in which socialists and neoconservatives alike so ardently

seek to drape themselves; it also evokes the evil black of "1984," in which adversaries so resourcefully attempt to envelop one another.

The point is a crucial one. The perversion of Orwell's own name not only reflects the ransacking of his legacy but also has had important, and neglected, consequences in its own right for the making and claiming of his reputation. Close scrutiny of the word's variable contexts, especially in adjectival form, in which it appears so frequently, will allow distinctions about Orwell's life and work to emerge which have failed to do so thus far because of the characteristic inattention of literary criticism to "marginal" reception materials, like newspaper and magazine articles devoted to or referring to the writer. The following examination of "Orwellian" at these wider spheres of reception makes clear that George Orwell has been assimilated in diverse ways in our culture. The canonization of the man and the works, and of the saint and the prophet, have sometimes proceeded along diametrically opposed lines; and the ambiguous and contradictory application of Orwell's name and proper adjective symbolize the incongruous oddity of Orwell's saintly-sinister cultural status today. To see this is to understand better the interrelations between the life and work and times of George Orwell. Perhaps we cannot clear up all the confusions about Orwell's life and work, but we can at least see those confusions clearly.

## V

The words "reputation" and "name" are frequently used interchangeably, and in Orwell's case certain ambiguities about his "name" drive to the heart of issues connected with his mixed heritage. Indeed no word better points up the significance and essential conflict of Orwell's cultural place today than his own name in adjectival form: "Orwellian." Perhaps no man's literary name as proper adjective has been so often cited and so widely apprehended (and misapprehended) in the Anglo-American press. "Like Xerox and IBM," one journalist wrote in 1984 (and with no discernible irony), " 'Orwellian' has joined the vocabulary of every educated person."[62] Implausible as this sounds, a concordance of the pages of Anglo-American daily newspapers since the mid-1950s might confirm the assertion. I have uncovered hundreds of uses of "Orwellian" merely during 1982–84; it must have appeared thousands of times in this period alone. And not only is the word headlined, it's institutionalized: *Webster's Dictionary* has carried it since the early 1960s. Shakespearean, Rabelaisian, Swiftian, Johnsonian, Byronic, Joycean, Kafkaesque—all these have their usages. But even though many people would recognize the *names* behind the adjectives of several of these authors, it is likely that relatively few people who are not literary-minded would grasp these adjectives' allusive meanings. And among more widely recognized proper adjectives, even outside the literary domain, possibly no adjective so defies neat linguistic bracketing and undermines itself with contradiction as does "Orwellian." Augustan, Christian, Machiavellian, Elizabethan, Marxian (-ist), Victorian, Freudian, Stalinist. Some of these

adjectives are casually bandied, abused in political discussion, and/or hard to pin down quickly because their references (e.g., historical periods or movements) resist easy characterization. Yet most of us would probably agree on some roughly consistent semantic correspondence between an historical figure and an adjective's cultural usage. Machiavelli was rather "Machiavellian," Queen Victoria was essentially "Victorian," and Marx was "Marxian" (if not finally, as he insisted, "Marxist").

But was Orwell, "the social saint," "Orwellian"? The word, as we have seen with "Orwell," constitutes a supremely ironic instance of doublespeak. On the one hand, it calls to mind unimpeachable integrity and plain-spoken common sense, "Johnsonian" with a venomous dash of "Swiftian." But the better-known and infamous meaning of "Orwellian" is "demonic," "terrifying," even "totalitarian." Here it signifies diabolical deceit and brutal force, a hideous amalgam of "Machiavellian" and "Stalinist"—the very reverse of what the man is supposed to have embodied and championed. A third usage is as a simple descriptive referent to Orwell himself, without intention (or perhaps even awareness) of his character or work.

Is there any contextual guideline through which to approach the word? What in fact does "Orwellian prose" "mean" in ordinary usage? Or "Orwellian journalism"? Our first impulse is to think of the corrupted language of *Nineteen Eighty-Four,* Newspeak, and then of Winston Smith's fabrications at the Ministry of Truth. Yet if we pause and recall Orwell's own journalism and his adages about writing ("Good prose is like a windowpane"), the phrases take on a noble bearing. This second, positive sense is precisely how one writer used the phrase in a 1974 editorial entitled "Orwellian Journalism." "His professional life was an example of much that is lacking in modern journalism," the writer said of Orwell. To him, the phrase signified "integrity" and "sensitivity," as opposed to "commercialism."[63] The editorial revealed no awareness of the phrase's ironic or negative implications. The same title could easily have served as an alternate headline for a 1984 letter titled "Journalists Are Elite of 1984." In the letter, a newspaper reader castigated editorial writers speaking on public morality "from the journalist-elitist viewpoint" and "imply[ing] that we 'proles' are indifferent to civil liberties as compared to better-educated, more affluent and more powerful opinion-leaders."[64]

Still, it may seem at a glance that "Orwellian" is negative when applied to objects, institutions, and events ("Orwellian technology," "Orwellian government," "Orwellian history") and positive when referring to Orwell himself. But what *is* "Orwellian character"? Or "Orwellian leadership"? Is it Gandhi or Genghis Khan? Or, for that matter, George Orwell or Big Brother?

The wish to demarcate the adjective's zone of meaning is based on the understandable urge to separate Orwell's work from his life, so that "Orwellian" means "horrible" when referring to the writer's vision and "honest" when referring to the man's character.[65] But to which, work or life, does "Orwellian journalism" or "Orwellian prose" naturally refer? What, for instance, is suggested by "an Orwellian turn of phrase"? Or "another flight of

Orwellian prose"? Or further, "an Orwellian style of describing and evaluating the world"?

For two journalists, the first two phrases referred not to Orwell himself but to language distortion, specifically the Pentagon's use of the euphemism "air support" for bombing and the Polish government's use of "Operation Calm" for its crackdown on the Solidarity movement. Solidarity leader Lech Walesa applied the third phrase with similar negative intent. Appearing in his 1981 Harvard University commencement address, Walesa's statement is another instance of "Truthteller" Orwell implicitly and unwittingly inverted into Winston Smith at the Ministry of Truth: "Someone who has lived for many years hearing *an Orwellian style of describing and evaluating the world* cannot comprehend how beautiful and communicative the ordinary language of truth can be."[66]

Nor are these uses just isolated examples. Take the following sample of instances, most of them headlines, in which "Orwellian" appeared during the early 1980s. The range of subjects alone frustrates any attempt to pin down a single meaning for the word:

(1)  "Lee Sets the Tone on a Team of Orwellian Stature"
     "Orwellian ideas are tied to freedom, decency and continuity."

(2)  "Reagan Wins Orwellian Prize"
     "Orwellian Child Testimony Decision"
     "Orwellian Nightmare Thwarted by Travel Industry"
     "Cable TV an Orwellian Plot"
     "An Orwellian Reagan Plan"
     "Afghan Education: Orwellian"
     "1999: A Year So Dreadful It Shames the Orwellian Vision"
     "Official Calls State Fire Code Imposition Orwellian"
     "We're Doing Orwellian Things to Ourselves"
     "Snoop Force Called Orwellian"
     "Orwellian Example in Poland"
     "Baby Jane Doe Case Called 'Orwellian Tragedy' in Court"

(3)  "Where Will the Orwellian Fascination End?"
     "TVA Power Control Center—An Orwellian Enchantment"
     "Orwellian Technology Turns Into Satellite Art"[67]

Thus do observers variously (1) exalt Orwell's character and the writer's prose, (2) denounce linguistic perversion and attempts to curtail personal freedom, or (3) merely refer descriptively to Orwell's work or life.

The confusion in usage is not limited to the press or attributable solely to popularization or vulgarization of *Nineteen Eighty-Four*. Even literary critics and Orwell's biographer have used "Orwellian" in all three of the senses above. And so a critic discusses Orwell's politics favorably under the chapter title "Orwellian Socialism,"[68] and a speaker at an academic conference praises Bernard Crick's "excellent Orwellian biography." In a reminiscence of Orwell, T.R. Fyvel blithely calls Oceania "Orwellian" on one page, fondly

remembers his old friend's "Orwellian remarks" on another, and on a third criticizes images of "an Orwellian hero" conflicting with his own image of Orwell. Of course, such variable usages of "Orwellian" (both of Fyvel's latter phrases apply not to *Nineteen Eighty-Four* but to Orwell himself) are just the sort of thing that has enabled such a conflicting diversity of "Orwellian" images to develop.[69]

Some writers insist on one meaning of "Orwellian" or another, and not just the word but *arguments* about the word have even filtered down into the editorial pages and letter columns of daily newspapers. Protesting a columnist's remark that the public was being "George Orwelled" by Ronald Reagan's "Orwellian tactics," one *Boston Globe* reader insisted on the sharp distinction between the man and the works, between Orwell and *Nineteen Eighty-Four:* "Orwell was one of the most straight-talking men who ever lived," the reader fumed. "We need another George Orwell not afraid to call an arms race an arms race, or an MX [missile] an MX."[70] Another *Globe* reader angrily criticized a fellow correspondent for doing "a great disservice to the legacy of George Orwell" by describing an incomprehensible passage in a Massachusetts death penalty bill as "Orwellian in timbre." Headlined "If It's Orwellian, It's Not Obfuscatory," the critical letter deserves quoting at length, for it tries to elucidate some of the confusions I have already identified, even as it vainly seeks to disallow what has become—as the preponderance of headlines listed above under (2) demonstrates—the predominant usage of "Orwellian":

> I would like to know why [another correspondent] thinks that the sort of garble-speak he found objectionable in the death penalty bill is "Orwellian."... The outstanding characteristic of Orwell's writing was the clarity with which he expressed his thoughts.... In stylistic terms, it is hard to imagine a less appropriate comparison. Perhaps he means "Orwellian" in the sense of something threatening and oppressive, which the death penalty certainly is. But if [he] wants to conjure up images of *Nineteen Eighty-Four* and Newspeak, he is still off-base in describing obfuscatory language as Orwellian.[71]

But in fact "Orwellian" has in some cases come to mean precisely "obfuscatory language"—and has become an example of obfuscatory language in its own right. Much of the obfuscation arises from the fact that, like "1984," "Big Brother," and "doublethink," "Orwellian" has become a useful word for tarring political opponents. So much so that in 1984 observers were arguing over who had the proper *claim* not just to Orwell but to these words—quite apart from their reference to the man or the works and as if they were fixed and determinate, with no history of use.

Or, more frequently at the level of popular use, adversaries vied to see who could *disclaim* Orwell's coinages—and pin them on opponents. One exchange during congressional hearings to which I have already alluded— on the (later abandoned) Reagan "squeal rule" proposal—is illustrative. Headlined "Orwell Would Have Loved It," a 1981 newspaper story re-

ported criticisms of the proposal (mandating that authorities notify parents after giving teenagers contraceptives) worked out by Richard Schweiker, then Secretary of Health and Human Services. The key difference with the intellectuals' battles is that, unlike the efforts by radical and conservative intellectuals to appropriate noble 'St. George' for their side, the campaign waged here is to associate the opposing political party with totalitarian "Big Brother." Defending his proposal by going on the offensive, Schweiker declaimed: "You would put Big Brother government between the parent and the child." Countered a Democratic congressman: "This is Big Brother getting into the bedrooms of people."[72]

Notice that each man was implying that, inasmuch as *Nineteen Eighty-Four* is a *roman à thèse*, it opposes his adversary's interpretation of the Administration's proposal. And, of course, each man was right. The book *does* attack the family's disintegration; likewise it *does* condemn the invasion of personal privacy. But, in warning against the totalitarian dangers of state collectivism, it nowhere makes explicit whether family or individual interests have priority should the two conflict. Both are suppressed so completely in *Nineteen Eighty-Four* that the need for such a distinction seems remote: Oceania children become enemies of their parents in organizations such as The Spies, like Parsons' innocently traitorous daughter; and the Thought Police and telescreens make personal privacy impossible. The need for such a distinction seems remote, that is, until we get to 1984 America and are confronted with standard policy problems like that of the Reagan squeal rule (the tag itself was, not surprisingly, labeled a piece of Democratic Newspeak by Republicans), in which the state claims to be stepping in to protect the integrity of the family against the socially (and self-) destructive individual. Similar disputes during the early 1980s involving relations among the state, family, and individual, specifically on the issues of abortion and euthanasia,[73] also invoked Orwell's name and slogans toward various ends.

The Schweiker example should leave no doubt: "Big Brother," "1984," "doublethink," "Newspeak," "Orwellian," and even "Orwell" *are* obfuscatory language—and they have served to obfuscate Orwell's reputation. Whether hurled with intent to confuse or in ignorance of Orwell's life and work, they have become charged code words, easily manipulated to call up reflexively all sorts of (often widely exaggerated) associations with a police state.

The result for Orwell is that he has become the Dr. Frankenstein of the twentieth century. And as has happened with the good doctor, one wonders if we will one day forget the man George Orwell and associate his name exclusively with his brilliant, horrible creation. A 1983 *Time* cover gives pause to the possibility: it featured a drawing of Orwell with a peeping eye behind him and under it the headline: "Big Brother's Father."[74] Indeed even the wax figure at Madame Tussaud's unwittingly contributes to Orwell's Dr. Frankenstein reputation. Orwell is seated at his typewriter with a Thought Police agent towering over him, as if he were Winston Smith

Orwell at the Ministry of Truth? George Orwellski of Moscow News rectifies the
facts after the Soviet shootdown in February 1983 of Korean airliner 007.

A workman puts finishing touches on a sculpture of Orwell—or is it Winston at
Minitrue under the eye of the Thought Police?—at Madame Tussaud's
Wax Museum.

working at his speakwrite at the Ministry of Truth. "George Orwell" runs the simple caption behind them.

Obviously, much of the confusion stems from the muddled association of "Orwellian" with George Orwell, the adjective intertwined with the man's name. "There is definitely an Orwellian cast to what was once a showcase of democracy as the government places unreal labels on things," wrote one journalist in 1981, noting that the government Newspeak of Philippine President Ferdinand Marcos now included "tactically immobilized" (i.e., imprisoned). The article's headline, which I have already mentioned— "Orwell Takes Over As Philippine Society Crumbles"—shows how an imputation of "Orwellian behavior" easily slides into a mistaken verdict of "*being like* George Orwell," thereby confounding the man and the work.[75]

Like the attempt to discuss Orwell's politics torn from his sociohistorical context, then, a broad semantic guideline for "Orwellian" isolated from the word's immediate linguistic context will not hold. Such semantic difficulties as that posed by "Orwellian" frequently gain coherence on examination of Orwell's complex history of reputation. But the sources of some of the confusions, though often hard to pinpoint, lie not only in postwar politicking or passing cultural fashions. They also reside in the tensions of Orwell's work and life that have figured so importantly in the growth of his reputation.

Some readers have sought to evade grappling with the tangled interrelations among Orwell's life, work, and reputation by simply labeling them a "paradox" or "dilemma." Critics have been pronouncing Orwell a "paradox" for more than a quarter-century now, and simply walking away. "George Orwell was the most paradoxical writer of his time," declared Richard Vorhees in *The Paradox of George Orwell* (1961). The "contradictions" are what are finally important in Orwell, concluded Raymond Williams in *George Orwell* (1971), urging that we see Orwell as a "paradox." "Profile of a Paradox," Peter Lewis titled the opening chapter of his *George Orwell* (1982). Predictably, the press has embraced and bannered these characterizations. "Orwell's Life Full of Paradox" ran one press headline in 1984.[76]

But such characterizations, rather than serve as starting points for exploring the interconnections between the life and legacy, have functioned as resigned stopping points and evasive abstractions for avoiding the nasty trench work of investigating such detailed interrelations. Calling Orwell a "paradox" is critical alchemy: it trades the unease of hard, alloyed distinctions for the dim comfort of an unanalyzable complex.

The proper starting point for understanding Orwell's reputation is the recognition of a series of tensions—not contradictions—emerging from a simple fact: George Orwell is the author of *Nineteen Eighty-Four*. That is to say, the nightmare state of social uniformity empowered by the systematic destruction of language was written by a man who insisted that political reform start by ensuring that language ("the verbal end") draw precise individual distinctions and communicate social truths. The writer who loved

the richness and nuances of Oldspeak was also the one who advocated clarity, directness, and simplicity even to the point of offering six easy writing "rules" which he expected "will cover most cases."⁷⁷ The writer who was once an enthusiast for C.K. Ogden's pared-down Basic English later opposed artificial languages and took them as a model for Newspeak. The writer who denounced emotion-laden jargon and doublespeak through the charged slogans of *Nineteen Eighty-Four* did the same through the temperate persona of "Politics and the English Language." Perhaps all this is "paradoxical"; but it certainly need not render Orwell's life and work an opaque, essential "paradox."

For the second simple fact is that Orwell was also the author of the famously plain-spoken essays, documentaries, and journalism. His relation to language—a prime source of the "paradox" of Orwell—must be seen in light of both achievements. Orwell sought fresh, powerful figures of speech *and* precise expression ("to write less picturesquely and more exactly"). He wanted, as it were, the simplicity and economy of Newspeak without its distortions and semantic impoverishment. He was both an engaged pamphleteer and an immaculate stylist.

Certainly the consequences of these twin roles have had enormous importance for Orwell's reputation. But the tensions which the roles themselves represent are, in a sense, everyday ones, those of a man who aspired to be an artist and a polemicist, who strove during his mature years "to make political writing into an art." It was not that others have not had similar goals, or that their lives or works do not consist of deep tensions; rather, Orwell succeeded better than practically anyone else of our time in "fusing political purpose and artistic purpose into one whole," and partly as a result he has been more coveted as an ideological patron and his work more aggressively mined to yield commercial payoffs.⁷⁸

If George Orwell had really written no more than plain, straightforward prose according to his six simple rules, his work might resemble much of the tepid, long-forgotten reportage and mediocre fiction of the 1930s. (Much of Orwell's political journalism and documentary writing is polemical and sometimes violates several of his writing rules in "Politics and the English Language"—and characteristically, Orwell admits the same of this very essay.) And yet if his essays and persona had not exemplified the qualities of clarity and simplicity that his pronouncements on good writing advocated, the attraction of the man, and of the man in the writings, would not exist—and the debate about Orwell's work and legacy would surely be much more circumscribed and largely textual.

But what is "paradoxical" and slightly unsettling to many people is that Orwell achieved what is so complex so simply: to speak on paper with a clear, plain voice. One of his greatest accomplishments was the complicated feat of forging a persona and style of such appealing simplicity. The ambivalence expressed by readers toward this quality of man and style—the ideal of The Common Man airing plain common sense—probably issues not so much from doubts about Orwell's integrity or sincerity as it reflects our own

cultural assumptions. In a complicated world, simple truths which are simply stated alternately arouse admiration and scorn, especially among critics given to what Orwell called "The Lure of Profundity."[79] It is true that some radical critics have called Orwell's self-effacing persona of "the frank, disinterested observer" a deceptive "invention";[80] but other critics have exalted Orwell's "simplicity" as a prelude to knocking his "simple-mindedness." No doubt a friend of Orwell's exaggerated when he claimed that Orwell's "uniqueness" lay in his having "the mind of an intellectual and the feelings of a common man."[81] Yet some of the critical skepticism about Orwell's "character" seems directed less toward Orwell himself than it appears to stem from the casually held premise that the intellectual lacks the capacity for "average" response and that the average man lacks the intellect for "sophisticated" response.

And so the "paradox" of Orwell says much about ourselves as well as about him. Surely it is true that Orwell was a more complex and conflicted person than the caricatures of "Saint" or "Common Man" would suggest. Orwell was indeed "paradoxical"; but so are all of us. The life and work and times of George Orwell have constituted the admittedly singular and highly complicated confluence of a very private man, a gifted political writer, a selectively autobiographical essayist and novelist, a sudden rush of posthumous media attention, a series of abrupt shifts in political allegiances within the liberal-Left intelligentsia, and an apparent cultural need in the Cold War for a potential "propaganda missile"[82] like *Nineteen Eighty-Four* and in the intelligentsia for an anti-Stalinist of unimpeachable integrity like Orwell himself. But to say all that is to gloss much too easily Orwell's complex history of reputation. A brief historiography will help make better sense of the Orwell "paradox" by positioning Orwell's history in a wider temporal frame: the sixty-year transfiguration from Blair to Orwell to 'St. George.'

## VI

"All reputations," wrote Emerson in a notebook entry, "each age revises."[83] One can outline a general history of Orwell's critical/popular reputation marked by nine distinct stages of growth and change, four pertaining to his active writing career and five posthumous. A nascent stage is also identifiable, before the publication of his first book and his public reputation as a writer—what might be called Orwell's "pre-history" of reputation as "Eric Blair." Each of these ten stages bears the imprint of different political events and presents a slightly different conception of Orwell the man and writer.[84]

**1927–33.**    These were the writer's five years of struggle as "Eric Blair." Beginning with his return home from Burma in 1927, twenty-four-year-old Blair worked ceaselessly to improve his writing. Scraps of biographical evidence and letters referring to lost stories with titles like "The Sea God" and "The Man with Kid Gloves" suggest that during this time Blair was writing descriptive fiction somewhat along the lines of *Burmese Days*. Orwell also

refers to two novels written by Blair during 1928–29 in Paris, which he failed to sell and later destroyed. Blair reworked *Down and Out in Paris and London* several times. At least until 1931 his self-image was very much that of a literary man, not a political writer. As late as 1934 or 1935, he still seems to have entertained the notion of becoming a poet, rather in the style of Gordon Comstock in *Keep the Aspidistra Flying* (whose poem on "the money god" Orwell actually published under his pen name as "St. Andrew's Day, 1935").[85] Most of Blair's published writings during these early years were reviews in small London literary magazines like the *Adelphi* and the *New English Weekly*. This period produced only one effort of more than biographical interest, the superb, apparently autobiographical essay "A Hanging" (1931). Yet for Etonian Blair this was nonetheless a time of decisive *déclassé* experience, much of which he recast in later publications: his London tramping and Paris dishwashing (*Down and Out*), his hop-picking and schoolteaching (*A Clergyman's Daughter*), and his two weeks in a Paris hospital ("How the Poor Die").

**1933–36.**   In this first stage of his reputation (from the January 1933 publication of *Down and Out* through *Keep the Aspidistra Flying* [1936]), Orwell was little known outside London literary circles, even though his first three books were also published by Harper and Brothers in America (and *Down and Out* in a French edition by Gallimard). In London he was chiefly known as an "old-fashioned" Edwardian novelist and a regular contributor (until 1935 as "Eric Blair") to the *Adelphi* and *New English Weekly*, and his name was linked with that of Richard Rees, Cyril Connolly, and other young editor-writers of his generation. Reviewers of Orwell's work were primarily interested in his writings apart from his life or personality, and aside from his self-portrait in *Down and Out* they knew relatively little about the man. Prognoses differed as to his achievement and potential. Reviewing *Burmese Days* in 1935, Compton Mackenzie judged that Orwell's output established him as England's most promising young writer.[86] But Mackenzie, deprecated as a realist, was not highly regarded by the younger and modernist writers; his was not a widely held view. Sean O'Casey told publisher Victor Gollancz that Orwell had "about as much chance of reaching the stature of Joyce as a tit had of reaching that of an eagle."[87] During this period Orwell's books, published by Victor Gollancz Ltd. and Harper, all suffered a few hundred remaindered on their modest 3,000 print runs.[88] Except for *Down and Out*, Orwell's work was typically reviewed in passing with several other books, often casually and vaguely praised in the sort of short reviews which he mocked in "Confessions of a Book Reviewer" and hated to write himself.

**1936–39.**   With *The Road to Wigan Pier* (1937), Orwell's reputation quickly expanded and altered. Commissioned by Victor Gollancz in order to expose the plight of the jobless in the industrial North of England, *Wigan Pier* was selected as a Left Book Club choice for March 1937 and distributed in a first edition of 43,690 copies, a hardback circulation exceeding all of Orwell's combined sales until *Animal Farm*. *Wigan Pier* became a subject of debate on

the Left and far beyond intellectual circles. Within weeks of its publication, it established Orwell's reputation as a socialist critic of the Left. Orwell's personal differences with the fellow traveling Gollancz forced him to take *Homage to Catalonia* (1938) to the new house of Secker & Warburg. Though the book sold only 900 copies until its reprinting as part of the Uniform Edition in 1951, its many respectful reviews in the non-Communist press enhanced Orwell's image as a left-wing journalist critical of Stalinism and as an independent-minded, if idiosyncratic, socialist. *Homage to Catalonia* also marked the beginning of the misinterpretation of Orwell's work on the Right and Left. "Probably [it will] be abused both by Conservatives and Communists," predicted Orwell's friend Geoffrey Gorer, a forecast which turned out to be especially true on the publication of the first American edition during the Cold War in 1952.[89]

During this second stage of public reputation, therefore, Orwell became known for his reportage. *The Road to Wigan Pier* and *Homage to Catalonia* showed Orwell turning his attention away from general themes like poverty and imperialism toward political disputes on the Left over how to deal with workers' unemployment and the threat of fascism. Orwell's personality, as much as the social questions themselves, attracted much comment from reviewers. For the first time, the "Orwell persona" was at issue. Hostile radical critics sought to undermine Orwell's socialist credentials by drawing attention to his Eton schooling and Indian Imperial Police service.[90] Sympathetic Left critics focused on Orwell's thought-provoking but all-too-passionate *advocatus diaboli* stance against socialism in *Wigan Pier* and upon his integrity and humility in *Catalonia*.

**1939–45.** Though Orwell's reputation grew more slowly during the war years, it widened and deepened. As *Time and Tide*'s film and theatre reviewer (1940–41) and a BBC talks producer for India (1941–43), Orwell found less time for what he considered "serious" writing and turned more to journalism and the essay. With his regular "As I Please" *Tribune* column (1943–47) and *Observer* war reports (1945), he became known outside the London intelligentsia as a journalist. His essays in *Inside the Whale* (on Dickens, Henry Miller, and boys' newspapers) and throughout the war years (on penny postcards, thriller fiction, Wells, Dali, and P.G. Wodehouse) established him as an essayist of distinction and made clear his serious interest in popular culture. A flattering 1940 overview of Orwell's career by Q.D. Leavis in *Scrutiny* reflected the growing respect of one sector of the literary Establishment for Orwell; her suggestion that he stick with nonfiction and abandon the novel was also probably the genesis of the frequently heard judgment in later years that Orwell was "really an essayist."[91] With his regular "London Letter" in *Partisan Review* (1941–46), Orwell also became known during this time in New York intellectual circles. His name became linked in America with anti- and ex-Communist European socialists, including Spender, Koestler, Silone, Gide, Malraux, Victor Serge, and Franz Borkenau, all of whom Orwell either met or praised in print. George Bowling's sentimental love of country and nostalgia for Edwardian England in

*Coming Up for Air* (1939), followed by Orwell's attacks on pacifism and foreign-leader worship in *The Lion and the Unicorn* (1941) and his affectionate *Tribune* columns on English habits, set the outlines for the image which *Tribune* colleague John Atkins later characterized as "The Patriot of the Left."[92] But *The Lion and the Unicorn*, in particular, confused Orwell's reputation as it broadened it: some war supporters on the Left saw him as a good socialist and "revolutionary patriot"; others further right viewed him as a Trotskyist; and Marxist and radical critics typically regarded his new-found patriotism as further evidence of his reactionary politics.

Probably the landmark event of the period, which signaled the beginning of Orwell's popular reputation, was the printing of 55,000 copies of *Down and Out* in a sixpenny Penguin edition.[93] Penguin misclassified *Down and Out* on its cover and in the trade lists as fiction, perhaps contributing to its sales. *The Lion and the Unicorn* also sold more than 10,000 hardback copies. Warburg estimated that, with reading matter scarce in wartime London, *The Lion and the Unicorn* was probably read by 50,000 people—and Warburg claimed that it contributed significantly to the change of public mind in Britain which brought the Labour Party to power in 1945. By contrast, *Coming Up for Air* did only slightly better than Orwell's earlier fiction, selling out its hardback print run of 3,000 copies within two years.

1945–50.   *Animal Farm* (1945) transformed Orwell's postwar reputation internationally almost as suddenly and decisively as had *The Road to Wigan Pier* within the British Left a decade earlier. The fable enhanced Orwell's reputation in intellectual circles and also made him a widely popular author. Concern about wartime ally Russia, along with Secker & Warburg's shortage of paper, delayed the book's publication more than seventeen months after Orwell's February 1944 completion date. (Several English publishers and a dozen or more American publishers apparently turned down *Animal Farm*, many of them on political grounds. One American house, Dial Press, innocently mistook the fable for "an animal story."[94]) Finally published in August 1945 by Secker & Warburg and August 1946 by Harcourt, Brace, *Animal Farm* was selected as a September 1946 Book-of-the-Month Club choice.

The Club's selection of *Animal Farm* is probably the single most significant event for expanding Orwell's reputation in his lifetime, and arguably the most important event in his entire American reputation-history. "The *Uncle Tom's Cabin* of our time," announced one member of the Club's selection committee. Extolling the fable's "worldwide importance," Club president Harry Scherman issued a special statement: "Every now and then through history, some fearless individual has spoken for the people of a troubled time . . . . Just so does this little gem of an allegory express, perfectly, the . . . inarticulate philosophy of tens of millions of free men. . . . [W]herever . . . men are free to read what they want, this book and its influence will spread." As if to guarantee that outcome, Scherman also asked subscribers to pick *Animal Farm* rather than any alternate Club choice.[95] The fable sold 460,000 copies during 1946–49 through the Club and soon became a runaway best-seller.[96] By 1947 it had been adapted as a

BBC radio play and translated into nine languages (and titled *Comrade Napoleon* in at least one language). In 1941 Koestler had bet some literary friends five bottles of burgundy that Orwell would be "the greatest best-seller" among them in five years' time: *Animal Farm* was proving Koestler prescient.[97]

As for Orwell's nonfiction, it continued to be highly regarded in England and during this period attracted its first attention in America. Influential Anglo-American reviewers (Pritchett, Eric Bentley, Joseph Wood Krutch) greeted Orwell's 1946 volume *Critical Essays* (American title: *Dickens, Dali and Others*) enthusiastically. Middleton Murry judged that the collection confirmed Orwell (along with Cyril Connolly) as one of the two best English literary critics of his generation.[98] Edmund Wilson praised both the essay collection and *Animal Farm,* and concluded in *The New Yorker* that Orwell "is now likely to emerge as one of the ablest and most interesting writers that the English have produced in this period."[99] *Animal Farm* and *Critical Essays* occasioned comparisons of Orwell as political writer and literary critic with past masters and notable contemporaries, including Swift, Voltaire, Hazlitt, Anatole France, Chesterton, Koestler and Wilson himself. Wilson had also recommended in his *Animal Farm* review that publishers reprint Orwell's early works, and Secker & Warburg obliged by starting the Uniform Edition in 1948 with *Coming Up for Air.*

*Nineteen Eighty-Four* also received a powerful boost as a July 1949 choice of the Book-of-the-Month Club. "Great Books Make Themselves," proclaimed the August 1949 *Book-of-the-Month Club News,* in a headline running over ecstatic tributes from Bertrand Russell, Arthur Schlesinger, Jr., and others. Nothing, of course, could have been wider of the mark than the headline's declaration. Already in July the new Club president had predicted *Nineteen Eighty-Four* would become "one of the most influential books of our generation," a view which the *Book-of-the-Month Club News* now repeated. The Club acknowledged that it had solicited the opinions of "prominent persons" like Russell and Schlesinger about the book, who now confirmed the Club's "certainty that Mr. Orwell's book will be one of the most widely discussed books in recent years."[100]

Subsequent kudos for *Nineteen Eighty-Four* from other "prominent persons" on both sides of the Atlantic (Pritchett, E.M. Forster, Rebecca West, Trilling, Rahv, Reinhold Niebuhr, Paul de Kruif) helped ensure that result. Leading intellectuals compared Orwell with Dostoyevsky, Wells, Huxley, and others in the anti-utopian tradition. Within five months the novel had sold 22,700 hardback copies in England. Eventually it rose to #3 on the *New York Times* best-seller list during 1949. It sold 190,000 copies as a Book-of-the-Month Club choice during 1949–52 and became an American best-seller in 1951 when it appeared as a Signet paperback.[101]

**1950–56.**  Not until the year of his death in 1950 did Orwell's name appear in the British *Who's Who.* But within half a decade, Londoners were discussing "the Orwell legend." Indeed the writer who warned against the rewriting of history was having his own history thoroughly rewritten. "He

Became a Legend in His Own Lifetime," ran one headline on Orwell in a popular London weekly. Describing the romanticizing of Orwell's last years, another literary journalist wrote that, even as he was dying, Orwell was for many people "already a legend and prophet, the great rainmaker who, in *Animal Farm* and *1984,* washed away the Stalinist '30s." Novelist James Hilton admitted in 1953 that it was "hard to think of any writer of this century whose posthumous fame has expanded more than George Orwell's," and deservedly so, said Hilton, "for he did more, thought more, and knew more than most professional writers who live to be eighty. . . ." Statements like these inflated Orwell's reputation in the guise of describing it.[102]

Both the perceived split in Orwell's reputation between the man and the works and the view of Orwell as a "saint" emerged full-blown soon after his death. The former crystallized almost immediately upon the appearance of *Nineteen Eighty-Four.* The latter image took shape starting with the acclamatory obituaries of the man from Pritchett, Koestler, Julian Symons, and other acquaintances. In the wake of the success of *Animal Farm* and *Nineteen Eighty-Four,* Harcourt, Brace had scheduled an early 1950 publication date for the first American editions of Orwell's early works. By coincidence these books (*Down and Out, Burmese Days, Coming Up for Air*) were published in the month of Orwell's death. So fresh was the image of the man in critics' minds that reviews of these works more closely resembled new obituary tributes. In June 1950 *The World Review* devoted a special number to Orwell, featuring excerpts from his wartime diaries and more praise from acquaintances like Muggeridge, Spender, Tom Hopkinson, and Bertrand Russell. The essay collection *Shooting an Elephant* appeared later that same year, bringing yet another round of reminiscences and salutes. Soon Harcourt, Brace issued American editions of *Homage to Catalonia* (1952) and *Keep the Aspidistra Flying* (1956), along with a 1953 essay collection, *Such, Such Were the Joys* (U.K. title: *England Your England*).

Orwell's popular reputation soared. *Nineteen Eighty-Four* sold 1,210,000 copies during this period as a New American Library paperback, 596,000 copies as a Reader's Digest Condensed Book, and several hundred thousand copies in Britain as a Penguin paperback. It was adapted for radio by Martin Esslin. CBS-TV (1953), BBC-TV (1954), and Columbia Pictures (1956) produced screen versions. Meanwhile, *Animal Farm* was readapted for BBC radio in 1952 and made into the first serious full-length feature cartoon in 1954. The adaptations in turn boosted sales of all Orwell's books. The popularity of *Animal Farm* and *Nineteen Eighty-Four* helped put *Burmese Days* and *Down and Out* on the U.S. best-seller paperback lists during 1952 and 1954, respectively.[103] Four Orwell acquaintances also published biographical-critical studies on him during the period. The Orwell ascension had become the Orwell cult and, by 1956, the Orwell industry.

Orwell's critical and popular reputation reached their twin peaks in the mid-1950s. "Orwell" was an ideological issue and cultural phenomenon. As Orwell's *Tribune* friend T.R. Fyvel bemoaned his "canonization on the Right," an American critic was concluding that "from now on, one cannot be

a really educated man without knowing a little of him." Although Orwell's Marxist contemporaries continued to attack him as a "Prisoner of Hatred" and "Maggot of the Month," some younger socialists (Raymond Williams) and former Party members (Philip Toynbee) eulogized him extravagantly. Writers of nearly all ages and political allegiances looked to him as an intellectual hero. "Any intellectuals who may submit to having a list of their heroes wrung from them," wrote Kingsley Amis in 1956, "are likely to put him in the first two or three whatever their age (within reason), whatever their other preferences, and—more oddly at first sight—whatever their political affiliations, if any."[104] Robert Conquest, Amis' friend and a fellow Movement writer, didn't need to be "wrung"; to him the quixotic Orwell was

> A moral genius. And truth-seeking brings
> Sometimes a silliness we view askance,
> Like Darwin playing his bassoon to plants.
> He too had lapses, but he claimed no wings.[105]

**1956–67.**   The next stage of Orwell's reputation was one of distancing, revision, and reconsolidation. The Orwell industry suffered a mild recession. Orwell's prominence in the media declined noticeably and his public reputation dipped accordingly. As the Cold War entered a new and calmer phase, Orwell's best-known works, *Animal Farm* and *Nineteen Eighty-Four,* lost their immediacy for the media and for many readers. Still, both works were adapted for the stage in the early 1960s;[106] and *Animal Farm* became standard reading in Anglo-American classrooms by the mid-1960s.

British critical opinion also revalued Orwell's achievement slightly downward. As if to compensate for their overestimations and embarrassingly unbridled paeans a few years earlier, British critics felt the need by 1960 to clip his wings. "I once heard him called a twentieth-century Socrates," sneered one 1958 reviewer of *Wigan Pier.*[107] An anti-Orwell cult soon arose, manned by former admirers of varying political stripes (e.g., Amis, Williams). In a 1961 poll of Labour Party M.P.s, not a single one mentioned Orwell's name when asked which recent intellectuals had exerted influence on them and on the party's outlook.[108] Noting the revisionist turn, Philip Toynbee accurately remarked that among British intellectuals Orwell had suffered the fate of Aristides: they had tired of hearing him called "The Just."[109] English critic Anthony West set off a flurry of psychoanalytic speculation about Orwell's "sadomasochistic" prep school years with his controversial 1956 *New Yorker* essay. Although books of literary-biographical criticism by admiring Orwell friends like Richard Rees and George Woodcock continued to appear, memories of Orwell the man were receding. Critics turned to scrutinize Orwell's writings without reference to his life. Typically they found the novels lacking in formal excellence and the nonfiction short on political acumen.

In America, Orwell's popular reputation faded after 1956, but his critical standing remained high. American intellectuals had not known the man, and so from the start they had looked primarily at the writings, or at the

man in the writings. American academics began writing scholarly articles and books on Orwell, sometimes claiming this distance as an advantage. American readers had not identified with Orwell to the extent of his English contemporaries and younger English intellectuals; no disillusion with and revision of Orwell thus occurred in the U.S. to match the British reaction. Moreover, many of Orwell's books published in America in the early 1950s were U.S. first editions. Orwell's work had been practically unknown outside literary New York before *Animal Farm*. Whereas British critics felt uneasy that they had overvalued Orwell after neglecting him for so long, American critics received him free from such guilt, generally seeing him rather as an established writer. Still, approaching him through the lens of *Animal Farm* and *Nineteen Eighty-Four* produced many overestimations. For example, whereas *A Clergyman's Daughter* had received lukewarm or dismissive reviews on its first American printing in 1935, the *New Yorker* hailed it as a distinguished work on its republication in 1960.[110]

On both sides of the Atlantic, critics gave increasing attention to Orwell's essays on culture and language, and less to *Animal Farm* and *Nineteen Eighty-Four*, though both books continued to be widely quoted (and to show up in some unexpected contexts).[111] Key intellectual spokesmen for the British New Left, such as Williams and Richard Hoggart, acknowledged the strong influence of Orwell's popular culture essays on their work. By the early 1960s, the focus of critical attention had shifted away from Orwell's life, back to Orwell the writer. An image of a depoliticized, "cultural" Orwell had replaced the Cold War image of an "ideological" Orwell.

**1968–80.** Both the *Collected Essays, Journalism, and Letters of George Orwell* (*CEJL*, 1968) and the two-volume biography by Peter Stansky and William Abrahams (*The Unknown Orwell*, 1972; *Orwell: The Transformation*, 1979) renewed critical interest in the man, especially in his prewar years. Even a play was written dramatizing Orwell's life.[112]

*CEJL* contained most of Orwell's major essays, a majority of the *Tribune* columns, and many other forgotten short pieces (though there were some significant omissions). Although *CEJL* did not settle any disputes about Orwell's work, it provided a more rounded picture of Orwell's life and enabled scholars to understand his development better. It also exposed the thinness of much of the pre-1968 Orwell criticism, which had usually been based only on the fiction and already collected essays. Reviewing the volumes, prominent literary men and writers of the Left and Right (George Steiner, Anthony Powell, Malcolm Muggeridge, Irving Howe, Alfred Kazin, Conor Cruise O'Brien, Hilton Kramer) judged Orwell one of the century's finest journalists and prose stylists. The distance he had traveled since Sean O'Casey's 1935 snub could be measured by the tribute in *Time:* "One of the most notable lives of the twentieth century."[113]

Orwell's *oeuvre* also became the object of pluralistic critical attention. Scholars studied the "art" of his fiction and his use of language, instead of approaching his work from political, biographical, and psychoanalytic standpoints, as they had in the '50s. More than a dozen books of Orwell criticism

appeared. Orwell's use of symbolism, his place in the literary tradition, and his narrative technique all received critical scrutiny. *Animal Farm* and *Nineteen Eighty-Four* also continued to sell. More than 20 million paperback copies had been sold by 1971; the two books were selling at a phenomenal rate of almost one million copies per year in the U.K. and U.S. by the early 1970s.

Orwell also became a subject of political debates in the late '60s as the Anglo-American Left entered a new phase of radical politics. Several observers (Mary McCarthy, Richard Rees, Noam Chomsky) expressed conflicting opinions as to "where Orwell would have stood" on the Vietnam War. An "ideological" Orwell figure re-emerged on the Left, though now variously described as radical, reactionary, and "responsible." These images were set alongside the "formalist" Orwell which academic critics of the fiction were presenting. The Vietnam War and the Watergate Affair presented countless opportunities for the press and "jargon experts" to attack "government Newspeak." Several words and phrases which do not appear in *Nineteen Eighty-Four* (doublespeak, Haigspeak, nukespeak, killspeak, Big Sister, Big Momma) were coined and often mistakenly credited to Orwell, or advanced with the claim to his authority.

**1980–85.** Bernard Crick's long-awaited, authorized biography, *George Orwell: A Life* (1980), cleared up much of the confusion about Orwell's early career. But it upset Sonia Orwell and some old Orwell friends (Rayner Heppenstall, George Woodcock) with its purported inaccuracies and "lifeless" portrait of the man;[114] and some conservative intellectuals (Norman Podhoretz, Leopold Labedz) with its allegedly partisan Left stance.

The 1984 "countdown"—the word itself a culminating product of several years of reputation-building—began. Attention not only to *Nineteen Eighty-Four* but also to George Orwell and his entire *oeuvre* increased dramatically. During 1983 and 1984, what the mass media called "Orwellmania" spurred *Nineteen Eighty-Four* alone to sales of almost 4 million copies. A new stage play of Orwell's life, a new film adaptation of *Nineteen Eighty-Four*, and numerous screen documentaries and specials appeared. The "puritanical" Orwell once satirized in a friend's novel as railing against the danger that "scanty panties" posed to the stability of the English family was now the subject of feature stories in *Playboy* and *Penthouse*.[115] Not just intellectuals and editorial writers but also political leaders like Margaret Thatcher, Neil Kinnock, Gerald Kaufman, Walter Mondale, John Glenn, and Jesse Jackson contested or applauded Orwell's "warning." At least among English-language readers, the 1981 judgment of a conservative critic that Orwell "arouses fiercer pro and anti- reactions than any writer since Marx" was arguably right.[116]

Two new critical perspectives on Orwell also emerged. Feminist critics examined the gender politics of Orwell's work; phenomenological critics investigated in detail the reading experience of Orwell's fiction.[117] The year also witnessed the publication of *Nineteen Eighty-Four, the Facsimile*, a reproduction of approximately half of the original manuscript (all that is known to survive), edited by Peter Davison and introduced by the manuscript's

American owner, Daniel Siegel. In 1984 Davison also began editing *The Complete Works of George Orwell*. This massive project, the first several volumes of which were published in 1986–87, includes expurgated passages from several Orwell novels (e.g., a rape scene in *A Clergyman's Daughter*) and a new nine-volume *CEJL*, featuring hundreds of letters and journalistic pieces omitted from the 1968 *CEJL*.

New primary material was also uncovered in Britain and America. More than ninety letters were found at Indiana University, apparently sold at auction in the early '50s and since forgotten. William West also discovered 62 radio scripts and 250 Orwell letters misfiled in the BBC archives. This material was later published in two volumes, accompanied by inflated claims as to its significance, as *The War Broadcasts* (1985) and *The War Commentaries* (1986).

1985–    . The political battles over Orwell's work continue,[118] but with the passing of 1984 Orwell's reputation has entered a new phase. Possibly it will compare with the period of the late 1950s and early '60s, during which his overall reputation suffered because of a perception that the Orwell "industry" had overheated and that Orwell had reached a "saturation level" of critical and popular attention. Yet while Orwell's public prominence in the media has already significantly declined since the early months of 1984, it is unlikely that reappraisals of his work will follow the tendency in the '50s toward a downward revaluation *en bloc*, or that a division between British and American judgments will be so pronounced. More probable is that, with the publication of Davison's new *CEJL*, attention will again shift from *Nineteen Eighty-Four* to Orwell's nonfiction and life, a trend that had begun in 1968 and was deflected only by the approach of 1984.

Looking back from the 1980s, it is clear that the decade immediately following Orwell's death constituted the crucial period in the making (and partial freezing) of his reputation. The oft-quoted critical commonplaces (and myths) about Orwell the man, the entry of Newspeak into the political lexicon, the introduction of his work into school curricula, the mass media adaptations of *Animal Farm* and *Nineteen Eighty-Four*, the political abuses of Orwell's name and work: all of these developments were well under way by the late 1950s. They are among the main causes and consequences of Orwell's present-day reputation.

## VII

Up until now, we have been examining the main issues and contingencies in Orwell's history of reputation. It will be advantageous to withdraw briefly from the specific matter of Orwell's literary repute to inquire into the making of literary reputations generally and their institutional basis, with the aim of returning better fitted to discuss the formation of Orwell's reputation.*

*Readers less interested in reputation as a conceptual issue and more interested in the formation of Orwell's own reputation may prefer to move directly to Chapter Two, Section 3, Approaching Orwell's Reputation: Distinctive Features (p. 93).

For, as we have seen, what is strikingly distinctive about Orwell's posthumous history is his multifaceted, conflicted history of repute among popular, intellectual, political, generational, and professional groups. Thus one glaring incongruity in Orwell's overall reputation is that the work of probably the most widely read and most highly "valued" recent political writer in English is apparently insufficiently "reputed" for inclusion in most college classes in modern British literature. A study of Orwell's reputation therefore invites inquiry into the roles of institutional audiences, which of course overlap and interact, in making evaluations, reputations, and canons.

The larger point, whose theoretical import literary critics have not yet squarely confronted, is that the reputation of the artist and his art are not simply matters of individual achievement and intrinsic value, respectively. Value and repute are relational phenomena, shaped according to the dynamics of interpersonal and institutional histories. Accordingly, given that the transmission of literary value judgments is a complex social process operating through innumerable personal and professional networks, it should not be surprising that, even within a single, apparently homogeneous audience, what is *valued* is not always what is *reputed,* and vice versa. But the "ideology of repute" is such that we do regularly equate the two, forgetting to ask, Evaluated and reputed by and for whom? When? For what? Under what conditions? Our unreflective tendency to assume that the equation holds is what I am referring to as "the problem of reputation."

Such observations about the "ideology" of repute may seem commonplaces. But their implications are not. In any event, the need is not to assert the observations but to pursue them: to make them concrete within sociohistorical contexts and to specify how particular social formations arise in and exert influence upon *particular* histories of repute. A reputation is no more an object of contemplation than it is an eternal monument. It emerges through lived social practices.

To approach Orwell's history of reputation strictly by way of a chronology of literary and popular verdicts on his work, therefore, without reference to the institutions of criticism which make for reputations, would be shallow and evasive. Orwell's own work was sometimes censored; often he fought with English publishers and reviewers, sometimes with the anger of a Gordon Comstock. "A writer isn't judged by his status," Orwell once fired back in *Partisan Review* when a London pacifist tried to misrepresent him to their American audience, "he is judged by his work."[119] Orwell's remark here was polemical; he and Gordon Comstock knew full well that the reverse was often the case. Time and again Orwell railed against London's literary-political cliques, and worried half-seriously about "selling my literary reputation" after providing friends with a few quotes as promotional blurbs.[120] It is interesting (and yet another indication of Orwell's protean reputation) that Richard Kostelanetz, in his two harsh studies on postwar American literary politics (featuring attacks on Orwell champions like Trilling and Howe), opened several of his chapters with epigraphs from Orwell's work, casting himself as Orwell's true American successor. "I admire

Orwell so much, and quote him so frequently," wrote Kostelanetz, "[because of] his willingness to expose problems which others would prefer to ignore."[121]

In this spirit, Chapter Two addresses the "problem" of reputation and explores the terms on and in which literary reputations are negotiated and disseminated.

# TWO

# Terms of Repute:
# Conditions, Constraints

## 2. Literary Studies and the Problem of Reputation*

### I

"Who makes or breaks a writer's reputation?" asked *Esquire* during the mid-1960s. The editors' answer, titled "The Structure of the Literary Establishment," came in the form of a multicolored "chart of power." The chart named names. Included was "virtually everyone of serious literary consequence," whether "writer, editor, agent, or simple hipster." The center of power was indicated, noted the editors, by "the hot red blob in the middle," which oozed over the names of the chief literary makers and breakers.[1]

In 1977 *Esquire* drove to the heart of the blob, asking a long list of "knowledgeable" writers, academic critics, and journalists the question, "Which American writers of this century do you consider the most over- and under-rated?" Running below the responses across four pages was a sketch of Father Time, busily at work inflating and bursting bubbles bearing the images of various candidates. No consensus was sought, though Dreiser and Willa Cather fared well, and Pound, Eliot, Hemingway, Mailer, and Edmund Wilson less well. The editors acknowledged that their respondents generously volunteered a number of non-Americans too (and stretched "writers of this century" back to the Venerable Bede), "proving that once you get started on this kind of thing, it's hard to know where to stop."[2]

Unfortunately, reflection on the matter seems to stop at the doorstep of literary studies. "Reputation" is one of those subjects that readers, critics,

*I am grateful to Michael Levenson for his generous assistance with this section.

and scholars love to talk about, but to which serious attention is rarely paid, even by sociologists of literature, and not at all by literary critics. William Goode notes in *The Celebration of Heroes,* his study of prestige as a system of social control, that sociology has not even proposed satisfactory concepts and a body of general hypotheses for what he calls "prestige processes,"[3] let alone formulated how "interlinkages" within the social structure affect such processes. Separate disciplines are devoted to the study of wealth and power, yet none to honor or reputation—the third chief category of class systems and human motivation.[4] A few cultural critics have drawn attention to the ways in which the "institution of criticism"—book publishing, book reviewing, literary journalism, scholarly criticism—has exerted influence on public literary taste or the profession of literary studies. But their work has typically castigated "the culture industry" or "the literary-industrial complex," rather than addressed the making of authors' and books' reputations.[5] Although semesterly reading lists and even whole libraries testify to the exalted reputations of a few "canonized" authors, a near-total silence has prevailed in the academy on reputation as a literary issue in its own right.[6]

That such a central dynamic of literary life—in a sense *the* defining, controlling category for an essentially honorific activity like literature and literary criticism—should go virtually unattended by critics of literature might seem at first glance almost a professional conspiracy by *Esquire*'s "Blob." Yet the academy's neglect of "the problem of reputation" is hardly due to outright professional collusion, but rather to a joint matter of epistemological, institutional, and historical factors. These have partly to do with the elusiveness of reputation as a concept, which has accommodated the more important repressive factors: the academy's preoccupation with literary interpretation and its persistent tendency to avert its eyes from its own institutional history.

## II

The "problem" of literary repute is essentially the problem of justice in literary terms: how and why do writers and literary works of "value" receive or not receive their due "repute" in society and in literary history? Any extended answer would necessitate a treatise in political theory or the sociology of knowledge, but the immediate issues are worth indicating.

The problem of reputation is first the ancient philosophical one of knowledge and opinion. Reputation (Gk. *doxa,* opinion, glory) is the estimation in which a person or thing is commonly held. "Commonly" here indicates that the concept refers to an intersubjective public domain. "Public" reputation therefore suggests a judgment extending beyond one's immediate range of relations with others, an "opinion" of character or performance held by influential sections of the community at-large. Reputation or "recognition" is an act of cognition on the part of the Other. It is gained variously through a perception of one's power, wealth, achievement, or character. But it can be

"won" or "lost" only through the acknowledgment of others. Others *confer* repute. One is "reputed" or "thought to be" (L. *re-putare*, to think again) as specified, e.g., one "has" a reputation "for integrity" or "for stealing." In such usages, a public "image" signifies the Other's perception of the subject as an embodiment or type of the stated quality, e.g., he is "the image of" integrity or graft. To talk about reputations is therefore to talk about images, which are ordinarily taken as "imitations" (L. *imago*) of the "real" person or thing. Typically an image is cast as a visual representation—"a picture made out of words," in C. Day Lewis' definition in *Poetic Image*.[7]

Reputation and image are linked through speech acts, through discourse as social action. To "possess" a reputation is to "have a good name," and the act of naming itself ("honest man," "thief") ascribes a motive and thereby generates a concrete image. An image is always relational, as Sartre emphasized in his *Psychology of Imagination*, indicating a relationship between perceiver and perceived.[8]

"Reputation, reputation, reputation!" wailed Cassio after his dismissal from Othello's army on account of Iago's craftiness. "I have lost the immortal part of myself!" Like other sorts of personal income, reputations may indeed be earned or unearned. "Oft got without merit and lost without deserving," Iago consoles Cassio philosophically. A change in others' attitudes, even if provoked by events independent of the subject's behavior, can cause a gain or loss of reputation. A person is "reputed to be" honest, to "possess" the attribute of honesty. The frequent passive voice of the usage shows how unstable and easily misunderstood or overlooked that ownership is. One possesses only the precarious, nonbinding *title* to a reputation, the "name" of being someone of some sort. "All reputation is hazardous," wrote Hazlitt, "hard to win, harder to keep."[9]

Corporations and political candidates—and publishers—trust the truth of Hazlitt's remark. They spend millions of dollars to improve, maintain, or change their reputations and their products' images, resources which might otherwise be devoted to improving the things themselves. These advertisers assume—and with much market research to support their beliefs—that advertising promotes a favorable public perception of them and their wares, and thus aids their success, perhaps more so than their products' actual quality. Publications like the popular *Consumer Reports* magazine aim to unmask this advertising and reveal products' "true value." Especially when a matter of public currency, with little or no chance for direct personal verification, the attribution of reputation is an act of perception about a property which may or may not inhere in the object.

It is here that the "problem" of reputation converges with the venerable aesthetic problems of taste and value, closely related issues of evaluation prominent in eighteenth- and twentieth-century debates in aesthetics. Their distinction from reputation is important and usually elided. Reputation is what *other* people prefer and value. "A good reputation," wrote Aristotle, "consists in being *considered* a man of worth."[10] Whereas reputation as *doxa* is a matter of cognition, supposition and approval, taste (L.

*taxare,* to feel, judge) and value (L. *valere,* to be strong, be worth) are matters of knowledge, assessment, and the good. Evaluation asks, What is good? And why? Reputation asks, What do "they" *say* is good? And why?

We cannot evaluate what we do not independently know: we cannot "taste" an object without experiencing it personally or "evaluate" a book without having read it. To evaluate is to be able to specify those features in our experience of the object which justify our judgment. Not mere sensory perception but *intellectual apprehension* of the object constitutes an evaluative experience.

On the other hand, people do regularly "approve" authors and books without having evaluated them personally, often expressing their opinion as a "notion" which they hold for reasons sometimes unclear even to themselves. For we cannot evaluate everyone and everything. For better or worse, we must rely for most of our opinions upon the judgments of others. Of course, as Socrates reminded Meno, *doxa* (opinion) serves just as well as knowledge in many daily affairs: the guide who only "supposes" that this is the road to Larissa yet is quite right gets us there just as effectively as if he "knew" it. But the reputable and the disreputable are not always what they are judged to be. Moreover, there is no guarantee that judgments of a certain quality will emerge through social networks as reputations of a comparable quality. "Reputability gaps" between (not always) informed private judgments and received public opinion may be minuscule or immense. At times we all judge our "renowned" colleagues "overrated," our "admired" friends "overestimated," and our own "unnoticed" selves sorely "deserving."

"Reputation" is an elusive concept partly because of the equivocations in its usages, traceable to its origins in *doxa.* Although "reputation" technically refers to both favorable and unfavorable estimations, we commonly reserve it for the former, as in *doxa* (opinion), e.g., one "gains" or "loses" a (good) reputation. *Doxa* as opinion actually suggests much more than personal or communal opinion, but rather any seeming or appearing ("The earth is flat"), and most journalism on reputations has approached the subject explicitly as deceptive appearance, false opinion.[11] Discussion easily slips from the description of institutionally affiliated, value-laden opinion to its indictment, often in favor of some fondly imagined, untainted value-free opinion. The pejorative tinge of the word "prestige" is rooted in its Latin origins (*praestringere,* to dazzle the eyes), where it was associated with the illusions of jugglers.[12] The adjectives "reputed," "putative," and even "recognized" also carry negative connotations.[13] In the wine industry, a "reputed" pint is only one-twelfth of a gallon, whereas an "imperial" pint is one-eighth of a gallon. A "putative" marriage is a formalized marriage rendered invalid because of impediments like consanguinity. It is notable that to "recognize" a state is not commonly to judge it *excellent* as a state. It is rather to acknowledge, sometimes reluctantly, its status as a state, a decision frequently prompted by influential acknowledgments from other members of the international community.

The two-edged semantics of reputation and the popular press's im-

pulse to sensationalize or trivialize the subject, all three represented in articles like *Esquire*'s, have facilitated academic disregard of reputation as a serious topic of inquiry. On those rare occasions when journals like *The American Scholar* have taken up literary reputation as an issue, they have politely asked only the first of *Esquire*'s questions (about underrated books and authors), characterizing their discussion as "the game" of "rediscovering" "Neglected Books."[14] Few readers and critics would probably deny that authors' reputations bear heavily on practices in publishing and literary journalism, or even question *Esquire*'s buried point that reputations get made through institutional networks which exchange and distribute information. Yet the literary academy has traditionally relegated the subject to the slick magazines and, more recently, to the sociology of art and occupations,[15] where it has received scant attention and where literary canons are not made.

Indeed the topic may well strike a bit too close to home, as observers as opposed in their literary politics as Norman Podhoretz and Richard Kostelanetz seem to agree.[16] For elite institutions and "star" reputations exist in academe and in the literary industry just as in other spheres of activity: the "image" of a writer or critic is surely in some cases as or more important than the "substantive achievement" of his writings. And these images emerge not only through the "qualities" of an author's writings but also as a result of institutional and social affiliations. Nor is this either necessarily to be deplored or denigrated: the image of the remembered living man, and of the man in the writings, will inevitably interact with institutional history to enlarge or limit reputation. Norman Mailer has sought to justify (and exploit) this necessity at great length in *Advertisements for Myself* and elsewhere, and it may well be that the reputations of writers like Mailer and Orwell, and also (as Kostelanetz insists about Lionel Trilling[17]) critics of celebrated personal style, are due as much to favorable or well-known recognition of them in and outside their work (and to their institutional affiliations and those of their champions) as to their written outputs.

But to study reputation risks reputations: we may conclude to the writer's disadvantage that public esteem is grossly at variance either with the "substantive achievement" of his work or with informed private judgment. Reputation typically makes for more reputation (the so-called Matthew Effect[18]) and vice versa, in many instances irrespective of merit. For instance, speaking of his journal's "star system," *Critical Inquiry* editor W.J.T. Mitchell concedes that "we sometimes print essays by famous writers which do not come up to our normal standards" in order to "interest those in other specialties" and because "[o]ne of our goals is to give our readers a sense of what recognized writers are up to . . . even when we do not think that they are up to much good."[19] Mitchell seems strangely unaware that *Critical Inquiry* (which proudly advertises itself, quoting a *Times Literary Supplement* comment, as " 'consistently the best of the academic journals—NEED WE SAY MORE? SUBSCRIBE TODAY' ") *makes* writers "recognized." Indeed, short of a disclaimer identifying those articles in its pages which "aren't up

to much good," one would assume that *an appearance* in "the best academic journal" by itself legitimates an author's work as "of interest" to those inside and outside his special field.

Professional reluctance to self-reflect upon how the literary industry and academy help build and maintain literary reputations is therefore strongly motivated. Viking Press was more than slightly embarrassed upon learning in the late 1970s that a book it had rejected as "inferior" was none other than a typed copy of a novel it had already published which had sold more than 400,000 copies and won the 1969 National Book Award. The novel was Jerzy Kosinski's *Steps,* submitted (as an experiment) under another name by a young author. (Fourteen other publishers and fifteen agents also rejected the retyped *Steps.*)[20] One report claims that Viking has published only one unsolicited fiction manuscript out of 135,000 submissions over 27 years.[21] And yet, a book published privately or by a small press typically goes unreviewed and little-noticed.[22] Richard Kostelanetz has drawn attention to the canonical authority of the *New York Review of Books* and the *New York Times Book Review,* and in particular to the high correlation between advertising space and review space in their pages. His own struggles to publish two books highly critical of the literary industry indicate the depth of resistance to a no-holds-barred discussion of the basis of reputations.[23] Quoting faculty comments on the academy's hiring practices and emphasis on scholarship over teaching, Richard Ohmann argues in *English in America* that "quality" is often sacrificed to "reputation" in that a "quality" department's self-image and future are typically determined by national rankings based on "the subjective perceptions of the department's reputation by those . . . who can know little or nothing of the department's quality." Such perceptions, what Ohmann calls "the myths of prestige," easily become regarded as self-evident facts.[24] (Half of *Esquire*'s academic "makers and breakers" in "The Literary Establishment" of the mid-1960s were drawn from four institutions.) To question literary repute is therefore to question perceptions: and to admit that perceptions are conditional and perspectival is to grant that other than the prevailing view is not only possible but possibly more "valid."

Reflection on these institutional realities does not require castigating institutions *per se,* or indeed mean that reputations do not, in many or even most instances, correlate with their claimed values. It does mean recognizing that value itself is not objectively self-evident but radically contingent. It does require abandoning the idea that reputations and values, any more than literary works themselves, emerge from a pure autonomous realm untainted by social-institutional affiliations, a persistent illusion which has facilitated the dismissal of the discussion of reputation as a mere matter of "leisure-class gossip," in Northrop Frye's memorable words.[25] Indeed it has been more comfortable for the academy to see itself as an aesthetic object— and to exchange political withdrawal for the respected status of museum of culture—than to risk the loss of this secure prestige through a severe and possibly compromising self-examination of its own institutional practices.

Yet an "anatomy of reputation" is not necessarily, and probably should not be, a wild debunking spree—any more than it should be an uncritical affirmation of existing institutional practices. Authority derived from intellectual achievement and institutional position may or may not coincide; but the two are roughly distinguishable, given certain criteria. Reputations and the study of their making, in other words, depend upon people making careful distinctions. The need is to make the criteria for the distinctions open and clear, rather than authoritarian and secretive, and to enforce the criteria consistently in the drawing of the distinctions. Selection processes are the way that institutions make judgments and establish opinions. Institutions not only limit but also enable opportunities, and the task is to see the operative ideology of existing processes: how they are organized, in whose interests they function, and what sorts of alternatives they give rise to. Repute is intimately bound up with what Kenneth Burke has called "the sin of hierarchy." Embedded in our discourse and in the realities of life, it is no doubt impossible to efface completely (" 'Tribally,' one inherits *status*," says Burke), yet it is always open to critical scrutiny and institutional restructuring.[26]

## III

Ironically, if perhaps predictably, the motive force for the official disparagement of reputation as a subject of serious inquiry came partly from the modern literary academy's urge to secure a better reputation for itself. The idea was to model "criticism" on the sciences (with "literature" its laboratory object of study) and to settle on a set of "masterpieces" (like formalizing the chemical elements chart) which would provide endogenous authority and disciplinary stability. Frye's *Anatomy of Criticism* (1957) vigorously expressed what was once (and in many quarters remains) the academy's prevailing view toward reputation. "[A]ll the literary chit-chat which makes the reputations of poets boom and crash in an imaginary stock-exchange," declared Frye in a passage quoted earlier, bears no connection with "real criticism."[27]

An example of "real criticism," explained Frye, was T.S. Eliot's pronouncement that the monuments of literature form an ideal order among themselves, an observation whose "solidity is indicated by its consistency with a hundred other statements that could be collected from the better critics of all ages." "Criticism" as a discipline, maintained Frye, was still in a state of "naive induction," ignorant of "its materials, the masterpieces of literature." Not yet "born as an individual science," it was "still an embryo within the body" of other subjects. Understandably exasperated with the imperial moral criticism of F.R. Leavis and Yvor Winters, and with some critic-reviewers' penchants for marking authors up and down according to ideology or literary politics (a practice still widespread), Frye insisted that "the first step" toward putting literature on a scientific basis was to stop bothering about reputations and the history of taste, "where there are no facts, and where all facts have been split into half-truths to sharpen their cutting edges. . . . [A]s the history of taste has no organic connection with

criticism, it can easily be separated." Criticism's second step, advised Frye, was to exercise extreme caution toward its "neighboring disciplines," which had traditionally exploited its lack of any systematic inductive approach to its masterpieces and "moved in" given the "power vacuum." The wary critic should "enter into relations with them in [a] way that guarantees his own independence." Shifts in critical and public taste, whatever their "attach-[ment] to contemporary social values," struck Frye as simply a matter of "combinations of promotion and demotion," a topic "totally devoid of content" and "too relative and subjective ever to make any consistent sense," "an anxiety neurosis prompted by a moral censor":

> This sort of thing cannot be part of any systematic study, for a systematic study can only progress: whatever dithers or vacillates is merely leisure-class gossip. The history of taste is no more a part of the structure of criticism than the Huxley-Wilberforce debate is part of the structure of science.[28]

And yet, it is hard to see how, based as it is upon the "consistency" of the "better" critics, the "solidity" of "real criticism" is determinable apart from attention to the issue of reputation. Or how criticism as a truly "systematic study" of literature could ignore "contemporary social values" and the "half-truths" of the history of taste, since this embryonic science's "materials," the "masterpieces of literature," would presumably owe their status in some measure to such factors.

Perhaps almost as much as by covert anxiety or overt disciplinary hostility, however, the academy's inattention to reputation is explained by the discourse in and by which literary studies and the history of criticism have inscribed more traditional, immediately accessible literary problems (especially taste, value, endurance, and validity). Even as the postwar literary academy's preoccupation with *interpretation* was leading to what Barbara Herrnstein Smith has called "the exile of evaluation" and to the severe circumscription of these other long-established problems, with critical discussion about them often limited to their proper place (if any) in literary studies, what passing attention these problems did receive served to obscure and absorb the problem of reputation.[29] Thus, in their chapter entitled "Evaluation" in *Theory of Literature* (1949), René Wellek and Austin Warren conflate endurance ("survival") with reputation and then make reputation a criterion for value. Their chapter reflects the common fallacy about the correspondence of reputation to value.[30] The authors write as if there existed a distributive "law of reputation" on the model of perfect economic competition, in which judges had access to all conceivably relevant information bearing on judgments and which worked flawlessly to reward merit with due esteem.[31] "T[he] largest reputations," note the authors, "survive generational tastes: Chaucer, Spenser, Shakespeare, Milton—even Dryden and Pope, Wordsworth and Tennyson—have a permanent though not fixed reputation."[32]

But "permanent" repute is not explainable by the tautology that certain

authors "survive generational tastes": such authors gain and maintain reputations at least partly because the literary industry and academy institu-
tionalize a fixed range of reputation within which authors and works are
more likely to endure, i.e., they become "major" authors. The practice of
dividing authors into "major," "minor," and "ephemeral" has reinforced the
idea of a single top tier of "canonical" literature, the Great Tradition. Current academic and publishing practices virtually guarantee that a recognized "major" author will not fall into "minor" status, where oblivion over
time threatens. Indeed as Wellek and Warren's usage (referring to great
*names* rather than great *works*) suggests, conferral of the status of "major"
(sometimes awarded for a single "masterpiece" or withheld for absurd reasons like the old notion that a major poet must have succeeded in epic) may
ensure attention to an author's lesser works or even keep his entire *oeuvre* in
print. Awarding the honorific "major" to a few dozen authors may simplify
literary studies and reading lists, but it makes for a ridiculous overattention
to the canon. Likewise it makes for personality cults honoring great *authors,*
rather than for the study of great books. Canon-worship also frustrates
classroom learning, since the second-tier writers get shoved out and students therefore rarely compare the well-made play with Ibsen or measure
George Eliot against Bulwer-Lytton—and thus rarely judge *for themselves*
which of the two is superior and why. Obviously the academy's preoccupation with a few authors has also discouraged the rediscovery of many worthwhile "neglected" books.[33]

Wellek and Warren's discussion of reputation under the category of
"evaluation" reflects an historical confusion traceable at least as far back as
the neoclassical debates on taste, in which words pertaining to reputation
like "greatness," "approbation," "honor," "fame," "acclaim," "admiration,"
"approval," and "renown" were confusedly mixed with terms pertaining to
evaluation, including "quality," "excellence," and "merit."[34] The tendency
to entangle endurance and reputation together as criteria for value is also
nothing new, as in Dr. Johnson's view in his *Preface to Shakespeare* that
"length of endurance and continuance of esteem" were the "only measure
of excellence." This blurring frustrated Johnson's immediate goal in the
*Preface,* which was actually to inquire into the relation between value and
reputation: Johnson was investigating "by what peculiarities of excellence
Shakespeare has gained and kept the favour of his countrymen." Johnson's
use of endurance to cover evaluation both by the passive "test of time" and
by active personal judgment is also a characteristic sleight-of-hand when
dealing with the subject of repute. Johnson insists that endurance is both,
by wide consent, "the test of literary merit," whereby Shakespeare already
warrants "prescriptive veneration" as "an ancient"; and also that "ancient"
works gain and retain value because they are continually subject to explicit
re-examination, comparison, and revaluation: "The reverence due to writings that have long subsisted . . . is the consequence of acknowledged and
indubitable positions, that what has been longest known has been most
considered, and what is most considered is best understood."[35] Approaches

like Johnson's indicate how a canon (Gk. *kanne,* rod), originally a measuring instrument, can ossify into a law or monument open only to deciphering.

Reputation obviously does not become problematic so long as the tastes of "everyone who matters" are roughly uniform. The consensus about such uniformity was gradually breaking down during the eighteenth century under the weight of accumulating historical and anthropological evidence of the diversity of cultural (and even European upper-class) tastes. In *Of The Standard of Taste,* Hume addressed the problem of taste, proposing that all aesthetic objects contain certain qualities ("particular beauties") which produce aesthetic pleasure for all humans. Practically speaking, however, the "joint verdicts" of an elite group of "true judges" would best decide aesthetic merit, Hume thought. His use of endurance and repute ("durable admiration") is, however, little different from Johnson's. "Authority and prejudice" may give "temporary vogue" to a bad author (like Bunyan), Hume maintained, but "his reputation will never be durable or general": "When his compositions are examined by posterity or by foreigners . . . his faults appear in their true colors."[36]

The conjoining of "posterity" with "foreigners" here is revealing, for Hume aims, like Johnson, to equate the *de facto* judgments of posterity with the active judgments of foreign audiences. But the movement of works across space is only superficially correspondent to their movement in time: a single "foreigner" can be multicultural and multilingual, and "foreigners" can and do exchange opinions with natives, whereas Shakespeare the Elizabethan and Hume the neoclassical man cannot possibly bridge their historical gulf. It is interesting that, although Hume and the other eighteenth-century British moralists were directly concerned with "approval" as a "moral sentiment," they were not concerned with sociological or epistemological distinctions between value and repute. Hume's psychologism in his major philosophical works disposed him to collapse approval into value and to argue that a thing's value consisted entirely in its being the object of approval.[37]

## IV

As we have seen, to talk about literary reputation and canonized authors inevitably leads to discussion about the literary canon itself. And the tendency for questions of literary evaluation to beg, blur, and devour reputation as an independent issue is perhaps best illustrated in the recent and long-overdue attention to canon-formation, an issue usually approached by way of taste and value.[38] Though canon-formation is of course a subject profitably approached via such traditional questions and from a number of disciplinary perspectives, it is most obviously one important subdivision of the problem of reputation.

Canon-formation is usually discussed narrowly to involve the reputation of works alone, the "masterpieces." Probably canon-formation has attracted recent attention partly because it directly bears on an inescapable pedagogi-

cal task: required reading lists. But genres, historical periods, national literatures, movements, and schools also possess reputations, all of which directly
influence the reputations of works and authors as well as one another. The
institutions of criticism and publishing (agents, publishing houses, critics,
review journals) also possess reputations which can weigh heavily in the
reputations gained or missed by books and authors, as the fate of Kosinski's
*Steps* minus his name suggests. The same observation holds for some extra-
literary phenomena (national prestige, language of composition, prevailing
aesthetic theories). Each of them is a "canon" with its own history and
dynamics. By tacit agreement, these canons too are usually scaled (typically
into "major" and "minor," though sometimes, as with genres and national
literatures, graded more precisely), though critics like Yvor Winters, accused of "enact[ing] a wholesale holocaust of twentieth-century reputations,"[39] did not hesitate to rank-order genres, periods, and whole traditions
explicitly and with sweeping finality.

The reputations of these categories and their sub-categories by no
means necessarily coincide: any of them may raise or lower and enlarge or
shrink the reputations of each other or of member works. Consider Orwell's
own case. *Nineteen Eighty-Four* certainly possesses a public reputation much
wider than Orwell's, and his last two works have undoubtedly extended, if
not directly raised, the standing in which his journalism is regarded—
indeed his journalism would probably never even have been republished if
it had not been for the success of *Animal Farm* and *Nineteen Eighty-Four*.
That Orwell wrote during the last years of the British Empire and in English also has weighed heavily, if uncertainly, in his reputation. Conor
Cruise O'Brien justly asked in the 1960s if Orwell's work, with its "An-
glocentric world view," would have commanded nearly so much attention
during the years of Britain's clear decline as a world power.[40] And surely
Orwell would be less well known today to the international reading public,
no matter how appealing his prose style, if he had written in Bulgarian, a
language with no internationally recognized literary tradition and whose
linguistic community is without power or status.[41]

Other categories of literary repute have also interacted to shape Orwell's
status. Prominent reviewers like Edmund Wilson and Lionel Trilling exerted significant positive influence on Orwell's reputation, as have master-
critics like T.S. Eliot and F.R. Leavis on Donne's and D.H. Lawrence's,
respectively. "George Orwell" is much better known and more highly esteemed than "the *Tribune* writers" of the 1940s as a group, though the same
may not be true for the Beat poets and their members. Some of Orwell's "As
I Please" columns are arguably superior as journalism to his early novels as
novels, but certainly none of them has received the critical attention (and
acclaim) of *Coming Up for Air*. *Nineteen Eighty-Four,* however, though often
judged a mediocre novel by certain intrinsicalist principles, has sometimes
been argued to be a superior political novel or novel of ideas, thereby
raising these lesser genres.

To speak of *the* canon, therefore, whether as a line of masterworks, or

even as limited to literary works exclusively, serves the restrictive view that the traditional high canon of great books is the only canon. Florence Howe's call for increased attention to hitherto little appreciated genres (the folk, the episodic, the polemic), for more culturally diverse anthologies (co-educational, multi-class and -racial), and for "truth in labeling" of academic courses ("American Male Writers of the Nineteenth Century" for a survey of Melville, Whitman, Emerson, Thoreau, etc.) is intended to break the illusion of a single, unrevisable canon exclusively composed of poetry, novels, and drama by certain authors.[42] To label such suggestions to "open up" the canon "special interest politics" and to dismiss them accordingly is just another instance of how the ideology of reputation enforces a globalizing hegemony. Here the pretense of aesthetic purity is staked out as moral high ground from which to obscure the fact that all canons are to some degree political, and to veil the connections between the politics of literary reputation and the politics of the academy and publishing industry.[43] Recent efforts in canon-formation which would define a "canonical" work through prescriptive intrinsic criteria deny implicitly the radically contingent nature of reputation and foster the high canon's hegemony.[44]

For the notion that the high canon contains "the best that has been thought and said" begs the crucial questions: thought and said by, for, and to whom? when and where? for what immediate task? to what larger ends? under what conditions? Thus when J. Hillis Miller expresses his support for the "established canon" on the grounds that "it is more important to read Spenser, Shakespeare, or Milton than to read Borges in translation, or even, to say the truth, Virginia Woolf,"[45] one is entitled to ask: more important for whom? for what? when? The works of Shakespeare, Spenser, and Milton are undeniably *historically significant*, but by what criteria are they always and necessarily more important? One can easily imagine audiences, occasions, and tasks for which the works of Borges and Woolf are the more suitable and "important." For canons legitimate authors as *auctores* (authorities) and books as models, and there are potentially as many pertinent authorities and fit models as there are institutional settings. Traditional or "standardized" reading lists testify to the fact that literary canons exist for all educational levels (from pre-schoolers' Dr. Seuss books to Ph.D. modern literature exams featuring Eliot and Faulkner), in all subjects (*Uncle Tom's Cabin* is a staple of ante-bellum history classes), and outside the academy (James Michener's novels are frequent selections by neighborhood library clubs). Most of the recent work in canon-formation, even by so-called "vigorous canonizers" like Harold Bloom and Paul de Man,[46] has worked within the assumption of "the" canon and the major/minor partition, at most shifting the order of the existing monuments.[47]

Thus, books and authors and other categories of repute possess esteem for many reasons other than endurance or "literary" value, i.e., reasons of *extrinsic* value, whether moral, pragmatic or economic. Some works enjoy high repute less because they are critically respected than because they are "historically significant" as period, style, or genre exemplars, or because

they were regarded as significant by their original audiences. Or works are esteemed for their influence upon authors of more "valued" works, or for their innovations in form, theme, or subject matter. Or because they are valuable social documents, or offer insight into a major writer's personal history or creative process.

Literary works gain and lose reputations, that is to say, partly from the various ways in which literary discourse gets structured, which is itself part of literary history. Some works gain reputations for unusual reasons, e.g., they enter anthologies primarily because they are *bad* instances of a genre, or add diversity, or are short. Some works gain reputations because they are widely taught as fitting examples of pedagogical approaches to literary study, either historical (periods, traditions), topical (genres, stylistic forms, national/regional literatures), biographical or interpersonal (literary "influences"), or theoretical (various critical methods). Literature courses taught in English Romanticism, the epic poem, the pastoral, Wordsworth and Coleridge, autobiography, and narrative theory might all include *The Prelude*, whole or in part. But each would doubtless focus on different passages and highlight different themes, presenting at least a slightly different poem.

## V

Unlike the case of evaluation, then, the history of repute is one of repression, not of one-time prominence and subsequent exile. Inhibited by semantic, professional, and historical factors from emerging into the full day of the academy's consciousness, the reputation process has nevertheless exerted dynamic force, influencing the course of literary history and the practices of the literary academy.[48] Conservative in tendency, the repression of reputation has operated to endorse existing reputations and the institutional arrangements whereby they gained status. By condensing literary issues of value, repute, and meaning into a single term—interpretation—it has also facilitated the preoccupation of the literary academy with exegesis and its quietist illusion of an impartial "test of time"or ideal sphere separable from institutional authority, through whose passive agencies "great" works infallibly emerge.

One might describe the circle of interrelations among the three activities of evaluation, reputation, and interpretation—activities directed toward the respective ends of establishing meaning, worth and opinion—in this way: acts of evaluation (based on overt or covert criteria) serve as the ostensible basis for reputations (and canons), which are then elucidated and (implicitly or explicitly) justified by repeated acts of interpretation. Reputation is thus a concealed link between evaluation and interpretation. If in interpreting a person asks, "What does it mean?" and in evaluating one asks, "What is it worth?" one asks in the passive activity of "reputing," "What do 'they' say it means and is worth?"

Yet this formulation—accurate enough so far as it goes—abrades the finer distinctions involved. Reputation is indeed "what *other* people prefer and value"—but the issue begins, not ends, there. Reputation is not simply

reducible to "second-hand value." For many aforementioned literary and extra-literary factors—most of them impossible to weight precisely yet which certainly condition critical judgments and shape reputations—lie far beyond what we normally consider the act of literary evaluation. Seldom, for instance, does the critic or reviewer of "serious" literature attend, even impressionistically (at least not in print), to how the institutional status of certain publishers, agents, universities, journals, and "esteemed" critics may figure in his or others' verdicts. Or to how the stature of prevailing aesthetic theories and literary movements influence his or others' criticism. Or to the significance of interpersonal networks of affiliations, mechanisms of literary promotion and celebrity, or the prestige of a genre or national literature in his or others' evaluations. And yet, however much these issues are treated as if they lie "beyond" value, they do not lie beyond reputation. Indeed they constitute, acknowledged or not, much of the *stuff* of reputations—of which "evaluation," in any relatively "pure" or "disinterested" sense, forms only a part. All these numerous factors probably *cannot* be given due consideration in judicial acts: the infinite complexity of the task defies detailed treatment. But that even the most decisive factors, in any particular judicial verdict, are almost invariably ignored as if "context-free" evaluations were possible or desirable, testifies less to the formidable nature of the task than to the academy's collective repression of it.

"What do 'they' say it means and is worth?" is therefore both a more subtle and a more resonant question than is immediately apparent. Unlike evaluating and interpreting, "reputing" is a *passive* activity; its complicated relation to them is asymmetrical. Unlike them, reputation is not really an "act"—and, as we have seen, its passive character has surely facilitated its subsumption and obscuring as a literary issue. Thus "value" and "repute" are much more than names for different stages of the same social process, but are also formally and epistemologically distinct. Evaluation (indeed reception itself) is active; reputation is passive. "Evaluation" is a private act; "reputation" is the cumulative, ultimate *consequence* of innumerable acts of receiving and approving (or disapproving). Reputation is therefore a cultural "condition" in which every receiver participates whether or not he himself interprets or evaluates: we all "assimilate" reputation. It is therefore essentially a social, not an individual, phenomenon. Edmund Wilson and Lionel Trilling did not singlehandedly "create" Orwell's American reputation by virtue of their favorable estimations: it is only because *others were influenced* by their judgments that Orwell's reputation grew. And the major difference between their estimations and those of other readers is the difference between a broadly social and a private (or restricted interpersonal) event.

To see these interrelations among interpretation, evaluation, and reputation is to see the role that reputation plays in our literary—and daily—lives.[49] To neglect conceptual consideration of reputation often *in practice* eliminates deliberate evaluation and makes for *de facto* evaluations; critics aim simply to yield appreciation for works which they already assume are "great." Or, even worse, they fail ever to examine those works which they

assume are secondary or "noncanonical." Put another way, one can "exile" evaluation, but one cannot exile reputation. Reputations and the existing canons remain. To repress reputation is merely to confirm and exalt standing judgments by ritualistic acts of exegesis, an abdication all the more inviting and easily committed in literature because of the existence of institutions designed to pre-judge for us: book review pages, literary academies, writing prizes, book clubs, best-seller lists. We often inherit literary opinions of educated taste long before we have the wherewithal to judge confidently ourselves. In the weak version of the process, the received opinions come merely by way of the practices of selection and exclusion (e.g., reading "the" canon). In the strong version, personal or institutional authorities legislate specific judgments about inferior and superior taste.

The critical perspective on reputation which follows is intended to lift the repression of reputation by asking questions about the making of literary reputation, both in general and in the specific case of Orwell. We have already seen how Orwell's reputation has varied widely across audiences and over time, and yet how the illusions of universality and fixity which characterize the ideology of repute have affected his reputation too. Since all reputations are adventitious and conditional, we need to ask, Reputed for what? By whom? When, where, and under what conditions? In no sense do the ensuing concepts constitute a literary "doxology," a counterpart in literary sociology to systems of thought proposing themselves as philosophical axiology or literary hermeneutics. Nor is this an attempt to devise a set of prescriptive "principles of literary reputation," let alone either a large-scale system designed to apply to some category called "literary figure" or a full-scale sociological "theory" of reputation which would restructure the canon and Orwell's place in it. A massive, hermetic construct is much too coarse an instrument for approaching the multiple interpersonal and institutional contingencies bearing on the formation of any single reputation. Instead my aim is to offer a set of questions and concepts in which the fragmentary evidence recoverable about authors' reputations can attain greater intelligibility and broader significance. Possessing instrumental power and aspiring to coherence, these related "terms of repute" may thereby illumine the processes of "reputation-formation" and generate questions appropriate for case studies of Orwell's (and other writers') history of reputation.

## 3. A Critical Perspective

### i. *From Aesthetic to Rhetoric*

I

Seeing reputation as process means seeing it as a certain kind of process, one different from the "reception" process. I have spoken of *reputation-formation* and *reputation-history*. The usage is deliberate, for "reputation" and

"reception" warrant further distinction as social *processes*. "Reception" can mean, as it does in German empirical reception theory and traditional *Wirkungsgeschichte* (the history of impact), a temporal stream of responses, or, as in *Rezeptionsästhetik* (the aesthetics of reception), an arbitrary selection of historical responses for analysis.[50]

"Reputation," as it is understood here, refers to the selection, codification, and characterization of responses into key moments, stages, and audiences. It is meta-reception. Not all reception evidence is equally important in the formation of a reputation: invariably some statements, moments, stages, and audiences are more influential—and more sociologically or historically revealing—than others.

Our ordinary discourse about reputations reflects the reception/reputation distinction and these critical categories: reputations, not receptions, "build," "culminate," and "fall off"; "grow," "skyrocket," "lag," "freeze," "spiral" upward or downward; and are "confined," "expanding," "limited," or "far-ranging." Reception refers to the flow of events; reputation consists in the discovery and presentation of *patterns* in the responses.

To pursue this distinction, it will prove useful to consider briefly a common metaphor when speaking of reputation, one that is suggestive of the reputation process and which in turn recommends a controlling concept for the dynamics and variabilities of the process. We often speak of reputations as "bright" or "dim," "enduring" or "short-lived," "big" or "small." Some especially highly reputed people, groups, and institutions are said to be "stars."

Reputations are indeed somewhat like stars. Reputations vary in luminosity, duration, and size. Some stars radiate brighter, longer, and farther than others. Some "superstar" reputations do likewise: images of and opinions about certain people are more intense, more abiding, and more widespread than others. Reputations "radiate" before us as individual perceivers of images, and these images radiate in time and through the social structure.

The *radiation* of a reputation is a way of speaking about the interpersonal dynamics and societal dissemination of reputation. The term usefully applies to these two dimensions of reputation. On these two "axes," depth and breadth, reputations "radiate." Images radiate over time in our memories; images radiate or "circulate" through the "coils" of the social structure. They alter as they travel in time and through social networks. As they move, they permute. The reputation process, that is to say, operates on the "micro" level of individual experience and on the "macro" level of large institutional publics—and on numerous "levels" in between.[51] One must recognize these different levels of cultural analysis, for they are patterned differently. The reputation process is not merely an overarching set of institutional interactions on the level of "reading publics" within the social structure, but also a series of expressive, symbolic forms of personal experience. At the "high" level of institutional "publics" or "organs" (the Soviet Union, Germany, the academy, the advertising industry, *Newsweek* readers), we are usually talking about the author's range of reception and impact. At the

"low" level of individual receivers, we are talking about the single reader's "texture of experience" of the author and his work.

Between these two "levels" stands the social group. Attention to the individual reader's reference group(s)—to the sociohistorical affiliations of concrete historical receivers within identifiable groups—often provides insight into his or her reading experience. Such information about reference group relations preserves real reader experience yet allows for broader cultural conclusions. With data about reference group relations, it is sometimes possible to reconstruct the sociohistorical context of a reader's response and in turn to see how the reader's group was influenced by the member's response. The study of the reader's group relations may therefore illumine not only how a selected reader's response is more than merely private—how it may reflect the responses of larger groups and institutions to which he or she belongs—but also how and why this particular response gained wider currency.

What concerns us in a sociology of literary repute, then, is the literary component of what C. Wright Mills called "the cultural apparatus," "the means by which [literary] work is made available to circles, publics, and masses."[52] Generally speaking, literary reputations radiate through smaller circles to the public at-large. Every person and institution is a potential "radiator" and "mediator," in and through whom images and information emerge and get passed on. Typically, however, judgments of influential critic-reviewers shape the outlines of an author's image. Groups and the mass media in turn distribute a version of that image, thereby helping expand a critical reputation into a public one. On literary issues, articulate opinion usually gets formed in print, and the mass media and educational authorities determine which opinions gain currency. Groups often "mediate" critical and popular reputation by distributing critical judgments (via little magazines, academic journals, university curricula) to a wider audience, or directly to the mass media, though prominent critic-reviewers often have direct access to institutional organs with large audiences.[53]

Roughly speaking, we can demarcate three spheres of literary repute.[54] "Academic" reputation institutionalizes the author in school curricula. His or her work becomes a "classic" or pedagogical staple, lectured about, set for examinations, anthologized in school and college readers. "Intellectual" or "avant garde" reputation often precedes reputation in the academy; it may or may not lead to it—usually depending on whether the avant garde becomes "the Establishment" (whether by transforming it or being coopted by it). Here the author is respected by other writers and receives attention chiefly in the non-specialist "intellectual" quarterlies or "advanced" magazines, rather than in the specialist academic journals. Not infrequently, his work is a direct challenge to those with exalted academic reputations; he may become a cult figure among the young. "Popular" or "public" reputation involves sales and public recognition. The author's books sell beyond academic and intellectual circles; often his name or personal history gets publicized by the mass media. There are various degrees of "popular" re-

pute; the mass-market writer or "blockbuster" seller will rarely achieve much of an academic or intellectual reputation, while the "serious" writer who sells a few hundred thousand copies may be regarded by academics and intellectuals as a "popular" writer. Orwell has acquired all three kinds of reputation, and Part Two will examine in some detail each of these spheres of his repute and their overlapping areas.

## II

Unlike the case with most discussions of literary reception, then, our chief concern is not with the phenomenology of the reading experience or with literary hermeneutics or social science, but rather with the sociology and historiography of reputations. This distinguishes our approach from the text-oriented West German reception aesthetics associated with the work of Hans Robert Jauss and the University of Konstanz theorists, who formulate an "ideal historical" reader, whereby a selected reader is designated as a hypothetical "reader-norm" which changes over time. Our interest, by contrast, is in the actual historical receiver. Whereas the reading public of the formalist-phenomenological *Rezeptionsästhetik* remains single, unified, and abstract, our shift in focus toward real readers aims to appreciate reception audiences in their multiplicity, discreteness, and concreteness. German reception aesthetics treats historical reception materials as mere accessory evidence for buttressing conclusions already arrived at through analysis of the phenomenology of the reading experience; we make the historical reception materials primary.[55]

The term *institutional reader* is meant to emphasize that the reading process does not occur in a vacuum: our responses to literature, as to everything else, are influenced by our historical-institutional affiliations. In a trivial sense, all of us are institutional readers, living our lives within and through institutions—the family, church, school, government, military, corporation, and many sub-institutions, according to a variety of ascribed and achieved social characteristics. For there is no need to quantify the concept of the institutional reader: the reader's decisive frames of reference are what concern us, however narrowly or broadly they may be drawn. An institutional reader need not, then, be linked formally to an institution (e.g., the members of one's "generation" or a magazine's readership also constitute an "institutional" group). Usually, however, we can determine audiences according to ascribed or achieved social characteristics (race, sex, ideological or political or religious affiliations, etc.), and some members will identify themselves—and be identified by outsiders—by these categorical labels.

This move away from literary texts and toward historical audiences, from a phenomenology of reading toward a sociology of reputation, could be termed a "rhetorical" approach toward literary reception, a *rhetoric of reception*. In the tradition of classical rhetoric, we focus upon actual historical audiences and situations. Following Kenneth Burke's post-Freudian conception of rhetoric, we approach reception as an act of speaker-listener

identification. With Burke, we view rhetoric as symbolic action and cultural images as forms of symbolic action.[56] Thus we pay special attention to the identifications of real historical readers with authors, to the resultant images (radiant or dim, far-ranging or local, enduring or momentary, stable or fluctuating) which readers have possessed of authors, and to the radiation of these images throughout the social structure. In focusing upon readers as receivers within institutional networks of relations, rather than upon texts as constitutive objects of consciousness, we also attend to the oral dimension of reception. For all of us are also "institutional auditors," forming our opinions partly (and sometimes largely) from verbal exchanges and electronic broadcasts. Our methodological starting point is traditional *rhetorica utens,* rhetoric as language in use. The idea, in short, will be to treat material instantiations of readers' responses as public, institutional discourse in order to reconstruct the context in which reception acts have occurred, thereby disclosing aspects of the author's changing public image and radiating impact.[57] To see how reception is *used* means to see how the act of reception also is often a rhetorical act of donation, appropriation, rejection, restitution, reprisal, or reconciliation—reception *as* gratitude, confiscation, contempt, etc. The form and substance of the reception act may vary. Receivers are also givers, lenders, borrowers, searchers—giving thanks, bestowing largesse, deriving glory, seeking authority. To receive, then, can be also to take, to challenge, to affirm, to deny: to exalt or vilify the Other as one risks or protects the self.

Thus a study of "reputation" is not merely a literary influence study (as in *Wirkungsgeschichte*), or the arbitrary selection of historical responses for study (as in *Rezeptionsästhetik*), or a statistical survey of the responses of contemporary readers (as in empirical reception theory).[58] All such approaches, whatever light they shed on literary reception, have had little to say about "reputation" because they have failed to acknowledge the need for the selection, codification, and characterization of reception materials. Likewise, they have often lacked sufficient self-consciousness about their theoretical assumptions and empirical limitations. Any discussion of *reputation* must include a frank weighing and sifting of the reception materials.

The case studies in Part Two which codify Orwell's history of reputation make use of a variety of materials associated with the two chief "levels" of literary reception already noted. For reputation is variously manifested. At the level of individual readers, it may involve seeing how readers (and especially writers) model themselves on an author. Or how an author's work influences the work of later writers, whether in theme, subject matter, style, or other ways. At the level of institutional publics (the academy, Germany), "reputation" may involve examining allusions to the author or his work, quotations from his *oeuvre,* or use of his coinages. Or it may involve information about his book sales, about media adaptations of his work, or about schools or movements indebted to him. All of these constitute "influence,"[59] though the influence is a matter of cultural effect, rather than merely literary effect.[60]

To talk about reputations, we have noted, is to talk about images, which exist only in and through language, as symbolic form. The plain historiographical fact, which nevertheless bears periodic emphasis, is that our images of Orwell are not the man himself but representations of "the real," made available only in and through language as symbolic form and chiefly through written materials. Nor are there any "groups" or "institutions." Of course, there was a George Orwell who wrote during the 1940s for the London left-wing weekly *Tribune*. But any such group or institution as *Tribune* is a social construction of reality: there are only persons and real relations among persons. Aggregates of people, assigned roles which sometimes possess socially recognized authority, are without metaphysical status. But persons do live *through* social groups and institutions, and often perceive one another (or even themselves) first or primarily as members of larger units, according to ascribed or achieved social categories.

A theoretical investigation of the relations between self-concept and group identity is far beyond the scope of this project. But I should make clear here the sharp distinction between an "institutional" reader and a "real" reader. The two are by no means identical. Inasmuch as all readers are affiliated with institutions and groups, all readers are institutional readers. But not all of a reader's experience can be interpreted exhaustively by sociological concepts and according to social-institutional affiliations: some residue of the uniquely *personal* element in the response remains. Persons can and usually do transcend their class and institutional categories. For example, we cannot fully assimilate the "Orwell" of the mid-'40s to his *Tribune* setting. However much Orwell may at that time have seemed "the voice of *Tribune*," either inside or outside the *Tribune* group, certain distinctively individual factors separated him from his *Tribune* colleagues. The same is true for any member of any social-institutional group. To a significant extent Orwell's work did reflect "the *Tribune* outlook" and "represented" *Tribune*. But neither he nor his work are reducible to "*Tribune*."[61] Still, in admitting that there are regions of experience in a particular reception act which lie beyond institutional description—and for which written materials, ordinarily the only reception evidence available, may not exist or survive—the critic's task remains worth doing: trying to understand what is pertinent to the reputation process, paraphrasable, and susceptible to analysis and generalization.[62] Difficulty and imprecision in literary sociology, as Jeffrey Sammons reminds us, should not be equated with impossibility and futility.[63] It is not necessary to know everything in order to understand something.

The point is, therefore, that reception is a concrete, individual, irreducible act, part of which stands beyond the limits of any sociological description or concept. One can never recapture the full individuality of a reader's reception, or of the reader himself. Nevertheless, by focusing on elements of the reader's background and situation which he shares with other receivers—by attending to his generational, political, professional, and other group affiliations—the concept of the institutional reader discloses

much of the reception experience of the "real" reader and yet possesses much broader sociological implications. Yet it does so not by presenting "*the* Marxist response" or "*the* neoconservative response" to Orwell; but rather *Raymond Williams'* and *Norman Podhoretz's* responses, influential institutional readers of Orwell with identifiable left- and right-wing affiliations.

"An institution," wrote Emerson, "is but the lengthened shadow of a man."[64] Our aim in studying the reception act of selected individual readers is to follow, where possible, the shadow of Orwell's reputation beyond individuals into wider circles and publics. Certainly, reading done within different institutions—the executive in the corporation, the scholar in the academy, the intellectual within the political group—usually conditions the reading experience in different ways. Because of his significance in shaping Orwell's reputation, Part Two will devote chief attention to this last sort of institutional reader.

Our shift from *Rezeptionsästhetik* is not, then, toward rhetoric as ornament (stylistics), which would simply be another poetics of reception and leave "the reader in the text," as per the title of one anthology of "audience-oriented" reception criticism.[65] "Audience-oriented" criticism is, inevitably, institution-oriented criticism. It is seeing, where pertinent, "the reader in the group," and seeing how institutional readers make and are influenced by literary "figures."[66] The case study which follows illustrates this process in one receiver's experience of Orwell during the formative period of Orwell's reputation, the early 1950s. I introduce it here because it serves as a "model" case history of those which will follow in Part Two and for three related reasons: 1) historical significance: it is one of the most influential statements ever made about Orwell; 2) sociological value: it is a "site" which raises numerous issues that the case studies in Part Two will confront singly, and it sheds light especially on the two main aspects of literary reputation as social process—i.e., how a reader's response contributes to the development of a writer's reputation and how a reader "relates" to and gets influenced by a writer; and 3) conceptual advantages: it offers the opportunity to introduce the chief "terms of repute" with which we will be working in Part Two.

ii.  *Between Literary Figure and Institutional Reader*

III

In his introduction to *Homage to Catalonia*, Lionel Trilling characterized Orwell memorably as "a virtuous man," "a figure in our lives." "We," Trilling said, could be like him if only . . .

> . . . if we but surrendered a little of the cant that comforts us, if for a few weeks we paid no attention to the little group with which we habitually exchange opinions, if we took our chance of being wrong or inadequate, if we looked simply and directly. . . . He liberates us . . . . He frees us from the need for the inside dope. He implies that our job is not to be intellectual, certainly not intellectual in this sense or that, but merely to be intelli-

gent according to our lights—he restores the old sense of the democracy of the mind. . . . He has the effect of making us believe that we may become full members of the society of thinking men. That is why he is a figure for us.[67]

And yet, despite Trilling's characteristically graceful prose and skillfully elastic use of first-person pronouns, all "that" may be no more than "why" Orwell was a figure for Lionel Trilling—not necessarily "why" also for his "little group" of New York Intellectuals* writing for *Partisan Review* or even for his Columbia graduate student who first called Orwell "a virtuous man"—let alone for "us," past or present.

For a *figure,* simply put, is one who somehow "figures" in the life of the Other(s). Persons figure conditionally and intermittently in our lives—or in certain people's lives, in certain forms, at certain times and in certain places, for certain reasons, given certain needs and aspirations. A figure for whom? of what? when and where? for what stated and unstated reasons?

When Trilling saw Orwell as "the man who tells the truth," "the figure . . . of the virtue of not being a genius,"[68] he was using the word "figure" as a rhetorical figure. To Trilling, literary figures were "intellectual heroes."[69] And although his use of the plural "we" was imprecise, he was trying to convey his sense of Orwell as a special presence in his life, and indeed the essay's "re-presentation" of Orwell (whom Trilling never met) helped make him a figure in some of "our lives."

Anyone can be a *presence* figuring in another's life, possessing, as Orwell temporarily did for Trilling at mid-century, a moral and imaginative immediacy which can act to shape one's values. Sometimes an individual becomes intensely, vividly "present" in the life of sections of a community. To call someone "a figure" is to imply such a shared communal consciousness of imagined presence. The sharing is inevitably uneven and fluctuating even within the most homogeneous groups. But there is no need to bound the "we" of communal presence. Orwell did not figure strongly for all, perhaps even many, of the writers at *Partisan Review* in the early 1950s, let alone for most of "us." The light of someone's presence, like a star, may pulsate with as many degrees of intensity as there are variations in personal relationships, from ignorance or dim awareness of an Other's existence to vague knowledge, name recognition, nodding acquaintance, friendship, and radiant presence. In this last, special form, a person can shine as a communal "figure in our lives."

Of course, there is no inherent property characterizing figures, any

---

*The term has been in currency since the 1940s. It designates a loose, predominantly Jewish group of New York-based writers (c. 1935–65), most of them contributors to *Partisan Review.* I follow Alexander Bloom in designating these writers with a capital I, thereby to distinguish them as a "group" distinct from other postwar intellectuals in New York. I also use the term interchangeably with "the New York writers" and "*Partisan Review* writers." See Bloom's *Prodigal Sons: The New York Intellectuals & Their World* (New York, 1986). Also Irving Howe's essay, "The New York Intellectuals: A Chronicle & A Critique," *Commentary,* October 1968, 29–51.

more than for identifying "star quality." We value people for many different qualities and see them in many different guises.[70] ("Figure" is in fact derived from the mask and costume of Greek actors, who uttered different speeches under different guises.) A person attains "stardom" upon the fortuitous convergence of his characteristics and a subject's projected desires: the person is somehow perceived as satisfying a personal, group, or cultural desire, though the "filling" may be experienced as near-total or partial, loose-fitting or exact, durable or fleeting.

The responses of audiences therefore "make" persons stars or figures. But not all persons will do. Which of the many potentially suitable figure "candidates" achieves such status depends heavily upon the particulars of the local historical-institutional setting, or *reception scene*. A "literary" figure is first and chiefly recognized and valued by persons familiar with the "literary" scene, and so forth. What distinguishes these scenes is what primarily "matters" to them: intellectual/literary achievement (the literary/intellectual scene), dress (the fashion scene), athletic prowess (the sports scene), and so forth. A London novelist-essayist like Orwell is, of course, more likely to figure on the London intellectual scene than on the American sports scene. But Orwell's reputation has radiated unusually far and wide for a modern literary figure. As we saw in the last chapter, he has managed the exceptional feat of figuring, brightly or dimly, for members of many different groups within many cultural scenes—literary, intellectual, academic, political, journalistic, commercial, religious.

The background of Lionel Trilling's reception of Orwell was the intellectual-academic scene of postwar New York, especially the *Partisan Review* contributors and some Columbia University faculty. It has gone unnoticed that Trilling's oft-quoted view of Orwell as "the virtuous man" directly reflected Trilling's exalted position within the New York-*Partisan Review* intelligentsia, and so we approach his reception act sensitive to the "little group" with which he "habitually exchanged opinions." The strong, warm responses to Orwell by other members of the New York writers' circle will receive further discussion in Part Two.* The immediate point here is that Trilling's image of Orwell emerged against a particular scene, was shaped by it and in turn reshaped it as it gained currency within it, and eventually radiated far beyond it into the wider public sphere.

The passion of Trilling's prose, his choice of details about Orwell, and indeed the very title of his Orwell essay—"The Politics of Truth: Portrait of the Intellectual as a Man of Virtue"—make clear that Trilling saw Orwell, however temporarily, as an intellectual ideal, the figure as intellectual hero. To Trilling, Orwell stood as a man of "truth" and "simple courage." By virtue of his remarkable "directness of relation to moral . . . fact,"[71] Orwell seemed, thought Trilling, to have miraculously resolved the problem of political commitment and intellectual integrity, the liberal intellectual's—

*See Chapter Six, Section 20, Socialist "intellectual hero," neoconservative "guiding spirit": Irving Howe, Norman Podhoretz, and the New York Intellectuals' Orwell (pp. 336–62).

and Trilling's—agonized "politics of truth." First published in the March 1952 *Commentary*,[72] edited by Trilling's friend and mentor Elliot Cohen, the essay strikes one as nothing less than an exalted portrait of the would-be first-generation New York Intellectual as "man of virtue," "liberated" from his "little group," his comforting "cant," his "need for the inside dope," his intellectual "fashions"—indeed very much like a sketch of Trilling's ideal self.

To Trilling, Orwell was "the figure of not being a genius." An odd way of characterizing the keynote to a man's reputation. Since when is "not being a genius" a virtue in itself? And yet, approached from within the perspective of the New York group in the 1950s, the phrasing becomes comprehensible. "He is the figure of not being a genius, of fronting the world with nothing more than one's simple, direct, undeceived intelligence. . . ." Orwell was not a genius. ("What a relief. What an encouragement.") He was just an extraordinary ordinary man. He was the ordinary man's thinking man. He "stood" for "plainness of mind" and "telling the truth." And in this "he communicates to us the sense that what he has done, any one of us can do."[73]

"Or could do if we but made up our minds to do it," Trilling added, as if to remind himself. For when Trilling the New York Intellectual looked at Orwell the London intellectual, he saw a man who had first of all renounced "intellectualizing" for plain, humble thinking. His Orwell had rejected respectable ideas, fashionable opinion, endless analysis, elaborate theoretical constructs—and stood instead for personal conviction and intuition, energy and nonconformity, open and nontechnical exchange, and intellectual freedom and passion. Orwell seemed to have achieved what Trilling was still struggling to achieve. The "great word" during his student days at Columbia, Trilling once recalled, had been "*intelligence*," which "did not imply exceptional powers of abstract thought" but rather "a readiness to confront difficulty and complexity" and "an ability to bring thought cogently to bear upon all subjects to which thought might be appropriate." Trilling conceived "the intelligent man" as exemplified not by erudition and scholarship but as possessing "an intelligence of the emotions and of task." His teacher John Erskine's motto "The Moral Obligation To Be Intelligent" became Trilling's too.[74] To Trilling, Orwell's "not being a genius" meant all this. It meant renouncing from the start the image of the intellectual as a self-important "thinker" trafficking in lofty abstractions and disdainful of the daily, earthbound routines of "ordinary" people. It meant being "far removed from the Continental and American type of intellectual." Orwell was "an intellectual to his fingertips," said Trilling, but he was none of this. For Orwell "implies that our job is not to be intellectual, at least not in this fashion or that, but as a man intelligent according to our lights."[75] Trilling's Orwell, "the portrait of the intellectual as man of virtue," was simply an honest, intelligent man.

And yet, Trilling found Orwell exceptional. "It is hard to find personalities in the contemporary world who are analogous to Orwell." In him "there

was indeed a quality of an earlier day," Trilling lamented, for Orwell was "an unusual kind of man, with a temper of heart and mind which is now rare."[76] Even his student's characterization of Orwell as "a virtuous man" seemed to Trilling an archaism especially appropriate for describing Orwell. "Somehow to say that a man 'is good,' or even to speak of a man who 'is virtuous,' is not the same thing as saying, 'He is a virtuous man.'" That sentence's simple phrasing, by some quirk of the English language, thought Trilling, brought out "the private meaning of the word virtuous, which is not merely moral goodness but fortitude and strength." *Homage to Catalonia* was imbued with virtue in this most sturdy and old-fashioned sense, "a genuine moral triumph written in a tone uniquely simple and true." Orwell was no genius, just a man who renewed in one "a respect for the powers that one does have, and the work one undertakes to do."[77]

Indeed Trilling's own reputation was not founded on brilliance. Even mutually antagonistic critics agree[78] that he was already by the early '50s viewed as, and doubtless knew it, the younger generation's example of humanist-critical intelligence and instinctive good judgment. Like Orwell, he was regarded as a "different" sort of intellectual, different even in the eyes of his fellow New York writers. Trilling belonged, said critic-friend and former Columbia classmate Clifton Fadiman, not to "the party of the party" but to "The Party of the Imagination."[79] Especially to outside observers critical of the *Partisan Review* writers for their parochialism and brashness, Trilling seemed a thinker independent of coteries, broadly humane and catholic in his tastes. Leslie Fiedler marveled at his "remarkable aura of respectability not granted to any of his colleagues." Unlike them, Trilling was "modesty itself," and yet he somehow also seemed to "embod[y] and modify the *PR* spirit."[80] Philip Toynbee noticed a strong resemblance between Orwell and Trilling as "liberal-democratic critics,"[81] and the *Partisan Review* group considered the London-*Horizon* literary circle to be a virtual mirror image of their New York enclave, with Cyril Connolly's *Horizon*—to which Orwell was a contributor—regarded as "*Partisan Review*'s English brother."[82] Already by the early '50s Trilling's name was associated with the names of his published and forthcoming books: Matthew Arnold, E.M. Forster, "The Liberal Imagination," and (opposed though the two concepts were in Trilling's vocabulary) "Sincerity and Authenticity."[83]

One senses that recognition of these similarities in position and temper between Orwell and himself did not pass Trilling's eye unnoticed. In his obituary of Trilling, Steven Marcus closed by naming five authors whom his onetime teacher "most admired." Orwell was the only contemporary writer on the list.[84] Significantly, of Orwell's many attributes, Trilling seized on Orwell's apparent "plainness of mind" and truth-telling. Trilling might well have focused on other attributes of Orwell, as so many other critics have done. But plainness and truth-telling were, of course, the very attributes which Trilling felt that most Left intellectuals lacked—especially when it had come to the equivocations about the Left's behavior in the Spanish Civil War—and which cut them off, unlike Orwell, from "the familial common-

place," "the stupidity of things." Orwell had never committed "the prototypi-
cal act of the modern intellectual" which marked the New York writers' rise
to cultural prominence and assimilation: "abstracting himself from the life
of the family."[85]

Of course, whatever his writings may suggest, Orwell was not fully integrated into the "life of the family," as his strained relations with his family
over his own struggle to be a writer attest.[86] Trilling was more accurate than
he realized when he spoke of Orwell's "fronting the world" with his "simple,
direct, undeceived intelligence." Orwell's persona was, partly, a front,
though that is not to say it was deceptive. In any case it achieved its aim;
Trilling, like others, *perceived* Orwell to be a "plain" man. Trilling's image of
Orwell was a moving, fully convincing portrait of a virtuous intellectual,
read by Americans just as interest in Orwell's life was growing. Much of
what made this portrait so convincing was Trilling's own passionate homage
to Orwell. Indeed the way Trilling describes Orwell and what he describes
about him are charged with identification, amounting almost to an effort
within the essay itself to extend a resemblance in position to one of character and destiny. And to some extent this destiny was realized: Trilling's
image of the "virtuous" Orwell came, at least in some instances, to be the
*Partisan* writers' image of Trilling himself. "He was, to use the old-fashioned
term, a virtuous man," William Barrett has written, "and moreover, a virtuous man without any touch of the prig. And in the particular environment
of New York in which we moved that was indeed an accomplishment."[87] If
Orwell was Trilling's Common Man and Man of Truth, Trilling himself was
"The Whole Critic," "The Intelligent Man's Guide to Literature," "modesty
itself."[88]

*Authoritative voices* like Trilling are special institutional readers, often
perceived from the outside as not only reflecting but representing their
groups.* As the *Partisan Review* writers' "single most influential member in
the 1950s, the only one . . . whose influence extended far beyond the confines" of their circle,[89] Trilling's eminence sprung from his "father figure"
status among the New York writers and yet his influence extended far
beyond New York. He "embodied" and yet "modified" the "*PR* spirit." He
was immediately associated in intellectual-academic circles with *Partisan Review*, and yet he was also recognized as a personality in his own right.

Frequently, as with Trilling, the authoritative voice is not just an influential or major critic, but rather possesses group-related authority.[90] Whether
or not he sees himself as a member of a group or school or movement,

---

*All institutional readers, of course, belong to several groups, each of which will vary in size,
sense of self-identity, physical proximity, and duration as a "we." All individuals (and groups)
have multiple frames of reference, including ascribed characteristics (sex, age, race, religion),
roles and memberships (occupation, class, political affiliation), and many other categories and
activities (education, hobbies). Usually a few persons and groups, however, are identifiable as
significant influences. Especially if addressing a defined audience in a journal or magazine, a
writer will have them chiefly "in mind" when communicating. It is with these decisive frames of
reference that we are mainly concerned.

he is perceived by many outsiders as affiliated with a definable political or cultural group, and often with a certain publication. His authority may be primarily organizational (like *Partisan* editor Philip Rahv), or chiefly charismatic and symbolic, like Trilling (and Orwell). Inside the group, he may be regarded with respect or hostility, or as just another member. Outside the group, he is often perceived as "speaking for" the group, and therefore speaks "loudly" or "authoritatively," as if with the voice of many. From far outside, he may seem even the voice of a class or nation, as from Britain Trilling seemed to Ernest Jones in 1956 nothing less than "intellectual America."[91]

The authoritative voice is of special interest to a sociology of literary reputation because of his close identification with and revealing location within a group. He or she is a "well-located" institutional reader, a reception "nodal point," so positioned that his or her personal response can be interpreted, using information about the group, to represent far more than a private, idiosyncratic response. A reader closely identified with a group also helps disclose the diverse radiations of a reputation, the variations in a writer's reputation at the group level. I have spoken of "Trilling's Orwell." The usage is intended to make clear that Lionel Trilling's image of Orwell did not coincide exactly with that of other New York Intellectuals;[92] one could speak of a "Rahv's Orwell," a "Howe's Orwell," and a "Diana Trilling's Orwell," all of them similar to yet distinct from Lionel Trilling's Orwell.[93] Selecting for study an authoritative voice within a group allows us to "trace" his Orwell image down through the history of the group, so that we can see how the image of "the virtuous man" fragments in the next generation of New York Intellectuals, between "Howe's Orwell" on the Left and "Podhoretz's Orwell" on the Right, with each man emphasizing different aspects of this image as he highlights his political affinities with Orwell.[94] Selecting for study those readers (partly) guided by ideological politics, like Trilling, also allows us to spotlight how Orwell the political writer has elicited passionate, politically tinged responses, and how a receiver tends to rewrite in his own image (or negative) a writer with whom he strongly identifies (or disagrees). Such receivers do not merely *report* an image of Orwell; they *recast* Orwell as they interpret his work. Thus, in this case study of Trilling's Orwell—and in many of the others in Part Two—we are not primarily concerned with "isolated" institutional readers possessing general authority apart from a group, even when (like Edmund Wilson and V.S. Pritchett) they have been influential in shaping Orwell's overall reputation. In order to see how Orwell has "figured" in the lives of readers, we focus upon authoritative voices so situated within groups as to disclose the radiations of reputation at the group level, voices whose prominent affiliations permit the reconstruction of a dense sociohistorical context in which to interpret their reception acts. By understanding the context of a response like Trilling's, we can see how a reader may seize upon certain aspects of an author and rewrite him, often as an attempt to resolve his own problems of identity.

## IV

With special authority come special burdens. Already by 1952 Trilling felt the tensions of his singular place in New York and American intellectual life. His powerful attraction to Orwell was to a romanticized figure who seemed to occupy, posthumously, a similar place and to have resolved his own "politics of truth" in a way Trilling had not. In Trilling's case, the politics were cultural and personal. Long after the battle lines of the 1930s had been drawn and erased, Trilling was still seeking to reconcile the dilemma of what William Barrett called "the two M's," Marxism and Modernism, wanting to champion both, and yet ambivalent because he felt that the political tendency of modernism generally ran counter to progressive thought. How to have high art and "the old sense of the democracy of the mind"?[95] Trilling saw that the dilemma was the form in which his century had chosen to present the age-old question of the proper relations of the aesthetic, the political, and the ethical. According to Barrett, Trilling "worr[ied] about this question for the rest of his life," "returning to it again and again yet leaving it finally unsolved" except to recommend that one practice the openness of mind to consider the "possibilities" of both choices.[96]

Inevitably, for an intellectual leader like Trilling, such a question also posed a dilemma of personal action. And this converged with another, apparently enduring worry of Trilling's: his own reputation. Podhoretz, who knew him intimately, suggests that Trilling had two sides, one that unusually craved honor and another that yearned for action. What Trilling wanted all his life, and increasingly in his later years, Podhoretz judged, was "to achieve what might be called a position of venerability."[97] Alfred Kazin recalls similarly Trilling's insistence in the 1940s that he would not write anything which would not "promote my reputation," with the phrase "my reputation" seeming to Kazin "to resemble an expensive picture on view. 'My reputation' was to be nursed along like money in a bank. It was capital."[98] Trilling was carefully composing his own intellectual portrait, in both senses of the verb. He would squander no resources in the effort.

Nevertheless, however much he sought "venerability," Trilling also did not want to remain above the political fray. Even in the '50s, when his authority was seldom questioned in print by the New York writers, these tensions between unsullied intellectual reputation and political action gripped him. In trying to criticize the Left from a liberal standpoint, Trilling found himself attacked by fellow liberals within and outside the New York writers. He found himself cast as an exponent of what Joseph Frank memorably called "the conservative imagination."[99] Trilling's once-admired sensitivity to "the conditioned nature of life," his careful and deliberate "qualifications," and his constant reminders of how "complicated" everything was, were already being interpreted by the mid-'50s, even within the *Partisan* circle, as indecisiveness, hair-splitting, even verbiage.[100] The New York group was breaking apart even before the *Catalonia* essay appeared, and members would split in the 1960s into rival political camps—liberal, radical, neoconservative, quietist—

as stands on the Vietnam War and communism divided the group generationally and ideologically. Trilling found it hard to take any firm stand at all.[101] At least as a type, Orwell was so attractive to Trilling because he seemed an example of the man who had achieved renown yet had remained "authentic" and politically active—the type of the writer *and* man of action who "was what he wrote"—and was widely recognized for it. But whereas Orwell had won admiration by diving into the political muck and somehow remaining clean, Trilling had always seemed simply to rise up and transcend all local, internecine New York battles. Already in the early '50s this posture was becoming more and more difficult to maintain.

Orwell thus combined in character and reputation the best of what Podhoretz described as "the two exemplary roles" Trilling saw immediately before him, in the reputations and political stances of his friends Isaiah Berlin and Sidney Hook. "If he had been English," Podhoretz mused after Trilling's death, comparing him to Berlin, Trilling would have become known as "Professor Sir Lionel Trilling, resting on his laurels, admired by all, and already in his own lifetime seeming not for the age but for the ages." Trilling desired the eminence of Berlin without becoming like him a benevolent, apolitical, and even-handed friend to radicals and anti-radicals alike; and he wanted the joys and satisfactions of Hook's fighting political commitment and concrete achievements, without suffering like him the crude labeling and fixed identifications which came with outspoken activism. Trilling sought both lasting and undisputed distinction and yet passionate political and intellectual engagement in the issues of his time. Orwell as intellectual hero is therefore comprehensible, finally, as the type of a third model for Trilling, a Hook in life and a Berlin afterwards. But in the '60s Trilling could commit himself fully neither to his Berlin nor Hook role model—feeling "torn" between the two, in Podhoretz's view, "unable to become the one and afraid of becoming the other."[102]

For unlike Orwell, Trilling as "virtuous man" was not a figure of "plainness" and "fortitude and strength" to his contemporaries, but rather one of "gracefulness," "subtlety," and "modesty."[103] Trilling seized upon Orwell at a time when he needed precisely more strength, less subtlety. *Homage to Catalonia* had spoken to Trilling in the way it did because it seemed to him a gutsy, unpopular book, written by "a man who tells the truth" and takes a stand. To Trilling (whose mother was English and whose Anglophilia was exceptional among the New Yorkers), Orwell stood forth as the last representative of a great nineteenth-century liberal tradition of English men of letters, an alternative tradition to both Marxism and the abstruse, anti-democratic modernism then being hailed in New York. Orwell had managed to be rooted in family values and to "praise such things as responsibility, order in one's personal life, fair play, physical courage"; yet he was also a relentlessly questioning "man of intelligence."[104] The writer had managed to preserve his "love affair with the English language" and yet exemplify "the old democracy of the mind."[105] Looking from both within and atop the New York intellectual world, Trilling understandably pointed to Orwell and

his example in *Homage to Catalonia* and felt, "He liberates us." "We," Trilling mused, could be like him "if only . . . ."


## V

However accurate may have been Trilling's explanation of Orwell's effect upon "us" as readers of *Homage to Catalonia,* "Trilling's Orwell" soon became a widely held image of Orwell for reasons having little to do with the essay's explicit argument, and only partly connected with the much-esteemed qualities of Trilling's (and Orwell's) prose. The chief determinants making for its far-ranging distribution were professional factors having to do with Trilling's own practically unrivaled intellectual-academic authority at mid-century.

For the making of a public literary figure is in large measure an institutional matter. And the fact is that it was Lionel Trilling's imagination and spirit that Orwell engaged.[106] (What became, one wonders, of the Orwell essay which Trilling says his nameless Columbia graduate student, who first called Orwell "a virtuous man," was also writing at the time?[107]) Acquaintances testify that much of Trilling's authority in New York circles derived simply from his urbane manner and rare gift for dramatizing his personality on paper.[108] Of course, it is always hard to distinguish intellectual versus institutional authority, or literary achievement from social-institutional affiliations, but the affiliations seem at least to have acted as professional bridges enabling Trilling's unusual, smooth traversing of the academic, intellectual, and publishing scenes (e.g., his status as the first tenured Jew in Columbia's English Department; his membership on the *Partisan Review, Commentary,* and *Kenyon Review* editorial boards; his heading both the Reader's Subscription and Mid-Century book clubs; his select membership in the National Institute of Arts and Letters and the Academy of Arts and Sciences; and his influence over and championing of young editor-intellectuals like Podhoretz at *Commentary* and Jason Epstein at Anchor Books.)[109] During the 1950s Trilling too was a "figure" on the American intellectual and academic scenes, "a veritable version of the *PR* writer as a belated Matthew Arnold."[110]

None of this is to say that Trilling singlehandedly created the image of Orwell as "man of truth." He was certainly not the first American intellectual to comment on Orwell's integrity and plainness, not even within the *Partisan Review* circle. Instead the essay was the culmination of the New Yorkers' extolling of Orwell for almost a decade and of a growing interest among American intellectuals in Orwell's life. Trilling's response crystallized and lent special authority to the image of Orwell as "the model liberal." Unquestionably, it also established the phrase "virtuous man" as a characterization of Orwell. Trilling's tributes soon inspired the magazine headline "Homage to Orwell," a phrase which continued to serve as a popular headline into the 1980s.

Much more than Trilling's explanation of Orwell's special appeal, then, the institutional reception accorded Trilling's essay (already guaranteed

prominence as the introduction to the first American edition of *Homage to Catalonia*) contributed to Orwell's stature. Reviewers have repeated Trilling's phrases almost ritually;[111] some critics have even gone so far as to attribute *Catalonia*'s success in the 1950s mainly to Trilling's introduction.[112] Trilling's characterizations have radiated outward and have become established views of Orwell, as in *Newsweek*'s 1968 headline "The Truthteller."[113] The telling irony is therefore that, whereas Trilling's explanation of Orwell's "figure" status is symptomatic of the misleading impression that criticism often (unintentionally) imparts—that writers gain literary reputations because their works possess self-evident, inherent qualities of "great" literature to which "we" all spontaneously assent—the actual explanation for how Orwell's reputation was made is much different. "Great Books" do not "Make Themselves." Contrary to the Book-of-the-Month Club's assertion about *Nineteen Eighty-Four,* reputations of books and authors get *made* because of the ballast which historical, material statements like Trilling's (and Russell's and Schlesinger's) carry—a weight attributable in large measure to the institutional reader's cultural authority.[114] Trilling, that is to say, helped fulfill by his authoritative pronouncement on Orwell what his essay already asserted as self-evident: Orwell's "figurehood."

Whether or not Trilling's blindness in his essay to his institutional authority was the price of his insight into Orwell's appeal, the irony is present in all of Trilling's widely scattered remarks on the "figure," a subject which apparently fascinated him.[115] Disingenuous or not, Trilling's introduction to *Homage to Catalonia* exemplifies in almost its pure form what I have discussed in this chapter as the *ideology of repute:* the casual tendency to universalize one's personal judgment and to overlook how the reading process takes place within and through institutional relations. The point is not that Trilling's was a private judgment, but rather that Trilling's was an influential yet limited, motivated, institutional "we."

In the end, however, to whatever extent George Orwell became, or now is, a figure in people's lives, it is due in no small part to the fact that he was once such in Lionel Trilling's. Trilling's attraction may have been temporary; there is no reference anywhere in his work to Orwell after 1957. But the attention and distribution afforded his *Catalonia* essay and 1949 *New Yorker* review of *Nineteen Eighty-Four* go far to explain why Orwell—and not other writers and potential "figure" candidates with whom Trilling compares Orwell, including Hazlitt, Cobbett, and Chesterton—came to figure in the '50s as an intellectual hero in many lives besides Trilling's. Given his special authority, Trilling's very act of naming Orwell a "figure"—of including him in the exalted company of recognized figures (Twain, William James, the two Lawrences, Shaw, Eliot) and pronouncing him the single writer "in our more recent literature" who "takes his place with these men as a figure"[116]—helped *make* Orwell a figure.

Similar acts accounted for Trilling's status. We are not, however, engaged in an exhaustive archaeology of reputation, which would only lead to an infinite regress. What concerns us here are those reception acts decisive

for, or revealing of, the emergence and radiation of reputations. Trilling's significant act "christened" Orwell a figure. It not only communicated a distinctively personal reading experience but formally nominated a writer (on behalf of intellectual America) to occupy a special cultural place. Trilling's identification with Orwell was, therefore, not only a private act of concretizing a text in consciousness. It was an institutional act, enabled and limited by social conditions.

### iii. *Identification and Identity*

### VI

Why is it that people sometimes respond so intensely to an Other that they drastically rewrite him, sometimes not even deliberately, in their self-images? Why, even within the same literary-political scene, does a writer stand as a radiant figure for one reader and yet not at all for others? And why such a different sort of figure for even those who do see him in heroic terms?

As we have seen, Trilling responded strongly to Orwell, drawing a portrait of him in his own idealized self-image partly in order to bolster and legitimate (if only to himself) his own identity. *Homage to Catalonia* provided Trilling with the lived example and occasion for asking himself what kind of intellectual he was and wanted to become. And searching for the Orwell in himself, as it were, Trilling naturally spotlighted in the essay the Trilling which he saw in George Orwell, even going so far as to interpret Orwell's critique of the English radical intelligentsia in the exact language of *The Liberal Imagination.* Trilling explained that Orwell's indictment was that radicals "refused to understand the conditioned nature of life." Such an identification with Orwell has not been unusual. Many other intellectuals have also responded to Orwell so strongly that they too have rewritten him as a way of addressing their own needs and aspirations. "Open [Orwell's books] anywhere," wrote one reviewer of *CEJL,* "and you touch a man very close to your best self, that self that exists for most of us only in wistful imaginings."[117] It was this self in Trilling about which Orwell provoked reflection.

It is not enough, however, to say that a figure "fills" personal and cultural needs in his receivers. Instead we must be aware that, in casting him as a model, the figure's admirers often lay emphasis on a few of his features—as Trilling did with Orwell's plainness and truth-telling—as a rhetorical strategy (calculated or not) for shoring up their own self-images. The receiver accents his model's strengths and downplays or rationalizes his shortcomings—and does the reverse with his cautionary anti-model.[118] Identifications of readers toward authors vary in force and duration, and often focus upon a single attribute. Most of the time we construct composite models, with a mixture of different (and sometimes conflicting) features of different persons constituting our version of the heroic, of our ideal selves.

But between a reader like Trilling and a figure like Orwell the identification, however momentary, is sweeping, direct, and passionate. As Ernest Becker explains it, such a fascination of the perceiver for the admired is an attempt to "address our performance of heroics" to another single human being. First as children "blowing up" our parents, and later (and typically more moderately) with spouses, teachers, mentors, political leaders, and writers, we beatify the Other so that we can know whether our performance is good enough. Our model guides us, and if our performance is inadequate, we can look to him or her and change. *Contra* Freud, Becker sees transference as natural, healthy projection, a reaching out for plenitude, and he terms this localized, intense charge of affect *transference beatification,* or *transference heroics.* The choice, Becker stresses, is not between independence and servitude. We all need models. Rather, it is between self-actualizing and demeaning models, between creative and slavish hero-worship. While no human being can "bear the burden of godhood," the challenge is to select life-enhancing models who will offer us the most freedom, dignity, and inspiration so as to outgrow them toward realizing our best selves.[119]

But the choice is not entirely the perceiver's or reader's. The model invites a certain kind of identification, or limits it, by his behavior. By assuming a certain rhetorical stance and tone, the writer as model takes on a certain role—and "pressures" or "guides" his readers into roles of his choosing. Teacher and student, confessor and confidant, exhibitionist and voyeur, criminal and co-conspirator: these are only a few of the roles which writers assume and in which readers get cast. In *Homage to Catalonia* Orwell, however self-consciously, occupied the role of honest witness and cast his readers into roles as sympathetic allies and outraged anti-Stalinist judges; and the informal language and plain-man persona which Orwell assumed in his essays, often slipping into the second person, cast his readers as colleagues and friends. A writer's effectiveness in inviting or thrusting readers into roles of his choosing weighs heavily, if imprecisely, in the making of reputation.[120] Trilling presented himself as an ally and admirer of Orwell "the man of virtue" in the *Catalonia* introduction, and invited his readers to do the same: to see themselves as "intelligent men" like Trilling struggling to reconcile virtue and action, fellow members of Trilling's elastic "we."

Surely Trilling realized, however obliquely, as he drew his self-portrait through Orwell, that Orwell stood before him as an inspirational model. It may be, in fact, that the great dead writer, the posthumous literary figure, is the type most amenable to idealization as a secure model, and for reasons which sharply distinguish the literary figure from other sorts of figures. For not only is the dead writer incapable of compromising himself in our eyes by further actions, but his living "voice" brings his image fully present before us and "re-presents" him at his best. One can select as many facets of him to admire and to imitate as there are passages in his immortal *oeuvre.* One can measure one's values and aspirations by his nonfictional pro-

nouncements and the ethos of his coherent imaginative world. The nature of his accomplishment also distinguishes the literary figure from other sorts—military, political, religious, athletic. For the work of the writer is, barring accident and vandalism, imperishable and unalterable. His "deed" is obviously less subject to distortion or confusion with legend: the original "exploit" of the writer "survives."[121] One can examine it, just as it was. One is sure: he did it exactly this way. The man is dead, but the work—and the man within the work—cannot die.

Moreover, whereas the fate of other persons of achievement (including judgments about musicians and artists) depends largely upon "what others wrote of them," the writer has a strong voice in the continuing historical conversation about him. In addition, the characteristic relation of the critic or historian to the writer is closer, and it is understandable that the former will tend to relate especially to someone who excelled at his own craft. Two of Carlyle's six heroic types in *Heroes and Hero-Worship* are writers, the poet and the man of letters.[122] It may even be that the comparative inattention of novelists and biographers to the lives of inventors, engineers, and captains of industry is attributable largely to their "not appealing to the literary type of mind."[123] Whether true or not, writers have certainly glorified the writer's lonely battles far more often than the struggles of persons in other essentially non-public arenas of imaginative effort, like musicians and scientists. Finally, in the person of the literary-academic critic (and art critics generally), the literary figure has a sort of professional public relations agent, or figure-maker, whose job, especially after the writer's death, has become not so much to evaluate his work as to demonstrate continuously and in new ways its greatness.

## VII

The special tendency of writers to identify with literary men, added to the fact that writings and style of life contribute significantly to "literary" reputation, necessitates close attention to the nature of the figure-institutional reader identification. An open, impassioned act of identification like Trilling's frequently presents one or two striking features of the figure. Often the figure is cast as the incarnation of a single attribute. Trilling's observation that figures "stand" always "for something," though inadequate, is right in the main.[124] More precisely, the author must be perceived to "stand" not merely "for something," but for a concrete attribute or attributes. Typically the attribute is identifiable via a single word or phrase, like Trilling's association of Orwell with "plainness" and "truth."

The sharper the perception of the author's image, the more readily special words epitomizing him will come to mind. These words are usually nouns and adjectives, and sometimes self-characterizations or favorite phrases of the author, so frequently invoked when his name comes up that the two practically constitute a collocation. After a time, their repetition often oversimplifies and debases them into a summary judgment about

him. Thus with Swift we think immediately of "misanthropy," with Dr. Johnson "common sense," with Franklin "self-made man," with Byron "rebel," with Poe "macabre" and "satanic," with D.H. Lawrence "passion." Orwell's name calls up quite a variety, not only his own words "honest" and "decent," but also the critics' "saint," "conscience," "man of truth," "rebel," "plain-spoken," "common sense," "common man," and—drawing from *Nineteen Eighty-Four*—"prophet," "nightmarish," "pessimist," "doomsayer."

The elements of this descriptive nomenclature, or *watchwords,* operate as names which characterize a figure's radiance and suggest a program of action toward him. A watchword is a word repeated, emphasized, foregrounded, linked to central themes. Such a word imputes a property to the author as it conveys the attitude of the receiver. Watchwords often provide a clue to the distinctive patterning of a reception act. For a word is a rhetorical act, and watchwords in effect become different acts when placed in different reception scenes, furnishing what Burke calls "perspectives by incongruity."[125] Burke confines himself to an examination of such incongruous perspectives in literary texts. But as we have seen with Trilling's reception of Orwell on the New York academic-intellectual scene, our rhetoric of reception begins by reconstructing scenes of an author's reception as "thickly described" cultural "texts."

In this ethnography, or, following our metaphor, "cosmography" of repute, the institutional reader is not just a stargazer reporting his view of the author but a plotter and shaper of the author's evolving reputation. The various watchwords will sometimes call up not a single image but a constellation of more-or-less distinct images. Especially for a multifaceted literary figure like Orwell, this means that his reputation radiates not like a single star but more like a galaxy with no fixed center. For each watchword associated with an author may generate a different image or images. Inevitably, as in Orwell's case, some watchwords ("truth," "decency," "prophet," "nightmarish") will be more commonly heard than others. Not surprisingly, more images orbit around these watchwords than some others, and more readers usually see an "Orwell" in these images and according to these signal words than via others.

The watchwords most frequently heard and fully developed in the materials of the author's reception history—e.g., in Trilling's introduction to *Homage to Catalonia*—constitute the orienting points and organizing frame for reception scenes which will develop, refine, and transform them. For watchwords, as it were, "entitle" complex scenes. To "read" Trilling's Orwell, we must flesh out the densely textured web of his response—derived from studying his *Catalonia* introduction, his other writings on Orwell and various related subjects, and the writings about Trilling himself. In Trilling's essay, "truth" is the radiant, essential quality of his Orwell as "virtuous man."[126] But Trilling did not discern in Orwell a self-effacing or diffident truth. His Orwell embodied a "primitive" virtue, "not merely moral goodness, but fortitude and strength." From here one could begin again to unfold the scene of Trilling's reception around the watchword "truth."

Moving back and forth between Trilling's essay and the image cluster generated by "truth," one could reconstruct at greater length how Orwell's "simple" truth evoked Trilling's "liberating" reading experience of an "intelligent" man who stood opposed to cliquish "intellectuals." The character of Orwell's "simple courage" and "plainness of mind" as an upholder of "family commonplaces," as a defiant anti-Stalinist leftist, and as a Catalonia militiaman struck Trilling as "old-fashioned"—just like the "old-fashioned" phrase "virtuous man"—and so refreshingly, humanly different from the "fashionable," morally bankrupt "American liberal" writers who "made the cause of civil liberties their own" and yet in whose work "one can find no mention of the [Stalinist] terror [in Catalonia during the Spanish Civil War]."[127]

Orwell and *Homage to Catalonia* spoke not only to a need in Trilling, but also to one in the fiercely anti-Stalinist *Partisan Review* group and the neo-liberal American intelligentsia generally in 1952. Published amid growing anti-Communist sentiment and at the height of the Korean War, *Homage to Catalonia* filled a cultural need for an anti-Communist champion of impeccable intellectual integrity, for a witness and fighter who "had been there" and "did it," and for a beautifully written and easily accessible historical record ("one of the most important documents of our time," said Trilling)[128] of Communist abuses in Spain. *Homage to Catalonia* appealed to the Left precisely because it contained no note of self-recrimination: one could pretend that one's position had always matched "clear-sighted" Orwell's, as Trilling implied of himself. Unlike the many books by ex-Communists then appearing, Trilling noted, Orwell in *Catalonia* had nothing about which to be embarrassed or ashamed. *Homage to Catalonia* was about "disillusionment with Communism, but it is not a confession." Trilling took the book as a guide for nothing less than how to live an honest life. *Catalonia* was "a testimony to the nature of political life" and "a demonstration on the part of its author of one of the right ways of confronting that life."[129] And Trilling, like so many others wondering about truth and politics, found himself seeking another, similarly honest, virtuous, "right" way.

We might finally characterize Trilling's Orwell—as others have done—as the man of simple honesty, "the plain man," "the man of truth," "The Truthteller." This *face* is the title which best sums up the constellation that is Trilling's essential, radiant image of Orwell—and the task of naming it is very much like putting a name on a constellation that the receiver (and also the reputation critic) has mapped from a certain standpoint, yet which could have been interpreted in other ways. The reconstructed face is reductionist in the sense of a Weberian ideal type. It is a stereotype selectively oversimplified to promote understanding. Faces "almost talk in concepts," to use Burke's phrase.[130] Invariably correlated with one or more watch-words, faces name a perceived quality of the figure and encapsulate an image, summing up the complexity of a reader's response in a word. But presented through case histories as *facial histories,* faces are not "caricatures." For the task is not to see faces in the abstract, divorced from the

author's rich history of reputation and reduced to a set of archetypes without substantial content, but rather to see in context those particular facial features which observers have profiled and to what ends.

To see these features, one must pay special attention to the constellation of images which the watchword contains, since watchwords allow for "mapping" or "plotting" in various ways according to the observer's standpoint. In Orwell's case, V.S. Pritchett's esteem for him as a "rebel" against Left orthodoxy was quite different from Communist fellow-traveler Sean O'Casey's contempt for the false, bourgeois-imperialist "Rebel Orwell," "a sergeant in the Burma police all right."[131] Sometimes rhetorical replacements even within a single reception audience indicate shifts in attitudes. Trilling's admiration for Orwell's intelligent "common sense" was quite different from *Partisan Review* editor Dwight Macdonald's castigation of Orwell's "common-sense philistinism."[132] Understanding the reasons for the two critics' different applications of "common sense" to Orwell goes a long way toward understanding the nature of *Partisan Review*'s wartime policy rifts between Deweyan pragmatism and Marxist ideology. Similarly, exploring in detail the circumstances of Pritchett's and O'Casey's different applications of "rebel" to Orwell illumines the split between the Labour Party and the Marxist Left in postwar Britain. When watchwords change, the author's "being" changes. A change in watchwords is an act of transubstantiation. Such words therefore bear special watching. For "nearly all human beings feel that a thing is different if you call it by a different name," Orwell once remarked, noting how successful propaganda exemplified "the magical properties of names."[133]

Watchwords return us to the larger question of the receiver's position vis à vis the author, for to name or to designate is always to do so from some point of view. An image is relational, expressing an attitude on the part of the subject and a perceived trait possessed by the object. The critic of reputation must be especially aware of the sociohistorical perspective from which he and other receivers see the author and his work. For the critic is the observer looking at observers looking at the author. This is the problem of *critical location*.

Every institutional reader confronts—and poses for the critic of repute—the problem of critical location, the problem of where and how to stand in relation to a person, group, issue and ultimately the world. Where is the institutional reader standing in relation to the figure? Where is the authoritative voice located within his group? Where is the critic of reputation himself? And what are the consequences of these placements? Inside or outside, above or below, near or far, behind or ahead? Firm or breezy, tense or relaxed? Location is partly within and partly outside (generation, race, sex, class of birth) one's control. Where and how institutional readers find themselves and position themselves—the spatio-temporal fact of critical location—largely shape their reception acts. As with stars, "where" the observer is in relation to the figure strongly affects how brightly and big and long the figure shines before him.

The repression of the study of reputation has contributed to the illusion that one need not take a position, that the problem of placement is merely a syntactic one, as if there were objective positions available if only "criticism" would become sufficiently "scientific." "There are no definite positions to be taken in chemistry or philology," writes Frye, "and if there are any to be taken in criticism, criticism is not a genuine field of learning. . . . One's 'definite position' is one's weakness, the source of one's liability to error and prejudice. . . ." To this we can only reply that one's "definite position" is also one's strength, the source of one's potential for insight and well-argued conviction. Even a "disinterested critic" like Frye possesses, whether he realizes it or not, "a color-filter."[134] The task is not to attempt to become color-blind, but to become aware of one's filter, to understand its implications, and to reveal and justify it insofar as possible. In studying literary reputation and image-making, the problem of re-presentation is always a problem of place, which is in turn a problem of identity—the institutional reader's identity and the reputation critic's own identity.

One's critical location is always, in some measure, a choice. One can't pretend the filter isn't there; it is. For instance, my own professional-historical-religious affiliations obviously have influenced my approach to Orwell in Part Two (e.g., the selected case studies I have devoted, as a student of mass communication, to Orwell's popular reputation; my attention to certain domains of Orwell's reputation, e.g., his treatment by the mass media and by the academy, his Anglo-American reputation, his reception in Catholic circles and during the 1980s), and indeed my choice of Orwell himself as a subject worthy of study.

iv. *The Reading Experience and the Writer's Public Image*

VIII

However "institutional" Trilling's reading experience of *Homage to Catalonia,* his deeply felt response was obviously much more than that, as we have seen. Nor was Trilling's response due simply to *Catalonia*'s artistic excellence, or even to Orwell's attractive literary personality. Richard Rees has pointed out that the appeal of Orwell for many observers is "partly due to the fact that 'first he wrought and afterwards he taught.' The reader knows that the man who wrote the books lived and acted in a certain way, and it reacts upon his feelings about the books."[135]

Surely this is so, and not only in Orwell's case. Most of us probably have a different, and less moving and powerful, experience of "Shooting an Elephant" or "How the Poor Die" if we approach them simply as short stories. To know, or assume, that Orwell lived them *does* make a difference.

And yet, for all its attention to the reading experience and despite its spawning of personality cults of authors through canon-worship, literary studies has not inquired as to how readers' perceptions of the real author within and behind the work affect their reading experience of the work.

Recoiling from the possibility of committing intentional, affective, and other fallacies, literary critics have defined attention to the life and personality of the author as "extrinsic" and thereby excluded a vital aspect of the reception act. This makes it all the more understandable that literary studies has had no vocabulary through which to approach reputation as a literary issue.

What *kind* of difference does it make—both for the experience of the work and the writer's reputation—if, as so many readers have casually done, we read "Such, Such Were the Joys" as the autobiographical account of Eric Blair?[136] What difference does a strong public "personality" have upon the reading experience and public reputation?

Writers themselves have testified that a concrete public image can enormously increase the chances of an artistic reputation crossing what one sociologist calls Fame's "inter-generational divide."[137] And it may be that what we have termed a *face*—the clear image of the literary (and sometimes private) personality—is an essential factor for gaining the attention of the mass media and achieving a reputation which radiates beyond literary circles and beyond the present moment. James Michener has discussed the plight of the image-less writer like himself and lamented his own lack of a public literary image:

> A writer, painter, or actor is indeed fortunate when a public image of himself is established early and is one whose confines he has the talent to fill. All sorts of advantages must accrue to this position in the public eye, and they are large and honorable ones. . . . [138]

Like Michener, and in contrast to Orwell, most writers—even many major writers—call to mind no arresting watchwords, anecdotes, or graphic images. They may command name recognition and critical respect, but their names evoke few or vague associations. They do not possess, in any sense, like Crick's Orwell, "a name to set argument going wherever books are read." With pre-modern writers, the lack derives partly from natural historical tendency. History tends to "bleach" images and reduce direct bequests. A "figure in our lives" is not necessarily a figure in the next century's or generation's. Still, although some writers are rediscovered, lasting reputation ordinarily depends a great deal on the verdicts of contemporaries.[139] The standard nomenclature making for Orwell's present-day images virtually all comes from characterizations in early postwar reviews, such as Trilling's "man of truth," Cyril Connolly's "revolutionary in love with 1910," and Pritchett's "saint," "conscience of his generation," and rebel "gone native in his own country."[140]

Some writers, like Hemingway and Mailer, not only acknowledge the value of a prominent public image but set about aggressively to construct it for themselves. Mailer's direct attempt in *Advertisements for Myself* (1959) to cast himself as Hemingway's successor is one unusually blatant instance:

> . . . for years [Hemingway] has not written anything which would trouble an eight-year old or one's grandmother, and yet his reputation is firm—he

knew in advance, with a fine sense of timing, that he would have to campaign for himself, that the best tactic to hide the lockjaw of his shrinking genius was to become the personality of our time. And here he succeeded.

. . . I give credit to the man, he's known the value of his own personality and he fought to make his personality enrich his books. Let any of you decide for yourselves how silly would be *A Farewell to Arms* or better, *Death in the Afternoon,* if it had been written by a man who was five-four, had acne, wore glasses, spoke in a shrill voice, and was a physical coward. . . .

An author's personality can help or hurt the attention readers give his books, and it is sometimes fatal to one's talent not to have a public with a clear public recognition of one's size. The way to save your work and reach more readers is to advertise yourself. . . .[141]

But just as the literary figure is not simply a "great writer," so too a literary celebrity or public writer like Hemingway or Mailer—known by far more people than his readers and honored as much for what he says and does as for what he writes[142]—is not necessarily a "figure." For, as I have stressed, not merely an image's size but its *content* is vitally important to "figure" status. Not mere public attention but the *quality* of the relation between author and reader is the mark of the figure. Self-promotion may gain one "clear public recognition," but it may also tarnish an image. Of course, figures need not actually be (as Orwell noted of Dickens' allegedly brutal treatment of his wife) authors who, in Trilling's phrase, "are what they write." But a sense of a calculated effort to win public recognition can adulterate the *perception* of authenticity between work and life so often necessary to a radiant image. As the sharply downward revisions of Hemingway's critical and popular reputation after his death (e.g., the 1963 *Esquire* survey) show, Mailer was not the only one well aware that Hemingway's feat of becoming "the personality of our time" could not mask his meretricious later work. Nor will Mailer's comparable success likely prove helpful to his own posthumous reputation, whereas Orwell's (apparent) self-effacement of his personality has ironically established him as an enduring culture hero.

Yet even the fame of the hero has its price. A writer of many faces like Orwell may find his reputation confused and distorted as a consequence of this multiplicity. In one sense, some distortion is the price of cultural irradiation. The wider distribution and popularization of works—translations, abridgments, adaptations—are inevitably different from the original. Strictly speaking, these different versions are "perversions," but they bring the writer's work to new audiences in essentially the same spirit as the original. Such a natural byproduct of societal irradiation must be sharply distinguished from radiation via calculated distortion or careless vulgarization. For *defacement* of his work and image also brings the author before new audiences, albeit in badly mangled form. The line between popularization and vulgarization cannot be drawn precisely, but blatant instances of defacement are usually identifiable. The East-West distortions of Marx, the caricatures of Freud's thought inside and outside psychoanalysis, the monstrous twisting of

Bergson's *élan vital* into a direct-action politics ("Bergsonism") before World War I, the abuse of Sorel by Stalin and Mussolini: all these are demonstrable examples of defacement. In Part Two we will explore further how Orwell has suffered similar abuses in ideological and commercial contexts, with the democratic socialist being made to appear a neoconservative, or "progressive," or Christian, or a capitalist promoter of "1984" gimmickry.

Not all such misreadings are malicious or even intentional: they may simply arise due to works entering new reception scenes, or from wishful thinking, as probably happened in some conservative reception scenes, at least outside Britain, with *Nineteen Eighty-Four*. Defacement may be a matter not of misrepresentation but simple misrecognition. Moreover, not all uses are abuses, not all distortions are equal in degree or scope. What may seem from one angle to be "appropriation" may from another angle be simply to achieve "acceptance" within a new reception scene or from a formerly indifferent or hostile group. The distinctions are important. And, as we have seen with Orwell, sometimes the author himself inadvertently contributes to his defacement. For neither saintly nor monstrous figures are created or chosen arbitrarily: there is invariably a meeting of the object's properties and the subject's or culture's needs. Given the many candidates "available" for disfiguration, some get chosen as especially "well worth stealing," in Orwell's phrase on Dickens—and not for reasons entirely separable from the character of their works and lives. Orwellian *facecrime* has occurred partly because of Orwell's association with "decency" and "truth," partly because the catchwords of *Nineteen Eighty-Four* could be easily turned back on him, partly because of his aggressive "conscience of the Left" stance, and partly because of his journalist's bent for addressing a variety of rapidly changing subjects about which he could not possibly be expert. Of course, it is not a simple question of blaming an author for his "lack of foresight" as to the uses and abuses to which his work are put after his death. Nor is it a matter of taking sides, certainly not of producing a "left" or "right" reading, but rather of getting down to particulars and seeing how writers sometimes invite or participate in their own appropriation. It is distinguishing the simple sketch from the gross caricature and seeing why a writer was so susceptible to defacement. "All Orwell faces are equal," we might say, "but some are more equal than others."

### v.   *Approaching Orwell's Reputation: Distinctive Features*

### IX

To this point I have been discussing general factors involved in the making of literary reputations, and looking at Orwell's reputation chiefly via a single, sharply focused reception scene. But there are distinctive features of and factors bearing on Orwell's reputation which it may be useful to summarize here, several of which will be explored in some detail in Part Two. For

as authors' works enter different reception scenes, different issues of critical location shape their reputations.

First, Orwell was "a political animal," a man "who could not blow his nose without moralising on conditions in the handkerchief industry," as Cyril Connolly once remarked.[143] It is not surprising, then, that Orwell has elicited strong politically motivated responses from readers. He was a socialist and a journalist deeply involved in the issues of his time, and, in turn, ideological and generational politics have figured heavily in the formation of his reputation. By contrast, issues of race have had virtually no bearing on his reputation's development, unlike Faulkner or James Baldwin; only recently, in the 1980s, has gender politics come to exert some influence, unlike the cases of Hemingway and Mailer.

Second, the claims of literary-cultural groups to Orwell as a model or forerunner (e.g., the *Partisan Review* writers, the so-called Angry Young Men, the cultural critics of the British New Left) have influenced the development of his reputation. With other writers, like Edith Sitwell or T.E. Hulme, links with the fine arts or with avant garde *littérateurs,* rather than with Left/Right politics, are more prominent. The association of Orwell's name not only with liberal or dissident Left writers (Dickens, Wells, Butler, Silone, Koestler, Camus, Malraux) but also with conservative and/or explicitly religious writers (Swift, Johnson, Kipling, Gissing, Chesterton, Waugh) has helped confuse his reputation and highlight its conservative aspects.

Third, Orwell has been the object of selective critical attention: Marxist and psychoanalytic criticism has influenced the emergence of certain issues about him and his work but, doubtless because of his reputed "plain" style and "straightforward" meaning, structuralist and post-structuralist critics have largely ignored Orwell. And as we have seen, *Animal Farm* and Orwell's essays are widely installed in pedagogy and literature canons, though seldom are his works taught elsewhere in the academy, contributing (along with the media's preoccupation with *Animal Farm* and *Nineteen Eighty-Four* and its relative neglect of his other works) to the odd split in his reputation between critical and public reception.

Certain distinctive aspects of his reputation-history associated with the man-versus-works issue constitute a fourth reason why Orwell, rather than another writer or another contemporary, has been the occasion for such acclaim and argument. His attention to language abuse anticipated and has fed the preoccupation with the topic today, and has kept his writings current. The delay of a full biography until 1980 facilitated the development of confusions about his work. His practice of compartmentalizing his relationships, and often behaving quite differently with one group of politically minded friends than with another, has also contributed to the controversies about his politics and the variety of Orwell images. His singular yet plain style has drawn intellectual admirers to the man while simultaneously making him an anthologized "model stylist" for beginning writers. The physiognomic fallacy, according to which "the style is the man," has operated to let Orwell the plain stylist be taken, perhaps too readily, for an honest and

open man. Good prose is like a mirror: it reflects the man who writes it—or so some critics assume. Orwell's much-praised style has even made some observers uneasy about criticizing him, as if they felt, "How can I criticize a writer of such wonderful prose in my pedestrian English?"[144]

The timing of Orwell's death is a fifth factor decisive in the formation of his reputation, as we saw in Chapter One. Orwell's early death made him especially inviting for canonization and claiming. (Perhaps his posthumous celebration reminds some hostile critics of his own comment about Lenin's saintedness: "one of those . . . who win an undeserved reputation by dying prematurely."[145]) Orwell's image as a Quixotic idealist made him an intellectual youth hero, especially in Britain in the 1950s, even as (like Kipling and Dickens) his Sancho Panza side seemed to speak to his reader's deepest desires and to voice clichés which grip so many of us (the "good bad" book, love of country, defense of the underdog).

But it was not so much that Orwell died "young": he died at precisely the "right" historical moment. Indeed, if Orwell had lived even until 1955 or certainly into the 1960s, he would not have been spared the agony of taking sides on numerous political issues: the Cold War, McCarthyism, de-Stalinization, Hungary, Suez, Algeria, the Campaign for Nuclear Disarmament, the New Left, Vietnam, the student movement. Inevitably, as happened with Bertrand Russell, Koestler, Sartre, Camus, and others in the 1950s and '60s, his positions (or lack thereof) on such issues would have compromised him in the eyes of some groups which today claim him as a patron saint. His patriotism, his democratic socialism, his anti-Communism: these and other aspects of his work would all have come under attack. Never could he have won or maintained his current stature on so many different fronts. "If Orwell Were Alive Today" would never have become a press headline, perhaps never much of a speculation at all.

The diversity of Orwell's work has further contributed to the development of different images of him, for it has in some ways lent support to the impression that there are many different Orwells. When adolescent readers outgrow the "amusing" *Animal Farm,* they can turn to the gruesome *Nineteen Eighty-Four,* then return to both works in more mature years and fully appreciate them as political satires. One also encounters the plain man of the essays, the truthteller of *Homage to Catalonia,* the vehement devil's advocate of *The Road to Wigan Pier,* and the salty journalist of the "As I Please" columns. Yet numerous writers have written in many forms and are known by different books. What is truly unusual in Orwell's case is the disagreement among readers as to which is "the best" of his works, or even as to what criteria to apply in reaching such a decision, a dispute which probably says as much about variable aesthetic standards as about Orwell's work. *Nineteen Eighty-Four* is widely regarded as Orwell's "towering" but "flawed" masterpiece; *Animal Farm* is his "best executed" book, a little gem, though often criticized as ending in a sterile negation; *Homage to Catalonia* is described as his "moving" and "inspiring" book; *Burmese Days* is called his "best novel." There are even votes for his other books. To Henry Miller, *Down and Out*

was Orwell's "best book"; to John Wain, *Coming Up for Air* is Orwell's "central book"; to *Time,* Orwell in *Keep the Aspidistra Flying* "never wrote a kinder or more human novel." Still other critics have considered Orwell's essays his finest work.[146]

Finally, perhaps the single most important factor accounting for the size of Orwell's reputation, has, fittingly enough, to do with a date. George Steiner has noted that, in titling his last book *Nineteen Eighty-Four,* Orwell became the only writer in history ever "to put his signature and claim on a piece of time."[147] If Orwell had named his dystopia "The Last Man in Europe," as he had originally planned, it quite probably would have had less impact, at least in the long run. The title invited correlations between world events and the book's events, produced an immediate association in the public mind between "Orwell" and a date in the near future, and generated the "countdown to 1984" mentality. Although the reputations of many writers have benefited from posthumous events like centennial celebrations, the long countdown to 1984 kept public attention continuously, if intermittently, focused on Orwell, reaching a climax as 1984 approached. Certainly, given a different book title, there would have been much less likelihood of such a sensationalized countdown. In seizing a calendar year as his own, Orwell not only etched his own name in history but blackened a segment of time. This unprecedented feat is undoubtedly a significant and overlooked reason why *Nineteen Eighty-Four* has probably had, as *U.S. News & World Report* believes, "greater impact than any novel since *Uncle Tom's Cabin.*"[148]

### X

The question of Orwell's distinctive reputation also raises more complicated questions about how historical "emergence" and artistic originality bear on the making of reputations. When does a writer's work "enter" History? How does one's "biological opportunity" and artistic "moment of entrance" relate to reputation?[149]

The processes are more complicated than they might seem, for the relationship of the writer's work to his reputation-history is not just a matter of dates. Books which seem to appear "at the same time" frequently enter history framed by radically different patterns and conditions. For instance, though *Animal Farm* and H. G. Wells' *Mind at the End of Its Tether* both appeared in 1945 and talked gloomily about the future, the two books' preoccupations and approaches indicate that they really belonged to different eras, the pre- and post-totalitarian, reflecting the fact that Wells was more than thirty-five years older than Orwell. Or consider *Nineteen Eighty-Four* and James Burnham's *Struggle for the World* (1947). Both appeared at roughly the same postwar moment and both depicted the same superpower alignments. Both had tremendous initial impacts. Yet Burnham's book was soon forgotten. The reverse is true if one compares any of the popular books on the Spanish Civil War with *Homage to Catalonia,* originally remain-

dered even before Secker & Warburg recovered its advance and yet a classic since its 1952 republication. Or compare *The Road to Wigan Pier* with James Agee's *Let Us Now Praise Famous Men* (1941). Both dealt with "invisible" poverty in outlying areas. Orwell's book had an immediate impact; Agee's book was little noticed. Yet both are classics of their kind today.

Thus, we need to see "spatial time" not merely as a concept applicable to fictional worlds and to literary criticism, but to our own world and to cultural criticism. The foregoing differences in historical emergence lend force to Edward Said's injunction against "an irreducibly serial, filiative conception of sociohistorical time." Cultural phenomena are "a family of ideas emerging . . . in discourse," not best understood as if they were "human beings born on a certain day; the past is not a set of such births, and time does not move like a clock, in discrete movements."[150]

There is, in other words, a synchronic dimension to reputation, what George Kubler in *The Shape of Time* calls "the mechanics of fame." Kubler concerns himself chiefly with how morphological problems of duration in series and sequence bear on the artist's achievement, e.g., by "inserting" him into a phase (early, middle, late) of a reigning aesthetic mode (whether genre, style, national/regional tradition, *Zeitgeist,* etc.). Kubler sees art history and artistic style not as uniquely individual accomplishments, but as "a linked succession of prime works with replications, all being distributed in time as recognizably early and late versions of the same kind of action." "[W]ithout a good entrance," says Kubler, even the gifted artist is "in danger of wasting his time as a copyist, regardless of temperament or training." Thus a Renaissance "great man" is less a "universal genius" than simply a highly talented person "bestriding many new tracks of development at a fortunate moment in that great renovation of Western civilization, and traveling his distance in several systems without the burdens of rigorous proof and extensive demonstration required in later periods."[151]

One might speculate whether the success of Orwell's plain-man style, so welcome as a refreshing change from the aestheticism of the 1920s and in line with American tastes for "tough-guy" writers like Henry Miller and Hemingway in the 1930s, helped make writers similarly styled in the 1950s (e.g., the Angry Young Men) seem, given Orwell's priority, artificial and worn. To discuss the mechanics of Orwell's historical entrance systematically would require extensive comparison and contrast with other "candidates" of a similar kind for literary repute, a difficult task beyond our intentions here. The *synchrony of repute* also raises large questions of historical "mood" and social structure, important to acknowledge yet hard to investigate empirically. It is clear, for example, that intellectuals continue to quote Orwell not just because of the timing of his death but for other reasons associated with his "moment of entrance," among them the enduring fascination of Left intellectuals with the Thirties as a golden age of idealism and political commitment, and with Orwell's attractive dual image as an opponent of right- and left-wing totalitarianism and as a conservative defender of native traditions.

vi.  *"The Faces Behind the Page": Images of Orwell*

## XI

The argument throughout this chapter has been directed toward two ends: the creation of a context in which to talk about literary image-making generally and Orwell's reputation in particular. With the foregoing critical concepts and distinctive features of Orwell's history in mind, we now enter the Orwell portrait gallery.

"When one reads any strongly individual piece of writing," Orwell said in "Charles Dickens," "one has the impression of seeing a face somewhere behind the page." It is not perhaps "the actual face of the writer" but "the face that the writer ought to have."[152] Orwell felt this on reading not only Dickens but also many other writers, and he implied that this feeling was a matter of the writer's distinctive style and clear speaking voice. Numerous readers have likewise offered their conflicting versions of the face Orwell "ought" to have. Orwell once considered titling *Critical Essays* "The Face Behind the Page," after the famous closing to his Dickens essay.[153] That title, in the plural, might serve as an alternative one for this book.

For the Orwell "figure" is like a rotating prism of faces. As it winds through history and among institutional audiences, it shows a series of profiles to the world. The form of these images is always a joint and haphazard reconciliation of the constant dynamic between Orwell's self-characterizations and his audiences' characterizations of him. And like the aim to impose unity on the conflicting usages of "Orwellian," the temptation to impose a false congruity upon Orwell's several faces is strong yet misleading. Instead his history of reputation constitutes a spinning top jointly rotated by Orwell's own acts of self-creation and by the hand of history, dispersing images like the coral glass paperweight in *Nineteen Eighty-Four*.

Trilling's "virtuous man" image is only one of the top's refracting images, presented from one critical location—indeed only one version of Orwell as "the man of truth." From other critical locations observers have cast other images of Orwell. Turn the prism one way and see The Rebel, the self-described "loner" and "failure" in prep school, the endearing and iconoclastic Quixote, the maverick within and against the London Left, the romantic "outsider." Flip it another way and spot The Common Man, the "quintessential Englishman," the aficionado of popular culture, the lovable Sancho Panza. Incline it again and behold The Prophet, the author of *the book,* the intellectual Jeremiah warning against the evils of totalitarian thinking, the "doomsday prophet" of the press headlines, the "prescient" or "blind" or "gloomy" seer so often argued to have been heading before his untimely death in the direction of wherever a special interest has happened to need him. Invert it a fourth way and witness The Saint, 'St. George' Orwell, a face encompassing many of the others: the Left's saintly truthteller, the Right's noble anti-Communist patriot, the Christians' would-be believer, the model stylist, the outspoken Defender of the King's English.

These faces, presented in Part Two, are what I have found to be the dominant images in Orwell's reputation-history. They are not my reification or groundless invention, but are carefully reconstructed from the many thousands of books, articles, reviews, and press references constituting the materials of Orwell's recoverable reception history. They are not discrete, but finally only methodologically divisible. They are not a complete set, but they constitute the "suns" around which related characterizations of Orwell orbit. And the more that is written about any one of these images without taking the others into account, the more elusive and slightly unreal the whole appears. All of them, even those defaced aspects of these images, are part of Orwell's history of reputation—and they must be understood rather than suppressed. To present merely a "dark prophet" image of Orwell from *Nineteen Eighty-Four* as observers have sometimes done—or to substitute any other single face for the whole figure—is to mistake the coral fragment broken at the novel's end for the resplendent paperweight glass. For Orwell is all of these historical images. And it is in this larger sense, as man, writer, and literary figure—and not just for his pellucid prose—that Orwell truly stands as, in the phrase of George Woodcock's book title, "The Crystal Spirit."

How, then, have I tried to make sense of this multifaceted reputation? Each chapter in Part Two is a different room in the portrait gallery. Each takes a title of one of Orwell's faces, culled from the watchwords historically applied to him and his work, and uses it as a point of departure for extensive facial analysis. What follows is a consideration of the epithet's fitness, limitations, and various versions. How did it emerge? In what directions has it pointed? Into what scenes have Orwell's name and work radiated and to what effect? The opening sections of Chapters Three to Six discuss the emergence and transformations of the face in question, primarily "from the outside," as seen by institutional readers, and periodically qualified with looks at Orwell's corresponding self-image. The succeeding three or four sections in each chapter constitute facial histories which scrutinize the portrait in question from various standpoints and distances, i.e., they are related yet distinctive "profiles" of the same face. They are case studies in literary reception as cultural history. Inevitably reputation-history is a personalizing of the historical and an historicizing of the personal. Just as Orwell was a witness to his time, I have used him as a far-seeing witness to events since his death, aiming through him to lend public events a personal voice and to make public a history visible only through the eyes of his ghostly presence.

Some of the following facial histories are tightly focused reception scenes, telescoped through the history of response to Orwell by an authoritative voice and his reference group (like the Trilling case study); others approach Orwell's reputation from a wider angle, exploring his impact in a domain of culture and treating his reputation-history as a lens through which to observe larger cultural currents; still others examine the role of a particular issue in his reputation-history. My choice of case studies has been guided by both

conceptual and practical matters: significance for illuminating reputation-formation in general and Orwell's reputation in particular; clarification of the many perspectives (especially political) from which Orwell has been viewed; and the availability of sufficient historical reception evidence to say something about such matters. Certainly other facial histories would have been possible (e.g., of Orwell's reception in France, by England's Movement writers of the 1950s, by the journalism profession, by ex-Communist writers, etc.).[154]

Thus the portrait gallery, though obviously not exhaustive, *is* meant to be a gallery, a panoramic survey of a reputation from a variety of critical locations: political (socialist, anarchist, conservative, Marxist, neoconservative), national (Anglo-American, Soviet, German), professional/cultural (academic, commercial, intellectual, popular), religious (Catholic), gender (feminist), and generational. Orwell's multifaceted reputation is best approached not as a long-erected monument but as a fitfully woven web. Its decisive transformations have occurred not only in time but across audiences, and we must therefore travel and traverse the complex ground of his reception, repeatedly moving through time and back and forth between critical and popular audiences.

"The face of Orwell," *Picture Post* once observed, "is the face of the mid-Twentieth Century. . . ."[155] Viewed from a series of well-chosen standpoints, Orwell's life and afterlife constitute a sprawling, still-unfolding, illustrated biography of the postwar world.

*Part Two*

# The Portrait Gallery

*Since the days of Homer one of the major consolations*
*of the literary life has been the belief in reputations....*
*"Not all of me shall die,"* Non omnis moriar.... *If*
*I were in a position to advise a writer who was*
*so ambitious as to desire recognition both in his lifetime*
*and after I would say:... "Set posterity a puzzle.*
*The living dislike puzzles: the unborn worship them....*
*Keep your contemporary success within bounds....*
*Above all, beware [not]...to deprive*
*posterity of all speculation, of its right to model you*
*in its own image."*
                              *Cyril Connolly, "Reputations," 1950*


*At 50, every man has the face he deserves.*
                              *George Orwell*

From *Saga: A Magazine for Men,* 1962. The cover headline: "George Orwell Vs. the World: The Rebel Who Invented Big Brother."

# THREE

# *The Rebel*

## 4. A Rebel's Progress

### I

In his *Observer* obituary, Arthur Koestler summed up Orwell's life as "A Rebel's Progress."[1] By the mid-1950s, Koestler's image of "Rebel Orwell" had radiated well beyond London intellectual circles. In 1960 Koestler told BBC-radio listeners:

> George was a rebel. . . . A revolutionary makes compromises to hang onto power; a rebel is a rebel, he is against; and he was against everything that stank in society, everything which was tripe and cabbage and decay and putrefaction, in himself and in society, and there was no compromise. . . . [F]or George, social injustice was physical pain, it smelt. . . .[2]

The uncompromising hater of "smelly little orthodoxies," the moralist with a nose for sniffing out his own side's hypocrisies, the scourge of the London literary intelligentsia, the Establishment "outsider," the sullen prep school boy, the "rebel of the Left": such was the "rebel" reputation George Orwell had acquired by the early 1950s. Since his death, critics have sometimes imposed this image of Orwell on his whole literary and private personality.

Rebel Orwell was not only the first face to emerge prominently in the development of Orwell's reputation, but also seems to have been the dominant self-image of Blair-Orwell himself. From the rebellious schoolboy "failure" to the adult critic of socialism "from the inside," Orwell came to see

himself in the late 1940s in terms approaching Crick's characterization, "the moral conscience of the Left." And so the inside and outside perspectives on this face of Orwell coincide fairly closely. Orwell would have agreed with Koestler and Richard Rees (who identified "the rebel Orwell" as his friend's most conspicuous "strain") that his first inclination was to react *against*. His self-described "natural hatred of authority" and "power of facing unpleasant facts" drove him to rebel against his "lower-upper-middle class" heritage and onto his road to Wigan Pier and democratic socialism.[3]

To chart the Rebel's Progress, then, is chiefly to trace a pattern of negative movement, the course of a man who, like Camus' rebel, said "no" before "yes." What concerns us, however, is less the man than his reputation, the public perceptions and self-perceptions of the man and his work. Not the raw biographical events in a life history but those events significant for his *reputation*-history command our attention. Prep school at St. Cyprian's, public school at Eton, police work in Burma, dishwashing and tramping in Paris and London, writing reviews in London in the early 1930s: these landmarks, though obviously decisive for Orwell's personal development and early, word-of-mouth reputation, became part of his published reception history only long after their occurrence. Not until publication of *The Road to Wigan Pier* in 1937 did Orwell's reputation as The Rebel begin to emerge clearly, whereupon Orwell's entire history was soon subjected to critical scrutiny and often reshaped to fit this face.

In tracing the evolution of this process, we need to be aware that

- certain significant, event-making moments have occurred in Orwell's reception history which have shaped the course of his reputation
- a few, identifiable authoritative voices often establish an image as prominent
- self- and public images interact to influence the course of a reputation
- images can evolve slowly and steadily or they can undergo major transformations over a short time and among different reception audiences
- various uses of watchwords in multiple contests often reveal different aspects of the developing image
- the formation of Orwell's faces can tell us much about the general processes of literary image-making

These, at any rate, are my major claims. In the introductory sections to each chapter in Part Two, these concerns, applicable not merely to the formation of Orwell's Rebel reputation but to the study of all his historical images, will guide us. Thus we are reconstructing in these opening sections the chronological unfolding of facial histories in order to illumine the development of Orwell's reputation and, where possible, the dynamics of the reputation process itself. Our aim is to make clear and make use of the broad outlines and certain distinguishing features of each face. We approach the formation of Orwell's reputation by way of the event-making moments and authoritative voices which established it.

II

The reception of *The Road to Wigan Pier* and the portrait of Blair-Orwell in Cyril Connolly's *Enemies of Promise* (1938) mark the emergence of Orwell's Rebel reputation in the late 1930s. Connolly was an old prep school friend and London literary intellectual; *Wigan Pier* was Orwell's first book to have a large readership and is the key work which established Orwell as "the rebel of the Left." That this image of Orwell is rooted specifically in his reception within the London intelligentsia indicates that there are not just certain individuals, but also certain audiences, like the London Left and the *Partisan Review* group, formative of or "authoritative" for a reputation.

"I was a stage rebel, Orwell a true one."[4] In hindsight, Cyril Connolly's remark about schoolmate Eric Blair in *Enemies of Promise* stands out as the earliest significant statement about Blair-Orwell, quoted so often in the 1940s that it took precedence over Orwell's unflattering self-characterizations of young Eric in *The Road to Wigan Pier,* thus making Orwell seem unduly modest. The comment also encouraged Orwell's new literary acquaintances, few of whom knew "Blair," to project indefinitely backwards in time an image of a defiantly rebellious "Orwell."

"Orwell alone among us was an intellectual," wrote Connolly. "He thought for himself and rejected not only Crossgates [St. Cyprian's] but the war, the Empire, Kipling, Success and Character." Not even so precocious a child as young Blair is likely to have protested all this at age eleven, and Connolly later conceded that he was probably thinking of his Eton days with Blair. (Connolly's repeated reference to "Orwell" also makes one wonder if his "Georgian Boyhood" memories of Blair weren't partly confused with his image of the adult Orwell.) Contrasting himself with the school's "philistines," Connolly described himself as a dilettante and aesthete merely "playing" a rebel role as he moved between his two role models, one of whom was "Orwell." Connolly's models represented his alternatives to school-approved "Character": "Orwell," the avatar of "Intelligence," and another schoolmate, Cecil Beaton, the incarnation of "Sensibility."[5]

Such a contrast certainly applied to the *adult* Orwell and Connolly in the 1940s, the combative *Tribune* pamphleteer and the cultivated editor of *Horizon*. In succeeding years, at least until the posthumous publication of "Such, Such Were the Joys," Connolly's image of young Blair was widely accepted. Acquaintances not only embraced it but introjected it into the present and inflated it into the verdict of a generation. To BBC colleague John Morris, in an otherwise harsh memoir of Orwell, Connolly's insight was the key to grasping Orwell's singular place among his contemporaries, if understood not merely as "a personal comparison" of the two men but as "valid for the whole of Orwell's generation." Koestler agreed in his *Observer* obituary that Connolly's statement actually described Orwell's relation "to his whole generation." Unlike other "*littérateurs* of social revolt" between the two wars, said Koestler, Orwell never allowed his rebellion to become conformist, joining

neither the "sham fraternity" of the Stalinist-dominated International Brigades in Spain nor the fashionable London literary Establishment.[6]

Among the many voices projecting an author's public image is, of course, that of the author himself, and surely the "rebel" persona of the author of *The Road to Wigan Pier* led readers to accept Connolly's characterizations as epitomizing both young Eric and George Orwell. Readers unfamiliar with "Blair" had no reason to think that he was unlike Orwell. Indeed Orwell had begun to craft a "true rebel" and "outsider" image for himself long before *Wigan Pier,* shortly after his return from Burma in 1927. His tramping and hop-picking were becoming known in London literary circles in the early 1930s, and he was already writing hard-hitting reviews of Catholic and Marxist books in the *Adelphi* and *New English Weekly.* The tendency to see Orwell as "a good hater," in Richard Rees's phrase, was well advanced by 1937;[7] the major change with *Wigan Pier* was its big audience and the fact that Orwell was starting to see himself not just as an Establishment outcast in solidarity with the poor but as a rebel *of* and *against* the Left, a man of the Left impatient with radical jargon and Marxist theory.

Readers also tend naturally to accept an author's self-presentations, and Orwell's straightforward style invited easy acceptance of his versions of himself. In the autobiographical section of *The Road to Wigan Pier* (Part II), he presented his former self as the snooty, iconoclastic Etonian ("an odious little snob" "against all authority"[8]) and ambivalent Empire policeman in Burma. He also cast himself as a skeptic and truth-seeker, "on the road" of rebellion away from Mandalay and toward Wigan Pier, thereby letting readers outside the left-wing fold identify with his new conversion to socialism. His language was inflammatory, calculatedly so. *Wigan Pier*'s extraordinary circulation as a recommended choice of the Left Book Club, the disputatious foreword by LBC co-director (and Orwell's publisher) Victor Gollancz, and Orwell's salty persona all combined to draw attention away from the socioeconomic issues of socialism and toward Orwell's character and relationship to the Left.

Critics on the Left agreed about little, except that *Wigan Pier* was cause for anger. Some critics were enraged about the material and spiritual deprivation which Orwell had detailed; others were angry with Orwell himself. Harry Pollitt, General Secretary of the British Communist Party, dismissed *Wigan Pier* in *The Daily Worker.* Orwell was "a disillusioned little middle-class boy . . . and late imperialist policeman." These characterizations soon became standard put-downs in Communist reviews. *Tribune,* the newly founded paper of the non-Stalinist Left, was alternately "infuriated" with Orwell's polemics and with the fact of the miners' poverty. The *New Statesman and Nation,* however, admired Orwell's "Gissingesque genius" unreservedly and acknowledged that it too had justly received Orwell's sting: "The honest Tory must face what he tells and implies, and the honest socialist must face him too. It may be hard for Mr. Orwell to accept such praise from such a notoriously snooty quarter. . . : it is fairly clear that the *New Statesman and Nation* is a pink rag compared to his bull-wrath.

But he must take it." Orwell was indeed coming to be seen both as a rebel of and against the Left.[9]

The Gollancz foreword deserves special mention. Reprinted in collections of Orwell criticism and published in the first American edition (1958) and later editions of *Wigan Pier,* the foreword helped shape Orwell's early reputation on the Left and is revealing for what it suggests generally about how certain prominent statements condition reputations. We have already spoken of authoritative voices, like Koestler and Trilling, who act as "reputation-builders"; Gollancz represents what might be thought of as a "reputation-suppressor," a contending voice literally "getting inside" Orwell's book with the effect of downplaying Orwell's criticisms of the Left and undercutting his credibility and "true rebel" persona.

Gollancz added to the effect of *Wigan Pier*'s autobiographical Part II by making Orwell's personality his focal point. A fellow-traveler who would soon be shocked by the Nazi-Soviet pact yet nevertheless remain loyal to Soviet Russia during the war, Gollancz introduced a line of argument in the foreword that the radical Left turned into a strategy for discrediting Orwell in the 1940s. Praising Orwell's intentions and bemoaning his judgment, Gollancz proceeded to psychologize Orwell in class terms. He admired Orwell's "complete frankness" and "burning indignation against poverty and oppression." But Orwell's criticisms of Marxism were "a patently outworn formula" traceable to "his general dislike of Russia. . . . The achievements of the Soviet Union are there for everyone to see." Gollancz criticized Orwell's devil's advocate stance against socialism. Orwell was "at one and the same time an extreme intellectual and a violent anti-intellectual," "a frightful snob . . . and a genuine hater of snobbery." (The "paradox" characterizations of Orwell by Raymond Williams and others may originate in these remarks.) For Gollancz the interest of Part II was chiefly psychological, an exposé of a middle-class mind in rebellion. "Still a victim" of his upbringing and public-school education, argued Gollancz, Orwell had declared himself a socialist and yet had partly succumbed to "the compulsion to conform to the mental habits of his class":[10]

> . . .the exhibition of this conflict is neither the least interesting nor the least valuable part of the book: for it shows the desperate struggle through which a man must go before . . . his mind can really become free—if indeed that is ever possible.[11]

Much of the influence of Gollancz's foreword was due precisely to the fact that it was a foreword. Unlike Trilling's introduction to *Homage to Catalonia,* Gollancz's fourteen pages were pedestrian criticism. But rarely is a piece of criticism more widely read than a book's introduction, not only reaching as many readers as the book itself but also, due to its position of priority, often shaping the individual reader's immediate experience and the course of subsequent criticism. The point calls attention to the importance of prefatory material for shaping reputations. A foreword may be the only piece of criticism that a reader, at least a non-specialist, ever reads.

Many readers, especially when they are unfamiliar with the author's past work or the subject area, read forewords first or even alone, never actually "getting through" that which comes after. Forewords are short: we usually assume they introduce, summarize, even handily (and favorably) "interpret" a book for us. Certainly Gollancz upset these expectations; his was not the standard introduction of vague praise one anticipates from a general editor. His foreword did, however, "pre-face" the Rebel Orwell. Its image of the man in the writings was a sharpened version of the developing Left view of Orwell as a heterodox radical.

Much as did Trilling, Gollancz spoke from a position of authority as LBC co-director. Moreover, his original 1937 audience, the 38,000 members of the LBC, were likely to be reliant on prefatory material. They were not chiefly "intellectual" readers familiar with the sectarian politics of the Spanish Civil War like many who read Trilling's introduction in *Commentary* and the first American edition of *Homage to Catalonia*. No doubt many of them were infrequent or nonreaders. *Wigan Pier* was a low-priced (2/6) LBC "discussion book" for March 1937, and so successful that Gollancz held it up as a model for running LBC discussions in the May 1937 LBC bulletin. Gollancz was quite pleased with Part I, a graphic description of Northern working conditions; he had originally tried to print Part I separately (Orwell objected) and later did issue it (along with the book's 32 grim photographs) to LBC members for a shilling. Not quite having expected or wanted Part II, Gollancz wrote his foreword to "greatly increase" the "value of the book" by giving "just a hint of certain vital considerations that arise from a reading of it." "Vital considerations," of course, meant undermining Part II; the "hint" occupied thirteen of Gollancz's fourteen pages. Gollancz addressed himself to LBC members and asked "the general public" to "ignore" the foreword, but, for reasons of economy, it also appeared in the regular edition.[12]

Unlike Trilling in 1952, Gollancz in 1937 certainly did not see young Orwell as a literary "figure." Gollancz regarded him as a promising young writer with a gift for detail to whom a generous publisher had advanced £500 for a report on Northern working-class conditions. For his part, Orwell was coming to see Gollancz as "part of the Communism racket."[13] Later Gollancz would reject *Homage to Catalonia* sight unseen and, as late as October 1938, laud the British Communist Party (BCP) in *Left News*, the LBC journal, for its "complete understanding" of the Hitler "peril." Once he had absorbed the shock of the Nazi-Soviet pact the next summer, Gollancz condemned it as "a base betrayal of socialist principles." In serving as a virtual mouthpiece for the BCP, the LBC had, Gollancz realized, "compromised our own values" and let "the end justify the means."[14] He was also speaking of himself. Soon he came around to a position on the war close to Orwell's "revolutionary socialism" in *The Lion and the Unicorn*, and the LBC ads for 1941 proclaimed "Win the War—And Win It By and For Socialism!" Gollancz had admired *Inside the Whale* (1940) and had asked Orwell to contribute to *Left News* in 1941 and to his collection *The*

*Betrayal of the Left* (1941), a harsh examination of Communist policy since 1939 which included an epilogue by Gollancz apologizing for the LBC's cooperation with the Communists during the prewar Popular Front years. But Gollancz, an intensely emotional man given to strong likes and dislikes, still felt a deep distaste for Orwell, whom he regarded as condescending and uncommunicative. Nor did Gollancz's basic sympathy for and trust in the Soviet Union alter. In later years Gollancz would become so frustrated with Orwell, seeing him as a prickly renegade, that he would turn down *Animal Farm*, phone other publishers to persuade them to do the same, and pronounce Orwell "intellectually dishonest" and "*enormously over-rated*."[15] So the Gollancz-Orwell relationship had its manifold tensions and complicated ups and downs, even in the 1930s. It was to become a microcosm of Orwell's mutually ambivalent, antagonistic relationship with the entire radical Left.

It bears emphasizing that the estrangement between Orwell and the Left was more than partly of his own doing. Even friendly critics have considered *The Road to Wigan Pier* marred by Orwell's focus on socialist intellectuals, his obsession with working-class smells and filth, and the implication, evident in his neglect of the trade-union movement, that workers lacked political consciousness. Tom Hopkinson, who wrote the first critical study of Orwell, made the much-quoted statement that *Wigan Pier* was Orwell's "worst book."[16] The judgment is questionable (Orwell himself once nominated, more plausibly, *A Clergyman's Daughter*), but whatever one's opinion, the significance of *Wigan Pier* for Orwell's reputation reminds us that an author's "worst" book is by no means necessarily his "least influential" book, either for his reputation or in its cultural impact. "Aesthetic value" often bears only an indirect relation to "influence." Accidents of history play their crucial part. What if *Wigan Pier* hadn't been selected as an LBC choice? (Orwell apparently expected this misfortune because the book was "too fragmentary and not, on the surface, very left-wing.") Certainly both the book's effect on Orwell's reputation and its wider social impact—and the same holds for the Gollancz foreword—would have been less. Although Orwell's wider fame stems from his last two books, *Wigan Pier* has had enormous importance for setting the outlines of Orwell's reputation, particularly the face of The Rebel.[17]

### III

After *The Road to Wigan Pier* and Connolly's *Enemies of Promise* established the basic contours of Orwell's Rebel image, *Animal Farm* and *Nineteen Eighty-Four* inflated and circulated it more widely. But what made this image a solid, richly textured, widely recognized public face—what we may say *crystallized* it—were the testaments of Orwell's influential literary friends after his death. Among the most significant of these were Koestler's *Observer* notice, from which we have already quoted, and V.S. Pritchett's *New Statesman* obituary. The latter is probably the single most widely quoted

piece of Orwell criticism, and its presentation of Orwell warrants extended consideration.

The importance not merely of Pritchett's obituary but of all his criticism for defining Orwell's whole literary reputation has not received its proper due. It cannot be overstated. To this date Pritchett has written no books, or even articles, on Orwell. Yet with his dozen short reviews of books by and about Orwell, and especially his British and American obituaries in early 1950, he has arguably had more influence than any other friend or critic in shaping the way people have seen Orwell. Such an influence is a subtle matter, easy to overlook. In no clear way does it sell any more books, capture film or TV contracts, or even permit substantive examination of Orwell's reputation within specific groups, as does the criticism of several other critics featured in case studies in this book. As I have noted, Pritchett is not one of those authoritative voices, like Trilling, who has ever been part of a group or has possessed a well-defined constituency.

Pritchett, the *New Statesman*'s book editor for two decades and an acclaimed short story writer, began calling Orwell a "rebel" as early as 1938;[18] his repeated and flattering characterizations of Orwell as a "rebel" and "conscience" reflect not only his high estimation of Orwell but also his penchant for memorable epithets. Connolly, Koestler, and Trilling, as we have seen, had a similar flair. In view of the general cultural authority of these critics, it is not surprising that their engaging formulations soon became established judgments.

It is worth dwelling for a moment on Pritchett's reviewing style, for it is on full display in the *New Statesman* obituary. Pritchett's bold descriptions of Orwell, not just his institutional authority, account for his characterizations gaining wide currency. Pritchett has tended in his criticism to congeal identified traits into essences. His inveterate habit, especially with Orwell but also with other writers whom he admires, has been to apply graphic epithets, like "saint" and "conscience." Pritchett aims to have readers see his version of his subject's "face behind the page." His criticism is provocatively worded and highly visual, designed to stick in the memory. And it does. "Saint" and "conscience" are lodged in historical memory as pregnant words in Orwell's reputation-history, words we have designated *watchwords*.

Pritchett is also fond of casting writers in terms of historical-mythical figures, like John the Baptist or Don Quixote, a practice which obviously highlights certain aspects of a reputation as it concretizes it. Other critics have invoked these two Pritchett allusions when describing Orwell too. And here it is possible to refine the notion of watchword, which we have discussed as typically a common noun or adjective reflexively associated with an author or work. Watchwords are also often proper nouns—names of persons, characters, places, etc.—which come up repeatedly in references to the author and whose associations influence his reputation.

Pritchett's admiring 1946 review of *Critical Essays*, titled "The Rebel," shows him linking Orwell as rebel with John the Baptist. Pritchett describes Orwell as "a John the Baptist who has returned from the wilderness." Or-

well's "noncomforming mind" makes him "different" from "the rest of the intelligentsia," says Pritchett. Orwell "stands apart from the imaginative writers of the Left: he spoils for trouble [and] dislikes his own side as much as the enemy."[19] Here we see, in Pritchett's gloss of Orwell as a John the Baptist returned from "the wilderness" of Wigan Pier and Spain, the iridescence of image-making, how faces shade into one another. The historical John the Baptist was not just a rebel but a prophet and saint. These meanings also resonate when "John the Baptist" is juxtaposed with "Orwell." In such ways, however subtly, aspects of faces, like prophet and saint, often protrude through other faces, like "rebel." Rich allusions like John the Baptist point up the prismatic character of reputation-formation, in which one hub of images anticipates, recasts, and merges with another, so that the foregrounded and clearly labeled face nevertheless contains within it certain features more immediately associated with other faces. One might, for instance, first think of the historical John the Baptist as a prophet, but Pritchett, using the allusion as a backdrop for a discussion of Orwell's position on the British Left, casts John as first and foremost a rebel.

In Pritchett's *New Statesman* obituary a more complex version of the same process of iridescent *image-shading* is at work. Take Pritchett's famous characterization of Orwell as "the conscience of his generation." A watchword in Orwell's reputation-history from virtually the moment the obituary appeared, the very word "conscience" consists of several pairs of image clusters not only linked with the borderline inside/outside stance of a rebel but also with the facial constellations of prophet and saint: sham rebel/true rebel, conformity/independence, accommodation/protest, compromise/integrity, inner-direction/other-direction, injustice/fairness, self-indulgence/self-denial.

Pritchett's obituary encapsulated these pairs and wove them into a striking portrait of the man. His notice presented Orwell as not just a "conscience of the Left" but as a conscience in a grander sense, as a symbolic, "saintly" rebel who stood against the vices of falsehood, hypocrisy, privilege, and self-interest. The constellation of features making up Pritchett's image of Orwell includes self-criticism, puckishness, extreme independence, "deadly pain," and "masochism."

Much of the force of Pritchett's obituary had to do with its circulation, timing, and span-of-career approach. Its impact can be measured by the fact that several of its ascriptions—"conscience of his generation," "saint," "rebel gone native in his own country," "Don Quixote"—almost immediately became watchwords applied to Orwell. Pritchett had already characterized Orwell in similar terms, but never before were such phrases collected together and given such eloquent expression—and precisely at the moment of the immediate posthumous revaluation of Orwell's achievement. In the major organ of Left intellectual opinion at mid-century—and then a week later in the major American review, the *New York Times Book Review*[20]—Pritchett was able, in effect, to gather up and consolidate several disparate images of "rebel Orwell" into a single compelling portrait. In this

light, Pritchett's obituary says much not just about Orwell but about the process of reputation-building. Pritchett's notice may be thought of as a charter document in Orwell hagiography, representing an early moment in the transfiguration of Orwell from "writer" into semi-mythical "literary figure." It began:

> George Orwell was the wintry conscience of a generation which in the 'thirties had heard the call to the rasher assumptions of political faith. He was a kind of saint and, in that character, more likely to chasten his own side than that of the enemy. . . . He prided himself on seeing through rackets, and on conveying the impression of living without the need for solace or even for the need of a single illusion. . . .
>
> In corrupt and ever-worsening years he always woke up one miserable hour earlier than anyone else and, suspecting something fishy on the side, broke camp and advanced alone to some tougher position in a bleaker place; and it had often happened that he had been the first to detect an unpleasant truth or to refuse a tempting hypocrisy. Conscience took the Anglo-Indian out of the Burma police, conscience sent the old Etonian among the down and outs in London and Paris. . . . His was the guilty conscience of the privileged and educated man . . . ; and this conscience could be allayed only by taking upon itself the pain, the misery, the dinginess, and the pathetic but hard vulgarities of a stale and hopeless period.[21]

As Malcolm Muggeridge noted in his diary, the obituary marks that moment when "the legend of a human being is created."[22] To etch an image in history, one must re-create a sense of lived *presence:* institutional authority alone is ordinarily necessary but not sufficient. And to re-create presence, one must arouse emotion and yet preserve distance, which necessitates being specific without being too concrete. Details increase the sense of actuality: metaphor allows for imaginative flight. Too much prosaic detail and the subject remains earthbound; no sense of magical presence results. Too much metaphor and the subject remains airy; no sense of reality emerges. Pritchett's obituary is a near-perfect balance, masterfully combining evocative detail with allusive grandeur.

But legends show no respect for their own genealogy. Like Trilling's "virtuous man" characterization, Pritchett's phrases about Orwell have been repeated (even on the dust jackets of Orwell's books) without acknowledgment or perhaps awareness of their author or source. Within the admittedly more circumscribed sphere of Orwelliana, these watchwords have become, like the catchwords of *Nineteen Eighty-Four,* hostages to popular repute, which so often grants fame to one's work only at the price of anonymity.

If we see Pritchett's obituary as one of those reception moments to which readers have repeatedly returned—like Trilling's introduction to *Homage to Catalonia* and Connolly's characterizations of Orwell in *Enemies of Promise*—it offers further insight into the reputation process. It illustrates how a climactic event helps establish a reputation. Such events can be viewed in our rhetoric of reception as *temporal topoi,* or *loci of the momentous.* They are historical places which, as a result of frequent reference and prominent

display, have become repositories of associations. Functioning like critical "spots of time," they stand out amid the flux and seem to grow in significance over time. One might also imagine these *topoi* as those places in a reputation which obtrude above the endless parade of reception events, towering like mountains above the vast flat terrain of a reception history, visible from great temporal distance. As with Pritchett's obituary, the vividness and impact of such "peak" events in later phases of a reception history often increase with time, for an episode can accumulate significance and meaning over the years as it gets repeated, embroidered, reapplied, and linked to other impressions. These *topoi*, usually containing oft-quoted watchwords, are therefore familiar reception ground, rhetorical landmarks which not only inscribe and direct a reputation but also somehow seem its destination and summit.

For the making of reputation is always a matter of selection, a highlighting of certain statements, events, and images. Like certain features in an image, certain moments in a history get foregrounded; in linking them in certain ways, we see certain stages and aspects of a reputation. In Orwell's case, this is merely to say that his reputation, like anyone's, is a cognitive matter of presence. What remains "present" from the past does so as a result of repetition and accent. Historical events do not recede in assembly-line fashion; some moments, like some features in an image constellation, impress themselves on our consciousness and retain a charged afterglow. They become the key, "window" events through which the past re-enters. To reconsider our metaphor of "star" reputations, we might say that, as we look backward in a reception history, we are looking upwards to a starry sky—and noticing over the reception horizon and against the black of the past certain luminous, enduring moments. The recurrence and formative power of such *peak* or *radiant moments* in a reputation-history remind us that some reception events are indeed, as it were, "event-making," truly more equal than others.

## IV

However significant his earlier obituary statements and posthumous reviews, Pritchett's consolidation did not hold. There are, of course, limits in range and firmness to any such consolidation—Pritchett's was really an image which held together for his generation of Left intellectuals. His suggestive "conscience" metaphor contained the seeds of its own transformation, and even as Pritchett repeated and extended the characterization in the early '50s, this new Rebel image was fragmenting. As Orwell's reputation grew during the decade (partly of course as a result of testaments like Pritchett's), and as the mass media and different intellectual groups approached him from different viewpoints and with different ends, his rebel face "split" into two distinct images: the "strong" and "weak" rebel, or the "manly" hero and the neurotic "failure." Broadly speaking, then, Orwell's posthumous reputation in the '50s and '60s split in two directions, develop-

ing into what could be considered two extreme, updated versions of the Gollancz-Connolly divergence of the late '30s, the false "rebel against the Left" and the "true" rebel. In effect, the split reflected a division of Pritchett's characterization of Orwell as "conscience," approaching it, in the case of Orwell as "failure," from the inside via psychoanalysis; and from the outside in the case of Orwell as the manly intellectual, in terms of the '50s cult of the tough-guy hero.

The new dimension of Orwell as a rebel failure emerged with the 1952 publication in *Partisan Review* of "Such, Such Were the Joys," collected in *Such, Such Were the Joys* (1953). The essay directed new, and often psychoanalytic, attention to Orwell's childhood.[23] That it could not be published in Britain (until 1968) for fear of libel also fit with Blair-Orwell's Rebel reputation. Described by Orwell in a letter to Connolly as a "pendant" to *Enemies of Promise,* the essay was part polemic and part autobiography, apparently a direct reply to Connolly. "I am anxious to make it clear that I was not a rebel, except by force of circumstance," Orwell wrote. "Potentially I was more of a rebel than most, but I never did rebel intellectually, only emotionally." Here again, as with *The Road to Wigan Pier,* we see Orwell as an authoritative voice contributing to the formation of his own reputation, this time speaking from the grave:

> I had no money, I was weak, I was ugly, I had a chronic cough, I was cowardly, I smelt. . . . I had won two scholarships, but I was a failure, because success was measured not by what you did but by what you were. . . . I did not possess character or courage or health or even good manners, the power to look like a gentleman. . . . There was time for a bit of happiness before the future closed in on me. But I did know that the future was dark. Failure, failure, failure—failure ahead of me, failure behind me—that was the deepest conviction I carried away.[24]

Orwell's self-images of "rebel" and "failure" thus competed in the early '50s with Connolly's image of Orwell as a triumphant rebel, which Koestler and others had just invested with generational significance. The new resultant image—"the rebel failure"—still presented Orwell as a true rebel, rather than a "stage" rebel. But now "truth" and "failure" were explicitly equated. Against prep school oppressors, Blair had maintained, wrote Orwell, his "incorruptible inner self."[25] Readers knew that Orwell had done the same in Burma and in literary London; the self-portrait of young Eric in "Such, Such Were the Joys" soon prompted critics to see the adult Orwell in the essay's terms. Critics began, that is to say, to do with "Such, Such Were the Joys" precisely the reverse of what they had done with *Enemies of Promise*: to project Blair's failure *forward* into Orwell's adulthood. Epitomizing the tendency was Anthony West's much-hailed psychoanalytic argument that the essay bared the "hidden wound" of Orwell's childhood and furnished the missing biographical link between Blair and Orwell, between the victimized child and the scarred author of *Nineteen Eighty-Four,* with O'Brien's tortures really a prep school beating and Big Brother none other than Blair's brutal prep school headmistress.[26]

This image of Orwell as a "rebel failure," like the 1930s image of him as a "true" political rebel rather than a dandy, was formed by and fit with the *Zeitgeist*. In vogue during the decade—in art as in life—was the alienated rebel. Especially popular was the misunderstood teenager, like Holden Caulfield and James Dean, both of whom made failure seem virtuous, even glamorous. Inevitably, some critics infused Blair/Orwell's life with an aura of romantic failure. The general mood made Orwell's life and premature death, much like that of Dean and James Agee and Camus, seem both a symbolic expression of the age and a tragic protest against it. Some young London writers specifically compared Orwell with Dylan Thomas, who died in 1953 at the age of 39, alcoholism seen as having laid waste to his great promise.[27] And so, while men of Orwell's generation like Richard Rees were still depicting him as a "Promethean" rebel championing the world's victims, younger writers were seeing Orwell as a "Loser" and "Victim."[28] As in the 1930s, the rebel heroes of Orwell's fiction were interpreted autobiographically, but this time it was noticed that most of his heroes—John Flory, Dorothy Hare, Gordon Comstock, Tubby Bowling, Boxer, Winston Smith—were failed rebels. Furthermore, because some of his characters' experiences were indeed Orwell's own, it was inviting to fill in the gaps in Orwell's history (since he had requested that no biography be written) by referring to his heroes. Even friends did this. So Orwell as "rebel failure" soon took on heroic proportions. The image had deep appeal for some intellectuals, as Andrew Sarris' confession of his and his brother's impassioned adolescent identification with Orwell makes clear:

> Orwell became our intellectual shield against both the hoggish complacency of the Right and the swinish connivance of the Left. Almost instantly, it seemed, we had already known Orwell. . .and we came to know him much better than we knew ourselves. Getting Out From Under Yourself is the favorite game of losers and outsiders, and all his life Orwell was something of a loser and outsider, and only other losers and outsiders could ever love Orwell as he deserved to be loved and could never love himself.[29]

Posed against this image was a new, "successful" Rebel Orwell. It had two aspects, one more moderate and "intellectual," the other more aggressive, manly, and popular. The first was the critical yet admiring image of Orwell as the great rebel writer of his generation, widely held especially by young leftists during the '50s and '60s, as Jenni Calder has recalled.[30] Many of them saw Orwell as the one honest, pragmatic radical from the 1930s. Their respect was evinced in the fiction of the decade: the sullen, alienated anti-heroes of the Angry Young Men were direct descendants of Gordon Comstock in *Keep the Aspidistra Flying*.

The second, more widely circulated image of Orwell as "triumphant" rebel also reflected, perhaps ironically, the cult of James Dean, as had Orwell as "failure." But this latter image celebrated the sullen, silent man. At its most absurd the image was a macho caricature of Connolly's image and of Orwell's self-presentation in *Wigan Pier*. A 1962 cover story in the

men's magazine *Saga,* titled "George Orwell Vs. The World: The Rebel Who Beat Big Brother," gives full play to this virile Orwell. On the magazine's cover appear numerous Orwells, sketched in harsh black strokes, confronted by enemies coming from all directions—Colonel Blimps, fascist snipers, verminous little lions. But Rebel Orwell stares them down, calm and resolute, virtually a comic book hero. Aware of the Cold War skirmishes for Orwell's mantle, this admirer (an ex-Marine) implied, in militantly sentimental language yet with more insight than most critics, that much of the Left-Right debate about Orwell's legacy was less an ideological dispute than a battle among male intellectuals periodically doubtful about their masculinity for the right to identify with a two-fisted culture hero, with Orwell the Spanish militiaman and blunt truth-teller. To some degree Orwell's "masculine" prose style invited both the debate and the following sort of response:

> Of the events which mark a man for greatness, one of the surest and most ironic comes immediately after his death when his enemies fall all over one another to claim him for a friend. [Since his death] almost all the frauds and phonies whom Orwell detested from the depths of a very deep reservoir of hatred for humbug—all of those pansy poets, culture kooks, rich liberals who love the poor. . . . All of these and more have flocked to the Orwell shrine to deposit unctuously one more identical wreath bearing the identical epitaph:
>
> "Here Lies Our Buddy"
>
> . . .But the fact is that no one can claim George Orwell, for he consistently "accepted no discipline". . . .The final obituary for George Orwell must be that he wore no man's collar, hated being top dog, and was, above all, an honest man. . . . He was that kind of man.[31]

With the *Saga* article, we see the Rebel face of Orwell enter the hazy penumbra of popular reputation, a dim region into which it is typically difficult to trace the radiation of a reputation with precision. In charting the permutations of this face further, we thus run up against the limits of rhetorical analysis of the Rebel's Progress. Indeed terms like "critical" and "popular" themselves fail to do justice to the variety and complexity of audiences which receive and transmit reputations. It is safe to say, however, that many images which originate in the critical sphere pass relatively unchanged, if simplified, into the popular sphere. Still, only with criteria such as the reappearance of watchwords at wider levels of repute can one trace the vicissitudes of images into those wider spheres. For example, by the late 1970s Connolly's "true rebel" characterization of Orwell was so well known that it could be cited (without reference to Connolly) in *The Encyclopedia Britannica* as a summary of Orwell's life and an indictment of his generation. Almost as precise a correlation between critical and popular treatments of Rebel Orwell occurred in one 1953 radio broadcast of Orwell as "The Outsider." The broadcast presented "an unhappy, dissatisfied man, poor Orwell. . .a perpetual outsider who stood apart from the crowd"—obviously a version of Orwell as

"failure." Images of an author also often pass relatively unchanged from the critical to popular spheres when authoritative voices present their images in mass circulation magazines or in broadcasts, as we have already seen with Koestler's 1950 obituary and 1960 BBC broadcast. Similarly, Pritchett's December 1946 BBC broadcast on Orwell is obviously an extension of his *New Statesman* review earlier that year, titled "The Rebel," from which we have already quoted. Pritchett describes Orwell in the broadcast as "the odd man out" among his contemporaries, who "belongs to no group, joins no side. . . . He is on his own." The broadcast concludes: "Rebel and diehard—in the English tradition—that is Orwell. . . ."[32]

## V

Thus far we have been chiefly concerned with those authoritative voices, significant statements, and radiant moments in Orwell's reception history which have decisively shaped his Rebel reputation across time and through to the popular sphere. Yet apparently marginal reception materials—what can be thought of as *minor voices*—are also worth examining, less for their impact on the course of a reputation than for what they reveal about how images permute as different institutional audiences receive them. The *Saga* article was an instance of such apparently marginal evidence. It indicated Orwell's reputation in a wider sphere than the critical and intellectual domains, giving us insight into the synchrony of repute. The remainder of this section explores both the easily overlooked heterogeneity of Orwell's reputation among different institutional audiences and the diverse uses of watchwords. And here we are as much concerned with investigating further the subtleties of the reputation process as with specifically tracing the unfolding of Orwell's facial history as The Rebel.

We have already noted that watchwords come in various sorts and form the spokes around which image clusters revolve. In the descriptions of Orwell by Pritchett, Sarris, and others, we notice a phenomenon which became common in the 1950s and '60s as Orwell received continued attention: the appearance of what we may think of as *secondary watchwords* (e.g., "outsider," "loser," "odd man out") generated from the primary, radiant watchword "rebel." Others included "pariah," "diehard," "guerrilla," "underdog," "dissenter," "gadfly," "maverick," "man of independence," and "individualist."[33] Secondary watchwords "densify" a face and often link it via an associational network to other faces. Typically the *primary watchword* is the point of departure for the evolution of the variants, but the variants may also serve as the basis for establishing the primary watchword. What distinguishes certain watchwords as "primary" is not temporal priority but centrality and frequency of occurrence in a reception history.

Invariably, secondary watchwords emphasize slightly different aspects of the primary watchword. For each watchword involves a change in critical location; each is a rhetorical act that remaps an image constellation and reflects (and invites) some movement in the reception scene. "Outsider"

foregrounds the ostracism often entailed in rebellion; "underdog" stresses the rebel's weak, disadvantaged position and suggests his hopeless and somehow virtuous opposition to Authority. But, as we saw in Chapter Two, the same watchwords are often turned by different institutional readers toward opposing ideological or critical ends. Examining this process—how the same watchword spins a different image cluster according to the critical location of the observer—discloses a "backroom" politics of reputation. For it shows how different images and issues often get organized around the same term, and how political disagreements sometimes really involve veiled dispute over a metaphor.

Consider the following two examples, the uses of "individualist" and "rebel" during the 1950s. We choose watchwords in reception material from the same historical period in order to underscore how, even when a face has been "consolidated" by an authoritative voice like Pritchett into one or two central images—e.g., Orwell as "conscience"—the image is not approached by all groups from the same vantage point. The consolidation is a superficial unity, holding together divergent perspectives under an umbrella image. Our goal is to show here how sharply distinct images can stem from the same watchword, thereby illustrating how many "rods" this umbrella image really has at any one time.

Notice how different estimates of Orwell on the Right and Left in the early to mid- '50s are nevertheless expressed through the same watchword "individualist." Despite the shared watchword, observers saw Orwell from different distances and addressed audiences of opposed political outlooks and literary tastes, as becomes apparent when one scrutinizes the contexts of "individualist Orwell." "Individualism" has traditionally had a quite different value and connotation for conservatives and radicals, and what is especially interesting is how "Orwell" is accommodated to the word's varied history, so that he becomes little more than a portable platform for airing different ideological views. In 1950 Henry Luce's conservative *Time,* for instance, cast Orwell as an "individualist" in the sense of being an anti-Communist, implicitly pro-capitalist champion of freedom and free enterprise. Orwell was "an individualist of a rare kind: he wanted other people to be individualists too." In what was purportedly a review of *Burmese Days* and *Coming Up for Air,* the *Time* reviewer devoted most of his space to lauding *Nineteen Eighty-Four* and *Animal Farm,* which he called "the best novel [*sic*] on the doublecross of Stalinism." English Conservative Laurence Brander, on the other hand, characterized Orwell in 1954 as "an individualist in an urban society." Brander's Orwell was a throwback to an earlier age, the preindustrial "English eccentric." Brander argued that Orwell "remain[ed] an individualist" because he rejected "acquisitive society":

> He lived as we sometimes dream we should like to live. . . . For most of us there is no escape. We hardly dare rattle the chains. But we are mightily attracted by the man who rattles off every chain that society attempts to load on him. That is why we like George Orwell.

Pointedly disputing this "we" and the appeal of Orwell's antagonistic relation to contemporary "Society" was James Walsh's 1956 essay in the *Marxist Quarterly,* sardonically entitled "An Appreciation of An Individualist Writer." *Nineteen Eighty-Four,* said Walsh, was "cold war propaganda" exhibiting Orwell's "neurotic hatreds" toward "the people"; Orwell himself was "a mouthpiece for some of the most deep-seated petit-bourgeois illusions and prejudices." Presenting "individualist" within a Marxist vocabulary which contrasts "bourgeois morality" unfavorably with collectivism, Walsh linked it negatively with capitalist profit-seeking and maladjustment. Between these conservative and radical uses of the word was a Canadian liberal's 1955 estimation of Orwell as "two things above all: an individualist and a preacher." This reviewer, Edith Fowke, admired Orwell as an old-fashioned liberal and moralist; she placed "individualist" within a context of shared liberal-Christian values, wherein it was linked with "decency, justice and liberty," "the goals he fought for with all his resources of intelligence and humour." Her Orwell was less a rebel fighting against something than a model liberal championing certain ideals. So we see that those watchwords (and secondary watchwords) particular to an author's history of reputation sometimes say less about him than about their own histories. And, of course, their etymologies become, in turn, part of an author's history of reputation. Watchwords, then, can generate very different images; the value and meaning of "individualist" depends on its use in a particular context, and it means different things to different groups.[34]

Now consider a diversity of laudatory ascriptions of "rebel" to Orwell during the postwar period. Again the responses are ideologically motivated. But one notices here that "Orwell" is the controlling mechanism for how the watchwords get applied, rather than the other way around. Though "Orwell" is still being claimed and dismissed by ideological groups, his life and work provide the basis for the images which unfold; modifiers are employed so as to present Orwell's allegiances as the observer's own. "Orwell" therefore becomes the battleground, rather than the word "rebel." This is, of course, largely because "rebel," unlike "individualist," has not been a linguistic site of contention between the Right and Left. So we see that, for critics of the Right, Orwell is a "thinking," "original," "uncontaminated" rebel disgusted with the shallow, dishonest Left; for most Left critics Orwell is a "responsible" rebel serving the traditional radical role of political conscience.

Thus, for Labour Party supporter Pritchett, Orwell's "spirit of nonconformity" resembles that of fellow dissidents like Milton, Defoe, Cobbett, Mill, and Wells. Orwell is critical of the Left, says Pritchett, but also clearly behind "his own side." For the right-wing American journal *The Freeman,* however, Orwell is "The Thinking Rebel," a conservative in all but name who brilliantly saw through socialism—not just communism—and finally attacked it from the Right in *Nineteen Eighty-Four.* A conservative critic for the *Atlantic Monthly* went even further, arguing that Orwell had turned rightward well before *Nineteen Eighty-Four* and exalting him as "an original kind of rebel. . ., miraculously uncontaminated. . .[and] one of the few men on

the far Left who did not unconditionally surrender to dogma." In Britain too, Peter Quennell in the conservative *Daily Mail* welcomed Orwell's anti-Soviet emphasis. Calling Orwell a "born rebel—one of those courageous, rebellious, irresponsible, intractable, obstreperously independent Englishmen"—Quennell noted that, however much Orwell "might protest against orthodox Toryism," he found "hidebound Stalinism" and "the dogmas of the extreme Left wing" "far more obnoxious to his sense of right and decency." Meanwhile young radical A.J.P. Taylor, who succeeded Orwell in introducing the second volume of *British Pamphleteers,* talked about him in terms similar to Pritchett's. Taylor cast Orwell as an independent radical, "a rebel all his life" in the tradition of the great English pamphleteers from Milton to Mill. But other radicals did not admire Orwell's rebelliousness. Unlike the case of "individualist," however, which possessed a pejorative status in James Walsh's Marxist lexicon, the Communist Left valued the word "rebel" and did not attack Orwell *as* a rebel. Rather, it simply denied him the honorific. "Rebel indeed!" said Sean O'Casey. "Rather a yielding blob that buried itself away from the problems of living. . . ." Titling his diatribe "Rebel Orwell," O'Casey described Orwell as a false rebel, an escapist and fatalist who pandered to public taste and whose reputation was engineered by Establishment insiders. His view is representative of the hard Left line toward Orwell. A softer, less direct approach, in the tradition of Gollancz's foreword, was to praise Orwell's character and intentions, thereby making dismissal of his judgment appear fair-minded. Herbert Matthews' 1952 review of *Homage to Catalonia* in *The Nation* exemplified this tack. Matthews, a *New York Times* correspondent during the Spanish Civil War, saw Orwell as "a passionate rebel at heart," "wonderfully brave, and as patient, decent, honest. . .as a human being can be." Unfortunately, Matthews' Orwell was also "misled," "confused," and "ignorant" about the war.[35]

The point here is to indicate how a reputation can come to be fought over, with different groups warring with the same words for very different kinds of heroes. Although many different observers may invoke the same watchword, by no means do they all see through it the same image. Indeed just the opposite. Terms like "individualist" and "rebel," which can generate substantially different images as they radiate into different contexts, do invite a battle among contending parties as to who "by right" may enlist heroic Orwell in his cause. In the case of Orwell as rebel, with the exception of certain observers on the far Left, the reasoning goes: If Rebel Orwell is against the same smelly little orthodoxy that I am, isn't he then on my side? Most of the responses suggest that this has been a typical assumption. O'Casey's essay, which seeks to undercut Orwell's reputation as a rebel, shows further that we automatically tend to regard "rebel" as a flattering characterization. To admire another's rebellion is to participate in it in some way, to be something of a rebel oneself. Indeed it is partly because Orwell criticized "his own side" so severely that he carries so much moral prestige today. If *Nineteen Eighty-Four* had been written by a John Bircher, or *Bur-*

*mese Days* by a Burmese nationalist, would many people bother to read them? Orwell's books possess tremendous conviction partly because they were actually written by a socialist and Empire policeman.

Still, however conveniently overlooked, to be anti-Establishment or anti-Stalinist is not necessarily to support a particular political faction or ideological position. (How many postwar groups do *not* claim to be on the side of "the foes of totalitarianism"?) Special interests of all sorts have downplayed their differences with Orwell, seizing on the fact of their shared enemies. Or they have generalized from a single prominent aspect of his reputation for "liberty, justice, decency" to a variety of positions which they associate with such values, often implying not only a general affinity between Orwell and themselves but also imputing to him doctrinal positions (even on issues which have arisen only since 1950) identical to their own. Part of the difficulty, of course, is that a rebel is, as Koestler noted, chiefly "a man against." Observers can agree with Orwell about what they are *against*—without ever getting down to saying what they are *for*. Since Orwell was a critic of socialism, not a system-builder or social planner, it is also easy to dwell on one's shared antagonists and extrapolate from his criticism and satires some imagined positive resemblances on all sorts of issues. Surely Orwell's stance as "the perpetual outsider," Pritchett's "odd man out" to every group, has facilitated these tendencies. Ironically, if understandably, within less than a decade of his death, the "odd man out" had become, as one *Time* headline put it, "Odd Man In."[36]

To four case studies which conditioned and illustrate this transformation we now turn.

## 5. "Knight Errant of Social Justice": Orwell As Don Quixote

### I

Few of literature's "odd men out" are better loved than Don Quixote. And few modern writers have been more dearly cherished than George Orwell. In no small part, the affection and admiration which Orwell has aroused in his readers not only is reflected in but also stems from his frequent comparisons with Quixote. "Don Quixote" has become a watchword in Orwell's reception history, and some of Quixote's popularity and ascribed characteristics have become features of Orwell's "Quixotic" reputation. We have already touched on the significance of analogies for reputations when we examined Pritchett's treatment of Orwell as a rebellious John the Baptist, where we noted how the casting of a literary figure in terms of a well-known historical-mythical figure can shape a writer's public image. This facial history of "Orwell as Don Quixote" affords an extended opportunity to explore this important aspect of the reputation process. It takes us far beyond the matter of a critic's allusive style to a study of the dense configuration of cultural meaning contained within a portrait. For we are not just examining

faces, but faces *in portrait*. In the case studies in this chapter, we must imagine the Rebel Orwell assuming various expressions—all of them recognizably the same face and yet each possessing a different "air" and "character." Here we encounter a portrait of The Rebel as Quixotic idealist.


## II

Before his death, Orwell's acquaintances had often remarked on his ascetic temper, eccentric habits, deep nostalgia, and raw-boned, even cadaverous frame. In numerous memoirs in the '50s and '60s they depicted him as an endearing and poignant and utterly unworldly character, again and again sallying forth, often ignorant of political realities and unrealistically attempting singlehandedly to combat evil and rescue the oppressed. To friends and admirers Orwell was nothing less than "the English Don Quixote." The resemblance was purportedly both physical and spiritual.

"Imagine Don Quixote without his horse and his drooping whiskers, and you will get a fair idea of what George Orwell looked like," George Woodcock opened a 1953 memoir of Orwell.[37] Woodcock later dwelt on the comparison in the first pages of his graceful book on Orwell, *The Crystal Spirit:*

> When I remember George Orwell, I see again the long, lined face that so often reminded one not of a living person, but of a character out of fiction. It was the nearest I had seen in real life to the imagined features of Don Quixote, and the rest of the figure went with the face. For Orwell was a tall, thin, angular man, with worn Gothic features accentuated by deep vertical furrows that ran down the cheeks and across the corners of the mouth. The thinness of his lips was emphasized by a very narrow line of dark moustache; it seemed a hard, almost cruel mouth until he smiled, and then an expression of unexpected kindliness would irradiate his whole face. The general gauntness of his looks was accentuated by the deep sockets from which his eyes looked out, always rather sadly. In contrast to the fragile, worn-down look of the rest of him, his hair grew upward into a kind of brown crest, vigorous and until the end untouched by grey.

"And however much he might on occasion find himself in uneasy and temporary alliance with others," Woodcock concluded, Orwell "was—in the end—as much a man in isolation as Don Quixote. His was the isolation of every man who seeks the truth diligently, no matter how unpleasant its implications may be to others or even to himself."[38]

In this description of the Quixotic Orwell we see more fully how a rich allusion contains within itself numerous associations which generate various images and how these associations serve to "densify" reputations. We devote a separate section to Orwell as Quixote because this analogy, as much as any other single comparison, has decisively contributed to Orwell's reputation.

The Quixote analogy has deepened the fondness which readers feel toward the man within the writings and has served as one basis for what

friends have termed "the Orwell myth."[39] Moreover, quite plainly, the Quixote allusion partly accounts for the man, and the man within the writings, being so loved. Many warm-hearted anecdotes about Orwell rest on some analogy between him and the naive, chivalrous, perseverant Quixote. The myth of the Quixotic Orwell is that of the romantic in a world of cynics, the self-dramatizing idealist amid a crowd of pseudo-sophisticated pragmatists.

The Quixotic Orwell is a man of many faces. First and foremost, he is The Rebel, Paul Potts's "proud man apart," "a knight errant . . . of social justice." But he is also, as Woodcock's last sentence quoted above suggests, the saintly Truth-seeker, the "virtuous man." The bony physique and pained "underdog" stance of the Quixotic Orwell remind other friends, like Malcolm Muggeridge and Anthony Powell, of particular saints, like St. Francis. But whether saint or mere romantic, their Quixotic Orwell is always, if sometimes ambivalently, a man against; and his quest is always a rebel's progress. "Like most people 'in rebellion'," Powell has written, Orwell "was more than half in love with what he was rebelling against. What exactly that was I could never be sure. Certainly its name was legion. . . ."[40]

We now explore the facial history of the Quixote image. We will be attending especially to the transformations which the image has undergone, how it has been used and has modified Orwell's reputation, variabilities in its reception among different audiences, the relation of Orwell's self-image to his public image as Quixote, and the significance of the allusion for the politics of Orwell's reputation.

### III

Acquaintances had commented on Orwell's physical and temperamental resemblance to Don Quixote in the 1940s. But as with the faces of The Rebel and The Saint, the image of the Quixotic Orwell did not crystallize until V.S. Pritchett's *New Statesman* obituary, which we have already examined. Pritchett linked Orwell's saintliness with his quixotism, much as Powell would do more explicitly in the next decade. Pritchett compared Orwell to Quixote not only as a man of conscience but also as a crazily lovable character who would expound passionately on the "alluring disadvantages" of his art of living:

> Conscience . . . drove him into the Spanish civil war and, inevitably, into one of its unpopular sects, and there Don Quixote saw the poker face of Communism. . . .
>
> He would be jogged into remembering mad, comical and often tender things which his indignation had written off. . . . He was an expert in living on the bare necessities and a keen hand at making them barer. There was the sardonic suggestion that he could do this but you could not. He was a handyman. He liked the idea of a bench. I remember once being advised by him to go in for goatkeeping, partly I think because it was a sure road to trouble and semi-starvation; but as he set out the alluring disadvantages, it seemed to dawn on him that he was arguing for some

country Arcadia, some Animal Farm he had once known; goats began to look like escapism and, turning aside as we walked to buy some shag at a struggling Wellsian small trader's shop, he switched the subject to the dangerous Fascist tendencies of the St. John's Wood Home Guard who were marching to imaginary battle under the Old School Tie.[41]

Pritchett's image of the Quixotic Orwell is probably the best-known one, and a version of it has persisted to the present day. When acquaintances talk about Orwell, they often mention his endearingly daft proclamations, his weirdly funny idiosyncrasies, his odd mix of cynicism and childlike innocence.

But mention the idealistic Don and one also immediately thinks of his fat little squire, Sancho Panza. To Bernard Crick, "Don Quixote" corresponds to Orwell "the writer" and Sancho Panza to Orwell "the man."[42] Although Orwell himself does not seem to have split his self-image along such lines, he did see life as more or less a constant battle between concupiscence and conscience, between Sancho and the Don, "the voice of the belly protesting against the soul."[43] Orwell considered them to be an archetypal pair, and referred to them often in his journalism. The famous instance is in "The Art of Donald McGill," in which Orwell discusses the cultural import of the Don/Sancho dualism, a passage often quoted by critics discussing Orwell as Quixote. As we saw with Trilling's introduction to *Homage to Catalonia*—which, because of the documentary's first two words, invited headline reviews paying "Homage to Orwell"—the quoting of this essay's reflections on Quixote constitutes an example of how a writer's remarks can directly, if inadvertently, shape his reputation when they get turned back upon him. "If you look into your own mind, which are you," Orwell once asked, "Don Quixote or Sancho Panza?" "Don Quixote," most readers of Orwell have answered about him. Orwell's own response was less flattering, and his answer reflects the puritanical side of his complicated nature and his ambivalent desire for a life of heroic renunciation:

> Almost certainly you are both. There is one part of you that wishes to be a hero or a saint, but another part is the little fat man who sees very clearly the advantages of staying alive with a whole skin. He is your unofficial self, the voice of the belly protesting against the soul. His tastes lie toward safety, soft beds, no work, pots of beer, and women with voluptuous figures. He it is who punctures your fine attitudes and urges you to look after Number One, to be unfaithful to your wife, to bilk your debts, and so on and so forth. Whether you allow yourself to be influenced by him is a different question.[44]

This split between the Don and Sancho suggests how quixotism constitutes a particular form of rebellion, making explicit the relation between Quixote and the Rebel Orwell. The Don rebels against the prosaic life lived by the ordinary man; the image thus inevitably stands in tense opposition to Orwell as The Common Man. Indeed, as we shall see, the image of the Quixotic Orwell raises the whole problem of how to be an individualist

in a standardized, rationalized, safe, "soft" age, a hero in an unheroic world.

Some observers have invoked the Quixote allusion by way of spotlighting the romantic, even ludicrous aspect of Orwell's reputation for patriotism, making him into a dreamy 'St. George'. Malcolm Muggeridge, dubbing him "The Knight of the Woeful Countenance," has a fond image of Orwell in battle fatigues as a World War II correspondent in Paris. Muggeridge touchingly describes the zany side of Orwell, looking somehow distinguished in his shabby "proletarian fancy dress," "always noticeable as Orwell. . . , a dear oddity," and so much like Quixote in characteristic outbursts like "All tobacconists are fascists," or extravagant pronouncements like his puckish declaration that Kipling's "Mandalay" was the best poem in the English language. Like Quixote, Orwell struck Muggeridge and others as a kindly country gentleman who, when exercised by an injustice, sometimes believed himself called upon to redress the problems of the world. Other tales about Orwell "in combat" leaven Muggeridge's Quixote image. Pritchett tells about Orwell's preference for top-floor flats because one could more easily get out on the roof to put out fire bombs. Muggeridge and Fredric Warburg joke about how "Sergeant Blair" in the St. John's Wood Company of the Home Guard posed a greater threat to England than did the enemy.[45]

An eyewitness account of "Sergeant Blair" in action by Orwell's handpicked corporal justifies this gentle mockery. "Corporal Fred Warburg," Orwell's publisher by this time, bemusedly recalls that Orwell viewed the Home Guard as the "ideal" fighting force. It was "unprofessional," "volunteer," "inefficient," "anti-fascist and anti-Nazi," and "animated above all by a deep affection for the England he loved above all else." Fittingly, Orwell and Warburg, a kind of Don and Sancho in the Home Guard, were put in charge of what became known as the Home Guard's "Foreign Legion," the foreign refugee recruits—who were unable to perform correctly even the simplest movements of close-order drill and whose "love of indiscipline amounted to genius." Among Warburg's favorite memories of Sergeant Blair was the day Orwell, forgetting to make sure that an inert, non-firing charge was in place for a routine drill, ordered "Fire!"—whereupon a practice (though non-explosive) bomb went whizzing past dozens of men. No one was badly hurt, though one man lost all his false teeth, top and bottom, and another was unconscious for twenty-four hours. Appearing before a Court of Inquiry a few weeks later, Orwell was not disciplined, though he was informed that a new set of dentures had cost £100. He was not charged the money, but was nevertheless angered. The cost of new dentures, he told Warburg, was altogether excessive.[46]

Several stories involving Orwell's Spanish adventures seem almost as if they were pre-designed to establish the Quixote image. Stafford Cottman, an eighteen-year-old soldier in Orwell's unit, recounts how Orwell "rejoiced" over his "luck" in being six-foot-three after a sniper's bullet hit him in the throat (i.e., not the head). (Others report that, if Orwell hadn't been

so tall, his head would not have stuck out over the parapet.) Bob Edwards, Orwell's company commander, recalls two hilarious stories of Orwell's knight-errantry on the Aragon front, either one of which could make his reputation as Quixote. Gallantly holding a bleeding soldier on a donkey through the night, Orwell and Edwards accidentally went to a fascist-held village instead of the designated Loyalist one—and then had to sneak out. (Meanwhile the wounded man had stopped bleeding, "due to either fright or natural causes.") In another episode, Orwell, who reportedly hated rats as much as Winston Smith, shot one and caused the whole militia to begin firing at supposed fascists. Machine-gun nests and night patrols flew into action. The end result was that the cookhouse and two buses were destroyed. None of this, however, should obscure the fact of Orwell's genuine bravery in battle, which both his English and Spanish comrades have attested to.[47]

Each of these amusing incidents brings Orwell alive before us; collectively they make clear the importance of anecdote for establishing presence—and *figurehood*. For figuration stems from acute perception and sharp recollection in tranquillity of radiant moments. "Telling a story" about a person fuses image with moment ("I remember the time when he. . ."), animating selected aspects of personality and giving listeners a clear "idea" of a person. Unlike those radiant moments in a reception history repeatedly cited by critics (e.g., Pritchett's eulogistic phrases), however, anecdotes constitute what we may call *personal moments*. No one else looked or behaved as *this* person did; and no one but *me* as anecdotist (except other first-hand witnesses) knows *this* about him or her. An anecdote places a person in a running narrative, thereby capturing him "in action"—and often seeming thereby to capture his "essence" too. The storyteller gains authority because his anecdotes furnish unique, direct, and privileged access to that essence. Personal moments—ordinarily biographical events severed from a writer's reception history until an association or occasion ("I know a story about him too") triggers their retrieval—individuate and humanize a person. They turn him from an abstraction into an idiosyncratic character to whom we can easily relate. Our picture of The Quixotic Orwell, then, should be considered a motion picture. As in other portraits—only more so—we are seeing Orwell in an action scene. This is a lively, not a lifeless, gallery.

Despite the purported physical resemblance, it is questionable whether Orwell would have become so closely associated with Quixote if not for the numerous entertaining and revealing anecdotes about his quixotic behavior. We might speculate that, when a writer's reception history becomes widely remarked *anecdotal history*, it marks a new stage in his reputation. It indicates that readers feel close to him, and that the image of the man, and the man in the writings, has become a significant dimension of his literary reputation. And because curious, funny anecdotes almost invite embroidery into "tales" and "yarns," anecdotal history also points beyond reputation to the ultimate stage of the figurative process—the fuzzy world of legend and myth.

Quite unwittingly, it would seem, Orwell himself has provided some of the most comic and memorable anecdotes grounding his Quixote legend. Indeed Warburg's and Edwards' testimony seems hardly necessary to establish Orwell's quixotism when military adventures loomed. Orwell's own reports of his war experiences are evidence aplenty—like his refusing on principle to shoot at an escaping enemy soldier struggling to hold his trousers up, or the fact that he required size 12 boots which could not be gotten in Spain and had to be shipped from England ("that Trotskyite with big feet," H.G. Wells later tagged him), or that the Spaniards accepted Orwell's authority as a commanding officer only after "the big Englishman" had drunk them under the table.[48] It is, without question, fitting that Spain—the land of Don Quixote—always fascinated Orwell, as he realized fully when walking the streets of Barbastro shortly before his return home:

> I seemed to catch a momentary glimpse, a sort of far-off rumour, of the Spain that dwells in everyone's imagination. White sierras, goatherds, dungeons of the Inquisition, Moorish palaces, black winding trains of mules, gray olive trees and groves of lemons, girls in black mantillas, the wines of Malaga and Alicante, cathedrals, cardinals, bullfights, gypsies, serenades—in short, Spain. Of all Europe, it was the country that had had the most hold upon my imagination.[49]

## IV

What has so fired the imaginations of Orwell's readers has been precisely these stories of the quirky, sometimes victorious, sometimes hapless, Quixotic Orwell. The two types of stories reflect a divergence which Orwell's Quixote image underwent in the 1950s, partly as a result of the publication of "Such, Such Were the Joys." Pritchett's image of the endearing, idiosyncratic Orwell gave way to two images, a development roughly parallel to the split between the "true" rebel portrayed in the *Saga* article and the "failed" rebel of Andrew Sarris and others. In the case of the Quixote image, the split can be characterized as between Orwell the Man of Action and Orwell the Fated Victim. Both images are closely tied to Orwell's experience in Catalonia.

The first image presents Orwell not just as any man of action, but in the image of the intellectual as man of action. A useful contrast of this "successful" Quixote is the withdrawn, "literary" Hamlet, a distinction first drawn by Turgenev.[50] Faced with the chasm between the real and the ideal, Hamlet's will to action is paralyzed; Quixote's is energized. Hamlet, overcome by the limitations imposed by the real, cannot make up his mind; Quixote, entranced by the possibilities of the ideal, simply wills his vision and imagines it as the *already*-real—and acts accordingly.

In an age in which action in any direction seems on reflection fraught with innumerable tradeoffs—and all the more so for the modern intellectual inclined to labor over the cost-benefit ratios to the final decimal place—the attraction of such a figure as the Quixotic Orwell is enormous. For he

acts, not agonizes. Even considering that Orwell had already made the courageous decision to go to Spain and fight Franco, it seems almost fantastic that any intellectual could actually have simply landed in the middle of what seemed to him a paradisiacal "workers' state" in 1936 Barcelona, "recognized it immediately as a state of affairs worth fighting for," and so automatically joined the militia "because at that time and in that atmosphere it seemed the only conceivable thing to do." Perhaps Orwell's description of the circumstances surrounding his arrival and first days in Spain is partly a pose designed for rhetorical purposes. But whatever its truth, the effect *is* liberating. Here is a man, we find in *Homage to Catalonia,* who acted resolutely and without guilt, who chose without the burden of doubt. As did Trilling, we feel somehow uplifted, that "what he has done, anyone of us could do."[51]

The fullest expression of this triumphant Quixote image is found in Paul Potts's 1957 memoir, "Don Quixote on a Bicycle." Dedicated to Richard Blair, Orwell's adopted son, the memoir is a soaring panegyric to the rebellious Orwell as "the man of independence." "He carried independence to such a length that it became sheer poetry," wrote Potts about his friend. "There indeed may be a Red Indian language somewhere on the northern borders of Manitoba in which the word for independence is George Orwell."[52] Potts's essay is studded with flights of this sort. Potts takes the Quixote allusion to absurd lengths:

> This always sick man made his typewriter take on the suggestion of a white steed. In his hand the biro he used for corrections could never quite help looking a bit like a drawn sword. . . . In his company a walk down the street became an adventure into the unknown. . . . In short his life was a duel fought against lies; the weapon he chose, the English language.
>
> On thinking of him a certain Don Quixote de la Mancha rides into mind on his horse Rosinante. . . . On him a tweed jacket wore the air of knightly armour. A cup of tea was wine before a battle. He carried no shield, used for a weapon plain facts loaded into simple English prose.[53]

Potts seems to have considered his relationship with Orwell the single bright spot of his life. "The happiest years of my life were those during which I was a friend of his," recalled Potts. "I would have rather known him than have won the Nobel Prize." If there was little chance of the latter, Potts nevertheless did come to know Orwell as well as most literary friends in the late '40s. A penurious poet in the Fitzrovian literary world who used to publish his poetry in broadsheets and was often mocked in wartime London intellectual circles, Potts was befriended by Orwell shortly after they met in 1944. Potts never forgot the act of kindness. His memories of Orwell, if expressed in flowery language, are nevertheless genuine and stirring. Orwell evidently trusted him sufficiently to consider publishing *Animal Farm*—before Secker & Warburg accepted it—with the tiny Whitman Press, with which Potts was associated. To his own life, which he dramatized as a romantic, virtuous "failure" in love and work, Potts counterposed Orwell's, his model of the

gifted, generous, and successful writer.[54] His identification with Orwell is a clear instance of what we have termed "transference heroics," though, unlike Trilling, Potts seems to have crossed the line from healthy to slavish hero worship. His response to Orwell exemplifies reception as prostration, not self-actualization.

Other writers, however, have identified precisely with an Orwell not unlike Potts himself. Their Orwell is the failed, "unsuccessful" Quixote. This second Quixote image fixes on Quixote's course at a later point in time—the moment of outcome, not the instant of decision-making. The issue is therefore "the bottom line," not the capacity to act: results, not resolution. From this angle, the first, "successful" Quixotic Orwell is an aestheticized moral figure, approached strictly in terms of self-realization and evaluated simply according to whether or not he entered the fray. The second Quixote is measured in hard social and political terms. What was his solid accomplishment? That is the question. Juxtaposed with Hamlet, the intellectual as Don Quixote may seem decisive, even successful; but contrast him with a pragmatic man of action like bold Prince Hal and his practical failures are evident. And judged according to concrete results, Don Quixote will always fail, ultimately. For not only are he and Sancho pathetically ill-equipped to do battle—for so was Henry V—but his very aspirations are beyond realization in this world. They are the stuff of romance. All the efforts of Cervantes' wandering knight errant to champion the world's underdogs—whatever military skill and nobility of spirit he may exhibit in the course of his adventures—are destined to fail. He is Sancho's Knight of the Woeful Countenance. He will defy all odds and be broken in the attempt.

And so too, in the myth of the Quixotic Orwell, was the rebellious Orwell. For just as Orwell was about to enjoy the taste of success, goes the story, he no longer possessed the capacity to taste at all. As soon as he had earned some money with *Animal Farm*, adopted a son, bought a peaceful hideaway off the Scottish coast, and married the beautiful young Sonia Brownell, we find him on his deathbed. "The tragedy of Orwell's life," wrote Cyril Connolly, was that "he had had fame and was too ill to leave his room, money and nothing to spend it on, love in which he could not participate."[55]

However accurate Connolly's judgment, it sums up one dimension of the myth of the Quixotic Orwell accurately enough. The myth is largely the work of Orwell's friends who, knowing the man, originally compared him to Quixote because of the uncanny physical resemblance. These comparisons were often later extended into perceived affinities in character and temper. It is thus understandable that the image of the Quixotic Orwell is chiefly an image of the man, and of the man in the writings; it is not closely tied to the writer or to aspects of his work.

Rarely have non-acquaintances alluded to Orwell as Quixote. But it was really an aspect of this image which Bernard Crick pointed to in his remark that Orwell was a proud member of "God's great awkward squad of unorthodox, dissident Englishmen," a sardonic rebel forever hurtling himself

against careerists and courtiers, making Establishment lions look small or slightly silly when they attack him. We love the Quixotic Orwell for the enemies he has made.

Partly on account of its origin in the memories of friends, partly due to Orwell's much greater influence on British intellectuals, and partly stemming from the linking of the Quixote image to Orwell's "quintessential Englishness," the Quixotic Orwell is mainly a British image. American critic-reviewers have not projected a radiant, explicit image of Orwell as Quixote. In romanticizing him as the Establishment "outsider" and the Catalonia militiaman "on the losing side of the losing side," however, some American critics have nevertheless identified with a key aspect of the Quixotic Orwell, in the image of "unsuccessful" rebel. As one American critic has described the appeal:

> The Orwell who attracts me is the unsuccessful Orwell, the man who is trapped between tradition and the modern world, between love of his country and hatred of the privilege rooted in it, between a passionate nature and a strange bent toward restraint. It is an attraction for a man who takes a side only to see it dissolve before his eyes, who comes to a conviction only to have it disappear in the morning headlines, who simply cannot find the heart's ease in its delight.[56]

We see here how a general description of the Quixotic Orwell, not reducible to the watchword itself, can nevertheless contribute to its development.

It is worth mentioning that the nature of observers' attachments to Orwell resonates strikingly with his effort to understand Hitler, exceptional on the Left during World War II. We are not concerned here with psychologizing Orwell, but rather with his own acute insight into the psychology of Hitler's mass appeal. Orwell certainly considered Hitler no noble Quixote. But his remarks are not without relevance to an appreciation of his own wide popularity. Orwell's diverse characterizations of Hitler also suggest the multiformity of the Quixote figure:

> The fact is that there is something deeply appealing about him. One feels it again when one sees his photographs. . . . It is a pathetic doglike face, the face of a man always suffering under intolerable wrongs. In a rather more manly way it reproduces the expression of innumerable pictures of Christ crucified, and there is no doubt that this is how Hitler sees himself. The initial, personal cause of his grievance against the universe can only be guessed at; but at any rate the grievance is there. He is the martyr, the victim, Prometheus chained to the rock, the self-sacrificing hero who fights single-handed against impossible odds. If he were fighting a mouse he would know how to make it seem like a dragon. One feels, as with Napoleon, that he is fighting against destiny, that he *can't* win, and yet that somehow he deserves to. The attraction of such a pose is enormous. . . .[57]

The attractions of Orwell and Hitler are alike in this single respect: to their admirers, they are heart-rending whether they succeed *or* fail—and in fact often precisely *because* they seem to fail.

Like the saga of the high-minded Quixote, struggling so earnestly yet vainly against his giants and windmills, the legend of Orwell's one-man battles against totalitarianism, political orthodoxy, and literary cliques have impressed, even in failure, many observers as struggles so noble and honest yet endearingly eccentric as to be inspiring. For the Quixotic Orwell is perceived to be an authentic rebel, a modern existential hero. He is true to himself. For many readers, this is the Quixotic Orwell's glory and his "success." He is heroic regardless of the outcome of his struggle, and his life and writings are inspirational precisely because they remind one that the dream will never die. This image of Orwell is that of a Kierkegaardian Knight of Faith, albeit secularized, possessing a quiet, secret trust in himself and in the rightness of his ultimate aim, whether or not that aim succeeds in terms understandable to a world bent on quantifiable results.

## V

Surely both reflecting and contributing to Orwell's cult status, the latter Quixote image underwent a final modification in the 1960s. "The twentieth century Quixote," Wayne Burns dubbed Orwell, remarking that by the late 1960s the myth of the Quixotic Orwell seemed no more capable of being undercut than the ideals of "passion," "honesty," and "decency" which the name "Orwell" had come to signify.[58] In this last incarnation the Quixote myth moved beyond pragmatic, moral, and existential categories altogether. Neither results nor resolution were at issue. The new category was religious. There was no "successful" or "unsuccessful" Orwell; the image was now a transcendent metaphor for the Good, the Right. Now Orwell was no longer in a battle or on a quest. The gap between the real and ideal was magically closed. It was closed not by reaching past the real to embrace the ideal. Rather, the Quixotic Orwell was imagined to have obliterated the real and *incarnated* the ideal. As Burns put it:

> He has been through so much, and is willing to admit so much, about himself as well as others, that he expresses to the full the doubts that have been plaguing his readers, and in fact all those who he was pleased to call "decent people.". . . For Orwell convinces them that he knows whereof he speaks (after all he is an intellectual, accepted by intellectuals, and can speak up to them and answer them in their own terms); and besides he has been there (in the Spanish war; down and out in Paris and London, etc.); and more than that he is a man of integrity, a fearless man of integrity. So they feel they can trust him, as well as what he says. He is their champion, and as their champion he cannot be defeated. If some anarchist intellectuals bring forth evidence to show that he is wrong, the evidence they adduce is just a matter of evidence. No matter what they argue, or prove, it is still not really a defeat for Orwell, any more than Don Quixote's encounter with the windmill was a defeat for Don Quixote. For decent people know that there are Giants and Subversives who may take the form of windmills and intellectuals, and they know that, so disguised, these subversives may seek to undermine the whole of Western Civilization. . . .

> [T]hey know too that Orwell cannot be wrong or defeated just as they know that "truth" and "justice" and "decency" cannot be wrong or defeated. Such is Orwell's mythic image—an image that Orwell in his last years tried in vain to deny. . . . Saints and Don Quixotes cannot, however, be permitted to deny their own images.[59]

What many of Orwell's detractors have not unfairly attacked as the "orthodox" intellectual admiration for Orwell is partly attributable to the power of this Quixote myth. So all-embracing has the myth become that, placed within its framework, even acquaintances' memories of Orwell's weaknesses—his very real prejudices (toward gays, Indians, Irish, Scots, Catholics) and genuine fanaticisms (his knee-jerk suspicions about "fascists")—are invariably presented with the effect of *enhancing* his reputation, by rendering Orwell more fallible and therefore (like Quixote) more "the virtuous man," the "man of truth," the loser, the outsider, the victim, the martyr, the self-sacrificing hero. This too reflects the role of anecdote in shaping Orwell's reputation. The Quixotic Orwell of the anecdotes is a dynamic, full-bodied *vision* of Truth, Justice, Decency. Only an equally compelling counter-vision, which portrays him as indecent and untruthful and unjust—and which the empirically minded critic rarely sees as his task to project—can undermine it. "Facts" which show Orwell to be intolerant or ignorant just bounce off—the critic's evidence is "just evidence." That the Quixotic Orwell was "wrong" doesn't matter: we still love him. And, moreover, anecdotes ground his myth: What will ground the debunkers' anti-myth? The would-be demythologizer must unearth new, unflattering biographical material or persuasively reinterpret the old material. All this testifies not only to the force of Orwell's quixotic appeal, but also to the power of anecdote itself as evidence in the rhetoric of reception. Reception as anecdotage reflects and generates keenly *felt* response. And the emotions know depths which reason cannot plumb.

In this last permutation of the Quixote myth, another important feature of Orwell's reception and of the politics of literary reputation becomes clear. It is that the skirmishing over a writer's legacy is often only apparently or superficially about him and his work. What is really being contested is what the writer is presumed to "represent." And perhaps strangely, despite the Left-Right arguments about Orwell, what he represents *is* to a large extent merely *presumed*, not argued—the values of Truth, Justice, Decency. The battle for "Orwell" among intellectuals is thus not so much a fight for the mantle of "Orwell" as over what lies under the mantle. Not "Orwell" but the claim to Truth, Justice, and Decency is what is coveted.

Without doubt, much of this is in the nature of the making and claiming of reputations. For if a reputation is "the image of" X or Y, the image itself may be considered mere Platonic packaging; what is valued is the underlying Form—Truth, Justice, Decency—represented in the image. The capital letters themselves make the point. And Truth, Justice, and Decency are hardly fixed images in our minds. Orwell may have known what he meant by them, and perhaps we can discern more or less consistency in his usage

of the terms after scrutiny of his work; but we do not all mean the same thing by them. In their polemical wars, the Left and Right quote Orwell to their purpose; generally they have cared little about having "George Orwell" on their side. "Orwell" becomes enmeshed in cultural politics chiefly because he is seen as an intellectual figure who embodies these virtues more attractively that practically anyone else. These ideals, not "Orwell," are at stake; and it is actually these, not "Orwell," which "cannot be defeated." Other historical figures have been mythicized as Orwell has been, almost in the style of Comrade Ogilvy at the Ministry of Truth. And it is in this sense that Orwell as 'St. George,' or the Quixotic Orwell, cannot "deny" his own image—for it is not "his" image at all, but a myth into which he has been fitted. So it is actually not the Giants and Subversives who have been disguised; rather it is Orwell himself. Orwell's image as the saintly Don Quixote therefore constitutes an instance of what we have described as defacement, the deformation of an authorial image. But it is a haloed defacement, unusual in that it is of the hagiographic sort.

That Orwell is perceived to incarnate virtues like Truth, Justice, and Decency is also a main reason for his protean reputation. For if most ideological and political groups care little about having "Orwell" on their side, they nevertheless care very much about having Truth, Justice, and Decency on their side. What better way to lay claim to Truth and Justice and Decency than by laying claim to Trilling's "man of truth," to Richard Rees's "just man," to Martin Green's "decent man"?[60] But if such categories are notoriously vague, as indeed they are, then one will never resolve either who "the decent people" are or what stance on specific issues a man who stands for Truth, Justice, and Decency should take. No dearth of groups claim to be "the decent people" and to have Truth and Justice with them. And so, in claiming these virtues through identification with Orwell, readers have sometimes made him seem a transilient talisman, a man for all seasons and stratagems.

The linking of Orwell's history with powerful, polysemous cultural images like Quixote provides a final clue to his continuing hold upon the imaginations of Anglo-American intellectuals, and in a larger sense, it suggests how we respond not just to anecdotes but to richly detailed portraits: how images grip and move us. Images give form and substance to sentiment, express emotion as well as idea. The demonstrative responses of friends and readers to the Quixotic Orwell testify to the charged complex of personal and cultural feeling which an image can introject and release. For the myth of the Quixotic Orwell speaks to our inexhaustible urge for idealistic culture heroes: not all of us are content to be skeptics and materialists like Sancho. The myth touches a human desire for rebels willing to stand up and be counted as individuals, to buck the system, and to aim for something beyond the Self. And in that light, it is quite true that Orwell's greatest character creation was himself, the whole literary and private personality, however transparent or opaque this persona really was. Even peers like Muggeridge have admitted that they have seen him as a rebel hero. "I always think of him as a hero," Muggeridge has written. "He stood alone in

every sense. . . . He was by nature the most truthful man who ever lived. . . ."[61] So strong is the identification between Orwell's many passionate defenders and their modern Quixote that they will defend him regardless of his sins or even his success or failure, for to distrust him would be to disbelieve not just in a vital part of themselves but in those very ideals which his image brings to life. And the need is precisely for "a man of flesh and bone" to bring these ideals to life. To imagine Orwell's life as an incarnation of or an extraordinarily noble quest for Truth, Justice, and Decency is to hold out the chance of achieving the same oneself. However foolish and idealistic, anachronistic and chivalric, lofty and impractical the ideals which Orwell represents, readers believe that they are for the most part ideals which the man *lived*. So long as these ideals are valued, the memory of the man who lived them and the voice of the writer who championed them will engage his readers' spirits.

## 6. "Permanent Outsider" Among Friends: Orwell's Compartmentalized Life

### I

"Tell me thy company," says Don Quixote, "and I'll tell thee what thou art."[62] Perhaps, but in the case of "the twentieth-century Quixote" neither side of the equation is so easily calculated as the formula implies. Nevertheless the line points directly to the main aim of this case study: to scrutinize The Rebel from the inside, exploring how Orwell's personal behavior as a self-willed "outsider" conditioned both this face specifically and the portrait gallery generally. We grapple with a complicated biographical question: How does a man's conduct of his personal life influence his reputation? And here we are working not with the writer's books or with literary reviews or criticism at all, but strictly with the thorny problem of interpreting autobiography and acquaintances' testimonies.

Still, what emerges is a portrait of The Rebel as passive resister. Friends' accounts of Orwell's personal life—and neither memoirs nor biographies have explored the significance of this testimony—produce striking unanimity on two points: Orwell's company was remarkably heterogeneous and he partitioned different groups of acquaintances rigidly. In virtually every instance, these observations are delivered with a note of wonder, because most acquaintances had no idea of the range and variety of Orwell's contacts until years after his death. "True and good friends are still surprised to discover whom else he knew," Bernard Crick discovered in the 1970s when he conducted interviews for his biography.[63] Orwell was the rebel *par excellence*, "a permanent outsider" to every group, even to his circles of friends, as Julian Symons has observed.[64] Or as the last line of Crick's biography puts it: "As odd in himself and as varied in his friends as man can be."[65] It is a tribute, but the odd compartmentalizing and diversity of Orwell's relation-

ships constitute a more complex matter than the sentence implies—and one crucial to an understanding of the basis of his multifaceted reputation.


II

Julian Symons, a good friend of Orwell's from about 1944, was one of the first people to draw attention to his practice of dividing friends into groups and then keeping the groups apart. A onetime Trotskyist who shared Orwell's anti-Stalinist views and wrote a moving obituary of him in *Tribune*, Symons opened his warm reminiscence of Orwell in *The London Magazine* with the caution that Orwell, like many people, "kept his life and friends in compartments shut off from one another. . ., but few seal off the compartments as fanatically as Orwell."[66] T.R. Fyvel, a fellow *Tribune* writer, and Anarchist George Woodcock have seconded this opinion.[67] Woodcock characterizes the way Orwell segmented his groups of friends as "almost obsessive." Yet he also speaks admiringly of Orwell's ability to juggle different kinds of relationships, getting "everyone [to] accept him on his own eccentric terms"—as if his aim were to keep a number of balls in the air at once, all within what Woodcock calls "the inner Orwell circle," each of which would bear a slightly different relation to the master juggler and none of which would collide. "He abandoned neither family nor friends," Woodcock wrote approvingly in *The Crystal Spirit*, "but managed to keep going a surprising number of guarded and carefully compartmentalized relationships."

> [R]elatively few of the many people he knew were invited to his North London flat. He even managed to segment [his] inner Orwell circle, as one might call it, so carefully as to keep its various strangely assorted members separated from one another. One of his regular visitors at this time was an irascible verse-writer who had vowed deadly hatred to me for a review I had written of his poems; Orwell managed things so adroitly that we never met in his flat.[68]

Surely this behavior, not commented on in print until Symons' 1963 memoir, has contributed to the conflicting posthumous images of Orwell, which were largely generated in the early 1950s by the writings of groups of his friends isolated from one another. And as these divergent images developed, it became evident to Orwell's acquaintances that no one—not even "true and close friends" like Symons, Woodcock, Fyvel, Richard Rees, Cyril Connolly, David Astor, or Sonia Orwell—had any more than a very limited, partial view of George Orwell. Even in literary London, let alone in Burma and Spain, different political and cultural groups of acquaintances— affiliated with the Labour Party, *Tribune, Adelphi, Horizon*, the anarchist Freedom Press, Fitzrovia—formed radically different impressions of Orwell, and many of the prominent literary men who wrote about him did not become friendly with him until the middle '40s. And so, when the posthumous myth of 'St. George' suddenly arose a few years later—partly on account of lavish memoirs by his literary acquaintances—the most that any-

one felt able to say was that the images promoted by other groups did not correspond to *"my* Orwell." Woodcock, for example, admits that he saw "only a facet" of Orwell, "how he responded to anarchists."[69] One also senses in friends' posthumous memoirs of Orwell that their deep admiration for him, and their tendency to rewrite him in their own images, is partly a result of Orwell's carefully maintained *distance* from them—they wished, after they realized his specialness (and observed his growing reputation) that they had been closer friends with him than they actually were. And so, a few acquaintances bridged the gulf posthumously and through the printed word, aiming to cement a bond that never was.[70]

Orwell's various groups of literary friends could therefore only contribute to, not reconcile, the rival images which they had produced. For Orwell had been extraordinarily successful—perhaps too successful for the good of his posthumous reputation—at "keep[ing] his small worlds apart."[71]

## III

Why did Orwell partition his worlds? Autobiographical and biographical evidence points to three reasons, all of them associated with Orwell's rebel stance.

First, it seems that young Eric Blair discovered that, in sealing off his worlds, he could protect himself. In *The Road to Wigan Pier* Orwell says that he considered the working people his "heroes" as a child, but when his mother discovered that he was playing with the daughter of a plumber, "I was told to keep away."[72] Orwell returns to this little incident at least four times in his work, and it obviously had great significance for him as a symbol of the English class barrier. He even scribbled a poem about his plumber's daughter while in hospital in 1949. Instead of "keeping away" from people that his family and "respectable" friends would not approve, however, Blair-Orwell seems to have simply learned to keep the two apart. Probably the practice began at prep school. Friends' memoirs establish that young Eric seemed different to schoolmates like Connolly and neighborhood playmates like the Buddicom children. Likewise, however much it may be polemic rather than memoir, "Such, Such Were the Joys" makes equally clear that Blair coped with the acutely discrepant worlds of St. Cyprian's and his "loving" home by developing separate selves, a silent, sullenly rebellious "school" self and a happy if sardonic "home" self. As we have seen he refers to his stifled yet "incorruptible inner self" at St. Cyprian's.[73] Already the young rebel is protesting against an "invasion" of the self. Apparently Blair felt that he could not openly show his "true," iconoclastic self at school and that he could not talk negatively about St. Cyprian's at home. His rebellion takes the form of *resistance:* he withholds part of himself, keeps it secure "within."

Young Eric's practice became Blair-Orwell's habit. "If he didn't like something," David Astor once observed, "he just withdrew." By the time Blair arrived in Burma, he was behaving not unlike John Flory in *Burmese*

*Days*, moving between his police colleagues and renegade friends with their Indian wives, always feeling compelled to keep the two worlds apart. And also apart from a third world: virtually none of Blair's fellow policemen seem to have known that he had a grandmother and close relatives in Burma. Back in England in the '30s, if reports are true that Orwell "compartmentalized his women friends" carefully, carried on affairs with married women in the early 1930s, and was not entirely faithful to Eileen, his structured life may also have served other purposes.[74]

Here, then, we see The Rebel in a new, defensive pose: the rebel as resister, recalcitrant, seditionist. Rebels not only attack but also protest, retreat, hide. Against powerful forces, the defenseless "outsider" and "individualist" may resist an invasion of the self by silence and noncompliance. "Compartmentalization," then, can constitute a passive-aggressive mode of rebellion, rebellion as self-restraint, self-withdrawal. One refuses to allow others to enter into the inner sanctum of his life. In effect Orwell came to spatialize his silence through willed isolation, keeping to himself by keeping distant, even from his family.

A second, related reason for Orwell's tendency to partition relationships was his temperament. Although he was a tolerant and open man on many subjects, his cast of mind tended to label and categorize with a vengeance, and he appears to have applied it energetically to that end in organizing his personal life. Symons, for instance, has said that he sensed that Orwell saw him as "a *Tribune* friend," not "a home friend"[75]—suggesting that the rigid school/home pattern of prep school persisted into adulthood. Orwell never even mentioned his wife Eileen's name to Symons before she died. Symons believes that he knew Orwell as well as anyone else did during Orwell's last years, and it seems clear that Symons was at least among Orwell's closest friends. But "close" and "friend" are perhaps misleading terms with Orwell's relationships. Acquaintances agree that Orwell neither sought nor permitted any intimates. As Symons admits, "because of the way in which [Orwell] shut off the various parts of his life, nobody knew the whole of him."[76]

Of course, nobody knows "the whole" of another person. Nor was Orwell unique in dividing up groups of friends—to some extent we all do that. What was unusual and needs emphasis here is that Orwell closed the circles with such care, so much so that some acquaintances were puzzled that such an apparently "open" friend was really quite guarded. Symons' observation on Orwell's rigid categories of "home" and "*Tribune*" friends touches on the matter, and his memoir makes clear Orwell's extreme reticence. Symons notes that Orwell "detested people asking questions about his life and background"—unusual in a writer whose work is so obviously autobiographical, even in some cases confessional—and Symons and Woodcock say that they never did ask for fear of losing Orwell's friendship. "Home" friends like Woodcock and Fyvel (also a *Tribune* colleague, the lone member of both Orwell categories) have also remarked on Orwell's "complete" and "fanatical" "reserve" about his personal affairs. Crick calls it "abnormal." Richard Rees terms it Orwell's "*pudeur*."[77]

Or was Orwell's guardedness really another manifestation of his open-mindedness? Or just tact? Woodcock and Symons think so, and both have written sympathetically about Orwell's strenuous efforts to keep them at a distance. "One did occasionally say or hear others saying, 'I don't know what Orwell sees in X'," Woodcock has recalled. "What he did see, almost certainly, was an interestingly individual personality."[78] Symons has observed similarly:

> George presented different faces to different people. I don't think he did so quite consciously, or intentionally. He simply tended to talk to people about things that he knew would interest them. He had a good deal more tact, of a kind, than is generally attributed to him. For instance, I think the reason that he probably never invited me to Jura was that he knew I was a pretty urban character—I just wouldn't have made out very well up there, that's all.[79]

And yet there seems more to it than that. Like Prufrock, we all prepare the face to meet the faces that we meet, but getting "everyone to accept him on his own eccentric terms," in Woodcock's phrase about Orwell, may have also served complicated literary and psychological ends related to Orwell's self-image as a writer and rebel. This marks a third possible factor accounting for his practice of segmenting groups of friends.

However deliberately or self-consciously Orwell lived it, his structured existence as outsider to every group was a most effective stance for the writer as English "anthropologist," in Pritchett's words, "gone native in his own country."[80] For a compartment can also be a "room of one's own," a liberating space for self- and social exploration. The native "anthropologist" Orwell could observe people in their "natural" state, in the circles in which they normally lived; and he could in turn withhold aspects of himself, not needing to concern himself with reconciling mixed audiences' expectations of him. By making sure that members of different groups didn't see him together in a situation, he could play different roles, preserving or changing them as he saw fit, a freedom which would have been compromised had he brought a mixed group together. "Blair" could experiment more easily with the new "George Orwell," with different versions of himself. With some groups of friends, like Woodcock and the anarchists, Orwell apparently talked in long monologues; other acquaintances report that he usually said little in their company. (Crick notes that, among those who did not get to know Orwell until the mid-1940s, "there is the most remarkable conflict of testimony as to whether he was talkative or silent" in their meetings.[81]) If members of opposed literary-political groups never met in his presence, Orwell did not need to worry himself with appearing inconsistent. Also he could readily assume another identity, as he learned to do in telling his life's story to the tramps and down-and-outs. He could revise his past in line with the needs of the present situation, and so achieve the direct experience of life for which he hankered and from which he wrote best. "I have often been struck by how

easy it is to get people to take you for granted if you and they are really in the same boat, and how difficult otherwise," Orwell wrote Jack Common from Morocco in 1938. "[Here] I am in the position of a tourist. The result is that it is quite impossible . . . to make any contact with the Arabs, whereas if I were here, say, on a gun-running expedition, I should immediately have entree to all kinds of interesting society."[82]

Indeed, by making separate peaces with members of various political and literary groups, Orwell may have been groping toward his ideal of the political writer. To the extent that it was a conscious choice, his compartmentalizing may have represented his enacted solution to the "painful dilemma" of the relation of the writer to politics: the split self. Note Orwell's exact words in "Writers and Leviathan": the writer "must split his life into two compartments," the "inviolate" self as "artist" and the "ordinary, dirty" self as "citizen." The passage merits quoting at length:

> When a writer engages in politics He should do so as a citizen, as a human being, but not as a writer. . . . He should make it clear [to politicians] that his writing is a thing apart. . . . He should [write] as an individual, an outsider, at the most an unwelcome guerrilla on the flank of a regular army. . . . If you have to take part in [politics]—and I think you do have to, unless you are armoured by old age or stupidity or hypocrisy—then you also have to keep part of yourself inviolate. For most people, the problem does not arise in the same form, because their lives are split already. They are truly alive only in their leisure hours, and there is no emotional connection between their work and their political activities. Nor are they generally asked in the name of political loyalty to debase themselves as workers. The artist, and especially the writer, is asked just that—in fact, it is the only thing that politicians ever ask of him. If he refuses, that does not mean that he is condemned to inactivity. One half of him, which is in a sense the whole of him, can act as resolutely, even as violently, if need be, as anyone else. But his writings, in so far as they have any value, will always be the product of the saner self that stands aside, records the things that are done and admits their necessity, but refuses to be deceived as to their true nature.[83]

Is this argument a rationalization for Blair-Orwell's instinctive need to resist impending invasions of his self? It is hard to say. Whereas young Eric sought to preserve his "incorruptible inner self," the adult Orwell strove to guard his "inviolate" artistic self.

From Orwell's standpoint, of course, his notion of the "split self" was not a half-conscious habit but a professional conviction. It rested on his idea of the need for a hard-and-fast distinction between the "writer" and the "citizen." Orwell felt strongly that the writer could and should "in times of conflict" compartmentalize his personal and public life. It might seem "defeatist or frivolous," he admitted, but "in practice I do not see what else he can do."[84] The writer had to rebel against the politicizing of his calling, he had to resist both getting turned into a party hack and drifting into a despairing quietism. And yet, added Orwell, he should also recognize that politics was not the whole of life. Thus, especially given the climate of

hatred in Left circles in the '30s and '40s, when political attitudes toward the Soviet Union and the war largely determined and restricted personal relations, Orwell's compartmentalizing may have served a pragmatic function: it may have been another example of his recognizing that one's choice of friends, like one's judgments about good literature, need conform to no political criteria. Indeed it may also have conveniently served a tactical function: by dividing his worlds, Orwell could, as it were, conquer them. If acquaintances were not aware of his background and the range of his relations, he had, in effect, the upper hand, secure in the knowledge that they did not know more about him than they let on and that he probably knew more about them than the reverse. Julian Symons expressed surprise on finding out from a third party, after he and Orwell had discussed the work of Rayner Heppenstall several times, that Orwell and Heppenstall were former flatmates and old friends. Orwell had never even mentioned that he knew Heppenstall personally. Orwell's contact with Juan Negrín, Prime Minister of the Spanish Republic during Orwell's seven months in Catalonia, is another example. Exiled in England during World War II, Negrín recalled thinking that Orwell, during their several conversations about Spain, was an editorialist for the *Observer* who had been in Spain as a reporter during the civil war. Whether from modesty or secretiveness or shrewdness (surely Orwell knew that Negrín had been Stalin's handpicked premier), Orwell never mentioned to Negrín that he fought with the Loyalist POUM or had written *Homage to Catalonia*. By keeping his relationships separated, therefore, Orwell could maintain his distance, always holding back important parts of himself and therefore—as with Symons and Negrín—never dealing from a position of "weakness" or allowing any betrayals.[85]

It would be simplistic to insist, however, that Orwell calculatedly designed his life to fulfill any of these ends. Reserve about personal matters was a Blair family trait. Orwell's reticence was also probably connected with his thinly veiled assumption that "manliness" meant silence and distance. Some acquaintances have described Orwell as shy and others as gregarious, but all agree that he was a man almost impossible to get to know well. Evidently Orwell was not disposed to trust people easily; in both the humorous sense that Pritchett and Muggeridge speak of Orwell's quixotism, and also in a slightly paranoid sense, he was indeed always on the lookout for conspiracies, suspecting them almost everywhere. Probably this combination of diffidence, caution, and cynicism is what has led even admiring friends like Woodcock to wonder about Orwell's "proneness to secrecy." Other friends have voiced Anthony Powell's impression that Orwell always seemed to him to be "acting a part." Powell did not mean that Orwell was a phony, but that he left the impression of a man not quite at ease with himself, "cut off from the world." Still others like Geoffrey Gorer report that, before Orwell met Eileen, he was "a very lonely man," "convinced that nobody would like him"—and many acquaintances report that he appeared the same after Eileen's death. To a large degree, as "Such, Such Were the Joys" and "Why I Write" suggest, Blair-Orwell's quixotic isolation was self-

chosen. He was a natural loner, literally a permanent outsider. As a young-ster, he withdrew into a self-created private literary world; his "dream of Jura" was obviously, in part, an adult retreat.[86]

## IV

What have been the effects of Orwell's tendency to partition groups upon specific portraits in the Orwell gallery? Whatever his intentions, Orwell's compartmentalizing behavior, combined as it was with his disarmingly di-rect personal manner with acquaintances, functioned to promote precisely those public faces Orwell worked most energetically to establish: The Rebel and The Common Man, the fumigator of smelly orthodoxies and the plain-spoken plebeian-intellectual. William Phillips, co-editor of *Partisan Review,* was struck with Orwell's directness, with how refreshingly "serious" he seemed, in contrast to rest of the London intelligentsia whom Phillips met on a 1949 visit.[87]

Orwell's straightforwardness eased his movement in and out of new situations. Indeed, it was precisely the odd disjunction between his forth-right manner and segmented life that so surprised old friends years later, when they heard about his compartmentalizing habits. Like his prose, Or-well's conversation had left upon acquaintances the impression of openness, naturalness, even naiveté. They had felt no urge to penetrate behind the Orwell exterior. There didn't seem to be one. Symons says that one of Orwell's chief characteristics was "an utter lack of formality" whereby he "by-passed entirely [the] getting-to-know-you procedure."[88] Symons' re-mark is merely in apparent conflict with reports of Orwell's diffidence and reserve, for Orwell talked politics and culture, not about himself. His "get-ting to know you" strictly cordoned off personal discussion. (A main reason why Orwell liked him, Symons says, was his "incuriosity" about Orwell's private life.[89]) Orwell's aversion to any talk about the private was bound up with his idea of intellectual integrity and dignity: one should go one's own way, without need for explanation or justification. His friends respected this view. In consequence they honored his request for no biography—in a fashion, as we shall see.

## 7. Lives of Independence: The History of Orwell Biography

### I

How do biographies shape an author's public image(s)? How does bio-graphical history interact with reputation-history? This case study explores these questions. How the behavior of the man who led what the *Observer* eulogized as "A Life of Independence"[90] influenced his biographies—how the life conditioned the Lives—is another development emergent from the stance of The Rebel and vital to an understanding of Orwell's overall critical and public reputation. It is another profile, drawn first from the outside

and then moving inside, which turns on Orwell's identity as an individualist, and it is directly linked to Orwell's practice of compartmentalizing his relationships. Indeed it is another portrait of The Rebel as passive resister—this time resisting his would-be biographers, once again through a mixture of silence, exile, and cunning.

Ironically, the man who asked in his will for no biography has gotten several, most of them presented as literary criticism yet written by acquaintances with quite different versions of his politics and including biographical comments. The story is a complicated one. But the three key large-scale effects of the perplexing history of Orwell biography on his reputation may be stated immediately: the blurring of the distinction between the man and the work, the muddling of Orwell's political stands, and the proliferation of the number of Orwell images. While Part Two explores these confusions in other contexts, in this section we investigate how Orwell's biographical history has helped generate them.

## II

The history of Orwell biography suggests from a dual vantage point—from the angles of biographer and subject—how personal relations affect the writing of biography, and how in turn biographies help shape reputations. First, many memoir-writers of Orwell have fallen into different forms of "the biographical fallacy"—e.g., misreading a literary man's works as if they were transparent autobiography; projecting elements of one's own life into the life of another; or, worst of all, using the biographical subject as an occasion for writing one's own autobiography. Second, the thirty-year lapse between Orwell's death and the publication of Bernard Crick's full, authorized *Life* allowed some myths about Orwell to grow and persist, especially in regard to his days as Eric Blair, which might have been quashed if a biography had appeared in the 1950s. Crick did a heroic job of digging up scraps of information about Blair and tracking down old friends of Orwell. The difficulty of rediscovering Blair was partly Orwell's own doing: his taking of a pseudonym, his request for no biography, his disputable autobiographical testimony. And typically, with each passing year, the historical record thins: letters get lost, memories fade, old friends die. Up against these difficulties, Malcolm Muggeridge, designated in the early 1960s by Sonia Orwell as Orwell's "official biographer," admitted that "the project defeated me." Muggeridge claimed that Orwell had set down a great "smoke-screen" between himself and any biographer "who tried to invade the privacy in which he lived and died." Woodcock has similarly suggested that Orwell's misgiving about a biography arose partly from his conviction that "his own creative persona had already reshaped the details of his life into writings with a deceptively autobiographical appearance. He did not want anyone to spoil the results of this interplay between his two selves."[91]

Woodcock may be right. But Orwell never explained in print why he requested no biography. His onetime housekeeper Susan Watson claims that

Orwell told her that only he could write his *Life* accurately—and that he would never do it.[92] On hearing reports of Dickens' alleged brutality to his wife, Orwell replied that Dickens was an admirable writer and that the writer's "literary personality" and "private character" were and should be of separate interest.[93] One guesses that Orwell had a low opinion of biography as a genre. Richard Rees, who served as Orwell's literary executor along with Sonia Orwell, told biographer Peter Stansky that Orwell's request reflected a fear that he might be written up "extravagantly or luridly."[94]

If so, the anxiety was not entirely unfounded. Lytton Strachey's anti-heroic *Eminent Victorians* (1918) and the popularity of Freud among intellectuals had given rise in the 1920s and '30s to what Virginia Woolf initially heralded as "The New Biography" and what detractors soon termed "Stracheyism." Less gifted followers of Strachey soon gave biography a bad name. In severe reaction against the tendencies of nineteenth-century biographers toward hagiography, the "new" biographers became self-appointed idol-smashers or amateur psychoanalysts. Often proceeding on the flimsiest of evidence, they went far beyond Dr. Johnson's advice to explore "domestic privacies." Instead they muddied their subjects' characters, trumpeted ill-founded or even false scandals, made wild use of literary devices like symbolism and irony, conducted psychoanalytic autopsies, and crudely proselytized the dead for various ideological camps. Doubtless Orwell's hostility in "Charles Dickens" to the attempts by Chesterton and T.A. Jackson to convert Dickens into a 1930s Christian and radical, respectively, stemmed from such biographical abuses as the last. It was the age of "biografiction" and what Joyce angrily called "the biografiends." The negative associations of biography with debunking and sensationalism probably stayed with Orwell into the '40s—as late as 1949 he was advising Julian Symons not to let his publisher pick a catchpenny title for the biography of his brother, A.J.A. Symons—and may have further motivated his request for no biography. (Other English writers prominent during Orwell's lifetime—Auden, Eliot, Hardy, Kipling, Somerset Maugham, Jean Rhys—also took steps to prevent biographies, probably similarly revolted by denigrating treatment of literary figures of the stature of Wordsworth, Scott, Arnold, and Tennyson during the interwar period.[95])

### III

Whatever Orwell's reasons for requesting no biography, and however determined his intention to prevent one—Rees evidently believed that Orwell would have withdrawn his objections if he had lived to witness the higher standard of postwar biography[96]—the request was, of course, like these others cited above, doomed from the start. By the early '50s, critics and reviewers had already transformed Orwell into a symbolic figure—and therefore an irresistible biographical subject to friend and scholar alike.

All of Orwell's acquaintances have respected his wish to have no formal biography written. Yet several of them have been so strongly drawn to the

man that they have felt compelled to write about him. George Woodcock
has remarked on this attraction and, in the context of the previous case
study, we should note here how Orwell's practice of sealing off his circles of
acquaintances inadvertently influenced the writing of six critical studies on
him in the 1950s and '60s. Again what is striking is how, whatever Orwell's
views about their relation, the "private" life has had unforeseen consequences for the "literary" reputation; and how an author has very limited
control, not only over how writings get received, but on how his behavior
affects his reputation. Orwell's life of independence arguably paved the way
for his posthumous lives of independence. Wrote Woodcock:

> Yet in a way all [six of] our books were intensely biographical even if they
> did not seem so. To begin, we were motivated by a sense that we had to
> preserve and transmit what we knew of this haunting and remarkable and
> perhaps great man. All of us included a great deal of personal recollec-
> tion, and each of us, I think, recognized that he had seen only a facet of
> Orwell—the facet Orwell wished him to see—but had seen it very in-
> tensely. Each of us tended to stress that aspect of Orwell's work which
> reflected his own basic outlook: Hollis, for instance, saw Orwell as the
> essential conservative; Atkins as the left-wing socialist, while I saw how he
> responded to anarchists. . . . And though we devoted major parts of our
> books to discussing what Orwell wrote, our discussion was modified by the
> fact that we had listened to him talking out the subjects of his essays and
> the themes of his novels, so that we felt we knew what he meant, right
> from the horse's mouth.[97]

Some of what Woodcock describes here is common to *all* biography: no
two biographers will see a subject exactly alike. To forget this is to fall into the
opposite extreme of the biographical fallacy, the myth of total objectivity.
The variety of selves emergent from several biographies testifies not so much
to the protean complexity of a subject's inwardness as it does simply to the
inevitably different relationships formed between him and his biographers.
Still, the distinctive features which Woodcock marks in his discussion of
Orwell biography are remarkable: the veiled yet unmistakable re-presentation of a man into several opposing, politically tinged images by his friends
within just a few years of his death—ironically the direct outcome of a writer
who (of all people) exerted through his vigilant widow a form of "thought-
control from the grave," in Woodcock's phrase.

One is left to speculate as to whether, as Woodcock implies in the same
essay, Orwell's request for no biography was a determined attempt on his
part to shape the course of his posthumous reputation. Was it a conscious
effort to make his posthumous public image conform to his carefully constructed, developing image? Did it reflect that last infirmity of noble mind?
(Here one cannot help recall young Eric's resolve as early as prep school. "It
was always 'When I am A FAMOUS AUTHOR . . .'," in capitals, his childhood friend Jacintha Buddicom recalls, an opening apparently chanted
again and again with the refrain "which nobody can deny." And the "popular subject" of the pair's talks was Eric's boyhood "dream" to have a Uniform

Edition of his *Collected Works*, bound in dark blue leather and silver lettering, and signed "E.A. Blair," which he thought "more dignified" than "Eric"
and "could keep people guessing."[98]) Woodcock notes that although Orwell
was no more capable than any of their friends of belief in personal immortality, he was much occupied in his criticism with the question of literary
immortality. He made no secret of his view that the single test of literary
merit was survival, and that survival turned on one's ability—not good
fortune—to tap the psychic depths of one's national culture, if not civilization itself. He admired writers like Shakespeare and Dickens above all, who
"lived" because they had touched the keenest public nerve and thereby—as
if in compensation and venerable recognition—were "assumed" into the
English popular consciousness.[99] Woodcock thinks it symbolically significant that Orwell's gravestone bore the name "Eric Arthur Blair," with no
mention at all of "George Orwell."

> This, I cannot help but feeling from what I remember of Orwell and his
> conversation, was because he felt that though Blair would die, Orwell
> might not. The private man would be no more; the literary personality
> could carry on, sustained on the wings of his own creation.[100]

Woodcock's prose is fanciful. But he is one of Orwell's most astute critics.
Aware of how his own relationship to Orwell has shaped his image of him,
Woodcock explicitly refers to *Orwell*'s fanciful "notions" about his chances
for literary survival and to his half-aware participation in his own "personal
myth."[101] The suggestions are tantalizing. Blair—even "E.A. Blair"—might
die. But the dream of the specially bound Uniform Edition translated into
numerous languages could come true under a different name. The "body"
of Orwell's *work* might transcend death. The FAMOUS AUTHOR would
live.

Woodcock's remarks gain in persuasiveness and plausibility when approached in accordance with Orwell's dominant self-image as a rebel. From
this angle, Orwell's request for no biography and its aftermath bear direct
affinity with his compartmentalized behavior as the outgrowth of Blair-
Orwell's lifelong struggle to resist would-be probers and pillagers of the self.
For biography may be seen as the literary invasion of the self, the peeling
away of layer upon layer of a (sometimes) carefully constructed identity—an
identity which an autobiographical writer has labored hard to build. The
memoirs of Muggeridge, Woodcock, and Symons suggest that this is just
how Orwell saw it. And in this light, Orwell is a rebel so thoroughgoing that
he will deny all efforts to enter his private sanctuary, an individualist so
resolute that he is determined not just to live but to be remembered in *just
this way*—and to the absolute end. To request no biography—and for literary executors to refuse quotation rights to all those who ignore the
request—is a writer's ultimate mode of rebellion as silence and noncompliance. And perhaps at this point Orwell's literary rebellion passes into an
existential one, as a protest against the dissection of a life.

Or perhaps only his life as "Eric Blair." "It took me thirty years to work

off the effects of being called 'Eric,' " Orwell once told Rayner Heppenstall, obviously relieved that the name and much of its history no longer stalked him.[102] It is interesting to note that some of Blair's acquaintances from home, school, and Paris apparently have read or heard about Orwell's work—even into the 1970s and '80s—without realizing that "Orwell" was "Blair." Blair-Orwell occasionally spoke about officially changing his name to "George Orwell," but he seems to have enjoyed the way in which his two names allowed him to keep apart his public and private lives, his new writer's life and his old family and colonial life. The possibilities in a separate literary identity may not have dawned on Blair when he adopted "Orwell" at the age of thirty, but he surely appreciated them later. Much of his autobiographical writing is understandable as Orwell's attempt to forge a new plain-man identity by rewriting his past as Blair—a "rectified" history which a biography would have undermined. For a writer who used his past as literary material and went in search of experience from which to write (even in Spain he identified himself as "Blair," a "grocer"[103]), the two names provided great flexibility. With the name change, it was less likely that anyone would find out (and think less of) the down-and-out for not mentioning that he had a favorite aunt in Paris, made regular stops at home, and took baths and got food at friends' houses in London. And less likely that readers would be pricked to question how much the events in "Shooting an Elephant" and Part II of *The Road to Wigan Pier* were reshaped for polemical effect. Combined with his compartmentalizing behavior and exceptional self-restraint, the name change virtually guaranteed that friends' views of Orwell's early years would be restricted and short-term. Few reports of "Eric" would surface; and since much of what gave the essays and *Wigan Pier* their power and even notoriety was the assumption by readers that they were unreconstructed autobiography, the effacement of "Blair" by "Orwell" was useful: it ensured the effect—an effect which a biography would have disturbed.[104]

## IV

Yet the biographical act not only strips and dismantles a self-portrait; it also puts another portrait in its place. Biographers and biographical critics have approached Orwell in numerous ways, reflecting and contributing to the diversity of his public images. Early biographers often searched for the "essence" of his life. This involved finding "the key" to Orwell, how he was "essentially" an "individualist" (Brander), a "Left-wing Patriot" (Atkins), or a defiant seeker after Justice, a "Fugitive from the Camp of Victory" (Rees). Some subsequent critic-biographers of Orwell presented his "life's battle." They pinpointed the "central conflict" of his life and polarized it. Thus they found "the Englishman" battling "the exile" (Raymond Williams), or the man of "rebellion and responsibility" at war with himself (Vorhees)—only to conclude finally that Orwell was "a paradox." A third approach was the "dramatic" life, exemplified in the two-volume biography by Peter Stansky

and William Abrahams. They chose two disjunctive events in Orwell's life and read them as "milestones" or "conversion" experiences. For Stansky and Abrahams, the name change from Blair to Orwell and Orwell's trip to Spain were the two turning points of his life. A fourth approach, which we have already discussed, was the "tableau" of a life. It resembled the first approach and is the most frequently used with Orwell, sometimes explicitly, as in short biographical essays on "The Outsider" or "The Prophet of '1984'." Observers identified a characteristic pose or image of Orwell, presented it as the whole, and froze it. This approach is distinguished from the first only in that it is not so much a reduction and condensation of Orwell by way of a single key as it is the symbolizing of him in a single image—an image often identifiable as a reflection and projection of the memoirist himself. Still other biographers have, according to their own interests, stressed the political context of Orwell's work (Crick), taken an analytical and interpretive approach (Woodcock), or treated Orwell as a rival polemicist (Hollis).[105]

The range alone of these approaches suggests that Orwell's biographers have played a significant role in generating the diverse Orwell imagery. And given the centrality of the "portrait" metaphor for this study and its traditional correlation with the act of writing biography, the moment is opportune for exploring via the language of portraiture how the history of Orwell biography has borne on the history of Orwell's overall reputation. Woodcock has distinguished a few phases of Orwell's biographical history up through the mid-'70s; he has aptly remarked that the first literary-critical books on Orwell, including Orwell's own autobiographical references and the first volume of the Stansky-Abrahams biography, add up to a "phantom biography."[106] With the subsequent publication of Miriam Gross's *The World of George Orwell*, the second volume of the Stansky-Abrahams biography, the Crick full biography, and two new biographical introductions to Orwell, we may now extend Woodcock's observations and speak of "seven ages" of Orwell portraiture.

1. *The Self-Portrait, 1933–1952.*    Orwell the autobiographer and rebel. The main documents here are Orwell's direct remarks on his background in Part II of *The Road to Wigan Pier* and in essays like "Why I Write" (1946) and "Such, Such Were the Joys" (1952). The chief image which emerges, which we have already met, is that of the schoolboy rebel and mature writer "daring to stand alone." This rebel stance, and Orwell's writings, serve as the point of departure for all subsequent biographies.

2. *Profiles By Friends, 1953–66.*    Six full-length books of "biographical criticism." These works reflected and contributed to the proliferation of Orwell imagery. Referred to by Woodcock earlier, all were written by Orwell acquaintances of various literary and political affiliations. Except for the anarchist Woodcock and Richard Rees, these authors were no more than friendly colleagues (socialist John Atkins at *Tribune*, Conservative Laurence Brander at the BBC) or slight acquaintances (Tom Hopkinson, Eton contemporary and Conservative M.P. Christopher Hollis) of Orwell.

With the exception of the last book of the set, Woodcock's *Crystal Spirit*, all of these studies explicated Orwell's writings in chronological order, took his scattered autobiographical remarks at face value, and added recollections of the man from conversation and hearsay. The memory of the man guided all six studies, and yet the authors were constrained (legally and out of respect for Orwell's wishes) from delving further into his personal life than the limits of their acquaintance. Thus most of the books teetered uneasily between criticism and biography, hobbled by Sonia Orwell's determination to carry out her late husband's last request. She allowed no putative "biographer" to quote from Orwell's writings—a literary executor can refuse permission to quote all copyrighted material, including published and unpublished letters—though she did grant quotation rights to authors of "critical" studies. The result was that Orwell's friends focused on his writings, called their books "criticism," and helped establish the view that Orwell's writings were straight autobiography. To fend off pressure from Orwell's publisher and from his friends for a biography, Mrs. Orwell first authorized Malcolm Muggeridge to do the job, expressing to friends the conviction that she knew Muggeridge would never get around to it. (She was right.) Frustrated with the delay, Secker & Warburg approached Julian Symons about a biography in the late '60s. But Mrs. Orwell refused quotation rights and Symons—though he now believes that he might have done an excellent job even under Mrs. Orwell's restrictions—abandoned the project as hopeless.[107]

3. *The "Stopgap" Portrait, 1968.*    *The Collected Essays, Journalism, and Letters of George Orwell* (*CEJL*), edited by Sonia Orwell and Ian Angus. *CEJL* constituted a failed attempt to "fix" Orwell's reputation. Mrs. Orwell's wish, expressed on *CEJL*'s jacket cover, was that the four volumes would "stand in for a biography." She underlined the impression that *CEJL* was a substitute biography by organizing her husband's writings in chronological order. Orwell's request for no biography, she argued in her introduction, was "probably in part due to his natural reticence" and also to his "knowledge that there was so little that could be written about his life—except for psychological interpretation—which he had not written himself." Mrs. Orwell aimed to "give a continuous picture of Orwell's life as well as of his work" and said "the autobiographical aspect" of Orwell's *oeuvre* invited such an approach. Wanting to establish her own plain-man image of her husband as the final one and yet not be accused of erecting an "academic monument," Mrs. Orwell said that *CEJL* constituted not "The Complete Works" but "The Definitive Collected Works."[108]

To her chagrin, reviewers took Mrs. Orwell only too literally at her word. "Monument to George Orwell," trumpeted *Books and Bookmen*. "A Victorian life-and-letters monument," declared the *New York Times Book Review*. Intended or not, the volumes touched off an academic boom in secondary literature on Orwell, which has not abated since 1968. The availability of Orwell's letters and journalism made him of much greater interest not just to literary scholars but also to historians, political philosophers,

sociologists, and others. Yet even though it was not possible to make a full assessment of Orwell's achievement until *CEJL* appeared, the volumes did not alter most critics' opinions: by 1968 many critics had committed themselves to a certain view of Orwell and they continued to defend entrenched positions.

Appearing near the height of the Vietnam War, *CEJL* also "revived" Orwell—who had come to seem something of a dated figure—as a subject of ideological dispute on the Left, quickly fueling long-simmering debates about his politics. Two anti-war intellectuals critical of *CEJL,* Mary Mc-Carthy and Conor Cruise O'Brien, drew attention to its pretensions to definitiveness. McCarthy attacked it as "very sparse in letters" and showing "a blank" during the early months of World War II, provoking an angry defense from Mrs. Orwell that she was not "hiding" any letters. O'Brien criticized it as "not what it appears to be," and derided it not only as "an academic monument" but "a contribution to a cult." Taking note of Mrs. Orwell's remark that Orwell was "a dedicated anti-Communist," O'Brien pointed out that *CEJL* was specifically an Anglo-American edition, which was fitting since Orwell was chiefly an anti-Communist to "his American admirers."[109]

4. *New Sketches, 1971.   The World of George Orwell,* edited by Miriam Gross, a friend of Sonia Orwell. Part of the Weidenfeld and Nicolson "The World of. . ." series, the Gross collection reflected and contributed to the inflation of the man and writer's reputation. Chronologically ordered with individual essays devoted to each period of Orwell's life, the volume was in effect a condensed, updated version of the biographical "Profiles by Friends" of the '50s and '60s. There were, however, two changes. The collection broke new ground in giving attention to Eric Blair in five essays. Also, the contributions evinced the growth in Orwell's reputation in two decades. Only one-third of the essays were personal memoirs. Most were written by men one or two generations younger than Orwell and two essays directly addressed the question of Orwell's reputation in the 1970s. Too short to be substantial, the collection's essays did not fulfill Gross's aim of presenting Orwell "both in terms of what he means today and as a man whose achievement very much needs to be set in the context of his own period."[110] But the book's 98 illustrations, some of them photographs of major international events and figures of the '30s and '40s, helped foster the impression that the "world" of George Orwell cut across nations, races, and classes, as if Orwell bestrode the planet.

5. *The Stansky-Abrahams Diptych: An Acting Portrait, 1972, 1979.   The Unknown Orwell* and *Orwell: The Transformation.* With this first formal attempt at a biography, we are at last fully introduced to "Eric Blair." Even as *CEJL* appeared, Stanford historian Peter Stansky and New York editor William Abrahams were at work on their Orwell biography, with the encouragement of Richard Rees and the cooperation of Avril Blair and Orwell's schoolfriends. Sonia Orwell, however, refused quotation rights from Orwell's *oeuvre,* and so what Woodcock called the Americans' "protobio-

graphy"[111] was an album of others' memories, unfortunately deprived of the one voice which would have breathed life into it.[112]

Stansky and Abrahams continued the tendency to look behind "Orwell" for "Blair." In *The Unknown Orwell*, they diligently traced the development of Eric Blair to the age of thirty and amassed a wealth of information to support the little-known fact that Blair was quite a literary man with no political orientation before he became George Orwell. But the authors marked the Blair/Orwell division somewhat too sharply, implying that "Orwell" suddenly came into being with his pen name. Their thesis that "Blair was the man to whom things happened; Orwell the man who wrote about them" was an oversimplified dichotomy of the intricate relation between the man and the writer, neither of which was always or necessarily congruent with "Blair" and "Orwell." *Orwell: The Transformation* followed Orwell up to the writing of *Homage to Catalonia*. It likewise uncovered valuable new details about Orwell's relationships. But its cause-effect presentation of Blair's transformation into "Orwell" sometimes overstressed the suddenness and finality of the change, making it too baldly and mechanically the result of his trips to Wigan Pier and Spain—and leaving the (surely unintended) impression that "Orwell" was fully formed by the age of thirty-four.

6. *The "Commissioned" Portrait, 1980.*    Bernard Crick's *George Orwell: A Life.* The story of the long-postponed "official" biography of George Orwell ends, predictably, in a snarl of confusion. Among other things, it raises the whole thorny question—quite unanswerable—of how literary executors sometimes direct, by a mix of design and accident, authors' posthumous reputations.[113]

Outraged that Stansky and Abrahams had violated her late husband's last request, Sonia Orwell took the unprecedented step in 1972 of writing the *Times Literary Supplement* before publication of *The Unknown Orwell*, warning readers that the biography was "written against my approval" and "contains mistakes and misrepresentations." Not wishing to "let it stand as the only existing biography of George Orwell," she turned in frustration to London University Professor of Politics Bernard Crick, editor of *The Political Quarterly* and author of *In Defense of Politics*, among other books.[114] (Like most other events in the saga, the selection of Crick was odd. As he tells it, he had just written a book review of the Gross collection in 1972 and Mrs. Orwell, pleased with it, rang up Secker & Warburg and said, "That's the man to do it—who is he?"[115]) Mrs. Orwell granted Crick unrestricted access and quotation rights to all of Orwell's published and unpublished papers. Later, dissatisfied with his emphasis on Orwell's radicalism and his questioning of Orwell's literal veracity in several "autobiographical" passages, Mrs. Orwell tried to revoke Crick's commission. She was unsuccessful. (The biography was advertised as an "authorized," rather than an "official," biography.) Apparently sharing Mrs. Orwell's reservations, however, Harcourt Brace Jovanovich, Orwell's American publisher, refused to publish the biography (and forfeited a $20,000 advance). It appeared through Atlantic Monthly Press.[116]

As one might have expected, "The First Complete Biography of George Orwell" (as the dust jacket billed it) came in for some harsh reviews. Old friends like Woodcock rejected it as "An Unwanted Biography." Conservative organs like the *Sunday Telegraph* hammered it as "a fate worse than death." Even the liberal-Left *Village Voice* damned it as "an appalling biography."[117]

It was nothing of the sort. Crick's biography was a rich and often brilliantly insightful work of scholarship, admirably avoiding the recent trend toward bloated "megabiographies" of literary men. Many of the criticisms from the Left and Right were partisan objections to Crick's "right-wing socialism."[118]

One difficulty, however, was with Crick's objectivist biographical method. Unlike Stansky and Abrahams, Crick presented his biography as a contribution to biographical theory and practice. In many ways recoiling from the same excesses—Stracheyism and Freudianism—as did the writers of Orwell's age, Crick denounced in a substantial introduction "the English biographical tradition" grounded in the "empathetic" fallacy of being able to enter a subject's mind and plumb his motivations. Crick offered instead his Brechtian biography of "externality" as not only suitable to Orwell but as the model for an alternate biographical tradition. To avoid any pretence of omniscience, Crick insisted, the biographer should always stand "outside" the subject, "interpreting" him but not putting him on the psychiatrist's couch.[119]

Here again, we can see the invisible hand of Rebel Orwell behind Crick's choice of approach and some readers' disparagement of it. Arthur Koestler's review of the biography provides the telling clue. Koestler complained that he was "unable to get Crick's image of Orwell into focus" and "to blend [it] with the image of Orwell in my memory."[120] Precisely. For "Crick's Orwell" was a man of many images. Each of Orwell's friends had related "only a facet" of Orwell to Crick, leaving him, as it were, to resolve the conflicting images or to present them all. Crick fairly judged that readers deserved some indication of them all. And to do justice to them all he felt compelled to stay "outside," and not to overrule persons actually acquainted with Orwell with presumptuous, second-hand, categorical pronouncements as to Orwell's essential character. "I didn't want to pretend to be any kind of super-friend who could pull all this together," Crick later said.[121] What both Koestler and Rayner Heppenstall castigated as Crick's "Blurred Portrait"[122]—revealingly, each with his own very different "clear" profile in mind—was actually Crick's "honest" portrait. Unfortunately, Crick never explained how Orwell's behavior and reputation had conditioned his approach, or why a scrupulous Orwell biography might necessarily wind up seeming a "blurred portrait."

Yet the real problem was not Crick's empiricist approach, but rather the rigidity with which he held to it. Given that Orwell's writings were so copiously autobiographical and so suffused with admissions of guilt and self-flagellation, it was not only legitimate but necessary to step occasionally "inside," to explore with care Orwell's psychology. For a biographer must

interpret the "facts" in order to assess character and states of mind—must use his facts imaginatively, which entails no obligations to invent interior monologues or theorize about a subject's "essence." Crick's reluctance to grapple in psychological terms with Orwell and his stress on "externality" implied the Rankean claim to historical objectivity—the opposite extreme of Freudianism and of the empathetic fallacy. "Really I think I have written an annotated bibliography," Crick explained modestly, arguing that the story of Orwell was not his "character" but how his books came to be written. True enough, replied his critics, but an "annotated bibliography" does not a biography make.[123]

7. *"Retouched" Portraits.*    The latest phase of Orwell biography reflects and has contributed to the hyper-inflation of his reputation. After Crick's biography, and with the approach of 1984, writers rushed to dig up biographical scraps about Orwell and furnish new introductions to his life. Peter Lewis' copiously illustrated *George Orwell: The Road to 1984* (1981) and T.R. Fyvel's *George Orwell: A Personal Memoir* (1982) were two of the best. Lewis, another personal friend of Mrs. Orwell, included photographs of figures like Trotsky, Lenin, and Stalin, continuing the trend begun in the Gross anthology to transform Orwell into a world-historical figure retroactively. Fyvel spent several chapters "re-reading" Orwell, revaluing his books and discussing their relationship in light of Orwell's growth in reputation. At least two composite biographies also appeared, Stephen Wadham's *Remembering Orwell* and Audrey Coppard and Bernard Crick's *Orwell Remembered* (whose back cover promised "to shed light on this complex and sometimes secretive man"). These volumes were nothing if not thorough, with remarks included from various neighbors in Wallington and Jura, from the nurses at Orwell's sanitoria, and from his tailor. Apparently somewhat dissatisfied with the Crick biography, in 1988 the Orwell Estate also commissioned Michael Sheldon to write a new biography.

During 1984, a retouched "self-portrait"—an expanded eleven-volume *CEJL* edited by Peter Davison—was also under way. It forms the most substantial part of the massive twenty-volume *Complete Works of George Orwell*, the first nine volumes of which were published in 1986–88. The new *CEJL* will contain all of Orwell's uncollected published journalism and many previously unpublished letters. Apparently the lust to uncover Orwell's "secrets" knows no bounds; and a dead man cannot seal off intrepid biographers from his private life. The new *CEJL* will doubtless make no pretense to being a "substitute" biography. But whatever its claims, its exhaustiveness testifies to the fact that, as much as any other modern literary figure, the ephemera of Orwell's work and life have become subjects of consuming interest.

## V

The history of Orwell biography points to important issues beyond Orwell's own case, raising not only legal but also cultural, ethical, and professional

questions about the writing of biography in the post-Stracheyan age. Probably the legal right to personal privacy (and personal property) should have prior claim when disputes between author/executor and scholar/biographer arise, but as George Simson notes in an incisive editorial in *Biography,* it is outrageous that authors and executors "passionate for glory" often "flirt" with biographers (e.g., initially granting permission to quote from works or use unpublished materials), only to balk when faced with "the consequences of turning loose an honest scholar."[124]

The case of Orwell suggests why and how, when a figure achieves a certain stature, the writing of his or her biography can only be delayed by restrictive measures, not prevented. Biographical treatment reflects, not just builds, reputation; a "FAMOUS WRITER" will eventually receive either a good or poor biography, not avoid one. Perhaps, at first, both biographers and executor will play along together in a genre game, calling their books "critical studies" rather than "biographies." Potential biographers may even initially collude further and agree to "merely read" but not "quote from" private papers (often tantalizingly deposited in public or university libraries, like the Orwell Archive at the University of London, founded in 1960). But inevitably someone—as in the instance of Stanksy and Abrahams—will "break the rules." (The history of Orwell biography has an unusual twist, in that Stansky and Abrahams claim to have begun their biography on the suggestion of Richard Rees, who thought that "the story of Blair" would make an excellent book.) With such carrot-and-stick games, as Simson observes, scholars are "teased" "into being thieves, sneaks, or shills."[125] Thus is the craft of biography triply compromised. Not only is history impoverished and authors and/or executors tainted by their ultimately futile exercises in silence, exile, and cunning. The otherwise "honest" scholar may, in response, turn "biografiend" and resort to similarly unsavory machinations—thereby compromising his own integrity and, just as sad, reinforcing the bad reputation from which the genre of biography has traditionally suffered and which fine and forthright scholars have labored so hard in recent decades to improve.

## 8. "Always Fighting Against Something": George Woodcock and the Anarchists' Orwell

### I

We have already touched on George Woodcock's relationship with Orwell in the last two sections. In this facial history we are exploring an aspect of Orwell's Rebel reputation not via an issue in his reception history, but through a sustained examination of one reader's history of response to Orwell. We are specifically concerned with how Woodcock's criticism illumines Orwell's anarchist affinities and has shaped his postwar reputation, and with how Orwell has "figured" in Woodcock's life.

Woodcock's writings about Orwell are roughly divisible into two periods. His early criticism on Orwell, beginning in the 1940s, was chiefly biographical. His more recent work, including *Orwell's Message: 1984 and the Present* (1984), has been critical and meta-critical. Woodcock's intellectual biography of Orwell, *The Crystal Spirit* (1966), contains both kinds of commentary and bridges the two phases of his reception. Still, it is fair to characterize "Woodcock's Orwell" as he described Orwell in 1983, "always the odd man out—the maverick writer defying fashion in the name of plain speaking, the radical rebel who never fitted in with any left-wing movement."[126]

Generally speaking, then, Woodcock's image of Orwell has remained stable over the years. Its variabilities arise not from any explicit change of view toward Orwell by Woodcock, but rather from shifts in Woodcock's own literary-political preoccupations, from his gradual evolution toward a new cultural and professional identity, and from his deepened critical insight into Orwell's achievement. For these reasons, it will be advantageous first to survey the shifting modulations of "Woodcock's Orwell," note a few of its larger implications for the making of reputations, and then return to consider the import of his entire reception history for our concept of the institutional "reader in the group" and with respect to Woodcock's relationship to Orwell.

## II

Woodcock's December 1946 article in Dwight Macdonald's *Politics* was the first serious essay about Orwell. Published after the first American edition of *Animal Farm* that August, the article provided an assessment of Orwell just as his reputation was emerging beyond New York intellectual circles. Equally significant, it included a biographical introduction to Orwell, marking the first time that an American audience had received detailed information about Orwell's background. Given that Orwell had not published a book in America in a decade, some of Woodcock's material was probably unfamiliar even to Orwell's New York intellectual readers, notwithstanding that Orwell had been the chief London correspondent for *Partisan Review* since 1941. In 1948 the essay also appeared in Britain in Woodcock's collection *The Writer and Politics*.

A friend of Orwell's since their 1942 dispute over pacifism conducted in *Partisan Review*, Woodcock effectively established his authority to speak about Orwell by drawing on their conversations to explain how Orwell had evolved differently from other writers of the 1930s generation. Possibly, however, these conversations misled Woodcock into taking Orwell's autobiographical works too much at face value. Woodcock had not known "Eric Blair" and he exaggerated the depths and duration of Orwell's "poverty," e.g., asserting that Orwell's few weeks of tramping had been sometimes "from necessity" and "for long periods." Such rumors about Blair's background were already in circulation in England, but Woodcock's essay gave them impetus and prominent display in New York.[127]

Woodcock saw Orwell as "essentially the iconoclast." Titled "George Orwell, 19th Century Liberal," Woodcock's essay ended by quoting Orwell's now-famous closing lines in "Charles Dickens":

> It is the face of a man who is always fighting against something, but who fights in the open and is not frightened, the face of a man who is generously angry—in other words, of a nineteenth-century liberal, a free intelligence— a type hated with equal hatred by all the smelly little orthodoxies which are now contending for our souls.[128]

Woodcock's essay helped make these lines famous—and helped transform them into well-known characterizations of Orwell himself. Added Woodcock immediately: "The open fighting, the generous anger, the freedom of intelligence are all characteristics of Orwell's own writing." Partly due to the shaping influence of Woodcock's article, the profile of Orwell as the "triumphant rebel"—his image as the Angry Young Man of the '30s "always fighting against something"—became firmly established in the '50s.

Here we may note the interplay of two common, already observed processes of reputation-building: 1) how writers get received in terms of one another and 2) how writers' remarks shape the terms in which they are approached. Earlier we saw instances of each process at work separately. Of course, comparisons between two authors function similarly to shape reputations—by calling attention to common aspects of the analogous pair—e.g., between an author and a mythical figure like Don Quixote or John the Baptist. The one difference for our purposes is that, whereas investigation of the latter is often difficult because the comparisons are usually no more than passing allusions, critics frequently do conduct extended comparative analyses of authors, which inevitably shape their reputations in terms of each other. A second difference exists when we consider reputation as self-image, approaching the author "from the inside." Unsurprisingly, authors do often identify with each other quite self-consciously— which is less common between writers and mythic figures like Quixote or John the Baptist. In Orwell's case, we find him openly identifying with Dickens in "Charles Dickens." We have spoken at length about how ideological and commercial interest groups have sought to claim Orwell; here we see how, in a certain sense, Orwell, who opened "Charles Dickens" railing at those who "stole" Dickens, manages by its end to appropriate Dickens for himself—not by distorting Dickens' work but by so identifying himself with Dickens in subject and style that he invited flattering comparisons like Woodcock's. One might think of this as "weak claiming"; it too plays a role, if less spectacularly than outright confiscation, in the politics of reputation. It occurs whenever a person aligns himself strongly with an Other, so that, intentionally or not, he basks in the reflected glory of the Other. Without doubt, some measure of the warmth that English readers have felt toward Orwell has derived from their reflex association of him with Dickens, the most beloved English writer since Shakespeare.

One can similarly observe what amounts to "weak claiming" by Woodcock toward Orwell in this 1946 essay. A struggling thirty-four-year-old writer with his first book just published, Woodcock stressed the similarities between Orwell and the younger London anarchists. First and foremost, Orwell and they had both possessed the courage, said Woodcock, to criticize Communism when it was highly popular in England during the war years. "Ask any circle of anarchists or independent socialists who regard opposition to totalitarian communism as an important task," wrote Woodcock, "and you will find Orwell's name respected. . . . Ask any Stalinist today who is the greatest danger to the Communist cause, and he is likely to answer 'Orwell'."[129] This emphasis was likely to be well received in New York by the militant anti-Stalinist writers associated with *Politics* and *Partisan Review*.

And yet, Woodcock's essay may also have paved the way for subsequent confusions which American and even British readers—including Diana Trilling and V.S. Pritchett—developed about Orwell's libertarianism.[130] Significantly, the early announcements that Orwell had "turned anarchist" were all made by critics outside the anarchist fold and with no intention of "claiming" him. (Not long after his death, however, socialists hostile to Orwell like Isaac Deutscher were disclaiming him as "a simple-minded anarchist."[131]) Such misreadings of Orwell's works (and perhaps of essays like Woodcock's) further illustrate how a reputation may undergo distortion when it radiates outside a very small circle and accretes false rumors; and the problem of distinguishing "rumor" from "reputation" runs us up against that fuzzy line where the report of literary gossip ends and the serious study of literary reputation begins. Is there any hard-and-fast distinction? Not absolutely, for what is idle chatter to one person may be pertinent information to another. Even a man's list of guests to tea, as Woodcock himself suggests in his story about Orwell's careful compartmentalizing of visitors coming in and out of his apartment, may reveal much about him. "Gossip" and "reputation" (as public opinion) intermesh finely. Gossip reflects and contributes to the making of reputation, reputation derives from and modifies gossip. Exactly how private "notions" become public "rumors," just how rumors move from individual to group and beyond, and precisely how they attach themselves to reputations or form their basis: these large questions about the circulation of reputation within the social structure cannot be answered here. Indeed, with most rumors such questions are never clearly answerable, for either the basis of the rumor is indeterminate or it has gone unrecorded and is lost to history. Still, where possible, the critic of reputation should distinguish between accurate and inaccurate information, just as between reasonably drawn portraits and caricatures.

Whatever the basis of the rumor that Orwell had embraced anarchism, a careful reading of Woodcock's *Politics* essay would have given no grounds for it. Woodcock noted that Orwell was "by no means" an anarchist, terming him "an independent socialist with libertarian tendencies." Yet at the same time Woodcock did mention that Orwell's old-style liberalism resonated with "the anarchism of the future." The essay was not celebratory. From an

anarchist-pacifist standpoint Woodcock deplored Orwell's shallow understanding of the causes of social evils, his vague conception of the socialist
state, and his misplaced belief in the value of patriotism. Finally, however,
Woodcock could "readily forgive [Orwell's] inconsistencies and [the] occasional injustices that accompany them."[132] Both Orwell's liberalism and his
own anarchism shared, Woodcock noted, in opposition to state socialism, a
respect for the freedom and dignity of the individual.

Appearing as they did in *Politics* and *The Writer and Politics*, such comments about Orwell's "libertarian tendencies" and respect in "anarchist circles" probably at least contributed to erroneous impressions in the late '40s
that he had become a radical libertarian in the tradition of philosophical
anarchism. Formerly a Trotskyist and an editor of *Partisan Review*, Macdonald was by the mid-'40s a pacifist and soon-to-be anarchist. By 1948
Woodcock was known in New York as the regular English correspondent
for *Politics* and in London as the editor of the anarchist paper *Freedom;* his
Orwell essay appeared in *The Writer and Politics* next to articles on Godwin,
Proudhon, and Kropotkin.

No doubt what really incited the gossip that Orwell had "turned anarchist," however, was his friendly association with the *Freedom* writers during his final years. While this includes the fact of his occasional contributions to Macdonald's *Politics* and to the literary magazine *Now* and the
anarchist papers *War Commentary* and *Freedom* (all three edited at various
times by Woodcock), one suspects that Orwell's close personal contacts
with Woodcock and his colleagues affiliated with the Freedom Press—and
the anarchists' glowing testaments to Orwell after his death based on this
association—chiefly fueled the rumors.[133] This likelihood testifies again to
the inextricable relation between the man and the works in Orwell's history of reputation. For certainly with respect to this issue—Orwell's alleged
anarchism—the conduct of the life, as much as the content of the works,
accounts for the confusions.

Orwell's friendship with the *Freedom* writers blossomed suddenly. During
the war, Orwell had often criticized what he termed their "Parlour Anarchism." But when Scotland Yard raided the offices of *War Commentary* (*Freedom*'s predecessor) in late 1944, Orwell characteristically sprang to the anarchists' defense. After three of the paper's four editors were convicted for
sedition, Woodcock became co-editor. To combat such violations of free
speech, Woodcock organized the Freedom Defence Committee in 1945, persuading Herbert Read to serve as chairman and Orwell as vice-chairman. It
was the only office Orwell ever held in any political or civic organization.[134]

Of course, this in itself is no reason to interpret Orwell as having adopted
anarchist views. As we have seen, he moved freely among various political
groups without embracing their doctrines. The same is true, if more complicated, in the case of the Freedom Press anarchists. For Orwell arguably had a
long history of "libertarian sympathizing" that could have been, and apparently was, interpreted (by Pritchett, among others) as having culminated in
his being at least a fellow-traveling anarchist by the time of his death. Before

going to Wigan Pier and Spain, Orwell had called himself, in a phrase he later used of Swift, a "Tory anarchist."[135] His soldiering in Catalonia brought him together with many anarchists in the radical, anti-Stalinist POUM militia. As a result Orwell always felt a deep emotional bond with anarchism; and he acknowledged in *Homage to Catalonia* that, if he had understood Spanish politics before his arrival, he would have joined the better-equipped Anarchist militia. Even before his trip, however, Orwell had noted the growing resemblance of communism and fascism, which had convinced him of the anarchist tenets that the centralized state was evil and that liberty was a human being's first, inalienable birthright.

Orwell further agreed with the anarchists, and against the Marxists, that power was psychologically addictive and inherently corrupting. On returning home to England, he became an active sponsor of the International Anti-Fascist Solidarity Committee launched by the Spanish anarchists, whose English section was organized by Emma Goldman and through whom he met the *Freedom* writer Vernon Richards, among many other anarchists and pacifists. Before the outbreak of World War II, Orwell wrote for *Peace News* and joined the anti-war Independent Labour Party (ILP), the only political party he ever formally joined; after the war, with the *Freedom* writers no longer war-resisters, he not only befriended them and contributed to *Freedom* and *Now* but made a substantial donation to the latter in a vain attempt to stem its losses. Some hostile critics have interpreted Orwell's switch from a vocal anti-war position in early 1939 to active support for the war when it broke out in September as a move from pre-war "pacifism" to wartime "jingoism"; but likely the switch arose because, ever the English Quixote, Orwell felt that one could no longer be pro-Peace as well as pro-Victim and pro-England. With the German army on the march, the bulldog had become the underdog.[136]

This attitude represents the characteristic expression of our portrait of The Rebel as anarchist. It bares the connection between anarchism and rebellion, and it links this case study to our previous portraits of The Rebel. The anarchist stance is at base a rebel's stance. Anti-authoritiarian, anti-corporatist, and anti-bureaucratic, the anarchist holds that the individual should not yield self-autonomy to the state and that one must act not according to law but conscience. Resistance, revolt, disobedience, spontaneity, theoretical flexibility, withdrawal of cooperation from institutions, and obstinate or even quixotic independence ("Flowers For the Rebels Who Failed" goes the anarchist hymn) are key components of the anarchist ethos.

Much of this ethos was Orwell's too. His temperamental affinity and friendship with anarchists, however, never led to any formal or philosophical allegiance. Indeed he announced as late as June 1949, when *Nineteen Eighty-Four* was being misinterpreted in America as not just an anarchist but a Conservative tract, that he was a "supporter"—he was careful not to say "member"—of the British Labour Party.[137] His Quixotic side was attracted to the anarchists on account of their high ideals—they are, as Woodcock once admitted, History's proudest losers, the one political sect still un-

tainted, having never been tested by getting to power. But Orwell's pragmatic streak dismissed anarchism as hopelessly utopian. Anarchism "aimed
at the impossible feat" of human "perfectibility." Orwell shared the anarchists' belief in the virtues of community and of decentralized government.
Yet the shortcomings of the modern state, he thought, were not ineradicable but lay primarily in its class structure.[138]

Unlike the anarchists, Orwell did not believe in the innate goodness of
human beings. Nor did he advocate a return to a pre-industrial world or
imagine that a complex, technological society could function on the basis of
strictly voluntary association. The communal "cooperation" that anarchism
envisioned, Orwell feared, might actually amount to thought control by
censure, to an oppressive, moralistic tyranny in which physical coercion was
merely supplanted by the power of Public Opinion. As for the Freedom
Press anarchists themselves, Orwell judged that during the war their attacks
on the British government exemplified Pecksniffery and power hunger—
not the renunciation of power at all. "For if you have embraced a creed
which appears to be free of the ordinary dirtiness of politics—a creed from
which you yourself can be expected to draw no material advantages," wrote
Orwell, "—surely that proves that you yourselves are in the right? And the
more you are in the right, the more natural that everyone else should be
bullied into thinking likewise."[139] Orwell did distinguish, however, between
the older and younger generations of pacifists and anarchists. He respected
Herbert Read as a writer and for his "realistic" acceptance of the machine;
but he criticized severely the militant, romantic pacifism of Alex Comfort
and D.S. Savage, whom he considered smug ingrates unappreciative of the
fact that they could dissent against the war effort only because they sat
safely behind the guns of the British navy.

### III

The latter-day history of Woodcock's reception of Orwell is the story of a
deliberate and constructive disengagement from a powerful personal and
literary presence in a life, from the influence of "a haunting and remarkable
and perhaps great man."[140] (As we will see in Chapter Five, Raymond
Williams' complicated reception history of Orwell provides the counter-
example.[141]) The forced detachment has been carried out largely through
Woodcock's criticism on Orwell. He has sought to understand Orwell and
his relationship to him by writing about both; his tone has remained consistently sympathetic yet critical.

Woodcock began to extricate his personal memories of the man from his
literary judgments of the writer's work in a few short essays in the 1950s.[142]
*The Crystal Spirit* shows him facing the task directly and at length. Before
addressing Orwell's achievement, Woodcock feels compelled to open his
book with an extended memoir, "The Man Remembered." By writing about
the man, his haunting crystal "spirit," Woodcock comes to terms with their
relationship:

I had intended to write merely a critical study of Orwell's books, but I found that until I had—as it were—exorcised the memory of the man by committing my recollections to paper, I could not approach his writings with any degree of objectivity. But once those recollections had been put on paper, they seemed to take their place naturally with the other aspects of Orwell. . . . I have written my introductory section on Orwell out of a sense of inner necessity . . . [and] have exposed the attitude, affectionate but at the same time critical, which I have developed toward Orwell a quarter of a century ago and from which the rest of the book naturally develops. . . .[143]

This attitude had not changed substantially over a quarter-century. What did change, however, was Orwell's cultural status. Within a decade of their wartime lunches in London, Orwell's story had become what Woodcock describes as that familiar romantic "myth" of "Life Against Odds," of "the tortured, tragic writer who died in his prime after a life of heroic hardships and left as his testament the haunting and admonitory nightmare of a future dominated by communism."[144]

Woodcock ridiculed this myth, what we have identified as the image of Orwell the Quixotic "failure." But in undercutting it, Woodcock inadvertently contributed to the development of another aspect of the Quixote myth by titling his book *The Crystal Spirit*—Orwell the "pure" writer and "saintly" man. Woodcock's title was taken from Orwell's romantic poem memorializing the illiterate Italian militiaman with whom, wordlessly, he had shaken hands on arriving in Spain and whom he never saw again. Just as Woodcock had turned the closing paragraph of "Charles Dickens" back upon Orwell in his tribute to him as a "19th Century Liberal," so too with *The Crystal Spirit* did Woodcock apply the closing line of Orwell's poem to Orwell himself. One notices this tendency to invert Orwell upon himself at work throughout *The Crystal Spirit*. It is a critical habit of Woodcock's much like Pritchett's allusive style. Woodcock frequently shows in *The Crystal Spirit* how Orwell was able in his literary criticism to analyze penetratingly such writers with whom he strongly identified as Swift, Dickens, and Tolstoy precisely because through them he was engaging in deep, if veiled, self-criticism. As we will see shortly, the same is true of Woodcock's own criticism of Orwell.

For the immediate purpose of tracing Orwell's developing reputation, however, what chiefly concerns us is Woodcock's book title. Of course, the myth of Orwell's "saintliness" was already well developed by 1966: what Woodcock did, in one fell rhetorical stroke, was to capture in a phrase what many people had felt about Orwell and, most engagingly, to do so in Orwell's own words. Probably this is Woodcock's single greatest contribution to Orwell's reputation. So often is the phrase "The Crystal Spirit" quoted that it too has become a watchword in Orwell's reputation-history, now so firmly entrenched as a characterization of Orwell that most people think it originated as a judgment about Orwell himself.

Certainly the televised documentaries about Orwell would give one that

impression. Melvyn Bragg ended his 1970 BBC-TV special, *The Road to the Left,* by acclaiming Orwell "the crystal spirit." The phrase was also used as the title and theme for a 1984 BBC-TV dramatization of Orwell's last years (*Orwell on Jura: The Crystal Spirit*), in which the reticent Richard Rees delivers a preposterous speech exalting his friend as "the crystal spirit." The unintentional obscuring of the source and meaning of the phrase by the broadcast media is an everyday example of defacement. The example illustrates how an image inevitably undergoes some distortion as it radiates into wider spheres of repute and loses definition. But as in the case of the Quixote myth generally, the effect of the facecrime is hagiographic rather than contaminating.

In his Orwell criticism of the 1970s and '80s Woodcock has taken an interest in Orwell's critical reputation. The main, if rather slight, work of this period is *Orwell's Message: 1984 and the Present,* which devotes an entire chapter to disputes and speculations on the Right and Left about Orwell's politics. Not to be outdone, Woodcock weighs in with his own forecasts. Had Orwell lived into the '70s and '80s, Woodcock predicts, he might well have "changed his mind" about Gandhi and pacifism.[145]

While warning against accepting the versions of Orwell proferred by putative "neo-Orwellians" of the Left like the "ex-Trotskyists" at *Partisan Review* and of the Right like Christopher Hollis, Woodcock has also forthrightly admitted that anarchists too have sometimes sought to claim Orwell for their own side.[146] As Woodcock's hopeful guess about Orwell's possible change of heart toward Gandhi suggests, he is open to the same charge himself. In fact, John Wain has delivered it in the bluntest terms, accusing Woodcock of being "out to steal [Orwell], to kidnap him and keep him in the anarchist and libertarian menagerie." Woodcock's review of *CEJL* in *Commentary,* wrote Wain, constituted "a flagrant example of the intellectual vice [dishonesty] Orwell hated most and denounced all his life." Wain's language is extreme; but Woodcock's repeated, pointed characterizations of Orwell's "libertarian" and "decentralized" socialism—adjectives never used by Orwell, who identified himself explicitly with Aneurin Bevan's and the *Tribune* writers' "democratic" socialism—is puzzling. It is not, as we have seen, that Orwell's politics do not exhibit "libertarian tendencies." Rather, whatever Woodcock's intentions, his stressing of the word "libertarian" as a characterization of Orwell's political position reflects his occasional habit of implying covertly what he broadly dismisses—that Orwell ever formally espoused a radical libertarian politics like his own.[147]

The same uncomfortable impression comes across in Woodcock's *Anarchist Reader* (1977), in which excerpts from *Homage to Catalonia* are placed alongside the work of self-declared anarchists. Most disconcerting of all is the British edition of *The Crystal Spirit.* Whereas the American-Canadian edition contained extensive discussion about Orwell's anarchist (and socialist) ties, much of this material was excised from the shorter British edition. It does seem questionable that so many of the thirty or more significant cuts in the latter were passages discussing little-known and controversial aspects

of Orwell's politics, rather than literary criticism of Orwell's *oeuvre*. One critic has suggested that Woodcock toned down his claims about Orwell's radicalism before a British audience well informed about the politics of literary London.[148] Of course, the cuts may be quite innocent; perhaps Woodcock hoped that *The Crystal Spirit* would serve as an introduction to Orwell. Still, one does notice throughout Woodcock's work an undertow toward an "anarchist Orwell," already evident in his 1946 essay and operating to pull Orwell toward the radical libertarian camp—or at least to make it easy for others, inside or outside the anarchist fold, to misunderstand Woodcock, or pretend to do so.

IV

To appreciate how a reputation forms, and why a reader casts a writer in a certain image, one must go beyond the evident contribution the reader makes to a figure's reputation. One must also examine the figure-reader relationship. To understand the reputation *process*, that is, one needs to see what particular features in a writer's work and life have appealed to the institutional reader, and why they have done so. For the portraits in the Orwell gallery are not contextless images, but reception *scenes* in which we see Orwell against a detailed background. We are not always looking at a close-up of a figure's face; we must also at times imagine Orwell standing variously with a friend or a group of admirers, or against the backdrop of postwar Germany or the Soviet Union or feminism or Catholicism or popular culture studies. In the present scene we find Orwell next to Woodcock and the *Freedom* writers, institutional readers whom we must not airbrush out of the canvas of Orwell's reputation-history.

Put another way, we must not merely take the portraits at "face value," but inspect also their deep structure and the texture of personal and cultural experience which they represent. Thus, we shift our attention here from the influence which Woodcock's writings have exerted on Orwell's reputation to the influence which Orwell himself has exerted on Woodcock's life and to those personal and political factors which have conditioned his anarchist image of Orwell. And immediately we return to Woodcock's memory of the man. "Always," Woodcock has admitted, "that gaunt, gentle, angry, and endlessly controversial image intervenes."[149]

Woodcock is the only friend of Orwell to acknowledge how subjective and limited has been "his" version of this "endlessly controversial image." However strong the anarchist undertow of "Woodcock's Orwell," Woodcock has recognized, at least since the '70s, that all along he has presented "only a facet" of Orwell and has "tended to stress that facet. . .which reflected [my] basic outlook. I saw how he responded to anarchists, if not to anarchism as a dogmatic structure."[150] His conversations with the man, Woodcock has come to realize, have always guided his interpretations of the writer's work. "Always the man" has intervened. It is, then, with Woodcock's

relationship to the man that one must begin in order to see how Orwell has "figured" in Woodcock's life.

Although Woodcock has become sensitive to the fact that "his" Orwell is merely a partial one, he has seemed less aware as to how his own evolution has shaped the Orwell he has seen. Having in effect "gained control" of his memories of Orwell through writing *The Crystal Spirit,* Woodcock has subsequently used "the man remembered" as a mirror and lamp, through whom he puts to himself his hardest questions of political commitment and professional aspiration. For Woodcock, as much as for any other friend and writer, Orwell has served as a touchstone and "conscience."[151]

One senses throughout Woodcock's Orwell criticism and in his autobiography, *Letter to the Past* (1982), that Woodcock feels, beneath all their apparent differences, he and his quixotic socialist friend are much alike. Although he has said that he "regards heroes with distrust," Woodcock excepts "the hero shaming a corrupt society." It is clear in *The Crystal Spirit* that, as with many of his other choices of biographical subjects (Godwin, Kropotkin, Wilde, Proudhon, Gandhi, Merton), Woodcock finds Orwell an admirable hero of this sort, "a good and angry man who sought for the truth because he knew that only in its air would freedom and justice survive."[152]

Like Orwell, young Woodcock came to his politics via direct experience and after seeing the abuses of power from the inside. Orwell's road to socialism through Burma, Wigan Pier, and Spain was more dramatic and tortuous, but Woodcock's quieter route was no less painful or real. Orwell embraced socialism after his unhappy schooldays and Burma police service, victimized by school authorities and then victimizing Asians; Woodcock arrived at his anarchism in reaction to his twelve years as a clerk and supervisor in a London railway office, first laboring under and then wielding modest bureaucratic authority. Both hated the lives which they were leading. Orwell's self-described "baptism" in his late twenties was his being taken for a "mate" by a tramp.[153] Woodcock's more prosaic, though similarly fateful, moment of salvation occurred when he came into a small inheritance at the age of twenty-eight in 1940. He daringly quit the railroad to pursue writing full time. Both men, then, entered on their literary careers comparatively late. Likening himself in his autobiography to a slow but sure and solid tortoise, Woodcock prides himself on his late-blooming, much as Orwell congratulated himself on having succeeded in literary London without having attended Oxbridge.[154]

The attraction of Orwell for young Woodcock was fundamentally the appeal of a rebel, of a man who stood alone and took risks. For in the 1930s, Woodcock, an ambitious lower-class youth whose family could not afford to send him to university, found himself caught between two literary worlds. On the one side were the contributors associated with Geoffrey Grigson's *New Verse,* a leftish magazine of Oxbridge Londoners. On the other side was the group around Julian Symons' *Twentieth Century Verse,* a magazine of more radical, lower-middle-class, grammar-school men from the suburbs and provinces. Woodcock identified with the latter group; Orwell, though

from a slightly older generation, seemed to him cut from the same cloth. Like the autodidact Symons, Woodcock became friendly with Etonian Orwell because Orwell showed no upper-class or university pretensions. Orwell struck Woodcock as a rare exception among writers of the preceding generation, entirely different from "the Spenders and Audens in their college rooms and parental country rectories" whose adherence to socialism was "mental." Equally important, Orwell seemed one of the few writers "of real significance" who had not "become deeply involved with the Communist party and suffer[ed] a subsequent disillusionment which drove him into an unrealistic social situation."[155] Unlike Auden, Orwell never adopted a quietist politics or retreated into Art.

Reviewing Woodcock's autobiography, a critic commented in passing that Woodcock had "found in Orwell his alter ego."[156] The remark is shrewd, but it does injustice to the complex truth behind it. Both Woodcock and Orwell aspired to be poets as young men, possessing in strong doses what Orwell characterized in "Why I Write" as "aesthetic enthusiasm" and "political purpose." The first impulse asserted itself more forcibly in Eric Blair, the second in young Woodcock; in their mature careers the reverse is the case. Orwell the apolitical young man turned into a writer balancing political commitment with party detachment; Woodcock the party activist became a man of letters. Woodcock entered militant anarchist politics at the age of thirty. He left it after almost a decade, exhausted by the parochial bickering of a moribund movement.

Orwell and Marie Louise Berneri, Woodcock's anarchist friend who died a few months before Orwell, had stood before Woodcock during the postwar period as living examples of how he might resolve his crucial dilemma, the wrenching conflict facing many writers of the 1930s and '40s: the relation of the writer to politics. The choice before Woodcock was plain: Orwell's commitment or Berneri's militancy. Woodcock had been co-editor (with Berneri) of *War Commentary* and *Freedom* from 1942 to 1948. But by 1949, at the age of thirty-seven, he had reluctantly arrived at a position not far from Orwell's own. He had concluded that "the infection of [anarchist] orthodoxy would kill me" if he did not leave militant politics. "I found myself agreeing more and more (against my will) with George Orwell" about the need for the writer to keep some distance from partisan politics, Woodcock later wrote. Orwell had pointed out to Woodcock that the anarchists' fanatical insistence that their members toe a party line not only resembled the Communist mentality but also directly contradicted their professed ideal of freedom. Finally Woodcock parted from Berneri and in effect chose Orwell's path. He decided to become "a freewheeling radical of my own kind, or perhaps of the same kind as Hazlitt and Orwell and Cobbett."[157] He saw the need for the writer to be, in Orwell's words, "an individual, an outsider, [a] guerrilla on the flank of a regular army."[158] Orwell struck him as a truly libertarian spirit, "a free mind";[159] his example nurtured Woodcock's rebellion and ultimately liberation from anarchist zealotry, so that Woodcock could find his way to become the kind of libertar-

ian and writer he aspired to be. Note the similarity of Woodcock's introduction to *The Writer and Politics* and Orwell's "Writers and Leviathan," both published in 1948. These essays mark the moment of the two men's political convergence before Woodcock's emigration to Canada and Orwell's death. Though he presents it as a philosophical statement, Woodcock's essay is obviously a defense of his impending leavetaking from London and anarchist politics for Canada and a writing career, a decision severely criticized by his anarchist friends:

> As long as [the writer] work[s] according to an internally valid creed, [his] work will have real significance and will contribute to the destruction of falsehood. . . . In so far as he subordinates the internal to the external values, his work loses significance. Instead of being subversive, he becomes subservient, an intellectual slave instead of a liberator of the mind. . . .
>
> The very nature of political groups. . .makes it impossible for the writer to remain within them and to keep his integrity. Either he must secede and do what he can individually, or he must stay and degenerate into the inanity and corruption of the party hack writer. Nevertheless, the writer who is forced to end his connection with organized political activity need not become socially useless. . . . The task of the writer is to. . .realiz[e] and portray the truth. . . . This function does not mean that the writer steps aside from the crude realities of life. On the contrary, it is these very crude realities which he must elucidate and give meaning.
> —Woodcock, *The Writer and Politics*[160]

> To accept an orthodoxy is always to inherit unresolved contradictions. . . . [A]cceptance of any political discipline seems to be incompatible with literary integrity. . . .
>
> Group loyalties are necessary, and yet they are poisonous to literature, so long as literature is the product of individuals. . . . No thinking person can or genuinely does keep out of politics, in an age like the present one. I only suggest that we should draw a sharper distinction than we do at present between our political and our literary loyalties. When a writer engages in politics, he should do so as a citizen, as a human being, but not *as a writer*. . . . Whatever else he does in the service of his party, he should never write for it. . . .
>
> But does this mean that he should refrain from writing *about* politics? Once again, certainly not. There is no reason he should not write in the most crudely political way if he wishes. Only he should do so as an individual, an outsider, at the most an unwelcome guerrilla on the flank of a regular army.          —Orwell, "Writers and Leviathan"[161]

Both Woodcock and Orwell refer to the tug of group loyalties, and by 1949 Woodcock realized that the pull of the Freedom Press group was self-compromising and, finally, waning: he no longer wanted a life of political activism and no longer needed a community of friends to sustain himself and his writing. He could and wanted to stand alone. He notes in *Letter to the Past* that no one in the Freedom Press group supported or really even comprehended his urge to return to Canada, his birthplace. How could he,

they asked, give up a budding literary career for an uncertain future and subsistence in the wilderness? Orwell was one of only three friends who understood and supported the move—and the only one whose opinion seems to have mattered to Woodcock.[162] Orwell looms large in these chapters of *Letter to the Past,* and his sympathy for Woodcock's decision, the most difficult of Woodcock's life, is obviously another source of and justification for Woodcock's deep identification with him. Orwell had helped Woodcock bridge the vocational, temporal, and continental divides of his life—art/politics, youth/adulthood, England/Canada. Orwell had confronted him— at a younger age, face-to-face, and in a more visceral way than he did Trilling—with "the politics of truth"; and Woodcock's answer reshaped his life's calling. His history of response has therefore amounted to reception as gratitude, self-affirmation, and fascinated looking-glass immersion. Although Woodcock does not say so, he implies that Orwell could appreciate his yearning to get away from the dreariness of postwar London because he shared it, so clearly did it resonate with his own "dream of Jura," his Hebrides retreat; and giving up a nascent London literary career was the kind of Quixotic venture likely to appeal to Orwell's romantic side.

Woodcock had his own "dream" of Canada. "My rosy and romantic vision of Canada," Woodcock later explained, was linked with "a Thoreau-like picture of the ideal writer's life." "Canada" held out to Woodcock the opportunity to come to terms with his familial, cultural, and vocational identity in a single grand gesture. By returning to Canada, he felt, he could not only become his ideal writer but also fulfill "the personal myth which told me that Canada was the one place where I could perhaps live out some of my father's unlived life." And so Woodcock emigrated to Vancouver, "the edge of the edge" of Canada, his own Jura, becoming fully an outsider, even geographically.[163]

The roles of Woodcock's friends vis á vis his emigration decision and his reception of Orwell allow us to pursue further a conceptual issue connected with our notion of the institutional "reader in the group." Not only does the reading process occur with reference to group relations; there are also "reference individuals," perceived "carriers" of group norms (like Berneri). Orwell became such a reference point when Woodcock began to reorient himself to a group not his own, those "freewheeling radicals" like Hazlitt and Cobbett. Our self-appraisals thus flow not simply from our *membership* in a group, but from where we find ourselves within the group, inside or outside, center or periphery. As the 1940s wore on, Woodcock found himself more and more an outsider among the Freedom Press anarchists, a literary man among party activists. Notable is the differing influence of what Woodcock terms "the Freedom Press group" on him in his Orwell criticism: the 1946 essay is obviously shaped in line with the group's basic outlook; Woodcock's later Orwell criticism is shaped partly *in reaction to* the group.

The core of the Freedom Press group consisted of Woodcock, Vernon Richards (*né* Vero Reccioni, son of anarchist revolutionary Enrico Mala-

testa) and his wife Marie Louise Berneri (daughter of anarchist writer Camillo Berneri, who was murdered in the May 1937 fighting in Barcelona which Orwell recounts in *Homage to Catalonia*). Herbert Read and Alex Comfort were peripheral members. Woodcock has described the group as a cooperative association constructed according to anarchist principles:

> The Freedom Press group was an almost classic example of the "affinity group" that had been developed among Latin-European anarchists as the ideal framework for propaganda of both the word and the deed: a group cemented by both personal friendship and shared sensibilities and ideals. The real nucleus of the group when I entered it [1942] was Marie Louise Berneri, whose beauty, personality, and filiation made her as near as one could get to an anarchist princess. . . . For the most part we were intellectuals who had not been attracted by the romantic Marxism that drew so many artists from earlier anarchist movements; and this may explain why so many of George Orwell's friends in his last years. . .were drawn from this circle.[164]

Woodcock related to Orwell, then, not only as a friend but also as a member of an anarchist circle, and Orwell responded to Woodcock partly in terms of this group affiliation. Woodcock's history of response has been "anarchist," but as his background makes clear, his response was also social, generational, and finally idiosyncratic. George Woodcock, then, is not just an institutional reader; his reception history of Orwell is uniquely his own, far richer than the sum of his institutional affiliations. We must not obliterate the irreducibly personal character of this response. Indeed our rhetoric of reception is fundamentally concerned with the real responses of real readers in real situations. The concept of the institutional reader is potentially useful for an understanding of reputation-formation, but no analysis can capture the individuality of a reader's response. For the conditions of any reception act involve numerous communal commitments. Occasionally, as with an authoritative voice like Woodcock or a Trilling, these affiliations are so well defined that they become institutionally determinate. In such cases, real readers possess special sociological value as influential institutional readers, whose reception acts render transparent what might otherwise remain obscure about the complexities of the reputation process.

"Woodcock's Orwell," therefore, is not reducible to "the anarchists' Orwell." The other Freedom Press anarchists did not respond to Orwell as warmly, strongly, or abidingly. Their responses had also emphasized Orwell's hatred of the centralized state, his championing of personal liberties, his "fierce honesty" and "humanitarianism," and above all his rebellious individualism.[165] But even within a group "cemented by personal friendship and shared sensibilities and ideals," a person possesses a slightly different reputation from individual to individual. And here we see how a reputation radiates variably at the group level, even within a small circle. Berneri, for instance, was less disposed than Woodcock to permit friendship to intrude on politics; when Woodcock proposed to her, as managing editor of Freedom Press, that the house publish *Animal Farm*, she rejected it categori-

cally, unwilling to forget Orwell's attacks on the anarchists during the war years.[166] Like Woodcock, twenty-two-year-old Alex Comfort was able to bury his differences with Orwell after their controversy over pacifism in *Partisan Review;* D.S. Savage, forty years later, still has not.[167] Herbert Read, two decades older than the others, was already a distinguished literary man when he and Orwell met. Theirs was not an antagonists' or apprentice-model relationship, but a peer relationship, something like a senior and a junior man of letters.[168]

Of course, though it is impossible to weight them quantitatively, it deserves mention that the responses of members within a group are not all equally influential—nor are all groups equally influential. Woodcock did not occupy the same position of influence within the Freedom Press circle in the late '40s as did Trilling among the *Partisan Review* writers, let alone the same position of pre-eminence in London and New York. (If any anarchist approached that status, it was Read.) Likewise the Freedom Press group certainly lacked the cultural authority of the New York Intellectuals. It was a smaller and tighter group—truly a "group"—and also less literary and avant-garde, more interested in journalism and organizational politics. But unlike the *Partisan* group, which survived, however loosely, through the 1960s, internal politicking and the loss of key members had fractured the Freedom Press group by 1950. All these factors help explain why Trilling's image of Orwell as "the virtuous man" was so widely known in academic-intellectual circles in the '50s, and why we can trace with some precision the effect of his introduction to *Homage to Catalonia* and yet cannot do so for Woodcock's *Politics* essay. (Academic critics of the 1970s have acknowledged its importance.[169])

The theoretical point, however, is that for understanding how an author's reputation "circulates" at the group level of reception and what role a figure can play in an institutional reader's life, an authoritative voice like Woodcock, speaking to and for a definable institutional audience, need not be a major critic or celebrated cultural commentator like Trilling. Nor even need he be the leading voice within his own group. (Berneri, not Woodcock, was the charismatic and organizational leader of the Freedom Press group.) It is enough that he is a member who is recognized, inside and outside the group, as affiliated with it and as somehow representing it.

Today, especially in Canada, Woodcock's name is firmly intertwined with Orwell's. During 1984 it was clear that Woodcock reigned in Canada as the undisputed spokesman for Orwell, "his partner in a storied friendship and the writer with whom he has perhaps most in common," as the editor of *The George Woodcock Reader* has picturesquely phrased it.[170] Certainly Woodcock has nurtured the comparison: in 1984 he hosted a five-hour radio biography of Orwell sponsored by the Canadian Broadcasting Corporation, the most expensive radio program in Canadian history; *Orwell's Message* focused on the specific relevance of *Nineteen Eighty-Four* for present-day Canada ("How 'Orwellian' Is Canada?" asked the cover); and *The George*

*Woodcock Reader* includes not only an essay on Orwell but also a long passage from *The Crystal Spirit*, the only book excerpted. Indeed, of Woodcock's fifty books, *The Crystal Spirit* (which received Canada's highest literary award) is his best-known work (and personal favorite).[171] It is a measure of Woodcock's talent and drive that, starting out in his forties in a new country, he has managed to climb to a position of eminence in Canadian intellectual circles comparable to Trilling's status in mid-century America.

In some striking respects the current positions of Orwell and Woodcock in their native countries are also alike. Just as the name "Orwell" evokes "England" for some readers, Woodcock's name is near-synonymous in Canadian intellectual circles with "Canadian Literature," the title of the journal he founded in 1959, the year he crossed his "personal Rubicon" from "English expatriate writer" to "Canadian writer."[172] Critic, journalist, biographer, historian, poet, polemicist, political essayist, editor, even playwright and translator: Woodcock is today justly celebrated as "a Renaissance man," "a national literary asset," "Canada's Ranking Man of Letters."[173] Since *The Crystal Spirit*, Woodcock has published all his books with Canadian houses, and he describes his evolution as one from "international anarchist" to "Canadian patriot" "deeply concerned with securing and preserving the independence of my country."[174] (Not surprisingly, given his new self-image, Woodcock now respects Orwell's wartime patriotism, which he dismissed as "reactionary" in 1946.)

Indeed, though Woodcock has proceeded to move away from activism and anarchism and toward literature and freewheeling radicalism, he has continued to draw attention to Orwell's anarchist affinities. Nostalgia and ambivalence are part of the reason. Much of the original and continuing appeal of anarchism for Woodcock—as it probably was for Orwell—is romantic and historical: its roots, from Winstanley to Godwin, are English, and many of the great anarchist agitators (like Kropotkin) worked in England for much of their lives. Woodcock looks back fondly, though not without anxiety, across the Rubicon. Even in 1984 in *Orwell's Message*, beneath and between all the pages of exegesis, the ghosts of Orwell and Berneri still seem to be stalking him, provoking him to ask aloud all over again his great never-quite-buried question of vocation and identity—Committed Writing or Direct Action?—which gripped him decades ago and a continent away. "Is what Orwell did as a writer. . ., combating in words the affronts against human decency and freedom. . ., all that can be done?" Woodcock wonders. "Are there not more direct means of arousing general consciousness and translating it into general action?" Woodcock points to Gandhi and Lech Walesa, and the implication is clear. Still, writing too can be a form of action, Woodcock implies, and writers like him and Orwell furnish "the message," without which resistance by "Gandhian methods" could never succeed.[175] Whatever his sectarian label, Woodcock insists elsewhere, he currently holds "anarchist attitudes," not "anarchist theories."[176] On pragmatic grounds he allows for some laws and government to restrain those who would violate their neighbors' freedoms[177]—a rationale and con-

cession which makes him sound not so much an anarchist as what one friend has called a "libertarian socialist"[178]—or perhaps a "19th Century Liberal," not a great deal unlike, one might say, his youthful image of George Orwell.

In the four case studies of this chapter, we have witnessed the Rebel Orwell in different poses, in different settings, from different angles, and from different distances. In one sense we have inspected distinctive expressions of rebellion, various ways and contexts in which "to be a rebel"—e.g., through quixotism, self-withdrawal, and libertarianism. Each room in the portrait gallery reflects a similarly multivalent diversity. For issues get variously embodied in images, and images get variously expressed in issues. Our task is to identify elective affinities among portraits, not erect categorical enclosures betweeen them. We must respect the multiple forms which a reputation takes, the many countenances which a face assumes. There are no doors in the Orwell gallery, only passageways.

# *The Common Man*

## 9. Decency and Democracy: The Aspiring Plebeian

### I

We now enter a second, adjoining room in the gallery rubricated "The Common Man." Even more so than with The Rebel, this face is self-crafted, derived from Orwell's own repeated use of favorite phrases like "common decency," both halves of which have become watchwords often linked with his name. Orwell used this particular phrase to evoke a great variety of attributes which he held in high esteem: simplicity, honesty, homey coziness, warmth, cleanliness, respectability, stoicism, grit. And in the years since his death the phrase has in turn attracted these and other associations to his name, giving him a reputation as a sort of intellectual's "common man." Intellectuals of all sorts have hailed Orwell's own "common decency." A month after Orwell's death *The New Republic* announced: "Today, without fear of contradiction, we can say that England never produced a novelist more honest, more courageous, more concerned with the common man— and with common sense." Unlike most left-wing intellectuals, countered *The Spectator* a few months later, "He never lost the common touch from which faith springs." "Orwell himself was a common man," maintained a Catholic critic in 1966. "Like Lord Jim, he was one of us." By the 1970s, Jeffrey Meyers had dubbed Orwell "The Honorary Proletarian." Declared *TV Guide* in 1984: "Orwell believed in the common sense of common humanity. He would have loved *Cheers*."[1]

Would Orwell have loved
*Cheers?*

Orwell as Honorary
Proletarian?

Certainly Orwell was deeply concerned with the plight of the underprivileged, as even his pre-socialist writings like *Down and Out in Paris and London*
make clear. (Given what he wrote about trendy pubs in *Coming Up for Air*
and elsewhere, however, one doubts he would have loved the NBC sitcom
*Cheers* and its stylized yuppie neighborhood bar.[2]) No more than Dickens, as
he said of his favorite English novelist, was Orwell "a champion of the
proletariat." But Orwell did come to see himself as an ally of, and often a
mouthpiece for, "the common man." The distinction is important, both for
understanding Orwell's self-image and for tracing the development of his
public image. He did practice, often ostentatiously and sometimes satiri-
cally, odd little proletarian affectations—cooling his tea in the saucer like a
working man, rolling his own shag cigarettes, drinking his beer from a
straight glass, wearing the blue shirt of the French working class, donning
what Malcolm Muggeridge calls his "proletarian fancy dress" (a tattered old
tweed coat and corduroy trousers) even on a few formal occasions.[3] Orwell
did, as he noted of Dickens, "admire" the working classes, even "romanti-
cize" them; but he too, finally, did not wish to "resemble" them. He realized
during his trip to Wigan Pier that he could not. On the other hand, Orwell
despised intellectual pretension and impractical theorizing. It is actually
more his rancor *against* the English intelligentsia than his positive identification *with* the English working man that shaped his self-image and reputation as an intellectual's common man.

And here we should pause to note how the faces of The Rebel and The
Common Man are linked, and to refine our notion *face*. For how can a man
be seen both as The Rebel and also as The Common Man? The capital
letters are intentional, for we are not merely speaking here of Orwell as a
"plebeian rebel" or "rebellious common man"—the *faces* of George Orwell
are not just loose collections of imbricated *attributes,* but rather distinct
*coherences.* They are faces, not facets. In this sense we can talk of *The* Rebel,
*The* Common Man, *The* Prophet, *The* Saint—each of which has a different, if
interacting and often overlapping, repertoire of features associated with it.
In the end, of course, all of them *are* faces "of Orwell." But what remains
striking and significant—and constitutes the foundation of this study—is
precisely their multiplicity: an image of one personality has resolved into
several distinct patterns. This is an easily observed dimension of Orwell's
history of reputation and not just a reflection of my theoretical framework.
The critic of Orwell's reputation, therefore, must be sensitive to the particular configuration of features which constitutes each face, and to the changing images in which they present themselves. For we are not examining The
Common Man as objectified essence, but the facial history of *Orwell as*
Common Man, with its own proportions and expressions, and seeing its
particular *relationship to* his other faces. And so, although each face is the
physiognomy of "Orwell," each amounts to a different visage of him distinguished by its own peculiar form, aspects, and *facial language.* Shared features between two or more of Orwell's faces, like the "Englishness" of The
Rebel and The Common Man, do not imply that these two faces lack distinc-

tiveness. D.H. Lawrence, also known as a "rebel" and for his "Englishness," is not regarded as a "common man." Dr. Johnson is well known for his individualism and "English common sense," but few people think of him as a "rebel," let alone a "common man." Both writers are often and fairly compared with Orwell according to these particular attributes—but it is important not to generalize casually (as so often happens) from a single striking similarity of feature to an overall resemblance. Two people with moustaches are not identical: to share a feature is not to exhibit the same face.

One can also formulate the oppositions and incompatibilities between The Rebel and The Common Man in another way: whereas The Rebel tends to be a distinctly negative archetype, defined chiefly by its antagonisms and characterized by defiance, The Common Man allows for affirmations and accommodations. However much the dual images of Orwell as a hero and anti-hero—as a successful and failed rebel, and as a tragic Promethean rebel and a Quixotic comic rebel—widened and intensified his appeal, his image as the intellectual's "average guy" allowed his reputation to broaden much further. For if Don Quixote keeps the flame of our pure intentions alive, Sancho takes account of the deficiencies of average people. If we reject Quixote, we deny our dreams; but if we reject Sancho, we deny our everyday selves.

Thus the Rebel and Common Man images of Orwell have interacted in subtle ways to deepen and widen Orwell's appeal, each speaking to different sides of Orwell's readers. The passionate Rebel ignites our imagination; the pragmatic Common Man checks our impetuousness. The Rebel incites the accepting Common Man; the Common Man tempers the fiery Rebel. Orwell's reputation as a passionate writer has probably grounded his reputation, but without his reputation for pragmatism he might not have won a hearing outside the ranks of the already converted. And yet, though Orwell's reputation has already radiated very widely, his "outsider" image helps gain him continued entry into new groups because it saves him from close identification with the Establishment. Perhaps the passionate and pragmatic Orwells also speak to different age-groups and temperaments. The Rebel is an idealist's and young man's hero, a pure figure challenging Authority and agitating for a just world. The Common Man is a realist's and mature man's hero, an experienced, skeptical, even worldly figure bluntly dismissing revolutionary change and other idealistic notions with his sardonic humor.

If we inquire again, then, how The Rebel also became The Common Man, the answer is twofold: 1) Orwell's fundamental self-image as a rebel, "a man against," asserted itself "against the Left" intelligentsia. It took the form of identification first with the down-and-outs and later with "the common people": the direction of Orwell's rebellion was socially downward. 2) As with the face of The Rebel, Orwell's self-presentations soon became public perceptions: his self-image, to a large degree, became his public reputation. And because Orwell is the chief architect of his Common Man reputation—

probably even more so than in the case of The Rebel—we must periodically scrutinize the relation of Orwell's self-image to his developing public image, the inside to the outside. In part, Orwell's embrace of "the common people" stemmed from his habit of mind, which was curiously antinomial and schematized on certain subjects. His Manichean strain is especially evident in his radically polarized oppositions of "intelligentsia" and "common man." He worked out an elastic, essentially negative definition of "common man" for himself: a "common" man was simply a man who was not an intellectual. Orwell did not restrict his use of the phrase to the working classes, then, but employed it as a catch-all term for non-intellectuals when deriding the Left intelligentsia. It could then embrace all "the people," especially Orwell's virtuous underdogs, whether tramps like Bozo the pavement artist in *Down and Out*, working girls like Rosemary Waterlow in *Keep the Aspidistra Flying*, or lower-middle-class salesmen like George Bowling. "Common man" was a plaudit in Orwell's vocabulary. If not an "honorary proletarian," he was at least an "aspiring plebeian."

Orwell's definition of "common man" by negation was also partly an attempt to resolve for himself a problem of identity and of writer's stance: How could he avoid being one of his despised, effeminate Cambridge intellectuals in *Keep the Aspidistra Flying* who write for each other? How instead could he be a "normal" man and a writer with a public following? Orwell realized that he could never be a "worker"; but he could distinguish himself as a "common man" among intellectuals. And some of his acquaintances did come to see him this way*—as the non-university, ex-Burmese policeman who was attractively different from themselves. But significantly, Orwell has not been held up by English workers or by his closest acquaintances as a "worker's hero"; mostly Anglo-American intellectuals who knew him little or not at all have exalted him as such. Their Common Man image has not only made Orwell more appealing to non-intellectuals, however; it has also spoken to their own longing for social acceptance—for a "common man" in their own image.

The Common Man, the second face to emerge clearly in Orwell's reputation-history, crystallized during the wartime period, between *The Lion and the Unicorn* (1941) and the weekly columns for *Tribune* (1943–45). To talk of its crystallizing, however, is somewhat misleading. For despite Orwell's rather straightforward anti-intellectual conception of his "common man," the face of Common Man Orwell is a protean image, probably the most complex face of Orwell. Indeed the very phrase "common man" has

---

*As he may really have done so himself. In 1984 David Astor related to BBC-2 viewers a conversation at Orwell's funeral which he had with Orwell's sister Avril. "Who did George admire?" asked Astor. "Did he have any heroes?" Astor expected her to name a famous literary or political figure. "The working-class mother of ten," she replied. Astor took her to mean that Orwell admired the way "ordinary people" get over "extraordinary difficulties, and keep sane and good-natured." His interpretation points up how much Orwell's democratic socialism was based on the conviction of the extraordinary possibilities of ordinary people. There is something of Don Quixote, Orwell believed, in all of us.[4]

come to encapsulate a wide variety of ideas associated with Orwell: common sense, decency, plain-speaking, accessible writing, justice for all, defense of the underdog. We have already seen this face from one angle, Lionel Trilling's "intelligent" man whose "plainness of mind" made him seem to the New York Intellectuals an extraordinary "ordinary" man. But Common Man Orwell is actually a number of discrete yet related images with shared features—the images of the down-and-out, the democratic socialist, "the quintessential Englishman," the common-sense critic, the plain stylist, the "popular" serious writer, the "patriot of the Left," the anti-intellectual pragmatist, "the decent man," the "vulgar" anti-aesthetic Sancho Panza. The present task is to see how a face expresses a range of attitudes and meanings, and to avoid impoverishing the rich image of The Common Man by reducing and hypostatizing its cluster of associations to a single one, such as "populist," "patriot," or "pragmatist."

We have already touched on the second difficulty involved in our tracing the emergence and history of this image. Orwell's reputation as The Common Man is a complicated joint creation of his style of life and writing, and of numerous indirect influences. As we saw with The Rebel, the author himself is among the authoritative voices responsible for shaping his reputation, and nowhere is this more the case than in Orwell's reputation as The Common Man. To a greater extent than elsewhere, as I have already stressed, the shape and complexity of this face is of Orwell's own making. Orwell's well-known contact with lower-class life, his constant repetition of many variants of the phrases "common decency" and "common man," his self-presentation in *Homage to Catalonia* and elsewhere as a man of action, his down-to-earth prose style, his plain-man persona, his attacks on the intelligentsia and warnings about "The Lure of Profundity," his patriotism and love of "England," his self-conscious association of himself with "English" writers (Lawrence, Johnson, Blake, Wells, Kipling) and lower-class writers (Jack London), his affinities with radicals like Cobbett and Dickens who championed the common man, his interest in popular culture and affection for "good bad poetry" like Kipling's, and his *Tribune* columns on small treasures of nature (the "common" toad, the rosebush) and everyday subjects (the ideal pub, how to make a good cup of tea): all of these factors have contributed to Orwell's Common Man reputation. And they in turn have given rise to many myths about Orwell's proletarian background (some of them possibly supported by Orwell himself), e.g., his impoverished working-class origins, his "years" spent tramping. Even his first wife Eileen is fit into the idyll as "a woman of the people."[5]

These complexities notwithstanding, this introductory section of Chapter Four chronicles the emergence of the most prominent images cited above which are associated with Orwell's reputation as The Common Man. As in our discussions of the development of Orwell's reputation as The Rebel, we aim not only to chart the progress of Orwell's reputation as The Common Man but also to disclose something of the process of image-

making itself. We will be paying close attention to the special relation between Orwell's self- and public images, to those authoritative voices and radiant moments significant for his history of reputation, and to a few minor voices whose responses illumine certain features of Orwell's reputation and/or the differences among his reception audiences.

## II

The face of Common Man Orwell undergoes several transformations both during Orwell's writing career and posthumously. Even before publication of *Down and Out in Paris and London,* the face is identifiable as the "down-and-out." In this image, the Rebel and Common Man faces meet, reflecting Orwell's developing reputation as an opponent of injustice and a defender of the weak. Reviewers immediately lauded the author of *Down and Out* for his "great sympathy with the man on the street." Indeed the well-known London tramp W.H. Davies (*Autobiography of a Super-Tramp,* 1908) praised Orwell's account as "all true to life, from beginning to end." The considerable achievement of *Down and Out,* said *The Listener,* was that it "help[s] us see things from below instead of from above." Sounding a note that would soon become prominent with the publication of *Wigan Pier,* a reviewer for *Time and Tide* concluded: "It is not only George Orwell's experiences that are interesting; George Orwell himself is of interest." In 1934, the co-director of Gollancz Ltd., Norman Collins, was convinced that the sufferings of Dorothy Hare in *A Clergyman's Daughter* were Orwell's own.[6] As the 1930s progress, readers gradually begin to accept, participate in, and elaborate Orwell's successive identifications with the poor, the working class, and all those "below."

One notices this interplay between Orwell's self-presentations and observers' re-presentations of him in the rumors about Eric Blair's tramping that began circulating in London as early as 1930. One friend's recollections of young Blair as a reviewer for Middleton Murry's *Adelphi,* though hindsight, makes clear that some quarters of literary London took Blair for an English Jack London:

> Already a legend was shaping up about him. He was not as other Blooms-bury souls, they said, he was an outsider, a rebel, a tramp, he lived and wrote in the bottom-most underworld of poverty. A man to look out for, then, a man to meet. . . . [With his] scrub of hair and curiously ravaged face, he looked the real thing: outcast, gifted pauper, kicker against authority, perhaps near-criminal. . . . [But] right away, manners—and more than manners—showed the process euphemistically called "breeding" through. A sheep in wolf's clothing, I thought. He was an Eton man, I learned later, one of a kind that often stray into contexts not their own to become catalysts of change, extra consciences to the "movement," whatever it is. All the same this man Blair was a letdown to me that day. . . . Was Eric just a phoney then?[7]

This memoir is by Jack Common, at this time *Adelphi*'s twenty-seven-year-old circulation manager and a working-class writer from Newcastle. Common expected to find a genuine proletarian in Blair, not an upper-class public school man like the other *Adelphi* writers. Whether or not Blair was really slumming, we can see here the origins of his "common man" reputation among bourgeois intellectuals unfamiliar with lower-class life. Notably, a working-class writer sees Blair not as a "rebel" and "common man" but as a "phoney" and an "amateur pauper" still playing a role. Biographical evidence suggests that the judgment is probably fair.[8] It also calls attention to how the image of the down-and-out relates to Orwell's Common Man myth. The distinctive appeal of the myth is that it held out a way of transcending class differences: Orwell first aspired to the ordinary *by way of* the down-and-out. The obvious strain—and self-admitted failure (in *Wigan Pier*)—of his melodramatic choice is later relieved by a related myth: the man of "common culture," which represents an ordinariness not necessarily limited to a particular class but is rather a matter of sensibility, a style of dress and tea-drinking and cigarette-smoking available to anyone. The power of this latter myth reflects the urge and difficulty of being a "common man" and also a "rebel"—i.e., being a "common" man without being a "mass" man: the desire to fit in and be ordinary and yet also be an individual.

In the early 1930s, then, Blair's revolt remained aesthetic and dandified, not yet political. His plan for getting thrown into prison one Christmas by starting a bonfire in Trafalgar Square struck Jack Common as "an undergrad stunt" that "mocked the rebellions of the truly destitute." And so it was: Blair was still coming to grips with his "outcast" role. Explaining why he preferred titling his first book "Confessions of a Dishwasher," he told his agent in 1932, "I would rather answer to 'dishwasher' than 'down and out'. . . ."[9] His anxiety had less to do with a concern for literal accuracy than with the tensions between his private self and his emerging public persona.

Orwell began to see himself first and foremost as a political writer in the aftermath of his two-month trip to the industrial North in January 1936, when he investigated the poverty of the unemployed and the miners. Richard Rees later expressed on BBC-TV what most of Orwell's acquaintances sensed about the "transformation" Orwell apparently underwent in 1936: his rebellion was taking the form of a descent into the social underworld. "There was the extraordinary change in his writing and, in a way also, in his attitude after he'd been to the North and written that book. [I]t was almost as if there'd been a fire smouldering in him all his life which suddenly broke into flame at that time. But I can't understand it or explain exactly what happened. I just don't know."[10]

Indeed the fire is smoldering in Orwell's writings even before the trip. In *A Clergyman's Daughter* and *Keep the Aspidistra Flying* we see his self-presentations as a writer evolving. Although his authorial stance toward his respective protagonists Dorothy Hare and Gordon Comstock is partly ironic, the characters' main activities in both novels match Blair's own *curriculum*

*vitae* in the early '30s: tramping, hop-picking, schoolteaching, clerking in a bookshop, poetry writing, reviewing for little magazines. These experiences, combined with public knowledge that *Down and Out* was autobiographical and that "A Hanging" and *Burmese Days* derived from Blair's police service in Burma, led some London readers to assume, much too casually, that Orwell's novels were straight autobiography—i.e., that Orwell himself had literally undergone the same events as did his fictional characters. This premise set a pattern of response for Orwell's subsequent reception history: his novels, as well as his documentaries, began to be taken as a transparent record of his life. Indeed Orwell's direct transposition of his personal experience in his early fiction reflects not only the essentially reportorial, rather than highly inventive, nature of his fictional imagination in the early '30s; it also discloses his changing self-image. Orwell is moving toward what will soon become his mobile definition of "common man": a non-intellectual. No longer is he sympathizing strictly with the scullions and tramps, Jack London's "lowest of the low," but also with the mainstream of society's underprivileged, the working and lower-middle class—soon to be his beloved "ordinary people." The shift is most apparent in *Keep the Aspidistra Flying*, whose hero Gordon Comstock, the penurious rebel poet, was taken by some reviewers in 1936 as a thinly veiled autobiographical character."[11] Comstock's epiphany, which leads him to abandon Art and marry Rosemary Waterlow, has often been read as Orwell's endorsement of the bourgeois "aspidistra" values of his "common man":

> A typical lower-middle-class street. . . . He wondered about people in houses like those. They would be, for example, small clerks, shop assistants, commercial travellers, insurance agents, tram conductors. . . . It mightn't be a bad thing, if you could manage it, to feel yourself one of them, one of the ruck of men. Our civilization is founded on greed and fear, but in the lives of common men the greed and fear are mysteriously transmuted into something nobler. . . . They contrived to keep their decency. . . . They had their standards, their inviolable points of honour. They "kept themselves respectable"—kept the aspidistra flying.[12]

The impassioned tone of the narrative voice suggests, as critics have argued, Orwell's own desire to be "one of the ruck of men"—"if you could manage it." Orwell can't—as he finds out, definitively, during his trip to Wigan. (Precisely the same wish, even more hopefully expressed, is delivered in Orwell's own voice at the close of Part I of *The Road to Wigan Pier*). But in the novel's juxtaposition of the common man with the snooty Cambridge intellectual, we see the beginnings of Orwell's characteristically negative approach toward describing the common man. The English common man possesses, in Orwell's descriptions, the virtues which the intellectual lacks: patriotism, spontaneity, love of nature, knowledge of the world outside books, skepticism, preference for the concrete.

A second public image of Common Man Orwell thus emerges in *Keep the Aspidistra Flying, Wigan Pier,* and *Coming Up for Air*—The People's Tribune.

This is an encompassing, multi-featured image that will unite and subsume the image of the down-and-out with other images of Orwell discernible in the late '30s and '40s—the man of action, the "democratic" socialist, the anti-intellectual pragmatist, the "quintessential Englishman," and "the patriot of the Left."

We see all these images brought together in Orwell's writings between 1938 and 1945. *Homage to Catalonia* shows Orwell as a man of action, fighting to save the Spanish Republic alongside soldiers like his illiterate Italian militiaman. Tubby Bowling in *Coming Up for Air* is, of course, one of England's "ruck of men," a lower-middle-class commercial traveler. But the key works of this period for Orwell's common man reputation are *The Lion and the Unicorn* and his "As I Please" column for *Tribune*. Once again, as the importance of *The Road to Wigan Pier* for building Orwell's Rebel reputation demonstrated, we see that an apparently minor work can heavily influence the shaping of an author's public image.

In *The Lion and the Unicorn* and his minor journalism of this time, Orwell assumes his self-appointed role of "The People's Tribune." He makes his opinions about "the common man" clear, framing "the intellectuals" and "common people" in almost diametrically opposed terms. The common man is "English," democratic, and commonsensical; the intellectual is "Europeanized," exhibits totalitarian habits of mind, and traffics in idiotic abstractions and conspiracy theories. The common man is ready to rush to England's defense against Hitler, the intellectual is frequently pacifist or anti-war. What Orwell hated most about the intelligentsia was their lack of patriotism and what he saw as their power-worship of Hitler and Stalin. "The really important fact about so many of the English intelligentsia," Orwell wrote in *The Lion and the Unicorn,* is "their severance from the common culture of the country. . . . In the general patriotism . . . they form an island of dissident thought. England is perhaps the only great nation whose intellectuals are ashamed of their country." Remarking in *Tribune* on the left-wing rumor that America had entered the war to crush a budding English socialist revolution, Orwell wrote in exasperation: "One has to belong to the intelligentsia to believe something like that. No ordinary man could be such a fool." One notices here how Orwell's anti-intellectualism, a characteristically English bias, gets explicitly tied to his version of "Englishness"—and how both of these work in tandem to distance him from the Left intelligentsia and *unite* him with "the people."[13]

And yet by half-conscious habit or shrewd design, Orwell presents this overgeneralized either/or as if it is the handiwork of "the intellectuals." The "cultural unity" of the English is primarily a matter of a shared, bedrock faith in "the idea of freedom and equality," Orwell says, which "the intellectuals" do not share. It is this loose, impressionistic criterion of "Englishness"— rooted in Orwell's justifiable contempt for some of the Left intellectuals of his generation—which serves as the basis for his woolly, expansive definition of "the common man." And Orwell recognized as much, and seems to have

considered this breadth a positive factor—a way to unify "England" (and perhaps cordon off "the intellectuals"). "People of very different types can be described as 'common' " when a nation's identity rests on the foundation of liberal belief, wrote Orwell in his essay on Dickens.[14]

The image of The People's Tribune suggests more fully how the interaction of the Rebel and Common Man images has facilitated the broadening of Orwell's reputation. By linking the call for "revolution" with "Englishness," "patriotism," and "decency," Orwell's rebellious fury—calculatedly or not— was successfully draped in the conventional pieties. We may note here how iconoclastic notions get clothed in traditional categories and thereby become acceptable or even right-minded thinking. This indicates another dimension of the rhetoric of reception: how the new is legitimated by way of the familiar. Thus Orwell's radicalism is legitimated via so-called conservative or moral categories. Orwell always advanced the political claims for socialism in ethical terms that all Englishmen could sanction ("justice," "liberty," "honesty," "decency," "fair play"). While his rhetoric was often criticized as soft-headed by fellow socialists, it doubtless contributed to the ultimate judgment (demonstrated in the 1945 Labour Party victory) that "fair-minded, decent sorts" who believed in "England" should favor some form of socialism. This willingness to make political claims on society by way of moral claims led Richard Rees to conclude that Orwell was not a political writer at all, but a "metapolitical" writer for whom politics was "the education of the human soul."[15]

With the 1940 publication of three essays of culture criticism, *Inside the Whale*, another related image of Orwell developed alongside The People's Tribune. This was, as it were, its literary version, for the man who speaks for the people must speak their language. Here Orwell's Common Man myth underwent its crucial modification: If it was not ultimately possible for a lower-upper-middle-class Etonian to surmount the class barrier and live as a "common man," it was at least possible to *write* common prose. If one could never truly become a "worker," one could nevertheless aspire to and master the plain style. One could write to and for the common *reader*—the non-university, public library reader of the lower-middle class.

Unlike the earlier images, the aspects of this literary image—the common-sense critic, the plain stylist, the critic of popular culture—derived chiefly from Orwell's literary criticism rather than as a response to Orwell's pamphleteering or to the man himself. And like "pragmatist," "quintessential Englishman," and "patriotic," "common sense," "plainness," and "populist" have become oft-quoted secondary watchwords in Orwell's history of reputation. The style and content of the essays in *Inside the Whale* promoted all of these images and associations. In "Boys' Weeklies," Orwell discussed boys' twopenny papers; in his Dickens essay he directly identified himself with Dickens, who did not cut himself off from everyday life but was "a popular novelist and able to write about ordinary people"—much like George Orwell, as reviewers noted. And in his title essay on Henry Miller,

Orwell lauded Miller for showing how "the man in the street" speaks and behaves.

The innovative treatment of popular culture, the fresh appreciation of Dickens, and the qualified praise of Miller marked Orwell as being quite different from most Left critics. His common-man style and persona were widely and favorably noted. Wrote V.S. Pritchett in *The New Statesman*: "His style is the English of the common man, cured of the common man's stutter and addressed to him."[16]

High praise also came from unexpected quarters. In the first general assessment of Orwell's *oeuvre*, Q.D. Leavis in *Scrutiny* praised Orwell's values, his straightforward thinking, and his blunt style. "Innately decent (he displays and approves of bourgeois morality)," she said, "he is disgusted with the callous theorising inhumanity of the pro-marxists." Perhaps unaware that Orwell's spleen for intellectuals extended to the "game of back-scratching . . . between tiny cliques of highbrows" at *Scrutiny,* Mrs. Leavis applauded Orwell's attacks on the Left intelligentsia. Orwell wrote from experience, she said approvingly, and "because what he knows is live information, not card-index rubbish, his knowledge functions." Her emphasis on Orwell's common sense, plain style, and "outsider" position in London linked features of what we have identified as characteristic of Orwell the Rebel and Common Man. She noted that Orwell belonged "by birth and education" to "the right Left people," yet that he seemed to stand apart from them. Orwell had "emancipated himself . . . by force of a remarkable character" from the Left intelligentsia and "sees them accordingly from the outside." Mrs. Leavis' observations were acute. And perhaps semi-autobiographical; no doubt she saw her own (and her husband's) position in the academy in a similar light. Despite their political and cultural differences, Mrs. Leavis felt an affinity with Orwell as a rebel against literary-political orthodoxy. She liked what she saw in Orwell, and much of what she chose to see was a refraction of herself.[17]

Mrs. Leavis' response represents an early instance in Orwell's reception history of a critic casting Orwell in her own image. Of course, she is not, unlike later critics, taking Orwell as a model; rather she is addressing her own concerns, and seeing in Orwell what she chooses to see. Uninterested either in popular culture or sociological criticism, Mrs. Leavis did not even mention "Boys' Weeklies" and admitted that "a lot of" the essay on Dickens was "beside the point from *Scrutiny*'s point of view." She respected Orwell's "special kind of honesty," which by implication the Leavises shared; the Leavises and Orwell also met on the broad ground of hostility to Marxist aesthetics. She had little time for Orwell's "dreadful" novels, and some critics have speculated that her essay directly influenced Orwell to abandon the realistic novel after *Coming Up for Air*. If so, her review illustrates the power of criticism to reshape an author's self-image, which then in turn affects his self-presentation and subsequent public image. Fond of the imperial "we" like her husband, Mrs. Leavis allowed that, although Orwell was certainly no "artist," "if the revolution were to hap-

pen that he wants . . . , he would be the only man of letters we can imagine surviving the flood undisturbed."[18]

## III

By the mid-1940s, Orwell's common man persona had been widely accepted by the critics. And, as we saw when discussing the formation of Orwell's Rebel face, once solidly formed, a face tends to add secondary features and yet retain its established shape. With the publication of *Animal Farm* (1945), which brought Orwell to the attention of a vast new audience and established him as a "popular" serious writer, and *Critical Essays* (1946), which showed him at his best as a literary essayist, the dual profile of The Common Man as The People's Tribune and as the plain stylist and common-sense critic began to be known by the literate public.

This latter image of Orwell as a writer—the plain stylist and common-sense critic—has remained essentially unchanged to this day. But in the early '50s, the former image, pertaining chiefly to Orwell's life, became conflated with the new face of The Saint, brought to prominence by Pritchett's obituary. The inflated treatment of the Common Man face during the decade indicates how, if not in life then finally afterwards, an author inevitably loses control of even a carefully crafted image.

The new incarnation of The Common Man was Stephen Spender's "extra-ordinary ordinary man" which we have already seen in Trilling's 1952 introduction to *Homage to Catalonia*. "Ordinary" now became a radiant watchword in discussions about Orwell, orbited by "decency," "common sense," "Englishness," "patriotism." It is this image that has had such enormous appeal for readers of Orwell. The implied message behind the image is that what Orwell did was nothing extraordinary; any ordinary man could have done what he did. His achievement, one could believe, was a matter of will, of dedication to an ideal—his "Englishness" could be one's own too, for unlike English rebels from Milton to Lawrence, he was no genius and no mystic or proselyte. Or at least, in Spender's view, no impossibly unattainable paragon of virtue. To be an intellectual rebel or a saint is beyond almost all of us. But to be a common man? The life he led, we could too. Or at least "we intellectuals." Unlike most intellectuals, declared Spender—anticipating Trilling—Orwell rejected that intellectualist orientation which all too often encloses one within a system of ideas and blinds one to ordinary feelings. Spender's Orwell was an intellectual who had stayed in touch with common humanity—and "we" could too.

This inspirational message was the undercurrent of Spender's revaluation of *Homage to Catalonia* in the Orwell memorial issue of the *World Review* (June 1950). Even before Trilling, then, Spender set the main outlines of this image. Emerging just months after Orwell's death and in the memoir of a friend, the image which Spender presented included praise of the writer but emphasized the man. Spender's review—indeed the entire *World Review*

issue—is another radiant moment in Orwell's reputation-history which helped launch his reputation and has been repeatedly quoted.

Spender's essay was comparable in its effect on Orwell's reputation in Britain to what Trilling's essay would soon achieve in America: it decisively boosted the critical estimate of *Homage to Catalonia* and Orwell's overall reputation.[19] To Trilling, Orwell was a "man of truth"; to Spender, Orwell was "an example of 'the lived truth'," of "the sacredness of truth [in] an individual life." As in Trilling's case, much of the impact of Spender's essay derived from his personal authority as a man of letters. Moreover, although here an early target of Orwell's "pansy Left" salvoes, Spender had become a friend of Orwell in the 1940s. The essay collected all of the features we have already associated with Common Man Orwell—decency, Englishness, ordinariness— and linked them with integrity, authenticity, humility, sanctity. These last features are highlighted by allusions to historical-mythic figures like Christ and Candide. One notices here how Spender's tribute to Orwell as "an Innocent" like Candide inevitably effaces another aspect of Orwell's Common Man reputation—the pragmatist. In this Spender was reflecting his own political odyssey toward Orwell's anti-Stalinism—and perhaps also his nostalgia. The university graduate who toyed with Communism in the late 1930s was soon to be the anti-Communist contributor to *The God That Failed* and editor of *Encounter*. Spender saw Orwell as a version of the ideal to which he once aspired—"really classless, really a socialist," the man whom young Spender himself once pretended to be and never was. Even as he claimed to deny Orwell sainthood, Spender proceeded to sanctify him.

> George Orwell was not a saint—although he was one of the most virtuous men of his day—and he was not a hero—although he was a man of outstanding courage. He was an Innocent, a kind of English Candide of the twentieth century. The Innocent is ordinary because he accepts the values of ordinary human decency; he is not a mystic, nor a poet. Ordinary, and yet extraordinary, because his faith in qualities of truth and decency drives like a drill through the façade of his generation. He is a drill made of steel driving through ordinary things. He happens to believe that two and two are four; and that what happens, happens. The consequences of *really* believing this are shattering. Christ was brought up as a carpenter in a carpenter's shop.
>
> Orwell was *really* what hundred of others only pretended to be. He was really classless, really a Socialist, really truthful. . . . He was what he was out of good faith and honesty, not out of neurosis or ecstasy or a sense of mystery.[20]

We have noted that most reputations are difficult to trace into the popular sphere of reception. Spender's image—like Pritchett's and Koestler's of The Rebel—is an exception, because a few years later Spender himself was discussing Orwell in near-identical terms on BBC radio. "The qualities of truth which showed in his writing he also practiced in his life," Spender said. "He

judged everything, every movement, every chord, by the standard of what it ought to be in terms of living."[21]

## IV

The facial history of each Orwell portrait should be seen as a gleaming palimpsest which, given changing reader responses, alters and accumulates new meanings even as old associations persist. This description pertains in particular to the profile of Common Man Orwell, which underwent one more major transformation in Britain in the next decade. Much as happened with The Rebel during this period, the "extraordinary ordinary man" image of Orwell inflated to symbolic dimensions and then split in two directions. Unlike the case of The Rebel, however, the second of these images was hostile, an inversion of Spender's image.

The first image was perhaps a natural culmination of Spender's rhetoric. "Orwell" got blown up into a national archetype, "the decent man." Martin Green, a young expatriate academic living in America, argued in a 1959 essay (reprinted in *A Mirror for Anglo-Saxons,* 1961) that this image, which Orwell represented, should be a new ideal—not only for British intellectuals but for all Britons. Quoting Trilling's observation of Orwell as a "figure in our lives," Green urged the generation of British writers coming of age to self-consciously *make* Orwell a figure in their lives. His call points up the fact that public images are prescriptive as well as descriptive, that culture heroes are means of social direction and control as well as personal models.

Green argued that the psychological hold of the two old models in British life—the Victorian aristocratic ideal of the gentleman and the 1920s aesthetic ideal of the dandy—was fast eroding. The gentleman and dandy, Green thought, were unhealthy national types, promoting values associated with the elegant, the sensitive, the amoral, and the maladjusted. Orwell represented a new, more vital national model, associated with responsibility, order, fair play, physical courage, and respect for privacy. "It is only decent men like Orwell who can restore to these qualities their wholly natural glamour which is valid under the keenest scrutiny," said Green. "My contention is that Englishmen must accord these qualities and these men a primary place in their imaginative lives." Included with Orwell among "these men" were Lawrence, Leavis, and Amis—further indicating how notoriously vague the word "decent" could be and how broadly Green meant to define his "decent man." Green saw his task as polemical: his aim was to have intellectuals take men like Orwell as their heroes, much as the Angry Young Men had done, so as to make "the decent man" into "the dominant image" in British cultural life. Orwell was to be an upraised mirror image, through which young Englishmen could strive to refashion themselves.[22]

The second new image of Orwell the man was a negative archetype, undercutting Spender's image—and Orwell's own. The People's Tribune turned into a sort of anti-model, The Enemy of The People. Chiefly the

Ziggy as a prole: not even the Thought Police care.

Orwell as the People's Tribune? Or an Enemy of the People?

work of Marxist intellectuals, the image was nothing new. Since *The Road to Wigan Pier,* Marxist critics had been advancing a negative image of Common Man Orwell: Orwell the petit bourgeois. Until the 1950s, however, this image achieved little prominence; no Marxist critic got "inside" Orwell's developing Common Man image and became a *reputation-suppressor,* as did Victor Gollancz in his *Wigan Pier* foreword—which became the basis for the "traitorous rebel" image of the 1940s. Instead, most Marxist critics were reputation-suppressors speaking from far outside, in papers and journals with modest circulations. So Orwell's positive Common Man image went relatively uncontested. What changed in the 1950s was that the Marxists gained the opportunity to promote their anti-populist image of Orwell beyond Communist circles in wider critical and popular spheres of repute. The occasion for the broadened exposure of The Enemy of the People image was the controversy over the BBC-TV adaptation of *Nineteen Eighty-Four* in December 1954. Among other things, the furor illustrates how a single major event can suddenly extend an image into the public arena and lead to all kinds of misunderstandings once a reputation moves far beyond literary circles.

The British Communist Party (BCP) apparently promoted the image of Orwell as Enemy of the People both indirectly and directly. The BBC suspected the BCP of organizing a protest campaign of letters and phone calls against the program—many of which also attacked Orwell's "despair," "fatalism," and "sadism." An official response to the BBC accusation came from the highest echelons of the BCP when Vice-Chairman R. Palme Dutt, an old antagonist of Orwell, wrote two letters to *The Manchester Guardian* in January 1955. Dutt castigated the BBC telecast by way of deploring "the philosophy of Orwell" that "violence, lies and torture can enslave humanity." A graduate of Balliol, a socialist theoretician, a conscientious objector during World War II, and an ideologue who toed Moscow's line through every shift and turn, Dutt was precisely the sort of Oxbridge left-wing intellectual whom Orwell had detested. Dutt's first *Guardian* letter immediately triggered a flurry of letters supporting Orwell. His attacks on Orwell represented a last-gasp *cri de coeur* from the Communists of Orwell's generation. They sought to undercut his standing with the public at the moment his reputation was at its height, just as *Animal Farm* and *Nineteen Eighty-Four* were appearing on the screen.[23]

Since the 1950s both negative and positive images—the Enemy of the People and various versions of The People's Tribune—have competed to represent Common Man Orwell. Each section in Chapter Four is a facial history of "ordinariness" as a site of struggle. Throughout, "Orwell" remains the star around which the case studies revolve, conditioning their perspectives and imposing the bounds on their irregular historical orbits. Forms of the first, anti-populist image have appeared in diverse, though chiefly intellectual and left-wing, reception audiences, and are discussed in Sections 10,11,12. In Section 13 we return to a version of The People's Tribune, via Orwell's relation to popular culture.

## 10. "An Ex-Socialist": Raymond Williams and the British Marxists' Orwell

I

Coincident with the denunciation of Orwell by the BCP in official Communist organs as the cold war of words heated up was his rising status as a youth hero for left-of-center British writers coming of age in the 1950s. In this period Orwell became popular as an intellectual model for such Angry Young Men as Kingsley Amis, John Wain, and John Osborne. Ideological and generational attachments tugged uneasily at each other for young Marxist intellectuals, some of whom found Orwell appealing precisely because of official disapproval. This case study addresses how the tensions of such divided allegiances have manifested themselves in the ambivalent reception of Orwell by radical British intellectuals. The most significant member of this group was Raymond Williams (1921–88), and in this section we again approach Orwell as a figure through a single reception history, though here we follow the making and *dis*claiming of his reputation, the evolution of his disfiguration among British radicals. Their finished sketch of Orwell is a defaced portrait of The Common Man as socialist turncoat.

The impassioned, mercurial response to Orwell by Williams, the leading literary leftist and Marxist culture critic of his generation, exemplifies the Left's shifting relation to him since the mid-1950s. In this respect Williams was unlike George Woodcock, whose history of response to Orwell shows little variation and whose emigration to Canada began a gradual migration away from anarchism itself—and whose latter-day reception of Orwell therefore is more strictly personal than group-specific. Of course, "the Freedom Press writers" is a smaller, more easily defined group than "the British radical Left," and Williams had indeed been affiliated with subgroups within the Left, e.g., the group around the *New Left Review*. Nevertheless such differences in size and dynamics further illustrate the variability of groups; and given Williams' stature on "the far Left" between the late 1950s and 1980s, it is surely reasonable to speak of him as an authoritative radical voice, one who was regarded inside and outside Left circles as representative of radical intellectual opinion. His running history of response to Orwell may thus be read not just as a personal chronicle but as a sharply focused intellectual biography of the postwar English radical Left.

This reception history is codifiable into four stages. It moves from the young intellectual's admiration for Orwell, to the culture critic's qualified sympathy, to the New Left spokesman's "questioning respect"[24] combined with debunking efforts, to the elder Marxist theoretician's distanced stock-taking spiraling downward into disillusion and contempt. The trajectory is identifiable from the Orwell landmarks in Williams' work: the essay-review "George Orwell" (1955); the chapter on Orwell in *Culture and Society* (1958); the monograph *George Orwell* (1971); and finally, two more recent essays

(1974, 1984) plus the Orwell chapter in *Politics and Letters* (1979). Again unlike Woodcock's reception history, each of these stages of Williams' and the Marxist Left's response to Orwell is specifically shaped in reply to different sociohistorical events: the Cold War, the early "cultural" phase of the British New Left, the Vietnam War, and the pre-Gorbachev era of renewed East-West hostility. Each stage also reflects responses to different aspects of Orwell's work and reputation, and each discloses distinct versions of "Williams' Orwell."

## II

As the twenty-six-year-old co-editor of the Cambridge University journal *Politics and Letters,* Williams had some slight contact with Orwell. The editors published Orwell's "Writers and Leviathan" in 1948 and accepted "George Gissing," though the journal folded before the essay could appear. Williams' 1955 article in *Essays in Criticism* reflects his and the young Left's still strong and affectionate attachment to Orwell. The Orwell chapter in *Culture and Society* is obviously the same essay revised. The difference in the first two stages of Williams' response to Orwell can be seen by contrasting the first and last paragraphs of the two pieces:

> "It is not so much a series of books, it is more like a world." This is Orwell, on Dickens. "It is not so much a series of books, it is more like a hero." This, today, is Orwell himself. . . . We look elsewhere [than to bravery in war] for a different mode of virtue; we emphasize one of the alternative definitions of hero—"a clear-seeing, self-reliant, valiant man." Orwell is our most common illustration. (1955)

> "It is not so much a series of books, it is more like a world." This is Orwell, on Dickens. "It is not so much a series of books, it is more like a case." This, today, is Orwell himself. . . . It is not that he was an important thinker. . . . It is not that he was a great artist. . . . His interest lies almost wholly in his frankness. (1958)

> If . . . [Conservative Laurence Brander's *George Orwell*] introduces new readers to Orwell's work, it will have served a useful purpose. And it may be seen also as a kind of memorial to the man; to one who was kindly, brave, frank and good, and whom we should long remember. (1955)

> I maintain, against others who have criticized Orwell, that as a man he was brave, generous, frank and good, and that the paradox of his work is not to be understood solely in personal terms, but in terms of the pressures of a whole situation. . . . His conclusions have no kind of general validity, but the fact is . . . that good men are driven again and again into this kind of paradox. . . . We have to try to understand . . . how the instincts of humanity can break down under pressure into an inhuman paradox; how a great and humane tradition can seem at times . . . to disintegrate into a caustic dust. (1958)[25]

Williams' "hero" worth remembering in 1955 became his "case" worth "understanding" in 1958. His clear-sighted "hero as exile" became "the

good man" caught in an historical paradox. This second formulation was an extension of the radical Left strategy practiced by Gollancz, Kingsley Martin, and Herbert Matthews in earlier years: in *Culture and Society*, Williams lauded Orwell's character while delicately knocking his judgment, thus patronizing his work with faint praise as "frank" and well intentioned even as he dismissed it as naive and misguided.

No doubt Williams' change of attitude toward Orwell between the time of the essay and the *Culture and Society* chapter, first drafted in 1956,[26] had much to do with the events of that year: Khrushchev's "Secret Speech" in February denouncing Stalin, Moscow's brutal suppression of the Hungarian uprising in October, and Britain's mishandling of the Suez crisis that same month. After the BCP extended official support for the Soviet intervention in Hungary, eleven *Daily Worker* journalists quit, Party membership dropped one-third in 1957, and Young Communist League membership fell by 70 percent. Intellectual defectors included E.P. Thompson, Doris Lessing, Ronald Meek, Randall Swingler, and Christopher Hill.[27] Meanwhile, the Labour Party's initial acquiescence to and subsequent lame protest against Anthony Eden's Suez mission also made clear to independent radicals the hopelessness of reformist parliamentary politics and rendered Khrushchev's declaration of "peaceful co-existence" all the more unconscionable.

Amid this crisis of faith, the official BCP turned to attack the one socialist intellectual with a mass readership, the renegade whose work had seemed to set the stage for the stampede out of the Party. The 1954 BBC adaptation of *Nineteen Eighty-Four* had been followed by film adaptations of *Animal Farm* in 1955 and *Nineteen Eighty-Four* in early 1956: the anti-totalitarian catchwords of Orwell's work were familiar to millions. As we have seen, the BCP energetically, and with some success, promoted in 1955–56 an anti-populist image of Orwell as The Enemy of the People, whose "neurotic hatred" of "the people" led him to become a "mouthpiece" for "petit-bourgeois illusions and prejudices."[28]

It was this passage from the 1956 *Marxist Quarterly* which Williams quoted and criticized as "shallow, arrogant and crass" in the final paragraph of his Orwell chapter in *Culture and Society*. For the events of 1956 pulled Williams in opposite directions. A member of the BCP during his early undergraduate days at Cambridge (1939–41), Williams let his membership lapse on entering the army and did not rejoin the party on his return home in 1945.[29] Still, during the war and thereafter, his stance was identifiable as that of an independent-minded, anti-Stalinist, active fellow-traveler. The Orwell chapter in *Culture and Society* reflects the tension between Williams' official Communist reading of Orwell and his still-deep attraction to his heroic image of Orwell as a hater of orthodoxy and the intellectual's Common Man. Looking more critically and less admiringly at Orwell than in 1955, Williams felt torn in 1958 between affection for Orwell the man and distaste for Orwell "the propagandist." Now in his mid-30s and from a generation once-removed from Orwell's, Williams split "the man" and "the writer" as a way of preserving his attachment to Orwell. He sought in

*Culture and Society* a middle course between acceptance and condemnation of Orwell, striving instead to sympathetically "understand" Orwell's "situation." Orwell saw the working classes as "not yet conscious," Williams argued. "One day they will be so, and meanwhile [Orwell] keeps the truth alive."[30] Indeed Orwell's influence is directly reflected throughout *Culture and Society,* the book that launched Williams' own reputation, imprinted in its very aim and sensibility. Begun in 1948 and written in response to the high culture programs of T.S. Eliot (especially *Notes Toward the Definition of Culture,* 1948) and of his teacher F.R. Leavis,[31] *Culture and Society* was the first book-length effort to examine the concept of "culture" in support of populist and socialist aims. The book might be said to systematize Orwell's scattered remarks on culture in *Inside the Whale* and *Critical Essays* and to culminate with Orwell himself, the subject of the last chapter before the conclusion. Clearly the Orwell chapter, like Williams at this time, moved in two directions, reflecting both the Cold War preoccupation with Orwell's politics and the early New Left's interest in Orwell's culture criticism.

By the late 1950s, Williams and Richard Hoggart (*The Uses of Literacy,* 1957) had shifted Left attention away from *Animal Farm* and *Nineteen Eighty-Four* and toward Orwell's popular culture essays on boys' newspapers, crime thrillers, and penny postcards. A depoliticized "cultural" Orwell thus replaced the "ideological" Orwell of the Cold War in this second stage of postwar Left reception. During what became known as the "cultural" phase of the New Left (1957–62), Orwell seemed, Williams later wrote, the one intellectual from an older generation who had "tried to live and feel where the majority of English people were living and feeling, reporting, understanding, respecting, beyond the range of Establishment culture."[32]

The connection between Orwell and the emergence of the British New Left is tangled and indirect yet vital. A "central feature" of the movement's development, Williams has admitted, was "a complicated relationship with Orwell and with the climate that incorporated him."[33] The relationship was complicated partly because of the New Left's radical turn in the early 1960s and partly because of the complex relationship between Orwell and leading New Left thinkers like Williams, Hoggart, and E. P. Thompson. It was primarily through these three that Orwell exerted influence on the New Left's tone and agenda, particularly during the movement's cultural phase. Years later Williams summarized the picture which the young radical of the period held of Orwell, a portrait which suggests Williams' own enduring anxiety of influence:

> In the Britain of the Fifties, along every road that you moved, the figure of Orwell seemed to be waiting. If you tried to develop a new kind of popular culture analysis, there was Orwell; if you wanted to report on work or ordinary life, there was Orwell; if you engaged in any kind of socialist argument, there was an enormously inflated statue of Orwell warning you to go back. Down into the Sixties political editorials would regularly admonish younger radicals to read their Orwell and see where all that led to.[34]

Williams' casual use of the plural "you" resembles the imperial "we" of Trilling and Mrs. Leavis and reflected his confidence, at least by the '70s, about casting himself as a representative figure for his generation of radicals. But in fact the imagined warnings to reverse course echoed loudest in Williams' ears: Orwell straddled every road *he* wanted to move on. Williams says he disagreed with the young Left's inflated image of Orwell in the 1950s. Nevertheless he felt fascinated by it. He realized that his and Orwell's careers had crisscrossed even as their interests had dovetailed. Williams, son of a railway signalman, was the lower-class Welsh boy moving up into Cambridge circles and the "snooty" journals (as editor of the *Cambridge University Journal* and *Outlook*) which Orwell derided; Orwell was the lower-upper-middle-class Etonian plunging (temporarily) into the world of the tramps and miners. Both Williams and Orwell would spend much of their careers looking over their shoulders at the classes which they left.[35]

## III

By the time of the New Left's radical turn in 1962 and the escalation of the Vietnam War, many Left intellectuals had concluded that "reading their Orwell" had led to political passivity and resignation. More than any other work of the 1940s, contended E. P. Thompson in 1960, Orwell's essay "Inside the Whale" had turned a younger generation of radicals into disillusioned Jimmy Porters. Orwell had issued "an apology for quietism" by which "the aspirations of a generation were buried; not only was a political movement, which embodied much that was honorable buried, but so also was the notion of disinterested dedication to a cause." By praising as "honest" Henry Miller's politics of withdrawal, said Thompson, Orwell branded causes as "swindles" and made revolutionary idealism seem foolish—and willed passivity sophisticated, even necessary.[36]

Thompson's stance toward Orwell at this time was much harder than Williams' or Hoggart's. The differences among the three illustrate well how the variability of Orwell's reputation on the Left at the group level corresponded to a British radical's overall outlook in the early 1960s. Generally, the more "left" and "internationalist" his stance, the less enthusiasm a radical seems to have maintained for Orwell. Thompson, a BCP member until 1956 and the most politically oriented of the trio from the start, was the leading force in the Movement's activist turn and the most hostile to Orwell. Hoggart, who belonged to the "literary" and moderate wing of the New Left and was never a member of the BCP, remained chiefly interested in English cultural criticism during the decade and has continued to admire Orwell.[37] In the middle was Williams, who shared Hoggart's literary-cultural interests yet gradually found himself moving in the direction of Thompson's politics and disaffection with Orwell.

Thompson's indictment signaled a shift in Left attention back to Orwell's brand of socialism. Orwell the cultural commentator gave way to a re-politicized Orwell figure. But the concentration on various of Orwell's

works (not only *Animal Farm* and *Nineteen Eighty-Four* but also the documentaries and essays) made the radical Left's image of Orwell during this third period of reception (c. 1963–72) even more complicated and fragmented than during the Cold War. Many leftists wondered aloud: If Orwell were alive today, where would he stand on Vietnam? The contradictory answers further indicate the variety of critical locations from which even institutional readers similarly positioned "on the far Left" approach a figure. For many other factors besides political affiliation or ideological stance may bear on a reader's response; or, a reader may not approach the author "whole" but instead focus upon *parts* of his work and *project* them for the whole, thus constructing "his" or "her" Orwell.

This was the case with the Left's balkanization, or "Vietnamization," of Orwell between 1967–71, when the politics of Orwell's reputation became explicit and sometimes rancorous. New Left supporters on both sides of the Atlantic cited *Homage to Catalonia* as evidence for their view that Orwell was a revolutionary who had fought against fascism and would likewise have denounced American imperialism in Vietnam. To some of them, Orwell's "simplicity" and dissident anti-Stalinist politics were congenial as a 1930s version of Maoism. One British radical saw Orwell as "an early Che Guevara" who fought with the Loyalists in Spain precisely "because a new social order was their first priority." Another admirer similarly described him as "a guerrilla, with all the revolutionary implications of that word." "The real Orwell" was the Catalonia militiaman, he insisted, urging fellow leftists to "liberate Orwell from his present grotesque role of chief propagandist for shareholders and dividend drawers everywhere." Some Movement heroes agreed. On a 1970 BBC-TV program, *The Road to the Left*, Noam Chomsky exalted Orwell as "unique, unfortunately" and argued that *Homage to Catalonia* defended "popular revolution." Chomsky's Orwell took "the side of the common man . . . against many kinds of repressive powers. . . . And the idea that his writings should be used for anti-Communist ideology would have been horrifying to him. At least I find it horrifying."[38]

Other radicals did too, though many of them blamed Orwell himself. His career was no exemplary "road to the Left" for Mary McCarthy or Tom Nairn. To D. A. N. Jones, Orwell was no "conscience of the Left" but "a bloody-minded nagger, a Mrs. Gummidge." Echoing Thompson, Jones concluded, "If you took Orwell's advice, you'd end up doing nothing."[39]

Williams, characteristically, took a middle course in *George Orwell* between both these views. In effect he constructed an admirable "young" Orwell, the tramp and Catalonia militiaman, and a disillusioned "mature" Orwell of *Animal Farm* and *Nineteen Eighty-Four*. Though apparently unaware of the parallel, Williams thus split Orwell much as German anti-Stalinist socialists in the 1930s had divided Marx into the "good" "young" humanist of the 1844 Paris Manuscripts and the "bad" "old" violent revolutionary and materialist of the *Communist Manifesto* and *Capital*.[40] Williams depicted an admirable young Orwell going among the tramps, writing bitter anti-bourgeois novels, reporting on the miners, and finally becoming in

Spain a "revolutionary," a "militant socialist," "what would now, from the outside, be called an 'ultra.' " But Orwell's maudlin myth of England as a "family" and his Trotskyist notion of a People's Revolution won via wartime social transformations perverted his thinking during the early 1940s, said Williams. These illusions gave rise to a "stale revolutionary romanticism" and then to reaction and "despair" when the expected revolution failed to occur. The "older" Orwell of *Animal Farm* and *Nineteen Eighty-Four* thus became, Williams agreed with Thompson, the fatalistic archetype for their generation: "We can write Berlin, Algiers, Aden, Watts, Prague in the margins of Orwell's passivity. . . . What in Orwell was a last, desperate throw became for many others, absurdly, a way of life."[41]

Williams' new, hard stance toward Orwell came with his support for the shift within the British New Left from culture criticism to radical politics. And in the factional infighting which finally issued forth in this shift we can see how Williams' reception during this period both reflected his complex group affiliations and influenced the groups he represented. Born out of a marriage between the *Universities and Left Review* and the *New Reasoner,* the early *New Left Review,* of which Williams was an editor, consisted of two factions separated generationally and ideologically: the Oxford-based *ULR,* composed of searching young university graduates; and the *New Reasoner,* edited by former BCP members (like co-editor Thompson) outraged about Stalin's crimes and the Soviets' invasion of Hungary. Williams belonged by age to the *New Reasoner* group, yet he favored less their preoccupation with Cold War debates and the international Marxist tradition and more the *ULR* postgraduates' attention to popular culture, English socialism, and the contemporary British scene. "The younger generation . . . on the whole had my interests," Williams later recalled, "and yet the older generation had really much more my experience and style."[42]

Experience and style won out in Williams and in the Movement. The New Left adopted Thompson's activism, and Williams in turn gradually adopted a version of Thompson's position on Orwell. As Thompson became a new, if much less exalted, intellectual model for Williams, Orwell gradually became Williams' anti-model. Equally significant, Williams himself by 1971 had become a model for younger radicals; and one can observe in the tensions of his response to Orwell hereafter a subtle feature of the dynamics of the reputation process: how the audience which the authoritative voice represents not only influences him and is influenced by him in more obvious senses, but how he may also begin to shape his message and identity in accord with what he believes his constituency wants him to say. In a very real sense he can become captive to his followers, for the model is drawn to scrutinize their responses to him, and the more he watches their responses, the more likely he in turn begins to model himself on them—or to feel paralyzed, the victim of his own fame. We saw how Trilling suffered from precisely this quandary as an intellectual figure in the New York of the 1950s, and how Orwell appealed to him partly as a way out of the dilemma posed by his own exalted reputation. Sartre and Camus, in different ways,

are perhaps even better examples of the misfortune of the intellectual who is hoisted upon the petard of his own virtue—and then, having been exalted as a public "conscience" and "voice," feels himself at the mercy of this outsized image. For it is in his followers that the model begins to see an attractively enlarged image of himself—which may or may not coincide with his self-image, yet which by his behavior he may reduce or expand further; and often he will feel compelled to seek his followers' approval as a way of affirming himself to himself. Orwell's early death meant that he largely avoided the problem of living out his role as model; he became an "inflated statue" posthumously. Williams, as we shall soon see, had to deal—if perhaps to a lesser extent than Sartre, Camus, or even Trilling—with this aspect of figure status by the mid-1970s.

## IV

By the close of Williams' 1971 monograph, Orwell's individuality has evaporated in Williams' ideological categories. Orwell the India-born "exile," public school boy from a "lost class," and Burma policeman embraces the "illusion" that "capitalist democracy" was becoming "social democracy" during the war and inevitably slips into a period of "radical pessimism" after it. *Animal Farm* and *Nineteen Eighty-Four* constitute an "overadjustment" to capitalism's wartime "contradictions."[43] The overadjustment, however, seems more like Williams' own. *Culture and Society* sought to "understand" Orwell's historical "situation"; the monograph makes Orwell's historical situation and social structure the determinants of his work. And so the "paradox" motif of 1958 becomes the thesis of 1971. Paradox and contradiction are "paramount" in Orwell's history; the Marxist categories leave us here, with Orwell himself a vexing "paradox." Williams, however, stopped short of drawing the conclusion to which his own analysis had driven him: that ideology cannot provide a total explanation of Orwell, no more than it could, say, for "working-class," "Cambridge-educated" "Professor" Raymond Williams. The fact is that "Eric Blair" and "George Orwell" transcend ideological categories; the individual residue—that which finally made *this* India-born Etonian and policeman into "Orwell"—remains. Williams' closing words to the New Left generation sound like an agonized reminder to himself, as if he were struggling to achieve some critical distance and break, finally, the old attachment to his heroic Orwell:

> The thing to do with his work, his history, is to read it, not imitate it. . . .
> We are acknowledging a presence and a distance: other names, other
> years; a history to respect, to remember, to move on from.[44]

Williams' attempts to disengage himself from Orwell were obviously part of a longer and even more traumatic process of dissociating himself from the Labour Party and "pragmatic" leftism altogether, a lengthy divorce whose "final break" took place in 1966, when his "long-looked-for" Labour Party parliamentary majority turned Britain not toward socialism or social

democracy but "into an actual and necessary agency of the mutation of capitalism by the representative incorporation of the working class."[45] The turgid language reflected Williams' turn not only toward New Left activism but toward Marxist theory in response to this disappointment; both his new politics and sensibility were reflected in the 1967 *May Day Manifesto* and its revised version of 1968, most of which he wrote, which severely criticized Harold Wilson's Labour government and expressed solidarity with the student rebellions in Paris and America.

What had especially attracted Williams and the early New Left to Orwell was their joint commitment to a moral critique of society, their interest in "the ordinary man," and their disavowal of "Establishment" politics. Like Orwell, the pre-radicalized New Left offered no systematic criticism of class or culture and no analysis of social structure. By the early '70s, Williams came to see this as a deficiency in his own work and in Orwell's. Calling himself a "Marxist" and a "cultural materialist," Williams found himself, as he moved further away from Orwell, moving further left and further toward the ideas of some European Marxists. For example, Williams' concepts of "structures of feeling" and of "dominant," "residual," and "emergent" cultures were derived from the work of Gramsci on hegemony, Lukács and Goldmann on reification, and Sebastiano Timpanaro on surplus consciousness.[46]

Given these turns toward radicalism and Marxist theory in the mid-'60s, it is unsurprising that Williams' estrangement from Orwell finally erupted into open hostility in the late '70s. In this fourth stage of reception, which was also reflected in the increasingly hostile attitude of the *New Left Review* toward Orwell, Williams concluded that what had originally drawn him to the heroic Common Man Orwell—his sense of Orwell's plainness, decency, and honesty—was a sham. Orwell's style was widely "received as wisdom, achievement, and maturity," Williams said in his Orwell interview in *Politics and Letters*, obliquely referring to his own response, "although it was false to the core." Williams felt duped; Orwell's deceit, rather than the exaggeratedly heroic image of Orwell projected by his younger self, was to blame. Prodded throughout the interview by the editors of the *New Left Review*, Williams admitted that Orwell's "impression of consistent decency and honesty" was "an invention." *Animal Farm* and *Nineteen Eighty-Four* could only have been written by "an ex-socialist." Because of his new awareness of Orwell's false plain-man persona and "defeatism," Williams said, he could not even affirm his reserved judgment of 1971. *George Orwell* had been "the last stage of working through a sense of questioning respect" for Orwell and now "a very much harder assessment" was due. But even this task seemed overburdening. "I am bound to say, I cannot read him now. . . ."[47]

This pronouncement brings us full circle to the BCP verdict on Orwell from the 1930s and '40s. For the exasperated scorn toward Orwell expressed by Williams the elder Marxist intellectual echoed the derision voiced toward him by his Marxist contemporaries during his lifetime. Williams' "questioning respect" in his 1971 monograph slid in the later essays into outright rejection; his careful slighting gave way to resigned dismissal. Thus Williams'

erstwhile "hero" became a historical "case" and then "paradox," and finally—
as Orwell seemed to BCP chiefs Harry Pollitt and R. Palme Dutt—a capitalist
accommodator. Though the sociopolitical factors conditioning Orwell's reputation on the far Left in the 1930s and '80s differ, the central features and
final shape of the two Enemy of The People images are remarkably similar.
Williams' attitude toward Orwell resembled A.L. Rowse's, an exact contemporary of Orwell's who has been condemning Orwell's "deformation of the
spirit of man" for four decades.

In 1984 Williams reissued his 1971 monograph, adding a closing chapter originally published in *Marxism Today*, "*Nineteen Eighty-Four* in 1984."
Persisting in his tendentious reading of the novel as literal historical prophecy, Williams castigated Orwell's "totalitarian" tactics of warning against
totalitarianism. "In the very absoluteness of the fiction," Orwell "committed
himself to [the] submissive belief" of the historical inevitability of socialism's
triumph. Orwell's salutary caution that "the world could be going the way"
of Hitler and Stalin transformed itself, argued Williams, into an "imaginative submission to power and privilege." Like Isaac Deutscher exactly thirty
years earlier, Williams concluded that Orwell's warning in *Nineteen Eighty-
Four* defeats itself. But whereas Deutscher attributed the defeat to Orwell's
"boundless despair," Williams went one step further and judged that Orwell's warning failed because Orwell himself had ironically become the very
victim he had so warned against: a pessimistic power-worshiper like James
Burnham who could only imagine that "present trends" would continue.[48]

## V

Although Williams' changing relationship to Orwell may strike one as very
nearly a personal obsession, it is of much more than merely private significance. It is characteristic of the ambivalence felt toward Orwell by many
British leftists, among whom Williams' stature has been undeniable.[49] Some
observers have even compared Williams' respected position among young
leftists in the 1970s and '80s with Orwell's cult status in the 1950s.[50] When
dismantling old statues, one often finds it useful to save the pedestals.*

Williams himself certainly never drew such a comparison. Nevertheless,
he struggled for three decades both to cast himself as Orwell's successor and
to withdraw from Orwell's shadow. Increasingly in the last decade Williams
pleased younger radicals by criticizing Orwell for what they had previously
argued was deficient in Williams' own work. *Politics and Letters* as self-
commentary was nothing less than a comprehensive joint attempt by Williams and the *New Left Review* editors to recast Williams' intellectual history
in line with radical postwar New Left ideology. To efface may be to escape: by renouncing his youthful empiricism in exchange for ideology and
social theory, his inherited Welshness and acquired Englishness for Euro-

---

*As, apparently, does Thompson, the 1980 recipient of *New Society*'s George Orwell Memorial
Prize.[51]

peanness, and his young man's Bevanite socialism for New Left Marxism, Williams might get out from under Orwell's ever-lengthening shadow. And so the interview subject of the 1979 *Politics and Letters* struggled to efface the youthful editor of the 1948 *Politics and Letters*—to abolish, as it were, the Orwell in himself. In these last, strenuous efforts to (in Williams' phrase) "work through"[52] Orwell—apparently to exorcise the demon—Williams embraced the generational iconoclasm of the New Left and applied it first and foremost to Orwell, the only individual accorded a separate chapter and treated negatively in *Politics and Letters*.

It is in the context of Williams' own history, then, that his conclusion in *George Orwell* gains special significance. Williams argued there that the main "key" to "the paradox of Orwell" was "the problem of identity."[53] This is clearly the problem which intrigued Williams himself about Orwell; he saw it as a "class" problem, the "India-born" Blair being reared to a life which he felt compelled to renounce. But the problem of identity, as it relates to Orwell, was also acutely Williams' own: how not merely "to imitate" but "to move on" from Orwell. And here one notices the deeper resemblances in the two men's histories: their pained renunciations of parts of themselves, their thoroughgoing explorations of their origins, their rewriting of their pasts as a way of redefining their social and professional selves. Orwell's "transformation" has been much discussed, but Williams', if less conspicuous and from a different starting point, was nevertheless comparable. For just as Orwell dropped "Eric Blair" to become the writer and democratic socialist "Orwell," Williams dropped his childhood nickname "Jim" at Cambridge to become "Raymond" the left Leavisite, and then moved steadily left in the 1960s and '70s—further away from "Jim."[54]

The identity "problem," then, is one of filiation and affiliation, and inasmuch as it is a class problem, it is the general problem of leaving one's class to become an "intellectual"—a person of no determinate class affiliation, who may identify with an elite, or with the workers, or with "the intellectuals" as a separate class. And in Williams' case, the problem was even more specific: the problem of how to find solidarity with "the common man"—i.e., how to be a socialist intellectual, invariably torn between political quietism and activism, between "feeling useless" and committing *la trahison des clercs*, between *embourgeoisement* and radicalization. In this broad sense, however different the form in which each manifested itself, the problem was not only Williams' but also Trilling's and Woodcock's—and yes, Orwell's "problem" too. But for Orwell (and later Woodcock) the tensions were mitigated. Orwell remained a "guerrilla on the flank of a regular army," never more than an outsider to any particular literary-political group—and so therefore able to take an idiosyncratic course, forging his own identity apart from the pressures of institutional elites and radical orthodoxies. On two counts, then, the problem of reconciling the intellectual life with political activism was especially severe for Williams. For not only did he belong to the radical Left during the 1950s and '60s; he also became an academic intellectual during the early days of the New Left,

affiliating with the elite of the elite, Cambridge University. Yet Williams' problem of "moving on" was not merely one of class but also generation—the more important issue in his case. Even Williams' fiction bore the mark of his self-conscious relation to Orwell's generation (e.g., *Second Generation*). Despite his embrace of radical politics and Marxist theory, Williams' ambivalent reception of Orwell—indeed, perhaps Williams' entire corpus—testifies to the personal truth of his observation in 1960, written when he was torn between Orwell's way and Thompson's—that generation, not class, constituted "the essential factor in any reading of contemporary British opinion."[55] Orwell, the untainted model socialist from the older generation whom the young Williams and Left needed in the '50s, served, a decade later, as the blameworthy elder on whom a radicalized Williams and New Left could lay the dashed dreams of their generations.

So Williams "moved on from" Orwell, but to—where? To become "the Orwell of our generation," in the phrase of Martin Green, a Cambridge contemporary.[56] In the end, Williams was unable merely to "acknowledge" Orwell as "a presence and a distance": the proximity remained too close, the radiance too bright. And perhaps even blinding; for given Williams' history of response to Orwell, one comment in *Politics and Letters* leaps out as especially ironic: "A pathetic aspect of the literary world of the fifties and early sixties . . . was the imaginary competition to be the heirs of Orwell in the next generation."[57] If Williams became a figure for the contemporary Left, Orwell nevertheless remained a figure for Williams. Williams' model of the '50s became his anti-model—and rival—of the '80s. Imitation, confrontation, condemnation—all provoked only renewed comparison, another round of imaginary competition. "The figure of Orwell" remained still there, tangibly, waiting at the end of the road, ever waiting.

In Williams' attempt to find a road around Orwell is reflected the entire postwar Left's frustrated struggle to forge a program and vision beyond the first Labour government under Attlee: the achievements and large personalities of the 1940s still tower before socialists of the 1980s as a standard and judgment. Orwell, the young Left's intellectual model in the 1950s, is now often perceived as its obstacle and foe. And, for some, one suspects that Orwell as Enemy of The People became a personal enemy. For by dislodging Orwell, Williams could clear space for himself—and for his own reputation—and so "move on" in more than one sense. His history of response to Orwell was reception as anguish and displacement; it illustrates what happens when a reader tries to salvage a hero who has become increasingly objectionable. First Williams took Orwell whole, seeing his weaknesses as the price of his strengths, then he carved him up to minimize the "late" Orwell of *Animal Farm* and *Nineteen Eighty-Four*, but finally he judged him "false to the core" and rejected him as unbearable. Thus does the inspiration of the heroic become the anxiety of influence. Unlike Woodcock, Williams eventually found Orwell a confining rather than a liberating presence; he felt the need to break *from* Orwell in charting his own road to the

Left, not break with and through him to his new political identity. Nor was Williams' break clean and gradual like Woodcock's; it was jagged, convulsive, and obviously painful.

Just as in the 1940s and 1960s, then, so too in the last decade: the more fiercely the Left has insisted on a radical orthodoxy, the less patience and sympathy it has had with Orwell.[58] Indeed, in recent years, for young and old radicals alike, lining up to revile Orwell has functioned as a ritual of solidarity and norm-making. Much as Thompson argued in 1960 before his disillusionment with the New Left's politics, some present-day radicals treat Orwell as a scapegoat for the failure of Left politics. The "political arguments" for the tepid, moderate Labourism of the 1950s and '60s "can be traced to Orwell's essays," Williams concluded in *Politics and Letters,* adding that *Nineteen Eighty-Four* "seem[s] to introduce a period of really decadent bourgeois writing."[59] And it likewise "seems," one should add, that this revised image of Orwell— along with the exaggeration of Orwell's impact on the Gaitskell Labourites— "can be traced" to Williams' uneasy accommodation to an ideology he reluctantly and only relatively lately grafted onto his own history. Much like Sartre with the young French Communists, Williams acquiesced to, more than led, the Left—as if in return for its fealty. One result was that Williams' and the young Left's balanced, if critical, portrait of Orwell in the late 1950s gave way to statue-bashing in the 1970s and '80s. Or as one *New Statesman* writer summed up the feeling: "Orwell is, in a sense, in the way."[60]

More than a decade ago, Williams wrote that Orwell's influence on the British Left was "diminishing" and would continue to do so.[61] The countdown to 1984 proved Williams' forecast premature; but he may turn out to be right in the long run, as Orwell's literary contemporaries die and as *Nineteen Eighty-Four* comes to be viewed more as an historical document than a doomsday book or political prophecy. Nevertheless, that events since the late 1970s have temporarily invalidated Williams' prediction is not only attributable to the media hoopla over Orwell during the 1984 countdown. It is also partly due to the repeated, agonizing, backward glances ("there was Orwell") by Williams and others of his generation.

## 11. "Enemy of Mankind?": The Soviet Union's Orwell

### I

The portraits in the Orwell gallery come in different sizes. Some reception scenes are cameos, featuring Orwell's life and his circles of acquaintances; others, like the Woodcock and Williams case studies, examine Orwell from a greater distance and depict wider scenes, like the British anarchist and Marxist traditions. Still others, like the present section, are giant murals, in which Orwell's reception history is set against the massive landscape of a nation's cultural and political history.

The "Soviet Union's Orwell" might be said at first glance to be "all politics, no letters." But on closer examination the Soviet portrait of The

Common Man begins, as we shall see, where Williams' ended and ends where Williams' began, i.e., the Stalin-era Enemy of mankind turns into Comrade Orwell in the 1980s.

Needless to say, however, Orwell "the man" has never been in any sense a radiant presence to Soviet writers and critics (unlike, say, Gorky) and they display nothing of the personal ambivalence of Williams and other Anglo-American radicals in their shifts of attitude toward him. To Soviet critics, Orwell has been only a rhetorical peg on which to hang well-worn ideological laundry, never a figure. In large part because of the susceptibility of his catchwords to abuse as propaganda, references to Orwell in the Communist world have appeared chiefly in the popular press, rather than in the literary journals; unsurprisingly, "Orwell" and "1984" have been treated more as topical political issues than as strictly literary or historical ones. A major difference between the treatments of Orwell by the British Marxists and the Soviet literary journalists is that, for the latter, Orwell has been essentially a one-book writer. For reasons of cultural distance and ideological politics, the Soviet response to Orwell has focused, almost exclusively, on *Nineteen Eighty-Four*. The prevailing Soviet image of him has thus been a caricature, consisting of a few broad strokes, rather than a detailed portrait.

In tracing the image of Orwell promoted by a state-controlled press, this case study affords the opportunity to examine his reputation not merely at the level of the reception group but at a national level. Heretofore we have stressed that the ideology of repute promotes the false view that reputations are homogenous; instead we have noted the pluralistic range of opinion which usually appears within institutional audiences according to observers' critical locations. Even within the Anglo-American radical Left, therefore, various prominent Marxists—often representing the opposing "official" and "unorthodox" wings of Marxist opinion—have presented sharply different images of Orwell, with some of them castigating him as a villain and others exalting him as a hero. No such diversity exists in the Soviet Union's historical reception of Orwell. The qualifying theoretical point here, then, is that the Soviet national reception of Orwell does not reflect a variety of contending voices—unlike "Germany's Orwell."* The *only* Soviet public image has been a monolithic "official" image. Still, though uniformly structured at each point in time, the "Soviet Union's Orwell" is not a fixed, unchanging image. A few elements of the militantly hostile criticism of Orwell in the Soviet press which began during the Cold War have persisted to the present day; but Soviet critics have also reinterpreted *Nineteen Eighty-Four* in interesting ways over the last quarter-century to fit political exigencies.

Thus a look into how Soviet commentators have seized upon different aspects of *Nineteen Eighty-Four* and applied different rhetorical strategies in their criticism of it offers a sharply focused history—from the Soviet side— of the postwar propaganda battle between East and West. It also illumines

*See Chapter Five, Section 17, The Spectre of *Der Grosse Bruder:* West Germany's Orwell, pp. 288–303.

the roles of ideology, state cultural policy, and international relations in the politics of literary reputation, illustrating what can happen to an author when his work gets received by a hostile audience and its interpretations become subject to a strict party line. As in the case of Anglo-American intellectual groups, one can also observe how a polemical writer like Orwell comes to be used and abused in ways which eerily evoke *Nineteen Eighty-Four*. For not the least of the many ironies of Orwell's Soviet reception is that, despite the frequent and loud denunciations of his work in Soviet government organs, none of his books has ever been officially published in the Soviet Union or in any East European nation aligned with Moscow.

This, however, will soon change. The Soviet media announced plans in the spring of 1988 to publish a complete edition of *Nineteen Eighty-Four* in 1989–90. One of the many cultural initiatives in the phenomenal reform campaign of Mikhail Gorbachev, Politburo head since 1985, this literary event inaugurates a new era for Soviet cultural policy as well as for Orwell's reputation in the Communist world. Numerous references to and even reviews of *Nineteen Eighty-Four* have long appeared in Soviet newspapers and journals, but for many years customs officials have confiscated copies of his novel from Western tourists, librarians have followed instructions to keep his books off their shelves, and publishers have banned his work from their book shows. Indeed, until 1988 there was even an official import ban on *Nineteen Eighty-Four*. Like "Goldstein" in Oceania, "Orwell"—at least until the early 1980s—had been a bogeyman word in official Communist organs. Communist reviewers had therefore been in the curious position, much like Winston Smith, of falsifying history even as they discussed a book about the falsification of history—and of referring to a work which their audiences had surely never read (except as *samidzat*).

Four stages in Orwell's postwar history of reception in the Soviet Union are identifiable.


## II


The publication of *Animal Farm* brought Orwell to the unfavorable attention of the Soviet press. At the request of the U.S.S.R., American authorities in Munich seized copies of a Ukrainian translation of the fable in 1947 and turned them over to Soviet repatriation officials in Germany.[62] Nevertheless, Orwell continued his efforts to get *Animal Farm* the widest possible international audience. Without asking for any fees, he licensed translations and radio broadcasts of *Animal Farm* in Eastern Europe and elsewhere*—

*The U.S. government was heavily involved in these translations. At the State Department, Dean Acheson authorized payment for the translation rights to *Nineteen Eighty-Four* in 1951. Beginning with the Korean edition of *Animal Farm* in 1948, the U.S. Information Agency sponsored translations and distribution of Orwell's books in more than thirty languages. The Voice of America also broadcast *Animal Farm* (1947) and *Nineteen Eighty-Four* (1949) in East Europe. Indeed, a vice-president of Orwell's American publisher, Harcourt Brace, went so far as to request a blurb for *Nineteen Eighty-Four* from J. Edgar Hoover, urging Hoover that he would thereby "be helping to halt totalitarianism." (Hoover declined.)[63]

and encouraged Arthur Koestler and others to do the same with their anti-Stalinist writings.[64]

Orwell's and Koestler's names were quickly linked in the Soviet press. In 1948 the literary journal *October* labeled Koestler a "literary agent *provocateur*" and identified Orwell as a former "police agent and yellow correspondent," a "charlatan," and "a suspicious individual" who passes in England for a writer "because there is a great demand for garbage there."[65] This harsh language reflected the dawning of the Soviet Union's new, aggressively anti-Western cultural program launched in August 1946 by unofficial cultural commissar and Stalin's onetime likely successor Andrei Zhdanov (who has "about as much knowledge of literature as I have of aerodynamics," said Orwell).[66] More belligerent than even the Kremlin's anti-Nazi propaganda during World War II, the campaign was in fact chiefly aimed at the U.S., and Orwell's popularity with "American capitalists" was soon pointed out by Soviet critics and British Communists. *Zhdanovshchina* ("Zhdanovism"), as the repressive policy and sterile art of the period (1946–53) were soon called, put literature in the forefront of the campaign for ideological orthodoxy. "Every successful literary work is comparable to a battle won or to a great victory on the economic front," declared Zhdanov in one celebrated speech. "Literature must be for the Party! . . . Down with non-Party writers!"[67] Stalin himself labeled Party writers "engineers of human souls." The language, of course, frighteningly echoes the duckspeak of Party members in *Nineteen Eighty-Four*.

By 1949, Glebe Struve, a Russian expatriate and friend of Orwell—whose *25 Years of Soviet Russian Literature* Orwell greatly admired—could write that literature had become a form of "Soviet thought-control." "Rabid anti-Westernism," said Struve, was "the most important characteristic of Soviet letters."[68] The anti-Western animus manifested itself clearly in *Pravda*'s May 1950 review of *Nineteen Eighty-Four*, titled "Enemies of Mankind." In a phrase popularized by Stalin, Orwell became an "enemy of the people."

[I]n describing a most monstrous future in store for man, he imputes every evil to the people. He is obliged to admit that in 1984 . . . capitalism will cease to exist, but only for opening the way to endless wars and the degradation of mankind, which will be brought down to the level of robots called "proles". . . . But the people are not frightened by any such fears of the instigators of a new war. The people's conscience is clearer today than ever before. The foul maneuvers of mankind's enemies become more understandable every day to millions of common people.[69]

The review coupled *Nineteen Eighty-Four* with Aldous Huxley's *Ape and Essence*, two "monstrous" works of "misanthropic fantasy" which are "fervently advertised and published in every place corrupted by the activity of American capitalism." *Pravda* characterized the authors as "Anglo-American cosmopolitans." (Equivalent in the Party lexicon to treason, "cosmopolitan" signified the disparagement of native Russian culture and adulation of everything foreign: "rootless cosmopolitan" was often used as a euphemism for

"Jew" during the Kremlin's anti-Semitic campaign of 1948–52, when dozens of Jewish writers were executed.[70]) Probably the linking of Orwell's name with "America" also anticipated the intensification of *Zhdanovshchina* in Stalin's last years, represented best by the "Hate America" campaign (again, the name inescapably recalls Oceania's "Hate Week" and "Two-Minute Hate"), which began in January 1951. The campaign, which coincided with the rise of McCarthyism and followed the Berlin blockade and start of the Korean War, introduced a shift in Soviet propaganda tactics, away from mostly general attacks on "The West" and "capitalism" toward exclusive and focused assaults on American policies and ideas. Orwell's popularity in the U.S. made him a prominent target on "the cultural front." *Pravda* saw him as one of "a whole army of venal writers on the orders and instigation of Wall Street." *Nineteen Eighty-Four* was "a filthy book in the spirit of such a vital organ of American propaganda as *Reader's Digest,* which published this work, and *Life,* which presented it with many illustrations."[71] In the next decade, Communist reviewers stopped calling Orwell "Anglo-American" and simply misidentified him as an American warmonger.[72] Once again—though this time, obviously, with deliberate polemical intent—Orwell's image was being defaced by linking him to enthusiasts whose views he by no means largely shared.

### III

By the late 1950s, Orwell and *Nineteen Eighty-Four* had entered a second phase of Soviet reception. Not only had *Nineteen Eighty-Four* become "an ideological superweapon" (in Isaac Deutscher's phrase)[73] in the West's offensive propaganda arsenal, but in the Soviet Union's too. Soviet critics had described *Nineteen Eighty-Four* previously as an anti-Stalinist polemic, and had simply damned it or denied its relevance. In a diabolical example of doublethink, this treatment now gave way to a clever recasting of the book into a portrait of the American future and a wholesale attack upon present-day American life. A 1959 issue of the Soviet newspaper *Return to the Homeland* referred to Orwell's novel as a picture of "America in 1984." Run by a repatriation organization known as the Committee for a Return to the Homeland and aimed at persuading Russians to return "home," the newspaper twisted *Nineteen Eighty-Four* into a tract on the day-to-day horrors of American life. In doing so, it also conflated (or, more likely, confused) details of *Nineteen Eighty-Four* with one of its main literary inspirations, Zamyatin's *We* (1924), another terrifying police state utopia, whose citizens live without privacy in glass apartments:

> Orwell predicted that by [1984] the private life of Americans will be viewed by means of secretly placed television screens. . . . Already today Americans live, so to speak, under a glass cover, and are viewed from all sides.[74]

The article, "Under the Hood of Mr. Hoover," claimed that the FBI was the special object of Orwell's satire. The power of "the Hoovers" to tap Ameri-

cans' telephones and invade their privacy, declared the Soviet newspaper, "has reached fabulous heights in the United States." Articles in the government newspaper *Izvestia* during the 1960s repeated these charges against America in general and Hoover in particular, while acknowledging that Orwell was "one of the most vicious haters of communism."[75]

The Soviet press also presented *Nineteen Eighty-Four* as a model of sexual corruption in class-ridden capitalist society. In this characterization one notices at work not only official Soviet *political* disapproval. For Soviet critics also saw *Nineteen Eighty-Four* as a deplorable example of "naturalism"—in Marxist aesthetics, a reactionary mode of art which remains at the level of appearances, sees things "as they are" rather than as "they should be," does not understand History "developmentally," and engages in "morbid" exploration of the depressing in order to distract The People from the class struggle. And yet not only the aesthetic "errors" of *Nineteen Eighty-Four* but also its moral offensiveness—its violation of the respectable Victorian sensibility of post-Zhdanov Russia—evidently account for the unusual tirade targeted at it in *Kommunist,* the Communist Party theoretical journal. Winston's loveless marriage to his wife Katharine and joyous adultery with Julia, argued *Kommunist* in 1960, typified "the amorality which flourishes in some strata of bourgeois society . . . , the growth of all kinds of temporary extramarital and family relations and open prostitution." We have spoken about how analogues shape reputations, and here again we find Soviet critics coupling Orwell and Huxley, this time pairing *Nineteen Eighty-Four* with *Brave New World* (and confusing the two, e.g., in the claim that Orwell portrays reproduction "by artificial means"). Both books reflected family life under American capitalism, said *Kommunist.* "Orwell, Huxley, and their ilk" possess "a primitive understanding of love itself, of motherhood and fatherhood, reducing these lofty and above all moral feelings to the level of animal instincts."[76]

Given that, following the Russian Revolution and the Civil War, the 1920s Soviet ideal of anarchistic "free love" had been replaced by rigid laws on divorce and abortion in the 1930s—and by the elevation of "Soviet motherhood" to a position strikingly similar to that of spiritualized Victorian "womanhood"—the Soviet assault on such "bourgeois" habits was most ironic. But in official Soviet eyes *Nineteen Eighty-Four* and *Brave New World* were logical extensions of the behavior detailed in the Kinsey Reports of the 1940s and '50s, which horrified Soviet critics as a revelation of the sexual depravity of Americans. By the mid-1930s, as one Russian expatriate put it, "Stalinist Virtue" had supplanted "Communist Free Love." The result was that "love for love's sake" became "treasonable," since such "self-sufficient activities" "detract from the sole purpose of human existence: service to the state."[77] The official view of sexual intercourse was, in other words, not far removed from Oceania's "Our Duty to the Party"—and "love for love's sake" was *sexcrime.*

Thus, despite the Kremlin's relaxation of ideological standards for literature after Stalin's death in 1953—especially following the period of cultural

liberalization ushered in by Khrushchev's 1956 "Secret Speech" at the Twentieth Communist Party Congress, which denounced Stalin for his "cult of personality" à la Big Brother[78]—the assault against anti-totalitarian writers like Orwell continued. The new Soviet policy of "peaceful co-existence" allowed for mild internal criticism and amnesty for certain loyal Communists proscribed by Stalin (e.g., Vsevlod Meyerhold and Alexander Tairov), but not for sympathy toward victimized non-Communists or foreign critics of the U.S.S.R. The mid-'50s intellectual ferment—which included Yevgeni Yevtushenko's poetry, Ilya Ehrenberg's *The Thaw* (1954), and Boris Pasternak's *Dr. Zhivago* (1956)—was in any case short-lived. Literary and international affairs—the 1957 attack on *Dr. Zhivago,* the U-2 affair, the erection of the Berlin Wall, the Cuban missile crisis—exacerbated East-West tensions. After Soviet intellectuals began clamoring for more freedom of expression following the sensational impact of Solzhenitsyn's *One Day in the Life of Ivan Denisovich* (1962), Khrushchev reopened "the cultural front," reintroducing a strict pro-Soviet and anti-American line for literature. With Khrushchev's downfall in 1964 and Brezhnev's accession to power, Soviet cultural controls tightened further, driving even mildly dissident literature underground. A 1966 *Izvestia* article, "For Society Means for Oneself," which attacked Orwell ("a disseminator of glaring falsehoods") for suggesting the difficulty of reconciling state collectivism with intellectual liberty, thus ironically confirmed the need for the warning of *Nineteen Eighty-Four.*[79] Surely to Orwell, the formula propounded in such a headline equaled the death of freedom;[80] the headline suggests one crucial point of difference between Bolshevism (e.g., Lenin's "democratic centralism," in which "factionalism" is forbidden) and democratic socialism. It thus highlights the tensions between being a rebel and a common man. In the government lexicon, an individual was officially a social being, and "individualism" was a form of social pathology. To be "for oneself" and be also a critic of Society was, virtually by definition, to be against the collective—and therefore against "the common man."

## IV

The "countdown to 1984" witnessed a third stage in Orwell's reputation-history in the U.S.S.R. Although Soviet commentators continued to discuss *Nineteen Eighty-Four* as a portrait of American society, the interpretations were fuller and more explicitly tied to current events. For the first time, lengthy quotations from *Nineteen Eighty-Four* appeared in reviews in the official press. One review in a 1983 issue of the *Literary Gazette,* the weekly newspaper of the Soviet Writers' Union, reflected the rise of a new Cold War era between the Kremlin and the Carter and Reagan administrations. The newspaper referred to the Pentagon as the "Ministry of Peace" for its arms buildup and to the Defense Department as the "Ministry of Truth" for its efforts to persuade Europe to accept deployment of middle-range nuclear weapons. While allowing that Americans are "not robots as

Orwell predicted," the article noted that "there is a striking similarity between what [Orwell] described in *Nineteen Eighty-Four* and what is going on in the U.S.!"

> History frequently jokes. What Orwell predicted before the coming of the monstrous 1984 has in many degrees turned out to be reality in just the same "free world" to which he himself belonged.[81]

*Izvestia* elaborated in succeeding months on the application of Newspeak and "1984" to America: Big Brother was, of course, Ronald Reagan; "War Is Peace" was embodied in the U.S. Air Force motto "Peace Is Our Profession"; Hate Week was exceeded by the American "month of hate" after the U.S.S.R. shot down a "spy provocateur flight" of Korean Air Lines flight 007 in 1983; Radio Liberty and Radio Free Europe were American "radio-sabotage centers" broadcasting Newspeak; and Thought Police surveillance was slipshod when compared with "the real telescreen of Uncle Sam," who "opens your mail, follows your movements, and most important, your thoughts." The incarnation of the slogan "Ignorance Is Strength," said the weekly *Moscow News* of Reagan, citing the American media's own loud doubts about Reagan's competence and about his "strong" defense posture. Addressing the Reagan administration's call, after the 1981 silencing of Lech Walesa's Solidarity workers' movement, for international sanctions against Poland's Communist government, *Izvestia* declared: "Let us hope that experience and realism will withstand pressure from 'Big Brother'."[82] The Soviet press also dismissed the Reagan Administration's proposals for disarmament in 1983 as "the fruit of doublethink" and attacked America's 1983 "rescue mission" in Grenada and "peacekeeping mission" in Lebanon as transparent examples of Newspeak. Meanwhile, in a classic instance of socialist realism, *Izvestia* portrayed the forthcoming global utopia of 2084. Headlined "A World That Will Be Lovely," the article depicted a climate-controlled planet in which all people will live to a healthy old age and have plenty of time for creative pursuits. "Naturally the new society will be Communist," *Izvestia* concluded.[83]

Even Orwell himself underwent "rehabilitation" in some Soviet press accounts during 1984. In a 2500-word review in the weekly *New Times*, a Soviet critic did what ideologically motivated Anglo-American critics have long been doing with Orwell's work: he quoted selectively from Orwell's corpus, identified Orwell's opponents as the Kremlin's own, and then claimed Orwell for the Soviet camp. Titled " '1984': Full Circle," the review praised Orwell's artistry and gave a flattering biographical summary, casting him as a worker's hero who "shared dry crusts with the clochards of Paris." Orwell saw through "the falsehoods of bourgeois democracy." In *Nineteen Eighty-Four* he took "the exact measure . . . of capitalism." Orwell's (remarkably prescient) message, the reviewer concluded, was that "B.B. is R.R."[84] With this review, one might say, the "mutability of the past" was complete. The line on Orwell himself had come "full circle." The man who ranked high in Soviet literary demonology was now a candidate for hagiog-

raphy. The erstwhile Enemy of Mankind had become, *mirabile dictu*, Friend of The Common Man.[85]

*New Times* did acknowledge that it would be an "exaggeration" to say that Orwell was "a convinced adherent of the communist outlook." But the reviewer attacked those who sought to "fit the tight 'suit of totalitarianism' " in *Nineteen Eighty-Four* "onto real socialism." Instead, Orwell's harsh criticism of England and bourgeois habits, said *New Times*, proved him a fellow traveler (a discovery which no doubt would have come as a distinct surprise to Raymond Williams, A.L. Rowse, and other British Marxists).[86] This Soviet conversion of Orwell was capped by an astonishingly blatant misreading of Orwell's famous July 1949 letter, published in *Life* and the *New York Times Book Review*, in which he explained that his intentions in *Nineteen Eighty-Four* were to "show up" the totalitarian "perversions to which a centralized economy is liable," already "partially realized in Communism and Fascism."[87] But Orwell added that his novel was set in Britain "in order to emphasize that the English-speaking races are not better than anyone else and that totalitarianism, *if not fought against*, could triumph anywhere." The Soviet reviewer seized on this last sentence:

> . . . what Orwell seems to be saying is: "If you don't take care, if you don't wake up, here is what, in caricature form, We run the risk of getting." WE—i.e., the West. We—i.e., capitalism. In a letter to a friend [*sic*] the author himself said that in placing the action of the novel in Great Britain he was prompted, above all, by the desire to emphasize that the English-speaking peoples are no whit better than others, and that totalitarianism, if not fought against, may triumph anywhere. He was writing, he said, because there was a lie that had to be exposed.[88]

The Soviet reviewer was drawing most selectively from Orwell's 1949 letter. For the "lie," as Orwell made clear in "Why I Write" and in the Ukrainian preface to *Animal Farm*, was "the belief that Russia is a Socialist country." "[E]xposing the Soviet myth," Orwell wrote, was his goal ever since his return from Catalonia.[89] Nevertheless " '1984': Full Circle" fittingly concluded:

> Not a single [Western journalist] has had the wisdom, the courage, or the honesty to acknowledge at long last that George Orwell with his prophetic gift diagnosed the syndrome of present-day capitalism with which we must co-exist today for lack of something better, restraining with all our might its pathologically militaristic, nuclear-missile ambitions.[90]

## V

With the publication in May 1988 in the *Literary Gazette* of a full-page extract from *Nineteen Eighty-Four*—beneath a stunning half-page drawing of a boot stamping on Winston Smith's upturned face—Orwell's Soviet reputation entered a fourth, unprecedented stage of official recognition. No longer is he being castigated by the Soviet press as a "troubadour of the Cold War"

and his novel treated as a "nonbook," noted the anonymous introduction to the excerpt in the *Literary Gazette*. Indeed the introduction not only conceded, if somewhat obliquely, that Stalinist Russia had served as a model for *Nineteen Eighty-Four,* but also frankly criticized the Party for its long-standing proscriptions against the novel.

> Of all the old taboos relating to foreign literature, this was one of the most stable and unproblematical. . . . And what the taboo derived from is not hard to guess. . . . [O]n the novel's first pages, the reader gets a portrait of a person with a moustache looking at other citizens from each corner. This panicky moment was sufficient to make the book, which was read by the whole world, illegal in our country.
>     . . . [S]uggestions to translate the novel (it is reliably reported that there were suggestions [in the 1970s]) were, as before, swept aside without discussion.
>     And why, exactly? . . . It should have been translated and analyzed a long time ago, no matter whether Orwell's dissenting political position was flawed or whether he slandered socialism (this was the most widespread accusation). . . . Alas, in the cacophony of the Cold War, the dying voice of the author was not heard. Year after year, his novel became distorted by myths and commentaries to the myths, as if it had fallen into a hall of crooked mirrors. And if one is not afraid to call things by their names, one must admit: By virtue of our biased relationship to Orwell, with all our prohibitions and labels against him, we did not at all hinder—but rather helped—this. The time has come to free ourselves from the stagnant prohibitions, to discard the myths, to shatter the crooked mirrors, and to read George Orwell thoughtfully and without prejudice. . . .

The announced intention to issue an unabridged, unexpurgated edition of *Nineteen Eighty-Four* in the literary monthly *Novy Mir (New World)* in 1989 follows the serialization in 1987–88 of several other long-suppressed works, including Zamyatin's *We,* Pasternak's *Dr. Zhivago,* Vasily Grossman's *Life and Fate,* Andrei Platonov's *Chevengur,* and Anatoly Rybakov's *Children of the Arbat,* all of them printed entire as part of Gorbachev's extraordinary crusade to re-evaluate the Stalin era and enlist intellectual and popular support for a systematic revamping of the Soviet bureaucracy and the Communist Party. As of 1989 it therefore seems likely that Orwell's status will alter drastically if the cultural thaw in the Gorbachev era of *glasnost* and *perestroika* continues. Unlike the case of Orwell's earlier phases of reputation, the Soviet intelligentsia today appears open to approaching *Nineteen Eighty-Four* less as a propaganda sheet, simply to be attacked or claimed, and more as a politically committed artwork inviting the Soviet Union to criticize itself along with the novel.

But how thoroughgoing will Soviet self-criticism be? The answer—as in the case of the question of Orwell's future reputation in the U.S.S.R.—remains speculative. Old habits die hard. For example, even as the introduction to the *Literary Gazette* extract, titled "The Ministry of Truth," acknowl-

edged that *Nineteen Eighty-Four* bore relevance to Stalinist Russia, it suggested that Orwell's main target was fascism. ("He asked a difficult question: Couldn't fascism find fertile ground in England and, if so, how soon? How will it appear? What shape will it take? Thus arose the form of the novel.") Indeed neither Stalin nor Stalinism is specifically mentioned in the *Literary Gazette* introduction, although—*mutatis mutandis*—Big Brother is likened to Chairman Mao, Minitrue fabrication of national heroes is associated with the Chinese Cultural Revolution (with Comrade Ogilvy explicitly compared to Ley Fen), Hate Week is identified with Islam, and the "totalitarian shadowing" of the population by means of "the newest electronic equipment" is called "a reality precisely in the advanced countries of the West, most of all America." One may therefore justly suspect the implied denial of Sergei Zalygin, editor of *Novy Mir,* that any parallels between the present-day Soviet Union and *Nineteen Eighty-Four* apply. Wrote Zalygin disingenuously in the same issue of the *Literary Gazette:*

> It's possible that Orwell wrote his book with a concrete address—the address of socialism. But the time has passed when the book frightens (or to put it delicately) embarrasses us. . . .[91]

Has it?

## VI

Outside the Soviet Union, official Communist reaction to Orwell has also varied somewhat over the years, but no sharp deviation from the traditional anti-Western Soviet line has yet occurred. For instance, radio broadcasts of a Czech version of *Animal Farm* were scheduled in 1948 and 1968, before *Zhdanovshchina* was imposed in Soviet satellites and before the suppression of the Dubček government began, respectively. The fable was never aired.[92] In the 1980s, Orwell has generally been presented in Eastern Europe as a vicious anti-Communist, though some critics have also argued that America is the realization of *Nineteen Eighty-Four.* Possibly with this latter strategy in mind, Polish authorities allowed copies of *Nineteen Eighty-Four* into book fairs under a "liberalized" cultural policy in 1983, shortly before yet another crackdown on Walesa and Solidarity. The novel remains outlawed in East Germany, Bulgaria, Hungary, and Czechoslovakia. In 1984 the East German press charged that *Nineteen Eighty-Four,* "the best seller of the Cold War," was gaining renewed attention in the West because "an Orwell renaissance" was being orchestrated "to provide the ideological background for the rebirth of the Cold War." The Budapest literary weekly *New Mirror* attacked Orwell's anti-Communism in its New Year issue. A Bulgarian journal described Orwell as "one of the intellectual victims of the real Oceania of modern imperialism."[93]

Among dissident Soviet and Eastern European intellectuals, however, Orwell has been admired as a brilliant satirist and a courageous artist in the

mold of Pasternak, Solzhenitsyn, and Milosz. In *The Captive Mind,* Milosz noted that dissident intellectuals are "amazed" that a writer who never lived in Russia should understand the system so well.[94] Even though they have been officially banned, Orwell's last two books have been translated into most Eastern European languages. Thousands of copies of *Nineteen Eighty-Four* were printed in the underground Polish press as "The Orwell Year" approached. Indeed Western intellectuals have periodically reported that Orwell's dystopia, translated into Hungarian and secretly circulated among the writers of the Petofi Club of Budapest, was a catalyst of the 1956 Hungarian uprising.[95]

*Nineteen Eighty-Four* has been especially esteemed by young dissidents in the Communist world. During the 1960s, Andrei Amalrik went to prison for his bitter analysis of the U.S.S.R., titled *Will the Soviet Union Survive Until 1984?* (1970). In 1983 one Rumanian refugee intellectual told me how, in the mid-1950s, he had procured a smuggled copy of *Nineteen Eighty-Four* on condition that he read it overnight and pass it on through the dissident underground. Like Milosz and others, he was astounded that an Englishman who had never set foot in Eastern Europe could describe with such horrifying accuracy the climate of terror which he then felt as a young man in rebellion against the state. For these intellectuals and for many other dissidents, *Nineteen Eighty-Four* crosses the line from dystopian fiction to living nightmare. "This book made perhaps the greatest impact on my life," the Lithuanian writer Tomas Venclova, who emigrated to the U.S. in 1977, has said. "That I am here and not there—for this I am grateful to Orwell."[96]

## 12. "A Sexist After All?" The Feminists' Orwell

### I

The feminist reception of Orwell affords us the opportunity to examine his reputation from a distinctly different critical location than in our previous case studies—from a gender perspective. Whereas the Marxist Left has focused on Orwell's socialism, feminists have concentrated their attention on his sexual politics. And while leftists have argued over the years as to whether Orwell is a "friend" or "enemy" of the common man, most feminists of the 1980s have agreed that Orwell is no comrade of women.

The countdown to 1984 coincided with the rise of feminist literary criticism in the academy, thereby bringing Orwell to the attention of feminist critics. Until the 1980s, unlike the case with other political and generational reception audiences whose response to Orwell we are surveying, Orwell had no distinctive reputation among women, let alone within any identifiable feminist group.

The feminists' Orwell is, then, a recent phenomenon, and no single feminist authoritative voice has responded to Orwell both over an extended

period of time and in identifiably individual terms.* Thus we will be exploring here not the *evolution* of Orwell's reception and the personal response of a select reader, but rather the key points of the feminist critique. Of course, the "feminists" are not a tiny group like Woodcock's Freedom Press writers. "Feminism" is a broad term representing a wide diversity of viewpoints; therefore we shall pay close attention here to how secondary factors of critical location bear on this gender-based image. Whereas, in the instance of Orwell's reception by Raymond Williams and the British Marxists, such a task meant focusing additionally on generational issues, this facial history invites supplemental scrutiny of feminist readers' political, national, and professional affiliations.

## II

Most feminists have found Orwell's affection for the traditional, male-dominant family and his chivalrous attitude toward women dated at best, misogynistic at worst. Marxist and radical feminists have written especially harshly about Orwell. Apart from citing several isolated remarks of Orwell that belittle women, they point out, accurately, that his writings consistently reflect the sexist assumption that the male is the human norm. They also deplore his occasional disparagement of feminism,[97] his derogatory remarks about "the pansy Left," and his aversion to contraception and abortion. In addition, many feminists criticize the emotional, sometimes convention-bound and puritanical female characters in his fiction as unflattering stereotypes—Elizabeth Lackersteen and her mother in *Burmese Days,* Dorothy Hare in *A Clergyman's Daughter,* Rosemary Waterlow in *Keep the Aspidistra Flying,* and Julia and the prole washerwoman in *Nineteen Eighty-Four.*[98]

One can distinguish Orwell's reception between American and British left-wing feminists. British feminists have typically come to Orwell's work via Marxism. Their hostility to Orwell is therefore unsurprising, given his current low reputation among the post-New Left generation of writers. Non-Marxist British feminists have expressed respect for Orwell, however, and in some ways his overall feminist reception in 1980s Britain is not unlike his split reception in the early 1950s on the Left, when the BCP denounced him and younger radicals exalted him. A few sympathetic, non-Marxist feminists coming of age in the 1970s, wanting to "understand" Orwell yet not compelled by his presence as was the young Raymond Wil-

*This circumstance also explains why the case studies in this book that spotlight the reception histories of individual institutional readers within groups—Trilling, Woodcock, Williams, Fyvel, Howe, Podhoretz, Hollis, and Wicker—feature male readers. Most critic-readers who have cast Orwell as an intellectual model and have played major roles in the making of his reputation have been men. And these facts of Orwell's reception history suggest, in turn, much about how writers become figures—i.e., not just because they stand as political or generational exemplars, but for unstated, less visible reasons too, e.g., because they also are inspirational gender models. Male critics have been peculiarly silent as to the significance of Orwell's reputation among male intellectuals and his special masculine appeal.

liams, have approached him in formalist and phenomenological terms.[99] In contrast, Marxist feminists, determined to "judge" Orwell and restrained by no filial bond like the mature Williams, have sought to demonstrate the relation between his socialist criticism and allegedly reactionary sexual politics.[100] Indeed the Marxist feminists' charges of Orwell's "misogyny" and "contempt for women"[101]—which equate his scattered comments dismissive of feminism with woman-hatred in general—may be taken as the newest line of attack against Orwell from the radical Left. From another vantage point, however, the feminist critique also exemplifies what happens to an author when he is interpreted, out of his own time, by a relatively new perspective—here a gender-sensitive one.

The key work in Orwell's *oeuvre* for most British feminists, again reflecting his continuing hold on the imagination of the Left, has been *The Road to Wigan Pier*. Inasmuch as Marxist feminists see the capitalist system and the institution of private property, rather than men collectively, as the source of women's oppression, their indictment of Orwell as sexist derives from their critique of his anti-populism and anti-socialism, not the other way around. One feminist journalist, Beatrix Campbell, has argued that Orwell's "big brotherly view of the working class" conditions his paternalistic attitude toward women.[102] In her contribution to *Inside the Myth* (1984), a collection of radical essays, she voices agreement with Raymond Williams that "the problem with Orwell is his representation, or rather misrepresentation, of the working class." Her Orwell is no People's Tribune, let alone a common man himself. "What he feels for the common people edges on contempt. Actually, he thinks they're dead common." Ignoring the fact that Orwell was commissioned by Victor Gollancz to investigate life among the Northern jobless and that he came to study the miners' working conditions through introductions which he fortuitously received, Campbell concludes: "As the misogynist he is, it is not surprising to find that he has chosen [to write about] the most masculinised profession."[103]

American feminists have focused on *Nineteen Eighty-Four*. Usually radical and liberal feminists, rather than Marxists, they have been more concerned with Orwell's depiction of sex roles and his system of values than with class issues. Their approach to his work has been less sociological and ideological than literary and textual. Probably these differences from the British feminists have to do not only with the topicality of *Nineteen Eighty-Four* in the early 1980s, but also with professional and cultural differences. The American Left, understandably, has generally had much more psychological distance from Orwell than has the British Left; and his American feminist critics have without exception been literary academics, some of whom also have a scholarly interest in the history of the feminist utopia.[104] Interestingly, Orwell probably also came to the attention of American feminists because the countdown to 1984 happened to coincide with what literary historians have recognized as a new, third historical phase in American feminist criticism beginning in the early 1980s, away from near-exclusive specialization in the study of women authors (or "separatism") and back

toward gender-sensitive critiques of male authors in the tradition of Kate Millett's *Sexual Politics* (1970).[105]

Such a critique is Daphne Patai's *The Orwell Mystique: A Study of Male Ideology* (1984). The book's title evokes Betty Friedan's *The Feminine Mystique*. The "Orwell Mystique" is the "masculine" mystique, the sexist myth, incarnated by Orwell, that to be "manly" is to support a gender hierarchy in which males are supreme. An American academic interested in Latin American literature, the feminist utopia, and the relation of myth and ideology to literature, Patai does not confine herself to *Nineteen Eighty-Four;* she contrasts Orwell's writings with feminist works and subjects all of his major books, and some of his journalism, to a thoroughgoing radical feminist reading. Unlike other radical feminists, Patai does not merely find Orwell guilty of "profound misogyny." The "startling unifying thread" running through all his work, says Patai, "can be expressed in one word: androcentrism." Patai's term defines the "ideological cluster" at the heart of Orwell's *oeuvre,* marked by an "insistent adherence to a gender polarization that assumes male centrality and supremacy." The concept of androcentrism "unifies Orwell's diverse pet peeves, his fear of socialism and the machine, his nostalgia for the past, his misogyny, his attraction to the experience of war, and the conservatism apparent in his carefully circumscribed challenge to hierarchy and authority."[106]

The value of *The Orwell Mystique* is that, given Patai's gender-conscious perspective, she calls attention to a significant and little-noticed dimension of Orwell's work. She links his anti-Communism with his androcentrism. Patai argues that "the Orwell myth" developed in the 1950s because Orwell's political position of the 1940s as an anti-Communist radical became increasingly "respectable" among intellectuals. "It protected one from the charge of simpleminded anti-Communism . . . and allowed one to be high-minded, a defender of justice and fairness for all. . . ." The point is valid and well taken; but *The Orwell Mystique* exaggerates the importance of this factor in Orwell's reputation and makes no mention why other anti-Communist writers never achieved Orwell's level of "respectability." Patai continues:

> But is this all? How does such a writer signal to his readers that he is indeed safe, that he does not mean to deprive them of cherished ideas, habits, and beliefs? One suitable technique would seem to be to show in some way that there is agreement between himself and his readership about fundamentals. . . . I believe that Orwell does this through his cultivation of a traditional notion of masculinity, complemented by a generalized misogyny. . . . Orwell reassured his readers that even a man who depicted himself as a great challenger of the powers-that-be could be counted on not to rock the boat.[107]

Here and elsewhere, Patai's often acute insight into Orwell's—and our culture's—patriarchal values is sometimes phrased in such a way as to distort it, so that the reader is tempted to reject the hard-won perception with the exaggerated accent. Orwell's tough-guy posturing in some of his work cannot

be denied, and its appeal in the conservative '50s was great. But the specific connections between the writer's work and his reception go unargued. Instead, Patai merely asserts in a note: "Nor can one argue that Orwell is 'not responsible' for the conservative uses made of his work." This pronouncement is supported not by a careful study probing which of Orwell's works and features of his reputation have been "used" by conservatives and how and why, but rather, remarkably, by a quotation from Althusser.[108] She thereby sidesteps the complex dynamics of reputation-formation, blurs the distinction between "the Orwell myth" and Orwell's own work, and conflates historical truth with the imputation of base motive. It is incontestable, for instance, that the Cold War contributed significantly to the rise in Orwell's reputation. But the contention that Orwell compromised the integrity of his work to conform to the Cold War climate is dubious.[109] I have already explored to some extent in Part One the difficult problem of Orwell's "complicity" in his Cold Warrior reputation, and I do so further in Chapters Five and Six. Patai, however, simply asserts that Orwell "signal[ed]" liberal and conservative intellectuals that he was "safe" by virtue of his "generalized misogyny." No biographical or historical evidence linking Orwell's alleged misogyny to his reception is adduced to support this claim, exemplifying the frequent tendency among literary critics to let textual analysis do the work of historical and biographical investigation. No mention is made of the fact that Orwell was criticizing Communism harshly a decade before *Animal Farm* appeared, or that *Wigan Pier* and *Homage to Catalonia* merely won him enemies on the Left in the 1930s, not friends on the Right. (The Right made no claim to Orwell until just before his death, after the publication of *Nineteen Eighty-Four*.) No comparisons of the sexual politics and receptions of any other writers of the period are offered, though Orwell's anti-feminism is alleged to be "exceptional even for his time."[110] Why then hasn't it been commented upon until now, unlike Hemingway's and Mailer's misogyny? Patai attributes this to "received opinion" about Orwell and the subtle role of androcentrism in "the Orwell mystique." Yet the formation and extent of this vague "received opinion" is not explored; and the phrase "the Orwell mystique" impedes rather than promotes investigation. Nowhere does *The Orwell Mystique* distinguish clearly, let alone show the interaction, between what *Orwell* did and what others have done *to* him. Many critics have suggested that some postwar radical intellectuals were attracted to the posthumous Orwell because his position lent respectability to rightward "retreat";[111] that his work and reputation were abused by the Left as well as the Right is not what is at issue here. But this fact does not justify the casual equation of Orwell with his disingenuous Left supporters (of which there were some), or the implication that postwar criticism of Stalinism from a "democratic" socialist or social democratic standpoint was somehow necessarily illegitimate or casuistic, or the suppression of Orwell's occasionally sympathetic and respectful comments about feminism,[112] or the conclusion that Orwell himself was a deceitful writer, posturing as a socialist but really aiming to "assure" his readers that he meant business-as-usual.

The energy of the prose in *The Orwell Mystique* suggests that Patai's has been far more than merely a scholarly reassessment of Orwell. Apart from her insistence on Orwell's sexism and misogyny, however, only the two-page Preface bears any direct trace of the author's personal engagement with Orwell. She reports that what "drew me to Orwell" was "his passion and his honesty," but that she came to realize that her view reflected merely "a general assent to received opinion about Orwell."

> I have reread earlier drafts of this book and note that I was often, at that point, still writing in what I now call the "honorific," carefully couching criticism in words of praise. . . . Something else struck me as well: that the critic who praises Orwell for his "honesty" is saying not only, "Orwell is honest," but also, "I am honest too." . . . I initially set out to explain Orwell's pessimism and eventual despair in terms that were compatible with his general reputation and the honor that is routinely done him. As I became more and more aware of the profound misogyny and preoccupation with manhood in his works, I still tried to hang onto an interpretation that would not so much challenge earlier views as complement them or register a small disclaimer.[113]

But on the far Left, "received opinion" has long been that Orwell died in "pessimism" and "despair." (Notably, even at the start, this was the premise of *The Orwell Mystique*, not its argument; it is based on reading *Nineteen Eighty-Four* psychobiographically, not on the recollections of acquaintances or the letters and journalism of 1948–49 in *CEJL*.[114]) And here we see again how reference group relations shape reading responses: Patai cites with approval not a single favorable critical comment about Orwell in her book, though she quotes not just published criticism but personal letters to her from Orwell's Marxist and radical critics. And so she exchanges the larger, amorphous reference group of "Orwell's uncritical admirers" for this smaller, more intense reference group, thereby trading one sort of received opinion for another. Coterie politics allow her to claim a higher "honesty." For her equation about Orwell's admirers is easily recast: by praising Williams and others for *their* rare "honesty" about Orwell—and declaring that their criticisms do not go far enough—one is saying not only, "They are honest," but "I am honest too." But not only "honest"—also beleaguered, thereby adding victimization to virtue. Dissatisfied about finding an all-too-human Orwell beneath and beyond all the honorifics, Patai seems, like the mature Williams, to have overadjusted. Although her academic book is not personal and transparently autobiographical like Williams' history of reception, one senses that she too, like Williams in his revisionist monograph *George Orwell*, has "worked through" Orwell via her study, only to wind up betrayed by a "pure" Orwell who never was. Her original, "tragic" Orwell was the incarnation of "passion" and "honesty"; she blames her failure to notice his not inconsiderable shortcomings on Orwell rather than herself. But unlike Williams, being unimpeded by a powerful attraction to Orwell "the man," she has not gotten stuck in an intermediate stage of "questioning respect," but rather gone straight to his final stage of anger and hostility

toward Orwell. Her criticism makes clear that, even with a textual critic, the act of reception is personal and developmental, not only an analytical but also an autobiographical act.

## III

*The Orwell Mystique* warrants considerable, and critical, attention not only because it fairly represents Orwell's left-wing feminist reception and has been well-received by feminist academics,[115] but also because it stands as the most substantial feminist critique of his work to date. Moreover, like many readers in the 1980s, I find Orwell's conventional attitudes toward gender and his uninterest in, even condescension toward, women's rights issues a notable deficiency in his work. The special contribution of the feminist response is to make us more gender-conscious about Orwell's writings; their unfavorable reception is, however, also an excellent example of the difference between taking a "hard" versus "sympathetic" stance toward a subject, between judging him by the present or trying to understand him in his own historical moment.

And so one pauses at the very phrasing of one feminist's question, "Is . . . Orwell . . . a sexist after all?"[116] Its scholastic, verbal nature—much like the onetime Soviet obsession with the epithets "naturalist" and "formalist"— gives a hint of the schematized approach dictated when one sifts a writer's work through the ideologically orthodox filter of what could be termed "feminist realism." Whatever the wording, however, the question of Orwell's attitude toward women cannot be answered merely within the terms of present-day critical ideologies, or by textual and autobiographical readings of his work.[117]

What is disheartening about the radical and Marxist feminist critique of Orwell is how a genuine insight of restricted scope is magnified into an *idée fixe* and then applied like a blanket to an author's work. Some feminist critiques present Orwell in a new light, but they often focus down too narrowly, ultimately falsifying his sexual politics. It is hard to see the value of conclusions such as, "Orwell altered the record of the past, so far as women are concerned, as efficiently as if he had been in the employ of Minitrue."[118] Likewise, though *The Orwell Mystique* fairly insists on judging a moral critic like Orwell "by the standards he proclaimed—honesty, decency, egalitarianism, [and] justice"—Patai doesn't finally judge Orwell in those terms. Instead she hypostatizes "honesty," "decency," "egalitarianism," and "justice" according to a 1980s feminist standard which swamps the political complexities and historical situation in which he found himself.[119] Certainly, Orwell was not sensitive to women's rights (or gay rights or the special needs of the aged either), but relative to the issues of race and class which gripped literary London in the 1930s and '40s—and despite his mild lifelong antipathy toward Catholics, Irishmen, and Scotsmen (and his early prejudice toward Jews, reflected in *Down and Out*)—he is, on the whole, a witness to his time.

Verdicts like those above reflect disdain (most ironic from Marxists) for the (admittedly laborious) task of gathering historical and biographical data, through which one might partly recover the social conditions of an author's writing and reception. In their rush to label Orwell a "sexist," some feminists have been blind to the extent to which Orwell's attitudes toward femininity and social roles were conventional for his time, among socialists as well as non-socialists. Although Patai denies in passing that her approach is anachronistic, she in effect concedes it when she admits that Orwell's "identification of the male with the human norm is among the conventions of an androcentric society that is only now being seriously challenged." She seems not to have considered that the "neglect" of Orwell's "exceptional" sexism might be due precisely to the fact that it was not "exceptional" for his time.[120]

Biographical testimony from acquaintances does not support the charge.[121] Moreover, nowhere do any of the radical and Marxist feminists explore Orwell's positive reception by left-wing women contemporaries, or explain why his misogyny went unmentioned even among female Communists until the 1980s. It is evasive to dismiss the silence as merely the "received opinion" of an "androcentric" culture. Likewise, to slight the "gender-less" criticism of a liberal feminist sympathetic to Orwell such as Jenni Calder as that of a "male-identified reader" is patronizing.[122] Liberal feminists like Calder, whose criticism reflects a keen awareness of the historical situation in which Orwell found himself, have pointed to his concern for the poor, his opposition to British imperialism, his anti-fascism and anti-Stalinism, and his defense of personal freedoms. Having grown up in postwar Britain and written a dissertation on Orwell in 1963 (later published as *Chronicles of Conscience,* 1968) before feminism became part of the Anglo-American consciousness, Calder grants Orwell the limitations of his era.

> Orwell simply didn't see feminism as a larger issue. On that particular issue, he was part of his time, certainly not ahead of it. But I think it noteworthy that he never distanced himself from ordinary, domestic life either. He thought family life was important. He didn't feel that "domesticity" was "low" and he was "above" it. In *Wigan Pier* he tells about the ambivalent reaction of the miners to his washing dishes in their homes—certainly not many writers of his time concerned themselves with washing dishes. And although he did get a nurse for his child, he was capable of doing all the practical things of looking after him when his wife died—he didn't denigrate that as "woman's work" either. The practicalities of living were important to Orwell. I don't say that he was a feminist, of course. . . . But he remains in many ways a model socialist for me.[123]

Any feminist critique should take into account Orwell's relatively modern attitude toward child-rearing and domesticity.[124] Calder's response makes clear that feminists as a group do not hold any single view of Orwell, reminding us again of the variability and perspectival nature of reader reception within any institutional audience.

Some American liberal feminists go much further than Calder in defending Orwell. Despite his conservative sexual politics, they see him as an opponent of authoritarianism first and last. "The best thing about Orwell," Gloria Steinem has said, "is that he remained an advocate of individual rights." Steinem speculates that Orwell might eventually have appreciated how the patriarchal family perpetuates racism and class oppression as well as sexism—and might have supported the main goals of feminism in the 1970s and '80s if he had lived to see it become a broad-based, society-wide movement.[125] Such conjectures are, of course, fruitless, but they do reflect an appreciation of the difference between English feminism in the 1930s and the 1980s. And a brief consideration of those differences is apposite here.

If Orwell never pondered much the implications of a gender-differentiated society, neither did any other leading left-wing male intellectuals of his generation writing between 1930 and 1950—e.g., Herbert Read, Graham Greene, Laski, Priestley, Koestler, Spender, John Strachey, G.D.H. Cole (whose wife Margaret was a leading member of the Fabian Society). Even women socialists of Orwell's acquaintance like Ethel Mannin and Jennie Lee, wife of Aneurin Bevan, turned their attention in the 1930s and '40s toward what seemed the "larger" issues of class and race. In the face of the hunger marches, the campaign for socialism, the rise of Hitler and Mussolini, and the war, feminism faded before seemingly more pressing problems. "After 1926," as Sheila Rowbotham has written, "there was little enough bread; the roses seemed no more than a distant memory."[126]

The prevailing left-wing outlook of the period is summed up in Simone de Beauvoir's recollection of her politics before writing *The Second Sex* (1949): "I used to think that the class-war should take precedence over the struggle between the sexes."[127] In his autobiography Irving Howe, who belonged to a splinter Trotskyist sect in the late 1930s, tries to account for the absence of feminist consciousness:

> Didn't the women feel they were suffering discrimination within the movement? Weren't they irked by our readiness to fall back onto the modes of condescension that prevailed in the outer world?. . . Decades later I did ask and was told that young women in the movement had now and again talked among themselves, disturbed by feelings of their own inadequacy and resentful of the roles to which they were often confined. Yet they had not complained openly or strongly—why? Because it was unrealistic to hope to change everything; because it would be unsporting to make trouble in those difficult years; because it seemed possible that some of their deficiencies were their own fault.[128]

The answers would be much the same in Britain. The period 1930–60 constitutes the nadir of the campaign for women's rights in Britain in this century. Suffrage having been secured in 1920, feminism turned gradualist and parliamentary in the following decades. Liberal, parliamentary advocates for women's rights (like Eleanor Rathbone, for whom Orwell arranged

a BBC talk) dominated the movement and put Fabian social reforms above radical goals, e.g., by campaigning for equal pay and protective family legislation. The radicalism of some pioneers (like Viscountess Rhondda) seemed to a younger generation "a sentimental attachment of older women."[129] If Orwell had little interest in or sympathy toward feminism, he was not alone. "Modern young women," wrote Ray Strachey in her introduction to *Our Freedom and Its Results* (1936), "show a strong hostility to the word 'feminism' and all which they imagine it to connote."[130]

Some feminists have criticized Orwell's offhand reference in *Wigan Pier* to "birth control fanatics." As a characterization of the movement's rank and file, the phrase is totally unfair. But it is no exaggeration to say that the chief publicists of the British contraception campaign in the 1920s and '30s, Marie Stopes and the American Margaret Sanger, were widely regarded as crazed "zealots."[131] One Marxist feminist remarks that Orwell saw birth control "as some Malthusian plot to limit the lower orders."[132] Actually, Stopes and Sanger, and sometimes the Neo-Malthusian League, were not beneath eugenicist appeals. Stopes belonged to the British Eugenics Society and called her own organization "The Society for Constructive Birth Control and Racial Progress." She proposed sterilization for the poor, the feeble-minded, and half-castes in order to curb breeding of the "C 3 population." By the mid-1930s, her "race betterment" rhetoric was attracting support from fascists like Oswald Mosley and his Blackshirts. Stopes regarded herself as "the sexual messiah."[133] "Stopery," as Germaine Greer has written, was an apt name for "the piddling activities of the Stopeses and Sangers and their radical, liberal, upper-class, do-gooder friends, together with the muddleheaded altruism of the socialists and the earnestness of the Malthusians. . . ."[134] Moreover, all this was going on when dire predictions were being made about the population decline; Britain's birthrate in the 1930s was at an all-time low at the same time that Nazi Germany's military buildup and pro-family population policies were generating fears of impending war.[135] It is vital to remember that Orwell's anti-contraception stand existed within this larger context and not only, as one feminist deplored, "when birth control campaigners were fighting hard to set up clinics throughout Britain."[136]

Orwell did oppose contraception firmly. He never argued his case in his work. No evidence suggests that his opposition derived from anti-feminism. Or because, as Patai suggests, he was obsessed with the idea that "potency proves manhood."[137] Rather, like most Britons, Orwell evidently equated the movement with Marie Stopes and Margaret Sanger (much as "the Catholic Church" meant to him the clergy and a few intellectual apologists, not millions of Irish laborers) and saw a practical need for a population increase.[138] His disparagement of "fanatics" like Stopes and her movement's homosexual mentor Edward Carpenter, theorist of the "intermediate sex" of "Uranians"—along with the rest of his *Wigan Pier* catalogue of fruit-juice drinkers, sandal-wearers, and vegetarians—stemmed not only from Orwell's sometime intolerance of others' idiosyncrasies but also from a

genuine (and not unjust) belief that they were crackpot special interest groups less committed to democratic socialism than to political fashion and self-promotion.[139]

## IV

The foregoing sketch of the political climate in which Orwell lived and wrote in the British 1930s and '40s is intended not only to suggest his complicated historical position or to salvage his reputation from feminist revisionism. The ahistorical approach of his radical and Marxist feminist critics points beyond his own case to significant issues in the current practice of feminist criticism. In so doing it invites close attention to the concerns voiced by several self-critical feminists within and outside the literary academy. Indeed the feminist Left's response to Orwell validates Judith Shapiro's anxiety "about the extent to which we have been projecting our own historically specific situation onto the lives and experience of those we study. . . ." It also makes manifest the continuing relevance of Catherine R. Stimpson's forthright acknowledgment that feminist critics "whose literary training has been in texts and textualities have frequently been ignorant of history's massive details. . . . So erring, feminist critics (I among them) have used literature as proof simple of patriarchal squalors."[140]

Of course, feminist critics are, as we have seen, hardly alone in their sometime tendency to gloss or even "rectify" the past. But insofar as it still constitutes as much an impassioned moral and political commitment as it does a well-developed critical method, feminist criticism seems particularly liable, in Jean Bethke Elshtain's words, to "a de-historicizing sweep that deflects from cultural particularities in search of the 'root' of all ways of life."[141] "Not yet fully evolved as a critical mode," as Patricia Meyer Spacks has noted, feminist criticism "can encourage practitioners to make texts into pretexts for expounding personal predilections" and "can appear to trivialize the critical enterprise."

> It commits its practitioner to passionate concerns but not to specific methodology. . . . The strengths I have mentioned—methodological flexibility, passionate commitment, insistence on relating art to life—imply corresponding weaknesses. Flexibility can lead to lack of discipline, to self-indulgence. . . . The passionate criticism which underlies the best feminist criticism sometimes supports the worst. Such commitment can confuse critical and political activity.[142]

The result, concludes Spacks, is on occasion "a kind of one-note criticism," in which "[r]eaders newly aware of the injustices perpetrated on one sex find evidence of such injustice everywhere—and sometimes, *only* evidence of this sort."[143]

Left-wing feminist criticism of Orwell, especially *The Orwell Mystique*, has unfortunately inclined in this direction. Thus *Burmese Days* is not primarily about imperialism but "reveals the extent to which an androcentric view of

the world . . . can be adapted to imperial purposes." *A Clergyman's Daughter* and *Keep the Aspidistra Flying* "enable us to study Orwell's gender ideology and its constraints on him as a writer of realistic fiction." *Down and Out* and *Wigan Pier* are not "examples of progressive and polemical reporting" but rather "narratives of a process of masculine self-affirmation." *Wigan Pier* is completely vitiated by its omission of "any reference to that key analytical tool, the sexual division of labor." Tubby Bowling in *Coming Up for Air* is no symbol for the English people, but rather "a spokesman for a misogyny ever more frantic in the face of changes threatening men's sense of being in control." *The Lion and the Unicorn* reflects neither "patriotism" nor any real anti-fascist convictions on Orwell's part but "is much more simply explained by his adherence to the myth of the warrior, which makes military prowess an essential part of the conventional notion of manhood and therefore something men want and need." "The Art of Donald McGill" is a flawed essay because "Orwell was not able to analyze the ideology of gender roles depicted in McGill's postcards." Orwell's democratic socialism was hopelessly simple-minded and romantic because he failed to "anticipate how sexuality would become the apotheosis of commodity fetishism"; his analysis of political language was disabled by his "masculine linguistics," his use of "he" rather than "he/she." *Animal Farm* is marred by "gender hierarchy" because the pig leaders "are not just pigs but boars." *Nineteen Eighty-Four* is not chiefly about the postwar international political scene but is properly understood (via the "conceptual apparatus" of "game theory") as "an allegory of hypertrophied masculinity" given the centrality of the homoerotic Winston-O'Brien relationship.[144]

Thus feminist ideology, which enabled original insights by feminist Left critics into Orwell's dismaying *machismo* and regressive gender politics, also blinds many of them to the complexity of his *oeuvre* and of his historical situation. Their *own* obsession with gender politics—what Frank Lentricchia has termed "essentialist feminism"—has prevented them from appreciating legitimate concerns other than gender (e.g., class, race, nation) which Orwell did address explicitly and effectively. As Lentricchia suggests, when "the sexual difference is [treated as] the only difference that makes a difference," criticism moves precipitously and "directly to the literary level . . . sans all mediation."[145] The consequences for literary criticism and historical scholarship are impoverishing.

As it evolves as a critical mode, therefore, feminist criticism confronts the work of intellectual maturation: to preserve the energy of its passions while insisting on complexity and richness in its analyses. Part of the latter task entails appreciating always "cultural particularities" and "history's massive details," distinguishing (though not separating) "critical and political activity," and avoiding "one-note criticism." The "new feminist intellectual," in Elshtain's phrase, must resist the impulse to "conflate difference with inequality," the "implicit, if not explicit, calls to solidarity," and "the creation of nothing but positive images of the movement," so that her work

gets "neither stuck in gendered categories nor [is] driven to deny the truth of gendered histories."[146] Susan Sontag puts the challenge of balancing feminist passion with intellectual complexity more pointedly in her still-pertinent 1975 exchange with Adrienne Rich, who criticized Sontag's inattention to feminist issues in the latter's essay on Leni Riefenstahl. Sontag replied:

> Applied to a particular historical subject, the feminist passion yields conclusions which, however true, are extremely general. Like all capital moral truths, feminism is a bit simple-minded. That is its power and, as the language of Rich's letter shows, that is its limitation. Fascism must also be seen in the context of other—less perennial—problems. Rich wants to persuade me I'm haggling, afraid to take the moral plunge. "What are these but masculinist, virilist, patriarchal values?" she asks. The trouble with *what-are-these-but* arguments is that they lead not just to devaluation of the complexity of history, but to aspersions upon its very claim on our attention. . . . Rich refers to a "phenomenon called fascism" as if she were in some doubt about its reality—as indeed she is—since, according to her view, all that epiphenomenal trash is nothing "in the light of" the real stuff, patriarchal history.[147]

Indeed the tendency to cast aspersions upon the very claim of the complexity of history to our attention has been, as the two previous case studies evince, the long-standing procedure of many of Orwell's unsympathetic, ideologically straitened left-wing critics. The search for motives, not the establishment of contexts. That, in a phrase, has been the approach of the Marxist and feminist Left toward Orwell. "Her Orwell," proclaims the blurb on the back cover of *The Orwell Mystique,* "like the Emperor in the fairy-tale, stands unveiled before us." Having punctured "the Orwell mystique," having gotten "inside 'the Orwell myth,' " nothing remains. Having dethroned the emperor, there is nothing left but to disrobe him. This stance of disillusioned loathing represents a main line of continuity between the attitudes voiced toward Orwell by the Stalinists of his generation, Williams and the *New Left Review,* and the post-structuralist Left (Christopher Norris) and post-New Left feminists of the 1980s.

Ironically, one of Orwell's most severe critics, E.P. Thompson, provided sharpest insight into the fashionable critical practice of ahistorical unmasking, which he discussed in his already cited hostile 1960 essay on the baneful "legacy of Orwell": "The disenchanted," wrote Thompson, speaking of those 1950s Labourites who rejected political utopianism, "fastened on the problem of motive. All the obstinate questions of actual context . . .—these could be set on one side." Thompson was lashing out at Orwell's "quietism" in "Inside the Whale," written during the dark days of England's looming defeat in 1940, an essay which allegedly "buried" the radical aspirations of the postwar generation.[148] Unwittingly, however, Thompson's sentences fairly summarize Orwell's far Left reception, yesterday and today: not contexts discovered, but motives uncovered.

V

To contextualize, however, is not—and should not be—to radically his-
toricize. Historians must walk the fine, unmarked line between contex-
tualizing to understand and historicizing to whitewash. As we strive to
understand the past, we need not—and should not—renounce the task of
historical judgment, only maintain a keen awareness of the implications
and responsibilities of judicial criticism. This entails neither rationalizing
nor condoning the newly perceived shortcomings (sexism, racism, imperialism) of figures of the past, only the injunction to see their limitations and
achievements in the light of their situation and that of their contemporaries. Interestingly, the situation of Orwell's reception by feminist radicals
presents an analogous challenge: to appreciate the complicated context of
*their* criticism and yet not recoil from noting its tendencies toward anachronism and essentialism.

Such sensitivity to Orwell's and his readers' historical situations is especially necessary given that his chilly reception by the feminist Left exemplifies the role of the history of ideas in shaping reputations, i.e., what happens to an established reputation when it collides with a belief system in
direct conflict with the values which helped enshrine and sustain it. Orwell's
reputation ascended in the non-feminist '50s; the feminist revisionism of
the '80s represents not only the newest but also the strongest challenge to
his reputation, at least in the academy and among intellectuals.

How can one be a truly "popular" hero and not stand as the champion of
half of humanity? feminists across the political spectrum ask, justly, about
Orwell. Their question pointedly exposes the limitation of the very title of
this room in the gallery: "The Common Man." What about the "common
woman"? A real champion of "decency and democracy" should recognize
that "the people" include women too! His egalitarian call should extend to
everyone; feminism, after all, is humanism.

In one sense, however, the impulse behind the "feminist Orwell" represents yet another ideal image of Common Man Orwell. Fairly or not, feminists have expected more of Orwell than of his contemporaries; they have
wanted him to be Trilling's and Spender's "extraordinary ordinary man" on
women's issues too. In effect they have wished that The Common Man were
The Prophet, a feminist trailblazer. "If Orwell were alive today," some
feminists dream, he might be different; and yet they hold him to his past:
he should have been different *then* too. The case of Orwell and the feminists
indicates how history can overtake an author, so that he becomes judged by
standards he could not have anticipated in his own day. He must, therefore,
not be merely a man of his time if he is to remain a figure; subsequent
generations of readers must be able to project *their* bedrock values as *his*.
When a figure can no longer accommodate his readers' idealized self-
images, his status is in jeopardy. For most readers seem to feel that a figure
must somehow guide them; when they sense that they have "overtaken"
him or her, their responses often turn from gratitude to contempt.

Indeed Orwell's exalted status only increases the urge to make him an "extraordinary" ordinary man on all issues, which in turn heightens the frustration when he cannot finally be remolded into the figure one desires. And there *is* recalcitrance: the gender gap is there. Many women cannot "read themselves into" Orwell very easily. They come to him with the expectation that he speaks to "the common reader," only to find the dialogue virtually closed. His reader seems to be the common *male* reader, and the disappointment is keen. His defaced "anti-woman" image held by some feminists thus arises partly from the pain of seeking to identify with a figure, only to be deflected. Their feeling of letdown, which their high expectations deepen and sharpen, points to the large problem of heroic identification across gender. This process of heightened anticipation and painful disenchantment suggests the dynamics of what might be called *figural recalcitrance*—and the spectrum of response available when one encounters it. The range of Orwell's fractured reception within the radical/ liberal feminist audience reflects variously the urge for a heroism that transcends gender modeling, the longing for intellectual heroes who are heroines too, the acquiescence to gradual social change, and the recognition or evasion of the differences between present and past.

In part "the Orwell cult" *is* a "cult of masculinity." As we have already seen, the images of Orwell as The Rebel and The Common Man—especially as iconoclast, plain speaker, and tough-minded pragmatist—have even been portrayed on the covers of popular men's magazines. The masculine voice of Orwell's prose, his association of moral courage with physical courage, his own "manly" example that socialism is something to fight and die for, his railing against the "softness" of a machine civilization, his emphasis on "hard" experience rather than theory and jargon, his conviction that one could be a socialist and yet be an "ordinary" man, his Quixotic capacity to *act*: Orwell the man and writer projected a virile image, especially attractive to radical male intellectuals of a generation naively worshipful of "common" men of action. Indeed part of his appeal has always been his capacity to make intellectual life seem manly, not effeminate, a calling of unusual adventure, larger than life. Male intellectuals have therefore projected their own dreams onto him, romanticizing his life as the saga of a world-historical individual somehow managing to touch all the major currents of his age, from poverty to imperialism to fascism. In all this Orwell has seemed the quintessential public writer—and the public sphere is the one to which men have traditionally felt called and compelled. Patai is wrong to suggest that Orwell has appealed especially to "British males of his own class";[149] as this study makes clear, his attractiveness to readers has transcended class and nationality, if not gender.

As far as gender is concerned, however, that process of highly selective perception which we have discussed as "the ideology of repute" has indeed operated; and it has not only contributed to the diverse imagery of Orwell's reputation but also helped elevate his reputation. The tendency to take the part for the whole has in this case meant to take the male for the human, so

that readers, male and sometimes female, have treated Orwell's slighting remarks about women as beneath mention. One reason why "the feminist Orwell" emerged only in the 1980s is that, until the 1970s feminist issues were typically subsumed under other topics. Orwell was as guilty of this as anyone. On the other hand, reflexively imposing contemporary moral-political standards on figures of the past often trivializes issues (e.g., to criticize Orwell's use of "he" rather than "he/she").

That the literary culture of the 1980s could receive Orwell's fictional women without feminist comment is, however, extremely unlikely. (Witness the furor during the last decade over Kingsley Amis' allegedly misogynistic fiction.) It is noteworthy that the first full-length revisionist study of Orwell has been Patai's feminist critique. Just as the Cold War climate was crucial for establishing certain aspects of Orwell's multifaceted reputation, then, the emergent feminist consciousness among intellectuals will probably play a large role in further reshaping his reputation, if not to some degree undermining it.

## 13. Critic and Object of Popular Culture

### I

One of the images of Common Man Orwell which arose in the 1940s and to which we have already alluded is "the critic of popular culture." Still another of the distinctive aspects of Orwell's reputation, however, is that he has come to stand not only as a pioneering critic but also as a commercial object of popular culture. Probably no other writer's work has both so decisively contributed to the development of popular culture studies as a formal domain of academic inquiry and so widely penetrated the international imagination that it qualifies as a substantial body of material for popular culture analysis.

This facial history explores the origins and nature of this unusual achievement, which is partly attributable to the variety of Orwell's *oeuvre*. For different works have accounted for his dual status as culture "critic" and culture "object." Whereas his essay collections (especially *Inside the Whale* and *Critical Essays*) and some of his journalism have exerted influence on postwar culture critics, *Animal Farm* and *Nineteen Eighty-Four* have been mined in diverse ways, particularly during the recent countdown to 1984, by commercial and ideological interest groups.

### II

When the history of popular culture studies comes to be written, Orwell should figure prominently in its early chapters. He was far from the only English intellectual in the 1920s and '30s interested in popular art. But he was one of the few who was truly receptive to it and who made it his

business to explore "the emotional overlap between the intellectual and the common man."[150] Accustomed to treating affection for the popular arts as obvious evidence of poor or lower-class taste, and deeply influenced by F. R. Leavis' impassioned defense of "minority culture" and by the elitist assumptions of T. S. Eliot and literary modernism, most English intellectuals before Orwell paid attention to popular art chiefly in order to denigrate it. In his *Principles of Literary Criticism* (1927), I. A. Richards urged the development of a theory of criticism which would explain the wide appeal of the popular arts "and give clear reasons why those who disdain them are not necessarily snobs."[151] Q. D. Leavis in *Fiction and the Reading Public* (1932) ridiculed the notion that P. G. Wodehouse and Edgar Wallace (two of Orwell's favorite "good bad" writers) merited serious attention. Like Orwell, Mrs. Leavis characterized her approach to the study of the history of English bestsellers as "anthropological." Yet unlike him, she was unsympathetic to her hostage subjects. She emphasized in particular that "an essential part of taste" was the pedagogical task of inoculating the public against the attractions of mass and popular culture.[152] Practical suggestions for such acculturation were soon forthcoming in F. R. Leavis and Denys Thompson's *Culture and Environment* (1933), which was circulated widely in English schools in the next two decades. It featured numerous examples of commercial exploitation by advertisers and middlebrows, asked questions virtually designed to reinforce taste snobbery ("What sort of person would likely respond to this type of advertisement?"), and recommended other anti-populist reading (e.g., *Instincts of the Herd, England and the Octopus*).[153] The Leavises and their fellow *Scrutiny* contributors drew the battle lines as "high" versus "low." They left no doubt about where they stood: Good taste = high art.

More than anything else, then, Orwell differed from these and most other English intellectuals of his day in that he genuinely liked "that stuff," popular culture. Orwell's onetime flatmate Rayner Heppenstall, later head of the BBC Third Programme, makes clear how different the Sancho Panza side of thirty-two-year-old Eric Blair was from most intellectuals of their time. Orwell casually suggested in "The Art of Donald McGill" that most people harbored a "secret" "vulgar" taste for popular art; Heppenstall says he and his literary friends certainly didn't:

> I had assiduously read *The Magnet* until [the age of eleven], and at Blackpool long ago had been amused by the picture-postcards, but I thought it odd to make a cult of these things. It did not seem to me to matter very much whether Edgar Wallace was a Fascist or not, since I was not tempted to read his books. . . . The fondness for country parsonages, comic postcards, anecdotes about Queen Victoria and bishops, all betrayed something quite inaccessible to us.[154]

The list is a representative inventory of Orwell's lifelong popcult favorites, and here again we see the iconoclastic Orwell rebelling against "the intellectuals" in the direction of his "common man." For despite his very strong aesthetic preferences for "old-fashioned" realistic Edwardian novels

like those of H. G. Wells, Orwell was a true liberal and democrat, and a defiant pluralist. All cultural products, he thought, merited sociological attention, if not aesthetic admiration. His anthropological sensibility toward popular literature is apparent in a 1936 letter to British anthropologist Geoffrey Gorer:

> I have often thought it would be very interesting to study the conventions etc. of books from an anthropological point of view. I don't know if you ever read Elmer Rice's *A Voyage to Purilia*. It contains a most interesting analysis of certain conventions—taken for granted and never mentioned—existing in the ordinary film. It would be interesting and I believe valuable to work out the underlying beliefs and general imaginative background of a writer like Edgar Wallace. But of course that's the kind of thing nobody will ever print.[155]

Orwell himself deserves some of the credit for the fact that his last sentence sounds so absurd to us today. It is easy to forget that his anthropological temper was rare among literary people in the mid-'30s; although a documentary interest in the everyday life of "the public" was part of a general, Left-inspired trend during the decade (best exemplified by the social scientific research of the "Mass-Observers"[156]), radicals gave relatively little attention to popular art. In both his culture criticism and his documentary writing (e.g., *Down and Out in Paris and London*), Orwell became well known in the 1930s as the writer who, in V. S. Pritchett's later phrase, "went native in his own country."[157] Orwell's popular culture essays heralded a new, more open way of looking at one's native culture. Accordingly, his effect on popular culture studies has been more cognitive than methodological. Orwell never systematized his approach to popular culture, yet he helped liberate Anglo-American intellectuals to *see* "ordinary" culture. He contributed toward the emergence of a wider, more inclusive stance toward cultural phenomena in the 1940s and '50s, rather than toward any formal method or aesthetics of popular culture. He was original insofar as he was one of the first critics to demonstrate how popular art offered insight into the public mind.

Much of Orwell's influence on popular culture studies has also to do with the mere fact that his essays are among the most widely read criticism on the subject. In addition to enjoying his journalism and occasional pieces on popular songs, jokes, and detective stories,[158] millions of readers have admired Orwell's three widely reprinted wartime essays: "Boys' Weeklies" (1940), dealing with boys' twopenny papers; "The Art of Donald McGill" (1941), an analysis of the vulgar penny postcard; and "Raffles and Miss Blandish" (1944), a discussion of the crime thriller.[159] The significance of the three essays, all collected in *Critical Essays* in 1946, was immediately recognized by intellectuals on both sides of the Atlantic. Evelyn Waugh compared Orwell to Edmund Wilson as "outstandingly the wisest" English representative of "the new humanism of the common man," which Waugh described as being characterized in criticism by the abandonment of "the

hierarchic principle." V.S. Pritchett hailed Orwell as "the first critic of real popular commercial culture, this uncouth and fertile field." In America, Henry Levin praised Orwell's essays as "pioneering" examples of "trenchant analyses of the patterns of popular culture," and Eric Bentley singled them out as "little masterpieces," also correctly forecasting that they would stimulate American critics to study comic strips and the pulp magazines. Wilson himself pronounced Orwell "the only contemporary master" of popular culture analysis.[160]

Subtitled "Studies in Popular Culture," *Critical Essays* also included pieces on Dickens, Kipling, Wells, Wodehouse, Yeats, Koestler, and Dali. Although these last three did not treat "popular" authors or subjects as did the other essays, the overall effect of the volume was to showcase Orwell's sociological, textual approach toward literature and culture. All of the essays were examples of "semi-sociological literary criticism," the phrase Orwell once used to characterize *Inside the Whale*.[161] Indeed "Charles Dickens" and "Boys' Weeklies" had already appeared in *Inside the Whale*, and more examples of such criticism were soon to follow in *Shooting an Elephant* (1950), *England Your England* (1953), *The Orwell Reader* (1956), and *Collected Essays* (1961). These essays and journalism exerted enormous influence on the direction and tone of postwar Anglo-American culture criticism. Indeed *Inside the Whale* and *Critical Essays* could be interpreted in retrospect as the opening salvoes of the cultural debates about "midcult" and "masscult" which raged in the 1950s and '60s, between heterogeneous groups of liberal-radical intellectuals open to mass culture (Bernard Rosenberg, David Manning White) or celebrating it as the triumph of a new "democratic" aesthetic (Marshall McLuhan, Susan Sontag, Leslie Fiedler), and of conservative-radical intellectuals trying to "defend standards" (Ernest Van den Haag) or exposing mass "opiates of the people" (Dwight Macdonald, Harold Rosenberg, Max Horkheimer, Theodor Adorno, Herbert Marcuse). In the 1920s and '30s, the intellectual debate consisted largely of advocates of "high" culture (Eliot, Leavis, Clive Bell) magisterially explaining the corrupting effects of "low" culture. Orwell's cultural essays appeared at a timely moment; the ideological-cultural split among radical, liberal, and conservative intellectuals in the 1950s made them receptive to new ideas about culture.[162] His criticism helped provoke a healthy exchange among intellectuals about the value and significance of "low" culture; partly as a result of essays like "Boys' Weeklies" and "Raffles and Miss Blandish," in which Orwell distinguished between popular and mass art, the simple, oppositional 1920s dichotomy of "high" versus "low" art had expanded to at least four categories a decade later—highbrow, middlebrow, popular, and mass. The essays helped widen the intelligentsia's Arnoldian conception of what constituted art and culture—indeed they helped break down rigid distinctions among "high," "middle," and "low" art altogether. As we shall soon see, Orwell himself was no enthusiast of mass culture—witness how he excoriates "Yank mags" in "Boys' Weeklies"—but his essays did stimulate many critics to look seriously at popular and mass art. Equally important, his criticism also probably gave impetus to the rise of the

"literary" mode of popular culture analysis in the American academy and on the British Left.

For Orwell's description of *Inside the Whale* was apt; he was indeed doing "semi-sociological literary criticism." His work had a sociological component, but it was basically *literary* criticism. Orwell *assumed* that "popular" material like boys' papers and penny postcards reflected popular attitudes. Rather than take an external approach to his material which would have tested such a premise by placing the work within a broad social setting, Orwell preferred an internal, textual approach which took the work as a world of its own, assumed it to be a representative text, and excavated whatever of cultural value seemed contained within it. (If the external approach sometimes does violence to the subtleties of cultural material by imposing sociological categories and abstractions on it, the textual approach sometimes leads to false generalizations about the representativeness of the cultural material—as Orwell's errors about the authorship of the boys' papers, exposed in the riposte to "Boys' Weeklies" by author Frank Richards, demonstrates.)[163]

So Orwell took essentially the same literary-sociological approach to popular art criticism as he had to literary criticism. In effect he adapted his high culture criticism to popular materials. Probably his essays have had an indirect influence in establishing sociologically oriented textual analysis as the chief current mode of popular culture criticism—and toward the prevalent academic view in America that an "aesthetics" of popular culture should be derived by adapting already-established aesthetic approaches toward elite art, rather than be formulated *sui generis* as if "popular art" constituted a unique, autonomous discipline warranting its own aesthetics. Orwell's "semi-sociological literary criticism" also resembles much of the American "literary" criticism of popular culture of the 1960s and '70s, such as has appeared in *The Journal of Popular Culture,* founded in 1967. It is in these respects that Mary McCarthy's grand, unargued assertion that Orwell "virtually invented" popular culture criticism as a genre has some validity.[164] And yet one strongly suspects that Orwell, like his friend Julian Symons, another aficionado of popular culture and a well-known author of detective stories, would find current intrinsicalist approaches toward popular culture—which, as Symons says in one caustic discussion of "Fiedlerism," sometimes wind up lavishing attention on comic strips as if they were *King Lear*—more than faintly ridiculous.[165]

Orwell's influence on cultural criticism—not only in subject matter but also in mood and style—is especially clear in the seminal English criticism of Richard Hoggart and Raymond Williams in the late 1950s, whose work has served as the foundation for the brand of left-wing social criticism known in Britain today as "cultural studies." Hoggart's *The Uses of Literacy,* which chronicled the twentieth-century changes in English working-class culture, devoted attention to sex-and-violence novels, boys' stories, "Peg's Paper," and popular songs—all subjects treated by Orwell. Williams' *Culture and Society* traced England's "common tradition" from Burke and Cobbett

through to Lawrence and Orwell. In both books there is a strong undercurrent of nostalgia, suggesting that England's old ways and values are somehow superior to the new.[166] The Left's hostility toward "masscult" in the late 1950s also frequently manifested itself in warnings similar to Orwell's about the threat of "Americanization," a shorthand term popularized by Leavis to inveigh against "levelling down" cultural and educational standards. Already by 1962 *The Spectator* was announcing the birth of "the science" of "Culturology," identifying popular culture studies chiefly with "the new systematizers" Hoggart and Williams, and naming Orwell as one of their chief progenitors.[167] By the decade's close, some English critics were predicting that Orwell's popular culture criticism, rather than *Animal Farm* and *Nineteen Eighty-Four*, would "secure his future reputation." Orwell was "the true founder of the sociology of popular literature," who had "blazed the trail of the academic empires of Hoggart & Co."[168] Indeed the "close cultural readings" of literature developed by Hoggart and others at Birmingham University's Centre for Contemporary Culture Studies since the mid-'60s bear unmistakable affinities to Orwell's culture criticism.[169]

### III

Even as we acknowledge Orwell's broad influence on contemporary popular culture criticism, however, we should not glance over the large area of his overlap with the thinking of intellectuals of the 1930s and '40s on cultural matters. Although Orwell's critical interests ranged perhaps more widely than those of any other literary intellectual of his day, from *Ulysses* to *The Gem* and *The Magnet*, he never pretended that the two were of comparable *aesthetic* value.[170] In this conviction he was very much an intellectual of his time. Orwell was indeed a defiant, not a radical, pluralist. By no means did he advocate that culture critics *totally* abandon what Evelyn Waugh referred to as "the hierarchic principle." Instead he condemned, in Paul Fussell's phrase, "generic snobbery," believing that literature, like society, had its underclasses.[171] Postcards, comics, thrillers, and pamphlets deserved attention too, Orwell held, since the business of the critic was language and its relation to human beings.

Orwell's governing attitude toward culture was therefore a rebel's; he did not so much proselytize the worth of penny postcards as he opposed the mandarin school of art and aesthetic pretentiousness in general. Largely as a result of his boyhood immersion in popular culture, and unlike even the most sympathetic Anglo-American intellectuals in the postwar period, Orwell seems to have felt no deep conflict between the claims of "culture" and "democracy," or any doubts about the value of popular culture. He could comfortably assert in one breath the immense *sociological* value of boys' papers while conceding in the next the aesthetic superiority of traditional, "high" culture—and do all this while feeling neither the intellectual's guilt for his "elitist" tastes nor the intellectual's shame for his lowbrow preferences. For many readers, Orwell's easy embrace of popular

culture has constituted another powerful source of his Common Man appeal, seeming an accessible, immediate way to bridge the gulf between the intellectual and the public—another possible way to be an intellectual's common man.

Unlike radical culture critics of the 1960s and '70s, then, Orwell did not hold that the works of writers like Edgar Wallace had any particular literary merit. In essence Orwell believed that "high" art could be treated as a complex individual vision or aesthetic structure, whereas popular art possessed value merely as cultural data. His outlook was, for instance, far removed from the radical cultural pluralism of Herbert Gans, who argued in *Popular Culture and High Culture* (1974) not only that the public should tolerate all "taste cultures," but that all such cultures are essentially of "equal" merit.[172] For however much Orwell was fond of vulgar postcards or seemed to younger writers in the 1940s an admirable example of an open-minded culture critic, his cultural outlook was Arnoldian insofar as he was first and last an old-fashioned literary intellectual, for whom poetry and the novel were the canonical forms of verbal art and for whom "culture" was the criticism of life. One can little imagine his participating in what Susan Sontag hailed as "the new sensibility" of the 1960s, which exalted Andy Warhol, the Temptations, and Happenings as art.[173]

Orwell also shared his literary contemporaries' distaste for most of the products of mass technology—of the radio, film, and the "slick" magazines. He associated them with "decadent" "modern," often "American" life. He had special contempt for Hollywood films, which he saw as a form of American cultural imperialism. As film critic for *Time and Tide* in 1940–41, Orwell railed again and again at the escapism of most American films, their absurd plots and empty urbanity, and their vaguely "fascist background." Like the Leavises, he generally saw film as "prolefeed" and feared its rise was part of the approaching "machine-culture."[174] But unlike the *Scrutiny* writers, Orwell did not see the radio and film as inherently corrupting; often he emphasized instead their potential power to elevate British culture.[175] The admittedly difficult task, Orwell said, was to raise the mass media's intellectual and aesthetic standards. And, as he showed in discussing crime thrillers in "Raffles and Miss Blandish," he was generally much more concerned to discover what social trends mass art reflected than to condemn mass culture itself.[176] And more interested too in showing the possible continuities among art forms than in counterposing "high" and "low" art—which is why he could think of the popular music hall comedian Max Miller as the Dickens of interwar England.[177]

His lifetime of uninhibited pleasure in reading papers like *The Gem* and *The Magnet* is evident everywhere in Orwell's fiction, which is filled with references to popular culture. In fact Orwell's novels constitute interesting culture criticism in their own right, and they may be read for their sharply differing verdicts on the value of popular and mass art. George Bowling's simple boyhood joy of lying on his belly and dreamily reading the penny-weekly *Chums* ("I'm up the Amazon, and it's bliss, pure bliss") in *Coming Up*

*for Air* contrasts pointedly with Gordon Comstock's disgust with the trashy books in Mr. Cheesman's mushroom library (marked "Sex," "Crime," and "Wild West") in *Keep the Aspidistra Flying*. In *Nineteen Eighty-Four* the old nursery rhyme about the London churches ("Oranges and lemons, say the bells of St. Clements") gives way to versificators belching out consoling jingles for the proles ("It was only an 'opeless fancy"), pornosec and novel writing machines, violent "flicks," and Hate Week telescreen features.

Orwell's conception of popular art was open and elastic. In practice "popular culture" meant for him the range of his own idiosyncratic cultural interests, from the oral traditions of folklore (e.g., the Vicar of Bray) to "good bad" poetry like Kipling's verse to Dickens' novels.[178] All of these were deeply rooted in the culture of his "common man." Orwell also drew a sharp distinction in practice, if never theoretically, between "popular" and "mass" culture. "Natural" versus "artificial," rather than high-middle-low, were his implicit distinguishing criteria. "Popular" art consisted of the artifacts, often traditional and communitarian, of folkways; "mass" art reflected commercialization and modernity. Max Miller's music hall performances, P. G. Wodehouse's school stories, Conan Doyle's detective stories, Frank Harris' boys' papers, village cricket, and the corner pub were immensely and self-evidently different, Orwell felt, from the "gangster 'Yank' mags," glossy American women's fashion magazines, racy bestsellers, and most radio programs and Hollywood films. To Orwell, the two groups belonged to different centuries and different worlds. As he argued in "Raffles and Miss Blandish," the peaceful Edwardian "schoolboy atmosphere" of gentlemen thief Raffles contrasted glaringly with the violent "modern" American world of James Chase's *No Orchids for Miss Blandish*. (Although he was not wholly aware of it, Orwell's fondness for many of the products of English popular culture was nostalgia; he associated them with his Edwardian childhood, that decade before World War I which George Bowling rosily remembers as a time of "endless summers.")

In "Boys' Weeklies" Orwell also offers an ideological justification for his preferences. Radio and the film industry are monopolies which need not study their readership closely, and bestsellers typically aim at the £4-per-week market and above. But papers like *The Gem* and *The Magnet* have specialized subject matter and cost tuppence. They continue to exist only because there is a demand for them. Thus they furnish "the best available indication of what the English people really feels and thinks."[179] Rayner Heppenstall was probably not exaggerating about Orwell's curiosity as to whether the work of Edgar Wallace reflected a fascist outlook; another of Orwell's legacies to popular culture criticism was to alert readers to the ideological slant of popular art. In "Boys' Weeklies" Orwell argues that popular boys' papers like *The Gem* and *The Magnet* are conservative in political tendency. They are "consistently and cheerfully patriotic" and project a world view *circa* 1910.[180] Much of the Marxist and feminist culture criticism of the 1960s and '70s (on comic strips, elementary school readers, romances, etc.) echoes (and sometimes even quotes)[181] the close of "Boys'

# $19.84

## By Einstein Moomjy.

WAR IS PEACE.
FREEDOM IS SLAVERY.
IGNORANCE IS STRENGTH.
And our crisp new Sisal-like look in wool broadloom is $19.84 a sq. yd.*

At $19.84 it's well worth watching, Big Brother. For although the past doesn't exist and we could be vaporized for committing a thoughtcrime, we'll just tell you that it was $39.99.

$19.84 for a revolutionary new carpet with a tight, low, fashionably flat look and a wide (13'9") selection of colors that are as crisp and heathery as a day in autumn: blue, beige, taupe, white linen (for people dreaming of an off white crispness) and to coin a phrase, fraise.

Perfect for the Ministry of Love or Truth or Peace or whatever ministry you work in. Also very much at home at home.

In 100% wool. So it'll be around for lots of 1984's to come.

But we're also ringing out the Oldspeak and bringing in the Newspeak in our Oridep (Newspeak for Oriental Department) where it's $1984. for our Indo Persian collection of Tabriz, Kashan and Kerman designs.

It was (ooops, a thoughtcrime again) $3249. for them.

So it's the best price in over a millenium.

All hand knotted, all approximately 9'x 12', all 100% wool. In uncold colors like red, brick and (tusk...tusk...) ivory.

All made by the master weavers of East Asia.

Ooops, we forgot. Sorry Big Brother. Only Oceania has master weavers. Uh-oh, they're coming to get us. Be speedwise and get to Einstein Moomjy before it's no longer $19.84. Or $1984. Before...it's ...too...late...

## Einstein Moomjy
## The Carpet Department Store®

*Padding and installation not included.
IN NEW YORK: 150 EAST 58TH ST., (BET. LEXINGTON & THIRD AVENUES) A&D BLDG., (212) 758-0900 STORE OPEN 9:30 AM TO 6:30 PM INCL. SAT., MON. & THURS. TILL 9 PM.
IN NEW JERSEY: PARAMUS, 526 ROUTE 17 (201) 265-1100 N. PLAINFIELD, 934 ROUTE 22 (201) 755-6800 WHIPPANY, 265 ROUTE 10 (201) 887-3600 LAWRENCEVILLE, 2801 BRUNSWICK PIKE (ALT. U.S. 1) (609) 883-0700. ALL N.J. STORES OPEN DAILY TO 9 PM, SAT. TO 6 PM. WE ACCEPT VISA, MASTER CARD AND AMERICAN EXPRESS

PURE WOOL PILE

Socialist writer as capitalist money-maker:
"19.84 for a revolutionary new carpet."

The 1984 hoopla exhausted even Snoopy.

# We're betting $2.3 billion Orwell was wrong.

We see a sunnier future today than George Orwell did in 1948, which is one reason we've launched our most ambitious capital investment program ever.

If all goes according to plan, we'll have invested $2.3 billion in our operations by the time 1984 arrives, and we'll have doubled our company's size.

There's more to this investment than growth, though. It's also designed to help us produce more wood and paper products *more efficiently.*

Our $2.3 billion will buy the innovations we need to continue to provide what all of us want: rewarding jobs, affordable products, growing profits *and* thriving trees.

At least, that's what we're betting on. And, with all due respect to a fine writer, we like the odds.

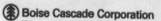

**Boise Cascade Corporation**
Wood and paper for today, trees for tomorrow.

Down the memory hole: draining Orwell of his identity and filling him with our hype.

"So when Farmer Bob comes through
the door, three of us circle around
and . . . Muriel! Are you chewing
your cud while I'm talking?"

Gary Larson's cartoons and those
of Boynton's Animal Farm line
are two popular products which
have made extensive use of
animal personification, sometimes
borrowing an idea or two from
*Animal Farm*.

Weeklies," including Orwell's charge that the papers (owned by Lord Camrose and the right-wing Amalgamated Press) reflect a calculated conservative and capitalist bias:

> Personally I believe that most people are influenced far more than they would care to admit by novels, serial stories, films, and so forth, and from this point of view the worst books are often the most important, because they are usually the ones read earliest in life. It is probable that many people who consider themselves sophisticated and "advanced" are actually carrying through life an imaginative background which they acquired in childhood from (for instance) Sapper and Ian Hay. If that is so, the boys' twopenny weeklies are of the deepest importance. Here is the stuff that is read somewhere between the ages of twelve and eighteen by a very large proportion, perhaps the majority, of English boys, including many who will never read anything else except newspapers; and along with it they are absorbing a set of beliefs which would be regarded as hopelessly out of date in the Central Office of the Conservative Party. All the better because this is done indirectly, there is being pumped into them the conviction that the major problems of our time do not exist, that there is nothing wrong with *laissez-faire* capitalism, that foreigners are unimportant comics and that the British Empire is a sort of charity-concern which will last forever. Considering who owns these papers, it is difficult to believe that this is unintentional.[182]

Orwell goes on to suggest that the Left no longer leave the field of popular literature to the Right ("*All* fiction from the novels in the mushroom libraries downwards is censored in the interests of the ruling class"[183]). He advocates the creation of boys' and women's papers with a left-wing slant. A few months later, in early 1940, he attempted to launch a left-wing comic with the children's story writer Geoffrey Trease, but the project fell through.[184]

Orwell's essay on Dickens reflected his conviction that the best popular art was politically subversive. "One of the marks of popular culture is a good-tempered antinomianism rather of Dickens' type."[185] Here Orwell, once a member of an Eton schoolboy faction known as "The Antinomians," is again sketching his self-portrait by way of doing literary criticism.[186] His assessment of Dickens' popularity is a fair estimate of important aspects of his own wide appeal. To Orwell, Dickens' "decency" is linked to his radicalism and rebelliousness; Dickens' continued popularity is due to his remarkable affinity with the Victorian mind, significant features of which had lingered on into Orwell's adulthood. Orwell sees that Dickens' work (as has Orwell's own in our day) fitted the needs of his age and those of several generations to follow. Orwell also notes that Dickens' artistic limitations are great. And yet Dickens possesses "a native generosity of mind" which "is probably the central secret of his popularity."[187] In literary terms, observes Orwell, the secret is revealed in Dickens' capacity to express "in comic, simplified, and therefore memorable form the native decency of the common man," who even in the 1930s—partly due to the power of Dickens'

imagination—is "still living in the mental world of Dickens." Like other artifacts of popular culture—folk stories and comic strips, Mickey Mouse and Popeye the Sailor, working-class socialism—Dickens' work embodies, according to Orwell, "the feeling that one is always on the side of the underdog, on the side of the weak against the strong."[188] The impression of severe artistic limitations, the sense of decency, the feeling of impassioned sympathy for the underdog—most readers of Orwell find his work characterized by these very same shortcomings and strengths.

## IV

By the early 1980s, Orwell the public writer had gone a step beyond Dickens. Not only had his writings "entered even into the minds of people who do not care about" books;[189] his work had also come to serve as the raw material for popular and mass cultural artifacts. And here we shift focus from Orwell as "critic" to "object" of popular culture, and from his reception by literary intellectuals to his use by commercial and ideological interest groups.

In Part One we discussed the variety of allusions to "Orwell" and "Orwellian" in the mass media and their implications, and in Chapter Five we will consider the impact of screen adaptations of *Animal Farm* and *Nineteen Eighty-Four* on his reputation as a "prophet." But Orwell's incorporation by contemporary mass culture has been even more pervasive than these developments indicate. Here our chief concern is not with media adaptations of Orwell's books or the entry of his catchwords into the political lexicon, but with the formal use of his name and work in all kinds of promotional activities.

The extraordinary degree to which "Orwell" was employed in such promotional campaigns, sometimes even before the 1980s, is yet another indication of his enormous public reputation—and a comment upon Orwell's own writing practices. For Orwell himself liberally used the popular and mass art of his day as background and motif for his fiction; reciprocally, his work itself has in turn become part of popular and mass culture. For example, the well-known Animal Farm greeting cards, featuring a piglet straddling a wall (caption: "Some cards are more equal than others"), have been popular since the early 1970s. Orwell wrote about postcards and comic strips; the 1984 countdown witnessed Orwell postcards, comic strips, T-shirts, pop songs (Laurie Anderson's "Good Morning, Mr. Orwell," Van Halen's "1984"). Campaign buttons ("Orwell in '84!!") came from a Pennsylvania advertising company, which launched the Orwell for President campaign in 1983–84, nominating their favorite-son candidate on April Fool's Day, 1983.[190]

Some spinoffs pegged to "1984" laced their humor with political invective. The left-slanted *Big Brother Book of Lists,* with a sinister Thought Police agent in a black trench coat on the cover, used "1984" as a handy hook for its numerous compilations (e.g., J. Edgar Hoover's eight ways to spot a car driven by a Communist[191]). *The 1984 Calendar: An American History* similarly

noted about 250 dates in history which the creators considered anniversaries of government intrusion into the lives of individuals.[192] In addition, the national campaign committees of both the Democratic and Republican parties sent out cover letters referring to the "Orwellian spectre" in soliciting funds from party supporters, on issues ranging from defense spending to abortion.

So in 1984 the socialist author was exploited not only as an ideological patron but also as a capitalist money-maker. "Orwell" was a hot item; the date's approach ignited a conflagration which lasted for several months. Orwell's popular reputation blazed like a shooting star, radiating into numerous spheres outside the literary-academic scene. An in-depth analysis of his treatment in hundreds of popular periodicals in 1983–84—quite possibly unprecedented for a literary figure—would probably offer insight into the relation between commercial fanaticism and celebrity. Just a partial list of the specialized magazines and trade journals which ran stories on Orwell and "1984" in late 1983 and early 1984, some of them with utterly outlandish angles of interest,[193] gives a hint of the phenomenal range of Orwell's reception among non-intellectual audiences during this time.

| | |
|---|---|
| *Roofing Spectator* | *Four Wheeler* |
| *Art Material Trade News* | *Cruising World* |
| *The National Clothesline Monthly* | *Ohio Farmer* |
| *Racing Wheel Times* | *Tennis Monthly* |
| *Construction Equipment Distribution News* | *Cablevision* |
| *Computer Decisions Monthly* | *Hospitals* |
| *Electronic Packaging and Production Monthly* | *Metal News* |
| *American Medical News* | |
| *Insulation Outlook Monthly*[194] | |

The presentation of Orwell and *Nineteen Eighty-Four* in these organs indicates how a writer's image can alter—sometimes beyond recognition— as his name and work radiate beyond the sphere of the serious literary community into the wider public. Take, for example, the following banal use of *Nineteen Eighty-Four* by *The Welding Journal*. Addressed to industry employees, the February 1984 article ("1984 Is Here!") began by confusing *Nineteen Eighty-Four* with *Animal Farm:*

> *Are you more equal than others?* This is your chance to become one who is more equal than others, more expert in the welding field. . . .
> Is Big Brother watching you? If to you Big Brother is your boss, a board of directors, a steering committee, or a review board, they too will be watching—and they will be wondering if you are keeping aware of today's fast-moving welding technology.[195]

Such hilarious examples of commercial defacement suggest the difference between the popularization and vulgarization of a work of art, a line hard to draw conceptually yet often quite identifiable in practice. Because its title

was a date, *Nineteen Eighty-Four* is probably unique in the way it was used by commercial and ideological interest groups. But the general process of its incorporation into commercial culture nevertheless broadly illustrates how the reputation of a relatively popular writer inevitably alters in response to changes in the time and place of his reception. Two trade journal editorials in 1983–84 underline this last point even more clearly. They also show how Orwell's public image as a "dark prophet" readily served as a pretext for industry spokesmen to counterpose themselves as "true," optimistic prophets. Their treating *Nineteen Eighty-Four* as a historical forecast, rather than as a warning against totalitarian thinking, allowed them to "trump Orwell" with sunny counter-forecasts about their own industry. The first editorial is from *The Casual Living Monthly;* the second is from *The Shooting Industry:*

> If I were to play George Orwell for one brief fleeting moment, I would predict a bright future for the casual furniture industry in 1984. My prediction is based strictly on fact and empirical observation, leaving fantasy and hypothesis to Orwell and his like.
>
> Unless George Orwell's predictions come true and 1984 sees Big Brother remove the accessibility of handguns from the majority of citizens, the handgun business should recover at least as fast as the general economy.[196]

As one might expect, however, the commercialization of Orwell and *Nineteen Eighty-Four* was carried out chiefly by the major Anglo-American mass media. By late 1983, the American press was shrieking that "Orwellmania!" has seized the U.S. and Britain.[197] One headline in January 1984 summed up the ubiquity of Orwell's name: "Where Will the Orwellian Fascination End?"[198] In the opening months of the year, gratefully christened "The Year of the Book" by Penguin Books, *Nineteen Eighty-Four* made publishing history, topping the *New York Times* and *Publisher's Weekly* lists of best-selling mass market fiction for five weeks, the first time any book several years old (let alone thirty-five) had ever risen to occupy the #1 position.[199]

The promotional campaigns associated with *Nineteen Eighty-Four* and the book's sales explosion in 1983–84 were actually the culmination of a decade-long trend.[200] By 1979, popular magazines like *Time* and *Playboy* were warning readers that "1984" was "only" five years away. The first signs that the countdown was turning *Nineteen Eighty-Four* into a mass culture object came in 1980–81. The 1980 Yale University's freshman "facebook" for the class of 1984 featured dozens of photographs of George Orwell, included to replace those "faceless" student "unpersons" who had failed to include a snapshot with their college applications.[201] In the next year "Orwell" and "1984" appeared in several advertisements. "We're betting $2.3 million that Orwell was wrong" ran an ad headline in early 1981 in *Time* for the Boise Cascade paper company. The full-page ad pictured a scene reminiscent of the Golden Country in *Nineteen Eighty-Four.* A husband, wife, and little boy stroll arm-in-arm through a quiet

glen, and then step lightly through the pages of a titanic calendar labeled "1984": "We see a sunnier future than George Orwell did in 1948," the ad copy begins, "which is one reason why we've launched our most ambitious capital investment program ever."[202] In succeeding months other firms and stores spun ambitious ad campaigns off "1984." One of the most audacious was Einstein Moomjy Carpet Store in New York (see p. 234). On New Year's Day, 1984, Apple Computers kicked off its Macintosh computer promotion using *Nineteen Eighty-Four.* The firm's controversial $500,000 one-week TV spot, probably seen by 60 million football fans on New Year's Day alone, stopped just short of labeling arch-rival IBM "Big Brother." A television image of rows of marching, chanting, zombie-citizens ("We are one people with one will, one resolve, one cause!")— presumably IBM patrons tutored in Room 101—was shattered when a beautiful woman in Olympic uniform hurled a sledgehammer through the screen. *Advertising Age* noted that no commercial in recent memory had aroused such widespread public and industry discussion.[203]

Yet nothing recedes like success. "Orwellmania" proved to be short-lived. With the exception of the Animal Farm cards and a few promotions associated with *Nineteen Eighty-Four,* the gimmickry was over by March 1984. By the date on which Winston Smith makes his first fateful diary entry, 4 April 1984, the "Orwellian fascination" had finally ended. The mutability of the present had rendered "1984" obsolescent as a masscult object.

O'Brien's declaration to Winston is a fit line on which to close this chapter: "We shall squeeze you empty, and then we shall fill you with ourselves." The line could very well serve as a gloss on the making of Orwell into a culture object, and indeed on Orwell's entire reputation-history. For "Orwell" and "1984" have been molded to fit nearly every conceivable commercial promotion and political cause, according to changes in the cultural climate. His recent reception history exemplifies how one gets "unpersoned" in a new way: not by primitive speakwrites but by the ravenous maw of commodity fetishism. Under advanced capitalism you go down the memory hole by becoming your claimant's rhetorical billboard or effigy. You are drained of your identity—and then filled with our hype.

That Common Man Orwell became "common property" in the 1980s, of course, says less about Orwell and *Nineteen Eighty-Four* than about our culture, especially about the nature of celebrity and the price—"unpersonhood"—at which it is bought. During the 1984 countdown, The Common Man became a "mass man." Society gave Orwell transitory fame in exchange for annexing and depersonalizing his name and work. The barter clarifies the terms of his peculiar dual status as culture critic and object. Partly because of his fascination with ordinary culture, Orwell had shaped his work from it, and partly on that account it had been highly assimilable and serviceable to societal reappropriation. In 1983–84 the "vast circle"[204] connecting writer and culture was completed. Orwell had drawn on the

cultural life and materials of his day, remolding them to forge his uniquely personal, searing vision of the future, *Nineteen Eighty-Four;* at last Society "reclaimed" the cultural materials, now brilliantly transformed and exalted in the finished work, and universalized itself through the work in the process of trivializing and exhausting it in and through new, ephemeral cultural artifacts—and granted its author, in return, a moment of collectivized glory.

# FIVE

# The Prophet

*... I don't see myself ever writing a best seller.*
                                        Eric Blair, 1936

## 14. Author of *the book*

### I

The commercialized Prophet Orwell and what a critic once caustically dubbed the "Profit Orwell" bear some resemblances, as the last section of Chapter Four suggested. We shall pursue their relation later in this chapter.* But what we should first notice about The Prophet is that, unlike The Rebel and The Common Man, this face and that of The Saint are cast in explictly religious imagery. This shift from secular to sacred metaphors not only reflects the expansion of Orwell's reputation and the hagiographic treatment of him toward his life's close and afterwards; it also helped trigger that sudden growth and set the stage for the rise of "the Orwell myth"—and facilitated the commercializing of Orwell's name and work. For The Prophet and The Saint—again unlike Orwell's first two faces—did not emerge over the span of Orwell's career. The Prophet crystallized after the 1949 publication of *Nineteen Eighty-Four;* The Saint emerged only posthumously.

And yet, this distinction between the religious and the profane is somewhat puzzling, for Orwell is typically discussed as a "secular prophet" or a "secular saint."[1] The language represents an effort both to recognize that Orwell considered himself an atheist and that, nevertheless, his behavior has led some admirers to call him a "lay saint." Much of the confusion in Orwell's reputation has in fact stemmed from variable uses of the "prophet"

*See Section 16, "Media Prophet": Orwell on the Telescreen, pp. 273–87.

NOVEMBER 28, 1983       $1.75

# TIME

## 1984
## Big Brother's Father

NUCLEAR ARMS
Troubled Talks
And Angry
Protests

Author
George Orwell

Orwell as Dr. Frankenstein, the Man Who Invented Big Brother.

and "saint" metaphors, with some observers approaching them within religious and sectarian traditions and others interpreting them according to contemporary secular usage.

Orwell, of course, however much he may have considered himself a "rebel" or "common man," would have disavowed the characterizations "prophet" and "saint." Still, to consider only the former here, Orwell did make clear that *Nineteen Eighty-Four* was a potentially prophetic warning to readers in the 1940s, bluntly declaring in a post-publication press release: *"The moral is: Don't let it happen. It depends on you."*[2] He was keenly interested in predictions too, and he had great admiration for the early work of H.G. Wells, whom he regarded as the "prophet" of his boyhood.[3] But Orwell also would have associated "prophet" with Christian and Jewish "fanatics," as he once described Christ and the Old Testament prophets;[4] his self-image in the late 1940s was still chiefly that of a whistleblowing rebel and anti-totalitarian dissenter, not a prophet.

But glimmerings of a grander, Wellsian image of himself occasionally appear in Orwell's writings. In "The Prevention of Literature," he cast himself as a reincarnated Old Testament prophet. Chastising the Left intelligentsia for cliquishness and implicitly holding himself up as a model of temerity, Orwell began the essay with lines from an old Revivalist hymn:

> Dare to be a Daniel,
> Dare to stand alone;
> Dare to have a purpose firm,
> Dare to make it known.[5]

Orwell obviously considered his allusion here to Daniel, the Hebrew prophet who heralded the coming of the Messiah and whose faith saved him from the lions' den, less an identification with Daniel as "prophet" than with Daniel as "rebel" and "conscience," a man who "dared to stand alone." Orwell goes on:

> In the past, . . . the idea of rebellion and the idea of intellectual integrity were mixed up. A heretic—political, moral, religious, aesthetic—was one who refused to outrage his own conscience. . . . To bring this hymn up to date one would have to add a "Don't" at the beginning of each line. For it is the peculiarity of our age that the rebels against the existing order, at any rate the most numerous and characteristic of them, are also rebelling against the idea of individual integrity. "Daring to stand alone" is ideologically criminal and practically dangerous.[6]

Much as we noted when discussing John the Baptist, we see here in Orwell's self-congratulatory criticism how a rich figure like Daniel suggests a constellation of features—daring, integrity, willed isolation—applicable both to a "true" rebel and to a prophet.

The fact is, however, that a "prophet," almost by definition, *must be* a man who "stands alone"—though, of course, not all rebels are prophets. The distinction redirects our attention to what it means for Orwell to be

spoken of as a prophet and how this face relates to the others we have identified as most prominent in his history of reputation.

For it is significant that Orwell is not merely a generic prophet. As we saw with Orwell's Rebel reputation, Orwell's image as prophet is partly derived from comparisons of him with other historical/mythical figures. He is not just *a* prophet but the prophets Daniel and John the Baptist. Perhaps the author of *Nineteen Eighty-Four* has most often reminded readers of the Old Testament prophet Jeremiah[7]—the man of peace called by God to prophesy strife for his people, unpopular in his lifetime and then lionized posthumously when his message was borne out. Even more so than Daniel, this analogue also calls to mind the notions of populism and rebellion— Jeremiah is in fact sometimes referred to as "The Rebel Prophet." The myth of Orwell as Prophet—as Daniel, John the Baptist, or Jeremiah—is that of a rebellious hero speaking out for "the people." In this conception, "prophet" evokes a train of associations pertinent to the recurring historical clash between prophet and priest—the conflict between the institution and the individual, between the elite and the people, between the Establishment and the outsider. The prophet renounces organizational power, and often the world itself. A prophet is also usually thought of as a man who not only predicts the future but passes on a divine revelation of Truth to the people. He possesses "the prophetic vision" (the title of one critical study of Orwell's work).[8] Finally, in communicating The Word, the prophet speaks with "the prophetic voice." And with the ideas of "divine revelation," "truth," and "intellectual integrity," shadings of Orwell as Saint intrude—whether we consider the image in religious or secular terms.

Acquaintances of Orwell have identified all of the above characteristics in their image of him as prophet: in his renunciation of creature comforts and desire to live the hard life in Jura (Pritchett, Rees); in his prose as the voice of "truth" (Spender) and his talk as "the voice of Jeremiah" (Woodcock); in his life of willed isolation, as "a prophet on his own" (Fyvel); and in the fiery writing of an otherwise mild-mannered man, for "when he wrote, he was possessed" (Atkins).[9] Thus the "message" of Orwell as secular prophet becomes, unsurprisingly, a moral one not unlike Jeremiah's, with *Nineteen Eighty-Four* his Book of Lamentations. The promise of a better, socialist world will be realized only if people heed the covenant's moral force: Socialism means "justice and liberty."

Once again, it is evident that the face of The Prophet possesses a family resemblance with the other three faces. Nevertheless it is a fully distinguishable face, with its own repertoire of features. For instance, though usually linked, "prophet" and "saint" are distinct coherences. St. Francis and many prophets may live simple lives or be ascetics, but we do not associate St. George with superhuman clairvoyance, or even necessarily with speaking with the power and word of God. Likewise with "rebel": there is, if subtle, something quite different about a "rebellious" and a "prophetic" voice and vision. Perhaps a rebel can sometimes be thought of as an immature or

apprentice prophet; the prophetic voice is revelatory and admonitory, angry yet never petulant. And the fact that a prophet projects a *vision,* usually detailed and horrifying, means that he is not simply "a man against," even if, like Jeremiah, his vision is essentially negative and disastrous. Nor, of course, does a rebel necessarily forecast the future as the prophet typically does, though a rebel's opposition may certainly take that form. Finally, while Orwell's democratic socialism and "Englishness" are essential to his prophetic vision and special relationship to the "English people," his love of nature and interest in popular culture and plain-man persona have little to do with his reputation as a prophet.

The configurations of Orwell identifiable as *The* Common Man and *The* Prophet turn on distinctions like these, which in turn point to other distinguishing features among the faces. For instance, without suggesting that the faces are divisible into separate Orwell personalities, Orwell's romanticism toward the proles in *Nineteen Eighty-Four* can be interpreted as the nostalgia of The Common Man, a gesture which stands in tension with the satiric warning of The Prophet. Still another distinction between The Common Man and The Prophet rests on the simple fact that there is ultimately a major difference between a man who *leads* the people and who is *one of* the people (though Orwell has been regarded as both). Orwell as Rebel and Common Man often presented himself as "the voice in the wilderness" and "the voice of the people," respectively, but one can be an outsider and a commoner without achieving the following necessary to be treated as a prophet. For there is no shortage of jeremiads to be heard in the name of "the people": one identifies a prophet finally not by his own claims, but by how his disciples treat him.

This is invariably the case with reputation-formation, as we have seen, and it also applies to the other three faces. A reputation is granted by Others; it cannot be merely asserted by the subject himself. But because "prophet" is a religious metaphor and has been so significant for building Orwell's posthumous reputation—a pre-inflated image, as it were—it deserves special mention that there is no property, or set of properties, which sums up "prophethood." If figurehood is in the eye of the beholder, "prophethood" is in the ear of the listener. It is finally Orwell's readers—notwithstanding Orwell's own self-image and whatever his superficial resemblances to the Judeo-Christian prophetic tradition—who have conferred the prophetic wreath upon him. Of course, most readers have used the term rather loosely in Orwell's case, but this also reflects how freely, in contemporary usage, the word "prophet" has been bandied about.

Given both the haphazard use of the word and its charged associations, it will come as no surprise that Prophet Orwell is the most visible and easily misinterpreted portrait in the Orwell gallery. In particular, the wide circulation of *Nineteen Eighty-Four* has made for the prominence of and confusion surrounding this face; the special circumstances of its composition and timing have only added to the misunderstandings. Focusing on it as his last book, readers become preoccupied with the question of "Orwell's legacy"

and "final vision." They ignore or downplay his earlier work and the variety of his *oeuvre*. Focusing on the image itself of Orwell as "prophet," observers exalt, extend, modify, or explain away Orwell's work as "prediction." As we saw with Raymond Williams, they treat *Nineteen Eighty-Four* as a literal historical prediction which testifies to Orwell's deep pessimism and despair. Or, as we shall see later in this chapter, they ask the question, "If Orwell Were Alive Today. . . ," and proceed to answer it, usually to their advantage, by forecasting where their forecaster would stand on the issues of the day. And perhaps most ironically, even when *Nineteen Eighty-Four* has been read—properly, I think—as a warning rather than as a prophecy, Orwell sometimes comes off seeming even more a prophet—since unexpected events can undermine a claim to prophecy, whereas they merely change the way in which we read a warning.

Prophet Orwell is unlike Orwell's other faces not only in its distinctive configuration but also in other respects. Unlike the others, its formation is due almost exclusively to wide and impassioned response to one work— *Nineteen Eighty-Four*. The press and broadcast media have sometimes treated it as if it were Orwell's only work; similarly The Prophet, bloated to gigantic size and reduced to a caricature by the mass media, is sometimes presented as if it constituted the whole Orwell figure—as if Orwell were indeed a Dr. Frankenstein, "The Man Who Invented Big Brother."[10]

The disproportionate impact of *Nineteen Eighty-Four* on Orwell's reputation, then, has sometimes made him seem, at least in the sphere of popular reception, a one-book author. Because the face of Orwell as prophet has radiated so widely, we will pay more attention here than in previous chapters to Orwell's popular reputation. *Nineteen Eighty-Four* will be our focal point. Because the book raised controversial questions about Orwell's politics and because it immediately circulated widely outside literary circles, the early images of Orwell as prophet did not consolidate but simply splintered and multiplied, fracturing along several lines according to the varied preoccupations of the book's huge audience. Readers belonging to widely divergent reception groups have consequently disagreed about the basic terms on which to discuss *Nineteen Eighty-Four*, as to whether it is a dystopia, a techno-political fantasy, a satire, or a novel. They have disagreed too about whether it is a portrait of a writer's state of mind, of a totalitarian society, of the gadgetry of the future, or of the world's end. In effect, summing up these two sets of four possibilities, they have finally asked: Is *Nineteen Eighty-Four* a writer's political warning, an unconscious projection of a death wish, a historical/technological prediction, or a brilliant apocalyptic message?

I should make clear that I consider Orwell's book primarily a satirical dystopia, directed chiefly at the Soviet Union though not excluding the West, a warning to his contemporaries of a possible totalitarian state thirty-five years away. For purposes of exploring Orwell's *reputation*, however, the answer to the questions above is that *Nineteen Eighty-Four* has been discussed according to all four possibilities: all of them are part of Orwell's reputation-history.

We now turn to discuss the four images of The Prophet—two of them emergent from within literary circles and two from outside—as they have developed over time and in relation to specific reception groups. Prophet Orwell is the most fragmented face of Orwell, and often we rely upon general descriptions of an image, not traceable to a specific critical statement or reducible to watchwords. Given these constraints, and because these four images are so easily correlated with particular institutional audiences, these images are best reconstructed as they have developed within identifiable audiences. By indicating how institutional audiences often concentrate on a single prominent dimension of a book, our audience-based imagery also suggests the numerous ways in which a work may unwillingly participate in its defacement—and how impossible it is to avoid such distortion altogether.

## II

The first image of Orwell to appear was The Cautionary Prophet, which suddenly crystallized when major Anglo-American critics reviewed *Nineteen Eighty-Four*. "A Prophet in the Making," headlined the *New York Herald Tribune Review*.[11] Although many of the major reviewers did not explicitly refer to Orwell as a prophet, they did agree—V.S. Pritchett in *The New Statesman*, Harold Nicolson in *The Observer*, Lionel Trilling in the *New Yorker*, and Philip Rahv in *Partisan Review*—that *Nineteen Eighty-Four* was a satirical warning to the present.

After Orwell's death, family, friends, and other literary critics echoed this view, and the label "prophet" became widely applied to Orwell. Unintentionally, many critics who wrote books and articles with titles like "The Road to Airstrip One," *The Road to Miniluv*, and *The Road to 1984* have probably contributed to the dominance of Orwell's Prophet face and to the rigidly teleological view that his *oeuvre* amounts to little more than a preparatory run at *Nineteen Eighty-Four*—a notion which has sometimes led people to think that once they've read *Nineteen Eighty-Four*, no more need be said about Orwell.[12] Furthermore, like any book, *Nineteen Eighty-Four* itself is capable of being used and abused in many ways for various ends. Even when it is treated as a "warning," disagreement can exist as to precisely what it is warning against. This was exactly the confusion which arose with the publication of *Nineteen Eighty-Four* and Orwell's untimely death a few months later. The image of Orwell as Prophet became politically tinged, and partisans of the Right and Left disagreed as to what kind of prophet Orwell actually was. Much as we saw with the watchword "rebel," Prophet Orwell became an ideological battleground, turned to different political ends depending on the observer's intentions. Orwell was presented as an embittered ex-socialist, a cautionary socialist, or a naive anti-communist, depending on the reviewer's politics. "On Logical Socialist Development, Orwell Is A Bitter Prophet," headlined one conservative magazine in its review of *Nineteen Eighty-Four*. On the liberal Left, the *New Republic* memori-

alized Orwell as the common man's voice, "the cautionary prophet of The People," who "loved the Bowlings so well [and] loathed and feared 'the streamlined men' so much [that he] felt no cry of warning could be uttered too loud." Here we can see a problem developing similar to the one we saw with Orwell as The Rebel: What is he *for*? Both the Right and Left agree that Orwell opposes "totalitarianism," but they differ on whether he supports capitalism or democratic socialism. Even the Communists called Orwell a "prophet," though using the word as a pejorative. *The Daily Worker* labeled Orwell the leading "prophet" of "that unhappy band" of anti-Stalinist intellectuals who insisted on an unreal " 'pure' Socialism unsullied by the mire of awkward reality." In the *Daily Worker*'s vocabulary, to be a "prophet" was to be a tender-minded idealist. So again we observe, as we did with the secondary watchword "individualist" in Chapter Three, how the same watchword can generate very different images by tailoring an author's reputation-history to its own history.[13]

General characterizations of Orwell as a prophet and secondary watchwords—like "clairvoyant" and "forecaster"—were important for building his reputation as a prophet throughout the 1950s. Well-known critics like Wyndham Lewis on the Right and George Elliott on the democratic Left welcomed Orwell as one of their own. Devoting the last five chapters of *The Writer and the Absolute* (1952) to a discussion of Orwell, Lewis praised Orwell's "burst of clairvoyance" in his last years. "With *Animal Farm*, he led the wavering lefties out of the pink mists of Left Land into the clear daylight," said Lewis, who interpreted *Nineteen Eighty-Four* as Orwell's effective break with socialism. Orwell was a "natural Rightist" whose socialism was "skin-deep," said Lewis, and in *Nineteen Eighty-Four* he showed his true colors. "Had Orwell been of German nationality who can doubt that he would have been an S.S. man?" Like so many other critics, Lewis, an admirer of Hitler until 1938, seemed throughout *The Writer and the Absolute* to be imputing to Orwell much of his own preference for the hardness of the "spatial mind" and of his tendencies toward leader-worship.[14]

Likewise George Elliott's 1957 characterization of Orwell as "the secular prophet of socialism"—and finally "a failed prophet" because he was "a slight artist"—partly reflects his own political and literary values. Because Elliott's essay-review collects most of the associations of Prophet Orwell to which we have alluded—and also is the first piece to refer to Orwell as a Jeremiah—it deserves quoting at length.

> . . . he *is* a sort of prophet—at least he is viewed as one, the secular prophet of socialism . . . . Prophets [speak] the truth, the experienced and reasoned-upon moral truth, the truth behind the confusion and lies of events, the steady truth. Prophets do not systematize, are no theologians, no philosophers even; Orwell sticks to his experience as faithfully as any Jeremiah to the word of God, and if it leads him into anti-socialistic or self-contradictory statements he is unconcerned, as are his readers. Prophets use satire as one of their scourges, and Orwell is excellent at satire. . . . Prophets tell the people, especially the mighty and chosen, what they

> ought to have done and ought to do, and boldly promise actual punish-
> ments for their trangressions and dreamlike rewards for their obedience
> to the right; all this Orwell does. Prophets want you to hear the word, not
> their delivery of it; in Orwell's plain, public prose, you never detect a
> murmur of vanity even when his own experiences are the subject. Proph-
> ets want you to change the way you think and act; and I am sure that
> politically, we, his readers, now think and act as we do in some measure
> because of what Orwell wrote.[15]

This conclusion has the ring of a personal testament. Although he finally
judges Orwell, rather oddly, to be a "failed prophet" on aesthetic grounds
because "a true prophet does not deal with the sorts of truth that fit into
prose," Elliott's admiration for Orwell's prose achievement is evident. And
in his detailed consideration of Orwell as Prophet, Elliott touches on many
of the features we have acknowledged as more characteristic of other Orwell faces: the "truth-telling" Saint, the "bold" Rebel, the "plain-speaking"
Common Man. Elliott's essay is a good example of how a watchword can
serve as a hub around which a constellation of features orbits and from
which images get generated. Elliott's qualification of Orwell as a "secular"
prophet shows him explicitly marking off the "prophet" from the "saint."
For in Elliott's view "secularism" possesses "no analogues to saints," so that
men like Orwell who were

> splendidly virtuous, honorable, upright, courageous, honest and con-
> cerned with right behavior are not necessarily in any special connection
> with God as saints are; but it has its analogue with prophets, who speak,
> and are thought of as speaking, the truth.[16]

This distinction, though real enough, is largely a matter of perspective.
Pritchett's and Rees's versions of Orwell as "a wintry saint" and "a lay saint,"
respectively, are what Elliott considers necessarily a "prophet."

Elliot's confidently drawn distinction between "prophet" and "saint,"
therefore, also raises a conceptual problem, one on which we have touched
before: If the "same" features belong to more than one face, how are faces
distinguished? One might offer two criteria, both observable in Elliott's
essay. First, *emphasis*. Although, following our metaphor of reputations as
stars, Elliott's Orwell could be "plotted" from a different standpoint and
yield a "saint" or "rebel" image constellation, the watchword "prophet" is
repeated and highlighted throughout. It is clear that it is the sun around
which other features orbit. Actually, no two faces ever exhibit exactly the
"same" feature. The proportion and distribution of features, what might be
called the *character* of a face, will always be different (though sometimes
trivially so), inasmuch as no two observers will describe an Other in exactly
the same words. The face is always more than the sum of its facets, though
the textual difference may be one of tone and resonance. Second, *titling*.
Names reflect perspectives; this essay is titled "A Failed Prophet." Again,
like a constellation, the essay could bear a different name. But an image is
always a relationship; this is "Elliott's Orwell." Titles are not excrescences: a

virtual twin with a different family name is not a sibling but a remarkable look-alike. Though a title can mislead us as to the image presented in the text itself, it too should be considered an exhibited feature. Indeed it is often the single most important shaping feature of an image.

III

A second image of Prophet Orwell, advanced especially by psychoanalytic and Marxist critics, grew up within a few months of Orwell's death: The False Prophet. This image did not replace or efface the first image; rather, promoted by a different institutional audience and given impetus by some acquaintances' memoirs and by new editions of Orwell's books during the '50s, it developed alongside the image of The Cautionary Prophet.

Unlike the first group of critics, many psychoanalytic and Marxist critics were hostile to Orwell; likewise they discussed *Nineteen Eighty-Four* not via politics but psychology. Thus they explained the monstrosity of Oceania by way of Orwell's psychopathology. To these critics, the book was not really about the outer world of the 1940s—or of the 1980s—but about Orwell's inner world. Although a few recent critics have used *Nineteen Eighty-Four* and Orwell's other prose writings to explore, tentatively and suggestively, his psychology,[17] most of the early psychoanalytic criticism was irresponsibly speculative, jargon-ridden, and reductive. Notions that Orwell "despaired," that *Nineteen Eighty-Four* represented his mental "nightmare" and "death wish," were tossed about freely. By 1955, Delmore Schwartz was pushing Orwell's death wish all the way back to 1944, describing *Animal Farm* as "the parable of an author who wrote with the feeling that he no longer wanted nor had any reason to live."[18] The general argument of these critics amounted to an assertion that Orwell "lost hope" in socialism, in his life, in man's future; and that his was a delusive and counterfeit despair: *Nineteen Eighty-Four* was not a response to the rise of Hitler's Germany or Stalin's Russia, but the projection of a diseased mind. The origin and blackness of the book's horrors were variously ascribed to Orwell's tubercular condition and to his sufferings as a schoolboy.[19] Even Marxists like Isaac Deutscher conducted psychoanalytic autopsies. To Deutscher, *Nineteen Eighty-Four* was not a "warning" but "a Cassandra cry" pervaded by "the mysticism of cruelty." Orwell himself was a "fanatical" author consumed by sadistic urges and conspiracy theories.[20]

Orwell himself had very little to do, directly at least, with the formation of this image. Probably, however, his oft-quoted remark to a friend that *Nineteen Eighty-Four* "wouldn't have been so gloomy if I hadn't been so ill," contributed to it.[21] But if Orwell had not died shortly after the publication of *Nineteen Eighty-Four,* it is doubtful whether this image of him would ever have arisen; almost certainly it would not have achieved such prominence. In itself, this is, to be sure, a pointless speculation. Nevertheless, we are reminded of the importance of such contingent events for a writer's reputation. For the "death wish" speculations obviously were advanced because Orwell died soon

after the appearance of *Nineteen Eighty-Four*. (No reviewer in 1949 mentioned any such idea.) The simple point is that Orwell might well have survived a few more years—or might have died before *Nineteen Eighty-Four* was completed—in which case it is unlikely that friends and critics would have been writing about his "passionate pilgrimage" toward death.[22] In any case, the reverse of what happened with the image of The Rebel once "Such, Such Were the Joys" was published—when reviewers projected Orwell's childhood traumas forward into his adult years and saw a "failed rebel"—occurred with The Prophet when Orwell died after *Nineteen Eighty-Four*. Instead of the work getting ransacked for insight into the life, now the life was used to illumine the work; and instead of projecting evidence from the life forwards, "evidence" now "available"—given the fact of Orwell's death—was projected backwards. Orwell's "death wish" and "masochism," that is, were now introduced to explain the horrors of *Nineteen Eighty-Four*.[23]

Such conclusions cannot be proven wrong, but neither can they be proven correct in the terms advanced—and the logical leaps are disconcerting, to put it mildly. This is also not to say that the psychology of Orwell, as I emphasized when discussing the history of Orwell biography, does not need exploring. It does. But such claims need to be researched by carefully investigating Orwell's life, not asserted solely by way of his writings. Many of the early psychoanalytic critics like Isaac Rosenfeld, Schwartz, and Anthony West, who apparently considered "Freud" a tool to be "applied" and were accustomed to doing literary exegesis, wrote about Orwell as if there were no problematical relation between the man and the works. As a consequence, they were much too ready to engage in psychobiography of Orwell's writings and to pin on him simplistic labels like "neurotic" and "sadomasochist"—and too complacent to follow up the memoirs by his friends so as to better understand the complex relationship between the man and the work. Because Bernard Crick disdained such a task in his otherwise well-researched biography, it remains to be done.

## IV

As *Nineteen Eighty-Four* radiated beyond literary circles into the popular sphere of reception, these two biographically based images of Orwell—the "cautionary" and "false" prophets—did not gain sway with many non-literary audiences. For these new audiences knew little or nothing about Orwell as man or writer. Probably most people who read *Nineteen Eighty-Four* and who encountered it via the TV and film adaptations of the mid-1950s had not read any other book by Orwell and were uninformed about his politics. Thus, new and distinctive images of Orwell began to emerge in the popular sphere in the 1950s and '60s, held by reception groups who knew George Orwell simply as "the author of *Nineteen Eighty-Four*." Whereas the literary critics' images were founded, in the first instance, on Orwell's statements and on the politics of postwar literary London, and in the second, on an exploration of Orwell's psychology, many of the new images developed in response to exter-

nal events and were little connected with either postwar England or George Orwell himself. And here we may stress the importance of the critical location from which an institutional audience sees an image: the new audiences were situated so far from literary circles that they did not treat *Nineteen Eighty-Four* as a work of imaginative literature at all.

One of these many images of Prophet Orwell, widely held by the public at-large at least until 1984, was The Fallible Prophet. It is easily documented because it was advanced primarily by a definable group of science writers and futurologists, whose image of Orwell was widely publicized by the mass media. These institutional readers were concerned near-exclusively with the technological dimension of *Nineteen Eighty-Four*, resulting in what might be called the "fetishizing" of Orwell's reputation. Fixating on the book's gadgetry, they blew up a small part of *Nineteen Eighty-Four* into the whole, inevitably projecting a caricature of Prophet Orwell composed of just a few simple features.

This image arose from treating *Nineteen Eighty-Four* as a forecast. As in the previous images of Prophet Orwell we have examined, we can see here that not just individuals but entire reception groups bring their own questions to a work and see in it what they are looking for—in this case, chiefly the technocratic aspects of *Nineteen Eighty-Four*. Beginning in the 1960s, the above group of readers focused mainly upon the futuristic inventions and sociopolitical "predictions" of *Nineteen Eighty-Four*. As the clock began to run down, they measured Orwell's vision against the march of history. A few of these readers marveled at Orwell's prescience as to technological developments; most criticized his vision as technically naive and historically inaccurate. And so The Fallible Prophet is, as it were, a monocled soothsayer, possessing one clairvoyant and one myopic eye.

The most comprehensive defense of Orwell as a gifted technocratic prophet has been advanced by a contributor to *The Futurist*, a popular magazine. By 1978 California neuroscientist David Goodman had identified 137 "predictions" in *Nineteen Eighty-Four*, of which almost one hundred had already been realized, he maintained. Most of the "predictions" dealt with inventions or technical developments already under way in 1949 and described only crudely or suggestively in *Nineteen Eighty-Four*. Still, the sheer size of Goodman's list, quickly reported in the press, was impressive: in the West during the 1970s we had closed-circuit "snooper" cameras in banks and department stores, a premonition of the haunting telescreens; we had military think tanks like Oceania's huge "teams of experts . . . planning the logistics of future wars"; we used defoliant poisons (e.g., Agent Orange), resembling the Party's "search for new and deadlier gases" and for "soulble poisons capable of . . . destroy[ing] the vegetation of whole continents"; we had mammoth electronic government data banks, like the large Oceania information banks on Party members; and we manipulated the weather for military purposes (e.g., the Vietnamese monsoons), resembling the efforts of the *Nineteen Eighty-Four* superstates to engineer "artificial earthquakes and tidal waves by tapping the heat at the earth's center." Goodman concluded that, while "an

Technocratic visionary or naive forecaster? The fallible prophet.

**OLIVETTI M20 PERSONAL COMPUTER**

# 1984:
# ORWELL WAS WRONG

According to Orwell, in 1984 man and computer would have become enemies. But his pessimistic outlook was wrong. Today, the computers produced by the world's leading companies are man's most reliable aid. And the Olivetti M20 personal computer proves it. But then you couldn't expect less from a manufacturer who has installed tens of thousands of machines in offices world-wide. Olivetti now brings you the M20D model with a memory thirty times larger than the basic version. And when there's a need for even greater power and coordination in office jobs, the Olivetti M20 can manage a group of M20s working in conjunction with one another, integrated into a local area network. So from today there is a family of Olivetti personal computers with different storage capacities and a wide choice of operating systems (MS-DOS, CP/M-86, PCOS, UCSD-P) to satisfy different needs. And with their 16-bit technology and communication capabilities they are designed to keep abreast of change. Olivetti protects your investment in equipment and software. With the M20 your office's problem solving becomes a more productive function. Olivetti's personal computers embody all of the company's leadership in ergonomics and design which have become a consolidated part of its success in the office throughout the world.

MS-DOS is a trademark of Microsoft Inc.
CP/M-86 is a trademark of Digital Research.
UCSD-P system is a trademark
of the Regent of the University of California.

**olivetti**
brains & beauty

Through the myopic eye of Prophet Orwell: was George wrong about the personal computer?

Orwellian future" was not yet an immediate threat, "not one of Orwell's predictions is beyond the range of possibility."[24]

That conclusion seemed foolish to a subsequent board of editors of *The Futurist*, when they reviewed Orwell's predictions in 1983. Goodman had been far too precious with the evidence, the editors agreed. Whereas Goodman's procedure was to ferret out passages from *Nineteen Eighty-Four*, especially from Goldstein's *book*, which described minor technical and historical details of Oceania, the editors focused on Orwell's larger vision. The different approach—predictions versus vision—may point to a basic difference between "forecasting" and "prophecy." In any case, the editors found Orwell's vision sorely lacking. Orwell was "so wrong" about the future, said *The Futurist*'s editors, that they would consider making him "into an 'unperson'!" Orwell was wrong on just about everything that mattered': no atomic wars occurred in the 1950s, the world was not divided into three warring superstates, sexual satisfaction had not declined or become outlawed, no two-way television systems existed in any country, London bore no resemblance to Airstrip One, authoritarian communism had been abandoned even in the Soviet Union, and language had evolved toward the prolix and away from the bareness of Newspeak. "No work of fiction has so powerfully influenced man's view of the future," *The Futurist* acknowledged. But strictly as a forecaster, Orwell was "a laughingstock," not "the great prophet of the modern age."[25]

Not only scientists and futurologists have contributed to Orwell's standing as a technological prophet. *Nineteen Eighty-Four* is sometimes thought of as science fiction, and science fiction writers have also described Orwell as a prophet. Some (Isaac Asimov) have dismissed *Nineteen Eighty-Four* as technically inept; others have considered it brilliant (Ray Bradbury, Ursula LeGuin, Robert Silverberg).[26] Much of the New Wave science fiction of the 1950s and '60s is directly indebted to *Nineteen Eighty-Four*, and some literary historians believe that the book exerted great influence upon the postwar shift in the genre—away from the construction of technocratic fantasy worlds set in the distant future and toward naturalistic worlds set in the near-future and featuring immediate planetary dangers (atomic destruction, worldwide tyranny, ecological disaster).[27] In this view, although Orwell did not invent a genre as did Wells and Verne, his generic innovations in *Nineteen Eighty-Four*—the depiction of graphic violence, the creation of Newspeak, and the near-future setting—have been comparable in their impact on postwar science fiction.

Of several other external factors responsible for promoting Orwell's image as a historical prophet, the most important has been the popularity of "1984" (that is, until 1984) as an all-purpose target date, "the favorite year for speculation," as *Time* once noted.[28] As a combination of "forecast" and vague warning, the date's targets have allowed for endless revision. As Cold War tensions cooled, commentators in the mid-'60s began to play up a "Halfway to 1984" theme. Even serious book-length studies used the date as a jumping-off point. *Halfway to 1984* was the title of a book of speculations

about the international economic situation of the 1980s by Lord Gladwyn, former British representative to the United Nations. *Britain 1984* was a comprehensive set of economic projections of British life in the 1980s, dedicated "with apologies—and corrections—to George Orwell!" Some forecasters intentionally sidestepped "1984"—revealing its sinister symbolic power as a target date. The U.S. military circumspectly titled its 1964 bulletin of 20-year projections *The United States and the World in the 1985 Era.* The 1974 World Food Conference used 1985 to set its dire scenarios of possible famines a decade away—forecasts which, alas, have turned out to be all too depressingly accurate. In the 1970s the "Halfway to 1984" motif gave way to the "Countdown to 1984" theme. Comparisons between *Nineteen Eighty-Four* and political and technological developments multiplied, typified by trade books like *Who's Afraid of 1984?* and *The Real World of 1984.*[29]

## V

A fourth, related image, which did not arise until the mid-'70s and has since largely disappeared, is of The Doomsday Prophet. Again, the image has not displaced the other three, but has developed alongside them within a different reception audience altogether. Actually it has two aspects, corresponding to the interests of two distinct audiences, both of which have treated *Nineteen Eighty-Four* as an "omen." The first group is a small number of secular "apocalypticians," a few of whose doomsday forecasts are represented in *The World in 1984.* The press, often using talk of military or ecological misfortunes as a news tag, has also promoted this image of Orwell, with headlines like "Eternal Pessimist" and "Doomsday Prophet." Even Horus, the "chief stargazer" for *Horoscope Magazine,* got into the act in 1984, allowing that Orwell ("strangely prophetic in his vision of the future") had outperformed many professional astrologists.[30]

The second group is the religious millennialists, many of whom have taken *Nineteen Eighty-Four* (again, at least until 1984) as a symbolic, or in some instances literal, doomsdate. I can think of no other serious contemporary work of literature which has occasioned anything comparable to the extraordinary, bizarre observations of the millennialists; their response is yet another testament to the unique impact of *Nineteen Eighty-Four* on Anglo-American culture. The millennialists have pointed to the book's supposed verisimilitude to the Book of Revelation: continuous wars, a false Antichrist worshiped by millions, outpourings of hate against the virtuous, chronic shortages of nearly everything, and the capacity to "get inside you" as only Satan and the Thought Police can. One associate of Billy Graham has made some end-time observations in connection with the book.[31] Other preachers have called *Nineteen Eighty-Four* a "warning," but said that it warned about the evils of the world and the Second Coming. In a 1981 symposium aiming to provide "an evangelical perspective" on the book, some evangelists used it as a point of departure to warn that the Second Coming was near at hand.[32] Herbert Armstrong's *The Plain Truth* asked in January 1984, "Was Orwell's

*1984,* warning of a new terrible dark age, a genuine human insight into the final stages of this world's civilization?" The writer answered:

> Orwell would have been astounded if he had known how suppressed and how profound is the answer to Winston Smith's problems! This suppressed knowledge centers on government—the government of God that we announce in the pages of *The Plain Truth.* Do you know what it would be like if this world were ruled by the government and laws of God instead of modern variations on INGSOC? . . . Indeed, the Orwellian INGSOC will appear in form. The Bible prophesies a terrible time soon to come (Matt. 24:21)—a short dark age of religious and political persecution. . . . This prophesied period of pain and persecution soon to come will be cut short in a series of events that will convince humanity of the folly of rejecting God. Humanity will learn, as Orwell faintly glimpsed, that man is indeed "unable to cope with the demands of his history."[33]

Moreover, neither Christian nor Jewish fundamentalists have missed the potential theological significance of the title date. Speaking of its "potentially shocking significance in light of prophetical truth," one evangelical minister said in 1982: "The circumstances surrounding [the dating] may have been providential in spelling out the rule of Antichrist. . . . Time will tell."[34] Some Christian evangelicals spot the "hand of Providence" in the synchronicity of the completion of *Nineteen Eighty-Four* and the founding of Israel: the year 1948. These fundamentalists consider the establishment of Israel significant because it is taken as marking the date of Armageddon's approach. Christ's promise that "this generation will not pass away until all these things take place" (Matt. 24) is generally interpreted by fundamentalist preachers to mean that the "last events" (the rise of the Antichrist, etc.) will be set in motion within thirty or forty years of 1948: thus "1984" is in the prophetic target range.

The Jehovah's Witnesses, however, interpret Matthew 24 to mean that the generation of baptized Witnesses alive in 1914 will not die before the End. They believe that Jehovah set up his kingdom in 1914, the date of Christ's invisible return or Second Coming, when God cast Satan to earth and concluded the so-called Gentile Times. The Watch Tower publications of the Witnesses have long held that within "seventy or eighty years" after 1914 God will extend His Kingdom to earth. Indeed the upper echelons of the Witness leadership, including President Frederick W. Franz, preached for decades that autumn 1984 was the deadline for Armageddon: just as Jerusalem was destroyed seventy years after the First Coming of Christ, the entire world would be destroyed seventy years after his Second Coming. One former Witness couple, Heather and Gary Botting, has devoted an entire book to parallels between the "theocracy" of the Witnesses and of the Party in Oceania (*The Orwellian World of Jehovah's Witnesses,* 1984).[35]

In a separate though related development (and a concern that has apparently run its course), experts in Jewish mysticism wondered aloud during the early 1980s about the year 1984 and its corresponding date in the Hebrew calendar, 5744. Working from a Kabalist number-letter system

which assigns letters to each digit in a date, mystics found that "5744" spelt *tashmad,* "destruction." At one international conference of Jewish mystics, a respected Kabalist argued that it was "obvious" that Orwell, who had many Jewish friends, was aware of the correspondence when he titled his novel. The Hebrew calendar is actually used in Israel, and some Knesset members took the danger so seriously—believing that the use of "5744" was inviting "destruction" by Jehovah—that they introduced legislation to change the calendar year. (It did not pass.) "Could it be that the numbers are telling us something important?" asked one Jewish journalist in 1983. "Could this be, finally, the year of the end?"[36]

The millennialists' Orwell shows *Nineteen Eighty-Four* taken to a ridiculously literal length that would have made Orwell furious—or provoked his sardonic laughter. Their image is one of this study's most remarkable examples of defacement, illustrating what can happen to a work when it radiates far beyond its original circles of reception.

The following four facial histories enable us to explore in greater detail all but this outlandish last image of Prophet Orwell, which has been entirely confined to the millennialists' reception. As in previous chapters, we approach a face by analyzing selected issues bearing on Orwell's reputation or by examining institutional audiences in which his work has been received. In doing so we go beyond sloganeering and again explore the rich configuration of cultural meaning which each Orwell portrait represents.

## 15. "If Orwell Were Alive Today. . ."

### I

In Part One we touched on the tendency of readers to wonder aloud "If Orwell Were Alive Today," but given the shaping influence of their musings on Orwell's reputation, the speculations about Orwell's posthumous politics warrant systematic study. To an extent probably unequaled by any other modern writer, Orwell has induced both admirers and detractors to prophesy about his likely opinions on events since his death. It is common to ask, say, upon the centennial of a writer's birth, what he would think about the present-day world or about an issue close to his heart. But readers have done this with Orwell near-continuously since his death and on a spectrum of issues, with each new edition of his works or book about him serving as an occasion for critics to wonder about *Orwell Redivivus* all over again.

Remarkably, readers have not advanced their predictions only in general terms or merely as asides; some conjectures have been elaborated in great detail, have concerned not only general political positions but specific issues and even party affiliations, and have led partisans to wrangle with one another as to "where Orwell would have stood." Moreover, although Orwell's own speculations about the future in *Nineteen Eighty-Four* have provoked many of the forecasts about him, the tendency to ruminate about

the "would-have-been Orwell" derives also from the ongoing topicality of Orwell's journalism and his enduring hold upon the imaginations of Anglo-American writers as an intellectual model. Indeed the prophecies represent an integral part of the politics of Orwell's reputation. For the practice of "extending" Orwell's work and predicting his posthumous stands has not been an innocent pursuit; it represents one of the main instances of the claiming of Orwell, largely conducted via selective citation from Orwell's corpus. This case study looks at the history and range of speculation about Orwell's posthumous politics. It offers insight not only into how a controversial posthumous figure can serve as a barometer of attitudes toward issues of the day, but also into the process of constructing intellectual genealogies. It is a portrait of The Prophet as political necromancee.

## II

"[I]f one imagines him as living into our own day," wrote Orwell about Jack London in 1945, "it is very hard to be sure where his political allegiance would have lain. One can imagine him in the Communist Party, one can imagine him falling victim to Nazi racial theory, and one can imagine him the quixotic champion of some Trotskyist or Anarchist sect."[37]

The would-be political legatees of the quixotic Orwell sometimes go by different names in this postwar era, but they have advanced a plethora of claims to him even more extraordinary than Orwell's speculations about London. Pacifist, militarist, liberal, neoconservative, militant socialist, Vatican II Catholic—the list could go on. Indeed Gracie Field's vaudeville refrain from the 1930s, "He's dead but he won't lie down"—which Orwell chose as the epigraph for *Coming Up for Air*—might well serve as his own epitaph. "Today [1971], reading his reactions to events," wrote W. H. Auden, once a victim of Orwell's attacks on "the pansy Left," "my first thought is: Oh, how I wish that Orwell were still alive, so that I could read his comments on contemporary events." Auden, after pronouncing Orwell a "true Christian," ran through his list: drugs, trade unions, birth control, nationalization, student demonstrations. "What he would have said I have no idea. I am only certain he would be worth listening to."[38]

Many readers have shared Auden's sentiments. Usually they have been less hesitant with their predictions. McCarthyism, the Suez Crisis, the Soviet invasion of Hungary, Britain's Campaign for Nuclear Disarmament (CND), Vatican II, Vietnam, Czechoslovakia, Watergate, Afghanistan and Poland, the Falkland Islands invasion, the nuclear freeze campaign, the Grenada invasion: scarcely a major Anglo-American issue has gone by since 1950 that has not moved someone to ask "what Orwell would have said." The enduring radiance of Orwell as a literary figure is perhaps best exemplified by the insistent recurrence of this conditional headline, variously voiced as lament, wish, challenge, and tactic. The phrase reflects and has promoted Orwell's many-sided reputation, especially his image as The Prophet.

It needs emphasis that it is the subject of Orwell himself and his would-

be verdicts—and not only the historical accuracy of *Nineteen Eighty-Four* set against the much-publicized countdown to his "doomsdate"—that has occasioned widespread discussion. For until the 1980s, the speculations as to "where Orwell would have stood" were advanced exclusively by intellectuals engaged with "the man" and familiar with not just *Nineteen Eighty-Four* but his *oeuvre*. What would Orwell have said about this crisis, readers asked. What would his politics be today? Numerous "old friends" implied that Orwell would have gone the way that they did. In Britain, within a few years of Orwell's death, as Raymond Williams once remarked, "Father Knew George Orwell" had become a tired joke.

Of course, in at least one sense, questions about a man's posthumous politics are manifestly absurd. The fact is that Orwell has been dead for more than three decades, and it is impossible to extrapolate from a man's writings what he would say about events after his death. But what is futile can nevertheless sometimes be enlightening, at least for sociological purposes—and sometimes precisely because of its obvious futility. Many observers continue to pose questions about Orwell into the late 1980s. That they do so—even while frequently admitting straight off that their conjectures are frivolous—testifies to the persisting appeal of the Orwell persona and the ongoing relevance of Orwell's work. The recurrence of the question has helped keep Orwell's reputation "alive" and controversial—and illustrates, more generally, the rhetorical advantages of claiming a sizable figure's mantle and the crucial influence of news events on a reputation's shape and size. From the Cold War to the peace movement of the 1980s, Orwell has proven a writer "well worth stealing."

## III

In the early 1950s, some former radicals "wondered" what Orwell would have had to say about the course which the Cold War—and they—had taken. To Granville Hicks, Communist Party member until the Nazi-Soviet pact and one of Orwell's leading American champions in the early 1950s, Orwell was his "Generation's Conscience." In the *New York Post* Hicks, quoting Pritchett, held up Orwell in 1953 as the exemplary "tough-minded" intellectual who would have "come out into the open" and opposed both Stalin and Joseph McCarthy.

> As an ex-Communist, I have a particular respect for [Orwell], for he saw through Communism when I didn't and should have.
> Yet he has none of the self-righteousness of so many anti-Stalinists. I wonder what Orwell would make of anti-Communism in America today. As I have said, he was tough-minded, and he would recognize that, in order to protect ourselves, we have to do many things that we don't like to do. But he would also see through the people who, in pretending to fight anti-Communism, are fighting something else. And it would not matter to him whether what they were really fighting was good or bad. The great evil for him would be their refusal to come out into the open, their willing-

ness to hide their personal views behind a worthy and popular cause, their contempt for truth.

And he would have little patience with the prevailing mood of fear. . . .[39]

With Orwell's reputation sharply on the rise in the early '50s, many intellectuals concluded that History was proving *Animal Farm* and *Nineteen Eighty-Four* prophetic. Hicks's reception reflects the desire to be on the side of a perceived "winner," a frequent feature of the politics of reputation. (Even ex-Communists like to stay on the "right side" of History.) A cold war liberal during the 1950s, Hicks imagined that Orwell would have stood with him, and against ferocious anti-Stalinists like Sidney Hook, whom Hicks suspected of promoting conservative ideas in the guise of attacking Communism. What Left-liberals and socialists of the 1950s would have thought of Orwell's private list of eighty-six people whom he suspected of Communist affiliations or sympathies—compiled in 1949 and found among his papers though still unpublished—is hard to say. The list has served as ammunition for some radicals (and neoconservatives) to predict that Orwell would have turned into a fiercely anti-Communist liberal or neoconservative.[40]

While Orwell's generation was still wondering about his Cold War stand, a younger generation began asking "where Orwell would have stood" on the Campaign for Nuclear Disarmament. "We would debate about Orwell's stand in the early '60s, but we couldn't really make up our minds," recalled Jenni Calder about herself and her socialist friends at Cambridge University. "Some of us, including me, would cite Orwell's 'decency' and 'pragmatism,' convinced that the whole tendency of his being would have been to oppose those weapons as nonsensical." And yet, Calder concedes, in essays like "You and the Atom Bomb" (1945) the "tough-minded" Orwell seemed to support deterrence. Moreover, Orwell's democratic socialist politics had been close to Labour leader and friend Aneurin Bevan's, who sided with Hugh Gaitskell in a controversial 1957 speech and supported, with qualification, the Labour Party's decision to deploy nuclear weapons. And yet (again), *Tribune* bitterly criticized Bevan's decision—perhaps Orwell would have too. A former member of CND's Committee of 100, Calder argues out these possibilities, also noting that students of the 1950s and '60s, probably unlike observers at the time of the 1945 Labour government, did not especially link Orwell's name with Bevan's. Young non-Communist leftists like Calder saw Bevan in 1960 as an accommodator to Gaitskell's gradualism, whereas they viewed Orwell as a "loner" who "stood outside the traditions that had led the Labour Party into a blind alley." They linked Orwell with Camus, seeing both of them as rebels against Left orthodoxy. "Orthodoxy" meant not only the British Communist Party but also Gaitskell and equivocation on CND.[41]

Partisans of a different politics and from an older generation, however, also wondered about Orwell's would-be attitude toward Suez, CND, and the New Left. But whereas Calder was uncertain how Orwell would have viewed CND, Raymond Williams, who arrived at Cambridge as a don at the

same time that Calder matriculated, felt surer about Orwell's likely opposition to the Bomb and sympathy for the "early" New Left.

> Th[e] New Left respected Orwell directly, especially in its early years. The invasion of Suez was an open exercise of the British imperialism he had so insistently attacked. The Hungarian revolution, a popular and socialist rising against a bureaucratic and authoritarian communism, was at once a confirmation of what he had said about Stalinism and a demonstration of the authentic movement to which he had paid homage in Catalonia. The danger of the Bomb—"either we renounce it or it destroys us"—was as he had seen it: the Bomb was not only the weapon that could destroy civilization but the shadow under which a new authoritarian war economy would grow and extend.[42]

As the '60s wore on, more readers speculated about and wished for the pronouncements of the posthumous Orwell, especially after the publication of *CEJL* in 1968. Sighed the *Tribune* reviewer: "Orwell, thou shouldst be living at this hour. England hath need of thee." The Right voiced similar sentiments. Said a reviewer for *The Financial Times:* "It would be impossible to count the occasions in the eighteen years since his death that I and many others have asked the question, 'What would Orwell think about that?' He was, in life, and has remained, part of our conscience as twentieth century citizens, and very especially, part of our consciousness as Englishmen."[43]

We have already referred to the Left's "Vietnamization" of Orwell in the late 1960s, with radicals disagreeing as to whether Orwell would have supported or opposed their stands against the Vietnam War. The convergence of *CEJL*'s appearance with the growing opposition to the War brought the predictions as to "where Orwell would have stood" on Vietnam center-stage—and turned "Orwell and Vietnam" into an intellectuals' mini-war in its own right. For the first time, the battle for Orwell's mantle took place not only between rival ideological traditions but over a current political issue. As the Old Left, Orwell's generation of the 1930s, split over Vietnam, intellectuals argued as to what direction Orwell would have taken: Radical? Moderate? Quietist? Mary McCarthy touched off a firestorm of predictions when she implied in her mixed review of *CEJL* that Orwell would have sided with Kingsley Amis, Bernard Levin, and other war supporters and against fashionably "current, squealing 'pinks' " like herself. The review first appeared in the January 1969 *New York Review of Books* (which had taken a radical stand against the war and had even given instructions on one issue's cover on how to construct a Molotov cocktail) and was twice reprinted within the year.

McCarthy initiated an approach toward Orwell's politics which has since become popular among unsympathetic critics of his work. She linked Orwell to some vocal followers, in this case hostile to her position on Vietnam, and proceeded from there, "wishing" that he might be different yet fearing the worst. To McCarthy, Orwell was a "political failure" because he left "no fertile ideas behind him to germinate." McCarthy's Orwell was mired in

nostalgia. In this he was "typical of the whole generation of middle-class radicals (myself included), whose loudest spokesman was Orwell." Mc-Carthy's essay amounted to a review and grand summary of the "If Orwell Were Alive Today" musings since the mid-1950s. Like Williams' entire reception history yet in more concentrated form, it reflected the sharp anxiety of influence which some members of the Old Left felt toward their generational "spokesman," their ambivalent urge both to embrace and break with him. Indeed her response constituted a running commentary on practically every issue which had troubled the Left since the days of Joseph McCarthy, issues which Orwell would have had to confront had he lived. But though Mary McCarthy felt the urge to pose the "if," she was no more certain than Auden or Jenni Calder about the "then":

> It is impossible, at least for me, to guess how he would have stood on many leading questions of the day. Surely he would have opposed the trial and execution of Eichmann, but where would he be on the war in Vietnam? I wish I could be certain that he would not be with Kingsley Amis and Bernard Levin (who with John Osborne seem to be his main progeny), partly because of his belligerent anti-Communism, which there is no trying to discount, and partly because it is modish to oppose the war in Vietnam: we are the current, squealing "pinks." I can hear him angrily arguing that to oppose the Americans in Vietnam, whatever their shortcomings, is to be "objectively" totalitarian. On the other hand, there was that decency. And what about CND? He took exception on the atom bomb, but as a "realist" he accepted the likelihood of an atomic confrontation in a few years' time and computed the chances for survival. . . . I cannot see him in an Aldermaston march, along with long-haired cranks and vegetarians, or listening to a Bob Dylan or Joan Baez record or engaging in any of the current forms of protest.* The word "protest" would make him sick. And yet he could have hardly supported Harold Wilson's government. As for the student revolt, he might well have been out of sympathy for a dozen reasons, but would he have sympathized with the administrators? If he had lived, he might have been happiest on a desert island, and it was a blessing for him probably that he died.[45]

Sonia Orwell was so upset with McCarthy's review that she wrote a reply ("Unfair to George"), the only essay which she ever wrote about her husband.[46] She defended Orwell's integrity and the portrait of Orwell presented in *CEJL* (which she had co-edited). Mrs. Orwell did not address McCarthy's conjectures about Orwell's posthumous politics. McCarthy's predictions did, however, provoke a rejoinder from the normally reticent Richard Rees, just a few weeks before his death. Rees, a conservative, went even further than McCarthy, suggesting that Orwell would have generally supported America's conduct of the war. Writing in late 1969, Rees allowed

---

*But pacifist-anarchist Nicolas Walter could. Proclaiming Orwell "the best anti-militarist we ever had," Walter sidestepped discussion of Orwell's severe criticism of pacifists after 1939 and suggested that, in the shadow of the Bomb, Orwell might have "returned to his old anti-militarism." "It is not so hard to believe that he might have joined the marchers, though scarcely the sitters. Might he have become one of us again?"[44]

that Orwell would have criticized America. But he would first have put the Left's own house in order, Rees said. Orwell would have stressed the yawning difference between America and the Communists, much as his later writings did the difference between Churchillian "imperialism" and Stalinist "totalitarianism."

> I knew Orwell intimately for the last twenty years of his life, but I always hesitate, after a friend's death, to make public guesses, based on the privilege of friendship, about his probable views on current events. But since Miss McCarthy has perceived, and had the rare honesty to state, something that should be obvious to every reader of Orwell, I feel justified in adding a further word about it. In my opinion it is practically certain that Orwell would have considered much of the propaganda against American involvement in Vietnam to be, at best, politically and morally imbecile. No doubt he would have disagreed with some of America's handling of the problem, but it is certain that he would have had much more to say about the Soviet Union's handling of Czechoslovakia; and as for all those who talk about American "imperialism" and equate it, and even compare it unfavorably, with Chinese and Russian tyranny, they should congratulate themselves that he is no longer here to give them a piece of his mind. He was a pessimist, no doubt, but he would not have compared the Western world of 1969 with the communist world. He would have known that 1969 is not yet *1984*.[47]

## IV

During the months before and during 1984, the speculations about Orwell's posthumous pronouncements went even further, extending beyond the intellectual reviews and into the popular sphere of reception. Here the focus was often on *Nineteen Eighty-Four;* entertainment, rather than politics, dominated. The headlines themselves from daily newspapers in 1983–84— "George Would Cheer," "If Orwell Were Here," "If he lived today, what would Orwell say?"—make clear the high level of interest in what the author of *Nineteen Eighty-Four* would have had to say about the 1980s.[48] One Associated Press story ("If Orwell Were a New Yorker") furnished his likely Monday-to-Friday diary for the opening weeks of 1984, which featured his pronouncements on herpes, jogging, and women's skirt lengths.[49] As if to top that, so anxious was one "awed admirer" to have Orwell "alive today" that he resuscitated his hero for two imaginary interviews—much as Orwell had done with Swift in a wartime BBC program. Questions touched on the British economy, Margaret Thatcher, and the Falkland Islands invasion. "You wouldn't describe yourself as a great man?" the "interviewer" asked. "A good gardener, perhaps," replied the modest Orwell. "But a great man? No."[50]

Many political intellectuals implicitly disagreed with that judgment; their claiming of Orwell reached new heights of brashness in 1983–84 as neoconservatives, socialists, and liberals "stole" Orwell back and forth from one another. The most controversial essay during the 1984 countdown,

which raised a ruckus even louder than McCarthy's during the Vietnam era, was by Norman Podhoretz. "If Orwell Were Alive Today," ran the headline of the January 1983 *Harper's,* atop a full-cover drawing of Orwell. What earlier readers, including McCarthy, had done as a secondary part of their discussions of Orwell, Podhoretz made primary: his essay was a concerted, sustained attempt to claim Orwell for the neoconservative camp, of which he had become one of the leading spokesmen. Podhoretz proceeded as if he were the first person to ask such a question; he was unaware that musings about "If Orwell Were Alive Today" already had a lineage. Unlike McCarthy and others, however, Podhoretz built his case systematically rather than impressionistically. Podhoretz made much use of Orwell's minor journalism—which, of course, was not collected until the 1968 *CEJL*. Citing Orwell's opposition to pacifism during World War II, his English patriotism, his loathing of the Soviet Union, and above all his relentless criticism of his fellow leftists, Podhoretz argued that Orwell's overall politics and stands on specific issues like the nuclear freeze would have resembled . . . well, Norman Podhoretz's. Orwell would have surely castigated the "peace" movement as pacifist-neoisolationist, and he would have stood fast against detente as an accommodation to "Soviet imperialism." He would probably have also allowed that democratic socialism had failed and should be abandoned, for he might well have accepted, like the neoconservatives, that "the aims of what *he* meant by socialism [had been] realized to a very great extent under capitalism, and without either the concentration camps or the economic miseries that have been the invariable companions of socialism in practice." Podhoretz concluded:

> . . . I find it hard to believe that Orwell would have allowed an orthodoxy to blind him [to socialism's failure] more than he allowed any other "smelly little orthodoxies" to blind him to the truth about the particular issues involved in the struggle between totalitarianism and democracy: Spain, World War II, and Communism.
>
> In Orwell's time, it was the left-wing intelligentsia that made it so difficult for these truths to prevail. And so it is too with the particular issues generated by the struggle between totalitarianism and democracy in our time, which is why I am convinced that if Orwell were alive today, he would be taking his stand with the neoconservatives and against the Left.[51]

Podhoretz was aiming here at nothing less than providing neoconservatism with an unimpeachable intellectual pedigree. He was well aware of what he was doing, noting that to have "the greatest political writer of the age on one's side" gave "confidence, authority, and weight to one's own political views." By emphasizing Orwell's hatred for "the left-wing intelligentsia" of his time, Podhoretz was also skillfully providing the present-day Left with an undesirable family tree, traceable to the British pacifists and Communists of Orwell's day. Podhoretz's essay pointed up the fact that the "If Orwell Were Alive Today" speculations were not merely intellectual ancestor-worship. For cultural politics has much to do with political origins. Eminent ancestors

make one's causes and programs respectable; disreputable ancestors taint and disgrace. (Distinguished and embarrassing offspring do the same: hence Mary McCarthy's tarring Orwell with supporters of the Vietnam War as "his main progeny.") Virtue- and guilt-by-association are central to the politics of reputation. Other intellectual leaders of the American Right besides Podhoretz also began tracing pedigrees in the '70s and '80s. As Podhoretz was seizing on Orwell and Lionel Trilling as the forerunners of American neoconservatism,* George Will was exalting Edmund Burke as the grandfather of American cultural conservatism.

Meanwhile socialist admirers of Orwell were disputing Podhoretz's claims and engaged in a reclamation process of their own. Selecting different quotations from *CEJL,* and filling in Podhoretz's questionable elisions, British socialist Christopher Hitchens argued that Orwell, since he had helped found the anarchist-sponsored Freedom Defence Committee, would have opposed "the McCarthy persecutions" "unequivocally." Hitchens, however, disagreed with Mary McCarthy about Orwell on Vietnam. Orwell "hated colonialism," said Hitchens, and he "would have seen the essential continuity of American intervention with the French colonial presence. . . . He would have seen through the obfuscations (lies, actually) of the Kennedy and Johnson administrations." Hitchens closed:

> I wish Orwell were alive today. The democratic socialist camp needs him more than ever. I would also dearly like to have his comments on the sort of well-heeled power worshiper who passes for an intellectual these days.[53]

So the pitched battle for Orwell's mantle between socialists and neoconservatives in 1983–84 turned personal and nasty. It should be noted, by the way, that neither Podhoretz's nor Hitchens' claim to Orwell is without its difficulties. Podhoretz, for example, elides the fact that Orwell, unlike virtually all neoconservatives from the generation of the '30s, was not a former Trotskyist or Stalinist or fellow traveler disillusioned by "the god that failed." Nor is Orwell's anti-imperialism or his support of the libertarian Freedom Defence Committee any indication as to how he would have acted during the McCarthy or Vietnam eras, as Hitchens supposes.

Meanwhile, as these disputes on the Left and Right about his politics continued, the resurrected Orwell sat on a pedestal above the fray, beyond criticism. Argument about Podhoretz's article lasted for three months in *Harper's* letter columns, even spilling into the pages of other magazines and newspapers. No consensus emerged as to whether Podhoretz or Hitchens made more sense; readers variously agreed with Podhoretz, found him "appalling," and concluded that Orwell would have abandoned politics alto-

---

*Indeed the conservative *New York Tribune,* which reprinted Podhoretz's essay, went even further than he did, calling Orwell not only the "forerunner" but also (in a subheadline) the "father" of neoconservatism. The *New York Tribune's* reference, whether accidental or otherwise, illustrates a later phase of the "claiming" and "genealogical" process—how a pedigree is invented and then embellished, especially as argument about it moves from the critical into the popular sphere of reception.[52]

gether. Some readers thought that even Podhoretz's hero worship of Orwell was disingenuous; others lampooned the whole exercise as ridiculous:

> I think that if Orwell were alive, he would long since have been dismissed as a loon by people like Podhoretz. He had a most unfortunate habit of wanting to look at political questions from the ground up, rather than from the generalization down. He might well have visited Guatemala and El Salvador, to see whether it made any real difference to the inhabitants which gang of thugs was putting on the squeeze. Perhaps he would dilate upon the difference between "totalitarian" Yugoslavia and "authoritarian" Argentina.
>
> Why not, in the interests of fair play and the American way and all that, open your pages to other equally impartial and honorably motivated students of the late master? Why not Lee Iacocca on why George would be driving a Chrysler? Or maybe Jerry Falwell on why Orwell would support the banning of his own books? No reason to be sectarian about all this. Bella Abzug might like to write a piece on why, if Orwell were alive today, he might be a woman.[54]

Yet even letters like these last two indicate, by their references, the import of the "If Orwell Were Alive Today" conjectures. For juxtaposing "Orwell" and his concerns with contemporary issues points to an experiential truth about figure-making and intellectual genealogies which underlies the soon-forgotten polemics: there is a "pastness" in the present; figures continue to speak to us, to irradiate our lives and our traditions. This is the meaning of a living Tradition, as Eliot realized. For we are not only ourselves, but also, in some sense, our ancestors; and they, in some sense, are we.

The question of heritage was an especially vexing one for some British intellectuals during the 1984 countdown, especially after the birth of the Social Democratic Party in Britain in 1981, which was formed in the wake of a Labour Party split and the departure of several of its leading moderate M.P.s. On the liberal-Left, Noel Annan emphasized that Orwell was no Social Democrat during his lifetime and would have supported the Labour Party in the 1980s.[55] Edward Crankshaw agreed, though he felt that Orwell would be assailing the Labour-supported "closed shop and the block vote with all the vigour that in the 1930s and '40s he brought to the attack on capitalists and fellow-travelers."[56] Feeling "entitled to do what racing correspondents do habitually," Orwell's old friend John Atkins devoted an entire article in 1984 to "where Orwell would stand" on contemporary issues. Orwell would have opposed unilateral disarmament as the stance of smug moralists, thought Atkins, though he probably would not have been "taken in" by the Social Democrats, who were nothing more than "Labour Party members who could no longer accept the activities of the Left."[57] On the Right, Orwell's even older friend Rayner Heppenstall attacked "atheistical socialists" like Bernard Crick and maintained that the *Tribune* of the 1980s was so far left that it wouldn't have even considered printing articles by an Orwell.[58] John Wain expressed views similar to Podhoretz in his 1982 "Dear George Orwell" letter.

Proud to remember that he was once touted by critics as "Orwell's natural successor" ("one strand in the rope that seems to connect me directly to you"), Wain argued that Orwell would have opposed anti-Zionism, the "anti-democratic Left," Scottish and Welsh nationalists, noisy pubs, and especially the militant leadership of the British miners' union.

> The new breed of trade-union leader is not like the one you saw in action and heard speak at meetings. . . . As I write, the National Union of Mineworkers has got itself under the leadership of a man [Arthur Scargill] who spouts Marxist clichés as copiously as Fidel Castro; he has already announced [that] . . . the strike weapon will be used not as means for getting the miner a fair day's work . . . but as a political battering ram in the service of the anti-democratic Left. Now, what would you, George Orwell, make of this? Would you say, "The miners forever—the common man right or wrong?" But then, who, nowadays, is the common man? Isn't it the case that highly organized key workers, in a position to bring the economy to a standstill and wreck everybody's hopes, form an aristocracy, in the sense of power handed on from generation to generation and unanswerable to the moral authority of a democratic state?[59]

However fair Wain's conclusions, his invocation of Orwell is typical of the intellectual gyrations which some long-time Orwell admirers routinely perform, compelled as they feel to petition their dead hero along the lines of his own arguments of four decades ago. They appeal to their patron saint to bless their present-day position, less by arguing it in its own terms than by explaining it in such a way that it appears to fit Orwell's anachronistic pronouncements on related subjects.

Wain's appeal is also typical of how readers use figures in *argument from authority*. Known in classical rhetoric as argument *ad verecundiam*, or argument "from shyness," it constitutes an appeal to revere the recognized status of an Other. It is often highly effective because it puts an antagonist in the awkward position of potentially committing a sin of pride: to disagree implies disrespect for the eminent authority invoked. As this case study illustrates, a significant dimension of the politics of reputation involves argument from authority. Argument *ad verecundiam* helps sanctify a reputation and then lays claim to it. The onset of the argument's appearance—as in Orwell's case in the early '50s—frequently signals a new stage in the reputation process, during which a person is transformed into an icon. Its appearance also indicates that a reputation has become so large and prestigious that groups see advantages to having it "on our side."

## V

Insofar as the "If Orwell Were Alive Today" predictions were partly tied to the 1984 countdown, they will probably dwindle as the century advances—as has already happened. But the arguments about Orwell's posthumous politics first arose when the ideological battle lines for the postwar era were drawn in the Cold War—and then flared again when lines were redrawn in

the 1960s over the New Left and Vietnam and, to a lesser extent, yet again in the 1970s and '80s over the issues of the welfare state and the peace movement. Another major realignment may well provoke a new round of speculations. One might expect that the crisscrosses and flipflops made through these three periods of altered allegiances by Orwell's coevals and followers— including not only former Communist Hicks but also former Left-liberal Wain and former socialist Podhoretz—would serve as object lessons about the futility of wondering about the political stands of the posthumous Orwell. And yet it is precisely these shifts which have tempted intellectuals to speculate; their predictions have been attempts to secure their own precarious positions amid the shifting tides of intellectual fashion. The rougher the waters, the greater has been the tendency of intellectuals to look to Orwell as anchor, compass, and weather prophet.

And so younger admirers have looked to him as a generational guide, just as his peers came to look to him as a generational spokesman. But there is at least one great difficulty in approaching Orwell as a "conscience," whether of his generation or later ones. As demonstrated by the multiple, conflicting directions his onetime left-wing intellectual allies have taken, a writer's political vision does not lead to any straightforward, single, definite future. There are many roads from Wigan Pier to 1984 and beyond. Orwell's early death has meant that many intellectuals of his generation have assumed the right to speak in his name as his generation's spokesman—a role, by the way, which Orwell never claimed for himself. One therefore sometimes finds critics arguing about Orwell's politics largely by way of analogy to the postwar politics of his prominent left-wing contemporaries, on the shaky grounds that, because their outlooks once resembled his and they have outlived him . . . .

Yet no matter how cleverly one tries to apply the political trajectories of Orwell's contemporaries to his own case, the conclusions will be ill-founded—just as they will be if one conducts the process by applying quotations from Orwell's *oeuvre* to current events. The fact is that some of Orwell's Anglo-American contemporaries and near-contemporaries on the Left, many of them personal acquaintances, veered rightward into liberal anti-Communism (Trilling, Spender), turned sharp right into conservatism (James Burnham, John Dos Passos, Will Herberg) or neoconservatism (Sidney Hook, Lionel Abel, Hilton Kramer, Irving Kristol, Lewis Feuer, William Barrett) or even toward the Catholic (Muggeridge) or Anglican (Auden) churches; others stayed (or were born again) far Left or center-Left as pacifist anarchists (George Woodcock, Dwight Macdonald), radical socialists or quasi-Marxists (Graham Greene, Mary McCarthy, Philip Rahv, William Phillips, Fred Dupee), or democratic socialists (T.R. Fyvel, Aneurin Bevan, Julian Symons, John Atkins, Alfred Kazin, Irving Howe); and still others resigned from politics altogether (Koestler). In which of these or other political directions Orwell might have gone it is impossible to say. What is likely is that, had he lived, it would not have been so easy to claim him as an all-purpose patron

saint. Nor, surely, would he have been turned, by the mid-1950s, into a "media prophet."

## 16. "Media Prophet": Orwell on the Telescreen

### I

More than any other single factor, film and television treatments of Orwell's work and life are responsible for the prominence of the face of Orwell as The Prophet. Their wide circulation has also done much to establish Orwell as a "public" writer, one whose name and work are known by far more people than merely those who have read his books.[60] Even before the release of a new film adaptation of *Nineteen Eighty-Four* in late 1984, 21 percent of Britons and 10 percent of Americans claimed in a 1984 Gallup Poll to have seen a televised or movie version of the novel.[61] In movie theatres, in schoolrooms, and on television, millions more have also seen the animated cartoon adaptation of *Animal Farm*—and, in 1983–84, the well-publicized television documentaries and specials devoted to Orwell himself.

How media adaptations and documentaries help shape a literary reputation, particularly a writer's standing outside literary and academic circles, is the subject of this case study. Anglo-American screen treatments of Orwell have clustered in three periods: the mid-1950s, the mid- to late 1960s, and 1983–84. This broadcast material not only illumines the politics of Orwell's reputation; it also yields insight into a popular reputation in formation, a glimpse of how a "serious" writer gets known beyond intellectual circles by the wider public. In a process especially pertinent for the making of literary reputations in the 1980s, we can appreciate how one big media event transformed Orwell into a public personality in the 1950s, and how subsequent events consolidated his reputation even as they reshaped it. We can also further explore, as we did in the preceding case study, how the reputation of a public writer like Orwell, one who continues to speak to readers long after his death, evolves in response to changes in the political and cultural climate.

### II

*The Fifties: Cultural Politics and the Cold War*

The most important period for our attention is the mid-1950s. Radio adaptations of *Animal Farm* (1947, 1952) and *Nineteen Eighty-Four* (1950) for the Third Programme, the BBC cultural channel, had circulated Orwell's work widely among the literary-minded in postwar Britain. But it was not until four adaptations of *Animal Farm* and *Nineteen Eighty-Four* (or, significantly, as the media men invariably abridged it, *1984*) reached the screen between

1953 and 1956 that Orwell's coinages began to appear regularly outside the literary pages of the press.

**The NBC *1984*.**    In September 1953 NBC's Studio One opened its fall season with the first screen adaptation of *Nineteen Eighty-Four*. Hailed by television critics as "masterly" and "stunning," the one-hour play starred Eddie Albert as Winston, Norma Crane as Julia, and Lorne Greene as O'Brien. It reached a viewing audience of 8.7 million homes (a 53 percent share of the market), making it the highest-rated Studio One program for 1953. It also did well with the critics. "I cannot recall seeing any other television drama so imaginatively and effectively presented," wrote the *New Yorker* critic. "The new television season has come alive," said the *New York Times* reviewer, who praised the play for depicting "with power, poignancy, and terrifying beauty the destruction of the human soul."[62]

NBC's *1984* made no explicit reference to the Soviet Union or Joseph Stalin, who had died just months before, but with the Cold War and McCarthyism dominating the news, it was inevitable that the play would get enmeshed in Cold War cultural politics. As they had done with the novel, Henry Luce's magazines boosted the TV adaptation as an anti-Communist warning. *Life* devoted a two-page picture spread to the TV play about "Big Brother and the terrifying totalitarian state."[63] The anti-Communist implication was clear. Abner Dean's drawings of Oceania and Winston Smith, which had appeared in a special issue of *Life* in 1949, were by 1953 gracing paperback covers of *Nineteen Eighty-Four*. Increasingly, Orwell was being taken in some quarters of the popular press as an exponent of Luce's conservative, anti-socialist politics.

**The BBC *1984*.**    Much more controversial and politicized, however, was BBC-TV's adaptation of the novel the following year. It is probably unusual that one can point to a single moment from which a writer's popular reputation is "launched." But in Orwell's case the date is clear: Sunday, 12 December 1954. Directed by Nigel Keale, the two-hour evening program appeared during prime time, on what was then Britain's only television channel. It starred Peter Cushing and Yvonne Mitchell, among the small screen's two most popular actors.

Most critics hailed the teleplay as an intelligent adaptation and praised the BBC's courage in presenting it. Thousands of viewers, however, protested that the show was "sadistic" and "horrific," characterizations which the tabloid press bannered on Monday morning, 13 December. A debate over the "propriety" of the telecast quickly took shape and soon escalated into a classic confrontation concerning the proper function of art in the state and, more particularly, on the role that the emergent medium of television should assume in British society. Conservatives intent on limiting the presumed "adventurism" of the state-supported BBC, and parents who were outraged over the graphic depiction of violence on an "entertainment" medium, ranged themselves against socialists preaching free speech and

literary men defending the production's naturalism and fidelity to Orwell's book. Within the space of a single week, the BBC *1984* became what the *New York Times* called "the subject of the sharpest controversy in the annals of British television."[64] Some observers compared the BBC row to the furor in America over Orson Welles's 1938 radio hoax, *War of the Worlds*.[65] When it was telecast again the following Thursday, 16 December, the second showing of the play attracted the largest audience in BBC-TV history to that date.[66] Editorialized *The Times* of London at the week's close: "The term 'Big Brother,' which the day before yesterday meant nothing to 99 percent of the population, has become a household phrase."[67]

BBC announcements before and during the program had made clear that the TV play would not be "light entertainment." The telecast opened with the image of a mushroom cloud (suggesting the atomic war fought in the '50s, as related in Goldstein's *book*) and the warning: "This program is unsuitable for children or those with weak nerves." The violence was mild by present-day BBC standards, and even by American standards of 1954—a major reason why the BBC production aroused so much more argument than the NBC show. The British stage had traditionally observed social proprieties, and the British public in 1954 was quite unprepared for graphic on-stage violence. Most objectionable to some viewers were the torture scenes in which Peter Cushing, his face streaked with blood and his body reduced to a shell, was brainwashed in a coffin with electric shocks and then, in Room 101, confronted with a cage of ravenous rats. One Sunday night viewer collapsed of a heart attack after the torture scenes. On Monday the *Daily Express* ran the story ("1984: WIFE DIES AS SHE WATCHES") on its front page:

> A forty-year-old mother of two children collapsed and died while watching the TV horror play *1984*, it was disclosed last night. She was Mrs. Beryl Kathleen Mirfin. Mrs. Mirfin, a local beauty queen of 1936, was watching the play on Sunday night at her home in Carlton-Hill, Herne Bay. With her was her husband, who is a real estate agent, and two friends. In the early part of George Orwell's nightmarish fantasy of a Police State Future, Mrs. Mirfin collapsed. A doctor who was called asked at once: "Was she watching the TV play?"[68]

The *News Chronicle*'s front-page story ("1984 SHOCKS VIEWERS") gives more fully the flavor of the tabloid press's coverage of the controversy:

> Hundreds of angry viewers telephoned the BBC and newspaper offices last night after the TV presentation of George Orwell's *1984*—the story of a nightmare era. All complained that it was too ghastly for television. Not one caller praised the play. The BBC view: "We televised *1984* as a masterpiece of our time."
>
> Mrs. Edna Burgess of Holborn rang the *News Chronicle* to say: "I trembled with fear as I watched; it was not fit for ordinary decent-minded human beings. It was nothing but unoriginal bits of horror put together."
>
> Mrs. Vivienne van Kampen of Muswell Hill demanded an immediate campaign to prevent the BBC from repeating the play—due to be shown

1954 - OR "1984"?

The month-long controversy over the BBC *1984* in December 1954 permanently established Orwell's popular reputation, raised searching questions about the future of the new medium of television, and witnessed numerous examples of ferocious anti-Communist Cold War propagandizing.

The Child Spies of Oceania: the Parson family and Winston, from the BBC *1984*.

again on Thursday. "Some of the scenes are the most ghastly things I've ever seen," she said.

It was not only women viewers who were upset. Mr. Frederick Poate of Woking was looking in with Canadian friends. "None of us is particularly squeamish, but we found the torture scene . . . more than we could stand," he said. Callers told the BBC that the play was worse than horror comics and not fit for public viewing.[69]

So began the tumult. By Monday afternoon, the chairwoman of the British Housewives League was condemning the play as "sadistic and horrible."[70] Later that day Malcolm Muggeridge joined the head of the BBC drama division on the BBC-TV program *Panorama* to defend the telecast on literary grounds against a Tunbridge Wells alderman. The alderman predicted "a tremendous increase in crime" if more telecasts like *1984* were shown.[71] His claim of a firm link between television violence and criminal behavior may well mark one of the earliest appearances of the argument in public debate.

By Wednesday the fracas had reached the floor of Parliament. Cultural Conservatives upset with the BBC's depiction of violence (deemed especially deplorable on a Sunday) faced off against libertarian Conservatives and Labourites insisting on viewers' freedom of choice and on the value of the drama as a thunderous warning against totalitarianism. Five Conservative M.P.s sponsored a motion decrying "the tendency evident in recent BBC programmes, notably on Sunday evening, to pander to sexual and

sadistic tastes." Labour countered with an amendment lamenting "the tendencies of honourable Members to attack the courage and enterprise of the BBC in presenting plays and programmes capable of appreciation by adult minds." One Conservative sympathetic to the Labour motion added a clever amendment expressing thanks to Winston Churchill's government for preserving that "freedom of the individual [which] still permits viewers to switch off." Finally, a counter-amendment proposed by more Conservatives pointed out that "many of the practices depicted [in the telecast] are already in common use under totalitarian regimes" and applauded "the sincere attempts of the BBC to bring home to the British people the logical and soul-destroying consequences of the surrender of their freedom."[72]

The Thursday repeat provoked yet another round of breast-beating— and of sensational headlines. "MORE PROTESTS OVER 'H' PLAY," shouted *The Daily Mirror*. Again viewers wrote and phoned:

> I NEVER WANT TO SEE IT AGAIN. . . says Betty Tay. "I had a basinful of TV's Big Brother last night—and if that's the sort of thing the BBC is going to give us as entertainment they can keep my license for one."[73]

> My husband and I watched "1984" and were appalled. "Horror comics" could be no more damaging in their influence on many people. The sadism and sordidness of the play certainly would not be helpful to the youth of today, who have quite a struggle to discover the true values of life among the things they see and hear around them.[74]

In succeeding weeks the posthumous Orwell was, predictably, dragged into the controversy. Complicating the British response—again unlike the situation in 1953 America—was the still-palpable presence of Orwell felt by British intellectuals. The immediate memory of the man among his acquaintances, unresolved disputes about his political position during his final years, and his radiance as an intellectual youth hero: all these factors influenced the course of the BBC controversy. Just as had already occurred in the intellectual organs and literary pages of newspapers and magazines, competing arguments began appearing in the political pages of newspapers of the Left and Right about Orwell's legacy. Newspapers on the Right hailed the BBC production as a welcome Cold War salvo. Lord Beaverbrook's *Daily Express,* a Conservative organ, began serializing a severely abridged *Nineteen Eighty-Four,* explaining that "the *Express* version will keep a vital argument going in every home where love and truth and honour are cherished." Lord Rothmere's *Daily Mail,* another Conservative paper, devoted two front-page editorials to a defense of the BBC play, praising it for exposing "the beastliness of Communism— . . . something that we must fight with all our strength of mind and will." One *Daily Mail* columnist even spoke of Orwell's "saintliness," provoking a Labour M.P. to accuse the Tories of "stealing" Orwell. The body-snatching of Orwell had entered the official realm.[75]

Thus the television audience found it just as impossible to discuss the

man apart from the work as literary critics had during Orwell's life. Sonia Orwell, Fred Warburg, and several of Orwell's friends explained his politics in press interviews, arguing that he remained a socialist until his death.[76] But many viewers simply believed that O'Brien was Orwell's mouthpiece in *Nineteen Eighty-Four*. People who had seen only the BBC telecast or read no other books by Orwell saw him as a prophet of despair, not as a desperate dissenter against totalitarianism. "Orwell was accused in letter after letter," wrote a BBC official in 1955, "of having a diseased and depraved mind."[77] Viewers did not mince words with the BBC:

> The BBC cannot acquit itself by warnings to children and old ladies. As a front-line soldier throughout the war with no regrets, I do not think I can be charged with squeamishness, and I suggest there is a limit, and that Orwell has overstepped it here . . . . [It was] horrible filth, which suits the taste of only the sadistic type of viewer.[78]

> You [the BBC and Orwell] have endeavoured to open the gates of Hell to millions of people only just recovering from two diabolical wars and who are painfully seeking a tranquil mind with which to inspire the coming generation.
> We who lived through the last war know of the depths to which human beings descended—it is still unbelievable—and we want to make sure it is a nightmare which will never be repeated. The best way is to endeavour to *uplift* public thought to better and higher things, not drag it down in filth and godlessness.[79]

The prediction of one critic after the second telecast was turning out to be true: "Orwell will probably acquire an undeserved reputation as the first of a new generation of literary horror-mongers."[80]

Other viewers, however, simply found Orwell's message unsuitable for "ordinary everyday folk" or his warning exaggerated:

> Perhaps for a select intellectual audience some subtleties may have emerged from the plot, but I feel sure that for the countless millions of ordinary everyday folk it is not suitable for them to be confronted with the frightening possibility of the loss of all human dignity, and I find it quite immoral that we should be left at the end of the play by the fact that evil has triumphed over good.
> The play is an overstatement of its case, and as it proceeded I found myself believing in its possibilities . . . less and less. . . . In Orwell's grim conception, the spirit of man has no reality, and instead of glowing from an eternal source, it can be snuffed out like the flame of a candle. That surely is just not true.[81]

But some viewers defended the production, its implicit warning, and Orwell in particular:

> The outcry against the TV presentation of George Orwell's novel, *1984,* seemed to me most unjust. A minority of viewers, including myself, have to turn off the majority of plays because they are too trivial and moronic. Surely the BBC must also cater to a small public who occasion-

ally want to think? Its title is 40 years out of date. Just after the liberation of Paris, I was allowed to enter the infamous Gestapo headquarters there. I saw a contraption wired for electric shock and torture, almost identical to the "coffin" used in the TV version of *1984*. Do the British people still not know what dictatorship means? . . . Or do they not want to know?

There has not in our generation been a better writer of English, for his chief article of belief was that clear language indicated clear thinking, and that clear thinking was the best safeguard against totalitarianism. The language and the thought of some of the objectors to the broadcast of *1984* bear him out.[82]

Like the telephone calls already quoted, the letters to the BBC and press prove interesting not only in themselves but also for what they suggest about Orwell's reputation among "the wider public." As did his intellectual audience in New York and London, many of the TV viewers misjudged him as a cynical defeatist; but others with some familiarity with his life or work saw him as an anti-totalitarian prophet. The letters indicate that Orwell's reputation among "ordinary folk" was also not monolithic: some people saw him as a fearful Jeremiah, others regarded him as a brilliant polemicist and visionary. Clearly these letters—presumably marginal reception evidence—demonstrate that a "public" writer like Orwell speaks far beyond an intellectual audience. They also testify to the importance of oral and visual reception in forming a popular reputation.

In the mid-'50s, then, Orwell's reputation as a public writer extended not only to institutional readers but also to *institutional viewers.* How the viewer's —or listener's—reception of an author or work differs from that of a reader is a complex matter. Most BBC viewers had not already read *Nineteen Eighty-Four;* evidence indicates that non-readers found the BBC production even more horrifying than readers did. Moreover, in 1954 Britain, TV viewing—especially on Sunday night—was a family event, as the above phone calls and letters suggest. (Viewers were immediately reminded of "the sanctity of the Sabbath" following the telecast. Ironically, or perhaps appropriately, next on the air was the traditional evening hymn, "Come, thou long-expected Jesus."[83]) Unlike reading the book, then, viewing the play was not a private but a family and neighborhood experience. The BBC *1984* was therefore "judged by its suitability to the youngest member of the family present," as the *New Statesman* observed.[84]

In fact, in a very real sense, the TV viewer's reception of the BBC *1984,* unlike the reader's, was not just a family and neighborhood event but a national, public one. This reception context must be kept in mind. The BBC *1984* was simultaneously experienced by millions and expected to adhere to certain social standards (most strict during prime time on Sunday). Clearly, given the visual and auditory power of the exciting new medium, the TV play produced a far greater *collective* impact on Britons than had heretofore occurred with the book. We should not, then, speak of the 1954 adaptation as a "sensationalizing" of Orwell's book—even though it caused a sensation.

Rather, we should note that a work which might or might not leave a deep imprint on an individual reader may, when put on the stage or screen, cause social upheaval if encountered by a pluralistic public audience—as happened with the BBC *1984*. The protests against the program demonstrated, in the *New Statesman*'s rueful words, that "the cultural rifts between us are revealed as greater than we had supposed."[85]

Indeed the BBC *1984* controversy raised for the first time in Britain numerous issues of social policy, some of which continue to be debated to this day. Should television be exclusively an entertainment medium or also a vehicle for social criticism? Should television portray graphic violence (and sex)? Does television have a special responsibility, particularly to youth, to furnish family programming at prime time? Or should viewers simply be entrusted—and expected—to "switch off"? Parliament resolved some of these decisions in opting for diversity: in 1955 the "serious" BBC-2 and the "light" ITV were born. Although parliamentary legislation for the new channels had already been passed by the time of the *1984* hubbub, the national uproar quelled most doubts about the need for more variety in British programming. The telecast had demonstrated, noted *The Times* of London, "the tremendous possibilities of television."[86] Henceforth it would be acceptable on British telecasts to arouse audiences in the service of artistic ends or a good cause. But whatever its liberating effect on BBC policy, the production's legacy, like Orwell's, was not without its conservative implications. Programmers made one prime-time concession to traditional mores: no more would Britons' Sunday evenings be disturbed by "BBC sadism."

Perhaps the most tangible effect of the BBC telecast was its immediate and enormous impact on sales of *Nineteen Eighty-Four*. In mid-1954 the Secker & Warburg hardback edition was selling 150 copies per week. A new Penguin paperback edition had just been published. During the week following the first telecast, 1,000 hardback and 18,000 paperback copies were sold.[87] *Nineteen Eighty-Four* was catapulted into what the book industry has since dubbed "supersellerdom." Equally significant, the sale of Orwell's *oeuvre* was permanently boosted.

It should be emphasized that NBC's 1953 telecast, despite its 8 million viewers and excellent ratings, produced no such impact; it did not turn Orwell overnight into "a household word" or boost sales of *Nineteen Eighty-Four* sharply. We see, then, that it is not audience numbers alone that make a public reputation; the *controversy* over the BBC telecast was crucial. If not for it, Orwell might well have remained strictly a literary figure and never have entered the political pages and letter columns of the press. Thus, it is no exaggeration to pinpoint December 1954 as the moment when the language of Orwell's novel entered the popular imagination and when the book became, as Isaac Deutscher characterized it after the telecast, "an ideological superweapon" in the Cold War of words.[88] The date marks the firm establishment of Orwell's status as a "public" writer.

And yet the event has gone unremarked in Orwell criticism, quite unlike those temporal *topoi,* or peak moments (e.g., Trilling's and Pritchett's

encomia), to which the critics repeatedly return. Instead we may think of December 1954 as a *volcanic moment* with explosive and permanent (and, arguably damaging) impact on Orwell's reputation, but which quickly faded into the general terrain of his reception history—thus becoming another forgotten, indistinguishable reception "crater." (On a lesser scale, August 1946—when *Animal Farm* was selected as a Book-of-the-Month Club choice—represents the same.) Volcanic moments are also *loci* of the momentous, but they are important for enlarging the *size* of a reputation; they are sometimes dimly recalled after their eruption because they leave no durable, quotable "traces" in print for critics to enshrine.

**Halas and Batcheler's** *Animal Farm.*    Although the BBC-TV ruckus soon left the news, Orwell did not. The 1954 Christmas season brought to the screen an animated cartoon version of *Animal Farm*. The cinema posters warned: "Pig Brother Is Watching You." To celebrate the event, the *Illustrated London News* began serializing an unabridged version of *Animal Farm*.

Created by the British husband-and-wife team of John Halas and Joy Batcheler, *Animal Farm* was the first non-American feature-length cartoon and the first animated cartoon of a "serious" work of art. Halas and Batcheler were touted as cinematic pioneers. One critic wrote a book about the film's production;[89] the film also received an award at the 1955 Berlin Film Festival. But *Animal Farm* was not technically innovative, little more in fact than derivative Disney. Nevertheless some educators praised it highly.[90] Despite its weaknesses, I found it a helpful pedagogical aid when I used it in a tenth-grade high school class in the 1970s.

Although no public outcry over *Animal Farm* occurred to match the BBC *1984* controversy, the sudden shift of opinion against Senator Joseph McCarthy made the politics of the film a subject of heated discussion in intellectual organs, particularly in America. McCarthy had been officially censured by the Senate in November 1954 for questionable financial dealings and persistent vilification of fellow senators. The move followed thirty-six days of televised hearings in April–June 1954 on McCarthy's largely groundless charges that the U.S. Army "coddled Communists." McCarthy's fall from grace was as meteoric as his ascension. For many, the spectre of "McCarthyism" had been "The Great Fear"[91]; now the media branded McCarthy's formerly popular anti-Communist crusade a "witchhunt."

The public's ambivalent attitude toward McCarthyism was reflected in the confused reception of *Animal Farm*. Perhaps because it portrayed Orwell's story as a general fable about the evils of power and lifted it clean from its historical context, the adaptation was assaulted in political organs from one end of the ideological spectrum to the other. On the far Left, the *Nation* used the film as an occasion to reopen the attack on Orwell and judged it a crude anti-Communist polemic. Conservative and anti-Communist critics, possibly still caught up in McCarthy's accusations about Communist control of Hollywood, implied that the British directors harbored "Trotskyite" sympathies. One reviewer suspected that Halas (an anti-Nazi war refugee from

Poland) and Batcheler, who together had made numerous anti-Nazi propaganda films for the British government during the war, had engaged in leftist subversion of Orwell's message and deliberately redirected the fable's satire away from the Bolshevik Revolution. Noting the lack of any clear historical correspondences in the film to Russia under Lenin and Stalin, the reviewer asked, "Has truth become a luxury no longer available to liberals?" Delmore Schwartz observed in *The New Republic:* "To a Rip Van Winkle or a Martian Man, the film might seem to be on the British Labour Party." Another critic did mistakenly describe the film as "a bitter satire on the Welfare State."[92]

Admittedly, Halas and Batcheler made no attempt to remind viewers of the special relevance of Orwell's fable to Soviet history. One pig clearly resembled recently deceased Labour leader Ernest Bevin. In promotional ads, a fat-bellied pig wearing a string tie and smoking a cigar was clearly a caricature of a U.S. political boss, apparently a southern senator cut in the mold of Huey Long. Old Major was given the voice and face of Winston Churchill, and a pig with bushy eyebrows and a rude scowl resembled Joseph McCarthy. There was also a porcine Hermann Goering, prompting at least one critic, in apparent ignorance of the book, to write that *Animal Farm* was a direct attack on fascism.[93]

Other cinematic decisions by Halas and Batcheler were also read as ideologically motivated, and found questionable. Only the pigs talked, giving ammunition again to the Communist charge that *Animal Farm* (and Orwell) considered "the People" mere "dumb beasts."[94] Widely deplored was the film's happy ending, implying that popular revolutions can succeed. The film closes with Benjamin leading animal revolutionaries from the far reaches of the globe in a triumphant march to oust the pigs from power. But I found that when Benjamin and the other animals join hands in the final frame, the film inadvertently evokes memories of the opening scenes and the solidarity of the first Animal Revolution led by the pigs—thus reawakening, rather than refuting, Orwell's doubts about the inevitable course of violent revolution.

Whatever the political motives of Halas and Batcheler, their adaptation served to confuse people further about Orwell's politics. *Animal Farm* was obviously a commercial film meant to cater to children. In effect the directors transformed Orwell's political allegory into an ahistorical fantasy. For instance, the elimination of Frederick and Pilkington completely effaced the fable's origins in the events leading up to World War II and obscured its fierce lampooning of the Nazi-Soviet pact and other of Soviet communism's "accommodations" with capitalism. The omission of certain minor characters like Clover, the mare who remains loyal to the Revolution even after Boxer's death, and Mollie, the pretty dray-horse who deserts the Revolution for lump-sugar and ribbons, further robbed the fable of its historical moorings and its complexity. Politics aside, in light of the cuts and inverted ending, one could with justice resent what one reviewer called "the transformation of the prophet Orwell into the profit Orwell."[95]

The Columbia *1984*.  The commercial "transformation"—or castration—of Orwell culminated in Columbia Pictures' *1984* in 1956. Advertised (in something of an understatement) as "freely adapted" from the novel, the film was a slapdash mix of science fiction and horror film—typical of the sci-fi genre of the period. One critic in 1955 had deplored the earlier adaptations of *Animal Farm* and *Nineteen Eighty-Four* "into forms for which they were never intended,"[96] but the Columbia *1984* was a far worse film and illustrates how mass media "translation" of a literary work of art often entails commercial (rather than ideological) defacement.[97]

The American-financed, British-made production starred two Americans, a miscast Edmond O'Brien as Winston and a nondescript Jan Sterling as Julia. Columbia Pictures tried to puff up the film into a romantic tragedy. The love angle and the torture scenes were played up; the politics was all but dropped. O'Brien and Sterling, whose accents clashed with those of the English cast, were reportedly included to "get the American audience," since the British producer feared that, after the ruckus over the BBC *1984*, Columbia's production might receive an "X" (over 16 only) rating in Britain. (It did.) The BBC-TV flap also prompted Columbia to shoot two endings, one faithful to the novel and the other more hopeful.[98] The American version (originally intended for the American market and switched over the director's protests[99]) showed the lovers overcoming their brainwashing and dying, clutching for each other, in a hail of Thought Police bullets as Winston shouts, "Down with Big Brother!!" Once again arguments about Orwell's life and politics dominated the film's reception. Producer Peter Rathvon defended his ending as "more logical," one which Orwell himself "would have written" if he hadn't been dying during the novel's composition. Sonia Orwell publicly castigated the film as a desecration of her husband's intentions.[100] Concluded *The Times* of London: "[T]hose moguls with their finger on the pulse of [the] public . . . are convinced that we cannot take the truth twice. . . . What kind of a people do they think we are?"[101]


III

*"Halfway to 1984": New Interest in Orwell's Life*

Orwell disappeared from the screen for almost a decade. But as social critics began comparing the British welfare state of the 1960s with Orwell's Oceania, BBC-2 responded in 1965 with a documentary of Orwell's life and three dramatizations of his works. *1984* was revised by Nigel Keale. But this time it provoked little interest; British intellectuals were no longer involved in the public hysteria and feverish ideological battles of the Cold War. Indeed, the new production left some viewers "amazed" that an adaptation of the novel could ever have "caused so much fuss" in 1954.[102] *The Times* of London pointed out that the intervening decade had "done little to support Orwell's prophecy," so that the teleplay seemed to refer less to a possibly

terrifying near-future than to a rather hazy past. The show now seemed "insignificantly theatrical," little more than "commonplace science fiction."[103] American reviewers agreed that the play was "curiously lacking in suspense."[104] In truth, however, the production was little changed from 1954. What had changed was history: Keale could no longer rely, as he had in the aftermath of World War II, on a frightening world offstage to give viewers a vivid sense of Oceania's horrors. History had outrun *Nineteen Eighty-Four* as prediction; fears about totalitarianism seemed in 1965 primarily a topic of historical interest. The change underscores the significance of the *Zeitgeist* in making a public reputation—and suggests how much Orwell's suddenly inflated reputation of the '50s owed to the Cold War.

The decision by BBC-2 to present a documentary of Orwell's life and adapt two of his minor novels (*Keep the Aspidistra Flying* and *Coming Up for Air*) also reflected the new turn in his reputation.[105] Falling interest in the writer's totalitarian vision was balanced by heightened interest in the man's life. Now Orwell himself was becoming a subject suitable for popular historical treatment. Telecast in November 1965 and narrated by Malcolm Muggeridge, the BBC-2 documentary was a frank contribution to a cult. Featuring recollections of Orwell by his wife Sonia, his sister Avril Blair, and old schoolmate Cyril Connolly, the show's tone was reverential.[106] By 1970 still more old acquaintances (Richard Rees, Geoffrey Gorer, Michael Foot), along with more recent admirers (Angus Wilson, Norman Mailer, Noam Chomsky), had joined the chorus in the BBC-TV special *The Road to the Left*, most of them praising Orwell in nothing less that superlatives.

IV

*"Countdown to 1984": The Public Writer*

Numerous documentaries, adaptations, skits, and spinoffs[107] were produced during the "countdown to 1984." Orwell seemed to dominate British television during late 1983 and early 1984, and many of these programs were subsequently aired in the United States. BBC-2 ran a five-part documentary of Orwell's life produced by Arena TV (*Orwell Remembered*), a two-part exchange about Orwell among literary critics, and a two-hour TV drama (starring Ronald Pickup) about Orwell's years on Jura. Granada Television broadcast *The Road to 1984*, which re-enacted the pilgrimage of Orwell's life as the camera traveled with old Orwell friends down a Wigan mine and across a Catalonia battlefield. Thames Television of Schools sponsored four dramatizations in which young writers spun contemporary tales off the names of Oceania's ministries: "Truth," "Peace," "Plenty," and "Love." ("Peace" turned out to be a case for disarmament; "Plenty" satirized modern anxieties about consumerism.[108]) Most of the programs, like the two-hour CBS special hosted by Walter Cronkite, *1984 Revisited*, consisted of interviews with scientists, critics, and acquaintances of Orwell, who compared the worlds of "1984" and the 1980s. The approach of *1984 Revisited*

reflected the continued inflation of Orwell's reputation. As in 1965 and 1970, most of the interviewees were open admirers of Orwell.

The main event on the big screen was a new *1984*. Facing production difficulties, Virgin Films, the independent British company underwriting the project, delayed its London release until September 1984. But the timing proved fortunate, ensuring that the film would get proper critical attention in Britain and not be lost amid the media barrage and ephemera of the previous twelve months.

Like the adaptations of the 1950s, the production reflected the times. Winston and Julia were cast as sexual revolutionaries and one Party meeting discussed new advances toward the elimination of the orgasm. Yet unlike earlier adaptations, the new celluloid *1984* was an intelligent interpretation of Orwell's book. John Hurt played a consumptive Winston, and Richard Burton, in his last screen performance before his death, was a convincingly diabolical O'Brien. Rather than conjure a vague fantasy world of the future, Director Michael Radford presented Oceania in grittily naturalistic terms, treating it as a satire on wartime London. (The Two-Minute Hate even included footage from a frightening anti-Nazi propaganda film scripted by Dylan Thomas.) Most effective was Radford's use of the telescreen as an all-pervasive "evil eye," always watching Party members. The only weakness of the film was the single major concession it made to commercialism. Running over its projected budget, Virgin Films decided the movie needed to appeal to the youth market. And so the Eurythmics, a popular British rock group, were hired (at a cost of $600,000 for a slipshod, one-week jam on a Caribbean island) to do the musical score, which turned out to be a strangely psychedelic sound much better suited to Columbia's futuristic *1984* than to Radford's postwar England. Unfortunately, some of the fears about movie audiences expressed in the 1950s proved all too true: despite the Eurythmics, Virgin Films found its *1984* hard to sell to American distributors, who explained that the bleak ending was "too depressing."[109]

Disappointingly, no film or television program pegged to Orwell tackled the question of his political legacy or the difference of opinion on the Right and Left as to his intentions in *Nineteen Eighty-Four*. Instead journalists and TV entertainers made explicit what they had already done in practice: they ordained Orwell a "media prophet." "The first media prophet," one television critic said of Orwell, praising him for envisioning the abuses of mass communication "when the technology was mostly theory." After Walter Cronkite seconded Orwell's warning in his introduction to the new Signet edition of *Nineteen Eighty-Four* and Phil Donahue devoted four programs to "1984" on his talk show in January 1984, Orwell's anointing as a pop prophet was official.[110]

The media overkill about *Nineteen Eighty-Four* as a prophecy of the present, as if Orwell were a modern Nostradamus, led mostly to burlesques of the novel and puns on Orwell's coinages. Although many of the jokes had long since been worn out by the new year, what was surprising and signifi-

cant was that television writers assumed the public's familiarity with the language, plot, and themes of *Nineteen Eighty-Four;* knowledge of *Nineteen Eighty-Four* had become a measure of cultural literacy. For example, a bizarre spoof of Oceania's telescreen exercise sessions appeared on *The New Show,* a CBS comedy hour. Studio 54 became the "Ministry of Fun," with a hip disk jockey shrieking, "Fellow Citizens, Do the Pony!!" But most of the skit's jokes fell flat.[111] Thus, even as the TV documentaries continued to applaud Orwell, the book which established his public reputation had reached a cultural saturation point. Already by January 1984, with "Orwellian" vengeance, the televising of *Nineteen Eighty-Four* had come full circle: from a horrifying prophecy about a Communist future in the '50s, to an outmoded prophecy in the '60s, to a mocked prophecy in the '80s. The evolution of Orwell's treatment on TV illustrates how a social prophet, when the course of events undercuts his "predictions," can be cut down to size by the media that created him—from a feared to an enfeebled to a frivolous prophet.

V

The treatment of Orwell's life and work by the broadcast media points to much larger questions than Orwell himself, ultimately taking us to the line where literary history and the history of publicity start to blur. In doing so it raises the enormous and fascinating question of how the modern electronic media, especially television, have altered the basic conditions on and in which public reputations are formed. In 1983–84, Orwell moved a step beyond "literary figure" and "public author" to, briefly, the status of "celebrity." We touched on the subject when we discussed Orwell as an ephemeral "masscult" object; here we place the phenomenon of Orwell's celebrity in an historical context.

Celebrity is a modern notion, no older than a few decades. The film critic Richard Schickel has argued in his stimulating book about celebrity, *Intimate Strangers,* that the concept of fame began to change only in the 1920s and '30s with the beginnings of film, and that it did not alter fundamentally until the 1950s, with the introduction of nationwide network television. Until then, fame was still chiefly the byproduct of concrete achievement. The "famous" person was someone of significant accomplishment in a certain field. But with the rise of "image technology"—especially television at mid-century—"celebrity-hood" was born. The West entered a new age of the person "known for being known," characterized by the media's creation of the isolated image, the celebrity divorced from achievement and even history.[112] It is noteworthy that the rise of "the Orwell myth" and the popular success of *Nineteen Eighty-Four* occurred just at the moment when this age was dawning, for as this case study suggests, it is most doubtful that the rapid international circulation of words like "Orwellian," "Big Brother," and "doublethink" could have occurred without the TV plays of the 1950s—before, that is, the era of the telescreen.

## 17. The Spectre of *Der Grosse Bruder:* West Germany's Orwell

I

Most Anglo-American readers of Orwell are surprised to learn that not only the Anglophone world but also West Germany subjected *Nineteen Eighty-Four* to a "media overkill" during the early 1980s. The Federal Republic of Germany (FRG) had its own countdown to 1984, which even extended to promotions of "Orwell" much like those in Britain and the United States, including special media events and mass culture gimmickry. For almost two years running, between 1982 and 1984, Orwell's dystopia was on *Der Spiegel's* best-seller lists.[113]

In no other non-Anglophone country does Orwell's standing even begin to approach his enormous reputation in the *Bundesrepublik*. Although Orwell is read and respected by intellectuals in France, Spain, Italy, and Japan, only in West Germany have leading intellectuals identified with him and only there has the literary public read him avidly. Indeed the total sales of Orwell's books in West Germany are exceeded only by his sales in the U.S. and Britain; he is the most popular twentieth-century British writer of serious fiction in the *Bundesrepublik*.[114] Some of his coinages have even entered the West German media—e.g., *der Grosse Bruder, Neusprache* (Newspeak), *Zweidenken* and *Doppeldenken* (doublethink), *die Gedankenpolizei* (Thought Police), and even *Orwellisch*. (The East German press and intelligentsia had nothing to say in print about Orwell until the 1980s; as in the case of the Soviet Union, apparently none of Orwell's works has been published in the German Democratic Republic (GDR).)

With the exception of our look in Chapter Four at Orwell's official standing in the U.S.S.R., this book has addressed the history and politics of Orwell's Anglo-American reputation. This emphasis is deliberate and appropriate; Orwell's favorable postwar reception in Britain and America not only launched his reputation but also continues to constitute its foundation. Nevertheless, that a so-called quintessentially English writer should become a role model for some German intellectuals and an object of German mass culture is itself a development worthy of attention.

Inquiry into the phenomenon illumines three important conceptual issues dealing with audience response and literary-cultural politics. First, it raises the question of the distinctive conditions of the foreign writer's reception. Secondly, it allows us to balance and contrast the Soviet case study by examining Orwell's reputation among non-Anglophone *Western* receivers. Here again, then, in observing Orwell's reception in view of Germany's tumultuous postwar history, we encounter a huge wall portrait of Orwell, necessarily drawn in broad brush strokes. Until the 1960s, it was virtually a black-and-white, "official" portrait; but in recent years West Germans have held a more variegated, densely textured image of Orwell. And significantly, the German scene prominently includes Orwell and some FRG admirers in

the foreground, rather than featuring *Nineteen Eighty-Four* alone. Unlike the case of the U.S.S.R., then, in West Germany Orwell himself—not just *Nineteen Eighty-Four*—has been a distinctive, if limited, presence in the nation's cultural and intellectual life since the late 1940s. Finally, Orwell's politicized German reception illustrates both how a literary figure becomes implicated in what American journalists have called "international *Kulturkampf*" and how an author inadvertently contributes to his own defacement.

One can reconstruct four phases in Orwell's history of reputation in postwar West Germany. Chronicling these stages opens large cultural questions, for the changes in Orwell's reception in the FRG provide a sharply focused glimpse into an ongoing effort by FRG writers to reinterpret their national identity.


## II

What one historian has called the West German "fascination"[115] with Orwell is traceable, in no small part, to the fact that his work entered and shaped the German intellectual scene when the new nation was still "in the womb," immediately after the Third Reich's collapse in 1945 and well before the formal birth of the FRG in May 1949. The years 1945–50 constitute the opening phase both of Orwell's reception in West Germany and of the Cold War. Until 1950 many Western policymakers feared that the western zones might be invaded by Soviet troops, and in this climate *Animal Farm* and *Nineteen Eighty-Four* were exploited as powerful propaganda weapons in the Allies' cultural arsenal. But, apart from whatever anti-Stalinist uses to which the Allies put *Nineteen Eighty-Four,* its resonances with Nazi Germany (whose occupation by the Allies Orwell witnessed in April 1945[116]) were inescapable for German readers: Oceania with the Reich, "The Party" with the National Socialists, Big Brother with Hitler ("*Das Reich ist der Führer!*"), Goldstein and his Brotherhood with European Jewry and the Resistance movements, the Thought Police with the SS, Winston's diary with the "inner emigration" of German intellectuals, the Ministry of Truth with Goebbels' Ministry of Popular Enlightenment and Propaganda, the Two Minute Hate with the grotesque spectacles of Nazi leader-worship, The Spies with Hitler Youth, duckspeak with Goebbels' goal of *Gleichschaltung* ("coordinating the gears" of Germans' thoughts), and doublethink ("Ignorance Is Strength") with Nazi slogans ("Strength Through Joy").[117] Historian Golo Mann fittingly compared *Nineteen Eighty-Four* in his 1949 review in the American-sponsored *Frankfurter Rundschau* with Max Picard's *Hitler in uns selbst* (*Hitler Within Ourselves,* 1946). "Especially for Germans," Mann admitted, *Nineteen Eighty-Four* is "like a fantastic nightmare. . . . [P]erhaps more than any other nation, [we] can feel the merciless probability of Orwell's utopia."[118]

In crucial respects, Orwell's early postwar reception in West Germany resembled the American, rather than the British, response. As in the U.S., Orwell burst on the German scene with *Farm der Tiere* (*Animal Farm*), first

published in Zurich in October 1946. We see again how, because his German reputation started with his last works, his reputation quickly inflated and all his works were subsequently read backwards from *Animal Farm* and *Nineteen Eighty-Four*. This is somewhat typical with an author who gains success only late in his career: he enters foreign reception scenes with no previous history of response to constrain misinterpretation and misuse. Whereas Orwell's work before *Animal Farm* was at least slightly known to Americans, in New York, however, none of his books had appeared in German translation before this time. Thus, even more than was the case with American readers, Orwell's early image in West Germany was shaped solely in response to *Animal Farm* and *Nineteen Eighty-Four*. In the wake of Hitler and in the context of massive anti-Soviet propaganda, literate West Germans encountered a near-official image of Orwell, promoted energetically by the Western occupying powers, as a heroic Cold Warrior, an exponent of "liberal" values who stood firm against "fashionable" leftism and the corruptions of "totalitarianism"—a word which applied equally to Nazism but was widely understood as a code word for communism. This rigid, monochromatic image of Orwell circulated by the Allies during 1945–50 may be roughly equated with the one-dimensional Enemy of Mankind portrait "state-crafted" by the Soviet national press: Orwell's work, like that of many other Western authors, became part of official Allied cultural policy.

Unknown in Germany before the war, after 1946 Orwell's work was eagerly sought by anti-Communist publishers,* probably with the support of *Amerikadienst,* the translation bureau and news service of the U.S. High Commission in Germany. Not only German translations appeared in the western zones. Between 1946 and 1951, anti-Communist Frankfurt and Munich publishers brought out Russian and Ukrainian translations, respectively, and two editions of *Nineteen Eighty-Four* appeared. Radio plays of *Animal Farm* and *Nineteen Eighty-Four* were also aired in 1948–49; even a ballet of *Animal Farm* was performed in Berlin. Minor journalism like *The English People* was translated too, and some of Orwell's shorter pieces were published in the anti-Communist *Stuttgarter Rundschau*.[120]

---

*Orwell gave these efforts his full support. His agent, Leonard Moore, corresponded with Russian anti-Stalinists in the Soviet zone about how to smuggle copies of *Animal Farm* into the eastern zones; Orwell even expressed his willingness to subsidize its distribution, telling Moore in 1947 that it was the right moment for such an effort since "the U.S. is altering its policy, and doing more anti-Russian propaganda. . . ." Orwell was also a sponsor of the Books in Germany program organized by the British Foreign Office. (*Animal Farm* and *Coming Up for Air* were on the Foreign Office list.) Concerning the translation of *Animal Farm* by an anti-Communist Ukrainian refugee, representing Prometheus Press in Munich, he told Arthur Koestler: "I am sure we ought to help these people all we can, and I have been saying ever since 1945 that the DPs [Displaced Persons] were a godsent opportunity for breaking down the wall between Russia and the West. If our government won't see this, one must do what one can privately."

Whatever the implications for the controversies about his posthumous politics, Orwell's cooperation with these translations discloses how tirelessly he fought Stalinism behind the scenes as well as frontally—and how directly his own actions contributed to the formation of his Cold Warrior reputation in Germany.[119]

As East-West tensions escalated in quadripartite Germany, *Animal Farm* and *Nineteen Eighty-Four* were widely circulated in the three Western (American, British, French) zones and smuggled into the Soviet eastern zone as anti-Stalin propaganda.[121] In accordance with *Entnazifizierung* ("denazification")—the Allies' paternalistic program of German political "re-education"—all German publishers were "licensed" until 1949. But anti-Stalinism and anti-Americanism soon replaced denazification as respective priorities for the Western and Soviet occupation authorities, and the western and eastern zone presses reflected this change. Thus did the separate states of a partitioned Germany come to mirror the divisions between the two great occupying powers and to reflect their opposing ideologies; Germany occupied the front line of the emerging bipolar Cold War, and Orwell's work was promoted in West Germany and attacked in East Germany in almost exactly the same terms as it was in the U.S.-U.K. and in the U.S.S.R.

Two other interrelated factors during the Cold War contributed heavily to the popularity of *Animal Farm* and *Nineteen Eighty-Four* in the western zones during the late 1940s: the poverty of German postwar intellectual life and the championing of Orwell by the American-sponsored *Der Monat*. An intellectual desert from 1933 to the early 1950s, Germany in the early postwar period suffered from what has been called *Lesehunger*. This "book famine" was particularly severe in the western zones, which together produced only one-third as much newsprint as the Soviet zone. During 1945–47 only the Soviet zone had daily newspapers. Fearing that its German readers would soon be dominated by Soviet propaganda, the Western powers rejected a Soviet proposal to circulate German publications throughout all four zones and instead in 1947 banned Soviet newspapers altogether from their zones. In view of the paralyzing newsprint shortage in the western zones, the publishing of *Animal Farm* and *Nineteen Eighty-Four* during these years is special testimony to the high value which the Allies, particularly the Americans, attached to it as an anti-totalitarian tract.[122]

Moreover, *Der Monat,* a monthly regarded in the West during the early postwar era as the finest *Kulturzeitschrift* in all of Germany,[123] devoted nearly one-half of its pages in 1949–50—230 densely packed pages in all—to full reprints of *Animal Farm* and *Nineteen Eighty-Four*. In its first number (October 1948), *Der Monat* proudly advertised Orwell as "our London correspondent"; in the next fifteen months it printed in separate issues his journalism, two critical articles about him, and two full-page photographs of him. *Der Monat* presented both *Animal Farm* (translated, apparently to emphasize the reactionary nature of Soviet socialism, *Hofstaat* [feudal state, or court] *der Tiere*) and *Nineteen Eighty-Four* as exclusively pertaining to the tyranny of Stalin.[124] The closing line of V.S. Pritchett's 1949 *Der Monat* profile of Orwell typified the reverential tone of the magazine's treatment of its anti-Communist champion: "He is the most honest writer of our time."[125]

Through organs like the liberal anti-Communist *Der Monat* and the *Frankfurter Rundschau,* the Federal Republic was becoming the most "American-

ized" of all European countries, touted in the West as Europe's new "model" democracy—and Orwell was one of the Western writers held up to FRG intellectuals as an exemplary guardian of democratic values. Published in West Berlin and considering itself "Western" rather than specifically "German," *Der Monat* was the *Partisan Review* of postwar Germany—an even clearer instance in which an organ, rather than any single individual, served as the authoritative voice promoting Orwell's reputation. Edited by an American, Melvin Lasky, *Der Monat* leaned heavily on established reputations and featured numerous contributions by prominent Anglo-American and European refugee anti-Communists, including Koestler, Bertrand Russell, Franz Borkenau, Friedrich Hayek, Bertram Wolfe, Ruth Fischer, Sidney Hook, Arthur Schlesinger, Jr., Peter Viereck, and James Burnham. Indeed, given Lasky's editorship and the international authority of such foreign writers, Orwell's early reputation in West Germany was largely shaped by non-Germans. Orwell's association with the above names in *Der Monat* established his initial postwar image as an "anti-Communist prophet," warning West Germans about what a future under Stalin might be like. (East Germans caught with copies of *Der Monat* faced imprisonment.[126]) Lasky, a fringe member of the New York Intellectuals and later an editor of *Encounter*, organized and promoted the inaugural Congress for Cultural Freedom in Berlin in June 1950 under the auspices of *Der Monat*. Its role as an official front-line anti-Communist organ became clear in the 1960s when it was discovered that the CIA, through Lasky, had funded Congress publications.[127]

Timing thus proved just as important in the making of Orwell's West German reputation as it did in the cases of the Anglo-American intelligentsia and mass media. *Animal Farm* and *Nineteen Eighty-Four* appeared in the pages of the most prestigious, Berlin-based German magazine at precisely the moment which has been regarded as the turning point in German postwar history, 1948–49, when the western zones merged into one unit and the Soviets blockaded Berlin, resulting in the Berlin airlift and permanently foreclosing serious discussion of reunification between the eastern and western zones. Heightened U.S.-U.S.S.R. tensions resulting from the Soviet invasion of Czechoslovakia in February 1948, from the formation of N.A.T.O. in April 1949, from North Korea's invasion of South Korea in June 1950, and from the onset of McCarthyism in 1950 and the Soviet "Hate America" campaign in January 1951 further increased hostilities between East and West Germany. With the outbreak of the Korean War, both Germanys began to rearm. Under such circumstances it is hardly surprising—despite Golo Mann's emphatic insistence that *Nineteen Eighty-Four* was "not merely anti-Russian"[128]—that Orwell's work was used in West Germany and assaulted in East Germany as capitalist propaganda.

## III

*Der Monat*'s publication in March and April 1950 of six glowing encomia to Orwell (from Koestler, Pritchett, Trilling, T.R. Fyvel, Julian Symons, and

the Swiss journalist François Bondy) shifted attention for the first time to Orwell the man and writer, thereby opening a second phase of Orwell's West German reception. Ideological discussion widened to include biographical and literary considerations. In the next decade, West German writers read Orwell not only through the lens of anti-Communism, but also for his "significance for our time" as a socialist and intellectual.[129] In many quarters, however, intellectual discussion remained riveted on *Nineteen Eighty-Four*.[130]

Perhaps predictably, the immediate effect of the new interest in Orwell's life—ironically provoked by his death—was to send critics back to *Nineteen Eighty-Four*. Eulogists differed as to whether Orwell's personality was the source of Orwell's "pessimism"; they wrangled about what kind of "prophet" Orwell was. Thus, as in Britain and America, the man was used to explain the masterwork. In 1950 the liberal Protestant paper *Christ und Welt* saw *Nineteen Eighty-Four* as lacking hope and its socialist author as a disillusioned "Prophet of Despair";[131] others, like Bondy, the first translator of *Animal Farm*[132] and one of Orwell's major continental champions, maintained that Orwell was "not a prophet of doom" but "a man of true epic talent, behind whose NO! stands not merely steel-like conviction but a rich imagination and a warm and genuine humanity." *Nineteen Eighty-Four*, insisted Bondy, was "not a gloomy vision but an invitation to reflection from a man of robust psychic health, a disturbing call to those of us who live on, issued from a fraternal voice which death has silenced."[133]

Of course, both these images say at least as much about the mood and anti-Communist politics of German intellectual life in 1950 as about Orwell. German intellectuals were themselves in "a hopeless state of mind. . . in the depths of despair,"[134] as one expatriate reported after a 1949 visit, and so *Nineteen Eighty-Four*, appearing at such an historical moment, resonated powerfully for them, in some instances reinforcing that despair. On the other hand, Bondy, a regular *Der Monat* contributor who would soon become editor of the Congress for Cultural Freedom's Paris magazine *Preuves*, promoted the Anglo-American intellectuals' image of him as a cautionary prophet. *Christ und Welt* suggested that Orwell, like Koestler and Silone, had despaired in the Communist god that failed; Bondy identified Orwell with anti-Communist socialists like Camus and Silone as a man of "intellectual courage and a critic of every sort of power."[135]

Both *Nineteen Eighty-Four* and Orwell deeply influenced West German intellectuals in the 1950s. Koestler had proclaimed Orwell "the missing link between Swift and Kafka," a verdict widely quoted and quickly elaborated.[136] Soon German intellectuals were pursuing the comparisons between *Nineteen Eighty-Four* and Kafka's *The Trial* and *The Castle*.[137] The themes and neo-realistic style of much of the West German *Trümmerliteratur* ("rubble literature") of the 1950s, best associated with the work of Heinrich Böll, are broadly indebted to *Nineteen Eighty-Four*: whereby through a leap of imagination Orwell had created a nightmarish state of the near-future, German writers needed only to recall their personal expe-

rience of the recent past. One of the most obvious examples of a German writer starting from Orwell's NO! and investing it with Kafkaesque eeriness is Walter Jens's *Nein—Die Welt der Angeklagten* (*No—The World of the Accused*, 1950), a vision of a brutal, depersonalized, collectivist world comprised only of judges, defendants, and witnesses.[138] Along with Günter Grass, Jens was one of the early members of *Gruppe 47* (Group 47), a cluster of politically aware young writers opposed to all illusions and isms in art, who first came together in 1947.[139] Much the same as did young Anglo-American writers, this postwar generation of German intellectuals took Orwell and Camus as personal models, as Grass has recalled.[140] But whereas Orwell appealed to younger American and British intellectuals specifically as a rebel against the Old Left, he appealed to Grass's generation more generally as an *engagé* writer of extraordinary literary and political integrity, one who did not flinch from depicting the grimness of modern life and who stood apart from all orthodoxies, parties, and ideologies. Comparisons with Brecht were perhaps inevitable; but Orwell was not only admired by the younger generation of socialists. Even *Hochland,* the organ of West Germany's Catholic elite, praised him as an example of a selfless modern intellectual willing to struggle, however vainly, for truth and social equality.[141]

Other critics, however, still linking Orwell with Koestler and Silone, continued to stress that *Nineteen Eighty-Four* satirized Soviet Russia and that Orwell was primarily a pamphleteer against Stalinism.[142] The Cold War generally became more temperate as the 1950s progressed, especially after Stalin's death in March 1953 (as exemplified by the Soviet Union's decision to recognize West Germany in late 1955). But the Soviet suppressions of workers' uprisings in East Berlin (June 1953) and Budapest (October 1956) and the erection of the Berlin Wall (August 1961) also produced something of a roller-coaster effect in East-West relations, doubtless exacerbated by Adenauer's strong friendship with John Foster Dulles, Eisenhower's aggressively anti-Communist Secretary of State. To some degree the alternations between ideological and literary readings of *Nineteen Eighty-Four* by West German intellectuals during the 1950s seem to reflect not only their personal and ideological predilections but the warming and cooling of East-West relations. Understandably so, for with the threats of Soviet invasion and nuclear war directly across the border, *Nineteen Eighty-Four* remained "real" for West Germans in a deeper way than for Americans and Britons, as Johanno Strasser, a democratic socialist and former vice chairman of the West German Young Socialists (linked to the Social Democratic Party) has argued. Certainly this is partly why *Nineteen Eighty-Four* remained a high-selling book in West Germany in the 1950s and '60s. But one will search in vain for pointed German reminders like Golo Mann's (who wrote his *Nineteen Eighty-Four* review from distant California) that Orwell's warning of *Nineteen Eighty-Four* also pertained to Nazism. Before 1982, not a single critic, so far as I can discover, ever mentioned that *Nineteen Eighty-Four* bore any relevance to Germany's own recent history. Even into the 1970s, con-

spicuously absent from German criticism of *Nineteen Eighty-Four* is any attempt by Germans to treat *Nineteen Eighty-Four* as an opportunity for coming to terms with the Nazi past. In this sense *Nineteen Eighty-Four* was also part of what Walter Kaufmann, as late as 1957, called West Germany's attempted "dodge" of the past, its "repression of any memory of the Hitler years."[143]

The silence, as one critic has noted, did not mean that Germans were unaware of the parallels between Oceania and Nazi Germany; they were only too aware.[144] And here we should point to the deeper, elective affinities between Nazism and Prophet Orwell. To FRG intellectuals of the 1950s and '60s, Hitlerism and *Nineteen Eighty-Four* were rival and yet complementary prophecies. *Nineteen Eighty-Four* appeared a terrible prophecy of what Hitlerism could have become. In the heady early days of German battle victories in 1940–41, Nazism had confidently heralded a *Weltzeitalter* (new world age), a German and national socialist future in which *das Herrenvolk* (the German master race) would rule over a hierarchy of subordinate peoples. But then the so-called *Götterdämmerung* came in 1945. Orwell's German readers in 1949 saw their utopia in his anti-utopia: the Thousand Year Reich would have led—and in some ways did lead—straight to *Nineteen Eighty-Four*. Orwell was therefore in the curious position of being a prophet in a country in which his warning had come too late—or, rather, where his prophecy had already come true. The horrifying myth of *Nineteen Eighty-Four* thus displaced the shattered myth of the Reich. The Germans were already condemned by popular international opinion and by themselves as "diseased" and "evil." Seeking to evade the indictment and bury their past, troubled German intellectuals projected Orwell as a cautionary, not a reproving, prophet; they closed their eyes to his book's immediate referents and pointed far east and to the future. But their shame and anxiety were palpable: talk about the Stalinist future conditional inescapably evoked memories of their own past imperfect.

German intellectuals, unlike Soviet writers, did not so much strive to censor or rewrite the past as to submerge it. Theirs was a skewed portrait of Prophet Orwell as oracular amnesiac. Their very attempt to pronounce the past dead, however, indicates the power which "the living past" exerts on a people—and on a reputation. The long period from the 1940s to '70s may be thought of as a single, protracted moment in Orwell's German reputation history, which conditioned the "climate" of his postwar reputation. Such a moment is another kind of temporal *topos*, but it is unlike those oft-forgotten volcanic moments (e.g., the BBC *1984*) or long-remembered peak moments (the Pritchett obituary) in the reception terrain. Rather, it is a "place" where time seems indefinite or stopped—a *still moment*, less substantial than these other two, more like the ocean depths out of which a reputation wells up, inheres, and abides. We might refer to it as a *locus of the subsistent*, a submerged condition of cultural consciousness ("the living past") forming the general environment in which a reputation subsists. As long as the "repression of the Hitler years" continued, the interpretation of *Nineteen Eighty-Four* as an anti-

Stalinist but not anti-Nazi book was sustained. Not until the 1980s, after the Eichmann trial and the televising of *Holocaust,* would West Germans fully confront "1984," The Big Brother Within Ourselves. Into the 1970s "the burden of the past" oppressed the German consciousness, impossible to ignore and yet impossible to deal with. The "spectre of Big Brother"—from without and within—remained.

### IV

The split between an "ideological" and "literary" Orwell also manifested itself in the pedagogical and academic spheres of Orwell's reception during the 1950s and '60s, a third scene of his West German reception. By the mid-'50s, *Nineteen Eighty-Four* had entered the German *Gymnasium* ("a beloved school lesson," one German writer has sardonically recalled),[145] sometimes over the protests of parents who decried it—much as did the adult viewers of the 1954 BBC-TV *1984*—as "a shameless and lascivious book that is not suitable for young minds."[146]

*Gymnasium* teachers invariably taught *Animal Farm* and *Nineteen Eighty-Four,* at least until 1962, from an anti-Communist standpoint. After West Germany's 1962 Guidelines for Treatment of Totalitarianism were issued, pedagogical approaches to both books became more historical and broadly political.[147] Teachers used *Nineteen Eighty-Four* in courses on comparative political systems and often explored through it various theories of totalitarianism, a subject made popular by the work of Hannah Arendt. Beginning in the 1960s, some of Orwell's essays (especially "Politics and the English Language") also became standard introductions to English expository writing.[148] Writing in *Merkur,* the influential Stuttgart *Kulturzeitschrift,* Richard Schmid held up Orwell in 1972 as "the model" for writers of English. Schmid's essay makes clear that Orwell was being touted, for young Germans just as for young Anglo-Americans, as a model not only of good style but also of the good man:

> . . . Clarity was Orwell's great ambition and his special talent. Neither in his books nor in his letters will you find imprecision, pretentiousness, lies, or fads. Every thought is his own, thought through to the end by him and made as simple as possible. . . .
>
> Orwell deserves most of the credit for the fact that the English have been spared most of the constipated academic language of our political and social writers. . . . His clarity comes through even in German translations . . . , and not only linguistically. Orwell is also a moral guide. His honesty, his directness, his contempt for expediency, his capacity to speak passionately out of his personal experience—all this invests his work with such an intensity that one feels moved even where his arguments are flawed. . . . Orwell today is nearly omnipresent in English literature. You can meet him around every corner. To have been his friend is a great distinction. To have not acknowledged the worth of his books—or to have rejected them—is a black mark on the past of many important Englishmen, e.g., T.S. Eliot, Kingsley Martin, and Victor Gollancz.[149]

Schmid closed by comparing Orwell to Karl Kraus (1874–1936), the much-respected satiric moralist who attacked the shams of Austrian culture and insisted, as did Orwell, that a writer's use of language was a direct reflection of his character.

Other literary critics also addressed Orwell's use of language in the late 1950s and '60s. The widespread attachment of West German *Germanistik* to the *werkimmanente Methode* gradually shifted academic and intellectual attention away from the ideological aspects of *Nineteen Eighty-Four* and toward questions about Orwell's stylistics and his place in various literary traditions. Similar in conception to American New Criticism, which had emerged in reaction against the ideological orthodoxies imposed by Marxist and historicist criticism in the 1930s, the postwar flourishing of *Werkinterpretation* until the 1960s was in part a response to the *Blut und Boden* of Nazi *Literaturwissenschaft;* the method involved a focus on the language of individual literary works, with little consideration given to their social and historical contexts. Its influence is apparent in Orwell criticism of the 1950s and '60s (e.g., in articles analyzing how *Keep the Aspidistra Flying* raises basic questions of poetic theory or how *Nineteen Eighty-Four* constitutes a "defense" of "Language").[150]

More historically minded German critics discussed the place of *Nineteen Eighty-Four* within the traditions of the utopia and the political novel, comparing it to German-language works such as Hertzka's *Freiland* (*Freeland,* 1891) and Erik von Kühnelt-Leddihn's *Moscow 1997* (1949).[151] With the German translations of *Coming Up for Air* (1953), *Homage to Catalonia* (1964), and some of Orwell's essays, interest in Orwell's life and admiration for his literary achievement also continued to grow. One German historian of English literature, after quoting tributes to Orwell from Trilling, called him "a fearless seeker and witness to the truth."[152] Another critic, while acknowledging that he was "a good prophet," emphasized that Orwell should be looked at not as a "prophet" but as a "writer."[153]

## V

*"1974: der Countdown für 1984 hat begonnen."*[154] *Merkur*'s announcement in October 1974 opened a fourth stage of Orwell's West German reception. In the next decade, more than one million copies of *Animal Farm* and *Nineteen Eighty-Four* were sold in the Federal Republic; and all of Orwell's books, including *CEJL,* were translated into German. During what came to be known as *Das Orwell Jahr, Nineteen Eighty-Four* was adapted for the stage[155] and promoters sold "1984" calendars, videos, even murals. The novel also became a sacred text of the German peace movement and of the Green Party, which used it to campaign against the deployment of American missiles. Many newspapers and magazines ran special features on Orwell. By January 1983, when *Der Spiegel* devoted a twenty-page cover story to *Der Orwell Staat,* complete with several photographs from the 1956 Columbia film adaptation of *Nineteen Eighty-Four,* Orwell's reputation had

clearly emerged far beyond intellectual circles. "Prophet As Man of the Year" ran one of *Der Spiegel's* captions under a photograph of Orwell.[156] If Richard Schmid had exaggerated about Orwell being "nearly omnipresent" in 1972 Britain, a dozen years later his remarks fairly applied to West Germany.

During this phase of Orwell's reception, *Nineteen Eighty-Four* was discussed more in technological and broadly political terms than ideologically, more as a prophetic warning to West Germans and less as a diatribe against the Soviet Union. Yet, if anything, this meant that the horror of "1984" was even greater. In the 1970s, one critic noted, "1984" became a date filled with terror for West Germans because its implications could no longer be deflected by vigorous finger-pointing at East Germany or Russia. Especially after Willy Brandt's *Ostpolitik* had culminated in the mutual recognition of the two Germanies in 1972—and even in the wake of the Soviet Union's 1979 invasion of Afghanistan and 1981 silencing of the Solidarity movement in Poland—West Germans were disposed to looked at "the 1984 within."[157] The "spectre of *der Grosse Bruder*," said many intellectuals and journalists, was now represented by threats like the computer state, the West German intelligence agencies, the nuclear stockpiles, the right-wing politics of Franz Josef Strauss: all these signaled the latent potential in German society for 1933 to happen all over again. As Johanno Strasser put it in 1983:

> In the fifties and sixties Orwell's book [*Nineteen Eighty-Four*] was a bestseller in Germany. . . . We transplanted his pessimistic visions of the future to the East, across the border separating the two "systems." There was hardly anyone who seriously believed that something of the sort could develop here in the West. . . . We must indeed read Orwell quite differently nowadays. . . . The greatest danger does not threaten us from reactionaries, from unenlightened powers of the past, but from the most modern achievements of our technological and economic lifestyle.[158]

According to a 1980 poll, Strasser noted, only 33 percent of West Germans still believed that technological progress would lead to greater freedom; 56 percent thought that it was likely to erode their freedom. Strasser went on to list eleven threats to democracy posed by the tendency of technological advance to lead to bigger bureaucracies and more centralization. He also called practices like the West German policy of "interrogating" all candidates for civil service positions and conscientious objectors about their political beliefs "a first step toward Orwell's Thought Police."[159]

Similar cries about "Orwellian" privacy invasion and language corruption were heard in newspapers and periodicals during 1983–84. "The danger of 'Big Brother' is no longer mere literature," warned Horst Herald, former head of the Federal Bureau of Criminal Investigation, the West German FBI. "Given the present state of technology, the threat is real." In its special feature in January 1983 ("On the Threshold of the Orwell Year"), *Der Spiegel* cautioned against "creeping Orwellianism" and listed the following items on

*Das Orwell-Jahr* in West Germany: Orwell's books have sold more than any other **serious** modern English-language writer in the Bundesrepublik.

its back cover: "Data Banks, Computerized Dragnets, MX Missiles, Gene Technology, Bureaucracy, Nuclear State."[160] "Big Brother has become electronic," *Der Spiegel* said about *Bundesrepublik* plans to issue computerized identity cards to all citizens.[161] *Der Spiegel* and other periodicals both deplored and poked fun at German *Neusprache*, e.g., *die Lohnpausen* ("salary pauses," i.e., wage cuts), *die Gastarbeiter* ("guest workers," i.e., second-class citizens), *der Entsorgungspark*, ("a neglected park," i.e., an atomic dump). FRG journalists found East-West *Neusprache* a mine of satirical gems, especially characterizations of East Germany (known as "the one-party state" in the West, "the popular front" in the East) and of the Berlin Wall (known as the "Wall of Shame" in the West, the "Freedom Wall" or "Peace Wall" or "Anti-Fascist Wall of Protection" in the East).

The main difference between the journalists' and intellectuals' discussions of *Nineteen Eighty-Four* was in the latter's greater awareness of the relationship between German postwar history and the book's reception. Radical critics stressed "the dual application" of *Nineteen Eighty-Four*,[162] though they sometimes emphasized near-exclusively its relevance to the *Bundesrepublik*, ostensibly as a counterbalance to the anti-Soviet polemics launched via Orwell in the 1950s. One critic noted that, whereas even West German leftists had rejected Soviet arguments in 1950 that *Nineteen Eighty-Four* applied to the "free" world, in the 1970s West German liberals largely accepted such charges—though they did not, as the Soviets did, exempt the U.S.S.R. from the same charges. The early postwar reception of *Nineteen Eighty-Four* in Germany, the critic added, had "occurred almost exclusively according to the instructions of the American occupying forces. . . . *Der Monat* ignored the Nazi past . . . , employing Orwell's warning solely as an anti-Communist propaganda instrument that was also directed against English socialism."[163] Thus to radical German critics, *Vergangenheitsbewältigung* ("overcoming the past") demanded at least as much a neutralizing of the effects of American postwar anti-socialist propaganda as it required coping with German guilt about Nazism and the Holocaust.

François Bondy was one of those who had promoted the American line in *Der Monat*, and the dramatic shift in Orwell's German reception since the 1950s is perhaps best reflected in Bondy's contemporary comments on Orwell. In 1983, Bondy noted with implicit approval that West Germans saw *Nineteen Eighty-Four* as pertaining less to the East-West confrontation than to the invasions of privacy posed by their own government. "In the *Bundesrepublik*, Orwell is no longer talked about in terms of competing ideologies," Bondy wrote. "Rather he has become the warning call against the coming of the technocratic state, which threatens to turn us all into glass men."[164] In his preference for applying Orwell's warning to threats posed by technological determinism in present-day Germany rather than to the U.S.S.R. and to East-West politics, Bondy exhibited the same self-critical tendency of many liberal-left Anglo-American critics toward *Nineteen Eighty-Four* in the early '80s.

Given the anti-nuclear and anti-technology stances of many German

intellectuals, and of the Green Party, the new interpretation of *Nineteen Eighty-Four* was understandable and justified: the threats posed by technocracy and nuclear stockpiling are real. And certainly the present generation of West Germans is far more willing to confront the Nazi past than were previous ones; indeed, unlike the 1950s, critics of the 1980s sometimes do discuss the application of *Nineteen Eighty-Four* to Hitlerism. But insofar as the new "end of ideology" attitude toward *Nineteen Eighty-Four* entails recasting its referents near-exclusively in terms of technocratic issues—thus depoliticizing and, to some degree, dehistoricizing the novel—it carries with it its own dangers. For narrowing down the discussion of *Nineteen Eighty-Four*—thus averting, intentionally or unintentionally, the explicit anti-totalitarian meaning of this political icon—may ease painful German memories by sedating collective, existential guilt; but inevitably it triggers a delayed, fiercer "return of the repressed," as demonstrated by the national uproar in the last decade over the televised *Holocaust,* over Germany's exclusion from the Allies' D-Day celebrations in 1984, over Ronald Reagan's visit to the Bitburg military cemetery that same year, over the (temporarily aborted) staging in November 1985 of the late Rainer Werner Fassbinder's allegedly anti-semitic play, *Trash, the City of Death,* and over the alleged attempt by neo-conservative German historians in 1986–87 to minimize the significance of the Nazi years and to deny the singularity of the Holocaust. Germans continue to find that the *Hitler in uns selbst* is not so easily exorcised.

One former German soldier (and American prisoner-of-war) who has repeatedly called attention to the peril of forgetting the ideological-historical context of *Nineteen Eighty-Four* has been Günter Grass. Although Heinrich Böll, Adolf Muschg, Gyorgy Konrad, and other figures in the German intellectual world have written short pieces about Orwell,[165] Grass has mentioned Orwell in many of his books and essays; his identification with Orwell seems only to have intensified since the 1950s.

Grass is one of few prominent intellectuals outside Britain and America who has taken Orwell as a personal and literary model. Probably Orwell's "Englishness" has served to limit his figure status outside Britain. (Though in America, given the Anglophilia of many readers [e.g., Lionel Trilling], Orwell's "quintessential Englishness"—like Churchill's—has probably aided his reputation.) But more general factors conditioning the reputation process place this explanation—as to why Orwell is not taken as an intellectual hero by non-Anglophone intellectuals—in proper context. It seems likely that, when institutional readers look to political writers as models, they are constrained by linguistic and national-cultural factors. The writer's voice must speak to them, and even the best translations rarely capture the model's pure tones. And both readers and writers tend to identify most easily with their own country's writers, since national problems which earlier writers have faced often confront the admirer in similar form. For all his attention to totalitarianism, Orwell's immersion in the English events of the 1930s and '40s sometimes seems insular to foreign writers. I suspect, moreover, that the brilliant artist typically has a better chance than the "extraordinary ordinary"

political writer of becoming an international culture hero, since whereas the battles political writers fight frequently do not capture the imaginations of foreign readers, the creative struggles of a gifted artist are deemed to be the common experience of struggling artists everywhere.

In any case, the German political writer who became most widely identified with Orwell during the countdown to 1984 was Grass. *"Orwells Jahrzehnt"* ("Orwell's Decade"), Grass titled two campaign speeches which he frequently used in the 1980 and 1983 West German elections, during which he campaigned for the Social Democratic Party and attacked, among other things, deployment of American missiles and Franz Josef Strauss's politics.[166] In *Der Butt* (*The Flounder*, 1977), Grass's narrator admits in a poem ("Too Much") that he is reading *Nineteen Eighty-Four* "in a very different frame of mind" than he first did in 1949.[167] Grass is referring to his worries about Third World poverty here; in *Kopfgeburten oder Die Deutschen sterben aus* (*Headbirths, or The Germans Are Dying Out,* 1980), a meditation contrasting the Third World's exploding birth-rate with Germany's declining one, another autobiographical narrator re-emphasizes this theme and discusses "1984" in other contexts. The narrator fantasizes beginning his next book by telling "dear George" that, as his decade dawns, "good old capitalism and good old communism . . . are becoming (as you predicted, dear George) more and more alike: two old evil men whom we have to love, because the love they offer us refuses to be snubbed. Big Brother has a twin. The only point to be argued is whether the Big Brother twins who watch over us are uni- or di-ovular." Later the narrator, standing at a nuclear power plant site near Hamburg, identifies "Big Brother" as his government's insistence on technological progress regardless of popular opposition or the danger to its citizens' welfare: "The Yes to Progress. The perpetually self-perpetuating Yes. The Yes to the eighties. Big Brother's Yes, somewhat, but not excessively, incommoded by Orwell's never-recanted No."[168]

As we have seen, it was this Orwell who shouted NO!, the rebel and prophet, who first attracted Grass, Bondy, Jens, and their generation in the 1950s. In the 1980s, Grass, a democratic socialist and the example *par excellence* of the writer as political activist, has self-consciously, audaciously embraced Orwell and Camus as intellectual heroes, balancing foreboding against hope and, as it were, setting the two writers in dialogue with each other. Orwell is Grass's dark and admonitory prophet, Camus his fortifying one. Orwell warns, says Grass, whereas Camus urges us to take action even in the most desperate circumstances. Orwell's never-recanted No, Grass believes, needs to be supplemented by Camus's murmured Yes. "And how will Sisyphus react to Orwell's decade?" Grass asks in *Headbirths*. "Should his stone be rationalized, will his stone be rationalized away?" For Grass, the stone (or, really, the boulder) is "Harm," the accumulated weight of human foibles and ills, beneath which lie beauty, freedom, love, justice. Bearing the stone—confronting "1984"—is a never-ending, Sisyphean task. Or as Grass concluded his 30 January 1983 campaign speech, "The Right to Resist," delivered on the fiftieth anniversary of Adolf Hitler's ascent to Reich Chancellor:

Orwell's decade demands that we not yield miserably to the inclination toward catastrophe but try to stem the downward trend. . . . What did Sisyphus say when he had rolled the stone uphill and it rolled right down again? He called out: Have no fear, you stone. I will also be down again. Every political effort which makes injustice smaller and peace safer, which preserves or even extends freedom and protects nature from the destructive arrogance of man, I say, each of these efforts is always part of the labors of Sisyphus. For the stone will never remain up there. For this rolling of the stone which seems in vain is part of human existence. Only if we were to give up and let the stone lie at the foot of the hill and would no longer want to be Sisyphus, only then would we all be lost.[169]

The allusions undeniably evoke Camus; but the same thoughts might well have come from the pen of the English democratic socialist after whom Grass named the decade of the '80s, perhaps from some of the inspiriting passages of *The Lion and Unicorn* or *Tribune,* where Orwell not only warned but also affirmed. The sentiments voiced in Grass's credo do indeed fit with the memory of another Orwell admirer, Swiss-born and German-speaking T.R. Fyvel, the *Tribune* friend who persuaded Orwell to write *The Lion and the Unicorn* and whose reception history of Orwell we now address.

## 18. "Friend and Prophet": T.R. Fyvel and the *Tribune* writers' Orwell

### I

Before us now is an intimate group portrait. The scene features Orwell, arguing heatedly, though respectfully, with Fyvel and a few colleagues at the *Tribune* office in the Strand. Much smaller than "Germany's Orwell," this cameo does not highlight international events. Such events do form a crucial part of the setting, but the scene lets them emerge gradually as it presents in detail this small group friendly with Orwell and the newspaper they edited.

The *Tribune* writers were the only literary group with which Orwell ever formally identified himself, serving as a wartime literary editor (1943–45). Of course, as our discussion in Chapter Three of Orwell's tendency to compartmentalize relationships indicated, he always appeared, even to his *Tribune* colleagues, an outsider. Nonetheless his association with *Tribune* has been treated by many observers, among them Bernard Crick and Michael Foot, as a key to understanding his politics.[170] This is justifiable but Orwell's relationship with *Tribune* varied during his decade of association with it, and attention should be given to the *shifting* pattern of their relations, to the dynamics of political affiliation and disaffiliation.

This case study explores how a group in which the figure himself is an authoritative voice receives him and conditions his reputation outside the group. It also discusses how Orwell's association with "democratic socialism"

and "Englishness" form part of his reputation as The Prophet. Nowhere is this truer than with the figure whom Crick has called "the *Tribune* Orwell."[171] This Orwell is not only Crick's "Dr. Johnson of the *Tribune* Left"[172]—the socialist visionary and "revolutionary patriot" of *The Lion and the Unicorn*—but also the pessimistic prophet of *Nineteen Eighty-Four*.

Although several of Orwell's former *Tribune* colleagues have written or been interviewed about him, none has devoted so much energy to the task as T.R. ("Tosco") Fyvel. The following pages approach the *Tribune* writers' image of Orwell primarily through Fyvel's reception history, and, secondarily, through Julian Symons' and John Atkins'. All three men knew Orwell chiefly on account of their *Tribune* journalism. Fyvel succeeded Orwell as literary editor and Atkins preceded him; Symons penned Orwell's obituary for *Tribune*.

The threefold aim of this section, then, is to reconstruct from the inside and outside the context of what Fyvel has called Orwell's "special relationship"[173] with *Tribune* in the 1940s, to explore those larger political and theoretical issues which emerge from it, and to explain not only *Tribune*'s image of Orwell but also Orwell's special place in the lives of Fyvel and *Tribune* as "Friend and Prophet."[174]

## II

"One's relations with a newspaper or magazine are more variable and intermittent than they can be with a human being," Orwell wrote about *Tribune* in his "As I Pleased" column in the tenth anniversary issue in 1947.[175] Whatever the general truth of this maxim, it does clue us to Orwell's flexible attitude about *Tribune*'s changes in editorial policy in the preceding decade. Orwell goes on to note in the same column that *Tribune* had already, by 1947, gone through two or three distinct lives and that his own attitude toward it had "varied sharply"[176] since its early years, when it had been a frankly pro-Soviet organ. Indeed one can demarcate three *Tribune* "lives" between 1937–47 and three periods of Orwell's relations with *Tribune*, roughly corresponding to the years before, of, and after his "As I Please" column (1943–47).

An extended look at *Tribune*'s history and Orwell's place in it is apposite here: the complex background of *Tribune* will put its contribution to Orwell's reputation in proper perspective. If numbers mean anything—e.g., volume of contributions and length of association—Orwell did consider *Tribune* "special." Beginning with brief book reviews in March 1940, he made more than one hundred contributions to *Tribune* in the next seven years. His seventy-one "As I Please" columns appeared weekly throughout his term as literary editor, November 1943 to February 1945, and then irregularly from November 1945 until April 1947. Thus his close relationship with *Tribune* spanned the latter half of the first decade of its life, when both he and it emerged as the cranky consciences of the Labour Left. Even the title of Orwell's column, "As I Please," suggests how he used *Tribune* as a

platform from which he spoke as *tribunus populi* and as a sometimes prophetic, sometimes merely strident, voice of democratic socialism. It is this
middle period of Orwell's association with *Tribune* to which socialists
friendly to Orwell usually refer; but one should remember that these four
years are surrounded on both sides by a *Tribune* and an Orwell somewhat
different from their wartime selves.

Born as a threepenny broadsheet in January 1937, *Tribune* began—and
has remained—a small, generally respected left-wing paper and a shoe-
string operation. It was "a fluke that came off," in Fyvel's words.[177] Orwell
said that he had never even heard of "the *Tribune*" (it eventually dropped
the article) until 1939.[178] Had he seen *Tribune* during its first two years, he
would surely have found its Soviet sympathies objectionable—as late as
December 1939 it did no more than protest weakly the Russian invasion of
Finland. Founded as a socialist weekly by Sir Stafford Cripps, a militantly
left-wing Labour M.P., *Tribune* (dubbed "Cripps' Chronicle") was intended
to serve as the voice of Cripps's fledgling Unity Campaign.[179] This was an
ill-fated and short-lived attempt to bring about a united front of Labourites,
Communists, and members of the Independent Labour Party (ILP) behind
issues of broad concern like unemployment and the government's policy of
non-intervention in Spain. Cripps was joined by a group of left-wing Labour M.P.s, including Bevan, George Strauss, and Ellen Wilkinson, all of
them inspired by the success of Victor Gollancz's Left Book Club, which had
started a few months earlier. Like the Club, *Tribune* was at first an unabashed defender of Stalin. It failed even to mention the show trials and
awkwardly rationalized both the Molotov-Ribbentrop pact and Stalin's take-
over of the Baltic nations and partitioning of Poland with Hitler.

The Unity Campaign soon died, but by 1939 *Tribune* had survived and
boasted a circulation of 30,000. During 1942–43, when it entered its "second life" under Bevan's editorship, it became the only paper to attack
Churchill's coalition government openly and the only left-wing paper to
criticize the Soviet Union. These twin distinctions have marked the war
years in *Tribune* history as the paper's finest hour. Even latter-day radical
Tribunites hostile to Orwell invoke his name warmly when *Tribune*'s early
history is recalled. This ready association is one of the chief reasons why
what Symons has called "the *Tribune* connection"[180] has figured importantly
in Orwell's posthumous reputation.

The connection is, of course, quite real after 1940, whatever its tensions.
Above and beyond all their disagreements throughout his association with
the paper, Orwell shared *Tribune*'s "mission"—to find a middle way between
Marxism and welfare state capitalism, to transform the Labour Party into a
truly socialist party. Along with sharing *Tribune*'s left-wing Labour stance,
Orwell agreed strongly with *Tribune*'s loud and persistent calls for full independence for India. Looking back over his editorship in 1947, he praised
*Tribune* as "the only existing weekly paper that makes a genuine effort to be
both progressive and humane—that is, to combine a radical socialist policy
with a respect for freedom of speech and a civilised attitude towards litera-

ture and the arts. . . ."[181] This judgment might also have summed up Orwell's high opinion of Aneurin Bevan, also a romantic Left rebel and in some ways his counterpart in party politics. If Orwell was *Tribune*'s "prize writer"[182] and the iconoclastic Etonian who had descended into the tramps' underworld in order to understand lower-class life better, Bevan was the much-loved (and -hated) Labour leader who rose from the Welsh coal mines to become an orator the equal of Churchill. Especially in the 1950s, when Bevan and Orwell were well-known names, they were often linked in the press. Like Orwell, Bevan possessed a populist reputation: probably no politician, even Churchill, was more loved by ordinary Britons in the early '50s than "Nye" Bevan.[183] Quite arguably Bevan was, as the *New Statesman* proclaimed posthumously, "the greatest figure the British Labour movement has produced."[184]

Bevan was virtually the only national politician whom Orwell admired.[185] In his biography of Bevan, Michael Foot points out that Orwell's reputation was only a modest one in 1943 when he took over as *Tribune* literary editor, and that, although Bevan and Orwell never became close, Bevan was the only wartime editor who would give Orwell "complete freedom" to write as he wished.[186] Likely this is true. And as literary editor, Orwell practiced a similar liberal policy. He invited contributors of diverse political views, concerned that *Tribune* not become a little magazine "unintelligible to outsiders."[187]

Probably most important for Orwell's fraternal relations with the wartime *Tribune* was that he could essentially agree with the paper on what to fight against. After Bevan became editor (January 1942), the paper began criticizing Soviet policy harshly, as did Orwell in its pages. In the same 1947 column, he noted that *Tribune* was "not perfect, as I should know, having seen it from the inside," but that during the war it was at least "the one paper in England that had neither supported the Government uncritically, nor opposed the war, nor swallowed the Russian myth."[188] The triple negative suggests once again that the wartime *Tribune* appealed to Orwell not only because it stood for democratic socialism, but because, like him, its style was that of an outspoken "rebel against the Left." *Tribune* was a paper of and for intellectual outsiders, casting itself as speaking to and for the working man. Whatever Orwell's differences with the wartime politics of the paper, many observers have agreed that "As I Please" represents the best of the pugnacious, iconoclastic *Tribune* spirit.[189]

The years following Orwell's last contribution to *Tribune* in April 1947 constitute a third stage of his relationship with the paper. During this phase of the paper's editorship under Jon Kimche and Evelyn Anderson, and later Michael Foot and Anderson, Orwell became increasingly critical of *Tribune*, primarily due to what he saw as the editors' "overemphasis" on Zionism and their virulent anti-Americanism. In letters and journalism in early 1948, Orwell lamented that *Tribune* "gets worse and worse" and criticized its failure of radical nerve with Labour now in office. Elsewhere he denounced its numerous "equivocations" about British foreign policy to-

ward the Soviet Union.[190] (A few months later, *Tribune* launched a harsh attack on the U.S.S.R., after Stalin's invasion of Czechoslovakia and blockade of Berlin.)

Even as Orwell was becoming increasingly critical of *Tribune,* however, *Tribune* was becoming ever more admiring of him. He joked in 1947 that the paper first caught his eye when it gave him a bad review, and it is true that its reviews of his early work were mixed. But during Fyvel's tenure as literary editor (1945–50), the kudos for *Animal Farm, Critical Essays,* and *Nineteen Eighty-Four* were lavish. Fyvel himself touted *Animal Farm* and *Critical Essays,* pronouncing Orwell, upon publication of the latter, "a national figure as a critic, satirist and political journalist." Fyvel's one negative note was directed at Orwell's "savagely pessimistic" conclusions about the Labour Party's chances of introducing socialism. Fyvel and *Tribune* were still bright with the glow of the 1945 Labour victory, after which Bevan, George Strauss, and Ellen Wilkinson had gained Cabinet posts. What Orwell saw as *Tribune*'s accommodation to politics-as-usual at home and "fashionable" anti-Americanism abroad,[191] Fyvel and *Tribune* saw as the practical politics of a radical paper sympathetic to a left-wing government.

Between 1946 and 1949, Orwell's *Tribune* acquaintances lauded him in and outside of the paper's pages. The most revealing sign of Orwell's status among his former colleagues was their serious treatment of *The English People,* a contribution to the Britain in Pictures series which Orwell considered no more than a piece of spirited journalism. In fact, Orwell went so far as to gently reprimand Symons—who had just succeeded Orwell, on his recommendation, as book reviewer for the *Manchester Evening News*—for his extravagant 1947 review of "that silly little *English People* book" in the *MEN.*[192] Especially appealing to the *Tribune* writers were lines such as, "England can only fulfill its special mission if the ordinary English in the streets can somehow get their hands on power."[193] Much as in *The Lion and the Unicorn,* Orwell cast himself as the anti-intellectual pragmatist and optimistic prophet of democratic socialism. Symons' generous praise reflected precisely this self-image:

> He always tells the truth—as he sees it. He has remarkably few prejudices, theories or preconceived notions about anything. He simply observes and records; and the truth he records is often very different from that recorded by statisticians and philosophers. They know what *should* happen: George Orwell tells you what *is* happening, according to the evidence of his eyes and ears.[194]

With the publication of *Nineteen Eighty-Four, Tribune*'s secondary emphasis on Orwell as a "prophet" became explicit and was inverted, highlighting his "pessimism." Alongside the image of the optimistic populist prophet in *Tribune* criticism, an image derived from *The Lion and the Unicorn* and *The English People,* there arose a darker Orwell, already suggested by Fyvel's focus on Orwell's "pessimism" in *Critical Essays.* "George Orwell is a prophet of the larger pessimism," wrote *Tribune*'s reviewer of *Nineteen Eighty-Four,*

calling the book "a picture of the world after the Bomb" and a warning about "the liquidation of the human will."[195] As we shall see, *Tribune* writers have continued into the 1980s to present these two images of Orwell, the optimistic and pessimistic socialist visionary.


III

I have sketched the story of Orwell's "sharply varied" relations with *Tribune* because ignorance of this history has facilitated posthumous left- and right-wing claims to his mantle. Both socialists and neoconservatives have pointed to Orwell's *Tribune* days, though the former mainly cite *The Lion and the Unicorn* and the *Tribune* writings from the 1940–47 period and the latter refer chiefly to the periods 1937–40 and after 1947. The differences are another example of the selectivity which Orwell's admirers exercise when they quote him to their purposes.

And so one finds Michael Foot hailing Orwell as "the *Tribune* socialist" and praising Bernard Crick for placing the "As I Please" columns of 1943–47 "at the very center" of his biography.[196] And Crick himself stresses the overriding importance of *The Lion and the Unicorn* for judging Orwell's politics, making it the basis of his judgment that Orwell was "a revolutionary and an egalitarian, a revolutionary in love with the past, but a revolutionary none the less. . . . His own [radical] values, whether capable of realization or not, were plainly stated and can only wilfully be misunderstood (as when he is claimed for the camp of the Cold War, *Encounter* magazine and the CIA)."[197]

But to dehistoricize and generalize about "the *Tribune* days," or to fix *The Lion and the Unicorn* as the centerpiece of "the *Tribune* Orwell," is perhaps a hazardous practice. "The camp of the Cold War" can—and indeed does—quote Orwell's *Tribune* writings to its purpose, presenting him as a *critic* of revolution. Of course, this "neoconservative Orwell" is reconstructed from a variety of references, among them passages from *The Lion and the Unicorn* and Part II of *The Road to Wigan Pier*, which reflect (in Norman Podhoretz's phrase) Orwell's "wholehearted patriotism"[198] and disgust with left-wing intellectuals. But neoconservatives have also cited Orwell's letters from 1947–48 critical of *Tribune*, and also "In Defence of Comrade Zilliacus" (1948), in which Orwell castigates *Tribune* and expresses his preference for an alliance with America over the Soviet Union.[199] Podhoretz puts Orwell's comments within the context of bipolar geopolitics and concludes: "Despite Crick's sophistical protestations, there can be no doubt that Orwell did belong in 'the camp of the Cold War' while he was alive."[200] Leopold Labedz agrees with Podhoretz, quotes also from pre-1940 *Tribune* columns, and addresses "the *Tribune* connection" frontally. For example, he argues that *Tribune*'s wartime criticism of Communism was an aberrant moment in its history. *Tribune* is therefore "clearly not in 'the Orwell tradition'," though the paper "claims him for its own"[201] by including pieces like Orwell's 1947 "As I Pleased" column in

the anniversary anthology *Tribune 40* (1977), says Labedz. (Foot also included several pieces by his "*Tribune* socialist" in the 1958 anthology *Tribune 21.*) Labedz admits that Orwell never "fell out" with *Tribune*. But the cumulative effect of his ahistorical approach to Orwell's "persistent differences" with *Tribune* (e.g., Labedz's speculations about Orwell's disapproval of *Tribune*'s and Foot's support for unilateral disarmament) understates their closeness during 1943–47 and implies that what amounted to a break between them did occur at some unspecified time.[202]

These Left-Right skirmishes over Orwell's mantle spotlight a different aspect of the argument from authority, raising conceptual issues about rival legitimacy claims to a figure, or involving what Robert Nozick has called the rhetoric of "historical entitlement."[203] No matter how different a figure of the past may *seem* from his contemporary claimants, they can search history for various kinds of "process" and "value" continuities that will link them to the figure—and thereby root their positions in a distinguished tradition. Radical admirers of Orwell have mostly linked themselves to him through process continuities. Though *Tribune* in the 1980s takes positions very different from Orwell's in the 1940s, the paper has undergone a natural evolution in response to events to which Orwell would also have had to adjust, Tribunites like Michael Foot argue. So Orwell was and remains a fellow Tribunite, regardless of *Tribune*'s apparent present-day differences with him. Some socialists, however, as Crick just did, stress value continuities, arguing that Orwell and socialism continue to share the same underlying values: the socialist belief in decency and justice for all. Neoconservative admirers like Labedz exclusively emphasize value continuities. They argue that "progressive" socialists of the 1980s do not share Orwell's "fundamental" (i.e., anti-collectivist) convictions; and that, even though the self-description "neoconservative" was not Orwell's, the values and policy stands of neoconservatism fairly characterize his views from the standpoint of the present. These Left/Right arguments then get linked to arguments about the formal/value continuities or discontinuities in Orwell's career. Liberal-Leftists typically seek to minimize the extent of Orwell's "evolution." And so they argue that Orwell has not changed, or that the change is only apparent, or that he did change but not significantly. Neoconservatives usually maintain that Orwell changed significantly—either midway or near the end of his career. They do so because the argument from authority is persuasive only if one can lay claim either to the whole man or to the "final" man. Typically, the Left claims the "whole" Orwell, the neoconservatives the "final" Orwell. The claim to the whole man is obviously preferable, but implausible when ostensibly sharp career shifts are hard to play down or reconcile. The claim to the "final" man can be effective if it can be demonstrated that the figure himself "saw the light" and ultimately arrived at a "new" position.

I save my further remarks on the socialist-neoconservative "debate" over Orwell for Chapter Five. Having established the fact of Orwell's checkered relationship with *Tribune* in the 1940s, I want here to pursue a more intricate question concerning the politics of Orwell's reputation, specifically how

the sharp points of political difference between Orwell and *Tribune* were obscured after his death and how the socialists' image of "the *Tribune* Orwell" became a received public image.

Three reasons stand out. One was that the differences between Orwell and the post-1947 *Tribune* were not publicly known, since they were expressed primarily in letters to Symons (not published until 1963)[204] and in the unpublished "In Defence of Comrade Zilliacus" (not available until *CEJL* in 1968). Moreover, the *Tribune* journalism went uncollected until *CEJL*, and few critics, with the exception of John Atkins, looked back over it when writing about Orwell. All this suggests again the importance of distinguishing between public and private (or intra-group) reputation, and of approaching a reputation developmentally.

A second, still-persisting reason lies in the ignorance of outsiders as to the nature of "the *Tribune* writers" as a group. And here we should return for extended consideration to the question of Orwell's self-image as a *"Tribune* writer."

Symons and Atkins point out that any notion of a public identification between Orwell and *Tribune* is exaggerated and largely hindsight if it implies, as Foot's remarks about Orwell do, that Orwell saw himself as a *"Tribune* writer."[205] Certainly he was not viewed as such by friends or reviewers. Although much posthumous criticism has emphasized the so-called *"Tribune* connection"—for purposes not only of convenient, neutral description but also for polemical reasons—there is almost no mention in book reviews of Orwell's work in the 1940s either that he contributed to or edited *Tribune*. Nor did Orwell himself mention the fact in postwar articles written for American magazines in which he discussed the British press, even when he hailed *Tribune* in 1948 (in a little-known article written after his private letters critical of *Tribune*) as "the best, and certainly by far the most independent, of the left-wing periodicals."[206]

Symons has wisely cautioned that "the *Tribune* writers" is a problematic term.[207] For *Tribune* not only passed through two or three distinct phases during its first decade; there were also two distinct sides to *Tribune* in the 1940s, the political and the literary. Orwell's own liberal, meritocratic editorial policy on the literary side allowed for poetry and reviews by Conservatives, Communists, anarchists, pacifists, and other writers whose politics the "political side" opposed. As Symons explained:

> As a "group" we were very loose indeed. It would probably be wrong even to call us "the *Tribune* writers" if one means by that a formal group which saw itself as a group. We were a left-wing cluster, but *Tribune* had its political and literary sides. The political writers [e.g., Aneurin Bevan, Frank Owen, Michael Foot, Tom Driberg] were close-knit; the literary contributors were quite heterogeneous in our politics—usually left-wing and Labour Party, but with some exceptions. On both sides, some knew and agreed with Orwell, others did not. Far more important in literary London at the time than simply the *Tribune* connection was whether one was an orthodox or a dissident socialist. Orwell and I, among other con-

tributors, were regarded in the mid-40s as "pre-mature anti-Stalinists"—
not a fashionable left-wing position to hold.[208]

To some extent, of course, Orwell bridged the literary and political sides
of the paper—old colleagues like Foot and George Strauss can't even remember whether "As I Please," which appeared on the fold of *Tribune's*
center-spread between the political front half and the arts back half, was
edited by the literary or political editor.[209] But apart from his political
writing, Orwell, unlike Foot or Bevan, was chiefly a literary man. He had no
taste for parliamentary political maneuvering; most of his friends were
other literary men.

Symons' remarks also remind us of the inevitable conceptual difficulties
in talking about "the figure in the group," namely that not only are there
differences of opinion within groups toward certain other members—as we
have already seen in earlier case histories—but that there are "groups within
groups." Someone may be identified as a member of a group when he or she
does not "belong" to it, or when "it" doesn't even exist in any sense which its
"members" experience as real. That writers contribute to the same political
weekly does not necessarily mean they constitute a "group" with the same
aims and assumptions, or if they do, that the groups are constituted along the
lines which outsiders perceive (e.g., the three *Tribune* writers whose receptions of Orwell we have been discussing varied not only in their attitudes
toward him but also somewhat in their politics during the 1940s: Symons was
a Trotskyist, Fyvel a Labour Party socialist, Atkins chiefly a literary man). All
this is understandable, for the "group" is often named not by those who are
taken to be its representatives, but by outsiders, whether opponents or journalists or historians, who give a name to what they regard as a resemblance or
trend in order to exalt or attack or describe it.

Of course, "editor" constitutes a much closer affiliation to a paper than
"contributor." In Orwell's case, the characterization "*Tribune* writer" during
the mid-1940s is fair and useful, provided that one understands by it that
Orwell spoke *through* the paper and helped shape *Tribune's* developing image, not merely reflected it. Orwell did support most of *Tribune's* political
stands during the mid-1940s. But even during his editorship, he apparently
was never politically "reliable." His freewheeling relationship with *Tribune* is
well captured in Bevan's reported remark: "George has alighted on our
desk, and he'll be when he leaves, free as a bird. We'll be glad when he's with
us. We'll accept the fact that there will be times when he will fly off."[210]
Orwell remained an outsider on a paper for outsiders, or in Fyvel's phrase,
a man who "rigidly went his own way, a prophet on his own."[211]

The timing of *Animal Farm's* appearance doubtless also affected Orwell's
self- and public images with regard to *Tribune*. He began the fable in the
same month that he took over as literary editor; it was published in August
1945, just six months after he resigned from the job. In later years, a
tendency arose to associate *Animal Farm* with the *Tribune* days, and partly on
the basis of the fable to link "premature anti-Stalinist" with "Orwell" and

"*Tribune* writer." In the late 1940s, however, not "*Tribune* writer" but "anti-Stalinist"—whether premature or timely—was the characterization of Orwell usually heard, to some degree because his reputation grew so quickly after *Animal Farm* that the phrase "*Tribune* writer" seemed inadequate for containing it, at least outside London literary circles.[212]

Indeed Symons and Atkins also admit that they never regarded themselves as "*Tribune* writers" either. Unlike, say, the postwar *Partisan Review*, the paper wasn't a prestigious organ which established a writer's reputation or claimed his identity. This is not to dispute Fyvel's view that, to the journalist in Orwell, even after he left his editorship, "*Tribune* was still his first love."[213] But, as we have seen, "love" was a relative term with Orwell: with neither persons nor periodicals did he develop intimate relationships. Fyvel's qualification—that Orwell felt allegiance to *Tribune* as a *journalist*—needs emphasis. *Tribune*, which paid its contributors little or nothing, meant weekly journalism to its staff too, not "literature" or even "criticism." Although he enjoyed writing "As I Please" and sometimes raised journalism to art, Orwell's real writing self, like that of Symons and Atkins, lay elsewhere, in fiction and criticism.

A third reason for the rise of the image of "the *Tribune* Orwell" was that, upon Orwell's death, his former *Tribune* colleagues were among his most prominent eulogists. Fyvel, Symons, Atkins, and Koestler (an occasional contributor to *Tribune* during the period of Orwell's closest association) all emphasized his socialist convictions in obituary notices. Sometimes their tributes read as if they were much closer to Orwell than mere acquaintances. They emphasized "the *Tribune* connection" because it was *their* connection. Orwell was their own—unlike the case with his other reception groups in this study—and stressing the connection kept it alive.

Their farewells burnished and elaborated the heroic image of The People's Tribune already begun by Fyvel and Symons. Now, in addition to Symons' obituary in *Tribune*, this image was carried far beyond *Tribune*'s pages. For example, in his influential *Observer* obituary Koestler singled out *The Lion and the Unicorn* as the finest political essay by any British writer during the war, "a minor classic." In *The World Review*, Fyvel acknowledged Pritchett's characterization of Orwell as a "saint," admitting that Orwell probably had "a touch of this quality," best represented in his ineradicable "faith in 'ordinary people'." The authoritativeness of Fyvel's biographical essay, the first one written about Orwell, was enhanced not only by his personal reminiscences but also by Atkins' pronouncement, delivered the following month, that Fyvel's memoir represented "very much what Orwell himself would have written about himself if he had got outside to have a look in."[214]

These panegyrics represented the beginning of a new relationship between Orwell and his former *Tribune* colleagues. If in the 1940s the *Tribune* writers were Orwell's collaborators and friends, in the 1950s and '60s they became his defenders and champions. The image of The People's Tribune was essentially the same, but in the face of right-wing and psychoanalytic

revisionism, this image required not only upkeep but advocacy. "Left-wing Patriot," Atkins titled the last chapter of his *George Orwell* (1954). "Orwell believed in ordinary people," wrote Atkins in his final paragraph, "and he also believed that the true traditions of the country were in their keeping, and not in that of the rich. He was also prepared to trust the common people, which few others, of whatever political persuasion, were prepared to do." Here we see how the image of The People's Tribune converges with The Prophet, for Atkins' heroic Orwell is not only a Common Man but also a tribune of the "common people"—and a willing participant in their suffering, an aspect of Orwell which shades off into another face in this study, The Saint.[215]

Fyvel defended Orwell against Conservative appropriation and generational attack more directly, deploring his "canonization on the Right" by Christopher Hollis as well as his "debunking" by Anthony West, Kingsley Amis, and other younger writers. Fyvel's recounting of personal conversations and habits of Orwell, respectfully though not uncritically, in memoirs like "Wingate, Orwell and the Jewish Question" (1951) and "George Orwell: Glimpses of a Dual Life" (1959) constituted not only final gestures of friendship from a longtime admirer but also signaled the beginning of three decades of inquiry into the transformation of his friend into an "international prophet." We conclude this case study by examining Fyvel's specific contribution to Orwell's reputation and how and why Orwell "figured" in Fyvel's life, thereby to better understand both the dynamics of the reputation process and why Fyvel saw Orwell as he did.[216]

## IV

"Given the reputation of *Nineteen Eighty-Four,*" Fyvel began his keynote address at the 1983 Smithsonian Institution symposium on Orwell, "I feel a little as though I were asked about the prophet Jeremiah: But what was he like as a personal friend?"[217]

Fyvel, the last person to talk with Orwell, spent a good deal of time pondering that question in *George Orwell: A Personal Memoir* (1982) and "Orwell As Friend and Prophet" (1983). Indeed the countdown to 1984 inaugurated a third phase of Orwell's reception by Fyvel and Orwell's other old *Tribune* colleagues, who shifted their attention to *Nineteen Eighty-Four,* to Orwell's reputation as a prophet, and to their memories of him. In one memoir Fyvel recalled conversations with Symons in which they marveled at how, before their eyes in the '50s and '60s, a picture of Orwell as "a completely eccentric, slightly saintly and slightly absurd, major prophet" was sketched, in which it was hard to recognize "the very different and much more ordinary figure of the Orwell we had known."[218]

Fyvel (1907–85) did not possess the national stature among intellectuals of a Trilling or Woodcock or Williams. Yet the impact of his work on Orwell's reputation has been notable. By the 1980s, Fyvel was the *Tribune* acquaintance most widely identified with Orwell, as suggested by his role as

honorary chairman of the Smithsonian's 1983 symposium on Orwell, where he delivered "Orwell As Friend and Prophet." His self-presentation as a sometime spokesman for Orwell since the 1950s has had much to do with this status, as have his use of reminiscence about Orwell and the sheer volume of his writings about his famous acquaintance. Indeed, except for a few memoirs in 1983–84, most of Orwell's *Tribune* acquaintances—except for Fyvel—have had little to say about Orwell in print since the early 1950s. This redirects our attention to the variability of reader response at the group level of reception. Why did Orwell hold such an unusually strong, if somewhat ambivalent, attraction for Fyvel, of all Orwell's *Tribune* colleagues, across more than four decades?

The immediate and obvious explanation is that Fyvel, who first met Orwell in 1940, knew him earlier and much better than other *Tribune* colleagues. They lived near each other for a time, worked together as co-editors of Searchlight Books in 1940–41,* and belonged at that time to Fredric Warburg's "little group" of "like-minded people" concerned with promoting progressive British war aims. So, well before Fyvel and Orwell became part of the *Tribune* writers, they participated in an even smaller collaborative group—a tighter group, which saw itself as such and met regularly at Warburg's house. This association resulted in Fyvel's becoming (to use Symons' categories) not only Orwell's "*Tribune* friend" but also a "home friend."[219] No one else bridged the two categories. Still, Fyvel acknowledges that Orwell, though "a lovable person" and "a gentle and considerate friend," was "remote" even with him. In truth, the relationship was probably warmer on Fyvel's side than Orwell's; and Fyvel might better be considered an "acquaintance" than "friend"—as the skimpiness of the personal recollections of Orwell in the 1982 memoir suggests. Nevertheless, all this notwithstanding, one sign of Fyvel's familiarity is that he did get to know Eileen Blair; he is the only male acquaintance of Orwell's to have written about her.[220]

But what seems to have so fascinated Fyvel about Orwell is precisely how his onetime "ordinary" friend *became* a "Jeremiah," how a man apparently much like himself—a fellow left-wing intellectual and Labour Party supporter, a *Tribune* writer, a BBC broadcaster, a British culture critic—deliberately "stepped right outside his British class" to "transcend" his history, defined and re-defined himself from "Blair" into "Orwell" into a superlative "political writer." Fyvel does not address himself to the numerous institutional factors which, as this book makes clear, have contributed to Orwell's reputation as a prophet. Rather, he meditates on Orwell's role in shaping his own reputation, on how a man of such major personal and artistic shortcomings—schooldays filled with trauma, poor health, "social and emo-

---

*At Fyvel's behest, Orwell wrote the first of the Searchlight series, *The Lion and the Unicorn*— surely Fyvel's single most important "contribution" to Orwell's reputation as an "optimistic prophet" and "revolutionary patriot." (Significantly, both Fyvel and Atkins close their books on Orwell by quoting the last sentence of *The Lion and the Unicorn:* "I believe in England and I believe we shall go forward.")

tional limitations," a "blinkered gaze" on popular culture and issues of political morality, an inability to create rounded characters, a lack of interest in the avant-garde, and a virtual ignorance of the fine arts—surmounted his drawbacks and made the most of his abilities, so that his narrowness issued forth in acute penetration, and finally even gave the appearance of openness and breadth. "Were I personally to venture a one-sentence judgement," wrote Fyvel in *George Orwell*, "I would say that more than any writer I can think of, Orwell by sheer concentration and drive transcended the limitations which he partly inherited but also partly created."[221]

Orwell was a "prophet," Fyvel thought, particularly in the sense that he was determined to *make* things happen; Fyvel's view of Prophet Orwell is an image which merges the faces of The Common Man and The Prophet. Indeed Fyvel's wonderment is really at the phenomenon of encountering a "prophet" in the secular, skeptical "century of the common man"—that his "ordinary" friend did become something of a prophet. His Orwell is a man blessed by ordinariness. Orwell's "prophetic touch" was altogether human, a matter of will and a "commonsense approach" to politics, said Fyvel.[222] For unlike most of their intellectual contemporaries, Fyvel argued, Orwell simply looked the implications of Stalinism in the eye and disowned both the collectivist god and the Christian one. And so he became "the great anticipator of our modern dilemma," the dilemma posed by the lack of any alternative to an unjust capitalism and a failed Marxism. Caught in this dilemma, Orwell responded in the only way possible, by calling for the reassertion of the "simple virtues"—the use of truthful language, observance of freedom of speech and equality before the law, and above all the practice of compassion and "common decency." Implicitly disagreeing with Trilling's either/or characterization of Orwell as "not a genius" but rather "a virtuous man," Fyvel argued that Orwell's genius lay in his commonsense awareness that the "simple virtues" were all that modern man had left for coping with the emergent problems of the post-liberal-Christian age.[223]

One "partly created" limitation of Orwell especially absorbed Fyvel's interest—and caused a slight tension in their relationship. To Fyvel, a Swiss-German Jew and a committed Zionist, one of the greatest deficiencies which Orwell had to "transcend" even to conceive *Nineteen Eighty-Four* was his paucity of knowledge about and even interest in Hitler and Nazism, "the supreme revolutionary force for evil active in his lifetime."[224] This brings us to the question of Orwell's attitude toward Zionism and Jews, a leitmotif throughout Fyvel's Orwell criticism,* obviously because of Fyvel's background.

---

*The London *Jewish Chronicle*, the official organ of Anglo-Jewry which Fyvel edited for many years, suggested that Fyvel wrote *George Orwell* to fill a gap on this score in Bernard Crick's *Life*. Largely on account of Fyvel's memoir, "Orwell and Zionism" was yet another topic during the countdown to 1984 which got caught up in the crossfire between neoconservatives and socialists vying for Orwell's mantle. See, e.g., the exchange between Norman Podhoretz and Christopher Hitchens in the February 1983 *Harper's*.[225]

It is significant that Fyvel wrote his 1951 memoir of Orwell, "Wingate, Orwell, and the Jewish Question," in response to a *Commentary* essay about Jewish "authenticity" and the problem of "the relation between Jews and non-Jews."[226] Possibly Fyvel's reflections about Orwell in 1951 were so formulated because of the popularity in London in the late 1940s of Sartre's *Anti-Semite and Jew* (1948), which Orwell had reviewed harshly. (In *George Orwell* Fyvel recalls one of their arguments over anti-Semitism, which sounds as if it may have derived from Sartre's book.[227]) In any case, it is the question of "authenticity"—as a Jew, as a socialist, and as an intellectual— that Orwell provocatively raised for Fyvel, in the 1980s as in the 1950s. One reviewer of *George Orwell* complained that Fyvel talked almost as much about himself as about Orwell.[228] Precisely so: Fyvel constantly circled back to himself because his identification with Orwell was so deep. Orwell confronted Fyvel—like so many other readers—with troubling questions of political and personal identity. And like theirs, Fyvel's response possessed, as we shall see, far more than merely private significance.

In his 1951 memoir, Fyvel compared Orwell with a fervent Zionist, Major General Orde Wingate (1903–44), the famed Chindit Commander who led Allied forces into the Burmese jungles behind Japanese lines and perished there in an aircraft accident. Fyvel mused on the "strange similarity"[229] between Orwell and Wingate: the two men (who never met) were of exactly the same age, were Englishmen of Scottish ancestry, had a Puritan streak, and possessed strong "opposition" temperaments and unshakable, almost monomaniacal convictions. Both men were extraordinarily acute, and sometimes blind and impersonal: principles, more than people, concerned them. "Chance brought me into contact" with Orwell and Wingate in the late 1930s, men "whose like I shall hardly encounter again." The passion with which Fyvel speaks of his two slightly older friends, even thirty years later in *George Orwell*—he freely called them each "hero," "prophet," "genius"—testifies to their indelible mark on him.[230] Orwell and Wingate are the two "legends" who touched Fyvel's life.[231] In turn he used them as touchstones by which he continued to question the relations between non-Jews and Jews; and their diametrically opposed positions on Zionism challenged him, even in the 1980s, to examine his own political allegiances.

Not unlike young Cyril Connolly, who in prep school, as we have seen, exalted Eric Blair as the incarnation of "Intelligence" and another boy as "Sensibility," Fyvel seems to have cast Orwell as one half of his ideal self, his "literary" hero. Wingate represented the other half, a "Bible and sword" man of action. Wingate struck Fyvel as "the man of destiny," Orwell equally "bold in the world of ideas." As Fyvel talked excitedly with Wingate in Palestine about Zionism in his *annus mirabilis* 1938, he also "agonizingly identified" with the Republican cause in Spain and read with admiration *Homage to Catalonia*. Orwell became "the English writer whom upon my return to England I would above all love to meet." In January 1940 Fred Warburg introduced the thirty-two-year-old author of *No Ease in Zion* (1938) to the thirty-six-year-old Orwell, already one of the Fyvel's "literary heroes."[232]

And so Orwell became Fyvel's literary hero, Wingate his military one. Wingate's "inspirational certainties" about Zionism and Orwell's "sharp [socialist] vision of the world" apparently exerted a similar stabilizing force upon Fyvel's "wavering," "conventional" left-wing views. Inevitably, Fyvel's two heroes, themselves both recent "converts" to their politics—Orwell to democratic socialism, Wingate to Zionism—clashed over Palestine. Orwell considered it a form of "nationalism"; Wingate believed that *Eretz Israel* was an absolute necessity. Fyvel, of course, met Wingate first and "fell under his spell" in Palestine.[233] But the implications of Fyvel's embrace of Zionism for his relationship with Orwell must be understood within the larger context of his and *Tribune*'s history.

Born of a Russian Jewess and a Zionist leader from Austria who had worked with Theodor Herzl, the founder of Zionism, Fyvel (*né* Raphael Joseph Feiwel) had felt very much a German Jew during World War I and "hated England."[234] Coming to Britain at the age of twelve in 1919, he attended an English prep school and Cambridge University, but was never a fully assimilated English Jew. He traveled in the Middle East in the 1920s, and in 1935–36 he lived in British-mandated Palestine, where he worked as an assistant to Golda Meir in the Histadrut at the time of the Arab Rebellion in 1936. Meanwhile, Captain O.C. Wingate had arrived in Palestine in September 1936 and, within a month, had reacted violently against the prevailing Arabophile view among the British (which he had shared) that the Arabs were simple, noble peasants and the Jews were well-heeled exploiters with friends in powerful places. Wingate concluded that exactly the reverse was the case: the Jews were the oppressed victims of Arab land swindlers and needed protection. He became, as his biographer puts it, a Zionist "extremist even among extremists."[235]

A "fairly skeptical" person when he met Wingate in 1938,[236] Fyvel was soon "at least half converted" to Wingate's conspiratorial opinion that the British Foreign Office intended to "crush" Zionism and that the Jews in Palestine should prepare for war with the Arabs, even if Britain armed the Arabs, as they might do. Fyvel had heard such "warlike views expressed only from the less respectable wildcat Zionist fringe."[237] To hear them from a British officer was "staggering." Listening, shamefacedly, to the zealous Wingate, a Christian willing to "devote my life" to Jewish liberation, Fyvel rediscovered his father's political Zionism and his own ethnicity: he rediscovered Raphael Joseph Feiwel. Much as Orwell returned home from Spain in 1937 imbued with a vision of democratic socialism, Fyvel returned to London in 1938 an impassioned Zionist intent on campaigning for Wingate's list of progressive war aims in the anticipated European war, first and foremost among them the creation of a Jewish state in Palestine. *No Ease in Zion* was soon followed by *The Malady and the Vision* (1941), an internationally-minded socialist program for Britain's future, written "roughly on Wingate's formula."[238]

Although Fyvel once said in an interview that his difference of opinion with Orwell over Zionism "wasn't a *major* theme in our relationship,"[239] it

emerged on the very first day that the two men met. "I felt enormously drawn towards him," Fyvel recalled of their initial encounter in 1940, though he sensed that Orwell must have seen him as something of a "stranger" because of his Zionist politics. Still, this strangeness seems also to have energized their relationship, providing the basis for many arguments. And the fact that "we agreed in nearly all our [other] political opinions made up" for the difference over Palestine, Fyvel said.[240]

But not completely, particularly after Fyvel succeeded Orwell as *Tribune*'s literary editor in mid-1945. For Fyvel joined an editorial staff dominated by Jews with whom Orwell had already clashed over Zionism during his own editorship (e.g., Kimche was managing editor [1942–46] and co-editor [1945–48]; Anderson, a Jewish refugee from Nazi Germany, also co-edited [1945–52]; Bevan and Foot [co-editor with Anderson, 1948–52] were also pro-Zionist[241]). Under Kimche and Anderson, *Tribune* devoted itself chiefly to foreign policy and gave more space to news of Palestine than to all the other ex-colonies combined;[242] and during this time Fyvel himself worked also on the paper's "political" side and contributed many pro-Zionist editorials. Although 1945–48 constituted the turbulent period of the U.N. partition of Palestine, the declaration of the state of Israel, and the outbreak of the first Arab-Israeli war, Orwell considered *Tribune*'s Palestine coverage and Zionist partisanship excessive. He criticized *Tribune*'s preoccupation with post-Holocaust Jewish needs and what he saw as its "anti-Bevinism"—its "personal feud" with and vilification of Foreign Secretary Ernest Bevin as "Public Enemy Number One" for his anti-Zionism.[243] According to one non-Jewish *Tribune* editor of the time, when Orwell found him revising the badly written prose of a Jewish Middle East correspondent, he [Orwell] asked: "What do you expect with all these Middle European Jews running the paper's politics?"[244]

Remarks like these have lent support to the belief of some Orwell acquaintances, like Malcolm Muggeridge, that he was anti-Semitic. Fyvel disagrees. He allows that Orwell was "anti-Semitic by education" and "a convinced anti-Zionist," but he maintains that Orwell was unprejudiced in his personal relations with Jews and notes that some of Orwell's closest English acquaintances were Jewish (Kimche, Warburg) or half-Jewish (Symons, Koestler) and that many of his early American supporters at *Partisan Review* were too (e.g., Trilling, Rahv, Rosenberg, Howe). Certainly Orwell's published work marked him as an opponent of anti-Semitism, and in *Tribune* and elsewhere he expressed concern for the refugee victims of the Holocaust, even suggesting in 1946 that Attlee grant 100,000 European Jews immediate entry into Britain.[245] (Though, in conversation, Fyvel considered Orwell "fearfully insensitive" and "curiously distant" on the subject of the Holocaust.[246]) Intellectually, Fyvel believes, Orwell rejected all prejudices; as his *Partisan Review* reception suggests, he certainly succeeded in eliminating anti-Semitic traces from his mature writings. Emotionally, however, Orwell did have a touch of anti-Semitism and "the conflict in him was never quite resolved," in Fyvel's view.[247]

Probably Orwell did have, as Fyvel puts it, "a blind spot" about Jews.[248] But the Quixotic Orwell saw Zionism as *"de rigeur"*[249] among English intellectuals and the Palestinian Arabs as the "underdogs." To him, the Jews were invading white settlers, much like the British in Burma.[250] (Orwell deplored what he saw as the anti-Arab prejudice of English Jews, even writing in *Partisan Review* that "many Zionist Jews seem to me to be merely anti-Semites turned upside down."[251]) Thus, like Wingate in Palestine, Orwell in London was reacting against the established view of his own reference group, the intelligentsia. Yet in the wake of the Holocaust and with 500,000 Jews in overcrowded European refugee camps, the *Tribune* editors saw a Jewish state as an urgent need. The 1894 Dreyfus case had convinced Herzl that assimilation would never work; Hitler had taught postwar Jews, many of them opposed to Zionism before the war, a similar lesson. *Tribune*'s editors objected especially to what they regarded as the Labour Government's refusal to honor its 1945 pre-election pledge to lift restrictions on Jewish emigration to and land-purchases in Palestine.[252]

Given the radiance of Orwell's presence in Fyvel's life, their differences over Zionism constituted for Fyvel much more than merely a political disagreement. Instead Orwell and Wingate raised for Fyvel "the whole problem" of how Jews can communicate the meaning of "the Jewish tradition" to non-Jews.[253] And to a large extent Fyvel's posthumous dialogue with Orwell seems to have been driven by a continuing effort to explain that tradition to a friend from a bygone age whose acquaintance, "even with the dimming of memory, left an impression unlike any other, of an historic era which has already become remote and of a writer who saw into its essence and understood it."[254] Indeed it is as if Fyvel were, all along, attempting to unite two poles of his own thinking, represented by two men dead almost four decades, the "virtuous" author of *Homage to Catalonia* and the indomitable "Lawrence of Judea."[255]

Partly because Orwell and he did have so much in common politically and partly because of the constraining influence of Wingate, Fyvel tended less to rewrite his socialist friend in his own image than to ask, through Orwell, those questions of identity begun in their conversations forty years earlier. To what degree is an assimilated Jewish intellectual "still different, still a Jew"? Fyvel presented this "puzzling question" as Orwell's but it obviously had also been Fyvel's.[256] From his side too, emotionally if not intellectually, the "conflict" over Zionism was never quite resolved. Fyvel recalled that, whereas he was willing in 1940 to support even Stalin so long as the Soviet Union fought Hitler, Orwell "by contrast seemed incorruptible" in his uncompromising opposition to accepting the legitimacy of either dictator.[257] And in *George Orwell* Fyvel forthrightly conceded his own insensitivity in the 1940s to the rights of Palestinian Arabs, his "obsessive" postwar campaigning for Zionism, and Orwell's uncanny foresight in anticipating that Zionism might lead to "Israeli militarism."[258]

And in their differing prognoses of the Zionist future lies the heart of Fyvel's differences with Orwell, and also the link in this case study between

issue and multivalent image—among Zionism, socialism, and prophecy. Zionism and socialism, once united in Herzl's vision, had split and become competing prophecies—and Fyvel's generation experienced the split viscerally. Jewish socialists of his youth held that the Diaspora would end with the international triumph of socialism. Zionists had maintained that it would conclude with the ingathering of the Jews into the ancestral homeland. To many non-Jewish socialists like Orwell, Zionism and socialism were irreconcilable: a socialist could not be internationally minded about most of the globe and nationalist toward one special corner.

Zionism or democratic socialism? A "chosen" people or "*The* People"? Special interest politics or intellectual integrity? Chauvinism or internationalism? Jewish consciousness or human consciousness? This was how the "puzzle"[259] of an unassimilated Jew's place in the West looked from Orwell's vantage point.[260] But unlike Orwell and Woodcock, Fyvel never saw himself faced with an absolute choice between personal authenticity and support for a militant politics. Instead, as if living out Sartre's argument in *Anti-Semite and Jew*, he seems to have viewed his Jewishness as a persistent *choosing* of identity, a heroic self-assertion—i.e., Zionism as the *means* to Jewish authenticity. Aware of a Socialist Zionist tradition which fused the promise of Zion with revolutionary socialism and which stretched back to Moses Hess and Ber Borokhov, Fyvel in effect rejected the stark terms in which Orwell posed the "puzzle" of Zionism. Instead Fyvel approached the issue of divided allegiances as a socialist Jew for whom twentieth-century Jews comprised a unique "national" underclass, a specially oppressed group. To reconcile loyalty to one's Jewish heritage with loyalty to one's adopted country was, for Fyvel, to see his "Jewishness" much as Orwell saw his own "Englishness." Thus Fyvel's choice became one of patriotism over uprooted cosmopolitanism. Rather than surrender his Jewishness, he would embrace it. The editor of the *Jewish Chronicle* chose to integrate himself in Britain as a Jewish intellectual with cosmopolitan interests rather than as an English intellectual of Jewish origin.

In so confronting his own "politics of truth," Fyvel enacted personally his proposed cultural "solution" to the problem of relations between Jews and non-Jews in the Diaspora: the forging of a "contemporary Jewish tradition" receptive both to Western acculturation *and* Jewish identity and achievement.[261] Orwell's anti-Zionism had challenged Fyvel's very "Jewishness"; Orwell was the half, but only the half, of the ideal to which Fyvel aspired. To accept Zionism in the aftermath of the Holocaust was, for Fyvel, to accept a fundamental part of his Jewish identity, to accept that he was "still different, still a Jew." It was no accident, then, that Raphael Joseph Feiwel had been fascinated by Orwell's repeated acts of "self-definition" and "transcendence" since, for a Jew of Fyvel's generation who did not become a citizen of Israel, the dilemma of divided allegiances—"Jewishness" or assimilation?—will always persist.

And yet, the side of Orwell whom Fyvel preferred to "remember" did fit with Fyvel's revolutionary cultural vision. The "other side of Orwell" is the

Orwell whom he first met, in "an admittedly uncharacteristic moment of general optimism, in the magic year 1940." This uplifting Orwell is not the author of *Nineteen Eighty-Four* but of *The Lion and the Unicorn,* the book which "to my credit," Fyvel writes proudly, "I managed to extract from Orwell . . . , the only positive . . . book he ever wrote." *The Lion and the Unicorn* is "Orwell as he might have been," prophesies Fyvel, "if there had been no war, if he had not been sick." Fyvel closes his *George Orwell* by quoting the final paragraph of *The Lion and the Unicorn,* implying that what Orwell envisions for the English contemporary tradition, he holds for the Jewish tradition: "By revolution we become more ourselves, not less. . . . We must add to our heritage or lose it."[262]

As we exit this room of the portrait gallery, the *Tribune* writers' responses to Orwell remind us of an integrant of the reputation process which we tend all too easily to lose sight of: the *human* dimension of reputation. For it is just not figures and receivers we are discussing in this study, but the relationships among people. Tosco Fyvel and the *Tribune* writers had a personal, not merely a literary, relationship with Orwell; they experienced not just the man in the writings, but the man in the flesh. And unlike George Woodcock and the London anarchists, they periodically met after Orwell's death and renewed their memories of the man. They and Orwell once worked together, lunched together, drank together, argued, laughed, commiserated. Reputation emerges not only from literary response but also from human interaction. It is not abstracted faces and images we are examining, but ways of seeing, modes of receiving, forms of imagining Orwell by unique human beings. The fabric of reputations is dyed the color of our lives.

# SIX

# *The Saint*

## 19. 'St. George,' The Halfway Saint

### I

The final room in the Orwell gallery consists of another set of religious, or "sacralized" portraits. And, looking back through the gallery, one notices a change which seems to reflect the reputation process: the steadily increasing metaphoric aspect of the faces, with The Rebel being the most literal and The Saint the most figural. For while it is clear that many people have viewed Orwell as a "rebel" and some have also seen him as a "common man" and perhaps even in some sense as a "prophet," one doubts whether anyone has really seen him as a "saint," in the literal sense of the word. This shift from the literal to the figural, as our discussion of the word "prophet" as a pre-inflated image suggested, may be a frequent feature of reputation-building.

Figuration, that is to say, tends to entail the metaphoric reinterpretation of a life. The subject's habits and perceived character traits are then treated metonymically: Orwell's poorly rolled shag cigarettes recall The Common Man; the "pure" prose suggests The Saint. But the progressively metaphorical character of Orwell's faces also alerts us to even more important conceptual matters: our metaphorical terminology ("face," "portrait gallery") and the partial metaphorical structuring involved in reputation-formation. What I have tried to do throughout this book is to make some sense of the reputation process via an eclectic figural vocabulary derived, as needed, from portraiture, cosmography, and geography: to capture, how-

"Orwell's Bedroom," by Richard Rees. Was Orwell a "self-mortifying saint who kissed the souls of lepers"?

ever partially, the elusive figure-making process in figures of my own. Some of my figures, like the notion of "star" reputations, pervade our thinking about status and have entered our everyday speech. Indeed a special metaphorical vocabulary is not merely justified but necessitated, since the concept of reputation is fundamentally metaphorical and metonymic. As we saw in Chapter Two, perceivers typically focus on certain aspects of the object; one perceived to "possess" the property of "truthfulness" is often hypostatized into "a man of truth." The concept "face" also has a metonymic, or synechdochal, character: the "face" stands for "the person." In fact the idea of the portrait is essentially metonymic: we look at pictures of faces, not of limbs and torsos, when we want to find out what a person looks like.

My own metaphors, then, have framed this study of Orwell's reputation. And the metaphors in which images of him have been cast, like "saint," have helped structure his reputation-history insofar as they have highlighted certain of his features and veiled others, leading observers to form their responses in accord with the metaphor. When a man is named a "prophet" or "saint," the figural dimension of reputation is especially pronounced, for through a coherent network of entailments the metaphor constructs social reality and guides action. And this power of metaphor to shape perceptions is rhetorical, embracing the diverse conceptions of rhetoric as ornament, persuasion, and identification. Within the scheme of our rhetoric of reception, we may speculate that the more completely the literal is collapsed into the metaphorical—the man Orwell into the metaphor "saint" and ultimately the figure 'St. George'—the greater the power of the image and the stronger the identification invited between perceiver and perceived. Personification is a special kind of metaphor which breathes personality into an abstraction. To personify a person in terms of a figure—to "characterize" Orwell as Don Quixote or St. George—is to provide that person with a new character, a new identity; it is pushing metaphor to its limit. When the structural "fit" between metaphor and subject becomes exact, one passes from reputation into full-fledged myth.

No such precise fit has occurred with Orwell, but the question nevertheless presents itself: How did George Orwell come to be seen as "Saint" George Orwell? Not even Prophet Orwell could have anticipated that, within a week of Orwell's death, the personal history of the resolute atheist would be revised and edited for literary canonization. On January 28, seven days after Orwell's death, V.S. Pritchett's *New Statesman* obituary appeared; within another week it was being quoted in other British newspapers[1] and a condensed version had appeared in the *New York Times Book Review;* and by the year's end passages from it were being showcased on the dust jackets of English and American editions of Orwell's own books. "A kind of saint," Pritchett called Orwell, a phrase intended to allow for Orwell's atheism yet which was followed by descriptions of his spiritual fervor and self-torment. Orwell was not simply his generation's better conscience, but its "wintry" conscience, who by turning his cold, skeptical eye on the false god of state collectivism had awakened fellow 1930s writers from their dogmatic Marxist

slumbers, alerting them to "the rasher assumptions of political faith." Even Orwell's physique reminded Pritchett of the martyrs and, of course, Don Quixote. Orwell was a consumptive martyr, "a tall emaciated man with a face scored by the marks of physical suffering." "There is the ironic grin of pain at the end of the kind lips," the eyes "gentle, lazily kind, and gleaming with workmanlike humour." Pritchett returned again and again to this image in later years, pronouncing Orwell "the comfortless saint of the Left and its only religious figure," for whom politics were "an opportunity for redemption, salvation and martyrdom."[2]

Tributes to the "saintly" Orwell from Richard Rees and others soon followed. To Rees, writing in 1951, Orwell was "one of those self-mortifying saints who kissed the sores of lepers, for he had only to think of something that would be beyond endurance and he could not rest until he had set himself to the task of enduring it." He possessed "a mind and heart of exceptional purity and nobility." A few years later Rees termed Orwell "a religious or 'pious' atheist." Orwell was not really an atheist at all, Rees contended, but rather a believer in "impersonal religion." Orwell's denial of the possibility of the soul's immortality, said Rees, meant that he believed in a religion "so pure and disinterested" that it did not depend for its appeal upon the promise of personal immortality.[3] In effect Rees claimed that his puritanical friend had outdone Christianity by insisting that the truly saintly man practiced virtue for itself, with no expectation of ultimate reward.*

"I always thought there might be a lot of money in starting a religion," Orwell joked to Jack Common in 1936.[5] Little did he realize that the cult would one day be his own. By the 1960s, memoirs like those by Pritchett and Rees, the two chief architects of Orwell's reputation as a saint, had given way to hosannas by literary journalists. "[A] considerate friend; an affectionate husband; a controversialist always chivalrous toward his foes; a man who wished passionately for children and was devoted to his son; an invalid remarkably free of self-pity; a writer who was badly used by publishers and editors, but who never lost his will to work or his craving for perfection." Thus did Orwell appear to one *New Statesman* critic, who could only affirm unreservedly "the reputation for utter integrity, for sheer goodness, that has prompted Orwell's canonization."[6] With such testaments, the road past Airstrip One was quickly re-routed straight to the gates of the Celestial City. The legend of 'St. George' Orwell was under way.

Indeed the hagiographers have been quick to fit Orwell's history to the saga of St. George, often presenting him as traveling a glorious unmarked road to wherever their special interests have happened to lead. The tale of the knight who became England's patron saint by converting to Christianity, killing the dragon, saving the princess, urging the kingdom to accept baptism, and riding off after refusing rewards resonates for his champions with Orwell's own life story. There seems something in it for nearly everybody. 'St.

---

*Or as Mr. Warburton tells Dorothy in *A Clergyman's Daughter:* "Your verminous Christian saints are the biggest hedonists of all. They're out for an eternity of bliss."[4]

George' Orwell undergoes a self-described "baptism" among the lowly, castigates pacifists and Communists opposed to the British war effort (and gets wounded fighting Spanish fascists before that), pays repeated tribute to the natural and moral beauty of his "England," urges the kingdom to accept socialism, denounces Stalinism with a horrible deathbed warning, saves the Anglo-American Left from the permanent taint of identification with Trotsky and Stalin, and rides off to his grave without ever truly enjoying the riches and renown of his exploits. Of such stories are legends—and figures—made.

It is, to be sure, the "tragic" dimension of Orwell's early, untimely leavetaking which has had such a strong hold on his admirers' sympathies and imaginations. He died, in effect, before postwar intellectuals, especially repentant former Marxists, could tell him that he was right on many scores and assuage their guilt with offers of fame and fortune. Orwell's parallels with St. George thus extend beyond the episode with the dragon: the saintly knight was repeatedly slain, only to return again and again until he was finally mutilated, cut into small pieces, and set to burn and scatter in the wind. From his martyrdom a cult eventually grew until his name became a synonym for his country and his cross inscribed on the English flag. The mutilation of 'St. George' Orwell by the press and by a spectrum of political factions, his confiscation on all sides since his death, and his emergence as a cult figure among intellectuals: the material for the mythmakers is there.

We will return to scrutinize a less storied version of Orwell as St. George, but here we note simply that this allusion is yet another instance of Orwell's getting cast in terms of an historical/mythic figure. We have already seen how such analogies (e.g., Don Quixote, John the Baptist, Daniel, Jeremiah) shape reputation by highlighting certain features of the object of comparison. This has also been the case with St. George, perhaps the most fertile of the historical/mythical metaphors in Orwell's case, and, along with the Don Quixote analogue, the most significant for Orwell's complex reputation. As we saw in Part One, the posthumous claiming of his reputation has been carried on through a circular process of left- and right-wing intellectual groups canonizing him as their 'St. George' Orwell and then fighting one another for title to his halo.

St. George is the most frequent personification of The Saint. It does not always indicate esteem: some critics have jeered 'St. George' Orwell as "the super-patriot."[7] Unlike the Quixote analogy, however, the St. George characterization is usually cited only in passing and rarely receives extended elaboration in criticism or memoirs. Probably the difference owes chiefly to the perceived physical resemblance between Orwell and Quixote.

The literary canonization of Orwell as "saint" by Pritchett, Rees, Atkins, Fyvel, and others in the early 1950s surely gave rise to the 'St. George' characterization, but the link is impossible to document. No doubt the personification fit Orwell's name and history so well that it soon became a catchy, memorable tag. Of course, 'St. George' was probably also taken up so readily for reasons apart from Orwell, e.g., because "saint" is customarily coupled with a Christian name—which is not ordinarily the case with

"rebel," "common man," or "prophet." But the particular effect of the title upon Orwell's reputation has been also to humanize the "saint" and highlight his Englishness and common man appeal, making him a more attractive figure—as if 'St. George' were a nickname. For the image of Orwell as the model socialist and good man, if not specifically "saint" or 'St. George,' has been the one cherished by those most acquainted with Orwell's life, especially those familiar with the man and the essayist, just as The Prophet has been the most widely recognized by readers of *Nineteen Eighty-Four* and by the general public.

I treat 'St. George' as a special image of the face "saint." In this introductory section we will find ourselves repeatedly moving back and forth between these two, between the generic saint and its most frequent personification, between the more literal and the more figural. As we shall soon see, the 'St. George' figure is such a rich generative metaphor that it has spawned images of its own apart from the traditional idea of saint. Not only the peculiar significance of 'St. George' for this last face, then, but also for the whole multifaceted Orwell figure will engage our attention later in this section. But first, a more basic question arises, prompted by our attention to the concept "face" and by the fact that the Prophet and Saint are both religious images: How does The Saint relate to the other portraits in the Orwell gallery?

We should begin with the relation between inside and outside views, for more than any other face, The Saint is the handiwork of Orwell's literary acquaintances and runs counter to Orwell's own apparent self-image. Although Orwell sometimes paraded his integrity and certainly considered himself a more honest writer than many of his contemporaries, even his enemies have never claimed that he pretended to be any paragon of virtue. If he was "puritanical," it was in his hatred of softness, his boyish relish of minor hardships,[8] his sometimes excruciating literary integrity,[9] and his love of simple living. Of course, as Richard Rees's painting "Orwell's Bedroom" suggests (see p. 323), what Orwell regarded as simplicity, others might regard as self-mortification. But Orwell evidently had no aversion to sexual pleasure.[10]

Orwell appears to have felt deep hostility to the very word "saint," which was a pejorative in his lexicon. In his essay on Gandhi, he defined it in contradistinction to his beloved "common man": "the essence of being human is that one does not seek perfection. . . . [S]ainthood is a thing which human beings must avoid." To Orwell "saintliness" and "ordinariness" were irreconcilable, for the former was "anti-human and reactionary." One could not be a saint and a socialist: "One must choose between God and Man, and all 'radicals' and 'progressives,' from the mildest Liberal to the most extreme Anarchist, have in effect chosen Man."[11] For Orwell the humanist, man was not only the measure but the end. "Saintliness" was not merely superhuman but *in*human. Still, Orwell's negative definition of "saint" via "common man" appears at first glance rather ironic, since, as we have seen, his working definition of "common man" was itself a negative, catch-all one, meaning "non-intellectual." But it is precisely here, in Orwell's basic self-image as

a "rebel against the Left," that his approach to the "common man" and the "saint" becomes understandable. Orwell reacted against the Left intelligentsia, and "intellectual" is the filter through which he understood both "saint" and "common man." In his vocabulary, the "saint" was an otherworldly, ascetic, often cowardly and hypocritical intellectual—at best a Gandhi, at worst a pacifist like the young literary "halfway saints" who refused to fight Hitler,[12] or an "official" holy man of the authoritarian Catholic Church—just as a "common" man was nothing more than a man who was not an intellectual.

Given that Orwell rejected saintliness as an ideal and contrasted it explicitly and unfavorably with ordinariness, it may seem surprising, to say the least, that he has not only been exalted as a saint but precisely as an ordinary man's saint. Indirectly, however, the formation of this face had much to do with Orwell's self-presentation. For just as The Prophet is clearly a mutant form of his root self-image as a rebel, The Saint is closely related to Spender's memorial image of the Christ-like "extraordinary ordinary man," which itself derived from Orwell's energetically crafted Common Man persona.

And here we should move to an outside view. The Saint was the last face of Orwell's to crystallize, not emerging until the obituaries. In the developing myth of the good man and visionary writer, this face became distinct by attracting, in a new configuration, many of the attributes which we have identified with the other faces: authenticity, plainness, decency, honesty, purity, passion. "Saint" and "conscience" encapsulated and sanctified these attributes, which were already being exaggerated and burnished during the last months of Orwell's life as a result of his growing fame after *Nineteen Eighty-Four*. For "saint" could re-organize the features in a new pattern partly because the features themselves facilitated such a reshaping. The rebel against intellectual pretension, modern indulgence, and Establishment conformity was cousin to the old-fashioned moralist; the common man intellectual with the clear, clean prose was a humble relative of the celebrated "virtuous man" and "pure" stylist, The Crystal Spirit; and the visionary writer with the burning hatred of oppression and the prophetic voice bore a fraternal relation to the Truthteller and passionate pamphleteer.

These are resonances and congruences, however; to exhibit a kinship relation is not to possess the same identity. All these faces are "Orwell," but even a family resemblance permits a great deal of variation among faces. Although Orwell was memorialized as a saint partly because his friends perceived him as a rebel against the world's indulgent standards of virtue and need, we do not necessarily think of a rebel as especially virtuous. And though, as religious images, "prophet" and "saint" are cognate, Orwell as Prophet is the Author of *the book;* Orwell as Saint is the man, and the man in the writings. Whereas Orwell's reputation as a prophet is based upon a single work, his reputation as a saint is founded on a perception that he incarnated what Spender called "lived truth," that the man lived the writings and wrote out of the depths of his experience. The Prophet is the

"public" Orwell, publicized by the media and known to an audience of millions; The Saint is the Orwell familiar only to those knowledgeable about his life. Orwell's "voice" has shaped both images, but whereas the prophetic voice of *Nineteen Eighty-Four* cries out in warning, the voice of the nonfiction is plain and sincere. Finally, although traditionally the prophet and saint are often represented in the same person (e.g., John the Baptist, Joan of Arc), the prophet is typically known by what he is heard to say, the saint by how he is seen to live. The shift is from Old to New Testament, from lawgiver's agent to surrogate model. To imitate Yahweh would be blasphemous. But *imitatio Christi* is the Pilgrim's Way. We do not speak of "false" or "fallible" or "doomsday" saints; sainthood has to do with holy living, not with claims to divine guidance or prophecies about the future. Not "Prepare ye the way," but "Live as He did" is the saint's message. And the many readers who have taken Orwell as an intellectual hero have implicitly delivered a similar lay epistle about Orwell's own life.

Although The Saint does share some features in common with the other portraits, then, it warrants "a room of its own" in the gallery because it too has coalesced into a *Gestalt,* an integrated whole greater than the sum of its attributes. Some aspects of The Saint are distinctive to it, a fact attested to by the literary comparisons which Orwell invites. Chesterton, H.G. Wells, and Jack London have all been frequently compared with Orwell. Each was a rebel, and arguably even a prophet and an intellectual's common man. But none of them has a reputation for saintliness, religious or secular. Conversely, though she was certainly a rebel and perhaps even something of a prophetess, the pious Simone Weil, who is often called saintly and compared with Orwell, is not regarded in the least as an "ordinary" woman.

The characterizations of Orwell as Saint are also attributable to the peculiar circumstances in which this watchword originated, which help account further for the discrepancy between acquaintances' memories of him and his own autobiographical self-presentations. The first tributes to Orwell's saintliness were obituary treatments and posthumous reviews which paid respect to a friend's memory. Although it is probably true, as one admirer said, that no other writer of Orwell's generation would have been memorialized so warmly in 1950,[13] the critics' hyperbole becomes more understandable within the pious tradition of the panegyric. What made The Saint into a distinct face, however, were not the tributes themselves, nor merely its congruence with the other Orwell imagery, but chiefly the timing of the testaments,* which were repeated and adorned as Orwell's reputation radiated outside London literary circles. In America, even deni-

---

*For example, although the great influence of Pritchett's obituary is surely partly attributable to its anecdotes and vivid imagery, this was not the first—nor the last—time that Pritchett had exalted Orwell as the exceptional figure of their generation and referred to him as a "saint." As early as 1946 he had called Orwell "the most honest writer of our time." In July 1949, reviewing *Nineteen Eighty-Four* in the *New York Times Book Review*, he called Orwell "a saint," praising him as a man who quietly lived his words and contrasting him with Lawrence, a moralistic "Sunday school teacher." By 1953 Pritchett was pronouncing Orwell—in yet another hallowed personification—"a Saint Augustine convicted of sin. . . ." Unlike *The New Statesman* obituary, however, none of these remarks has been widely quoted.[14]

als of Orwell's sanctity began to assume a hagiographic tone, as the quotation blazoned in large black letters across the cover of the *The Orwell Reader* (1956) suggests: "Orwell, thank God, was no saint. . . ."[15] The special conditions which gave rise to the lavish farewells were almost immediately obscured. Instead the tributes laid the foundation for the gathering legend of The Saint.

This legend, as I have suggested, represented not merely the development of another face. Rather, it recast all the faces. Not only did its posthumous crystallization coincide with and partly cause the dramatic upward revaluation of Orwell, but its formation also marked the culmination of a tendency, observable in the other three faces since the publication of *Nineteen Eighty-Four*, toward radiance and overinflation. Thus, just as The Prophet "dominated" Orwell's reputation in the popular realm, overshadowing the other images and becoming the image known to those familiar with *Nineteen Eighty-Four* alone, The Saint "capped" the critical realm for a few years after Orwell's death and was widely known to readers informed about Orwell's life.

The images of The Prophet and The Saint also gained and maintained prominence because even their very sound was a bit sensationalist; a watchword like "saint" was, like "prophet," pre-inflated. Unlike "rebel" and "common man"—which, perhaps because of our democratic age, seem invested with special rhetorical power only when capitalized and preceded by definite articles—the religious metaphors of "prophet" and "saint" seem to possess such force even without these additions. Such *pre-inflated watchwords* seem to be ready-made cornerstones for laying a "monumental" reputation. These are subtle and admittedly impressionistic observations about watchwords and reputation-building, perhaps not empirically supportable beyond Orwell's case. But it is more than coincidence that Orwell's critical reputation ascended at the moment when the Prophet and Saint faces crystallized, between the 1949 publication of *Nineteen Eighty-Four* and the 1952 American edition of *Homage to Catalonia*.

In drawing attention to these three factors—the configuration of Orwell's reputation around 1950, its likely interplay with the posthumous characterizations of Orwell as saint, and the sensationalist "ascension" effect such words understandably had—we are led back to the fact that George Orwell was not merely described as a saint but sometimes cast specifically as 'St. George' Orwell. To a fuller consideration, then, of "saint" and its personifications we now turn. In analyzing them, we are not taking them at face value, but are engaged in what religious and art historians would call iconology and critical hagiography, respectively. We are plumbing the symbolic implications of the image and establishing, where possible, its validity.


II

On closer examination, one notices a striking similarity between the two Orwell "legends" significant for his reputation, both of which emerged in

the early 1950s: the legends of Orwell as St. George and as the English Don Quixote. The two seem to have mutually influenced each other; one finds that friends like Pritchett and Paul Potts, drawn both to the heroic and mock heroic aspects of Orwell, conflated details of the legends in their memoirs of him.

Yet perhaps this is not so surprising. For insofar as *Don Quixote de la Mancha* satirizes the chivalric romance, one can, broadly speaking, view the legend of Quixote as a parody of the story of St. George, the archetypal crusader. St. George and Quixote are both knights errant who insist on redressing injustices and on leading lives of scrupulous integrity in a world usually run on a lower plane. George, a Roman military tribune, exchanges his soldier's uniform for Christian garb; Alonso Quijano, a kindly country gentlemen, dons moldering armor and a cardboard helmet. But whereas St. George, "the White-horsed Knight," rides a fine steed and slays his dragon, The Knight of the Woeful Countenance sallies forth on a bony nag and flails haplessly at windmills. The Legend of St. George is the story of Christianity's triumph over Evil, with George a glorious martyr; the myth of Don Quixote is the tale of a deluded romantic devoured by his illusions, who dies pathetically, though his unflinching dedication to an idealistic vision so colorful and honorable nevertheless confers on him a moral grandeur.

At first this contrast between the two figures may seem to represent them merely as another version of the "triumphant" and "failed" rebel images of Orwell which we encountered in Chapter Three. But the fact that George's pilgrimage is a Christian and explicitly spiritual one means that his quest is different in nature from Quixote's. The difference is not merely spiritual versus secular, however, but also private versus communal. George's sainthood is not merely a token of his success, like a hero's wreath, but the testament of his faith in God. For unlike Quixote, his task is not to be faithful to a personal dream which no one else may grasp, but to God's vision—which in the myth of 'St. George' Orwell is transmuted back into secular terms: the vision of democratic socialism.

But the difficulty of making sense of the St. George myth for Orwell's reputation only begins here, for as history sadly attests, "democratic socialism," like Orwell's values "justice" and "liberty," has by no means meant the same thing to all socialists, nor have all socialists been disposed to practice the values they preached. Yet Orwell is one socialist intellectual reputed for having gone far in living out his socialist ideals. Since the reputation of The Saint is based chiefly on the perception of his exceptional life, we should look closely at some of the hagiographic memoirs. And directly we are led to the essentially dualistic character of Orwell's reputation for sainthood. The memoirs depict a "human" and an "inhuman" saint. 'St. George,' as we shall see, is mainly associated with the former image.

The relation between Orwell's socialist vision and the duality of his saintly reputation is best pointed up by an incident which took place on BBC-TV in 1970. Richard Rees quoted and glossed the following passage

from "Looking Back on the Spanish Civil War." "All that the working man demands," Orwell asserted, is

> the indispensable minimum without which human life cannot be lived at all. Enough to eat, freedom from the haunting terror of unemployment, the knowledge that your children will get a fair chance, a bath once a day, clean linen reasonably often, a roof that doesn't leak, and short enough working hours to leave you with a little energy when the day is done.[16]

Probably such modest demands would have satisfied few working men, then or now, but in any case the socialist bill of particulars was Orwell's. Remarked Rees only half-jestingly: "He doesn't say whether he means a hot bath or a cold bath. I hope he means a hot bath." No hedonist himself, Rees, arguably Orwell's closest friend, added: "One would have to conclude that Orwell was . . . essentially a sort of ascetic."[17]

And so, ironically, in the way in which Orwell lived out his conception of socialism—often doing without his rations in World War II, cheerfully subjecting not only himself but also Eileen and sometimes his friends to a bare, almost spartan life in London before and during the war—we have a figure much like the ascetic whom Orwell railed at in his essay on Gandhi. Two images of The Saint therefore recur in acquaintances' memoirs. First there is a secularized, popular hero, Atkins' "social saint," an idealized version of Orwell's ordinary man. Second, there is an otherworldly, nearly inhuman figure very much the opposite of this ideal: Rees's "strenuous and self-martyrising man."[18]

Aspects of the two images are often mingled in memoirs of Orwell. But where this is the case, the tension between the two images is palpable. Evidently the moral force exerted by the image of an idealized ordinary man and of an uncompromising extremist is very different, the first typically arousing deep affection and the second discomfort, even exasperation. Both the "ordinary" and the "extreme" were part of Orwell's nature. And they are part of his history of reputation. Clarifying the relation between the two images, the "human" and the "inhuman" saint, may help illumine the relation between the life and the reputation.

It was the first image which David Astor held when he told BBC-TV: "He was a most lovable person . . . , somebody who never failed you, never disappointed you. . . . [And he had] this wonderful independence and wonderful dignity as a human being. 'Above all unto thyself be true' is somehow what you felt with Orwell. . . ."[19] Wrote John Atkins: "Orwell believed there was a social duty and he was nothing if not dutiful. In some ways he tried to live the ideal life for a modern man, which is why some of his friends have actually used the term 'saint' to describe him."[20] This image of the great-souled friend and "real" socialist has inspired admiration and even love in acquaintances and readers—and the urge to imitate and to follow. And this "ordinary," non-intellectual Orwell is also the one, with just a touch of Quixote, so often observed in the well-known photographs of the amateurish carpenter sawing a board with a cigarette dangling from his mouth, of

the unhurried smoker rolling his own awful shag tobacco, of the tender father dressing baby Richard or towering above him as he pushes the baby stroller. It is this Orwell who embodies the humanistic values so eloquently defended in "Reflections on Gandhi": to be fully human is to be "prepared in the end to be defeated and broken up by life, which is the inevitable price of fastening one's love upon other individuals."[21]

And yet the second image of Orwell is very Gandhian, that of a man who fastened little love upon friends and family and did "push asceticism" to the limit, "possessed" as he was "by a kind of mania of the same sort that you find in a Tolstoy or Dostoyevsky or in a Kierkegaard," in Richard Rees's words. Rees believed that Orwell was driven by an "idealistic urge" so strong that he was "rather unaware of other people."[22] Several acquaintances have agreed. Orwell himself confessed an "aesthetic distaste" for Gandhi,[23] and unsurprisingly, many people have similarly felt awe, respect, and slight revulsion toward this puritanical image of Orwell. "The key to his personality," Arthur Koestler once explained, was "his ruthlessness toward himself." Orwell was "unkind" toward himself, and equally "unkind" to his friends, said Koestler. Orwell's ardor was inversely proportional to his distance from people: "the greater the distance . . . , the more warming became the radiations of this lonely man's great power of love. . . . He was merciless towards himself, severe upon his friends, unresponsive to admirers, but full of understanding sympathy for those on the remote periphery."[24] The closer somebody was to Orwell, the more Orwell felt entitled to treat that person as he treated himself. Coldness signified respect and "love." Insofar as Orwell clearly spared Eileen Blair none of his travails, took an impersonal attitude toward his own health, and almost relished adversity, Koestler's theory contains some truth. It explains both Orwell's seeming reluctance to extend his friendship with literary peers like Koestler, Rees, and Connolly to intimacy, and also his evident warmth to young David Astor and the struggling Paul Potts.

These two spiritualized images of Orwell, the "human" and the "inhuman" ideal, have formed the bases of his reputation as a secular and near-Christian saint. The lovable, ordinary, secular saint is Trilling's liberating image of "the virtuous man"; the ascetic is Rees's otherworldly saint. "Saint," of course, is a word we no longer use much to characterize our culture heroes. Still, the difference between these two images is roughly that between the saint as warrior and as monk, between the public life and the contemplative life, between the man on a mission who would save the world through action and the man on an inner journey who would break with this world for a "higher," "other" world. Orwell, as most of us do, was thinking of the latter type when he criticized Gandhi. Like Atkins and Trilling, most readers have understandably been drawn to the first, naturalized image of Orwell. For the great majority of us live "ordinary" lives and tend to cherish what we can approach, what we can see as our best selves projected before us; and we recoil at a level of spiritual development which we cannot, or will not, make our own. Nevertheless, Rees is not alone in acknowledging the

ascetic Orwell as his "spiritual hero." Rees's identification reminds us again that reputation is one's *perception* of an Other, a relationship between Subject and Object. Our personal ideals and level of self-development will determine how each of us responds to the two images of the saintly Orwell, as well as to his other images.

But one need not sharply oppose the two images; one can, as Rees did, admire both. From the standpoint of the traditional, ecclesiastical conception of sainthood, Orwell as "virtuous man" is a *stage* on the way to the ascetic saint. For the will to altruism, which is still part of the ordinary moral being, can be intensified by a will to self-denial, self-punishment, self-martyrdom. This movement from the natural to the supernatural corresponds in moral terms to the aesthetic evolution from the literal to the metaphorical. The good man who carries altruism to the ultimate becomes a man of goodness, or "saintliness"; as he flays the natural self, he passes beyond the circle of his immediate ties and widens his sphere of concern to embrace all humanity.

But whether the "human" and "inhuman" saints are viewed as opposed ideals or placed on a continuum of virtue, their appeals are quite distinct. And the fact of their distinctive appeals returns us to the matter of Orwell's personification—not only as St. George but also as another saint, St. Francis. "The closest parallel I can find to George Orwell is Francis Bernardone," wrote John Atkins in the final paragraph of his *George Orwell*.[25] Indeed the legend of St. Francis, another knight errant, leavens the legend of 'St. George' Orwell. It helps explain further the "doubleness" of Orwell's reputation as The Saint and the special appeal of his St. George legend, the two points on which we conclude this section.

What if the historical St. George had given up crusading? We might imagine that he would have become a retiring Francis. For Francis too loved chivalry and participated in at least one crusade before foreswearing soldiering for a life of action in the service of the poor. Whereas St. George personifies the "human" saint, St. Francis exemplifies both "human" and otherworldly sanctity. Francis was both a man of action and an ascetic. He was born a nobleman and voluntarily renounced his birth in the service of his "Lady Poverty" (interestingly, Blair's first proposed title for *Down and Out in Paris and London*). His asceticism, then, had nothing to do with monastic living. His uniqueness lay in his public identification with the poor, precisely what Mary McCarthy has singled out as Orwell's greatest achievement, not in the fact that he abandoned a life of privilege for one of extreme poverty—well-born monks had practiced poverty for centuries. Francis is the non-ecclesiastical saint who spurned corporate standards for a personal way, just as the prophet traditionally rejected the priests. But Francis repudiated institutionalized poverty, not his faith or calling. The legend of the man who knew all Nature for a friend, who could even talk to the birds and the beasts, is the example of a Christian who served not his Church first, but his God and God's creatures. He is perhaps best known as the prototype of the "ordinary" saint. But while we may feel the nearly

irresistible charm of his communion with Nature and his passion for freedom, most of us are nevertheless repelled by his extraordinary austerity and deliberate self-punishment.

And similarly with Orwell, Atkins' "social saint," in whom there evidently co-existed a zest for life with a puritanical insistence on expiating his "sins" by going down-and-out, a feeling for the common man with a categorical rejection of the basic comforts which the common man so values. "He shared the taste of the ordinary man for life in this world," wrote Atkins, "yet he seemed to go out of his way to endure its pains. He did not wish to cut himself off from life but appeared to have the conviction that he could help recreate a better life." Combining facets of the rebel and common man with the saint, this archetype of a socialist Francis is a version of what may be, as R.W.B. Lewis suggests, the emergent form that sainthood must take in our modern, secular age: "the picaresque saint," the good man whose sanctity is manifested not in private communion with God but in urgent communion with his fellow man.[26]

Of course, what admirers like Atkins have called Orwell's "devotion" to his principles, critics like Isaac Deutscher have termed his "fanaticism."[27] Both agree, in any case, that Orwell had his extreme side. "All or nothing might well have been Orwell's motto," Richard Rees once said[28]—hardly the slogan of the ordinary man. But even here, if the "all" has to do with effort rather than natural gifts—with the idea of a man putting all of himself into his ordinary faculties and so achieving something extraordinary—"All or nothing!" as a call to arms is inspiring rather than repellent.

"All or nothing!" was certainly the call to arms of the crusading warrior-saint George. And while the legend of the meek Francis probably better captures the dualistic nature of Orwell's reputed saintliness,[29] most of us identify more easily with St. George, which is probably another reason why warring intellectuals have preferred to idealize Orwell in St. George's image.

And here we shift our attention away from the image of Orwell as saint and back, for a final time, to his personification as 'St. George.' We have noted that the hope of a halo effect from associating oneself with "Orwell" (and one's adversary with "Orwellian") has had much to do with Orwell's reputation as the intellectual hero of many factions—and with turning his legacy into a Chancery case. Some observers who have downplayed talk of "saintliness" altogether have nevertheless discussed Orwell, explicitly or implicitly, via imagery associated particularly with St. George—patriotism, Englishness, boldness, courage, dragon-fighting, the pen-as-sword. So on the Left Orwell gets cast as the unbeliever's model socialist, the socialist "saint" or Trilling's "virtuous man," St. George the Political Paragon. On the Right he enters the lists as the champion of England and the anti-Communist (or anti-socialist) dragon-slayer and martyr, St. George the patriotic Cold Warrior. To the Christian believer he is Richard Rees's "pious" atheist, St. George the Unwilling Convert. In a fourth incarnation, Orwell "the writer" is also accommodated to the metaphor, becoming a campaigner against language abuse

and the schoolchild's model stylist, St. George the Defender of the King's English.

What is extraordinary in all this, as I indicated earlier, is how fertile a generative metaphor is 'St. George' Orwell. No other historical/mythic allusion to Orwell has organized and thematized ideological disputes around itself as this one has done; the metaphor has fully taken on a life of its own, suggesting how a watchword can itself become a multifaceted face, with its images of Orwell as Cold Warrior and Model Stylist having little to do with the man's "virtue" and reaching far outside the limits of even secular conceptions of sainthood.

Indeed, in at least one sense 'St. George' Orwell *is* a full-fledged portrait. Technically, it is a broken image which never cohered. For much as we saw in tracing the emergence of Orwell's fractured image as The Prophet, the image of Orwell as 'St. George' is also fragmented and identifiably linked to specific audiences. We have already discussed its first and third forms in some detail: Trilling's and Atkins' secular saint of the Left and Rees's Christian saint. The second and fourth images of the Cold Warrior and The Model Stylist are held by the intellectual Right and the academic-journalistic community, respectively.

The following sections address versions of all four images as they have evolved within segments of these four institutional audiences.

## 20. Socialist "intellectual hero," neoconservative "guiding spirit": Irving Howe, Norman Podhoretz, and the New York Intellectuals' Orwell

I

In Chapter Two we discussed how the Orwell exalted by Lionel Trilling in his 1952 introduction to *Homage to Catalonia,* the radiant image of "the virtuous man," became a "figure in our lives." Historical and conceptual reasons return our attention in this chapter to "the New York Intellectuals' Orwell." No other group's reception of Orwell has borne so decisively on the growth and shape of his American, and even international, reputation, and for this reason we attempt further to locate the group's reception history within its rich and complicated intellectual history.

But here we are chiefly concerned with the response to Orwell by the second generation of *Partisan Review* contributors. As we noted in Chapter Two, however influential "Trilling's Orwell" was in and beyond his "little group" of New York writers, his has not been the only image of Orwell held by the *Partisan Review* circle. Trilling may well have "embodied" yet "modified" the "*PR* spirit" as its authoritative voice in the early '50s, its widely acknowledged elder statesman of letters. Still, regardless of how expansive the referential reach of his pronouns, Trilling's "we" was strictly time-bound. Indeed just as "the politics of truth" was conditioning Trilling's response to

Orwell in 1952, it was also sundering the *Partisan Review* group in the 1950s and '60s—over the issues of McCarthyism, the Eichmann trial, the New Left, and the Vietnam War. By the 1970s Trilling's "model liberal" image of Orwell had itself split into clearly distinguishable—and admiring—"radical" and "neoconservative" images, held by the second generation of New York writers, many of them affiliated with *Dissent* and *Commentary*, respectively. The two biggest Orwell admirers—probably the two most prominent New York writers of their generation—were in fact the editors of these magazines, Irving Howe and Norman Podhoretz, now squared off against each other on the Left and Right. Like Trilling in the '50s, each man has discerned in Orwell an ideal image of himself, and each man has drawn via Orwell his own "Portrait of the Intellectual As Man of Virtue." Yet, as we shall see, the Orwell portraits which Howe and Podhoretz have sketched are very different from Trilling's and from each other's; likewise the *Dissent* and *Commentary* Orwells are very different from Trilling's and Philip Rahv's *Partisan* Orwell. To Howe, Orwell is the "intellectual hero" of his generation of radicals; to Podhoretz, Orwell is the "guiding spirit" of neoconservatism.[30]

How does an image radiate within an ideologically polarized group down through history? In our case studies of the images of Orwell held by the London anarchists, British Marxists, Anglo-American feminists, and *Tribune* writers, we pointed to *contemporaneous* variations in Orwell's reception at the group level, and our attention was limited to a *single* image held by a *single* receiver and group. In discussing how the second-generation New York Intellectuals have responded to Orwell in the 1980s, however, we close this section with a double focus on "the readers in the groups," comparing Howe's "socialist" Orwell with Podhoretz's "neoconservative" Orwell. Here and throughout we also examine how Trilling's radiant figure of "the man of truth" has been recast in later years. This overall approach enables us both to indicate the substantial shaping influence of Orwell on a younger generation of New York writers and of their criticism on his reputation, and to identify a few of the complexities of multiple, concurrent, and shifting group affiliations on institutional reader response.

We should imagine this scene, then, as an "extended Family" (chiefly a Jewish family) portrait. Perhaps the occasion is a testimonial dinner honoring the posthumous Orwell for receiving the first Partisan Review Award. Orwell is in the center of a crowded canvas, dominated by the New Yorkers though including a few European contributors to *PR*. The New Yorkers are jostling for position, with Howe on Orwell's left, Trilling and Podhoretz on his right, and the others grouped around them accordingly. Or it may be seen as a diptych, a fascinating double profile of the Left-liberal and neoconservative Orwells. Either way, the portrait is extraordinarily intricate and wide-ranging: like the *Tribune* scene, it depicts a complicated intellectual "family" of which Orwell is usually considered a distant cousin;[31] and like such larger scenes as the "Soviet Union's Orwell" and "Germany's Orwell," its immediate background touches many of the major international issues of the postwar years.

II

Anti-Stalinist in their politics and polemical by nature, both Irving Howe and Norman Podhoretz first met Orwell in his quarterly "London Letter" in *Partisan*'s pages (1941–46). Podhoretz wrote *Making It* (1968) "in large part with [Orwell's] example in mind" but had little to say explicitly about Orwell until the 1980s.[32] For Howe, Orwell has been a major influence and near-constant presence since the 1950s. We therefore begin with and devote most attention to Howe's history of reception, which can be roughly demarcated into four phases.

A fiercely anti-war Trotskyist activist and contributor to the theoretical organ of Max Shachtman's Independent Socialist League, *The New International*, Howe first castigated Orwell in its pages as "pro-imperialist." Orwell's insistence in *PR* in 1942 that pacifism was "objectively pro-fascist" outraged the 22-year-old Howe. By 1949, however, when he read *Nineteen Eighty-Four*, Howe's Trotskyism was fast dissolving. Nevertheless, though the *Partisan* and ISL circles moved in overlapping orbits (already by 1947 Howe was writing for *Partisan*), Howe still saw himself chiefly as a political man and his primary reference group was the Shachtmanite sect. "Half in . . . and half out" of "our little group" of dissident Trotskyists—ISL membership at mid-century numbered no more than 1,000, a tiny faction within a faction of the American Left—Howe's primary reference group in the late 1940s was not the *Partisan* writers but the Shachtmanite sect, which had split with the mainline Trotskyists in 1940 over whether Stalin's betrayal of the Russian Revolution deprived the Soviet Union of its status as the workers' fatherland. Trotsky said no, blaming Stalin alone for Stalinism; the Shachtmanites insisted yes, arguing that the real revolution had not yet happened. To them, Russia was no "degenerate workers' state" and Stalinism was no "transition" to socialism—but rather a new form of class rule.[33]

It was in the context of these intramural Marxist disputes and practical problems of revolutionary action that Howe responded to *Nineteen Eighty-Four,* unlike Orwell's other vocal *Partisan* admirers (e.g., the Trillings, Rahv, Alfred Kazin, Daniel Bell, Dwight Macdonald, Arthur Schlesinger, Robert Gorham Davis).[34] Although many of the older *Partisan* writers were Trotskyists in the 1930s (and Macdonald and Rosenfeld were Shachtmanites in the early 1940s), they had already shed their revolutionary socialism and Marxist scholasticism for social democratic politics; Howe was responding to Orwell from a stance the *Partisan* writers no longer shared. Howe's 1950 essay-review of *Nineteen Eighty-Four* was largely a meditation on whether, deliberately or inadvertently, socialism could be "twisted into something as horrible as '1984,' " even by "we, the good people, the good socialists." Howe concluded that Orwell had answered, somberly, in the affirmative. Howe emphatically agreed. *Nineteen Eighty-Four* was a ghastly picture of what socialism could become, "not merely from Stalinism" but even from "genuine socialist efforts." The lesson of *Nineteen Eighty-Four,* said Howe, concerned precisely how to conduct the transition to socialism. Howe de-

fended Lenin's "completely democratic aspirations" and his view that economic centralism was the material prerequisite for socialism; but Orwell's
valuable warning was that democratic practices could not automatically be
taken for granted after a revolution. Democracy would more likely be preserved during the transition to socialism if workers shared political and
social power with other classes.[35]

From the start, then, as we can see, Howe's image of Orwell was a more
radical, polemical, ideologically tinged image than Trilling's quiet, wistful,
liberal figure. In his 1949 *New Yorker* review of *Nineteen Eighty-Four,* Trilling
had spotlighted Orwell's moral stance, his old-fashioned integrity, his "fairness, decency, responsibility."[36] No doubt young Howe saw this as a quaint,
rather bourgeois image. In his *New International* essay Howe noted his "numerous disagreements" with Orwell's democratic socialism and approved
Lenin's criticisms of gradualist Eduard Bernstein.[37] Yet even by 1950 Howe
was moving toward his conclusion of a few years later that workers had
much more to fear from Leninism than from social democracy. Already he
was a wearied veteran of a dozen years of Marxist infighting, feeling the
same sense of exhaustion and despair about the Shachtmanites as did Woodcock in London about his clique of militant anarchists. A socialist at the age
of fourteen, an editor at twenty of the Trotskyist paper *Labor Action,* and
one of the original organizers of the ISL in 1942, Howe had felt his commitment to revolutionary socialism waning ever since his return to New York
after four years of military service in Alaska. Capitalism was not crumbling,
he realized, and America was not Nazi Germany. By the late 1940s this
Jewish son of an immigrant grocer found himself slowly "drifting away
from a movement that has held [my] deepest feelings. . . ." And yet Howe
was still unable to undergo the final "wrench of faith."[38]

The break eventually came, without fanfare, though Howe remained an
inactive member of the Shachtmanites until the mid-'50s. As it gradually
occurred, Howe discovered, much as had Woodcock, that his true vocation
was that of a writer and literary critic. Already by 1949 he had co-authored
(with B. J. Widick) an insightful, pro-labor study on the rise of the industrial
unions, *The UAW and Walter Reuther.* This volume was soon followed by two
books of literary-biographical criticism, *Sherwood Anderson* (1951) and *William Faulkner* (1952). And as he began to see himself less as an activist and
political journalist and more as a literary man, Howe began to exchange his
old reference group of the Trotskyists for the larger, cultivated world of the
*Partisan* writers, a group he at first imagined would be an intellectual utopia, "another world, a community bright with freedom, bravura and intimate exchange."[39] But the *Partisan* circle, young Howe soon realized, would
never be his yearned-for close-knit community of mutual learning and help.
Unlike the Shachtmanites, the New York Intellectuals were "a loose and
unacknowledged tribe," "a gang of intellectual freebooters."[40] Yet the *Partisan* writers were also a more confident, more cosmopolitan, more dialecti-
cally daunting "we" ("the herd of independent minds," in Harold Rosenberg's notorious phrase[41]). During the war years Orwell had been one of the
very few writers whom most of the first-generation herd—including *Parti-*

*san*'s pacifist, revolutionary wing (Macdonald, Clement Greenberg) and more moderate, culturally oriented wing (Rahv, Phillips, Trilling)—had admired.[42] Their estimations grew enormously after *Animal Farm, Dickens, Dali, and Others, Nineteen Eighty-Four*, and the posthumous essay collections. Now, with his full entry into the *Partisan* circle and his transition to "writer," Howe's own admiration for Orwell intensified and the range of questions which he brought to his thinking about Orwell broadened and diversified.

## III

From the mid-'50s to the early '60s, Howe came increasingly to identify with Orwell, and this second stage of his reception (c. 1955–63) is marked less by ideological and more by historical, literary, and personal concerns, some of which he shared with other *Partisan* writers.

Chief among the former was the nature and development of totalitarianism. *The Origins of Totalitarianism* (1951), that brilliant and controversial masterpiece of Hannah Arendt, an "elder" member of the New York Intellectuals, had an enormous impact on the thinking of the *Partisan* writers and the intellectual world generally. Especially during the period of "de-Stalinization" in the mid-1950s, when debate raged about the possibility that the Soviet system was altering fundamentally, Arendt's book sparked numerous historical and theoretical discussions as to whether totalitarianism was the form of authoritarian government characteristic of the modern bureaucratic, collectivist age. Howe's major contribution to Orwell's critical reputation in the 1950s was to help lift *Nineteen Eighty-Four* above mere Cold War polemics and place it within the context of these discussions. Partly as a result of Howe's widely reprinted essay, "Orwell: History as Nightmare" (1956), *Nineteen Eighty-Four* was soon being treated by journalists and political scientists alike as a work of political theory, an abstract model of the totalitarian state (or, in Howe's phrase, "the post-totalitarian" state[43]). Howe maintained that *Nineteen Eighty-Four* fit no established literary categories. But this argument had a liberating, rather than a limiting, effect on critics: if *Nineteen Eighty-Four* belonged to no genre, it could belong to any genre. Following Howe's declaration that "no other book has succeeded so completely in rendering the essential quality of totalitarianism" and his detailed examination of Orwell's "view of the dynamics of power in a totalitarian state," critics treated *Nineteen Eighty-Four* as the fictional counterpart to theoretical studies on totalitarianism by Arendt, Richard Lowenthal, Carl Friedrich, and Zbigniew Brzezinski.[44] Here, then, is another genre in which *Nineteen Eighty-Four* was placed in the 1950s, in addition to the four (satire, novel, techno-historical fantasy, dystopia) which we discussed in Chapter Five: political treatise.

We have already noted the role of intellectual genealogies in the politics of reputation; here we see an instance of how a newborn genre can lend prestige to an older, if sometimes distant, "relative" (even as, though perhaps less so, *Nineteen Eighty-Four* was lending its own prestige to the work of

Arendt and other theorists of totalitarianism). Indeed, because *Nineteen Eighty-Four* antedated *The Origins of Totalitarianism* and similar political treatises, some critics saw it as *inaugurating* this emergent tradition and suggested that it had inspired Arendt and later theorists. Howe contributed to this tendency in his *Nineteen Eighty-Four: Text, Sources, Criticism* (1963). His edition included a supplemental section on "the politics of totalitarianism" which featured extracts from the work of Arendt and Lowenthal designed to present *Nineteen Eighty-Four* as a "typology" of a totalitarian world.[45] By 1983, when Howe edited *1984 Revisited: Totalitarianism in Our Century,* he could fairly write that Orwell's book "occupies a central place" in "the vast literature concerning totalitarianism." It was a place which Howe himself, with his praise of Orwell's "theoretical grasp" of totalitarianism, had done much to establish.[46]

If "genre genealogy" operated to invest *Nineteen Eighty-Four* with the dual prestige of "theory" and of priority of place in an emergent tradition, it also acted to raise the book's artistic standing—and did so by way of the opposite historical direction. "Orwell: History As Nightmare" was published as the closing chapter of Howe's *Politics and the Novel* in 1957, probably Howe's best-known work of literary criticism. Howe placed *Nineteen Eighty-Four* last in a distinguished line of political novels, following works by recognized masters including Stendhal, Dostoyevsky, Conrad, James, Turgenev, Malraux, Silone, and Koestler—and grandly pronounced that *Nineteen Eighty-Four* "brings us to the end of the line."

> Beyond this—one feels or hopes—it is impossible to go. In Orwell's book the political themes of the novels that we have been discussing in earlier chapters reach their final and terrible flowering. . . .[47]

As we saw in our discussion of canon-formation in Chapter Two, the relation between literary categories and member works is interactive and complex. Some readers, for instance, might argue that *Nineteen Eighty-Four* has raised the reputation of the contemporary *political* novel; but to call *Nineteen Eighty-Four* the "terrible flowering" of a novel tradition deriving from *The Red and the Black* and *The Possessed* is surely to enhance its stature as a political *novel.*

"Orwell: History As Nightmare" also had an even more direct—though inadvertent—influence on *Nineteen Eighty-Four* and on the faces of Orwell as The Prophet and The Saint. This essay was the germ of the "nightmare" interpretation of *Nineteen Eighty-Four.* Howe argued against critics like Anthony West who viewed *Nineteen Eighty-Four* "primarily as a symptom of Orwell's psychological condition." The key word here is "primarily"; Howe was advancing a subtle, syncretistic, psycho-social interpretation of *Nineteen Eighty-Four.* The work referred not only to Orwell's personal history, insisted Howe, but also to the history of the twentieth century; it was not just a private nightmare but part of "the social reality of our time."[48] Howe was not the first to discuss *Nineteen Eighty-Four* as a "nightmare"; but earlier characterizations were made in passing and were narrowly political: *Nine-*

*teen Eighty-Four* as "the nightmare of the future." Writing shortly after the publication of "Such, Such Were the Joys" and amid growing psychobiographical interest in Orwell, Howe tried to fuse psychology and politics in discussing Orwell's "nightmare." But the unintended effect of his essay was to give hostile psychological critics of *Nineteen Eighty-Four* another catchword to sling. Following unsympathetic Marxist and psychoanalytic critics, journalists and reviewers began to describe *Nineteen Eighty-Four* as a "nightmarish" projection of a dying prophet's childhood terrors, rather than as a satiric political novel. Likewise, unexpectedly, admirers used Howe's "nightmare" characterization to bolster their psychological argument that Orwell "died" for *Nineteen Eighty-Four,* and that the "nightmare" of tubercular agony he endured to complete his gift to the world testified all the more to his nobility of spirit and love of humanity.[49]

Howe closed "Orwell: History As Nightmare" on a benedictory note:

> There are some writers who live most significantly for their own age; they are writers who help redeem their time by forcing it to accept the truth about itself, and therefore saving it, perhaps, from the truth about itself. Such writers, it is possible, will not survive their time, for what makes them so valuable and so endearing to their contemporaries—that mixture of desperate topicality and desperate tenderness—is not likely to be a quality conducive to the greatest art. But [this] should not matter to us. . . . We know what they do for us, and we know that no other writers, including the greater ones, can do it.[50]

One notices the same adroitly elastic use of first-person pronouns that Trilling employed; Howe "knows" what books like *Nineteen Eighty-Four* do for "us," and what should and should not matter to "us." But the concerns here and throughout this essay are Howe's: Orwell and *Nineteen Eighty-Four* are significant and valuable and endearing because they speak to Irving Howe as a writer and radical—and, as we shall see, because they had helped redeem and force *him* to accept "the truth" about his political self and about the little intellectual groups in New York in whose identities lay part of his own.

For the "we" of this essay's close is not Trilling's *Partisan* "we" but mainly Howe's own. By 1954 Howe had founded (with Lewis Coser) the bimonthly *Dissent,* and had "part[ed] company with most of the New York intellectuals I had admired," including Trilling, once a "spiritual mentor."[51] "The *Dissent* group"—a cluster of unaffiliated radicals dedicated to democratic socialism—was but "a tiny minority within the intellectual world," "turn[ed] in upon ourselves" and at times sustained by nothing more than "the animating ethic of socialism."[52] Howe's relationships with several of the early *Dissent* writers (including Meyer Schapiro, Michael Harrington, C. Wright Mills, and Paul Goodman) are profiled in his autobiography, *A Margin of Hope* (1983). The *"Dissent*ers" still considered themselves Socialists (with a capital "s") in the '50s.[53] They agreed with the *Partisan* writers and other ex-radicals that Stalinism was the major danger internationally, but they held

that in domestic life it was necessary to focus energies against McCarthyism. "[T]he debacle of socialism" stood forth as a "central event in their lives," and they took it upon themselves to (in Howe's italics) *"salvage the honor of the socialist idea."*[54] Howe was the intellectual leader of this small, tight, yet independent-minded group, and thus, by the late 1950s, an authoritative voice of American radicalism. And quite obviously, it is the *Dissent* circle, not the *Partisan* writers, who have most influenced (and been influenced by) Howe's politics in the last three decades.

These waxing and waning cross-influences upon Howe in the mid-'50s— the Shachtmanites, the *Partisan* writers, the *Dissent* group—remind us that a multiplicity of reference groups operates in a life, and that one's relations with each group usually alter with time. But Howe's reception history of Orwell is distinctive in that the groups with which he has affiliated have come to differ sharply through a series of ideological shifts and splits into the 1980s, and these variations in turn have had a bearing on his evolving relationship to Orwell. Even more so than in the case of Raymond Williams, modulations in partisan political and personal loyalties—rather than direct acquaintance, as in the cases of Woodcock and Fyvel—have constituted the decisive determinant of Howe's reception history of Orwell and have conditioned key changes, at least in tone and emphasis, in his responses.

But groups rarely claim the whole of our being or cease to influence us altogether; Howe certainly continued to share *Partisan*'s uneasy allegiance to modernism in the 1950s, even as he deplored its rightward political drift during the McCarthy years. Indeed the essayistic style and critical sensibility characteristic of *Partisan Review,* which Howe brought to his Orwell criticism in the 1950s, remain part of his work to this day: clarity, directness, brilliance, briskness, verve. No doubt certain of these values were formed from reading Orwell in *Partisan*'s pages. For, taking stock of his verbal resources, Howe searched at this early moment of his writing career for suitable literary models—and settled on Orwell. "I decided to work hard to write like Orwell—not, heaven knows that I succeeded, but it made sense to try, since whatever strength of style I had lay in a certain incisiveness." Orwell and Edmund Wilson became Howe's literary benchmarks.[55]

And yet, even before his *Dissent* years, Howe had felt himself growing far apart from the *Partisan* writers on political matters. This became especially evident to him in *Partisan*'s 1952 symposium, "Our Country and Our Culture," in which Howe dissented from the *Partisan* near-consensus that American intellectuals should disavow their "alienation" and become "part of American life." "Consensus," "pluralism," and "end of ideology" were becoming buzzwords in liberal intellectual circles in the mid-'50s; like Trilling, whom Howe now regarded as one of his "intellectual adversaries," the *Partisan* writers were to Howe "intellectuals in retreat" espousing "a liberalism increasingly conservatized."[56] They had abandoned their minimum commitment to "the idea of socialism as a problem and a goal."[57] Amid the "Cold War chauvinism,"[58] several of them had joined the executive board of the single-mindedly anti-Communist American Committee for Cultural

Freedom, which later became *Partisan's* publisher and whose European affiliates were discovered to have been secretly funded by the CIA. In Howe's view, most of the New York Intellectuals had lost their radical nerve.[59] In the phrase of his controversial *Partisan* contribution of 1954 that temporarily severed his relationship with Trilling, they had succumbed to "This Age of Conformity." Moderation in temper had slid into moderation in politics and principle.

All this lay behind Howe's "we"—and behind his insistence on the quality of "desperation" in Orwell's work—at the close of "Orwell: History As Nightmare." The resonances were already clear from Howe's 1955 *Partisan* article on Orwell, "A Moderate Hero." Howe rejected the view of most liberals that Orwell should be seen as a "good" man, a "conscience," or a "saint." Such characterizations, Howe thought, softened or spiritualized Orwell's angry radicalism. Too "cozy" with the conservative spirit of the mid-'50s, liberal critics like Trilling, Pritchett, and John Atkins were unnerved by the gritty, irascible, even ill-tempered side of Orwell, claimed Howe. Unable to fathom Orwell's "desperation," they sought to remake him into "a moderate hero," "a down-at-the-heels Boy Scout who voted Labour." Likewise, lacking Orwell's own "fiery" imagination, they were incapable of understanding Orwell's passion for justice and decency, so they recast it in moral terms as a species of "sainthood."[60]

At issue here were not just competing views of Orwell. What these two images reflected were nothing less than rival visions of the limits of politics and the proper role of the intellectual in the decade of the American 1950s. The hopeful radical ethos of a Howe maintained faith in the efficacy of political action to alleviate human suffering and declared that the prevailing spiritual malaise was merely the temper of the time—and could be overcome. The skeptical liberal ethos of a Trilling implied that the crisis of alienation cut much deeper than political action could reach, that human suffering was not entirely or necessarily traceable to a particular form of government or economic organization, and that large areas of human experience should be held apart from the realm of politics. Howe saw such a compromise as self-compromising; to him the liberal spirit was one of opportunistic reasonableness, smug *mésure*—and now it was also compromising his image of a combative Orwell, his refreshingly *im*moderate hero. Chafing at what struck him, accurately, as the overcautious neoliberalism of the *Partisan* crowd and clearly speaking for the embattled radicalism of his new group around *Dissent;* Howe scorned the liberals' "modified" Orwell, averring that Orwell was no moderate and no saint. Trilling's "virtuous man" became Howe's "revolutionary personality"; Trilling's "man of truth" became Howe's "truculent" man, befitting Howe's own more aggressive, less guardedly urbane personality.

> The more one learns about Orwell, the more one begins to doubt that he was unusually virtuous or good. . . . Neither the selflessness nor the patience of the saint, certainly not the indifference to temporal passion that

would seem a goal of sainthood, can be found in Orwell. As a "saint" Orwell would not trouble us, for by now we have learned how to put up with saints: we canonize them and thus are rid of them. In fact, one sometimes suspects that, behind the persistent liberal effort to raise Orwell from the mire of polemic to the clear heavens of sainthood, there is an unconscious desire to render him harmless. It is as a man and a writer that Orwell makes his challenge to the writers who follow him. He stirs us by his example, by his all too human and truculent example. For he stood in basic opposition to the modes and assumptions that have since come to dominate American and English literary life. He was a writer who rejected the middle-class pattern . . . . He knew how empty, and often how filled with immoderate aggression, the praise of moderation could be. . . . He wasn't a Marxist or a political revolutionary. He was something better and more dangerous: a revolutionary personality.[61]

"One must choose between God and Man," Orwell had maintained in an already-quoted passage from his essay on Gandhi, "and all 'radicals' and 'progressives' . . . have in effect chosen Man."[62] Orwell had rejected belief in "sainthood" because he had resolutely chosen "Man"; Howe, also an atheist, repudiated literary and spiritual canonization in Orwell's name. One must, Orwell insisted, choose: to wait for Sugarcandy Mountain above or work for a socialist utopia below. Howe drew the necessary conclusion as to the corollary choice: "the clear heavens of sainthood" or "the all-too-human" political "mire." For Howe, as for Orwell, sanctity meant non-attachment; sainthood and communitarianism were mutually exclusive.

Yet Howe's main reservation actually concerned the likely *political consequences* flowing from use of the term "saint": moderation, gradualism, quietism. His Orwell, Howe insisted, was no "man of truth"—he was a political figure: an honest radical. Not a "political revolutionary"—but, at this nadir of American socialism, an image of a "revolutionary personality" who could help radicals keep the spirit of revolution alive was "something better." "Saint" and "virtuous man," however, would not do. They evoked in Howe not Atkins' and Trilling's inspiring images of the fully committed, extraordinary ordinary man (Atkins' "social saint"), but Richard Rees's "self-mortifying saint." It is the latter image which sometimes seems almost inhuman, which is indifferent to temporal passion, which is so exceptionally difficult to follow, which cannot serve as the model for those who would launch a political movement, which seems so far from human capacity that it ceases to "challenge" "us."

Here again we see Howe speaking with plural pronouns. And, once again, it is Irving Howe who was not "stirred" by a "virtuous," "saintly" Orwell—as Trilling, Atkins, Pritchett, and Rees had been. One could well ask, as Richard Rovere, another liberal, soon did in *The Orwell Reader*: "But what is [a 'revolutionary personality'] except another term, one with secular and socialist overtones, for a saint? A 'revolutionary personality' is what the Ethical Culturalist calls Jesus Christ."[63]

In their own minds, these liberals did not "canonize" Orwell in order to

"rid" themselves of him, as Howe alleged; rather, they elevated him to engage him all the more fully as a moral beacon, to see him from the angle they needed to. Trilling's Orwell as "virtuous man" had been a "liberating" figure. But Trilling, as we saw, encountered Orwell as he grappled with questions of personal authenticity and reputation from a similar social position (and "always keeping one eye on posterity," in Podhoretz's phrase[64]) atop the New York Intellectual world. Howe approached Orwell on a lower plane, as a young disciple rather than a peer. Still, in another sense, he was wrestling with the same problem—and the one that Woodcock and Williams were also confronting: the relation of the writer to politics. Torn like Trilling between "the two M's," Marxism and modernism,[65] Howe found in Orwell, as did these other writers, what he needed in the mid-1950s: not just a literary model but a model of the radical writer. Trilling had tried to cope with the tension of "the two M's" by aestheticizing his politics into ethics, thereby focusing on Orwell's "truth" and "virtue." Howe refused to do this. He had always believed that action in the public world was "a moral necessity"; to him, Trilling's liberalism "eased a turning away from all politics."[66] Howe's politics of truth thus lay in the stark choice between the liberal imagination and (in the title of an essay collection Howe later edited) "the radical imagination."

And in this choice lay the revelatory personal truth couched in the closing lines of "Orwell: History As Nightmare"—a truth about the relation of writer to politics—which the author of *Nineteen Eighty-Four* and *Homage to Catalonia* helped not only "us" but also Irving Howe, at a "desperate" moment in American radicalism in the mid-'50s, to accept. For Orwell reaffirmed Howe's conviction that "some writers" are indeed "valuable" precisely *because* they "live for their own age," "help redeem their time," acquiesce to an ephemeral and "desperate topicality," force their generation "to accept the truth about itself"—whether or not their work "survives" or is "great art." And Orwell reminded Howe that his own fate and task might be to join the ranks of such writers, the ranks of Orwell and Ignazio Silone. Socialism might one day re-emerge as a viable movement in America if dissenting intellectuals preserved a sense of their calling, preserved "a margin of hope." "I bridled at the notion that the literary life was inherently more noble than the life of politics," Howe recalls. "I bridled because acknowledging this could have been politically disabling at a time when politics remained essential, but also because I knew that it held a portion of obvious truth—otherwise, how explain my inner divisions?" Striving for literary excellence and yet to keep alive socialism's "animating ethic," Howe found in Orwell the political self which he believed, fairly, Trilling and the *Partisan* ex-radicals had forsaken. Howe wanted "instances of that poise which enables a writer to engage with the passions of the moment yet keep a distancing skepticism." Trilling "spoke for part of what I wanted, yet another perhaps larger part of me had to speak against him."[67] Trilling spoke for the skeptical Howe, Orwell for the passionate Howe. "I saw Orwell," Howe recalls, "as a fellow spirit—a radical and engaged writer."[68]

Trilling would not have described Orwell this way. Nor as a "revolutionary" personality. Nor, given his valuation of Orwell's respect for "the familial commonplace" and the "stupidity of things,"[69] as a rebel against middle-class life. But Howe needed a more unbridled, more iconoclastic figure. For Howe, an Orwell hemmed in by the conventional bourgeois pattern was "empty," politically "harmless." "Dangerous" was "better": only a recognizably radical image could truly "challenge" and "trouble" "us."


## IV

No less than his evolving allegiances to groups, a writer's variable relationships with his models reflect his own intellectual development. In the mid-'60s, partly in strong reaction to the authoritarian radicalism of the New Left, Howe felt impelled "toward a liberalizing of radicalism"—and toward the hesitant renewal of his relationship with Trilling.[70] But Howe's respect and admiration for Orwell remained constant—as did his dissatisfaction with American liberalism, which had merely emerged from "a contagion of repressiveness" in order to enter "a time of structured deceit":[71] a maniacal stockpiling of arms, a senseless war in Vietnam. Looking back in 1969 on Orwell's reception during the Cold War, Howe felt vindicated in his 1955 judgment that the liberals' moderate image of Orwell "tells us a great deal more about the historical moment than about Orwell."[72]

The same might be said for Howe's revised image of Orwell in the late '60s. But what changed in this third stage of his reception (c. 1965–73) was not Howe's esteem but the content and context of his image of Orwell. By this time, after the 1963 publication of *Nineteen Eighty-Four: Text, Sources, Criticism,* Howe was coming to be regarded as Orwell's main American defender and radical champion. Now, however, Howe was defending Orwell not from appropriation by liberals but from denigration by radicals. Imperialist, jingoist, warmonger—the charges against Orwell from the American New Left spewed forth, variously based on random passages from *Burmese Days, The Road to Wigan Pier, Animal Farm, Nineteen Eighty-Four,* or a *Tribune* column.* "The Artist As Imperialist," one young academic dubbed the author of *Burmese Days,* calling him "an embittered old man" "trapped in the house that Kipling built." Another Movement writer explained the point of *Animal Farm* this way: "Man is a pig. . . . But this trash can't withstand the rising revolution. . . . How can you assert that revolutionary leaders are just pigs, as Orwell does, in the face of Malcolm X

---

*Thus, unlike the case with the British New Leftists, who accepted Williams' split between a "good" "young" Orwell (a would-have-been "ultra" in the '60s), and a "bad" "mature" Orwell of *Animal Farm* and *Nineteen Eighty-Four,* American leftists swallowed Orwell whole. Theirs was a cruder politics of reputation. But theirs could be, for their movement was not indebted to Orwell. Williams and the *New Left Review* felt compelled to acknowledge a "good" "young" Orwell because Orwell's cultural criticism was a formative influence on Williams and Richard Hoggart in the early, "cultural" phase of the British New Left.

and Ho Chi Minh?"[73] In *Mr. Sammler's Planet* (1970), Saul Bellow, a friend of Howe's and a fringe member of the *Partisan* circle, imagined the hostile response to Orwell from some of Mark Rudd's SDS followers at Columbia. Sammler, the Old Left guest lecturer brought in to talk about the 1930s, could well have been Irving Howe.

> "Old Man! You quoted Orwell before."
> "Yes?"
> "You quoted him to say that British radicals were all protected by the British navy. . . ."
> "Yes, I believe he did say that."
> "That's a lot of shit."
> Sammler could not speak.
> "Orwell was a sick counterrevolutionary. It's good he died when he did."[74]

But Howe could speak and did. "[S]omething within me—sentimentality, conscience, stubbornness—kept murmuring that I had an obligation to speak."[75] Writing in January 1969, in the wake of the Columbia student uprisings and near the height of the Movement's influence, Howe declared acridly that, when it came to sharing and understanding the experience of workers, the student Left and its older enthusiasts like Murray Kempton had much to learn from Orwell.

> He saw them and liked them as they were, not as he or a political party felt they should be. He didn't twist them into Marxist abstractions, nor did he cuddle them in the fashion of the New Left populism. He saw the workers neither as potential revolutionaries nor savage innocents nor stupid clods. He saw them as ordinary suffering human beings; quite like you and me, yet because of their circumstances radically different from you and me. When one thinks of so much of the falseness that runs through so much current writing of this kind—consider only the "literary" posturings of Murray Kempton—it becomes clear that Orwell was a master of the art of exposition. . . . Orwell's deepest view of life [was] his faith in the value and strength of common existence: "The fact to which we have got to cling, as to a life-belt, is that it *is* possible to be a normal decent person and yet to be fully alive." Let *that* be inscribed on every blackboard in the land![76]

Whereas in the '50s he had felt caught between *Partisan*'s neoliberalism and his own liberal radicalism, Howe now felt boxed in between the New Left's "kamikaze radicalism" and his own Left-liberalism. Pilloried by the New Left as a "dastardly"[77] opponent and tired old liberal for his blunt critiques of their unworkable decentralized politics ("participatory democracy"), their anti-democratic attacks on individual freedoms ("liberal fascism," "repressive tolerance"), their indulgence in violence ("confrontationism"), and their naive leader-worship of Mao and Ho and Castro, Howe nevertheless felt driven continually to speak out against their romantic-nihilistic "politics of the deed," which threatened to destroy his "steady work" (the title of his 1966 collection of political essays) of the past three

decades. By the end of the '60s, feeling "politically beleaguered" and "emotionally entangled," Howe was realizing his need to pull back from "the competitiveness and the clamor." He had "overreacted, being at times harsh and strident."[78] What the "larger part" of Howe had sought and found in Orwell during the moderate '50s was passion; but the larger part of him, frustrated and outraged with the excesses of the young radicals, needed Trilling's "distancing skepticism" by the close of the '60s.

This too Howe eventually came to find in Orwell. "I came to appreciate more deeply the side of Orwell that wanted and needed to get away from politics."[79] Howe found himself unable to yield "full allegiance" to any political movement and "settled into an ambivalence toward politics that would remain with me to the end—an ambivalence perhaps rooted in any democratic persuasion."[80] This "outsider" stance, as we saw, was the one Orwell and Woodcock arrived at too, and one notices that in his 1969 essay Howe now spotlights those qualities in his model which he had previously downplayed. Howe now stresses the nonpolitical dimension—the moral, literary, and even spiritual aspects—of Orwell, though he rails once more against those who call Orwell a "saint." Howe gives emphasis to the nonpolitical in Orwell not by tempering Orwell's radicalism, however, but rather by proclaiming Orwell's rugged virtuousness: "He is the greatest moral force in English letters during the last several decades: craggy, fiercely polemical, sometimes mistaken, but an utterly free man." Orwell achieved a "state of grace" in his prose by "sloughing off the usual vanities of composition," which enabled him to speak "as a voice of moral urgency."[81] As in the '50s, responding to the political climate and his personal situation, Howe remolds Orwell as he assimilates him, bending him into the figure he needs, not without a touch of exaggeration and sentimentality. Howe imagines that, as a writer living with workers and speaking to readers, Orwell "solved the problem of narrative distance" involved in sharing and communicating his experience. In "Hop Picking" and *The Road to Wigan Pier* Orwell understood the necessary balance between proximity and distance: he neither "cuddled" the workers nor "twisted" them into "Marxist abstractions." He was "driven to plunge into every vortex of misery or injustice that he saw," but he retained sufficient perspective to "see what looms in front of his nose."[82] Howe's Orwell of 1969 is the figure Howe wished he might have been in the '60s. To plunge in without getting sucked into the vortex: this is what both the young leftists and Howe had not done, why they and he needed a distancing skepticism to check centripetal passions.

Generational distance prevailed instead. To the New Left, Orwell and Howe belonged to an Old Left "scarred by the past," bearing "marks of corrosion and distrust," "skeptical of Marxism," "rigidly anticommunist," in Howe's words.[83] And "middle-aged Socialists" like himself, Howe admitted, though respectful of the early achievements of the New Left (e.g., the civil rights campaigns, the SDS community action projects) resented the young for repeating their elders' pro-Communist follies of the 1930s—and for depriving them of "the role of mentor to the young."[84] Orwell had per-

formed that role for Howe in the postwar years, the role Howe himself might have inherited in the 1960s. But in an anguished, heartfelt tribute, Howe insisted, as if he were Bellow's Sammler giving the student Left a history lesson of a forgotten era, that Orwell was and remained "a model for every writer of our age."[85] And Howe allowed himself, in closing, to imagine that "if he had lived," Orwell would have steered a course similar to his own, lambasting both Establishment politicians and apocalyptic populists:

> For a whole generation—mine—Orwell was an intellectual hero. He stormed against those English writers who were ready to yield to Hitler; he fought almost single-handed against those who blinded themselves to the evils of Stalin. More than any other English intellectual of our age, he embodied the values of personal independence and a fiercely democratic radicalism. Yet, just because for years I have intensely admired him, I hesitated to return to him. One learns to fear the disappointment of fallen heroes and lapsed enthusiasms.
>
> I was wrong to hesitate. . . .
>
> It is depressing to think that, if he had lived, he would today be no more than sixty-five years old. How much we have missed in those two decades! Imagine Orwell ripping into one of Harold Wilson's mealy speeches, imagine him examining the thought of Spiro Agnew, imagine him dissecting the ideology of Tom Hayden, imagine him casting a frosty eye on the current wave of irrationalism in Western culture!
>
> The loss seems enormous. . . . He was one of the few heroes of our younger years who remains untarnished. Having to live in a rotten time was made just a little more bearable by his presence.[86]

And yet: the plural pronouns notwithstanding, not all socialists of Howe's generation agreed. It was not so simple as Old Left = pro-Orwell; New Left = anti-Orwell. Some of the *Dissent* and *Partisan Review* intellectuals of Howe's generation—and Orwell's—did indeed find Orwell a "lapsed enthusiasm." We spoke of the British Left's "balkanization" or "Vietnamization" of Orwell, and this occurred within the much smaller circle of the New York Intellectuals to an even greater extent—and, to a degree, for reasons similar to those which accounted for his divergent receptions by the British and American New Left.

Orwell had not been a continuous presence in the previous decade for the New York Intellectuals any more than he had for the American New Left. (Not even for the *Dissent* writers, except Howe.) Whereas the British Left had "grown" with Orwell, developing a close familiarity with and selective affection for his work, the New York writers encountered him in the late '60s as if he were an acquaintance unseen for fifteen years. No doubt their responses were bound to be more extreme. Equally responsible for the "Vietnamization" of Orwell was that the New York writers not only disagreed about *Orwell's* politics but also—unlike the British Left—about the War and the New Left itself. We see here, then, how internal disputes within a group not only about the figure himself but also about issues far removed from his time complicate his reception. Thus, political and histori-

cal factors, from within and without the New York group, conditioned responses to Orwell in 1968–69 which were, if anything, even more complex and contradictory than in the case of the British Left.

Just as *CEJL* was being published in September 1968, arguments about the New Left and the anti–war movement were splitting the old *Partisan* group into opposing factions, generationally and ideologically, with several New York writers (e.g., Rahv, Phillips, Macdonald, Mary McCarthy, Fred Dupee, Leslie Fiedler, Susan Sontag) sympathetic to or supportive of the New Left (and some even becoming New Left celebrities, e.g., Mailer, Paul Goodman, and the posthumous Mills), and the majority hostile like Howe or reserved (e.g., Bellow, Podhoretz, Hilton Kramer, Sidney Hook, Daniel Bell, Irving Kristol, Nathan Glazer, Alfred Kazin).[87] For most in the latter group, Orwell did indeed remain "untarnished." Lamenting that the counterculture represented the very antithesis of "the age of Orwell," Kazin lashed out at "Mark Rudd, Leonid Brezhnev, the Beatles, Marshall McLuhan, Timothy Leary and all those sordid activists, swingers, and hippies. . . ."[88] Likewise Hilton Kramer, then beginning his rightward turn into neoconservatism, exalted Orwell's "genius for decency," which itself explained why "the more comfortable intellectual factions of the current New Left" disowned him.[89] Pro-Movement writers, on the other hand, were divided on Orwell, just as the British Left had been. Orwell was no longer an intellectual hero for Hanoi sympathizer Mary McCarthy, as we have seen. Mailer, however, who was hailed as "the American counterpart to Orwell," called Orwell "one of my favorite writers" and even claimed that *Keep the Aspidistra Flying* had "given me charity and compassion for the poor."[90]

Yet for no socialist of Howe's generation was Orwell more a "fallen hero" than for Raymond Williams, whose reception in comparison with Howe's warrants final comment, given the two men's sharply differing attitudes toward Orwell during the Movement years and after. Their receptions of Orwell disclose a phenomenon in the politics of reputation which we have already touched on in other case studies: how readers sometimes "contest" each other's image of their shared figure (e.g., "Howe's Orwell" vs. "Trilling's Orwell," "Wain's Orwell" vs. "Woodcock's Orwell"). Here we should note that Howe and Williams—unlike Howe and Trilling—approached Orwell from roughly similar ideological and professional locations until the late '60s. This bears notice, for it alerts us to the fact that authoritative voices not only dispute each other's images, but also see each other as *versions* of their shared figure. They relate indirectly to each other through their shared model (or anti-model), and then, as in the case of Williams and Howe, their conflicting judgments of their hero-rival bear on how and whether their images get disseminated within their respective groups.

Reviewing Howe's *Steady Work* early in 1969, in the afterglow of the May uprisings in Paris and Britain's biggest anti-war demonstration in October 1968, Williams criticized Howe's "wholly unjustified superiority" toward "the young American left." Howe did not engage in sustained socialist criticism of dangerous American government policies, but rather in sus-

tained criticism of "other people and other groups on the Left." Howe's criticism, said Williams, was negative, destructive, and rooted in dated Cold War fears. But Williams confessed a "prolonged hesitation" to say all this and "part company" with Howe. For Howe was "a once friendly man," to whom he had "felt close"; yet now he was "not moving, ready to cut one down with a phrase." "This," Williams concluded, "is what made and makes me so reluctant to criticize Howe: that I have stood where he stands, and I think I know how it feels; that his arguments against movements now being made, on quite different bearings, are as familiar as yesterday, but are only yesterday; that it would be better, really to say nothing, but just wave and turn away, across a growing distance."[91]

The language, spatial metaphors, and verdict of this final paragraph echo the already quoted closing lines of the 1971 monograph *George Orwell*, in which Williams advised the young Left not to "imitate" Orwell but to "acknowledge a presence and a distance: other names, other years; a history . . . to move on from."[92] Even in his critique of Howe, one glimpses, as it were, the figure in the carpet: Williams' Orwell. To Williams, Irving Howe came to seem a basher of the Left, an extreme version of "ex-socialist" Orwell—"alive today." Williams had stood where Howe now was—Orwell had been his generational hero too. But Howe was "not moving," his "steady work" was to stand still and glance backwards. Williams had "moved on," had gone beyond yesterday to today, beyond negation to affirmation, beyond Howe and Howe's Orwell, finally to support and lead—or be led by?—the Movement.

For it is closer to the truth to say that *Williams* kept glancing backwards ("there was Orwell") even as he was hurtling forward, and that Howe saw, all too accurately, the difficult radical course ahead—and looked upward to Orwell and backward to the radical tradition for guidance. The middle-aged Williams became the "mentor of the young" that Howe never did. In turn, Williams' Orwell soon became the accepted far Left image, whereas Howe's heroic Orwell was ignored or disparaged by young radicals.

Thus the trajectories of the two men's reception histories of Orwell rise and fall in opposite directions. Howe came to see Orwell as a model for his generation and for the next, a voice of moral urgency calling him on, a political mentor challenging him to follow in his footsteps—and "the loss seems enormous."[93] But for Williams, Orwell became "an enormous statue warning you to go back"[94]—a roadblock, not a guide. Williams excavated his personal Obstacle, "working through" Orwell by 1971, and yet not working him out of his system—but nevertheless enabling himself to "move on" to become, in the already cited phase of a contemporary, "the Orwell of our generation."[95] Meanwhile Howe, in his "search for a moral style" which could enable American socialism "an honorable style of survival in a time of moral confusion,"[96] remained open to Orwell's voice, and thereby noticed another, eventually more personally valuable, temperate side of Orwell. Howe stayed more or less put, returning to Orwell's example, trying against the Left/Right undertows to "hold fast to the socialist vision,"[97] aware that

enacting a gradualist politics claiming a utopian vision is slow and steady work.


V

"We could be like him," Trilling had wondered in 1952, "if only . . . ."

"If Orwell Were Alive Today," his former student Norman Podhoretz responded, as it were, in 1983.[98]

Yet many observers who had assented to Trilling's musings balked, as we have already seen, at Podhoretz's answer. Trilling had "nominated" Orwell a figure and model liberal; Podhoretz, acknowledging Orwell's stature and obvious rhetorical value to any cause, boldly "elected" Orwell to the ranks of the neoconservatives. Both Trilling and Podhoretz spoke as authoritative voices within their intellectual communities. But Podhoretz's tone was more strident, his range limited to his title question, his sympathetic audience smaller. Trilling's gesture, as we saw in Chapter Two, given his eminence and his essay's status as the introduction to the first American edition of *Homage to Catalonia*, was immediately received as a disinterested, quasi-official, almost ceremonial act performed not just by a *Partisan* writer but made on behalf of the American intelligentsia. Podhoretz's response, however, appeared to many readers, both neoconservative opponents and others, a political play for a distinguished addition to the Right's ideological arsenal, the work of a clever and unabashed polemicist. Both men drew self-portraits. Institutional conditions and Trilling's prose style made his sketch seem Orwell's likeness; whereas the ideology of repute was nakedly apparent in Podhoretz's essay. Trilling's remarks seemed simply a grateful, overflowing tribute, a hymn to "the man who told the truth," reception as restitution; Podhoretz's statement came across as a narrowly self-interested argument, reception as acquisition—or confiscation. "Kidnapping Our Hero," Howe characterized Podhoretz's claim to Orwell, insisting that "to the end of his life Orwell remained a writer of the Left."[99]

In addressing the neoconservative vs. Left "debate"[100] on Orwell in 1983–84, we now turn our attention to "Podhoretz's Orwell." For although a leftist was actually the first to suggest (and bemoan) that Orwell was an erstwhile neoconservative,[101] the Right/Left arguments about Orwell were largely triggered by Podhoretz's controversial essay, "If Orwell Were Alive Today," which we examined in a case study of that title in Chapter Five. We dealt there, however, exclusively with the essay's impact on Orwell's reputation; here our focus widens to consider both author reputation and reader response. We now approach reputation-formation, that is, not only from the side of the figure but also the receivers, i.e., Podhoretz and, secondarily, Howe.

The Right/Left dispute about Orwell in the early 1980s occurred against a complicated background, traceable to the rift in the *Partisan* group during the McCarthy years between mildly progressive, "hard" anti-Communist

liberals (e.g., Hook, Irving Kristol) and Left-liberals (e.g., Howe). This early fissure widened in the next decade and ended in the breakup of the *Partisan* writers in the late '60s, as political differences (over the Vietnam War, the Movement, the situation of Israel and American Jewry, the 1966–67 revelations about CIA funding of the Congress for Cultural Freedom, the 1968 New York schoolteachers' strike), intellectual-aesthetic clashes (over avant-garde and popular art vs. traditional "high" culture), and personal grievances (the negative reception of Podhoretz's *Making It*, the rivalry between the pro-Movement *New York Review of Books* and anti-Movement *Commentary*) all seemed to converge at once. In his 1968 essay "The New York Intellectuals," Howe had pondered whether to call the *Partisan* writers "we" or "they";[102] but by then, with the "herd" rampaging in all directions, the question was academic. Both pronouns were soon being bandied angrily to mark off rival pro- and anti- Movement factions of writers. At first, a number of anti-Movement Left-liberals joined forces with rightward-veering Podhoretz to bombard the New Left and counterculture in *Commentary*'s pages; Howe wrote for *Commentary* as late as 1973. But as the Movement withered away, this alliance dissolved too. Each side moved to its present position, Howe veering left and Podhoretz right. Hostile liberal-Left and neoconservative camps now formed. The battle lines were soon drawn, with Howe and Coser's *The New Conservatives* (1974) constituting one of the early salvos. Neoconservatives, in turn, argued their views skillfully and to a wide intellectual audience in *Commentary* and in Bell and Kristol's *The Public Interest* (and later in Kramer's *The New Criterion*). Against the liberal-Left, neoconservatives generally argued for welfare state capitalism, vigilant maintenance of the national interest, a strong military, and the social value of traditional religious belief.[103] Soon the Right and Left had taken up antagonistic positions on almost every topical political and social issue, ranging from busing to prisoners' rights to affirmative action to feminism to— during the 1984 countdown—the legacy of George Orwell.

Although several leading neoconservatives (Bell, Kristol, Kramer, Epstein, Lewis Feuer) have expressed admiration for Orwell, no one on the Right has done so more outspokenly than Podhoretz. "A literary and political model," Podhoretz calls Orwell, explaining that he feels "a deep affinity" with Orwell because "we share a common history as critics of the Left intelligentsia."[104] A decade younger than Howe, Podhoretz never underwent the "god that failed" experience of '30s socialists; his radical period came later, at the age of thirty, when he began editing *Commentary* in 1960 and, influenced by soon-to-be Movement spokesmen like Mailer and Goodman, turned the magazine sharp left. Yet by the mid-'60s, after the 1964 student protests at Berkeley and with the Movement's rising anti-American (and anti-Zionist) rhetoric in 1966–67, Podhoretz found his doubts about the New Left growing. The snide and hostile response to *Making It* by the *Partisan* writers—whom Podhoretz, evoking all the (Jewish) resonances of the phrase, dubbed "The Family"—hurt him deeply; the term itself indicates how much his membership in the group and position as the desig-

nated male "star" of his generation bore on his self-image.[105] And now he was the Family's black sheep. But the Family's outrage in 1968 over *Making It*, a confessional story of his and the *Partisan* group's "lust" for Success, did not so much chasten Podhoretz as persuade him of the accuracy of his contention that Ambition was the intellectual's "dirty little secret." And throughout, he saw Orwell as an inspirational and sustaining presence:

> I tried in that book [*Making It*] to tell the truth about the values of my intellectual community, and to do so without embellishment or deception. And Orwell was a presence at the time. I saw him as a writer unafraid to criticize unpleasant realities, even when they endangered his own standing within his circle. Orwell snuffed out the "smelly little orthodoxies" of the London Left; I tried to expose the "dirty little secret" of my New York world.[106]

That secret was the hunger for Success. Podhoretz wrote not to destroy but to celebrate Success. "The gospel of anti-success" was, in his view, the prevailing orthodoxy.[107] And here, certainly, Podhoretz differed from Orwell, for the "incorruptible inner self"[108] of Rebel Orwell despised worldly success. But we construct the Orwells we need. In this first stage of reception, Podhoretz saw in Orwell an aestheticized version of Trilling's "man of truth," less the author of *Homage to Catalonia* than a cocksure, self-absorbed Gordon Comstock, evidently more concerned with the personal than the social consequences of disclosure, more so too with moral heroism than the immediate issues at hand. The Orwell behind *Making It* was not a figure who harangued against politically significant lies, but one who revealed (and endorsed) the professional code which Podhoretz and other New York writers silently lived by. Podhoretz saw *Making It* as daring, salutary cultural pornography: he possessed the fortitude of an Orwell up against the Stalinists of the '30s, fighting superstition and cant; he was a D.H. Lawrence of Manhattan, exposing and neutralizing the dirty little secret's power to shame and thereby maim, disclosing the prudish, hypocritical attitude of his fellow New York Victorians toward the pursuit of Money, Power, and Fame. "That Last Infirmity," Podhoretz titled his final chapter, and *Making It* was indeed a book about "the whole business of reputation,"[109] told from the inside, the story of how to "make it" and how to enjoy "it." It was thus a case study in the politics of reputation in its own right. It was also, as Podhoretz was hardly unaware, an effort to reshape his reputation in a new direction.

Podhoretz foresaw too that *Making It* might unleash "the terror"[110] of literary New York on his head. But if the book was in any sense his bid to become the Orwell of *his* generation, the attempt misfired: "the higher calculus of fame"[111] was more complex than he realized. What Podhoretz had seen in Orwell as truth-telling and fearlessness, his critics saw in him as self-display and tastelessness, an embarrassing airing of "Family" laundry.

Although *Making It* dealt with literary politics, it did not so much affect Podhoretz's political development in the broader sense as "liberate me to speak my mind"[112] about the New Left and to inveigh against what he saw

as the Family's embrace of radical chic. Just as the loose *Partisan* group was breaking up, then, its liberal-Left faction became an important negative reference group for Podhoretz, provoking him to attack its and the Movement's politics more unreservedly than he might otherwise have done. Podhoretz had come to see the New Leftists as "the spiritual children of the Stalinists," and so now viewed first-generation New York writers like Rahv and Phillips as betraying their decision of the 1930s to break with the Communists.[113] Podhoretz thus came full circle, back to the "hard" anti-Communist liberalism of his twenties. Soon, however, this "passionate anti-Communist"[114] would go even further and reject liberalism for neoconservatism, thereby "breaking ranks" (the title of his 1979 memoir about the '60s) with most of the *Partisan* writers. In the early '70s, the editor of *Commentary* had no ready-made positive reference group; like Howe in the '50s, he and a few others forged a movement and a group on their own. And here again, Podhoretz has acknowledged Orwell as an example, the solitary figure who acted on his convictions.

> If you break with the Left, you are read out of existence. That's the price you must pay: you no longer can hope to have influence in that world. That's the way it was for the neoconservatives in the early '70s—and though it's changed today because we've built up a community of our own, the Left still dominates intellectual life. . . .
>
> Certainly Orwell wasn't ready in the late '40s to break. Nevertheless he would have understood that this was the price he would have to pay. He knew very well what had happened to [James] Burnham. . . . Burnham became an object of ridicule. He was simply *out*. Orwell knew that and he knew it could happen to him. In fact, to an extent, it had already happened with *Homage to Catalonia* and *Animal Farm*. I don't know if Orwell would have ever broken—he cherished his identification with the Left. Though he clung so tenaciously to his identity as a man of the Left that I've wondered if he may have simply done so because he was aware that it added authority to his criticism. . . . But he was, above all, an honest man, and I do think it's possible that, if he had seen the recent history of socialism—and seen his socialist goals being realized under capitalism—he would have been able to acknowledge that. Then he would have sided with the neoconservatives and against the Left.[115]

One can, of course, point to remarks of Orwell's in which he explicitly supports the Labour Party and dissociates himself from an anti-Communist Conservative group of his day.[116] But the neoconservatives have seized on the question of *motive,* whereby any such passages can be interpreted as the strategic stance of a literary mole. Of interest here is that Podhoretz searches for motives and applies the psychology of the conversion experience to Orwell, thereby reaffirming his own political conversion, his own traumatic decision to "break ranks." Podhoretz and most neoconservatives long resisted the label, continuing to see themselves, in opposition to the liberals of the '60s who had gone left, as the true guardians of the "liberal" tradition.[117] *They* "clung tenaciously" to *their* identities as "liberals," until, in

time, they formed a new intellectual "family" of their own; and they hope that Orwell too might have acted for such tactical reasons. In *Breaking Ranks,* Podhoretz criticizes Howe's "compulsive need to maintain his credentials as a radical";[118] Orwell, "an honest man," might have realized with Podhoretz that "the choice lay between radicalism and intellectual integrity."[119] Here Podhoretz does seem unable to appreciate the radical temper, though not because he fails to possess the requisite "desperation" or "passion"—as Howe had suggested in 1955 about the neoliberals' view of Orwell. Rather, Podhoretz's passion runs so powerfully counter to the radical ethos that he cannot understand Orwell's devotion to the *ideals* of socialism. Orwell's criticism was almost always directed at social*ists*, not social*ism*: and he mercilessly assaulted their lies and orthodoxies because he wanted socialists to be worthy of socialism. A "conscience of the Left," in Atkins' phrase, does criticize from within; and though Orwell may sometimes have been a guilty or excessively scrupulous conscience, he flayed the Left in order to strengthen it, not to weaken or abandon it.

Podhoretz's audacious claim to Orwell also reflects the rhetorical stance of a movement struggling to build *ex nihilo* a reputable intellectual genealogy. Unlike traditional conservatives, neoconservatives believe that in an inescapably ideological age like our own, the Right must not merely stand by as a complacent supporter of the status quo. It must fight the Left with its own program of ideas and forge an attractive political tradition and vision.[120] It must therefore be willing, Podhoretz insists, to "claim" ancestors like Orwell.

> I don't think it's necessary or proper to look for ancestors who aren't your ancestors, and if I believed that Orwell were not what I've portrayed him—anti-pacifist, anti-neutralist, and on America's side in the Cold War—I'd give him up. But Orwell *is* an ancestor on the issues that concern me: democracy versus totalitarianism. So is Trilling; but Camus, for instance, is not, and I've never pretended otherwise.[121]

Not false relatives, then, should be claimed, Podhoretz notes. Even though Camus' *The Rebel* pointed rightward, he argues, Camus is no neoconservative forebear because he could not summon up "the full courage" to become a man of the Right "and thereby los[e] his standing as a secular saint" of the Left.[122] Trilling is an ancestor, however, representing a line between the conservative liberals of the '50s and the neoconservatives of the '70s. But one gathers that Trilling is too small, too narrowly academic, too "gracious" a figure to serve as neoconservatism's "guiding spirit": waging ideological warfare requires a belligerent figure whose reputation goes far beyond literary and New York circles. 'St. George' Orwell thus seems perfect: he provides neoconservatives with the ideological compatibility of a Trilling and the stature and sanctity of a Camus—and also a potent arsenal of catchwords already battle-certified from previous wars against the Left.

Podhoretz maintains, then, that *he* hasn't "kidnapped" Orwell. Rather, Left-liberals and radicals (e.g., Howe, Crick, Christopher Hitchens) have

done so. They, Podhoretz charges, have de-emphasized Orwell's anti-Communism, rationalized away his distinction between "authoritarian" and "totalitarian" governments, downplayed his "wholehearted patriotism"[123] during and after the war, ignored his anti-pacifism, and bowdlerized his writings to justify "neutralism" between America and Russia—as if there were no difference between the Communist world and the democratic West and as if one needn't choose between them. Podhoretz has seen himself as *re*claiming Orwell the Cold Warrior, the "real" Orwell whom he knew in the 1940s and '50s.

> I think I have more in common with Orwell than Irving Howe and certainly the likes of Christopher Hitchens—the idea that the children of Kingsley Martin should be claiming to stand in the tradition of Orwell is so bizarre that I can't believe it. . . . If someone asked you in the '50s who Orwell was, you would say—not to put too fine a point on it—"an anti-Communist." No one in New York really knew him otherwise. When you said "Orwell" to a radical, he replied, derisively, "That anti-Communist." And after all, not conservatives but Soviet sympathizers like Kingsley Martin and Isaac Deutscher were the critics you'd think of as Orwell's enemies. . . . So the name "Orwell Press" adopted by the Committee for the Free World is accurate: it's an anti-Communist organization and Orwell was the patron saint of anti-Communism. He is the neoconservative "guiding spirit" in that he was one of the first to fight the lies of the Communists.[124]

Yet Orwell was not known exclusively as an anti-Communist in New York or elsewhere in the '50s—witness the reception histories of Howe, Williams, Woodcock, Fyvel, and others. And again, one could cite statements in which Orwell the Little Englander hopes for a "third way" between America and Russia, notes that Ingsoc refers both to socialism and "hundred percent Americanism," and makes clear the compatibility between patriotism and socialism.[125] But, although one may disallow Podhoretz's *claim* to a "neoconservative" Orwell, it is simplistic to brand his image of Orwell "false." It is a caricature in its overemphasis of certain features (e.g., Orwell's anti-Communism and anti-pacifism)—much as a cartoon of pointy-headed intellectuals is a distortion—but this is not to say that these features, differently proportioned, are not part of the Orwell physiognomy. Orwell was unequivocal in his opposition to totalitarianism; and, though anti-war in 1938, he was strongly anti-pacifist during World War II. Like the other views of Orwell in this study, Podhoretz's is the partisan view of a partisan viewer; he holds a partial image of Orwell—to which he is extremely partial.

And so Podhoretz frames Orwell's history to fit his own. His political odyssey—from Center to Left to Right—is "not unlike"[126] Orwell's, Podhoretz argues. Orwell underwent "several major political transformations,"[127] from self-declared "Tory anarchist" in the '30s to quasi-Trotskyist in Spain to—the crucial stage for Podhoretz—"Orwell the English Patriot" at the outbreak of the war. This "new Orwell"[128] remained a patriot to the end, but his vision grew darker as he turned his guns on totalitarian Russia; the

author of *Animal Farm* and *Nineteen Eighty-Four* was a disillusioned socialist: St. George, the Cold Warrior.[129] And since his trajectory from Left to Right is common among the first- and second-generation New York Intellectuals, most of whom are former Trotskyists or independent radicals (Hook, Kramer, Bell, Lionel Abel, William Barrett, Nathan Glazer, Seymour Martin Lipset), Podhoretz concludes that Orwell's development resembles the general course taken by neoconservatives in the '80s. At the same time, reluctantly accepting that its defining tradition entails an "unshakable commitment" to the "utopian Left," Podhoretz disavows the *Partisan* legacy, making clear—as Leopold Labedz has made equally clear about *Tribune*— that its fundamentally progressivist tradition is not George Orwell's.[130] Thus, like Williams, Podhoretz splits Orwell into phases, an unregenerate and a "new" or "late" Orwell. But unlike Williams, Podhoretz stakes his claim to the late Orwell: he welcomes as "breaking ranks" what Williams castigated as breaking faith.

In this second stage of his reception of Orwell, therefore, as a neoconservative of the '80s, Podhoretz has embraced a much more political figure. Podhoretz's Orwell is an English version of the cold war liberal of the '50s, the "patron saint of anti-Communism," a guiding spirit not only personally but also politically. And yet, though he has returned to his politics of the '50s, Podhoretz has not become the Orwell of his generation, but rather, as he noted in *Breaking Ranks,* a younger version of the best-known American Cold Warrior of the '50s, that "cautionary figure" whom Trilling had feared to become—the Sidney Hook of his generation. Podhoretz admired enormously Hook's willingness to remain for decades "on the field of political and ideological combat" against the Stalinists, the fellow-travelers, and the New Left;[131] and he deplored the timidity of his "intellectual father" Trilling, who, though anti-radical by temper and conviction, distanced himself from Podhoretz's anti-Movement campaign, fearing that controversy would deprive him of "a position of venerability."[132]

Orwell thus represented for Podhoretz in the '70s, as he had also for Trilling two decades earlier, a composite of the "two exemplary roles" *he* saw immediately before him, in the elder generation of New York Intellectuals. And in the process of rejecting his "father" Trilling and choosing the path of Hook ("the one who had gone too far in the rebellion against radicalism"[133]), Podhoretz also recast and politicized Orwell via Hook's image, turning the aestheticized Truthteller who had guided *Making It* into the fierce "guiding spirit" of neoconservatism. Clearly, Hook is the figure in this Orwell carpet—though with a touch of Trilling, as evidence of the Orwell who remains a literary model for Podhoretz, woven in too.

In *Breaking Ranks,* Podhoretz called a yearning for "venerability" Trilling's "English" side, whereas the image of the battle-scarred Hook represented Trilling's "New York or Jewish side." His English side was stronger, Podhoretz believed; Trilling wanted to be "admired by all." But the stronger side of Podhoretz, as of Hook, is the combative New York Jew. And perhaps these impressionistic differences between Trilling and Podhor-

etz suggest reasons beyond their differing historical contexts why their responses to Orwell have so diverged—why Trilling, by sensibility and sympathetic imagination, has seemed to most readers to have captured a "truer," more "authentic" image of the Englishman Orwell, and why Podhoretz's Orwell has seemed a caricature, a set of propositions in a case.

Yet if Podhoretz has become the Hook of his generation, the distinction of the American Orwell of his generation has not gone unawarded. Howe's 1983 autobiography even brought the accolade of "virtuous man" from the formerly antagonistic *New York Review of Books*.[134] Campus speeches on Orwell, conference talks and radio interviews about Orwell, a *New Republic* cover story, a new and expanded edition of *Nineteen Eighty-Four: Text, Sources, Criticism,* the edited volume *1984: Totalitarianism in Our Century*: in 1983–84 Howe seemed to be the designated American keeper of the Orwell flame. In this fourth stage of Howe's reception of Orwell, then, he has been increasingly identified with Orwell, even as he himself has gained a reputation beyond intellectual and academic circles as a result of his widely acclaimed bestseller *World of Our Fathers* (1977).

With the neoconservative challenge to Orwell in 1983–84, Howe assumed, once again, the role of defender of the radical Orwell. As in the '50s, Howe was guarding Orwell on his right flank, but by the 1980s Howe's own radicalism had attenuated to "radical humanism."[135] His highly critical *Leon Trotsky* (1978) made clear that the liberal social democrat of the 1970s had traveled a long way from the young Shachtmanite of four decades earlier. No longer was *Dissent* subtitled "A Quarterly of Socialist Opinion"; and in his elegiac *Socialism and America* (1985) Howe pondered whether socialism had outlived its historical moment. Still, though he now puts more emphasis on the "conservatism of feeling" in *Nineteen Eighty-Four,* Howe strongly affirmed Orwell's own socialism, branding Podhoretz's argument "vulgar."[136]

> Neither Trilling nor I ever said that Orwell "is me" or "is like" me. My construction of Orwell is just that—a construction—and of an admittedly self-serving kind. But it is a clearer and more openly acknowledged image than Trilling's in the '50s, and I make no claims about a "posthumous" Orwell as Podhoretz does. . . .[137]

But what is vulgarity to one man may be clarity—and integrity—to another. ("[C]larity is courage," insisted Podhoretz in *Breaking Ranks*.[138]) What Trilling and Howe do not say outright, they do say between the lines: Orwell is "like me." Their constructions *are* constructions, and, yes, self-serving ones—as are, unavoidably if subtly, my reconstructions of their constructions. Still, one does sense that, of the readers of Orwell featured in this study, Howe, along perhaps with Woodcock, *is* most "like" him. And Orwell is one of "the writers who have meant most to me," one of "the crucial witnesses," Howe says at the close of his autobiography. "It is with their witness that, along the margin, I want to identify," a witness to witnesses. If, in the end,

one affirms with Howe that Orwell died a "democratic socialist," it is in no small part, I think, also to pay witness—and final respect—to a perception of Orwell's integrity, intelligence, and self-knowledge.

The aim here, however, is not to adjudicate claims to paternity or custody, thereby to award Orwell to the liberal-Left rather than to the neoconservatives. One notices that these rival claims are being staked to different images of Orwell as 'St. George' anyway. And they are images which reach far beyond "Orwell," amounting finally to arguments and self-justifications for how to live the intellectual life. The radical claim is chiefly to the rebel-saint Quixote, the crusading moralist who dreams of a better way and protects his integrity above all. The neoconservative claim is to St. George the Cold Warrior, the responsible pragmatist who dirties his hands to get results. Quixote is an "intellectual hero" for us if we share his passionate commitment to his ideals. But he is prone to self-delusion, self-absorption, and self-righteousness—just as utopian ideology can give way to totalitarian pathology. The pragmatic Cold Warrior is a "guiding spirit" for us if we share his assessment as to what must be done and how to do it. Yet he is liable to cynicism and smugness—just as *Realpolitik* can lead to expedient relativism.

Orwell once criticized the London Left in *Partisan Review* for not being "true intellectuals." Characteristically, he never explained what he meant by the phrase. And indeed, what is a "true intellectual"? Is he chiefly the critic or the guardian of his country, the dissenter against or the defender of his culture? Is his main obligation to struggle for a different and radically better future? Or to protect and preserve the present order? Is his first duty to agitate for the best of all possible worlds? Or to choose among the best of available worlds? To Howe, "the intellectual calling" means that "either we . . . live by some value or ideal, or we're not worth a minute's notice." To Podhoretz, to be an intellectual means to judge, to face "the hard truth about the limits of the possible, which very often means choosing a lesser evil." To Howe, the visionary shapes the practical and the far guides the near, and "utopia . . . speaks for our sense of what might be." To Podhoretz, "if you believe in utopian possibilities, you don't act, you focus on your dream and evade the actual choices presented by reality in the here-and-now, all of which seem by comparison undesirable." To Howe, neoconservatism is a philosophized "Making It," a small-spirited realism generated by bitter disillusion and the attractions of power. To Podhoretz, socialism is a fashionable pseudo-religion for intellectuals, a deluded and dangerous idealism rooted in an obsession with authenticity and a weakness for heroic posturing.[139]

And yet, at what Trilling called the "bloody crossroads where literature and politics meet,"[140] these two political writers have shared, with Trilling, an allegiance to "the intellectual calling" as a spiritual vocation—and to Orwell as a moral guide. "What Trilling, Howe and I have in common," as Podhoretz puts it, "is that, in our different historical moments, we have found ourselves at odds with the times and with our intellectual communi-

ties. And for all of us, Orwell has been the great model of how to swim against the current: with integrity, with courage, with honor. We disagree on *what* is involved, but not on *how* to do it."[141] One would hope for hard-headed utopianism or great-souled pragmatism. But the "how" is a beginning. Indeed, that writers of the Left and Right and Center have all imagined Orwell as incarnating their ideals is not only a tribute to Orwell's achievement but also in itself points beyond the "how." For it testifies to the human urge for figures approaching Max Weber's "genuine man," those who live by both "an ethic of ultimate ends" and "an ethic of responsibility,"[142] and to the all-too-human need of political writers for self-portraits of the intellectual as a man of right action and virtue.

## 21. The Religious Fellow-Traveler: Christopher Hollis, Brian Wicker, and the British Catholics' Orwell

### I

The *Partisan* writers were not the first intellectual group to project images of Orwell as a man of both the Right and Left. Two separate, antagonistic subgroups of English Catholic intellectuals, associated with the conservative London *Tablet* and with *Slant,* the organ of the Catholic New Left, have also engaged Orwell. But unlike the Left-liberals and neoconservatives in New York, the *Tablet* and *Slant* writers' images of Orwell emerged in different decades and in distinctive political contexts. The *Tablet* Orwell was a conservative, pre-Vatican II image of the 1940s and 1950s; the radical Catholics' Orwell was a "baptized" version of Raymond Williams' and Richard Hoggart's socialist image of Orwell from the early 1960s.

Also unlike the New York Intellectuals, these two English Catholic groups did not directly contest each other's images of Orwell—instead they argued with Orwell himself. For though certain intellectuals associated with *The Tablet* and *Slant* identified strongly with Orwell, none of them ever responded to him openly and unreservedly as a hero or guide. The *Partisan* writers had been able to overlook Orwell's anti-Zionism and mild anti-Semitism; but *Tablet* writers like Christopher Hollis regarded Orwell's fierce anti-Catholicism and socialism as a major shortcoming; and Catholic radicals like Brian Wicker found Orwell's anti-Marxism a serious deficiency.

This case study, then, explores how religious concerns may condition the literary reputation of an unbeliever. Whereas in several previous case studies we have discussed Orwell's reputation among groups of political intellectuals, here we examine his standing within Christian circles, focusing upon the pre- and post-conciliar images of Orwell held by the Catholic Right and Left, respectively. Thus, this section presents another diptych of Orwell. But this time we encounter a religious scene, the only ecclesiastic portrait in the gallery. Familiar Church imagery dominates the *Tablet* scene. The Saint is treated less metaphorically, if not quite literally, than elsewhere. Yet even

here the hagiography is critical; The Saint is not haloed. The *Slant* Orwell is a thoroughly modern portrait, with traditional Catholic themes downplayed and the question of Orwell's sanctity not even raised. With both portraits, in addition, we must pay special attention, as we did with the British Marxists' and the feminists' images of Orwell, to how secondary factors of critical location have shaped his reputation among Catholics. Hence not only sectarian but also ideological and generational affiliations concern us in this case history. Our attention to the theological/ideological/generational divisions within English Catholicism in the 1960s will disclose further complexities of reference group relations: how, when an institutional audience with a shared identity (like "Catholic") experiences tensions due to sharp secondary differences, subgroups within the larger group who come to see each other as rivals will identify much more strongly with "outside" reference groups. Thus the traditionalist English Church, supported by the older *Tablet* writers, disapproved of the radicalism of the *Slant* writers, who, though remaining "Catholic," eventually aligned themselves more with the secular far Left than with the English Church—and in turn saw Orwell, unfavorably, much more through Marxist than Catholic spectacles.

## II

In the spring of 1931 Orwell explained to fellow Old Etonian Christopher Hollis why he read the Catholic press: "I like to see what the enemy is up to."[143] Typically, Orwell found that "the enemy" was up to no good, and he pulled no punches in his war of words with Catholics, especially Catholic intellectual apologists like Hollis. Orwell considered the Church's political tendency plainly fascist, distinguishing it from Anglicanism, which did not "impose a political 'line' " on its followers.[144] The collaboration of the Spanish Church with Franco in the Spanish Civil War permanently hardened his attitude, though his bitter, and sometimes obsessive, anti-Catholicism[145] is evident throughout his work. Orwell mocked notions of heaven and the Catholic (and Anglican) priesthood in *Down and Out in Paris and London* and *A Clergyman's Daughter,* denounced "Romanism" as the ecclesiastical equivalent of Stalinism in *The Road to Wigan Pier,* compared "orthodox" Catholic intellectuals to Communist Party writers throughout his journalism, satirized religious belief via the figures of Moses the Raven and Sugarcandy Mountain in *Animal Farm,* and linked religious with political orthodoxy in O'Brien's power-crazed speech in *Nineteen Eighty-Four.* Guerrilla campaigns against "the enemy" pleased Orwell. After spotting a Bible Society sign noting that the local Protestant shop did not carry the Catholics' Douay Bible, he wrote to a friend: "Long may they fight, I say; so long as that spirit is in the land we are safe from the RCs."[146]

And yet, ironically, Orwell's own reputation proved not to be so safe. "Mr. Orwell is a man we Catholics ought to get on reading terms with," one Catholic reviewer advised his readers in the 1940s, "for he is very definitely on our side." Soon Orwell's passing comment to a socialist friend that Gra-

ham Greene "might become our first Catholic fellow traveller" was being posthumously applied, with a sharp shift in emphasis on the phrase's last two words, to Orwell himself.[147] "There is no reason why, at least in Chestertonian geography," eulogized a Catholic critic in 1950, "one should not travel the path to Rome by way of the road to Wigan Pier. . . . In this vale of tears we are all fellow travelers."[148]

Tributes like these from believers—and posthumous conversions of Orwell into a would-be Catholic St. George—became frequent in the 1950s. "People are already beginning to speak of him as a saint," wrote a Jesuit admirer in 1957. "They use the word in no ordinary sense, but it is easy to understand and to sympathize. . . . He believed in freedom and truth and he was ready to die for his belief."[149]

One could well understand it if Orwell were merely being reclaimed posthumously as an Anglican or a radical Dissenter in the Protestant tradition. He saw himself as an atheist and freethinker, and he was confirmed in the Anglican Church and requested an Anglican burial service.[150] Unsurprisingly, many Protestants, uninterested in "Chestertonian geography" and "the path to Rome," have also saluted Orwell as a pilgrim Christian without faith.[151] But not only have Christians greeted him as a fellow-traveler. Stressing Orwell's hard-headed, this-worldly orientation and his concern with individual human dignity, some Personalists, Humanists, and Rationalists have also embraced Orwell as one of their own.[152] Nowhere in his work, however, does Orwell make specific reference to any of these philosophies. Socialism was his "religion of humanity"; common decency was his secular faith.* Despite unmistakable affinities between his apparent religious thinking and these philosophies' outlooks, Orwell never bothered formally to align himself with these groups or to call himself by these or any other sectarian labels. This disregard doubtless made it more possible even for groups toward which Orwell was openly antagonistic, like Catholics, to interpret his occasional religious pronouncements as reconcilable with their own central preoccupations.

The attempts to "press-gang Orwell" for "the papists," in the *New Statesman*'s angry words,[154] culminated in the mid-1950s with the work of Christopher Hollis, which we will address shortly. But Hollis devoted little attention in print to Orwell until the late 1940s; certainly he was not the first Catholic intellectual to praise Orwell's work. Reviewers of Orwell's early work, however, made no strong efforts to "convert" him. Instead, throughout this first stage of Orwell's Catholic reception, in the 1930s and '40s, Catholic intellectuals engaged mainly in what might be termed *claiming by acclaiming.*

---

*In Orwell's post-Enlightenment view, intellectual disburdenment of religion was in effect a stage in the progress of the species toward maturity. To be a skeptic was to be "grown up." (In a deathbed journal entry, Orwell remarks of Evelyn Waugh: "One cannot really be a Catholic & grown up.") "Religion," which Orwell often discussed in the singular as a monolithic and anachronistic institution, amounted to "pie in the sky," an otherworldly evasion of the here-and-now's problems. When he thought of believers he dealt in stereotypes like Mr. Pithers in *A Clergyman's Daughter,* who says to his wife at the end of each suffering day, "Never you mind, my dear, we ain't far off from heaven now."[153]

While sometimes expressing sharp disagreement with Orwell's skepticism and anti-Catholicism, critics stressed Orwell's similarities to certain Catholic writers and lauded those aspects of his work and literary personality which bore clear affinity with Catholic positions (anti-Communism) and values ("honesty," "decency").[155] This treatment gave Catholic readers the impression that Orwell was indeed "on our side."

Most responsible for Orwell's warm reception among Catholics were the Oxbridge intellectuals affiliated with England's leading Catholic weekly, *The Tablet*. Reviewing *Homage to Catalonia* in 1938, editor Douglas Woodruff acknowledged Orwell as "a patently honest man" and "an impressive witness" against the case for fascism.[156] Orwell had written that he could conceive only of "millionaires or Romantics" supporting Franco, but most of Orwell's *Tablet* admirers (Hollis, Woodruff, Waugh, Father C.C. Martindale, Sir Arnold Lunn, Monsignor Ronald Knox), like English Catholics generally, strongly backed the Nationalists. Cardinal Hinsley protested the murder of several hundred Spanish clergy by the Loyalists and hailed the fascist rebellion against the Second Spanish Republic as a "crusade" by the forces of Christ against Antichrist, the latter represented by an atheistic Communism which had been recently condemned by Pius XI in a papal encyclical.[157] To many English Catholics, Franco was fighting a holy war to save Christendom; some English Catholic intellectuals wrote pro-Franco tracts and a few even assisted Franco directly in the military rising of July 1936.[158] This overall situation formed the context for Woodruff's regret that Orwell lacked "the inclination" to understand both "the ideas behind the Nationalist movement" and "the aspirations of the men against whom he went to fight." Woodruff's displeasure was mild. Instead he emphasized Orwell's anti-Communism. In castigating the Spanish Communists, he noted, Orwell "joins hands with people at the other extreme of political thought from his own."[159]

A few months later Father Martindale was even more gracious. "Why Not Our Ally?" asked Martindale, responding to Orwell's hostile anti-Catholic remarks in *The Road to Wigan Pier*. Martindale suggested that Orwell "ought to find us his reliable allies" and reasoned that he didn't simply because "we don't know one another." The Jesuit added:

> The advantage would be mutual if we did. He would give us more facts, and something of his fervour. And we, perhaps, could offer him a more firm philosophy.[160]

It has gone little-noticed that this 1939 essay was the first full-length article ever written about Orwell. It is not a radiant moment in Orwell's reputation-history, being undistinguished by its style or argument. But as the recently appointed editor of *The Tablet*, the forty-one-year-old Woodruff was rapidly becoming one of England's most prominent Catholic laymen; and among the generation of priest-intellectuals influential in the Catholic community in the early decades of the century, Martindale alone remained. Their conciliatory attitude to Orwell fit with their sharp departure from the combative apologetic stance formerly taken toward anti-

Catholic opponents,[161] and on account of their stature as the authoritative voices of the English Catholic laity and clergy, their reception established the tone and pattern for subsequent Catholic response. In the next decade, the *Tablet* writers welcomed each of Orwell's new publications, though Waugh himself lamented Orwell's "ignorance of Catholic life" and his view that "few thinking people" still believe in life after death: "I can only answer," said Waugh, "that all the entirely sane, learned and logical men of my acquaintance, and more than half of those of high intelligence, do in fact sincerely and profoundly believe in it."[162]

Waugh's reference to "all . . . the men of my acquaintance" suggests the narrowness of his circle and points to an important feature of Catholic intellectual life in England during the pre-Vatican II years: its parochialism. Having only entered what Cardinal Newman heralded as its "Second Spring" with the restoration of the ecclesiastical hierarchy in 1850, British Catholicism remained defensive and inward-looking for more than a century afterwards. Not only were Catholics a small, embattled minority within the English population at large (fewer than four million, or 6 percent in 1950), but the great majority were also working-class, Labour-voting, urban Irish immigrants. Thus the tiny upper-class elite of landed, English Tory Catholic intellectuals around *The Tablet* felt doubly cut off—both from the non-Catholic Left intelligentsia and also from their fellow Catholics. And there was even a further cause for their aggressive insecurity within "our small world":[163] though a few Catholic intellectuals were members of the old recusant families (e.g., Woodruff) who had anxiously preserved the faith since the Reformation, most (including clergy like Martindale and Knox) belonged to a still tinier group of converts, some of them never entirely convinced of their full membership in their new community and restlessly eager to prove their piety and loyalty. This is often true of converts. But the *Tablet* writers' feeling of exclusiveness was also more than half-willed and tinged with pride: the conversions of Waugh, Hollis, and others in the 1920s had followed a distinguished nineteenth-century line, including members of the Oxford Movement (Newman, Gerard Manley Hopkins) and the Lord Acton–Baron von Hügel circle of Liberal Catholics. The most famous and influential of the twentieth-century apologists were Hilaire Belloc and convert G.K. Chesterton. The anti-Protestant, ultramontane "Chesterbelloc" tradition reached its pugnacious peak with the writers of Woodruff's generation, especially those interwar converts (Waugh, Greene, Christopher Dawson) whose literary achievements were hailed as "the Catholic intellectual renaissance."[164]

Of chief interest for our purposes among this generation is Christopher Hollis (1902–77), whose history of response to Orwell was decisively shaped by his 1924 conversion to Catholicism.

### III

Hollis was one of Orwell's oldest literary acquaintances and his chief Catholic and Conservative admirer. Conservative M.P. for Devizes in Wiltshire

(1945–55), chairman of the educational publishing house Hollis & Carter, and a member of *The Tablet*'s board of directors for three decades, Hollis was one of England's prominent postwar Catholic laymen. His *Study of George Orwell* (1956), published just after he left Parliament, is probably his best-known work. It opened a second phase of Orwell's reception in English Catholic circles, within which it exerted a significant shaping influence on Orwell's reputation in the 1950s and early '60s. Inside and outside the Catholic intelligentsia, Hollis' detailed report of Blair's schooldays at Eton was received as authoritative, even more so than was Connolly's *Enemies of Promise* in the 1930s. Except for Connolly, "no one knows more of [Orwell's] early years than I," said Hollis, noting that only he among Orwell's memoirists had met Blair in Burma and had read Orwell's work in the order it had appeared, without the distortions of Orwell's later fame.[165] Until Stansky and Abraham's *The Unknown Orwell* and Bernard Crick's biography, Hollis' personal account of Blair's Eton and Burma years was generally accepted as the final word. Hollis' book also coincided with and facilitated attempts by postwar American Catholics and "cultural" conservatives (e.g., Russell Kirk) to turn Orwell into an anti-socialist champion.[166] Indeed, although Orwell himself noted that Catholicism and conservatism should not be automatically equated, his cordial reception by Anglo-American Catholics did mirror in microcosm the wider pattern of his favorable reception among conservatives in the '50s[167]—just as, in the '60s, as we will soon see, Orwell's mixed reception among Catholic New Leftists reflected the shape of his severe Left reception generally.

"All differences of opinion," England's Cardinal Manning once declared, "are at bottom theological." Hollis opened one essay about Orwell with this pronouncement, and it fittingly summarizes Hollis' own belief and his reception history of Orwell. For Hollis, whether or not everything began in *politique*, it ended in *mystique*. "More and more I am convinced that it is as a theologian that Orwell will be considered important," Hollis told Catholic readers, adding ingenuously that such a view was "the last thing [Orwell] would have guessed himself." Widely quoted on both sides of the Atlantic have been Hollis' judgments in *A Study of George Orwell* that Orwell "half-understood" that "God is Truth" and that Orwell was not against Conservatism as a "philosophy" but only against Conservatives who "failed to conserve."[168]

Repeatedly Hollis objected in *A Study of George Orwell* and elsewhere to Orwell's religious and political stands, and then either tried to refute Orwell's criticisms directly, or argue them out of existence, or translate them into agreement with Hollis' ideas. For example, citing Orwell's view that modern man required "something to believe in," Hollis concluded that Orwell's thought rested on a subconscious Christian foundation. Orwell's outcry against the "unspeakable wrongness" of capital punishment in "A Hanging," insisted Hollis, was "only tenable on the basis of a theology" since secularists hold that man is mortal anyway.[169] Orwell's descent into the underworlds of Paris and London was "a search for a particular religious

experience" comparable to that sought by "ascetical Spanish saints," said Hollis, which Orwell predictably failed to find because he violently denied the reality of all religious experience.[170] *Keep the Aspidistra Flying* was "interesting as Orwell's first attack on contraception."[171] *Nineteen Eighty-Four* ends in despair and futility, argued Hollis, because Orwell did not point out that the only way to prevent "the stream-lined men" from coming was to recognize that "the essential belief of Man . . . has been his belief in God and in some form of future life where in some way the injustices of this world will be corrected."[172] Hollis' conclusion was clear: "Orwell never doubted that man was fundamentally a moral being and that this world was a testing place. . . . Just as socialists were the obstacle to socialism, Christians were the main objection to Christianity."[173]

Likewise, Orwell was not against "Conservatism" properly understood, maintained Hollis, but only against the corruption of Conservatism by men like Joseph Chamberlain, whose radicalism, secularism, and imperialism turned the Conservative Party away from its ideals of respect for continuity and for traditional institutions. Pointing out that one of Orwell's highest values was individual liberty, Hollis foisted on Orwell the additional belief that the best way to safeguard personal freedom was to maintain class divisions.[174] Essentially Hollis' 'St. George' Orwell was a dual image, the Unwilling Convert and the English Patriot. Hollis' Orwell resembled an old and "true" Conservative like Hollis himself—almost a Catholic Cobbett, a Christian "Tory Radical." Implying that Orwell's patriotism reflected his Conservatism—even though Orwell in *The Lion and the Unicorn* explicitly argued that patriotism "is actually the opposite of Conservatism"[175]—Hollis depicted Orwell as a lover of the land who espoused a Toryism sharply distinguishable from "big business" Conservatism: pre-capitalist, agrarian, favoring small economic units, and disinclined to scramble for money.

> His main complaint against the Conservative Party was that it failed to conserve. Man, he thought, if he was to be happy, needs a stable environment. He needs the ownership of property, in a simple, straightforward way, to know, to see and to handle what was his own. . . . Whatever the indefensible relics of feudalism that it might try to defend, there was at any rate something to be said for the earlier Conservatism, which was suspicious of capitalism as a corrupting and liberal business. . . . When the later Conservatism surrendered to its arch-enemy, Joseph Chamberlain . . . , and came to boast that it was the party of progress and capitalism, there was no force left in the country that could fight for decency.

> He was against those who called themselves Conservatives and had captured the Conservative machine. His complaint against them was that they were at once too arrogant and too compromising. They were too arrogant in so far as they tended to claim their privileges as something which they had deserved and to arrogate to themselves the airs of superior people. These very claims obscured the true case for Conservatism which was that society had to be arranged ideally well, that it was fatally easy for men to fritter away all their energies in agitation and scheming for its rearrange-

ment, and that therefore there was always something to be said, within limits, for accepting society broadly as it is and getting on with the business of living. It may very well be that there would be more liberty that way than down a more revolutionary, more ideally perfectionist road—and liberty was what really mattered . . . . [T]he Conservatives in practice, he complained, had shown themselves always only too ready to do a deal with the new philosophies of the "stream-lined men". . . . They did a deal with the Fascists before the war and with the Communists in the Anglo-Russian alliance during the war. Orwell despaired of the Conservatives because the Conservatives despaired of Conservatism. They were without principle.[176]

I quote at length Hollis' very partial image of a "Conservative Catholic Orwell" not only because certain of his tendentious claims about Orwell have gained wide currency, but also because his response represents the process of defacement as it has typically been conducted with Orwell in literary journalism and in the popular press, especially by conservative journalists and commercial interests in 1983–84.[177] Hollis rewrote Orwell's convictions often without reference to Orwell's writings, minimized their differences, and then praised Orwell's good sense. Throughout *A Study of George Orwell* he summarized Orwell's views in terms congruent with his own and then "elaborated" Orwell's position by interspersing personal opinions so that the line between his and Orwell's ideas blurred. Frequently Hollis acknowledged Orwell's opposition to Catholic or Conservative positions, only to undercut Orwell's views as either misunderstandings or matters of minor detail. Or Hollis underlined the spiritual or preservative streak in Orwell's temper, and he suggested that Orwell's ideas really "point in the direction" of Christianity and Conservatism. Nowhere did Hollis quote any passage of Orwell's which implied a belief in the sanctity of private property—nor, indeed, for any of his other assertions in the passages above. We are left to suppose, charitably, that Hollis was reporting private conversations—though he rarely said so, apparently relying instead on the persuasive authority of his personal relationship with Orwell. These practices render Hollis' "claim" to Orwell, though it was never explicitly stated as such and involves no lengthy speculations about Orwell's posthumous opinions, more audacious than even Podhoretz's. If one were to read only Hollis' account of Orwell and not Orwell's writings, one might conclude that Orwell was a well-intentioned, if misguided, disciple of Burke and Robert Peel, insisting on reason rather than majority will as the foundation for law, on possession of private property as the basis for individual self-determination, on legislation from nature rather than from disputable "ideals," on the sacred importance of tradition, and on the moral free agency of the individual.

This is not to say that Hollis' image was "false." Rather, the fact is that English radicalism has characteristically possessed a backward-looking, rustic strand, traceable to Cobbett and Morris.[178] That Orwell valued personal liberty and certain English customs highly, and opposed birth control strongly, is clear. But this does not mean that he subscribed to these other

Conservative views, nor that he *was* a "Conservative" or "Christian" in any sense. Edward Thomas captures the distinction nicely in clarifying the relation between Orwell the revolutionary patriot and nostalgic moralist.

> . . . he was not a root-and-branch man. He belonged, not to the minority who want to topple an entire civilization, but to the larger number who would eradicate the chief injustices of their society but do not desire to abandon altogether the traditional moulds of life. Where Orwell wanted change, he wanted it whole-heartedly and actively. Evolutionary and historical theories of society are not his chief concern, and people who think in these terms are inclined to see in him a heroic dead end. Political writing was for him not a branch of knowledge but a form of action in defence of standards of which he felt reasonably certain, and this certainty seems to have been rooted in an unequivocal reaction to concrete experience. Just as his conservatism is founded on love of concrete objects and ways from the past, not on abstract veneration for tradition, so it is a feeling for particular injustices, not a doctrine of progress, that makes him a revolutionary.[179]

Kingsley Amis' remark that Hollis "cannot resist drawing Orwell in his own image" is exactly right.[180] *A Study of George Orwell* consists so much of Hollis' opinions and experiences, introduced and justified as a counter-standard to Orwell's own, that the book amounts to a self-study; its title could very well have appended the phrase "and Christopher Hollis." And here we recall Woodcock's astute observation that each of Orwell's old literary friends saw "only a facet" of him, but saw that facet very intensely.[181] Hollis obviously saw a version of Orwell's nostalgic and Quixotic side. And because their outlooks diverged so completely and their relationship began so early, this side of Orwell whom Hollis projected for the whole man is of even greater significance than in the case of left-wing friends who got to know him in the 1940s. Unlike Woodcock, Fyvel, Atkins, and Symons, Hollis obviously felt that he needn't rely on Orwell's writings for his knowledge of Orwell's early development, an assumption which partly carried over to his assessments of Orwell's mature work too. Moreover, all these other friends were Orwell's juniors, and all except Fyvel by a decade. By contrast, Hollis, two classes (or "elections") ahead of Blair at Eton, saw him as a peer and fellow Etonian, not as a model man of letters or his generation's shining example. Although Hollis felt a "deep respect" for Orwell,[182] he regarded him as a surprising success story. At least until *Animal Farm*, Hollis had made a much bigger mark in the world than Orwell. Thus, whereas Woodcock and the *Tribune* writers looked up to Orwell, Hollis looked at Orwell with a level gaze—or perhaps, for a time, slightly downward.[183]

Of course, by the time of the publication of Hollis' study of Orwell in 1956, the two men's fortunes had reversed. Hollis had retired from Parliament, having been passed over for the post of Minister of Education in the incoming 1951 Conservative government; Orwell was at the height of his critical and popular fame. And in part Hollis' book demythologizes Orwell, especially the heroic "true rebel" image of schoolboy Blair spawned by

Connolly's *Enemies of Promise*.[184] Yet Hollis did not seek—as did Rayner Heppenstall in his memoirs of the '50s[185]—to cut Orwell down to size. The timing of his book's appearance had little to do with his judgments therein. (Hollis said the same things in the same relentless way from the mid-1940s through the 1970s.[186]) Certainly recourse to the book's date does not take us beyond Amis' observation, to understand *why* Hollis found doing self-portraiture through Orwell so irresistible.

But Hollis' description of their Burma meeting provides a clue. The two Eton skeptics had gone their separate ways, and now Blair the tough Empire policeman and atheist faced off against Hollis the former Oxford Union president and recent Catholic convert. Hollis recalled thinking in 1925 that there was "no trace of liberal opinions" in "the imperial police-man" Blair. Later, he realized that Blair, in arguing with him, "was in some sense arguing with his second self," and as a result "exposed, in the complexity of his character, his imperial creed in a manner more crude and brutal than the truth demanded."[187]

One suspects similarly from *A Study of George Orwell* that, in arguing with Orwell over the years, Hollis was in some sense arguing with a second self, his former skeptical self at Eton so vividly evoked in the person of school-mate Blair-Orwell. Throughout Hollis's writings on Orwell it is indeed as if we are encountering one side—and merely the print version—of a lifelong running battle between these two College Pop debaters from Eton,[188] with each man's dominant side now confronted by his long-dormant secondary side in the arguments of his opponent. Orwell, as Crick suggests, may have flirted briefly in the early 1930s with Anglicanism;[189] and certainly for Hollis, Orwell's skepticism and radicalism must likewise have awakened echoes of a past self. For Hollis had, to use Bishop Blougram's widely quoted lines, exchanged "a life of doubt diversified by faith/For one of faith diversified by doubt."[190] Orwell obviously was a lifelong presence who pro-voked Hollis to defend his decision. Hollis even conceded in his introduction to *A Study of George Orwell* that he stood as a partial "convert" to Orwell's "doctrines." Clearly he considered his shadow-boxing book a last chance in turn to convert Orwell—a sort of final rebuttal, crammed with countless debater's points, to a lifetime of cordially contentious dispute:

> . . . the years were years of continuing friendly argument. . . . If as a result of all this I had been an obedient convert to every doctrine Orwell champi-oned, [this] book would have been tedious. If I had rejected and quarreled with every one of his doctrines, it would have been again as tedious. I should not think it justifiable to write such a book save about a man whom I deeply respect—about one to whom I thought it worthwhile to pay the final tribute of respect which is to explain the reason of difference where one differs. But we had, with a somewhat curious exactness, I fancy, enough in common and enough in difference to make argument between us stimulating.[191]

Both Hollis and Orwell came from families of moderate means, received scholarships to attend strict and fashionable prep schools, and attended

Eton College as King's Scholars. The years immediately following Eton were the dividing ones: both men underwent conversions, Blair to socialism after Wigan and Spain, Hollis to Catholicism at Oxford. If John Flory in *Burmese Days* is Orwell "as he imagined he might have been had he stayed in Burma," as Hollis puts it,[192] *A Study of George Orwell* reads as if Orwell were Christopher Hollis as *he* might have been if he had not gone to Oxford. For at Oxford Hollis became an "ardent disciple" of "the Chesterbelloc," adopting Belloc's ideas about the Church's magnificent European cultural tradition and Chesterton's Distributist notions about the dignity of small property and the need for the wide distribution of property.[193]

"Chesterbelloc" was the common intellectual legacy which Orwell and Hollis inherited as young men, and Hollis spends several pages in *A Study of George Orwell* defending Chesterton in particular against Orwell's attacks.[194] Indeed the key to Hollis' Catholic self-portrait of Orwell lies in his attempt to return Orwell to his Chestertonian roots—to his Christian "second self." Much as Podhoretz rewrote Orwell in his image through Sidney Hook, thus bolstering his political conversion to neoconservatism, the Catholic Hollis recast Orwell in his image by recasting him in Chesterton's, thereby reaffirming his religious conversion. The use of such a *mediating figure* is frequent in the rhetoric of reception. Usually a more familiar, closer, cherished presence for the receiver, the proximate figure serves a dual function. He helps bridge the gulf between the receiver and the Other because he shares features common to both of them, thus facilitating the receiver's urge (or assuaging his hesitancy) toward identification with (or appropriation of) the Other. And, perhaps paradoxically, the bridge figure enables the receiver to maintain necessary distance and better "control" his relationship with the Other, since through the bridge figure the receiver can more securely craft and define the new, mediated relationship.

One striking difference between Hollis' and Podhoretz's responses to Orwell, however, is that the link between Orwell and Chesterton is direct and conspicuous, not veiled. Orwell wrote about and admired Chesterton, and did resemble him in many ways—especially in his patriotism and his strong feeling for the commonplace and the common man, as Trilling noted in his introduction to *Homage to Catalonia*. Hollis, however, projects onto Orwell also those features of Chesterton which he himself shared: "love of small property," a "liking for rural life," "hatred of industrialism and big cities," opposition to monopolistic practices and big business. Some of these features are arguably Orwell's literary and personal attributes too—*in toto* they might amount to what Conor Cruise O'Brien once called Orwell's "Tory growl"[195]—but Hollis' emphases here implied that Orwell was an unreconstructed Distributist:

> Chesterton's essential case [in *The Napoleon of Notting Hill*]—the case that there was a grave danger in the growth of gigantic impersonal units—that there was an urgent necessity, if anything was to be saved, to give men "a thing to love"—was exactly Orwell's case. His quarrel with Chesterton was that Chesterton did damage to his own case by dressing it up in these

pantomime trappings, preaching it but preaching it as if it were a joke rather than a matter of urgency. It was necessary, thought Orwell, seriously and grimly to face the ugly dangers. . . . What was wanted in fact was the serious *1984* to rebuke the flippant *Napoleon of Notting Hill;* but Orwell's criticism of Chesterton was not that he had not asked a real question, but that he had not given a real answer.[196]

Hollis also set aside Orwell's objections to Chesterton's anti-Semitism and his inveterate tendency to take the Catholic side in every dispute, replying that Orwell did not understand how Chesterton's "deep and sincere Catholic faith" acted as an obligation to support the Church's positions.[197] Whereas Orwell thought Chesterton subordinated his intellectual integrity to an orthodoxy, Hollis saw him as a fellow convert and admirable Defender of the Faith whose passion occasionally resulted in bad judgments but which also "carried him far beyond the boundaries of politics and controversy and brought him in the end to something not very far short of sanctity." What Orwell saw as Chesterton's moral sell-out, Hollis regarded as his "depth of faith."[198] These differences over Chesterton constitute the heart of the difference between Orwell and Hollis, the socialist "outsider" and the Church apologist, on the writer's identity and the possibility of party allegiances. Once again, as has been the case with several other Orwell admirers, we confront the issue of the relation of the writer to politics—though this time the "party" is an organized religion. To the antinomian Orwell, Catholic "orthodoxy" was group conformity; to the churchman Hollis, "orthodoxy" meant "right reason." Orwell could not abide what struck him as Chesterton's betrayal of particular truths for an ideology; Hollis agreed with Chesterton that God is Truth, and that orthodox loyalty to the Church was humility before His earthly voice. And in defending Chesterton, Hollis was of course defending himself; his own loyalty to the Church had led him also to rationalize support for Mussolini, Franco, Father Coughlin, and even (most equivocally) the onetime Catholic Hitler.[199] The choice was indeed, as Orwell had said of Gandhi, "between God and Man," and Hollis and Chesterton had chosen their Church and their God.

Thus, whereas Chesterton remained a lifelong intellectual hero for Hollis, he was, in Hollis' words, "a hero of Orwell's youth, of whose hero-worship he afterwards grew a little ashamed."[200] Nevertheless there remained much of the Chesterbelloc in Orwell, whose *Nineteen Eighty-Four* is partly indebted not only to Chesterton's *The Napoleon of Notting Hill* but also to Belloc's *Servile State.* In any case, Hollis, coming to Belloc's and Chesterton's works in his teens as a disillusioned Anglican, never underwent Orwell's reaction.[201] Hollis was an admitted "hero-worshiper" of Belloc,[202] and his *Mind of Chesterton* (1970) is a glowing appreciation of the man and writer. A line from a Chesterton poem served as the title for Hollis' first volume of autobiography, *Along the Road to Frome.* If Orwell's was the road to Wigan Pier and Chesterton's common man, Hollis' was the road to Frome and Chesterton's Catholicism.

To Hollis, Orwell was a victim of the skepticism of the 1920s, which

Hollis had reacted against when he met Oxford's "facile" agnostic dons.[203] Possessing "little sense of history," Orwell was, said Hollis, an example of "the atheism of our generation," a modern intellectual who could not accept a belief in immortality because he associated it with Wordsworthian romanticism. Orwell was "the creature of a particular generation in which educated people thought less about a future life than people do since his day or than they ever did before it." Like the other *Tablet* writers, Hollis regarded Orwell as (in Chesterton's phrase) a "good agnostic," though also a "tragedy."[204] And here, in his resigned conclusion that Orwell was in the end an unbeliever, Hollis' Catholic-tinged reception of Orwell also differed from Podhoretz's. Whereas Podhoretz's response constituted reception as confident acquisition, Hollis' response was reception as ambivalent acknowledgment, as abandoned proselytism. Unlike Podhoretz, despite all his dialectics and wrangling, Hollis stopped just short in their debate's closing round of formally converting his absent opponent, ultimately refusing to go all the way and turn the Unwilling Convert into a Crusader-by-impressment. Hollis' Orwell remained a foot-dragging religious fellow-traveler. However jesuitical, it is a distinction, at least for Hollis, with a difference: the Catholic apologist would not finally "elect" Orwell a Catholic, or a Conservative, as Podhoretz had inducted Orwell into the neoconservative ranks. For a soul is "received" into the Church. Salvation cannot be self-willed or given by a friend; the redemptive act is the reception of grace. Hollis' Orwell was "a man of great integrity," even "a virtuous man." But he was not a Christian for the same reason that he was not a "saint." For a saint, though not necessarily an ascetic like Gandhi, concluded Hollis, was one who "has attained a special relationship with God, and it is hard to see how the word can bear any meaning to one who does not believe in God or in the possibility of a personal relationship with Him."[205]

## IV

Yet to some of the university-educated, working-class, "born" Catholics coming of age in 1960, Hollis and his generation of "Chesterbelloc" Catholics were themselves casualties of the 1920s, victims of reactionary political and theological dogmas of a bygone age. Radical Catholics in their twenties and thirties, many of them members of the Campaign for Nuclear Disarmament and the New Left, believed that they had little in common with the conservative English hierarchy and with *Tablet* churchmen like Hollis. More distant than their elders from the struggles through which English Catholicism had gone to survive, the younger generation also felt no pride in being different from other Englishmen or, often, even that they were possessors of "the one true Faith." Initially enthusiastic with the spirit of ecumenism and call for *aggiornamento* ("updating") by the Second Vatican Council (1962–65), by the mid-'60s most radicals also came to regard the Vatican II reforms as bourgeois and superficial. These so-called Catholic New Leftists or Catholic Marxists or Slantists, some of whom attended Cambridge University and

were strongly influenced there by Raymond Williams, proferred their own ecumenism, an idiosyncratic synthesis of Christianity and Marxism, with the emphasis being placed on the latter. *First the Political Kingdom* (1967), Brian Wicker's short history of those radicals who wrote for *Slant* and for the Dominican journal *New Blackfriars*, summarized the movement's priorities in a phrase. Militant Catholics ranged the Church on the side of revolutionary socialism, supported worker control of industry, urged the election of bishops and more power to the laity, and opposed the "segregated" system of "ghettoized" Catholic parishes and church schools. The Catholic leftists were certainly not the first European group to try to wed socialist and Christian thought. But they were the first to do so via Marx and to call themselves Marxists, and the rise of their movement owed at least as much to the recent history of English anti-nuclear activism and to the New Left as to Vatican II and the debates within the institutional Church over the vernacular liturgy and contraception.

The Catholic New Leftists were a disparate group. They included pacifists and nuclear disarmers (Walter Stein), Dominican theologians (Father Charles Davis, Father Herbert McCabe, Father Charles Boxer, Father Laurence Bright), and lay theologians with literary and linguistic interests (Wicker, Terry Eagleton, Adrian Cunningham, Neil Middleton, Martin Redfern, Hugo Meynell). This last-named faction, especially Wicker and Eagleton, devoted most attention to Orwell, who, though he exerted less influence upon Catholic leftists than other radicals, was nevertheless a presence. Probably the intellectual father of the *Slant* writers was Wicker, though the inspiration for his theological innovations came from Williams[206]—and so it was indirectly through Williams that the Catholic New Left first responded to Orwell, just as in the case of the secular New Left.

The Catholic New Left may be dated to Wicker's *Culture and Liturgy* (1963), in which the thirty-four-year-old Wicker reworked Williams' *Culture and Society*, arguing that any Church renewal of the liturgy was merely formalist unless it was accompanied by a political renewal of society. The Catholic liturgy, argued Wicker, was the Church's cultural life; and the Church was not meant to be a community unto itself but a mission to the world. The Mass was the vehicle of the Church's mission, and it belonged not to the clergy but to all God's people. Williams' idea that "culture is ordinary"[207] was recast into Wicker's call, "Liturgy is ordinary." As one of the first socialists to discuss "ordinary culture," Orwell was "extraordinarily relevant" to contemporary Catholicism, said Wicker.[208] For Orwell realized that an English political revolution had to be rooted in the national culture, in a patriotic sense of "Englishness"—just as a religious revolution within English Catholicism needed to emerge, whatever Catholicism's aspirations to ecumenism or transcendent unity, from within a living English culture.[209] And yet, said Wicker, although Orwell was "a great writer," he was also "par excellence the tragic figure."[210] But unlike Hollis, Wicker did not see Orwell's "tragedy" as his lack of faith, but rather his obsession with personal integrity and the fate of the individual, which disabled his social-

ism. Placing Williams' Orwell of *Culture and Society* within a theological context, Wicker saw Orwell as "the non-religious socialist" whose "no-nonsense outlook was unconsciously shaped by the acceptance of a naive empiricism."[211]

Unlike Hollis and the *Tablet* writers, then, Wicker was more troubled by Orwell's philosophical credulity than his atheism, in part because he believed that the main weakness of the early, "cultural" New Left was that it "tackled social and moral problems without an adequate philosophy of man."[212] Wicker hoped that Christian theology might fill this gap, and in *Culture and Theology* (1966) he discussed how it might do so—and why the tradition represented by English "empiricists" like Orwell would not serve. As had the New Left by 1962 when it evolved from its "cultural" to its "radical" phase, Wicker judged the English cultural tradition confining, and he therefore widened his concept of culture to embrace contemporary continental philosophy.[213] Wicker's liberation theology consisted of an odd congeries of Marcel, Eliade, Merleau Ponty, the early Marx and the later Wittgenstein, through whom he explored parallels between the Fall and alienation, sin and exploitation, salvation and emancipation, and the body of Christ and the community of Man.

Wicker's judgment of Orwell also grew harsher. In such philosophical company, Orwell appeared to Wicker a vulgar pragmatist. And here we notice that, whereas Hollis and the *Tablet* conservatives had seen a spiritualized image of Orwell as Chesterton's "good agnostic," the Catholic radicals saw a version of Williams' anti-populist image of Common Man Orwell. Two generations removed from Orwell and Hollis, young radicals in this third stage of Orwell's Catholic reception did not talk about Orwell's "saintliness" or "goodness"; they responded, for the most part, not to the man but to his work (or to the man as a social type). Indeed, to have discussed Orwell in Hollis' terms would have run counter to the basic critique of the Church by the Catholic Left, which was that the liberal-minded Church gave too much attention to the sanctity of isolated individuals and not enough to the material and social environment.

Wicker's Orwell was not an "ex-socialist" like Williams. Nor was he a saintly "extraordinary ordinary" man like Atkins' or Spender's Orwell. He was "a naive realist," an "ordinary" man in the sense of exemplifying "the average nonphilosophical Englishman." Orwell's epistemology was mere common sense. He thought he could simply look at the world as wholly other and record it via his "saner self." But his Cartesian presuppositions led him, fatally, to a form of self-exile, said Wicker. Orwell's radical philosophical dualisms between observer and world, language and thought, word and object made communion with his fellow man impossible, for he imagined that the writer could split himself in two and "stand apart." According to Wicker, although Orwell was rightly suspicious of the tyrannical caprice of public opinion and believed in the values of authority and law, he did not see that his empiricism disposed him to reject as "orthodoxy" those doctrines, like Catholicism, which grounded such values. Whatever could not be sup-

ported by concrete evidence was "orthodoxy." "Emotionally and morally," Orwell remained a socialist, Wicker conceded, but his common-sense outlook was inadequate to secure his socialist ideals of brotherhood and equality. For he mistakenly thought that socialism could retain the "ethic" of Christianity without some "theology." Unable to fathom "the substance of things unseen," Orwell did not realize that the need was not to reject metaphysics altogether but to find an orthodoxy in which personal integrity and conscience were integral to the creed itself. Christianity is that creed, Wicker said. Thomas More showed that "sanity is not statistical": he was the "last man" whom Winston Smith should have been.[214]

Orwell was indeed "a heroic dead end" for an admirer so theoretically minded as Wicker, as Edward Thomas had forecast. Wicker failed to grasp Thomas' insight that Orwell's empiricism was the *source* of his specially "English" radicalism—that Orwell's love of concrete experience inspired and enflamed his feeling for particular injustices. Nonetheless, this academic treatment of Orwell's limitations by Wicker, a Birmingham University English instructor (and, like Williams, a teacher in adult education, from which many Catholic radicals emerged), marked a sharp departure from that of the *Tablet* writers. So, of course, did his and the more militant Slantists' reliance on non-Christian and Marxist authorities. "The Church's Red Guards," Woodruff labeled the Slantists, dismissing their attempts to "impose" a political program on Catholicism as "nefarious nonsense." "The cult term of the decade," Waugh characterized the Slantist call for a "priesthood of the laity." Wicker's focus on philosophical and linguistic issues also dismayed secular New Left critics like Williams, who worried that Wicker was merely engaged in an internal Church argument and was "appropriating" the radical critique.[215]

Though a convert himself, Wicker was clearly a new breed of English Catholic. Like Hollis, he argued at length with Orwell, but he felt no impulse to "convert" Orwell posthumously; his self-appointed task was ecumenical, not apologetic. Wicker admitted that the Church did represent an oppressive force historically, as Orwell charged. If Orwell needed a theology, Wicker suggested, Catholics needed a humane politics. Less defensive than Hollis, Wicker emphasized not that unbelievers needed to remain open to God's grace but that the Church needed to change. If Wicker sought to convert the world to Catholicism, his approach was to convert Catholicism to the world. Catholics needed to be more conspicuous on the road from Wigan Pier to Aldermaston.

> Only a radical adjustment of the Church's practical posture toward the modern world, through the development of a constructive theology of toleration, will be able to convince honest disbelievers like Orwell, who are concerned for the survival of decency and truth, that it has the answer to their problem.[216]

From one angle "their problem" was epistemological, but from another side it was intensely personal—and also Wicker's own: the problem—and

one of this study's recurrent leitmotifs—of the writer's relation to politics. Given that Wicker endured charges from the Left that he was emasculating socialism and from his co-religionists that he was bleaching the distinctive character of Catholicism and turning it into a hodgepodge, it was perhaps inevitable that, in an act of self-scrutiny, he would be drawn to grapple with "the problem"—and to assert, *pace* Orwell, that honest writing and full political commitment *were* possible. Orwell's compartmentalized "double life" was "simply a confession of failure," said Wicker.[217] Caught between two worlds, the political and the religious, Wicker tried—valiantly but without success—to suture them together.

The Church could answer Orwell's fears that group allegiances and personal integrity were incompatible, said Wicker. In effect the answer was that the Church become a group to which an individual could give his allegiance and not give up the world or his integrity—that Catholicism become, as it were, an ideal orthodoxy. Trying to "update" the Church, Wicker strove to reconcile Church authority with freedom of thought and speech, to make the Church an open, pluralistic society to which "honest disbelievers like Orwell" could belong. In Wicker's political and spiritual kingdom, the man of letters who entered politics would not have to split himself in two. Orwell had declared that the Church's existence "made true socialism impossible, because its influence is and always must be against freedom of thought and speech, against human equality, and against any form of society tending to promote earthly happiness."[218] But Wicker argued that the Church and the world had changed sufficiently by 1965 to make a Christian-Marxist humanism possible:

> It is perhaps possible in this post-Orwell, post-John XXIII world to believe that the saner self does not have to stand aside in sceptical honesty, but can once more take part in the world's activity. Such activity is not necessarily dirty business, as Orwell thought it was; but we must show unmistakably that being a Catholic is not itself a dirty business, a subservience to a smelly little orthodoxy.[219]

Essentially, Wicker was trying to perform the same roles for Catholic intellectuals that Orwell had assumed for socialists: critic and conscience. Ironically, while rejecting Orwell's analysis of the writer's relation to politics, Wicker adopted his "outsider" stance. But the struggle of slanting Catholics toward the Left and the Left toward Catholicism proved too much for the nascent movement, which collapsed not long after *Slant*'s demise in 1970. Its efforts to restructure the Church, to revitalize Catholic culture through the liturgy, and to articulate a Christian-Marxist humanism had barely begun.[220]

Unlike Williams, Wicker has never turned hostile toward Orwell. More temperate in his politics and less passionate in his response to Orwell than Williams, Wicker and most Catholic leftists never admired Orwell so wholeheartedly nor repudiated him so completely. Instead the more moderate Wicker has been, in the phrase of one historian, a "Catholic Richard Hoggart."[221] Like Hoggart, Wicker grew more sympathetic toward Orwell as

the '60s progressed. Just as Williams was experiencing Orwell as an onerous presence, Wicker was growing convinced that Orwell's criticism of the Old Left as "over-theoretical" and intolerant also applied to the New.[222]

If there was a "Catholic Raymond Williams," it was his student Terry Eagleton, the twenty-one-year-old undergraduate co-founder of *Slant* in 1964, editor (with Wicker) of the 1966 *Slant Manifesto*, author of *The New Left Church* (1966), and a contributor to Williams' 1967 *May Day Manifesto*. In Williams' view, the Catholic radicals were valuable to the New Left because it was easier for Catholics than for socialists to criticize liberalism, since socialists had always to answer for the abuses of freedom by "socialist" regimes like Russia.[223] Decrying its moral callousness and expedient reformism, Eagleton pamphleteered vigorously against "liberal paternalism"—and against paternalist liberals like Orwell.

Like Williams, Eagleton grew more disaffected with Orwell as he accompanied the New Left on its far leftward travels in the late '60s—but like E.P. Thompson, his engagement with Orwell was never so personal as Williams', and he too has had little to say about Orwell in recent years. Eagleton first appreciated essays like "Politics and the English Language" for their "demystification" of political language.[224] But as he moved from Catholic radicalism through "Catholic leninism" to Althusserian Marxism—a shift roughly contemporaneous with Williams' evolution from culture critic to Marxist theoretician—his interest in Orwell diminished. In *Exiles and Émigrés* (1970), published at the moment of his transition from theological Leninist to structural Marxist,[225] Eagleton advanced a Lukácsian sociology of the novel, including analyses of Orwell's early novels. Great writers, Eagleton argued, "totalize" and thereby "transcend" their experience. But Orwell was too much the bourgeois skeptic to believe that socialist theory could provide such a "totalization." According to Eagleton, whereas a Catholic novelist like Graham Greene possessed a "structure" which rendered routine experience intelligible down to its smallest details, the liberal Orwell, like Dorothy Hare, was left with the raw material of experience on the one hand and a scorned "ideology" on the other, with neither viable. The first was too much the stuff of the emotions and the ephemeral; the second, detached from the first, was a "pansy" abstraction. Like Flory, Dorothy, Comstock, and Bowling, Orwell was a man caught between defiant moral gesture and the embrace of "drably normative life," said Eagleton. Adjusting this biographical reading of Orwell's fiction to the conclusions about Orwell in Williams' *Culture and Society*—and anticipating the "paradox" thesis of Williams' *George Orwell*—Eagleton argued that his characters' failings constituted Orwell's own "paradox." But whereas Williams approached Orwell's situation historically, seeing Orwell as a man trapped in a contradiction of advanced capitalism, Eagleton, working from the novels, treated the "paradox" more strictly in terms of social class. Eagleton's Orwell represented the paradox of the lower-middle-class hero generally, the dilemma of a class marooned between "orthodox decencies and deprivation, unable either to fully accept or reject the social system and so critical of common life and its alternatives."[226]

Much as for Williams, Orwell "got in the way" of Wicker and Eagleton. But Orwell was a different, relatively minor obstacle for Catholic radicals. If he was a towering statue lodged massively in the path of the leftward-marching secular radicals, a figure whom Williams and the New Left could hardly avoid, he was more like a tunnel overpass, with toll charge, for the Catholics—a constricting, conscience-pricking presence insofar as he represented the liberal English tradition and yet, finally, a writer who could be circumnavigated. Catholic radicals mainly sought out Orwell, rather than felt enveloped by his shadow. They found him suitably illustrative of what they aimed to move past, rather than central to it; he posed, more disturbingly than anyone else, the problem of the intellectual's involvement in politics, but otherwise he was not difficult to detour around—there were, after all, numerous alternate ways to exemplify parochial Englishness and shallow liberalism.

Thus, however relevant they occasionally acknowledged Orwell to be, the Slantists chiefly found him inconvenient or impeding. Dedicated to accelerating the post-conciliar *aggiornamento*, Catholic leftists typically found Orwell "out of date," as Martin Green, a Slantist sympathizer, explained to Catholic readers.[227] In a decade whose intellectuals embraced the flamboyance and melodrama of what Green called the "Faustian" temperament, Orwell stood for the "old-fashioned" values of the "Erasmian" temperament—moderation, modesty, decency, irony, exactness.[228] Catholic radicals were looking for a Luther, not an Erasmus; much as in the case of the New York Intellectuals' reception of Orwell, whereas in the '50s Orwell was too radical for Catholic intellectuals, in the '60s he seemed too moderate.

V

The "Erasmian" temperament was back in vogue two decades later, but no longer was Orwell a discernible presence of any sort for Catholic intellectuals, even though numerous tributes to him appeared in the Catholic press during the 1984 countdown. But these differed not at all from those in the secular press; they were not identifiably *Catholic* responses at all.[229] Unlike Wicker in 1969, no English Catholic wondered about what Orwell's attitude toward the Church would be "in the post-Vatican II and post-*Humanae Vitae* age."[230] And in this we are reminded that a wide variety of institutional affiliations condition reader response. A sign of the weakening through time of a group's identity may be the disappearance of its special imprint in its later reception history of figures. A figure like Orwell, then, may still be admired, but he is no longer recast in the group's image. By the 1980s, English Catholic intellectuals were no longer defensive and exclusivist. But the price of their full assimilation into the secular world was the loss of their traditional "Chesterbelloc Catholic" identity.[231] That English Catholicism had become more pluralistic, ecumenical, and catholic, if less Catholic,

was perhaps the most significant, albeit little-noticed, legacy of the '60s Catholic radicals.

The unusual inversion which Orwell's Catholic reputation underwent within a decade, first shaped by the Right and then the Left, not only points up the sea change in the Catholic intellectual environment but also illumines two larger conceptual issues. First, it further clarifies the relation between reputation-formation and secondary factors of critical location. In the 1960s, political factors assumed priority over religious concerns for Catholic intellectuals, and accordingly, the terms in which they discussed Orwell shifted from the moral to the populist. That is, to reverse Hollis and Cardinal Manning: most differences of opinion in the '60s turned out to be at bottom not theological but ideological. And yet, theology conditioned Orwell's reception indirectly: the Slantists' leftist ideology transformed the Catholic image of Orwell, but their theological concerns proved sufficiently important to reorient the Slantists outside the main line of Orwell's influence, so that he never became a radiant figure for them and never blocked them from moving in new directions.

Secondly, Orwell's Catholic reception sheds additional light on the intricate connections between image-making and the dynamics of reference groups and subgroups in literary reception. The case study makes explicit a fact about group identity which we touched on in discussing the *Partisan* Orwell of the late '60s and the *Tribune* writers' Orwell—that there are groups within groups within groups, and that members of different subgroups often experience a communal identity like "Catholic," or even "Catholic intellectual," very differently. The Slantist response to Orwell indicates how a subgroup, ostensibly working out of a certain larger group's tradition ("English Catholicism") yet which considers the tradition's current intellectual leaders (the *Tablet* writers) irrelevant to its vision, may relate to an outsider figure like Orwell without even an awareness of his previous reception history within the tradition—even as, all along, the subgroup advances claims to its legitimate inheritance of the tradition. Rather than formally repudiate the image presented by those Establishment intellectuals generally seen as representing the larger group, the subgroup, trying to build a tradition of its own, may respond to a visible, broadly influential figure like Orwell via the preoccupations of a more like-minded tradition and group (the New Left). The Slantists, that is, simply ignored the *Tablet* image of Orwell, continued to call themselves "Catholics" (indeed, "true" Catholics[232]), and approached Orwell from the angle of his alternate reception history by the New Left. The counter-instance of a subgroup contesting the prevailing image of Orwell was the case of the New York neoconservatives, who disputed the Left's view of Orwell, eventually broke with the Left, disclaimed the "utopian" *Partisan Review* heritage, inaugurated themselves as an independent group with their own emergent tradition, and started devising a pedigree in which Orwell figured as a distinguished ancestor. Like the neoconservatives, of course, though less self-consciously, the

Slantists had also begun to construct an intellectual genealogy for their movement—but their secular heroes were the early Marx and the later Wittgenstein, not Orwell.

Which perhaps was just as well. For whether they charted their missionary route to the Kingdom according to Chestertonian or Marxist geography, it is not easy to imagine the Unwilling Convert concurring with "the enemy" that his road to Wigan Pier was also their path to Rome.

## 22.  Canonization and the Curriculum: Orwell in the Classroom

I

"Canonization" and 'St. George' have served as fertile organizing metaphors throughout this chapter on The Saint. In this last case study we examine another institutional sphere which has been conditioned by these two terms. Here we explore not attempted annexations of Orwell's name to any litany of religious or secular "saints," but rather a subject which we touched on in Part One: the place of *Animal Farm, Nineteen Eighty-Four*, and the essays in school curricula. This section is a portrait of The Saint as canonized author.

'St. George' Orwell's reputation as The Model Stylist and The Defender of the King's English arises primarily from images of the writer rather than the man. Yet to a large degree Orwell's status as a "pure stylist" is based upon the essays and documentaries, genres in which the writer speaks directly in the man's name and about his real-life experiences—and which therefore spotlight Orwell's "inspiring" literary personality and "authentic" voice. At least insofar as Orwell's place in school curricula is attributable to his nonfiction, the image of the man, and of the man within the writings—and the assumption of the transparency between the two ("the style is the man")—have been crucial to his "canonization." In recent years, however, more than one teacher has protested the hosannas. Criticizing the inflated reputation of "Politics and the English Language" as "the Classic-Statement-About-the-Abuse-of-Language-by-Politicians," an angry English composition teacher in the late '70s bemoaned that schools had "canonized Orwell as a certified Good Guy, Freedom Fighter, Lover of the People, [and] popular instructor of the masses . . . about the evils of totalitarian socialism. . . . In brief: *Saint George*."[233]

Certainly the fitness and power of 'St. George' as an encapsulating, generative watchword "summing up" Orwell's reputation is partly due to the history of Orwell's prominent place in Anglo-American schoolrooms and to the homage which his work has often received from teachers. Even if there are no Orwell societies or journals, two awards sponsored by the National Council of Teachers of English (NCTE) testify to Orwell's checkered *blackwhite* reputation and his curious dual role as prose guardian and laureate. Following Orwell's "intention to expose inhumane, propagandist uses of

language," the NCTE's Committee on Public Doublespeak presents the ironic tribute of the Doublespeak Award to a deserving public figure; and the NCTE also annually bestows the George Orwell Award for Distinguished Contribution to Honesty and Clarity in Public Language. No other English or American writer has prompted the establishment of tributes to his legacy by an official national body like the NCTE; and certainly no other author's work has inspired positive and ironic awards in his name.[234]

Who can doubt that the widespread and lasting entry of an author's work into formal school and university curricula is of monumental importance to his reputation? If his work becomes "required reading" in school syllabuses, it reaches countless readers at an early age, receives support from the publishing industry, and tends to attract increased critical attention. But one critic's caustic observation that the "Orwell 'phenomenon' " would not exist if Orwell's work had not gone through the "mills of the institutions of 'learning' and 'taste' " takes us little way in explaining how in fact an author gets canonized and how the process can help make him a literary figure. Understanding the story of Orwell's academic reputation is not merely a matter of "dissect[ing]" his "sacred place in the school curriculum."[235] For that place, however sacred, is also highly ramified; Orwell's educational status is a puzzling mix of elevations and exclusions, what we might call reception as selective official enshrinement. Again we see the ideology of repute in operation, for if one focuses on a single educational level alone, one mistakes Orwell either as ubiquitously "sacred" or altogether absent in Anglo-American curricula. In fact, secondary school and introductory college composition courses make much use of *Animal Farm*, *Nineteen Eighty-Four*, and the essays; but rarely do advanced undergraduate and graduate students encounter Orwell's work in their English courses.

Such discrepancies in academic reputation, though they are by no means unique to Orwell, nevertheless warrant emphasis, as does the unusual variability of his reputation across intellectual, popular and academic spheres of reception, which we noted in Part One. Previous case studies in Part Two have drawn attention to the diverse images of Orwell projected by literary-political intellectuals and by the mass media and advertising industry; here we discuss the heretofore little-examined third major sphere of his reputation, the academy. Likewise, whereas prior reception scenes featured attention to ideological, generational, national, and gender contexts of institutional reader response, this case study approaches Orwell chiefly from the standpoint of readers' professional affiliations: i.e., readers as students, classroom teachers, and academic critics. In this section, then, the institutional setting of the reading act is more sharply defined: we look at how Orwell is being read in the academy, "in the classroom." Before us, we should imagine, is a mammoth "school portrait" of Orwell. Its background is the postwar Anglo-American educational scene, but the setting is peopled by countless students and teachers of Orwell's work. The scene focuses on them and their "curricular" Orwell, rather than on the Orwell of the scholars and specialized journals.

Our attention in this facial history is therefore directed less toward the various scholarly interpretations of Orwell's writings by academic "critic-readers" than toward his reputation among classroom "teacher-readers" and "student-readers." This emphasis will allow us to pursue further, beyond our suggestions in the case studies on Orwell's image in popular culture and the mass media, the dynamics of reputation-formation. Most case studies in Part Two have focused on the reception of Orwell's work; here we attend also to the historical-institutional context of its production, distribution, and transmission in the schools and in educational publishing.

We will return to these conceptual points as we relate the anomalies of Orwell's present-day educational institutionalization and their implications for canon- and reputation-formation to the development of his curricular reputation. This history has evolved on three distinct educational levels (junior and senior high school, and college) and in four phases since the early 1950s.*

## II

How and when do books and authors become canonized in British and American schools and universities? Amid all the calls in the 1970s and '80s to "open up" the canon and the fine studies on the theoretical issues involved in canon-formation, this practical question has gone unexplored in the literary academy. And indeed, there is no simple or systematic way to answer it. The several plurals in the question rightly imply, however, that distinctive canons obtain for educational levels and nations. This reminds us that, as we saw in Part One, quite apart from the "high" canon taught in upper-division university literature courses (The Great Tradition), a multiplicity of canons—pertaining to books, authors, genres, periods, national and regional literatures, institutional levels, and many other categories of literary repute—exists, formally or informally scaled according to aesthetic and other criteria.

Like most countries, neither the U.S. nor Britain has a national syllabus of required school texts. In the U.S., individual schools, or school districts, usually establish curricula. Only elementary school textbooks are chosen at the state level (and only in 22 states).[236] The traditional British "set book" policy, however, in which readings are "set" for external examinations by regional Examination Boards in cooperation with their Local Education Authorities, introduces a greater measure of uniformity and consensus about appropriate school texts—though by no means a "national canon." Orwell's work—specifically *Animal Farm*—first entered English O[rdinary]-level (15 to

---

*I base this historical reconstruction on teachers' discussions of curricula in British and American education journals, on personal correspondence with British and American education officials, on American study guides of *Animal Farm* and *Nineteen Eighty-Four*, on the contents of anthologies and composition textbooks, on personal conversations with instructors who have taught Orwell, and on my own experience as a college and high school teacher of English and composition.

16-year-olds) classes in the 1950s. Composed of examiners and teachers, Examination Boards for O-level (and sometimes for the AO (Alternative Ordinary) level) began prescribing *Animal Farm* as a set book every three or four years after 1958. (The fable is often read in British classes before the O-level year, at the age of thirteen or fourteen, whether or not it is studied for the external examinations.[237]) *Animal Farm* appears to have entered American eighth- to tenth-grade classrooms at roughly the same time.

Why did *Animal Farm* join *Silas Marner* and *Great Expectations* as a standard fiction assignment in many Anglo-American schoolrooms in the late 1950s? "It is such a useful teaching text for pupils of a wide range of ability," wrote one British education official. "It is short, entertaining, makes a suitable impact, and is acceptable at a variety of levels."[238] Surely brevity, readability, perceived literary merit, and sufficiency to the assigned task and grade level have been significant considerations—as in the case of such mainstays as *Silas Marner* and *Great Expectations.* But politically wary teachers might justly cast a cold eye on talk about the "usefulness" and "suitable impact" of *Animal Farm.* Indeed many interacting and overlapping factors, impossible to weigh precisely—some quite routine and others historically specific and particular to *Animal Farm*—obviously contributed to its acceptance in the 1950s: its wide availability in cheap paperback editions, the turn by American high schools away from anthology selections and back toward "high quality" paperback books, the shift toward contemporary literature in American secondary schools, the new orientation of the NCTE toward a balance of socially relevant and artistically respected fiction in the late '50s, the convenient existence of the 1954 cartoon film, the effects of the Cold War on Anglo-American curricula, the easy use of *Animal Farm* as an anti-Communist and anti-revolutionary "lesson"—all these factors, plus Orwell's rising status among intellectuals and the TV public's growing familiarity with Orwell's work in the wake of the 1953 NBC and 1954 BBC television adaptations of *Nineteen Eighty-Four,* doubtless helped lay the groundwork for the fable's canonization (and for the adoption of *Nineteen Eighty-Four* as a school novel a few years later).[239]

Equally important is the related question of how *Animal Farm* was actually taught in the 1950s and '60s. It is clear that the Cold War affected some English school programs, especially in the U.S.,[240] but hard to determine its precise impact on Orwell's work. Scattered evidence suggests that teachers, then and now, have veered between two pedagogical approaches. Some have presented *Animal Farm* as an entertaining story, tacking on the bromide that "Power corrupts" but downplaying the Russian parallels (as does the Halas-Batcheler film). Other teachers have taught it point-by-point as a horrifying "animallegory" of Soviet despotism. Study guides dating from the mid-'60s (e.g., Cliff's Notes and Monarch Notes) take the latter approach, usually offering chapter-by-chapter summaries of the correspondences between Russian history and the fable's characters and events. Among the guides' sample "test questions" are the following, each of which receives a two-paragraph "model" answer:[241]

- Whom do Snowball and Napoleon represent?
- How may the character of Boxer be interpreted?
- Assemble details which obviously refer to characteristic aspects of Russian society. The decorations given and the naming of battles are two. Find as many as you can.

O-level exam questions in England, though more sophisticated, have been similarly phrased and have leaned in the same political direction, as the three questions below from two 1964 exams illustrate:[242]

- Give an account of the building of the Windmill and its interruptions; show how far this affected the animals and what, in real life, it is meant to represent.
- Describe the origins of the seven commandments, and give an account of the changes they underwent later. What was Orwell's satire directed against in this part of the book?
- Write an essay defending *Animal Farm* against a reader who tells you that it is "merely anti-communist propaganda." Illustrate your answer with detailed reference to the book.

Questions like this last one instruct students to "defend" *Animal Farm* by way of subtly inculcating a standard of political taste; the very tone of the question disposes the examinee to imagine that any radical critic of Orwell is invariably a tiresome nuisance, a "mere" propagandist himself. (One easily forgets Orwell's oft-declared view that "all art is propaganda.") Such questions do indeed verge on "a manipulative form of 'thought policing'," in one radical's phrase,[243] and their ideological thrust is transparent. Another leftist, D.A.N. Jones, a teacher of Nigerian children in the 1950s, has written that his Commonwealth text of *Animal Farm* stressed Orwell's anti-Communism and passed over his socialist convictions altogether.* The fable was chosen as a set book for the colonies, Jones has claimed, because it was "a clear-cut expression of the anti-Communist orthodoxy."[245] Such a claim is impossible to verify. The preface to the special Overseas edition of *Animal Farm* by Longman in 1960, however, treats the fable as a general satire on revolution and makes no mention of Russia, Marx, Lenin, or Stalin.[246]

Still, the prevalence of questions like those above since the 1950s suggests the structural "fit" between the demand, whether overt or implicit, for anti-Communist propaganda and a "simple lesson" like *Animal Farm*. Just as *Homage to Catalonia* filled a social-psychological "need" within the liberal American intelligentsia for an unapologetic moral and political condemnation of 1930s Communism in Spain, *Animal Farm* filled, as probably no other contemporary work could, a public need during the Cold War era

_____

*If so, it would come as little surprise. The preface to the 1956 Signet paperback edition of *Animal Farm*, which has sold several million copies, does the same. It quotes from "Why I Write": "Every line I have written since 1936 has been written, directly or indirectly, against totalitarianism. . . ."—thus vaporizing the last clause ("and for democratic socialism, as I understand it") and Orwell's radicalism too. Such flagrant use of ellipses is, unfortunately, an all-too-common practice in the politics of reputation.[244]

to wipe out the Communist menace, especially in the schools, and thereby safeguard impressionable youth.[247] Alan Brown has argued persuasively that the fable has typically been taught since the 1950s as a "simple equivalence" between Soviet history and the book's events, with the students then eagerly mining the allegory for parallels. The correspondences then become the basis for rote-learning, with students "regurgitat[ing] the equations of Cold War wisdom."[248] My own experience in teaching *Animal Farm*, along with the film adaptation, to tenth grade students in the 1970s, partly confirms Brown's indictment: I found my own teaching tending toward these reductive practices, despite my attempts at nuance. Sometimes students concluded (guided by their study guides) that the fable's version of history constituted the whole story; a few student essays slid into anti-Soviet tirades. And yet such dangers are hard to avoid entirely if *Animal Farm* is actually taught as a satiric allegory. I discovered that much of the excitement of the re-reading experience for my students lay in their realizing that the book *was* an allegory with a serious subtext (of which many were unaware until class discussion). With 14- and 15-year-old students who have never even heard the names Lenin and Stalin, it may not be possible to present the intricacies of socialist theory and Soviet history. Once again, the plain style masks the intricate context. Indeed it may be that this little book, so simple on the surface, should be saved for the eleventh and twelfth grades. I have found that college freshmen discuss well all the issues which *Animal Farm* raises—e.g., the Russian Revolution, Bolshevism, utopianism, the rewriting of history, the allegory and fable as literary forms.

## III

Although a 1955 secondary school survey showed that *Nineteen Eighty-Four* was one of thirty novels most commonly read by college-bound seniors,[249] it was not widely taught in schools until the early 1960s. Its entry into senior high school classrooms at this time marks a second stage and level of Orwell's canonization. (The timing should make clear that, although Cold War politics doubtless conditioned *how* Orwell's work was taught, it was not the prime determining factor in the *selection* of Orwell's books for classroom use.)

*Nineteen Eighty-Four* occupies a different, and less secure, place than *Animal Farm* in school canons. Invariably, it is read at more advanced grades; it belongs to what could be called the "senior high school canon," whereas *Animal Farm* would normally be classed in the "junior high school canon." In the U.S., *Nineteen Eighty-Four* is most frequently read in the twelfth grade, sometimes as a science fiction novel. In England it has sometimes been a set book for A [dvanced] -level (17 to 18-year-olds) students, though it has never been so popular an examination text as *Animal Farm* (except during 1983–84).[250]

Numerous reasons account for *Nineteen Eighty-Four* being less frequently taught than *Animal Farm* in schools. In America, its greater length has

probably deterred teachers from assigning it. Whereas teachers not bound to anthologies are frequently encouraged to innovate in their selection of poems, plays, and short fiction for syllabuses, curricular guides often advise caution in the choice of full-length novels, since a month or more of class time may be required for a novel.[251] Parents and educators have also found the love scene between Winston and Julia objectionable; a few school boards have even banned *Nineteen Eighty-Four*. Controversy about its sexual content was probably a key factor in its delayed entry into American schoolrooms. Even during the McCarthy era, parental opposition to *Nineteen Eighty-Four* on moral grounds was evidently more powerful than anti-Communist support for it on political grounds.[252]

In England, where censorship in the schools is rarely a community issue, the examination structure largely explains why *Nineteen Eighty-Four* is less often set as an exam book than *Animal Farm*. *Nineteen Eighty-Four* does not easily fit examiners' expectations for texts at either O- or A-level. Understandably, it is often regarded as too difficult to be an O-level set book. One A-level paper for which it could be assigned is the Practical Criticism exam, where traditional critical standards (organic unity, character development, etc.) have often made it appear inappropriate, a "failed" novel possessing insufficient literary merit. As the following three A-level questions from 1972–73 illustrate, the judgment of the book's failure is usually advanced indirectly. Students are invited to "agree" with rather than contest, the authoritative statements (enshrined in quotation marks) by anonymous examiners that *Nineteen Eighty-Four* is "diminished" as literature by its political purpose:[253]

- "*1984* is unashamedly a book with a message." Do you consider that this diminishes its merits as a novel?
- "The political message is constantly getting in the way of the story, and this diminishes its interest and excitement." Do you agree with this view of *1984*?
- "Characterisation in this novel is negligible. It is completely subordinated to the political message." Do you agree?

The very idea of testing readers about a book indicates how the conditions of the institutional student-reader differ from those of most other institutional readers. And this raises the large, elusive question of how the institutional reading experience of Orwell—as a classroom assignment—has conditioned his public reputation. But we should distinguish between those books set for examinations and those suggested as "outside" reading. Studies show that students strongly prefer books they choose to read, and that they enjoy a book less once it becomes an examination subject.[254] *Nineteen Eighty-Four* is possibly read more outside class than for class by students; reading surveys show that it is one of the few "classics" many students buy for leisure reading. This element of student choice probably has contributed to its popularity among students. In a 1969 survey, university-bound British and American students ranked *Nineteen Eighty-*

*Four* among their most "personally significant" books. British students also listed Orwell in fourth position as "the author who had greatest influence on them."[255] A 1971 survey among A-level students found Orwell, after Lawrence, the most popular "serious" author (with Hardy third, and Shakespeare fourth).[256] Orwell was also the only author with two books among students' top twenty "favorites," as judged by a 1975 survey of American teachers.[257] Asked to suggest titles which should be added to the required English program, both British and American students also cited *Nineteen Eighty-Four* among their first choices. (One wonders whether such a curricular change would undercut *Nineteen Eighty-Four*'s appeal, particularly since most of the students' suggested additions were "forbidden fruit," in the survey editor's phrase—e.g., *Catcher in the Rye* and *Brave New World*.)[258]

A great deal of reading is conducted, of course, within the school as a social institution, with numerous attendant advantages and constraints. Certainly many teacher-readers and critic-readers return to Orwell, not always eagerly, with a professional purpose (to teach, to write criticism). The student-reader, however, is in a slightly different situation. For perhaps the majority of students, even their first reading of Orwell's work is not self-initiated: they encounter *Animal Farm* and *Nineteen Eighty-Four* as "required reading." Possibly the vast majority of young readers would never otherwise read Orwell, and doubtless many of them profit from reading him under the guidance of teachers. Surely a large number, however, do not enjoy reading Orwell in class, and find the experience vulgar with purpose in that its end is examination performance. One 1979 British educational report found that reading had been "impoverished" in secondary schools by a concentration on exam requirements.[259] Another report showed that Practical Criticism is the exam most frequently failed at A-level.[260] (One recalls the attitude of the author of "Such, Such Were the Joys" toward exams.) The situation may be even worse in Britain than in the U.S., at least during the O- and A-level years, when the small number of set books are sometimes analyzed in excessive detail, critical terminology is drummed into students, and classes are turned into cram sessions—all directed toward an artificial situation, in which the student has an hour, without the text, to deal with topics like "the merits of *Nineteen Eighty-Four* as a novel." Exams, of course, may be among the necessary evils of student life. But there is no need that student answers be mired in the overuse and misuse of critical terms—or that exam questions, as exemplified by those about *Nineteen Eighty-Four* mentioned above, impose categories on students' reading experiences, thereby constricting, rather than awakening, their responses to books.

IV

While both British and American schools have each accorded Orwell's fiction a place of comparable significance and taught it similarly, the same

cannot be said for Orwell's nonfiction. Only occasionally have English schools set Orwell's documentaries and selections of his essays as exam books (variously at O-level, AO-level, and A-level[261]); and English teachers have taught his essays as much for their subject matter as style.[262] By contrast, in the U.S. Orwell's essays are standard reading, being taught in introductory college composition courses as prose models. Because most British universities do not have courses comparable to these American writing courses, British students do not normally encounter Orwell's essays in class at the post-secondary level.

Indeed, so widely used are Orwell's essays in American composition courses that it may be a more common experience for an American to read Orwell's essays in college than to read either *Animal Farm* or *Nineteen Eighty-Four* in high school. Most frequently anthologized are "Politics and the English Language" and "Shooting an Elephant," both of which began to enter composition readers in the early 1950s.[263] After the 1956 publication of *The Orwell Reader,* composition anthologies also began to include some selections from *Down and Out, The Road to Wigan Pier,* and *Nineteen Eighty-Four.*[264] This development illustrates the interaction between publishing and canon-formation. By making handily available "pre-packaged" excerpts from an author's *oeuvre,* a well-edited collected volume can facilitate the institutionalizing of new works and the growth of a reputation.[265]

Orwell's essays acquired the status of composition classics in the 1960s. Per the Matthew Effect, which postulates that the status system operates to award recognition disproportionately to those who already possess it, anthology editors aiming to avoid "overfamiliar" essays like "Politics and the English Language" and "Shooting an Elephant" often turned not to other essayists but to less familiar essays by Orwell himself (e.g., "Marrakech," "A Hanging," "Why I Write," "Such, Such Were the Joys," "Writers and Leviathan," "The Art of Donald McGill"), with even minor journalism ("The Moon Under Water") entering anthologies after *CEJL*'s publication in 1968.[266] Authors of composition handbooks excerpted "exemplary passages" of Orwell's plain style, sermonized on prose style via "Politics and the English Language," and added luster to grammatical rules by name-dropping "Orwell."[267] (The last practice indicates another context in which Orwell is routinely invoked in argument from authority.) Some composition handbooks of the 1960s and '70s quote Orwell more frequently than any other "authority"; in some composition readers of this period Orwell is represented by more selections than any other writer.[268]

Questions in instructors' manuals often serve as the basis of class discussion, suggesting even more clearly than in the case of the exam questions how images of an author radiate throughout an institutional audience—e.g., from editor to teacher to student. Biographical questions dominate some manuals' approaches to Orwell's essays, as in the following questions on "Marrakech" in the manual for William Smart's widely used *Eight Modern Essayists:*

- Discuss the qualities you most admire in George Orwell.
- Based on "Shooting an Elephant" and "Marrakech," discuss V.S. Pritch-ett's statement that Orwell was "the conscience of his generation."[269]

Such questions place Orwell's personality center-stage, spotlighting his "virtue" and "integrity."*

Orwell's distinctively plain style has obviously had much to do with the canonization of his essays as composition models. And the ascension of his reputation as an essayist, in turn, is surely linked to the rise of the plain style in our postwar "information age." As late as the 1940s Cyril Connolly could speak well of the latinate mandarin style of Gibbon, but by the 1960s the tradition of which Orwell has been regarded as the twentieth-century master, the tradition of the "familiar" style represented by Dryden, Swift, Defoe, and Hazlitt—informal, conversational, clean, fast-moving—had won the allegiance of most educators and intellectuals. Prose had come to imitate journalism, and journalism had become artistic and professional.

Yet Orwell's essays would probably never have been so widely adopted in introductory composition courses had it not specifically been for the changing conception of the college course during the 1950s. Until then, most freshman composition courses were literature survey courses, with selections from the established literary canon serving as prose models. English departments saw their mission as the teaching of literature, not writing. "Error-Comp," which emphasized the ability to write "correct" English in the plain style according to certain modes (description, narration, exposition, argumentation) joined traditional "Lit-Comp" during the decade as the prevailing pedagogy;[271] the resultant combination of the two approaches and the fortuitous timing proved highly favorable to Orwell's work. Writing instructors discerned the pedagogical advantages of using Orwell's essays, which encourage good writing by both precept and example: "Politics and the English Language" and "Why I Write" discuss the how and why of writing; "Shooting an Elephant" and "Marrakech" present themselves as the finished models. (Many composition anthologies of the '60s through the '80s suggest student assignments such as "Evaluate 'Shooting an Elephant' according to Orwell's advice in 'Politics and the English

---

*The study guides do likewise, uncritically identifying the writer's "pure" style with the man's "saintliness." "Orwell's style shows the simple, self-conscious quality of his own personality," declares the Cliff's Notes for *Animal Farm.* The Monarch Notes for *Animal Farm* calls Orwell "a sort of modern-day saint" and asserts that Orwell and Eileen had "an ideal relationship," since both of them were "saintly ascetics." The Cliff's Notes for *Nineteen Eighty-Four* likewise personalizes the prose craftsman, calling him a "lumberjack" who used words for an "ax" and a "magician" who wove a "spell" in language. It also asks the student to imagine, in inviting him to compare *Nineteen Eighty-Four* with the international political scene of the 1980s, that he is George Orwell. That these emphases on Orwell's character come within the context of discussions of *Animal Farm* and *Nineteen Eighty-Four* makes clear that his reputation as The Model Stylist and Defender of the King's English is not founded solely on the essays. The former image is partly based on the simple, economical style of *Animal Farm;* the latter image is significantly indebted to Newspeak and the Ministry of Truth.[270]

Language'.") Also, Orwell wrote a sufficient number of varied, short essays that his work offered instances of the standard prose modes of Error-Comp: description ("Marrakech," "A Hanging"), narration ("Shooting an Elephant"), exposition ("The Art of Donald McGill," "England Your England"), and argumentation ("Why I Write").

It was perhaps inevitable that, after the NCTE's institution of the Doublespeak Award (1973) and George Orwell Award (1974), the pedagogical worth of Orwell's essays would be subject to reassessment in the late '70s and '80s. Revisionist judgment centered on "Politics and the English Language," on which one teacher archly bestowed "the golden essay award for 'most anthologized essay in college texts'."[272] Teachers of the '50s and '60s had valued the essay for its discussion of economy and honesty in writing and its attention to the connection between good writing and good citizenship. Even as the Watergate Affair was providing fresh material for use in teaching the essay, however, liberals and radicals began disagreeing sharply about its merit—and about the wisdom of elevating Orwell and his plain style as writing models. Liberal-Left defenders praised the populism of the plain style and its fitness for a variety of tasks. Wrote Irving Howe: "And when my students ask, 'Whom shall I read in order to write better,' I answer, 'Orwell, the master of the plain style, that style which seems so easy to copy and is almost impossible to reach'."[273] Radicals saw such views as part of "the Orwell myth" and stressed getting beyond "the fifties relic" represented by Trilling's uncritical image of Orwell.[274] Deriding Orwell's "fetishizing of the particular" and aversion to system, one teacher argued that the "liberal empiricism" of the plain style served to mask the interrelations between individualism and capitalist hegemony. The "immense academic prestige" of "Politics and the English Language" helped perpetuate the notion that the plain style was the only style, he added, urging that the plain style be taught *as* the plain style (i.e., with attention to its ideological implications) rather than as "good English."[275]

Other teachers discussed the practical difficulties of teaching Orwell's essays in freshman composition. Cleo McNelly noted that "Politics and the English Language," though a fine essay, presumes far more than one should in speaking to beginning student writers, many of whom simply do not possess the level of cultural literacy and range of prose techniques necessary to benefit from the essay's advice: e.g., choose short words, avoid dead metaphors, and cut unnecessary words out. Many freshmen can't follow these and other "rules" of Orwell, argued McNelly, because they possess limited lexicons, can't distinguish between live and dead metaphors, and can't even meet word limits. Orwell's famous sixth rule ("Break any of these rules sooner than say anything outright barbarous") doesn't help them because they often just can't recognize barbarisms. Most of her freshmen, said McNelly, responded to this and other Orwell essays "with a neutral or negative stare." "Orwell's essays," she concluded, "are prime examples . . . of how not to teach composition'."[276]

Having taught several of Orwell's essays in freshman composition, I find

myself in unfortunate agreement with McNelly's analysis,[277] though my conclusions differ. To start off, the problem is not Orwell's essays but the poor writing skills of college students. Beginning student writers, especially those who do not read much and are from disadvantaged backgrounds, do find it difficult to model their work on Orwell's. They don't hear Orwell's "living voice." Asked to evaluate the prose of an editorial or public speech in light of Orwell's "Politics and the English Language," beginning students often ape the outraged, doubting tone of Orwell, but without his clarity and insight.*

A different problem emerges when writing teachers take a non-rhetorical, literary approach to Orwell's narrative essays. Writing instructors frequently teach an essay like "Shooting an Elephant" not as a prose model but as a short story—and engage chiefly in exegesis or biographical criticism rather than in rhetorical analysis. They conclude class sessions by giving students a comparative assignment in personal narrative, e.g., "Relate an incident in which you acted solely to 'avoid looking a fool.' Use concrete detail." Such courses no doubt heighten students' critical appreciation of Orwell's essays; but students' writing skills, especially in the area of their greatest weakness, analytical argument, remain undeveloped.[279] The fact is that introductory composition courses should place more emphasis on analysis and argument, for which essays like "Shooting an Elephant" are inappropriate models.[280]

Orwell's essays, then, are indeed examples of how not to teach composition *to beginning students*. This is a pedagogical, not ideological, point. Model essays should be sufficiently accessible to allow readers to imitate the author's writing strategies and to identify with his writing situation; and more

---

*Orwell's "rules" almost invite beginning writers to take a "detective" approach toward such an assignment, and to confuse the use of idioms with politically distorted language, as in the following student paper on a Reagan speech:

Ronald Reagan: Contributing to the Decline
of the English Language

It is evident that Ronald Reagan, through his use of dying metaphors and meaningless words, is contributing to the decline of the English language. . . . Reagan uses dead (or dying) metaphors a lot. I was able to identify eight without even looking very hard. The president says "disaster hangs over our lives." I've never seen disaster hang, what does it look like? Later he says that when America decreased defense spending, Soviet spending "forged ahead." Forged ahead? I may sound like Andy Rooney, but George Orwell wouldn't forgive me if I hadn't mentioned it. Reagan's most obvious use of a dead metaphor occurs when he says he will "leave no stone unturned in the effort to reinforce peace." Does Mr. Reagan plan on finding a reinforcement for peace under a rock? One of Orwell's bad language categories that Reagan abuses most routinely is meaningless words. I stopped counting after I found twenty examples. . . .[278]

This is a lively paper. But beginning students rarely possess the verbal and intellectual resources to engage in Orwell's skillful rhetorical analysis, so instead they reduce writing to rules and Orwell to a rules-monger. They seize on the "don'ts" and "nevers" of "Politics and the English Language." They mechanically apply Orwell's "rules"—but with little sense of appropriateness or audience, so that Orwell's caveats obstruct rather than promote effective writing.

models of fine argument (and less devotion to the procrustean categories of Error-Comp) are needed. (Outstanding student essays would probably serve as better argumentation models.) Nevertheless, I have found several Orwell essays useful for advanced composition, where students usually do appreciate "Politics and the English Language" and are sufficiently skilled in prose argument to justify focusing on narration and description via Orwell's other essays. I have also discovered Orwell's essays fitting for introductory literature courses which include the short story. (Here again one notices the ironies in Orwell's canonical status: his firm place in freshman composition, where his work is not well suited, and its exclusion from upper-class English literature courses, where he should, arguably, be better represented.)

But the issue of whether or not Orwell's essays are appropriate as prose models probably says more about American education than about Orwell's work per se. Moreover, we should remember that Orwell wrote for literate London audiences and never considered himself a "proletarian" writer, let alone a juvenile writer. "Politics and the English Language" originally appeared in *Horizon*. The essay assumed one could write, if badly, not that one needed to learn *how* to write. As editor of the London *Observer*, David Astor circulated the essay as a model to reporters in the late '40s.[281] But that "Politics and the English Language" commends itself as a model to journalists and teachers does not mean that it is a composition model fit for beginning student writers. Orwell freely admitted that the essay's advice was meant for himself as much as anyone else. His six "rules" were really based on his awareness of his own bad habits, which he constantly struggled to ward off. Indeed the essay should be read as a companion piece to "Why I Write" (written a few months later), showing an experienced writer with an irrepressible "joy of mere words" reminding himself and others to resist "purple passages" and write "less picturesquely and more exactly." Good prose is like window-washing: the writer as craftsman strives to wipe clean his smudges so that his clear pane of prose will let his meaning shine forth.

## V

During the 1984 countdown an enormous surge of interest in Orwell's work occurred at all educational levels. In England, Longman issued special school editions of *Animal Farm* and *Nineteen Eighty-Four* in 1984. Orwell's dystopia was taught on all levels, with some schools even requesting that special O-level exams be devised at school expense. Orwell's essays were also set for A-level exams by many boards in 1983–84.[282] The loudest dissenting voice was D.S. Savage's diatribe in *The New Pelican Guide to English Literature*. This essay was the only hostile critique of a writer in the eight-volume series and most unusual in a literary history intended as a reference work.[283]

Meanwhile, in the U.S., entire college courses were devoted to *Nineteen Eighty-Four* during the title year.[284] Political theory, sociology, and history courses also made increasing use of *Burmese Days, Keep the Aspidistra Flying,*

and *Coming Up for Air.* Whereas in the 1970s British radicals were charging that *Animal Farm* was used in high schools as anti-Soviet propaganda, in the 1980s neoconservatives were protesting that *Nineteen Eighty-Four* was being taught as if it applied not just to totalitarian states but also (or primarily) to the Western democracies.[285] Lobbying efforts by right-wing and religious groups to proscribe the book on sexual grounds intensified, with the ironic result that it was one of the most widely assigned *and* most widely banned books in American schools in 1983–84. (In its 1983 list of Top Ten classics, the Association of American Publishers ranked *Nineteen Eighty-Four* first (and *Animal Farm* third); meanwhile the American Booksellers Association included *Nineteen Eighty-Four* on its 1983 list of books which libraries and bookstores had recently been pressured to remove from their shelves. Inevitably, civil libertarians like the editors of *Penthouse* used the occasion to warn against the coming spectre of a right-wing "1984."[286])

With the passing of 1984, Orwell's fiction and nonfiction once again largely disappeared from upper-division college literature courses. The absence of Orwell's work from most classes in British literature is an interesting phenomenon. It is the result of an odd confluence of received truths: *Animal Farm* and *Nineteen Eighty-Four* are "high school reading," the essay is not really "literature," and the realistic tradition of the modern British novel is inferior. How these three judgments have solidified and interacted, and how they have structured Orwell's academic reputation by level and genre, merits attention here. And on this discordant note, indicating how the canon-formation process has operated to *exclude* as well as include Orwell as a canonized author, we take our leave of the Orwell gallery's final portrait.

First of all, probably the rapid entry of *Animal Farm* into school curricula in the 1950s served to fix an image of Orwell as a "school" author. For authoritative voices speak from "on high," not from below, and, as we have seen, it is typical for a reputation to radiate outward and downward. The reverse, given the dynamics of reputation-formation, is less common. Moreover, just as critics' first impressions of an author continue to weigh heavily in subsequent evaluations of him, how an author makes his institutional debut—into the schools, media, or any other sphere of repute—often buoys or burdens him for years to come. For better or worse, revaluation usually lags behind reality. This tendency has operated both to win Orwell an enduring place in the schools and to frustrate his entry into university syllabuses. As one examination board official explained, once an author gets "set" in Britain, he tends to stay set. "Schools have only limited funds available for buying textbooks, and there is considerable pressure, therefore, on us to set texts that schools already possess."[287] The same is true in American high schools. Economic considerations may outweigh literary and pedagogical ones. (Which is another reason why *Silas Marner* and *Great Expectations* become school fixtures.[288]) When a high school has purchased 600 copies of a book, it will not only use them year after year, but often assign them, round robin, to several different grades throughout

the year, thus maximizing their economic value through continuous use. (Hence the practical payoff of investing in an author "acceptable at a variety of levels.")

Such practices keep authors out as well as in. *Animal Farm* and *Nineteen Eighty-Four* are still taught in schools in the 1980s, sometimes for the reasons cited above. But I also suspect that *Animal Farm*'s institutionalization at the secondary school level in the 1950s—when the values of Matthew Arnold, T.S. Eliot, and the New Critics were dominant in Anglo-American academic criticism—added legitimacy to the dismissal of Orwell by some academic critics as a "lightweight" or "teenage" author. The entry of *Nineteen Eighty-Four* into British and American schools in the early 1960s probably reinforced this impression, as did the adoption of Orwell's essays in freshman college composition courses.

In none of these cases did Orwell's work enter college *literature* courses. The essays were not treated as literature. No widely used English literature anthologies of the '50s and '60s included Orwell's essays, though pieces by Chesterton, Maugham, Max Beerbohm, W.H. Hudson, H.M. Tomlinson, Lawrence, Woolf, David Cecil, C.P. Snow, and others appeared. Not until the 1973 edition of the massive two-volume *Oxford Anthology of English Literature* did an anthology include a short excerpt (from "England Your England") of Orwell's prose. And here we should, strictly speaking, qualify our characterization of his essays as "canonical." Technically, they have been canonical as "prose models" but not as "essays." However widely they are anthologized and presented in freshman composition as prose models, they are rarely taught as essays and do not really belong to any formal essay canon. For by defining periods and genres, *curricula* establish formal, exclusivist, stable, professionally recognized canons. English curricula feature period courses in poetry, fiction, and drama—and even in "minor" genres like lyric, epic, romance, etc.—but not in the essay. Considered an amorphous genre, "a catch-all term for nonfictional prose of limited length,"[289] the essay is treated as a sundry, grab-bag category, into which is thrown "subliterary" prose like editorials, humorous sketches, and occasional journalism—anything that doesn't "belong" elsewhere.

The exclusion of *Animal Farm, Nineteen Eighty-Four,* and the essays from the "high" canon further illumines the dynamics of reputation-formation in the academy. It first demonstrates that levels of canonization can and do conflict. In particular, entry into a "lower" canon often constrains, rather than facilitates, admittance into "higher" canons—usually according to some variant of the notion that an accessible, popular author cannot be "serious" too. "Generic hierarchy" plays a determining role in the making of reputation.[290] Where an author gets placed in the generic class-system—as "novelist" versus "literary journalist" or "essayist"—is crucial to the development of his reputation. Some genres get exiled from or discriminated against in the high canon. So even distinguished achievement in a genre of mediocre or vague literary status (the essay, the fable, the utopia) may doom a writer to exclusion from the high canon.

Furthermore, just as curricula establish formal canons, educators establish curricula. That is, literary academics—though admittedly influenced greatly by literary-political intellectuals, publishers, and others—ultimately "make" the university canon. Literary-political intellectuals do not. They may shape cultural opinion through their journals and books, "leading the way" for institutional acceptance, but they do not directly establish curricula. And so the fact that leading intellectuals of the Left and Right unite in their admiration for Orwell does not guarantee his entry into university literature classrooms. Intellectuals are often reputation-makers and even "figure-makers," but they are not necessarily canon-makers. (Nor do historians or other academics exert great influence on the *literary* canon.) All this helps explain the apparent paradoxes of Orwell's eclectic educational canonization, especially his "relative absence from the literary scene," in Cleo McNelly's words. McNelly suggests that Orwell was too radical in the 1950s and '60s to be brought "above stairs" into college literature classrooms.[291] But this seems doubtful. (Non-experimental writers of Orwell's generation, like Waugh, fared little better; Auden's early work was widely taught.) The crucial fact is that postwar literary academics, beholden to Arnoldian and modernist principles, approached Orwell according to formalist criteria—and judged his works "simplistic," with the meaning of books like *Animal Farm* just "there," lamentably "on the surface," and requiring no labor of exegesis. They therefore relegated Orwell to the schools as an admirably "accessible" author, but not "a major writer." (The verdict has persisted. Orwell was not an eligible choice for the "major author" category of my English Ph.D. examinations in the 1980s.) I suspect that Orwell's relatively lower standing with English professors than with politically minded intellectuals has much to do with the differing identities of the two groups. Literary academics as a group have not expressed intense personal or professional admiration for Orwell. On the other hand, although George Woodcock, Raymond Williams, and Irving Howe have each taught for years in the academy, each has also seen himself as an intellectual rather than an English professor, and has seen Orwell in turn as a model writer and man.

This difference bears on the third reason for Orwell's exclusion from the high canon, namely the devaluation of the realistic or social-political novel of the twentieth century. In effect, Henry James won the so-called Great Debate against H.G. Wells on the purpose of the novel during the war years, and the Great Tradition of the modern British novel has been shaped accordingly. Orwell's absence from the high canon is partly explained by his fiction's lying outside the Jamesian-Eliotic-Leavisite tradition, which has retrospectively restructured not only authors but also periods into "major" and "minor" in terms favorable to itself. Its influence has been especially marked upon the reputations of authors and works of the late nineteenth and twentieth centuries; its version of The Tradition has largely won acceptance as "modern English literary history." Orwell is not alone among its prominent victims. (For instance, period courses in British literature often skip from the Victorians to modernists, giving little or no attention to the years of the Decadents,

Edwardians, and Georgians, since these do not constitute "major" periods.)
In this respect Orwell's exclusion from The Great Tradition of the British
novel takes on much larger implications than his own case. It points to the
existence of a severely restricted canon ignoring another "great tradition,"
one which Orwell himself identified in his review of Leavis' enormously
influential The Great Tradition. Orwell pointed to the realistic or rhetorical
tradition, traceable to Defoe, Fielding, Smollett, and Dickens, which continues, albeit with little curricular acknowledgment, on through Butler, Gissing,
Wells, Bennett, Galsworthy, Orwell, and Amis. "But surely a book on the
English novel," Orwell concluded in his review, titled "Exclusive Club,"
"ought at least to mention Smollett, Surtees, Samuel Butler, Mark Rutherford, and George Gissing?"[292]

Silence, of course, is a major instrument of the politics of reputation. For
reputations in the rarified high canon live or die on the oxygen of classes,
criticism, and new editions. The point returns us by a different path to the
value-status nexus. But this study has not set itself the task of arguing the
upward or downward revaluation of Orwell's reputation.[293] Instead we will
merely note here that the banishment of an entire line of historically (and
artistically) significant writers—a line of writers who, moreover, obviously
derive more directly than Joyce and Woolf from the original "great tradition" of the British eighteenth-century novel—has reflected and reinforced
Orwell's own exile.[294]

"Nature didn't intend him to be a novelist," Q. D. Leavis pronounced in
her 1940 essay-review on Orwell. One doubts that Animal Farm and Nineteen
Eighty-Four would have broadened her categories or changed her mind. Yet
she could hardly have pondered the consequences for the Leavisite Great
Tradition when she concluded:

> Perhaps the best thing for him and the best thing for us would be to export
> him to interpret English literature. . . . Everyone would benefit. . . .[295]

How inclusive she meant her "us" and "everyone" to be is hard to say. But
not the least of the beneficiaries, one imagines, would be The Model Stylist
and Defender of the King's English himself—and his "only seemingly simple"[296] last works of fiction, Animal Farm and Nineteen Eighty-Four.

# Conclusion

## *"Tuppence for the Opinion of Posterity":*
## *The Intellectual Hero in History*

I

If Orwell had not existed, it might have been necessary to invent him. A quixotic intellectual who could be idealized as a moral hero by readers across the political spectrum, a screaming bogeyman whose catchwords could be bannered and pinned to nearly every ism of the age, a commercial opportunity whose masterwork could be exploited by date-minded advertisers and media men, a writer whose very name could be used as a reversible emblem signifying both what he aspired to and warned against—indeed one almost suspects that someone *did* find it necessary to invent "George Orwell."

And so in fact someone did: Eric Blair did. And the further irony is that in time the fictional invention "Orwell" came to pass for the man "Blair"—and that, in yet another twist, by virtue of the writer's inventing an "ideological superweapon" which could be targeted anywhere and launched from any position, the pseudonym itself became, in many quarters, confused with or replaced by its nightmarish proper adjective. In this way, in a final irony, the posthumous "Orwell" could be reinvented to undergo the mythic fate which his protagonist, the fictional Everyman of *Nineteen Eighty-Four,* was willing to suffer for The Brotherhood and ultimately underwent in Room 101. As O'Brien says to Julia about Winston Smith:

> "Do you understand that even if he survives, it may be as a different person? We may be obliged to give him a new identity. His face, his movements, the shape of his hands, the color of his hair—even his

voice would be different.... Our surgeons can alter people beyond recognition."[1]

This study has found the pen sharper than the scalpel, for the defacement of George Orwell by critics and the media has resulted in his "surviving" in the form of multiple new identities. So much so that Orwell the man and writer has gradually come in these pages to seem that which he certainly never was nor sought to be: a human kaleidoscope whose variegated imagery has represented nearly all things to all people, or at least all political writers—the Zelig of modern intellectuals.

And yet, however strange and remarkable the phenomenon, it is unique to Orwell only in its iridescent diversity and labyrinthine ironies. For any figure whom a culture elevates and irradiates serves as a looking glass which it raises to itself—and tilts to suit itself as it pursues its self-image. The mirror can lie. Many ugly regimes have demanded homage to their fair, false Comrade Ogilvys. The search for the usable past easily becomes the quarry for the abusable past.

Whether they are accurate or distorting mirrors, however, figures invariably act as "lenses through which we read our minds" and whose "spirit infuses itself in concentric circles from its origin," as Emerson wrote in "Uses of Great Men." In giving voice here to those social processes we have termed *transfiguration* and *radiation,* Emerson reminds us that figure-making also entails figure-*using,* that reputation-building is not only a matter of reader identification but also reader projection. A "star" reputation is thus also a "moon," refracting—if through a glass darkly—the enlarged self imagined by an individual or group. "A hero of our time in the Lermontov style," Malcolm Muggeridge once called Orwell, intending the tribute to convey Orwell's quixotism. But the characterization assumes richer significance in Lermontov's own remark that *Hero Of Our Time* was not so much the portrait of an individual as of an age. The Orwell gallery is the same. We have fashioned the "usable Orwells" we need. We have met the images and they are ourselves.[2]

## II

But *if* he had never existed, what real difference would it have made? "The minds of all of us, and therefore the physical world, would be perceptibly different if Wells had never existed," wrote Orwell in 1941, though he granted that it was difficult to assess the influence of a writer. Forty years later, Nicholas von Hoffman made a similar claim about Orwell: "He, as much as any single person, has shaped our political vision of the landscape in which we dwell."[3]

The tributes are lavish. Yet it is not that, if Wells and Orwell had never existed, there would be no space travel, no science fiction, no Cold War, no popular culture studies. Surely not. Wells and Orwell did not so much "make" history as furbish the Western mindscape. In *The Hero in History,* Sid-

ney Hook distinguished between the "event-making hero," the Lenin or T.E. Lawrence who wills his vision of history as perhaps no one else could have done, and the "eventful hero," the boy near the dike who happens to have a finger handy when the tide of history is breaking.[4] We might think of a writer like Wells or Orwell as a third heroic type, the "event-shaping hero." He wills his private vision, utopia or nightmare, into literary form. His books constitute public acts. If his work speaks to and for the aspirations and anxieties of the historical moment, it may indeed alter the shape of things to come.

Yet the moment passes. And when it does, the event-shaping hero—as Wells discovered in his own lifetime—may pass too, rendered dated and irrelevant by events he helped effect, a perishable "hero of our time." The hero in history is by no means the hero throughout history.

Only Posterity can make you a hero for all time. Posterity alone can grant you the earthly semblance of immortality. "Posterity will decide." Or so we are told. By and large, Orwell agreed; he accepted these truisms with the same ambivalence as do most of us. He scoffed at the concern for posthumous reputation even as he recognized that to "go down in history" was to gain a form of immortality. Only "posterity," "survival," "the test of time," Orwell insisted, fairly proved literary merit. He rejected religious belief in an afterlife, but held that, in Richard Rees's words, "to care passionately about the fate of mankind after your death was an ethical imperative."[5] Perhaps it was also a psychological imperative: the urge to continue to be. *Non omnis moriar.* "Not all of me shall die." Such a hope, argued Cyril Connolly shortly after Orwell's death, constitutes "one of the major consolations of the literary life." For reputation differs from money or power in at least one crucial respect: You *can* take it with you. Life lasts no more than a few decades, but a reputation may endure for millennia.

However strongly he felt the pull of what T.E. Lawrence called "the historical ambition," Orwell scorned the pursuit of reputation, posthumous or otherwise. On the one hand, he declared that "no decent person cares tuppence for the opinion of posterity."[6] On the other hand, he acknowledged that "to be remembered after death" and "to find out true facts and store them up for the use of posterity" were among the chief motives for writing. A friend insists that "his sole ambition" was "to be a famous writer."[7] Her contention recalls again young Eric's chant, "To be A FAMOUS AUTHOR," the refrain accompanying his boyhood dream of a Uniform Edition of his *Collected Works* in blue leather and silver lettering: a dream which posterity granted. And yet who is posterity but we ourselves? Posterity is but a later present, and the "test of time" is administered by us all. *We* decide: a person "survives" only in the memories of the living. Only a posthumous author's *readers* can recognize his heroic identity.

But not just any readers: the heroic reputation can neither emerge nor endure without the heroic response. Intellectual hero-worship, or what we might term *the heroics of reception,* consists in the willingness of readers to acknowledge the heroic when it shows its thousand faces. Orwell acknowledged it when he extolled the face behind Dickens' pages, and he once

commended a biographer of Attlee for remaining "on the right side of hero worship"[8]—the phrase implying that Orwell recognized that there could be "right" and "wrong" sides. The wrong side entails explaining away the Other's weaknesses or glossing over his faults, whether out of misguided reverence for the hero or through fear of diminishing his stature. Orwell's readers have often engaged in just such whitewashing, which, in the long run, usually achieves just the opposite of the admirer's intentions. Reacting against the orthodoxies of the Orwell "cult" in 1955, Kingsley Amis fairly complained that the "unwillingness, or inability, to give one's hero less than ten out of ten for everything occasionally results in the alienation of more temperate admirers."[9] The right side of intellectual hero-worship insists neither on "ten out of ten" nor any other quota. It is the generous and discriminating, never self-abasing nor reflexive nor uncritical nor servile, honoring of someone fit to be an intellectual hero. Indeed, perhaps "the ethics of admiration"[10] demands precisely that we *not* insist on "ten out of ten," but rather that we accept our heroes "impure"—that we acknowledge their inevitable flaws and focus on their considerable strengths.

Passionately engaged in the conflicts of his time, the intellectual hero writes for the age rather than the ages. Unlike the artistic hero, he or she may or may not leave any works to "posterity," but he accepts this as the price of his commitment: he speaks to the moment and aims to shape the present. He considers silence in the face of social injustice or political tyranny a pact with evil, yearns to reaffirm "man's solidarity with man," hopes against hope that words may change the world, and enacts his self-chosen role of public "conscience" and "voice" with the dedication of a spiritual mission.[11] His vocation thus typically tends to find expression in versions of the images of Orwell encountered in this study: Rebel, Common Man, Prophet, and Saint.

Throughout this project I have attended to the institutional basis of reputations, but I have also tried to respect the admirer's (or detractor's) perception of Orwell's fitness (or unfitness) to be a hero, and thus avoid reducing Orwell's reputation to a purely institutional matter. For reader response not only occurs within an institutional context but also constitutes a relationship between reader and author. Nowhere is this clearer than in the impassioned responses to Orwell by many of the readers featured in these chapters. Ultimately the intellectual hero represents not just an aspiration but an ideal; he or she is thus not merely one whom readers admire but whom they can idealize. This means that he has somehow struck them as having reached beyond the limits of ordinary human capacity, and also that they have been able to surrender themselves sufficiently to grant his specialness.

To honor the heroic with disinterest is, however modestly, to share in it; those who recognize and idealize the worthy hero earn some small measure of heroism themselves. Idealize, not fabricate: hero-worship is not idolatry. Neither a celebrity nor a networking mentor, a hero like Orwell usually does possess in some form the attributes we perceive in him; but *we* endow them with the transfiguring personal significance that makes him

. . . a feeling, a man seen
As if the eye was an emotion,
As if in seeing we saw our feeling
In the object seen. . . .[12]

A feeling of human possibility, a momentary vision of an ideal self: this is the Orwell whom many readers have experienced, and through him have found their way to hidden resources within themselves.


## III

At Madame Tussaud's Wax Museum, the effigies of men and women who have "lost" their eminence or fame are melted down to make room for new figures. The practice raises the question of Orwell's future reputation as a widely known "public" writer, especially given that the museum installed its "George Orwell" in December 1983, the peak month of the 1984 countdown. Will the countdown soon be followed by a "meltdown"?

One may also speculate about the critical reputation. "Who controls the past controls the future," runs the Party slogan. "Who controls the present controls the past." The slogan points up the significance of the contemporary audience in shaping a reputation: who controls the present controls the past *and* the future. Orwell's literary contemporaries and near-contemporaries have been influential on the Anglo-American intellectual scene for years. Pritchett, Muggeridge, Powell, Woodcock, Howe, and Podhoretz have all regarded Orwell as a "conscience" of their generations and have kept his critical reputation high. With their deaths, will it decline? Or will he be regarded in future decades as, in the view of one French critic, "the most important writer of twentieth-century literature" and "the best loved"?[13]

The questions are of course impossible to answer. But the decisive "low-level" factors conditioning the course of Orwell's long-term reputation seem clear. As the year 1984 further recedes, many of the associations which *Nineteen Eighty-Four* has acquired will inevitably slip away. The face of The Prophet may, accordingly, become less dominant. Images moult as well as accrete. By contrast, increased attention to the essays and documentaries may raise the profiles of The Common Man and The Saint. Quite possibly, Orwell's public reputation will never again approach its level of the early 1980s, or perhaps even of the mid-1950s. It is unlikely that there will be any international "countdown to 2050" (the target date for the perfection of Newspeak). Nor does one expect the Orwell centennial in 2003 to be more than an academic affair. Yet so long as his works remain in school curricula and his slogans are quoted in the press, Orwell will remain a widely known author. As for the critical reputation, it could rise if Orwell's work enters the "high" literary canon. That succeeding generations of young intellectuals will take him as a model or rival—that he will continue to seem, in Michael Levenson's wry phrase, "almost every intellectual's big brother"—is, however, doubtful. Orwell may indeed have to "make room" for new figures.

But the unusual doubleness of his appeal—idealist and pragmatist, intellectual and common man, saint and socialist—will be hard to duplicate. Indeed, so long as these dualisms are still perceived, controversies about Orwell's life and personality will probably simmer.

But how these "low-level" factors function will to no small degree depend on certain "higher-level" factors. And here we touch on the larger issue of how reputation-history and world history interact.

For Orwell is "alive today" as a public literary figure partly because the political and technological developments of mid-century which initially conditioned his reputation—the Cold War, the Bomb, the specter of totalitarianism, the agonies of the Left, the advent of the "media age," the rise of the "organization man"—are themselves still "alive today." Orwell wrote about some of these issues, and he anticipated others; but all of them emerged in the early postwar era, in the years 1945–55, which Eric Goldman has called "the Crucial Decade."[14] This is precisely the period during which Orwell's reputation ascended and crystallized. His latter-day history, like contemporary history generally, is thus largely the result of events which "the crucial decade" set in motion. Unless these great issues of the last four decades alter drastically in form or substance, it is unlikely that Orwell's reputation will vaporize any time soon.

All this is to say that Orwell remains "in the present"—and will continue to do so in the foreseeable future—because he and his work have intertwined with a larger pattern of events whose own consequences are still in process. The pattern ranges from the rise of the plain style to the key international developments of the postwar West. The importance of an event (or the public reputation of an author), as Leonard Meyer has argued, is partly defined by the duration of the highest "hierarchic level" of which it forms a component. How long a reputation remains "in the present" will depend on whether or not it fuses with any "higher order" event, and if so, on how long it remains a constituent element and how long *this* greater event "resounds." Each event possesses what Meyer terms its historical "reverberation time"—which may be five seconds or five millennia.[15] The survival of a reputation thus turns on what it gets "attached to." If *Nineteen Eighty-Four* had not become enmeshed in ongoing East-West polemics, its reputation might be strictly literary, and it might today be regarded as a period piece. It possesses contemporary consequence, rather than mere historical significance, partly because it is conjoined to the still-relevant higher-order events of World War II and the Cold War.

Yet the future is not, after all, "foreseeable."

> Alien they seemed to be:
> No mortal eye could see
> The intimate welding of their later history,
> Or sign that they were bent
> By paths coincident
> On being anon twin halves of one august event. . . .[16]

History vouchsafes to no mortal eyes its plans to couple—or sunder—phenomena and events. How long a hero will stay "in" the mainstream of history is no more certain than the hour he will enter it or which remnants of his reputation will ultimately be salvaged from the shipwreck of Time. Wells was the "inspired prophet of the Edwardian age," wrote Orwell,[17] but Wells came to seem an anachronism soon after the watershed of World War I. His reputation had interwoven with events of 1895–1914 which were no longer perceived by the 1930s to have direct consequence. To us a half-century later, it seems hardly imaginable that Wells died just three years before Orwell. Wells seems to us a figure of the past, whereas Orwell's "pastness" is, in a sense, merely chronological.[18] Not all "pasts" are, then, equally usable—or abusable. Indeed a "live" figure like Orwell remains usable and abusable precisely because he is *not* perceived to be in the past but still "in the present."

Non omnis mortuus est. "Not all of him has died." Yet if Orwell remains "alive" and "present," it is not only because the world has not passed him by, but also because the writer spoke in a voice so plain and so insistent that he has continued to command the world's attention. Not only the age which has received Orwell, then, but also the literary achievement which has helped shape it account for his remaining "a figure in our lives." And so also do observers' discrepant perceptions of the adamantly unsainted man, so fiercely hated and so dearly loved.

# Acknowledgments

One of the great joys of writing this book has been the personal friends and intellectual companions acquired along the way. For reading the manuscript whole or in part and for the generosity of their responses, I am grateful to Bernard Crick, Jim Connors, Arthur Eckstein, Nicholas Edsall, Dante Germino, Thomas Helscher, Michael Hogan, Joli Jensen, Steve Longstaff, Jeffrey Meyers, Michael Moses, Dennis Rohatyn, Jonathan Rose, Jack Rossi, Tim Shutt, Henry Schmidt, Peter Stansky, and Renate Voris.

Several other people enriched my understanding by kindly granting me an interview, corresponding with me, or otherwise sharing their thoughts: Kingsley Amis, Ian Angus, John Atkins, Jenni Calder, Paul Cantor, Linda Cookson, Peter Davison, Mary Fyvel, Martin Green, Mark Hamilton, Irving Howe, Alfred Kazin, Russell Kirk, Steven Marcus, William Lee Miller, Merrill Peterson, William Phillips, Norman Podhoretz, Marion Scott, Julian Symons, John Wain, Ian Willison, and John Wesley White. I owe a large debt to Marvin Rosenblum, who graciously made available to me his vast private collection of Orwelliana. My deep gratitude also goes to the outstanding editorial staff of Sheldon Meyer, Rachel Toor, and Leona Capeless at Oxford University Press.

Four other friends, colleagues and teachers encouraged this project from its infancy and have been, over many years, my unflagging supporters and honest critics. I have valued them in all these roles; I could not have written this book without them. Austin Quigley tempered my will to systematize and relentlessly challenged me to think further for myself; Walter Sokel exemplified the engaged historian, tactfully reminding me that intellectual history is lived as well as written. Jim Aune's comradeship and rigorous self-questioning emboldened me to re-explore my own personal and political commitments; Michael Levenson radiated a quiet trust as he ingeniously steered me back on course, somehow eliciting my best self and helping me believe in him.

Support of a more intangible kind came from still other friends. The abiding confidence of John Buettler and the infectious good spirits of Kathleen O'Connor often adjusted my vision and gave me much-needed perspective. From Virginia Invernizzi I received the gift of herself; she was all that a friend could be.

Finally I thank my brothers and my parents, for their faith and for their love— and for always being there.

J.G.R.

# Notes

The main collection of Orwell material is in the Manuscripts and Rare Books Department of University College, London. This is referred to below as the Orwell Archive. It includes correspondence to and from Orwell, press cuttings, copies of radio and television programs devoted to him and his work, and transcripts of these programs. A private collection of more than 10,000 press cuttings, amassed by Marvin Rosenblum of Chicago, has also proven an invaluable resource. Cited as the Rosenblum Collection, it chiefly covers news events relating to Orwell and *Nineteen Eighty-Four* during the years 1980–85. Unpublished letters from Orwell have also been obtained from the Partisan Review Collection at Boston University and the Berg Collection, New York Public Library. Letters and memoranda pertaining to the translation and distribution of Orwell's work by U.S. government agencies from the 1940s through 1970s have also been obtained through the Freedom of Information Act, and they are cited FOIA.

### Preface

1. "Poet and Priest," review of W. H. Gardner's *G.M. Hopkins*, in *Observer*, 12 November 1944, 3.
2. These characterizations are from V.S. Pritchett, "George Orwell," *New Statesman and Nation*, 15 August 1953, 183; and "Slouching Toward Bethlehem," *Time*, 19 February 1983.
3. T. R. Fyvel, "George Orwell," *Picture Post*, 8 January 1955, 39–40.
4. See *Washington Post*, 1 April 1984.
5. David Bergman, "Orwell Becomes a Household Word," *Daily Variety*, 27 January 1984. Copy in Rosenblum Collection.
6. Malcolm Muggeridge, *Like It Was: The Diaries of Malcolm Muggeridge* (London, 1976), 376.

### Introduction

1. Lionel Trilling, Introduction to *Homage to Catalonia* (New York, 1952), viii. (Hereafter cited as Trilling.)

2. "The Writer's Dilemma," review of George Woodcock's *The Writer and Politics,* in *Observer,* 22 August 1948, 3.

3. See, for example, Diana Laurenson and Alan Swingewood, *The Sociology of Literature* (London, 1971); Robert Escarpit, *Sociology of Literature,* trans. E. Pick (Lake Erie, Ohio, 1965); Levin L. Schucking, *The Sociology of Literary Taste,* trans. Brian Battershaw (Chicago, 1966); Hans Robert Jauss, *Toward an Aesthetic of Reception* (Minneapolis, 1982).

4. Northrop Frye, *Anatomy of Criticism* (New York, [1957] 1967), 19.

5. Edmond de Goncourt, quoted in Henri Peyre, *The Failures of Criticism* (Ithaca, 1967), 268.

6. For an overview of the general issues involved in analyzing the "literary system," see Jeffrey L. Sammons, *Literary Sociology and Practical Criticism* (Bloomington, 1977).

7. "Orwell a Book Publishing Phenomenon," *Providence Journal* (R.I.), 20 January 1984. This figure does not include the thousands of copies of *Nineteen Eighty-Four* sold through the Book-of-the-Month Club and the Quality Paperback Club in 1983–84. *Nineteen Eighty-Four* also sold 430,000 copies in Britain between September 1983 and January 1984.

8. Quoted in Bernard Crick, *George Orwell: A Life* (New York, [1980] 1982), 358. All references are to Crick in the revised 1982 Penguin edition. (Hereafter cited as Crick.)

9. Thomas N. Franck and Edward Weisband, *Word Politics: Verbal Strategy Among the Superpowers* (New York, 1971).

10. George Orwell, *The Collected Essays, Journalism, and Letters,* ed. Sonia Orwell and Ian Angus, 4 vols. (New York, 1968), vol. 1, 528. All references are to *CEJL* in the Harcourt edition.

11. *CEJL,* Vol. 1, 503. John Atkins, *George Orwell: A Literary and Biographical Study* (London 1954), 306. (Hereafter cited as Atkins.)

12. Jean-Paul Sartre, *Search for a Method* (New York, 1968), 35–84; C. Wright Mills, *The Sociological Imagination* (New York, 1959), 6–7.

13. Crick, 34.

14. Mills, *Sociological Imagination,* 6, 226.

15. For an insightful, bitter, and at times paranoiac example of what could be called "the conspiracy theory" of literary reputation, see Richard Kostelanetz, *The End of Intelligent Writing: Literary Politics in America* (New York, 1974), and his sequel, *"The End" Appendix: "Intelligent Writing" Reconsidered* (Metuchen, N.J., 1979). See also William Goode, *A Celebration of Heroes: Prestige as a Control System* (Berkeley, 1980), esp. 127–30.

16. See Chapter Two.

17. *CEJL,* Vol. 1, 520.

18. Joseph Campbell, *The Hero with a Thousand Faces* (New York, 1949). Irving Howe, address delivered at West Chester State University, 7 October 1983. Ernest Becker, *The Denial of Death* (New York, 1973), 4.

19. Becker, *Denial of Death,* 6.

20. Lionel Trilling, *Homage to Catalonia,* xxiii. Irving Howe, "As the Bones Know," *Harper's,* January 1969, 97. Atkins, 123. Stephen Spender, "Homage to Catalonia," *World Review,* June 1950, 54. V. S. Pritchett, "George Orwell," *New Statesman and Nation,* 28 January 1950, 96. George Woodcock, "Orwell and Conscience," *World Review,* April 1950, 28. Alfred Kazin, telephone interview, 1 July 1986. Malcolm Muggeridge, "Books," *Esquire,* March 1969, 12. Richard Rees, *Brave Men: A Study of D.H. Lawrence and Simone Weil* (Carbondale, Ill., 1959), 145–47. John Wain, *A House for the Truth* (New York, 1973), 1.

21. Quoted in Crick, 367–68.

22. Quoted in "Orwell Remembered," Part 1 (of 5). Produced by Nigel Williams for BBC-Arena TV (Great Britain) and broadcast in America over the Arts and Entertainment Network, October 1984. Excerpts from the program appear in *Orwell Remembered,* ed. Audrey Coppard and Bernard Crick (London, 1984). W. Warren Wagar, "George Orwell As Political Secretary of the Zeitgeist," in *The Future of Nineteen Eighty-Four,* ed. Ejner J. Jensen (Ann Arbor, 1984), 177–200.

Part One. Anatomy of Reputation

*Chapter One. Orwell into the Nineties*

*1. Reputation, Legacy, Historiography*

1. *CEJL,* Vol. 4, 463.

2. V.S Pritchett, "George Orwell: An Appreciation," *New York Times Book Review,* 5 February 1950, 22.

3. See, for example, *The World Review,* June 1950, 3–60.

4. For samples of hostile Marxist criticism, see Samuel Sillen, "Maggot of the Month," *Masses and Mainstream,* August 1949, 79–81; also James Walsh, "An Appreciation of an Individualist Writer," *Marxist Quarterly,* January 1956, 25–39. The most influential psychoanalytic essay has been Anthony West, "Hidden Damage," *New Yorker,* 28 January 1956, 164–76. All three of these essays are reprinted in *George Orwell: The Critical Heritage,* ed. Jeffrey Meyers (London, 1975). (Hereafter cited as Meyers.)

5. Typical is the response of one reviewer to Bernard Crick's reports of Orwell's extramarital affairs: "Though happily married," Crick reminds us, "Orwell was not above an occasional infidelity." Dan Cryer, *Christian Science Monitor,* 9 March 1981. See also Crick, 473–86.

Acquaintances of Orwell have sometimes presented unflattering portraits of him. Occasionally, the negative reports have not just been ignored but suppressed. See, for instance, Humphrey Dakin's harsh comments about his brother-in-law Eric in Coppard and Crick's *Orwell Remembered,* 127–33, not broadcast on Melvyn Bragg's 1970 BBC-TV program, *The Road to the Left.*

Other negative memoirs include those by John Morris, "Some Are More Equal Than Others: A Note on George Orwell," *Penguin New Writing,* ed. John Lehmann, Vol. 40 (Harmondsworth, 1950), 90–97; Elisaveta Fen, "George Orwell's First Wife," *Twentieth Century,* August 1960, 115–26; and Rayner Heppenstall, *Four Absentees* (London, 1960). Also by Heppenstall, "Memoirs of George Orwell: The Shooting Stick" and "Orwell Intermittent," *Twentieth Century,* April/May 1955, 367–73, 470–83. Critics have given these views of Orwell relatively little attention, with virtually all unfavorable reaction to him focused on his perceived literary personality in *The Road to Wigan Pier* and *Nineteen Eighty-Four.*

6. Francis Russell, "Postscript to George Orwell," *Christian Science Monitor,* 19 March 1953, 12.

7. *CEJL,* Vol. 1, 160.

8. The warnings seem to have taken effect. A 1983 Gallup Poll in Europe, comparing our world with Oceania, found that 72 percent of Britons, 38 percent of West Germans, and 37 percent of Swiss believe that government agencies, East or West, "can learn anything they want about you." Sizable pluralities also agreed that their own governments routinely use "false words and statistics" in reporting their activities to the public. The poll was conducted in October 1983 and published in *The Philadelphia Inquirer,* 30 December 1983.

On the lighter side—though also reflecting anxieties about "1984"—a group of Swiss citizens proposed a constitutional amendment in 1983 to eliminate "the Orwellian year" from the calendar. Their petition, presented to the federal government in Berne, called for the Christian calendar to be divided into periods of 1,983 years. See Eddie Olsen, "Happy New Year: The Swiss Want to Abolish 1984," *Philadelphia Inquirer,* 31 December 1983.

9. *CEJL,* Vol. 2, 192.

10. The session was part of the conference, "The Road After 1984: High Technology and Human Freedom," held at the National Museum of American History, Washington D.C., 8 December 1983.

11. *Dickens, Dali, and Others: Studies in Popular Culture* (New York, 1946).

12. Robert Lee, *Orwell's Fiction* (South Bend, 1969).

13. See, for example, *Readings in Sociology,* ed. Edgar A. Schuler et al. (New York, 1960). Dwight Macdonald, "Varieties of Political Experience," *New Yorker,* 28 March 1959, 141–50.

14. See, for example, Harvey Zorbaugh, *The Gold Coast and the Slum* (Chicago, 1929) and Paul Cressey, *The Taxi-Dance Hall* (Chicago, 1932).

15. See, for example, Tom Wolfe's remarks on Orwell as a forerunner in *The New Journalism* (New York, 1973), esp. 45–46.

16. Notable studies of Orwell's political thought include: Michael Maddison, "1984: A Burnhamite Fantasy?," *Political Quarterly*, January–March 1961, 71–79; John Mander, "George Orwell's Politics," *Contemporary Review*, January–February 1960, 32–6, 113–19. Numerous articles in *College English* and *ETC: A Review of General Semantics* have discussed the importance of Orwell's essays for rhetoric and semantics. Nigel Calder's two-volume *The World in 1984* (London, 1964) uses Orwell's date as a springboard for speculations on the future by distinguished scientists and humanists. Leslie Johnson discusses Orwell's contribution to popular culture studies in *The Culture Critics: From Matthew Arnold to Raymond Williams* (London, 1979). Alan Sandison's *The Last Man of Europe* (New York, 1974) is a study of Orwell as *"Homo religiosis."* Other critics have discussed Personalism and Humanism in relation to Orwell's thought. See Max Cosman, "Orwell's Terrain," *Personalist*, Winter 1954, 41–49; and Peter Faulkner, "Orwell and Christianity," *Humanist*, December 1973, 270–73.

17. *CEJL*, Vol. 1, 159, 399.

18. John Casey, "Raymond Williams and Orwell," *Spectator*, March 1971, 349–50. T.A. Birrell, "Is Integrity Enough?," *Dublin Review*, Autumn 1950, 49–65.

19. Bruce Franklin, "Teaching Literature in the Highest Academies of the Amerikan Empire," in *The Politics of Literature: Dissenting Essays in the Teaching of English*, ed. Louis Kampf (New York, 1972), 116. Worst of all, thought Franklin, a Stalinist, was that such a "reactionary tract" should have gained wide currency in secondary schools.

20. Yale University, however, sponsored the George Orwell Forum (c. 1957–65) devoted to discussion of contemporary political issues connected with "democratic socialism." Its activities, which included hosting speakers such as Bayard Rustin and Raya Dunayevskaya (Trotsky's onetime secretary), were monitored by the FBI during 1958–60. FBI memo to J. Edgar Hoover, 10 November 1960. FOIA. In 1987 Dennis Rohatyn at the University of San Diego also began a Society for Orwell Studies newsletter.

21. "Professors Rate *1984* A Good Book, But Say It's Not an Outstanding Novel," *Binghamton Sun Bulletin* (N.Y.), 30 December 1983. Copy in Rosenblum Collection.

22. Richard Rovere, Introduction to *The Orwell Reader* (New York, 1956), xii.

23. Casey, "Raymond Williams and Orwell," 349.

24. *Nineteen Eighty-Four* is #4 on a list of books most frequently banned from U.S. schools, according to a summary of six censorship surveys conducted between 1965 and 1982. "Alleged obscenity" is the reason. (Ahead of *Nineteen Eighty-Four* are *Catcher in the Rye*, *Go Ask Alice* (anonymous), and *Of Mice and Men*). Reported in Barbara Nellis, "The Dirty Thirty," *Playboy*, January 1984, 262.

25. Kevin Hyland, "Orwellmania Getting Off to Fast Start Across Land," *Syracuse Herald Journal*, 16 January 1983. Copy in Rosenblum Collection.

26. "Do You Know Who George Orwell Is?," *People Magazine*, 9 January 1984.

27. Crick, 27. Paul Potts, "Don Quixote on a Bicycle: In Memoriam, George Orwell, 1903–50," *London Magazine*, March 1957, 42, 44. Jacintha Buddicom, *Eric and Us: A Remembrance of George Orwell* (London, 1974), 148. George Woodcock, *The Crystal Spirit* (Boston, 1966), 355.

28. Woodcock, *Crystal Spirit*, 289–355. Isaac Deutscher, *"1984—*The Mysticism of Cruelty," *Russia in Transition and Other Essays* (New York, 1960), 230–45. Walsh, "An Appreciation . . . ," 30.

29. Muggeridge, *Like It Was*, 375. Woodcock, *Crystal Spirit*, 53. "Penguin Celebrates with Orwell," *The Bookseller*, 26 July 1975, 288–89.

30. *CEJL*, Vol. 1, 415.

31. "Guerrilla," *Time*, 13 November 1950, 113. "Honest Witness," *Time*, 16 March 1953, 126. James Stern, "Homage to George Orwell," *New Republic*, 20 February 1950, 18. "Orwell at War," *Newsweek*, 26 May 1952, 102–3.

32. See, for example, Fredric Warburg, *All Authors Are Equal* (London, 1973), 106; and Bertrand Russell, "George Orwell," *World Review*, June 1950, 5.

**33.** Isaac Rosenfeld, "Decency and Death," *Partisan Review*, May 1950, 514–18.

**34.** Jeffrey Meyers, *A Reader's Guide to George Orwell* (London, 1975). Woodcock has also claimed that Orwell went to Jura with the awareness that *Nineteen Eighty-Four* was to be his last testament. "Recollections of George Orwell," *Northern Review* (Montreal), August–September 1953, 25–26. The idea that Jura's winters are "bleak," Crick has argued in his biography, drawing on climatological evidence, is "an isothermic fantasy" (p. 511). Nevertheless, it was surely rash of Orwell, given his fragile health in 1947–48, to go to a place where he was 25 miles from a doctor and without a telephone.

**35.** John Dahlburg, "Consumed by His Book, George Orwell Died for It," *Fort Myers News Press* (Va.), 1 January 1984. See also "Each Day's Work Brought Author Closer to His Death," *Pensacola Journal* (Fla.), 22 December 1983. Copies in Rosenblum Collection.

**36.** See, for example, Malcolm Muggeridge's discussion of *Burmese Days* as a transparently autobiographical novel. "Revaluation—*Burmese Days*," *World Review*, June 1950, 45–48. Muggeridge did not meet Orwell until 1944.

**37.** Even Sonia Orwell innocently believed that the autobiographical sections of *The Road to Wigan Pier*, published well before she met Orwell around 1940, were "straight autobiography." When Bernard Crick, specially authorized by her to write Orwell's life, speculated that Orwell might have freely reconstructed or even invented material in the essays and documentaries for polemical effect, Mrs. Orwell protested against Crick's "doubting his word." Bernard Crick, "Orwelliana," *New Statesman*, 17 September 1982, 20.

**38.** See the July 1949 *Book-of-the-Month Club News*, 8.

**39.** K. A. Jelenski, "The Literature of Disenchantment," *Survey*, April 1962, 114. Italics supplied. Milton Blau, "Pig's Eye View," *New Masses*, 10 September 1946, 24–25.

**40.** Stephen Spender, "The Truth About Orwell," *New York Review of Books*, 16 November 1972, 4. Malcolm Muggeridge refers to his frequent conversations with Orwell on this subject in *Chronicles of Wasted Time*, Vol. 1 (London, 1972), 272–73. See, for example, Joseph Evans, "The Bookshelf," *Wall Street Journal*, 16 June 1949, 4.

**41.** Unpublished letter from Orwell to his agent Leonard Moore, 9 January 1947. Berg Collection, New York Public Library.

**42.** See Les K. Adler and Thomas G. Paterson, "Red Fascism: The Merger of Nazi Germany and Soviet Russia in the American Image of Totalitarianism, 1930s–1950s," *American Historical Review*, 1970, 1046–64.

**43.** But it seems likely that, although Orwell's main assault was directed against the totalitarian Left's cooptation of the word "socialism," he meant "Ingsoc" to reflect the doublespeak of the Stalinists *and* the Nazis (the National *Socialists*). That Ingsoc is sometimes taken to signal Orwell's abandonment of *democratic* socialism is another illustration of his being victimized by the very forces he attacked.

**44.** Warburg, *All Authors Are Equal*, 104.

**45.** *CEJL*, Vol. 4, 502.

**46.** George Malcolm Thomson, "I Choose George Orwell," *Evening Standard*, 7 June 1949.

**47.** Frank O'Connor, "It's Fiction All Right, But Is It Political?," *New York Times Book Review*, 31 March 1957, 4.

**48.** "Nineteen Eighty-Four," *Reader's Digest*, September 1949, 129–57. "The Strange World of 1984," *Life*, 4 July 1949, 78.

**49.** See, for example, Kelsey Guilfoil, "How Thought Will Perish Under Red Rule," *Chicago Sunday Tribune Magazine*, 12 June 1949; and B.K. Sandwell, "On Logical Socialist Development, Orwell Is a Bitter Prophet," *Saturday Night*, 5 July 1949, 12.

**50.** "Re: Certain Liberals," *Freeman*, 19 November 1952, 119.

**51.** Atkins, 115.

**52.** Philip Rieff, "George Orwell and the Post-Liberal Imagination," *Kenyon Review*, Winter 1954, 49.

**53.** For the selling of *Nineteen Eighty-Four* as "a conservative novel," see "Birchites Open Office in White Plains," *New York Herald Tribune*, 16 December 1964, 9.

**54.** Deutscher, "*1984*—The Mysticism of Cruelty," 244.

**55.** "If Orwell Were Alive Today," *Harper's*, January 1983, 30–37. Robert de Camera,

"Homage to Orwell," *National Review*, 13 May 1983, 572. Irving Howe (ed.), "1984: Enigmas of Power," in *1984 Revisited: Totalitarianism in Our Century* (New York, 1983), 17. Alexander Cockburn, "Chronicles of a Decent Man," *Village Voice*, 1 February 1983.

56. In 1981 the anti-Sandinista newspaper *La Prensa* even serialized *Animal Farm*, presenting it as applicable to the allegedly corrupt Sandinista revolution. See Nick Frazier, "Sandinistas Testing in Ailing Nicaragua," *Wall Street Journal*, 4 May 1981.

57. "Grenada, By O'Neill, By Orwell," *New York Times*, 10 November 1983.

58. On military issues, see: "Soviet Union: The Threat from Within," *Toronto Star*, 21 December 1982; and Colin Colvert, "Stick Out Your Tongue and Say . . . ," *Detroit Free Press*, 7 January 1983.

On abortion, privacy, feminism, and social questions, see: Edwin Yoder, "Doublespeak Clouds Abortion Debate," *Chicago Sun-Times*, 7 December 1982. "1984 Is Legalized Murder," *The Lake Charles Catholic Calendar* (La.), 25 February 1984. Daniel Kagan, "Big Brother Is Closing In," *Penthouse*, January 1984. "Schweiker Defends Teenage Birth Control Plan," *New York Times*, 10 February 1982. Judy Goldsmith, "Feminists Challenge 1984," *Miami Herald*, 2 January 1983. Copies in Rosenblum Collection.

59. Podhoretz, *Making It*, 30–31. Howe, "As the Bones Know," 97. Crick, 26.

60. Leopold Labedz, "Will George Orwell Survive 1984?," *Encounter*, June 1984, 11–18. Irving Kristol, "There'll Never Be a 1984," *The Wall Street Journal*, 16 December 1983.

61. "Orwell Takes Over as Philippine Society Crumbles," *Washington Star*, 3 August 1981. Carole Hemingway, "Orwell Would Have Loved It," *Patriot-Ledger* (Quincy, Mass.), 28 June 1982. "Orwell in Warsaw," *Richmond Contra Costa Independent* (Calif.), 17 December 1982. Scott Langford, *Fort Wayne Journal Gazette*, 23 June 1982. Copies in Rosenblum Collection.

Rev. W. Donald Beaudreault, "Orwell in the Classroom," *New Orleans Times-Picayune*, 28 August 1981. "An Antidote to Orwell," *Travel Weekly*, 22 December 1983. Kennedy's speech was delivered 25 February 1983. The *Albequerque Journal* cartoon appeared in *Time*, 19 September 1983, 36. The second cartoon is from the *Philadelphia Inquirer*, 19 October 1986.

62. Frank Whelan, "George Orwell: Product of the Class System," *Allentown Morning Call* (Pa.), 2 February 1984. Copy in Rosenblum Collection.

63. Donald McDonald, "Orwellian Journalism," *Center Magazine*, September 1974, 72.

64. "Journalists Are Elite of 1984," *St. Paul Dispatch* (Minn.), 17 January 1984. Copy in Rosenblum Collection.

65. Except in his biography of Orwell, nowhere in print have I found Bernard Crick's suggested working distinction between "Orwell-like" ("moral seriousness") and "Orwellian" ("ghastly political future"). The distinction is Crick's own, not part of Orwell's reception history, as Crick implies. "He loved the land and he loved England and he loved the language of the liturgies of the English Church. 'Orwell-like' conveys all these things; Orwellian other things." Earlier Crick admits that "Orwellian" is indeed sometimes taken to signify Orwell's "manner" as well as Oceania's horrors (pp. 23, 488, 580).

66. Colvert, "Stick Out Your Tongue and Say. . . ." *Detroit Free Press*, 7 January 1983. "Still More Repression in Poland," *Newsday*, 22 February 1982. "Poland's New Consciousness," *Christian Science Monitor*, 21 June 1983.

67. Copies of these articles are in the Rosenblum Collection:

(1)

John Schulian, "Lee Sets the Tone on a Team of Orwellian Stature," *Everett Herald* (Wash.), 1 January 1984.

Jane Dubose, "Big Brother," *Knoxville News Centinel* (Tenn.), 11 February 1984.

(2)

Ellen Goodman, "Reagan Wins Orwellian Prize," *Fort Worth Star-Telegram* (Texas), 7 December 1982. Goodman awarded first prize in her "George Orwell War-Is-Peace Sweepstakes" to, "hands down, The Great Communicator himself, Ronald Reagan."

Barbara Shibels, "Orwellian Child Testimony Decision," *Middlesex Daily News* (Mass.), 18 November 1983.

"Orwellian Nightmare Thwarted by Travel Industry," *Meeting News*, October 1983.

"Cable TV an Orwellian Plot" (letter), *Batavia Chronicle* (Ill.), 16 September 1981.

"An Orwellian Reagan Plan," *Los Angeles Herald-Examiner* 28 July 1983.

"Afghan Education: Orwellian," *San Antonio Light,* 27 November 1981.

Robert Cross, "1999: A Year So Dreadful It Shames the Orwellian Vision," *Chicago Tribune,* 1 January 1984.

George Clay, "Official Calls State Fire Code Imposition Orwellian," *Ithaca Journal* (N.Y.), 11 November 1981.

Neal Skene, "We're Doing Orwellian Things to Ourselves," *St. Petersburg Times* (Fla.), 1 January 1984.

"Snoop Force Called Orwellian," *Windsor Star* (Ontario), 28 May 1983.

Anthony Lewis, "Orwellian Example in Poland," *Franklin News Herald* (Pa.), 1 March 1982.

"Baby Jane Doe Called 'Orwellian' Tragedy in Court," *Hayward Daily Review* (Calif.), 3 December 1983.

(3)

Kevin Hyland, "Where Will the Orwellian Fascination End?," *Syracuse Herald-Journal* (N.Y.), 16 January 1983.

"TVA Power Control Center—an Orwellian Enchantment?," *Nashville Banner* (Tenn.), 24 August 1981.

Scott Powers, "Orwellian Technology Turns into Satellite Art," *Chicago Sun-Times,* 1 January 1984.

68. Edward Thomas, *Orwell* (London, 1965).

69. T. R. Fyvel, *George Orwell: A Personal Memoir* (London, 1982), 138, 148–50. (Hereafter cited as Fyvel.)

70. "Where Is Orwell Now That We Need Him?," *Boston Globe,* 6 December 1982.

71. "If It's Orwellian, It's Not Obfuscatory," *Boston Globe,* 19 January 1983.

72. "Schweiker Defends Teenage Birth Control Plan."

73. See footnote 58 above.

74. *Time,* 28 November 1983.

75. "Orwell Takes Over as Philippine Society Crumbles."

76. Richard Vorhees, *The Paradox of George Orwell* (Lafayette, Ind., 1961). Raymond Williams, *George Orwell* (New York, 1971), 88–92. Peter Lewis, *George Orwell: The Road to 1984* (London, 1981), 1–18. Margaret Sullivan, "Orwell's Life Full of Paradox," *Buffalo Evening News* (N.Y.), 1 January 1984. Copy in Rosenblum Collection.

77. *CEJL,* Vol. 4, 139.

78. *CEJL,* Vol. 1, 6–7.

79. "The Lure of Profundity," *New English Weekly,* 30 December 1937, 235–36.

80. Raymond Williams, *Politics and Letters* (London, 1979), 391–92.

81. Atkins, 1.

82. William Salter, "Look and Listen," *New Statesman and Nation,* 18 December 1954.

83. Ralph Waldo Emerson, *Journals,* Vol. 5 (Boston, 1913), 312.

84. See also Jeffrey Meyers' discussion of Orwell's reputation in his introduction to *George Orwell: The Critical Heritage,* 1–36; Bernard Crick's discussion of *Nineteen Eighty-Four*'s critical reception in 1949 in his Clarendon edition of Orwell's *Nineteen Eighty-Four* (Oxford, 1984), 92–104; David Rankin, "The Critical Reception of the Art and Thought of George Orwell," Dissertation, University College, London University, 1965; and David Pryce-Jones, "Orwell's Reputation," in *The World of George Orwell,* ed. Miriam Gross (London, 1971), 144–52.

85. *Adelphi,* November 1935, 86.

86. Compton Mackenzie, *Daily Mail,* 12 March 1935.

87. Quoted in Crick, 258.

88. I.R. Willison, "George Orwell: Some Materials for a Bibliography" (Part III), School of Librarianship, University of London, 1953. All publishing data pertaining to Gollancz in Chapter One are from Willison.

89. Geoffrey Gorer, "A Really Important Book," *Time and Tide,* 30 April 1938, 599. Reprinted in Meyers, 121–23.

90. See Harry Pollitt, *Daily Worker,* 17 March 1937.

91. Q.D. Leavis, "The Literary Life Respectable," *Scrutiny*, September 1940, 173–76.

92. Atkins, 323–47.

93. Willison, . . . "Materials for a Bibliography," Part III.

94. Orwell comments on Dial Press's mistake in *CEJL*, Vol. 4, 110.

95. Harry Scherman, "A Statement," *Book-of-the-Month Club News*, August 1946, 1.

96. Publishing information about the sales of Orwell's books between 1946 and 1970 comes from Warburg, *All Authors Are Equal*, 35–59, 92–121.

97. Koestler's prediction is recounted in Crick, 395.

98. John Middleton Murry, "Orwell and Connolly," *Adelphi*, July–September 1946, 165–74.

99. Edmund Wilson, "Books," *New Yorker*, 25 May 1946, 82–83.

100. "Great Books Make Themselves," *Book-of-the-Month Club News*, August 1949.

101. Warburg, *All Authors Are Equal*, 116.

102. Kenneth Allsop, "He Became a Legend in His Own Lifetime," *Picture Post*, 8 January 1955, 39, 41; J. D. Scott, "Orwell," *Saturday Review*, 30 March 1957; James Hilton, review of *Such, Such Were the Joys*, in *New York Herald Tribune Book Review*, 1 March 1953, 3.

103. Kenneth C. Davis, *Two-Bit Culture: The Paperbacking of America* (Boston, 1984), 188–90.

104. T. R. Fyvel, "A Case for George Orwell," *Twentieth Century*, September 1956, 254–55. Donald Barr, "The Answer to Orwell," *Saturday Review*, 30 March 1957, 21. Kingsley Amis, "The Road to Airstrip One," *Spectator*, 31 August 1956, 292.

105. Robert Conquest, "George Orwell," in *George Orwell: Selected Writings*, ed. George Bott (London, 1958).

106. The adaptations reflected the times. The preface to Nelson Bond's *Animal Farm* (1961), first performed in Virginia, reads: "You will meet beasts whose prototypes have dominated news headlines for a half hundred years. . . . The entire action of the [play] takes place in England . . . . You may decide for yourself that the real scene is set several hundred miles further to the east." *Nineteen Eighty-Four*, meanwhile, was commercialized into a mawkish romance by Robert Owens, Wilton Hall, and William Miles (1963).

107. Eugene McNamara, *The Critic*, October–November 1958, 42.

108. K. W. Alexander and Alexander Hobbs, "What Influences Labour MPs?," *New Society*, 13 December 1962, 11–14.

109. Philip Toynbee, "Orwell's Passion," *Encounter*, August 1959, 81.

110. "Briefly Noted," *New Yorker*, 3 September 1960, 106.

111. At the 1964 Warren Commission hearings on President Kennedy's assassination, Marine Corps friends of Lee Harvey Oswald testified that *Nineteen Eighty-Four* was "one of his favorite books" and "our traditional meeting ground." So preoccupied was Oswald with the book that he would often compare the Marine Corps with Oceania and would sometimes refer to fellow Marines as "Smith, Winston" or "O'Brien." See *The President's Commission on the Assassination of President Kennedy* (Washington, D.C., 1964), vol. 8, 254–55, and vol. 11, 66–95.

112. Holman, *Outside the Whale*, 1976. Another dramatization of Orwell's life, *Eric Blair Tonight*, by Howard Slaughter, was performed in January 1984 at the University of Akron.

113. "Odd Man In," *Time*, 15 November 1968, 110.

114. Rayner Heppenstall, "A Blurred Portrait," *Encounter*, February–March 1981, 77–80. George Woodcock, "Unwanted Biography," *Canadian Forum*, April 1981, 24–26.

115. Orwell is affectionately satirized as Basil, an eccentric polemicist, in Stevie Smith's *The Holiday* (London, 1949), 67–69. Quoted in Crick, 424. See also E.L. Doctorow, "On the Brink of 1984," *Playboy*, January 1984; and "Big Brother Is Closing In," *Penthouse*, January 1984.

116. See, for example, "Orwell Quite Wrong on 1984 Predictions, Thatcher Tells U.S.," *The Globe & Mail* (Toronto), 31 December 1983. Also Anne Gottlieb, "Is 1984 Really Here?," *McCall's*, January 1984, 20, 96–101, 119.

**"any writer since Marx":** Dennis J. O'Keefe, review of Crick's *George Orwell: A Life*, in *Policy Review*, Summer 1981, 130.

117. See, for example, Daphne Patai, *The Orwell Mystique: A Study in Male Ideology* (Amherst, 1984). Lynette Hunter, *George Orwell: The Search for a Voice* (Suffolk, 1984).

118. In June 1986 the Theatre of Nations Festival, sponsored by the UN-supported International Theatre Institute, dropped *Animal Farm* from its playbill after pressure from East

European officials. An international outcry against the decision followed. Directed by Peter Hall and performed by the National Theatre of Great Britain, the adaptation had been a hit in London since 1984. See Jack Kroll, "The Politics of the Stage," *Newsweek*, 30 June 1986, 67.

119. *CEJL*, Vol. 2, 229.

120. From a BBC memorandum, quoted in Crick, 415; *CEJL*, Vol. 1, 310.

121. Kostelanetz, *"The End" Appendix*, 86.

### Chapter Two. *Terms of Repute: Conditions, Constraints*

#### 2. *Literary Studies and the Problem of Reputation*

1. Rust Hills, "The Structure of the American Literary Establishment," *Esquire*, July 1963, 40.

2. "American Writers: Who's Up, Who's Down?," *Esquire*, August 1977, 77–82.

3. William J. Goode, *The Celebration of Heroes: Prestige as a Control System* (Berkeley, 1978), 98–102.

4. Sociologists, following Max Weber's comments on social stratification in *Economy and Society*, have often addressed the subject under the category of "status," typically correlating it with class or professional position. See, for example, M.S. Larson, *The Rise of Professionalism: A Sociological Analysis* (Berkeley, 1977), esp. Part II ("The Collective Conquest of Status"), 66–144.

5. See, for example, Max Horkheimer and Theodor Adorno, "The Culture Industry: Enlightenment as Mass Deception," in *The Dialectic of Enlightenment*, trans. John Cumming (New York, 1972), 120–67; Peter Uwe Hohendahl, *The Institution of Criticism* (Ithaca, 1982).

6. The single academic discussion of the subject in conceptual terms is a short section entitled "Reputations" in Alistair Fowler's *Kinds of Literature* (Cambridge, 1982). The best descriptive essay on changing taste remains Henri Peyre's "The Search for Standards and the Myth of Posterity," in *Writers and Their Critics: A Study of Misunderstanding* (Ithaca, 1944), revised and retitled *The Failures of Criticism* (1967). Cyril Connolly's essay "Reputations" (1950), collected in his *Ideas and Places* (London, 1953), is an editor's witty suggestion on how to get the better of posterity and achieve lasting fame.

Many earlier essays deal with "reputation" by way of remarks on the vogue for (or neglect of) particular authors, or via reflections on literary taste. See, for example, E.E. Kellett, *The Whirligig of Taste* (London, 1929) and *Fashion in Literature: A Study of Changing Taste* (London, 1931). For two more general historical and sociological discussions of reputation, see Leo Braudy, *The Frenzy of Renown* (New York, 1986) and Pierre Bourdieu, *Distinction* (New York, 1985).

7. C. Day Lewis, *Poetic Image* (London, 1969), 18.

8. Jean-Paul Sartre, *The Psychology of Imagination*, trans. Bernard Frechtman (New York, 1966), 7.

9. William Hazlitt, *Table Talk* (London, [1821–22] 1869), 340.

10. Aristotle, *The Rhetoric*, trans. John Henry Freese (Cambridge, Mass., 1982), 12. Italics supplied.

11. See, for example, Jonathan Yardley, "The Faulkner Factor, Cont'd: On Making Writers' Reputations," *Washington Post*, 23 April 1984, C 1.

12. Harold Nicolson, *The Meaning of Prestige* (Cambridge, 1937), 7.

13. Latin etymology points up how the process of "gaining a reputation" emerges from canonical acts of selection and purification. The Romans often punned and conflated *putare* (primary meaning: to lop, prune, purify) with *putere* (to rot or stink as in "putrid"). *Putidus* was frequently applied to literary style, meaning "in bad taste." One could therefore reconstruct "re-puting" as an act of "pruning the branches," or "purifying the impure."

14. "Neglected Books," *American Scholar*, 38 (1970), 318–45. When solicited for his opinions, Wallace Stegner violated the genteel game and asked the editors of the *American Scholar* the question which seemed to be on others' minds: "Why don't you ask sometime for a list of books that get altogether too *much* attention for what they offer? Then we could all take out our

hatchets and have fun" (p. 345). For other treatments of the subject, see several articles in *Antaeus* under the headline "Neglected Books of the Twentieth Century," in the following issues: Summer 1975, 133–36; Autumn 1975, 136–40; Autumn 1979, 107–14.

15. The best discussion in the sociology of art is Howard Becker's chapter "Reputation" in *Art Worlds* (Berkeley, 1982), 351–71. Becker devotes his main attention to production and distribution networks in the fine arts.

16. See Podhoretz on "the whole business of reputation" in American intellectual life. *Making It* (New York, 1967), 352. See also Richard Kostelanetz's *The End of Intelligent Writing*, esp. "The Literary and Industrial Complex," 183–215.

17. See especially Mailer's "First Advertisement for Myself," *Advertisements for Myself* (New York, 1959); Kostelanetz, *The End of Intelligent Writing*, 51–53.

18. See Robert K. Merton, "The Matthew Effect in Science," *Science*, June 1968, 56–63.

19. W.J.T. Mitchell, "Critical Inquiry and the Ideology of Pluralism," *Critical Inquiry*, September 1982, 613, 616.

20. Chuck Ross, "*Steps*—Rejected," *New West*, 12 February 1979, 39–43.

21. *Ibid.* Random House's score, according to Ross, was one published manuscript out of 60,000 to 70,000 unsolicited submissions.

22. A celebrated case of neglect and discovery was Barbara Pym, who went unpublished for 16 years until Stephen Spender and Lord David Cecil included her in a 1977 list of "most underrated writers." A publisher called Pym immediately, and four of her unpublished works appeared in the next four years.

Nor is the Kosinski incident an isolated example. The so-called Doris Lessing Hoax was the same experiment conducted by the author herself under the pseudonym Jane Somers. She discovered, as Anthony Trollope had a century ago after engaging in a similar test in mid-career, that "merit" often counts for less than existing reputation towards the continued success of an established writer's books. (The reviews for "Lessing's" novels were noticeably warmer the second time around.) See "The Doris Lessing Hoax," *Washington Post*, 29 September 1984.

23. Kostelanetz, *The End of Intelligent Writing*, 107–23. The story of his difficulties in getting this book published is recounted in his sequel, *"The End" Appendix*.

24. Richard Ohmann, *English in America: A Radical View of the Profession* (New York, 1976), 213, 231.

25. Frye, *Anatomy of Criticism*, 18.

26. Kenneth Burke, *Permanence and Change* (Indianapolis, [1935] 1965), 274–94.

27. Frye, *Anatomy of Criticism*, 16, 18.

28. *Ibid.*, 16.

29. Barbara Herrnstein Smith, "Contingencies of Value," *Critical Inquiry*, September 1983, 1–34. Among the chief reasons for the decline of evaluation as a literary issue, Smith argues, have been the following: the academy's persistent, near-exclusive attachment to questions of meaning and interpretation (partly traceable to the modern philosophic preoccupation with language and language-centered theory); the conflicting disciplinary traditions of positivistic scholarship and humanistic pedagogy (generating the once widely practiced division of labor between "objective" scholars and "judicial" critics); and the attempts to "elevate" literature to the ranks of the sciences ("poetry as poetry") or to convert it into a secular religion. Obviously, these factors have also contributed to repress the emergence of reputation as a literary issue. Her essay is reprinted in *Canons*, ed. Robert von Hallberg (Chicago, 1984). For her fuller treatment of evaluation, see her *Contingencies of Value* (Cambridge, Mass., 1988).

30. René Wellek and Austin Warren, *Theory of Literature* (New York, [1949] 1970), 238–52. John Ellis also confuses them in his chapter "Evaluation," in *The Theory of Literary Criticism* (Berkeley, 1974), 83.

31. See Becker's discussion of this so-called law in *Art Worlds*, 362.

32. Wellek and Warren, *Theory of Literature*, 247.

33. For a critical anthology of "neglected" twentieth-century fiction which has been already published, see David Madden's *Rediscoveries* (New York, 1971).

34. For example, according to the *Oxford English Dictionary*, until the seventeenth century

"approve" and "approbate" were synonymous with "to value" in the sense of "to prove" (meaning "to demonstrate to be true").

35. Samuel Johnson, *Rasselas, Poems and Selected Prose*, ed. Bertrand Bronson (New York, 1952), 239–87.

36. David Hume, *"Of the Standard of Taste" and Other Essays*, ed. John W. Lenz (Indianapolis, 1965).

37. See John Laird's *The Idea of Value* (Cambridge, 1929) for a general discussion of the British moralists, approval, and value.

38. See, for example, von Hallberg's *Canons*.

39. Gabriel Pearson, quoted in Francis Murphy's introduction to Winters' *Uncollected Essays and Reviews* (Chicago, 1973), 20.

40. Conor Cruise O'Brien, "Orwell Looks at the World," in *George Orwell: A Collection of Essays*, ed. Raymond Williams (London, 1974), 160.

41. Cf. Charles A. Moser, "National Renown and International Reputation: The Case of Ivan Vasov," *Slavic and East European Journal*, Vol. 23 (1979), 87–93.

42. Florence Howe, "Those We Still Don't Read," *College English*, January 1981, 12–16.

43. And, of course, to veil the connections between literary canons and political imperatives outside education and publishing. For instance, concerns about Empire, working-class cultivation, and the dangers of female emancipation were apparently chief factors leading to the incorporation of English literature into the British school curriculum. Chris Baldick, *The Social Mission of English Criticism, 1848–1932* (Oxford, 1983), 59–83.

44. Charles Altieri, "An Idea and Ideal of a Literary Canon," *Critical Inquiry*, September 1983, 37–60. Also reprinted in von Hallberg's *Canons*.

45. Quoted in Christine Froula, "When Eve Reads Milton: Undoing the Canonical Economy," in von Hallberg's *Canons*, 152.

46. John Guillory, "Canon-Formation," *Critical Inquiry*, September 1983, 198.

47. The modern practice of shifting the monuments under the guise of canon-formation— what Frye referred to as the "work[ing] out . . . [of] combinations of promotion and demotion"— was first reflected in Cleanth Brooks's influential essay "Notes Toward a Revised Literary History." Brooks merely revised some lines of influence in the existing neoclassical and Romantic canons, not even raising the question as to whether those authors and works canonized merited their "major" reputations. The essay is collected in his *Modern Poetry and the Tradition* (Chapel Hill, 1939).

Even Marxist and post-structuralist critics, for all their attention to "marginality" and gestures of exclusion, have been curiously uninterested in actively "transvaluing" the canon in line with their theoretical assumptions (e.g., to include proletarian literature). Instead they have usually reinterpreted confirmed "major" authors.

Of all the movements in contemporary criticism, only feminists as a group have openly sought to revise the high canon. Even they seem to have done so less from theoretical principles than for cultural reasons of collective identity, arguing in effect for a retroactive affirmative action program which would increase "minority representation" in the high canon.

48. I have spoken throughout this section of "the" literary academy, but of course there is no such monolithic institution. For instance, continental literary theory has traditionally been more concerned with literary evaluation than has Anglo-American criticism, though no European critical movement has systematically studied literary reputation either.

49. To what extent may the repression of reputation by literary academics be related to what sociologist Helmut Schoeck refers to as the "the repression of envy" in the sociological literature? Envy is a frequent accompaniment of fame, and if Podhoretz's remarks in *Making It* on the importance of "the politics of literary envy and literary adulation" (p. 352) for literary repute have any basis in fact, the inattention to both subjects may be an expression of envy-avoidance. What Schoeck calls our "egalitarian mask" may be the counterpart to the mask of judicial objectivity governing verdicts about literary value and repute. Shoeck sees intellectual elites as especially prone to "prestige-avoidance," which he considers a form of envy-avoidance, since they feel they must, in an egalitarian society, avoid outward expression of their self-presumed innate superiority.

Adulation and envy touch very closely: to be reputed "successful" is to invite either the adoration of an inferior or the envy of a peer or superior. Which passion gets expressed is to some extent a matter of the perception of distance between the parties: when the distance is great enough, we stop envying and start adoring. To adore or envy openly is to admit one's "inferiority" openly. As Schoeck demonstrates, discussion of envy is avoided even in conversation; instead the word "jealousy" (the passionate endeavor to keep something that is by right one's own) is invariably substituted for envy (the desire for another's possession). We know that it reflects better on us to confess "jealousy": much "better" to be an Othello than a Iago. *Envy: A Theory of Social Behavior* (New York, 1969), esp. "The Eminent in a Society of Equals," 274–85.

### 3. A Critical Perspective

50. German literary theory on audience reception is pluralistic and goes by various names: *Wirkungsgeschichte, Wirkungsforschung, Wirkungsästhetik, Rezeptionsästhetik,* and others.

*Wirkung* is usually translated either as "effect" or "response"; *Wirkungsgeschichte* (the history of effect) is a sociohistorical approach to reception, usually identified with nineteenth- and early twentieth-century studies of influence of authors on subsequent writers. *Wirkungsforschung* (research on effects) is empirical reception theory, usually conducted via questionnaires and statistical analyses of the responses of "real" readers to texts. *Wirkungsästhetik* (the aesthetics of response) is a phenomenological treatment of the reading experience, typically associated with Wolfgang Iser's work at the University of Konstanz on reading as performance, i.e., on the reader's role in constituting texts. *Rezeptionsästhetik* (the aesthetics of reception), a combination of sociohistorical and phenomenological concerns (finally leaning more to formalism), is concerned with the history of reader response and is usually identified with the work of Iser's Konstanz colleague Hans Robert Jauss. Jauss's work in the aesthetics of reception has gained most attention in West Germany, and it is our chief point of reference in this chapter.

Although reception theory has dominated West German literary studies since the late 1960s, neither empirical nor phenomenological/hermeneutic reception theorists have distinguished "reception" from "reputation." From the outsider's viewpoint, the German focus on reception has not resulted in a sharpening of method, or indeed even in any consensus on what the aims of reception studies should be. Nor have empirical and phenomenological theorists engaged each other's work. Empirical reception studies have been theoretically impoverished, leading the Konstanz School to treat them as naive scientism; Jauss's work on historical reception has proven more impressive in concept than useful in method, inviting empiricists to write it off as grand theorizing.

For a useful overview of work in German reception studies, see Robert Holub, *Reception Theory: An Introduction* (New York, 1984), esp. 53–107, 134–47.

51. Spatial metaphors like "level," "link," "axis," "coil," and "network" are useful for suggesting the structural character of some interrelationships within the reputation process. But, like "group" and "institution," they suffer the danger of reification and the Whiteheadian fallacy of misplaced concreteness, the fallacy of assuming that our concepts precisely capture the content to which they are applied. For reputation involves an intersubjective relationship: no metaphor, structural or otherwise, can render its nuances and complexity. Moreover, groups and institutions are structured in a wide variety of ways. Mass communication theorists have, for example, discussed how groups structured as "wheels" (one person connected to all group members as "hub") operate differently from those structured in some sort of "chain" of persons with no center. Doubtless such differences influence reception patterns. But it is far beyond the scope of our intentions to investigate the geometrical character of reception groups.

52. C. Wright Mills, "The Cultural Apparatus," in his *Power, Politics and People,* ed. Irving Louis Horowitz (New York, 1963), 406.

53. Even this rudimentary characterization of cultural radiation—from author to critic to group to public—is, however, routinely contradicted. The radiation of reputation is not a simple "trickle-down" process: there is constant back-and-forth movement and inter-level interaction among people and institutions. Nor is the "average reader" a passive consumer of

elite and mass media opinions. Sometimes critic-reviewers will be influenced as much or more by a group or by the public as the reverse in a particular case. Thus the radiation of a reputation is not merely patterned in ever-widening circles. Images and opinions are exchanged from person to person and from small groups to large groups, each communication act modifying the image in different ways. While reputations usually dim as they radiate outward, this is by no means always so, especially given the mass media's capacity to create vivid (if often one-dimensional) public images.

54. Cf. Cyril Connolly, "Reputations," in *Ideas and Places* (London, 1953).

55. For our point of departure is the insistence that a study of historical reception start and end with the historical materials. Although we grapple with the formation of consciousness and ideology, our rhetoric of reception rests on an historical, rather than a phenomenological, grounding. Admittedly, this makes study of reputations in the distant past near-impossible. But if no actual reading responses can be discovered during a historical period, then, simply, an author's reputation during that time cannot be reconstructed. Although in many ways a notable methodological accomplishment, *Rezeptionsästhetik* has long resisted this plain fact. The consequence for Jauss's practical criticism is to render "reception history" a mere report of a contemporary critic-reader's response, making his "historical" reader little different in practice from Iser's "implied" reader.

*Rezeptionsästhetik* treats a reader's aesthetic experience in the act of processing a text (what goes on in his mind when "reading it fully"), and only secondarily a selected reader's historical response to the text. Jauss hypostatizes the reader on a sociohistorical basis as an "ideal historical" reader; his selected reader is effectively a text function rather than a concrete historical recipient. Nowhere in his practical criticism does Jauss indicate where his selected readers meet or depart from his historical reader-norm (the "horizon of expectations"), or even how to plot the norm. Instead Jauss begins his practical criticism with phenomenological considerations and never does give serious consideration to empirical, sociological problems of reception.

For an example of an application of *Rezeptionsästhetik*, see "The Poetic Text Within the Change of Horizons of Reading: The Example of Baudelaire's Spleen II," in *Toward an Aesthetics of Reception* (Minneapolis, 1982), 139–85. Jauss never explains in this essay how his chosen historical readers (Gautier, Paul Bourget, Huysmans, Sebastian Neumeister) possess authority as influential readers or as "reader-norms," or indeed how their responses constitute anything except their own idiosyncratic experiences.

56. See Kenneth Burke, *A Grammar of Motives* (Berkeley, 1945) and *A Rhetoric of Motives* (Berkeley, 1950).

57. Treating reception materials as institutional discourse further marks our difference in approach from *Rezeptionsästhetik*. Disdaining "pragmatic history," which "must reconstruct the life of the past from largely mute evidence or ideologically motivated statements," Jauss says that the "advantage" of "art history" is that it is constructed "from works that are still accessible to us—or can become so again—in aesthetic pleasure and understanding." This emphasis on aesthetic pleasure leads Jauss to abdicate the twin tasks of historical and aesthetic evaluation. Jauss renounces the literary historian's difficult and always imperfectly executed task of giving voice to mute evidence within specific contexts and of weighing ideologically motivated (i.e., "distorted") evidence. By contrast, a "rhetorical" approach is inevitably "pragmatic history." It is a judging and interpreting of the ideologically motivated discourse in which readers have responded to authors—and in and through which authors have presented themselves to the world. Jauss, "Art History and Pragmatic History," *Toward an Aesthetics of Reception*, 46–75.

58. See footnote 50 above.

59. In speaking of these various indices to a literary reputation, I should emphasize that empirical "measurement" of a reputation is near-impossible, even if it were desirable. For there are no opinion polls, and no elections. Likewise prizes are usually (or ostensibly) awarded according to aesthetic criteria, not popular acclaim. Judgments about public reputation based on an author's institutionalization are necessarily inexact and speculative. Critics and the media do "vote" in some sense, in a process far from democratic (with a voter like Lionel Trilling

exercising much more power than a classroom full of his Columbia students). But the votes are never (and cannot be) systematically weighted and tallied; even a Mailer is not officially running for literary office, and the prizes which get distributed (like Orwell's Partisan Review Award), whatever the apparent criteria, are themselves enmeshed in institutional history. Sales figures, reprints and foreign translations, broadcast adaptations, university courses on an author's work, academic publications—such quantitative criteria may or may not indicate accurately the size and shape of a reputation. What roughly identifies a "public" reputation is decisive entry of his work and biography into the institutions of education and the mass media, so that his name and work radiate beyond local circles.

60. Perhaps in this sense, our approach to reputation could be thought of as a broadened, self-aware *Wirkungsgeschichte*, conceiving of the writer's "impact" not merely in naive empirical or narrow biographical terms (i.e., as an indexing of responses or a classifying of literary influences), but rather as a wide-ranging cultural phenomenon in which the critic himself is also sensitive to his own position as an historical receiver. From another angle, a sociology of repute constitutes an effort to bridge the gap between the hermeneutical and empirical approaches through a case-history-as-method approach to reception.

61. There is, in other words, no "group reader-norm." To approach the institutional reader in terms of a "group mind" would be simply to hypostatize the reader on a different basis than does *Rezeptionsästhetik*.

62. In interpreting cultural material, we should not lose sight of the institutional practices and social forces which shape it. Often, however, these are not easily open to analysis. A few of the case histories in Part Two do touch on these practices and forces. But for the most part I do little more in this study than acknowledge their structuring influence. How publishers market books, how literary reviews and criticism get written, how educators select books for curricula, how certain books get chosen for media adaptation: these processes bear on the making of all reputations. Clearly the literary industry does interact as a sub-system within the institution of "culture" and with other institutions (education, publishing, the mass media, the church, the government, entertainment, etc.). Moreover, there are not only different "levels" of the reputation process, but also different "phases": literary reception and social formation constitute a dynamic, reciprocal process. Reception is the fourth and last phase of this institutional process, following creation, production, and distribution. While I focus almost exclusively on the conditions of Orwell's reception, conditions of his books' production and distribution (e.g., *de facto* political censorship and paper shortages during World War II, the birth of the paperback book, the development of a postwar literary canon of "modern masters") have obviously influenced his reputation in ways hard to document. It is important to note that these logically prior factors are necessary to the actualizing of a reputation. If a book is not published and distributed, it will have no "reception"—and its author no (literary) reputation.

For a short discussion of the phases of the literary industry, see Priscilla Clark, "The Comparative Method: Sociology and the Study of Literature," *Yearbook of Comparative and General Literature*, 23 (1974), 5–13.

63. Jeffrey Sammons, *Literary Sociology and Practical Criticism* (New Haven, 1977), x.

64. Ralph Waldo Emerson, "Self-Reliance," *Selected Writings of Ralph Waldo Emerson*, ed. William Gilman (New York, 1965), 265.

65. *The Reader in the Text: Essays on Audience and Interpretation*, ed. Susan R. Suleiman and Inge Crosman (Princeton, 1980), vii.

66. At "higher" levels of reader reception, of course—where we will be more concerned with the author's cultural impact than with the texture of experience which individual readers possess of him—our focus is on how supra-individual entities (nations, professions, etc.) have responded to Orwell.

67. Trilling, *Homage to Catalonia*, viii–xi.

68. *Ibid.*, viii.

69. Lewis Nichols, "Talk with Lionel Trilling," *New York Times Book Review*, 13 February 1955, 21.

70. See Chaim Perelman, *The New Rhetoric: A Treatise on Argumentation* (South Bend, 1969), 168.

71. Trilling, "Orwell on the Future," *New Yorker,* 18 June 1949, 78.

72. The essay first appeared under the title "George Orwell and the Politics of Truth: Portrait of the Intellectual as a Man of Virtue," in *Commentary,* March 1952, 218–27.

73. Trilling, *Homage to Catalonia,* xi.

74. Trilling, *The Last Decade: Essays and Reviews 1965–75,* ed. Diana Trilling (New York, 1979), 230–31.

75. Trilling, "Orwell on the Future," 80–81. Trilling, *Homage to Catalonia,* xi.

76. *Ibid.,* vii–viii.

77. *Ibid.,* vii–xi.

78. See Podhoretz's *Making It, passim*; and Kostelanetz's *The End of Intelligent Writing,* 51–53.

79. Clifton Fadiman, "Lionel Trilling and the Party of the Imagination," *New Yorker,* 22 April 1950, 109–10.

80. Leslie Fiedler, "*Partisan Review:* Phoenix or Dodo?" (1956), in *Collected Essays* (New York, 1971), 53. "Those who condemn all else about [*Partisan Review*]," Fiedler went on, "specifically exempt him from the general blame. Yet he is in most ways not untypical: Jewish, a New Yorker who refuses to leave that city, an exploiter of the themes of anguish and alienation" (pp. 53–54).

81. Philip Toynbee, "An Attack on Our Cultural Idols," *New York Times,* 9 April 1950, 13.

82. The characterization is by the New York poet Harvey Breit. Connolly himself in turn proclaimed *Partisan Review* "by far the most interesting and progressive literary magazine in America, as well as politically the most far-sighted." Both comments are quoted in James Gilbert, *Writers and Partisans: A History of Literary Radicalism in America* (New York, 1968), 247.

83. Comparisons with Arnold and Forster come up repeatedly in reviews of Trilling's work; and so do the adjectives "liberal," "gracious," "courtly," "sincere," and even "authentic." See Morton Zabel, "The Straight Way Lost," *Nation,* 18 October 1947, 415–16. Milton Watson, "Turning New Leaves," *Canadian Forum,* October 1950, 160. John Holloway, "Sincerely, Lionel Trilling," *Encounter,* September 1973, 68.

84. Steven Marcus, "Lionel Trilling, 1905–75," in *Art, Politics, and Will: Essays in Honor of Lionel Trilling,* ed. Quentin Anderson, Stephen Donadio, and Steven Marcus (New York, 1977), 278.

85. Trilling, *Homage to Catalonia,* xvi.

86. See Crick, esp. 176–219.

87. William Barrett, *The Truants: Adventures Among the Intellectuals* (New York, 1982), 162.

88. The first two characterizations are from Dennis Donoghue, "The Critic in Reaction," *Twentieth Century,* October 1955, 377. The third is from Fiedler, "*Partisan Review. . . .*"

89. Podhoretz, *Making It,* 126.

90. If one were studying Henry Miller, for example, Orwell's authority on the British Left and the influence of his essay "Inside the Whale" would render him an authoritative voice in the formation of Miller's reputation.

91. Ernest Jones, *The Life and Work of Sigmund Freud,* ed. and abridged by Lionel Trilling and Steven Marcus (New York, 1961).

The variabilities of the reception groups which we will examine inevitably defy rigid formalizing. These groups vary in members' degree of group-identity and group-commitment; where pertinent, we will call attention to the implications of diverse group norms for a study of audience reception, mindful that people who commit themselves to professional (and other) groups rarely do so totally; their identities are not distilled essences of "the" group-identity; and the several groups with which they affiliate often have contradictory values, which a member usually reconciles only partially and not without conflict.

From roughly the '30s to the early '50s, however, many members of the *Partisan Review* group apparently considered themselves "we" in the sense of a contentious extended family. Howe in fact takes pains to emphasize the *Partisan* writers' sense of shared identity as a "we," the group as "tribe." Podhoretz describes the group as "a Jewish family" complete with non-Jewish "kissing cousins" and intra-family feuds. From the outside, Kostelanetz has referred to the New York writers' "group-aggrandizement," calling them "the mob," "the literary Mafia."

Considered with reference to the New York writers, then, Trilling's homey "we" is understandable, and it makes clear that Trilling's *Catalonia* essay was not only a portrait reflecting the London Orwell but creating the New Yorkers' Orwell.

See Podhoretz, *Making It*, 109; Howe, "New York Intellectuals," 30; and Kostelanetz, "Militant Minorities," *Hudson Review*, Autumn 1965, 480.

92. The fact that one is "a liberal New York Jewish intellectual of the generation of the '30s," in other words, does not mean that he or she will always respond identifiably *as* a Jew, liberal, etc. His or her response *may* be identifiably sectarian—and these "institutional" responses are the ones with which we are most interested. To paraphrase Sartre on Valéry in *Search for a Method*, Lionel Trilling was a liberal New York Jewish intellectual, but not all liberal New York Jewish intellectuals were Lionel Trilling.

93. For instance, whereas Trilling in his review of *Nineteen Eighty-Four* emphasized Orwell's affiliation with the liberal tradition, Rahv in *Partisan Review* stressed Orwell's anti-Communism. Diana Trilling in her *Nation* review, however, was bothered by Orwell's "implacable tone" and the "extreme pressure it exerts upon the reader." Philip Rahv, "The Unfuture of Utopia," *Partisan Review*, July 1949, 749. Mrs. Trilling's essay is in *Reviewing the Forties* (New York, 1978), 265.

94. See Chapter Five, Section 20, 336–62.

95. Barrett, *The Truants*, 124; see also 161–86.

95. Trilling, *Homage to Catalonia*, xi.

96. Barrett, *The Truants*, 169–72.

97. Norman Podhoretz, *Breaking Ranks: A Political Memoir* (New York, 1979), 300. One should note that, as they have done with Orwell, many of the New York Intellectuals have measured themselves against Trilling and claimed him as one of their own in the post-Vietnam era. Judgments differ between neoconservatives (Podhoretz, Barrett) and Left-liberals (William Phillips, Howe, Mark Krupnick) as to whether the main tendency of Trilling's political thought in the 1960s and '70s was conservative or liberal. For a critical view of Podhoretz's Trilling, see Mark Krupnick, "The Neoconservative Imagination," *Salmagundi*, Winter–Spring 1980, 202–8.

98. Alfred Kazin, *New York Jew* (New York, 1978), 43. "He seemed," concluded Kazin, "intent on not diminishing his career by a single word."

99. Joseph Frank, "Lionel Trilling and the Conservative Imagination" (1956), collected in *The Widening Gyre* (New Brunswick, N.J., 1963), 253–74.

100. The most vocal critic within the group was Delmore Schwartz. See his "The Duchess' Red Shoes," *Partisan Review*, January 1953, esp. 63–70. See also Podhoretz, *Breaking Ranks*, 299–301.

101. Podhoretz, *Breaking Ranks*, 300.

102. *Ibid.*

103. Barrett, *The Truants*, 161–62.

104. Trilling, *Homage to Catalonia*, vii, xxiii.

105. *Ibid.*, xiii.

106. Thus the making of a "hero" is neither necessarily so bankrupt and without valid psychosocial foundation as Max Horkheimer and Theodor Adorno's attacks on "the culture industry" would have it, nor so much purely "the communicative achievement of art" as Hans Robert Jauss maintains. Jauss rightly criticizes Adorno's *Aesthetic Theory* for claiming that the existence of heroes, real or fictional, as figures with which to identify, always seeks and serves to preserve ruling-class interests. But Jauss's idealist aesthetics ignores the institutional basis of hero-making, why one "hero candidate" rather than another is identified with and exalted to satisfy a community's needs. See Adorno, *Aesthetic Theory*, trans. C. Lenhardt (London, 1985). Jauss, "Levels of Identification in Hero and Audience," *New Literary History*, Winter 1974, 283–317.

107. The essay was never published, but the student has gone on to become an associate editor of *Partisan Review* and a professor at Columbia. The nameless graduate student was Steven Marcus. Letter to the author from Steven Marcus, 16 December 1986.

108. See Kazin, *New York Jew*, 42–43; Barrett, *The Truants*, 161–65; and Podhoretz, *Making*

*It,* 126, and *Breaking Ranks,* 300. On Trilling's elastic use of the first person plural, see George Elliott, "Who Is *We?*," in *A Piece of Lettuce: Personal Essays* (New York, 1964).

109. See Podhoretz, *Making It, passim;* and Kostelanetz, *The End of Intelligent Writing,* 51–53. Other indications of Trilling's stature at mid-century, within and outside the group, included his selection by Rahv and Phillips to introduce the *Partisan Review Reader* (1946) and his appearance on the cover of the *Saturday Review* upon publication of *The Opposing Self* (12 February 1955). Kostelanetz also notes Trilling's and *Partisan Review*'s proximity to the New York-based national media; surely this proximity contributed to the wide circulation of their opinions.

110. Fiedler, *"Partisan Review . . . ,"* 53.

111. Often the phrase "virtuous man" is quoted without any attribution to Trilling: the characterization has become part of Orwelliana. See, for example, Gayle Golden, "Orwell: Man vs. Myth," *Dallas Morning News,* 1 January 1984.

112. See, for example, Edmund Fuller, "No Middle Stool," *Saturday Review,* 12 July 1952. "Without this interpretive help, the book probably would not carry its proper weight today" (p. 17).

113. Paul Zimmerman, "The Truthteller," *Newsweek,* 28 October 1968, 120.

114. In addition to the essay's appearance in *The Opposing Self,* it has been reprinted in Irving Howe's *Nineteen Eighty-Four: Text, Sources, Criticism* and in Raymond Williams, *George Orwell: A Collection of Essays.* Its appearance in these collections has widened its influence and enhanced its stature. It has in turn lent lustre to these collections, and become itself the subject of flattering introductions. Thus are institutional influences reciprocal and mutually reinforcing. Williams calls it in his introduction "a classic statement" of "the general judgment of Orwell that shaped his initial literary reputation: the man who told the truth. The case is better put by Trilling than by anyone else I know" (p. 6). In *George Orwell: The Critical Heritage,* editor Jeffrey Meyers also calls Trilling's introduction "probably the most influential essay on Orwell" (p. 34).

115. See especially "Why We Read Jane Austen," *The Last Decade,* 204–25.

116. Trilling, *Homage to Catalonia,* ix.

117. Richard Schickel, "Orwell Emerges Stronger and More Interesting Than Ever," *Chicago Sun-Times,* 20 October 1968.

118. See Perelman's section, "Model and Anti-Model," in *The New Rhetoric,* 362–71.

119. Becker, *The Denial of Death,* 127–58.

120. For a fuller discussion of these possible roles, see Walter J. Ong, "The Writer's Audience Is Always a Fiction," *PMLA,* January 1975, 9–21.

121. Indeed, another difference between artistic and nonartistic reputation is that even the "finished" exploit is *revisable.* Wordsworth tinkered with *The Prelude* for almost a half-century, and today readers usually read the final 1850 version, rather than the 1805 *Prelude.*

122. Thomas Carlyle, *On Heroes and Hero-Worship* (Boston, [1841] 1913).

123. Charles Cooley, *Social Process* (Carbondale, Ill., 1966), 118.

124. Trilling, *Homage to Catalonia,* viii.

125. See Burke, *Permanence and Change,* esp. 89–97.

126. "Truth" is the coordinating point of Trilling's reception scene of Orwell; the word is repeated no less than eight times in the last two paragraphs of Trilling's introduction. The essay ends with an emphasis on the man within the work. "He told the truth, and told it in an exemplary way, quietly, simply, with due warning to the reader that it was only one man's truth. . . . He was interested only in telling the truth . . . . And what matters most of all is our sense of the man who tells the truth" (Trilling, *Homage to Catalonia,* xxiii).

127. *Ibid.,* v–xvii. Thus, not only do watchwords enable the description of images, but also contribute to their transformation and deformation. For the original watchwords will invariably generate related others, linked semantically and phonically to earlier watchwords, and thereby adding to the image constellation. The resultant transformations, either of the image itself or its sociohistorical context, often exert great influence on the size and configuration of a reputation, especially during periods of consensus-forming and critical revaluation. The late '40s and early '50s, as we have seen, were such a time for Orwell.

128. *Ibid.,* v.

129. *Ibid.,* v–vi.

130. Burke, *Permanence and Change,* 251.

131. V. S. Pritchett, "The Rebel," *New Stateman and Nation,* 16 February 1946, 124. Sean O'Casey, "Rebel Orwell," *Sunset and Evening Star* (New York, [1954] 1961), 138–39.

132. Dwight Macdonald, review of *The Lion and the Unicorn,* in *Partisan Review,* March 1942, 166.

133. *CEJL,* Vol. 3, 165–66.

134. Frye, *Anatomy of Criticism,* 19, 7.

135. Richard Rees, *George Orwell: Fugitive from the Camp of Victory* (Carbondale, Ill., 1961), 130.

136. One prep school classmate of Orwell's wrote in the margins of his copy: "Not true! You sod!! Libel!!!" Would a reader who took "Such, Such Were the Joys" as fiction have reacted this way? The issue is not so much, as some critics have argued, whether Orwell would be a more honest man if the essay were found largely true or a more gifted writer if it were found largely false, but rather our premises as readers that it is autobiography or fiction. Its fame has derived from the set of expectations about Orwell (as an "honest witness") which audiences have traditionally brought to it. What has made the essay so powerful is the widespread assumption that it *is* straight reportage, the literal truth. Crick is certainly right to suspect in his biography that the essay is semi-fictional (pp. 66–80), but the point is that if it were approached as a short story by its early readers, it likely would have aroused less controversy, both about Orwell's personality and about the English boarding school. A change of genre usually changes the author-reader relationship.

137. See Orrin Klapp, *Symbolic Leaders: Public Drama and Public Men* (Chicago, 1964), 52–65.

138. James Michener, "A Writer's Public Image," in *Book Publishing: Inside Views,* ed. Jean Spealman Kujoth (Metuchen, N.J., 1971), 201.

139. For example, empirical investigations on literary review practices indicate that the "older" the writer, the less frequently cited and quoted, even when he may be a more suitable allusion or comparison than more contemporary authors. See Karl Eric Rosengren, *Sociological Aspects of the Literary System* (Stockholm, 1968).

140. Connolly's characterization is the opening line of his *Animal Farm* review in *Horizon*; Pritchett's remarks appeared in several places, most notably his *New Statesman* obituary. Both are collected in Meyers, 199–201, 204–6. The standard nomenclature for Orwell's present-day images all come from characterizations in wartime and postwar reviews. The rounded development of Orwell as a "figure" was roughly complete by the mid-'50s. In this sense we can thus speak of the partial freezing of his *reputation* despite the continued flow of attention (or "reception").

141. Mailer, *Advertisements for Myself,* 23.

142. For a discussion of "the public writer," see John Raeburn, *Fame Became of Him: Hemingway as a Public Writer* (Bloomington, 1984), 1–12.

143. Cyril Connolly, *The Evening Colonnade* (New York, 1973), 345.

144. Several reviewers criticized Bernard Crick's biography as an "injustice" to Orwell, often attacking Crick's politics by ridiculing his prose style. See, for example, Labedz's discussion of Crick's biography in "Will George Orwell Survive Until 1984?," *Encounter,* July 1984.

145. *CEJL,* Vol. 4, 168.

146. See, for example, Henry Miller, "The Art of Fiction," *Paris Review,* Summer–Fall 1962, 146. John Wain, *Essays in Literature and Ideas* (London, 1963), 199. *Time,* 2 February 1956, 98.

147. George Steiner, "Killing Time," *New Yorker,* 12 December 1983, 171.

148. George Jones, "1984: How Close to Reality?" *US News & World Report,* 5 February 1979.

149. George Kubler, *The Shape of Time: Remarks on the History of Things* (New Haven, 1962), 87–88.

150. Edward Said, *The Text, the World, and the Critic* (New York, 1981), 32–33.

151. Kubler, *Shape of Time,* 88.

152. *CEJL*, Vol. 1, 460.

153. Unpublished letter from Orwell to his agent Leonard Moore, 1 December 1945. Berg Collection, New York Public Library.

154. Cf. my "Down and Out in Paris? George Orwell's Reputation in France," unpublished manuscript; and my " 'The Rope That Connects Me Directly with You': John Wain and the Movement Writers' Orwell," *Albion*, Vol. 20, No. 1 (Spring 1988), 59–76.

155. Kenneth Allsop, "He Became a Legend in His Own Lifetime," 41.


**Part Two. The Portrait Gallery**

*Chapter Three. The Rebel*

*4. A Rebel's Progress*

1. Arthur Koestler, "A Rebel's Progress," *Observer*, 29 January 1950, 4. Reprinted in Meyers, 296–99.

2. Reprinted in Coppard and Crick, *Orwell Remembered*, 170.

3. Crick, 364. Rees, *George Orwell: Fugitive*, 6. Orwell, *CEJL*, Vol. 1, 1–2.

4. Cyril Connolly, *Enemies of Promise* (London, [1938] 1948), 163.

5. *Ibid.*, 164–65.

6. John Morris, 90–97. Koestler, in Meyers, 297.

7. Richard Rees, review of *Keep the Aspidistra Flying*, in *Adelphi*, June 1936, 190. Reprinted in Meyers, 69.

8. *The Road to Wigan Pier*, 137, 140.

9. Harry Pollitt, *Daily Worker*, 17 March 1937. Walter Greenwood, *Tribune*, 12 March 1937. Hamish Miles, *New Statesman and Nation*, 1 May 1937. The *Tribune* and *New Statesman* reviews are reprinted in Meyers, 99–100, 110–12.

10. Victor Gollancz, Introduction to *The Road to Wigan Pier*, xi–xx.

11. *Ibid.*, xvi.

12. *Ibid.*, ix–x. Crick, 309–12.

13. *CEJL*, Vol. 1, 279.

14. Quoted in John Lewis, *The Left Book Club: An Historical Record* (London, 1970), 113.

15. Victor Gollancz, from a 1956 letter quoted in Sheila Hodges, *Gollancz: The Story of a Publishing House, 1928–78* (London, 1978), 111.

16. Tom Hopkinson, *George Orwell* (London, 1953).

17. *CEJL*, Vol. 4, 205; Vol. 1, 256.

18. V.S. Pritchett, review of *Homage to Catalonia*, in *New Statesman and Nation*, 30 April 1938, 734.

19. V.S. Pritchett, "The Rebel," *New Statesman and Nation*, 16 February 1946, 124.

20. The *New Statesman* obituary is far better known than the briefer notice in the *New York Times Book Review* of February 5. And yet, it is the *NYTBR* formulation—"conscience of his generation"—which is usually quoted. The *New Statesman* phrase was actually "the wintry conscience of his generation." The wide circulation of the *NYTBR* phrase may have reflected a desire among '50s intellectuals to cast Orwell as a less extreme, more moderate figure—a "good liberal" like Pritchett and Trilling.

21. *New Statesman and Nation*, 28 January 1950, 96. Reprinted in Meyers, 294–96.

22. Malcolm Muggeridge, *Like It Was*, 376.

23. See, for example, Charles Poore, "Books of the Times," *New York Times*, 26 February 1953.

24. *CEJL*, Vol. 4, 363.

25. *Ibid.*, 351.

26. Anthony West, "Hidden Damage," *New Yorker*, 28 January 1956, 86–92.

27. John Wain, interview, 14 March 1985. See also Granville Hicks, "Dylan Thomas and George Orwell—So Different Yet in One Way So Alike," *New Leader*, 26 December 1955, 16.

28. On Orwell as a "loser" or "victim," see also Rees, *George Orwell: Fugitive*, 6; John

Leonard, *This Pen for Hire* (New York, 1974), 80; Atkins' chapter "Victims," 119–29; and Hopkinson, *George Orwell*, 20.

29. Andrew Sarris, "George Orwell," *The Primal Scream* (New York, 1973), 287–88.

30. Jenni Calder, interview, 7 May 1984.

31. See Robert Leckie, "The Man Who Invented Big Brother," *Saga*, October 1962. The full title appears on the magazine's front cover.

32. George Woodcock, "Orwell, George," *Encyclopedia Britannica: Macropedia*, Vol. 13 (1974), 750. Gilbert Highet's broadcast is reprinted in *A Clerk of Oxenford* (New York, 1954). Pritchett's remark is from a 1946 BBC-radio broadcast, reprinted in "George Orwell," *Living Writers*, ed. Gilbert Phelps (London, 1947), 115.

33. To name just a few of these characterizations from *Time* and *Newsweek* reviews: "**odd man out**" and "**political pariah**": "Odd Man In," *Time*, 15 November 1968, 110. "**guerrilla**": "Guerrilla," *Newsweek*, 13 November 1950. "**Maverick Orwell**": "To the Heart of Matters," *Time*, 6 February 1950, 87.

34. "To the Heart of Matters," 87. Laurence Brander, *George Orwell* (London, 1954). Walsh's article is reprinted in Meyers, 289–90. Edith Fowke, review of John Atkins' *George Orwell: A Literary and Biographical Study*, in *Canadian Forum*, August 1955, 117.

35. V.S. Pritchett, "The Rebel," 124. Ben Ray Redman, "The Thinking Rebel," *The Freeman*, 20 April 1953, 536. Charles J. Rolo, "The Reader's Choice," *Atlantic Monthly*, March 1950, 78–80. Peter Quennell, "Mark of a Rebel," *Daily Mail*, 21 October 1950. *British Pamphleteers*, Vol. 2, edited by Reginald Reynolds with an introduction by A.J.P. Taylor (London, 1951). Sean O'Casey, "Rebel Orwell," *Sunset and Evening Star* (London, 1954), 124–43. Herbert Matthews, *Nation*, review of *Homage to Catalonia*, December 1952, reprinted in Meyers, 144–45.

36. "Odd Man In."

5. *"Knight Errant of Social Justice": Orwell as Don Quixote*

37. Woodcock, "Recollections of George Orwell," 17.

38. Woodcock, *The Crystal Spirit*, 3–4.

39. Fyvel, "George Orwell," *Picture Post*, 8 January 1955, 39.

40. Anthony Powell, *To Keep the Ball Rolling: The Memoirs of Anthony Powell*, Vol. 1, *Infants of the Spring* (London, 1976), 135. On Orwell as a "saint," see Vol. 2, 221. See also Potts's remark in *Orwell Remembered*, 248.

41. Pritchett, in Meyers, 294–95.

42. Crick, 29.

43. *CEJL*, Vol. 2, 163.

44. *Ibid.*

45. Pritchett, in *Orwell Remembered*, 167. Malcolm Muggeridge, "A Knight of the Woeful Countenance," in *The World of George Orwell*, ed. Miriam Gross (London, 1971), 170–71. Warburg, *All Authors Are Equal*, 37–39.

46. Warburg, *All Authors Are Equal*, 37–39.

47. Bob Edwards, Introduction to *Homage to Catalonia* (London, 1970), 6–10. Crick, 327. See also Edwards' reminiscences in 1960 about Orwell on BBC radio, in *Orwell Remembered*, 148. Crick has interviewed members of the Home Guard of St. John's Wood who respected Orwell's knowledge of weapons and street warfare. Crick, 400–401.

48. On Orwell's drinking with the Spaniards: Crick, 319–20. On the size 12 boots: Crick, 320. On H.G. Wells's remark: Crick, 290. On Orwell's head sticking out: Crick, 325. On the fascist bullet: Interview with Stafford Cottman by Karen Brown, for the 1984 BBC-Arena TV broadcast, 16 June 1983. Copy of transcript in Rosenblum Collection.

49. *Homage to Catalonia* (American edition), 203.

50. Turgenev, "Hamlet and Don Quixote," *Contemporary Review*, January 1860. See also Lionel Abel, *The Intellectual Follies* (New York, 1984), 134–40.

51. *Homage to Catalonia*, 4–6.

52. Potts, in *Orwell Remembered*, 249, 256.

53. *Ibid.*, 259.

54. *Ibid.*, 256–57.

55. Connolly, *The Evening Colonnade,* 377.

56. Thomas Stritch, "Art and Journalism," *Review of Politics,* April 1972, 240.

57. *CEJL,* Vol. 2, 13–14.

58. Wayne Burns, "George Orwell: Our 'Responsible Quixote'," *West Coast Review,* 1967, 13–21.

59. *Ibid.*, 19.

60. Trilling, *Homage to Catalonia,* xxiii. Martin Green, "British Decency," in *A Mirror for Anglo-Saxons* (London, 1961), 95–127. Rees, *George Orwell: Fugitive . . . ,* 4.

61. Muggeridge, "A Knight of the Woeful Countenance," 170.


*6. "Permanent Outsider" Among Friends: Orwell's Compartmentalized Life*

62. Miguel de Cervantes, *Don Quixote de la Mancha,* Part II, Book 11, Chapter 23.

63. Crick, 449. See also 447 and 39.

64. Julian Symons, interview, 13 March 1985.

65. Crick, 581.

66. Julian Symons, "Orwell, a Reminiscence," *London Magazine,* September 1963, 35.

67. T.R. Fyvel, "Orwell as Friend and Prophet," keynote address delivered at the Smithsonian Institution's conference, "The Road After 1984," Washington D.C., 7 December 1983, pp. 8–9. Copy of typescript in Rosenblum Collection.

68. Woodcock, *The Crystal Spirit,* 20. See also Woodcock, "The Man Who Invented 1984," *Quest,* December 1983, 32.

69. Woodcock, "Orwell, Blair and the Critics," *Sewanee Review* 83 (1975), 529.

70. Bernard Crick argues that Christopher Hollis in *A Study of George Orwell* (London, 1956) exaggerated his closeness to Orwell (Crick, 602). John Atkins has said the same of fellow *Tribune* writer T.R. Fyvel (John Atkins, interview, 15 March 1985).

71. Crick, 253.

72. *The Road to Wigan Pier,* 125.

73. *CEJL,* Vol. 4, 351.

74. In his chapter on Blair in Burma, Crick notes that people in later years were "astonished" to find out the acquaintances they (unknowingly) shared with Orwell. Crick argues that Burma may have been the place where Blair learned to compartmentalize his relationships. Crick, 167.

**"Compartmentalized his women friends":** Kay Ekevall, quoted in Peter Stansky and William Abrahams, *Orwell: The Transformation,* 99. See the entire chapter on "Eileen," 69–147. Mrs. Ekevall also claims in the 1984 BBC-Arena TV documentary "Orwell Remembered" that Blair engaged in affairs with a few married women in Southwold before wedding Eileen. On his extramarital encounters during the war, see Crick, 480.

75. Symons, "Orwell, a Reminiscence," 39.

76. *Ibid.*, 36, 37.

77. *Ibid.*, 40. Woodcock, *The Crystal Spirit,* 31.

78. Woodcock, *The Crystal Spirit,* 20; Crick, 253; Rees, *George Orwell: Fugitive,* 87.

79. Symons, interview, 13 March 1985.

80. See Pritchett, "George Orwell," in *Living Writers,* 112; and Pritchett, "George Orwell," *New Statesman and Nation,* 28 January 1950, 96.

81. Crick, 447.

82. *CEJL,* Vol. 1, 353.

83. *CEJL,* Vol. 4, 412–13.

84. *Ibid.*, 413–14.

85. Symons, "Orwell, a Reminiscence," 35. Juan Negrín is quoted in Herbert Matthews' 1952 review of *Homage to Catalonia,* reprinted in Meyers, 148–49.

86. **"Proneness to secrecy":** Woodcock, "Orwell, Blair and the Critics," 528. Powell, *Infants of the Spring,* 140–41. Gorer is quoted in Crick, 264–65. See also Crick on Orwell's behavior after Eileen's death (pp. 480–86).

87. William Phillips, *Partisan Views* (New York, 1983), 209–10.

88. Symons, "Orwell, a Reminiscence," 37.

89. *Ibid.*, 40.

### 7. Lives of Independence: The History of Orwell Biography

90. "George Orwell: A Life of Independence," *Observer*, 22 January 1950, 5.

91. Muggeridge, "Books," *Esquire*, May 1967, 23, 30. Woodcock, "Escaping Eric Blair," *New Leader*, 16 June 1980, 19–20.

92. Susan Watson, "Canonbury Square and Jura," in *Orwell Remembered*, 221.

93. *CEJL*, Vol. 1, 414.

94. Peter Stansky, "Thinking About Biography," *New Republic*, 19 April 1975, 28.

95. See Richard Altick, *Lives and Letters: A History of Literary Biography in England and America* (New York, 1960), 281–300, 317–50. "advising Julian Symons": *CEJL*, Vol. 4, 422.

96. Stanksy, "Thinking About Biography," 28.

97. Woodcock, "Orwell, Blair and the Critics," 529–30.

98. Buddicom, *Eric and Us*, 38, 76.

99. Woodcock, "Orwell, Blair and the Critics," 525.

100. *Ibid.*, 525.

101. *Ibid.* On Orwell's reticence, Woodcock also has written: "He treated his police career almost as if it had belonged to another person—as if Eric Blair had really been a different man from George Orwell." Woodcock, "Orwell: Imperial Socialist," *Mother Jones*, June 1976, 57–58.

102. *CEJL*, Vol. 2, 22.

103. Crick, 322.

104. Woodcock has suggested that "a desire to protect his white lies" may have been "at the bottom of Orwell's request" for no biography. See "Orwell's Changing Repute," *Queen's Quarterly*, Vol. 88 (1981), 251.

105. For a discussion of various modes of biographical writing along these lines, see Elizabeth Young-Bruehl, "The Writing of Biography," *Partisan Review*, 3 (1983), 413–22.

106. Woodcock, "Orwell, Blair and the Critics," 528.

107. *Ibid.*, 527. Symons, interview, 13 March 1985.

108. Woodcock, "Orwell, Blair and the Critics," 530. Sonia Orwell, Introduction to *CEJL*, Vol. 1, xvii–xix.

109. Oswell Blakeston, "Monument to George Orwell," *Books and Bookmen*, November 1968. Hilton Kramer, "A Passion for Honesty, A Genius for Decency," *New York Times Book Review*, 27 October 1968, 1. Mary McCarthy, "The Writing on the Wall," *New York Review of Books*, January 1969, 3–6. Sonia Orwell, "Unfair to George," *Nova*, June–July 1969, 20. Conor Cruise O'Brien, "Honest Men," *Listener*, 12 December 1968, 797–98.

These harsh judgments about Mrs. Orwell's motives were inaccurate. But Mary McCarthy and O'Brien had hit upon a big question mark about *CEJL*: Mrs. Orwell's editorial criteria. As Robert Klitzke has noted, the volumes have a "literary" bias, with much of Orwell's political pieces from 1941–43 (e.g., the Home Guard articles and the *Betrayal of the Left* and *Victory and Vested Interest* contributions), 1945–46 (e.g., the *Manchester Evening News* features on British intellectual life), and 1948–49 (e.g., "Britain's Struggle for Survival" in the October 1948 *Commentary*) excluded. These omissions "suppress Orwell's political commitment to the English Socialist tradition" and give his "revolutionary period—as it emerged from *The Lion and the Unicorn*—the character of a momentary mood." Quoted in Crick, 621.

But Mrs. Orwell's "suppressions" were not politically motivated. According to Crick, she believed that his "real character" was not political, and that in his desire to marry her he was "showing the dominance of his literary over his political self." Crick, "Orwell and Biography," *Biography*, Vol. 10, No. 4 (1987), 292.

110. Miriam Gross, "Foreword," *The World of George Orwell*, ix.

111. Woodcock, "Orwell, Blair and the Critics," 526.

112. See also Jeffrey Meyers' account of the circumstances surrounding Mrs. Orwell's

decision to authorize a biography, in his review of *The Unknown Orwell, Modern Fiction Studies,* Summer 1973, 250–51.

113. Crick has suggested, quite reasonably, that Sonia Brownell exerted relatively little influence on Orwell's life. It is clear, however, that in her role as executrix, Sonia Brownell Orwell significantly affected his posthumous reputation. Crick is quoted in Garrett Epps, "Satirical Orwell Tradition," *Baton Rouge Advocate,* 28 June 1981. See also Bruce Cook, "Protecting the Dear-Departed," *Detroit News,* 5 April 1981. Copies in Orwell Archive.

114. Letter from Sonia Orwell to the *Times Literary Supplement,* 13 October 1972, 1226.

115. Epps, "Satirical Orwell Tradition."

116. William Jovanovich, president of Harcourt Brace and a personal friend of Mrs. Orwell, apparently sided with her and against Crick on the biographer's taking a skeptical stance toward Orwell's essays and reportage. (Some reports claim that Mrs. Orwell also threatened Harcourt with the removal of Orwell's titles from Harcourt's list.) When Mrs. Orwell read the first three chapters of Crick's biography, she tried, according to Crick, to "back out of the deal." Crick, a socialist, also suspects "political dislike" toward him by Jovanovich, whom he describes as "a Cold War warrior." Crick suggests that both Mrs. Orwell and Jovanovich took exception to his view of Orwell as "a good old woolly English democratic socialist," seeing him instead as "a one-note anti-Communist." The conflict over the biography boiled over into Crick's next Orwell project. Harcourt Brace Jovanovich also refused to publish Crick's annotated edition of *Nineteen Eighty-Four* or to grant any other American publisher the rights to it, a decision which Crick termed "close to censorship." See Michael Slung, "The Annotated Orwell Affair," *Book World,* 15 April 1984, 15.

117. Woodcock, "An Unwanted Biography," *Canadian Forum,* April 1981, 24–26. Nigel Dennis, "Orwell Booby-Trapped," *Sunday Telegraph,* 23 January 1980. Laurie Stone, "George Orwell: Not a Nice Guy," *Village Voice,* 8 April 1981, 38.

118. For Crick's own view of his politics and Orwell's influence on him, see *London Review of Books,* 22 January–4 February 1981. See also Stella Saunders, "Homage to Orwell," *Kensington News and Post* (London), 19 December 1980. Copies in Orwell Archive.

119. Crick, 29–34.

120. Arthur Koestler, "A Blurred Portrait," *Observer,* 23 January 1980.

121. Epps, "Satirical Orwell Tradition."

122. See Koestler, "A Blurred Portrait"; and Rayner Heppenstall, "A Blurred Portrait," *Encounter,* February–March 1981, 77–80.

123. Stella Saunders, "Homage to Orwell."

124. George Simson, "Editorial: Fire and Flirtation," *Biography,* Vol. 9, No. 1 (Winter 1986), 93.

125. Stansky and Abrahams, *The Unknown Orwell,* x; Simson, "Fire and Flirtation," 93.


8. *"Always Fighting Against Something": George Woodcock
and the Anarchists' Orwell*

126. Woodcock, "The Man Who Invented 1984," *Quest,* December 1983, 25.

127. *CEJL,* Vol. 2, 223–30. Woodcock, "George Orwell, 19th Century Liberal," *Politics,* December 1946; reprinted in Meyers, 239.

128. *Ibid.,* 246.

129. *Ibid.,* 236.

130. Diana Trilling, *Nation,* 25 June 1949, reprinted in Meyers, 259–60. Reviewing *Shooting an Elephant,* Pritchett wrote: "He was a pure rebel and recalcitrant . . . , an anarchist and not a socialist (believing that doctrine led straight to tyranny)." *New Statesman and Nation,* 28 October 1950, 388. See also Pritchett, "Books in General," *New Statesman,* 15 August 1953, 183.

131. Isaac Deutscher, "*1984*—The Mysticism of Cruelty," 252.

132. Woodcock, in Meyers, 245.

133. The closeness extended to Orwell's sending his adopted five-year-old son Richard to the anarchist summer colony at Whiteway in 1949 (*CEJL,* Vol. 4, 507). It also deserves mention that, in Woodcock's judgment, "How the Poor Die" was the most famous essay ever to appear

in *Now*. "State of Letters," 410. See also Nicolas Walter, "Orwell and the Anarchists," *Freedom*, January 1981, 9–12.

134. **"Parlour Anarchism"**: *CEJL*, Vol. 2, 312. Also Woodcock, *The Crystal Spirit*, 15–33.

135. Crick, 174, 205, 211, 233, 239, 254, 256. Other friends have also characterized Orwell as an "anarchist." See the remarks of Jon Kimche and Richard Rees in *Orwell Remembered*, 254, 124.

136. On Orwell's anarchist connections: Crick, 351. **"some hostile critics"**: D.S. Savage, "The Fatalism of George Orwell," in *The New Pelican Guide to English Literature*. Vol. 8, *The Present*, ed. Boris Ford (Harmondsworth, 1983).

137. *CEJL*, Vol. 4, 502.

138. *Ibid.*, 48–52. See also Woodcock, *Orwell's Message: 1984 and the Present* (Madeira Park, British Columbia, 1984), 126–27.

139. *CEJL*, Vol. 4, 301–2.

140. Woodcock, "Orwell, Blair and the Critics," 529.

141. For Woodcock's criticisms of Williams' view of Orwell, see "Half-Truths on Orwell," *The Nation*, 11 October 1971, 341–42.

142. Cf. Woodcock, "Recollections of George Orwell," *Northern Review*, August–September 1953, 17–27; "Five Who Fear the Future," *New Republic*, 16 April 1956, 17–19; and "Utopias in Negative," *Saturday Review*, Winter 1956, 81–97.

143. Woodcock, *The Crystal Spirit*, vi.

144. *Ibid.*, 53.

145. Woodcock, *Orwell's Message: 1984 and the Present*, 186.

146. Woodcock, *The Crystal Spirit*, 53–54.

147. John Wain, "Controversy: On George Orwell," *Commentary*, June 1969, 28. Woodcock's reply is on p. 30. For Woodcock's *Commentary* review of *CEJL*, see the January 1969 issue.

**"Pointed characterizations"**: see the February 1969 *Canadian Forum*, in which Woodcock wrote that Orwell "carefully defined his socialism as libertarian" (p. 246).

148. Robert Weaver, "Remembering George Orwell," *Saturday Night*, June 1967, 33.

149. Woodcock, *The Crystal Spirit*, vi.

150. Woodcock, "Orwell, Blair and the Critics," 529.

151. Woodcock, "Orwell and Conscience," *World Review*, April 1950, 28–33.

152. **Woodcock on heroes:** "George Woodcock: 'I grew up with a rosy and romantic vision of Canada,' " *Quill and Quire*, August 1981, 10. **"good and angry man"**: Woodcock, *The Crystal Spirit*, 355.

153. *The Road to Wigan Pier*, 152.

154. Woodcock, *Letter to the Past* (Don Mills, Ontario, 1982), 207–36.

155. Woodcock, "George Orwell, 19th Century Liberal," in Meyers, 235. See also Woodcock, "Poetry Magazines of the Thirties: A Personal Note," *Tamarack Review*, October 1973, 68–74.

156. David Stafford, "Life on the Margin," *Books in Canada*, 19 May 1983, 18.

157. Woodcock, "Anarchism Revisited," *Commentary*, August 1968, 54. Woodcock, "The State of Letters: Half a Life of Editing," *Sewanee Review*, 89 (1981), 414. Woodcock, *Letter to the Past*, 281, 283.

158. *CEJL*, Vol. 4, 413.

159. Woodcock, *The Crystal Spirit*, 164.

160. Woodcock, *The Writer and Politics* (London, 1948), 18, 23–24, 27.

161. *CEJL*, Vol. 4, 412–13. Woodcock quotes this passage in *Letter to the Past*, 309–10.

162. Woodcock, *Letter to the Past*, 309–10. See also Woodcock, "The State of Letters," 414.

163. **"Rosy"**: Woodcock, "George Woodcock: 'I grew up with a rosy and romantic vision of Canada,' " 10. **"personal myth"**: *Letter to the Past*, 310. **"Edge of the edge"**: Stafford, "Life on the Margin," 18.

164. Woodcock, "The State of Letters," 411–12.

165. V. Richards, "Orwell—the Humanist," *Freedom*, 4 February 1950, 2–3. See also Vernon Richards, "Orwell's Unpublished Notebooks," *Freedom*, 10 June 1950, 2; L.A., "Seen in a Crooked Mirror," *Freedom*, 11 June 1949; Paul Potts, "Don Quixote on a Bicycle," *Freedom*, 26

October 1968; and Dwight Macdonald, "Varieties of Political Experience," *New Yorker*, 28 March 1959, 141–50.

166. Woodcock, *The Crystal Spirit*, 14.

167. Alex Comfort, "1939 and 1984: George Orwell and the Vision of Judgment," in *On Nineteen Eighty-Four*, ed. Peter Stansky (Stanford, 1983), 15–24. D.S. Savage, *op. cit.*

168. And yet Orwell must have become, in death if not in life, a conscience for Read too, a figure. Noting the influence Orwell still exerted on both of them, Woodcock quotes a letter from Read written fully sixteen years after Orwell's death: "His personality, which remains so vivid after all these years, often rises like some ghost to admonish me." Quoted in Woodcock, "Orwell, Blair and the Critics," 527.

Nicolas Walter's history of reception bridges the responses to Orwell from the anarchist Old Left and New Left, representing Orwell's continuing influence on a generation of anarchists younger than Read and Woodcock. Walter first praised Orwell in the early '60s as "one of the few real heroes our age has seen," and he has continued to admire Orwell into the 1980s. See his "George Orwell, An Accident in Society," *Anarchy*, October 1961, 246–55; and "Orwell and the Anarchists."

169. Cf. Meyers' remarks in *George Orwell: The Critical Heritage*, 23–24.

170. Doug Fetherling, Introduction to *The George Woodcock Reader* (Toronto, 1980), xiv.

171. "**Favorite book**": Woodcock, *Taking It to the Letter* (Montreal, 1981), 16.

172. Woodcock, "Narcissus Among the Snows: A Letter from Canada," *London Magazine*, June 1978, 37–38.

173. Woodcock, "George Woodcock: 'I grew up . . .'," 10. Julian Symons, "George Woodcock, an Old Friend," *Critical Observations* (New Haven, 1981), 199. R.P. Bilan, "Canada's Ranking Man of Latters," *Canadian Forum*, reprinted in *World Press Review*, January 1981, 61.

174. Woodcock, *The Rejection of Politics* (Toronto, 1972), xii. Woodcock, "George Woodcock: 'I grew up . . . ," 10.

175. Woodcock, *Orwell's Message*, 186, 13, 186–87.

176. Woodcock, "George Woodcock: 'I grew up . . . ," 10.

177. Woodcock, *The Rejection of Politics*, 20–29.

178. Doug Fetherling, editor of *The George Woodcock Reader*, states that Woodcock himself in 1980 "is what can only be called a libertarian socialist" (p. viii).

*Chapter Four. The Common Man*

*9. Decency and Democracy: The Aspiring Plebeian*

1. James Stern, "Homage to George Orwell," *The New Republic*, 20 February 1950, 18–20. R.D. Charques, "Books and Writers," *Spectator*, 15 December 1950, 702. Edward Jost, review of Woodcock's *The Crystal Spirit*, in *America*, 8 October 1966, 430. Jeffrey Meyers, "The Honorary Proletarian: Orwell and Poverty," in *A Reader's Guide to George Orwell* (London, 1975), 74–100. James Morrow, "Big Brother Isn't Watching—Yet," *TV Guide*, 28 January 1984, 10.

2. That, of course, doesn't mean he felt at ease in working-class pubs. Indeed relatives and friends report just the reverse. Their observations point to a paradox at the heart of Orwell's "common man" reputation: a man hailed as a "proletarian champion" was widely acknowledged by acquaintances to have been aloof from and uncomfortable with the "working man." (The phrase "proletarian champion" appears in Cyril Connolly, *The Evening Colonnade*, 339.)

On Orwell's pub presence (some regulars in a local Jura pub nicknamed him "Gloomy George"), see Lawrence Malkin, "Halfway to 1984," *Horizon*, 12 (1970), 38. See also the recollections of his brother-in-law Humphrey Dakin in Crick, 207; and of his brother-in-law Bill Dunn in Crick and Coppard's *Orwell Remembered*, 234; and Woodcock, *The Crystal Spirit*, 23.

3. Orwell on Dickens, *CEJL*, Vol. 1, 414. "**proletarian affectations**": Muggeridge, "A Knight of the Woeful Countenance," 170–71. See also Anthony Powell's story of Orwell's attending a formal party at Powell's in his "proletarian outfit." *Infants of the Spring*, 35–42. "**blue shirt of the French**": Fyvel, 99. See also William Empson's story about Orwell's mock Cockney accent, in "Orwell at the BBC," in *The World of George Orwell*, ed. Miriam Gross, 95–96. Orwell on Dickens, *CEJL*, Vol 1, 414–15.

4. Astor made these remarks in the 1984 BBC-Arena TV program "George Orwell." Astor repeats the story in *Remembering Orwell,* ed. Stephen Wadhams (Markham, Ontario, 1984), 218–19.

5. **"proletarian background"**: For example, by July 1949 *The Book-of-the-Month Club* was referring to Orwell's "several years of severe poverty as a dishwasher, tutor and in other odd jobs" (p. 8). See also Woodcock, "George Orwell, 19th Century Liberal," quoted in Meyers, 239. Crick also refers to the "legend" in the '50s that Orwell "had joined the tramps much as Count Tolstoy had joined the peasants" (p. 206). On erroneous ideas about Eileen's background, see the memoir by her friend "Elizaveta Fen" (a.k.a. Lydia Jackson), "George Orwell's First Wife," *Twentieth Century,* August 1960, 115.

6. Davies' *New Statesman* review is in Meyers, 44. Basil de Selincourt, *The Listener,* 22 January 1933. See also "Hard Up," *Time and Tide,* 14 (11 February 1933), 152. Norman Collins on *ACD:* see Crick, 257.

7. Quoted in Crick, 204.

8. On Brenda Salkeld's and Ruth Pitter's recollections that Orwell was just "slumming," see Crick, 205–6.

9. Jack Common on Orwell: Quoted in Crick, 204. Orwell to his agent: *CEJL,* Vol. 1, 107.

10. Quoted in Crick, 278.

11. **"subsequent reception history"**: On the Orwell-Comstock link, for example, see the reviews by Henry Popkin and Louis Simpson in Meyers, 81, 89–90.

**"some reviewers"** of *KAF:* See, for example, A.G. Macdonnell, in *Observer,* 19 April 1936; and Cyril Connolly, in *New Statesman and Nation,* 25 November 1936. Doubtless the Blair-Comstock associations were strengthened by the fact that the poem which Gordon Comstock struggles throughout *KAF* to complete was actually published a few months before the novel's appearance under the name Eric Blair. See "St. Andrew's Day, 1935," *Adelphi,* 11 (November 1935), 85.

12. *Keep the Aspidistra Flying* (London, 1936), 239.

13. **"the really important fact"**: *CEJL,* Vol. 2, 74–5. **"one has to"**: *CEJL,* Vol. 3, 379.

14. *CEJL,* Vol. 1, 459.

15. Richard Rees, "George Orwell," in *The Politics of Twentieth-Century Novelists,* ed. George Panichas (New York, 1974), 86, 88.

16. V.S. Pritchett, "Back to Jonah," *New Statesman and Nation,* 16 March 1940, 309.

17. Q.D. Leavis, "The Literary Life Respectable," reprinted in Meyers, 187. **Orwell on** *Scrutiny: CEJL,* Vol. 1, 253.

18. Leavis, in Meyers, 188–90.

19. One indication of its immediate influence was that John Atkins discussed it the following year on page one of his *George Orwell: A Literary and Biographical Study.*

20. Spender, "Revaluation—*Homage to Catalonia,*" *World Review,* June 1950, reprinted in Meyers, 134, 136–37.

21. Spender, BBC radio interview (7 May 1963), reprinted in Coppard and Crick's *Orwell Remembered,* 262.

22. Martin Green, "British Decency," *Kenyon Review.* Autumn 1959, 505–12. Reprinted in Green's *A Mirror for Anglo-Saxons* (London, 1961), 95–127. For his more recent views of Orwell, see *Children of the Sun* (London, 1972).

23. **"BBC letters"**: see David Sylvester, "Orwell on the Screen," *Encounter,* March 1955, 35. R. Palme Dutt, "Image in the Home," *Manchester Guardian,* 5 March 1955, 4. One BBC official called the controversy "a put-up job" by the BCP. See "Cries of Brutality and Horror Raised Over '1984' on British TV," *New York Times,* 14 December 1954, 50.

*10. "An Ex-Socialist": Raymond Williams and the British Marxists' Orwell*

24. Raymond Williams, *Politics and Letters* (London, 1979), 70.

25. Raymond Williams, "George Orwell," *Essays in Criticism,* January 1955, 44, 52; and *Culture and Society* (London, 1958), 285, 294.

26. Raymond Williams, Introduction to *George Orwell: A Collection of Critical Essays* (Englewood Cliffs, N.J., 1974), 3–4.

27. Cf. David Widgery, *The Left in Britain, 1956–68* (Baltimore, 1976), esp. 43–97. Neal Wood, *Communism and British Intellectuals* (New York, 1959).

28. James Walsh, "An Appreciation of an Individualist Writer," *Marxist Quarterly*, January 1956, reprinted in Meyers, 289, 291.

29. Williams, *Politics and Letters*, 42–43, 53, 65.

30. Williams, *Culture and Society*, 288.

31. Williams, *Politics and Letters*. 97.

32. Raymond Williams, *George Orwell* (New York, 1971), 87.

33. Williams, *George Orwell: A Collection of Critical Essays*, 6–7.

34. Williams, *Politics and Letters*, 384.

35. See Martin Green, "George Orwell: Contradictions and Paradoxes," 10–12. Unpublished paper, 1984. I am grateful to Professor Green for sharing with me his reflections on Williams and the British Left.

36. E.P. Thompson, "Outside the Whale," in *Out of Apathy* (London, 1960), 158–65.

37. See, for instance, Hoggart's "George Orwell and the Road to Wigan Pier," *Critical Quarterly*, 7 (1965), 72–85; "Walking the Tightrope: *Animal Farm*," in *Speaking to Each Other*, Vol. 2 (London, 1970); and "The Authorised Biography," *Punch*, 26 November 1980, 976.

38. The comparison with Guevara is from a letter in the *New Statesman*, 13 September 1968, quoted in D.A.N. Jones, "Arguments Against Orwell," in *The World of George Orwell*, 161. "a guerrilla": J.P. O'Flinn, "Orwell on Literature and Society," *College English*, 31 (1970), 610. Noam Chomsky, broadcast on BBC-TV's "Omnibus" program produced by Melvyn Bragg in 1970. Copy of transcript in Orwell Archive.

39. Mary McCarthy, "The Writing on the Wall," 6. Tom Nairn, "St. George," *New Statesman*, 14 July 1967, 53. D.A.N. Jones, "Arguments Against Orwell," 155.

40. See, however, Williams' interesting scattered references to Orwell in his review of the English translation of the Paris Manuscripts. "The Future of Marxism," *Twentieth Century*, July 1961, 128–42.

41. Williams, *George Orwell*, 96.

42. Williams, *Politics and Letters*, 361–66.

43. Williams, *George Orwell*, 1–3, 11–24, 90, 94–95.

44. *Ibid.*, 97.

45. Raymond Williams, *Problems in Materialism and Culture* (London, 1980).

46. *Ibid.*

47. Williams, *Politics and Letters*, 384, 388–91.

48. A.L. Rowse, "The Contradictions of Orwell," *Contemporary Review*, October 1982, 185–86. See also Rowse, "Pity the Poor English," *Sunday Times*, 19 October 1947, 3.

49. Raymond Williams, "*Nineteen Eighty-Four* in 1984," *Marxism Today*, January 1984, 16.

50. In their Foreword to *Politics and Letters*, the *New Left Review* editors refer to Williams as "the pre-eminent intellectual representative of socialism in contemporary Britain." They also note approvingly that his recent work has "rejoined a wider internationalist Marxist debate" (p. 9). The interviewers were Perry Anderson, Anthony Barnett, and Francis Mulhern, of the editorial committee of *New Left Review*.
Eric Homberger calls Williams "the only writer in England since George Orwell . . . whose description of himself as a revolutionary socialist is not greeted with yawns or derision." "Up from Leavisism," *Nation*, 8 December 1979, 601. See also Blake Morrison, "Jim, Raymond, Jim," *New Statesman*, 16 October 1979, 637.

51. "The Orwell Prize," *New Society*, 15 January 1981.

52. Williams, *Politics and Letters*, 391.

53. Williams, *George Orwell*, 90.

54. Cf. Morrisson, "Jim, Raymond, Jim."

55. Raymond Williams, "The New British Left," *Partisan Review*, Spring 1960, 341.

56. Green, "Contradictions and Paradoxes," 11.

57. Williams, *Politics and Letters*, 391.

58. One also notes the opposite tendency: Hoggart's continued high admiration for Orwell contrasts with his severe remarks on the radicalized Left. See, for example, his "1968–78, the Student Movement and Its Effects in the Universities," *Political Quarterly,* April–June 1979, 172–81.

59. *Ibid.*

60. Francis Hope, "My Country Right or Left," *New Statesman,* 19 December 1969, 892.

61. Williams, *George Orwell: A Collection of Critical Essays,* 8.

*11. "Enemy of Mankind?": The Soviet Union's Orwell*

62. *CEJL,* Vol. 4, 379–80.

63. State Department memorandum from Dean Acheson, titled "Participation of Books in Department's Fight Against Communism," 11 April 1951. *Animal Farm* and *Nineteen Eighty-Four,* the memo notes, "have been of great value to the Department in its psychological offensive against Communism. . . . [O]n account of the possible psychological value, the Department has felt justified in sponsoring translations, either overtly or covertly." Two 1950 memos from Acheson, dated 18 and 28 October, also discuss negotiations for the Chinese rights to *Nineteen Eighty-Four. Animal Farm* was also one of a half-dozen books which the FBI was vigorously promoting in the West in 1946–47, according to an FBI memo to J.Edgar Hoover, 8 May 1947. FOIA.

**On Hoover:** Letter from Eugene Reynolds to J. Edgar Hoover, 22 April 1949. Negative reply from Hoover, 29 April 1949. FOIA.

**On the foreign translations and Voice of America broadcasts:** Letter and enclosures to the author from Charles Jones, Jr., United States Information Agency, 18 July 1983. FOIA.

64. *CEJL,* Vol. 4, 379–80. August Rei, the former Prime Minister of Estonia, also wrote Orwell for permission to arrange for *Animal Farm*'s translation, which Orwell granted. Unpublished letter from August Rei to Orwell, 9 May 1946. Berg Collection, New York Public Library.

65. Glebe Struve, "Anti-Westernism in Recent Soviet Literature," *Yale Review,* December 1949, 222.

66. *CEJL,* Vol. 4, 266.

67. *U.S. Department of State Bulletin,* 25 (3 December 1951), 897.

68. Struve, "Anti-Westernism . . . ," 220. Struve, a professor at London University in the 1930s and '40s, was among those responsible for bringing Orwell to the attention of dissident Russian intellectuals. He reviewed *Nineteen Eighty-Four* flatteringly in the Russian journal *New Russian Wind* (10 July 1949) and wrote a sympathetic obituary in the same journal. The latter is translated and reprinted in Coppard and Crick's *Orwell Remembered,* 260–61.

69. I. Anisimov, "Enemies of Mankind," *Pravda,* 12 May 1950, 3. Translated in *Current Digest of the Soviet Press,* 1 July 1950, 14–15.

70. *Ibid.* Koestler was half-Jewish.

71. *Ibid.,* 15.

72. Victor Babish, "What Is Flourishing in the U.S.A.?" *Pravda Ukrainy,* 21 August 1962, 4. Translated in the *Digest of the Ukrainian Press,* October 1962, 24.

73. Deutscher, "*1984:* The Mysticism of Cruelty," 252.

74. "Under the Hood of Mr. Hoover," *Return to the Homeland,* Vol. 3 (January 1959). The FBI had obtained a copy of this periodical, and the quotation is from an FBI memorandum referring to it and titled "Smear Campaign" (31 March 1959). FOIA.

75. *Ibid.,* FBI memo. Also Melor Sturua, "What the U.S. Is Like: Sullen Eagle," *Izvestia,* 10 September 1969, 2. Translated in *Current Digest of the Soviet Press,* 8 October 1969, 19. (Sturua is a well-known Soviet journalist whose first name is derived from "Marx, Engels, Lenin, October Revolution.")

76. A.A. Kharchev, "The Soviet Family Now and Under Communism," *Kommunist,* May 1960, 57. Translated in *Current Digest of the Soviet Press,* 22 July 1960, 10.

77. Vera Sandomirsky, "Sex in the Soviet Union," *Russian Review,* July 1951, 199.

78. "Orwell That Ends Well," *The Times* (London), 29 February 1956, 9. Azary Messerer, a

Russian expatriate and former employee of Radio Moscow, has also suggested that the Two Minutes Hate blared on Oceania telescreens satirizes the "awe-inspiring ritual" of Stalin's war broadcasts of the 1940s. "All life would become still" when the broadcasts began, recalls Messerer. The broadcasts were delivered by Party functionaries with commanding voices, rather than by Stalin himself, who had a weak voice and spoke Russian with a heavy Georgian accent. Messerer believes that Stalin sustained his "God-like image" until his death partly because—like Big Brother—he never appeared in public. See Azary Messerer, "Orwell and the Soviet Union," *Et cetera*, Summer 1984, 131–33.

79. "For Society Means for Oneself," *Izvestia*, 11 September 1966, 5. Translated in *Current Digest of the Soviet Press*, 5 October 1966, 18.

80. Messerer has some observations relevant to the equation posited in the headline. Orwell surely would have appreciated them. Messerer insists that there is "no such word as privacy in the modern Russian language." Instead "privacy" is translated as "loneliness, intimacy, or secrecy," with no mention by Soviet lexicographers "about the right to freedom from interference in one's private life. In other words, the Soviet citizen cannot express his lack of privacy, just as inhabitants of Oceania are not able to express their lack of political or intellectual freedom" (Messerer, "Orwell and the Soviet Union," 132).

81. Quoted in "Soviet Compares U.S. to Orwell's '1984'," *New Orleans Times-Picayune*, 30 January 1983, 8. See also Michael Glenny, "Orwell's 1984 Through Soviet Eyes," *Index on Censorship*, August 1984, 15–17.

82. Melor Sturua, "An Orwellian America," *Izvestia*, 15 January 1984. Translated in *World Press Review*, March 1984, 53. See also "Soviets Say '1984' Portrays America," *Florida Times-Union* (Jacksonville), 18 January 1984; and "Reagan Called 'Big Brother' in Kremlin Anti-Sanction Bid," *Binghamton Evening Press* (N.Y.), 10 January 1982. Copies in Rosenblum Collection.

83. Reported in "Soviet Says Vision Is Alive in U.S.," *New York Times*, 8 January 1984.

84. Victor Tsoppi, " '1984': Full Circle," *New Times* (English edition), December 1983, 22–24.

85. Penalties were still in force for reading and circulating the newly rehabilitated Orwell, however. A Latvian translator convicted of possessing a copy of *Nineteen Eighty-Four* was sentenced to seven years' imprisonment in December 1983 on charges of "anti-Soviet agitation and propaganda." Reported in Karel Kyncl, "Is *1984* anti-Soviet?," *Index on Censorship*, April 1984, 16.

86. See, for example, Williams' *Politics and Letters* or Rowse's "The Contradictions of George Orwell."

87. Tsoppi, " '1984': Full Circle," 22–24. Orwell, *CEJL*, Vol. 4, 502.

88. Tsoppi, " '1984': Full Circle," 22.

89. *CEJL*, Vol. 1, 8; and Vol. 4, 504.

90. Tsoppi, " '1984': Full Circle," 24. As one would expect, the new approach of the Soviet press toward *Nineteen Eighty-Four* was received coldly by most American journalists. See Eric Waha, "Reds Rip 1984, But Don't Let Their People Read It," *Springfield Daily News* (Mass.), 9 January 1984; Tom Tiede, "To Russians, Big Brother Is Alive," *Macomb Daily* (Miss.), 15 October 1983; and Dusko Doder, "1984, Comrades, Is a Book About the West," *Washington Post*, 24 January 1984. Copies in Rosenblum Collection.

91. Sergei Zalygin, "Here Is What the Editor-in-Chief of *Novy Mir* Thinks About *Nineteen Eighty-Four*," *Literaturnaya Gazeta*, 11 May 1988, 15. See also the anonymous introduction, "About George Orwell and His Novel," on the same page. I am grateful to Mark Elson for his help with the translations. The *Nineteen Eighty-Four* extract features two short sections from the opening pages of the novel.

As this book was going to press, *Izvestia* also published two chapters of *Animal Farm* in its weekly supplement *Nedelya* in mid-September 1988. The anonymous introduction noted that Orwell's fable "does not make fun of socialist ideals as some of our critics maintained until recently," but rather "is aimed against those who make a mockery of these ideals, openly or in a disguised way, against political demagoguery and political adventurism." The self-criticism is unmistakable. Nevertheless, as with *Nineteen Eighty-Four*, nowhere did the *Izvestia* introduction specifically mention Lenin or Stalin. This is an even more grievous omission than with the case

of Orwell's dystopia, since *Animal Farm* is, quite transparently and unavoidably if not exclusively, a satirical allegory of the Russian Revolution. Quoted from "Soviet Newspaper Prints a Chapter of Formerly Banned Novel [*sic*] by Orwell," *Houston Post*, 17 September 1988, 2A. The *Animal Farm* extract appeared in *Izvestia*, 16 September 1988.

92. Cf. David Pryce-Jones, "Orwell's Reputation," in *The World of George Orwell*, 151. On State Department efforts to circulate a Czech translation of *Animal Farm*, see the State Department memo from Richard G. Johnson, vice consul, U.S. embassy in Prague, 11 May 1961. FOIA.

93. **On Poland:** Reported in *Addison Press Weekly* (Ill.), 1 February 1984. **On East Germany and Hungary:** Reported in "Communists Criticize Orwell's '1984' Novel," *Oshkosh Daily Northwestern*, 9 January 1984. Copies in Rosenblum Collection.

**On Bulgaria:** Plamen Georgiev, " '1984': Impudent Speculation with Wild Idea," *Otechestven Front*, 15 June 1984, 8. Translated in *Joint Publications Research Service*, July 1984, 5. See also Sonya Zalubrowski, "1984 in Rumania," *Chicago Sun-Times*, 1 January 1984.

94. Czeslaw Milosz, *The Captive Mind*, trans. Jane Zielonko (London, 1953), 42. See also Lewis Feuer's remarks about Orwell's stature among a secret group of dissident students at Moscow University in 1963. *A Conflict of Generations* (New York, 1969), 531.

95. **"Underground Polish press":** See Peter Stansky, "The Orwell Year," *DLB Yearbook*, ed. Jean W. Ross (Detroit, 1984), 52–62. **"Petofi Club":** Lawrence Malkin, "Halfway to 1984," *Horizon*, 12 (1970), 36–37.

96. Tomas Venclova, "I Am Grateful to Orwell," *Index on Censorship*, August 1984, 11.

### 12. "A Sexist After All?" The Feminists' Orwell

97. On Orwell's occasional derogation of women's intellectual capacities, see *CEJL*, Vol. 1, 63; *CEJL*, Vol. 4, 455. One should not, however, overlook Orwell's respectful comments about feminism and women's abilities (cf. footnote 112). The evidence from Orwell's journalism and letters supports Arthur Eckstein's view that Orwell's condescending or contemptuous remarks about feminism and women's capacities "diminished greatly in the 1940s, and are on the wane even earlier." Eckstein, "Orwell, Masculinity, and Feminist Criticism," *The Intercollegiate Review*, Fall 1985, 50.

98. Nevertheless it could be argued that Orwell's women are the noblest, most dignified characters in his fiction. Although Julia, the prole washerwoman, and Winston's mother are unintellectual, they represent the values of decency and humanity which Winston, O'Brien, and the world of Oceania have lost. Certainly Rosemary Waterlow is the most joyous, life-affirming character in all of Orwell's novels. Indeed *A Clergyman's Daughter*, though a weak novel, might easily be taken as a feminist statement of the 1930s if one did not know the author. It negatively portrays paternalism, sexual harassment, oppressive housework, lack of job opportunities for working-class women, and the inadequacies of girls' educations.

99. Lynette Hunter, "Stories and Voices in Orwell's Early Narratives," in *Inside the Myth*, ed. Christopher Norris (London, 1984), 163–82. See also her book, *George Orwell: The Search for a Voice* (Suffolk, 1984).

100. See, for example, Beatrix Campbell, "Orwell—Paterfamilias or Big Brother?" and Deirdre Beddoe, "Hindrances and Help-Meets: Women in the Writings of George Orwell," in *Inside the Myth*, 126–38, 139–54. This essay collection was published by Lawrence & Wishart, the BCP's regular house.

101. Campbell, 128, and Beddoe, 140.

102. Campbell, 126.

103. Campbell, 126–28. See also Campbell's book, *Wigan Pier Revisited: Poverty and Politics in the 1980s* (London, 1983), in which she discusses Orwell's "toxic scorn" toward women and working-class socialists (pp. 228–30).

104. This orientation leads some feminist critics to approach *Nineteen Eighty-Four* not as a warning against the totalitarian state Orwell witnessed in the 1940s, but as an historical prediction of the 1980s. See Marlene Barr's introduction to the special Orwell issue in 1984 of *Women's Studies International Forum*, Vol. 7, No. 2 (1984). On differences between British

and American feminism, see *The New Feminist Criticism,* ed. Elaine Showalter (New York, 1985), 8.

105. See also *The New Feminist Criticism,* 8.

106. Patai, *The Orwell Mystique,* x, 14.

107. *Ibid.,* 15–16.

108. *Ibid.,* 308.

109. Orwell made clear in a 1946 exchange with Communist Randall Swingler that he considered such a practice just as corrupt as a reflexive pro-Communism: "In five years it may be as dangerous to praise Stalin as it was to attack him two years ago. But I should not regard that as an advance. Nothing is gained by teaching a parrot a new word. What is needed is the right to print what one believes to be true, without having to fear bullying or blackmail from any side." Orwell, annotations to Swingler's "The Right to Free Expression," *Polemic,* September–October 1946, 53.

110. Patai, *The Orwell Mystique,* 272.

111. Conor Cruise O'Brien, "Orwell Looks at the World," in *Writers in Politics* (London, 1965), 32.

112. See, for example, Orwell's 1944 review of Hilda Martindale's *Sweated Woman Labour,* which concludes with the sentence: "Her own career, and the self-confidence and independence of outlook that she evidently showed from the very start, bear out her claim that women are the equals of men in everything except physical strength." "Sweated Woman Labour," *Manchester Evening News,* 29 June 1944, 2. See also his favorable reviews of Fortune and Burton's biography of Elizabeth Ney and of Woolf's *A Room of One's Own.* "Elizabeth Ney— Feminist and Mad King's Sculptress," *Manchester Evening News,* 17 February 1944, 3. "Front Sea View of Politics," *Manchester Evening News,* 2 August 1945, 3.

Significantly, all these positive statements are from the mid-1940s, lending support to the impression that Orwell's views on feminism and women's issues, though they hardly became progressive, were not static throughout his life. Perhaps his 1936 marriage to Eileen and his adoption of his son Richard in 1944 contributed to the evolution of his attitudes.

113. Patai, *The Orwell Mystique,* ix–x.

114. See *CEJL,* Vol. 4; and the numerous recollections by Orwell acquaintances in Coppard and Crick's *Orwell Remembered,* Wadhams' *Remembering Orwell,* and in Crick's *George Orwell: A Life.* Notably, the working title for *The Orwell Mystique* was *Orwell's Despair: Manhood and the Path to 1984.* See Patai, "Forum: Women in *1984,*" *PMLA,* 98 (1983), 257. The title of the Conclusion to *The Orwell Mystique* preserves this original premise: "Orwell's Despair" (p. 264).

115. See, for example, Patsy Schweickart's enthusiastic review. Schweickart praises Patai for her "thoroughness and cogency," even as she notes "the unrelieved negativity of her approach" and the fact that "she makes almost no use of biographical information" and that her study often reads like just "one more book about one more obnoxious male writer." "Orwell Revisited," *Women's Review of Books,* 2 (November 1984), 3.

116. Elaine Hoffman Baruch, " 'The Golden Country': Sex and Love in *1984,*" in *1984 Revisited: Totalitarianism in Our Century,* ed. Irving Howe (New York, 1983), 54.

117. For an example of "feminist realism," see the reading of *Animal Farm* as a "feminist fable" in *The Orwell Mystique,* 216–18. "**textual and autobiographical readings**": For a superb, critical assessment of Orwell which is chiefly textual, however, see Leslie Tentler, " 'I'm Not Literary, Dear': George Orwell on Women and the Family," in *The Future of Nineteen Eighty-Four,* 47–63.

118. Beddoe, "Hindrances and Help-Meets," 153.

119. Patai, *The Orwell Mystique,* 20.

120. *Ibid.,* 19, 263.

121. Stansky and Abrahams suggest in *Orwell: The Transformation* that Orwell may never have been entirely comfortable with women or have understood them well, having had no regular contact with them until his mid-20s, after Burma. But they write explicitly: "Misogynistic he was not" (p. 37). Although Brenda Salkeld insists that Orwell "didn't really like women," other women acquaintances disagree. Kay Ekevall calls him "old-fashioned." Celia Goodman relates a

story in which Orwell jokingly wishes he could be "irresistible to women." Lettice Cooper and Lydia Jackson have said that he did like and respect women, and they have attributed his lack of understanding toward Eileen to an obliviousness to the needs of friends generally, male and female. See the Salkeld, Ekevall, and Cooper reminiscences in Coppard and Crick's *Orwell Remembered*, 67–68, 102, 161–62. Lydia Jackson's remarks are in "George Orwell's First Wife," 113–17, and in Wadhams' *Remembering Orwell*, 66–68. Goodman's story is in *Remembering Orwell*, 163.

122.  Patai, *The Orwell Mystique*, 272.

123.  Jenni Calder, interview, 7 May 1984.

124.  See Celia Goodman's remarks on Orwell's "marvellous" caretaking of his adopted son Richard. Peter Lewis, *George Orwell: The Road to 1984* (London, 1981), 104. See also her comments in *Remembering Orwell*, 163.

125.  Many feminist political activists, probably familiar only with *Nineteen Eighty-Four*, have gone still further than Steinem. For instance, Judy Goldsmith, then president of the National Organization for Women, implied in a 1983 speech that Orwell was advocating feminism in *Nineteen Eighty-Four*. According to Goldsmith, what bothered Orwell most was how authoritarianism destroys human relationships. "George Orwell wrote *1984* as a warning. Feminism offers the hope of avoiding *1984*." Here we can see the difference between a feminist culture critic like Calder or Steinem interpreting Orwell's work and a feminist political leader using his work and reputation for immediate political ends. Goldsmith's use is a good example, from the Left, of how groups with which Orwell had little sympathy have strategically "deployed" him when it has suited them. Steinem's observations are in Anne Gottleib, "Is '1984' Really Here?," *McCall's*, January 1984, 98. See also Judy Goldsmith, "Feminists Challenge 1984," *Miami Herald*, 2 January 1983. For Phyllis Schafly's anti-Communist reading of *Nineteen Eighty-Four*, see *McCall's*, January 1984, 100.

126.  Sheila Rowbotham, *Hidden from History* (London, 1973), 166.

127.  Simone de Beauvoir, *All Said and Done* (New York, 1975), 470.

128.  Irving Howe, *A Margin of Hope: An Intellectual Autobiography* (San Diego, 1983), 44–45.

129.  Rowbotham, *Hidden from History*, 163.

130.  Ray Strachey, quoted in Rowbotham, *Hidden from History*, 163. Or as Rowbotham herself has observed: "These young women had been taught to despise their own movement by a culture which was anti-feminist. But this was not the whole of it. They inherited a feminism which had lost its glory, and forgotten its power, and thus saw little that could capture their feelings. . . . They were likely to be dismissive of feminism, because they only knew it as a limited movement and because they felt they no longer needed to be feminists. The women in Left political organizations, including the Labour Party, could feel that they worked as individuals and that a specific consciousness as women was a kind of indulgence" (p. 163).

131.  Germaine Greer, *Sex and Destiny: The Politics of Human Fertility* (New York, 1984), 159–61.

132.  Beddoe, "Hindrances and Help-Meets," 150.

133.  Greer, *Sex and Destiny*, 159–61. See also Rowbotham on Mosley, *Hidden from History*, 151.

134.  Greer, *Sex and Destiny*, 378.

135.  See Enid Charles, "The Effect of Present Trends in Fertility and Mortality Upon the Future Population of Great Britain and Upon Its Age Composition," in *Political Arithmetic*, ed. Lancelot Hogben (New York, 1938), 73–105; G.R. Searle, "Eugenics and Politics in Britain in the 1930s," *Annals of Science*, 36 (1979), 159–69; Rowbotham, *Hidden from History*, 144; and Ruth Adam, *A Woman's Place* (London, 1975), 130–31.

136.  Beddoe, "Hindrances and Help-Meets," 149.

137.  Patai, *The Orwell Mystique*, 287.

138.  On Orwell's worries about the declining birthrate, see *CEJL*, Vol. 3, 31–32, 192–93; and Vol. 4, 123–24, 238.

139.  Greer, *Sex and Destiny*, 357–58. Likely Orwell also objected to contraception for personal and temperamental reasons. He always wanted a child badly and felt vaguely guilty that

he may have been sterile (Crick, 269, 486). He idealized Nature and "the family," and contraception seems to have represented to him an offense against both (Hollis, "Keeping Up with the Joneses," *The Tablet,* 31 July 1954, 107). In *The Lion and the Unicorn,* England is also romanticized as "a family," albeit "with the wrong members in control (*CEJL*, Vol. 2, 68); at this level too—again unlike most left-wing socialists of his time—Orwell seems to have found birth control somehow running counter to his communitarian vision of socialism (see Woodcock, *George Orwell,* 262–64, 284). His radicalism was in many ways much like Robert Blatchford's, the nineteenth-century British socialist, who also idealized "the common people," cherished an already dated agrarian vision of England, and believed sentimentally that the nation should be "a family."

140. Judith Shapiro, "Anthropology and the Study of Gender," in *A Feminist Perspective in the Academy: The Difference It Makes,* ed. Elizabeth Langland and Walter Gove (Chicago, 1981), 126. Patricia Meyer Spacks, "The Difference It Makes," *ibid.,* 282.

141. Jean Bethke Elshtain, "The New Feminist Scholarship," *Salmagundi,* 70 (Spring–Summer 1986), 10.

142. Spacks, "The Difference It Makes," 11–12.

143. *Ibid.,* 13.

144. "sexual division of labor": Beddoe, "Hindrances and Help-Meets," 152. "commodity fetishism": Jenny Taylor, "Desire Is Thoughtcrime: *Nineteen Eighty-Four* in 1984," in *Autonomy, Control and Communication,* ed. Crispin Aubrey and Paul Chilton (London, 1983), 30. "he/she": quoted in Peter Kemp's report of the speeches delivered in the January 1984 Orwell symposium "Thoughtcrimes at the Barbican," a two-week festival of events linked to Orwell and organized by the Royal Shakespeare Company. *Times Literary Supplement,* 3 February 1984, 112. All other quotations are from *The Orwell Mystique,* 25, 96, 54, 194, 130, 205, 262.

145. Frank Lentricchia, " 'Patriarchy Against Itself'—The Young Manhood of Wallace Stevens," *Critical Inquiry,* 13 (1987), 784.

146. Elshtain, "The New Feminist Scholarship," 19; and in "Orwell's Legacy: A Discussion," *Salmagundi,* 70 (Spring–Summer 1986), 123.

147. Susan Sontag and Adrienne Rich, "Feminism and Fascism: An Exchange," *New York Review of Books,* 20 March 1975, 31.

148. E.P. Thompson, "Outside the Whale," in *Out of Apathy,* 162, 172.

149. Patai, *The Orwell Mystique,* 16.


*13. Critic and Object of Popular Culture*

150. *CEJL,* Vol. 2, 195.

151. I.A. Richards, *Principles of Literary Criticism* (London, 1927), 2.

152. Q.D. Leavis, *Fiction and the Reading Public* (London, 1932), 5, 11. *CEJL,* Vol. 1, 222, 528.

153. F.R. Leavis and Denys Thompson, *Culture and Environment* (London, 1933).

154. Rayner Heppenstall, *Four Absentees* (London, 1960), 60.

155. *CEJL,* Vol. 1, 222.

156. For more on the social scientific research organization known as Mass Observation, see Tom Jeffrey, *Mass Observation: A Short History* (Birmingham, 1980).

157. Pritchett first used the phrase in a December 1946 BBC Third Programme broadcast. Reprinted in "George Orwell," *Living Writers,* ed. Gilbert Phelps, 110. The phrase is widely known as a result of its appearance in Pritchett's much-quoted obituary of Orwell in the *New Statesman.*

158. See, for example, "Songs We Used to Sing," *Evening Standard,* 19 January 1946; and "Funny, But Not Vulgar," *New Leader,* 28 July 1945. The best example of Orwell's criticism of detective stories is his 2500-word article on Conan Doyle in the Free French review *Fontaine,* entitled "Grandeur et Décadence du Roman Policier Anglais." No English original is known to exist. See *Fontaine,* nos. 37–40 (Algiers, 1944), 213–75.

159. All three essays are reprinted in *CEJL:* "Boys' Weeklies," Vol. 1, 460–85; "The Art of Donald McGill," Vol. 2, 155–65; "Raffles and Miss Blandish," Vol. 3, 220–32.

160. The Waugh, Levin, Bentley, and Wilson reviews are reprinted in Meyers, 211–27. Pritchett's comment is from his 1946 BBC broadcast, reprinted in *Living Writers,* 113.

161. *CEJL,* Vol. 1, 528.

162. For an overview of the main participants and issues in these historic debates on culture, see *Mass Culture: The Popular Arts in America,* ed. Bernard Rosenberg and David Manning White (New York, 1957); and *Culture for the Millions,* ed. Norman Jacobs (Princeton, 1959).

163. Richards' essay, which originally appeared in the May 1940 *Horizon,* is reprinted in *CEJL,* Vol. 1, 485–93.

164. Mary McCarthy, "The Writing on the Wall," 5.

165. See Julian Symons' attack on "Fiedlerism" in "Viewpoint," *Times Literary Supplement,* 19 October 1973, 1278.

166. Williams, *Culture and Society;* Richard Hoggart, *The Uses of Literacy* (London, 1957).

167. Ronald Bryden, "Birth of a Science," *Spectator,* 25 May 1962, 691.

168. J.E. Miller, "Orwell and Koestler," *Tribune,* 17 January 1969, 5.

169. For illustrations of Hoggart's approach, see his "Humanistic Studies and Mass Culture," *Daedalus,* Spring 1970, 451–72.

170. For instance, Orwell says that Rupert Brooke's "Grantchester" is "something worse than worthless from an aesthetic point of view," but "as an illustration of what the thinking middle-class young of that period *felt,* it is a valuable social document." *CEJL,* Vol. 1, 503.

171. Paul Fussell, "George Orwell," *Sewanee Review,* Spring 1985, 232–43.

172. Herbert Gans, *Popular Culture and High Culture* (New York, 1974), x.

173. Susan Sontag, "One Culture and the New Sensibility," in *Against Interpretation* (New York, 1969), 294–304.

174. Orwell's film (and drama) criticism for *Time and Tide,* omitted from *CEJL,* was written (May 1940 to August 1941) during Britain's darkest days in World War II, when virtually all of Europe was occupied by German armies and it appeared that Hitler might soon conquer Britain. Much of Orwell's exasperation with Hollywood's escapism and self-absorption is obviously linked to his anger with America's isolationist politics—and to the frustration of his own repeated failures, on account of poor health, to enlist as a soldier.

175. See, for example, "Poetry and the Microphone," *CEJL,* Vol. 2, 334–36.

176. *Ibid.,* 222–23.

177. *Ibid.,* 162.

178. Indeed Orwell insisted that the novel was fundamentally "a popular form of art," which partly accounts for his preference for *Uncle Tom's Cabin* over Virginia Woolf. He recommended in "In Defence of the Novel" that critics abandon their highbrow "*Criterion-Scrutiny* assumptions" and become "elastic-brows." His neo-Aristotelian suggestion was that novels be evaluated comparatively as "good of their kind" within clearly stated categories since books "are 'good' at very different levels." *CEJL,* Vol. 1, 253–54.

179. *Ibid.,* 461.

180. *Ibid.,* 481.

181. See, for example, Bridget Fowler, "True to Me Always: An Analysis of Women's Magazine Fiction," *British Journal of Sociology,* March 1979, 90.

182. *CEJL,* Vol. 1, 482.

183. *Ibid.,* 484.

184. See Crick, 385.

185. *CEJL,* Vol. 1, 459.

186. Cf. Stansky and Abrahams on Orwell's "antinomianism" in *The Unknown Orwell,* 122–26.

187. *CEJL,* Vol. 1, 459.

188. *Ibid.,* 459.

189. *Ibid.,* 449.

190. For a report on the Orwell for President campaign, see my article "President Orwell?," *Philadelphia Inquirer Magazine,* 1 January 1984.

191. See Ron Givens, "Cramming for 1984," *Newsweek on Campus*, October 1983, 30.

192. Created by Tim Keefe and Howard Levine, the calendar aimed to "demonstrate the validity and relevance of Orwell's commentary regarding the U.S. in this century." "Obviously," note the authors in their introduction, "ours is not *exactly* the same as the society Orwell warned us of. We believe the differences are in degree rather than in kind" (italics added).

For a survey of some of the commercial gimmickry tied to Orwell's dystopia during 1984, see Kathy Booth, "Seeing 1984 as a Capitalist Opportunity," *Muncie Star* (Ind.), 2 January 1984. Copy in Rosenblum Collection. Also Nancy Mills, "Here's 1984: All's Well with Orwell," *Los Angeles Times*, 1 January 1984; and Peter Stansky, "The Orwell Year," *DLB Yearbook*, 1984, 52–62.

193. A prize for the most outrageous article should go to *Hydrocarbon Processing Monthly* for its discussion of "The Orwell Writing Success Number System," a "formula" to improve technical writing. Orwell's suggestions for good prose in "Politics and the English Language," along with "a component called the 'Superfluity Ratio'," serve as "the cornerstone" for "OSWN," as the formula is called. This exercise in Newspeak concludes with a perfect example of doublethink: "the OSWN is the only readability formula that encourages the development of a true style." D.L. Plung, "Add Style to Your Technical Writing," *Hydrocarbon Processing Monthly*, May 1983, 123. Copy in Rosenblum Collection.

A runner-up award for most absurd article should also go to investment counselor George Nicolson's newsletter featuring "the Orwell Thesis." Nicolson termed the 1984 national election "George Orwell Election #3." (The 1980 and 1982 elections were numbers 1 and 2.) "The great test of the Orwell Thesis will occur in the 1984 election," Nicolson prophesied in 1981. The 1980 and 1982 elections witnessed the decline of inflation, the reduced danger of "the Russian problem," and the Dow-Jones stock average topping 1000. Nicolson maintained that, if the Republicans could win both houses of Congress in 1984 and keep the Russians "down," "chances look good for the biggest bull market in 1984." These predictions appear in *Better Investing*, August 1981. Copy in Rosenblum Collection.

194. Copies of the articles on Orwell and "1984" in these publications are in the Rosenblum Collection.

Some trade spokesmen went so far as to credit their industry with heroically preventing the arrival of *Nineteen Eighty-Four*. See the article by the president of the New York Convention and Visitors Bureau, Charles Gillett, "Orwellian Nightmare Thwarted by Travel Industry," *Meeting News*, October 1983.

195. "1984 Is Here," *Welding Journal*, February 1984, 2. Copy in Rosenblum Collection.

196. Ralph Monti, "Casually Speaking: Here Comes 1984," *Casual Living Monthly*, January 1984. "The State of the Handgun Market Today," *The Shooting Industry*, October 1983. Copies in Rosenblum Collection.

197. Kevin Hyland, "Orwellmania Is Getting Off to a Fast Start Around Land," *Syracuse Herald-Journal* (N.Y.), 16 January 1983. Copy in Rosenblum Collection.

198. Mildred Tober, "Where Will the Orwellian Fascination End?," *Fort-Wayne Journal Gazette* (Ind.), 2 January 1984. Copy in Rosenblum Collection.

199. See "1984 Top Seller Again 35 Years After Publication," *Indianapolis Star*, 29 January 1984. *Nineteen Eighty-Four* was listed as #1 on the two lists between January 15 and February 19. *Nineteen Eighty-Four* is also possibly the only book ever to climb the bestseller lists on three separate occasions: 1949, with the original hardback edition; 1951, with the Signet paperback edition; and 1983–84.

200. See, for example, *Punch*'s cover story announcing "the Orwellian decade": "Big Sister Is Watching You: 1984, 10 Years to Go," 2 January 1974.

201. On the Yale facebook, see *The Philadelphia Inquirer*, 5 March 1983, 9A.

202. The ad appears in *Time*, 2 February 1981.

203. Nancy Millman, "Apple's 1984 Spot: A Love-Hate Story," *Advertising Age*, 30 January 1984, 2. Copy in Rosenblum Collection.

204. Otto Rank, *The Myth of the Birth of the Hero and Other Writings* (New York, 1959), 227. See his brilliant chapter, "Success and Fame" (211–27), excerpted from *Art and Artist* (1932).

*Chapter Five. The Prophet*

*14. The Author of* the book

1. "The Decent Dolorist," *Times Literary Supplement,* 2 June 1961, 342.
2. Quoted in Crick, 566.
3. Cf. *CEJL*, Vol. 2, 142–45.
4. *CEJL,* Vol. 4, 119.
5. *Ibid.,* 60.
6. *Ibid.*
7. See, for example, Crick, 248, 372, 386, 426; Meyers, 58; Stansky and Abrahams, *Orwell: The Transformation,* 199, 201–2.
8. Ruth Ann Lief, *Homage to Oceania: The Prophetic Vision of George Orwell* (Columbus, 1969). See also Steven Edelheit, *Dark Prophecies* (New York, 1977).
9. Spender, in Meyers, 137. Woodcock, *The Crystal Spirit,* 26. Fyvel, "George Orwell, Friend and Prophet," 6. Atkins, 4.
10. Robert Leckie, "The Man Who Invented Big Brother," 37–39, 88–89.
11. James Hilton, "A Prophet in the Making," *New York Herald Tribune Book Review,* 12 June 1949, 3.
12. Examples include Kingsley Amis, "The Road to Airstrip One," *Spectator,* 31 August 1956, 292–93; Christopher Small, *The Road to Miniluv* (New York, 1975); and Peter Lewis, *George Orwell: The Road to 1984.*
13. B.K. Sandwell "On Logical Socialist Development, Orwell Is a Bitter Prophet," 12. Stern, "Homage to Orwell," 18. Thomas Spencer, "Prisoner of Hatred," *Daily Worker,* 19 October 1950, 3.
14. Wyndham Lewis, "Orwell, or Two and Two Make Four," *The Writer and the Absolute* (London, 1952), 153–74.
15. George Elliott, "A Failed Prophet," *Hudson Review* (1957), reprinted in Meyers, 335–36.
16. *Ibid.,* 335.
17. See Richard Smyer, *Primal Dream and Primal Crime: Orwell's Development as a Psychological Novelist* (Columbia, Mo., 1979).
18. Delmore Schwartz, review of *Animal Farm* film, in *New Republic,* 17 January 1955, 23.
19. Isaac Rosenfeld, "Decency and Death," *Partisan Review,* May 1950, 514–18. Anthony West, "Hidden Damage," *New Yorker,* 28 January 1956.
20. Deutscher, "*1984*—the Mysticism of Cruelty," 250–65.
21. The comment first appeared in Tom Hopkinson, letter to the *New Statesman and Nation,* 29 August 1953, 234.
22. Fyvel, "A Writer's Life," 20.
23. See Rosenfeld, "Decency and Death"; and West, "Hidden Damage." See also C.M. Kornbluth, "The Failure of the Science Fiction Novel as Social Criticism," in *The Science Fiction Novel: Imagination and Social Criticism,* ed. Basil Davenport (Chicago, 1959), 87–95; and Gerald Fiderer, "Masochism as Literary Strategy: Orwell's Psychological Novels," *Literature and Psychology,* 20 (1970), 3–21.
24. David Goodman, "Countdown to 1984: Big Brother May Be Right on Schedule," *The Futurist,* December 1978, 345–55.
25. "An Inquiry into George Orwell's 1984," *The Futurist,* December 1983, 21.
26. Isaac Asimov, "Asimov vs. Orwell," *Science Digest,* August 1979, 16–20. Michael Robertson, "Orwell's 1984: Prophecy or Paranoia?" *San Francisco Chronicle,* 19 December 1983.
27. Mark Hillegas, *The Future as Nightmare: H.G. Wells and the Anti-Utopians* (New York, 1967), 123–32.
28. "Is There Any Future in Futurism?," *Time,* 17 May 1976, 51.
29. Lord Gladwyn, *Halfway to 1984* (London, 1966). Ronald Brech, *Britain 1984: An Experiment in the Economic History of the Future* (London, 1963). Richard Farmer, *The Real World of 1984* (New York, 1973). Jerome Tuccille, *Who's Afraid of 1984?* (New Rochelle, 1975).
30. "George Orwell: Eternal Pessimist," *Shreveport Journal* (La.), 30 December 1983.

"Horus": Reported in "Orwell Outshines Stargazers," *The Sun* (Vancouver), December 1983. Copy in Rosenblum Collection.

31. John Wesley White, *Re-Entry: Parallels Between Today's News Events and Christ's Second Coming* (Grand Rapids, 1971).

32. Cf. "1984 Symposium: The Future Becomes the Present," *Journal of the American Scientific Affiliation*, March 1981. See esp. Richard Perkins, "Freedom in 1984: Facing Up to Our Dilemma," 18–20.

33. Michael Snyder, "Is a New Dark Age Coming?," *The Plain Truth*, January 1984, 39, 41.

34. Letter to the author from The Reverend Jack van Impe of Royal Oak, Mich., 29 September 1982.

35. "seventy or eighty years": *Awake*, 22 September 1962; quoted in Heather and Gary Botting, *The Orwellian World of Jehovah's Witnesses* (Toronto, 1984), 168.

"parallels between the 'theocracy' ": For example, the Bottings argue that the "Orwellian theocracy" of the Witnesses closely resembles the organizational structure of Oceania: "the Governing Body" is Big Brother; "the Remnant," or Inner Party, are the first 144,000 baptized Witnesses (before 1935); "the Great Crowd," or Outer Party, are Witnesses who have been baptized since 1935. The Bottings also discuss how the Witnesses rewrite history, enforce youthful chastity (like the Junior Anti-Sex League), and indoctrinate their children and even encourage spying on fellow Witnesses (*à la* the Spies and Thought Police).

Acknowledging that the coincidental significance of "1984" for the Witnesses is "uncanny" and that the year has long been taken in the West as a numeral charged with anxiety toward the future, the Bottings conclude: "What much of the world has come to think of as an Orwellian metaphor, the Jehovah's Witnesses have come to think of in quite literal terms as the postulated end of the corrupt world" (p. 171).

36. Walter Reich, "Is the Apocalypse at Hand?," *Detroit News*, 19 October 1983. In reply to the Kabalist speculations, however, Tosco Fyvel said that the correspondence between *Nineteen Eighty-Four* and *tashmad* was "only coincidence." Fyvel, "1984: Year of Destruction?," *The Jewish Chronicle*, 30 December 1983. Nevertheless, Israeli Education Minister Zevulum Hammer proposed that the Hebrew calendar, which is a lunar calendar, be rearranged to *shadmat*, connoting "fields or birds," which Fyvel called "tantamount to changing 1984 to 1849 in the Western calendar." (Some Jews reportedly did change the date when issuing bar mitzvah invitations.) See the Associated Press stories: Gerald Nadler, "And the Prophets Met in Jerusalem, Declaiming Doom in '84," *Hollywood Sun*, 15 December 1983; and "Israelis May Blot Out Doomsday," *Gadsden Times* (Ala.), 23 October 1982. Copies in Rosenblum Collection.

*15. "If Orwell Were Alive Today . . ."*

37. *CEJL*, Vol. 4, 29.

38. W.H. Auden, "George Orwell," *Spectator*, 16 January 1971, 86.

39. Granville Hicks, "Orwell—a Generation's Conscience," *New York Post*, 1 March 1953, 1. See also Hicks's "George Orwell's Prelude in Spain," *New York Times Book Review*, 18 May 1952, 1, 30.

40. For a radical's response, see Patai's *The Orwell Mystique*, 8–9, 270–71. The list is in the Orwell Archive.

41. Jenni Calder, interview, 6 May 1984.

42. Williams, *George Orwell*, 87.

43. Anthony Arblaster, "Orwell: The Man Who Was Ahead of His Time," *Tribune*, 4 October 1968, 2. Philip French, "Bloody, But Alive," *Financial Times*, 3 October 1968.

44. Nicolas Walter, "Orwell and the Pacifists," *Peace News*, 1 November 1968.

45. Mary McCarthy, "The Writing on the Wall," *New York Review of Books*, 30 January 1969, 5–6.

Reprinted as "The Man Who Wanted Out," *Nova*, May–June 1969, 28, 30, 33, 34, 40, 46; and in *The Writing on the Wall* (New York, 1970), 153–71.

46. Sonia Orwell, "Unfair to George," *Nova*, June–July 1969, 18, 20, 22, 27, 29, 30.

47. Rees, "George Orwell," in *The Politics of Twentieth-Century Novelists*, 98.

48. Melvin Maddocks, "If He Lived Today, What Would Orwell Say?," *Chicago Daily Economist*, 20 January 1983. See also "George Would Cheer," *The Gazette* (Manitoba), 31 December 1983; and "If Orwell Were Here," *Rutland Herald* (Vt.), 16 June 1983. Copies in Rosenblum Collection.

49. Hugh Milligan, "If Orwell Were a New Yorker," *Holyoke Daily Transcript-Telegram* (Mass.), 7 January 1984. Copy in Rosenblum Collection.

50. "Interview with 'George Orwell,' " *Rochester Democrat and Chronicle* (N.Y.), 1 January 1984. Copy in Rosenblum Collection. See also the "interview" conducted with Orwell by two educational psychologists, in which Orwell, incredibly, pronounces on "behavioral disorders" and "deviance" problems in schools. James A. and Robert H. Zabel, "Reflections on Deviance in *Nineteen Eighty-Four:* A Conversation with George Orwell," *Behavioral Disorders*, August 1984, 264–76.

51. Norman Podhoretz, "If Orwell Were Alive Today, He'd Be a Neoconservative," *New York Tribune*, 29 December 1983, 37.

52. Norman Podhoretz, "Will Reason, Common Sense Prevail Now That 1984 Is Here?" *New York Tribune*, 5 January 1984. See also Podhoretz, "If Orwell Were Alive Today."

53. Christopher Hitchens, "An Exchange on Orwell," *Harper's*, February 1983, 56–57.

54. "Orwell Lives," *Harper's*, March 1983, 5.

55. Noel Annan, "Artist in Politics," *New York Review of Books*, 16 April 1981.

56. Edward Crankshaw, "The Documents in the Case," *Times Literary Supplement*, 26 December 1980, 1456.

57. John Atkins, "Orwell in 1984," *College Literature*, Vol. 11, No. 1 (1984), 36–37.

58. Rayner Heppenstall, "A Blurred Portrait," 77–80.

59. John Wain, "Dear George Orwell: A Personal Letter," *American Scholar*, February 1983, 30–31.

### 16. *"Media Prophet": Orwell on the Telescreen*

60. For an extended discussion of the "public" writer, see John Raeburn, *Fame Became of Him: Hemingway as a Public Writer* (Bloomington, 1984).

61. "Few Predictions True Despite Orwell's Grim Visions," *Fayetteville Observer* (N.C.), 9 February 1984. Copy in Rosenblum Collection.

62. The quotations are from Jack Gould, "TV in Review: Orwell's 1984," *New York Times*, 23 September 1953, 31; and Philip Hamburger, "Nineteen Eighty-Four," *New Yorker*, 3 October 1953, 84. The viewing statistics are from a telephone interview with the Department of Audience Measurements, National Broadcasting Company, 19 December 1985.

63. "Hour of Gloom," *Time*, 5 October 1953, 71. "A 1984 Spectre on 1953 Screens," *Life*, 5 October 1953, 115–16. See also "The Strange World of 1984," *Life*, 4 July 1949, 78–82.

64. "BBC Repeats 1984 Despite Objections," *New York Times*, 17 December 1954, 35.

65. "Terror by Television," *Newsweek*, 27 December 1954, 28.

66. Burton Paula, *British Broadcasting: Radio and Television in the United Kingdom* (Minneapolis, 1956), 275–76.

The December 12 showing reached approximately 4 million homes, and the December 16 telecast even more. James Thomas, "He Will Debate on TV Why He Wants *1984* Banned," *News Chronicle*, 14 December 1954, 3.

67. "1984," *The Times* (London), 15 December 1954, 5.

68. Quoted in John Sutherland, "The Drama Caused by the Camera in Room 101," *Times Educational Supplement* (London), 30 December 1983, 8.

69. *Ibid.*

70. "BBC Defies Horror Play Critics," *The Times* (London), 14 December 1954, 3.

71. *Ibid.*

72. See "Commons Split Over 'Sunday Sadism'," *Daily Mail*, 15 December 1954, 3.

73. Quoted in Sutherland, "The Drama Caused by the Camera . . . ."

74. Letter to the editor, *Daily Telegraph*, 16 December 1954.

75. "1984," *Daily Express,* 15 December 1954. " '1984' and All That," *Daily Mail,* 14 December 1954, 1. "The Lesson of '1984'," *Daily Mail,* 18 December 1954, 1. The quotation is from the second editorial. Peter Black, "Honest Orwell Did Not Write To Horrify, in Love with Freedom He Wanted To Warn," *Daily Mail,* 14 December 1954, 4.

76. *Ibid.*

77. David Sylvester, "Orwell on the Screen," *Encounter,* March 1955, 36.

78. Letter to the editor, *Daily Telegraph,* 15 December 1954.

79. Quoted in Sylvester, "Orwell on the Screen," 37.

80. Bernard Hollowood, "On the Air," *Punch,* 22 December 1954, 800.

81. Letter to the editor, *Daily Telegraph,* 26 December 1954. Letter, quoted in Sylvester, "Orwell on the Screen," 37.

82. *Picture Post,* 8 January 1955. *Daily Telegraph,* 21 December 1954.

83. William Salter, "Look and Listen," *New Statesman and Nation,* 25 December 1954.

84. *Ibid.*

85. *Ibid.*

86. "Understanding the Lesson," *The Times* (London), 3 January 1955, 2.

87. See Sutherland, "The Drama Caused by the Camera . . . ."

88. See Deutscher, "*1984*—the Mysticism of Cruelty," 252.

89. Roger Manville, *The Animated Film* (London, 1954).

90. See, for example, "Animal Farm," *Senior Scholastic,* 12 January 1955, 30.

91. Cf. David Caute, *The Great Fear: The Anti-Communist Purge Under Truman and Eisenhower* (New York, 1978).

92. See Robert Hatch's review of the *AF* film in *The Nation,* 22 January 1956, 85. Delmore Schwartz, review of *AF* film, *New Republic,* 17 January 1955, 23. The other references are quoted in Spencer Brown, "Strange Doings at Animal Farm," *Commentary,* February 1955, 157.

93. *Ibid.,* 160.

94. Robert Hatch's review of the *AF* film, 85.

95. Gerald Weales, "Films from Overseas," *Quarterly Journal of Film, Radio and TV,* Fall 1955, 13.

96. Ian Willison, "Orwell's Bad Good Books," *Twentieth Century,* April 1955, 354. There was not much "profit Orwell" in either *Animal Farm* or the Columbia *1984,* however. Neither film was listed during 1955–57 by *Variety,* which computes the box-office sales of all films that gross above $1 million. A spokesman for the Motion Picture Association of America in New York called Columbia's production "just a bomb" and attributed *Animal Farm*'s failure to poor distribution. "It was a serious cartoon, and the distributors didn't know what to do with it." Telephone interview, 19 December 1985.

The exact effect on book sales of the *Animal Farm* film and the other adaptations of *Nineteen Eighty-Four* is harder to measure than in the case of the BBC *1984.* Certainly, however, no comparable sales explosion occurred. Fredric Warburg has discussed the sales history of the book in some detail in his 1973 autobiography, *All Authors Are Equal* (pp. 54–56, 114–15). But Warburg does not provide year-by-year breakdowns. I was also not able to obtain such breakdowns from Orwell's publishers.

Other evidence relating the adaptations to Orwell's public reputation is more impressionistic yet probably no less significant a factor in its growth. When I taught the *Animal Farm* film to Philadelphia high school students in the 1970s, I found that it was one of the most frequently requested films, usually shown more than 150 times per year. Certainly it is likely that there is a dialectical relationship between literary and media reputation: Orwell's prior literary reputation probably prompted producers to exploit his artistic standing in promoting media adaptations of his books. The adaptations, in turn, reached large audiences, and this gradually broadened the base of Orwell's book sales—and the same interaction continued over time.

97. It need not, of course. A 1949 letter from Orwell to his agent, in which he granted a request for a stage adaptation of *Nineteen Eighty-Four,* suggests that he recognized the difference between "translation" and "defacement": "What I was afraid of was that the true meaning of the book might be seriously deformed, more than is unavoidable in any stage adaptation of a

novel." Unpublished letter from Orwell to Leonard Moore, 22 August 1949. Berg Collection, New York Public Library.

98. Stephen Watts, "Shaping the World of 1984 to the Screen," *New York Times*, 24 July 1955, 5. On the alternative endings, see Stephen Watts, "Orwell That Ends Well," *The Times* (London), 10 March 1956, 7.

99. *Ibid.*

100. *Ibid.* See also Edward Goring, " 'Happy' 1984 Film Shocks Mrs. Orwell," *Daily Mail*. 27 February 1956. Mrs. Orwell complained that Columbia Pictures "did not understand the book at all. I did make strenuous efforts to have the script altered, but I am afraid I am not used to dealing with movie people." She was so angered that she decided to withdraw all of the 1950s adaptations of *Nineteen Eighty-Four* from circulation when the rights expired in the mid-1970s (twenty years after their original release date). The adaptations became what *The Times* (London) called "unfilms." See "Ministry of Unfilms," 15 November 1983, 12.

My own experience with the "unfilms" bears out *The Times*'s tag. Both CBS and the BBC refused me permission to see their adaptations of *Nineteen Eighty-Four;* I happened to see a pirated version of the Columbia production (American ending) in 1982.

Indeed the restrictions may continue indefinitely. Marvin Rosenblum, the executive producer of the Virgin Films adaptation of *Nineteen Eighty-Four*, which appeared in late 1984, told me that one condition of his contract with Mrs. Orwell was that the old films would not be available.

101. "Orwell That Ends Well," *The Times* (London), 29 February 1956, 9. In a letter to the editor, Richard Rees expressed similar outrage, claiming that the adaptation undermined Orwell's intentions. See *The Times* (London), 2 March 1956, 9.

102. Philip Purser, "1984 in 1965," *New Statesman*, 3 December 1965, 900.

103. "1984," *The Times* (London), 14 December 1965, 12.

104. Stuart Hood, "Orwelliana," *Spectator*, 19 November 1965, 659–60. The American response is from George Gent, "TV: Big Brother Takes a Look at Channel 13," *New York Times*, 20 April 1968, 67.

105. On *KAF*, see Robin Chapman, "Rebel Poet's Decline and Fall," *The Times* (London), 8 November 1965, 6. On *CUA*, see "Repeat of Orwell Well Worthwhile," *The Times* (London), 19 September 1966, 6. Some critics approached these dramatizations autobiographically, once again reflecting the increased interest in Orwell himself. See, for example, Hood's review, which discussed Gordon Comstock as if he were George Orwell.

106. Malcolm Muggeridge, "Orwell and His Times," *Radio Times*, 18 November 1965.

107. "spinoffs": For example, the BBC-TV series *1990.* begun in 1977, was an updated rehash of *Nineteen Eighty-Four*. An all-powerful bureaucracy, the "Department of Public Control," rules England and supervises all aspects of citizens' lives. Only those with "privilege cards" are free, one of whom is a rebellious journalist who attempts to outwit the system.

108. See John Corry, "TV: 1984 Revisited," *New York Times*, 7 June 1983.

109. Misfortunes seem to accompany adaptations of *Nineteen Eighty-Four*. Radford spent more than twice his allotted $2.5 million budget, and (shades of 1956!) two different sound tracks—the Eurythmics' "synthetic" music and a classical score by Dominic Muldowney—were run. Radford claimed that Virgin's producers "foisted" the Eurythmics' "crass rubbish" on him after he had already opened the film in Britain with the Muldowney sound track. An "authorized" version first tried to mix some Eurythmics pieces with a few Muldowney ones. The Eurthymics protested, and after three weeks of public showings in Britain, Virgin Films agreed to use the complete Eurythmics sound track. See Cathy Booth, "Controversy and Anger Erupt over Eurythmics Score for '1984'," *The Philadelphia Inquirer*, 5 December 1984, 3.

For information about the financial and distribution problems experienced by Virgin Films, see James Park, "Orwell on Screen," *World Press Review*, January 1985, 58. The article originally appeared in the *Sunday Times* of London.

110. *Memphis Commercial Appeal*, 1 January 1984. Copy in Rosenblum Collection.

111. See "Mining Familiar Territory," *Time*, 16 January 1984, 81.

112. Richard Schickel, *Intimate Strangers* (New York, 1985), 15–87, 286–99.

*17. The Spectre of* Der Grosse Bruder: *West Germany's Orwell*

NOTE: Translations from the German are my own.

**113.** See the fiction bestseller lists published in the book review pages of *Der Spiegel,* 1982–84, *passim.*

**114.** Diogenes Verlag, Orwell's German-language Swiss publisher, reports that it has sold 730,000 paperback copies of *Animal Farm,* including 230,000 between 1982 and 1984. (Letter to the author from Diogenes Verlag, 8 October 1985.) Ullstein Verlag, Orwell's West German publisher, reports that it sold 1,210,000 paperback copies of *Nineteen Eighty-Four* between 1955 and 1983. (Letter to the author from Ullstein Verlag, 10 September 1985.) These figures do not include the many other editions of *Animal Farm* and *Nineteen Eighty-Four* by other German-language publishers, or the thousands of copies sold of his other works in German. As of 1984–85, all of Orwell's works were translated into German and in print, most of them available through Diogenes, Orwell's main German-language publisher.

**115.** Heinz D. Osterle, "An Orwellian Decade? Günter Grass and the Peace Movement in Germany," 2. Unpublished manuscript, Northern Illinois University. I am indebted to Professor Osterle for calling my attention to Grass's interest in Orwell. See also Osterle's "Interview with Günter Grass Concerning American-German Relations," *New German Critique,* Winter 1984, 125–43.

**116.** Orwell sent dispatches to the *Observer* from Cologne, Nuremberg, and Stuttgart, none of which appear in the *CEJL.* His reports are unexceptional, but they are of biographical interest.

**117.** Tosco Fyvel reports that he explained to Orwell on his deathbed how systematically Dr. Goebbels' propaganda ministry distorted language, implying that Orwell was not fully aware of it when he wrote *Nineteen Eighty-Four.* See Fyvel, *George Orwell: A Personal Memoir,* 189. Fyvel's claim, however, conflicts with the memories of the Austrian-born drama critic Martin Esslin, who worked with Orwell at the BBC during the war and later adapted *Nineteen Eighty-Four* into a BBC radio play. Esslin argues that Orwell was quite familiar with Goebbels' propaganda techniques, and that German radio broadcasts announcing Nazi victories always began with "lengthy bursts of martial music and fanfares, in exactly the same manner as described in *Nineteen Eighty-Four.*" Esslin adds that Orwell would probably have known George Weidenfeld, a member of the special BBC unit that analyzed Nazi propaganda, or that he would at least have known his book *The Goebbels Experiment.* See Martin Esslin, "Television and Telescreen," in *On Nineteen Eighty-Four,* ed. Peter Stansky, 129.

**118.** Golo Mann, review of *Nineteen Eighty-Four,* in *Frankfurter Rundschau,* 5 November 1949. Translated and reprinted in Meyers, 277.

**119.** On the smuggling of *Animal Farm* and the Books in Germany program: Unpublished letters from Orwell to Leonard Moore, 24 July 1947, 11 August 1947, and 10 April 1947. Berg Collection, New York Public Library.

**120.** *Der Monat* reported in January 1949 (inside front cover) on the radio plays of *Animal Farm* and *Nineteen Eighty-Four* and on the *Animal Farm* ballet. Golo Mann mentions the *1984* radio play in his review of the novel (Meyers, 277). *The English People* was published by Schlosser in December 1948. Ullstein (Vienna) and Diana (Zurich) brought out German editions of *Nineteen Eighty-Four* in 1950. The leading Viennese paper, *Die Presse,* distributed *Animal Farm* free to its subscribers in 1951. The Russian-language magazine *Possev,* edited in Frankfurt, published other works by Orwell (sometimes translated into Russian by Orwell's friend Glebe Struve). (For other publications by and about Orwell in *Der Monat,* see footnote 124 below. For general publishing information see Willison, *op. cit.,* 58–175.)

Translations of Orwell's "Letter to London" column for *Partisan Review* also appeared in the 1947 *Stuttgarter Rundschau,* whose editor corresponded with Orwell and whom Orwell met through their mutual friend Marjorie Springe. Unpublished letter from Dr. Fritz Eberhard to Orwell, 16 January 1948. Partisan Review Collection, Boston University.

**121.** The smuggling attempts did not always succeed, being sometimes thwarted by Allied

officials seeking to maintain good East-West relations. In a September 1947 letter to Koestler, Orwell reports that American authorities in Munich seized 1500 copies of the Ukrainian edition of *Animal Farm* (2500 got through to the eastern zone) and handed them over to the Soviet Repatriation Commission. *CEJL*, Vol. 4, 379–80.

122. Joachim Joesten reports that 67 percent of paper supplies were from Soviet-occupied Germany and Poland; the American, British, and French zones produced 15, 10, and 8 percent, respectively. For a discussion of *Lesehunger* and the differences between the Soviet and western zone presses, see Joesten's *The German Press in 1947* (New York, 1947); and Albert Norman, *Our German Policy: Propaganda and Culture* (New York, 1951), 44–53.

123. See "Der Monat," *Times Literary Supplement*, 15 December 1950. Also see G.L. Arnold (a.k.a. George Lichtheim), "The German Reviews," *The Nineteenth Century*, August 1950, 92. *Der Monat*'s circulation was 30,000.

124. The full-page pictures of Orwell appeared in the March 1949 issue (p. 49) and the March 1950 issue (p. 625). *Animal Farm* was serialized for three months from February to April 1949. *Nineteen Eighty-Four*, translated by Kurt Wagenseil, ran five months, from November 1949 to March 1950. The critical articles were by V.S. Pritchett (see footnote 125 below) and Hellmut Jaesrich, "Fünfunddreissig Jahre weiter," *Der Monat*, August 1949, 115–19.

125. V.S. Pritchett, "George Orwell," *Der Monat*, March 1949, 92. The essay is a translation of Pritchett's 1946 BBC Third Programme broadcast on Orwell, reprinted in *Living Writers*, ed. Gilbert Phelps.

126. Reported in *Time*, 20 September 1954, 48.

127. The Congress for Cultural Freedom (CCF) was set up in 1950 to promote the cultural politics of the West in opposition to the *Kulturbund* (Cultural League for the Democratic Renovation of Germany), the Communist-front group organized in Soviet-occupied Berlin in 1945. Both the CCF and the *Kulturbund* professed to be nonpartisan and nonpolitical.

For information about the CIA connection to the CCF, see Christopher Lasch, *The Agony of the American Left* (New York, 1970), 100–10; and Alexander Bloom, *Prodigal Sons: The New York Intellectuals & Their World* (New York, 1986), 259–73.

128. Golo Mann, in Meyers, 277.

129. Eugen Gurster, "George Orwells Bedeutung für unsere Zeit," *Hochland*, April 1958, 312–20.

130. See also Hanns Mukarovsky," "Die Welt im Jahre 1984," *Die Österreichische Furche* (1950), 8; Hansres Jacobi, "Der Swift unserer Zeit, zum Tode George Orwells," *Die Zeit*, Vol. 5, No. 6 (1950), 4.

131. "Prophet aus Enttäuschung," *Christ und Welt*, 2 February 1950, 9.

132. Published by Diana Verlag in Zurich (October 1946) under the pseudonym N. Scarpi. *Der Monat* also used this translation when it serialized *Animal Farm* in 1949.

133. François Bondy, "Gentleman und Streiter," *Der Monat*, March 1950, 567.

134. Ludwig Marcuse, "German Intellectuals Five Years After the War," *Books Abroad*, Autumn 1950, 350.

135. Bondy, "Gentleman und Streiter," 568.

136. Koestler, "A Rebel's Progress," 5. Reprinted as "Die Pilgerfahrt eines Rebellen," *Der Monat*. March 1950, 563–65.

137. Bruno Seidel, "Franz Kafkas Vision des Totalitarismus. Politische Gedanken zu Kafkas Roman 'Das Schloss' und George Orwells Utopie '1984'," *Besinnung*, June 1951, 11–14.

138. For a comparison of Orwell and Jens, see Helmut Wiemken, "Soziale Utopien: Bemerkungen zu Büchern von George Orwell und Walter Jens," *Deutsche-Universitäts-Zeitung*, Vol. IX, No. 12 (1954), 14–17. Jens, however, has claimed that he was unaware of Orwell's *Nineteen Eighty-Four* when he wrote his novel. See Sidney Rosenfeld, "*Nineteen Eighty-Four* in Germany: A Look Back," *World Literature Today*, Spring 1984, 199.

139. For a discussion of the role of *Gruppe 47* in the revival of postwar German intellectual life, see Walter Jens, *Deutsche Literatur der Gegenwart* (Munich, 1961).

140. Grass, in Osterle, "Interview with Günter Grass Concerning American-German Relations," 136.

141. Gurster, "George Orwells Bedeutung . . . ," 312–14, 318.

142. Gerd Krause, "George Orwells Utopie 'Nineteen Eighty-Four'," *Die Neueren Sprachen,* 3 (1954), 529–42.

143. Walter Kaufmann, "German Thought Today," *Kenyon Review,* 10 (1957), 15.

144. Rosenfeld, *"Nineteen Eighty-Four* in Germany," 203.

145. Heinz Ludwig Arnold, "Zur Wirkungsgeschichte von Orwells, '1984'," in *Der Orwell Kalendar: 1984,* ed. Johanno Strasser (Berlin, 1984), 170.

146. The outrage about *Nineteen Eighty-Four* in this German school, then, was not ideologically motivated but moral. The suit, brought by a mother who did not want her 15-year-old daughter reading *Nineteen Eighty-Four,* charged that the book "replaces children's fantasies with images of fear against which even adults are not shielded; at a time of spiritual and sexual awakening, this can lead to tremendous spiritual disturbances." The court ruled that *Nineteen Eighty-Four* was "art," but "not suitable for 15-year-olds." Thereafter the book was reserved for older *Gymnasium* students. See Georg Schulz, "Strafrechtliche Ermittlungen wegen Orwells '1984'," *Polizei/Polizei-Praxis,* April 1958, 93–94.

147. See Hans Ulrich Seeber, *Wandlungen der Form in der Literarischen Utopie* (Göttingen, 1970).

148. By the end of the decade, wrote Seeber in 1970, the German academy practiced four distinct "approaches" to Orwell. First was the anti-Communist Orwell, reflected in the continued tendency to take up *Animal Farm* and *Nineteen Eighty-Four* "against the German Left . . . as a tool against the Communists." In a second incarnation, Orwell was the political theorist, with his work (chiefly *Nineteen Eighty-Four*) discussed in courses on comparative government. A third figure was the "philosophical" or "existential" Orwell, with *Nineteen Eighty-Four* discussed as a story of "the fate of the individual under totalitarianism." Finally, there was the literary, even formalist, Orwell of the essays, which were studied as models of good writing. This list is perhaps not exhaustive, but it does show that German academics were well aware of the various uses to which Orwell was being put (pp. 55–90).

For a discussion of the second approach, see Alfred Wollman, "George Orwells *Nineteen Eighty-Four* als Klassenlektüre," *Anregung* (Munich), 5 (1959), 294–303.

149. Richard Schmid, "Versuch über George Orwell," *Merkur,* Vol. 26, No. 12 (1972), 1188–1202.

150. Cf. Wilhelm Fuger, "Wie entsteht ein Gedicht?," *Die Neueren Sprachen,* 14 (1965), 49–60. Helmut Müller-Tochtermann, "George Orwell und die Sprachpflege in England," *Muttersprache,* February 1961, 39–45.

151. Georg Huntemann, "Der Gedanke der Selbstentfremdung bei Karl Marx und in den Utopien von E. Cabet bis G. Orwell," *Zeitschrift für Religion und Geistesgeschichte,* 6 (1954), 138–46.

152. Roland Hill, *Lexikon der Weltliteraturen im 20. Jahrhundert,* Vol. 2 (Munich, 1961), 568.

153. Hans Joachim Lang, "Orwells dialektischer Roman: 1984," in *Rationalität—Phänomenalität—Individualität,* ed. Wolfgang Ritzel (Bonn, 1966), 301–41.

154. Harald Weinrich, "Warnung vor der Neusprache," *Merkur,* Vol. 28, No. 10 (1974), 997–1000.

155. The dramatization by Czech playwright Pavel Kohout was first performed in Vienna in early 1984.

156. *Der Spiegel,* 3 January 1983, 20–21.

157. West German discussion of the "1984 within" did not, however, avoid mention of the GDR altogether. See, for instance, Friedrich Uttitz, *"1984*—Der grosse Bruder steht vor der Tür," *Die Welt,* 29 December 1979, 3.

158. Johanno Strasser, "1984: Decade of the Experts?," in *1984 Revisited,* ed. Irving Howe, 151. See also pp. 150, 153.

159. *Ibid.,* 151.

160. *Der Spiegel,* 3 January 1983, 27–28.

161. *Ibid.,* 8 August 1983, 17–22.

162. See Arnold, in *Der Orwell Kalendar,* 170.

163. *Ibid.*

164. François Bondy, "Orwell und 'Orwell'," *Merkur,* Vol. 37, No. 12 (1983), 971.

165. See *Der Orwell Kalendar*.

166. Grass elaborated on the "Orwell theme" of his campaign speech in the *New German Critique* interview: ". . . two dangers particularly concern me because they remind one of George Orwell's novel, *1984*. . . . I am worried that we in the Federal Republic are in danger of creating a 'Big Brother' state in a clandestine manner through the systematic development of official computer systems and new devices for electronic surveillance. In this way we could give up democracy without a spectacular seizure of power. Fortunately there has been a great deal of resistance against the proposed new method of census-taking. . . . These identity cards could perfect the 'Big Brother' state in the Orwellian manner. . . . My speech is a warning as is Orwell's *1984*" (pp. 136–37).

167. I quote here from translations of Grass's work by Ralph Manheim. See *The Flounder* (New York, 1978), 189; and *Headbirths, or the Germans Are Dying Out* (New York, 1980), 67, 130.

168. *Ibid.*, 79.

169. Speech by Grass, 30 January 1983, printed in *Die Zeit* under the title "Vom Recht auf Widerstand," 11 February 1983, 18. Translated and quoted by Osterle in "An Orwellian Decade?," 18. A similar version of this speech is collected in Günter Grass, *On Writing and Politics, 1967–83*, trans. Ralph Manheim (New York, 1983), 141–49.

### 18. "Friend and Prophet": T.R. Fyvel and the Tribune *writers' Orwell*

170. Crick, 441–49. Michael Foot, "Working Words into Weapons," *Liverpool Daily Post*, 27 November 1980.

171. Crick, 444.

172. *Ibid.*

173. Fyvel, "The Years at *Tribune*," in *The World of George Orwell*, 113.

174. Fyvel, "George Orwell as Friend and Prophet." Keynote address delivered at Smithsonian Institution conference, "The Road After 1984," 7 December 1983. Copy in Rosenblum Collection.

175. Cf. *CEJL*, Vol. 4, 276.

176. *Ibid.*

177. Fyvel, "The Years at *Tribune*," 112.

178. *CEJL*, Vol. 4, 276.

179. For a concise history of *Tribune* during this period, see Douglas Hill, ed., *Tribune 40: The First Forty Years of a Socialist Newspaper* (London, 1977), 1–24.

180. Julian Symons, interview, 13 March 1985.

181. *CEJL*, Vol. 4, 280.

182. "Tribune's Ten," *Time*, 10 February 1947, 74.

183. Cf. Tosco Fyvel's observations in his review of Bevan's *In Place of Fear*, in the *New Republic*, 28 April 1952, 18–19. See also Kingsley Martin, "In Place of Fear," *New Statesman and Nation*, 5 April 1952.

184. John Freeman, "Aneurin Bevan," *New Statesman and Nation*, 26 October 1962, 571.

185. See Orwell's unsigned profile, "Aneurin Bevan," *Observer*, 14 October 1945.

186. Michael Foot, *Aneurin Bevan*, Vol. 1, *1897–1945* (London, 1963), 349.

187. *CEJL*, Vol. 3, 311.

188. *CEJL*, Vol. 4, 279–80.

189. For a different interpretation of Orwell's relation to the paper, see Paul O'Flinn, "Orwell and *Tribune*," *Literature and History*, 6 (1980), 210.

In *Tribune 40* Hill says that Orwell is "the man whom many have called the pre-eminent literary journalist of our time" (p. 39). See also Ben Pimlett, "*Tribune* and the Thirties," *New Statesman*, 7 January 1977, 8.

190. *CEJL*, Vol. 4, 394–400. Symons, "Orwell, a Reminiscence," *London Magazine*, September 1963.

191. T.R. Fyvel, "The Missing Middle," *Tribune*, 8 March 1946. Orwell on "fashionable" anti-Americanism: *CEJL*, Vol. 4, 394.

192. *Ibid.*, 380.

193. *CEJL,* Vol. 3, 37.

194. Julian Symons, "Ourselves as Orwell Sees Us," *Manchester Evening News,* 7 August 1947.

195. Bruce Bain, "After the Bomb," *Tribune,* 17 June 1949.

196. Foot, "Working Words into Weapons."

197. Crick, 408.

198. Podhoretz, "If Orwell Were Alive Today," 32.

199. Cf. Leopold Labedz, "Will Orwell Survive 1984?," *Encounter,* June and July 1984. Orwell's "In Defence of Comrade Zilliacus" is collected in *CEJL,* Vol. 4, 397–98. This piece was written between October 1947 and January 1948 but not published until it appeared in *CEJL* in 1968.

200. Podhoretz, "If Orwell Were Alive Today," 31.

201. Leopold Labedz, "Will George Orwell Survive 1984?," *Encounter,* June 1984, 23–24.

202. Leopold Labedz, "The Case of Julian Symons' Nostalgia," *Encounter,* November 1984, 76–77. See also the *Tribune* writers' responses: Symons, "The Beds That Don't Fit: On Labedz's Orwell," *Encounter,* November 1984, 74–75; and Fyvel, "Orwell and *Tribune,*" *Encounter,* December 1985, 68–69.

203. See Robert Nozick, *Anarchy, State and Utopia* (New York, 1975), 150–82, 199–200. See also Seymour Mandelbaum, "The Past in Service to the Future," *Journal of Social History,* Spring 1983.

204. See Julian Symons, "Orwell, a Reminiscence." *London Magazine,* September 1963.

205. Symons, interview, 13 March 1985. John Atkins, interview, 15 March 1985.

206. *The Progressive,* June 1948.

207. Symons, interview, 13 March 1985.

208. *Ibid.*

209. Peter Lewis, *George Orwell: The Road to 1984,* 88.

210. Crick, 445–46.

211. Fyvel, "George Orwell as Friend and Prophet," 8.

212. Symons, interview, 13 March 1985.

213. Fyvel, "The Years at *Tribune,*" 115.

214. T.R. Fyvel, "A Writer's Life," *World Review,* June 1950, 7–27. Atkins, "George Orwell," *World Review,* July 1950, 2–3.

215. Atkins, *George Orwell: A Literary and Biographical Study,* 347.

216. T.R. Fyvel, "Wingate, Orwell and the 'Jewish question'," *Commentary,* February 1951, 137–44. Fyvel, "George Orwell and Eric Blair: Glimpses of a Dual Life," *Encounter,* July 1959, 60–65.

217. Fyvel, "George Orwell as Friend and Prophet," 1.

218. Fyvel, *George Orwell: A Personal Memoir,* 173.

219. "little group": Fyvel, quoted in *Remembering Orwell,* 120. Symons, "Orwell, a Reminiscence," 39.

220. Fyvel, *George Orwell,* 68–69, 103–6, 134–38.

221. *Ibid.,* 176. Fyvel, "George Orwell as Friend and Prophet," 7–8.

222. "George Orwell as Friend and Prophet," 11–12.

223. *Ibid.*

224. Fyvel, *George Orwell,* 209.

225. "Orwell's Friend," *Jewish Chronicle,* 21 November 1980.

226. Fyvel, "Wingate, Orwell and the 'Jewish Question'," 137.

227. Fyvel, *George Orwell,* 180.

228. Herb Greer, "Orwell in Perspective," *Commentary,* March 1983, 53.

229. "Wingate, Orwell and the 'Jewish Question'," 141.

230. "chance brought me": *ibid.,* 137. " 'hero,' 'prophet,' 'genius' ": Fyvel, *George Orwell,* 98, 107, 93; and "Wingate, Orwell and the 'Jewish Question'," 137, 139.

231. "legends": *ibid.,* 203–10, 173–76, 106; and "Wingate, Orwell and the 'Jewish Question'," 138. See also Fyvel's remarks on Orwell in *Intellectuals Today: Problems in a Changing Society* (London, 1968).

232. Cf. Fyvel's *George Orwell*, 98, and "Wingate, Orwell and the 'Jewish Question'," 140–41.

233. Fyvel, *George Orwell*, 93. See also Tosco Fyvel, "Wingate in Palestine," *Encounter*, January 1985, 63–65.

234. T.R. Fyvel, *The Malady and the Vision* (London, 1941), 16.

235. Christopher Sykes, *Orde Wingate: A Biography* (New York, 1959), 109–10.

236. "Wingate, Orwell and the 'Jewish Question'," 140.

237. *Ibid.*, 139–40.

238. "staggering": *ibid.*, 139. "devote my life": Wingate, quoted in Sykes, *Orde Wingate*, 112. "roughly": Fyvel, *George Orwell*, 105–6.

239. Fyvel, quoted in *Remembering Orwell*, 122.

240. Fyvel, *George Orwell*, 102.

241. Kimche in particular is a well-known writer of Jewish history. The author of seven books on Jewish subjects, the best known of which is *Seven Fallen Pillars* (London, 1950), he left *Tribune* to become the first editor of *The Jewish Observer and the Middle East Review* (1952–67), the official organ of the Zionist Federation of the United Kingdom of Great Britain and Northern Ireland. Koestler, also a strong Zionist, served from 1945 to 1947 as an *Observer* correspondent in Palestine, from where he occasionally contributed to *Tribune* in 1945–46.

242. Cf. Hill, *Tribune 40*, 75–76.

243. *CEJL*, Vol. 4, 395–96. Walter Laqueur calls the years 1945–48 the "most critical period in the history of the Zionist movement." See his *History of Zionism* (New York, 1972), esp. 564–86.

244. Frederick Mullally, "1984: A Failed Prophecy," *Los Angeles Times*, 1 January 1984. Mullally remarks that Orwell was "gripped by romanticism, pessimism, and sadomasochism . . . ." Mullally was a *Tribune* editor from February 1945 to January 1947.

245. Muggeridge, *Like It Was*, 376. Fyvel, *George Orwell*, 178–79; also Fyvel, quoted in *Remembering Orwell*, 121–22, and "Wingate, Orwell and the 'Jewish Question'," 142. On Orwell's statement about 100,000 refugee Jews: *CEJL*, Vol. 4, 238. See also Orwell's essays "Anti-Semitism in Britain" and "Notes on Nationalism." Both condemn anti-Semitism and were known to the Jewish writers around *Partisan Review* as a result of their appearance in the 1953 essay collection *Such, Such Were the Joys*. In one "London Letter" in *Partisan Review*, Orwell also criticized anti-Semitism. See *CEJL*, Vol. 2, 290.

246. Fyvel, in *Remembering Orwell*, 122, and in his *George Orwell*, 182.

247. "Wingate, Orwell and the 'Jewish Question'," 142.

248. Fyvel, *George Orwell*, 86.

249. *CEJL*, Vol. 3, 336.

250. Fyvel, *George Orwell*, 142.

251. *CEJL*, Vol. 3, 340.

252. Cf. Fyvel, *George Orwell*, 142, 146.

253. Fyvel, "Wingate, Orwell and the 'Jewish Question'," 143–44.

254. Fyvel, *George Orwell*, 5.

255. Wingate, a distant cousin of T.E. Lawrence, earned the sobriquet "Lawrence of Judea" for his exploits in Palestine in the 1930s.

256. "Wingate, Orwell and the 'Jewish Question'," 143.

257. Fyvel, *George Orwell*, 102.

258. *Ibid.*, 178, 128, 204, and Fyvel in *Remembering Orwell*, 121–22.

259. "Wingate, Orwell and the 'Jewish Question'," 143–44.

260. For Orwell's views on the advantages of Jewish assimilation, see his little-known contribution to "A Symposium . . . Upon Professor John Macmurray's *The Clue to History*," *Adelphi*, July 1939, 469–73.

261. Fyvel, in *Remembering Orwell*, 120–21. Fyvel, *George Orwell*, 209–10.

262. Fitly, the last sentence of the last piece Fyvel ever completed, published posthumously, declared: "He should be seen as a writer with premonitions of genius, but also as a man with friends, with eccentricities, with his own contradictions, and not just as a walking political opinion to be quoted without context forty years on" ("Orwell and *Tribune*," *Encounter*,

December 1985, 69). See also Peregrine Worsthorne, "Remembering Tosco Fyvel," *Encounter*, December 1985, 76–77.

### Chapter Six. The Saint

#### 19. 'St. George,' The Halfway Saint

1. See, for example, H.McK., "Orwell—Conscience of a Generation," *Evening Standard*, 4 February 1950, 2. Orwell is "a kind of twentieth-century saint, in some respects a Don Quixote tilting at windmills, and now like so many saints and Quixotes, he will doubtless win the acclaim of a world that all too often passed him by." Copy in Orwell Archive.

2. Pritchett, "Books in General," *New Statesman and Nation*, 15 August 1953, 183.

3. Richard Rees, "George Orwell," *Scots Chronicle*, 26 (1951), 7–14.

4. *A Clergyman's Daughter* (New York, 1960), 308.

5. *CEJL*, Vol. 1, 304.

6. Angus Calder, "Orwell: The Rarer Animal," *New Statesman*, 4 October 1968, 429.

7. D.A.N. Jones, "Arguments Against Orwell," in *The World of George Orwell*, 158–59. See also Tom Nairn, "St. George," *New Statesman and Nation*, 14 July 1967, 53. For other references to Orwell as 'St. George,' see Isaac Rosenfeld, "Gentleman George," *Commentary*, June 1956, 589; Hugh Rank, "Mr. Orwell, Mr. Schlesinger and the Language," *College Composition and Communication*, 28 (1977), 159. Leopold Labedz uses "St. Orwell" in his "Will George Orwell Survive Until 1984?," *Encounter*, July 1984, 25.

8. Cf. Woodcock, *The Crystal Spirit*, 13.

9. Warburg relates how Orwell had refused to make the cuts requested by the Book-of-the-Month Club, thereby running the risk of losing a minimum of £40,000 if *Nineteen Eighty-Four* were not chosen as a Club edition. "Would every author have taken this risk?" Warburg asked rhetorically, "especially at a time of critical illness, when he feared he might be an invalid for the rest of his life?" Warburg, *All Authors Are Equal*, 110.

10. Cf. Alfred Ayer's recollections in *Orwell Remembered*, 211–12.

11. *CEJL*, Vol. 4, 467; see also 441.

12. *CEJL*, Vol. 2, 303.

13. Philip Toynbee, "Passionate Sanity," *Observer*, 3 December 1950, 7.

14. V.S. Pritchett, "Letter from London," *New York Times Book Review*, 3 July 1949, 13; and Pritchett, "Books in General," 183.

15. The quotation is taken from Richard Rovere's introduction to the collection, p. xx.

16. *CEJL*, Vol. 2, 265.

17. Rees, in *Orwell Remembered*, 125–26.

18. *Ibid.*, 122.

19. BBC-TV Arena program, "George Orwell," produced by Nigel Williams, broadcast in January 1984. The latter quote ("this wonderful . . . with Orwell") is also included in *Orwell Remembered*, 191–92.

20. Atkins, 110.

21. *CEJL*, Vol. 4, 467.

22. Rees, in *Orwell Remembered*, 126.

23. *CEJL*, Vol. 4, 470.

24. Koestler, delivered on BBC radio in 1960. Reprinted in *Orwell Remembered*, 169.

25. From the expanded edition of Atkins' *George Orwell* (London, 1971), 391. On Orwell as St. Francis, see Malcolm Muggeridge, Introduction to *Burmese Days* (London, 1967), xi; and Alain Besançon, "Orwell in Our Time," *Survey*, Spring 1984, 190–97.

26. Atkins (1954 edition), 115. R.W.B. Lewis, *The Picaresque Saint* (Philadelphia, 1956), 32.

27. Deutscher, "*1984*—The Mysticism of Cruelty," 253.

28. Rees, *George Orwell: Fugitive from the Camp of Victory*, 31.

29. One might also approach the "doubleness" of Orwell's saintly appeal by counterpointing it with that ascribed to the two literary contemporaries most often compared with him, one a "virtuous man" and the other known as a puritan. Curiously, despite Orwell's

celebrated "Englishness," both are French—Camus and Simone Weil. Like Orwell, and also for reasons having very much to do with a public perception of his moral courage and sheer goodness as a man, Camus is one of the few modern writers who has aroused the emotion of love among his readers, rather than mere admiration or respect. Camus' bravery in the French Resistance has been compared with Orwell's fighting in Spain, as have their defiant, anti-Stalinist postwar stances toward their respective Left intelligentsias. But Camus was not known as an ascetic; he grew up poor and did not insist in adulthood on living barely. Orwell did, however, and especially his sacrifice of his wartime rations not for relatives or friends but for faceless Englishmen invites comparison with Simone Weil, that wartime martyr whose fanatical, religious asceticism quite literally drove her to starve herself to death because her compatriots were going hungry.

20. *Socialist "intellectual hero," neoconservative "guiding spirit": Irving Howe, Norman Podhoretz, and the New York Intellectuals' Orwell*

30. Howe, "As the Bones Know," 97. Podhoretz, "If Orwell Were Alive Today," 31.

31. For a list of the members of the *Partisan* "Family," according to filial relation and generation, see Daniel Bell, "The Intelligentsia in American Society," in *The Winding Passage* (New York, 1980), 127–29.

32. Podhoretz, "An Exchange on Orwell," *Harper's,* February 1983, 57. See also Podhoretz's comments on Mary McCarthy's radical critique of Orwell in "A Minor Cultural Event," *Commentary,* April 1972.

33. **"pro-imperialist":** Irving Howe, "The Dilemma of *Partisan Review*," *New International,* February 1942, 24. See also Howe, "How *Partisan Review* Goes to War," *New International,* April 1942. **"Half in":** Howe, *A Margin of Hope* (New York, 1983), 114.

34. See the reviews of Orwell's work by Diana Trilling, Rahv, and Daniel Bell in Meyers. Kazin boosted *Nineteen Eighty-Four* in the July 1949 *Book-of-the-Month Club News;* Schlesinger reviewed *Animal Farm* enthusiastically on page one of the *New York Times Book Review* in August 1946. See also Robert Gorham Davis, "Forms of Popular Art," *New York Times Book Review,* 19 May 1946, 4.

35. Howe, "*1984*—Utopia Reversed," *New International,* November/December 1950, 366–68.

36. Trilling, "Orwell on the Future," *New Yorker,* 18 June 1949, 82.

37. Howe, "*1984*—Utopia Reversed," 366.

38. Howe, *A Margin of Hope,* 112.

39. *Ibid.,* 119.

40. Howe, "The New York Intellectuals: A Chronicle & A Critique," 39. *A Margin of Hope,* 120.

41. Harold Rosenberg, "The Herd of Independent Minds," *Commentary,* September 1948, 244–52.

42. On the wartime rifts among the *Partisan* editors, see S.A. Longstaff, "*Partisan Review* and the Second World War," *Salmagundi,* Winter 1979, 108–29.

43. Howe, "Orwell: History as Nightmare," *American Scholar,* Spring 1956, 193–207. Reprinted under the title "*1984:* History as Nightmare," in *Nineteen Eighty-Four: Text, Sources, Criticism,* ed. Irving Howe (New York, 1963), 188–96.

44. *Ibid.,* 190, 194.

45. *Ibid.,* 249.

46. Howe, Preface to *1984 Revisited: Totalitarianism in Our Century* (New York, 1983), ix.

47. Howe, "*1984:* History as Nightmare," 196.

48. *Ibid.,* 190.

49. For an example of the latter, see George Steiner, "True to Life," *New Yorker,* 29 March 1969. Reprinted in Meyers, 363–73.

50. Howe, "*1984:* History as Nightmare," 196.

51. Howe, *A Margin of Hope,* 211, 213–14, 229.

52. *Ibid.*, 242, 217–18, 238.

53. *Ibid.*, 293.

54. *Ibid.*, 205. The latter phrase is italicized in Howe's contribution to "Liberal Anti-Communism Revisited," *Commentary*, September 1967, 49.

55. Howe, *A Margin of Hope*, 146.

56. *Ibid.*, 237, 227–28.

57. *Ibid.*, 236–37.

58. *Ibid.*, 246.

59. *Ibid.*, 213.

60. Howe, "Orwell as a Moderate Hero," *Partisan Review*, Winter 1954–55, 105–6.

61. *Ibid.*, 106–7.

62. *CEJL*, Vol. 4, 449.

63. Richard Rovere, Introduction to *The Orwell Reader*, xx.

64. Podhoretz, interview, 1 July 1986.

65. Barrett, *The Truants: Adventures Among the Intellectuals*, 124.

66. Howe, *A Margin of Hope*, 231.

67. *Ibid.*, 232, 321–22.

68. Howe, interview, 8 October 1983.

69. Trilling, Introduction to *Homage to Catalonia*, xvi, xviii.

70. Howe, *A Margin of Hope*, 324.

71. *Ibid.*, 295.

72. Howe, "As the Bones Know," 102. Howe, "Orwell as a Moderate Hero," 104.

73. Jonah Raskin, *The Mythology of Imperialism* (New York, 1971), 46–52. Franklin, "Teaching Literature in the Highest Academies of the Amerikan Empire," 116.

74. Saul Bellow, *Mr. Sammler's Planet* (New York, 1970), 35.

75. Howe, *A Margin of Hope*, 314.

76. Howe, "As the Bones Know," 102.

77. **"kamikaze radicalism"**: Howe, *Steady Work: Essays in the Politics of Democratic Radicalism, 1953–66* (New York, 1966), 42. **"dastardly"**: Howe, *A Margin of Hope*, 315.

78. Howe, *A Margin of Hope*, 324.

79. Howe, interview, 8 October 1983.

80. Howe, *A Margin of Hope*, 321.

81. Howe, "As the Bones Know," 103.

82. *Ibid.*, 98–99.

83. Howe, *A Margin of Hope*, 291–92.

84. *Ibid.*, 315.

85. Howe, "As the Bones Know," 97.

86. *Ibid.*, 97, 103.

87. On the breakup of the New York Intellectuals in the 1960s, see Bloom, *Prodigal Sons*, 318–65.

88. Alfred Kazin, review of *CEJL*, in *Book World*, 27 October 1968.

89. Hilton Kramer, "A Passion for Honesty, a Genius for Decency," *New York Times Book Review*, 27 October 1968, 1.

90. **"American counterpart"**: *New York Times Book Review*, 1 December 1968. Mailer on *KAF:* Remarks transcribed but not broadcast on Melvyn Bragg's 1970 "Omnibus" program, *The Road to the Left*.

91. Raymond Williams, "Parting of the Ways," *Commentary*, February 1969, 74–75.

92. Williams, *George Orwell*, 97.

93. Howe, "As the Bones Know," 103.

94. Williams, *Politics and Letters*, 384.

95. Martin Green, "George Orwell: Contradictions and Paradoxes," 11.

96. The phrases, originally applied by Howe to the American literary tradition, are from his essay "The Quest for Moral Style," in *Decline of the New* (New York, 1970), 155–56.

97. Howe, "The First 25 Years," *Dissent*, Winter 1979, 6.

98. See Podhoretz, "If Orwell Were Alive Today," 30–37.

99. **"Kidnaping Our Hero":** Subtitle of address delivered by Howe at West Chester University, 8 October 1983.

100. According to Podhoretz, Michael Kinsley, then editor of *Harper's,* tried to arrange a "debate" between Podhoretz and Howe on the topic that became Podhoretz's title. Howe declined to participate. Podhoretz, interview, 1 July 1986.

101. Edward Said, "Tourism Among the Dogs," *New Statesman,* 18 January 1980.

102. Howe, "The New York Intellectuals," 30.

103. See Peter Steinfels, *The Neoconservatives* (New York, 1979).

104. Podhoretz, interview, 1 July 1986. For other neoconservative responses to Orwell, see: Kristol, "There'll Never Be a 1984," *Wall Street Journal,* 16 December 1983. Joseph Epstein, "*Partisan Review* and the Phillips Curve," *Encounter,* January 1985, 73. Lewis Feuer, "What Orwell Means for Our Time," *Survey,* June 1984, 155–64.

105. Podhoretz, *Making It,* 109–37.

106. Podhoretz, interview, 1 July 1986.

107. Podhoretz, *Making It,* xv–xvi.

108. *CEJL,* Vol. 4, 351.

109. Podhoretz, *Making It,* 351.

110. Podhoretz, *Breaking Ranks,* 220, 264.

111. Podhoretz, *Making It,* xvii.

112. Podhoretz, interview, 1 July 1986.

113. Norman Podhoretz, "The Future of America," *Partisan Review,* Winter 1984, 866.

114. Norman Podhoretz, *The Bloody Crossroads* (New York, 1986), 168.

115. Podhoretz, interview, 1 July 1986.

116. See Orwell's already quoted letter from 1949 explaining that *Nineteen Eighty-Four* is "NOT an attack on the British Labour Party." *CEJL,* Vol. 4, 502. See also Orwell's 1945 letter to the Duchess of Atholl in which he insists: "[I] cannot associate myself with an essentially Conservative body which claims to defend democracy in Europe but has nothing to say about British imperialism. . . . I belong to the Left and must work inside it, much as I hate Russian totalitarianism. . . ." *CEJL,* Vol. 4, 30.

117. Podhoretz himself long preferred the self-characterization "centrist liberal" or "old-fashioned liberal." See Bloom, *Prodigal Sons,* 371.

118. Podhoretz, *Breaking Ranks,* 305.

119. Podhoretz, interview, 1 July 1986.

120. See Irving Kristol, *Reflections of a Neoconservative* (New York, 1984).

121. Podhoretz, interview, 1 July 1986.

122. Podhoretz, *The Bloody Crossroads,* 47.

123. Podhoretz, "If Orwell Were Alive Today," 34.

124. Podhoretz, interview, 1 July 1986. Most of the publications under the "Orwell Press" imprint deal with East-West foreign policy issues. See, for example, Victor Bukovsky, *The Peace Movement and the Soviet Union* (New York, 1982).

125. Orwell on a **"third way":** *CEJL,* Vol. 4, 370–75; on **"hundred percent Americanism,"** see Crick, *op. cit.,* 566; on patriotism as **"revolutionary"** and the opposite of Conservatism, see *CEJL,* Vol. 2, 103. See also Gordon Beadle, "George Orwell and the Neoconservatives," *Dissent,* Spring 1984, 71–79.

126. Podhoretz, interview, 1 July 1986.

127. Podhoretz, "If Orwell Were Alive Today," 30.

128. *Ibid.,* 32.

129. *Ibid.* For a thorough discussion of Orwell's ambivalence toward capitalism, see Arthur Eckstein, "*1984* and George Orwell's Other View of Capitalism," *Modern Age,* 1985, 11–17.

130. Podhoretz, "The Future of America," 866–67.

131. Podhoretz, *Breaking Ranks,* 300.

132. Podhoretz calls Trilling his "intellectual father" in *Time*'s obituary, "A Sad Solemn Sweetness," 17 November 1975, 74. Podhoretz on Hook, in *Breaking Ranks,* 300.

133. Podhoretz, *Breaking Ranks,* 300.

134. Robert Brustein, "Ciao! Manhattan," *New York Review of Books,* 3 February 1983.

135. Howe, *A Margin of Hope,* 345.

136. Howe, interview, 8 October 1983.

137. *Ibid.*

138. "clarity": Podhoretz, *Breaking Ranks,* 302. "the writers": Howe, *A Margin of Hope,* 350.

139. Orwell, *CEJL,* Vol. 2, 229. Irving Howe, "Controversy: The New York Intellectuals," *Commentary,* January 1969, 16; and *A Margin of Hope,* 351. Podhoretz, interview, 1 July 1986.

140. Lionel Trilling, "Reality in America," in *The Liberal Imagination: Essays in Literature and Society* (New York, 1950), 11. Podhoretz muses on the phrase in his essay collection bearing the title (pp. 11–14).

141. Podhoretz, interview, 1 July 1986.

142. Max Weber, "Politics as a Vocation," in *From Max Weber: Essays in Sociology,* ed. H.H. Gerth and C. Wright Mills (New York, 1946).

*21. The Religious Fellow-Traveler: Christopher Hollis, Brian Wicker, and the British Catholics' Orwell*

143. Christopher Hollis, "George Orwell and His Schooldays," *Listener,* 4 March 1954, 383.

144. *CEJL,* Vol. 2, 148.

145. *CEJL,* Vol. 1, 50.

146. Charles Brady, "Virtuous Skeptic," *America,* 20 July 1946, 364.

147. *CEJL,* Vol. 4, 496.

148. T.A. Birrell, "Is Integrity Enough? A Study of George Orwell," *Dublin Review,* Autumn 1950, 51, 65.

149. John Kelly, S.J., review of Hollis' *A Study of George Orwell,* in *Studies: An Irish Review,* Summer 1957, 256.

150. Indeed Grandfather Blair had been vicar of Milbourne at St. Andrews in Dorset. Orwell also attended church regularly in the early 1930s, convincing the parish rector that he was a devout believer at the same time he was mocking religion in letters to Brenda Salkeld. For an insightful treatment of Orwell's views on Christianity, see James Connors, " 'Who Dies If England Live?': Christianity and the Moral Vision of George Orwell," in *The Secular Mind: Transformations of Faith in Modern Europe,* ed. W. Warren Wagar (New York, 1982), 169–86.

151. Wrote W.H. Auden: "If I were asked to name people who I considered true Christians, the name of George Orwell is one of the first that would come to mind." "W.H. Auden on George Orwell," *Spectator,* 16 January 1971, 87.

152. See, for instance, Peter Faulkner, "Orwell and Christianity," *The Humanist,* December 1973, 270–73; and Max Cosman, "Orwell's Terrain," *Personalist,* Winter 1954, 41–49.

153. Orwell on Waugh: *CEJL,* Vol. 4, 513. Belief in the supernatural, insisted Orwell, entailed conservatism and *contemptus mundi.* "In practice," Orwell wrote in 1939, "accepting the Catholic standpoint means accepting exploitation, poverty, famine, war and disease as the natural order of things." *CEJL,* Vol. 1, 385.

154. John Raymond, "Barrack-Room Lawyer," *New Statesman and Nation,* 15 September 1956, 314.

155. See, for example, Neville Braybrooke, "The Two Poverties: Léon Bloy and George Orwell," *Commonweal,* 14 August 1953, 449–51. Hollis compares Orwell with Chesterton in *A Study of George Orwell: The Man and His Work* (Chicago, 1956), 175–81.

The gap between Orwell and Catholicism was, however, much wider than most Catholic intellectuals realized. To Orwell, "common decency" and the religious concept of good and evil were fundamentally incompatible. He once upbraided Arnold Lunn (only half-jestingly) for his "pessimism," arguing that their basic difference centered on the unwillingness of Christians to allow that human nature could be improved through social change. See Arnold Lunn, "Revolutions and Conservatives," *Renascence,* Summer 1957, 212.

156. Douglas Woodruff, review of *Homage to Catalonia,* in *The Tablet,* 9 July 1938 reprinted in Meyers, 131.

157. See Thomas Moloney, *Westminster, Whitehall, and the Vatican: The Role of Cardinal Hinsley, 1935–49* (London, 1985), esp. 70–71.

158. On Douglas Jerrold's aid to Franco, see Luis Bolin, *Spain: The Vital Years* (London, 1938), 9–51. See also Arnold Lunn, *Spanish Rehearsal* (New York, 1937) and *Spain and the Christian Front* (New York, 1937). Among English Catholics, only Eric Gill and his Pax circle expressed pro-Republican sympathies.

159. Woodruff, review of *Homage to Catalonia*, 133.

160. C.C. Martindale, "Why Not Our Ally?" *The Month*, February 1939, 126.

161. For an concise overview of English Catholicism during the period, see Bernard Bergonzi, "The English Catholics," *Encounter*, January 1965, 19–30. See also Adrian Hastings, "Some Reflexions on the English Catholicism of the Late 1930s," in *Bishops and Writers*, ed. Adrian Hastings (Cambridge, 1977), 107–26.

162. Evelyn Waugh, review of Orwell's *Critical Essays*, in *The Tablet*, 6 April 1946. Reprinted in Meyers, 211–15. In an interesting letter to Orwell, Waugh later argued at length that "the disappearance of the Church" rendered *Nineteen Eighty-Four* "spurious." See *The Letters of Evelyn Waugh*, ed. Mark Amory (London, 1980), 302.

163. The reference is to Waugh's Catholic circle at Oxford, which included Hollis and Woodruff. See Waugh's autobiography, *A Little Learning* (London, 1963), 187. In the 1940s John Betjeman called this circle (which also included Catherine Asquith and Frank Pakenham) "the smart Catholic set." Quoted in *The Letters of Evelyn Waugh*, 253.

164. Alexander Calvert, *The Catholic Literary Revival* (Port Washington, N.Y., 1935), 283–84, 311–15.

165. Hollis, *A Study of George Orwell*, viii, 28.

166. Russell Kirk, *Beyond the Dreams of Avarice* (Chicago, 1956), 181–82. E. Merrill Root, "Orwell's Socialism," *Freeman*, September 1954, 104.

167. See my article, "Orwell on Religion: The Catholic and Jewish Questions," *College Literature*, Vol. 11, No. 1 (1984), 44–58.

168. Christopher Hollis, "George Orwell: His Thoughts on Religion," *Books on Trial*, August–September 1956, 506, 48–49. Hollis, "George Orwell and Swift," *The Tablet*, 4 December 1954, 541.

169. Hollis, *A Study of George Orwell*, 40.

170. Christopher Hollis, "George Orwell," *The Tablet*, 3 June 1961, 534.

171. Hollis, *A Study of George Orwell*, 74. According to Hollis, Orwell was so opposed to contraception that he considered the Church's position "on the safe period . . . not strict enough." "His view was that people who desired intercourse without desiring children were guilty of a profound lack of faith in life, and that a generation which slipped into the way of thinking such a desire legitimate was inevitably damned." Christopher Hollis, "Keeping Up with the Joneses," *The Tablet*, 31 July 1954, 107.

172. Hollis, *A Study of George Orwell*, 200.

173. *Ibid.*, 86.

174. Christopher Hollis, "The New Class Distinctions," *The Tablet*, 11 October 1947, 232.

175. *CEJL*, Vol. 2, 103.

176. Hollis, *A Study of George Orwell*, 114–15, 152–53.

177. See, for example, Robert C. de Camera, "Homage to Orwell," *National Review*, 13 May 1983, 566–73. Joseph Sobran, "1984 Reveals Orwell's Anti-Socialist Sentiments," *Charlotte News* (N.C.), 6 January 1984. Edward Feulner, "Verdict Still Out on Orwell's 1984," *Zanesville Times Recorder* (Ohio), 27 January 1984. John Chamberlain, "Looking Ahead to 1984," *Indianapolis News*, 22 December 1983. Copies in Rosenblum Collection.

178. See Martin J. Wiener, *English Culture and the Decline of the Industrial Spirit, 1850–1980* (Cambridge, 1981), 118–27.

179. Thomas, *Orwell*, 40.

180. Amis, "The Road to Airstrip One," 292.

181. Woodcock, "Orwell, Blair and the Critics," 529.

182. Hollis, *A Study of George Orwell*, viii.

183. See Jerome Archer, "Contemporary Catholic Authors: Christopher Hollis, Biographer and Social Critic," *Catholic Library World*, December 1942, 67–73. See also Hollis' recollec-

tion of his low estimation of Blair in 1931, when Hollis had already published four books and was recognized on both sides of the Atlantic as a leading young Catholic intellectual. *A Study of George Orwell*, 41–42.

184. Hollis, *A Study of George Orwell*, 1–26.

185. See fn. 5, p. 409.

186. See, for example, "The New Class Distinctions" (1947) and his second volume of autobiography, *The Seven Ages* (London, 1974), 17–18.

187. Hollis, *A Study of George Orwell*, 27–28.

188. Stansky and Abrahams, *The Unknown Orwell*, 130, 134.

189. Crick, 226–29.

190. Bishop Blougram, quoted in Hollis, *A Study of George Orwell*, 44.

191. *Ibid.*, viii.

192. *Ibid.*, 37.

193. Christopher Hollis, *Along the Road to Frome* (London, 1958), 77; see also 81–82, and *The Seven Ages*, 59.

194. Hollis, *A Study of George Orwell*, 175–81.

195. Conor Cruise O'Brien, "Orwell Looks At the World," in *George Orwell: A Collection of Essays*, 159.

196. Hollis, *A Study of George Orwell*, 179.

197. *Ibid.*, 177.

198. *Ibid.* See also Christopher Hollis, *The Mind of Chesterton* (London, 1970), 20.

199. See Christopher Hollis, "Mussolini," His Italy," *The Ave Maria*, 12 January 1938, 97–99. "An Alliance with Russia," *ibid.*, 10 June 1939, 721. "Father Coughlin and the Third Party," *The Tablet*, 19 September, 1936." "The German Stiuation," *The Ave Maria*, 24 April 1937. "Fascists and Nazis," *The Tablet*, 13 February 1937, 221–23. "Future Alignments with Spain," *The Ave Maria*, 2 January 1937, 9–11. Curiously, Hollis' autobiographies draw a veil over his political sympathies in the 1930s. Nevertheless, Hollis was never in any sense a fascist; he was a loyal churchman—and consequently a latinophile and an anti-Communist.

200. Hollis, *A Study of George Orwell*, 175.

201. Hollis, *Along the Road to Frome*, 77, 82.

202. Hollis, *The Seven Ages*, 51.

203. Hollis, *Along the Road to Frome*, 77–82.

204. Hollis, *A Study of George Orwell*, 161; and "George Orwell: His Thoughts on Religion," 49.

205. Hollis, *A Study of George Orwell*, 202–3.

206. Douglas Hyde referred to the Catholic Left as "the step-child" of the New Left, and the Catholic radicals were sometimes (unflatteringly) considered Williams' step-children. His influence was so great that Peter Hebblethwaite, S.J., could twit the young radicals for regarding Williams "with the veneration supposedly accorded Aristotle in the Middle Ages." Williams contributed to *Slant*, *New Blackfriars*, and *From Culture to Revolution* (*The Slant Manifesto*), ed. Terry Eagleton and Brian Wicker (London, 1968). See Hyde, "The New Catholic Left," *The Month*, December 1966, 318. Hebblethwaite, "The World of Wicker," *The Month*, December 1966, 324.

207. Brian Wicker, *Culture and Liturgy* (New York, 1963), 148.

208. *Ibid.*, 202.

209. Brian Wicker, "Liturgy and Politics," *New Blackfriars*, 47 (1965–66), 360–71.

210. Wicker, *Culture and Liturgy*, 106.

211. *Ibid.*, 142. See also Brian Wicker, *First the Political Kingdom* (South Bend, 1968), 49–55.

212. Wicker, *Culture and Liturgy*, 195.

213. Hence the point of the title in the American edition, *Toward a Contemporary Christianity* (New York, 1967).

214. Wicker, *Toward a Contemporary Christianity*, 21, 104, 64–70; and "An Analysis of Newspeak," *Blackfriars*, 43 (1962), 272–73, 282–85.

215. Douglas Woodruff, "The Church's Red Guards," *The Tablet*, 19 November 1966, 1297. Evelyn Waugh, "The Same Again, Please," *Spectator*, 23 November 1962, 785–88. Ray-

mond Williams, "New Left Catholics," *New Blackfriars,* November 1966, 77. Hollis was more sympathetic to Vatican II and the Catholic Left. See, for example, Hollis' *The Achievements of Vatican II* (New York, 1967).

216. Wicker, "An Analysis of Newspeak," 285.

217. Brian Wicker, "The Church: A Radical Concept of Community," in *The Committed Church,* ed. Laurence Bright, O.P., and Simon Clements, O.P. (London, 1966), 274.

218. *CEJL,* Vol. 4, 374.

219. Wicker, "The Church: A Radical Concept of Community," 279.

220. See Terry Eagleton's requiem on the Movement: "*Slant:* Intentions and Achievements," *New Blackfriars,* February 1971, 551–55. See also Brian Wicker, "The Aims and Hopes of Britain's New Catholic Left," *The Critic,* October–November 1967, 64–69; and "More Civilized, Less Interesting," *Commonweal,* 9 March 1973, 7–11.

221. George Scott, *The RCs: A Report on the Roman Catholics in Britain Today* (London, 1967), 227.

222. Brian Wicker, "Books," *Commonweal,* 10 January 1969, 474.

223. Raymond Williams, "The Catholic Crisis," *The Nation,* 17 July 1967, 77.

224. Terry Eagleton, *The New Left Church* (London, 1966), 82–83.

225. See Terry Eagleton, *The Body as Language: Outline of a 'New Left' Theology* (London, 1970), 81–82.

226. Terry Eagleton, *Exiles and Émigrés* (London, 1970), 84, 89, 91, 93, 104–7.

227. Martin Green, "Amis and Mailer: The Faustian Contract," *The Month,* February 1971, 48. See also his "Comment," *New Blackfriars,* October 1966, 2–5.

228. Green, "Amis and Mailer," 48–49.

229. See, for example, E.W.F. Tomlin, "Beware of Big Brother," *The Tablet,* 7 January 1984, 6–7.

230. Wicker, "Books," 475.

231. Wicker reflects on this development in "Adult Education," *The Tablet,* 24 February 1979, 185–87. One notes in this connection the sharp difference between the Catholic reception of Orwell in the 1970s and '80s and that of Tosco Fyvel, whose response to Orwell into the 1980s continued to be shaped by Jewish and Zionist concerns.

232. Cf. Herbert McCabe, O.P., "*Slant* and the *Tablet*," *The Tablet,* 26 November 1966, 1340.


*22. Canonization and the Curriculum: Orwell in the Classroom*

233. Hugh Rank, "Mr. Orwell, Mr. Schlesinger and the Language," 159.

234. William Lutz, "Scenario: Setting Parameters for a Task Force to Implement Language Enhancement," *Social Education,* March 1984, 177–79. Lutz also edits the *Quarterly Journal of Doublespeak,* which devotes itself to Orwell's concerns about language abuse in public discourse. Well-known "Doublespeak" awardees have included Yasir Arafat (1975), the nuclear power industry (1979), Ronald Reagan (1983), the U.S. State Department (1984), and Admiral John Poindexter and Lieutenant Colonel Oliver North (1987). Ted Koppel received the 1984 Orwell Award for his TV program "Nightline."

235. "the Orwell 'phenomenon' ": Alan Brown, "Examining Orwell: Political and Literary Values in Education," in *Inside the Myth,* ed. Christopher Norris, 39. "dissecting": See the paperback cover of *The Orwell Myth.*

236. But a set of recommended college-entrance books, the Uniform Lists, did serve as an effective national syllabus for the college-bound between 1874 and 1916 (and continued to exert strong influence into the 1930s). See Arthur N. Applebee, *Tradition and Reform in the Teaching of English: A History* (Urbana, 1974), 49–53, 128.

More recently, the Advanced Placement (AP) program, begun in 1952 and run today by the College Entrance Examination Board (CEEB), similarly promotes an informal high school canon. In the foreign languages, the AP regularly sets specific texts for examination. In English, the essay sections of AP tests sometimes suggest certain "recognized works of literary merit" appropriate to a response, but students usually are invited to choose their own text

when answering general thematic questions. Students "occasionally" feature *Animal Farm* and *Nineteen Eighty-Four* in their answers. Telephone interview with Eric Wimmer, AP English division of the CEEB, 4 November 1986.

237. **"after 1958"**: Letters to the author from several education boards, cited below. **"age of 13 or 14"**: James R. Squire and Roger K. Applebee, *Teaching English in the United Kingdom: A Comparative Study* (Urbana, 1969), 96.

238. Letter to the author from M.T. Fain, Associated Board for the General Certificate of Education, Hampshire, 7 July 1983.

239. On the turn by American schools toward paperbacks, contemporary literature, and "quality" fiction, see Arthur N. Applebee, *Tradition and Reform . . .* , 129, 170, 189, 204.

240. Cf. David Caute, *The Fellow Travellers: A Postscript to the Enlightenment* (London, 1973), 320; and *The Great Fear*, 404. Also William L. Neumann, "Historians in an Age of Acquiescence," *Dissent*, Winter 1957.

241. Questions one and two are from Ralph Ranald, *Monarch Notes to George Orwell's* Animal Farm (New York, 1965), 95–96, 98–99. Question three is from Frank Thompson, *Cliff's Notes to Orwell's* Animal Farm (Lincoln, 1967), 50.

242. Quoted in Brown, "Examining Orwell," 48–49. For a discussion of O-level exams and *Animal Farm*'s use, see H. Lionel Jackson, "Getting Involved with the Text," *Times* [London] *Educational Supplement,* 21 August 1970.

243. Brown, "Examining Orwell," 243.

244. D.A.N. Jones, "Arguments Against Orwell," in *The World of George Orwell,* 159.

245. C.M. Woodhouse, Introduction to *Animal Farm* (New York, 1956).

246. Laurence Brander, "George Orwell: His Life and Writings," Introduction to *Animal Farm* (London, 1960), v–xxii.

247. Brown, "Examining Orwell," 242, 243, 247, 252. Communists also betrayed a knee-jerk "Cold War wisdom" when it came to Orwell's work. See Donald Thomas' humorous story of Chinese students asking to drop his course when "Orwell" appeared on his syllabus. (Notably, the class was not reading *Animal Farm* or *Nineteen Eighty-Four,* but rather "Marrakech," "The Sporting Spirit," and excerpts from *Wigan Pier*.) "The Red Line in a Literary Setting," *Times* [London] *Educational Supplement,* 10 February 1967, 437.

248. Albert B. Friedman, "The Literary Experience of High School Seniors and College Freshmen," *The English Journal,* 44 (1955), 423.

249. On the suggestion that a "middlebrow" work like *Nineteen Eighty-Four* be taught, along with other science fiction, in order to "elevate" student taste, see Dwight Burton, *Literary Study in the High Schools* (New York, 1964), 46.

250. James Knapton and Bertrand Evans, *Teaching a Literature-centered English Program* (New York, 1967), 19–21.

251. One comprehensive survey reported that *Nineteen Eighty-Four* "never failed to appear" on postwar lists of censored books. "Censorship in the English Classroom: A Review of Research," *Journal of Research and Development in Education,* Spring 1976, 65–66.

252. Quoted in Brown, "Examining Orwell," 55–56.

253. Robert Protherough, *Developing Response to Fiction* (London, 1983), 131–32, 139.

254. Cecilia Algra and James Fillbrandt, "Book Selection Patterns Among High School Students," *Journal of Reading,* Vol. 14, No. 3 (December 1970), 157–62.

255. Squire and Applebee, *Teaching English in the United Kingdom,* 110–11.

256. G. Yarlott and W.S. Harpin, "1000 Responses to English Literature (2)," *Educational Research,* Vol. 13, No. 2 (February 1971), 92.

257. Theodore Hipple, "The Novels Adolescents Are Reading," *Research Bulletin of the Florida Educational Research and Development Council,* Vol. 10, No. 1 (Fall 1975), 23. Of course, students' reading preferences are surely influenced—indirectly, directly, or negatively—by teachers' preferences. A 1979 survey also showed *Animal Farm* among teachers' favorite books to teach. Stephen and Susan Judy, "English Teachers' Literary Favorites: The Results of a Survey," *The English Journal,* February 1979, 36.

258. Squire and Applebee, *Teaching English in the United Kingdom,* 110.

259. Reported in Protherough, *Developing Response to Fiction,* 10.

260. Margaret Mathieson, *Teaching Practical Criticism: An Introduction* (London, 1985), 21.

261. Orwell's essays were first set for examination in the early 1960s. Correspondence with ten exam boards indicates that selections from *Inside the Whale and Other Essays* or from Orwell's documentaries were set approximately every other year by at least one board. Letters to the author from H.F. King, Oxford and Cambridge Schools Examination Board, 10 June 1983; G.M. Lambert, University of Cambridge Local Examinations Syndicate, 13 June 1983; and letter from M.T. Fain.

262. George Bott, Introduction to Orwell's *Selected Writings* (London, 1951). Bott's collection, specially designed for sixth-form use, has been frequently assigned as a set book for Orwell's prose.

263. On PEL, see, for example: *Modern Prose: Form and Style*, ed. William van O'Connor (New York, 1954); and Wilfrid Stone and Robert Hoppes, *Form in Thought and Prose* (New York, 1954). On SAE, see: *Readings for Liberal Education*, ed. L.G. Locke (New York, 1952); and *The Meaning of Meaning*, ed. J. Hooper Wise et al. (New York, 1953).

264. For instance, after the publication of *The Orwell Reader*, excerpts identical to those in the collection from *Wigan Pier* appeared in *Thought in Prose*, ed. Richard Beal and Jacob Korg (New York, 1958), and from *Nineteen Eighty-Four* ("The Principles of Newspeak") in *Rhetoric and Reading*, ed. J.J. Kallsen and D.E. McCoy (New York, 1963).

265. The interaction among literary reputation, canon-formation, and the sociology of occupations is well illustrated by how the rise of the New York Intellectuals to national prominence in the 1950s led to Orwell's increased representation in composition readers. As the New Yorkers became more influential in the New York publishing world, they edited more anthologies and readers—and, understandably, excerpted themselves and their favorite writers, one of whom was Orwell. Apart from Howe's edition of *Nineteen Eighty-Four*, see, for example, Leslie Fiedler, *The Art of the Essay* (New York, 1958); Alfred Kazin, *The Open Form* (New York, 1960); and Lewis Coser, *Sociology Through Literature* (New York, 1963).

266. See, for example, *Reading for Rhetoric*, 2nd edition, ed. Caroline Shroder et al. (New York, 1967); *Eight Modern Essayists*, ed. William Smart (New York, 1967); *Prose Models*, 3rd edition, ed. Gerald Levin (New York, 1975); and *The Bedford Reader*, 2nd edition, ed. X.J. and Dorothy Kennedy (New York, 1985).

267. See John C. Hodges and Mary E. Whitten, *Harbrace College Handbook*, 7th edition (New York, 1972), 244. Also Wilfred Stone and J.G. Bell, *Prose Style: A Handbook for Writers*, 2nd edition (New York, 1977), 1.

268. "Orwell is quoted": See, for example, Stone and Bell, *Prose Style*. In my survey of sixty prose anthologies from the 1950s through the 1980s, Orwell's essays were among the most frequent selections. See, for example, the widely used *Borzoi College Reader* (shorter edition), ed. Charles Muscatine and Marlene Griffith (New York, 1968) and *The Voices of Prose*, ed. William Stafford and Frederick Candelaria (New York, 1966), both of which contain more essays by Orwell than by any other author.

269. Quoted from Instructor's Manual to William Smart's *Eight Modern Essayists*, 4th edition, p. 9.

270. Thompson, *Cliff's Notes to Orwell's Animal Farm;* Thompson, *Cliff's Notes to Orwell's Animal Farm;* Ranald, *Monarch Notes to George Orwell's Animal Farm;* Gilbert Borman, *Cliff's Notes to Orwell's 1984* (Lincoln, 1967), 44–45.

271. See Richard Lloyd-Jones, "The Study and Teaching of Writing," *PMLA*, 99 (1984), 981. Christopher Gould, "Freshman Composition as a Survey Course," *Journal of Education*, Vol. 34, No. 4 (1981), 308–18. See also Michael Shugrue, *English in a Decade of Change* (New York, 1968).

272. Albert J. Brouse, "A Negative Response," *College Composition and Communication*, 25 (1974), 218.

273. Howe, "As the Bones Know," 97–98.

274. Cleo McNelly, "On Not Teaching Orwell," *College English*, February 1977, 566.

275. Carl Freedman, "Writing, Ideology, and Politics: Orwell's 'Politics and the English Language' and English Composition," *College English*, April 1981, 337–40.

276. McNelly, "On Not Teaching Orwell," 553.

277. See also Mina O'Shaughnessy, *Error and Expectation: A Handbook for Teachers of Basic Writing* (New York, 1977), 553.

278. The essay was written for a basic composition course at the University of Viriginia in October 1982. I am grateful to the instructor, Patti Schroeder, for sharing it with me.

279. This is partly so because most introductory composition courses, at least in universities, are taught by graduate students, who aspire to teach literature—and so turn basic writing classes into "literary" courses. For a still-relevant critique of the problem, see Alfred Kitzhaber, *Themes, Theories and Therapy: The Teaching of Writing in College* (New York, 1963), 1–26, 73–82.

280. One of the difficulties is the anthologies themselves, which feature selections more appropriate to literary analysis than practice in expository writing. See Joseph Kersoes, "Anthologies of Prose Models and the Teaching of Composition," Ph.D. dissertation, Stanford University, 1983.

281. Crick, 495.

282. Examination boards differ widely in their judgments about suitable set books. One board reported that *Nineteen Eighty-Four* was being set at O-level for the first time in 1985; another board set *Nineteen Eighty-Four* for the fourth time in a dozen years in 1984. Letters to the author from K. Davidson, Schools Examination Department, University of London, 23 May 1983; K.M. Galvin, Joint Matriculation Board, Manchester, 12 May 1983; A.R. Davis, Oxford and Cambridge Schools Examination Board, 13 May 1983; and letters from H.F. King and G.M. Lambert.

283. D.S. Savage, "The Fatalism of George Orwell," in *The New Pelican Guide to English Literature*, Vol. 8, *The Present*, ed. Boris Ford (Harmondsworth, 1983).

284. "entire college courses": See, for example, Luther P. Carpenter, "1984 on Staten Island," in *1984 Revisited: Totalitarianism in Our Century*, 72–88.

285. "neoconservatives": Podhoretz, "1984 Is Here: Where Is Big Brother?," *Reader's Digest*, January 1984, 37–38. See also Arthur Eckstein, "An Orwellian Nightmare," *Chronicle of Higher Education*, 16 October 1984.

286. "Top Ten Classics": "Politics Dominates Classics' Top Ten List," *The College Store Journal*, January 1984. "American Booksellers Association": Fred M. Hechinger, "Censorship of Books on Upswing in U.S., Report Shows," *Lexington Herald* (Ky.), 2 November 1981. Copies in Rosenblum Collection.

See also L.J. Davis, "Onward Christian Soldiers," *Penthouse*, March 1982; and Barbara Nellis, "The Dirty Thirty," *Playboy*, January 1984, 262.

287. Letter to the author from G.M. Lambert.

288. In Hipple's 1975 survey of high school reading, *Silas Marner* and *Great Expectations* were the two most frequently anthologized novels and among the most frequently taught (p. 33).

289. "a catch-all term": Robert Scholes and Carl Klaus, *Elements of the Essay* (New York, 1969), 46.

290. Cf. Fowler, *Kinds of Literature*, 213–34.

291. McNelly, "On Not Teaching Orwell," 566, 554.

292. F.R. Leavis, *The Great Tradition* (London, 1948). Orwell, "Exclusive Club," *Observer*, 6 February 1949, 3.

293. For an explicit attempt at an upward revaluation, see Robert A. Lee, *Orwell's Fiction* (South Bend, 1969). For downward revaluations, see D.S. Savage, "Fatalism," and Daphne Patai, *The Orwell Mystique*.

294. Interestingly, even when social-political writers like Conrad, Forster, and Lawrence are admitted to the modern British novel canon, it is usually on tacit condition that they can be accommodated to the Arnoldian tradition. Instead of discussing these writers' treatments of imperialism or class tensions, that is, their work is characteristically approached by way of the formal and epistemological issues which it raises.

295. Speaking of *Ulysses*, Orwell bemoaned that "a novel is gradually being smothered by a lexicographer." Of *Finnegans Wake*, Orwell said, "The words have finally won . . . . The entire

book is written in a private language." "Elephantine Crossword or Masterpiece?," *Manchester Evening News*, 2 March 1944, 2. On Orwell's view of the novel as a "popular form of art," see footnote 169 in Chapter Four. Q.D. Leavis, "The Literary Life Respectable," in Meyers, 189–90.

**296.** Crick, "Readings, and Misreadings," *Times* [London] *Educational Supplement*, 3 June 1983.

### Conclusion

1. Orwell, *Nineteen Eighty-Four* (New York, 1961), 143.

2. Muggeridge, "A Knight of the Woeful Countenance," 170. Emerson, *The Works of Ralph Waldo Emerson* (Boston, 1883), vol. 4, *Representative Men* ("The Uses of Great Men"), 11, 36.

3. Orwell, *CEJL*, Vol. 2, 143. Nicholas von Hoffman, review of Crick's *George Orwell: A Life*, in *Saturday Review*, March 1981, 71.

4. Sidney Hook, *The Hero in History* (New York, 1943).

5. Richard Rees, "George Orwell," *Scots Chronicle*, 26 (1951), 11. Cyril Connolly, "Reputations," in *Ideas and Places* (London, 1953), 129.

6. *CEJL*, Vol. 3, 151.

7. Kay Ekevall, in *Remembering Orwell*, 60. Brenda Salkeld echoes similar thoughts on page 39.

8. "Prime Minister," *Observer*, 4 July 1948, 3.

9. Kingsley Amis, "One World and Its Way," *Twentieth Century*, 158 (1955), 169.

10. The phrase is Susan Sontag's, from her essay on Elias Canetti, "Mind as Passion," in *Under the Sign of Saturn* (New York, 1980), 182.

11. Victor Brombert, *The Intellectual Hero: Studies in the French Novel* (Chicago, 1974), 18–19.

12. Wallace Stevens, "To a Hero in a Time of Crisis," in *Collected Poems of Wallace Stevens* (New York, 1954).

13. Alain Besançon, "Orwell in Our Time," 190.

14. Eric Goldman, *The Crucial Decade—and After* (New York, 1960).

15. Leonard Meyer, *Music, the Arts and Ideas: Patterns and Predictions in Twentieth Century Culture* (Chicago, 1967), 91–103.

16. Thomas Hardy, "The Convergence of the Twain," in *Selected Poems of Thomas Hardy*, ed. John Crowe Ransom (New York, 1960), 42–43.

17. *CEJL*, Vol. 2, 143.

18. Meyer, 191–93.

# Index